AI CRITICAL NEW TESTAMENT
(AICNT)

NEUTRAL TRANSLATION

WITH ANNOTATIONS FOR

OVER 7000 TEXTUAL VARIANTS

Neutral translation by Artificial Intelligence (GPT)

Josiah E. Verkaik

Author

(Preface, critical apparatus, textual annotations, and curated arrangement)

Dustin R. Smith

Editor

INTEGRITY SYNDICATE LLC

integritysyndicate.com

BOISE | ID

First published in 2025

Published by Integrity Syndicate, LLC
1073 W Lake Hazel Rd. #64, Boise, ID 83709
integritysyndicate.com • info@integritysyndicate.com

Integrity Syndicate publishes critical resources at the core of the New Testament.

Library of Congress Control Number: 2025916896
ISBN 978-1-969070-00-6 (Hardcover Laminate)
ISBN 978-1-969070-05-1 (Hardcover Cloth)
ISBN 978-1-969070-10-5 (Paperback)
ISBN 978-1-969070-01-3 (EPUB)
ISBN 978-1-969070-03-7 (PDF)
ISBN 978-1-969070-04-4 (Kindle)

This edition is part of the AI Critical New Testament (AICNT) series, which presents a transparent, annotated translation with variant readings and critical apparatus to support deeper textual analysis.

Printed in the United States and other countries.
1 2 3 4 5   29 28 27 26 25

Preface Contents

About this Edition

The AI Critical New Testament (AICNT) is tailored for readers desiring a literal and transparent translation of the New Testament that aligns with the earliest known Greek manuscripts, with additional transparency into textual changes that occurred over time. As the name implies, the AICNT is a critical edition of the New Testament translated with AI for maximum transparency into the text.

A critical edition is a version of the text that is carefully edited and compiled based on an extensive review of the earliest available manuscripts. The primary objective of a critical edition is to reconstruct, as closely as possible, the original text of the New Testament books and letters. Additionally, when particular manuscripts and other critical editions vary with respect to the base text, these variations are documented extensively in what is called a critical apparatus, a system of notes and annotations accompanying the main text.

Critical editions of the New Testament are typically in Koine Greek and are not adapted for Bible students who rely solely on English resources. The innovative approach of compiling an English critical text serves to give those who have not studied biblical Greek a level of accessibility that was previously unavailable.

The AICNT further pioneers this new approach by offering a critical edition in English wherein all text is rendered by AI with the aim of a neutral and transparent translation. The translation of the AICNT is intended to be transparent and avoid human biases, as humans tend to interpret the text as they translate, rather than rendering the text in the most transparent way possible and leaving interpretation up to the reader.

The specific objectives of the AI Critical New Testament (AICNT) are as follows:

1. The Greek text used for translation is attested by one or more benchmark critical editions relied upon for modern Bible translations.
2. The translation incorporates, yet distinguishes, differences between early manuscripts and later textual traditions, including the Byzantine text-type and the Textus Receptus.
3. The use of braces {}, brackets [ ], and double brackets [[ ]] within the text identifies and differentiates textual variants.

4. The critical apparatus includes extensive footnotes documenting textual variants, including changes and additions in later manuscripts, differences between early manuscripts, and disagreements between critical editions.

5. The AICNT incorporates conventional notation for frequently cited witnesses in the critical apparatus, including:

   (a) Earliest manuscripts (up to the end of the 5th Century)

   (b) Traditional text-types (BYZ and TR)

   (c) Benchmark critical editions (NA28, SBLGNT, THGNT).

6. The authoritative BDAG lexicon constitutes the primary foundation for the English translation of Greek vocabulary.

7. Utilization of an AI large language model in accordance with specific instructions aimed at achieving an accurate, readable, transparent, and unbiased translation. The goal is essentially a machine translation with advanced contextual awareness for obtaining a neutral output.

8. The translation avoids editorializing through suggestive section headings and other types of suggestive formatting.

9. Frequent paragraph breaks are implemented to improve readability and comprehension, balancing large blocks of text and smaller text segments.

10. Additional footnotes are provided for clarity, including abridged BDAG definitions, cross-references, and notes pertaining to the neutrality of the rendered text.

By accomplishing these core objectives, the AI Critical New Testament equips English readers with a critical New Testament of unparalleled depth and transparency.

Preface Part I: Critical Edition, Rationale & Methodology

1. Understanding Textual Changes

Over the centuries, the text of the New Testament has undergone various kinds of changes as it was copied, translated, and transmitted. These changes range from unintentional errors like misspellings, omissions, and duplication to more deliberate alterations such as harmonization between Gospel accounts, adding words for clarification, streamlining the text, or the inclusion of marginal notes into the text.

Variants that enhance or embellish the story are often termed "expansions of the text" or "additive variants." These are instances where scribes might add phrases, sentences, or even entire verses to make the narrative more detailed, dramatic, or theologically rich. Such changes could include additional dialogue, descriptive elements, or interpretative remarks. Expansions of the text are essentially a layer of commentary by scribes aimed at clarifying or elaborating upon specific points for the reader or listener. In other instances, they might arise from later scribes incorporating the marginal notes of previous scribes into the main body of the text.

Several well-known passages are missing from the earliest Greek manuscripts. These include Mark 16:9–20 (the longer ending of Mark), John 7:53–8:11 (the story of the woman caught in adultery), and 1 John 5:7–8 (the Comma Johanneum, "there are three testify [[in heaven, the Father, the Word, and the Holy Spirit: and these three are one]]"). Also absent in early witnesses are Luke 22:43–44 (the angel strengthening Jesus and sweat like blood), Luke 23:34a ("Father, forgive them..."), and Acts 8:37 (the Ethiopian eunuch's confession of faith). Verses like Matthew 17:21, 18:11, 23:14, Mark 15:28, and Luke 24:12 are also omitted in early texts and often reflect harmonizations from other Gospels.

Among the variants in New Testament manuscripts, the most significant are those with theological or doctrinal implications. Such variants are not merely scribal errors or stylistic modifications; they can impact how a passage is interpreted and understood in the context of Christian beliefs. While most textual variants do not fall into this category, there are some that are theologically significant. For example, there are various substitutions of pronouns with the words "God," "the Lord," or "Christ," or substitution of the terms "God," "the Lord," or "Christ," when comparing manuscripts. A few examples of this are Acts 20:28, 1 Timothy 3:16, and Jude 5.

A consolidated list of theologically significant variants in the Gospel of John is 1:3-4, 18, 27, 34; 5:26; 8:58; 9:38; 12:28, 41, 45; 14:13-14; 16:28; 18:5. There are also many textual variants that have implications for other Christian doctrines.

The New Testament as we know it today is based on many ancient manuscript copies. Later texts exhibit the cumulative effect of over a thousand years of textual changes. For example, in comparing the Gospel text, the later manuscript witnesses of the 12th-16th centuries have thousands of additional words than seen in 3rd-5th century manuscripts. Since there are numerous variations between copies of the same book in different periods and regions, textual criticism must be employed in the process of figuring out what was most likely the original text.

The sheer number of manuscripts, spanning different periods and geographical locations, has resulted in a complex textual history with multiple text-types like Alexandrian, Western, and Byzantine.

Textual critics employ a range of methodologies to evaluate variations to reconstruct the most authentic version of the New Testament text. Studying and comparing these manuscript families and individual variants is crucial for understanding the New Testament's historical development, interpretation, and reliability.

2. What is a Critical Edition?

A critical text or edition is based on the best scholarly estimates of the original text as best reconstructed from the manuscript witnesses. A critical edition is a publication of a text designed to present the most accurate and authoritative version of that text. It is based on exhaustive research involving the collation of various manuscripts, fragments, and other primary sources. The edition typically includes a base text, considered the most reliable representation of the original, along with a critical apparatus that annotates textual variants.

In addition to offering a text as close as possible to the original, critical editions can serve to provide much insight into the history of textual transmission. These editions are essential tools in biblical scholarship. There have been numerous critical texts over the last 200 years. Many have been revised and updated as additional manuscript evidence has been discovered. Some differ in methodology or criteria for selecting between textual variants.

The critical apparatus of critical editions is an organized system of notations to represent, in a single text, the complex history of that text in a concise form. The apparatus typically includes footnotes with standardized abbreviations for the source manuscripts that indicate what manuscripts attest to specific readings. Differences with respect to the base text are referred to as textual variants.

For a further primer on textual criticism and how modern critical texts are determined, see Dirk Jongkind's *Introduction to the Greek New Testament* (Wheaton, IL: Crossway, 2019).

For a more detailed introduction to critical editions and the theory and practice of modern textual criticism, recommended books include:

- Kurt Aland and Barbara Aland, *The Text of the New Testament: An Introduction to the Critical Editions and to the Theory and Practice of Modern Textual Criticism*, translated by Erroll F. Rhodes, 2nd ed. (Grand Rapids: Eerdmans, 1989).
- Bruce M. Metzger and Bart D. Ehrman, *The Text of the New Testament: Its Transmission, Corruption, and Restoration*, 4th ed. (New York: Oxford University Press, 2005).
- D. C. Parker, *An Introduction to the New Testament Manuscripts and their Texts* (Cambridge: Cambridge University Press, 2008).

3. Braces and Brackets

In the AICNT we have endeavored to document all significant differences between the text of the early manuscripts, the current critical editions, and the later text-types. Text considered by the critical editions to be later improvements and additions is distinguished from the undisputed text with brackets.

Braces {}, brackets [ ], and double brackets [[ ]] are used within the body of the text to distinguish textual variants as follows:

- {} Braces, called curly brackets, indicate where textual variants occur with alternate wording. The variant is selected for the text that is most likely the original reading based on the critical editions. The variant reading is noted in the footnotes.

- **[ ]** Single square brackets pertain to text included in at least one of the critical editions but absent in one or more early manuscripts. Since the text in single brackets is not unanimously attested by all the early manuscript witnesses, this indicates some uncertainty about the text being in the original autographs.

- **[[ ]]** Double square brackets indicate words or series of words deemed later additions and interpolations by the Benchmark Critical editions. This material is either indicated with double brackets in the critical editions or only included in the notes of the critical editions, indicating that critical editions do not consider the text original. Double brackets separate supplementary or secondary content (later additions) from primary content (earliest text).

Brackets also indicate varying levels of certainty concerning the text's original wording. By using this formatting in the English translation, readers are given a clear indication of the extent of significant textual variants exhibited through centuries of reproduction. Readers can easily distinguish the critical text from manuscript changes that prevailed later in development.

4. Types of Variant Footnotes

There are several types of footnotes used for documenting variants. The following summaries are provided to clarify how to understand particular footnotes.

- *Some manuscripts read* "x" – This statement pertains to text in braces { } and indicates a variant of a different word or combination of words between manuscripts. The best-attested reading is the wording in the base text, and the alternative reading (considered a later variant) is provided in the footnotes. Usually, it is evident that the alternate reading is that of later manuscripts, but occasionally, there is also early manuscript support for the alternate reading. Sometimes more than one alternate reading is noted.

- *Some manuscripts include* – This statement pertains to text in double brackets [[ ]], which lacks support from any early witnesses. Often, but not always, the only support for the double-bracketed reading is BYZ and TR. Although there may be some support in early manuscripts, none of the benchmark critical editions accept it as original.

- *Absent from some manuscripts* – This statement pertains to text in single brackets [ ] absent in one or more early manuscripts. Although critical editions have incorporated the text based on significant early attestation, there remains some uncertainty about whether the text is original.

- ‖ - When the footnote includes witnesses supporting the base text and those pertaining to a variant, the contrasting statements and their corresponding witnesses are separated with ‖.

Footnotes serve as a valuable tool for further providing additional information about variant readings, including which particular manuscripts and additions affirm them. The variant footnotes include notations indicating the frequently cited witnesses that support the reading.

Typically, a statement is made, followed by notations indicating the textual witnesses that support the particular statement. Witnesses cited are listed in the section entitled "Frequently Cited Witnesses." Later and less relevant manuscripts are typically not noted so as not to overwhelm the general reader. When the word "manuscripts" is used in the footnotes, it typically refers to multiple manuscripts, even when only one witness is cited. In many cases, there may be a single manuscript that the note pertains to.

5. Exclusions to Documented Variants

The aim of the footnotes in this translation is not to document every minor variation. Instead, the focus is on documenting those variants that result in a significantly different English rendering. Variants that are generally not noted in the AICNT critical apparatus are as follows:

- **Orthographic variations**: Differences in the spelling of a Greek word that result in an identical rendering are generally not noted.
- **Abbreviations**: In various manuscripts, words are sometimes abbreviated, including some common, frequent words (e.g., man/human) and, more often, Nomina Sacra (sacred names or titles such as "God" or "Lord"). Variants pertaining to the use of abbreviations are not noted.

- **Transpositions**: Differences in word order where the different word order results in the same or equivalent rendering are generally not noted. (An exception to this is the noting variants of "Christ Jesus" and "Jesus Christ.")
- **Articular variations**: Differences where some manuscripts include the definite article "the" and some exclude it are generally not noted unless it may have a significant interpretative implication.
- **Conjunctional variations**: Differences in the use of conjunctions "and," "but," or "for," are not always noted.
- **Tense variations**: Differences in verb tenses in cases where the different tenses of the same word result in an identical or nearly equivalent rendering are generally not noted.
- **Word substitution**: When synonyms or near-synonyms are used in place of certain words, these differences are not noted unless they result in a different rendering.
- **Verse divisions**: Differences resulting from dividing text in verses are generally not noted. An example is when the text at the end of a verse in one edition is transposed to the beginning of the following verse in another. Verse divisions are more a matter of textual presentation and organization than textual integrity. The AICNT follows the verse divisions of the critical editions used as a benchmark.

Documenting the exclusions mentioned above would add tens of thousands of variants to the footnotes without adding much value to the general reader.

6. Manuscript Text-Types

The terms "Alexandrian," "Western," and "Byzantine" refer to the three primary text-types or families of manuscripts of the New Testament exhibited in the period up to the 6th century. These text-types are named after the regions where they were most commonly found or associated with and exhibit distinct textual characteristics. The following is an outline of these three major text-types.[1]

- **Alexandrian Text-Type**
  - Initially associated with Alexandria, Egypt
  - Generally dated to an earlier period, from the 2nd to 5th centuries

---

[1] Bruce M. Metzger and Bart D. Ehrman, *The Text of the New Testament: Its Transmission, Corruption and Restoration*, 4th ed. (New York: Oxford University Press, 2005), 276-78, 307-13.

- Known for a more concise and grammatically rigorous text. It is generally considered by many scholars to be closer to the original autographs. Alexandrian texts are often favored by scholars for their early dating and for exhibiting a shorter, more primitive text.

- **Western Text-Type**
  - In early textual criticism, this text-type was associated with the Western part of the Roman Empire, particularly centers like Rome and Carthage. It is now established that this text was found in the East as well as in the West, with correlation to Old Syriac manuscripts and quotes from Eastern church fathers.
  - Extends from the 2nd to the 9th centuries, although most manuscripts are from later periods
  - Known for significant paraphrasing, expansion, and omissions. It often includes additional explanatory material. It is generally not favored for establishing the original text by modern critical editions.

- **Byzantine Text-Type (BYZ)**
  - Associated with the Byzantine Empire, centered around Constantinople (modern-day Istanbul, Turkey)
  - Mostly dated to the 5th century and later, although some may exist from earlier periods
  - Known for a smoother, more polished text that sometimes includes explanatory phrases. It is the most numerous among the manuscript families. This text became the prevailing ecclesiastical form of the New Testament and eventually constituted the basis of the Textus Receptus.
  - Generally considered less reliable for critical text reconstruction due to its later dating and tendency toward textual expansion.
  - By the 6th century, the Byzantine (BYZ) text type became dominant and is commonly referred to in some critical editions as the Majority Text (MT)

Other minor subtypes, including the so-called "Caesarean" text-type and text families such as f^1 and f^{13}, exhibit distinctive characteristics. However, the three major text-types outlined above are the most significant when considering the textual history and transmission of the New Testament.

7. Categories of New Testament Manuscripts

Aland and Aland developed a system for categorizing the degree to which various text-types are exhibited in New Testament manuscripts.[2] The five categories are as follows:

- **Category I**: "Manuscripts of a very special quality which should always be considered in establishing the original text." These manuscripts have almost no Byzantine influence. Although most texts in Category I agree with the Alexandrian text-type, they are not necessarily Alexandrian.
- **Category II**: "Manuscripts of a special quality but distinguished from manuscripts of Category I by the presence of alien influences." These are generally Alexandrian texts with some Byzantine intrusion.
- **Category III**: "Manuscripts of a distinctive character with an independent text, usually important for establishing the original text, but particularly important for the history of the text." These are manuscripts with a large Byzantine component and many non-Byzantine readings."
- **Category IV**: "Manuscripts of the D text." The D text is the principal witness of the "Western" text-type and stands apart from the Alexandrian and Byzantine text-types.
- **Category V**: "Manuscripts with a purely or predominantly Byzantine text." This is often associated with the majority text-type, more developed than the texts of other categories.

---

[2] Kurt Aland and Barbara Aland, *The Text of the New Testament: An Introduction to the Critical Editions and to the Theory and Practice of Modern Textual Criticism*, translated by Erroll F. Rhodes, 2nd ed. (Grand Rapids: Eerdmans, 1989), 106, 332–336.

8. Frequently Cited Witnesses

Frequently cited witnesses are noted in the critical apparatus footnotes when applicable to indicate support for various types of textual variants shown in the footnotes. The frequently cited witnesses fall into three categories: (a) early manuscripts, (b) text-types of later tradition, and (c) benchmark critical editions.

a. Early Greek Manuscripts

Particular Greek manuscripts are noted using symbols and numbers, according to the system of Gregory-Aland. However, the general symbols are maintained here without more complex qualifying symbols (additional syntax) seen in some critical editions, which may not be apparent to the general reader.

The goal of the AICNT critical apparatus is to provide only the most essential information in the most intuitive way possible. Citations herein only pertain to the original version of the manuscripts. Citations pertaining to later corrections made by a second, third, or fourth hand are omitted. For the sake of simplicity, parentheses are not used as in other critical editions to indicate a particular witness that attests to a reading but with slight differences.

The frequently cited witnesses first include papyrus fragments and uncial manuscripts, up to about 500 CE. These are representatives of the most primitive forms of the text. In addition to early Greek texts, there are early texts translated into other languages from this same period, most notably Old Latin and Old Syriac versions of the Gospels.

- 𝔓: Papyrus fragments. This is the earliest type of Greek New Testament manuscripts. Below is a list of identification numbers of those Papyri dated up to about 500 CE, as reported by Aland:[3]

---

[3] Kurt Aland and Barbara Aland, *The Text of the New Testament: An Introduction to the Critical Editions and to the Theory and Practice of Modern Textual Criticism*, Translated by Erroll F. Rhodes, 2nd ed. (Grand Rapids: Eerdmans, 1989), 159-60.

These papyrus fragments are only cited when their text varies from the critical base text.

- ○ 𝔓 ≤ **200 CE:**
  Category I: 𝔓 32, 46, 52,[4] 64 + 67, 66, 77, 90, 104
- ○ **200 CE < 𝔓 ≤ 300 CE:**
  Category I: 𝔓 1, 4, 5, 9, 12, 13, 15, 16, 18, 20, 22, 23, 27, 28, 29, 30, 37, 39, 40, 45, 47, 49, 53, 65, 70, 72, 75, 78, 80, 87
  Category IV: 𝔓 48, 69
- ○ **300 CE < 𝔓 ≤ 400 CE:**
  Category I: 𝔓 10, 24, 35
  Category II: 𝔓 6, 8, 17, 19, 51, 57, 62, 71, 81, 82, 85, 86
  Category III: 𝔓 38
- ○ **400 CE < 𝔓 ≤ 500 CE:**
  Category II: 𝔓 14, 56
  Category III: 𝔓 54, 63

- **ℵ(01):** 4th century Greek uncial, *Codex Sinaiticus*. This is an Aland Category I text. It exhibits numerous singular readings and errors and was overrated by some early textual scholars (Tischendorf), as it is "distinctly inferior to B(03)."[5] Jongkind regards it as "a copy of a good text, but it is not a good copy of a good text."[6]

- **A(02):** fifth-century Greek uncial, *Codex Alexandrinus*. It is the most complete Greek Bible from before 1000 CE, and it contains most of the New Testament with only two parts missing. A(02) is of uneven value, inferior in the Gospels, where it is classified as Aland Category III, and good in the rest of the New Testament, where it is Aland Category I.[7]

---

[4] Brent Nongbri, a scholar in the field of papyrology, argued that the paleographical evidence for dating P52 to the early 2nd century is not as strong as previously thought and that a later date into the early 3rd century cannot be discounted. (Brent Nongbri, "The Use and Abuse of P52: Papyrological Pitfalls in the Dating of the Fourth Gospel." [Harvard Theological Review 98:1, 2005] 23-52.)

[5] Aland, *The Text of the New Testament*, 159-60.

[6] Dirk Jongkind, *An Introduction to the Greek New Testament* (Cambridge: Tyndale House, 2019), 54-6.

[7] Aland, *The Text of the New Testament*, 108-9.

- **B(03):** fourth-century Greek uncial, *Codex Vaticanus*. This is an Aland Category I text. The end of it, from Hebrews 9:14 to Revelation, is lost. Many scholars have considered *Codex Vaticanus* superior to all extant texts. Sir Frederic Keyton wrote, "Codex Vaticanus [is] the most valuable of all the manuscripts of the Greek Bible."[8] Professor Kurt Aland said, "Among the uncials, B has a position of undisputed precedence in the Gospels."[9] For this reason, Reuben J. Swanson used Codex Vaticanus as the exemplar text in several reference volumes featuring a critical apparatus for documenting variant readings of New Testament books.[10]

- **C(04):** fifth-century Greek uncial, *Codex Ephraemi Rescriptus*. This Aland Category II text contains most New Testament books, but with sizable portions missing. It originally contained the whole of both the Old and New Testaments. The biblical text was erased and overwritten with other material (a process known as palimpsesting), but modern recovery techniques have successfully reconstructed much of the original text beneath the later writing.

- **D(05):** fifth-century Greek uncial, *Codex Bezae*. This is an Aland Category IV text, defined as "Manuscripts of the D text," that contains the Gospels and Acts. It is the principal example of the "Western" text-type. Due to numerous peculiarities, *Codex Bezae* has been one of the most controversial New Testament uncials. Critical scholars generally regard it as a highly revised text, but the source text used is an outstanding example of a primitive text.[11]

---

[8] Sir Frederic Kenyon, *Our Bible and the Ancient Manuscripts* (London: Harper, 1958), 202.

[9] Kurt Aland, *Nestle-Aland Novum Testamentum Graece, 26th ed.* (Stuttgart: Deutsche Bibelgesellschaft, 1983), 49.

[10] Reuben J. Swanson, *New Testament Greek Manuscripts: Matthew* (Pasadena, CA: William Carvey Int'l Univ Press, 1995), vii-ix.

[11] Aland, *The Text of the New Testament*, 159-60.

Scholars have expressed the three primary views regarding D(05):

(a) It is heavily influenced by the Old Latin text.[12]

(b) It is heavily influenced by the Old Syriac text.[13]

(c) It is the earliest form of the text (most notably Luke and Acts) before efforts to streamline it.[14] [15] [16]

- **W(032):** fifth-century Greek uncial, *Codex Washingtonianus*. This Aland Category III text contains only the Gospels and is frequently characterized by independent readings. W(032) and $\mathfrak{P}$45 are the principal early examples of the hypothetical Caesarean text-type, used to characterize manuscripts with a pattern of variant readings not found in the other more widely recognized text-types. The term Caesarean is used because the particular variants match quotations found in the third-century works of Origen written in Caesarea.

About 50 other Greek uncial fragments are dated up to around 500 CE. Because most of these early uncial manuscripts only contain parts of a limited number of chapters, they are rarely noted unless they have a significant bearing in attesting to a variant reading. If the notation for a manuscript differs from those uncials frequently cited, it likely falls in this category.

---

[12] James R. Harris, *Codex Bezae: A Study of the So-called Western Text of the New Testament* (Cambridge, [Eng.]: University Press, 1891)

[13] Frederic H. Chase, *The Old Syriac element in the Text of Codex Bezae* (London: Macmillan and Co., 1893)

[14] James M. Wilson, *The Acts of the Apostles: Translated from the Codex Bezae with an Introduction on its Lucan Origin and Importance* (London: Society for Promoting Christian Knowledge, 1923).

[15] Albert C. Clark, The Acts of the Apostles: *A Critical Edition with Introduction and Notes on Selected Passages* (Oxford: Clarendon, 1970).

[16] J. Read-Hemimerdinger and J. Rius-Camps, *Luke's Demonstration to Theophilus: The Gospel and the Acts of the Apostles According to Codex Bezae* (London: Bloomsbury T&T Clark, 2013).

b. Early Latin and Syriac Manuscripts

A handful of Latin and Syriac manuscripts overlap the period before 500 CE. There are about fifty surviving manuscripts (or fragments). Metzger describes the most significant.[17] Those with substantial text dating from the early period of 350 to 500 CE are identified by the notation of a, b, d, e, ff², h, i, and k.[18] Of these, a, b, d, e, and ff² are characterized as exhibiting a "Western" text-type having similarities to D(05). Notation includes:

- **a, k**: indicates individual Latin manuscripts up to the end of the 4th century CE.
- **b, e, d, ff², h, i**: indicates individual Latin manuscripts up to the end of the 5th century CE.
- **it**: (Itala) Used when a reading is supported by the "all or majority of Old Latin witnesses as a group."

Early Syriac manuscripts from about or before 500 CE are noted as follows:[19]

- **sy^s**: *Syrus Sinaiticus* (Old Syriac manuscript of about 400 CE)
- **sy^c**: *Syrus Curetonianus* (Old Syriac manuscript being a revised form of *Syrus Sinaiticus*, 5th century CE)
- **sy^p**: Syriac Peshitta (5th century CE)
- **sy**: The entire Syriac tradition

---

[17] Bruce M. Metzger and Bart D. Ehrman, *The Text of the New Testament: Its Transmission, Corruption and Restoration*, 4th ed. (New York: Oxford University Press, 2005), 96-100.

[18] Institute for NT Textual Research, ed., *Nestle-Aland Novum Testamentum Graece*, 28th ed. (Deutsche Bibelgesellschaft: Stuttgart, 2012), 69-71.

[19] Metzger, *The Text of the New Testament*, 100-105.

c. Text-Types of Later Tradition

Secondly, the frequently cited witnesses include the Byzantine text-type and the Textus Receptus, representatives of enhanced textual traditions established in later periods of textual transmission.

- **BYZ**: The Byzantine text-type (its earliest form and not necessarily the majority of manuscripts). Used herein, BYZ is in reference to Robinson, Maurice A., and William G. Pierpont, *The New Testament in the Original Greek: Byzantine Textform* (Bellingham, WA: Logos Bible Software, 2005). "BYZ" has been used herein and is sometimes indicated by "RP" or "MT" in other critical editions. This text-type corresponds to Aland Category V, defined as "Manuscripts with a purely or predominantly Byzantine text."

- **TR**: The Textus Receptus ("the received text") is the name given to the series of printed Greek New Testament editions produced during the 16th and 17th centuries, beginning with Erasmus and continued by Stephanus, Beza, and the Elzevirs. It is not a single manuscript, but a tradition of printed texts that became the standard Greek New Testament of Protestant Christianity and the base for the King James Version (1611) and other Reformation-era translations. Later editions, including the Oxford 1873 Textus Receptus edited by F.H.A. Scrivener and his 1894 Cambridge reconstruction to reflect the KJV, further consolidated this tradition.[20]

In this work, references to the TR generally pertain to the Oxford 1873 edition, as also used in the CNTTS apparatus. The Oxford 1873 edition provides a carefully standardized presentation of the TR. However, this standardized TR does not always correspond exactly to the readings of the KJV, since textual variations exist among the different TR editions.

---

[20] F.H.A. Scrivener, *The New Testament in Greek According to the Text Followed in the Authorised Version, Together with the Variations Adopted in the Revised Version* (Cambridge: Cambridge University Press, 1894); Metzger, *The Text of the New Testament*, 137–164.

d. Critical Editions

Finally, the frequently cited witnesses include the following critical editions. These critical editions are described in more detail in a subsequent chapter entitled "Benchmark Critical Editions."

- **NA28**: Nestle-Aland 28th Edition
- **NA27**: Nestle-Aland 27th Edition (NA27 differs from NA28 only in the Catholic epistles and is only noted there.)
- **SBLGNT**: *The Greek New Testament: SBL Edition* (Society of Biblical Literature)
- **THGNT**: *The Greek New Testament, Produced at Tyndale House.*

When a witness is shown with brackets [ ] (for example, NA28[ ]), this indicates that the word is bracketed in the critical edition cited.

In select cases where there is significant doubt as to what the original text reads, the present work also compares four modern critical editions where they differ. In some cases where two or more critical editions disagree, the footnotes are accompanied by all the frequently cited references in what is likely the original reading.

Those variants not attested by any critical editions mentioned are assumed to be later changes or additions. These usually correspond to the Byzantine (BYZ) or the much later text-form known as *Textus Receptus* (TR).

9. "Western Non-Interpolations"

The Old Latin (a b d e ff[2] it) and Old Syriac versions (sy[s], sy[c]) before 500 CE often agree with the "Western" text of D(05) *Codex Bezae*. Because these are translations, they are not always accurate witnesses for the exact wording of the original Greek but are especially significant when they exhibit an absence of text as compared to other manuscripts, which may call into question whether the absent words, phrases, or even entire verses were part of the original text (autographs).

Some scholars have suggested that the combination of Old Latin and Old Syriac with D(05), in many cases, indicates the original New Testament text, especially when the text is shorter than other forms of the tradition.[21] That is, when the absence in Old Latin and Old Syriac text corresponds with D(05), the text of other manuscripts is not original but rather later interpolations (additions). Thus, the omissions in the "Western" text-type have been called "Western non-interpolations."

F. J. A. Hort affirmed that in many places, the Western text-type D's omissions were original, and that the absence of text attested by the combination of witnesses indicates a more primitive second-century text. Based on the tendency of the text to be expanded over time, he assumed that any significant omissions must represent the original form of the text. Prior generations of textual critics were trained in this perspective."[22]

Recent scholars, including Aland,[23] Metzger,[24] and Fitzmyer,[25] have maintained that new findings such as $\mathfrak{P}$75 have refuted Hort's hypothesis regarding text absent from D(05), the Old Latin, and Old Syriac manuscripts. Aland expressed the opinion that Hort's line of thinking "can only be regarded today as a relic of the past."[26] Scholars

---

[21] Brooke F. Westcott and Fenton J. A. Hort, *The New Testament in the Original Greek*, 2nd ed. (New York: Macmillan & Co., 1896), 175-77.

[22] Aland, *The Text of the New Testament*, 236.

[23] Aland, *The Text of the New Testament*, 236.

[24] Bruce M. Metzger, *A Textual Commentary on the Greek New Testament* (Stuttgart: United Bible Societies, 1971), 164-166.

[25] Joseph A. Fitzmyer, *The Gospel According to Luke (I-IX)* (Garden City, N.Y: Doubleday, 1981), 130-31.

26 Aland, *The Text of the New Testament*, 236.

have based this view on the reasoning that the papyri discovered over the last century, such as 𝔓75, have not lent additional support to the omissions of D(05).

In response to scholars who rejected Hort's views, Ehrman rebuts in his "Excursus on Western Non-Interpolations" and concludes that new findings such as 𝔓75 are consistent with what Hort expected. [27]

In this edition, we have enclosed "Western Non-Interpolations" in single brackets (except when NA28 uses double brackets). Single brackets indicate that the early manuscripts do not unanimously attest to the text. Based on the manuscript evidence and the nature of the omissions, we leave it to the reader to form their own opinion on whether they regard bracketed text as original.

10. Benchmark Critical Editions

The leading critical editions consulted for this translation as the authorities for the base text include the following:

- **SBLGNT**, *SBL Greek New Testament*, (Society of Biblical Literature & Logos Bible Software, 2010).
- **NA27**, *Nestle-Aland Novum Testamentum Graece*, 27th Edition, (German Bible Society, 1993).
- **NA28**, *Nestle-Aland Novum Testamentum Graece*, 28th Edition, (German Bible Society, 2012).
- **UBS5**, *United Bible Societies' Greek New Testament*, 5th Edition, (German Bible Society, 2014).
- **THGNT**, *Tyndale House Greek New Testament*, (Tyndale House Cambridge & Crossways, 2017).

The NA27, NA28, and UBS5 are published by the German Bible Society, which claims "the scholarly editions from the German Bible Society are the basis for almost all modern translations of the Bible."

---

[27] Bart D. Ehrman, *The Orthodox Corruption of Scripture: The Effect of Early Christological Controversies on the Text of the New Testament* (New York: Oxford University Press, 1996), 223–27.

NA26-NA28 are reflective of the leading critical editions used for modern Bible translations. For approximately 33 years, between 1979 and 2012, the NA26/27 text was the dominant critical edition. Only the apparatus (notation of variants) was changed in the publication of NA27 in 1993. With the publication of the NA28 in 2012, the text and the apparatus were revised in the catholic epistles with the implementation of a revised methodology as a first point of departure from NA26/27.

In these revised sections, the NA28 text is characterized as having more of a pro-Byzantine bias than the NA26/27, and it is not always clear how the selection of readings can be justified. Additional sections of NA29 and beyond will be updated according to the revised methodology in future publications. Future editions of the AICNT will compare NA27 and other critical editions with the latest edition of the Nestle-Aland text.

Scholars such as Dirk Jongkind have noted, "It was only the 26th Edition, published in the [19] 70s, that really marked a sort of independent look at all the variants. So then we have 26 and 27, which are identical, and then we are now at the 28th edition and have started a new method, highly dependent on statistics, and the text is sort of reflecting a slightly different approach in sections."[28] Others, such as Daniel Wallace, have noted that the NA28 has "actually taken a step backward in cooperative effort across 'denominational' lines (in a broad sense)."[29]

NA27 is only noted when it disagrees with NA28 (in the Catholic Epistles); otherwise, it is assumed that NA27 is consistent with NA28. The notation of NA28 also indicates UBS5, which is also noted separately.

The UBS5 critical text is identical to NA28. The difference between the two is the apparatus and some minor punctuation differences. The Open Greek New Testament (OpenGNT, opengnt.com) features an open license and differs from the NA28/UBS5 only in the spelling of 61 words and in the word order for three verses.

---

[28] Dirk Jongkind and Greg Pritchard, "Greek Textual Criticism" (foclonline.org, March 3, 2016), https://www.youtube.com/watch?v=usVtLIWvA4o

[29] Daniel B. Wallace, "Nestle-Aland 28: The New Standard in Critical Texts of the Greek New Testament" (danielbwallace.com, December 17, 2012), https://danielbwallace.com/2012/12/17/259/.

SBLGNT (*SBL Greek New Testament*) is edited by Michael W. Holmes, who did his Ph.D. work under Bruce Metzger. It uses a modern text-critical methodology and guidance from the most recently available articles, monographs, and technical commentaries to establish the text of the Greek New Testament. The SBLGNT differs from the wording of NA28 in about 540 variant units. Often, SBLGNT omits text bracketed in NA28, noting the questionable text in the footnotes.

THGNT (*Tyndale House Greek New Testament*) is a recent critical text developed by Dirk Jongkind and Peter Williams with a team of scholars from Tyndale House. They "have taken a rigorously philological approach to re-evaluating the standard text." This includes re-examining paragraph decisions and allowing more recent discoveries related to scribal habits to inform editorial decisions. A notable feature the AICNT shares with THGNT is more frequent paragraphing.

11. Deciding Between Critical Editions

All the noted critical editions agree in the vast majority of cases. In the relatively few instances where the critical editions don't agree, we follow these two additional principles for choosing between variants:

(1) A manuscript that exhibits a shorter and less embellished text is likely more primitive than one that is lengthier and more expressive. Usually, the more concise text is rendered as the base text, with the lengthier variant(s) documented in the footnotes.

(2) In the cases where variants have a significant theological implication consistent with developing orthodoxy, the text is selected that reflects the most neutral (less theologically charged) rendering. Theologically neutral readings are more likely original than those with more pronounced theological connotations. Variants bearing heightened theological significance are documented in the footnotes in such instances.

In significant places where critical editions differ, the variants are noted in the footnotes along with the respective critical editions (for example, SBLGNT, NA28, THGNT) that attest to each reading.

12. Software Resources

Various Bible software tools and resources were used. These include:

- Logos Bible Software
  - Comparison of Greek texts side by side with *Text Comparison Tool*:
    - NA28
    - SBLGNT
    - THGNT
    - BYZ (RP)
    - TR (TR1550MR)
    - Codex Sinaiticus
    - Codex Bezae
  - The Critical Apparatus for NA28, SBLGNT and THGNT
  - A Textual Guide to the Greek New Testament: An Adaptation of Bruce M. Metzger's Textual Commentary for the Needs of Translators.
- Accordance Bible Software
  - *Greek Pro Collection*
  - *CNTTS Apparatus* (3rd ed., 2021)
  - *The Comprehensive New Testament*
  - *Comprehensive NT Notes*
- Olive Tree Bible software
  - *ESV Greek-English Interlinear*
  - BDAG: *A Greek-English Lexicon of the New Testament and Other Early Christian Literature* (3rd ed.)
  - *UBS Handbooks for New Testament*

13. Methodology for Identifying Textual Variants

The method of identifying textual variants involved three primary steps as follows:

a. Text Comparison of Digital Editions

The first method utilized for identifying textual variants was to compare several texts using the *Text Comparison Tool* in Logos Bible software. These manuscripts include benchmark critical editions noted previously, the traditional text types of BYZ and TR, and the early manuscripts of *Codex Sinaiticus* and *Codex Bezae*.

Where differences were found between manuscripts, the different text was translated with AI into English. This included entire verses, phrases, or words depending on the number of words within the scope of the variant reading. The rendering in English was conducted to determine if the variants result in a different English rendering and to determine what the variant readings in English are.

b. Apparatus Review of Benchmark Critical Editions

Reference information on manuscript variations was supplemented by the critical apparatus of the benchmark critical editions, including the NA28, UBS5, SBLGNT, and THGNT. Of these, the NA28 documents the largest number of variants in the apparatus and includes notation of some early Latin and Syriac references.

Some limitations were seen in reviewing the apparatus of these critical editions. None of them (including the NA28) were found to document all significant variants determined through textual comparison and the rendering of differences in Step (a). NA28 often failed to note a variant associated with a single frequently cited witness if that manuscript was later corrected. Additionally, NA28 provides limited information about the early Latin manuscripts as compared to the CNTTS apparatus.

c. Review of the CNTTS Critical Apparatus

The final step in identifying and documenting variants was to review the extensive CNTTS, which is a textual database designed to include as much textual information from each manuscript as possible. The intent is to be an exhaustive computer database, with every manuscript reading, no matter how large or small, included. The database offers a great deal more information on any passage than is usually available to the reader through the apparatus of critical editions of the New Testament.

The CNTTS database is developed and maintained by the H. Milton Haggard Center for New Testament Textual Studies (CNTTS) and is under the direction of Dr. William Warren. Work on the database began in 2010 with the latest release of the 3rd edition in 2021, including corrections to numerous readings. Initially, the data for the MS readings relied on various sources; however, they now claim that the data is predominantly derived from fresh transcriptions and/or collations by CNTTS researchers.

Hundreds of additional variants were noted in the AICNT based on the CNTTS. The database also contributed to supplementing the witnesses noted for already documented variants. The CNTTS also includes data on early Latin manuscripts, significantly exceeding NA28. Despite their and our best efforts, the NA28 and CNTTS, and the AICNT may have occasional errors, which result in some inaccuracy in a small number of footnotes herein. We are committed to improving the apparatus and correcting any inaccuracies in future editions.

Preface Part II: AI Translation, Rationale & Methodology

14. AI As a Solution for Neutral Translation

The Bible is the best-selling book of all time, as it serves as the primary basis for many believers everywhere to understand God's revelation. However, widely used English versions often reflect the inherent biases of translators and editors. The textual biases are then combined with an additional layer of bias reflected by editorial decisions to lead readers down a predetermined interpretive path. The opacity in these translations can sometimes render them closer to a commentary on the meaning of the text instead of a neutral rendering.

Faced with the challenge of human bias in translating Scripture, the question arises: where can one find an impartial English Bible? Developments in the capacity of AI to provide neutral "machine" translation offer the answer. Given the proper input instructions and settings, Large Language Models starting with OpenAI's GPT-4 and later versions have demonstrated the ability to function as an accurate and consistent tool for translating biblical Greek under appropriate guidelines. The great advantage of the AICNT as a sophisticated machine translation is that it serves to convey the New Testament with optimal transparency, as opposed to exhibiting the gross interpretive bias that many human translations do.

Technologies serve as versatile instruments with the capacity to produce both beneficial and detrimental effects depending on how they are used. When deployed with ethical considerations and stringent guidelines, AI becomes a robust mechanism for enhancing human understanding across various disciplines. In the humanities, machine-learning models can assist in translating ancient texts with a level of consistency and impartiality that is difficult for human translators to achieve.

The AICNT is generated directly from the Greek text provided through OpenAI's API using GPT-4 and later Large Language Models (LLMs). The inputs provided included the system message (specific instructions), the API settings, and the selected Greek text. All text incorporated in the AICNT, including alternate readings of variant manuscripts provided in the footnotes, was rendered utilizing AI (none of it was human-translated).

Utilizing its comprehensive knowledge repository and state-of-the-art computational architecture, GPT LLMs demonstrated exceptional proficiency in accurately rendering biblical Koine Greek. Although no translation is 100% perfect, the AICNT generally provides a more neutral rendering of what the New Testament manuscripts say, as opposed to what human translators believe it means.

15. AI Rendering Methodology

To ensure the highest level of consistency and accuracy in the translated text, the parameters of the AI model were fine-tuned to minimize randomness. GPT-4 and later LLMs were used to render all the translated text.

Rather than use the web interface for ChatGPT, the API for Chat Completion, featuring additional controls, was utilized with custom Python code that defined specific parameters to yield a more deterministic and consistent output.

One such parameter is the *Temperature* variable. Higher values result in more random outputs, whereas lower values yield a more focused and deterministic result. For this translation, the minimum value 0 was utilized to generate the most deterministic output possible.

The custom API script developed for interacting with OpenAI GPT models included a system message to ensure the best quality output. The system message contained the instructions for translating the Koine Greek text provided. This had the instructions only to use the BDAG lexicon and to give a theologically neutral rendering to minimize interpretive bias.

It is well known that AI could give varying results if not prompted correctly with tight controls and specific instructions. For this reason, the previously described measures were taken to maintain tight parameters for the LLM to function. With such rules, the output was optimized for neutrality and repeatability. Once the program was developed, the only user input was the raw Greek text for generating the output rendering.

16. BDAG Lexicon

The system instructions was to use of the BDAG lexicon as the basis of the translation, BDAG is an acronym pertaining to *A Greek-English Lexicon of the New Testament and Other Early Christian Literature*, 3rd ed., edited by W. Bauer and based on previous contributions from F. W. Danker, W. F. Arndt, and F. W. Gingrich (Chicago: University of Chicago Press, 2001).

This comprehensive reference work lists thousands of references to classical, intertestamental, and early Christian literature. It is considered the most authoritative and widely used lexicon of the New Testament in the English-speaking world. BDAG contains a thorough and detailed analysis of the meanings and uses of every word in the Greek New Testament and other classical literature. The entries provide a range of information, including etymology, usage in various contexts, historical and cultural background, and cross-references to related words and concepts.

17. Rendered Word Equivalents

When rendering an English translation from the raw Greek text using the controls mentioned above, the GPT Language Model (LLM) output sometimes fluctuated between two equivalent English words (highly equivalent synonyms) when translating particular Greek words provided within a sentence or phrase. This was the primary variation observed when using GPT as a translation tool.

Some examples of these pairs in the output, with the word that is less frequently used in parentheses, are heavens (heaven), Gehenna (hell), beginning (start), taught (instructed), wealth (mammon), purchased (ransomed), gain (acquire), follow (go after), disturbances (insurrections), expectation (foreboding), and disciplined (punished).

In places where the output fluctuated between two equivalent words, it was observed that both word choices were always reasonable options, and those words with more familiarity to the general reader were usually selected. In cases where a less widely understood word choice is used for improved accuracy (for example, *Gehenna*), a clarifying footnote is added to give the reader a fuller understanding of the word's meaning.

18. Quality Assurance

When evaluating the output differences in providing GPT LLMs with entire chapters compared to a single paragraph or verse, we observed that the number of verses translated simultaneously influenced the output. In general, rendering more text at a time improved readability but reduced accuracy. Rendering a paragraph or sentence at a time typically resulted in the best combination of high accuracy and excellent readability. In instances when the Greek text is more complex or abstract, processing a single verse, phrase, or word at a time was employed to achieve an even more accurate output. Inaccuracies were generally resolved by translating smaller bits of Greek text at a time.

Dustin Smith, Ph.D., biblical scholar of Early Christianity at Spartanburg Methodist College (Spartanburg, SC), reviewed the translation for accuracy and readability. Professor Smith conducted a complete review of the rendered text but did not edit the translation. When an issue was identified, shorter lengths of Greek text were rendered to resolve the inaccuracy. In most cases, this resolved the issue without the need for a footnote. In some cases, a footnote was added to provide clarification.

The translated text was configured in a format suitable for use with various software applications, including those used by translators, to ensure the quality of translations. Such software features several quality checks to check punctuation, capitalization, and grammatical issues, among other things. The process of checking for consistency of translated words between Gospel parallels and re-rendering shorter text lengths with GPT LLMs to improve consistency resulted in an additional layer of quality assurance.

The accuracy was further improved during the process of meticulously reviewing every textual variant in constructing and examining the critical apparatus.

19. Clarifying Footnotes

In addition to the textual variants described in the footnotes, other types of footnotes were added to give clarification and greater transparency, as follows:

- Some added footnotes provide Scriptural references for the verses that quote the Old Testament and other texts. "LXX" in the footnote indicates references particular to the Greek Septuagint.

- Some added footnotes provide the abridged BDAG definition in places where the translated Greek word may have a wide range of meanings or may not be fully expressed by the English word rendered.
- Some added footnotes provide an alternative reading of a specific word or phrase. This applies in cases where the rendered word or phrase may pose difficulty in comprehension, such as idiomatic or cryptic expressions, or where the word or phrase can be expressed or understood differently.
- Some added footnotes provide an alternate rendering in those few cases where the AI output fluctuated between two significantly different renderings due to syntactical or textual ambiguity of the source text.
- Some added footnotes provide a clarifying explanation about the theological neutrality of how particular verses are translated.

20. Formatting

The AICNT does not use capital letters for pronouns that refer to God, as that would amount to an interpretive bias. However, words such as God, Lord, and Holy Spirit are capitalized as is customary in English translation. It should be noted that Hebrew does not differentiate between upper-case and lower-case letters. Additionally, the initial Greek manuscripts were composed entirely in capital letters. Capitalization (or lack thereof) in the AICNT is not intended to convey a particular theological position or bias.

The AICNT abstains from formatting conventions of modern translations used to distinguish and classify types of text, such as quotations, poetry, or red-lettered words attributed to Jesus. Italicized words are only used in cases where the AI model indicated that it added helper words in English that are not in the Greek text.

The early Greek manuscripts did not exhibit the suggestive formatting in most English Bible translations. Especially regarding explanatory section headings, the formatting exhibited in many popular translations adds a layer of subjectivity and editorial bias that is avoided here. Since section headings are not used, this translation relies on more frequent paragraphing (like the *Tyndale House Greek New Testament*) to help the reader navigate and search through chapters more efficiently.

Structuring the text in smaller, more frequent paragraphs also serves to enrich the reading experience. The paragraphing of the AICNT exhibits a balance between the conventional paragraph layout of Bible translations (exhibiting large paragraphs) and those translations that provide a verse-by-verse layout (placing each verse on a new line). Smaller groupings of text are also valuable for aiding in readability and comprehension by causing the reader to pause more often and digest a shorter length of text before proceeding.

21. Punctuation

The earliest manuscripts were written in uncial, essentially all capital script without punctuation or word separation. These features, including punctuation, were introduced into minuscule manuscripts (having text with both upper-case and lower-case characters), which began to appear in the 9th century. The earliest dated minuscule manuscript with lower-case Greek characters is the Gospel minuscule 461 from the year 835.[30]

The punctuation of this edition is generally consistent with one or more of the critical editions in the section entitled "Benchmark Critical Editions." In some cases, the punctuation is slightly modified to facilitate documenting multiple variants and incorporating the bracketed text of the critical apparatus.

Having provided an overview of the basis and methodology pertaining to the translation of its extensive critical apparatus, we are now pleased to present to you the AI Critical New Testament.

---

[30] Kurt Aland, and Barbara Aland, *The Text of the New Testament: An Introduction to the Critical Editions and to the Theory and Practice of Modern Textual Criticism*, translated by Erroll F. Rhodes, 2nd ed. (Grand Rapids: Eerdmans, 1989), 128.

Matthew[a]

1 [1] The book of the genealogy of Jesus Christ,[b] the son of David, the son of Abraham.

[2] Abraham fathered Isaac, Isaac fathered Jacob, Jacob fathered Judah and his brothers, [3] Judah fathered Perez [and Zerah by Tamar],[c] Perez fathered Hezron, Hezron fathered Ram, [4] Ram fathered Amminadab, Amminadab fathered Nahshon, Nahshon fathered Salmon, [5] Salmon fathered Boaz by Rahab, Boaz fathered Obed by Ruth, Obed fathered Jesse, [6] Jesse fathered David the king.

David [[the king]][d] fathered Solomon by the wife of Uriah, [7] Solomon, moreover, fathered Rehoboam, Rehoboam fathered Abijah, Abijah fathered {Asaph},[e] [8] {Asaph} fathered Jehoshaphat, Jehoshaphat fathered Joram, Joram fathered Uzziah, [9] Uzziah fathered Jotham, Jotham fathered Ahaz, Ahaz fathered Hezekiah, [10] Hezekiah fathered Manasseh, Manasseh fathered {Amos},[f] {Amos} fathered Josiah, [11] Josiah fathered Jeconiah and his brothers at the time of the deportation to Babylon.

[12] After the deportation to Babylon, Jeconiah fathered Shealtiel, Shealtiel fathered Zerubbabel, [13] Zerubbabel fathered Abiud, Abiud fathered Eliakim, Eliakim fathered Azor, [14] Azor fathered Zadok, Zadok fathered Achim, Achim fathered Eliud, [15] Eliud fathered Eleazar, Eleazar fathered Matthan, Matthan fathered Jacob, [16] Jacob fathered Joseph the {husband[g] of}[h] Mary, from whom was born Jesus, who is called Christ.

[17] So all the generations from Abraham to David are fourteen generations, and from David to the deportation to Babylon are fourteen generations, and from the deportation to Babylon to the Christ are fourteen generations.

---

[a] 1:0, **Title ("Matthew"):** Absent from ℵ(01) B(03) ‖ Latin(a b h) BYZ reads "According to Matthew." ‖ C(04) W(032) BYZ reads "Gospel according to Matthew." ‖ TR reads "The Holy Gospel according to Matthew."

[b] 1:1, **Christ:** The Greek word is defined by BDAG as: (1) fulfiller of Israelite expectation of a deliverer, *the Anointed One, the Messiah, the Christ,* (2) the personal name ascribed to Jesus, *Christ.* (BDAG, Χριστός).

[c] 1:3, **and Zerah by Tamar:** Absent from Latin(k).

[d] 1:6, **the king:** Included in C(04) W(032) Latin(h) BYZ TR ‖ Absent from 𝔓1 ℵ(01) B(03) NA28 SBLGNT THGNT.

[e] 1:7-8, **Asaph:** 𝔓1 ℵ(01) B(03) C(04) NA28 SBLGNT THGNT ‖ Some manuscripts read "Asa." W(032) BYZ TR.

[f] 1:10, **Amos:** ℵ(01) B(03) C(04) NA28 SBLGNT THGNT ‖ Some manuscripts read "Amon." W(032) BYZ TR.

[g] 1:16, **husband:** The Greek word is defined by BDAG as (1) an adult human male, *man, husband* (2) someone, *a person,* or (3) a transcendent figure. (BDAG, ἀνήρ).

[h] 1:16, **husband of:** Some manuscripts read "the to whom was betrothed the virgin." Latin(a b).

18 Now the {genesis}[a] of [Jesus][b] Christ took place as follows: [[For]][c] After his mother Mary was betrothed to Joseph, before they came together, she was found to be with child by the Holy Spirit.[d] 19 And Joseph her husband, being a just man and not wanting to {disgrace her},[e] planned to divorce her secretly.

20 But as he considered these things, behold, an angel of the Lord appeared to him in a dream, saying, "Joseph, son of David, do not be afraid to take Mary as your wife, for that which is conceived in her is from the Holy Spirit.[f] 21 She will bear a son, and you shall call his name Jesus, for he will save his people from their sins."

22 All this took place to fulfill what the Lord had spoken by [[Isaiah]][g] the prophet: 23 "Behold, the virgin shall conceive and bear a son, and they shall call his name Immanuel"[h] (which means, with us is God).[i]

24 When Joseph having risen from sleep, he did as the angel of the Lord commanded him: he took his wife, 25 and he did not[j] know her until she gave birth to {a son}[k] and he called his name Jesus.

2 1 Now when Jesus was born in Bethlehem of Judea in the days of Herod the king, behold, magi[l] from the east arrived in Jerusalem, 2 saying, "Where is the one who has been born king of the Jews? For we saw his star in the east and have come to worship[m] him."

3 And when King Herod heard this, he was troubled, and [all][n] Jerusalem with him, 4 and gathering together all the chief priests and scribes of the people, he inquired [of them][o] where the Christ was to be born. 5 And they said [to him],[p] "In Bethlehem of Judea; for thus it has been written by the prophet: 6 'And you, Bethlehem, land of Judah, are by no means least among the rulers of Judah; [for][q] [[to me]],[r] from you shall come a ruler who will shepherd my people Israel.'"[s]

---

a 1:18, **genesis:** 𝔓1 ℵ(01) B(03) C(04) NA28 SBLGNT THGNT ‖ Some manuscripts read "Birth." BYZ TR.

b 1:18, **Jesus:** Absent from W(032) Latin(a b h).

c 1:18, **For:** Included in BYZ TR.

d 1:18, **Spirit:** The Greek word is defined by BDAG as: (1) air in movement, *blowing, breathing*, (2) that which animates or gives life to the body, *breath, (life-)spirit*, (3) a part of human personality, *spirit*, (4) an independent noncorporeal being, in contrast to a being that can be perceived by the physical senses, *spirit*, or (5) God's being as controlling influence, with focus on association with humans, *Spirit, spirit*... (c) Because of its heavenly origin and nature this Spirit is called (the) Holy Spirit. (BDAG, πνεῦμα).

e 1:19, **disgrace her:** B(03) NA28 SBLGNT THGNT ‖ Some manuscripts read "put her to public shame." ℵ(01) C(04) W(032) BYZ TR.

f 1:20, **Spirit:** See the footnote for Spirit for Matt 1:18.

g 1:22, **Isaiah:** Included in D(05) Latin(a b h).

h 1.23, **Immanuel:** Or Emmanuel.

i 1:23, Isaiah 7:14 LXX.

j 1:25, **not:** Absent from B(03).

k 1:25, **a son:** Some manuscripts read "her firstborn son." C(04) D(05) BYZ TR.

l 2:1, **magi:** Or astrologers. The Greek word refers to a 1) Persian man and priest, who was expert in astrology, interpretation of dreams, and various other occult arts, 2) a magician (BDAG, μάγος).

m 2:2, **worship:** BDAG gives meaning of the Greek word translated "worship" as to express in attitude or gesture one's complete dependence on or submission to a high authority figure, *(fall down and) worship, do obeisance to, prostrate oneself before, do reverence to, welcome respectfully*. BDAG states "Frequently used to designate the custom of prostrating oneself before persons and kissing their feet or the hem of their garment, the ground, etc." (BDAG, προσκυνέω).

n 2:3, **all:** Absent from D(05).

o 2:4, **of them:** Absent from D(05).

p 2:5, **to him:** Absent from Latin(a).

q 2:6, **for:** Absent from ℵ(01).

r 2:6, **to me:** Included in C(04).

s 2:6, Micah 5:2.

7 Then Herod secretly called the magi and determined from them the exact time the star appeared. 8 And sending them to Bethlehem, he said [[to them]],ᵃ "Go and search carefully for the child; and when you have found *him*, report to me, so that I too may come and worship him."

9 And having heard the king, they went on their way, and behold, the star which they had seen in the east, led them until it came and stood over {where the child was}.ᵇ 10 And when they saw the star, they rejoiced exceedingly with great joy. 11 And entering the house, they {saw}ᶜ the child with Mary his mother; and falling down, they worshipedᵈ him; and opening their treasures, they presented to him gifts of gold, frankincense, and myrrh. 12 And having been warned in a dream not to return to Herod, they departed for their own country by another way.

13 Now when they had departed [[into their land]],ᵉ behold, an angel of the Lord appeared in a dream to Joseph, saying, "Arise, take the child and his mother, and flee to Egypt, and stay there until I tell you; for Herod is about to search for the child to destroy it." 14 So he arose, took the child and his mother by night, and departed to Egypt, 15 and was there until the death of Herod; that what was spoken by the Lord through the prophet might be fulfilled, saying, "Out of Egypt I called my son."ᶠ

16 Then Herod, seeing that he was mocked by the magi, was very angry, and sending forth, he killed all the children in Bethlehem and in all its borders, from two years old and under, according to the time which he had carefully inquired from the magi.

17 Then was fulfilled what was spoken {through}ᵍ Jeremiah [the prophet],ʰ saying, 18 "A voice was heard in Ramah, [[lamentation and]]ⁱ weeping and great mourning; Rachel weeping for her children, and she would not be comforted because they are no more."ʲ

19 Now when Herod had died, behold, an angel of the Lord appeared in a dream to Joseph in Egypt, 20 saying, "Get up, take the child and his mother, and go to the land of Israel; for those who sought the child's life are dead."

21 So he got up, took the child and his mother, and {entered}ᵏ into the land of Israel.

22 But when he heard that Archelaus was reigning [[over]]ˡ Judea in place of his father Herod, he was afraid to go there. Having been warned in a dream, he withdrew to the region of Galilee, 23 and he went and lived in a city called Nazareth; so that what was spoken through the prophets might be fulfilled, that he would be called a Nazarene.ᵐ

ᵃ 2:8, **to them:** Included in D(05).
ᵇ 2:9, **where the child was:** Some manuscripts read "the child." D(05) Latin(b).
ᶜ 2:11, **saw:** Some manuscripts read "found." TR Latin(b).
ᵈ 2:11, **worship:** See footnote for worship in verse 2.
ᵉ 2:13, **into their land:** Included in B(03).
ᶠ 2:15, Hosea 11:1 Masoretic text.
ᵍ 2:17, **through:** Some manuscripts read "by." D(05) BYZ TR.
ʰ 2:17, **the prophet:** Absent from W(032).
ⁱ 2:18, **lamentation and:** Included in C(04) D(05) W(032) BYZ TR ‖ Absent from ℵ(01) B(03) NA28 SBLGNT THGNT.
ʲ 2:18, Jeremiah 31:15. The wording of early manuscripts is from the Masoretic text and later manuscripts from the LXX.
ᵏ 2:21, **entered:** ℵ(01) B(03) C(04) NA28 SBLGNT THGNT ‖ Some manuscripts read "came." D(05) W(032) BYZ TR.
ˡ 2:22, **over:** Included in C(04) D(05) W(032) Latin(a b k) BYZ TR.
ᵐ 2:23, Unknown Scriptural reference. This may be a reference to a widely known prophetic tradition not preserved in the canonical Old Testament texts, reflecting a common Jewish understanding at the time. The Hebrew word) נֵצֶר(netzer), meaning "branch," occurs in Isaiah 11:1, potentially

3 1 [But][a] In those days John the
Baptist came, preaching in the
wilderness of Judea, 2 [and][b] saying,
"Repent, for the kingdom of the
heavens has come near." 3 For this is the
one spoken of {through}[c] the prophet
Isaiah, saying, "A voice of one crying
out in the wilderness: 'Prepare the way
of the Lord, make his paths straight.'"[d]

4 Now John himself had a garment
of camel's hair and a leather belt
around his waist, and his food was
locusts and wild honey.

5 Then Jerusalem and all Judea and
all the region around the Jordan went
out to him, 6 and they were baptized in
the Jordan [river][e] [by him],[f] confessing
their sins.

7 But when he saw many of the
Pharisees and Sadducees coming to
{his}[g] baptism, he said to them, "Brood[h]
of vipers, who warned you to flee from
the coming wrath? 8 Therefore, produce
fruit worthy of repentance 9 and do not
presume to say to yourselves, 'We have
Abraham as our father.' For I tell you
that God is able to raise up children for
Abraham from these stones.

10 "Indeed, the axe is already laid
at the root of the trees; therefore,
every tree not producing good fruit
is cut down and thrown into the fire.
11 [[For]][i] I indeed baptize you with
water for repentance, but the one
coming [after me][j] is more powerful
than I, whose sandals I am not worthy
to carry; that one will baptize you
with the Holy Spirit[k] [and fire].[l]
12 His winnowing fork is in his hand,
and he will clear[m] his threshing floor
and gather his wheat into {the}[n]
storehouse, but the chaff he will burn
with unquenchable fire."

13 Then Jesus comes from Galilee
to the Jordan to John, to be baptized
by him. 14 But [John][o] tried to prevent
him, saying, "I need to be baptized by
you, and you come to me?" 15 But Jesus
answered {and said to him},[p] "Allow
it now, for in this way it is fitting for
us to fulfill all righteousness." Then he
allowed him.

16 {But}[q] having been baptized,
Jesus immediately went up from the
water; and behold, the heavens were
opened [to him],[r] and he saw [the][s]
Spirit[t] of God descending like a dove
[and][u] coming upon him; 17 and behold,

---

referring metaphorically to the Messiah: "There shall come forth a shoot from the stump of Jesse, and a branch (netzer) from his roots shall bear fruit." Matthew might be employing a wordplay connecting "Nazarene" to "branch.".

a 3:1, **But:** Absent from D(05) Latin(b).

b 3:2, **And:** C(04) D(05) W(032) BYZ TR NA28[] SBLGNT THGNT || Absent from ℵ(01) B(03).

c 3:3, **through:** Some manuscripts read "by." BYZ TR.

d 3:3, Isaiah 40:3 LXX.

e 3:6, **river:** Absent from D(05) Latin(a b k) BYZ TR.

f 3:6, **by him:** Absent from ℵ(01).

g 3:7, **his:** Some manuscripts read "the." ℵ(01) B(03).

h 3:7, **Brood:** Or offspring.

i 3:11, **For:** Included in ℵ(01).

j 3:11, **after me:** Absent from 𝔓101.

k 3:11, **Spirit:** See the footnote for Spirit in Matt 1:18.

l 3:11, **and fire:** Absent from BYZ.

m 3:12, **clear:** Or clean.

n 3:12, **the:** Some manuscripts read "the." B(03) Latin(b).

o 3:14, **John:** Some manuscripts read "he." ℵ(01) B(03).

p 3:15, **and said to him:** Some manuscripts read "him and said." (missing πρὸς) 96 B(03) Latin(a b h).

q 3:16, **But:** B(03) C(04) NA28 SBLGNT THGNT || Some manuscripts read "And." D(05) BYZ TR.

r 3:16, **to him:** D(05) BYZ TR NA28[] THGNT || Absent from manuscripts. ℵ(01) B(03) SBLGNT.

s 3:16, **the:** Absent from ℵ(01) B(03) SBLGNT.

t 3.16 **Spirit:** See footnote for Spirit in Matt 1:18.

u 3:16, **and:** C(04) D(05) W(032) BYZ TR NA28[] THGNT || Absent from ℵ(01) B(03) Latin(a b h) SBLGNT.

a voice from the heavens said [[to him]],[a] "{This}[b] is my beloved Son, in whom I am well pleased."

4 [1] Then Jesus was led up into the wilderness by the Spirit to be tempted by the devil. [2] And after fasting forty days and forty nights, he was hungry. [3] And the tempter came [[to him]][c] and said [to him],[d] "If you are the Son of God, command these stones to become bread."

[4] But {he}[e] answered and said, "It is written, 'Man shall not live by bread alone [, but {on}[f] every word [that proceeds out of the mouth][g] of God].[h,][i]"

[5] Then the devil takes him to the holy city and stands him on the pinnacle of the temple [6] and says to him, "If you are the son of God, throw yourself down [[from here]];[j] for it is written, 'He will command his angels concerning you, and they will lift you up in their hands, so that you will not strike your foot against a stone.'"[k] [7] Jesus said to him, "Again it is written, 'You shall not put the Lord your God to the test.'"[l]

[8] Again, the devil took him to a very high mountain and showed him all the kingdoms of the world[m] and their glory, [9] And he said to him, "I will give you all these things, if you fall down and worship me."

[10] Then Jesus said to him, "Go away [[behind me]],[n] Satan! For it is written, 'You shall worship the Lord your God, and serve him alone.'"[o] [11] Then the devil leaves him, and behold, angels came and ministered to him.

[12] Now when {he}[p] heard that John was handed over,[q] he withdrew into Galilee. [13] And leaving Nazareth, he went and lived in Capernaum by the sea, in the region of Zebulun and Naphtali; [14] so that what was spoken through the prophet Isaiah might be fulfilled, saying, [15] "Land of Zebulun and [land][r] of Naphtali, the way of the sea, beyond the Jordan, Galilee of the Gentiles, [16] The people sitting in darkness saw a great light, [and][s] for those sitting in the region and shadow of death, a light has risen for them."[t]

[17] From then on, Jesus began to preach and to say, "Repent, for the kingdom of the heavens has come near."

---

[a] 3:17, **to him:** Included in D(05) Latin(a b).

[b] 3:17, **This:** Some manuscripts read "You are." BD(05) Latin(a b).

[c] 4:3, **to him:** Included in C(04) D(05) Latin(a b h k) BYZ TR.

[d] 4:3, **to him:** Absent from C(04) Latin(k) BYZ TR.

[e] 4:4, **he:** D(05) reads "Jesus."

[f] 4:4, **on:** Some manuscripts read "in." C(04) D(05).

[g] 4:4, **that proceeds out of the mouth:** Absent from D(05) Latin(a b k).

[h] 4:4, **but on every word..:** Absent from Latin(k).

[i] 4:4, Deuteronomy 8:3.

[j] 4:6, **from here:** Included in C(04).

[k] 4:6, Psalm 91:11-12.

[l] 4:7, Deuteronomy 6:16.

[m] 4:8, **world:** Or inhabited earth.

[n] 4:10, **behind me:** Included in D(05) Latin(a b h) BYZ.

[o] 4:10, Deuteronomy 6:13 LXX.

[p] 4:12, **he:** ℵ(01) B(03) C(04) D(05) NA28 SBLGNT THGNT ‖ Some manuscripts read "Jesus." W(032) Latin(a b h) BYZ TR.

[q] 4:12, **handed over:** Or arrested.

[r] 4:15, **land:** Absent from D(05) W(032).

[s] 4:16, **and:** Absent from D(05) Latin(a b h k).

[t] 4:16, Isaiah 9:1-2.

18 While walking by the Sea of Galilee, {he}[a] saw two brothers, Simon who is called Peter, and Andrew his brother, casting a net into the sea; for they were fishermen. 19 And {he}[b] said to them, "Come after[c] me, and I will make you [[become]][d] fishers of men." 20 And they, immediately leaving {the}[e] nets, followed him.

21 [Going on from there, he saw two other brothers, James the son of Zebedee and John his brother, in the boat with Zebedee their father, mending their nets, and he called them. 22 Immediately they left {the}[f] boat and their father and followed him.][g]

23 And {he}[h] went about in all of Galilee, teaching [[them]][i] in their synagogues and proclaiming the good news of the kingdom and healing every disease and every sickness among the people.

24 And the report about him went out into all of Syria; and they brought to him all those who were ill, afflicted with various diseases and torments, [[and]][j] those who were demon-possessed and moonstruck[k] and paralytics [and healed them][l] [[all]].[m] 25 And large crowds followed him from Galilee and the Decapolis and Jerusalem and Judea and beyond the Jordan.

5 1 And seeing the crowds, he went up on the mountain, and when he sat down, his disciples came to him. 2 And opening his mouth, he taught them, saying,

3 "Blessed are the poor in spirit, for theirs is the kingdom of the heavens.

4 "Blessed are those who mourn, for they will be comforted.

5 "Blessed are the meek,[n] for they themselves will inherit the earth.

6 "Blessed are those who hunger and thirst for righteousness, for they will be satisfied.

7 "Blessed are the merciful, for they will be shown mercy.

8 "Blessed are the pure in heart, for they will see God.

9 "Blessed are the peacemakers, for they will be called sons of God.

10 "Blessed are those who are persecuted for the sake of righteousness, for theirs is the kingdom of the heavens.

11 "Blessed are you when they insult you and persecute you say every evil [word][o] against you [[falsely]][p] because of {me}.[q]

12 "Rejoice and be exceedingly glad, for your reward is great in the heavens;

---

[a] 4:18, **he:** TR reads "Jesus."

[b] 4:19, **he:** Latin(a) reads "Jesus."

[c] 4:19, **come after:** Or follow.

[d] 4:19, **become:** Included in D(05) Latin(a b).

[e] 4:20, **the:** Some manuscripts read "their." W(032) Latin(a b h).

[f] 4:22, **the:** Some manuscripts read "their." ℵ(01) Latin(b).

[g] 4:22, Verses 21-22 are absent from some manuscripts. W(032).

[h] 4:23, **he:** B(03) Latin(k) NA28 SBLGNT ‖ Some manuscripts read "Jesus." ℵ(01) C(04) D(05) W(032) Latin(a b h) BYZ TR THGNT.

[i] 4:23, **them:** Included in ℵ(01).

[j] 4:24, **and:** Included in ℵ(01) D(05) W(032) BYZ TR NA28[] ‖ Absent from B(03) C(04) SBLGNT THGNT.

[k] 4:24, **moonstruck:** The Greek word is defined by BDAG as experience epileptic seizures, be an epileptic. In the ancient world, epileptic seizure was associated with transcendent powers of the moon. (BDAG, σεληνιάζομαι) .

[l] 4:24, **and healed them:** Absent from Latin(k).

[m] 4:24, **all:** Included in D(05) Latin(a b h).

[n] 5:5, **meek:** The Greek word for *meek* is defined by BDAG as: to not being overly impressed by a sense of one's self-importance, gentile, humble, considerate, meek (BDAG, πραΰς).

[o] 5:11, **word:** ℵ(01) B(03) D(05) NA28 SBLGNT THGNT ‖ Absent from C(04) W(032) BYZ TR.

[p] 5:11, **falsely:** Absent from D(05) Latin(b h k).

[q] 5:11, **me:** Some manuscripts read "righteousness." D(05) Latin(a b k).

for so they persecuted the prophets who were before you [[, your fathers]].[a]

13 "You are the salt of the earth; but if the salt becomes tasteless, with what will it be salted? It is good for nothing anymore, except to be thrown out and trampled underfoot by men.

14 "You are the light of the world. A city cannot be hidden when it is set on a hill; 15 nor do they light a lamp and put it under a basket, but on a lampstand, and it gives light to all who are in the house.

16 "In the same way, let your light shine before men, so that they may see your good [works][b] and glorify your Father who is in heaven.

17 "Do not think that I came to abolish the law or the prophets; I did not come to abolish but to fulfill.

18 "For truly I say to you, until heaven and earth pass away, not one iota or one stroke will pass from the law until [when][c] all is accomplished.

19 "Whoever, therefore, breaks one of the least of these commandments and teaches others to do so, will be called least in the kingdom of the heavens [; but whoever does and teaches them, this one will be called great in the kingdom of the heavens].[d]

20 ["For I say to you that unless your righteousness exceeds that of the scribes and Pharisees, you will not enter the kingdom of the heavens.][e]

21 "You have heard that it was said to the elders,[f] 'You shall not murder; and whoever murders will be liable to judgment.'[g] 22 But I say to you that everyone who is angry with their brother [[without cause]][h] will be liable to judgment; whoever says to their brother, 'Raca,'[i] will be liable to the council; and whoever says, 'You fool,' will be liable to the hell[j] of fire.

23 "So if you are offering your gift at the altar and there remember that your brother has something against you, 24 leave your gift there before the altar and go; first be reconciled to your brother, and then come and offer your gift.

25 "Be quick to settle matters with your adversary, while you are [still][k] with him on the way, lest your adversary hand you over to the judge, and the judge [[hand you over]][l] to the officer, and you be thrown into prison; 26 truly, I say to you, you will not get out until you have paid the last penny.

27 "You have heard that it was said [[to the elders]],[m] 'You shall not commit adultery.'[n] 28 But I say to you that everyone who looks at a woman with desire has already committed adultery with her in his heart.

---

a 5:12, **your fathers:** Included in Latin(b).

b 5:16, **works:** Absent from B(03).

c 5:18, **when:** Absent from B(03).

d 5:19, **but whoever does and teaches them, this one will be called great in the kingdom of the heavens:** Absent from some manuscripts including ℵ(01) D(05) W(032).

e 5:20, Verse 20 is absent from D(05).

f 5:21, **elders:** Or, to those of old.

g 5:21, Exodus 20:13; Deuteronomy 5:17.

h 5:22, **without cause:** Included in D(05) W(032) Latin(a b h k) BYZ TR ‖ Absent from 𝔓64-67 ℵ(01) B(03) NA28 SBLGNT THGNT.

i 5:22, **Raca:** An Aramaic insult.

j 5:22, **hell:** Greek "Gehenna," often translated "hell," was the name of a valley southwest of Jerusalem, where human sacrifices had once been offered and where garbage from the city was constantly burning. Later this picture was combined with the idea of God's judgment, and so the notion of a fiery hell developed. (UBS Handbooks).

k 5:25, **still:** Absent from D(05).

l 5:25, **hand you over:** Included in D(05) W(032) Latin(a b h) BYZ TR ‖ Absent from 𝔓64-67 ℵ(01) B(03) Latin(k) NA28 SBLGNT THGNT.

m 5:27, **to the elders:** Included in Latin(h) TR.

n 5:27, Exodus 20:14; Deuteronomy 5:18.

29 "But if your right eye causes you to stumble, remove it and throw it away from you; for it is better for you that one of your members should perish, and not your whole body be thrown into Gehenna.[a]

30 ["And if your right hand causes you to stumble, cut it off and throw it away from you; for it is better for you that one of your members should perish, and not that your whole body should {go into Gehenna}.][bc]

31 "It was said [[that]],[d] 'Whoever divorces his wife, let him give her a certificate of divorce.'" 32 But I say to you [that][e] everyone who divorces his wife, except for the reason of sexual immorality, makes her commit adultery [; and whoever marries a divorced woman commits adultery].[f]

33 "Again, you have heard that it was said to the elders,[g] 'You shall not swear falsely, but shall fulfill to the Lord your oaths.'[h] 34 But I say to you, do not swear at all; neither by heaven, for it is the throne of God, 35 nor by the earth, for it is the footstool of his feet, nor by Jerusalem, for it is the city of the great King, 36 nor shall you swear by your head, for you cannot make one hair white or black. 37 But let your word be 'Yes, yes' or 'No, no'; anything more than this is from the evil one.

38 "You have heard that it was said, 'An eye for an eye [and][i] a tooth for a tooth.'[j] 39 But I say to you, do not resist the evil one; but whoever {strikes}[k] you on {your}[l] [right][m] cheek, turn to him the other also; 40 and if anyone wants to sue you and take your tunic, let him have your cloak as well; 41 and whoever forces you to go one mile,[n] go with him two. 42 Give to the one who asks you, and do not turn away from the one who wants to borrow from you.

43 "You have heard that it was said, 'You shall love your neighbor and hate your enemy.'[o] 44 But I say to you, love your enemies, [[bless those who curse you, do good to those who hate you,]][p] [and][q] pray for those who [[mistreat you and]][r] persecute you, 45 so that you may be sons of your Father who is in the heavens; for he causes his sun to rise on the evil and the good, and sends rain on the righteous and the unrighteous.

---

a 5:29, **Gehenna:** See footnote for verse 22.

b 5:30, **go into Gehenna:** Some manuscripts read "cast into Gehenna." W(032) BYZ TR.

c 5:30, Verse 30 is absent from D(05), all Syriac versions and other manuscripts.

d 5:31, **that:** Included in W(032) BYZ TR.

e 5:32, **that:** Absent from D(05).

f 5:32, **and whoever marries a divorced woman commits adultery:** Absent from D(05) Latin(a b k).

g 5:33, **elders:** Or, to those of old.

h 5:33, Leviticus 19:12; Numbers 30:2.

i 5:38, **and:** Absent from D(05) Latin(a b k).

j 5:38, Exodus 21:24; Leviticus 24:20; Deuteronomy 19:21.

k 5:39, **strikes:** ℵ(01) ‖ Some manuscripts read "slaps." D(05) Latin(a b h k) BYZ TR.

l 5:39, **your:** B(03) D(05) Latin(b) NA28[] BYZ ‖ Some manuscripts read "the." ℵ(01) W(032) Latin(a h) SBLGNT THGNT.

m 5:39, **right:** Absent from some manuscripts D(05) Latin(k).

n 5:41, **mile:** Greek *million* equivalent to 4,854 feet.

o 5:43, Leviticus 19:18.

p 5:44, **bless those who curse you, do good to those who hate you:** Included in D(05) W(032) Latin(h) BYZ TR ‖ Absent from ℵ(01) B(03) Latin(a b k) NA28 SBLGNT THGNT.

q 5:44, **and:** Absent from W(032).

r 5:44, **mistreat you and:** Included in D(05) W(032) Latin(a b h) BYZ TR ‖ Absent from ℵ(01) B(03) Latin(k) NA28 SBLGNT THGNT.

46 "For if you love those who love you, what reward do you have? Do not even the tax collectors do {the same}?[a] 47 [And if you greet your {brothers}[b] only, what more are you doing? Do not even the {Gentiles}[c] do {the same}?[d]][e]

48 "Therefore, you shall be perfect, [[just]][f] as your {heavenly Father}[g] is perfect."

6 1 "Be careful [then][h] not to {practice your righteousness}[i] in front of men, in order to be seen by them; otherwise, you have no reward from your Father who is in the heavens.

2 "So when you give to the needy, do not sound a trumpet before you, as the hypocrites do in the synagogues and in the streets, so that they may be praised by men; truly [[truly]][j] I say to you, they have received their reward.

3 "But when you give to the needy, do not let your left hand know what your right hand is doing, 4 so that your giving may be in secret; and your Father who sees in secret [[himself]][k] will reward you [[openly]].[l]

5 "And when you pray, do not be like the hypocrites, for they love to [[stand]][m] praying in the synagogues and on the street corners, so that they may be seen by men; truly I say to you, [[because]][n] they have received their reward.

6 "But when you pray, go into your inner room, and having shut the door, pray to your Father who is in secret, and your Father who sees in secret will reward you [[in the open]].[o]

7 "And when you pray, do not use vain repetitions as the Gentiles do, for they think that they will be heard for their many words. 8 Therefore, do not be like them; for [[God]][p] your Father knows what you need before you ask him.

9 "In this manner, therefore, pray: Our Father who is in the heavens; let your name be sanctified;[q] 10 let your kingdom come; let your will be done, [as][r] in heaven, so also on earth. 11 Give us today our daily bread; 12 And forgive us our debts, as we also have forgiven[s] our debtors; 13 and do not lead us into temptation, but deliver us from the evil one [[, for yours is the kingdom and the power and the glory, forever. Amen]].[t]

---

a 5:46, **the same:** Some manuscripts read "thus." D(05).

b 5:47, **brothers:** Some manuscripts read "friends." W(032) BYZ.

c 5:47, **Gentiles:** ℵ(01) B(03) D(05) NA28 SBLGNT THGNT ‖ Some manuscripts read "tax collectors." W(032) BYZ TR.

d 5:47, **the same:** Some manuscripts read "so." BYZ TR.

e 5:47, **And if you…:** Verse 47 is absent from Latin(k).

f 5:48, **just:** Included in D(05) BYZ TR.

g 5:48, **heavenly Father:** Some manuscripts read "Father in the heavens." D(05) Latin(b h k) BYZ TR.

h 6:1, **then:** ℵ(01) NA28[] SBLGNT ‖ Absent from B(03) D(05) W(032) Latin(a b h k) BYZ TR THGNT.

i 6:1, **practice your righteousness:** Some manuscripts read "do your charitable deeds." W(032) BYZ TR.

j 6:2, **truly:** Included in ℵ(01).

k 6:4, **himself:** Included in D(05) W(032) BYZ TR.

l 6:4, **openly:** Included in W(032) Latin(a b h) BYZ TR.

m 6:5, **stand:** Included in D(05) Latin(a b h k).

n 6:5, **because:** Included in W(032) BYZ TR.

o 6:6, **in the open:** Included in W(032) Latin(a b h) BYZ TR ‖ Absent from ℵ(01) B(03) D(05) NA28 SBLGNT THGNT.

p 6:8, **God:** Included in B(03).

q 6:9, **Let your name be sanctified:** Or "Hallowed be your name."

r 6:10, **as:** Absent from D(05) Latin(a b k).

s 6:12, **have forgiven:** Some manuscripts read "forgive." D(05) W(032) BYZ TR.

t 6:13, **for yours is the kingdom and the power and the glory, forever. Amen:** Included in W(032) BYZ TR ‖ Absent from ℵ(01) B(03) D(05) NA28 SBLGNT THGNT.

¹⁴"[For]ᵃ If you forgive men their trespasses, your heavenly Father will also forgive you; ¹⁵but if you do not forgive men [their trespasses],ᵇ neither will your Father forgive your trespasses.

¹⁶"But when you fast, do not become [[just]]ᶜ like the hypocrites, with a sad countenance, for they disfigure their faces so that they may appear to men to be fasting. [[For]]ᵈ Truly I say to you [[that]],ᵉ they have their reward." ¹⁷But when you fast, anoint your head and wash your face, ¹⁸so that you may not appear to men as fasting, but to your Father who is in secret; and your Father who sees in secret will reward [you]ᶠ [[in the open]].ᵍ

¹⁹"Do not store up for yourselves treasures on earth, where moth and rust destroy and where thieves break in and steal; ²⁰but store up for yourselves treasures in heaven, where neither moth nor rust destroys and where thieves do not break in [nor steal];ʰ ²¹for where {your}ⁱ treasure is, there your heart will be [also].ʲ

²²"The lamp of the body is {the}ᵏ eye. [Therefore,]ˡ If your eye is clear,ᵐ your whole body will be full of light; ²³but if your eye is evil, your whole body will be full of darkness. If then the light that is in you is darkness, how great is the darkness!

²⁴"No one can serve two masters; for either he will hate the one and love the other, or he will be devoted to one and despise the other. You cannot serve God and wealth.

²⁵"Therefore I say to you, do not worry about your life, what you will eat [or what you will drink],ⁿ nor about your body, what you will wear. Is not life more than food, and the body more than clothing? ²⁶Look at the birds of the sky, that they do not sow, nor reap, nor gather into barns, and your heavenly Father feeds them. Are you not worth more than they?

²⁷"And which of you by worrying can add one cubit to his stature?

²⁸"And why do you worry about clothing? Consider the lilies of the field, how they grow; they neither toil nor spin; ²⁹yet I say to you [that]ᵒ even Solomon in all his glory was not arrayed like one of these [[of the field]].ᵖ

³⁰"Now if God so clothes the grass of the field, which today is, and tomorrow is thrown into the oven, will He not much more clothe you, O you of little faith?

³¹"Therefore do not worry, saying, 'What shall we eat?' Or, 'What shall we drink?' Or, 'What shall we wear?' ³²For all these things the nations seek;

ᵃ 6:14, **For:** Absent from D(05).
ᵇ 6:15, **their trespasses:** B(03) W(032) BYZ TR THGNT ‖ Absent from ℵ(01) D(05) Latin(a h k) NA28 SBLGNT.
ᶜ 6:16, **just:** Included in W(032) BYZ TR.
ᵈ 6:16, **For:** Included in ℵ(01).
ᵉ 6:16, **that:** Included in W(032) BYZ TR.
ᶠ 6:18, **you:** Absent from ℵ(01).
ᵍ 6:18, **in the open:** Included in some manuscripts. W(032) Latin(a b h k) TR ‖ Absent from ℵ(01) B(03) D(05) BYZ NA28 SBLGNT THGNT.
ʰ 6:20, **nor steal:** Absent from W(032) Latin(k).
ⁱ 6:21, **your (singular):** Some manuscripts read "you (plural)." W(032) BYZ TR.
ʲ 6:21, **also:** Absent from B(03).
ᵏ 6:22, **the:** Some manuscripts read "your." B(03) Latin(a b h k).
ˡ 6:22, **Therefore:** Absent from ℵ(01) Latin(a).
ᵐ 6:22, **clear:** Or healthy. The Greek word for *clear* is defined by BDAG as: being motivated by singleness of purpose so as to be open and aboveboard, without guile, sincere, straightforward, i.e. without a hidden agenda. (BDAG, ἁπλοῦς).
ⁿ 6:25, **or what you will drink:** Absent from ℵ(01) Latin(a b k) SBLGNT.
ᵒ 6:29, **that:** Absent from W(032).
ᵖ 6:29, **of the field:** Included in W(032).

for your [heavenly]^a Father knows that you need all these things.

³³"But seek first the kingdom [of God]^b and his righteousness, and all these things shall be added to you.

³⁴"Therefore, do not worry about tomorrow, for tomorrow will worry about itself. Each day has enough trouble of its own."

7 ¹"Do not judge, so that you may not be judged; ²for with the judgment you judge, you will be judged, and with the measure you use, it will be {measured}^c to you.

³"Why do you see the speck in your brother's eye, but do not notice the log in your own eye? ⁴Or how can you say to your brother, 'Let me remove the speck from your eye,' while the log^d is in your own eye? ⁵Hypocrite, first remove the log from your own eye, and then you will see clearly to remove the speck from your brother's eye.

⁶"Do not give what is holy to dogs, nor throw your pearls before swine, lest they trample them under their feet, and turn and tear you.

⁷"Ask and it will be given to you, seek and you will find, knock and it will be opened to you; ⁸for everyone who asks receives, and the one who seeks finds, and to the one who knocks it {will be}^e opened.

⁹"Or which one of you men, [[if]]^f whom his son will ask for bread, will give him a stone? ¹⁰Or [[if]]^g even he will ask for a fish, will give him a serpent?

¹¹"If you, being evil, know how to give good gifts to your children, how much more will your Father who is in the heavens give good things to those who ask him.

¹²"[Therefore,]^h Whatever you want men to do to you, do also to them; for this is the Law and the Prophets.

¹³"Enter through the narrow gate; for wide [is the gate]ⁱ and spacious is the road that leads to destruction, and many are those who enter through it; ¹⁴{how}^j narrow [is the gate]^k and constricted is the road that leads to life, and few are those who find it.

¹⁵"[But]^l Beware of the false prophets, who come to you in sheep's clothing, but inwardly are ravenous wolves. ¹⁶By their fruits you will recognize them. Do people gather grapes from thorns, or figs from thistles?

¹⁷"So every good tree produces [good]^m fruits, but the rottenⁿ tree produces evil fruits. ¹⁸A good tree cannot produce evil fruits, nor can a rotten tree produce good fruits. ¹⁹[[Therefore,]]^o Every tree that does not produce good fruit is cut down and thrown into the fire. ²⁰Therefore, by their fruits you will recognize them.

---

a 6:32, **heavenly:** Absent from ℵ(01) Latin(a b k).
b 6:33, **of God:** Absent from ℵ(01) B(03) Latin(k) SBLGNT.
c 7:2, **measured:** Some manuscripts read "measured back." Latin(h) TR.
d 7:4, **log:** Or beam.
e 7:8, **will be:** B(03) reads "is."
f 7:9, **if:** Included in W(032) Latin(k) BYZ TR.
g 7:10, **if:** Included in W(032) Latin(a b h k) BYZ TR.
h 7:12, **Therefore:** Absent from ℵ(01).
i 7:13, **is the gate:** Absent from ℵ(01) Latin(a b h k).
j 7:14, **how:** C(04) W(032) Latin(a b h k) BYZ NA28 THGNT ‖ Some manuscripts read "for." ℵ(01) B(03) SBLGNT TR.
k 7:14, **is the gate:** Absent from Latin(a h k).
l 7:15, **But:** Included in C(04) W(032) BYZ TR.
m 7:17, **good:** Absent from W(032).
n 7:17, **rotten:** Or bad.
o 7:19, **Therefore:** Included in Latin(h).

21 "Not everyone who says to me, 'Lord, Lord,' will enter into the kingdom of the heavens, but the one who does the will of my Father who is in {the heavens}[a] [[will enter into the kingdom of the heavens]].[b] 22 Many will say to me on that day, 'Lord, Lord, did we not prophesy in your name, and in your name cast out [[many]][c] demons, and in your name perform many miracles?' 23 And then I will confess to them, 'I never knew you; depart from me [[all of you]],[d] you who practice lawlessness.'

24 "Therefore, everyone who hears these words of mine and does them {will be like}[e] a wise man who built his house on the rock; 25 and the rain came down, and the rivers came, and the winds blew and beat against that house, and it did not fall, for it was founded on the rock.

26 "And everyone who hears these words of mine and does not do them will be like a foolish man who built his house on the sand; 27 and the rain came down, and the rivers came, and the winds blew and struck against that house, and it fell, and great was its fall."

28 And it happened when Jesus {finished}[f] these words, the crowds were astonished at his teaching; 29 for he was teaching them as one having authority and not as {their}[g] scribes [[and the Pharisees]].[h]

8 1 And when he came down from the mountain, large crowds followed him. 2 And behold, a leper came up and worshiped[i] him, saying, "Lord, if you are willing, you can make me clean." 3 And stretching out his hand, {he}[j] touched him, saying, "I am willing; be cleansed." And [immediately][k] his leprosy was cleansed. 4 And Jesus said to him, "See that you tell no one; but go, show yourself to the priest and offer {the}[l] gift that Moses commanded, as a testimony to them."

5 When {he}[m] entered Capernaum, a centurion approached him, pleading with him, 6 [and][n] saying, "[Lord,][o] my servant is lying at home paralyzed, terribly tormented." 7 And {he}[p] said to him, "I will come and heal him." 8 {And}[q] the centurion replied, "Lord, I am not worthy for you to come under my roof, but only say the word, [and my servant,][r] he will be healed. 9 For I too am a man [[being appointed]],[s] under authority, having soldiers under me, and I say to this one, 'Go,' and he goes, and to another, 'Come,' and he comes, and to my servant, 'Do this,' and he does it."

---

a 7:21, **the heavens:** Some manuscripts read "heaven." W(032) BYZ TR.

b 7:21, **will enter into the kingdom of the heavens:** Included in W(032) Latin(b h k).

c 7:22, **many:** Included in ℵ(01).

d 7:23, **all of you:** Included in Latin(b).

e 7:24, **will be like:** Some manuscripts read "I will liken him to." C(04) W(032) BYZ TR.

f 7:28, **finished:** Some manuscripts read "ended." BYZ TR.

g 7:29, **their:** Some manuscripts read "the." BYZ TR.

h 7:29, **and the Pharisees:** Included in C(04) W(032) Latin(a b h k).

i 8:2, **worship:** See footnote for worship in Matt 2:2

j 8:3, **he:** Some manuscripts read "Jesus." W(032) Latin(b h) BYZ TR.

k 8:3, **immediately:** Absent from ℵ(01).

l 8:4, **the:** The TR reads "your."

m 8:5, **he:** TR reads "Jesus."

n 8:6, **and:** Absent from B(03) Latin(b h k).

o 8:6, **Lord:** Absent from ℵ(01) Latin(k).

p 8:7, **he:** ℵ(01) B(03) NA28 SBLGNT THGNT ‖ Some manuscripts read "Jesus." C(04) W(032) Latin(a b h) BYZ TR.

q 8:8, **And:** C(04) W(032) BYZ TR NA28 SBLGNT THGNT ‖ Some manuscripts read "But." ℵ(01) B(03).

r 8:8, **and my servant:** Absent from Latin(a k).

s 8:9, **being appointed:** Included in ℵ(01) B(03) Latin(a b h k).

10 When Jesus heard this, he marveled[a] and said to those following him, "Truly, I tell you, {I have not found such great faith in Israel}.[b] 11 And I tell you that many will come from the east and the west and will recline at the table with Abraham, Isaac, and Jacob in the kingdom of the heavens, 12 but the sons of the kingdom[c] will be thrown into the outer darkness; there will be weeping and gnashing of teeth." 13 And Jesus said to the centurion, "Go, as you have believed, let it be done to you." And {the}[d] servant was healed in that hour. [[And the centurion, having returned to his house in that very hour, found the servant restored to health.]][e]

14 And when Jesus came into Peter's house, he saw his mother-in-law lying down and suffering from a fever; 15 and he touched her hand, and the fever left her, and she got up and served {him}.[f]

16 When evening came, they brought to him many who were demon-possessed; and he cast out the [[unclean]][g] spirits with a word, and healed all who were ill, 17 so that what was spoken through the prophet Isaiah might be fulfilled, saying, "He took our weaknesses, and he bore the diseases."[h]

18 And when Jesus saw {a crowd}[i] around him, he ordered to go to the other side. 19 And one scribe came up and said to him, "Teacher, I will follow you wherever you go." 20 And Jesus said to him, "The foxes have dens and the birds of the sky have nests, but the Son of Man has nowhere to lay his head."

21 But another of {the}[j] disciples said to him, "Lord, allow me first to go and bury my father."

22 But {Jesus}[k] {says}[l] to him, "Follow me and let the dead bury their own dead."

23 And when he got into {a}[m] boat, his disciples followed him. 24 And behold, a great earthquake[n] occurred in the sea, so that the boat was being covered by the waves, but he was sleeping. 25 And {they}[o] came and woke him, saying, "Lord, save us, we are perishing." 26 And he said to them, "Why are you afraid, you of little faith?" Then he got up and rebuked the winds and the sea, and there was a great calm.

27 And the men marveled, saying, "What sort of man is this, that [even][p] the winds and the sea obey him?"

---

a 8:10, **marveled:** Or was amazed.

b 8:10, **I have not found such great faith in Israel:** B(03) W(032) Latin(a k) NA28 SBLGNT THGNT ‖ Some manuscripts read "Not even in Israel have I found such great faith." ℵ(01) C(04) Latin(b h) BYZ TR.

c 8:12, **the kingdom:** Or this kingdom. Sons of the kingdom is a Semitic idiom meaning "people (here, the Jewish people) who belong to the kingdom." (UBS Handbooks).

d 8:13, **the:** ℵ(01) B(03) SBLGNT THGNT ‖ Some manuscripts read "his." C(04) W(032) Latin(a b h k) BYZ TR NA28[].

e 8:13, **And the centurion...:** Included in ℵ(01) C(04).

f 8:15, **him:** TR reads "them."

g 8:16, **unclean:** Included in Latin(a b h).

h 8:17, Isaiah 53:4.

i 8:18, **a crowd:** ℵ(01) B(03) NA28 ‖ Some manuscripts read "great crowds." C(04) W(032) Latin(a b h k) BYZ TR SBLGNT THGNT.

j 8:21, **the:** ℵ(01) B(03) Latin(a b h) SBLGNT THGNT ‖ Some manuscripts read "his." C(04) W(032) Latin(k) BYZ TR NA28[].

k 8:22, **Jesus:** Some manuscripts read "he." ℵ(01) Latin(a k).

l 8:22, **says:** ℵ(01) B(03) C(04) NA28 SBLGNT THGNT ‖ Some manuscripts read "said." W(032) BYZ TR.

m 8:23, **a:** B(03) C(04) SBLGNT THGNT ‖ Some manuscripts read "the." ℵ(01) W(032) BYZ TR NA28.

n 8:24, **earthquake:** The Greek word means a violent shaking or commotion, most commonly *earthquake* (BDAG, σεισμός).

o 8:25, **they:** ℵ(01) B(03) ‖ Some manuscripts read "his disciples." C(04) W(032) Latin(b h) BYZ TR.

p 8:27, **even:** Absent from C(04) Latin(a b h).

28 And when he came to the other side, to the country of the {Gadarenes},[a] two demon-possessed men met him, coming out of the tombs, extremely fierce, so that no one could pass by that way. 29 And behold, they cried out, saying, "What have we to do with you, [[Jesus,]][b] Son of God? Have you come here to {torment}[c] us before the time?" 30 Now there was a herd of many pigs feeding at a distance from them. 31 The demons begged him, saying, "If you cast us out, {send us}[d] into the herd of pigs." 32 And {he}[e] said to them, "Go." So they came out and went into the [[heard of]][f] pigs; and behold, the whole herd [[of pigs]][g] rushed down the steep bank into the sea and died in the waters.

33 The herdsmen fled, and going into the city, they reported everything, including what had happened to the demon-possessed men. 34 And behold, the whole city came out to meet Jesus; and when they saw him, they begged him to depart from their region.

9 1 And entering into {a}[h] boat, {he}[i] crossed over and came to his own city. 2 And behold, they brought to him a paralytic lying on a bed. And seeing their faith, Jesus said to the paralytic, "Take courage, child, your sins {are forgiven}."[j]

3 And behold, some of the scribes said to themselves, "This one blasphemes." 4 And {seeing}[k] their thoughts, Jesus said [[to them]],[l] "Why do you think evil in your hearts? 5 [For][m] Which is easier, to say, 'Your sins are forgiven,' or to say, 'Rise and walk'? 6 But so that you may know that the Son of Man has authority on earth to forgive sins" – then he says to the paralytic, "Rise, [[and]][n] take up your bed and go to your house." 7 And rising, he went to his house.

8 But when the crowds saw this, they {were filled with awe}[o] and glorified the God who had given such authority to men.

9 And as Jesus passed on [from there],[p] he saw a man sitting at the tax booth, called Matthew, and said to him, "Follow me." And rising up, he followed him. 10 And [it happened][q] as he reclined at the table in the house, [and][r] behold, many tax collectors and sinners [came and][s] were reclining with Jesus and his disciples. 11 And the Pharisees, having seen this, said to his disciples, "Why does your teacher eat with tax collectors and sinners?"

---

a 8:28, **Gadarenes:** Some manuscripts read "Gergesenes." W(032) BYZ TR.

b 8:29, **Jesus:** Included in W(032) Latin(a b h) BYZ TR ‖ Absent from ℵ(01) B(03) C(04) Latin(k) NA28 SBLGNT THGNT.

c 8:29, **torment:** ℵ(01) reads "destroy."

d 8:31, **send us:** Some manuscripts read "allow us." C(04) W(032) Latin(h) BYZ TR.

e 8:32, **he:** C(04) reads "Jesus."

f 8:32, **heard of:** Included in W(032) Latin(h) BYZ TR.

g 8:32, **of pigs:** Included in TR.

h 9:1, **a:** Some manuscripts read "the." C(04) W(032) BYZ TR.

i 9:1, **he:** Some manuscripts read "Jesus." C(04).

j 9:2, **are forgiven:** Some manuscripts read "have been forgiven you." BYZ TR.

k 9:4, **seeing:** ℵ(01) C(04) D(05) W(032) NA28 BYZ TR ‖ Some manuscripts read "knowing." B(03) SBLGNT THGNT.

l 9:4, **to them:** Included in D(05) Latin(h).

m 9:5, **For:** Absent from Latin(a b).

n 9:6, **and:** Included in D(05) Latin(a h k).

o 9:8, **were filled with awe:** Some manuscripts read "were astonished." C(04) BYZ TR.

p 9:9, **from there:** Absent from ℵ(01).

q 9:10, **it happened:** Absent from ℵ(01).

r 9:10, **and:** Absent from ℵ(01) D(05) Latin(a b).

s 9:10, **came and:** Absent from ℵ(01) Latin(a).

12 But {he},[a] having heard, said [[to them]],[b] "Those who are strong have no need of a physician, but those who are ill. 13 Go and learn what this means: 'I desire mercy and not sacrifice.'[c] For I did not come to call the righteous, but sinners [[to repentance]]."[d]

14 Then the disciples of John came to him, saying, "Why do we and the Pharisees fast [often],[e] but your disciples do not fast?"

15 And Jesus said to them, "Can the sons of the bridechamber mourn as long as the bridegroom is with them? [But the days will come when the bridegroom will be taken away from them,][f] And then they will fast [[in those days]].[g]

16 "No one puts a patch of unshrunk cloth on an old garment; for the patch pulls away [from the garment],[h] and a worse tear occurs. 17 Nor do they put new wine into old wineskins; otherwise, the {wineskins burst},[i] the wine is {spilled, and the wineskins are ruined}.[j] But they put new wine into new wineskins, and both are preserved."

18 While he was saying these things to them, behold, a ruler [came and][k] worshiped[l] him, saying [that],[m] "My daughter has just died; but come and lay your hand on her, and she will live." 19 And Jesus got up and followed him, and so did his disciples.

20 [n]And behold, a woman who had been bleeding for twelve years came up from behind and touched the fringe[o] of his garment; 21 for she said to herself, "If [only][p] I touch his garment, I will be saved."

22 But {Jesus}[q] {having turned}[r] and saw her, and said, "Take courage, daughter; your faith has saved you." And the woman was saved from that hour.

23 And when Jesus came to the ruler's house and saw the flute players and the noisy crowd, 24 {he said},[s] "Go away, for the girl has not died, but is sleeping." And they laughed at him [[knowing that she had died]].[t] 25 But when the crowd had been put out, he went in and took her by the hand, and the girl arose. 26 And this report went out into all that land.

---

[a] 9:12, **he:** ℵ(01) B(03) D(05) ‖ Some manuscripts read "Jesus." C(04) W(032) Latin(a b h k) BYZ TR.

[b] 9:12, **to them:** Included in W(032) Latin(a h) BYZ TR.

[c] 9:13, Hosea 6:6 LXX.

[d] 9:13, **to repentance:** Included in BYZ TR.

[e] 9:14, **often:** Absent from ℵ(01) B(03).

[f] 9:15, **But the days will come…:** Absent from ℵ(01).

[g] 9:15, **in those days:** Included in D(05) Latin(a b h).

[h] 9:16, **from the garment:** Absent from Latin(a).

[i] 9:17, **wineskins burst:** Some manuscripts read "new wine bursts the wineskins." D(05) Latin(k).

[j] 9:17, **spilled, and the wineskins are ruined:** Some manuscripts read "wine is lost, and the wineskins as well." D(05) Latin(k).

[k] 9:18, **came and:** D(05) W(032) NA28 SBLGNT THGNT ‖ Some manuscripts read "approached and." ℵ(01) B(03) Latin(a b).

[l] 9:18, **worship:** See footnote for worship in Matt 2:2

[m] 9:18, **that:** Absent from ℵ(01) D(05).

[n] 9:20, **garment:** Or cloak.

[o] 9:20, **fringe:** Or hem.

[p] 9:21, **only:** Absent from ℵ(01) Latin(a h).

[q] 9:22, **Jesus:** Some manuscripts read "he." ℵ(01) D(05) Latin(a b k).

[r] 9:22, **having turned:** ℵ(01) B(03) NA28 SBLGNT THGNT ‖ Some manuscripts read "having turned back." C(04) W(032) BYZ TR.

[s] 9:24, **he said:** ℵ(01) B(03) D(05) Latin(a b h k) NA28 SBLGNT THGNT ‖ Some manuscripts read "he says to them." C(04) W(032) BYZ TR.

[t] 9:24, **knowing that she had died:** Included in ℵ(01).

27 And as Jesus passed on from there, two blind men followed [him],[a] crying out [and saying],[b] "Have mercy on us, [[Jesus]][c] Son of David." 28 {But}[d] when he had come into the house, the [[two]][e] blind men came to him, and Jesus said to them, "Do you believe that I am able to do this?" They said to him, "Yes, Lord." 29 Then he touched their eyes, saying, "According to your faith let it be done to you." 30 And their eyes were opened. And Jesus sternly warned them, saying, "See that no one knows about this." 31 But they went out and spread the news about him throughout that [whole][f] land.

32 As they were going out, behold, they brought to him [a man][g] who was mute and demon-possessed. 33 And when the demon had been cast out, the mute man spoke. And the crowds marveled, saying [[that]],[h] "Never has it been seen like this in Israel." 34 [But the Pharisees said, "By the ruler of the demons he casts out the demons."][i]

35 And Jesus went about all the cities and villages, teaching in their synagogues [and][j] proclaiming the good news of the kingdom and healing every disease and every sickness [[among the people]][k] [[and many were following him]].[l]

36 Seeing the crowds, {he}[m] had compassion for them because they were harassed and helpless,[n] like sheep not having a shepherd.

37 Then he said to his disciples, "The harvest is plentiful, but the workers are few; 38 therefore, ask the Lord of the harvest to send out workers into his harvest."

10 1 And calling to him his twelve disciples, he gave them authority over unclean spirits, so as to cast them out and to heal every disease and every infirmity.

2 The names of the twelve apostles are these: first, Simon who is called Peter, and Andrew his brother; and James the son of Zebedee, and John his brother; 3 Philip and Bartholomew, [Thomas and Matthew the tax collector,][o] James the son of Alphaeus, and [[Lebbaeus, who was called]] Thaddaeus;[p] 4 Simon the {Cananaean},[q] and Judas Iscariot, who [also][r] betrayed him.

5 Jesus sent out these twelve, instructing them, [saying,][s] "Do not go on the road to the Gentiles, and do not enter a city of the Samaritans; 6 [but][t] rather go to the lost sheep of the house of Israel.

---

a 9:27, **him:** Absent from B(03) D(05).

b 9:27, **and saying:** Absent from C(04) Latin(a k).

c 9:27, **Jesus:** Included in C(04).

d 9:28, **But:** Some manuscripts read "And." D(05) Latin(a b h k).

e 9:28, **two:** Included in ℵ(01) D(05) Latin(a b h).

f 9:31, **whole:** Absent from ℵ(01).

g 9:32, **a man:** Absent from ℵ(01) B(03).

h 9:33, **that:** Included in TR.

i 9:34, Verse 34 is absent D(05) and Syriac manuscripts.

j 9:35, **and:** Absent from ℵ(01).

k 9:35, **among the people:** Included in ℵ(01) Latin(a b h) BYZ TR.

l 9:35, **and many were following him:** Included in ℵ(01) Latin (a b h).

m 9:36, **he:** Some manuscripts read "Jesus." C(04).

n 9:36, **helpless:** Or scattered.

o 10:3, **Thomas and Matthew the tax collector:** Absent from Latin(a b).

p 10:3, **Lebbaeus, who was called:** Included in W(032) BYZ TR ‖ Absent from ℵ(01) B(03) NA28 SBLGNT THGNT.

q 10:4, **Cananaean:** Meaning Zealot. B(03) C(04) NA28 SBLGNT THGNT Some manuscripts read "Canaanite." ℵ(01) W(032) BYZ TR.

r 10:4, **also:** Absent from Latin(b e h k).

s 10:5, **saying:** Absent from ℵ(01).

t 10:6, **but:** Absent from D(05).

7 "As you go, proclaim this message [that],[a] 'The kingdom of the heavens has come near.' 8 Heal the sick, [raise the dead],[b] cleanse the lepers, cast out demons; freely you have received, freely give.

9 "Do not acquire gold, [or silver,][c] or copper for your belts, 10 nor a bag for the journey, nor two tunics, nor sandals, nor {a staff};[d] for the worker is worthy of his {food}.[e]

11 "And into whatever city [or village][f] you enter, inquire who in it is worthy; and stay there until you leave.

12 "As you enter the house, greet it [[saying Peace to this house!]];[g] 13 [and][h] if the house is worthy, let your peace come upon it, but if it is not worthy, let your peace return to you.

14 "And whoever does not receive you, nor listen to your words, as you go out of [that house or][i] city, shake off the dust from your feet.

15 "Truly, I say to you, it will be more bearable for the land of Sodom and [[land of]][j] Gomorrah in the day of judgment than for that city.

16 "Behold, I am sending you out as sheep in the midst of wolves; therefore, be wise as serpents and innocent as doves.

17 "But beware of men; for they will deliver you over to councils and in {their}[k] synagogues they will flog you; 18 and you will be brought before governors [and also kings][l] for my sake, as a testimony to them and to the nations.

19 "But when they deliver you up, do not be anxious about how or what you should speak; for it will be given to you in that hour what you should speak; 20 for it is not you who speak, but the Spirit of your Father speaks in you.

21 "And brother will deliver up brother to death, and a father his child; and children will rise up against parents and put them to death. 22 And you will be hated by all because of my name; but the one who endures to the end, [this one][m] will be saved.

23 "But when they persecute you in this city, flee to {the other},[n] [[and if they persecute you in the other, flee to another;]][o] [for][p] truly I say to you, you will not finish the cities of Israel until the Son of Man comes.

24 "A disciple is not above {the}[q] teacher, nor a servant above his master. 25 It is enough for the disciple to become like the teacher, and the servant like the master. If they have called the head of the house {Beelzebul},[r] how much more the members of the household!

---

a 10:7, **that:** Absent from B(03).

b 10:8, **raise the dead:** Absent from W(032) BYZ.

c 10:9, **or silver:** Absent from ℵ(01).

d 10:10, **a staff:** Some manuscripts read "staffs." C(04) W(032) Latin(a k) BYZ TR ‖ Some manuscripts read "a staff in your hands." Latin(b h).

e 10:10, **food:** Some manuscripts read "wage." Latin(a b h).

f 10:11, **or village:** Absent from Latin(a b h k).

g 10:12, **saying Peace to this house!:** Included in ℵ(01) D(05) W(032) Latin(a b h).

h 10:13, **and:** Absent from D(05).

i 10:14, **that house or:** Absent from D(05) Latin(a e h k).

j 10:15, **land of:** Included in ℵ(01) C(04).

k 10:17, **their:** Some manuscripts read "the." D(05).

l 10:18, **and also kings:** Absent from D(05) Latin(a b e h k).

m 10:22, **this one:** Absent from W(032).

n 10:23, **the other:** ℵ(01) B(03) W(032) NA28 SBLGNT THGNT ‖ Some manuscripts read "another." C(04) D(05) BYZ TR.

o 10:23, **and if they persecute you in the other, flee to another:** Included in D(05) Latin(a b e h k).

p 10:23, **for:** Absent from D(05) Latin(a b h).

q 10:24, **the:** Some manuscripts read "his." ℵ(01) W(032).

r 10:25, **Beelzebul:** Or "Beelzebub."

26 "So do not fear them; for there is nothing concealed that will not be revealed, and hidden that will not be known. 27 What I say to you in the darkness, speak in the light; and what you hear in the ear, proclaim on the rooftops.

28 "And do not fear those who kill the body but cannot kill the soul; rather fear the one who can destroy both [[the]]ᵃ soul and [[the]] body in Gehenna.ᵇ

29 "Are not two sparrows sold for a penny? And not one of them will fall to the ground apart from your Father. 30 But even the hairs of your head are all numbered. 31 So do not fear [[them]];ᶜ you are worth more than many sparrows.

32 "Therefore, everyone who acknowledgesᵈ me before men, I will also acknowledge him before my Father who is in heaven; 33 but whoever denies me before men, I will also deny them before my Father who is in [the] heavens.

34 "[[Therefore]]ᵉ Do not think that I came to bring peace on the earth; I did not come to bring peace, but a sword. 35 For I came to divide a {man}ᶠ against their father, and daughter against her mother, and a bride against her mother-in-law, 36 And the enemies of the person will be the members of their household.

37 "The one who loves father or mother more than me is not worthy of me, and the one who loves son or daughter more than me is not worthy of me; 38 and whoever does not take up his cross and follow after me is not worthy of me.

39 ["The one who finds their life will lose it, and the one who loses their life for my sake will find it.]ᵍ

40 "The one who receives you receives me, and the one who receives me receives the one who sent me.

41 "The one who receives a prophet in the name of a prophet will receive a prophet's reward, and the one who receives a righteous person in the name of a righteous person will receive a righteous person's reward. 42 And {whoever}ʰ gives one of these little ones a cup of cold water [only],ⁱ in the name of a disciple, truly I say to you, he will not lose his reward."

11 ¹ And it happened when Jesus finished giving instructions to his twelve disciples, he went from there to teach and preach in their cities.

2 Now when John heard in the prison the works of {Christ},ʲ he sent {by}ᵏ his disciples 3 and said to him, "Are you the one who is to come, or should we expect someone else?"

4 And Jesus answered and said to them, "Go and report to John what you hear and see: 5 the blind receive their sight, and [the lame walk,]ˡ lepers are cleansed, and the deaf hear, [and]ᵐ the dead are raised up, and the poor have good news preached to them.

ᵃ 10:28, **the:** Some manuscripts include in two places. BYZ.

ᵇ 10:28, **Gehenna:** "Gehenna," often translated "hell," was the name of a valley southwest of Jerusalem, where human sacrifices had once been offered and where garbage from the city was constantly burning. Later this picture was combined with the idea of God's judgment, and so the notion of a fiery hell developed. (UBS Handbooks).

ᶜ 10:31, **them:** Included in W(032).

ᵈ 10:32, **acknowledges:** Or "confess in."

ᵉ 10:34, **Therefore:** Absent from 𝔓19.

ᶠ 10:35, **man:** Some manuscripts read "son." D(05) Latin(a b h).

ᵍ 10:39, **The one who finds their life...:** Absent from ℵ(01).

ʰ 10:42, **whoever:** Some manuscripts read "if anyone." BYZ TR.

ⁱ 10:42, **only:** Absent from D(05).

ʲ 11:2, **Christ:** Some manuscripts read "Jesus." D(05).

ᵏ 11:2, **by:** Some manuscripts read "two of." BYZ TR.

ˡ 11:5, **the lame walk:** Absent from D(05).

ᵐ 11:5, **and:** Absent from C(04) Latin(h) TR.

6 And blessed is the one who is not
offended by me."

7 As these went away, Jesus
began to speak to the crowds about
John, "What did you go out into the
wilderness to see? A reed shaken by the
wind? 8 But what did you go out to see?
A man dressed in soft [[garments]]?[a]
Behold, those who wear soft clothing
are in the houses of kings. 9 But what
did you go out to see? A prophet? Yes, I
tell you, and more than a prophet.

10 "[[For]][b] This is about whom it
is written, 'Behold, I am sending my
messenger before your face, Who will
prepare the way before you.'[c]

11 "Truly I say to you, among those
born of women there has not arisen
anyone greater than John the Baptist;
yet the one who is least in the kingdom
of the heavens is greater than he.

12 "[But][d] From the days of John
the Baptist until now, the kingdom of
heaven has been forcefully advancing,[e]
and forceful men seize it. 13 For all
the prophets and the law prophesied
until John; 14 and if you are willing
to accept it, he is Elijah who is to
come.[f] 15 He who has ears [to hear],[g] let
him hear.

16 "But to what shall I compare this
generation? It is like children sitting
in the marketplaces {who call out}[h]
to [[their]][i] others, 17 [[and]][j] saying,
'We played the flute for you, and you
did not dance; we mourned [for you],[k]
and you did not lament.' 18 For John
came neither eating nor drinking, and
they say, 'He has a demon.' 19 The Son
of Man came eating and drinking,
and they say, 'Look, a glutton and a
drunkard, [a friend of tax collectors][l]
and sinners!' And wisdom is justified by
[[all]][m] [her {works}[n]]."[o]

20 Then {he}[p] began to denounce
the cities in which most of {his}[q]
mighty works had been done, because
they did not repent: 21 "Woe to you,
Chorazin! [[Woe to you,]][r] Bethsaida!
For if the miracles that were done in
you had been done in Tyre and Sidon,
they would have repented long ago
in sackcloth and [[sitting]][s] in ashes.
22 But I say to you, it will be more
bearable for Tyre and Sidon on the day
of judgment than for you.

---

a 11:8, **garments:** Included in C(04) W(032) Latin(b h) BYZ TR.
b 11:10, **For:** Included in C(04) W(032) Latin(h) BYZ TR.
c 11:10, Malachi 3:1 Masoretic text.
d 11:12, **But:** Absent from D(05).
e 11:12, **forcefully advancing:** Or "suffering violence." The verb is ambiguous so it could be passive or active.
f 11:14, Malachi 4:5.
g 11:15, **to hear:** Some Manuscripts include. ℵ(01) C(04) W(032) Latin(a b e h) BYZ TR THGNT || Absent from B(03) D(05) Latin(k) NA28 SBLGNT.
h 11:16, **who call out:** ℵ(01) B(03) D(05) NA28 SBLGNT THGNT || Some manuscripts read "and speaking to." C(04) W(032) BYZ TR.
i 11:16, **their:** Included in C(04) W(032) Latin(e ff² k) BYZ TR.
j 11:17, **and:** Included in C(04) W(032) BYZ TR.
k 11:17, **for you:** Included in C(04) W(032) Latin(a b e ff² h) BYZ TR || Absent from ℵ(01) B(03) D(05) Latin(k) NA28 SBLGNT THGNT.
l 11:19, **a friend of tax collectors:** Absent from Latin(a b).
m 11:19, **all:** Included in Latin(k).
n 11:19, **works:** ℵ(01) B(03) W(032) NA28 SBLGNT THGNT || Some manuscripts read "children." C(04) D(05) BYZ TR || Wisdom is often rendered with the pronoun "her."
o 11:19, **her works:** Absent from Latin(b).
p 11:20, **he:** Some manuscripts read "Jesus." C(04) W(032) Latin(h).
q 11:20, **his:** D(05) reads "the."
r 11:21, **Woe to you:** Absent from some manuscripts which read "and." D(05) Latin(a b ff² h).
s 11:21, **sitting:** Included in ℵ(01) C(04).

23 "And you, Capernaum, will you be exalted to heaven? You will {descend}ᵃ to Hades; for if the mighty works done in you had been done in Sodom, {it}ᵇ would have remained until this day. 24 But I say to you [that]ᶜ it will be more bearable for the land of Sodom on the day of judgment than for you."

25 At that time, Jesus answered and said, "I thank you, Father, Lord of heaven and earth because you have hidden these things from the wise and understanding and revealed them to infants; 26 Yes, Father, for such was your gracious will.

27 "All things have been handed over [to me]ᵈ by my Father, and no one knows the Son except the Father, nor does anyone know the Father except the Son and to whom the Son chooses to reveal him.

28 "Come to me, all you who labor and are burdened, and I will give you rest.

29 "Take my yoke upon you and learn [from me],ᵉ for I am gentle and humble in heart, and you will find rest for your souls; 30 For my yoke is easy and my burden is light."

12 1 At that time, Jesus went on the Sabbath through the grainfields; and his disciples were hungry and began to pluck heads of grain and to eat. 2 But when the Pharisees saw {them},ᶠ they said to him, "Look, your disciples are doing what is not lawful to do [on the Sabbath]."ᵍ

3 He said to them, "Have you not read what David did when he was hungry, [[he]]ʰ and those with him, 4 How did he enter into the house of God and eat the bread of the Presence, which it was not lawful for him to eat, nor for those who were with him, but only for the priests alone?

5 "Or have you not read in the law that on the Sabbath the priests in the temple profane the Sabbath and are guiltless? 6 {But}ⁱ I tell you that something greater than the temple is here.

7 "And if you had known what this means, 'I desire mercy, and not sacrifice,'ʲ you would not have condemned the guiltless. 8 For the Son of Man is lord [[even of]]ᵏ of the Sabbath."

9 And moving on from there, {he}ˡ came into their synagogue; 10 and behold, [[there was]]ᵐ a man with a withered hand. And they questioned him, saying, "Is it lawful to heal on the Sabbath?" - so that they might accuse him.

11 But he said to them, "Which of you [men],ⁿ having one sheep, and if [it]ᵒ falls into a pit on the Sabbath, will not take hold [of it]ᵖ and lift it out? 12 How much more valuable is a man than a sheep! Therefore, it is lawful to do good on the Sabbath."

ᵃ 11:23, **descend:** B(03) D(05) W(032) NA28 SBLGNT ‖ Some manuscripts read "be brought down." ℵ(01) C(04) THGNT BYZ TR.
ᵇ 11:23, **it:** Some manuscripts read "they." BYZ TR.
ᶜ 11:24, **that:** Absent from ℵ(01).
ᵈ 11:27, **to me:** Absent from ℵ(01).
ᵉ 11:29, **from me:** Absent from ℵ(01).
ᶠ 12:2, **them:** Included in C(04) D(05) Latin(a b h).
ᵍ 12:2, **on the Sabbath:** Absent from Latin(k).
ʰ 12:3, **he:** Included in Latin(b h) BYZ TR.
ⁱ 12:6, **But:** Some manuscripts read "For." D(05) Latin(k).
ʲ 12:7, Hosea 6:6 LXX.
ᵏ 12:8, **even of:** Included in TR.
ˡ 12:9, **he:** Some manuscripts read "Jesus." C(04) Luke(h).
ᵐ 12:10, **there was:** Included in D(05) Latin(a b ff²) BYZ TR.
ⁿ 12:11, **men:** Absent from Latin(a b).
ᵒ 12:11, **it:** Absent from D(05) Latin(b).
ᵖ 12:11, **of it:** Absent from ℵ(01) Latin(ff² h).

13 Then he said to the man, "Stretch out your hand." And he stretched it out, and it was restored, healthy [like the other].ᵃ

14 But the Pharisees [went out and]ᵇ took counsel against him, as to how they might destroy him.

15 But Jesus, knowing this, withdrew from there. And many [crowds]ᶜ followed him, and he healed them all, 16 [[And he healed all their ears,]]ᵈ and he admonished them not to make him known, 17 so that what was spoken through the prophet Isaiah might be fulfilled, saying, 18 "Behold, my servant whom I have chosen, My beloved, in whom my soul is well pleased; I will put my Spirit upon it, And judgment to the nationsᵉ he will proclaim. 19 He will not quarrel nor cry out. No one will hear its voice in the streets. 20 [A bruised reed]ᶠ He will not break, and a smoldering wick he will not extinguish, until he brings forth judgment to victory. 21 And in his name, nationsᵍ will hope."ʰ

22 Then a demon-possessed man who was [blind and]ⁱ mute was brought to him, and he healed him, so that the [[blind and]]ʲ [mute]ᵏ man [[both]]ˡ spoke and saw. 23 And all the crowds were amazed and said, "Could this be the son of David?"ᵐ

24 But when the Pharisees heard it, they said, "This one does not cast out demons except by {Beelzebul},ⁿ the ruler of the demons."

25 [[Jesus]]ᵒ Knowing their thoughts, he said to them, "Every kingdom divided against itself is laid waste, and every city or house divided against itself will not stand. 26 And if Satan casts out Satan, he is divided against himself; how then will his kingdom stand? 27 And if I cast out demons by Beelzebul, by whom do your sons cast them out? Therefore, they will be your judges. 28 But if I cast out demons by the Spirit of God, then the kingdom of God has come upon you.

29 "Or how can someone enter into the house of the strong man and plunder his goods, unless he first binds the strong man? And then he will plunder his house.

30 "He who is not with me is against me, and he who does not gather with me scatters.

ᵃ 12:13, **like the other:** Absent from ℵ(01).

ᵇ 12:14, **went out and:** Absent from W(032).

ᶜ 12:15, **crowds:** C(04) D(05) W(032) BYZ TR NA28[] THGNT ‖ Absent from ℵ(01) B(03) Latin(a b k) SBLGNT.

ᵈ 12:16, **And he healed all their ears:** Included in D(05) W(032) Latin(a b ff2 k).

ᵉ 12:18, **nations:** Or Gentiles.

ᶠ 12:20, **A bruised reed:** Absent from D(05).

ᵍ 12:21, **nations:** Or Gentiles.

ʰ 12:21, Isaiah 42:1-4 LXX.

ⁱ 12:22, **blind and:** Absent from C(04).

ʲ 12:22, **blind and:** Included in C(04) W(032) BYZ TR.

ᵏ 12:22, **mute:** Absent from Latin(a b ff2 h).

ˡ 12:22, **both:** Included in C(04) BYZ TR.

ᵐ 12:23, The Greek indicates that the question is not open-ended implying speculation rather than doubt.

ⁿ 12:24, **Beelzebul:** Or "Beelzebub."

ᵒ 12:25, **Jesus:** ℵ(01) B(03) NA28 SBLGNT THGNT ‖ Included in C(04) W(032) Latin(a b ff2 h) BYZ TR.

31 "Therefore I say to you, every sin and blasphemy will be forgiven men [, but the blasphemy against the Spirit will not be forgiven [[to you]][a] [[men]][b].[c] 32 And whoever speaks a word against the Son of Man, it will be forgiven him; but whoever speaks against the Holy Spirit,[d] it will not be forgiven him, neither in this [[present]][e] age nor in the one to come.

33 "Either make the tree good and its fruit good, or make the tree rotten[f] and its fruit rotten; for from the fruit the tree is known.

34 "Offspring of vipers! How can you speak good things, being evil? For out of the abundance of the heart, the mouth speaks.

35 "The good person out of the good treasure [[of his heart]][g] brings forth good, and the evil person out of the evil treasure brings forth evil.

36 "I tell you that for every idle word that people [[may]][h] speak, they will give an account of it on the day of judgment; 37 for by your words you will be justified, {and}[i] by your words you will be condemned."

38 Then some of the scribes [and Pharisees][j] answered [him],[k] saying, "Teacher, we want to see a sign from you."

39 But he answered them, "An evil and adulterous generation seeks a sign, and no sign will be given to it except the sign of Jonah the prophet. 40 For just as Jonah was in the belly of the great fish for three days and three nights, so [[also]][l] will the Son of Man be in the heart of the earth for three days and three nights.[m]

41 "Men of Nineveh will rise up in the judgment with this generation and condemn it, for they repented at the preaching of Jonah, and behold, something greater than Jonah is here.

42 "The queen of the South will rise up[n] at the judgment with this generation and will condemn it, for she came from the ends of the earth to hear the wisdom of Solomon, and behold, something greater than Solomon is here.

43 "When the unclean spirit goes out from a person, it passes through waterless places seeking rest and does not find it. 44 Then it says, I will return to my house from which I came, and when it comes, it finds {it}[o] empty, swept, and put in order. 45 Then it goes and takes with it seven other spirits more evil than itself, and they enter and dwell there; and the last state of that person becomes worse than the first. So it will be also with this evil generation."

46 [[But]][p] While he was still speaking to the crowds, behold, his mother and his brothers were standing outside [, seeking to speak to him].[q] 47 [Someone said to him, "Behold, your mother and your brothers are standing

---

a 12:31, **to you:** Included in B(03).

b 12:31, **men:** Absent from C(04) D(05) W(032) Latin(ff[2]) BYZ TR.

c 12:31, **but the blasphemy…:** Absent from Latin(a).

d 12:32, **Spirit:** See footnote for Spirit in Matt 1:18.

e 12:32, **present:** Some manuscripts include. BYZ.

f 12:33, **rotten:** Or bad.

g 12:35, **of his heart:** Included in TR.

h 12:36, **may:** Included in C(04) W(032) BYZ TR.

i 12:37, **and:** Some manuscripts read "or." D(05) Latin(a).

j 12:38, **and Pharisees:** Absent from B(03).

k 12:38, **him:** Absent from W(032) BYZ TR.

l 12:40, **also:** Included in D(05) W(032) Latin(a b ff[2] h k).

m 12:40, Jonah 1:17.

n 12:42, **rise up:** Or be raised.

o 12:44, **it:** D(05) reads "the house."

p 12:46, **But:** Included in C(04) D(05) W(032) BYZ TR SBLGNT.

q 12:46, **seeking to speak to him:** Absent from ℵ(01).

outside, seeking to speak with you."][a]
48 But he, having responded, said [to
the one speaking to him],[b] "Who is
my mother, {and}[c] [who are][d] [my][e]
brothers?" 49 And stretching out his
hand toward his disciples, he said,
"Behold, my mother and my brothers!
50 For whoever does the will of my
Father who is in the heavens, he is my
brother and sister and mother."

13 1 [[But]][f] In that day, Jesus
went [out of the house][g] and sat
by the sea. 2 And large crowds gathered
to him, so that he got into a boat and
sat down, and all the crowd stood on
the shore.

3 And he spoke to them many things
in parables, saying, "Behold, the sower
went out to sow [[his seed]].[h] 4 [And as
he was sowing,][i] Some seeds fell by the
road, and the birds came and ate them
up. 5 Other seeds fell on rocky ground,
where they did not have much soil, and
they sprang up quickly because they
had no depth of soil. 6 But when the sun
rose, they were scorched, and because
they had no root, they withered away.
7 Other seeds fell among thorns, and
the thorns grew up and choked them.
8 Other seeds fell on good soil and
produced fruit, some a hundredfold,
some sixty, some thirty. 9 He who has
ears [[to hear]],[j] let him hear."

10 And {the}[k] disciples approached
[[him]][l] and said to him, "Why do
you speak to them in parables?"
11 But in response, he said [to them],[m]
"Because it has been given to you to
know the mysteries of the kingdom [of
the heavens],[n] but to them it has not
been given. 12 For whoever has, to him
more will be given, and he will have
abundance; but whoever does not have,
even what he has will be taken away
from him.

13 "Therefore I speak to them in
parables, because seeing they do not
see, and hearing {they do not hear, nor
do they understand}.[o] 14 And [[then]][p]
the prophecy of Isaiah is fulfilled [in
them],[q] saying, '[[Go and say to this
people,]][r] You will hear with your ears
and will not understand, and seeing you
will see and will not perceive. 15 For the
heart of this people has become dull,
and with their ears they hear with
difficulty, and their eyes were blinded,
lest they should see with their eyes and
[hear][s] with their ears and understand
with their heart and turn, and I would
heal them.'[t]

16 "But blessed are your eyes
because they see, and your ears because
they hear.

---

a 12:47, **Someone said to him...:** Verse 47 is absent from some manuscripts. ℵ(01) B(03) Latin(k) Syriac(sy^s sy^c).
b 12:48, **to the one speaking to him:** Absent from W(032).
c 12:48, **and:** Some manuscripts read "or." D(05) W(032) Latin(a ff^2 h k).
d 12:48, **who are:** Absent from W(032).
e 12:48, **my:** Absent from B(03).
f 13:1, **But:** Included in C(04) D(05) W(032) BYZ TR.
g 13:1, **out of the house:** Absent from D(05) Latin(a b ff^2 k).
h 13:3, **his seed:** Included in Latin(b h).
i 13:4, **And as he was sowing:** Absent from C(04).
j 13:9, **to hear:** Included in C(04) D(05) W(032) Latin(b ff^2 h) BYZ TR.
k 13:10, **the:** Some manuscripts read "his." C(04) Latin(a b e h k).
l 13:10, **him:** Included in C(04).
m 13:11, **to them:** Absent from ℵ(01) C(04) Latin(k).
n 13:11, **of the heavens:** Absent from Latin(a b ff^2).
o 13:13, **they do not hear, nor do they understand:** Some manuscripts read "Lest they hear and understand and perhaps turn back." D(05) Latin(a b e ff^2 h k).
p 13:14, **then:** Included in D(05) Latin(h k).
q 13:14, **in them:** Absent from Latin(a).
r 13:14, **Go and say to this people:** Included in D(05) Latin(a b e ff^2 h k).
s 13:15, **hear:** Absent from C(04).
t 13:14-15, Isaiah 6:9-10 LXX.

17 "[For]^a Truly, I say to you, many prophets [and righteous ones]^b desired to see what you see and {did not}^c see, and to hear what you hear and did not hear.

18 "Therefore, hear the parable of the sower. 19 When anyone hears the word of the kingdom and does not understand, the evil one comes and snatches what has been sown in his heart; this is the one sown along the path. 20 The one sown on rocky ground, this is the one who hears {the}^d word and immediately takes and receives it [[and]]^e with joy, 21 yet has no root in themselves but is temporary; when tribulation or persecution comes because of the word, they immediately fall away.^f 22 But the one sown among the thorns, this is the one who hears {the}^g word, and the worry of {the}^h age and the deceit of wealth choke the word, and it becomes unfruitful. 23 But the one sown on the good ground, this is the one who hears {the}^i word and understands it, who indeed bears fruit and produces, some a hundredfold, some sixty, and some thirty. [[He who has ears to hear, let him hear.]]"^j

24 He put before them another parable, saying, "The kingdom of the heavens is like a man who sowed good seed in his field. 25 But while the men were sleeping, his enemy came and sowed weeds among the wheat and went away. 26 When the wheat sprouted and produced grain, then the weeds also appeared. 27 The servants of the master of {the}^k house came and said to him, 'Sir, did you not sow good seed in your field? Where then did the weeds come from?' 28 He said to them, 'An enemy has done this.' The servants said to him, 'Do you want us to [then]^l go and gather them?' 29 [But]^m He said [[to them]],^n 'No, lest in gathering the weeds you uproot [the wheat along with them].^o 30 Allow both to grow together until the harvest, and at the time of the harvest I will tell the reapers, First gather the weeds and bind [them]^p in bundles to burn [them],^q but gather the wheat into my barn.'"

31 He put before them another parable, saying, "The kingdom of the heavens is like a mustard seed, which a man took and sowed in his field; 32 which indeed is smaller than all the seeds, but when it has grown, it is larger than [[all]]^r the garden plants and becomes a tree, so that the birds of the sky come and nest in its branches."

33 [He spoke to them]^s Another parable: "The kingdom of the heavens is like leaven, which a woman took and hid in three measures of flour until it was all leavened."

34 Jesus spoke all these things in parables to the crowds, and without a parable, he spoke nothing to them, 35 so that what was spoken through the prophet might be fulfilled, saying, "I

---

a 13:17, **for:** Absent from ℵ(01) Latin(a b h).

b 13:17, **and righteous ones:** Absent from ℵ(01).

c 13:17, **did not:** Some manuscripts read "were not able." D(05).

d 13:20, **the:** Some manuscripts read "my." W(032).

e 13:20, **and:** Included in W(032).

f 13:21, **fall away:** Or stumble.

g 13:22, **the:** W(032) reads "my."

h 13:22, **the:** Some manuscripts read "this." C(04) W(032) Latin(b) BYZ TR SBLGNT.

i 13:23, **the:** W(032) reads "my."

j 13:23, **He who has ears to hear, let him hear:** Included in Latin(b).

k 13:27, **the:** Some manuscripts read "that." D(05).

l 13:28, **then:** Absent from D(05).

m 13:29, **But:** Absent from D(05) Latin(a h k).

n 13:29, **to them:** Included in D(05) Latin(a f h k).

o 13:29, **the wheat along with them:** Absent from Latin(a b e ff2 h).

p 13:30, **them:** Absent from D(05).

q 13:30, **them:** Absent from D(05) Latin(a b e ff2).

r 13:32, **all:** Included in Latin(a b e ff2 h k).

s 13:33, **He spoke to them:** Absent from D(05) Latin(k).

will open my mouth in parables; I will utter things hidden since the foundation [of the world]."[ab]

36 Then, leaving the crowds, {he}[c] came into the house. And his disciples approached him, saying, "Explain to us the parable of the weeds of the field."

37 But he answered and said [[to them]],[d] "The one who sows the good seed is the Son of Man, 38 and the field is the world, and the good seed, these are the sons of the kingdom; and the weeds are the sons of the evil one, 39 and the enemy who sowed them is the devil, [and the harvest is the end of the age,][e] and the harvesters are angels.

40 "Just as the weeds are gathered and burned with fire, so it will be at the end of {the}[f] age. 41 [[And]][g] The Son of Man will send {his}[h] angels, and they will gather out of his kingdom all the stumbling blocks and those who practice lawlessness 42 and will throw them into the furnace of fire; there will be weeping and gnashing of teeth. 43 Then the righteous will shine like the sun in the kingdom of their Father.

The one who has ears [[to hear]],[i] let him hear.

44 "[[Again,]][j] The kingdom of the heavens is like treasure hidden [in a field],[k] which a man found and hid; and from his joy he goes and sells all that he has and buys that field.

45 "Again, the kingdom of the heavens is like [a man,][l] a merchant, seeking fine pearls;

46 "And having found {one}[m] very valuable pearl, he went and sold [all][n] that he had and bought it.

47 "Again, the kingdom of the heavens is like a net that was thrown into the sea and gathered fish of every kind; 48 when it was full, they drew it ashore, sat down, and put the good into containers, but threw out the bad. 49 So it will be at the end of the age; the angels [[of God]][o] will come out and separate the evil from among the righteous 50 and throw them into the furnace of fire; there will be weeping and gnashing of teeth." 51 [[Jesus says to them,]][p] "Have you understood all these things?" They said to him, "Yes [[Lord]]."[q]

---

a 13:35, **of the world**: ℵ(01) C(04) D(05) W(032) NA28[] BYZ TR ‖ Absent from B(03) Latin(e k) SBLGNT THGNT.

b 13:35, Psalm 78:2.

c 13:36, **he**: Some manuscripts read "Jesus." C(04) W(032) Latin(h) BYZ TR.

d 13:37, **to them**: Included in C(04) W(032) Latin(h) BYZ TR ‖ Absent from ℵ(01) B(03) D(05) Latin(a b ff² k) NA28 SBLGNT THGNT.

e 13:39, **and the harvest is the end of the age**: Absent from ℵ(01).

f 13:40, **the**: ℵ(01) B(03) D(05) NA28 SBLGNT THGNT ‖ Some manuscripts read "this." C(04) W(032) Latin(h) BYZ TR.

g 13:41, **And**: Included in W(032).

h 13:41, **his**: Some manuscripts read "the." ℵ(01).

i 13:43, **to hear**: Included in C(04) D(05) W(032) Latin(ff² h) BYZ TR ‖ Absent from ℵ(01) B(03) Latin(a b e k) NA28 SBLGNT THGNT.

j 13:44, **Again**: Included in C(04) W(032) Latin(h) BYZ TR.

k 13:44, **in a field**: Absent from ℵ(01).

l 13:45, **a man**: Absent from ℵ(01) B(03).

m 13:46, **one**: Some manuscripts read "a." D(05) Latin(a b e h k).

n 13:46, **all**: Absent from D(05) Latin(a h).

o 13:49, **of God**: Included in C(04).

p 13:51, **Jesus says to them**: Included in C(04) W(032) Latin(k) BYZ TR ‖ Absent from ℵ(01) B(03) D(05) Latin(b e ff² k) NA28 SBLGNT THGNT.

q 13:51, **Lord**: Included in C(04) W(032) Latin (a b e h) BYZ TR ‖ Absent from ℵ(01) B(03) D(05) Latin(ff² k) NA28 SBLGNT THGNT.

52 [But]^a {he}^b said to them, "Therefore every scribe who has been trained {for}^c the kingdom of the heavens is like a master of a house, who brings out of his treasure what is new and what is old."

53 And when Jesus had finished these parables, he went away from there. 54 And coming to his hometown, he taught them in their synagogue, so that they were astonished, and said, "Where did this one get {this wisdom}^d and these mighty works? 55 Is not this the carpenter's son? Is not his mother called Mary? And are not his brothers James and {Joseph}^e and Simon and Judas? 56 And are not all his sisters with us? Where then did this one get all these things?" 57 And they took offense at him. But {Jesus}^f said to them, "A prophet is not without honor except in his [[own]]^g hometown and in his own household." 58 And he did not perform many miracles there because of their unbelief.

14 1 At that time, Herod the tetrarch heard the report about Jesus, 2 and said to his servants, "[[Surely]]^h This is John the Baptist [[who I beheaded]];ⁱ he has been raised from the dead, and [for this reason]^j these powers are at work in him."

3 For [[then]]^k Herod had arrested John, bound [him]^l [and put him]^m in prison on account of Herodias, the wife of his brother [Philip];ⁿ 4 for John said [to him],^o "It is not lawful for you to have her." 5 And although he wanted to kill him, he feared the crowd because they regarded him as a prophet.

6 But when Herod's birthday came, the daughter of Herodias danced in the midst and pleased Herod, 7 so he promised with an oath to give her whatever she might ask. 8 And she, prompted by her mother, said, "Give me here on a platter the head of John the Baptist." 9 And the king, being distressed [because of the oaths]^p and those reclining at the table with him, ordered it to be given, 10 and he sent and had John beheaded in the prison. 11 And his head was brought on a platter and given to the girl, and she brought it to her mother.

12 And his disciples came and took {the}^q body and buried it, and they went and reported to Jesus.

13 Now when Jesus heard this, he withdrew from there in a boat to a deserted place by himself; and when the crowds heard it, they followed him on foot from the towns. 14 When [{he}^r went]^s ashore, he saw a great crowd; and he had compassion for them and cured their sick.

---

^a 13:52, **But:** Absent from D(05) Latin(a e k).

^b 13:52, **he:** Some manuscripts read "Jesus." C(04).

^c 13:52, **for:** Some manuscripts read "in." D(05) Latin(a b ff² h) BYZ TR.

^d 13:54, **this wisdom:** W(032) reads "these things, and what is this wisdom."

^e 13:55, **Joseph:** ℵ(01) B(03) C(04) W(032) NA28 SBLGNT THGNT ‖ Some manuscripts read "Joses." W(032) BYZ TR.

^f 13:57, **Jesus:** ℵ(01) reads "he."

^g 13:57, **own:** Included in ℵ(01) C(04).

^h 14:2, **Surely:** Included in D(05) Latin(b f h).

ⁱ 14:2, **who I beheaded:** Included in D(05) Latin(a b h).

^j 14:2, **for this reason:** Absent from B(03).

^k 14:3, **then:** Included in B(03).

^l 14:3, **him:** Absent from ℵ(01) B(03) Latin(h).

^m 14:3, **and put him:** Absent from D(05) Latin(a b e k).

ⁿ 14:3, **Philip:** Absent from D(05) Latin(a e k).

^o 14:4, **to him:** Absent from ℵ(01).

^p 14:9, **because of the oaths:** Absent from Latin(a b ff² h).

^q 14:12, **the:** Some manuscripts read "his." ℵ(01) D(05) Latin(h).

^r 14:14, **he:** Some manuscripts read "Jesus." C(04) W(032) Latin(h) BYZ TR.

^s 14:14, **he went:** Absent from Latin(a b ff²).

15 When it was evening, {the}[a] disciples came to him and said, "This is a deserted place, and the hour is now late; [[therefore]][b] send the crowds away so that they may go into the {villages}[c] [[around]][d] and buy food for themselves."

16 But [Jesus][e] said [to them],[f] "They do not need to go away; you give them something to eat." 17 They replied, "We have nothing here but five loaves and two fish." 18 But he said, "Bring them [here][g] to me."

19 And having ordered the crowds to recline on the grass, [[and]][h] taking the five loaves and the two fish, looking up to heaven, he blessed and broke and gave the loaves to the disciples, and the disciples to the crowds. 20 And all ate and were filled; and they took up what was left over of the broken pieces, twelve baskets full. 21 And those who ate were [about][i] five thousand men, besides women and children.

22 And [immediately][j] {he}[k] compelled {the}[l] disciples to get into the boat and go ahead [of him][m] to the other side, while he dismissed the crowds. 23 And [having dismissing the crowds,][n] he went up on the mountain by himself to pray. When evening came, he was there alone.

24 But the boat was already {many stadia away from the land},[o] being battered by the waves, for the wind was against it. 25 In the fourth watch of the night, {he came}[p] to them [walking on the sea].[q]

26 And when {the disciples}[r] saw him walking on the sea, they were troubled, saying, "It is a ghost!" and they cried out in fear. 27 But immediately [Jesus][s] spoke to them, saying, "Take courage, it is I; do not be afraid."

28 And Peter answered [him],[t] "Lord, if it is you, command me to come to you on the water." 29 And he said, "Come." And Peter, getting down from the boat, walked on the water and came to Jesus. 30 But seeing the [strong][u] wind, he became [[greatly]][v] afraid [[to come]],[w] and beginning to sink, he cried out, saying, "Lord, save me!"

31 Immediately Jesus, stretching out his hand, took hold of him and said to him, "You of little faith, why did you doubt?"

---

a 14:15, **the:** Some manuscripts read "his." C(04) D(05) W(032) Latin(a ff² h) BYZ TR.

b 14:15, **therefore:** Included in ℵ(01) C(04).

c 14:15, **villages:** Some manuscripts read "land." ℵ(01).

d 14:15, **around:** Included in C(04).

e 14:16, **Jesus:** Absent from ℵ(01) D(05) Latin(k).

f 14:16, **to them:** Absent from Latin(a ff² k).

g 14:18, **here:** Absent from D(05).

h 14:19, **and:** Included in ℵ(01) C(04) W(032) TR.

i 14:21, **about:** Absent from W(032).

j 14:22, **immediately:** Absent from ℵ(01) C(04).

k 14:22, **he:** Some manuscripts read "Jesus." Latin(a b ff² h) BYZ TR.

l 14:22, **the:** Some manuscripts read "his." B(03) Latin(a b ff² h) TR.

m 14:22, **of him:** Absent from D(05) Latin(a b e ff² h).

n 14:23, **having dismissing the crowds:** Absent from ℵ(01).

o 14:24, **many stadia away from the land:** Some manuscripts read "in the middle of the sea." ℵ(01) C(04) D(05) W(032) Latin(a b ff² h) BYZ TR. A stadia is about 190 meters.

p 14:25, **he came:** Some manuscripts read "Jesus went." Latin(a b e ff² h) BYZ TR.

q 14:25, **walking on the sea:** Absent from Latin(b).

r 14:26, **the disciples:** Some manuscripts read "they." ℵ(01) Latin(a b e ff² h).

s 14:27, **Jesus:** Some manuscripts read "he." ℵ(01) D(05).

t 14:28, **him:** Absent from Latin(a).

u 14:30, **strong:** Absent from ℵ(01) B(03).

v 14:30, **greatly:** Included in W(032).

w 14:30, **to come:** Included in W(032).

32 And when they had climbed into the boat, the wind ceased. 33 And those [[having come]]ᵃ [in the boat]ᵇ worshipedᶜ him, saying, "Truly, you are the Son of God."

34 And crossing over, they came to the land of Gennesaret. 35 And recognizing him, the men of that place sent word to the whole surrounding region and brought to him all those who were suffering. 36 And they were begging [him]ᵈ that they might only touch the fringe of his garment; and as many as touched it were made well.

15 1 Then {Pharisees and scribes}ᵉ from Jerusalem come to {Jesus},ᶠ saying, 2 "Why do your disciples break the tradition of the elders? For they do not wash {when they eat bread with their hands}."ᵍ

3 But he answered [them],ʰ "Why do you also break the commandment of God for the sake of your tradition? 4 For God {said},ⁱ 'Honor your father and mother,' and, 'Whoever speaks evil of father or mother must be put to death.'ʲ 5 But you say, 'Whoever says to his father or mother, "Gift, whatever you might benefit from me," he need

not honor his father [or his mother]."ᵏ 6 Thus you nullify the {word}ˡ of God for the sake of your tradition.

7 "Hypocrites,ᵐ Isaiah prophesied well about you, saying, 8 'This people [[draws near to me with their mouth and]]ⁿ honors me with their lips, but their heart is far from me; 9 But they worship me in vain, teaching doctrines, commandments of men.'"ᵒ

10 And calling the crowd to him, he said to them, "Listen and understand: 11 {It is not what}ᵖ goes into the mouth that defiles a person, but what comes out of the mouth; this defiles a man."

12 Then {the} q disciples came and said to him, "Do you know that the Pharisees were offended when they heard this saying?"

13 He answered, "Every plant that my heavenly Father has not planted will be rooted up. 14 Let {them}ʳ alone; they are blind guides [of the blind].ˢ If a blind person leads a blind person, both will fall into a pit."

15 But Peter said to him, "Explain {this}ᵗ parable to us."

16 And {he}ᵘ said, "Are you also still without understanding? 17 Do you not

---

ᵃ 14:33, **having come:** Included in D(05) W(032) Latin(a b e ff² h) BYZ TR.

ᵇ 14:33, **in the boat:** Absent from C(04).

ᶜ 14:33, **worship:** See footnote for worship in Matt 2:2

ᵈ 14:36, **him:** Absent from B(03).

ᵉ 15:1, **Pharisees and scribes:** Some manuscripts read "scribes and Pharisees." C(04) W(032) Latin(a b ff² h) BYZ TR.

ᶠ 15:1, **Jesus:** Some manuscripts read "him." D(05) Latin(a b ff²).

ᵍ 15:2, **when they eat bread with their hands:** Some manuscripts read "their hands when they eat bread."

ʰ 15:3, **them:** Absent from D(05) Latin(e).

ⁱ 15:4, **said:** Some manuscripts read "commanded them saying." ℵ(01) C(04) W(032) BYZ TR.

ʲ 15:4, Exodus 20:12, Leviticus 20:9, Deuteronomy 5:16, Exodus 21:17.

ᵏ 15:5, **or his mother:** Included in C(04) W(032) Latin(b ff²) BYZ TR.

ˡ 15:6, **word:** Some manuscripts read "law." ℵ(01) C(04) ‖ Some manuscripts read "commandment." W(032) BYZ TR.

ᵐ 15:7, **Hypocrites:** "Hypocrites" is in the vocative indicating the Pharisees and scribes are being addressed.

ⁿ 15:8, **draws near to me with their mouth and:** Included in C(04) W(032) BYZ TR.

ᵒ 15:8-9, Isaiah 29:13 LXX.

ᵖ 15:11, **It is not what:** D(05) reads "Not everything that."

q 15:12, **the:** Some manuscripts read "his." C(04) W(032) Latin(a b ff² h) BYZ TR.

ʳ 15:14, **them:** D(05) reads "the blind."

ˢ 15:14, **of the blind:** Absent from ℵ(01) B(03) D(05).

ᵗ 15:15, **this:** Some manuscripts read "the." ℵ(01) B(03).

ᵘ 15:16, **he:** Some manuscripts read "Jesus." C(04) W(032) BYZ TR SBLGNT.

see[a] that whatever goes into the mouth enters the stomach and is expelled into the latrine? 18 But what comes out of the mouth proceeds from the heart, and this defiles a person. 19 For out of the heart come evil thoughts, murders, adultery, fornications, thefts, false witnesses, blasphemies.[b] 20 These are what defile a person; but eating with unwashed hands does not defile a person."

21 And going out from there, Jesus withdrew to the regions of Tyre and Sidon. 22 And behold, a Canaanite woman from those borders came out and cried out [[to him]],[c] saying, "Have mercy on me, Lord,[d] Son of David; my daughter is severely demon-possessed."

23 But he did not answer her a word. And his disciples came and asked him, saying, "Send her away, for she cries out after us."

24 But he answered and said, "I was not sent except to {the}[e] lost sheep of the house of Israel."

25 But she came and worshiped[f] him, saying, "Lord,[g] help me."

26 And he answered and said, "It is not {good}[h] to take the children's bread and throw it to the dogs."

27 But she said, "Yes, Lord,[i] [for][j] even the dogs eat the crumbs that fall from their masters' table."

28 Then {Jesus}[k] answered and said to her, "O woman, great is your faith! Let it be to you as you desire." And her daughter was healed from that very hour.

29 And moving on from there, Jesus came by the Sea of Galilee, and going up on the mountain, he sat down there. 30 And many crowds came to him, having with them the lame, the blind, the crippled, [the mute],[l] and many others, and they laid them at {his feet},[m] and he healed them [[all]];[n] 31 so that the crowd was amazed, seeing [the mute [speaking],[o] [the crippled made whole],[p] the lame walking, and the blind seeing];[q] and they glorified the God of Israel.

32 And Jesus, calling his disciples to him, said [to them],[r] "I have compassion on {the}[s] crowd because they have been with me for three days now and have nothing to eat; and I do not want to send them away hungry [, lest they faint on the way]."[t] 33 And {the}[u] disciples said to him, "Where [[then]][v] can we get enough bread in the wilderness to satisfy such a large crowd?"

---

a 15:17, **see:** Or realize.

b 15:19, **blasphemies:** Or slanders.

c 15:22, **to him:** Included in D(05) W(032) BYZ TR.

d 15:22, **Lord:** "Lord" is in the vocative indicating that Jesus is being addressed.

e 15:24, **the:** D(05) reads "these."

f 15:25, **worship:** See footnote for worship in Matt 2:2

g 15:25, **Lord:** "Lord" is in the vocative indicating that Jesus is being addressed.

h 15:26, **good:** Some manuscripts read "lawful." D(05) Latin(a b ff²).

i 15:27, **Lord:** "Lord" is in the vocative indicating that Jesus is being addressed.

j 15:27, **for:** Absent from B(03) Latin(e).

k 15:28, **Jesus:** Some manuscripts read "he." D(05).

l 15:30, **the mute:** Absent from D(05).

m 15:30, **his feet:** Some manuscripts read "the feet of Jesus." C(04) W(032) BYZ TR.

n 15:30, **all:** Included in D(05) Latin(b ff²).

o 15:31, **speaking:** Some manuscripts read "hearing." B(03) Latin(e).

p 15:31, **the crippled made whole:** Absent from ℵ(01) Latin(b ff²).

q 15:31, **the mute speaking, the crippled made whole, the lame walking, and the blind seeing:** Absent from Latin(a).

r 15:32, **to them:** Absent from ℵ(01) C(04).

s 15:32, **the:** Some manuscripts read "this." D(05) Latin(b).

t 15:32, **lest they faint on the way:** Absent from D(05).

u 15:33, **the:** Some manuscripts read "his." C(04) D(05) W(032) BYZ TR.

v 15:33, **then:** Included in D(05) Latin(a b e ff² h).

34 And Jesus said to them, "How many loaves do you have? And they said [[to him]],ᵃ Seven, and a few small fish." 35 And he commanded the {crowd}ᵇ to sit down on the ground.

36 [[And]]ᶜ He took the seven loaves and the fish, [and after giving thanks,]ᵈ he broke them and gave them to {the}ᵉ disciples, and the disciples to the {crowds}.ᶠ 37 And they all ate and were satisfied. And they took up the leftover broken pieces, seven baskets full. 38 And those who ate were [[about]]ᵍ four thousand men, [apart from women and children].ʰ

39 And after dismissing the crowds, he got into the boat and came to the region of Magadan.

16 1 And the Pharisees and Sadducees came, and to test him they asked him to show them a sign from heaven.

2 But he answered [them],ⁱ "[When it is evening, you say, 'It will be fair weather, for the sky is red'; 3 [and in the morning, 'Today it will be stormy,]ʲ for the sky is red and threatening.' [[Hypocrites]],ᵏ you know how to interpret the appearance of the sky, but you cannot interpret the signs of the times?]ˡ 4 An evil [and adulterous]ᵐ

generation seeks a sign, and no sign will be given to it except the sign of [[the prophet]]ⁿ Jonah." And leaving them, he went away.

5 And when {the}ᵒ disciples came to the other side, they forgot to take bread.

6 But Jesus said [to them],ᵖ "[Watch and] q Beware of the leaven of the Pharisees [and Sadducees]."ʳ 7 And they were reasoning among themselves, saying, "We did not take any bread."

8 But Jesus, knowing this, said [[to them]],ˢ "Why do you reason among yourselves, you of little faith because you have no bread? 9 Do you not yet understand [, nor remember]ᵗ the five loaves of the five thousand and how many baskets you took up? 10 Nor the seven loaves of the four thousand and how many baskets you took up? 11 How do you not understand that I did not speak [to you]ᵘ concerning bread? [But]ᵛ Beware of the leaven of the Pharisees and Sadducees."

12 Then they understood that he did not tell them to beware of the leaven [of the bread],ʷ but of the teaching of the Pharisees [and Sadducees].ˣ

13 Now when Jesus came into the region of Caesarea Philippi, he asked

---

ᵃ 15:34, **to him:** Included in D(05).

ᵇ 15:35, **crowd:** Some manuscripts read "crowds." C(04) W(032) Latin(a e) BYZ TR.

ᶜ 15:36, **And:** Included in C(04) W(032) Latin(a b e ff² h) BYZ TR.

ᵈ 15:36, **and after giving thanks:** Absent from C(04).

ᵉ 15:36, **the:** Some manuscripts read "his." C(04) W(032) Latin(a b e ff²) BYZ TR.

ᶠ 15:36, **crowds:** Some manuscripts read "crowd." C(04) D(05) W(032) Latin(a b ff²) BYZ TR.

ᵍ 15:38, **about:** Absent from ℵ(01) B(03).

ʰ 15:38, **apart from women and children:** Absent from Latin(k).

ⁱ 16:2, **them:** Absent from D(05) Latin(a).

ʲ 16:3, **and in the morning, today it will be stormy:** Absent from W(032).

ᵏ 16:3, **Hypocrites:** Included in Latin(b e) BYZ TR.

ˡ 16:2-3, **When it is evening...:** Absent from ℵ(01) B(03).

ᵐ 16:4, **and adulterous:** Absent from D(05) Latin(a e ff²).

ⁿ 16:4, **the prophet:** Included in C(04) W(032) Latin(a b e ff²) BYZ TR.

ᵒ 16:5, **the:** Some manuscripts read "his." W(032) Latin(a b ff²) BYZ TR.

ᵖ 16:6, **to them:** Absent from ℵ(01).

q 16:6, **Watch and:** Absent from Latin(a b ff²).

ʳ 16:6, **and Sadducees:** Absent from Latin(a).

ˢ 16:8, **to them:** Included in C(04) Latin(a) BYZ TR.

ᵗ 16:9, **nor remember:** Absent from ℵ(01).

ᵘ 16:11, **to you:** Absent from D(05) Latin(a b ff²).

ᵛ 16:11, **But:** Absent from D(05) W(032) BYZ TR.

ʷ 16:12, **of the bread:** Absent from D(05) Latin(a b ff²).

ˣ 16:12, **and Sadducees:** Absent from Latin(a b).

{his}[a] disciples, saying, "Who do men say {the Son of Man is}?"[b] 14 And they said, "Some say John the Baptist, others Elijah, and others Jeremiah or one of the prophets." 15 {He}[c] said to them, "But who do you say I am?"

16 And Simon Peter answered and said [[to him]],[d] "You are the Christ,[e] the Son of the living God."

17 {But}[f] Jesus answered and said [to him],[g] "Blessed are you, Simon bar-Jonah, for flesh and blood has not revealed this to you, but my Father who is in the heavens. 18 And I also say to you that you are Peter, and on this rock I will build my church, and the gates of Hades shall not prevail against it. 19 [[And]][h] I will give you the keys of the kingdom of heaven, and whatever you bind on earth will be bound in heaven, and whatever you loose on earth will be loosed in heaven." 20 Then he {commanded}[i] {the}[j] disciples not to tell anyone that he is [[Jesus]][k] the Christ.

21 From that time Jesus [[Christ]][l] began to show his disciples that he must go to Jerusalem and suffer many things from the elders, chief priests, and scribes, and be killed, and on the third day be raised. 22 And Peter took him aside and began to rebuke him, saying, "God forbid it, Lord![m] This shall never happen to you."

23 But he turned and said to Peter, "Get behind me, Satan![n] You are a stumbling block to me, for you are not setting your mind on the things of God [, but on the things of men].'"[o]

24 Then Jesus said to his disciples, "If anyone wishes to follow me, let him deny himself and take up his cross and follow me. 25 For whoever wishes to save his life will lose it, but whoever loses his life for my sake will find it.

26 "For what will it profit a man if he gains the whole world and forfeits his soul? Or what will a man give in exchange for his soul? 27 For the Son of Man is going to come in the glory of his Father with {his}[p] angels, and then he will repay each person according to his deeds.

28 "Truly, I say to you [that],[q] there are some standing here who will not taste death until they see the Son of Man coming in his kingdom."

17 1 And [[it happened]][r] after six days Jesus took Peter, James, and John his brother, and leads them up a high mountain by themselves. 2 [And][s] {He}[t] was transfigured before them, and his face shone like the sun, and his clothes became white as {light}.[u] 3 And behold, Moses and Elijah appeared to them, talking with him.

---

[a] 16:13, **his:** D(05) reads "the."

[b] 16:13, **the Son of Man is:** Some manuscripts read "that I, the Son of Man, am." C(04) W(032).

[c] 16:15, **He:** Some manuscripts read "Jesus." C(04) Latin (b e ff²).

[d] 16:16, **to him:** Included in D(05).

[e] 16:16, **Christ:** See footnote for Christ in Matt 1:1.

[f] 16:17, **But:** Some manuscripts read "And." C(04) W(032) BYZ TR.

[g] 16:17, **to him:** Absent from D(05).

[h] 16:19, **And:** Included in C(04) W(032) Latin(a b e ff²) BYZ TR.

[i] 16:20, **commanded:** Some manuscripts read "rebuked." B(03) D(05) Latin(e).

[j] 16:20, **the:** Some manuscripts read "his." W(032) Latin (a b e ff²) BYZ TR.

[k] 16:20, **Jesus:** Included in C(04) D(05) W(032) BYZ TR.

[l] 16:21, **Jesus:** Some manuscripts include "Christ." ℵ(01) B(03).

[m] 16:22, **Lord:** "Lord" is in the vocative indicating that Jesus is being addressed.

[n] 16:23, **Satan:** "Satan" is in the vocative indicating that Peter is being addressed.

[o] 16:23, **but on the things of men:** Absent from Latin(e ff²).

[p] 16:27, **his:** Some manuscripts read "the holy." C(04) D(05) Latin(b).

[q] 16:28, **that:** Absent from C(04) D(05) W(032) Latin(a) BYZ TR.

[r] 17:1, **it happened:** Included in D(05) Latin(a b e ff²).

[s] 17:2, **And:** Absent from D(05).

[t] 17:2, **he:** Some manuscripts read "Jesus." D(05) Latin(a b e ff²).

[u] 17:2, **light:** Some manuscripts read "snow." D(05) Latin(a b e ff²).

4 Then Peter answered and said to Jesus, "Lord, it is good for us to be here; if you wish, {I will}[a] make three tents here, one for you, one for Moses, and one for Elijah."

5 While he was still speaking, behold, a bright cloud overshadowed them, and behold, a voice from the cloud said, "This is my beloved Son, in whom I am well pleased; listen to him." 6 {And}[b] when the disciples heard this, they fell on their faces and were greatly afraid. 7 And Jesus came near and having touched them, he said, "Rise, and do not be afraid." 8 And when they lifted up their eyes, they [[no longer]][c] saw no one but Jesus alone.

9 And as they were coming down from the mountain, Jesus commanded them, saying, "Tell no one the vision until the Son of Man is raised from the dead."

10 And {the}[d] disciples asked him, saying, "Why then do the scribes say that Elijah must come first?" 11 And {he}[e] answered and said [[to them]],[f] "Elijah indeed comes [[first]][g] and will restore all things; 12 but I say to you that Elijah has already come, and they did not recognize him, but did to him whatever they wished; so also the Son of Man is going to suffer at their hands." 13 Then the disciples understood that he was speaking to them about John the Baptist.

14 And when they came to the crowd, a man approached [[in front of]][h] him, kneeling down to him 15 and saying, "[Lord,][i] Have mercy on my son, for he is moonstruck[j] and suffers terribly; for he often falls into the fire and often into the water. 16 And I brought him to your disciples, but they could not heal him."

17 {Jesus}[k] answered and said [[to them]],[l] "O faithless and perverse generation, how long will I be with you? How long will I bear with you? Bring him here to me." 18 And Jesus rebuked him, and the demon came out of him, and [the boy][m] was healed from that hour. 19 Then the disciples came to Jesus privately and said, "Why could we not cast it out?" 20 {He}[n] said to them, "Because of your little faith; for truly I say to you, if you have faith as a mustard seed, you will say to this mountain, 'Move from here to there,' and it will move; and nothing will be impossible for you." 21 [[But this kind does not go out except by prayer and fasting.]][o]

22 As they were {gathering}[p] in Galilee, Jesus said to them, "The Son of Man is about to be handed over into the hands of men, 23 and they will kill him, and on the third day he will be raised." And they were greatly distressed.

24 When they came to Capernaum, those who collected the two-drachma tax approached Peter and said, "Does your teacher not pay the two-drachma tax?" 25 {He}[q] said, "Yes." And when he came into the house, Jesus spoke to

---

a 17:4, **I will:** Some manuscripts read "we will." D(05) W(032) Latin(a e) BYZ TR.

b 17:6, **And** D(05) reads "But."

c 17:8, **no longer:** Absent from C(04).

d 17:10, **the:** Some manuscripts read "his." B(03) C(04) D(05) Latin(ff²) BYZ TR.

e 17:11, **he:** Some manuscripts read "Jesus." C(04) BYZ TR.

f 17:11, **to them:** Absent from ℵ(01) C(04) BYZ TR.

g 17:11, **first:** Included in C(04) BYZ TR.

h 17:14, **in front of:** Included in D(05) Latin(e).

i 17:15, **Lord:** "Lord" is in the vocative indicating that Jesus is being addressed. Absent from ℵ(01).

j 17:15, **moonstruck:** Or, one who has seizures.

k 17:17, **he:** Some manuscripts read "Jesus." ℵ(01).

l 17:17, **to them:** Included in ℵ(01).

m 17:18, **the boy:** Absent from ℵ(01).

n 17:20, **he:** Some manuscripts read "Jesus." C(04) W(032) Latin(b e) BYZ TR.

o 17:21, Some manuscripts include verse 21. C(04) D(05) W(032) Latin(a b ff²) BYZ TR ‖ Absent from ℵ(01) B(03) Latin(e) NA28 SBLGNT THGNT.

p 17:22, **gathering:** Some manuscripts read "staying."

q 17:25, **He:** Some manuscripts read "Jesus." W(032).

him first, saying, "What do you think, Simon? From whom do the kings of the earth collect customs or taxes? From their sons or from others?" 26 And when {he said},[a] "From others," Jesus said to him, "Then the sons are free. 27 But so that we do not cause them to stumble, go to the sea, cast a hook, and take the first fish that comes up; and when you open its mouth, you will find [[there]][b] a shekel. Take that and give it to them for me and you."

18 1 At that time the disciples approached Jesus, saying, "Who then is greatest in the kingdom of the heavens?" 2 And calling a child, {he}[c] placed it in their midst 3 and said, "Truly I tell you, unless you turn and become like children, you will never enter the kingdom of the heavens. 4 For whoever humbles himself like this child, this one is the greatest in the kingdom of the heavens. 5 And whoever receives one such child in my name, receives me.

6 "But whoever causes one of these little ones who believe in me to stumble, it would be better for him to have a large millstone hung {around}[d] their neck and to be drowned in the depths of the sea.

7 "Woe to the world because of the stumbling blocks! For it is necessary for stumbling blocks to come, but woe to {the}[e] man through whom the stumbling block comes. 8 If your hand or your foot causes you to stumble, cut {it}[f] off and throw it away from you; it is better for you to enter life crippled or lame than to have two hands or two feet and be thrown into the eternal fire. 9 And if your eye causes you to stumble, gouge it out and throw it away. It is better for you to enter life with one eye than to have two eyes and be thrown into the Gehenna[g] [of fire].[h]

10 "See that you do not despise one of these little ones [[who believe in me]];[i] for I tell you that their angels [in heaven][j] always see the face of my Father who is in heaven. 11 [[For the Son of Man came to save the lost.]][k]

12 "What do you think? If a man has a hundred sheep and one of them goes astray, does he not leave the ninety-nine [[sheep]][l] on the mountains and go in search of the one that went astray? 13 And if he finds it, truly, I say to you, he rejoices over it more than over the ninety-nine that never went astray. 14 So it is not the will {before}[m] {your}[n] Father who is in the heavens that one of these little ones should perish.

---

a 17:26, **he said:** Some manuscripts read "Peter said to him." w(032) BYZ TR.

b 17:27, **there:** Absent from D(05) Latin(a b).

c 18:2, **he:** Some manuscripts read "Jesus." D(05) W(032) Latin(a b e ff²) BYZ TR.

d 18:6, **around:** ℵ(01) B(03) ‖ Some manuscripts read "on." D(05) Latin(a b e ff²) TR ‖ Some manuscripts read "to." W(032) BYZ SBLGNT.

e 18:7, **the:** Some manuscripts read "that." B(03) Latin(a b ff²) BYZ TR.

f 18:8, **it:** Some manuscripts read "them."

g 18:9, **Gehenna:** Often translated hell, Gehenna is a term derived from a place called the Valley of Hinnom, located near Jerusalem. In the Hebrew Bible (Old Testament), this valley was associated with practices of child sacrifice to foreign gods, notably the Canaanite deity Moloch. Because of these associations, the Valley of Hinnom was reviled and became a symbol of divine judgment and destruction.

h 18:9, **of fire:** Absent from D(05).

i 18:10, **who believe in me:** Included in D(05) Latin(b ff²).

j 18:10, **in heaven:** Absent from Latin(e).

k 18:11, Some manuscripts include verse 11. D(05) W(032) Latin(a b ff²) BYZ TR. ‖ Absent from ℵ(01) B(03) Latin(e) NA28 SBLGNT THGNT.

l 18:12, **sheep:** Included in B(03).

m 18:14, **before:** Some manuscripts read "of." ℵ(01).

n 18:14, **your:** Some manuscripts read "my." B(03) ‖ D(05) reads "our."

15 “If your brother sins [against
you],[a] go [[and]][b] reprove him between
you and him alone. If he listens to you,
you have gained your brother; 16 but if
he does not listen [[to you]],[c] take with
you one or two others, so that by the
mouth of two or three [witnesses][d]
every word may be established; 17 and if
he refuses to listen to them, tell it to the
church; and if he refuses to listen even
to the church, let him be to you as a
Gentile and [[as]][e] a tax collector.

18 “Truly I say to you, whatever you
bind on earth will be bound in heaven,
[and][f] whatever you loose on earth will
be loosed in heaven.

19 “Again [truly][g] I say to you, if
two [of you][h] agree on earth about
anything for which they ask, it will
be done for them by my Father in the
heavens. 20 For where two or three are
gathered in my name, there {I am}[i] in
their midst.”

21 Then Peter came up and said [to
him],[j] “Lord, how often will my brother
sin against me, and I forgive him? As
many as seven times?”

22 Jesus said to him, “I do not
say to you seven times, but seventy
times seven.

23 “Therefore the kingdom of the
heavens is like a man, a king, who
wished to settle accounts with his
servants. 24 When he began to settle,
one was brought to him who owed him
ten thousand talents. 25 And since he
could not pay, {the}[k] lord ordered him
to be sold, with {the}[l] wife and children
and all that he had, and payment to
be made.

26 “So {the}[m] servant fell on his
knees, imploring him, ‘Have patience
with me [[Lord]],[n] and I will pay [you][o]
everything.’

27 “And out of pity for him, the
lord of that servant released him and
forgave him the debt.

28 “But when that same servant went
out, he found one of his fellow servants
who owed him a hundred denarii, and
seizing him, he began to choke him,
saying, ‘Pay [[me]][p] what you owe.’

29 “So his fellow servant [[fell down
at his feet and]][q] pleaded with him,
saying, ‘Have patience with me, and I
will pay you [[all]].’[r]

30 “He refused and went and put
him in prison until he should pay
[[all]][s] what was owed. 31 When his
fellow servants saw what had taken
place, they were greatly distressed, and
they went and reported to their lord all
that had taken place. 32 Then his lord
summoned him and said [to him],[t] ‘You
wicked servant! I forgave you all that
debt because you pleaded with me.

---

[a] 18:15, **against you:** Absent from א(01) B(03).
[b] 18:15, **and:** Included in W(032) BYZ TR.
[c] 18:16, **to you:** Included in Latin(a b e ff^2 h).
[d] 18:16, **witnesses:** Absent from D(05).
[e] 18:17, **as:** Included in D(05).
[f] 18:18, **and:** Absent from א(01) D(05).
[g] 18:19, **truly:** Absent from א(01) D(05) W(032) Latin(ff^2) TR.
[h] 18:19, **of you:** Absent from Latin(a).
[i] 18:20, **I am:** D(05) reads “I am not.”
[j] 18:21, **to him:** Absent from א(01).
[k] 18:25, **the:** Some manuscripts read “his.” W(032) Latin(b e ff^2 h) BYZ TR.
[l] 18:25, **the:** Some manuscripts read “his.” D(05) W(032) Latin(a b e ff^2) BYZ TR.
[m] 18:26, **the:** Some manuscripts read “that.” D(05) Latin(a b e ff^2 h).
[n] 18:26, **Lord:** Included in א(01) Latin(ff^2) BYZ TR.
[o] 18:26, **you:** Absent from D(05) Latin(b e ff^2).
[p] 18:28, **me:** Included in C(04) Latin(e) BYZ TR.
[q] 18:29, **fell down at his feet:** Included in W(032) BYZ TR.
[r] 18:29, **all:** Included in W(032) TR.
[s] 18:30, **all:** Included in C(04).
[t] 18:32, **to him:** Absent from D(05).

33 [[Therefore,]]ᵃ Was it not necessary for you [also]ᵇ to have mercy on your fellow servant, as I also had mercy on you?' 34 And in anger his lord delivered him to the jailers, until he should pay [all]ᶜ his debt [[to him]].ᵈ 35 So also my heavenly Father will do to you, if you do not forgive your brother from your heart [[their trespasses]]."ᵉ

19 1 And it happened when Jesus finished these words, he moved from Galilee and came to the borders of Judea beyond the Jordan. 2 And many crowds followed him, and he healed them there.

3 And Pharisees approached him, testing him and saying [[to him]],ᶠ "Is it lawful [for a man]ᵍ to divorce his wife for any reason?"

4 But he answered and said [[to them]],ʰ "Have you not read that the one who {created}ⁱ them from the beginning made them male and female?ʲ 5 And he said, 'For this reason a man will leave {the}ᵏ father and mother and be joined to his wife, and the two will become one flesh.'ˡ 6 So they are no longer two but one flesh. Therefore, what God has joined together, let man not separate."

7 They said to him, "Why then did Moses command to give a certificate of divorce and to send [her]ᵐ away?"ⁿ

8 {He}ᵒ said to them, "Because of your hardness of heart Moses allowed you to divorce your wives, but from the beginning it was not so. 9 And I say to you [that],ᵖ whoever divorces his wife, except for [[the matter of]]�q sexual immorality, and marries another, commits adultery. [[And the one who marries a divorced woman commits adultery.]]"ʳ

10 {The}ˢ disciples said to him, "[If]ᵗ Such is the case of a man with his wife, it is better not to marry."

11 But {he}ᵘ said to them, "Not everyone can accept {this}ᵛ teaching, but only those to whom it is given. 12 [For]ʷ There are eunuchs who were born that way from their mother's womb, and there are eunuchs who were made eunuchs by men, and there are eunuchs who have made themselves eunuchs for the sake of the kingdom of the heavens. Let the one who is able to accept this accept it."

ᵃ 18:33, **Therefore:** Included in 𝔓25 D(05).

ᵇ 18:33, **also:** Absent from 𝔓25.

ᶜ 18:34, **all:** Absent from B(03).

ᵈ 18:34, **to him:** Included in ℵ(01) C(04) W(032) BYZ TR.

ᵉ 18:35, **their trespasses:** Included in C(04) W(032) Latin(h) BYZ TR.

ᶠ 19:3, **to him:** Absent from W(032) Latin(h) BYZ TR.

ᵍ 19:3, **for a man:** Absent from ℵ(01) B(03).

ʰ 19:4, **to them:** Included in C(04) W(032) BYZ TR.

ⁱ 19:4, **created:** Some manuscripts read "made."

ʲ 19:4, Genesis 1:27, 5:2.

ᵏ 19:5, **the:** Some manuscripts read "his." W(032).

ˡ 19:5, Genesis 2:24.

ᵐ 19:7, **her:** Absent from ℵ(01) D(05) Latin(a e h).

ⁿ 19:7, Deuteronomy 24:1.

ᵒ 19:8, **He:** Some manuscripts read "Jesus." ℵ(01) Latin(a b).

ᵖ 19:9, **that:** Absent from B(03) D(05) Latin(a b e ff² h).

q 19:9, **the matter of:** Included in B(03) D(05) Latin(a b e ff²).

ʳ 19:9, **And the one who marries a divorced woman commits adultery:** Included in B(03) C(04) BYZ TR SBLGNT THGNT ‖ Absent from ℵ(01) D(05) Latin(a b e ff² h) NA28.

ˢ 19:10, **The:** Some manuscripts read "his." ℵ(01) B(03) Latin(e) SBLGNT.

ᵗ 19:10, **If:** Absent from ℵ(01).

ᵘ 19:11, **he:** Some manuscripts read "Jesus." Latin(a b).

ᵛ 19:11, **this:** Some manuscripts read "." B(03) Latin(e).

ʷ 19:12, **For:** Absent from ℵ(01).

13 Then children were brought to him so that he might lay his hands on them and pray; but the disciples rebuked them. 14 Jesus said [[to them]],[a] "Let the children come to me, and do not hinder them, for to such belongs the kingdom of the heavens." 15 And he laid his hands on them and went on from there.

16 And behold, one came up to him and said, "[[Good]][b] Teacher, what good thing shall I do, that I may {have}[c] eternal life?" 17 {He}[d] said to him, "Why do you ask me about what is good? There is only one who is good [[except God alone]].[e] If you want to enter into life, keep the commandments."

18 He said to him, "Which ones?" {Jesus}[f] said, "You shall not murder, [You shall not commit adultery, You shall not steal,][g] You shall not bear false witness, 19 Honor your father and mother, and, You shall love your neighbor as yourself."[h]

20 The young man said to him, "All these I have kept [[from my youth]];[i] what do I still lack?"

21 Jesus said to him, "If you want to be perfect, go, sell your possessions and give to the poor, and you will have treasure in heaven; and come, follow me."

22 But when the young man heard [the word,][j] he went away sorrowful, for he had many possessions.

23 But Jesus said to his disciples, "Truly I say to you that a rich person will enter the kingdom of the heavens with difficulty.

24 "Again I say to you, it is easier for a camel to go through the eye of a needle than for a rich person [to enter][k] the kingdom of God."

25 When {the}[l] disciples heard this, they were greatly astonished [[and were afraid]],[m] saying, "Who then can be saved?" 26 But Jesus, looking at them, said, "[With men][n] This is impossible, but with God all things are possible."

27 Then Peter answered and said to him, "Behold, we have left everything and followed you; what then will be for us?"

28 And Jesus said to them, "Truly I say to you, you who have followed me, in the regeneration, when the Son of Man sits on his glorious throne, you also will sit on twelve thrones, judging the twelve tribes of Israel.

29 "And whoever has left [houses or][o] brothers or sisters [or father][p] mother [[or wife]][q] or children or fields for my name's sake, will receive a hundredfold and will inherit eternal life.

30 "But many who are first will be last, and the last [[will be]][r] first."

---

a 19:14, **to them:** Included in ℵ(01) C(04) D(05) W(032).

b 19:16, **Good:** Included in C(04) W(032) Latin(b ff² h) BYZ TR.

c 19:16, **have:** Some manuscripts read "inherit." ℵ(01).

d 19:17, **he:** Some manuscripts read "Jesus." Latin(a b ff²).

e 19:17, **except God alone:** Included in C(04) W(032) Latin(h) BYZ TR.

f 19:18, **Jesus:** Some manuscripts read "he." 𝔓71 Latin(e).

g 19:18, **You shall not commit adultery, You shall not steal:** Absent from ℵ(01).

h 19:18-19, Exodus 20:12-16; Deuteronomy 5:16-20; Leviticus 19:18.

i 19:20, **from my youth:** Included in C(04) W(032) Latin(a b e ff² h) BYZ TR.

j 19:22, **the word:** Absent from C(04) D(05) W(032) Latin(a b ff²) BYZ TR.

k 19:24, **to enter:** Absent from ℵ(01) Latin(a b e ff² h) SBLGNT.

l 19:25, **the:** Some manuscripts read "his." W(032) BYZ TR.

m 19:25, **and were afraid:** Included in D(05) Latin(a b e ff²).

n 19:26, **With men:** Absent from ℵ(01) D(05).

o 19:29, **houses or:** Absent from ℵ(01).

p 19:29, **or father:** Absent from D(05) Latin(b ff²).

q 19:29, **or wife:** Included in W(032).

r 19:30, **will be:** Included in W(032).

20 ¹ "For the kingdom of heaven is like a man, a householder, who went out early in the morning to hire workers for his vineyard. ² And having agreed with the workers for a denarius a day, he sent them into his vineyard. ³ And going out about the third hour, he saw others standing idle in the marketplace ⁴ and said to them, 'Go also into the vineyard, and whatever is right I will give you.' ⁵ So they went. {Again},ᵃ going out about the sixth and ninth hour, he did likewise. ⁶ And about the eleventh [[hour]],ᵇ going out, he found others standing [[idle]]ᶜ and said to them, 'Why have you been standing here idle all day?' ⁷ They said to him, 'Because no one has hired us.' He said to them, 'Go also into {the}ᵈ vineyard [[and whatever is right you will receive]].'ᵉ

⁸ "And when evening came, the owner of the vineyard said to his steward, 'Call the workers and give [them]ᶠ their wages, beginning from the last to the first.' ⁹ And those who came about the eleventh hour each received a denarius. ¹⁰ {And}ᵍ when the first came, they thought they would receive more; {and}ʰ they also received a denarius each. ¹¹ And when they received it, they grumbled against the householder, ¹² saying [that],ⁱ 'These last worked only one hour, and you have made them equal to us who have borne the burden of the day and the scorching heat.' ¹³ But he answered one of them and said, 'Friend, I am not doing you wrong; did you not agree with me for a denarius? ¹⁴ Take what is yours and go. But [[also]]ʲ I want to give to this last man the same as I give to you. ¹⁵ [Or]ᵏ Is it not lawful for me to do what I want with my own? Or is your eye evil because I am good?' ¹⁶ So the last will be first, and the first last. [[For many are called, but few are chosen]]ˡ"

¹⁷ And as Jesus was going up to Jerusalem, he took {the}ᵐ twelve [disciples]ⁿ aside privately and said to them [on the way],ᵒ ¹⁸ "Behold, we are going up to Jerusalem, and the Son of Man will be handed over to the chief priests and scribes, and they will condemn him [to death]ᵖ ¹⁹ and hand him over to the Gentiles to be mocked and flogged and crucified, and on the third day he {will be raised}."�q

²⁰ Then the mother of the sons of Zebedee came to him with her sons, kneeling and asking something from him.

²¹ But he said to her, "What do you want?" She said to him, "Declare that {these}ʳ two sons of mine will sit, one at your right hand and one at your left, in {your}ˢ kingdom."

ᵃ 20:5, **Again:** SBLGNT ‖ Some manuscripts read "But again." NA-28 THGNT.

ᵇ 20:6, **hour:** Included in C(04) W(032) Latin(e) BYZ TR.

ᶜ 20:6, **idle:** Included in C(04) W(032) Latin(h) BYZ TR.

ᵈ 20:7, **the:** Some manuscripts read "my." C(04) D(05) Latin(a b e ff² h).

ᵉ 20:7, **and whatever is right you will receive:** Included in C(04) W(032) Latin(h) BYZ TR.

ᶠ 20:8, **them:** Absent from ℵ(01) C(04).

ᵍ 20:10, **And:** Some manuscripts read "But." ℵ(01) W(032) BYZ TR.

ʰ 20:10, **and:** Some manuscripts read "but." D(05) Latin(a b e ff² h).

ⁱ 20:12, **that** Included in C(04) W(032) BYZ TR.

ʲ 20:14, **also:** Included in Latin(a b ff² h).

ᵏ 20:15, **Or:** Absent from B(03) D(05) SBLGNT.

ˡ 20:16, **for many are called, but few are chosen:** Included in C(04) D(05) W(032) Latin(a b e ff² h) BYZ TR.

ᵐ 20:17, **the:** Some manuscripts read "his." Latin(a e).

ⁿ 20:17, **disciples:** Absent from ℵ(01) D(05).

ᵒ 20:17, **on the way:** Absent from Latin(b ff²).

ᵖ 20:18, **to death:** Absent from B(03).

q 20:19, **will be raised:** Some manuscripts read "will rise." B(03) D(05) W(032) BYZ TR.

ʳ 20:21, **these:** Absent from C(04) Latin(a e).

ˢ 20:21, **your:** Some manuscripts read "the." D(05) Latin(b e ff²) TR.

22 But Jesus answered, "You do not know what you are asking. Are you able to drink the cup that I am about to drink [[and be baptized with the baptism that I am baptized with]]?"[a] They said [to him],[b] "We are able."

23 [And][c] {He}[d] said to them, "You will indeed drink my cup [[And the baptism with which I am baptized, you will be baptized]],[e] but to sit at my right hand {and}[f] at my left is not mine to give, but it is for those for whom it has been prepared by my Father."

24 {And}[g] when the ten heard this, they {were}[h] indignant about the two brothers.

25 But Jesus called them to him and said [[to them]],[i] "You know that the rulers of the Gentiles lord it over them, and their great ones exercise authority over them. 26 [[But]][j] It will not be so among you, but whoever wishes to become great among you will be your servant, 27 and whoever wishes to be first among you must be your slave; 28 just as the Son of Man did not come to be served, but to serve, and to give his life as a ransom for many. [[But you seek to grow from little and to be less from greater. But when you enter and are invited to dine, do not recline in the prominent places, lest someone more honorable than you comes, and the one who invited comes and says to you, 'Move down further,' and you will be put to shame. But if you recline in the lower place, and one lesser than you comes, the one who invited will say to you, 'Move up further,' and this will be beneficial for you.]]"[k]

29 And as they were going out from Jericho, a large crowd followed [him].[l] 30 And behold, two blind men sitting by the road, hearing that Jesus was passing by, cried out, saying, "Have mercy on us, [Lord,][m] [[Jesus]][n] Son of David."

31 But the crowd rebuked them so that they would be silent; yet they cried out {even}[o] more, saying, "Have mercy on us, Lord,[p] Son of David."

32 And Jesus, stopping, called them and said, "What do you want me to do for you?" 33 They said to him, "Lord,[q] that our eyes may be opened." 34 And Jesus, moved with compassion, touched their eyes, and immediately {they regained their sight and followed him}.[r]

21 1 And when they approached Jerusalem and came to Bethphage at the Mount of Olives, then Jesus sent two disciples, 2 saying to them, "Go into the village opposite you, and [immediately][s] you will find a donkey tied and a colt with her; untie them and bring them to me. 3 And if

---

a 20:22, **and be baptized with the baptism that I am baptized with:** Included in C(04) W(032) Latin(h) BYZ TR.

b 20:22, **to him:** Absent from D(05).

c 20:23, **And:** Included in C(04) W(032) BYZ TR Latin(h).

d 20:23, **He:** Some manuscripts read "Jesus." D(05) Latin(a b e ff² h).

e 20:23, **And the baptism with which I am baptized, you will be baptized:** C(04) Latin(h) BYZ TR.

f 20:23, **and:** Some manuscripts read "or." B(03) Latin(a b e ff² h).

g 20:24, **And:** Some manuscripts read "But." Latin(a b e ff² h).

h 20:24, **were:** Some manuscripts read "began to be." ℵ(01).

i 20:25, **to them:** Included in D(05) W(032).

j 20:26, **But:** Included in C(04) Latin(ff²) BYZ TR.

k 20:28, **But you seek to grow...:** Included in D(05) Latin(a b e ff² h).

l 20:29, **him:** Absent from some manuscripts 𝔓45 ℵ(01).

m 20:30, **Lord:** Absent from ℵ(01) D(05) Latin(a b e ff² h) "Lord" is in the vocative, indicating that Jesus is being addressed.

n 20:30, **Jesus:** Included in ℵ(01) Latin(e h).

o 20:31, **even:** Some manuscripts read "much." ℵ(01).

p 20:31, **Lord:** "Lord" is in the vocative indicating that Jesus is being addressed as such.

q 20:33, **Lord:** "Lord" is in the vocative indicating that Jesus is being addressed as such.

r 20:34, **they regained their sight and followed him:** Some manuscripts read "their eyes received sight and they followed." C(04) W(032) BYZ TR.

s 21:2, **immediately:** Absent from Latin(a b h).

anyone says to you {anything},[a] you shall say, 'The Lord needs them,' and immediately he will send them."

[4] Now [[all]][b] this took place so that what was spoken through the prophet might be fulfilled, saying, [5] "Say to the daughter of Zion: Behold, your king comes to you, gentle and mounted on a donkey, and on a colt, the foal of a beast of burden."[c]

[6] And the disciples went and did as Jesus had instructed them, [7] and brought the donkey and the colt, and laid their garments on them, and he sat on them. [8] But the majority of the crowd spread their own garments on the road, others were cutting branches [from the trees][d] and spreading them on the road.

[9] And the crowds that went before [him][e] and that followed him were shouting, "Hosanna to the son of David! Blessed is the one who comes in the name of the Lord! Hosanna in the highest!"[f]

[10] And when he entered Jerusalem, the whole city was stirred, saying, "Who is this?"

[11] And the crowds said, "This is the prophet [Jesus],[g] from Nazareth of Galilee."

[12] And Jesus entered the temple [[of God]][h] and drove out all who were selling and buying in the temple, and he overturned the tables of the money changers and the seats of those selling doves. [13] And he said to them, "It is written, 'My house shall be called a house of prayer,'[i] but {you make it}[j] a den of robbers.'"[k] [14] And the blind and the lame came to him in the temple, and he healed them. [15] But when the chief priests and the scribes saw the wonderful things that {he}[l] did, and the children crying out in the temple, "Hosanna to the Son of David!" they were indignant, [16] and they said to him, "Do you hear what these are saying?" And Jesus said to them [that],[m] "Yes; have you never read, 'Out of the mouth of infants and nursing babies you have prepared praise?'"[n]

[17] And leaving them, he went [out of the city][o] to Bethany and lodged [there].[p]

[18] In the morning, returning to the city, he became hungry. [19] And seeing a fig tree by the road, he came to it and found nothing on it but leaves only, and he said to it, "May no fruit ever come from you again into the age."[q] And the fig tree withered immediately. [20] And when the disciples saw it, they marveled, saying, "How did the fig tree wither at once?"

[21] Jesus answered and said to them, "Truly I say to you, if you have faith and do not doubt, not only will you do what was done to the fig tree, but even if you say to this mountain, 'Be lifted up and thrown into the sea,' it will happen. [22] And whatever you ask for in prayer, believing, you will receive."

---

a 21:3, **Anything:** D(05) reads "what is being done."

b 21:4, **all:** Included in B(03) W(032) BYZ TR.

c 21:5, Isaiah 62:11, Zechariah 9:9.

d 21:8, **from the trees:** Absent from W(032).

e 21:9, **him:** Absent from W(032) Latin(a b e ff² h) BYZ TR.

f 21:9, Psalm 118:25-26.

g 21:11, **Jesus:** Absent from Latin(a).

h 21:12, **of God:** Included in C(04) D(05) W(032) Latin(a e ff² h) BYZ TR.

i 21:13, Isaiah 56:7.

j 21:13, **you make it:** Some manuscripts read "you have made it." C(04) D(05) W(032) BYZ TR.

k 21:13, **robbers:** The Greek word is defined by BDAG as: (1) robber, highwayman, bandits or (2) revolutionary, insurrectionist, guerrilla (BDAG, λῃστής).

l 21:15, **he:** Some manuscripts read "Jesus." Latin(a b e ff² h).

m 21:16, **that:** Absent from ℵ(01) D(05) Latin(b e ff² h).

n 21:16, Psalm 8:2 LXX.

o 21:17, **out of the city:** Absent from ℵ(01).

p 21:17, **there:** Absent from C(04).

q 21:19, **into the age:** Or for eternity.

23 And when he came into the
temple, the chief priests and the elders
of the people approached him as he was
teaching, saying, “By what authority
are you doing these things? And who
gave you this authority?” 24 [But][a] Jesus
answered and said to them, “I will
also ask you one question, [which][b]
if you tell me, I likewise will tell you
by what authority I do these things:
25 The baptism of John, where was it
from? From heaven or from men?” And
they {reasoned among themselves},[c]
saying, “If we say, ‘From heaven,’ he
will say to us, ‘Why [then][d] did you not
believe him?’ 26 But if we say, ‘From
men,’ we fear the crowd, for they all
hold John as a prophet.”

27 And they answered Jesus and
said, “We do not know.” And {he}[e] said
to them, “Neither will I tell you by
what authority I do these things.

28 “What do you think? A man
had two children. [And][f] Coming
to the first, he said, Child, go today
and work in {the}[g] vineyard. 29 But he
answered and said, ‘I do not want to,’
but later, having regretted it, he went
[[to the vineyard]].[h] 30 {But}[i] {coming
to the other},[j] he said likewise. [But
he answered and said],[k] ‘{I will, sir,’
and did not go}.[l] 31 Which of the two
did the will of the father?” They say
[[to him]],[m] “the first.” Jesus says
to them, “Truly I say to you that the
tax collectors and the prostitutes are
going {first}[n] of you into the kingdom
of God. 32 For John came to you in the
way of righteousness, and you did not
believe him, but the tax collectors and
the prostitutes believed him; and you,
seeing [this],[o] did not even regret it
later to believe him.

33 “Listen to another parable. There
was a [[certain]][p] man, a householder,
who planted a vineyard and put a
fence around it and dug a winepress
in it and built a tower and leased it to
vine-growers and went on a journey.
34 When the time of the fruits drew near,
he sent his servants to the vine-growers
to receive his fruits. 35 The vine-growers
took his servants, one they beat,
one they killed, one they stoned.
36 [[Therefore]][q] Again, he sent other
servants, more than the first, and they
did the same to them. 37 Later, he sent
his son [to them],[r] saying, ‘They will
respect my son.’

38 “But when the vine-growers saw
the son, they said to themselves, ‘This
is the heir; come, let us kill him and
{obtain}[s] his inheritance.’ 39 Taking him,
they threw him out of the vineyard
and killed him. 40 Therefore, when the
lord of the vineyard comes, what will
he do to those vine-growers?” 41 They
said to him, “He will miserably destroy
those wicked men, and he will lease
his vineyard to other vine-growers,

---

[a] 21:4, **But:** Absent from Latin(a b ff^2 h).
[b] 21:24, **which:** Absent from D(05).
[c] 21:25, **among themselves:** Some manuscripts read “reasoned with themselves.”
[d] 21:25, **then:** Absent from D(05) Latin(a b e ff^2).
[e] 21:27, **he:** Some manuscripts read “Jesus.” ℵ(01) Jesus(e h).
[f] 21:28, **And:** Absent from ℵ(01) Latin(e) SBLGNT.
[g] 21:28, **the:** Some manuscripts read “my.” B(03) W(032) BYZ TR.
[h] 21:29, **to the vineyard:** Included in D(05) Latin(a b ff^2 h).
[i] 21:30, **But:** Some manuscripts read “And.” C(04) W(032) Latin(h) BYZ TR.
[j] 21:30, **coming to the other:** Some manuscripts read “he went to the second.”
[k] 21:30, **But he answered and said:** Absent from ℵ(01).
[l] 21:30, **I will, sir, and did not go:** Some manuscripts read, “I do not want to, but later, having regretted it.” C(04).
[m] 21:31, **to him:** Included in C(04) W(032) Latin(a b e ff^2 h) BYZ TR.
[n] 21:31, **first:** Some manuscripts read “last.” B(03) D(05) Latin(a b e ff^2 h).
[o] 21:32, **this:** Absent from D(05) Latin(e).
[p] 21:33, **certain:** Included in Latin(e h) BYZ TR.
[q] 21:36, **Therefore:** Absent from D(05).
[r] 21:37, **to them:** Absent from Latin(e).
[s] 21:38, **obtain:** Some manuscripts read “seize.” C(04) W(032) BYZ TR.

who will give him the fruits in their seasons."

42 Jesus says to them, "Have you never read in the Scriptures, 'The stone which the builders rejected, this has become cornerstone; this was the Lord's doing, and it is marvelous in our eyes'?ᵃ

43 "Therefore I say to you [that]ᵇ the kingdom of God will be taken away from you and given to a nation producing its fruits. 44 [[And the one who falls on this stone will be broken to pieces; but on whomever it falls, it will crush them.]]"ᶜ

45 And when the chief priests and the Pharisees heard his parables, they knew that he was speaking about them; 46 and seeking to seize him, they feared the crowds, since they held him to be a prophet.

22 1 And Jesus, answering [again],ᵈ spoke to them in parables, [saying,]ᵉ 2 "The kingdom of the heavens is like a man, a king, who made a wedding for his son. 3 And he sent his servants to call those who were invited to the wedding, and they did not want to come. 4 Again, he sent other servants, saying, 'Tell those who are invited, "Behold, I have prepared my dinner; my oxen and my fattened livestock are slaughtered, and everything is ready. Come to the wedding."' 5 But they disregarded it and went away, one to his own field, another to his business; 6 and the rest seized {his}ᶠ servants, mistreated them, and killed them. 7 {But the king was enraged},ᵍ and he sent his troops and destroyed those murderers and burned their city.

8 "Then he said to his servants, 'The wedding is ready, but those who were invited were not worthy. 9 Go therefore to the crossroads of the streets, and as many as you find, invite to the wedding.' 10 And those servants went out into the streets and gathered all whom they found,ʰ both bad and good; and the {wedding}ⁱ was filled with guests.

11 "And the king, having entered to look upon the guests reclining, saw there a man not wearing a wedding garment. 12 And he said to him, 'Friend, how did you come in here without a wedding garment?' And he was speechless. 13 Then the king said to the servants, 'Bind him hand and foot, [[take him away]]ʲ and cast him into outer darkness; there will be weeping and gnashing of teeth.' 14 For many are called, but few are chosen."

15 Then the Pharisees went and took counsel on how to trap him [in his words].ᵏ 16 And they sent to him their disciples with the Herodians, saying, "Teacher, we know that you are truthful and teach the way of God in truth, and you do not care about anyone; for you do not look at the face of men. 17 So [tell us then]ˡ what you think: is it lawful to pay taxes to Caesar or not?"

ᵃ 21:42, Psalm 118:22-23.
ᵇ 21:43, **that:** Absent from ℵ(01) B(03).
ᶜ 21:44, **And the one who falls...:** Verse 44 is absent from some manuscripts. D(05) Latin(a b e ff²).
ᵈ 22:1, **again:** Absent from W(032) Latin(a b h).
ᵉ 22:1, **saying:** Absent from Latin(ff² h).
ᶠ 22:6, **his:** Some manuscripts read "the." W(032).
ᵍ 22:7, **But the king was enraged:** Some manuscripts read "But when the king heard it, he was enraged." C(04) D(05) W(032) Latin(b h) BYZ TR.
ʰ 22:10, **all whom they found:** Some manuscripts read "as many as they found."
ⁱ 22:10, **wedding:** Some manuscripts read "wedding hall." ℵ(01) B(03).
ʲ 22:13, **take him away:** Included in C(04) W(032) BYZ TR THGNT ‖ Absent from ℵ(01) B(03) NA28 SBLGNT.
ᵏ 22:15, **in his words:** Absent from ℵ(01).
ˡ 22:17, **tell us then:** Absent from D(05) Latin(a b e ff²).

18 But Jesus, knowing their
wickedness, said, "Why do you test me,
hypocrites? 19 Show me the coin for the
tax." And they brought him a denarius.
20 And {he}[a] said to them, "Whose
image and inscription is this?" 21 They
said [to him],[b] "Caesar's." Then he said
to them, "[Therefore,][c] Give to Caesar
the things that are Caesar's, and to God
the things that are God's." 22 And when
they heard this, they marveled, and
leaving him, they went away.

23 On that day Sadducees came [to
him][d] saying there is no resurrection,
and they questioned him 24 saying,
"Teacher, Moses said, 'If someone dies
without having children, his brother
shall marry [his wife][e] and raise up
offspring for his brother.'[f] 25 [Now][g]
There were among us seven brothers;
and the first married and died, and not
having offspring, he left his wife to his
brother; 26 likewise the second and the
third, up to the seven. 27 But last [of
all],[h] the woman [[also]][i] died. 28 In the
resurrection, therefore, whose of the
seven will she be wife? For they all
had her."

29 But Jesus answered and said to
them, "You are mistaken, not knowing
the Scriptures nor the power of God;
30 for in the resurrection they neither
marry nor are given in marriage,
but they are like angels [[of God]][j]
in heaven. 31 But concerning the
resurrection of the dead, have you not
read what was spoken to you by God,
saying, 32 'I am the God of Abraham,
and the God of Isaac, and the God of
Jacob'?[k] {He}[l] is not the God of the
dead but of the living."

33 And when the crowds heard this,
they were astonished at his teaching.

34 But when the Pharisees heard
that he had silenced the Sadducees,
they gathered together, 35 And one of
them [a lawyer][m] asked him, testing
him, [[and saying]][n] 36 "Teacher, which
is the greatest commandment in the
Law?" 37 And {he}[o] said to him, "'You
shall love the Lord your God with
all your heart and with all your soul
and with all your mind,'[p] 38 this is the
great and first commandment. 39 And a
second is like it: 'You shall love your
neighbor as yourself.'[q] 40 On these two
commandments depend [all][r] the Law
and the Prophets."

41 Now when the Pharisees had
gathered together, Jesus asked them,
42 saying, "What do you think about the
Christ? Whose son is he?" They said to
him, "The son of David."

43 {He}[s] said to them, "How then
does David, in the Spirit, call him
'Lord,' saying, 44 'The Lord said to my
Lord, "Sit at my right hand, {until I

---

a 22:20, **he:** Some manuscripts read "Jesus." D(05) Latin(a b e ff^2 h).
b 22:21, **to him:** Absent from א(01) B(03).
c 22:21, **Therefore:** Absent from D(05) Latin(a b e).
d 22:23, **to him:** Absent from א(01).
e 22:24, **his wife:** Absent from D(05).
f 22:24, Deuteronomy 25:5.
g 22:25, **Now:** Absent from D(05).
h 22:27, **of all:** Absent from Latin(e).
i 22:27, **also:** Included in D(05) Latin(a b ff^2 h) BYZ TR.
j 22:30, **of God:** Included in א(01) W(032) BYZ TR SBLGNT THGNT || Absent from B(03) D(05) Latin(a b e ff^2 h).
k 22:32, Exodus 3:6, 15.
l 22:32, **He:** Some manuscripts read "God." BYZ TR.
m 22:35, **a lawyer:** Absent from Latin(e).
n 22:35, **and saying:** Included in D(05) W(032) Latin(b ff^2 h) BYZ TR.
o 22:37, **he:** Some manuscripts read "Jesus." D(05) W(032) BYZ TR.
p 22:37, Deuteronomy 6:5.
q 22:39, Leviticus 19:18.
r 22:40, **all:** Absent from א(01).
s 22:43, **He:** Some manuscripts read "Jesus."

put your enemies under your feet}?"[a] 45 If David [[in the Spirit]][b] calls him 'Lord,' how is he his son?" 46 And no one was able to answer him a word, nor did anyone dare from that day on to ask him any more questions.

23 1 Then Jesus spoke to the crowds and to his disciples, 2 saying, "The scribes and the Pharisees sit on Moses' seat. 3 Therefore, all things that they say [to you][c] [[to observe]],[d] do [and observe];[e] but do not do according to their works; for they say and do not do.

4 {But}[f] they tie up [[great and]][g] heavy [and hard to bear][h] burdens and lay them on people's shoulders, but they themselves are not willing to lift a finger to move them. 5 "But they do all their deeds to be seen by men; {for}[i] they broaden their phylacteries and enlarge the tassels [[of their garments]],[j] 6 and they love the place of honor at feasts and the best seats in the synagogues, 7 and the greetings in the marketplaces and to be called by men, 'Rabbi. [[Rabbi.]]'[k] 8 [But you are not to be called 'Rabbi,'][l] For you have one teacher, [[the Christ]][m] and you are all brothers.

9 "And do not call anyone on earth 'father,' for you have one {Father, the heavenly one}.[n] 10 Nor are you to be called instructors, for one is your teacher, the Christ. 11 [But][o] The greatest [among you][p] will be your servant. 12 Whoever exalts himself will be humbled, and whoever humbles himself will be exalted.

13 "[But][q] Woe to you, scribes and Pharisees, hypocrites, because you shut the kingdom of heaven in men's faces; for you do not enter, nor do you allow those who are entering to go in..

14 [["Woe to you, scribes and Pharisees, hypocrites, because you devour the houses of the widows, and for a show make long prayers; for this reason you will receive greater condemnation.]][r]

15 "Woe to you, scribes and Pharisees, hypocrites, because you travel over sea and land to make one proselyte, and when it happens, you make it a son of Gehenna[s] twice as much as yourselves.

---

a 22:44, **until I put your enemies under your feet:** Some manuscripts read "till I make your enemies your footstool." Psalm 110:1.

b 22:45, **in the Spirit:** Included in D(05) Latin(a b ff2 h).

c 23:3, **to you:** Absent from D(05).

d 23:3, **to observe:** Included in W(032) BYZ TR.

e 23:3, **and observe:** Absent from א(01).

f 23:4, **But:** Some manuscripts read "For." D(05) Latin(h) BYZ TR.

g 23:4, **great and:** Absent from א(01).

h 23:4, **and hard to bear:** B(03) W(032) BYZ TR NA28[] THGNT ‖ Absent from Latin(a b e ff2 h) SBLGNT.

i 23:5, **for:** Some manuscripts read "but." W(032) BYZ TR.

j 23:5, **of their garments:** Included in W(032) Latin(ff2 h) BYZ TR.

k 23:7, **Rabbi:** Some manuscripts include "Rabbi" a second time. D(05) W(032) BYZ TR.

l 23:8, **But you are not to be called Rabbi:** Absent from א(01).

m 23:8, **the Christ:** Included in BYZ TR.

n 23:9, **Father, the heavenly one:** Or heavenly Father. Some manuscripts read "Father, who is in the heavens." D(05) W(032) Latin(a b e ff2 h) BYZ TR.

o 23:11, **But:** Absent from D(05) Latin(a b e ff2 h).

p 23:11, **among you:** Absent from א(01).

q 23:13, **But:** Absent from א(01) W(032) Latin(h).

r 23:14 Verse 14 is included in some manuscripts. W(032) Latin(b ff2 h) BYZ TR ‖ Absent from א(01) B(03) D(05) NA28 SBLGNT THGNT.

s 23:15, **Gehenna:** Often translated hell, Gehenna is a term derived from a place called the Valley of Hinnom, located near Jerusalem. In the Hebrew Bible (Old Testament), this valley was associated with practices of child sacrifice to foreign gods, notably the Canaanite deity Moloch. Because of these associations, the Valley of Hinnom was reviled and became a symbol of divine judgment and destruction.

16 "Woe to you, blind guides, who say, 'Whoever swears by the temple, it is nothing; but whoever swears by the gold of the temple, he is obligated.' 17 Fools and blind men! For which is greater, the gold or the temple that sanctifies the gold? 18 And, 'Whoever swears by the altar, it is nothing; but whoever swears by the gift that is on it, he is obligated.' 19 [[Fools and]]ᵃ Blind men! For which is greater, the gift or the altar that sanctifies the gift? 20 Therefore, he who swears by the altar, swears by it and by everything on it; 21 and he who swears by the temple, swears by it and by the one who dwells in it; 22 and he who swears by heaven, swears by the throne of God and by the one who sits upon it.

23 "Woe to you, scribes and Pharisees, hypocrites, because you tithe the mint and dill and cumin, and have neglected the weightier matters of the law: justice, mercy, and faith; [but]ᵇ these things you should have done, without neglecting the others. 24 Blind guides, [those]ᶜ who strain out the gnat, but swallow the camel.

25 "Woe to you, scribes and Pharisees, hypocrites, because you clean the outside of the cup and the dish, but inside they are full of greed and self-indulgence [[and unrighteousness]].ᵈ 26 Blind Pharisee, first clean the inside of the cup [[and dish]],ᵉ so that the outside [of it]ᶠ may also become clean.

27 "Woe to you, scribes and Pharisees, hypocrites, because you are like whitewashed tombs, which outwardly appear beautiful to people, but inside they are full of dead men's bones and all uncleanness. 28 So you also outwardly appear righteous to men, but inside you are full of hypocrisy and lawlessness.

29 "Woe to you, scribes and Pharisees, hypocrites, because you build the tombs of the prophets and adorn the monuments of the righteous, 30 and say, 'If we had been in the days of our fathers, we would not have been partakers with them in the blood of the prophets.' 31 Therefore you testify against yourselves that you are sons of those who murdered the prophets. 32 Fill up, then, the measure of your fathers. 33 You snakes, offspring of vipers, how will you escape the judgment of Gehenna?ᵍ 34 For this reason, behold, I am sending [you]ʰ prophets and wise men and scribes; some of them you will kill and crucify, [and some of them you will scourge in your synagogues]ⁱ and persecute from city to city; 35 so that upon you may come [all]ʲ the righteous blood shed on earth, from the blood of righteous Abel to the blood of Zechariah, [son of Barachiah,]ᵏ whom you murdered between the temple and the altar. 36 Truly I say to you [[that]],ˡ all these things will come upon this generation.

ᵃ 23:19, **Fools and:** Included in B(03) C(04) W(032) BYZ TR.

ᵇ 23:23, **but:** Absent from ℵ(01) D(05) Latin(e ff²) BYZ TR SBLGNT.

ᶜ 23:24, **those:** Absent from B(03) D(05).

ᵈ 23:25, **and unrighteousness:** Included in W(032).

ᵉ 23:26, **and dish:** Included in ℵ(01) B(03) C(04) W(032) Latin(h) BYZ TR SBLGNT.

ᶠ 23:26, **of it:** Absent from Latin(ff² h).

ᵍ 23:33, **Gehenna:** Or hell. Often translated hell, Gehenna is a term derived from a place called the Valley of Hinnom, located near Jerusalem. In the Hebrew Bible (Old Testament), this valley was associated with practices of child sacrifice to foreign gods, notably the Canaanite deity Moloch. Because of these associations, the Valley of Hinnom was reviled and became a symbol of divine judgment and destruction.

ʰ 23:34, **you:** Absent from D(05).

ⁱ 23:34, **and some of them you will scourge in your synagogues:** Absent from D(05) Latin(a).

ʲ 23:35, **all:** Absent from ℵ(01).

ᵏ 23:35, **son of Barachiah:** Absent from ℵ(01).

ˡ 23:36, **that:** Included in C(04) W(032) BYZ TR.

37 "Jerusalem, Jerusalem, the one
killing the prophets and stoning those
sent to her, how often I wanted to
gather your children together, just as a
bird gathers its young under its wings,
and you were not willing. 38 Behold,
your house is left to you [desolate].[a]
39 For I tell you [[that]],[b] you will not
see me from now on until you say,
'Blessed is the one coming in the name
of {the Lord}.[c]'"[d]

24 1 And Jesus went out from
the temple and was going on
his way, and his disciples came [[to
him]][e] to show him the buildings of
the temple.

2 But he answering [[Jesus]][f] said to
them, "Do you not see all these things?
Truly I tell you, not a stone will be left
[here][g] upon a stone that will not be
torn down."

3 And as he was sitting on the
Mount of Olives [[opposite the
temple]],[h] {the}[i] disciples came to him
privately, saying, "Tell us, when will
these things be, and what will be the
sign of your coming and the end of
the age?"

4 And Jesus answered and said to
them, "See that no one leads you astray.
5 For many will come in my name,
saying, 'I am the Christ,' and they will
lead many astray. 6 And you will hear
of wars and rumors of wars; see that
you are not alarmed; for it must [[all]][j]
happen, but the end is not yet.

7 "For nation will rise against
nation, and kingdom against kingdom,
and there will be famines [[and
plagues]][k] and earthquakes in various
places; 8 [but][l] all these things are the
beginning of birth pains.

9 "Then they will deliver you up
to tribulation and will kill you, and
you will be hated by {all the nations}[m]
because of my name. 10 And then
many will fall away and will betray
one another {and will hate one
another};[n] 11 and many false prophets
will arise and will lead many astray;
12 and because lawlessness will increase,
the love of many will grow cold.
13 But the one who endures to the end [,
this one][o] will be saved.

14 "And {this}[p] gospel of the
kingdom will be proclaimed throughout
the whole inhabited earth as a
testimony to [all][q] the nations, and then
the end will come.

15 "So when you see the
abomination of desolation, spoken of
by Daniel the prophet,[r] standing in the
holy place, let the reader understand,
16 then let those who are in Judea flee
to the mountains, 17 the one on the roof
should not go down to take anything
out of his house, 18 and the one in the
field should not turn [back][s] to take
his cloak.

---

a 23:38, **desolate:** Absent from B(03) Latin(ff²).
b 23:39, **that:** Included in D(05) Latin(a b ff² h).
c 23:39, **the Lord:** D(05) reads "God."
d 23:39, Psalm 118:26.
e 24:1, **to him:** Included in Latin(a ff²).
f 24:2, **he answering:** Some manuscripts read "Jesus." C(04) W(032) BYZ TR.
g 24:2, **here:** Absent from W(032).
h 24:3, **opposite the temple:** Absent from C(04).
i 24:3, **the:** Some manuscripts read "his." C(04) Latin(h).
j 24:6, **all:** Included in C(04) W(032) Latin(a b e ff² h) BYZ TR.
k 24:7, **and plagues:** Included in C(04) Latin(h) BYZ TR.
l 24:8, **but:** Absent from Latin(a b).
m 24:9, **all the nations:** C(04) reads "all." || א(01) reads "the nations."
n 24:10, **and will hate one another:** א(01) reads "into tribulation."
o 24:13, **this one:** Absent from W(032).
p 24:14, **this:** Some manuscripts read "the." 𝔓70 D(05) Latin(a).
q 24:14, **all:** Absent from W(032).
r 24:15, Daniel 8:14, 9:27, 11:31, 12:11.
s 24:18, **back:** Absent from Latin(a b ff² h).

19 "Woe to those who are pregnant and to those who are nursing infants in those days! 20 Pray that your flight may not be in winter or {on}[a] a Sabbath. 21 For [then][b] there will be great tribulation, such as has not been from the beginning of the world until now, nor never will be. 22 And if those days had not been cut short, no flesh would be saved; but for the sake of the elect those days will be cut short.

23 "Then if anyone says to you, 'Look, here is the Christ,' or '[[Behold,]][c] There,' do not believe it; 24 for [false christs and][d] false prophets will rise and will give [great][e] signs and wonders, so as to deceive, if possible, even the elect. 25 Behold, I have told you beforehand. 26 So if they say to you, 'Look, he is in the wilderness,' do not go out; 'Look, he is in the inner rooms,' do not believe it. 27 For as the lightning comes from the east and is seen even to the west, so [[also]][f] will be the coming of the Son of Man. 28 [[For]][g] Wherever the {corpse}[h] is, there the vultures will gather.

29 "But immediately after the tribulation of those days, the sun will be darkened, and the moon will not give its light, and the stars will fall from heaven, and the powers of the heavens will be shaken.[i]

30 "And then the sign of the Son of Man will appear in {heaven},[j] and then all the tribes of the earth will mourn, and they will see the Son of Man coming on the clouds of heaven with great power and great glory. 31 And [[then]][k] he will send his angels with a great trumpet [[sound]],[l] and they will gather his elect[m] from the four winds, from the ends of the heavens to their ends. [[But when these things begin to happen, look up and lift up your heads because your redemption is drawing near.]][n]

32 "Now learn the parable from the fig tree: when its branch has already become tender and puts forth its leaves, you know that summer is near; 33 so also you, when you see all these things [[happening]],[o] know that it is near, at the doors. 34 Truly I say to you [that],[p] this generation will not pass away until all [these things][q] take place.

35 [Heaven and earth will pass away, but my words will not pass away.][r]

36 "But concerning that day or hour, no one knows, not even the angels in heaven [nor the Son],[s] but only {the}[t] Father.

---

[a] 24:20, **on:** Some manuscripts read "in."

[b] 24:21, **then:** Absent from Latin(b ff²).

[c] 24:23, **Behold:** Included in Latin(b e).

[d] 24:24, **false christs and:** Absent from Latin(h).

[e] 24:24, **great:** Absent from ℵ(01) W(032).

[f] 24:27, **also:** Included in Latin(b ff²) BYZ TR.

[g] 24:28, **For:** Included in W(032) Latin(ff²) BYZ TR.

[h] 24:28, **corpse:** Some manuscripts read "body." ℵ(01) Latin(a b e ff² h).

[i] 24:29, Isaiah 13:10, 34:4.

[j] 24:30, **heaven:** D(05) reads "the heavens."

[k] 24:31, **then:** Included in ℵ(01).

[l] 24:31, **sound:** Included in B(03) D(05) Latin(a b ff² h) BYZ TR.

[m] 24:31, **his elect:** Or his chosen ones.

[n] 24:31, **But when these things begin to happen...:** Included in D(05) Latin(b h).

[o] 24:33, **happening:** Included in Latin(a h).

[p] 24:34, **that:** Absent from ℵ(01) W(032) BYZ TR.

[q] 24:34, **these things:** Absent from Latin(b).

[r] 24:35, **Heaven and earth will pass away:** Verse 35 is absent from ℵ(01).

[s] 24:36, **nor the Son:** ℵ(01) B(03) D(05) Latin(a b ff²) NA28 SBLGNT THGNT ‖ Absent from W(032) Syriac(sy) BYZ TR.

[t] 24:36, **the:** Some manuscripts read "my." W(032) BYZ TR.

37 "{For}[a] just as the days of Noah were, so [[also]][b] will be the coming of the Son of Man. 38 For [[just]][c] as they were [in those][d] days {before}[e] the flood, eating and drinking, marrying and giving in marriage, until the day Noah entered the ark, 39 and they did not know until the flood came and took them all away, so will be [also][f] the coming of the Son of Man.

40 "Then two will be in the field; one will be taken and [[the]][g] one will be left. 41 Two women will be grinding at the mill; one will be taken and one will be left. [[Two will be on one bed; one will be taken, and one will be left.]][h] 42 Therefore, stay awake, for you do not know on what {day}[i] your Lord is coming.

43 "But know this, that if the master of the house had known in what {watch}[j] the thief was coming, he would have stayed awake and would not have let his house be broken into. 44 For this reason, you also must be ready, for the Son of Man is coming at an hour you do not expect.

45 "Who then is the faithful and wise servant, whom {the}[k] master has put in charge of his household to give [them][l] their food at the proper time? 46 Blessed is that servant whom the master finds doing so when he comes. 47 Truly I tell you, he will put him in charge of all his possessions.

48 "But if {that}[m] wicked servant says in his heart, 'My master delays [to come],'[n] 49 and begins to beat {his}[o] fellow servants, and eats and drinks with drunkards, 50 the master of that servant will come on a day when he does not expect him and at an hour he does not know, 51 and will cut him in pieces and assign him [a place][p] with the hypocrites; there will be weeping and gnashing of teeth."

25 1 "Then the kingdom of the heavens will be likened to ten virgins, who took their lamps and went out to meet the bridegroom [[and the bride]].[q] 2 Five of them were foolish and five were wise. 3 For the foolish, having taken {their}[r] lamps, did not take oil with them [[in their vessels]].[s] 4 But the wise ones took oil in {the}[t] vessels[u] with {their}[v] lamps. 5 And while the bridegroom was delayed, they all became drowsy and slept. 6 But at midnight there was a cry, 'Behold, the bridegroom [[is coming]]!'[w] Go out

---

a 24:37, **For**: Some manuscripts read "But." ℵ(01) W(032) Latin(a b ff² h) BYZ TR.

b 24:37, **also**: Included in D(05) W(032) Latin(a b e ff²) BYZ TR.

c 24:38, **just**: Included in D(05) W(032) BYZ TR.

d 24:38, **in those**: Absent from ℵ(01) W(032) Latin(a e) BYZ TR SBLGNT.

e 24:38, **before**: Some manuscripts read "of." Latin(a e).

f 24:39, **also**: Absent from B(03) D(05) Latin(a b h).

g 24:40, **the**: Included in W(032) BYZ TR.

h 24:41, **Two will be on one bed...**: Included in D(05) Latin(a b h).

i 24:42, **day**: Some manuscripts read "hour." Latin(a b h) BYZ TR.

j 24:43, **watch**: Some manuscripts read "hour." Latin(a b e ff² h).

k 24:45, **the**: Some manuscripts read "his." W(032) Latin(b) BYZ TR.

l 24:45, **them**: Absent from W(032).

m 24:48, **that**: ℵ(01) reads "the."

n 24:48, **to come**: Included in C(04) D(05) W(032) Latin(a b e ff² h) BYZ TR.

o 24:49, **his**: Some manuscripts read "the." W(032) BYZ TR.

p 24:51, **a place**: Absent from Latin(a).

q 25:1, **and the bride**: Included in D(05) Latin(a b ff² h).

r 25:3, **their**: Some manuscripts read "the." Latin(ff²).

s 25:3, **in their vessels**: Included in D(05).

t 25:4, **their**: Some manuscripts read "the." C(04) W(032) Latin(b ff²) BYZ TR.

u 25:4, **vessels**: Or flasks.

v 25:4, **their**: Some manuscripts read "the." C(04) Latin(ff²).

w 25:6, **is coming**: Included in D(05) W(032) Latin(b ff² h) BYZ TR.

to meet[a] [him].'[b] 7 Then all {those}[c] virgins got up and trimmed their lamps. 8 The foolish ones said to the wise, 'Give [[us]][d] some of your oil, for our lamps are going out.'

9 "But the wise answered, saying, 'No, lest there not be enough for us and you; [[but]][e] go rather to those who sell, and buy for yourselves.' 10 [But][f] {As they were going away}[g] to buy, the bridegroom came, and those who were ready went in with him to the wedding, and the door was shut. 11 Later the other virgins [also][h] came, saying, 'Lord, Lord, open to us.' 12 But he answered and said, 'Truly I say to you, I do not know you.' 13 Therefore, be alert, for you do not know the day nor the hour [[in which the Son of Man comes]].[i]

14 "[For][j] Just as a man going on a journey called his own servants and entrusted to them his possessions, 15 and to one he gave five talents, to another two, and to another one, to each according to his own ability, and he went away immediately. 16 [[But]][k] having gone, the one who had received the five talents worked with them [and gained][l] another five [talents];[m] 17 likewise [[also]],[n] the one with two gained another two [[talents]].[o] 18 But the one who had received the one [[talent]][p] [went away],[q] dug a hole [in the ground,][r] and hid his master's money. 19 Now, after a long time, the master of those servants came and settled accounts with them. 20 {And}[s] the one who had received the five [talents][t] came forward, bringing another five [talents][u] [[besides them]],[v] saying, 'Master, you entrusted me with five talents; see, I have gained [[with them]][w] another five [talents].'[x] 21 [[But]][y] His master said to him, 'Well done, good and faithful servant; you have been faithful over a little, I will set you over much; enter into the joy of your master.'

22 "But [also][z] the one {with}[a] the two talents came forward, saying, '[Lord],[b] you entrusted me with two talents; see, I have gained [[with me]][c] another two talents [[besides them]].'[d]

---

a 25:6, **meet:** Or, with the intention of escorting him to his destination.
b 25:6, **him:** Absent from ℵ(01) B(03).
c 25:7, **those:** Some manuscripts read "the." D(05).
d 25:8, **us:** Included in A(02).
e 25:9, **but:** Included in C(04) W(032) Latin(ff²) BYZ TR.
f 25:10, **But:** Absent from D(05) Latin(b ff²).
g 25:10, **As they were going away:** Some manuscripts read "Until they went." D(05) Latin(b ff²).
h 25:11, **also:** Absent from D(05) Latin(b h).
i 25:13, **in which the Son of Man comes:** Included in BYZ TR.
j 25:14, **For:** Absent from D(05) W(032).
k 25:16, **But:** Absent from C(04) D(05) W(032) Latin(ff² h) BYZ TR.
l 25:16, **and gained:** Absent from Latin(b ff²).
m 25:16, **talents:** Included in ℵ(01) A(02) C(04) D(05) W(032) BYZ TR.
n 25:17, **also:** Included in A(02) D(05) W(032) Latin(a h) BYZ TR.
o 25:17, **talents:** Included in D(05) Latin(a b ff² h).
p 25:18, **talent:** Included in A(02) Latin(a b ff² h).
q 25:18, **went away:** Absent from D(05) Latin(a b ff²).
r 25:18, **in the ground:** Absent from Latin(ff²).
s 25:20, **And:** Some manuscripts read "But." A(02).
t 25:20, **talents:** Absent from ℵ(01).
u 25:20, **talents:** Absent from W(032) Latin(h).
v 25:20, **besides them:** Included in A(02) D(05) W(032) Latin(h) BYZ TR.
w 25:20, **with them:** Absent from A(02) C(04) W(032) BYZ TR.
x 25:20, **talents:** Absent from C(04) Latin(a b ff² h).
y 25:21, **But:** Included in A(02) W(032) BYZ TR.
z 25:22, **also:** Absent from Latin(b ff²).
a 25:22, **with:** Some manuscripts read "having received." ℵ(01) D(05) Latin(a b ff² h) BYZ TR.
b 25:22, **Lord:** Absent from ℵ(01).
c 25:22, **with me:** Included in A(02) C(04) W(032) BYZ TR.
d 25:22, **besides them:** Included in A(02) C(04) BYZ TR.

23 His master said to him, 'Well done, good and faithful servant; you have been faithful over a little, I will set you over much; enter into the joy of your master.' 24 But [also]ᵃ the one who had received the one talent also came forward, saying, 'Master, I knew you to be a hard man, reaping where you did not sow and gathering where you did not scatter; 25 [[And]]ᵇ Being afraid, I went and hid your talent in the ground; see, you have what is yours.' 26 But his master answered him, 'You wicked and lazy servant! You knew that [[because I am a harsh man]]ᶜ I reap where I did not sow and gather where I did not scatter? 27 Then you should have invested my money with the bankers, and at my coming, I would have received what was mine with interest. 28 Therefore, take the talent from him and give it to {everyone}ᵈ who has the {ten}ᵉ talents; 29 for the one who has, more will be given, and he will have abundance; but [[from]]ᶠ the one who does not have, even what he has will be taken away. 30 And cast the worthless servant into the outer darkness; there will be weeping and gnashing of teeth.'

31 "When the Son of Man comes in his glory, and all the [[holy]]ᵍ angels with him, then he will sit on the throne of his glory;ʰ 32 and all the nations will be gathered before him, and he will separate them one from another, just as a shepherd separates the sheep from the goats, 33 and he will place the sheep on his right, but the goats on the left.

34 "Then the king will say to those on his right, 'Come, you who are blessed by my Father, inherit the kingdom prepared for you from the foundation of the world. 35 For I was hungry and you gave me food, [[and]]ⁱ I was thirsty and you gave me drink, I was a stranger and you welcomed me, 36 I was naked and you clothed me, I was sick and you visited me, I was in prison and you came to me.'

37 "Then the righteous will answer him, saying, 'Lord, when did we see you hungry and feed you, or thirsty and give you drink? 38 When did we see you a stranger and welcome you, or naked and clothe you? 39 When did we see you sick or in prison and come to you?' 40 And the king will answer them, 'Truly, I say to you, as you did it to one of the least [of these my brothers],ʲ you did it to me.'

41 "Then he will say to those on his left, 'Depart from me, you who are cursed, into the eternal fire [[my Father has]]ᵏ prepared for the devil and his angels. 42 For I was hungry and you gave me nothing to eat, I was thirsty and you gave me nothing to drink, 43 I was a stranger and you did not invite me in, [and]ˡ I was naked and you did not clothe me, I was sick and in prison and you did not look after me.'

44 "They also will answer [[him]],ᵐ 'Lord, when did we see you hungry or thirsty or a stranger or needing clothes or sick or in prison, and did not help you?'

45 "He will reply, 'Truly I tell you, whatever you did not do for one of the least of these, you did not do for me.' 46 Then they will go away to eternal punishment, but the righteous to eternal life."

ᵃ 25:24, **also:** Absent from D(05) Latin(a b).

ᵇ 25:25, **And:** Included in D(05) Latin(a b ff² h).

ᶜ 25:26, **because I am a harsh man:** Included in W(032).

ᵈ 25:28, **everyone:** Some manuscripts read "the one." D(05) W(032).

ᵉ 25:28, **ten:** Some manuscripts read "five." D(05).

ᶠ 25:29, **from:** Included in A(02) C(04) W(032) BYZ TR.

ᵍ 25:31, **holy:** Included in A(02) W(032) BYZ TR.

ʰ 25:31, **throne of his glory:** Or his glorious throne.

ⁱ 25:35, **and:** Included in W(032).

ʲ 25:40, **of these my brothers:** Absent from B(03) Latin(ff²).

ᵏ 25:41, **my Father has:** Included in D(05) Latin(a b ff² h).

ˡ 25:43, **and:** Included in 𝔓45.

ᵐ 25:44, **him:** Included in ℵ(01) Latin(ff² h) TR.

26 1 And it happened when Jesus
finished all these words, he said
to {his}[a] disciples, 2 "[You know][b] that
after two days the Passover takes place,
and the Son of Man is delivered over to
be crucified."

3 Then the chief priests and the
elders [of the people][c] gathered in the
courtyard of the high priest [[and the
scribes]],[d] who was called Caiaphas,
4 and they conspired to arrest Jesus by
deceit [and kill him];[e] 5 but they said,
"Not during the feast, lest there be an
uproar among the people."

6 Now when Jesus was in Bethany,
in the house of Simon the [[one called
the]][f] leper, 7 a woman came to him
with an alabaster jar of very expensive
ointment, and she poured it on his head
as he was reclining at the table. 8 When
{the}[g] disciples saw this, they were
indignant, saying, "Why this waste?
9 For this [[ointment]][h] could have been
sold for a high price and given to the
poor." 10 But Jesus, aware of this, said to
them, "Why do you trouble the woman?
[For][i] She has done a good deed for me.
11 For you always have the poor with
you, but you do not always have me.
12 For in pouring this ointment on my
body, she has prepared me for burial.

13 "Truly I say to you, wherever this
gospel is preached in the whole world,
what she has done will also be spoken
of in memory of her."

14 Then one of the twelve, the one
called Judas Iscariot, went to the chief
priests 15 and said [[to them]],[j] "What
are you willing to give me, and I will
hand him over to you?" And they set
for him thirty silver coins. 16 And from
then on, he sought an opportunity to
hand him over [[to them]].[k]

17 On the first day of Unleavened
Bread, the disciples came to Jesus,
saying [[to him]],[l] "Where do you want
us to [[go]][m] prepare for you to eat the
Passover?"

18 He said [[to them]],[n] "Go into
the city to a certain man and say to
him, '[The teacher says,][o] My time is
near; I will keep the Passover at your
house with my disciples.'" 19 {And}[p]
the disciples did as Jesus had directed
them, and they prepared the Passover.

20 When evening came, he
reclined at the table with the twelve
[[disciples]].[q] 21 And as they were
eating, he said, "Truly I tell you, one of
you will betray me." 22 And they were
very sorrowful and began to say to him
each one, "Is it I, Lord?"

23 He answered, "The one who has
dipped his hand in the dish with me
will hand me over. 24 [[Therefore]][r] The
Son of Man goes as it is written of him,
but woe to that man by whom the Son
of Man is handed over [[because of
this]]![s] It would have been better for
that man if he had not been born."

---

[a] 26:1, **his:** D(05) reads "the."
[b] 26:2, **you know:** Absent from D(05).
[c] 26:3, **of the people:** Absent from B(03).
[d] 26:3, **and the scribes:** Included in W(032) Latin(ff^{2} h) BYZ TR.
[e] 26:4, **and kill him:** Absent from B(03).
[f] 26:6, **one called the** Included in 𝔓45.
[g] 26:8, **the:** Some manuscripts read "his." A(02) W(032) BYZ TR.
[h] 26:9, **ointment:** Included in BYZ TR.
[i] 26:10, **For:** Absent from Latin(a).
[j] 26:15, **to them:** Included in D(05) Latin(a b ff^{2} h).
[k] 26:16, **to them:** Included in D(05) Latin(b h).
[l] 26:17, **to him:** Included in A(02) BYZ TR.
[m] 26:17, **go:** Included in W(032).
[n] 26:18, **to them:** Included in Latin(a b).
[o] 26:18, **The teacher says:** Absent from A(02).
[p] 26:19, **And:** W(032) reads "Then."
[q] 26:20, **disciples:** Included in ℵ(01) A(02) W(032) Latin(a b ff^{2} h) SBLGNT ‖ Absent from 𝔓37 𝔓45 B(03) D(05) BYZ TR.
[r] 26:24, **Therefore:** Included in D(05).
[s] 26:24, **because of this:** Included in D(05) Latin(a).

25 Then Judas, who would betray him, answered, "Is it I, Rabbi?" {He}ᵃ said to him, "You have said so."

26 While they were eating, Jesus took bread, And {having blessed},ᵇ he broke it and gave it to the disciples, saying, "Take, eat; this is my body." 27 [And]ᶜ Taking a cup, and after giving thanks, he gave it to them, saying, "[All of]ᵈ You Drink from it, 28 [for]ᵉ this is my blood of the [[new]]ᶠ covenant, which is poured out for many for the forgiveness of sins. 29 But I tell you [[that]],ᵍ I will not drink from this fruit of the vine from now on until that day when I drink it new with you in the kingdom of my Father."

30 And after singing a hymn, they went out to the Mount of Olives.

31 Then Jesus says to them, "All of you will be made to stumble because of me this night, for it has been written, 'I will strike the shepherd, and the sheep of the flock will be scattered.'ʰ 32 But after I am raised, I will go ahead of you into Galilee."

33 Peter answered and said [to him],ⁱ "Even if all stumble because of you, [[but]]ʲ I will never stumble."

34 [[And]]ᵏ Jesus said to him, "Truly I say to you that on this night, before the rooster crows, you will deny me three times."

35 Peter said to him, "Even if I must die with you, I will not deny you." Likewise, all the disciples said *the same.*

36 Then Jesus went with them to a place called Gethsemane, and he said to {the}ˡ disciples, "Sit [here]ᵐ while I go over there and pray."

37 And taking Peter and the two sons of Zebedee, he began to be grieved and distressed.

38 Then {he}ⁿ said to them, "My soul is deeply grieved, to the point of death; remain here and keep watch with me."

39 And going a little farther, he fell on his face, praying and saying, "[My]ᵒ Father, if it is possible, let this cup pass from me; yet not as I will, but as you will."

40 And he came to {the}ᵖ disciples and found them sleeping, and he said to Peter, "So, you could not keep watch with me for one hour?

41 "Keep watch and pray, so that you do not enter into temptation; the spirit is willing, but the flesh is weak."

ᵃ 26:25, **He:** Some manuscripts read "Jesus." 𝔓45 ℵ(01) Latin(a b ff² h).

ᵇ 26:26, **having blessed:** Some manuscripts read "gave thanks." A(02) W(032) BYZ.

ᶜ 26:27, **And:** Absent from C(04).

ᵈ 26:27, **All of:** Absent from D(05) Latin(a b).

ᵉ 26:28, **for:** Absent from Latin(a).

ᶠ 26:28, **new:** Included in A(02) C(04) W(032) Latin(a ff² h) ‖ Absent from 𝔓37 ℵ(01) B(03) NA28 SBLGNT THGNT.

ᵍ 26:29, **that:** Included in A(02) C(04) W(032) Latin(ff²) BYZ TR.

ʰ 26:31, Zechariah 13:7.

ⁱ 26:33, **to him:** Absent from 𝔓37 Latin(b ff²).

ʲ 26:33, **But:** Included in BYZ Latin(h).

ᵏ 26:34, **And:** Included in 𝔓37.

ˡ 26:36, **the:** B(03) BYZ TR NA28 SBLGNT THGNT ‖ Some manuscripts read "his." ℵ(01) A(02) C(04) D(05) W(032) Latin(a b ff² h).

ᵐ 26:36, **here:** Absent from ℵ(01) C(04).

ⁿ 26:38, **he:** Some manuscripts read "Jesus." Latin(a h) BYZ.

ᵒ 26:39, **My:** Absent from 𝔓53 Latin(a).

ᵖ 26:40, **the:** Some manuscripts read "his." D(05) Latin(a b ff² h).

42 Again, for the second time, he went away and prayed, [saying,]ᵃ "[My]ᵇ Father, if this [[cup]]ᶜ cannot pass away [[from me]]ᵈ unless I drink it, your will be done." 43 And coming again, he found them sleeping, for their eyes were heavy.

44 And leaving them [[again]],ᵉ he went away and prayed [for the third time],ᶠ saying the same word [again].ᵍ

45 Then he came to {the}ʰ disciples and said to them, "Sleep on now and take your rest;ⁱ [[for]]ʲ behold, the hour is at hand, and the Son of Man is handed over into the hands of sinners. 46 Rise, let us go; behold, the one who is handing me over has drawn near."

47 [And]ᵏ While he was still speaking, behold, Judas, one of the twelve, came and with him a great crowd with swords and clubs from the chief priests and elders of the people.

48 Now the one who was betraying him gave them a sign, saying, "Whomever I kiss, that one is he; seize him." 49 And immediately he went up to Jesus and said [[to him]],ˡ "Greetings, Rabbi," and kissed him.

50 But {Jesus}ᵐ said to him, "Friend, for what purpose have you come?" Then they came and laid hands on Jesus and seized him.

51 And behold, one of those with {Jesus}ⁿ having stretched out his hand, drew his sword and struck the servant of the high priest and cut off his ear.

52 Then Jesus said to him, "Put your sword back into its place; for all who take up the sword will {perish}ᵒ by the sword. 53 Or do you think that I cannot [[now]]ᵖ call upon my Father, and he will provide me [[here]]�q [now]ʳ with more than twelve legions of angels? 54 But how then would the Scriptures be fulfilled, that it must happen this way?"

55 At that hour, Jesus said to the crowds, "Have you come out as against a robber,ˢ with swords and clubs to capture me? Day after day I sat [[with you]]ᵗ in the temple teaching, and you did not seize me. 56 But all this has taken place that the Scriptures of the prophets might be fulfilled." Then all {the}ᵘ disciples left him and [[those who had seized Jesus]]ᵛ fled. 57 Those who had seized Jesus led him away to Caiaphas the high priest, where the scribes and the elders had gathered.

ᵃ 26:42, **saying:** Absent from B(03).

ᵇ 26:42, **My:** Absent from 𝔓37 Latin(a).

ᶜ 26:42, **cup:** Included in Latin(a h) BYZ TR.

ᵈ 26:42, **from me:** Included in A(02) C(04) W(032) Latin(ff²) BYZ TR.

ᵉ 26:44, **again:** Absent from 𝔓37 Latin(a).

ᶠ 26:44, **for the third time:** Absent from 𝔓37 A(02) D(05) Latin(a b ff²).

ᵍ 26:44, **again:** Absent from A(02) C(04) D(05) W(032) Latin(a b ff² h) BYZ TR.

ʰ 26:45, **the:** Some manuscripts read "his." D(05) W(032) BYZ TR Latin(a b ff² h).

ⁱ 26:45, **sleep on now and take your rest:** The verbs "sleep" and "take your rest" have ambiguous forms in Greek, they could be imperatives or indicatives that lead to a question being asked.

ʲ 26:45, **for:** Included in B(03).

ᵏ 26:47, **And:** Absent from Latin(a b ff² h).

ˡ 26:49, **to him:** Included in C(04).

ᵐ 26:50, **Jesus:** ℵ(01) reads "he."

ⁿ 26:51, **Jesus:** B(03) reads "him."

ᵒ 26:52, **perish:** Some manuscripts read "die." W(032) BYZ.

ᵖ 26:53, **now:** Included in A(02) W(032) Latin(a b ff² h) BYZ TR ‖ Absent from ℵ(01) B(03) NA28 SBLGNT THGNT.

q 26:53, **here:** Included in ℵ(01).

ʳ 26:53, **now:** ℵ(01) B(03) NA28 SBLGNT THGNT ‖ Absent from A(02) C(04) D(05) W(032) Latin(a b ff² h) BYZ TR.

ˢ 26:55, **robber:** Or revolutionary, insurrectionist.

ᵗ 26:55, **with you:** Included in A(02) C(04) D(05) W(032) Latin(a b ff² h) BYZ TR ‖ Absent from ℵ(01) B(03) NA28 SBLGNT THGNT.

ᵘ 26:56, **the:** Some manuscripts read "his." B(03) Latin(a h).

ᵛ 26:56, **those who had seized Jesus:** Included in B(03).

58 But Peter was following him at a distance, as far as the courtyard of the high priest; and going inside, he sat with the servants to see the end.

59 Now the chief priests [[and the elders]]^a and the whole council were seeking false testimony against Jesus so that they might put him to death, 60 but they found none, [[and]]^b though many false witnesses came forward [[, they did not find any]].^c But afterward, two [[false witnesses]]^d came forward. 61 and said, "{This one said},^e 'I am able to destroy the temple of God and in three days to build it.'" 62 And the high priest stood up and said to him, "Do you not answer? What is it that these testify against you?" 63 But Jesus was silent. And the high priest [[answering,]]^f said to him, "I adjure you by the living God, tell us if you are the Christ, the Son of [[the living]]^g God." 64 Jesus said to him, "You have said it; nevertheless, I tell you [[that]],^h from now on you will see the Son of Man seated at the right hand of Power and coming on the clouds of heaven."

65 Then the high priest tore his clothes, saying [[that]],ⁱ "[[See,]]^j He has blasphemed!^k What further need do we have of witnesses? See, now you have heard {the}^l blasphemy. 66 What do you think?" They [[all]]^m answered, "He deserves death."

67 Then they spat in his face and struck him; [but they slapped him,]ⁿ 68 saying, "Prophesy to us, Christ! Who is it that struck you?"

69 But Peter was sitting outside in the courtyard, and a servant girl came to him, saying, "You also were with Jesus the Galilean." 70 But he denied it before [them]^o all, saying, "I do not know what you are saying." 71 When he had gone out to the gateway, another [[servant girl]]^p saw him and said to those there, "This one was with Jesus the Nazarene." 72 And again he denied it with an oath [that]^q [[saying]],^r "I do not know the man." 73 After a little while, those standing by came up and said to Peter, "Truly you are also one of them, for your speech makes it clear [[you are a Galilean also]]."^s 74 Then he began to curse and swear, "I do not know the man." And immediately a rooster crowed. 75 And Peter remembered the word Jesus had said [[to him]]^t [that],^u "Before the rooster crows, you will deny me three times." And going out, he wept bitterly.

---

a 26:59, **and the elders:** Included in A(02) C(04) W(032) BYZ TR.

b 26:60, **And:** Included in A(02) W(032) BYZ TR.

c 26:60, **they did not find any:** Included in A(02) D(05) W(032) Latin(a) BYZ TR ‖ Absent from ℵ(01) B(03) C(04) Latin(a ff² h) NA28 SBLGNT THGNT.

d 26:60, **false witnesses:** Included in A(02) C(04) D(05) Latin(a b ff² h) BYZ TR ‖ Absent from ℵ(01) B(03) NA28 SBLGNT THGNT.

e 26:61, **This one said:** Some manuscripts read "We heard this one saying." D(05) Latin(b ff² h).

f 26:63, **answering:** Included in A(02) C(04) W(032) Latin(a b ff² h) BYZ TR ‖ Absent from ℵ(01) B(03) NA28 SBLGNT THGNT.

g 26:63, **the living:** Included in C(04) Latin(ff²).

h 26:64, **that:** Included in D(05).

i 26:65, **that:** Included in A(02) W(032) BYZ TR.

j 26:65, **See:** Included in ℵ(01).

k 26:65, **blasphemed:** The Greek word is defined by BDAG as: to speak in a disrespectful way that demeans, denigrates, maligns (BDAG, βλασφημέω).

l 26:65, **the:** Some manuscripts read "his." A(02) C(04) W(032) Latin(b ff²) BYZ TR.

m 26:66, **all:** Included in D(05) Latin(a b h).

n 26:67, **but they slapped him:** Absent from Latin(a b ff²).

o 26:70, **them:** Absent from A(02) C(04) W(032) BYZ.

p 26:71, **servant girl:** Included in D(05) Latin(a b ff² h).

q 26:72, **that:** Absent from ℵ(01) D(05) Latin(b ff²).

r 26:72, **saying:** Included in D(05) Latin(b ff²).

s 26:73, **you are a Galilean also:** Included in C(04).

t 26:75, **to him:** Included in A(02) C(04) W(032) Latin(b) BYZ TR.

u 26:75, **that:** Absent from D(05) Latin(a b ff² h).

27

¹Early in the morning, all the chief priests and the elders of the people took counsel against Jesus to put him to death; ²and having bound him, they led him away and handed [him]ᵃ over to [[Pontius]]ᵇ Pilate the governor.

³Then, when Judas, the one who handed him over, saw that he was condemned, he regretted it and returned the thirty silver coins to the chief priests and elders, ⁴saying, "I have sinned by handing over {innocent}ᶜ blood." But they said, "What is that to us? You see to it." ⁵And throwing the [[thirty]]ᵈ silver coins {into}ᵉ the temple, he withdrew, and going away, he hanged himself.

⁶But the chief priests, taking the silver coins, said, "It is not lawful to put them into the treasury, since it is blood money."

⁷So, after taking counsel, they bought with them the potter's field as a burial place for strangers. ⁸Therefore, that field has been called [[Akeldama, which means]]ᶠ the Field of Blood to this day.

⁹Then was fulfilled what was spoken through [Jeremiah]ᵍ the prophet, saying, "And they took the thirty silver coins, the price of the one who was valued, whom they valued from the sons of Israel, ¹⁰and they gave them for the potter's field, as the Lord directed me."ʰ

¹¹Now Jesus stood before the governor, and {the governor}ⁱ questioned him, saying, "Are you the king of the Jews?" And Jesus said [[to him]],ʲ "You say so." ¹²And while he was being accused by the chief priests and elders, he answered nothing.

¹³Then Pilate said to him, "Do you not hear how many things they testify against you?" ¹⁴And he did not answer him with regard to [not]ᵏ even one word, so that the governor was greatly amazed.

¹⁵Now at the feast the governor was accustomed to release for the crowd any one prisoner whom they {wanted}.ˡ ¹⁶And they had then a notorious prisoner called [Jesus]ᵐ Barabbas. ¹⁷{So}ⁿ when they had gathered, Pilate said to them, "Whom do you want me to release for you [[of the two]],ᵒ [Jesus the]ᵖ Barabbas or Jesus who is called Christ?" ¹⁸For he knew that it was out of envy that they had handed him over.

¹⁹While he was sitting on the judgment seat, his wife sent word to him, "Have nothing to do with that righteous man, for I have suffered much because of him today in a dream."

²⁰But the chief priests and the elders persuaded the crowds to ask for Barabbas and to destroy Jesus.

ᵃ 27:2, **him:** Included in A(02) W(032) BYZ TR.

ᵇ 27:2, **Pontius:** Included in A(02) C(04) W(032) Latin(a b ff² h) BYZ TR.

ᶜ 27:4, **innocent:** Some manuscripts read "righteous." Latin(a b ff² h).

ᵈ 27:5, **thirty:** Included in ℵ(01).

ᵉ 27:5, **into:** Some manuscripts read "in." A(02) C(04) W(032) Latin(a b ff² h) BYZ TR.

ᶠ 27:8, **Akeldama, which means:** Included in Latin(a b ff² h).

ᵍ 27:9, **Jeremiah:** Absent from Latin(a b).

ʰ 27:9-10, Zechariah 11:12-13, Jeremiah 19:1-3, 32:6-9.

ⁱ 27:11, **the governor:** Some manuscripts read "he." W(032).

ʲ 27:11, **to him:** Included in A(02) D(03) W(032) BYZ TR.

ᵏ 27:14, **not:** Absent from D(05).

ˡ 27:15, **wanted:** Some manuscripts read "entreated." BYZ TR.

ᵐ 27:16, **Jesus:** NA28[] SBLGNT ‖ Absent from ℵ(01) A(02) B(03) D(05) W(032) Latin(a b ff² h) BYZ TR THGNT.

ⁿ 27:17, **So:** Some manuscripts read "But." D(05) Latin(a b ff² h).

ᵒ 27:17, **of the two:** Included in Latin(a).

ᵖ 27:17, **Jesus the:** Absent from ℵ(01) A(02) D(05) W(032) Latin(a b ff² h) BYZ TR.

21 The governor again said to them, "Which of the two do you want me to release for you?" And they said, "Barabbas." 22 Pilate said to them, "Then what shall I do with Jesus who is called Christ?" They all said [[to him]],ᵃ "Let him be crucified." 23 [But]ᵇ {He}ᶜ said [[to them]],ᵈ "Why, what evil has he done?" But they shouted all the more, "Let him be crucified."

24 So when Pilate saw that he was gaining nothing, but rather that a riot was beginning, he took water and washed his hands before the crowd, saying, "I am innocent of the blood of this [righteous]ᵉ one; see to it yourselves."

25 And all the people answered, "His blood be on us and on our children!" 26 Then he released to them Barabbas, but Jesus, after having him flogged, he handed over to them to be crucified.

27 Then the soldiers of the governor took Jesus into the Praetorium and gathered the whole cohort around him. 28 And they stripped him and put on him [a purple garment and]ᶠ a scarlet cloak, 29 and having woven a crown of thorns, they put it on his head and put a reed in his right hand. And kneeling before him, they mocked him, saying, "Hail [[the]],ᵍ King of the Jews!" 30 And they spat on him and took the reed and struck him on the head. 31 And when they had mocked him, they stripped him of the cloak, put his own clothes on him, and led him away to crucify him.

32 As they were going out, they found a man from Cyrene [[to meet him]]ʰ named Simon; they forced him to carry his cross.

33 When they came to a place [called]ⁱ Golgotha, which is [called]ʲ Place of the Skull, 34 [[and]]ᵏ they offered him {wine}ˡ mixed with gall to drink; but after tasting it, he did not want to drink it. 35 And having crucified him, they divided his garments, casting lots, [[that it might be fulfilled which was spoken by the prophet: "They divided my garments among them, and for my clothing they cast lots,]]"ᵐ 36 and sitting down, they kept watch over him there.

37 They placed above his head the charge against him, written: "This is Jesus, the King of the Jews."

ᵃ 27:22, **to him:** Included in BYZ TR.

ᵇ 27:23, **But:** Absent from D(05) Latin(a b ff² h).

ᶜ 27:23, **he:** Some manuscripts read "the governor." A(02) D(05) W(032) Latin(a b ff² h) BYZ TR.

ᵈ 27:23, **to them:** Absent from D(05) Latin(a b ff² h).

ᵉ 27:24, **righteous:** Included in ℵ(01) A(02) W(032) Latin(ff²) BYZ TR.

ᶠ 27:28, **a purple garment and:** Included in D(05) Latin(a b ff² h).

ᵍ 27:29, **the:** Included in ℵ(01) A(02) W(032) BYZ TR.

ʰ 27:32, **to meet him:** Included in D(05).

ⁱ 27:33, **called:** Absent from D(05) Latin(a b ff² h).

ʲ 27:33, **called:** Absent from B(03).

ᵏ 27:34, **and:** Included in D(05) Latin(a b ff² h).

ˡ 27:34, **wine:** Some manuscripts read "vinegar." Or, sour wine. A(02) W(032) Latin(h) BYZ TR.

ᵐ 27:35, **that it might be fulfilled…:** Included in Latin(a b h) TR.

38 Then two robbers[a] were crucified with him, one on the right and one on the left. 39 But those passing by were blaspheming[b] him, shaking their heads 40 saying, "[[Aha!]][c] You who destroy the temple and build [it][d] in three days, save yourself! If you are the Son of God, [and][e] come down from the cross." 41 [And][f] Similarly, the chief priests, along with the scribes [and elders,][g] [[and Pharisees]][h] were mocking, saying, 42 "He saved others, he cannot save himself. He is the King of Israel; let him come down now from the cross, and we will believe {in him}.[i] 43 He trusts in God; let God rescue him now if he wants him, for he said, 'I am the Son of God.'"

44 The same was also the case with the robbers who were crucified with him, they were insulting him.

45 Now from the sixth hour darkness fell [over the whole land][j] until the ninth hour. 46 And about the ninth hour Jesus cried out with a loud voice, saying, "Eli, Eli, lema sabachthani?" that is, "My God, my God, why have you forsaken me?"[k]

47 Some of those standing there, when they heard it, said [that],[l] "This one is calling for Elijah." 48 And immediately one of them ran, and having taken a sponge, filled it with sour wine, and put it on a reed, and gave it to him to drink. 49 But the rest said, "Leave it, let us see if Elijah comes to save him." [[But another, taking a spear, pierced his side, and water and blood came out.]][m]

50 And Jesus, crying out [again][n] with a loud voice, yielded up his spirit.[o]

51 And behold, the curtain of the temple was torn in two from top to bottom, and the earth shook, and the rocks were split, 52 [and the tombs were opened,][p] and many bodies of the saints who had fallen asleep were raised, 53 and coming out of the tombs after his resurrection they entered the holy city and appeared to many.

54 Now the centurion and those with him who were keeping watch over Jesus, having seen the earthquake and what had happened, were greatly afraid, saying, "Truly this was the Son of God!"

55 There were many women there, watching from a distance, who had followed Jesus from Galilee, serving him; 56 among whom were [Mary Magdalene, and][q] Mary the mother of James and {Joseph},[r] and the mother of the sons of Zebedee.

---

[a] 27:38, **robbers:** Or revolutionary, insurrectionist.

[b] 27:39, **blaspheming:** The Greek word for *blasphemed* is defined by BDAG as: to speak in a disrespectful way that demeans, denigrates, maligns (BDAG, βλασφημέω).

[c] 27:40, **Aha:** Included in D(05) Latin(a b ff² h).

[d] 27:40, **it:** Included in Latin(a b ff² h).

[e] 27:40, **and:** Absent from B(03) W(032) Latin(ff²) BYZ TR.

[f] 27:41, **and:** Absent from ℵ(01) A(02) W(032) Latin(b).

[g] 27:41, **and elders:** Absent from D(05) W(032) Latin(a b ff² h).

[h] 27:41, **and Pharisees:** Included in D(05) W(032) Latin(a b ff² h) BYZ TR.

[i] 27:42, **in him:** Some manuscripts read "him." A(02) D(05) Latin(a b ff² h) TR.

[j] 27:45, **over the whole land:** Absent from ℵ(01).

[k] 27:46, Psalm 22:1.

[l] 27:47, **that:** Absent from ℵ(01) D(05) Latin(a b ff² h).

[m] 27:49, **But another, taking a spear, pierced his side, and water and blood came out:** Included in ℵ(01) B(03) C(04).

[n] 27:50, **again:** Absent from Latin(h).

[o] 27:50, **spirit:** Or breath.

[p] 27:52, **and the tombs were opened:** Absent from ℵ (01).

[q] 27:56, **Mary Magdalene, and:** Absent from ℵ(01).

[r] 27:56, **Joseph:** Some manuscripts read "Joses." A(02) B(03) BYZ TR.

57 When evening came, a rich man from Arimathea arrived, named Joseph, who also had become a disciple of Jesus. 58 This man approached Pilate and asked for the body of Jesus. Then Pilate ordered {it}ᵃ to be given.

59 And taking the body, Joseph wrapped it [in]ᵇ a clean linen cloth 60 and placed it in his new tomb which he had cut out in the rock, and, having rolled a large stone to the door of the tomb, he left. 61 There were Mary Magdalene and the other Mary sitting opposite the tomb.

62 Now on the next day, which is after the preparation, the chief priests and the Pharisees gathered together with Pilate, 63 saying, "Sir, we remember that this deceiver said while still alive, 'After three days I will rise.' 64 Therefore, command that the tomb be made secure until the third day, lest {his}ᶜ disciples come [[by night]]ᵈ and steal him away and say to the people, 'He has been raised from the dead,' and the last deception will be worse than the first."

65 [But]ᵉ Pilate said to them, "You have a guard; go, make it as secure as you know how." 66 And they went and made the tomb secure by sealing the stone along with the guard.

28 1 Now after the Sabbath, as it began to dawn toward the first day of the week, Mary Magdalene and the other Mary came to look at the tomb. 2 [And]ᶠ Behold, there was a great earthquake; for an angel of the Lord descended from heaven and came and rolled away the stone [[from the door]]ᵍ and sat upon it. 3 And his appearance was like lightning, and his clothing as white as snow. 4 And from the fear of him the guards shook and became like dead men.

5 [But]ʰ The angel answered and said [to the women],ⁱ "Do not be afraid; for I know that you are looking for Jesus who was crucified. 6 He is not here, for he has risen just as he said; come, see the place where {he}ʲ was lying. 7 And go quickly and tell his disciples that he has risen [from the dead],ᵏ and [behold,]ˡ he is going ahead of you into Galilee; there you will see him. Behold, I have told you."

8 And they quickly {departed}ᵐ from the tomb with fear and great joy, and ran to report to his disciples.

ᵃ 27:58, **it:** Some manuscripts read "the body." A(02) C(04) D(05) W(032) Latin(a b ff² h) BYZ TR.
ᵇ 27:59, **in:** B(03) D(05) Latin(a b ff² h) NA28[] ‖ Absent from ℵ(01) A(02) C(04) W(032) SBLGNT THGNT.
ᶜ 27:64, **his:** Some manuscripts read "the." N01 B(03).
ᵈ 27:64, **by night:** Included in BYZ TR.
ᵉ 27:65, **But:** Included in ℵ(01) A(02) C(04) D(05) W(032) BYZ TR.
ᶠ 28:2, **And:** Absent from ℵ(01) D(05) BYZ TR.
ᵍ 28:2, **from the door:** Included in A(02) C(04) W(032) Latin(h) BYZ TR.
ʰ 28:5, **But:** Absent from C(04) W(032).
ⁱ 28:5, **to the women:** Absent from ℵ(01).
ʲ 28:6, **he:** Some manuscripts read "the Lord." A(02) C(04) D(05) W(032) Latin(a b ff² h) BYZ TR.
ᵏ 28:7, **from the dead:** Absent from D(05) Latin(a b e h).
ˡ 28:7, **behold:** Absent from D(05) Latin(a b ff² h).
ᵐ 28:8, **departed:** Some manuscripts read "went out."

9 And [[as they went to tell his disciples,]]ᵃ behold, Jesus met them saying, "Rejoice!" And they, having approached, took hold of his feet and worshipedᵇ him.

10 Then Jesus said to them, "Do not be afraid; go and tell {my}ᶜ brothers to go to Galilee, and there they will see me."

11 Now as they were going, behold, some of the guard came into the city and reported to the chief priests all that had happened. 12 And when they had assembled with the elders and taken counsel, they gave a sufficient sum of money to the soldiers 13 and said, "Tell people, 'His disciples came by night and stole him away while we were asleep.' 14 And if this comes to the governor's ears, we will persuade [him]ᵈ and keep you out of trouble."

15 And those who had received the silver did as they were instructed. And this word was spread among the Jews until this day.

16 But the eleven disciples went to Galilee, to the mountain where Jesus had directed them.

17 And when they saw him, they worshipedᵉ [[him]],ᶠ but some doubted.

18 And Jesus came and spoke [to them,]ᵍ saying, "All authority has been given to me in heaven and on [the]ʰ earth. 19 [Therefore,]ⁱ Go and make disciples of all nations, baptizing them in the name of the Father and of the Son and of the Holy Spirit,ʲ 20 teaching them to observe all that I have commanded you, and behold, I am with you always, even to the end of the age. [[Amen]]"ᵏ

ᵃ 28:9, **as they went to tell his disciples:** Included in A(02) C(04) BYZ TR.

ᵇ 28:9, **worshiped:** See footnote for worship in Matt 2:2.

ᶜ 28:10, **my:** Some manuscripts read "the." ℵ(01).

ᵈ 28:14, **him:** Absent from ℵ(01) B(03) Latin(e).

ᵉ 28:17, **worshiped:** See footnote for worship in Matt 2:2.

ᶠ 28:17, **him:** A(02) W(032) Latin(a b e ff² h) BYZ TR ‖ Absent from ℵ(01) B(03) D(05) NA28 SBLGNT THGNT.

ᵍ 28:18, **to them:** Absent from ℵ(01).

ʰ 28:18, **the:** Absent from ℵ(01) A(02) W(032) BYZ TR.

ⁱ 28:19, **Therefore:** B(03) W(032) Latin(e ff²) TR NA28 SBLGNT THGNT ‖ Absent from ℵ(01) A(02) BYZ ‖ Some manuscripts read "Now." D(05) Latin(a b h).

ʲ 28:19, **Spirit:** See footnote for Spirit in Matt 1:18.

ᵏ 28:20, **Amen:** Included in Latin(a b ff²) BYZ TR.

Mark[a]

1 [1] The beginning of the gospel of Jesus Christ[b] [, Son of God].[c]

[2] As it is written in {Isaiah the prophet},[d] "Behold, I send my messenger before your face, who will prepare your way [[before you]][e];"[f]

[3] "The voice of one crying in the wilderness, 'Prepare the way of the Lord, make {his paths straight}.[g]"[h]

[4] [[And]][i] John {the baptizer came about in the wilderness, and was preaching}[j] a baptism of repentance for the forgiveness of sins. [5] And all the Judean countryside and all the Jerusalemites were going out to him, [and][k] they were being baptized {by him in the Jordan River},[l] confessing their sins.

[6] And John was clothed with camel's hair [and wore a leather belt around his waist][m] and ate locusts and wild honey.

[7] And {he preached, saying},[n] "After me comes he who is mightier than I, the strap of whose sandals I am not worthy to [stoop down and][o] untie. [8] [[Indeed]][p] I baptize you with water, {but he will baptize}[q] [you][r] in the Holy Spirit."[s]

[9] And it happened in those days that Jesus came from Nazareth of Galilee and was baptized in the Jordan by John.

---

a 1:0, **Title ("Mark"):** Absent from ℵ01 B(03). ‖ A(02) D(05) Latin(a b ff²) reads "Gospel According to Mark." ‖ TR reads "The Holy Gospel According to Mark."

b 1:1, **Christ:** The Greek word is defined by BDAG as: (1) fulfiller of Israelite expectation of a deliverer, the Anointed one, the Messiah, the Christ, (2) the personal name ascribed to Jesus Christ. (BDAG, Χριστός).

c 1:1, **Son of God:** A(02) B(03) D(05) W(032) Syriac(sy) Latin(a b ff²) BYZ TR NA28[] THGNT ‖ Absent from ℵ(01) SBLGNT.

d 1:2, **Isaiah the prophet:** ℵ(01) B(03) D(05) Latin(a b ff²) NA28 SBLGNT THGNT ‖ Some manuscripts read "the prophets." A(02) W(032) BYZ TR.

e 1:2, **before you:** Included in A(02) Latin(ff²) BYZ TR ‖ Absent from ℵ01 B(03) D(05) W(032) Latin(a b) NA28 THGNT SBLGNT.

f 1:2, Malachi 3:1 Masoretic text.

g 1:3, **his paths straight:** Some manuscripts read "straight the paths of God for yourselves." D(05) Latin (a b ff²).

h 1:3, Isaiah 40:3 LXX.

i 1:4, **And:** Included in ℵ(01) W(032).

j 1:4, **the baptizer came about in the wilderness, and was preaching:** ℵ(01) NA28 THGNT‖ Some manuscripts read "came baptizing in the wilderness and preaching." A(02) W(032) BYZ TR ‖ Some manuscripts read "came about, the one baptizing in the wilderness, proclaiming." B(03) SBLGNT ‖ Some manuscripts read "came about in the wilderness and baptizing, proclaiming." D(05) Latin(a b ff²).

k 1:5, **And:** Absent from ℵ(01) Latin(a).

l 1:5, **by him in the Jordan River:** ℵ(01) B(03) Latin(b ff²) NA28 SBLGNT ‖ Some manuscripts read "in the Jordan River, by him." A(02) D(05) W(032) Latin(a) BYZ TR.

m 1:6, **and wore a leather belt around his waist:** Absent from D(05) Latin(a b ff²).

n 1:7, **preached, saying:** Some manuscripts read "he said to them." D(05) Latin(a).

o 1:7, **stoop down and:** Absent from D(05) Latin(a ff²).

p 1:8, **Indeed:** Included in A(02) D(05) W(032) BYZ TR.

q 1:8, **but he will baptize:** D(01) reads "and he baptizes."

r 1:8, **you:** Absent from ℵ(01).

s 1:8, **Spirit:** See footnote for Spirit in Matt 1:18

10 And [immediately,]ᵃ as he was coming up out of the water, he saw the heavens being torn apart and the Spirit descending like a dove [[and coming]]ᵇ [in]ᶜ him. 11 And a voice [came]ᵈ from {the heavens},ᵉ "You are my beloved Son; in you I am well pleased."

12 And immediately the [[Holy]]ᶠ Spirit drives him out into the wilderness. 13 And he was [[there]]ᵍ in the wilderness forty days, being tempted by Satan, and he was with the wild animals, and the angels were ministering to him.

14 {But}ʰ After John was handed over,ⁱ Jesus came into Galilee, proclaiming the good newsʲ [[of the kingdom]]ᵏ of God 15 [and]ˡ [saying],ᵐ "The time is fulfilled, and the kingdom of God has come near; repent and believe in the good news."

16 And passing by the Sea of Galilee, he saw Simon and Andrew, the brother of Simon, casting {a net}ⁿ into the sea; for they were fishermen. 17 And Jesus said to them, "Come afterᵒ me, and I will make you fishers of men." 18 And immediately, leaving {the nets},ᵖ they followed him.

19 And going on [[from there]]�q a little further, he saw James the son of Zebedee and John his brother, and they were in the boat mending their nets. 20 And immediately he called them; and leaving their father Zebedee in the boat with the hired servants, they went after him.

21 And they went into Capernaum; and immediately on the Sabbath {he entered the synagogue and taught [[them]]ʳ}.ˢ 22 And they were astonished at his teaching; for he was teaching them as one having authority, [and]ᵗ not as the scribes.

23 And [immediately]ᵘ there was in {their}ᵛ synagogue a man with an unclean spirit, and he cried out, 24 saying, "{What is there between us and you},ʷ Jesus of Nazareth? [[Ha!]]ˣ Have you come to destroy us? I know who you are, the Holy One of God."

ᵃ 1:10, **immediately:** Absent from D(05) Latin(a b).

ᵇ 1:10, **and coming:** Included in ℵ(01) W(032) Latin(b ff²).

ᶜ 1:10, **in:** B(03) D(05) Latin(a b) NA28, SBLGNT, THGNT ‖ Some manuscripts read "upon." ℵ(01) A(02) W(032) Syriac(sy) BYZ TR.

ᵈ 1:11, **came:** Absent from ℵ(01) D(05) Latin(b ff²).

ᵉ 1:11, **the heavens:** W(032) reads "heaven."

ᶠ 1:12, **Holy:** Included in D(05).

ᵍ 1:13, **there:** Included in W(032) Syriac(syˢ) Latin(a) BYZ TR.

ʰ 1:14, **But:** Some manuscripts read "And." B(03) D(05) Latin(a) SBLGNT.

ⁱ 1:14, **handed over:** Or arrested.

ʲ 1:14, **good news:** Or Gospel.

ᵏ 1:14, **of the kingdom:** Included in A(02) D(05) W(032) Syriac(sy) Latin(a) BYZ TR ‖ Absent from ℵ(01) B(03) Latin(b ff²) NA28 SBLGNT THGNT.

ˡ 1:15, **and:** Absent from ℵ(01) A(02) D(05) Syriac(syˢ) Latin(ff²).

ᵐ 1:15, **saying:** Absent from ℵ(01) Syriac(syˢ).

ⁿ 1:16, **a net:** Some manuscripts read "the nets." D(05) Latin(a).

ᵒ 1:17, **come after:** Or follow.

ᵖ 1:18, **the nets:** ℵ(01) B(03) C(04) W(032) NA28 SBLGNT THGNT ‖ Some manuscripts read "their nets." A(02) Syriac(syˢ) BYZ TR ‖ Some manuscripts read "all." D(05) Latin(a b ff²).

q 1:19, **from there:** Included in A(02) C(04) BYZ TR.

ʳ 1:21, **them:** Included in D(05) Latin(a b e ff²).

ˢ 1:21, **he entered the synagogue and taught:** A(02) B(03) W(032) Latin(b) BYZ TR NA28 THGNT ‖ Some manuscripts read "he taught in the synagogue." ℵ(01) SBLGNT.

ᵗ 1:22 , **And:** Absent from D(05), Latin(b e).

ᵘ 1:23, **immediately:** ℵ(01) B(03) Syriac(sy) NA28 SBLGNT THGNT ‖ Absent from A(02) C(04) D(05) W(032) Latin(b e ff²) BYZ TR.

ᵛ 1:23, **their:** Some manuscripts read "the." D(05) Latin(b e ff²).

ʷ 1:24, **What is there between us and you:** Some manuscripts read "What have we to do with you." C(04) BYZ TR.

ˣ 1:24, **Ha!:** Included in A(02) C(04) BYZ TR.

25 And {Jesus}[a] rebuked it, [saying,][b] "Be silent, and come out of {him}."[c] 26 And the unclean spirit, {convulsing him}[d] and crying out with a loud voice, came out of him.

27 And they were all amazed, so as to discuss [among themselves, saying],[e] "{What is this? A new teaching with authority! He commands}[f] [even][g] the unclean spirits, and they obey him."

28 And his fame spread [immediately][h] [everywhere][i] throughout the whole region {of Galilee}.[j]

29 {And immediately}[k] after leaving the synagogue, they came into the house of Simon and Andrew, with James and John.

30 Now Simon's mother-in-law was lying down, suffering from a fever, and they [immediately][l] told him about her. 31 And approaching, he raised her up, taking her by the hand; and [[immediately]][m] the fever left her, and she served them.

32 And when evening came, after the sun had set, they brought to him all who were sick and those who were demon-possessed; 33 and the whole city was gathered together [at {the}[n] door. 34 And he healed many][o] who were sick with various diseases and cast out many demons [[from those who had them]];[p] and he did not allow the demons to speak, because they knew him [[to be the Christ]].[q]

35 And [very][r] early in the morning, [while it was still dark,][s] he [got up and][t] went out and departed to a deserted place, and there he prayed.

36 And Simon and those with him pursued him, 37 and {they found him and said to him}[u] [that],[v] "Everyone is looking for you."

38 And he said to them, "Let us go [elsewhere,][w] to the neighboring towns, so that I may preach [there also];[x] for this is why I came out."

---

a 1:25, **Jesus:** Some manuscripts read "he." D(05) W(032) Latin(b).

b 1:25, **saying:** Absent from ℵ(01). ‖ Some manuscripts read "and he said." W(032) Latin(b e).

c 1:25, **him:** Some manuscripts read "the man, unclean spirit." D(05) W(032) Latin(b e ff²).

d 1:26, **convulsing him:** Some manuscripts read "came out having convulsed him." D(05) W(032) Latin(e) ‖ B(03) reads "convulsed him."

e 1:27, **among themselves, saying:** Absent from Latin (b e ff²).

f 1:27, **A new teaching with authority! He commands:** Some manuscripts read "What is this new teaching, that with authority he commands." A(02) C(04) BYZ TR.

g 1:27, **even:** Absent from W(032).

h 1:28, **immediately:** A(02) B(03) C(04) BYZ TR NA28 SBLGNT THGNT‖ Absent from ℵ(01) W(032) Syriac(syˢ) Latin(b e ff²).

i 1:28, **everywhere:** B(03) C(04) W(032) Latin(b e) NA28 SBLGNT THGNT ‖ Absent from ℵ(01) A(02) B(05) Latin(ff²) BYZ TR.

j 1:28, **of Galilee:** ℵ(01) reads "of Judea."

k 1:29, **And immediately:** Some manuscripts read "But having gone out." D(05) W(032) Latin (e ff²).

l 1:30, **immediately:** Absent from W(032) Latin(b ff²).

m 1:31, **immediately:** Included in A(02) D(05) Latin(b ff²) BYZ TR.

n 1:33, **the:** Some manuscripts read "his." D(05) Latin(ff²).

o 1:33-34, **at the door. And he healed many:** Absent from ℵ(01).

p 1:34, **from those who had them:** Included in D(05) Latin(ff²).

q 1:34, **to be the Christ:** Included in B(03) C(04) W(032).

r 1:35, **very:** Absent from W(032) Latin(a b e ff²).

s 1:35, **while it was still dark:** Absent from Latin(b ff²).

t 1:35, **got up:** Absent from D(05) Latin(a).

u 1:37, **they found him and said to him:** Some manuscripts read "when they found him, they said." D(05) Latin(a ff²) ‖ Some manuscripts read "saying to them." W(032) Latin(b).

v 1:37, **that:** Absent from W(032) Latin(e).

w 1:38, **elsewhere:** Absent from A(02) D(05) W(032) Latin(a b e ff²) BYZ TR.

x 1:38, **there also:** Absent from W(032) Latin(e).

39 And he went, preaching in their synagogues throughout all Galilee [and casting out demons].[a]

40 And a leper came to him, imploring him [kneeling down][b] [[to him]][c] and saying [to him],[d] "[[Lord,]][e] If you are willing, you can make me clean." 41 And [[Jesus,]][f] {moved with compassion},[g] he stretched out his hand and touched him, and said [to him],[h] "I am willing; be cleansed." 42 And [[when he had spoken]][i] immediately the leprosy left him [, and he was cleansed].[j]

43 And he sternly warned him, [he immediately sent him away,][k] 44 and he said to him, "See that you tell no one anything, but go, show yourself to the priest and offer for your cleansing what Moses commanded, as a testimony to them."

45 But he went out and began to proclaim [much][l] and spread the word, so that he could no longer enter a city openly, but [was][m] in deserted places; and they came to him [from everywhere].[n]

2 1 And entering again into Capernaum after some days, it was heard that he was in a house. 2 And [[immediately]][o] many gathered, so that there was no longer room, not even at the door, and he spoke the word to them.

3 And [[behold,]][p] {they came, bringing to him a paralytic carried by four men}.[q] 4 And not being able to {bring him to him}[r] {because of}[s] the crowd, they removed the roof where {he}[t] was, and having dug through, they let down the mat {where}[u] the paralytic lay.

5 [And][v] seeing their faith, Jesus said to the paralytic, "[[Take courage,]][w] [[My]][x] Child, your sins {are being}[y] forgiven [[you]]."[z]

6 Now some of the scribes were sitting [there][a] and reasoning in their hearts, [[saying,]][b] 7 "Why does this

---

a 1:39, **and casting out demons:** Absent from W(032).
b 1:40, **kneeling down:** Absent from B(03) D(05) Latin(a b ff²).
c 1:40, **to him:** Included in A(02) C(04) BYZ TR.
d 1:40, **to him:** Absent from D(05) W(032) Latin(a b ff²).
e 1:40, **Lord:** Included in W(032).
f 1:41, **Jesus:** Included in A(02) C(04) BYZ TR.
g 1:41, **moved with compassion:** Some manuscripts read "having become angry." D(05) Latin(a ff²) SBLGNT ‖ Absent from Latin(b).
h 1:41, **to him** Absent from ℵ(01) W(032) Latin(b ff²).
i 1:42, **when he had spoken:** Included in A(02) C(04) BYZ TR.
j 1:42, **and he was cleansed:** Absent from (W032) Latin(b).
k 1:43, **he immediately sent him away:** Absent from W(032) Latin(b).
l 1:45, **much:** Absent from D(05) W(032) Latin(a b e ff²).
m 1:45, **was:** Absent from B(03) Latin(b e).
n 1:45, **from everywhere:** Absent from Latin(b e).
o 2:2, **immediately:** Included in A(02) C(04) D(05) Latin(a e ff²) BYZ TR.
p 2:3, **behold:** Included in W(032).
q 2:3, **they came, bringing to him a paralytic carried by four men:** Some manuscripts read "men were bringing to him a paralytic on a bed." W(032) Latin(b e).
r 2:4, **bring him to him:** Some manuscripts read "approach him." 𝔓84 A(02) C(04) BYZ TR ‖ Some manuscripts read "approach." D(05) Latin(b e).
s 2:4, **because of:** Some manuscripts read "from." D(05) W(032).
t 2:4, **he:** Some manuscripts read "Jesus." D(05) Latin(a e ff²).
u 2:4, **where:** Some manuscripts read "on which." 𝔓84 A(02) C(04) BYZ TR Latin(b e ff²).
v 2:5, **And:** Some manuscripts read "But." A(02) D(05) W(032) BYZ TR.
w 2:5, **take courage:** Included in C(04).
x 2:5, **my:** Included in ℵ(01).
y 2:5, **are being:** B(03) NA28 SBLGNT ‖ Some manuscripts read "are." 𝔓88 ℵ(01) A(02) C(04) W(032) Syriac(sy) BYZ TR THGNT.
z 2:5, **you:** Included in BYZ TR Latin (a).
a 2:6, **there:** Absent from Latin (b ff²).
b 2:6, **saying:** Included in D(05) W(032) Latin (a b e ff²).

man speak like {this? He blasphemes!}[a] Who can forgive sins but God alone?"

8 And [immediately][b] Jesus, recognizing in his spirit that they were reasoning in this way within themselves, says [to them],[c] "Why do you reasoning [these things][d] in your hearts? 9 [[For]][e] Which is easier, to say [to the paralytic],[f] 'Your sins {are being}[g] forgiven,' or to say, 'Rise, [[and]][h] take up your mat][i] and {walk}'?[j]

10 "But so that you may know that the Son of Man has authority {to forgive sins [on earth][k]}"[l] - he says to the paralytic, 11 "{I say to you, rise},[m] [[and]][n] pick up your mat and go to your house."

12 {And he rose and}[o] immediately took up the mat and went out before them all, so that they were [all][p]

amazed and glorified God, [saying,][q] "We have never seen anything like this!"

13 And he went out [again][r] {by}[s] the sea; and all the crowd came to him, and he taught them.

14 And as he passed by, he saw Levi the son of Alphaeus sitting at the tax office, and he said to him, "Follow me." And rising up, he followed him.

15 And it happened that {he reclined}[t] in his house, [and][u] many tax collectors and sinners were dining with Jesus and his disciples; for there were many and they followed him.

16 And the scribes {of}[v] the Pharisees, [seeing that he was eating with sinners and tax collectors,][w] said to his disciples, "[[Why is it]][x] That {he}[y] eats [[and drinks]][z] with tax collectors and sinners?"

---

a 2:7, **this? He blasphemes!:** Some manuscripts read "this, uttering blasphemies?" C(04) W(032) BYZ TR Latin (e).

b 2:8, **immediately:** Absent from D(05) W(032) Latin(b ff²).

c 2:8, **to them:** Absent from B(03) Latin(ff²).

d 2:8, **these things:** Absent from W(032) Latin (b e ff²).

e 2:9, **For:** Included in W(032).

f 2:9, **to the paralytic:** Absent from W(032) Latin(a e).

g 2:9, **are being:** 𝔓88 ℵ(01) B(03) D(05) Latin (a b e ff²) NA28 SBLGNT ‖ Some manuscripts read "are." A(02) C(04) W(032) BYZ TR THGNT.

h 2:9, **and:** Absent from C(04) D(05) Latin (a ff²).

i 2:9, **and take up your mat:** Absent from W(032) Latin (b e).

j 2:9, **walk:** Some manuscripts read "go." 𝔓88 ℵ(01) ‖ Some manuscripts read "go to your house." D(05) Latin (a ff²).

k 2:10, **on earth:** Absent from W(032) Latin(b).

l 2:10, **to forgive sins on earth:** 𝔓88 ℵ(01) C(04) Latin (e ff²) NA28 ‖ Some manuscripts read "on earth to forgive sins." A(02) BYZ TR SBLGNT THGNT.

m 2:11, **I say to you, rise:** Some manuscripts read "Rise, I say to you." 𝔓88 ℵ(01).

n 2:11, **and:** Included in A(02) W(032) BYZ TR.

o 2:12, **And he rose and:** Some manuscripts read "But having risen." W(032) Latin(b).

p 2:12, **all:** Absent from W(032) Latin (b e).

q 2:12, **saying:** Absent from W(032) Latin(b) ‖ D(05) reads "and said."

r 2:13, **again:** Absent from D(05).

s 2:13, **by:** Some manuscripts read "into." ℵ(01) Latin(a e ff²).

t 2:15, **he reclined:** Some manuscripts read "while reclining." A(02) C(04) BYZ TR.

u 2:15, **and:** Absent from D(05) W(032) Latin(a b e ff²).

v 2:16, **of:** Some manuscripts read "and." A(02) C(04) D(05) Latin(a e ff²) BYZ TR.

w 2:16, **seeing that he was eating with sinners and tax collectors:** Absent from W(032) Latin(e).

x 2:16, **Why is it:** Included in ℵ(01) A(02) D(05) W(032) BYZ TR ‖ Absent from B(03) C(04) Latin(a b e ff²).

y 2:16, **he:** Some manuscripts read "your teacher." ℵ(01) C(04).

z 2:16, **and drinks:** Included in 𝔓88 A(02) C(04) BYZ TR.

17 And when Jesus heard it, he said [to them],[a] [that][b] "Those who are well have no need of a physician, but those who are sick; I did not come to call the righteous, but sinners [[to repentance]]."[c]

18 And the disciples of John and [[the disciples]][d] of the Pharisees were fasting. And they came and said to him, "Why do the disciples of John [and {the disciples}[e] of the Pharisees][f] fast [, but your disciples do not fast]?"[g]

19 And {Jesus}[h] said to them, "Can the sons of the bridechamber[i] fast while the bridegroom is with them? [As long as {they have the bridegroom}[j] with them, they cannot fast.][k] 20 But the days will come when the bridegroom is taken away from them, and then they will fast in {that day}.[l]

21 "[[But]][m] No one sews a patch of unshrunk cloth on an old garment; if he does, the [new][n] patch tears away from [[it, the new from]][o] the old, and a worse tear is made.

22 "And no one pours new wine into old wineskins [[, but into new ones]].[p] If he does, the wine will burst the wineskins, and {the wine is lost as well as the wineskins}.[q] [But new wine {is for}[r] new wineskins.]"[s]

23 And it happened [[again]][t] that on the Sabbath he was passing through the grainfields, and {his}[u] disciples began to [make their way][v] plucking the heads of grain. 24 {And}[w] the Pharisees said [to him],[x] "Look, what {they}[y] are doing on the Sabbath which is not lawful?"

---

a 2:17, **to them:** Absent from 𝔓88 D(05) W(032) Latin(a b ff²).
b 2:17, **that:** 𝔓88 B(03) NA28[] SBLGNT || Absent from ℵ(01) B(03) C(04) D(05) W(032) Latin(a b e ff²) BYZ TR THGNT.
c 2:17, **to repentance:** Included in C(04) Latin(a) BYZ TR.
d 2:18, **the disciples:** Included in W(032).
e 2:18, **the disciples:** Some manuscripts read "those." D(05) W(032) Latin(a ff²) BYZ TR.
f 2:18, **and the disciples of the Pharisees:** Absent from A(02).
g 2:18, **but your disciples do not fast:** Absent from 𝔓88 Latin(ff²).
h 2:19, **Jesus:** Some manuscripts read "he." D(05) W(032) Latin(b).
i 2:19, **bridechamber:** Or wedding hall.
j 2:19, **they have the bridegroom:** ℵ(01) reads "the bridegroom is."
k 2:19, **As long as...:** Absent from D(05) W(032) Latin(a b e ff²).
l 2:20, **that day:** Some manuscripts read "those days."
m 2:21, **But:** Included in D(05) Latin(a ff²) || Some manuscripts read "And." BYZ TR.
n 2:21, **new:** Absent from 𝔓88 ℵ(01).
o 2:21, **it, the new from:** Included in 𝔓88 ℵ(01).
p 2:22, **but into new ones:** Included in W(032).
q 2:22, **the wine is lost as well as the wineskins:** 𝔓88 B(03) || Some manuscripts read "both the wine and the wineskins will be ruined." D(05) Latin(a b e ff²) || Some manuscripts read "the wine is poured out and the wineskins are destroyed." ℵ(01) A(02) C(04) W(032) BYZ TR.
r 2:22, **is for:** Some manuscripts read "should be put." 𝔓88 C(04) W(032) BYZ TR.
s 2:22, **But new wine is for new wineskins:** Absent from D(05) Latin(a b ff²).
t 2:23, **again:** Included in D(05) Latin (a e).
u 2:23, **his:** D(05) reads "the."
v 2:23, **make their way:** Absent from D(05) W(032).
w 2:24, **And:** Some manuscripts read "But." D(05) W(032) Latin(a b e ff²).
x 2:24, **to him:** Absent from D(05) Latin(e).
y 2:24, **they:** Some manuscripts read "your disciples." D(05) Latin (a b ff²).

25 And [[in response]][a] he says
to them, "Have you never read what
David did when he was in need and was
hungry, he and those [[who were]][b]
with him; 26 [how][c] he entered the
house of God [in the time of Abiathar
the high priest].[d] [And][e] He ate the
bread of the Presence, which it is not
lawful to eat except for the priests, and
also gave it to those [[who were]][f]
with him?"

27 {And he said to them,}[g] ["The
Sabbath was made for men][h] [, [and][i]
not men for the Sabbath;][j] 28 [so][k]
the Son of Man is lord even of the
Sabbath."

3 1 And he entered [again][l] into
the synagogue; and there was
a man there who had a withered
hand. 2 And they watched him closely,
whether he would heal [him][m] on the
Sabbath, so that they might accuse
him. 3 And he says to the man with the
withered hand, "Rise [[and stand]][n]
into the {middle}[o]."

4 [[And]][p] He says to them, "Is it
lawful on the Sabbath to do good or
[[rather]][q] {to do evil},[r] to save a life or
to kill?" But they were silent.

5 [And][s] looking around at them
with anger, [being grieved][t] at the
hardness of their hearts, he says to the
man, "Stretch out your hand." And
he stretched it out, and his hand was
[[immediately]][u] restored [[as whole as
the other]].[v]

6 {And}[w] the Pharisees went out and
[immediately][x] {took}[y] counsel with the
Herodians against him, how they might
destroy him.

---

a 2:25, **in response:** Included in D(05) Latin(a).
b 2:25, **who were:** Included in D(05).
c 2:26, **how:** Absent from B(03) D(05).
d 2:26, **in the time of Abiathar the high priest:** D(05) W(032) Syriac(sy^{s}) Latin(a b e ff^{2}).
e 2:26, **And:** Absent from W(032).
f 2:26, **who were:** Absent from D(05) W(032) Latin(a b e ff^{2}).
g 2:27, **And he said to them:** Some manuscripts read "But I say to you." D(05) W(032) Latin(b) || Absent from Lain (a e ff^{2}).
h 2:27, **The Sabbath was made for men:** Absent from D(05) Latin(a e ff^{2}).
i 2:27, **and:** Absent from A(02) D(05) W(032) Latin(a e ff^{2}) BYZ TR.
j 2:27, **and not men for the Sabbath:** Absent from D(05) W(032) Latin(a e ff^{2}).
k 2:28, **so:** Absent from D(05).
l 3:1, **again:** Absent from some manuscripts W(032) Latin(b i).
m 3:2, **him:** Absent from D(05) W(032) Latin(a b e ff^{2}).
n 3:3, **and stand:** Included in D(05) Latin(e).
o 3:3, **middle:** Or "midst."
p 3:4, **And:** Absent from B(03).
q 3:4, **rather:** Included in D(05).
r 3:4, **to do evil:** W(032) reads "or not."
s 3:5, **and:** Absent from W(032).
t 3:5, **being grieved:** Absent from W(032) Latin(b).
u 3:5, **immediately:** Some manuscripts include D(05) Latin(ff^{2} i).
v 3:5, **as whole as the other:** Included in Latin(b) BYZ* TR.
w 3:6, **And:** Some manuscripts read "But." D(05) W(032) Latin(b).
x 3:6, **immediately:** Absent from D(05) W(032) Latin(ff^{2} i).
y 3:6, **took:** B(03) NA28 SBLGNT THGNT || Some manuscripts read "made." ℵ(01) A(02) C(04) D(05) W(032) Latin(b e ff^{2}) BYZ TR.

7 And Jesus, with his disciples
withdrew to the sea, and a great
{multitude}[a] from Galilee [followed][b]
[[him]],[c] and from Judea 8 and from
Jerusalem [and from Idumea][d] and
[[those]][e] beyond the Jordan [and][f]
[[those]][g] around Tyre and Sidon, a
great multitude {hearing what he was
doing came to him}.[h]

9 And he told his disciples to have
a small boat ready for him because of
the crowd, so that they would not press
upon him [[greatly]];[i] 10 for he healed
many, so that they would fall upon him
in order to touch him, as many as had
afflictions.

11 {And}[j] the unclean spirits, when
they saw him, fell down before him
and cried out, saying [[that]],[k] "You
are [[the Christ,]][l] the Son of God."
12 And [many][m] he sternly warned them
not to make him known. [[For they
knew that he himself was the Christ.]][n]

13 And he went up to the mountain
and called to himself those whom he
wanted, and they went to him.

14 And he made twelve [whom
he also named apostles][o] so that they
would be with him and so that he
would send them to preach [[the
gospel]][p] 15 and to have authority
[[to heal sicknesses and]][q] to cast
out demons. [[And while traveling
around, they were proclaiming the
good news.]][r] 16 [And he appointed
the twelve,][s] And he gave the name
Peter to Simon, 17 [and James the son
of Zebedee and John the brother of
James, and he gave them the name[s]
Boanerges, which means Sons of
Thunder;][t] 18 and Andrew, and Philip,
and Bartholomew, and Matthew,
and Thomas, and James the son of
Alphaeus, [and Thaddaeus,][u] and Simon
the {Cananean},[v] 19 and Judas Iscariot,
who also betrayed him.

20 And he comes into a house; and
again the crowd gathers, so that they
could not even eat bread. 21 And when
those with him [[the scribes and
the rest,]][w] heard, they went out to
seize him; for they said, "He is out of
his mind."

---

[a] 3:7, **multitude:** D(05) reads "crowd."
[b] 3:7, **followed:** Absent from D(05) W(032) Syriac(sy^s) Latin(a b e ff^2 i).
[c] 3:7, **him:** Included in A(02) BYZ TR.
[d] 3:8, **and from Idumea:** Absent from W(032).
[e] 3:8, **those:** Included in D(05).
[f] 3:8, **and:** Absent from ℵ(01).
[g] 3:8, **those:** Included in D(05).
[h] 3:8, **hearing what he was doing came to him:** W(032) reads "followed him, hearing what he was doing."
[i] 3:9, **great:** Included in D(05) Latin(a ff^2).
[j] 3:11, **And:** W(032) reads "But."
[k] 3:11, **that:** Absent from D(05) W(032) Latin(a b e ff^2 i).
[l] 3:11, **the Christ** Included in C(04).
[m] 3:12, **many:** Absent from W(032).
[n] 3:12, **For they knew that He Himself was the Christ:** Included in C(04) Latin(a).
[o] 3:14, **whom he also named apostles:** ℵ(01) B(03) C(04) W(032) Latin(b e ff^2) NA28[] || Absent from A(02) D(05) Syriac(sy) Latin(a i) BYZ TR SBLGNT THGNT.
[p] 3:14, **the gospel:** Included in D(05) W(032) Latin(b e ff^2 i).
[q] 3:15, **to heal sicknesses and:** Included in A(02) D(05) W(032) Latin(a b e ff^2 i) BYZ TR || Absent from ℵ(01) B(03) NA28 SBLGNT THGNT.
[r] 3:15, **And while traveling around, they were proclaiming the good news:** Included in W(032) Latin(a e).
[s] 3:16, **and he appointed the twelve:** Absent from A(02) D(05) W(032) Syriac(sy) Latin(a b e ff^2) BYZ TR.
[t] 3:17, **and James the son of..:** Absent from W(032).
[u] 3:18, **and Thaddaeus:** Absent from W(032) Latin(e).
[v] 3:18, **Cananean:** "Cananean" is Greek for "Zealot." Some manuscripts read "Canaanite." A(02) W(032) BYZ TR.
[w] 3:21, **the scribes and the rest:** Included in D(05) W(032) Latin(a b e ff^2 i).

22 [And the scribes who came down
from Jerusalem,][a] They said, "He has
Beelzebul, and by the ruler of the
demons he casts out the demons."

23 And calling them to him, {he}[b]
spoke to them in parables, "How
can Satan cast out Satan? 24 And if a
kingdom is divided against itself, that
kingdom cannot stand. 25 [And][c] If a
house is divided against itself, {that
house}[d] will not be able to stand.
26 And if {Satan}[e] has risen up against
himself and is divided, {he}[f] cannot
stand, but has an end. 27 [But][g] No
one can enter the strong man's house
and plunder his goods, unless he first
binds the strong man; and then he will
plunder his house.

28 "Truly I say to you, all sins will
be forgiven the sons of men, and
blasphemies [, whatever they may
blaspheme];[h] 29 but whoever blasphemes
against the Holy Spirit[i] does not have
forgiveness [forever],[j] but is guilty of
{an eternal sin}."[k] 30 Because they said,
"He has an unclean spirit."

31 {And}[l] his mother and his
brothers come, and standing outside,
they sent to him, {calling}[m] him.
32 And a crowd was sitting around
him, and they say to him, "Behold,
your mother and your brothers [and
your sisters][n] are [[standing]][o] outside
seeking you."

33 And answering them, he says,
"Who is my mother {and}[p] [my][q]
brothers?" 34 [And][r] Looking around at
those sitting around him [in a circle],[s]
[[the disciples,]][t] he says, "Behold,
my mother and my brothers. 35 [For][u]
Whoever does the will of God, this one
is my brother and [[my]][v] sister and
[[my]] mother."

4 1 And again he began to teach by
the sea; and a very large crowd
gathered around him, so that he got
into a boat and sat in the sea, and
all the crowd was by the sea [on the
land].[w]

---

a 3:22, **And the scribes who came down from Jerusalem:** Absent from Latin(e).
b 3:23, **he:** Some manuscripts read "the Lord Jesus." D(05) Latin(a ff²).
c 3:25, **And:** Absent from W(032).
d 3:25, **that house:** Some manuscripts read "it." W(032) Latin(e).
e 3:26, **Satan:** W(032) reads "he."
f 3:26, **he:** Some manuscripts read "his kingdom." D(05) W(032).
g 3:27, **But:** Absent from A(02) D(05) W(032) Latin(b e i) BYZ TR.
h 3:28, **whatever they may blaspheme:** Absent from W(032) Latin(a b e ff² i).
i 3:29, **Spirit:** See the footnote for Spirit in Matt 1:18.
j 3:29, **forever:** Absent from D(05) W(032) Latin(a b e ff²).
k 3:29, **an eternal sin:** Some manuscripts read "eternal judgment." A(02) BYZ TR.
l 3:31, **And:** Some manuscripts read "So." A(02) BYZ TR.
m 3:31, **calling:** A(02) reads "seeking."
n 3:32, **and your sisters:** Absent from א(01) B(03) C(04) Syriac(sy) BYZ TR Latin(e).
o 3:32, **Standing:** Included in W(032).
p 3:33, **and:** Some manuscripts read "or." A(02) D(05) BYZ TR.
q 3:33, **my:** Absent from B(03) D(05).
r 3:34, **And:** Absent from B(03).
s 3:34, **in a circle:** Absent from D(05) W(032) Latin(a).
t 3:34, **the disciples:** Included in W(032).
u 3:35, **For:** Absent from B(03) W(032) Latin (b e).
v 3:35, **my:** Included in C(04) BYZ TR Latin(a).
w 4:1, **on the land:** Absent from D(05) W(032).

2 And he taught them [many
things][a] in parables and said [to them
in his teaching],[b] 3 “Listen. Behold, the
sower went out to sow. 4 {It happened
during}[c] the sowing, some seed fell by
the path, and the birds [[of the air]][d]
came and ate it. 5 {And}[e] other seed
fell on rocky ground where it did not
have much soil; [and][f] it sprang up
immediately [because it had no depth
of soil];[g] 6 {and}[h] when the sun rose, it
was scorched, and because it had no
root, it withered. 7 And other seed fell
among thorns, and the thorns grew up
and choked it, and it did not yield fruit.
8 And other seed fell into good soil and
produced fruit, growing and increasing,
and it bore thirtyfold, sixtyfold, and
a hundredfold.” 9 And he said, “He
who has ears to hear, let him hear.
[[And let the one who understands,
understand.]]”[i]

10 {And}[j] when he was alone, {those
around him with the twelve}[k] asked
him about the parables. 11 And he said
to them, “To you has been given [[to
know]][l] the mystery of the kingdom of
God; but to those outside, everything
is in parables, 12 so that [seeing][m] they
may see and not perceive, and hearing
they [may hear and][n] not understand,
lest they should turn and be forgiven
[[their sins]].”[o][p]

13 And he says to them, “Do you
not understand this parable? And how
will you understand all the parables?
14 The one who sows the word sows.
15 These are the ones by the road;
where the word is sown and when
they hear, immediately Satan comes
and takes away the word that was
{sown in them}.[q] 16 And these are
[[likewise]][r] the ones sown on the
rocky ground, [who,][s] when they hear
the word, [immediately][t] receive it
with joy, 17 and they have no root in
themselves but are temporary; then
when tribulation or persecution comes
because of the word, they immediately
fall away.[u] 18 {And there are others
who}[v] are sown among the thorns;
[these are the ones][w] who hear the
word, 19 and the worries of {the}[x] {age}[y]
and the deceitfulness of {wealth}[z] and
the desires for other things entering
in, choke the word, and it becomes

---

a 4:2, **many things:** Absent from W(032).
b 4:2, **to them in his teaching:** Absent from W(032).
c 4:4, **It happened during:** Some manuscripts read “In.” D(05) Latin (b e ff2).
d 4:4, **of the air:** Included in D(05) Latin(a) TR.
e 4:5, **And:** Some manuscripts read “But.” A(02) W(032) Latin(e ff2) BYZ TR.
f 4:5, **and:** Absent from W(032) Latin(e ff2).
g 4:5, **because it had no depth of soil:** Absent from W(032) Latin(b e).
h 4:6, **and:** Some manuscripts read “but.” A(02) W(032) BYZ TR.
i 4:9, **And let the one who understands, understand:** Included in D(05) Latin(a b ff2 i).
j 4:10, **And:** Some manuscripts read “But.” A(02) BYZ TR.
k 4:10, **those around him with the twelve:** Some manuscripts read “his disciples.” D(05) W(032) Latin(a b ff2).
l 4:11, **to know:** Included in D(05) BYZ TR Latin(a b ff2 i).
m 4:12, **seeing:** Absent from W(032).
n 4:12, **may hear and:** Absent from W(032) Latin(a).
o 4:12, **their sins:** Included in A(02) D(05) BYZ TR Latin(a ff2 i).
p 4:12, Isaiah 6:9-10 LXX.
q 4:15, **sown in them:** ℵ(01) B(03) C(04) W(032) NA28 SBLGNT THGNT|| Some manuscripts read “sown in their hearts.” A(02) D(05) Syriac(sy) Latin(a b ff2) BYZ TR.
r 4:16, **likewise:** Included in ℵ(01) A(02) B(03) C(04) BYZ TR SBLGNT THGNT || Absent from D(05) W(032) Latin(a b ff2) NA28.
s 4:16, **who:** Absent from W(032).
t 4:16, **immediately:** Absent from D(05) Latin(ff2).
u 4:17, **fall away:** Or stumble.
v 4:18, **And there are others who:** W(032) reads “But these.”
w 4:18, **these are the ones:** Absent from A(02) BYZ TR.
x 4:19, **the:** Some manuscripts read “this.” A(02) BYZ TR.
y 4:19, **age:** Some manuscripts read “life.” D(05) W(032) Latin(b e ff2 i).
z 4:19, **wealth:** Some manuscripts read “the world.” D(05).

unfruitful. 20 And {those}[a] are the ones sown on the good ground, who hear the word and accept it and bear fruit, thirty, sixty, and a hundredfold."

21 And he said to them [that],[b] "Is the lamp brought in to be put under a basket [or][c] under a bed? Is it not to be [put][d] on a lampstand? 22 For there is nothing hidden that will not be revealed, nor has anything been kept secret but that it should come to light. 23 If anyone has ears to hear, let him hear."

24 And he said to them, "Pay attention to what you hear. With the measure you use, it will be measured to you [[who hear]],[e] and more will be added to you. 25 For whoever has, to him more will be {given};[f] and whoever does not have, even what he has will be taken away from him."

26 And he said, "The kingdom of God is like [[this;]][g] a man who casts seed upon the earth. 27 And he sleeps and rises night and day, and the seed sprouts and grows, as he does not know. 28 [[For]][h] The earth bears fruit automatically, first grass, then the stalk, then full grain in the stalk. 29 {But}[i] when the fruit is ripe, [immediately][j] he sends forth the sickle, because the harvest has come."

30 And he said, "How shall we compare the kingdom of God, or in what parable shall we put it? 31 It is like a mustard seed, which, when sown upon the earth, is smaller than all the seeds [on the earth],[k] 32 [And when it is sown,][l] [It grows up][m] And it becomes larger than all the garden plants and produces large branches, so that the birds of the sky can nest under its shade."

33 And with [many][n] such parables, he was speaking [the word][o] [to them],[p] as they were able to understand; 34 but without a parable, he did not speak to them, and privately he explained everything to {his own}[q] disciples.

35 And he says to them on that day, when evening had come, "Let us go over to the other side." 36 And leaving the crowd, [[and]][r] they took him along as he was in the boat, and there were [many][s] other boats with him.

37 And a great windstorm arose, and the waves were breaking into the boat [, so that {the boat}[t] was [already][u] filling].[v] 38 And he was in the stern, sleeping on the cushion. And they woke him and said [to him],[w] "Teacher, do you not care that we are perishing?"

---

a 4:20, **those:** Some manuscripts read "these." A(02) D(05) W(032) BYZ TR.

b 4:21, **that:** Included in B(03).

c 4:21, **or:** Absent from Latin(i).

d 4:21, **put:** Absent from Latin(e).

e 4:24, **who hear:** Included in A(02) BYZ TR.

f 4:25, **given:** D(05) reads "added."

g 4:26, **this:** Included in A(02) C(04) BYZ TR.

h 4:28, **For:** Included in D(05) W(032) Latin(a b e ff² i) BYZ TR.

i 4:29, **But:** Some manuscripts read "And." D(05) Latin(a ff² i) ‖ Absent from W(032).

j 4:29, **immediately:** Absent from W(032).

k 4:31, **on the earth:** Absent from C(04).

l 4:32, **and when it is sown:** Absent from D(05) Latin(i).

m 4:32, **it grows up:** Absent from D(05) Latin(b i).

n 4:33, **many:** Absent from W(032) Latin(b e).

o 4:33, **the word:** Absent from Latin(b e).

p 4:33, **to them:** Absent from D(05) Latin(ff² i).

q 4:34, **his own:** ℵ(01) B(03) C(04) Latin(a b e) NA28 SBLGNT THGNT ‖ Some manuscripts read "the." Latin(ff² i) ‖ Some manuscripts read "his." A(02) D(05) W(032) BYZ TR.

r 4:36, **and:** Included in D(05) W(032) Latin(b e ff²).

s 4:36, **many:** Included in D(05) W(032).

t 4:37, **the boat:** Some manuscripts read "it." A(02) W(032) BYZ TR.

u 4:37, **already:** Absent from Latin(a b ff² i).

v 4:37, **so that the boat was already filling:** Absent from ℵ(01).

w 4:38, **to him:** Absent from W(032).

39 And having risen, he rebuked the wind and said to the sea, "[Be silent,]ᵃ Be still." And the wind ceased, and there was a [great]ᵇ calm.

40 And he said to them, "Why are you so afraid? Do you still have no faith?" 41 And they were filled with great fear and said to one another, "Who then is this, that [even]ᶜ the wind and the sea obey [him]?"ᵈ

5 1 And they came [to the other side]ᵉ [[and]]ᶠ [of the sea,]ᵍ into the country of the {Gerasenes}.ʰ

2 And when he had come out of the boat, [immediately]ⁱ a man with an unclean spirit met him from the tombs, 3 who had his dwelling among the tombs; and no one could bind [him]ʲ [anymore],ᵏ not even with a chain, 4 because he had often been bound with shackles and chains, and the chains had been torn apart [by him]ˡ and the shackles broken in pieces; and no one was strong enough to [subdue]ᵐ him. 5 And constantly, night and day, he was in the tombs and in the mountains, crying out and cutting himself with stones.

6 And when he saw Jesus [from]ⁿ afar, he ran and bowed down before him; 7 and crying out with a loud voice, he said, "What have I to do with you, Jesus, [Son]ᵒ of the {Most High}ᵖ God? I adjure you by God, do not torment me." 8 {For}�q {he}ʳ had been saying to him, "Come out of the man, you unclean spirit!"

9 And he asked him, "What is your name?" And {he said to}ˢ him, ["My name is Legion; for we are many."]ᵗ 10 And he begged him earnestly not to send them out of the country.

11 Now there was there near the mountain a [large]ᵘ herd of pigs feeding; 12 and they begged him, [[all the demons,]]ᵛ saying, "Send us into the pigs, that we may enter into them." 13 And [[immediately]]ʷ {he}ˣ allowed them [[into the pigs]].ʸ And the [unclean]ᶻ spirits, having come out, entered into the pigs, and the herd rushed down the cliff into the sea,

---

ᵃ 4:39, **Be silent:** Absent from W(032) Latin(b e ff²).

ᵇ 4:39, **great:** Absent from W(032).

ᶜ 4:41, **even:** Absent from W(032) Latin(b e ff² i).

ᵈ 4:41, **him:** Absent from D(05) Latin(ff² i).

ᵉ 5:1, **to the other side:** Absent from Latin(e ff²).

ᶠ 5:1, **and:** Included in D(05).

ᵍ 5:1, **of the sea:** Absent from D(05) Latin(b ff² i).

ʰ 5:1, **Gerasenes:** Some manuscripts read "Gadarenes," or "Gergesenes."

ⁱ 5:2, **immediately:** Absent from B(03) W(032) Syriac(syˢ) Latin(b e ff² i).

ʲ 5:3, **him:** Absent from W(032).

ᵏ 5:3, **anymore:** Absent from A(02) BYZ TR.

ˡ 5:4, **by him:** Absent from W(032) Latin (b e).

ᵐ 5:4, **subdue:** Absent from ℵ(01).

ⁿ 5:6, **from:** Absent from A(02) W(032).

ᵒ 5:7, **Son:** Absent from Latin(i).

ᵖ 5:7, **Most High:** A(02) reads "Living."

q 5:8, **For:** ℵ(01) reads "And." ‖ Absent from A(02).

ʳ 5:8, **he:** Some manuscripts read "Jesus." D(05) Latin(ff²).

ˢ 5:9, **said to:** Some manuscripts read "answered." D(05) Latin(a e ff² i) ‖ Some manuscripts read "answered, saying." BYZ TR.

ᵗ 5:9, **My name is Legion; for we are many:** Absent from Latin(ff²).

ᵘ 5:11, **large:** Absent from D(05) Latin(b e ff² i).

ᵛ 5:12, **all the demons:** Included in A(02) BYZ TR ‖ Some manuscripts read "the demons." D(05) Latin(e) ‖ Absent from ℵ(01) B(03) C(04) W(032) NA28 SBLGNT THGNT.

ʷ 5:13, **immediately:** Included in A(02) BYZ TR.

ˣ 5:13, **he:** Some manuscripts read "the Lord Jesus." D(05) Latin(a ff²) ‖ Some manuscripts read "Jesus." A(02) BYZ TR.

ʸ 5:13, **into the pigs:** Included in D(05) Latin(ff² i).

ᶻ 5:13, **unclean:** Absent from A(02).

about two thousand, [[and they were]]^a drowned in the sea.

14 And those who were feeding {them}^b fled and reported it in the city and in the fields; and they {came}^c to see [what had happened].^d

15 And they came to Jesus and saw the demon-possessed man [sitting, clothed and]^e in his right mind, [the one who had the legion,]^f and they were afraid. 16 And those who had seen it described to them how it had happened to the demon-possessed man and about the pigs. 17 And they [began to]^g beg him [[that]]^h to depart from their region.

18 And as he was getting into the boat, the man who had been demon-possessed begged him that he might be with him. 19 {And he}ⁱ did not allow him, but said to him, "Go to your home, to your own people, and report to them what the Lord has done for you and how he has had mercy on you."

20 And he went away and began to proclaim in [[all]]^j the Decapolis what Jesus had done for him, and everyone marveled.

21 And when Jesus had crossed over [in the boat]^k again [to the other side],^l a large crowd [was]^m gathered around him, and he was by the sea.

22 And [[behold]]ⁿ one of the synagogue leaders, [named Jairus,]^o comes [and seeing him,]^p falls at his feet 23 and pleads with him [greatly]^q saying [that],^r "My daughter is at the point of death. Come and lay your hands on her, so that she may be saved and live." 24 And he went with him.

And a large crowd followed him and they pressed upon him.

25 And [[there was]]^s a woman who had a flow of blood for twelve years, 26 and had suffered much under many physicians, and had spent all that she had, and was not helped at all, but rather having become worse, 27 having heard about Jesus, she [came up]^t behind him in the crowd and touched his garment; 28 {for she said}^u [that]^v "If I touch [even]^w his garments, I will be made well."

29 And immediately the source of her blood was dried up. [And]^x [[that]]^y She knew in her body that she was healed [from the affliction].^z

---

^a 5:13, **and they were:** Included in A(02) BYZ TR Latin(a i).

^b 5:14, **them:** Some manuscripts read "the swine." A(02) BYZ TR.

^c 5:14, **came:** Some manuscripts read "went out." ℵ(01) C(04) D(05) W(032) BYZ TR.

^d 5:14, **what had happened:** Absent from A(02).

^e 5:15, **sitting, clothed and:** Absent from W(032).

^f 5:15, **the one who had the legion:** Absent from D(05) Latin(b e i).

^g 5:17, **began to:** Absent from D(05) Latin(a).

^h 5:17, **that:** Included in D(05) Latin(a b e ff² i).

ⁱ 5:19, **And he:** Some manuscripts read "but Jesus." D(05) Latin(b ff² i) BYZ TR.

^j 5:20, **all:** Included in C(04).

^k 5:21, **in the boat:** Absent from 𝔓45 D(05) Syriac(sy^s) Latin(a b e ff² i).

^l 5:21, **to the other side:** Absent from 𝔓(45) Latin(a b e ff² i).

^m 5:21, **was:** Absent from D(05) Latin(b e ff²).

ⁿ 5:22, **behold:** Included in 𝔓45 A(02) C(04) W(032) BYZ TR.

^o 5:22, **named Jairus:** Absent from D(05) Latin(a e ff² i).

^p 5:22, **and seeing him:** Absent from D(05) Latin(e).

^q 5:23, **greatly:** Absent from D(05) Latin(b ff² i).

^r 5:23, **that:** Absent from D(05) Latin(a e).

^s 5:25, **there was:** Included in D(05) BYZ TR Latin(a).

^t 5:27, **came up:** Absent from W(032).

^u 5:28, **for she said:** Some manuscripts read "saying to herself." D(05) Latin(b ff² i).

^v 5:28, **that:** Absent from Latin(a b e ff² i).

^w 5:28, **even:** Absent from B(03) Latin(a b e ff² i) BYZ TR.

^x 5:29, **And:** Absent from Latin(e i).

^y 5:29, **that:** Included in D(05) Latin(b).

^z 5:29, **from the affliction:** Absent from Latin(b e).

30 And [immediately]^a Jesus, perceiving [in himself]^b that power had gone out [[from him]],^c turned around in the crowd and said, "Who touched my garments?"

31 {And}^d {his}^e disciples said to him, "You see the crowd pressing around you, and yet you say, 'Who touched me?'" 32 And he looked around [to see who had done this].^f

33 But the woman, fearing and trembling [[because of what she had done in secret]],^g [knowing what had happened to her],^h came and fell down before him and told him [[before all]]ⁱ the whole truth.

34 But {he}^j said to her, "Daughter, your faith has saved you; go in peace [and be]^k healthy from your affliction."

35 While he was [still]^l speaking, they came from the synagogue leader's house, saying [[to him]],^m "Your daughter has died; why do you still trouble the teacher?"

36 But Jesus, [[immediately]]ⁿ {overhearing}^o {the}^p word [being spoken],^q says to the synagogue leader, "Do not fear, only believe."

37 And he did not allow anyone to follow [with]^r him except [[only]]^s Peter, James, and John, the brother of {James}.^t

38 And they came to the house of the synagogue leader, and he sees a commotion and [many]^u weeping and wailing. 39 And entering, he says to them, "Why are you making a commotion and weeping? The child has not died but is sleeping." 40 And they laughed at him [[knowing that she died]].^v But he, having put {everyone}^w outside, takes the child's father and mother and those with him, and goes in where the child was [[lying]].^x

41 And [taking the child's hand,]^y he says to her, "[[Rabbi]]^z Talitha [koum],"^a which is translated, "Little girl, I say to you [, arise]."^b

---

a 5:30, **immediately:** Absent from Latin(a).

b 5:30, **in himself:** Absent from D(05) Latin(b e ff²).

c 5:30, **from him:** Included in D(05) Latin(a b e ff² i).

d 5:31, **and:** Some manuscripts read "but." D(05) Latin(e ff²).

e 5:31, **his:** Some manuscripts read "the." W(032) Latin(a).

f 5:32, **to see who had done this:** Absent from Latin(e) ‖ W(032) reads "to see."

g 5:33, **because of what she had done in secret:** Included in D(05) Latin(a ff² i).

h 5:33, **knowing what had happened to her:** Absent from Latin(a b e).

i 5:33, **before all:** Included in W(032).

j 5:34, **he:** Some manuscripts read "Jesus." C(04) D(05) Latin(a b ff² i).

k 5:34, **and be:** Absent from C(04).

l 5:35, **still:** Absent from Latin(a b ff² i).

m 5:35, **to him:** Included in D(05) Latin(b i).

n 5:36, **immediately:** Included in A(02) C(04) Latin(a b i) BYZ TR.

o 5:36, **overhearing:** Some manuscripts read "hearing." A(02) C(04) D(05) Latin(a b) BYZ TR.

p 5:36, **the:** Some manuscripts read "this." D(05) Latin(ff² i).

q 5:36, **being spoken:** Absent from D(05) Latin(a b ff² i).

r 5:37, **with:** Absent from A(02) W(032) Latin(a b ff² i) BYZ TR.

s 5:37, **only:** Included in W(032).

t 5:37, **James:** Some manuscripts read "him." D(05) Latin(a).

u 5:38, **many:** Absent from Latin(b).

v 5:40, **knowing that she died:** Included in W(032).

w 5:40, **everyone:** D(05) reads "the crowds." ‖ Absent from Latin(a).

x 5:40, **lying:** Included in A(02) C(04) W(032) BYZ TR ‖ Absent from ℵ(01) B(03) D(05) Latin(a b e ff² i) NA28 SBLGNT THGNT.

y 5:41, **taking the child's hand:** Absent from Latin(e i).

z 5:41, **Rabbi:** Included in D(05).

a 5:41, **koum:** Absent from W(032) Latin(a).

b 5:41, **arise:** Absent from W(032) Latin(a).

42 And immediately the girl got up and began to walk around; for she was [[about]]ᵃ twelve years old. And they were [[all]]ᵇ [immediately]ᶜ overcome with great astonishment. 43 And he [strictly]ᵈ ordered them that no one should know about this, and he said to give her something to eat.

6 ¹ And he went out [from there and came]ᵉ to his hometown, and his disciples followed him.

2 And [on the Sabbath [day],ᶠ]ᵍ he began to teach in the synagogue, and [many who heard,]ʰ they were astonished [[at his teaching]]ⁱ, saying, "From where does this one get [[all]]ʲ these things, and what is the wisdom given to him, that such powers being done through his hands? 3 Is not this the carpenter, the son of Mary and brother of James and {Joses}ᵏ and Judas and Simon? And are not his sisters [here]ˡ with us?" And they took offense at him.

4 [And]ᵐ Jesus said [to them],ⁿ "A prophet is not without honor except in his [[own]]ᵒ hometown [and among his relatives]ᵖ and in his household."

5 And he could not do any miracles [there],�q except that he laid his hands on a few sick people [, he healed them].ʳ 6 [And he marveled]ˢ because of their unbelief.

And {he},ᵗ went around the villages in a circuit teaching.

7 And he calls the twelve [[disciples]]ᵘ [and began]ᵛ to send them out [[again]]ʷ [two]ˣ by two {and gave}ʸ them authority over the unclean spirits, 8 and he commanded [them]ᶻ [that]ᵃ they should take nothing [for the journey]ᵇ except a staff only, no bread, no bag, no money in their {belts}, 9 but to wear sandals and not to put on two tunics.

ᵃ 5:42, **about:** Included in ℵ(01) C(04).

ᵇ 5:42, **all:** Included in D(05) Latin(ff² i).

ᶜ 5:42, **immediately:** ℵ(01) B(03) C(04) NA28[] SBLGNT THGNT ‖ Absent from 𝔓45 A(02) D(05) W(032) Syriac(sy) Latin(a b e ff²) BYZ TR.

ᵈ 5:43, **strictly:** Absent from D(05) Latin(b e i).

ᵉ 6:1, **from there and came:** Absent from W(032).

ᶠ 6:2, **day:** Included in D(05) Latin(ff²).

ᵍ 6:2, **on the sabbath day:** Absent from Latin(b e).

ʰ 6:2, **many who heard:** Absent from Latin(b).

ⁱ 6:2, **at his teaching:** Included in D(05) Latin(a b ff² i).

ʲ 6:2, **all:** Included in ℵ(01) C(04) Latin(a).

ᵏ 6:3, **Joses:** ℵ(01) reads "Joseph."

ˡ 6:3, **ere:** Absent from Latin(e).

ᵐ 6:4, **And:** Some manuscripts read "But." A(02) W(032) BYZ TR.

ⁿ 6:4, **to them:** Absent from W(032).

ᵒ 6:4, **own:** Included in A(02).

ᵖ 6:4, **and among his relatives:** Absent from ℵ(01) Latin(e).

q 6:5, **there:** Absent from W(032).

ʳ 6:5, **he healed them:** Absent from Latin(b).

ˢ 6:6, **And he marveled:** Absent from Latin(b e).

ᵗ 6:6, **he:** Some manuscripts read "Jesus." ℵ(01) Latin(ff²).

ᵘ 6:7, **disciples:** Included in D(05) Latin(b ff² i).

ᵛ 6:7, **and began:** Absent from D(05) Latin(a b e ff² i).

ʷ 6:7, **again:** Included in D(05).

ˣ 6:7, **two:** Absent from Latin(e).

ʸ 6:7, **and gave:** Some manuscripts read "giving." D(05) Latin(a b e ff² i).

ᶻ 6:8, **them:** Absent from A(02).

ᵃ 6:8, **that:** Absent from Latin (a b e ff² i).

ᵇ 6:8, **for the journey:** Absent from Latin(b).

10 And he said [to them],[a] "Whenever you enter [into a house],[b] stay there until you leave that place. 11 And {whoever}[c] [place][d] does not receive you, nor listen to you, as you depart from there, shake off the dust {that is under your}[e] feet as a testimony against them." [["Truly I say to you, it will be more bearable for Sodom and Gomorrah on the day of judgment than for that city"]][f]

12 And going out, they preached [[to them][g]] that people should repent, 13 and they cast out many demons and they were anointing with oil many who were sick and they were healing [[them]].[h]

14 And King Herod heard, for his name had become known, and {they}[i] said, "John the Baptist has been raised from the dead, and that is why miraculous powers are at work in him." 15 [But][j] others were saying, "He is Elijah." And others [were saying],[k] "He is {a prophet}[l] [like][m] {one of the prophets}."[n] 16 But when Herod heard, he said [[that]],[o] "John, whom I beheaded, this one has been raised [[from the dead]]."[p]

17 For Herod himself had sent and arrested John and bound him [[and threw him]][q] in prison for the sake of Herodias, [the wife][r] of his brother Philip, because he had married her. 18 For John had been saying to Herod [that],[s] "It is not lawful for you to have your brother's wife." 19 And Herodias had {a grudge}[t] against him and {wanted}[u] to kill him. But she could not, 20 for Herod feared John, knowing him to be a righteous and holy man, [and][v] he kept him safe. When he heard him, {he was greatly perplexed},[w] and yet he heard him gladly.

21 {And}[x] [when][y] the day became opportune, Herod made a feast for his birthday for {his}[z] high officials, and the commanders, and the leading men of Galilee. 22 For when Herodias's daughter came in and danced, {she}[a] pleased Herod and {his}[b] guests. And the king said to the girl, "Ask me for

---

a 6:10, **to them:** Absent from W(032).

b 6:10, **into a house:** Absent from D(05).

c 6:11, **whoever:** Some manuscripts read "as many as." A(02) D(05) BYZ TR.

d 6:11, **place:** Absent from A(02) C(04) D(05) Latin(a b ff² i) BYZ TR.

e 6:11, **that is under your feet:** Some manuscripts read "from." D(05) Latin(a b).

f 6:11, **Truly I say to you, it will be more bearable for Sodom and Gomorrah on the day of judgment than for that city:** Included in A(02) Latin(a) BYZ TR ‖ Absent from ℵ(01) B(03) C(05) D(05) W(032) Latin(b ff² i) NA28 SBLGNT THGNT.

g 6:12, **to them:** Included in ℵ(01).

h 6:13, **them:** Included in W(032).

i 6:14, **they:** Some manuscripts read "he." ℵ(01) A(02) C(04) BYZ TR.

j 6:15, **But:** Absent from BYZ TR.

k 6:15, **were saying:** Absent from ℵ(01) Latin(a b ff²).

l 6:15, **a prophet:** Absent from D(05) Latin(b ff² i).

m 6:15, **like:** Absent from D(05) Latin(a b ff²).

n 6:15, **one of the prophets:** Absent from Latin(a).

o 6:16, **that:** Included in 𝔓45 A(02) C(04) W(032) BYZ TR.

p 6:16, **from the dead:** Included in A(02) C(04) D(05) Latin(a ff² i) BYZ TR.

q 6:17, **and threw him:** Included in D(05) Latin (a ff²).

r 6:17, **the wife:** Absent from B(03).

s 6:18, **that:** Absent from D(05) Latin(ff² i).

t 6:19, **a grudge:** 𝔓45 reads "it."

u 6:19, **wanted:** C(04) reads "was seeking."

v 6:20, **and:** Absent from B(03).

w 6:20, **he was greatly perplexed:** Some manuscripts read "he was doing many things." A(02) C(04) D(05) Latin(a b ff²) BYZ TR.

x 6:21, **And:** Some manuscripts read "But." D(05) Latin(b).

y 6:21, **when:** Absent from D(05).

z 6:21, **his:** Some manuscripts read "the." D(05) Latin(a b ff²).

a 6:22, **she:** NA28 ‖ Some manuscripts read "and." SBLGNT THGNT.

b 6:22, **his:** Some manuscripts read "her." A(02) C(04) W(032) TR BYZ.

whatever you wish, and I will give it to
you." 23 {And he vowed to her [many
things],[a] "Whatever you ask me, I will
give you, up to half of my kingdom}."[b]

24 And she went out and said to her
mother, "What shall I ask for?" And she
said, "[[Ask for]][c] The head of John the
Baptist." 25 And entering [immediately
with haste][d] [to the king, she {asked
saying}[e]],[f] "[I want that you][g] Give me
at once on a platter [[here]][h] the head
of John the Baptist."

26 [And][i] The king, becoming deeply
distressed [[when he heard]],[j] but
because of the oaths and [because
of][k] those reclining at the table,
did not wish to reject her. 27 {And}[l]
[immediately][m] [the king],[n] having sent
a soldier, he commanded to bring his
head [[on a platter]][o]. [{And}[p] going
away, he beheaded him in the prison.
28 And he brought {his}[q] head on a
platter.][r] And he gave it to [her][s] the
girl, and the girl {gave it}[t] to {her}[u]
mother.

29 {And when his disciples heard of
it},[v] they came and took his body and
laid it in a tomb.

30 And the apostles gathered
together with Jesus and reported to
him all that they had done and taught.
31 And {he}[w] {says}[x] to them, "Come {by
yourselves, privately}[y] to a secluded
place and rest a little." For there were
many coming and going [, and they did
not even have the opportunity to eat].[z]

32 And they went [away in
the boat][a] to a deserted place by
themselves.

---

[a] 6:23, **many things:** 𝔓45 B(03) D(05) Latin(a b ff^2) NA28[] || Absent from ℵ(01) A(02) W(032) BYZ TR SBLGNT THGNT.

[b] 6:23, **And he vowed to her...:** W(032) reads "And he vowed to her up to half of the kingdom."

[c] 6:24, **Ask for:** Included in 𝔓45 W(032).

[d] 6:25, **immediately with haste:** Absent from D(05) Latin(a b ff^2 i).

[e] 6:25, **asked saying:** Some manuscripts read "said." D(05).

[f] 6:25, **to the king, she asked saying:** Absent from W(032).

[g] 6:25, **I want that you:** Absent from D(05).

[h] 6:25, **here:** Included in D(05).

[i] 6:26, **And:** Absent from D(05).

[j] 6:26, **when he heard:** Included in D(05) Latin(ff^2).

[k] 6:26, **because of:** Included in D(05) Latin(a b i).

[l] 6:27, **And:** Some manuscripts read "But." D(05) || Absent from Latin(a).

[m] 6:27, **immediately:** Absent from Latin(ff^2 i).

[n] 6:27, **the king:** Absent from D(05) W(032) Latin(a b ff^2 i).

[o] 6:27, **on a platter:** Included in C(04) W(032).

[p] 6:27, **And:** Some manuscripts read "But." A(02) D(05) Latin(b) BYZ TR || Absent from ℵ(01).

[q] 6:28, **his:** Some manuscripts read "the." D(05) Latin(a ff2 i).

[r] 6:27-28, **And going away..:** Absent from ℵ(01).

[s] 6:28, **her:** Absent from W(032) Latin(b).

[t] 6:28, **gave it:** C(04) reads "carried it."

[u] 6:28, **her:** Some manuscripts read "the." D(05) Latin (a ff^2 i).

[v] 6:29, **And when his disciples heard of it:** D(05) reads "But his disciples, having heard this."

[w] 6:31, **he:** Some manuscripts read "Jesus." D(05) Latin (a b ff^2 i).

[x] 6:31, **says:** ℵ(01) B(03) C(04) Latin (b ff^2) NA28 SBLGNT THGNT || Some manuscripts read "said." 𝔓84 A(02) D(05) Latin(a) BYZ TR.

[y] 6:31, **by yourselves, privately:** D(05) reads "let us go." || Latin (a ff^2 i) reads "you."

[z] 6:31, **and they did not even have the opportunity to eat:** Absent from Latin(a).

[a] 6:32, **away in the boat:** Absent from Latin(b).

33 And they saw {them}ᵃ going away, and many recognized [[them]],ᵇ and on foot from all the cities they ran together there [and went ahead of them]ᶜ [[and gathered to him]].ᵈ 34 And when {he}ᵉ went ashore, {he}ᶠ saw a great crowd, [and]ᵍ {he}ʰ had compassion on them because they were [like sheep]ⁱ without a shepherd, and he began to teach them many things.

35 And when it was already late, his disciples approached him and said, "This place is deserted, and the hour is already {late};ʲ 36 send them away so that they may go into the surrounding countryside and [[into the]]ᵏ villages and buy themselves {something to eat}.ˡ"

37 {But}ᵐ {he}ⁿ answered and said to them, "You give them something to eat." And they said to him, "Shall we go and buy two hundred denarii worth of bread and give it to them to eat? [[So that each may take a little.]]ᵒ"

38 {But}ᵖ {He}ۑ says to them, "How many loaves do you have? Go and see." And when they {found out},ʳ they said [[to him]],ˢ "Five [[loaves]],ᵗ and two fish."

39 And {he}ᵘ commanded them [all]ᵛ to recline [in groups]ʷ on the green grass. 40 And they reclined in groups [, in hundreds and in fifties].ˣ

41 And taking the [five]ʸ loaves and the [two]ᶻ fish, looking up to heaven, blessed and broke the [[five]]ᵃ loaves, and gave them to {his}ᵇ disciples to set before [them], and he divided the two fish among them all. 42 And they all ate and were satisfied, 43 and they picked

---

ᵃ 6:33, **them:** Some manuscripts read "the crowds." W(032) TR.

ᵇ 6:33, **them:** Included in ℵ(01) A(02) BYZ TR.

ᶜ 6:33, **and went ahead of them:** Absent from W(032).

ᵈ 6:33, **and gathered to him:** Included in A(02) BYZ TR.

ᵉ 6:34, **he:** ℵ(01) B(03) W(032) Latin (a b i) NA28 SBLGNT THGNT ‖ Some manuscripts read "Jesus." A(02) Latin(ff²) BYZ TR.

ᶠ 6:34, **he:** Some manuscripts read "Jesus." Latin(a b ff² i).

ᵍ 6:34, **and:** Absent from D(05) Latin(a b ff² i).

ʰ 6:34, **he:** Some manuscripts read "Jesus." A(02) D(05) Latin (ff²) BYZ TR.

ⁱ 6:34, **like sheep:** Absent from ℵ(01).

ʲ 6:35, **late:** Some manuscripts read "passed." W(032).

ᵏ 6:36, **into the:** Included in D(05) Latin(i).

ˡ 6:36, **something to eat:** Some manuscripts read "bread, for they have nothing to eat." A(02) BYZ TR Latin(b) ‖ ℵ(01) reads "food."

ᵐ 6:37, **But:** Some manuscripts read "And." D(05) Latin(a b ff² i).

ⁿ 6:37, **he:** Some manuscripts read "Jesus." D(05) Latin(ff²).

ᵒ 6:37, **So that each may take a little:** Included in W(032).

ᵖ 6:38, **But:** Some manuscripts read "And." D(05) Latin(a i) ‖ Absent from Latin(b).

ۑ 6:38, **he:** Some manuscripts read "Jesus." D(05) Latin(b).

ʳ 6:38, **found out: ,** ℵ(01) reads "came."

ˢ 6:38, **to him:** Included in A(02) D(05).

ᵗ 6:38, **loaves:** Included in D(05) Latin(a ff² i) Syriac(syˢ).

ᵘ 6:39, **he:** Some manuscripts read "Jesus." D(05) Latin(a b ff² i).

ᵛ 6:39, **all:** Absent from 𝔓45.

ʷ 6:39, **in groups:** Absent from Latin(a).

ˣ 6:40, **in hundreds and in fifties:** Absent from 𝔓45.

ʸ 6:41, **five:** Absent from 𝔓45.

ᶻ 6:41, **two:** Absent from 𝔓45.

ᵃ 6:41, **five:** Included in D(05) W(032).

ᵇ 6:41, **the:** 𝔓45 A(02) D(05) W(032) Latin(a b ff² i) BYZ TR SBLGNT THGNT NA28[] ‖ Some manuscripts read "the." ℵ(01) B(03).

up twelve baskets [full]ᵃ of [[excess]]ᵇ broken pieces and of the [[two]]ᶜ fish. ₄₄ And there were [[about]]ᵈ five thousand men who ate [the loaves].ᵉ

₄₅ And immediately [[having risen,]]ᶠ he compelled his disciples to get into the boat and go ahead [to the other side,]ᵍ to Bethsaida, while he [[himself]]ʰ dismissed the crowd. ₄₆ And after saying farewell to them, he went away to the mountain to pray.

₄₇ And when evening came, the boat was [[formerly]]ⁱ in the middle of the sea, and he was alone on the land. ₄₈ And seeing them straining at the oars, for the wind was [[exceedingly]]ʲ against [them],ᵏ about the fourth watch [of the night]ˡ {he}ᵐ came [to them],ⁿ walking on the sea, and he intended to pass by [them].ᵒ

₄₉ But when they saw him walking on the sea, they thought it was a ghost, and they cried out; ₅₀ [for they all saw him]ᵖ and were terrified. {But}�q [immediately]ʳ he spoke with them and said [to them],ˢ "Take courage, it is I; do not be afraid."

₅₁ And he got into the boat with them, and the wind ceased, and they were [exceedingly]ᵗ [beyond measure]ᵘ astounded [[and wondered]],ᵛ ₅₂ for they did not understand about the loaves, but their hearts were hardened.

₅₃ And crossing over to the land [[from there]],ʷ they came to Gennesaret [and anchored].ˣ ₅₄ And when they got out of the boat, immediately recognizing him, [[the men of that place,]]ʸ ₅₅ they ran around [[into]]ᶻ the whole [[surrounding]]ᵃ region [and]ᵇ they began {to carry around [all]ᶜ on mats those who were sick, wherever}ᵈ they heard {he}ᵉ was.

ᵃ 6:43, **full:** Absent from Latin(i).

ᵇ 6:43, **excess:** Included in Latin(a ff² i).

ᶜ 6:43, **two:** Included in א(01).

ᵈ 6:44, **about:** Included in TR.

ᵉ 6:44, **the loaves:** A(02) B(03) BYZ TR NA28[1] SBLGNT THGNT ‖ Absent from 𝔓45 D(05) W(032) Latin(a b ff²).

ᶠ 6:45, **having risen:** Included in D(05) Latin(a b ff² i).

ᵍ 6:45, **to the other side:** Absent from 𝔓45 W(032) Syriac(syˢ).

ʰ 6:45, **himself:** Included in D(05) Latin(a b ff² i).

ⁱ 6:47, **formerly:** Included in 𝔓45 D(05) Latin(b).

ʲ 6:48, **exceedingly:** Included in 𝔓45 W(032).

ᵏ 6:48, **them:** Absent from Latin(a b ff² i).

ˡ 6:48, **of the night:** Absent from 𝔓45.

ᵐ 6:48, **he:** Some manuscripts read "Jesus." D(05) Latin (ff² i).

ⁿ 6:48, **to them:** Absent from D(05) W(032) Latin(a b).

ᵒ 6:48, **them:** Absent from 𝔓45.

ᵖ 6:50, **for they all saw him:** Absent from D(05).

q 6:50, **But:** Some manuscripts read "And." A(02) W(032) Latin(b ff² i) BYZ TR.

ʳ 6:50, **immediately:** Absent from D(05) Latin(ff² i).

ˢ 6:50, **to them:** Absent from D(05) Latin(a b ff²).

ᵗ 6:51, **exceedingly:** Absent from D(05) Latin(a b ff² i).

ᵘ 6:51, **beyond measure:** Absent from א(01) B(03).

ᵛ 6:51, **and wondered:** Included in A(02) D(05) W(032) BYZ TR.

ʷ 6:53, **from there:** Included in D(05) Latin(b ff²).

ˣ 6:53, **and anchored:** Absent from D(05) W(032) Latin(a b ff² i) Syriac(syˢ).

ʸ 6:54, **the men of that place:** Included in A(02) W(032) Latin (a ff² i).

ᶻ 6:55, **into:** Included in W(032).

ᵃ 6:55, **surrounding:** Included in A(02) D(05) W(032) BYZ TR.

ᵇ 6:55, **and:** Absent from A(02) D(05) Latin (a b ff² i) BYZ TR.

ᶜ 6:55, **all:** Included in D(05) Latin (a b ff²).

ᵈ 6:55, **to carry around..:** Some manuscripts read "to bring all who were sick, carrying them on mats. For they were moving them around to." D(05) Latin(a b ff² i).

ᵉ 6:55, **he:** D(05) reads "Jesus."

56 And wherever he went, into villages [or cities]ᵃ or fields, they laid the sick [in the marketplaces]ᵇ and begged him that they might touch even the fringe of his garment; and as many as touched him were made well.

7 1 And the Pharisees and some of the scribes gathered to him, having come from Jerusalem.

2 And when they saw [that]ᶜ some of his disciples were eating bread with defiled hands, that is, unwashed, [[they complained]]ᵈ 3 (for the Pharisees and all the Jews do not eat [[bread]]ᵉ unless they wash their hands with a fist, holding to the tradition of the elders, 4 and when they come from the marketplace, they do not eat unless they wash themselves; and there are many other things that they have received to hold, washings of cups and pots and bronze vessels [and beds])ᶠ –

5 [And]ᵍ The Pharisees and the scribes asked him [[saying]],ʰ "Why do your disciples not walk according to the tradition of the elders, but eat bread with defiled [[and unwashed]]ⁱ hands?"

6 And he [[answering,]]ʲ said to them [[that]],ᵏ "Well did Isaiah prophesy about you hypocrites, as it is written [that]ˡ 'This people {honors}ᵐ me with their lips, but their heart is far away from me; 7 But they worship me in vain, teaching doctrines, [[and]]ⁿ commandments of men.'ᵒ

8 "[[For]]ᵖ Abandoning the commandment of God, you hold to the tradition of men [[washing of vessels and cups, and many other such things you do]]."�q

9 And he said to them, "You have a fine way of rejecting the commandment of God, in order to {establish}ʳ your tradition. 10 For Moses said, 'Honor your father and your mother,' and, 'Whoever {speaks evil}ˢ of father or mother must surely die.'ᵗ 11 But you say, If a man says to his father or mother, 'Corban, which means, "Gift," whatever you might benefit from me,' 12 [[and]]ᵘ you no longer allow him to do anything to {the father or the mother},ᵛ 13 nullifying the word [[the commandment]]ʷ of God by your [[foolish]]ˣ tradition which you

---

ᵃ 6:56, **or cities:** Absent from A(02) W(032) BYZ TR.

ᵇ 6:56, **in the marketplaces:** Absent from Latin(ff²).

ᶜ 7:2, **that:** Absent from A(02) D(05) W(032) BYZ TR.

ᵈ 7:2, **they complained:** Included in D(05) BYZ TR.

ᵉ 7:3, **bread:** Included in D(05) Latin(a b ff² i).

ᶠ 7:4, **and beds:** A(02) D(05) Latin (a b ff² i) BYZ TR NA28[] SBLGNT THGNT ‖ Absent from 𝔓45 ℵ(01) B(03) Syriac(syˢ).

ᵍ 7:5, **And:** ℵ(01) B(03) Latin(ab ff²) NA28 SBLGNT THGNT ‖ Some manuscripts read "Then." A(02) W(032) BYZ TR.

ʰ 7:5, **saying:** Included in D(05) W(032) Latin (a ff² i).

ⁱ 7:5, **and unwashed:** Included in 𝔓45.

ʲ 7:6, **answering:** Included in 𝔓45 A(02) D(05) W(032) Latin(a b ff² i) BYZ TR.

ᵏ 7:6, **that:** Included in 𝔓45 A(02) D(05) W(032) Latin(b) BYZ TR.

ˡ 7:6, **that:** ℵ(01) B(03) NA28[] SBLGNT THGNT ‖ Absent from A(02) W(032) Latin(a b ff² i) BYZ TR.

ᵐ 7:6, **honors:** Some manuscripts read "loves." D(05) W(032) Latin(a b).

ⁿ 7:7, **and:** Included in 𝔓45 Latin(a i).

ᵒ 7:6-7, Isaiah 29:13 LXX.

ᵖ 7:8, **For:** Included in A(02) BYZ TR.

q 7:8, **washing of vessels and cups, and many other such things you do:** Included in A(02) BYZ TR.

ʳ 7:9, **establish:** Some manuscripts read "keep."

ˢ 7:10, **speaks evil:** W(032) reads "disregard."

ᵗ 7:10, Exodus 20:12, Deuteronomy 5:16, Exodus 21:17.

ᵘ 7:12, **and:** Included in 𝔓45 A(02) W(032) Latin(b ff² i) BYZ TR.

ᵛ 7:12, **the father or the mother:** Some manuscripts read "to his father or to his mother." A(02) BYZ TR.

ʷ 7:13, **the commandment:** Included in W(032).

ˣ 7:13, **foolish:** Included in D(05).

have handed down. [And you do many similar things.]"ᵃ

₁₄ And calling [again]ᵇ the crowd to him, he said to them, "Listen [to me, all of you,]ᶜ and understand. ₁₅ There is nothing outside a man that by going into him can defile him, but the things that come out [of a man]ᵈ [[those]]ᵉ are what defile him. ₁₆ [[If anyone has ears to hear, let him hear]]"ᶠ

₁₇ And when he had entered the house and left the crowd, his disciples asked him about the parable. ₁₈ And he says to them, "Are you also without understanding in this way? Do you not seeᵍ that whatever goes into a person from outside cannot defile him. ₁₉ For it does not enter into the heart but into the stomach, and expelled into the latrine."

Thus cleansing all the foods.ʰ

₂₀ And he said, "What comes out of a person, that is what defiles him. ₂₁ For from within, out of the heart of men, come evil thoughts, fornications,ⁱ thefts, murders, ₂₂ adulteries, greed, wickedness, deceit, lasciviousness,ʲ an evil eye,ᵏ blasphemies,ˡ pride,

foolishness. ₂₃ All [these]ᵐ evil things come from within and defile a person."

₂₄ From there, having arisen, he went away to the region of Tyre [[and Sidon]].ⁿ And entering into a house, he wanted no one to know, but he could not escape notice; ₂₅ {but}ᵒ [immediately]ᵖ a woman heard about him, whose daughter had an unclean spirit, {came and fell}�q [at his feet];ʳ ₂₆ now the woman was a Greek, a Syrophoenician by birth; and she asked him to cast out the demon from her daughter.

₂₇ And {he}ˢ said to her, "Let the children be satisfied first, for it is not good to take the children's bread and throw it to the dogs." ₂₈ But she answered {and said}ᵗ [to him],ᵘ "[[Yes]]ᵛ Lord, [[for]]ʷ even the dogs under the table eat from the children's crumbs."

₂₉ And he said to her, "Because of this word, go; the demon has gone out of your daughter." ₃₀ And going away to {her}ˣ house, she found the child lying on the bed and the demon gone out.

ᵃ 7:13, **And you do many similar things:** Absent from W(032).

ᵇ 7:14, **again:** Absent from ℵ(01).

ᶜ 7:14, **to me, all of you:** Absent from ℵ(01) D(05).

ᵈ 7:15, **of a man:** Absent from A(02) BYZ TR.

ᵉ 7:15, **those:** Included in D(05) W(032).

ᶠ 7:16, **If anyone has ears to hear, let him hear:** Some manuscripts include verse 16. A(02) D(05) W(032) Latin(a b ff² i) BYZ TR ‖ Absent from ℵ(01) B(03) NA28 SBLGNT THGNT.

ᵍ 7:18, **see:** Or realize.

ʰ 7:19, This verse is likely a narrator's comment.

ⁱ 7:21, **fornications:** Or sexual immoralities.

ʲ 7:22, **lasciviousness:** Or sensuality.

ᵏ 7:22, **an evil eye:** Or envy.

ˡ 7:22, **blasphemies:** Or slanders.

ᵐ 7:23, **these:** Absent from W(032).

ⁿ 7:24, **and Sidon:** Included in ℵ(01) A(02) B(03) BYZ TR ‖ Absent from D(05) W(032) Latin(a b ff² i) NA28 SBLGNT THGNT.

ᵒ 7:25, **but:** Some manuscripts read "for." A(02) W(032) BYZ TR.

ᵖ 7:25, **immediately:** Absent from A(02) W(032) BYZ TR.

q 7:25, **came and fell:** Some manuscripts read "and coming, she fell." D(05) Latin(a ff²).

ʳ 7:25, **at his feet:** Absent from Latin(b i).

ˢ 7:27, **he:** Some manuscripts read "Jesus." A(02) W(032) BYZ TR.

ᵗ 7:28, **and said:** Some manuscripts read "saying." 𝔓45 D(05) W(032).

ᵘ 7:28, **to him:** Absent from 𝔓45.

ᵛ 7:28, **Yes:** Included in ℵ(01) A(02) B(03) Latin(a) BYZ TR THGNT ‖ Absent from 𝔓45 D(05) W(032) Latin(b ff²) NA28 SBLGNT.

ʷ 7:28, **for:** Included in A(02) Latin(a b ff² i) BYZ TR ‖ D(05) reads "but."

ˣ 7:30, **her:** Some manuscripts read "the." 𝔓45 D(05) W(032) Latin(b ff² i).

31 And again, going out from the region of Tyre, he came through Sidon to the Sea of Galilee, in the midst of the region of Decapolis.

32 [And]ᵃ They brought to him a deaf and mute man, and they begged him to lay his hand on him. 33 And taking him aside from the crowd privately, he put his fingers into his ears, and having spit, he touched his tongue, 34 and looking up to heaven, he sighed and said to him, "Ephphatha," which means, "Be opened."

35 And [immediately]ᵇ his ears were opened, and [[immediately]]ᶜ the bond of his tongue was loosed, and he spoke correctly. 36 And he ordered them {not to tell anyone};ᵈ but {the more he ordered them, the more [[exceedingly]]ᵉ they [themselves]ᶠ proclaimed it}.ᵍ 37 And they were exceedingly astonished, saying, "He has done all things well; he even makes {the deaf hear and [the]ʰ mute speak}."ⁱ

8 1 [[But]]ʲ In those days, when there was again a large crowd and they had nothing to eat, {he}ᵏ called {the}ˡ disciples and said [to them],ᵐ 2 "I have compassion for the crowd because they have been with me for three days and have nothing to eat. 3 And if I send them away hungry [to their homes],ⁿ they will faint on the way; {and}ᵒ some of them have come from a distance."

4 {His}ᵖ disciples say to him [that],ᑫ "From where will anyone be able to satisfy these people with bread in a desolate place?"

5 He asked them, "How many loaves do you have?" They said, "Seven." 6 And he commanded the crowd to sit down on the ground; and taking the seven loaves, he gave thanks, broke them, and gave them to his disciples to set before the people; and they set them before the crowd. 7 They also had a few small fish; and after blessing [them],ʳ [he said]ˢ {to set these also before them}.ᵗ 8 So they [[all]]ᵘ ate and were satisfied; and they took up the leftover [broken pieces],ᵛ seven baskets

---

ᵃ 7:32, **And:** Absent from 𝔓45 A(02) BYZ TR.

ᵇ 7:35, **immediately:** 𝔓45 A(02) W(032) Latin(a b ff² i) Syriac BYZ TR NA28[] ‖ Absent from ℵ(01) B(03) D(05) SBLGNT THGNT.

ᶜ 7:35, **immediately:** Included in ℵ(01).

ᵈ 7:36, **not to tell anyone:** D(05) reads "to say nothing to anyone."

ᵉ 7:36, **exceedingly:** Included in D(05) BYZ TR.

ᶠ 7:36, **themselves:** Absent from A(02) W(032) Latin(b ff² i) BYZ TR.

ᵍ 7:36, **the more he ordered them..:** Some manuscripts read "they proclaimed it all the more exceedingly." D(05) BYZ TR.

ʰ 7:37, **the:** Absent from ℵ(01) B(03).

ⁱ 7:37, **the deaf hear and the mute speak:** W(032) reads "to hear and speak."

ʲ 8:1, **But:** Included in D(05) W(032).

ᵏ 8:1, **he:** Some manuscripts read "Jesus." BYZ TR SBLGNT.

ˡ 8:1, **the:** Some manuscripts read "his." A(02) B(03) W(032) BYZ TR.

ᵐ 8:1, **to them:** Absent from W(032).

ⁿ 8:3, **to their homes:** Absent from Latin(b).

ᵒ 8:3, **and:** D(05) reads "because."

ᵖ 8:4, **His:** Some manuscripts read "The." ℵ(01) Latin(ff²).

ᑫ 8:4, **that:** B(03) NA28 SBLGNT THGNT ‖ Absent from A(02) D(05) Latin(a b ff² i) BYZ TR ‖ Some manuscripts read "they said." ℵ(01) W(032).

ʳ 8:7, **them:** Absent from D(05) BYZ TR.

ˢ 8:7, **he said:** Absent from ℵ(01) Latin(a b ff²).

ᵗ 8:7, **to set these also before them:** A(02) B(03) Latin(a b ff²) BYZ TR NA28 SBLGNT THGNT ‖ Some manuscripts read "to set before them." ℵ(01) W(032) ‖ D(05) reads "and he commanded them also to set before them."

ᵘ 8:8, **all:** Included in ℵ(01).

ᵛ 8:8, **broken pieces:** Absent from W(032) Latin(k).

[[full]].[a] ⁹And they [[who ate]][b] were [about][c] four thousand men. And he sent them away.

¹⁰[Immediately][d] he got into the boat with his disciples and [[Jesus]][e] came to the region of Dalmanutha.

¹¹And the Pharisees went out and began to debate [[with]][f] him, seeking from him a sign [[to see]][g] from heaven, {testing him}.[h]

¹²And sighing deeply in {his}[i] spirit, [he says,][j] "Why does this generation seek a sign? [Truly][k] [I say][l] to you, no sign will be given to this generation."

¹³And leaving them, he again got into the boat [[once more]][m] and went [to the other side].[n] ¹⁴And {they}[o] forgot to take bread, {[p]and except for one loaf, they did not have any} [with them][q] in the boat.

¹⁵And he was warning them, saying, "[Watch,][r] Beware of the leaven of the Pharisees and the leaven of Herod." ¹⁶And they reasoned with each other [[saying]][s] that they did not have bread. ¹⁷And knowing this, {he}[t] says to them, "Why do you reason [[in your hearts, you of little faith,]][u] that you have no bread? Do you not yet understand or comprehend? {Is your heart hardened?}[v] ¹⁸{Having eyes, do you not see},[w] and having ears, do you not hear? [And][x] Do you not [understand nor][y] remember? ¹⁹[[And]][z] When I broke the [five][a] loaves for the five thousand, how many baskets full of broken pieces did you pick up?" They said to him, "Twelve."

---

a 8:8, **full:** Included in W(032).

b 8:9, **who ate:** Included in A(02) C(04) D(05) W(032) Latin(a b ff² i) ‖ Absent from ℵ(01) B(03) NA28 SBLGNT THGNT.

c 8:9, **about:** Absent from ℵ(01).

d 8:10, **Immediately:** Absent from D(05) Latin(a b ff²).

e 8:10, **Jesus:** Included in ℵ(01).

f 8:11, **with:** Included in D(05) Latin(a b ff²).

g 8:11, **to see:** Included in ℵ(01).

h 8:11, **testing him:** Or tempting him.

i 8:12, **his:** Some manuscripts read "the." D(05) W(032) Latin(b i).

j 8:12, **he says:** Absent from Latin(ff²).

k 8:12, **Truly:** Absent from 𝔓45 B(03) W(032).

l 8:12, **I say:** Absent from 𝔓45 W(032).

m 8:13, **once more:** Included in 𝔓45 A(02) D(05) W(032) BYZ TR.

n 8:13, **to the other side:** Absent from Latin(b).

o 8:14, **they:** Some manuscripts read "his disciples." 𝔓45 D(05) W(032).

p 8:14, **and except for one loaf, they did not have any:** Some manuscripts read "having only one loaf."𝔓45 D(05) W(032).

q 8:14, **with them:** Absent from D(05).

r 8:15, **Watch:** Absent from D(05) Latin(a b ff² i).

s 8:16, **saying:** Included in A(02) B(04) BYZ TR.

t 8:17, **he:** Some manuscripts read "Jesus." ℵ(01) A(02) C(04) D(05) W(032) Latin(a b ff²) BYZ TR ‖ Absent from B(03) NA28 SBLGNT THGNT.

u 8:17, **in your hearts, you of little faith:** Included in D(05) Latin(a b ff² i) ‖ Some manuscripts read "in yourselves, you of little faith." 𝔓45 W(032) ‖ Absent from ℵ(01) A(02) B(03) C(04) BYZ TR NA28 THGNT SBLGNT.

v 8:17, **Is your heart hardened?:** Some manuscripts read "Your heart is hardened." D(05) W(032) Latin(a b i).

w 8:18, **Having eyes, do you not see:** W(032) reads "You have eyes, but do not see."

x 8:18, **And:** Absent from D(05) W(032).

y 8:18, **understand nor:** Included in 𝔓45.

z 8:19, **And:** Included in ℵ(01) A(02) C(04) D(05) W(032) Latin(a ff²) BYZ TR SBLGNT THGNT ‖ Absent from 𝔓45 B(03) NA28.

a 8:19, **five:** Absent from Latin(i).

20 "When I broke [the seven]ᵃ [for the four thousand],ᵇ [how many baskets [full]ᶜ [of broken pieces]ᵈ did you pick up?" And they said [to him],ᵉ "Seven."]ᶠ 21 And he said to them, " [[How]]ᵍ Do you not yet understand?"

22 And they come to Bethsaida. And they bring to him a blind man and they ask him to touch him. 23 And taking {the blind man by the hand},ʰ he led him out of the village; and after spitting on his eyes and laying his hands on him, he asked him, "Do you see anything?" 24 And looking up, he said, "{I see people, for I see them like trees walking around}."ⁱ 25 {Then he laid his hands on his eyes again, and he saw clearly, and his sight was restored, and he saw}ʲ everything clearly. 26 And he sent him to his house, {saying, "Do not even enter the village}ᵏ [[nor tell it to any in the village]]."ˡ

27 And Jesus went out, and his disciples, into [the villages of]ᵐ Caesarea Philippi; and on the way he asked {his}ⁿ disciples, saying [to them],ᵒ "Who do men say that I am?" 28 And they {said to}ᵖ him, saying [that]ᑫ "John the Baptist; and others, Elijah; but others, [that]ʳ one of the prophets." 29 And he {asked}ˢ them, But who do you say that I am? Peter answered and said to him, "You are the Christᵗ [[, the son of the living God]]."ᵘ 30 And he warned them not to tell anyone about him.

31 And he began to teach them that the Son of Man must suffer many things and be rejected by [the elders and]ᵛ the chief priests and the scribes and be killed, and after three days rise again. 32 And he spoke the word openly.

ᵃ 8:20, **the seven:** Absent from Latin(b).

ᵇ 8:20, **for the four thousand:** Absent from Latin(ff²).

ᶜ 8:20, **full:** Absent from D(05) Latin(a b ff²).

ᵈ 8:20, **of broken pieces:** Absent from W(032) Latin(b).

ᵉ 8:20, **to him:** B(03) C(04) NA28[] SBLGNT ‖ Absent from 𝔓45 א(01) A(02) D(05) W(032) Latin(a b ff²) BYZ TR THGNT.

ᶠ 8:20, **how many baskets…:** Absent from Latin(b).

ᵍ 8:21, **How:** Included in A(02) B(03) D(05) W(032) Latin(a ff²) BYZ TR ‖ Absent from א(01) C(04) NA28 SBLGNT THGNT.

ʰ 8:23, **the blind man by the hand:** Some manuscripts read "his hand." 𝔓45 W(032).

ⁱ 8:24, **I see people, for I see them like trees walking around:** Some manuscripts read "I see people; they look like trees walking around." D(05) W(032) Latin(a b ff² i).

ʲ 8:25, **Then he laid his hands:** Some manuscripts read "Then he again placed his hands on his eyes, and he made him look up, and his sight was restored, and he saw." A(02) BYZ TR ‖ D(05) reads "And again, placing his hands on his eyes, he began to see; and his sight was restored so that he could see."

ᵏ 8:26, **saying, Do not even enter the village:** Some manuscripts read "and said to him, 'Go to your house." D(05).

ˡ 8:26, **nor tell it to any in the village:** Included in A(02) C(04) D(05) Latin(ff² i)BYZ TR.

ᵐ 8:27, **the villages of:** Absent from D(05) Latin(a b ff² i).

ⁿ 8:27, **his:** A(02) reads "the."

ᵒ 8:27, **to them:** Absent from D(05) Latin(a b ff² i k).

ᵖ 8:28, **said to:** א(01) B(03) C(04) NA28 SBLGNT THGNT ‖ Some manuscripts read "answered." A(02) BYZ TR ‖ Some manuscripts read "they answered him, saying." D(05) W(032) Latin(a b ff² i).

ᑫ 8:28, **that:** א(01), B(03) C(04) NA28[] SBLGNT ‖ Absent from A(02) D(05) Latin(a b ff² i k) BYZ TR THGNT.

ʳ 8:28, **that:** א(01), B(03) C(04) NA28 SBLGNT THGNT ‖ Absent from A(02) D(05) W(032) Latin(a b ff² i k) BYZ TR.

ˢ 8:29, **asked:** א(01) B(03) C(04) D(05) Latin (a) NA28 SBLGNT THGNT ‖ Some manuscripts read "says to." A(02) W(032) Latin(b i k) BYZ TR.

ᵗ 8:29, **Christ:** See footnote for Christ in Matt 1:1.

ᵘ 8:29, **the son of the living God:** Included in W(032) Latin(b) Syriac(syᵖ) ‖ Some manuscripts read "Son of God." א(01).

ᵛ 8:31, **the elders and:** Absent from A(02).

And Peter took [him][a] aside and
began to rebuke him. 33 But [[Jesus]][b]
turning around and seeing his disciples,
he rebuked Peter {and said},[c] "Get
behind me, Satan ! For you are not
setting your mind on the things of God,
but on the things of men."

34 And calling the crowd together
with {his}[d] disciples, he said to them,
"If anyone wishes to follow me, let him
deny [himself and][e] take up his cross
and follow me. 35 For whoever wishes to
save his life will lose it, but whoever
loses his life [for my sake and][f] for the
gospel [[the same]][g] will save it.

36 "For what does it profit a man
{to gain}[h] the whole world and forfeit
his soul? 37 For what can a man give in
exchange for his soul?

38 "For whoever is ashamed of me
and my words in {this}[i] adulterous
and sinful generation, the Son of Man
will also be ashamed of him when he
comes in the glory of his Father with
the holy angels."

9 1 And he said to them, "Truly I say
to you, there are some standing
here [[with me]][j] who will not taste
death until they see the kingdom of
God having come with power."

2 And after six days Jesus took
Peter, James, and John, and leads
them up a high mountain alone by
themselves. And {he}[k] was transfigured
before them, 3 and his clothes became
dazzling white [[as snow,]][l] [as no
launderer on earth can whiten them].[m]

4 And [[behold]][n] Elijah appeared to
them with Moses, and they were talking
with Jesus. 5 And Peter answered and
said to Jesus, "Rabbi, it is good for us
to be here; [[if you want]][o] let us make
[[here]][p] three tents, one for you, one
for Moses, and one for Elijah." 6 For he
did not know what to say, for they were
greatly afraid.

7 And [[behold,]][q] it happened ,
a cloud overshadowed them, and [it
happened,][r] a voice came out of the
cloud [[saying]],[s] "This is my beloved
Son. Listen to him." 8 And suddenly,
looking around, they no longer
saw anyone but Jesus alone with
themselves.

9 And as they were coming down
from the mountain, he instructed them
not to tell anyone what they had seen,
until the Son of Man had risen from the
dead. 10 [And they kept the matter to
themselves, discussing what it meant to
rise from the dead.][t]

---

a 8:32, **him:** Absent from D(05) Latin(b ff^2 i k).
b 8:33, **Jesus:** Included in A(02).
c 8:33, **and said:** ℵ(01) B(03) C(04) Latin(ff^2) NA28 SBLGNT THGNT || Some manuscripts read "saying." A(02) D(05) W(032) Latin(a b i) BYZ TR.
d 8:34, **his:** Some manuscripts read "the." D(05) W(032) Latin(a b ff^2 i k).
e 8:34, **himself and:** Absent from W(032) Latin(b i).
f 8:35, **for my sake and:** Absent from 𝔓45 D(05) Latin(a b i k).
g 8:35, **the same:** Included in BYZ TR.
h 8:36, **to gain:** ℵ(01) B(03) NA28 SBLGNT THGNT || Some manuscripts read "if he gains." 𝔓45 A(02) C(04) D(05) W(032) Latin(a b ff^2 i k) BYZ TR.
i 8:38, **this:** Some manuscripts read "the." 𝔓45 W(032) Latin(a i k).
j 9:1, **with me:** Included in D(05) Latin(a b).
k 9:2, **he:** Some manuscripts read "Jesus." 𝔓45 W(032).
l 9:3, **as snow:** Included in A(02) D(05) Latin(a b ff^2 i) BYZ TR || Absent from ℵ(01) B(03) C(04) W(032) Latin(k) NA28 SBLGNT THGNT.
m 9:3, **as no launderer on earth can whiten them:** Absent from Latin(a).
n 9:4, **behold:** Included in W(032).
o 9:5, **if you want:** Included in D(05) W(032) Latin(a b ff^2 i k).
p 9:5, **here:** Included in 𝔓45 C(04) W(032).
q 9:7, **behold:** Included in W(032).
r 9:7, **it happened:** Absent from A(02) D(05) W(032) Latin(a b i k) BYZ TR.
s 9:7, **saying:** Included in A(02) D(05) W(032) Latin(a b ff^2 i) TR.
t 9:10, **And they kept the matter to themselves...:** Absent from Latin (ff^2).

11 And they asked him, saying,
"Why do the scribes say that Elijah
must come first?" 12 [And][a] He said
to them, "Elijah does come first and
restores all things. And how is it written
of the Son of Man that he should
suffer many things and be treated with
contempt? 13 But I say to you [that][b]
Elijah has [[already]][c] come, and they
did to him whatever they wished, just
as it is written of him."

14 And when they came to the
disciples, they saw a [great][d] crowd
around them and scribes arguing with
them. 15 And immediately all the crowd,
when the whole crowd saw him, they
were amazed and ran up to greet him.
16 And he asked {them},[e] "What are you
arguing about with them?"

17 And someone from the crowd
answered [him][f] [[and said]],[g]
"Teacher, I brought my son to you, for
he has a mute spirit. 18 And whenever it
seizes him, it throws him down, and he
foams and grinds his teeth and becomes
rigid. And I asked your disciples to cast
it out, and they were not able [[to cast
it out]]."[h] 19 And {he}[i] answered them,
"O faithless [[and corrupt]][j] generation,
how long am I to be with you? How
long am I to bear with you? Bring him
to me."

20 And they brought the boy [to
him].[k] And when the spirit saw him,
[immediately][l] it convulsed the boy,
and {he}[m] fell on the ground and rolled
about, foaming at the mouth.

21 And Jesus asked his father
[[saying]],[n] "How long has this been
happening to him?" And he said, "From
childhood. 22 [And][o] It has often cast
him into fire and into water, to destroy
him. But if you can do anything,
[[Lord]][p] have compassion on us and
help us."

23 And Jesus said to him, "'If you
can [[believe]]'![q] All things are possible
for one who believes." 24 [[And]][r]
[Immediately][s] The father of the child
cried out [[with tears]][t] and said, "I
believe [[Lord]];[u] help my unbelief!"

25 And when Jesus saw that a crowd
came running together, he rebuked
the [unclean][v] spirit, saying [to it],[w]
"You mute and deaf spirit, I command
you, come out of him and never enter
him again." 26 And after crying out and
convulsing him terribly, it came out
[[of him]],[x] and the boy was like a

---

a 9:12, **And:** Absent from Latin(a ff² i).
b 9:13, **that:** Absent from ℵ(01).
c 9:13, **already:** Included in C(04) W(032) Latin(i).
d 9:14, **great:** Absent from W(032).
e 9:16, **them:** Some manuscripts read "the scribes." A(02) C(04) Latin(a) BYZ TR.
f 9:17, **him:** Absent from A(02) W(032) BYZ TR.
g 9:17, **and said:** Included in A(02) C(04) Latin(i) BYZ TR.
h 9:18, **to cast it out:** Included in D(05) W(032) Latin(a b).
i 9:19, **he:** Some manuscripts read "Jesus." 𝔓45 W(032).
j 9:19, **and corrupt:** Included in 𝔓45 W(032).
k 9:20, **to him:** Absent from D(05) Latin(a b i k).
l 9:20, **immediately:** Absent from D(05).
m 9:20, **he:** Some manuscripts read "the boy." Latin(a b ff² i k).
n 9:21, **saying:** Included in W(032).
o 9:22, **And:** Absent from 𝔓45 D(05) W(032) Latin(b ff² i k).
p 9:22, **Lord:** Included in D(05) Latin(a b ff² i).
q 9:23, **believe:** Included in A(02) D(05) BYZ TR.
r 9:24, **And:** Included in 𝔓45 ℵ(01) A(02) C(04) D(05) W(032) Latin(a b i k) BYZ TR || Absent from B(03) NA28 SBLGNT THGNT.
s 9:24, **Immediately:** Absent from ℵ(01) C(04).
t 9:24, **with tears:** Included in D(05) Latin(a) BYZ TR.
u 9:24, **Lord:** Included in Latin(a b) BYZ TR.
v 9:25, **unclean:** Absent from 𝔓45 W(032).
w 9:25, **to it:** Absent from 𝔓45 Latin(a).
x 9:26, **of him:** Included in D(05) Latin(a b ff² i k).

corpse, so that {most}[a] of them said, "He is dead." 27 But Jesus took him [by the hand][b] and lifted him up, and he arose.

28 And when he had entered the house, his disciples {asked him privately},[c] "Why could we not cast it out?" 29 And {he}[d] said to them, "This kind cannot be driven out by anything but prayer [[and fasting]]."[e]

30 And from there they went out and {passed}[f] through Galilee, and he did not want anyone to know; 31 for he was teaching his disciples and saying [to them],[g] "The Son of Man is to be handed over to the hands of men, and they will kill him, and [after being killed,][h] he will rise {after three days}."[i] 32 But they did not understand the statement, and they were afraid to ask him.

33 And they came to Capernaum. And when he was in the house, he asked them, "What were you discussing [[among yourselves]][j] on the way?" 34 But they were silent; for [on the way][k] they had discussed with one another who [[among them]][l] was the greatest.

35 [And][m] Sitting down, he called the twelve and said to them, "If anyone wants to be first, he will be last of all and servant of all."

36 And taking a child, he placed it in their midst, and embracing it, he said to them, 37 "Whoever receives one of such children [in my name],[n] receives me; and whoever receives me, does not receive me but the one who sent me."

38 John said to him, "Teacher, we saw someone [[who does not follow us]][o] casting out demons in your name, and we tried to stop him because he was not following us."

39 But {Jesus}[p] {said},[q] "Do not hinder [him];[r] for no one who performs a miracle in my name will be able [soon][s] afterward to speak evil of me; 40 {for whoever is not against us is for us}.[t]

41 "For whoever gives you a cup of water to drink in my name because you belong to Christ, truly I say to you, [that][u] he will not lose his reward.

42 "And whoever causes one of {these}[v] little ones who believe [in me][w] to stumble, it would be better for him if a millstone were hung around his neck and he were thrown into the sea.

---

a 9:26, **most:** Some manuscripts read "many."

b 9:27, **by the hand:** Absent from W(032) Latin(k).

c 9:28, **asked him privately:** Some manuscripts read "came to him privately and asked him." W(032).

d 9:29, **he:** Some manuscripts read "Jesus." Latin(b).

e 9:29, **and fasting:** Included in 𝔓45 A(02) C(04) D(05) W(032) Latin(a b ff² i) Syriac(sy^s) BYZ TR ‖ Absent from ℵ(01) B(03) Latin(k) NA28 SBLGNT THGNT.

f 9:30, **passed:** Some manuscripts read "going."

g 9:31, **to them:** Absent from B(03) Latin(k).

h 9:31, **after being killed:** Absent from D(05) Latin(a k).

i 9:31, **after three days:** B(03) D(05) Latin(a b ff² i k) NA28 SBLGNT THGNT ‖ Some manuscripts read "on the third day." A(02) W(032) BYZ TR Syriac.

j 9:33, **among yourselves:** Included in A(02) W(032) BYZ TR.

k 9:34, **on the way:** Absent from A(02) D(05) Latin(a b i).

l 9:34, **among them:** Included in ℵ(01) D(05) W(032) Latin(a b ff² i k).

m 9:35, **And:** Some manuscripts read "Then." D(05) Latin(b ff² i) ‖ Absent from W(032).

n 9:37, **in my name:** Absent from Latin(k).

o 9:38, **who does not follow us:** Included in A(02) D(05) Latin(a b ff² i k).

p 9:39, **Jesus:** Some manuscripts read "he." D(05) W(032) Latin(a b ff² i).

q 9:39, **said:** Some manuscripts read "answered." A(02) C(04) D(05) W(032) Latin(b ff² i k) BYZ TR.

r 9:39, **him:** Absent from D(05) Latin(a b i k).

s 9:39, **soon:** Absent from W(032).

t 9:40, **not against us is for us:** Some manuscripts read "not against you is for you."

u 9:41, **that:** Absent from A(02) Latin(a i) BYZ TR.

v 9:42, **these:** Some manuscripts read "my." W(032).

w 9:42, **in me:** A(02) B(03) W(032) BYZ TR NA28[] SBLGNT THGNT ‖ Absent from ℵ(01) C(04) D(05) Latin(a b ff² i k).

43 "And if your hand causes you to stumble, cut it off; it is better for you to enter life crippled than having two hands to go [into Gehenna],^{ab} into the unquenchable fire 44 [[where their worm does not die, and the fire is not quenched]].^c

45 "And if your foot causes you to stumble, cut it off; [[for]]^d it is better for you to enter into life lame than having two feet to be thrown into {Gehenna}^e 46 [[Their worm does not die and the fire is not quenched]].^f

47 "And if your eye causes you to stumble, cast it out; it is better for you to enter the kingdom of God with one eye than having two eyes to be thrown into Gehenna [[of fire]],^g 48 where their worm does not die and the fire is not quenched.

49 "{For everyone will be salted with fire}^h [[and every sacrifice will be salted with salt]].^i

50 "Salt is good; but if the salt becomes unsalty, with what will you season it? [[You therefore]]^j Have salt in yourselves, and be at peace with one another."

10 1 And from there, getting up, he comes to the borders of Judea [and]^k {beyond the Jordan},^l and crowds gather [again]^m to him, and as he was accustomed, again he taught them.

2 And [Pharisees approached,]^n questioning him whether it is lawful for a man to divorce a wife, testing him. 3 But he, answering, said to them, "What did Moses command you?" 4 They said, "{Moses}^o allowed a certificate of divorce to be written and to divorce."^p

5 But Jesus said [to them],^q "Because of your hardness of heart he wrote [you]^r this commandment. 6 But from the beginning [of creation],^s {he}^t made them male and female. 7 [[And, he said]]^u For this reason a

---

a 9:43, **into Gehenna:** Absent from W(032).

b 9:43-47, **Gehenna:** Often translated hell, Gehenna is a term derived from a place called the Valley of Hinnom, located near Jerusalem. In the Hebrew Bible (Old Testament), this valley was associated with practices of child sacrifice to foreign gods, notably the Canaanite deity Moloch. Because of these associations, the Valley of Hinnom was reviled and became a symbol of divine judgment and destruction.

c 9:44, **where their worm does not die, and the fire is not quenched:** Some manuscripts include verse 44. A(02) D(05) Latin(a b ff² i) BYZ TR ‖ Absent from ℵ(01) B(03) C(04) W(032) Latin(k) Syriac(sy^s) NA28 SBLGNT THGNT.

d 9:45, **For:** Included in A(02).

e 9:45, **Gehenna:** Some manuscripts read "into the unquenchable fire." A(02) D(05) Latin(a b ff² i) BYZ TR.

f 9:46, **Their worm does not die:** Absent from ℵ(01) B(03) C(04) W(032) SBLGNT.

g 9:47, **of fire:** Included in A(02) C(04) BYZ TR.

h 9:49, **For everyone will be salted with fire:** Some manuscripts read "and every sacrifice will be salted with salt." D(05) Latin(a b ff² i k).

i 9:49, **and every sacrifice will be salted with salt:** Included in A(02) C(04) BYZ TR.

j 9:50, **You therefore:** Included in W(032).

k 10:1, **and:** Some manuscripts read "across." A(02) BYZ TR ‖ Absent from D(05) W(032) Latin(a b ff² i k).

l 10:1, **beyond the Jordan:** Some manuscripts read "by the far side of the Jordan."

m 10:1, **again:** Absent from W(032) Latin(b ff² i k).

n 10:2, **Pharisees approached:** Absent from Latin (a b ff² k) SBLGNT.

o 10:4, **Moses:** Some manuscripts read "he." Latin(a ff²).

p 10:4, Deuteronomy 24:1, 3.

q 10:5, **to them:** Absent from D(05) Latin(b k).

r 10:5, **you:** Absent from W(032) Latin(b).

s 10:6, **of creation:** Absent from D(05) Latin(b ff²).

t 10:6, **he:** ℵ(01) B(03) C(04) NA28 SBLGNT THGNT ‖ Some manuscripts read "God." A(02) D(05) W(032) Latin(a b ff² k) BYZ TR.

u 10:7, **And, he said:** Included in D(05) W(032).

man will leave {his}[a] father and [[his]][b] mother [and be joined to his wife],[c] 8 and the two shall become one flesh; so they are no longer two but one flesh.[d] 9 [Therefore,][e] What God has joined together, let no man separate."

10 And in the house again, {the}[f] disciples questioned him about this. 11 And he says to them, "Whoever divorces his wife and marries another commits adultery [against her];[g] 12 and if {she},[h] having divorced her husband, [marries another,][i] she commits adultery."

13 And they were bringing children to him so that he might touch them; but {the}[j] disciples rebuked {them}.[k] 14 But when Jesus saw this, he was indignant and said to them, "Let the children come to me; [[and]][l] do not hinder them, for the kingdom of God belongs to such as these.

15 "Truly I say to you, whoever does not receive the kingdom [of God][m] like a child will not enter it." 16 And he took them in his arms, blessed them, laying his hands on them.

17 As he was setting out on his journey, a [[certain rich]][n] man ran up and knelt before him, and asked [him][o] [[saying]],[p] "Good Teacher, what must I do to inherit eternal life?"

18 Jesus said to him, "Why do you call me good? No one is good except one, God [[alone]].[q]

19 "You know the commandments: 'Do not murder, [Do not commit adultery,][r] Do not steal, Do not bear false witness, [Do not defraud,][s] Honor your father and [[your]][t] mother.'" 20 And he [[answering]][u] said to him, "Teacher, I have kept all these things since my youth. [[What am I still lacking?]][v]

21 {Jesus},[w] looking at him, loved him and said to him, "You lack one thing; [[if you will be perfect]][x] go, sell all that you have and give to the poor, and you will have treasure in heaven; and come, [[take up the cross, and]][y] follow me." 22 But he was saddened by the word and went away grieving; for he had many possessions. 23 And looking around, Jesus says to his disciples, "How difficult it is for those who have wealth to enter the kingdom of God!"

---

a 10:7, **his:** Some manuscripts read "the." D(05).

b 10:7, **his:** Included in ℵ(01) D(05) Latin(a b ff²).

c 10:7, **and be joined to his wife:** Absent from ℵ(01) B(03).

d 10:7-8, Genesis 2:24.

e 10:9, **Therefore:** Absent from D(05) Latin(k).

f 10:10, **the:** Some manuscripts read "his." A(02) W(032) Latin(b ff²) BYZ TR.

g 10:11, **against her:** Absent from W(032).

h 10:12, **she:** Some manuscripts read "a woman." A(02) D(05) W(032) BYZ TR.

i 10:12, **marries another:** Absent from W(032).

j 10:13, **the:** Some manuscripts read "his." D(05) Latin(a ff² k).

k 10:13, **them:** Some manuscripts read "those that brought them." A(02) D(05) W(032) Latin(a b ff²) BYZ TR.

l 10:14, **and:** Included in ℵ(01) A(02) C(04) D(05) TR.

m 10:15, **of God:** Absent from D(05).

n 10:17, **certain rich:** Included in A(02) Latin(a b ff²).

o 10:17, **him:** Absent from W(032) Latin(a b k).

p 10:17, **saying:** Included in D(05) W(032) Latin(a k).

q 10:18, **alone:** Included in D(05).

r 10:19, **Do not commit adultery:** Absent from ℵ(01).

s 10:19, **Do not defraud:** Absent from B(03) W(032).

t 10:19, **you:** Included in ℵ(01) C(04) W(032) Latin(a b).

u 10:20, **answering:** Included in A(02) C(04) D(05) W(032) Latin(a b ff² k).

v 10:20, **What am I still lacking?:** Included in W(032) Latin(a).

w 10:21, **Jesus:** Some manuscripts read "he." A(02).

x 10:21, **if you will be perfect:** Included in W(032).

y 10:21, **take up the cross, and:** Included in W(032).

24 But {the}[a] disciples were amazed at his words. {Jesus},[b] answering [again],[c] says to them, "Children, how difficult it is [[for those who trust in riches]][d] to enter the kingdom of God! 25 It is easier for a camel to go {through}[e] [the][f] eye of [the][g] needle than for a rich person to [enter][h] the kingdom of God."

26 And they were exceedingly astonished, saying to themselves, "And who can be saved?" 27 [[But]][i] Looking at them, Jesus says, "With men it is impossible, {but not with God.}[j] [For all things are possible with God.]"[k]

28 [[And]][l] Peter began to say to him, "[Behold,][m] We have left everything and followed you. [[What, therefore, will be for us?]]"[n]

29 Jesus {said}[o] [[to him]][p] [[saying]],[q] "Truly I tell you, [[that]][r] there is no one who has left [house or][s] brothers or sisters or mother [or father][t]

[[or wife]][u] or children or fields [for my sake and for [the sake of][v] the gospel],[w] 30 who will not receive a hundredfold [now][x] in this time [[the one who has left]][y] [houses [and brothers][z] and sisters and mothers and children and fields, with persecutions][a] [and][b] in the age to come, [[will receive]][c] eternal life.

31 But many who are first will be last, and [the][d] last first."

32 They were on the way going up to Jerusalem, and Jesus was leading them; and they were amazed [, and those who followed were afraid].[e] And taking the twelve aside again, he began to tell them what was going to happen to him, 33 saying, "Behold, we are going up to Jerusalem, and the Son of Man will be handed over to the chief priests [and the scribes],[f] and they will condemn him to death and hand him over to the Gentiles, 34 and they will mock him

---

a 10:24, **the:** Some manuscripts read "his." D(05).

b 10:24, **Jesus:** Some manuscripts read "he." A(02).

c 10:24, **again:** Absent from A(02) W(032) Latin(a ff2).

d 10:24, **for those who trust in riches:** Included in A(02) C(04) D(05) Latin(b ff2) BYZ TR.

e 10:25, **through:** Some manuscripts read "into."

f 10:25, **the:** Absent from ℵ(01) A(02) C(04) D(05) W(032) TR.

g 10:25, **the:** Absent from ℵ(01) A(02) C(04) D(05) W(032) TR.

h 10:25, **enter:** Absent from D(05) Latin(a ff2 k).

i 10:27, **But:** Included in A(02) D(05) W(032) Latin(k) BYZ TR.

j 10:27, **but not with God:** Some manuscripts read "but with God possible." ‖ Absent from Latin(a b ff2 k).

k 10:27, **For all things are possible with God:** Absent from D(05).

l 10:28, **And:** Included in D(05) Latin (a b ff2 k) TR.

m 10:28, **behold:** Absent from W(032).

n 10:28, **What, therefore, will be for us?:** Included in ℵ(01) Latin(b).

o 10:29, **said:** Some manuscripts read "answered." A(02) C(04) D(05) Latin (a b ff2 k) BYZ TR.

p 10:29, **to him:** Included in ℵ(01).

q 10:29, **saying:** Included in A(02) C(04) W(032) Latin(a b ff2) BYZ TR.

r 10:29, **that:** Included in A(02).

s 10:29, **house or:** Absent from D(05) Latin(b).

t 10:29, **or father:** Absent from D(05) Latin(a ff2).

u 10:29, **or wife:** Included in A(02) C(04) BYZ TR.

v 10:29, **the sake of:** Absent from A(02) B(03) TR.

w 10:29, **for my sake and for the sake of the gospel:** Absent from ℵ(01).

x 10:30, **now:** Absent from D(05) Latin(a).

y 10:30, **the one who has left:** Included in D(05) Latin(a b ff2).

z 10:30, **and brothers:** Absent from W(032).

a 10:30, **houses and brothers...:** Absent from ℵ(01).

b 10:30, **and:** Absent from D(05) Latin(b ff2).

c 10:30, **will receive:** Included in D(05) Latin(a b ff2).

d 10:31, **the:** Absent from ℵ(01) A(02) D(05) W(032) BYZ.

e 10:32, **and those who followed were afraid:** Absent from D(05) Latin(a b) ‖ W(032) reads "following him."

f 10:33, **and the scribes:** Absent from ℵ(01).

and spit on him [and flog him and kill him],^{a} and {after three days}^{b} he will rise."

35 And James and John, the [[two]]^c sons of Zebedee, came to him, saying [to him],^{d} "Teacher, we want you to do [for us]^e whatever we ask of you."

36 [And he said to them, "{What do you want me to do for you?}"^{f}]^g 37 And they said [to him],^{h} "Grant [to us]^i to sit, one at your right hand [and one at your left],^{j} {in your glory}."^{k}

38 But [[having answered,]]^l Jesus said to them, "You do not know what you are asking. Are you able to drink the cup that I drink, {or}^{m} to be baptized with the baptism with which I am baptized?" 39 And they said [to him],^{n} "We are able."

[And Jesus said to them,]^o "The cup that I drink you will [[indeed]]^p drink, and with the baptism with which I am baptized, you will be baptized, 40 but to sit at my right hand or at my left is not mine to give, but it is for those for whom it has been prepared [[by my Father]]."^{q}

41 [And]^r When the [[other]]^s ten heard it, they began to be indignant at James and John.

42 [And]^t {Jesus}^{u} called them to him and said to them, "You know that those who are considered rulers of the nations lord it over them, and their great ones exercise authority [over them].^{v} 43 [But]^w It is not so among you, but whoever wishes to become great among you will be your servant, 44 And whoever wishes to be first [among you]^x will be the servant of all; 45 For even the Son of Man did not come to be served, but to serve, and to give his life as a ransom for many."

a 10:34, **and flog him and kill him:** Absent from D(05) Latin(ff^2 k).
b 10:34, **after three days:** Some manuscripts read "the third day."
c 10:35, **two:** Included in C(04) D(05).
d 10:35, **to him:** Absent from A(02) W(032) Latin(b ff^2 i k) BYZ TR.
e 10:35, **for us:** Absent from Latin(k).
f 10:36, **What do you want me to do for you:** Some manuscripts read "I will do for you." D(05).
g 10:36, **And he said to them...:** Absent from א(01) Latin(k).
h 10:37, **to him** Absent from א(01).
i 10:37, **to us:** Absent from א(01).
j 10:37, **and one at your left:** Absent from Latin(b ff^2 i k).
k 10:37, **in your glory:** Some manuscripts read "In the kingdom of glory." W(032) ‖ Absent from Latin(k).
l 10:38, **having answered:** Included in D(05) W(032) Latin(b ff^2 i).
m 10:38, **or:** Some manuscripts read "and."
n 10:39, **to him:** Absent from D(05) W(032) Latin (a b ff^2 i k).
o 10:39, **And Jesus said to them:** Absent from W(032).
p 10:39, **indeed:** Included in A(02) D(05) Latin(a b ff^2 i k) BYZ TR.
q 10:40, **by my Father:** Included in א(01) Latin(a).
r 10:41, **And:** Absent from D(05).
s 10:41, **other:** Included in D(05) Latin(a b i).
t 10:42, **And:** Absent from Latin(b ff^2 i).
u 10:42, **Jesus:** Some manuscripts read "he."
v 10:42, **over them:** Absent from א(01) Latin(k).
w 10:43, **But:** Absent from D(05) Latin(a b ff^2 i k).
x 10:44, **among you:** Absent from D(05).

46 [And they come into Jericho.]ᵃ {And}ᵇ As he was going out from Jericho, and his disciples and a considerable crowd, the son of Timaeus, [Bartimaeus,]ᶜ {a blind beggar, was sitting by the road}.ᵈ 47 And when he heard that it was Jesus the Nazarene, he began to cry out and say, "Son of David, Jesus, have mercy on me!" 48 [And many were rebuking him, that he should be silent; but he cried out all the more, "Son of David, have mercy on me!"]ᵉ

49 And Jesus stopped and said, "Call him." And they called the blind man, [saying to him],ᶠ "Take courage, get up, he is calling you." 50 And throwing off his cloak, he jumped up and came to {Jesus}.ᵍ 51 And Jesus answered him and said, "What do you want me to do for you?" The blind man said to him, "[[Master,]]ʰ Rabboni, that I may regain my sight." 52 And Jesus said to him, "Go, your faith has saved you." And immediately he regained his sight and followed {him}ⁱ on the way.

11 1 And when they approach Jerusalem, [[and]]ʲ to Bethphage [[and Bethany]],ᵏ at the Mount of Olives, he sends two of his disciples 2 and says to them, "Go into the village [opposite you],ˡ and immediately upon entering [into it]ᵐ, you will find a colt tied, on which no one of men has ever sat; untie it and bring it. 3 And if anyone says to you, 'Why are you {doing this}?'ⁿ say [[that]],ᵒ 'The Lord needs it, and will send it back here [again]ᵖ immediately.'"

4 And they went and found a colt tied near a door outside on the street, and they untied it. 5 And some of those standing there said to them, "What are you doing, untying the colt?" 6 And they said [to them]ᑫ just as Jesus had {said}ʳ [[to them]]ˢ and they let them go.

7 And they {brought}ᵗ the colt to Jesus and threw {their}ᵘ garments on it, and he sat on it.

ᵃ 10:46, **And they come into Jericho:** Absent from B(03).
ᵇ 10:46, **And:** Some manuscripts read "After." D(05) Latin(a b ff² i k).
ᶜ 10:46, **Bartimaeus:** Absent from W(032) Latin(k).
ᵈ 10:46, **a blind beggar, was sitting by the road:** Some manuscripts read "a blind man, was sitting by the road, begging." A(02) W(032) Latin(a b ff² i) BYZ TR.
ᵉ 10:48 Verse 48 is absent from W(032).
ᶠ 10:49, **saying to him:** Absent from D(05).
ᵍ 10:50, **Jesus:** Some manuscripts read "him." D(05).
ʰ 10:51, **Master:** Included in D(05) Latin(b ff² i).
ⁱ 10:52, **him:** Some manuscripts read "Jesus." BYZ TR.
ʲ 11:1, **And:** Included in A(02) D(05).
ᵏ 11:1, **and Bethany:** Absent from D(05) Latin(a b ff² i k).
ˡ 11:2, **opposite you:** Absent from ℵ(01).
ᵐ 11:2, **into it:** Absent from D(05) Latin(a b ff² i).
ⁿ 11:3, **doing this:** Some manuscripts read "untie the colt." D(05) ‖ Absent from W(032).
ᵒ 11:3, **that:** Included in ℵ(01) A(02) C(04) D(05) W(032) BYZ TR.
ᵖ 11:3, **again:** Absent from A(02) Latin(a b k) BYZ TR.
ᑫ 11:6, **to them:** Absent from D(05) Latin(b ff² i).
ʳ 11:6, **said:** Some manuscripts read "commanded." A(02) BYZ TR.
ˢ 11:6, **to them:** Included in D(05) W(032) Latin(a b ff² i) +.
ᵗ 11:7, **brought:** Some manuscripts read "lead."
ᵘ 11:7, **their:** Some manuscripts read "the." W(032).

8 And many spread {their}[a] garments on the road [, and others cut branches from the {fields}[b]].[c] 9 And those who went before and those who followed cried out [[saying]],[d] "[Hosanna!][e] Blessed is the one who comes in the name of the Lord! 10 [[And]][f] Blessed is the [coming][g] kingdom [[in the name of the Lord]][h] of our father David! Hosanna in the highest!"

11 And {he}[i] entered Jerusalem and went into the temple; and when he had looked around at everything, as it was already late, he went out to Bethany with the twelve [[disciples]].[j]

12 And on the next day, as {they}[k] went out from Bethany [, he was hungry].[l] 13 And seeing a [[single]][m] fig tree from a distance having leaves, he came [[to it]][n] to see if perhaps he would find something on it; and when he came to it, he found nothing but [[only]][o] leaves, for it was not the season for figs. 14 And responding, {he}[p] said to it, "May no one ever eat fruit from you again." And his disciples were listening.

15 And they come [[again]][q] to Jerusalem. And entering into the temple, {he}[r] began to drive out [[from there]][s] those who were selling [and those who were buying][t] in the temple, and he overturned the tables of the money changers [[he poured out]][u] and the seats of those who were selling the doves, 16 and he would not allow anyone to carry a vessel through the temple.

17 And he was teaching and saying [to them],[v] "Is it [not][w] written [that],[x] 'My house shall be called a house of prayer for all the nations'? But you have made it a den of robbers."

18 And the chief priests and the scribes heard it and were seeking how they might destroy him; for they were afraid [of him],[y] for all the crowd was astonished at his teaching.

19 And when evening came, they went out of the city.

20 And passing by in the morning, they saw the fig tree withered from the roots. 21 And Peter, remembering, said to him, "Rabbi, look! The fig tree that you cursed has withered."

---

a 11:8, **their:** Some manuscripts read "the." W(032).

b 11:8, **fields:** Some manuscripts read "trees, and spread them in the road." A(02) D(05) Latin(a b ff² k) BYZ TR.

c 11:8, **and others cut branches from the fields:** Absent from W(032) Latin(i).

d 11:9, **saying:** Included in A(02) D(05) W(032) Latin(a b i) BYZ TR.

e 11:9, **Hosanna!:** Absent from D(05) W(032) Latin(b ff²)P.

f 11:10, **And:** Included in A(02) D(05).

g 11:10, **coming:** Absent from Latin(a k).

h 11:10, **in the name of the Lord:** Included in A(02) D(05) BYZ TR.

i 11:11, **he:** Some manuscripts read "Jesus." A(02) BYZ TR.

j 11:11, **disciples:** Included in D(05).

k 11:12, **they:** Some manuscripts read "he." D(05) Latin(a b ff² i k).

l 11:12, **he was hungry:** Absent from ℵ(01).

m 11:13, **single:** Included in ℵ(01).

n 11:13, **to it:** Included in W(032).

o 11:13, **only:** Included in W(032) Latin(a).

p 11:14, **he:** Some manuscripts read "Jesus." W(032).

q 11:15, **again:** Included in Latin(b ff² i).

r 11:15, **he:** Some manuscripts read "Jesus." A(02) BYZ TR.

s 11:15, **from there:** Included in D(05) Latin(b).

t 11:15, **and those who were buying:** Absent from W(032).

u 11:15, **he poured out:** Included in W(032).

v 11:17, **to them:** Absent from B(03) Latin(a ff²).

w 11:17, **not:** Absent from D(05) Latin(b ff² i k).

x 11:17, **that:** Absent from C(04) D(05) Latin(a b i k).

y 11:18, **of him:** Absent from A(02).

22 [And]ᵃ Jesus, answering, said to them, "Have faith [in God].ᵇ 23 [[For]]ᶜ Truly I say to you [[that]],ᵈ whoever says to this mountain, 'Be lifted up and thrown into the sea,' and does not doubt in his heart but believes that he says is happening, it will be done for him [[whatever he says]].ᵉ

24 "Therefore I say to you, whatever you {pray and ask for},ᶠ believe that you {have received it},ᵍ and it will be yours. 25 And whenever you stand praying, forgive if you have anything against anyone, so that your Father [in heaven]ʰ may also forgive [you]ⁱ your trespasses. 26 [[But if you do not forgive, neither will your Father in heaven forgive your trespasses.]]"ʲ

27 And they came again to Jerusalem. And as he was walking in the temple, the chief priests, the scribes, and the elders [[of the people]]ᵏ came to him. 28 And they said to him, "By what authority are you doing these things? [{Or}ˡ who gave you this authority to do them?]"ᵐ

29 And Jesus [[answering,]]ⁿ said to them, "I will ask you one question; answer me, and I will tell you by what authority I do these things. 30 The baptism of John—was it from heaven or from men? Answer me." 31 And they discussed it among themselves, saying, "[[What shall we say?]]ᵒ If we say, 'From heaven,' he will say [[to us]],ᵖ 'Why [then]�q did you not believe him?' 32 But shall we say, 'From men?'" – they feared the {crowd},ʳ for they all held that John was [truly]ˢ a prophet. 33 So they answered Jesus, "We do not know." [And]ᵗ [[Answering,]]ᵘ Jesus said to them, "Neither will I tell you by what authority I do these things."

12 1 And he began to speak to them in parables, "A man planted a vineyard and put a fence around it and dug a winepress and built a tower and leased it to vine-growers and went on a journey. 2 And he sent a servant to [[the vine-growers]]ᵛ at the time, {in order to receive}ʷ [[from the vine-growers]]ˣ some of the fruits of the vineyard; 3 and taking him, they beat him and sent him away empty-handed. 4 And [again]ʸ

ᵃ 11:22, **And:** Absent from W(032).
ᵇ 11:22, **in God:** Absent from Latin(a k).
ᶜ 11:23, **For:** Included in A(02) C(04) W(032) BYZ TR.
ᵈ 11:23, **that:** Absent from ℵ(01) D(05) W(032).
ᵉ 11:23, **whatever he says:** Included in A(02) BYZ TR.
ᶠ 11:24, **pray and ask for:** Some manuscripts read "ask for in prayer." A(02) Latin(a b ff² i k) BYZ TR.
ᵍ 11:24, **have received it:** Some manuscripts read "are receiving it."
ʰ 11:25, **in heaven:** Absent from Latin(i).
ⁱ 11:25, **you:** Absent from Latin(a ff² i).
ʲ 11:26, **But if you do not forgive, neither will your Father in heaven forgive your trespasses:** Included in A(02) C(04) D(05) Latin(a b ff² i) BYZ TR ‖ Absent from ℵ(01) B(03) W(032) Latin(k) NA28 SBLGNT THGNT.
ᵏ 11:27, **of the people:** Included in D(05).
ˡ 11:28, **Or:** Some manuscripts read "And." D(05) Latin(k) ‖ Absent from C(04).
ᵐ 11:28, **Or who gave you this authority to do them?:** Absent from D(05) Latin(k).
ⁿ 11:29, **answering:** Included in A(02) D(05) W(032) Latin(a b ff² i) BYZ TR.
ᵒ 11:31, **What shall we say?:** Included in D(05) SBLGNT.
ᵖ 11:31, **to us:** Included in D(05) Latin(a b ff² i k).
q 11:31, **then:** Absent from A(02) C(04) W(032).
ʳ 11:32, **crowd:** Some manuscripts read "people." A(02) D(05) W(032) Latin(a b ff² i k) BYZ TR.
ˢ 11:32, **truly:** Absent from ℵ(01) Latin(k).
ᵗ 11:33, **And:** Absent from D(05).
ᵘ 11:33, **Answering:** Absent from A(02) D(05) W(032) Latin(i) BYZ TR.
ᵛ 12:2, **the vine-growers:** Absent from W(032).
ʷ 12:2, **in order to receive:** Some manuscripts read "so that they might give him." D(05) Latin(a b ff² i).
ˣ 12:2, **from the vine-growers:** Absent from D(05).
ʸ 12:4, **again:** Absent from W(032).

he sent another [servant]ᵃ to them; and they [[stoned that one,]]ᵇ struck him on the head and {dishonored him}.ᶜ ₅And [[again]]ᵈ he sent another [[servant]];ᵉ [and they killed him,]ᶠ [and many others, some they beat, and some]ᵍ they killed. ₆[[Yet]]ʰ {Still}ⁱ He had one, {a}ʲ beloved son; [[and]]ᵏ he sent [him]ˡ last [to them],ᵐ saying [that],ⁿ 'They will respect my son.' ₇But {those}ᵒ vine-growers said to themselves [that],ᵖ 'This is the heir; come, let us kill him, and the inheritance will be ours.' ₈And taking him, they killed [him]ۨ and threw him out of the vineyard. ₉What [then]ʳ will the owner of the vineyard do? He will come and destroy the vine-growers and give the vineyard to others.

₁₀"Have you not read this scripture, 'The stone which the builders rejected, this has become the cornerstone; ₁₁this was the Lord's doing, and it is marvelous in our eyes'?"ˢ

₁₂And they sought to seize him, but they feared the crowd, for they knew that he had spoken the parable against them. [And leaving him, they went away.]ᵗ

₁₃And they send [to him]ᵘ some of the Pharisees and of the Herodians, in order to catch him in his words. ₁₄And {coming, they say to him},ᵛ "Teacher, we know that you are truthful and do not care about anyone; for you do not look at the face of men, but teach the way of God in truth. [[So tell us,]]ʷ Is it lawful [[for us]]ˣ to pay taxes to Caesar, or not? [Should we pay, or should we not pay?]"ʸ

ᵃ 12:4, **servant:** Absent from ℵ(01).

ᵇ 12:4, **stoned that one:** Included in A(02) C(04) BYZ TR.

ᶜ 12:4, **dishonored him:** Some manuscripts read "sent him away dishonored." A(02) C(04) W(032) BYZ TR ‖ Absent from Latin(k).

ᵈ 12:5, **again:** Included in A(02) W(032) BYZ.

ᵉ 12:5, **servant:** Included in D(05) Latin(a b ff² i).

ᶠ 12:5, **and they killed him:** Absent from W(032).

ᵍ 12:5, **and many others, some they beat, and some:** Absent from Latin(k).

ʰ 12:6, **Yet:** Included in A(02) C(04) Latin(ff²) BYZ TR.

ⁱ 12:6, **still:** Some manuscripts read "but later." W(032) ‖ Absent from Latin(k).

ʲ 12:6, **a:** Some manuscripts read "his." 𝔓45 A(02) W(032) Latin(ff² i).

ᵏ 12:6, **and:** Included in A(02) C(04) BYZ.

ˡ 12:6, **him:** Absent from W(032) TR.

ᵐ 12:6, **to them:** Absent from D(05).

ⁿ 12:6, **that:** Absent from W(032).

ᵒ 12:7, **those:** Some manuscripts read "the." BYZ TR.

ᵖ 12:7, **that:** Absent from D(05) Latin(a b ff² i k).

ۨ 12:8, **him:** Absent from ℵ(01) A(02) D(05) W(032) Latin(b i) BYZ.

ʳ 12:9, **then:** Absent from B(03) Latin(k) SBLGNT.

ˢ 12:10-11, Psalm 118:22-23.

ᵗ 12:12, **And leaving him, they went away.:** Absent from W(032).

ᵘ 12:13, **to him:** Absent from D(05) Latin(a ff² i k).

ᵛ 12:14, **coming, they say to him:** Some manuscripts read "The Pharisees were questioning him." D(05) Latin(k) ‖ W(032) reads "Coming, they began to question him with deceit."

ʷ 12:14, **So tell us:** Included in C(04) D(05) W(032) Latin(a b ff² i k).

ˣ 12:14, **For us:** Included in D(05).

ʸ 12:14, **Should we pay, or should we not pay?:** Absent from D(05) Latin(a b ff² i k).

15 But knowing their hypocrisy, {he}[a] said to them, "Why do you test me [[hypocrites]]?[b] Bring me a denarius [[here]][c] so that I may see it." 16 And they brought it. And he says to them, "Whose image is this and the inscription?" And they said [to him],[d] "Caesar's." 17 {Jesus said}[e] [to them],[f] "Give to Caesar the things that are Caesar's, and to God the things that are God's." And they marveled at him.

18 And Sadducees come to him, who say there is no resurrection, and they questioned him, saying, 19 "Teacher, Moses wrote for us [that][g] if someone's brother dies and {leaves}[h] a wife, and leaves no {child},[i] the brother should take {the}[j] wife and raise up offspring for his brother.[k] 20 [[Now]][l] There were [[with us]][m] seven brothers; and the {first}[n] took a wife, and dying left no offspring; 21 and the second took her, and died {leaving no offspring};[o] [and][p] {the third likewise};[q] 22 [and][r] the seven [[took her]][s] [[also]][t] left no offspring. [Last of all,][u] [the woman also died.][v]

23 "In the resurrection [when they rise],[w] whose [wife][x] will she be? [For the seven had her as wife.]"[y]

24 [[And answering,]][z] Jesus said to them, "Is it not for this reason that you are mistaken, not knowing the Scriptures nor the power of God? [[You know.]][a] 25 For when they rise from the dead, they neither marry nor are given in marriage, but are like angels [[which are]][b] in heaven.

26 But concerning the dead, that they are raised, have you not read in the book of Moses, in the passage

---

a 12:15, **he:** Some manuscripts read "Jesus." D(05) Latin(a b ff² i).

b 12:15, **hypocrites:** Included in 𝔓45 W(032).

c 12:15, **here:** Included in ℵ(01).

d 12:16, **to him:** Absent from W(032) Latin(a).

e 12:17, **Jesus said:** Some manuscripts read "And Jesus, answering, said." 𝔓45 A(02) D(05) Latin(a b ff² i) BYZ TR ‖ W(032) reads "And answering, he said."

f 12:17, **to them:** Absent from B(03) D(05).

g 12:19, **that:** Absent from D(05).

h 12:19, **leaves:** Some manuscripts read "has." D(05) W(032) Latin(a b ff² i k).

i 12:19, **child:** B(03) W(032) Latin(a ff² k) NA28 SBLGNT THGNT ‖ Some manuscripts read "children." ℵ(01) A(02) C(04) D(05) Latin (i) BYZ TR.

j 12:19, **the:** Some manuscripts read "his." A(02) D(05) Latin(a b ff² i) BYZ TR.

k 12:19, Deuteronomy 25:5.

l 12:20, **Now:** Included in D(05) Latin(a b ff² i).

m 12:20, **with us:** Included in D(05) Latin(a b ff² i).

n 12:20, **first:** Some manuscripts read "the one." BYZ TR.

o 12:21, **leaving no offspring:** Some manuscripts read "and not even he left." A(02) D(05) Latin(a) ‖ Some manuscripts read "and not even he left offspring." BYZ TR.

p 12:21, **and:** Absent from W(032) Latin(b ff²).

q 12:21, **the third likewise:** , ℵ(01) B(03) C(04) W(032) Latin(a i) NA28 SBLGNT THGNT ‖ Some manuscripts read "Likewise, they took her." D(05) Latin(b ff²) ‖ Some manuscripts read "The third likewise, and they took her." BYZ TR ‖ A(02) reads "The third likewise, and they took her in the same way."

r 12:22, **and:** Absent from D(05) W(032) Latin(i) BYZ TR.

s 12:22, **took her:** Included in Latin(ff²).

t 12:22, **also:** Included in A(02) BYZ TR.

u 12:22, **Last of all:** Absent from ℵ(01) D(05).

v 12:22, **the woman also died:** Absent from Latin(k).

w 12:23, **when they rise:** A(02) Latin(a b ff² i) NA28[] SBLGNT ‖ Absent from ℵ(01) B(03) C(04) D(05) W(032) Latin(k) THGNT. In some manuscripts, this phrase "from the dead" is added to "when they rise" making explicit what is implicit in the term "rise."

x 12:23, **wife:** Absent from Latin(k).

y 12:23, **For the seven had her as wife:** Absent from Latin(k).

z 12:24, **And answering:** Included in A(02) D(05) W(032) Latin(b ff² i) BYZ TR.

a 12:24, **you know:** Included in D(05).

b 12:25, **which are:** Included in A(02) B(03) BYZ TR.

about the bush, {how God said to him saying},[a] I am [the]^b God of Abraham, and [the]^c God of Isaac, and [the]^d God of Jacob? 27 He is not [the]^e God of the dead, but [[God]]^f of the living; [[therefore]]^g you are greatly mistaken."

28 And one of the scribes came up, having heard [them disputing, and seeing that he had answered them well],^h asked him, [[saying "Teacher."]]ⁱ "What is the first commandment [of all]?"^j

29 [[But]]^k {Jesus}^l answered [[him]],^m "The first [[of all commandments]]ⁿ is this, 'Hear, O Israel, the Lord our God, [the Lord]^o is one; 30 and you shall love the Lord your God with all your heart, and with all your soul, [and with all your mind,]^p

and with all your strength.'^q [[This is the first commandment.]]^r 31 [[And]]^s The second is {this},^t 'You shall love your neighbor as yourself.' There is no other commandment greater than these."^u

32 [And]^v The scribe said to him, "Well said, teacher, you have spoken the truth, for there is one [[God]],^w and there is no [other]^x besides him;^y 33 and to love him with all {the}^z heart, and with all the understanding, [[with all the soul]]^a and with all the strength, and to love one's neighbor as oneself, is more than all the burnt offerings and sacrifices."^b 34 And Jesus, seeing [him]^c that he had answered wisely, said to him [that],^d "You are not far from the kingdom of God." And no one dared question him [any longer].^e

---

a 12:26, **how God said to him saying:** Some manuscripts read "as God said to him saying." A(02) D(05) BYZ TR ‖ W(032) reads "as God said, saying to him."

b 12:26, **the:** Absent from B(03) W(032).

c 12:26, **the:** Absent from B(03) D(05) W(032).

d 12:26, **the:** Absent from B(03) D(05) W(032).

e 12:27, **the:** Absent from A(02) D(05) W(032) NA28 SBLGNT THGNT.

f 12:27, **God:** Included in BYZ TR.

g 12:27, **therefore:** Included in A(02) D(05) Latin(a b i) BY TR.

h 12:28, **them disputing...:** Absent from Latin(k).

i 12:28, **Saying Teacher:** Included in D(05) Latin(b ff² i).

j 12:28, **of all:** Absent from D(05) W(032).

k 12:29, **But:** Included in A(02) C(04) D(05) Latin(a b ff² i k) BYZ TR.

l 12:29, **Jesus:** Some manuscripts read "he." W(032).

m 12:29, **him:** Included in A(02) C(04) D(05) Latin(a b ff² i k) BYZ TR.

n 12:29, **of all commandments:** Included in A(02) C(04) Latin(ff²) BYZ TR.

o 12:29, **the Lord:** Absent from Latin(a k).

p 12:30, **and with all your mind:** Absent from D(05) Latin(k).

q 12:30, Deuteronomy 6:4-5.

r 12:30, **This is the first commandment:** Included in A(02) D(05) Latin(i) BYZ TR ‖ Some manuscripts read "this is first." W(032) Latin(k).

s 12:31, **And:** Included in A(02) W(032) Latin(k) BYZ TR.

t 12:31, **this:** Some manuscripts read "like it." A(02) W(032) D(05) Latin(k) BYZ TR.

u 12:31, Leviticus 19:18.

v 12:32, **And:** Absent from C(04).

w 12:32, **God:** Included in D(05) W(032) Latin(a b ff² i) TR.

x 12:32, **other:** Absent from D(05) Latin(a k).

y 12:32, Deuteronomy 6:4, 4:35, Isaiah 45:21.

z 12:33, **the:** Some manuscripts read "your." א(01).

a 12:33, **with all the soul:** Included in A(02) Latin(a) BYZ TR.

b 12:33, Deuteronomy 6:5, Leviticus 19:18.

c 12:34, **him:** Absent from א(01) D(05) Latin(b ff² i k).

d 12:34, **that:** Included in W(032).

e 12:34, **any longer:** Absent from D(05).

35 And {Jesus}[a] answering, was teaching in the temple, "How do the scribes say that the Christ is the son of David? 36 [[For]][b] David himself {said}[c] by the Holy Spirit, 'The Lord said to my Lord, "Sit at my right hand, until I put your enemies {under your feet}.'"[d] 37 [[Therefore]][e] David himself calls him Lord; so how is he his son?" And the large crowd listened to him gladly.

38 And in his teaching he said, "Beware of the scribes who like to walk around in long robes and {receive}[f] greetings in the marketplaces, 39 and [have the best seats][g] in the synagogues and the places of honor at banquets, 40 who devour widows' houses and [[orphans]][h] for a show make long prayers; they will receive the greater condemnation."

41 And sitting down opposite the treasury, {he}[i] observed [[everyone]][j] how the crowd was putting {copper coins into the treasury}[k] [and many rich people were putting in large amounts].[l] 42 And a [poor][m] widow came and put in two small copper coins, which is a quadrans.[n] 43 And calling {his}[o] disciples to him, he said to them, "Truly I say to you [that],[p] this poor widow has put in more than [all][q] [of those who are contributing] to the treasury;[r] 44 for {they all}[s] contributed out of their abundance, but she out of her poverty has put in everything she had, her entire livelihood."

13 1 And as he was going out of the temple, one of his disciples said to him, "Teacher, [[teacher]][t] [look at][u] what stones and what buildings!"

2 [[Having answered,]][v] {Jesus}[w] said to him, "Do you see these great buildings? [[Truly, I say to you that]][x] There will not be left [here][y] a stone upon a stone that will not be torn down. [[And in three days, another will raise it up without hands.]]"[z]

3 And as he was sitting on the Mount of Olives opposite the temple, Peter and James and John and Andrew asked him privately, 4 "Tell us, when will these things be, and what will be

---

a 12:35, **Jesus:** Some manuscripts read "he." W(032).

b 12:36, **For:** Included in A(02) Latin(b ff2 i).

c 12:36, **said:** Some manuscripts read "says." BYZ TR.

d 12:36, **under your feet:** Some manuscripts read "as a footstool for your feet."

e 12:37, **Therefore:** Included in A(02) Latin(b ff2) BYZ TR.

f 12:38, **receive:** Some manuscripts read "make." D(05).

g 12:39, **have the best seats:** Absent from Latin(k).

h 12:40, **orphans:** Included in D(05) W(032) Latin(a b ff2 i).

i 12:41, **he:** Some manuscripts read "Jesus." A(02) W(032) Latin(ff2 i) BYZ TR.

j 12:41, **everyone:** Included in W(032).

k 12:41, **copper coins into the treasury:** Some manuscripts read "in many coins." D(05).

l 12:41, **and many rich people were putting in large amounts:** Absent from D(05) ‖ Latin(i k) reads "and many rich people."

m 12:42, **poor:** Absent from D(05) Latin(a b ff2 i k).

n 12:42, **quadrans:** Or "two lepta, which is a kodrantes."

o 12:43, **his:** W(032) reads "the."

p 12:43, **that:** Absent from W(032) Latin(ff2).

q 12:43, **all:** Absent from Latin(k).

r 12:43, **of those who are contributing:** Absent from W(032) Latin(b ff2 i k).

s 12:44, **they all:** Some manuscripts read "all of these." D(05).

t 13:1, **teacher:** ℵ(01) includes a second time. ℵ(01).

u 13:1, **look at:** Absent from W(032).

v 13:2, **having answered:** Included in A(02) D(05) W(032) Latin(a b ff2 i k) BYZ TR.

w 13:2, **Jesus:** W(032) reads "he."

x 13:2, **Truly, I say to you that:** Included in D(05) Latin(a b ff2 i).

y 13:2, **here:** Absent from A(02) BYZ TR.

z 13:2, **And in three days, another will raise it up without hands:** Included in D(05) W(032) Latin(a b e ff2 i k).

the sign [when][a] all these things are
about to be [completely][b] fulfilled?"

5 And Jesus {began to say}[c] to them,
"See that no one leads you astray.
6 [[For]][d] Many will come in my name,
saying, 'I am he,' and they will lead
many astray. 7 And when you hear of
wars and rumors of wars, {do not be}[e]
alarmed; [[for]][f] it must happen, but
the end is not yet.

8 "[For][g] Nation will rise against
nation, and kingdom [against
kingdom];[h] [[and]][i] there will be
earthquakes in various places [[and]][j]
[[there will be]][k] [famines][l] [[and
disturbances]].[m] [These are but the
beginning of birth pains.][n]

9 "[But see to yourselves;][o] [[For]][p]
They will deliver you over to councils,
and you will be beaten in synagogues,
and you will stand before governors
and kings for my sake, as a testimony
to them. 10 And the gospel must first be
proclaimed [to all nations].[q] 11 {And}[r]
when they bring you to trial and deliver
you over, do not be anxious [[or
premeditate beforehand]][s] what you are
to say, but say whatever is given you in
that hour, for it is not you who speak,
but the Holy Spirit.[t] 12 {And}[u] brother
will deliver brother over to death, and
the father his child, and children will
rise against parents and have them put
to death. 13 And you will be hated by all
for my name's sake. But the one who
endures to the end will be saved.

14 "But when you see the
abomination of desolation [[spoken
of by Daniel the prophet]][v] standing
where it[w] should not be (let the reader
understand [[what he reads]])[x] then
those in Judea should flee to the
mountains,[y] 15 the one on the roof
should not go down or enter [[into the
house]][z] to take anything out of his
house, 16 and the one in the field should
not [turn back to][a] take his cloak.

---

a 13:4, **when:** Absent from Latin(k).
b 13:4, **completely:** Absent from W(032).
c 13:5, **began to say:** Some manuscripts read "having answered, said." A(02) D(05) Latin(k) BYZ TR || Some manuscripts read "having answered, began to say." Latin(a b i).
d 13:6, **For:** Included in A(02) D(05) BYZ TR.
e 13:7, **do not be:** Some manuscripts read "see that you are not." ℵ(01).
f 13:7, **for:** Included in A(02) D(05) Latin(a i k) BYZ TR.
g 13:8, **For:** Absent from W(032).
h 13:8, **against kingdom:** Absent from ℵ(01).
i 13:8, **and:** Included in A(02) Latin(a b ff^{2} i k) BYZ TR.
j 13:8, **and:** Included in A(02) BYZ TR.
k 13:8, **there will be:** Absent from ℵ(01) D(05) W(032) Latin(a b ff^{2} i k).
l 13:8, **famines:** Absent from ℵ(01).
m 13:8, **and disturbances:** Included in A(02) W(032) BYZ TR.
n 13:8, **These are but the beginning of birth pains:** Absent from W(032).
o 13:9, **But see to yourselves:** Absent from D(05) W(032) Latin(a b ff^{2} i).
p 13:9, **For:** Included in ℵ(01) A(02) Latin(k) BYZ TR.
q 13:10, **among all nations:** This is added to the base text of some manuscripts. D(05) Latin(ff^{2}).
r 13:11, **And:** Some manuscripts read "but." A(02) W(032) BYZ TR.
s 13:11, **or premeditate beforehand:** Included in A(02) Latin(a).
t 13:11, **Spirit:** See footnote for Spirit in Matt 1:18.
u 13:12, **And:** Some manuscripts read "But." A(02) W(032) BYZ TR.
v 13:14, **spoken of by Daniel the prophet:** Included in A(02) BYZ TR.
w 13:14, **it:** Or "he."
x 13:14, **what he reads:** Some manuscripts include added to the base text. D(05) Latin(a).
y 13:14, Daniel 9:27, 11:31, 12:11.
z 13:15, **into the house:** Included in A(02) D(05) W(032) Latin(ff^{2} i) BYZ TR.
a 13:16, **turn back to:** Absent from Latin(i).

17 “[But][a] Woe to those who are
pregnant and to those who are nursing
in those days! 18 But pray that [[your
flight]][b] might not happen in winter,
19 for those days will be a tribulation
[such][c] as has not occurred from the
beginning of creation [which God
created][d] until now, and never will.
20 And if {the Lord}[e] had not cut short
{those}[f] days [[because of his chosen
ones]],[g] no flesh would be saved; but
for the sake of the elect [whom][h] he
chose, he cut short {the}[i] days.

21 “And then if anyone says to
you, ‘{Look,}[j] Here is the Christ,’ or
‘{Look,}[k] There he is,’ do not believe
it; 22 {for}[l] [false christs and][m] false
prophets will rise and will {give}[n] signs
and wonders in order to lead astray, if
possible, [[even]][o] the elect. 23 But you,
watch out; [[behold]][p] I have told you
everything.

24 “But in those days, after that
tribulation, the sun will be darkened,
and the moon will not give its light,
25 and the stars [will be falling from
heaven],[q] and the powers in the
heavens will be shaken.

26 “And then they will see the Son
of Man coming {in clouds}[r] with great
power and glory.[s] 27 And then he will
send {the}[t] angels and gather the elect
[of him][u] from the four winds, from the
ends of the earth to the ends of heaven.

28 “Now learn the parable from the
fig tree: when its branch has already
become tender and puts forth its leaves,
you know that summer is near; 29 so also
you, when you see [all][v] these things
happening, know that it is near, right at
the doors.

30 “Truly I say to you, this
generation will not pass away until all
these things take place.

31 “Heaven and earth will pass
away, but my words will not pass away.

32 “But concerning that day {or}[w]
hour, no one knows, not even the
angels in heaven, nor the Son, but only
the Father.

33 “Watch [[therefore]],[x] stay awake
[[and pray]];[y] [for][z] [[except the Father
and the Son]][a] you do not know when
the time is.

---

a 13:17, **But:** Absent from D(05).
b 13:18, **your flight:** Included in A(02) Latin(k) BYZ TR.
c 13:19, **such:** Absent from Latin(b ff^2 i k).
d 13:19, **which God created:** Absent from D(05) Latin(b ff^2 i k).
e 13:20, **the Lord:** Some manuscripts read “God.” Latin(b ff^2 k) || Absent from W(032).
f 13:20, **those:** Some manuscripts read “the.” Latin(b k).
g 13:20, **because of his chosen ones:** Some manuscripts include added to the base text. D(05).
h 13:20, **whom:** Absent from Latin(k).
i 13:20, **those:** Some manuscripts read “the.” Latin(b k).
j 13:21, **Look:** Absent from Latin(ff^2).
k 13:21, **Look:** Absent from C(04) Latin(ff^2).
l 13:22, **for:** Some manuscripts read “but.” א(01) C(04).
m 13:22, **false christs and:** Absent from D(05) Latin(i k).
n 13:22, **give:** Some manuscripts read “make.” D(05).
o 13:22, **even:** Included in A(02) C(04) BYZ TR.
p 13:23, **behold:** Included in א(01) C(04) D(05) BYZ TR.
q 13:25, **will be falling from heaven:** Absent from Latin(k).
r 13:26, **in clouds:** Some manuscripts read “in a cloud.” W(032) || D(05) reads “on the clouds.”
s 13:26, Daniel 7:13.
t 13:27, **the:** Some manuscripts read “his.” א(01) A(02) C(04) BYZ TR.
u 13:27, **of him:** Absent from D(05) Latin(a e ff^2 i k) SBLGNT.
v 13:29, **all:** Included in D(05) Latin(i).
w 13:32, **or:** Some manuscripts read “and.” א(01) D(05) W(032) Latin(a i k) TR.
x 13:33, **therefore:** Included in D(05) || W(032) reads “but.”
y 13:33, **and pray:** Included in א(01) C(04) W(032) Latin(ff^2 i) BYZ TR.
z 13:33, **for:** Absent from Latin(ff^2).
a 13:33, **except the Father and the Son:** Included in W(032).

34 "[[For]][a] It is like a man traveling
abroad, having left his house and given
authority to his servants, each with
their own task, and commanded the
doorkeeper to stay awake.

35 "Therefore, stay awake; for you
do not know when the lord of the house
is coming, whether in the evening, [or][b]
at midnight, or at the crowing of the
rooster, or in the morning, 36 lest he
come suddenly and find you sleeping.

37 "{And what}[c] I say to you, [I say
to all]:[d] stay awake."

14 1 Now the Passover [and the
Unleavened Bread were][e] after
two days. And the chief priests and the
scribes were seeking how, [by deceit],[f]
they might arrest him and kill him;
2 [for][g] they said, "[Not][h] During the
feast, lest there {will be}[i] an uproar
among the people."

3 And while {he}[j] was in Bethany,
in the house of Simon the leper, as he
reclined, a woman {came}[k] with an
alabaster jar of ointment [of pure nard,
very costly],[l] [[and]][m] breaking the
[alabaster][n] jar, she poured it on his
head. 4 But {there were some who were
indignant among themselves},[o] [[and
saying]][p] "{Why has this waste [of the
ointment][q] occurred}?[r] 5 [For][s] This
[ointment][t] could have been sold for
more than three hundred denarii and
given to the poor." And they scolded
her.

6 But Jesus said [[to them]],[u] "Leave
her alone; why are you causing her
trouble? [[For]][v] She has done a good
deed for me. 7 For you always have the
poor with you, and whenever you want,
you can [[always]][w] do good for them;
but you will not always have me. 8 What
she had, she did: she has anointed my
body beforehand for burial.

9 "[[But]][x] Truly [I say to you][y]
[[that]],[z] wherever {the}[a] gospel is
preached in the whole world, what
she has done will also be spoken of in
memory of her."

---

a 13:34, **For:** Included in W(032).
b 13:35, **or:** Absent from A(02) D(05) W(032) Latin(a e ff^2 i) BYZ TR.
c 13:37, **And what:** Some manuscripts read "But." D(05) Latin(a).
d 13:37, **I say to all:** Absent from D(05) Latin(a).
e 14:1, **and the Unleavened Bread were:** Absent from א(01) D(05).
f 14:1, **by deceit:** Included in D(05) Latin(a i).
g 14:2, **for:** Some manuscripts read "but." A(02) W(032) BYZ TR.
h 14:2, **Not:** Absent from D(05) Latin(a ff^2 i k).
i 14:2, **will be:** Some manuscripts read "might be." Latin(ff^2 i k).
j 14:3, **he:** Some manuscripts read "Jesus." D(05) Latin(ff^2 i).
k 14:3, **came:** W(032) reads "approached."
l 14:3, **of pure nard, very costly:** Absent from D(05).
m 14:3, **and:** Included in A(02) C(04) D(05) W(032) Latin(a ff^2 i k) BYZ TR || Absent from א(01) B(03) NA28 SBLGNT THGNT.
n 14:3, **alabaster:** Absent from Latin(k).
o 14:4, **there were some who were indignant among themselves:** Some manuscripts read "his disciples were indignant." D(05) W(032).
p 14:4, **saying:** Included in A(02) D(05) W(032) Latin(a ff^2 k) BYZ TR.
q 14:4, **of the ointment:** Absent from W(032) Latin(a).
r 14:4, **Why has this waste of the ointment occurred:** Some manuscripts read "Why this waste of the ointment." D(05) Latin(a ff^2 i).
s 14:5, **For:** Absent from D(05) Latin(k).
t 14:5, **ointment:** Absent from BYZ TR.
u 14:6, **to them:** Absent from D(05) W(032) Latin(a ff^2 i k).
v 14:6, **For:** Included in א(01) W(032).
w 14:7, **always:** Included in B(03).
x 14:9, **But:** Absent from A(02) C(04) W(032) Latin(ff^2 i k) TR.
y 14:9, **I say to you:** Absent from Latin(ff^2).
z 14:9, **that:** Included in W(032) Latin(a i k).
a 14:9, **the:** Some manuscripts read "this." A(02) C(04) BYZ TR.

10 And [[behold]][a] Judas Iscariot,
[one][b] [of the twelve],[c] went to the
chief priests in order to betray him [to
them].[d] 11 {But they},[e] [having heard,][f]
they were glad and promised to give
him money. And he sought how he
might betray him at an opportune time.

12 And on the first day of
Unleavened Bread, when they were
sacrificing the Passover lamb, his
disciples said to him, "Where do you
want us to go and prepare for you
so that you may eat the Passover?"
13 And he sent two of his disciples and
said [to them][g], "Go into the city, and a
man carrying a jar of water will meet
you; follow him. 14 And wherever he
enters, say to the master of the house
[that],[h] 'The Teacher says, "Where is
my guest room, where I may eat the
Passover with my disciples?"' 15 And he
will show you a large upper room [[of a
house]][i] furnished [and ready];[j] there
prepare for us."

16 And {the}[k] disciples went out [[to
prepare]][l] [and came][m] into the city and
found it just as he had told them, and
they prepared the Passover.

17 {And}[n] when evening came, he
arrived with the twelve. 18 And while
they were reclining and eating, Jesus
said, "Truly I say to you, one of you will
betray me, the one eating with me."
19 [[But]][o] They began to be distressed
and to say to him one after another,
"{Is it I?}"[p] 20 But [[answering]][q] he said
to them, "It is one of the twelve, the
one who is dipping bread into the dish
with me.

21 "For the Son of Man [[is being
handed over]][r] goes as it is written of
him, but woe to that man by whom [the
Son of Man][s] is betrayed! It would have
been better for that man if he had not
been born."

22 And while they were eating, he[t]
took bread, and after blessing it, he
broke it and gave it to them, and said
[[to them]],[u] "[Take,][v] [[Eat]][w] This is
my body."

23 And taking a cup, after giving
thanks, he gave it to them, and they
all drank from it. 24 And he said [to
them],[x] "This is my blood [of the
[[new]][y] covenant],[z] which is poured
out for many [[for the forgiveness of

---

a 14:10, **behold:** Included in W(032).
b 14:10, **one:** Absent from A(02) D(05) Latin(a ff^2 i k).
c 14:10, **of the twelve:** Absent from A(02).
d 14:10, **to them:** Absent from D(05) W(032) Latin(a ff^2 i k).
e 14:11, **But they:** A(02) reads "And."
f 14:11, **having heard:** Absent from D(05) Latin(a ff^2 i k).
g 14:13, **to them:** Absent from D(05) Latin(a ff^2 i).
h 14:14, **that:** Absent from Latin(a ff^2 i k).
i 14:15, **of a house:** Absent from D(05).
j 14:15, **and ready:** Absent from A(02) Latin(a).
k 14:16, **the:** Some manuscripts read "his." A(02) C(04) D(05) W(032) Latin(a ff^2 i k).
l 14:16, **to prepare:** Included in W(032).
m 14:16, **and came:** Absent from א(01).
n 14:17, **and:** Some manuscripts read "But." D(05) Latin(ff^2 i).
o 14:19, **But:** Included in A(02) D(05) W(032) Latin(ff^2 k) BYZ TR ‖ C(04) reads "And."
p 14:19, **Is it I?:** Some manuscripts read "Surely not I?" D(05) BYZ TR ‖ A(02) reads "Is it I, Rabbi?" and another, "Surely not I." ‖ Some manuscripts read "I." Latin(a ff^2 i).
q 14:20, **answering:** Included in A(02) W(032) Latin(k) BYZ TR.
r 14:21, **is being handed over:** Included W(032).
s 14:21, **the Son of Man:** Absent from D(05) Latin(a).
t 14:22, **he:** Some manuscripts read "Jesus." א(01) A(02) C(04) BYZ TR.
u 14:22, **to them:** Some manuscripts include. W(032) Latin(i k).
v 14:22, **Take:** Absent from Latin(k).
w 14:22, **eat:** Included in BYZ TR.
x 14:24, **to them:** Absent from B(03).
y 14:24, **new:** Included in A(02) Latin(a) BYZ TR.
z 14:24, **of the covenant:** Absent from Latin(ff^2).

sins]].[a] 25 Truly I say to you, no longer, [certainly not][b] will I drink. of the {fruit}[c] of the vine until that day when I drink it new in the kingdom of God."

26 And after singing a hymn, they went out to the Mount of Olives.

27 {And}[d] Jesus says to them [that],[e] "You will all be made to stumble [[because of me this night]],[f] for it is written [that],[g] 'I will strike the shepherd, and the sheep [[of the flock]][h] will be scattered.' 28 {But}[i] after I am raised [[from the dead]],[j] I will go ahead of you into Galilee."

29 But Peter [[answering]][k] said to him, "{Even if}[l] all are made to stumble [[because of you]],[m] but not I. [[I will not fall away.]]"[n]

30 And Jesus says to him, "Truly I say to you [today,][o] that on {this very}[p] night, before the rooster crows [twice],[q] you will deny me three times." 31 But {he}[r] spoke [[more]][s] emphatically, "Even if I must die with you, I will never deny you." And all were saying the same.

32 And they came to a place called Gethsemane, and he said to his disciples, "Sit here while I pray." 33 And he took Peter, [and] James, [and] John with him, and began to be greatly distressed and troubled. 34 {And}[t] he said to them, "My soul is very sorrowful, even to death; remain here and watch."

35 And going a little farther, he fell on [[his face to]][u] the ground and prayed that, if it were possible, {the}[v] hour might pass from him. 36 And he said, "Abba, [[my]][w] [Father, all things are possible for you; remove {this}[x] cup from me; yet][y] not what I will, but what you [[will]]."[z]

37 [And he came][a] And he found them sleeping, and he said to Peter, "Simon, are you asleep? Could you not watch one hour? 38 Watch and pray [that][b] you may {not}[c] enter into temptation; the spirit indeed is willing, but the flesh is weak."

---

a 14:24, **for the forgiveness of sins:** Included in W(032).

b 14:25, **certainly not:** Absent from ℵ(01) C(04) W(032) Latin(k).

c 14:25, **fruit:** Some manuscripts read "offspring."

d 14:27, **And:** Some manuscripts read "Then." BYZ TR.

e 14:27, **that:** Absent from Latin(a b ff²).

f 14:27, **because of me this night:** Included in A(02) W(032) BYZ TR ‖ Some manuscripts read "in me." Latin(a i k).

g 14:27, **that:** Absent from Latin(k).

h 14:27, **of the flock:** Included in Latin(a c).

i 14:28, **But:** Some manuscripts read "And." C(04).

j 14:28, **from the dead:** Included in W(032).

k 14:29, **answering:** Included in W(032).

l 14:29, **Even if:** D(05) reads "if ever."

m 14:29, **because of you:** Included in Latin(b).

n 14:29, **I will not fall away:** Included in D(05) Latin(b ff²).

o 14:30, **today:** Absent from D(05) Latin(a b ff² i). This is also absent from one early Sahidic or Bohairic witness. (NA28).

p 14:30, **this very:** Some manuscripts read "in this."

q 14:30, **twice:** Absent from ℵ(01) C(04) D(05) W(032).

r 14:31, **he:** Some manuscripts read "Peter." A(02) C(04) W(032).

s 14:31, **more:** Included in A(02) W(032) BYZ TR.

t 14:34, **And:** Some manuscripts read "then." D(05) Latin(a b).

u 14:35, **his face to:** Included in D(05).

v 14:35, **the:** Some manuscripts read "this." D(05) Latin(i).

w 14:36, **my:** Included in W(032).

x 14:36, **this:** Some manuscripts read "the." D(05).

y 14:36, **Father, all things are…:** Absent from Latin(k).

z 14:36, **will:** Included in D(05).

a 14:37, **and he came:** Absent from Latin(a).

b 14:38, **that:** Absent from D(05) Latin (a b).

c 14:38, **not:** Absent from Latin(ff² k).

39 And again he went away and
prayed [, having said the same word].[a]

40 And [[having returned]][b] {again
he came and found them sleeping},[c] for
their eyes were heavy, and they did not
know what to answer him.

41 And he came the third time and
said to them, "Sleep [on now][d] and
take your rest; it is enough; the {hour
has come};[e] behold, the Son of Man
is betrayed into the hands of sinners.
42 Rise, let us go [; behold, the one
betraying me has drawn near]."[f]

43 And [immediately],[g] while he was
still speaking, Judas [[Iscariot]],[h] one
of the twelve, came up, and with him a
[[large]][i] crowd with swords and clubs
from the chief priests [, the scribes, and
the elders].[j]

44 Now the one who was betraying
him had given them a sign, saying
[to them],[k] "Whomever I kiss, that
one is *the one*; seize him and lead him
away securely." 45 And [having come
immediately,][l] approaching him, he
says, [[Greetings]][m] "Rabbi, [[Rabbi]][n]"
and kissed him. 46 Then they laid their
hands {on}[o] him and seized him.

47 But [a certain][p] one [of those
standing by],[q] drawing his sword,
struck the servant of the high priest and
cut off his ear.

48 And Jesus, [answering,][r] said to
them, "Have you come out [as][s] against
a robber, with swords and clubs to
arrest me? 49 I was with you every day
in the temple teaching, and you did
not seize me; but *this has happened* so
that the Scriptures [[of the prophets]][t]
might be fulfilled." 50 And [[his
disciples]][u] leaving him, they all fled.

51 And a certain young man was
following him, wrapped in a linen cloth
[over his naked body],[v] and [[the young
men]][w] they seized him; 52 but leaving
the linen cloth, naked he fled [[from
them]].[x]

53 And they led Jesus away to the
high priest [[Caiaphas]],[y] and [all][z]
the chief priests and the elders and
the scribes gathered together [[with
him]].[a] 54 And Peter followed him from

a 14:39, **having said the same word:** Absent from D(05) Latin(a b ff2 k).

b 14:40, **having returned:** Included in A(02) C(04) W(032) BYZ TR || Absent from ℵ(01) B(03) D(05) Latin(a b ff2 k) NA28 SBLGNT THGNT.

c 14:40, **again he came and found them sleeping:** Some manuscripts read "He found them again sleeping." A(02) C(04) W(032) BYZ TR || D(05) reads "Having come, he found them sleeping."

d 14:41, **on now:** Absent from Latin(a b ff2 k).

e 14:41, **hour has come:** Some manuscripts read "end is near." D(05) Latin(a ff2) || Some manuscripts read "end is near, it has come." W(032) Latin(b).

f 14:42, **behold, the one betraying me has drawn near:** Absent from Latin(k).

g 14:43, **immediately:** Absent from D(05) W(032) Latin(a b ff2).

h 14:43, **Iscariot:** Included in A(02) D(05) Latin(a b ff2 k).

i 14:43, **large:** Included in A(02) C(04) D(05) W(032) Latin(k) BYZ TR || Absent from ℵ(01) B(03) Latin(a b ff2) NA28 SBLGNT THGNT.

j 14:43, **the scribes, and the elders:** Absent from Latin(b ff2).

k 14:44, **to them:** Absent from D(05) Latin(a ff2 k).

l 14:45, **having come immediately:** Absent from D(05) Latin(a b ff2 k).

m 14:45, **Greetings:** Included in W(032) Latin(a).

n 14:45, **Rabbi:** Some manuscripts include a second time. A(02) BYZ TR.

o 14:46, **on:** Some manuscripts read "upon." A(02) BYZ TR.

p 14:47, **a certain:** Absent from ℵ(01) A(02) D(05) Latin (a ff2 k).

q 14:47, **of those standing by:** Absent from D(05) Latin(a).

r 14:48, **answering:** Absent from D(05) Latin(a b ff2).

s 14:48, **as:** Absent from D(05).

t 14:49, **of the prophets:** Included in W(032).

u 14:50, **his disciples:** Included in W(032).

v 14:51, **over his naked body:** Absent from W(032) Latin(k).

w 14:51, **the young men:** Included in A(02) W(032) BYZ TR.

x 14:52, **from them:** Included in A(02) D(05) W(032) BYZ TR.

y 14:53, **Caiaphas:** Included in A(02) W(032).

z 14:53, **all:** Absent from C(04) Latin(ff2 k).

a 14:53, **with him:** Included in A(02) B(03) C(04) BYZ TR.

a distance, even {into}[a] the courtyard of the high priest, and he was sitting with the servants and warming himself by the fire.

55 Now the chief priests and the whole council were seeking testimony against Jesus to put him to death, but they found none. 56 For many bore false witness against him, but their testimonies were not equal.

57 And some stood up and bore false witness against him, saying, 58 "{We heard him say},[b] 'I will destroy {this}[c] temple made with hands, and in three days I will build another not made with hands.'" 59 Yet even in this way their testimony was not equal.

60 And the high priest stood up in the midst and questioned Jesus, [saying,][d] "[Do you not answer anything?][e] What is it that these men testify against you?" 61 But {he}[f] remained silent and did not answer anything.

[Again][g] The high priest [questioned him and][h] said to him, "Are you [the Christ,][i] the Son of {the Blessed One}?"[j] 62 And [[answering him,]][k] Jesus said, "I am, and you will see the Son of Man seated at the right hand of Power [[of God]][l] [and coming][m] {with}[n] the {clouds}[o] of heaven."

63 Then [[immediately]][p] the high priest tore his garments and said, "What further need [do we have][q] of witnesses? 64 [[Look]][r] You [[all]][s] have heard the blasphemy [[from his mouth]];[t] what does it seem to you?" And they all condemned him as deserving death.

65 And some began to spit on him and to cover his face and to strike him and to say to him, "Prophesy! [[to us, Christ! who hit you?]]"[u] And [the officers][v] received him with blows.

66 And while Peter was below in the courtyard, one of the servant girls of the high priest came, 67 and seeing Peter warming himself, she looked at him and said, "You also were with the Nazarene, Jesus." 68 But he denied it, saying, "I neither know nor understand what you are talking about." And he went out into the forecourt [and a rooster crowed].[w]

---

a 14:54, **into:** Some manuscripts read "to." D(05) Latin(a k).

b 14:58, **We heard him say:** Some manuscripts read "He said." ℵ(01) Latin(k).

c 14:58, **this:** Some manuscripts read "the." D(05) Latin(ff²).

d 14:60, **saying:** Absent from Latin(a k).

e 14:60, **Do you not answer anything:** Absent from W(032).

f 14:61, **he:** Some manuscripts read "Jesus." ℵ(01) A(02).

g 14:61, **Again:** Absent from D(05) Latin(a).

h 14:61, **questioned him and:** Absent from D(05).

i 14:61, **the Christ:** Absent from Latin(k).

j 14:61, **the Blessed One:** Some manuscripts read "of God." ℵ(01). ‖ A(02) reads "of God, the Blessed One."

k 14:62, **answering him:** Included in D(05) W(032).

l 14:62, **of God** Included in Latin(ff²).

m 14:62, **and coming:** Absent from D(05).

n 14:62, **with:** Some manuscripts read "on." Latin(a).

o 14:62, **clouds:** W(032) reads "power."

p 14:63, **immediately:** Included in W(032) Latin(a).

q 14:63, **Do we have:** Absent from Latin(a).

r 14:64, **Look:** Included in ℵ(01).

s 14:64, **all:** Included in W(032).

t 14:64, **from his mouth:** Included in W(032).

u 14:65, **to us Christ! who hit you?:** Included in W(032).

v 14:65, **the officers:** Absent from D(05) Latin(a k).

w 14:68, **and a rooster crowed:** Absent from ℵ(01) B(03) W(032).

69 And [again][a] the servant girl,
seeing him, {began again to say}[b] to
those who were standing there, "This
man is one of them." 70 [But he again
denied it.][c]

And after a little while, those
who were standing there again said to
{Peter},[d] "Truly you are one of them [,
for you are a Galilean][e] [[, and your
speech resembles]]."[f] 71 But he began to
curse and to swear, "I do not know this
man [you are talking about]."[g]

72 And [immediately][h] a rooster
crowed [a second time].[i] And Peter
remembered the word that Jesus had
said to him [, "Before the rooster crows
twice, you will deny me three times."][j]
And he broke down and wept.

15 1 And [immediately],[k] [in the][l]
morning, [the chief priests],[m]
with the elders and scribes and the
whole council, having made a plan,
bound Jesus, led him away [[in the
courtyard]],[n] and handed [[him]][o] over
to Pilate.

2 And Pilate questioned him
[[saying]],[p] "Are you the King of the
Jews?" He answered him, "You say
so." 3 And the chief priests accused him
of many things. [[But he answered
nothing.]][q]

4 But Pilate again questioned
him, [saying,][r] "Do you not answer
[anything]?[s] See how many things they
accuse you of."

5 But Jesus no longer answered
anything, so that Pilate was amazed.

6 Now at the feast {he}[t] was
accustomed to release for them
one prisoner for whom they asked.
7 But [[then]][u] among the rebels
in prison, who had committed [[a
certain]][v] murder in the insurrection,
there was a man called Barabbas.
8 And having gone up, the [[whole]][w]
crowd began to ask him as he used to
do for them.

9 But Pilate answered them, saying,
"Do you want me to release [for you][x]
the King of the Jews?" 10 For he knew
that it was out of envy that {the
chief priests}[y] had handed him over.
11 But the chief priests stirred up the
crowd to have him release Barabbas for
them instead.

12 Pilate spoke to them [again],[z]
"What then {do you want me to

---

[a] 14:69, **again:** Absent from D(05) W(032) Latin(a ff^2 k).
[b] 14:69, **began again to say:** B(03) reads "said."
[c] 14:70, **But he again denied it:** Absent from D(05).
[d] 14:70, **Peter:** Some manuscripts read "him." D(05) Latin(a).
[e] 14:70, **for you are a Galilean:** Absent from W(032) Latin(a).
[f] 14:70, **and your speech resembles:** SBLGNT || Absent from A(02) BYZ TR NA28 THGNT.
[g] 14:71, **you are talking about:** Absent from D(05).
[h] 14:72, **immediately:** Absent from A(02) BYZ TR Latin(a).
[i] 14:72, **a second time:** Absent from ℵ(01) C(04).
[j] 14:72, **Before the rooster crows twice, you will deny me three times:** Absent from D(05) Latin(a).
[k] 15:1, **immediately:** Absent from Latin(a).
[l] 15:1, **in the:** Absent from ℵ(01) B(03) C(04) D(05) Latin(a ff^2) k.
[m] 15:1, **the chief priests:** Absent from A(02).
[n] 15:1, **in the courtyard:** Included in D(05) Latin(a ff^2 k).
[o] 15:1, **him:** Included in W(032).
[p] 15:2, **saying:** Included in W(032) Latin(k).
[q] 15:3, **But he answered nothing:** Included in W(032) Latin(a).
[r] 15:4, **saying:** Absent from ℵ(01) Latin(a).
[s] 15:4, **anything:** Absent from B(03).
[t] 15:6, **he:** Some manuscripts read "the governor." W(032).
[u] 15:7, **then:** Included in W(032).
[v] 15:7, **a certain:** Included in ℵ(01).
[w] 15:8, **whole:** Included in D(05) Latin(a).
[x] 15:9, **for you:** Absent from D(05).
[y] 15:10, **the chief priests:** Some manuscripts read "they." B(03).
[z] 15:12, **again:** Absent from D(05) W(032) Latin(ff^2).

do}[a] [to the one you call][b] the King of the Jews?" 13 They shouted back, [[saying,]][c] "Crucify him!"

14 Pilate said [to them],[d] "Why, what evil has he done?" But they shouted [all the more],[e] [[saying,]][f] "Crucify him!"

15 So Pilate, [wishing to satisfy the crowd,][g] released Barabbas for them; and after having Jesus flogged, he handed him over to be crucified.

16 And the soldiers led him away inside the courtyard, which is the Praetorium, and they called together the whole cohort. 17 And they dress him in a purple robe, and place on him a [woven][h] crown of thorns; 18 and they began to greet him [[and say]],[i] "Hail, King of the Jews!" 19 And they struck his head with a reed and spat on him [and, kneeling down, they paid homage to him].[j] 20 And when [they had mocked him,][k] they stripped him of the purple and dressed him in his own clothes. And they led him out to crucify him.

21 And they compel a certain passerby, Simon of Cyrene, coming from the country, the father of Alexander and Rufus, to carry his cross. 22 And they bring him to the place called Golgotha, which is translated Place of the Skull. 23 And they offered him wine mixed with myrrh; but he did not take it [[to drink]].[l]

24 And they crucify him and divide his garments, casting lots [for them *to determine* who should take what].[m] 25 Now it was the third hour, and they crucified him. 26 And the inscription of the charge against him was written, "[[This is]][n] The King of the Jews."

27 And with him they crucify two robbers, one on the right and one on his left. 28 [[And the scripture was fulfilled, which says, And he was numbered with the transgressors.]][o]

29 And those passing by were blaspheming[p] him, shaking their heads and saying, "Aha! You who destroy the temple and build it in three days, 30 save yourself by coming down from the cross."

31 [Likewise,][q] the chief priests, mocking among themselves with the scribes, said, "He saved others; he cannot save himself. 32 Let the Christ, the King of Israel, come down now from the cross, that we may see and believe [[in him]]."[r]

And those who were crucified [with him][s] also reproached him.

---

a 15:12, **do you want me to do:** Some manuscripts read "shall I do." ℵ(01) B(03) C(04) W(032).

b 15:12, **to the one you call:** Absent from A(02) D(05) W(032) Latin(a ff² k).

c 15:13, **saying:** Included in A(02).

d 15:14, **to them:** Absent from ℵ(01).

e 15:14, **all the more:** Absent from Latin(ff²).

f 15:14, **saying:** Absent from ℵ(01).

g 15:15, **wishing to satisfy the crowd:** Absent from D(05) Latin(ff² k).

h 15:17, **woven:** Absent from D(05).

i 15:18, **and say:** Included in ℵ(01).

j 15:19, **and, kneeling down, they paid homage to him:** Absent from D(05).

k 15:20, **they had mocked him:** Absent from D(05).

l 15:23, **to drink:** Included in A(02) D(05) Latin(ff² k) BYZ TR.

m 15:24, **for them to determine who should take what:** Absent from Latin(ff² k) ‖ D(05) reads "for them."

n 15:26, **This is:** Included in D(05).

o 15:28, **And the scripture was fulfilled, which says, And he was numbered with the transgressors:** Included in BYZ TR ‖ Absent from ℵ(01) A(02) B(03) C(04) D(05) NA28 SBLGNT THGNT.

p 15:29, **blaspheming:** The Greek word for *blasphemed* is defined by BDAG as: to speak in a disrespectful way that demeans, denigrates, maligns (BDAG, βλασφημέω).

q 15:31, **likewise:** Absent from D(05) Latin(ff² k).

r 15:32, **in him:** Included in D(05) Latin(ff² k) BYZ.

s 15:32, **with him:** Absent from D(05).

33 {And}[a] when the sixth hour came, darkness fell over the whole land until the ninth hour. 34 And at the ninth hour, {Jesus}[b] cried out with a loud voice, [[saying,]][c] "Eloi, Eloi, lema sabachthani?" which is translated, "[My][d] God, [my God],[e] why have you forsaken me?"

35 And some of those standing nearby, [hearing this,][f] said, "[Behold,][g] He is calling for Elijah." 36 [And][h] Someone ran and filled a sponge with sour wine, put it on a reed, [and gave him a drink, saying,][i] "Let us see if Elijah comes to take him down." 37 But Jesus, having let out a loud voice, breathed his last.

38 And the curtain of the temple was torn in two from top to bottom. 39 And when the centurion, who was standing opposite him, saw that he [[cried out and]][j] breathed his last [in this way],[k] he said, "Truly, this man was a son of God."

40 There were also women watching from a distance, among whom were Mary Magdalene, [and][l] Mary the mother of James the Less and of Joses, and Salome, 41 who, when he was in Galilee, followed him [and served him],[m] and many other women who had come up with him to Jerusalem.

42 And when it was already evening since it was the day of preparation, which is the day before the Sabbath, 43 Joseph of Arimathea, a respected member of the council, who was also himself waiting for the kingdom of God, came and boldly went in to Pilate and asked for the body of Jesus.

44 Pilate was surprised that he was already dead, and summoning the centurion, he asked him if he had been dead for some time. 45 And when he learned [from the centurion],[n] he granted {the}[o] {corpse}[p] to Joseph.

46 And having bought a linen cloth, he took him [down],[q] wrapped him in the linen cloth, and laid him in a tomb that had been cut out of the rock, and he rolled a [[large]][r] stone against the door of the tomb [, he went away].[s]

47 [Mary Magdalene and Mary the mother of Joses were watching where he was laid.][t]

---

a 15:33, **And:** Some manuscripts read "But." A(02) C(04) BYZ TR.

b 15:34, **Jesus:** Some manuscripts read "He." D(05) Latin(i k).

c 15:34, **saying:** Included in A(02) C(04) BYZ TR.

d 15:34, **my:** Absent from A(02) Latin(i).

e 15:34, **my God:** Absent from B(03).

f 15:35, **hearing this:** Absent from C(04).

g 15:35, **Behold:** Absent from D(05) Latin(ff² k).

h 15:36, **And:** Absent from B(03) Latin(ff² i).

i 15:36, **and gave him a drink, saying:** Absent from D(05).

j 15:39, **cried out and:** Included in D(05).

k 15:39, **in this way:** Absent from D(05).

l 15:40, **and:** Absent from D(05) Latin(ff² k).

m 15:41, **and served him:** Absent from C(04) D(05).

n 15:45, **from the centurion:** Absent from Latin(k).

o 15:45, **the:** Some manuscripts read "his." D(05).

p 15:45, **corpse:** Some manuscripts read "body." A(02) C(04) W(032) Latin(ff² k) BYZ TR.

q 15:46, **down:** Absent from D(05).

r 15:46, **large:** Included in ℵ(01).

s 15:46, **he went away:** Included in D(05).

t 15:47, **Mary Magdalene...:** Verse 47 is absent from ℵ(01).

16 [1] {And [when the Sabbath had passed,][a] Mary Magdalene and Mary of James and Salome bought spices so that they might come and anoint him}.[b] [2] {[And very][c] Early on the first day of the week, they came to the tomb when the sun had risen}.[d] [3] And they were saying to themselves, "Who will roll away the stone for us from the entrance of the tomb?" [4] {And looking up, they saw that the stone had been rolled away; for it was very large.}[e]

[5] And entering the tomb, they saw a young man sitting on the right side, dressed in a white robe, and they were alarmed. [6] But he said to them, "Do not be alarmed; you are looking for Jesus [the Nazarene],[f] who was crucified; he has been raised; he is not here. See the place where they laid him. [7] But go, tell his disciples and Peter that {he is going ahead of you to Galilee; there you will see him, just as he told you}."[g]

[8] And {going out [[quickly]],[h]}[i] they fled from the tomb, for trembling and astonishment had seized them; and they said nothing to anyone, for they were afraid.[j]

The Shorter Ending of Mark

[[But they quickly reported all the instructions to those around Peter. And after these things, Jesus himself sent out from the east to the west, through them, the sacred and imperishable proclamation of eternal salvation. Amen.]][k]

---

[a] 16:1, **when the Sabbath had passed:** Absent from ℵ(01).

[b] 16:1, **And when the sabbath had passed…:** D(05) reads "And having gone, they bought aromatic spices so that they might anoint him."

[c] 16:2, **And very:** Absent from W(032).

[d] 16:2, **And very early…:** D(05) reads "And they come early on the first day of the week to the tomb, as the sun was rising."

[e] 16:4, **And looking up…:** Some manuscripts read "For it was very large, and they come and find the stone rolled away." D(05) Latin(ff²).

[f] 16:6, **the Nazarene:** Absent from ℵ(01) D(05).

[g] 16:7, **he is going ahead of you…:** Some manuscripts read "behold, I go before you into Galilee; there you will see me, just as I told you." D(05) W(032) Latin(k).

[h] 16:8, **quickly:** Included in TR.

[i] 16:8, **going out:** W(032) reads "And having heard, they went out and."

[j] 16:9-20, The last twelve verses (Mark 16:9-20), often called the "Long Ending" of Mark, are absent from some of the earliest and most reliable Greek manuscripts, such as Codex Sinaiticus ℵ(01) and Codex Vaticanus B(03). Some other manuscripts mark this section as doubtful or non-canonical. In place of the longer ending, some manuscripts feature a shorter ending, which is less well-known and not typically included in most modern Bible translations.

[k] 16:8, **But they quickly…:** Latin(k) contains only this shorter ending without the longer ending. The Sinaitic Syriac and Sahidic and Bohairic Coptic versions contain both the short and long endings. Some later Greek manuscripts also contain both the short and long endings.

The Longer Ending of Mark

9 [[And having risen early on the first day of the week, he appeared [first]ᵃ to Mary Magdalene, from whom he had cast out seven demons. 10 She went and reported to those who had been with him, as they were mourning [and weeping].ᵇ 11 And when they heard that he was alive and had been seen by her, they did not believe.

12 After this, he appeared in a different form to two of them as they were walking into the countryside. 13 And they went and reported it to the rest, but they did not believe them either.

14 [[But]]ᶜ Later, he appeared to the eleven as they were reclining at the table, and he rebuked their unbelief and hardness of heart because they had not believed those who had seen him after he had been raised [[from the dead]].ᵈ

15 {And he said to them,}ᵉ "Go into [all]ᶠ the world and proclaim the gospel to all creation. 16 Whoever believes and is baptized will be saved, but whoever does not believe will be condemned.

17 "And these signs will accompany those who believe: in my name they will cast out demons, they will speak in new tongues, 18 [and with their hands]ᵍ they will pick up snakes, and if they drink any deadly poison, it will not harm them; they will lay their hands on the sick, and they will recover."

19 [So]ʰ Then the Lord [[Jesus]],ⁱ after he had spoken to them, was taken up into heaven and sat down at the right hand of God.

20 And they went out and preached everywhere, while the Lord worked with them and confirmed the message by the accompanying signs. [[Amen]]ʲ]]ᵏ

ᵃ 16:9, **first:** Absent from W(032).

ᵇ 16:10, **and weeping:** Absent from W(032).

ᶜ 16:14, **But:** A(02) D(05) Latin(ff²) NA28 [] SBLGNT THGNT ‖ Absent from ℵ(01) B(03) C(04) W(032) BYZ TR.

ᵈ 16:14, **from the dead:** Included in A(02) C(04).

ᵉ 16:15, **And he said to them:** W(032) reads "But."

ᶠ 16:15, **all:** Absent from D(05).

ᵍ 16:18, **with their hands:** C(04) ‖ Absent from ℵ(01) A(02) B(03) W(032) Latin(ff²) BYZ TR.

ʰ 16:19, **So:** Absent from ℵ(01) B(03) C(04) W(032).

ⁱ 16:19, **Jesus:** Absent from ℵ(01) A(02) B(03) D(05) BYZ TR.

ʲ 16:20, **Amen:** Included in C(04) W(032) BYZ TR.

ᵏ 16:20, Mark 16:9-20 is absent from some manuscripts. ℵ(01) B(03).

Luke[a]

1 [1] Since many have undertaken to compile a narrative concerning the matters that have been fulfilled among us, [2] just as they were handed down to us by those who from the beginning were eyewitnesses and servants of the word, [3] it seemed good to me also, having followed everything carefully from the start, to write an orderly account for you, most excellent Theophilus,[b] [4] so that you may know the certainty of the things[c] you have been taught.

[5] In the days of Herod, king of Judea, there was a priest named Zechariah, of the division of Abijah, and {he had a wife}[d] from the daughters of Aaron, and her name was Elizabeth. [6] Both were righteous before God, walking in all the commandments and ordinances of the Lord blamelessly. [7] But they had no child, because Elizabeth was barren, and both were advanced in years.

[8] Now while he was serving as priest before God when his division was on duty, [9] according to the custom of the priesthood, he was chosen by lot to enter the temple of {the Lord}[e] and burn incense. [10] And the whole multitude [of the people][f] were praying outside at the hour of incense.

[11] And there appeared to him an angel of the Lord standing on the right side of the altar of incense. [12] And Zechariah was troubled when he saw him, and fear fell upon him.

[13] {But}[g] the angel [[of the Lord]][h] said to him, "Do not be afraid, Zechariah, for your prayer has been heard, and your wife Elizabeth will bear [you][i] a son, and you shall call his name John. [14] And you will have joy and gladness, and many will rejoice at his birth. [15] For he will be great before the Lord, and he shall not drink wine or strong drink, and he will be filled with the Holy Spirit,[j] even from his mother's womb.

---

[a] 1:0, **Title ("Luke"):** Absent from ℵ(01) B(03) ‖ BYZ reads "According to Luke." ‖ A(02) W(032) Latin(a b e ff²) reads "Gospel according to Luke." ‖ TR reads "The Holy Gospel According to Luke."

[b] 1:3, **Theophilus:** Related to the word θεοφιλής which means (be)loved by God or loving God (BDAG, θεοφιλής). There are numerous theories among scholars as to the identity of Theophilus. These include (1) a Roman official or nobleman, (2) a wealthy patron, (3) a generic title for believers, (4) a new convert (catechumen), (5) a Jewish priest or leader, or (6) a title used for literary purposes (literary device). Each of these theories has varying degrees of acceptance among scholars, and without concrete historical evidence, the true identity of Theophilus remains a matter of interpretation and conjecture.

[c] 1:4, **things:** Or "words."

[d] 1:5, **he had a wife:** Some manuscripts read "his wife was." BYZ TR.

[e] 1:9, **the Lord:** Some manuscripts read "God." C(04) D(05).

[f] 1:10, **of the people:** Absent from Latin(b).

[g] 1:13, **But:** Some manuscripts read "And." D(05) Latin(b e ff²).

[h] 1:13, **of the Lord:** Included in Latin(ff²).

[i] 1:13, **you:** Absent from D(05).

[j] 1:15, **Spirit:** The Greek word is defined by BDAG as: (1) air in movement, *blowing, breathing,* (2) that which animates or gives life to the body, *breath, (life-)spirit,* (3) a part of human personality, *spirit,* (4) an independent noncorporeal being, in contrast to a being that can be perceived by the physical senses, *spirit,* or (5) God's being as controlling influence, with focus on association with humans, *Spirit, spirit...* (c) Because of its heavenly origin and nature this Spirit is called (the) Holy Spirit. (BDAG, πνεῦμα).

16 "And he will turn many of the children of Israel to the Lord their God. 17 And he will go before him in the spirit and power of Elijah, to turn the hearts of the fathers to the children, and the disobedient to the wisdom of the just, to make ready for the Lord a people prepared."[a]

18 And Zechariah said to the angel, "How shall I know this? For I am an old man, and my wife is advanced in years."

19 And the angel answered him, "I am Gabriel, who stands in the presence of God, and I was sent to speak to you and to bring you this good news. 20 And behold, you will be silent and unable to speak until the day these things come to pass, because you did not believe my words, which will be fulfilled in their time."

21 And the people were waiting for Zechariah, and they were amazed at his delay in the temple. 22 And when he came out, he was unable to speak to them, and they realized that he had seen a vision in the temple; and he was making signs to them and remained mute.

23 And it happened that when the days of his service were completed, he went to his house.

24 And after these days, his wife Elizabeth conceived and hid herself for five months, saying 25 "Thus the Lord has done to me in the days when he looked upon me, to take away my reproach among men."

26 In the sixth month, the angel Gabriel was sent {from}[b] God to a city of Galilee [named Nazareth],[c] 27 to a virgin {engaged}[d] to a man whose name was Joseph, of the house of David; and the virgin's name was Mary.

28 And having entered, {he}[e] said to her, "Greetings [, favored one]![f] The Lord is with you. [[Blessed are you among women]]"[g] 29 But she [[seeing,]][h] was greatly troubled [at {the}[i] saying][j] and considered in her mind what sort of greeting this might be.

30 And the angel said to her, "Do not be afraid, Mary, for you have found favor with God. 31 And behold, you will conceive in your womb and bear a son, and you shall call his name Jesus. 32 He will be great and will be called the Son of the Most High; and the Lord God will give to him the throne of his father David, 33 and he will reign over the house of Jacob forever; and of his kingdom there will be no end."

34 And Mary said to the angel, "[How can this be, since][k] I do not know a man?"[l]

---

a 1:17, Malachi 4:5-6.

b 1:26, **from:** ℵ(01) B(03) L W(032) NA28 SBLGNT THGNT ‖ Some manuscripts read "by." A(02) BYZ TR.

c 1:26, **named Nazareth:** Absent from D(05).

d 1:27, **engaged:** Some manuscripts read "betrothed." C(04) BYZ TR.

e 1:28, **he:** B(03) W(032) NA28 SBLGNT THGNT ‖ Some manuscripts read "the Angel." A(02) C(04) D(05) BYZ TR.

f 1:28 , **favored one:** Absent from Latin(b).

g 1:28, **Blessed are you among women:** Included in A(02) C(04) D(05) BYZ TR ‖ Absent from ℵ(01) B(03) W(032) NA28 SBLGNT THGNT.

h 1:29, **seeing:** Included in A(02) C(04) BYZ TR ‖ Absent from ℵ(01) B(03) D(05) W(032) NA28 SBLGNT THGNT.

i 1:29, **the:** Some manuscripts read "his." BYZ TR.

j 1:29, **at the saying:** Absent from C(04).

k 1:34, **How can this be, since:** Absent from Latin(b).

l 1:34, **know a man:** Or sexually.

35 And the angel answered her, "The Holy Spirit[a] will come upon you, and the power of the Most High will overshadow you; therefore, the one being born [[from you]][b] will be called holy, the Son of God."[c]

36 "And behold, your relative Elizabeth in her old age has also conceived a son, and this is the sixth month with her who was called barren; 37 for nothing will be impossible with God."

38 [And Mary said, "Behold, I am the servant of the Lord; let it be to me according to your word." And the angel departed from her.][d]

39 And Mary, having arisen in those days, went into the hill country with haste, to a city of Judah, 40 and entered the house of Zechariah and greeted Elizabeth.

41 And it happened, when Elizabeth heard the greeting of Mary, the baby leaped in her womb, and Elizabeth was filled with the Holy Spirit,[e] 42 and she cried out with a {shout}[f] and said, "Blessed are you among women, and blessed is the fruit of your womb. 43 And why is this granted to me, that the mother of {my}[g] Lord should come to me? 44 For behold, when the sound of your greeting came to my ears, the baby in my womb leaped for joy.

45 And blessed is she who believed that there would be a fulfillment of what was spoken to her from the Lord."

46 And {Mary}[h] said, "My soul magnifies the Lord, 47 and my spirit rejoices in God my Savior, 48 for he has looked on the humble state of his servant. For behold, from now on all generations will call me blessed; 49 for the Mighty {One}[i] has done great things for me, and holy is his name. 50 And his mercy is for those who fear him from generation to generation. 51 He has shown strength with his arm; he has scattered the proud in the thoughts of their hearts; 52 he has brought down rulers from their thrones and exalted the humble; 53 he has filled the hungry with good things, and the rich he has sent away empty. 54 He has helped his servant Israel, in remembrance of his mercy, 55 as he spoke to our fathers, to Abraham and to his offspring forever."

56 And Mary stayed with her [about][j] three months and returned to her home.

57 Now the time came for Elizabeth to give birth, and she bore a son. 58 And the neighbors and her relatives heard that the Lord had shown great mercy to her, and they rejoiced with her.

---

a 1:35, **Spirit:** See footnote for Spirit in Luke 1:15.

b 1:35, **from you:** Included in C(04) Latin (a e).

c 1:35, **the one being born [[from you]] will be called holy, the Son of God:** Or "the one to be born holy will be called the Son of God."

d 1:38, Verse 38 is absent from some manuscripts. Latin(b e).

e 1:41, **Spirit:** See footnote Spirit in Luke 1:15.

f 1:42, **shout:** B(03) W(032) NA28 SBLGNT THGNT ‖ Some manuscripts read "loud voice." ℵ(01) A(02) C(04) D(05) BYZ TR.

g 1:43, **my:** W(032) reads "the."

h 1:46, **Mary:** Some manuscripts read "Elizabeth." Latin(a b). Elizabeth is also attested by Irenaeus, a variant reading of Origen, and Niceta.

i 1:49, **One:** D(05) reads "God."

j 1:56, **about:** Absent from D(05) Latin(a b e ff² it).

59 And on the eighth day they came to circumcise the child, and they would have called him by the name of his father, Zechariah. 60 But his mother answered, "No; he will be called; [[his name]]ᵃ John." 61 And they said to her, "There is no one [among your relatives]ᵇ who is called by this name." 62 And they made signs to his father, inquiring what he wanted him to be called. 63 And he asked for a writing tablet, he wrote [, saying]:ᶜ "John is his name." And all were amazed.

64 And his mouth was opened [immediately, and his tongue loosed,]ᵈ and he spoke, blessing God. 65 And [[great]]ᵉ fear came on all their neighbors and [all]ᶠ these things were talked about throughout the entire hill country of Judea. 66 And all [who heard them]ᵍ laid them up in their hearts, saying, "What then will this child be?" [For]ʰ The hand of the Lord was with him.

67 And Zechariah, his father, was filled with the Holy Spirit {and [prophesied,]ⁱ saying},ʲ 68 "Blessed is [the Lord,]ᵏ the God of Israel, for he has visited and brought redemption to his people, 69 and has raised up a horn of salvationˡ for us in the house of David, his servant, 70 just as he spoke through the mouth of his holy prophets from of old, 71 salvation from our enemies and from the hand of all who hate us, 72 to show mercy to our fathers [and]ᵐ to remember his holy covenant, 73 the oath that he swore to Abraham, our father, to grant us 74 to serveⁿ him without fear, having been rescued from the hand of [[our]]ᵒ enemies, 75 in holiness and righteousness before him all {our days}.ᵖ

76 "And you, child, will be called a prophet of the Most High; for you will go before [[the face of]]ۊ the Lord to prepare his ways; 77 [to give]ʳ knowledge of salvation to his people in the forgiveness of their sins, 78 because of the tender mercy of our God, by which the rising sun {will visit}ˢ us from on high, 79 to {appear}ᵗ to those who sit in darkness and in the shadow of death, to guide our feet into the way of peace."

80 And the child grew and became strong in spirit, and he was in the wilderness until the day of his public appearance to Israel.

ᵃ 1:60, **his name:** Included in C(04) D(05).
ᵇ 1:61, **among your relatives:** Absent from Latin(ff²).
ᶜ 1:63, **saying:** Absent from D(05) Latin(e) Syriac(syˢ).
ᵈ 1:64, **immediately, and his tongue loosed:** Absent from D(05) Latin(a b ff²).
ᵉ 1:65, **great:** Included in D(05) Latin(b c).
ᶠ 1:65, **all:** Absent from ℵ(01).
ᵍ 1:66, **who heard them:** Absent from Latin(e).
ʰ 1:66, **For:** 𝔓4 ℵ(01) B(03) C(04) D(05) W(032) Latin(latt) ‖ Absent from A(02) Syriac(syᴾ).
ⁱ 1:67, **prophesied:** Absent from D(05).
ʲ 1:67, **and prophesied saying:** D(05) reads "and said."
ᵏ 1:68, **the Lord:** Absent from 𝔓4 W(032).
ˡ 1:69, **horn of salvation:** Or "mighty Savior."
ᵐ 1:72, **and:** Absent from D(05).
ⁿ 1:74, **serve:** Or worship.
ᵒ 1:74, **our:** Included in A(02) C(04) D(05) BYZ TR ‖ Absent from ℵ(01) B(03) W(032) NA28 SBLGNT THGNT.
ᵖ 1:75, **our days:** Some manuscripts read "the days of our lives." BYZ TR.
ۊ 1:76, **the face of:** Included in BYZ TR.
ʳ 1:77, **to give:** Absent from W(032).
ˢ 1:78, **will visit:** ℵ(01) B(03) D(05) NA28 SBLGNT THGNT ‖ Some manuscripts read "had visited." A(02) C(04) D(05) BYZ TR.
ᵗ 1:79, **appear:** D(05) reads "reveal light."

2 1 Now it came to pass in those
days that a decree went out from
Caesar Augustus that all the world
should be registered. 2 This was the
{first registration}[a] when Quirinius was
governing Syria. 3 {And everyone went
to be registered, each to his own city}.[b]

4 So Joseph also went up from
Galilee, from the city of Nazareth, to
Judea, to the city of David, which is
called Bethlehem, because he was
of the house and lineage of David,
5 [to be registered][c] with Mary, his
{betrothed},[d] who was pregnant.

6 And {it came to pass, while they
were there},[e] the days were {fulfilled}[f]
for her to give birth. 7 And she gave
birth to her [firstborn][g] son, and she
wrapped him up and laid him in a
manger, because there was no place for
them in the inn.

8 And there were shepherds in the
same region, staying out in the fields
and keeping watch over their flock
by night. 9 And [[behold]][h] an angel
of the Lord appeared to them, and
the glory [of the Lord][i] shone around
them, and they were greatly afraid.
10 And {the angel}[j] said to them, "Do
not be afraid, for behold, I bring you
good news of great joy which will be
for all the people, 11 for today a Savior
has been born to you, who is Christ[k] the
Lord, in the city of David. 12 And this
will be a sign for you: you will find a
baby wrapped in swaddling cloths [and
lying][l] in a manger."

13 And suddenly there was [with the
angel][m] a multitude of the heavenly
host, praising God and saying, 14 "Glory
to God in the highest, and on earth
peace {among men of goodwill}."[n]

15 And it came to pass, as the angels
departed from them into heaven,
and {the shepherds}[o] spoke to one
another [[saying]],[p] "Let us go now to
Bethlehem and see this thing that has
happened, which the Lord has made
known to us."

16 And they came quickly and found
Mary and Joseph, and the baby lying in
the manger.

17 And when they saw it, they
understood about the word that was
spoken to them concerning {this}[q]
child. 18 And all who heard it wondered
at the things spoken by the shepherds
to them.

19 But Mary kept all these words,
pondering them in her heart.

20 And the shepherds returned,
glorifying and praising God for all they
had heard and seen, as it had been told
to them.

---

a 2:2, **first registration:** Some manuscripts read "registration first." ℵ(01) D(05).
b 2:3, **And everyone went...:** ℵ(01) reads "And each went to register in their own city."
c 2:5, **to be registered:** Absent from A(02).
d 2:5, **betrothed:** ℵ(01) B(03) C(04) D(05) W(032) Latin(it) (sy^p) || Some manuscripts read "betrothed wife." A(02) Latin(ff^2) BYZ TR || Some manuscripts read "wife." Latin(b) Syriac(sy^s).
e 2:6, **it came to pass, while they were there:** D(05) reads "as they were traveling."
f 2:6, **fulfilled:** D(05) reads "completed."
g 2:7, **firstborn:** Absent from W(032).
h 2:9, **behold:** Included in A(02) D(05) BYZ TR || Absent from ℵ(01) B(03) W(032) NA28 SBLGNT THGNT.
i 2:9, **of the Lord:** Absent from D(05) Latin(b ff^2). || Some manuscripts read "God." Latin(e).
j 2:10, **the angel:** Some manuscripts read "he." A(02).
k 2:11, **Christ:** The Greek word for *Christ* is defined by BDAG as: (1) fulfiller of Israelite expectation of a deliverer, *the Anointed One, the Messiah, the Christ,* (2) the personal name ascribed to Jesus, *Christ.* (BDAG, Χριστός).
l 2:12, **and lying:** Absent from ℵ(01) D(05).
m 2:13, **with the angel:** Absent from Latin(b).
n 2:14, **among men of goodwill:** Or "goodwill among men."
o 2:15, **the shepherds:** Some manuscripts read "the men keeping sheep." A(02) D(05) BYZ TR.
p 2:15, **saying:** Included in ℵ(01).
q 2:17, **this:** Some manuscripts read "the." D(05) Latin(a e f it) Syriac(sy^s sy^c).

21 And when eight days were completed for circumcising {him},ᵃ his name was called Jesus, the name given by the angel before he was conceived in the womb.

22 And when the days of {their purification}ᵇ were fulfilled according to the law of Moses, they brought him up to Jerusalem to present him to the Lord, 23 just as it is written in the law of the Lord, "Every male that opens the womb shall be called holy to the Lord,"ᶜ 24 and to offer a sacrifice according to what is said in the law of the Lord, "A pair of turtledoves or two young pigeons."ᵈ

25 And [behold,]ᵉ there was a man in Jerusalem whose name was Simeon, and this man was righteous and devout, waiting for the consolation of Israel, and the Holy Spirit was upon him. 26 And it had been revealed to him by the Holy Spirit that he would not see death before he had seen the Lord's Christ. 27 And he came in the Spirit into the temple; and when the parents brought in the child [Jesus],ᶠ to do for him according to the custom of the law concerning him, 28 he took him up [in {the}ᵍ arms]ʰ and blessed God and said, 29 "Now dismiss your servant, Master, according to your word in peace; 30 for my eyes have seen your salvation, 31 which you have prepared in the presence of all peoples, 32 a light for revelation to the nations,ⁱ and the glory of your people Israel."

33 And {his father}ʲ and {the}ᵏ mother marveled at what was said about him. 34 And Simeon blessed them and said to Mary his mother, "Behold, this child is appointed for the fall and rising of many in Israel, and for a sign that is opposed; 35 and a sword will pierce through your own soul also; so that evil thoughts from many hearts may be revealed."

36 And there was a prophetess, Anna, the daughter of Phanuel, of the tribe of Asher; she was of a great age, having lived with her husband seven years from her virginity, 37 and as a widow {until she was eighty-four}.ˡ She did not depart from the temple, worshiping with fasting and prayer night and day. 38 And coming up at that very hour she [[herself]]ᵐ gave thanks to {God}ⁿ and spoke of him to all who were waiting for {the redemption of} Jerusalem.ᵒ

ᵃ 2:21, **him:** Some manuscripts read "the child." D(05) Latin(e) Syriac(syˢ syᶜ) TR.

ᵇ 2:22, **their purification:** Referring to the time of purification according to the Law of Moses after Jesus' birth. ‖ Some manuscripts read "her purification," referring specifically to Mary. D(05).

ᶜ 2:23, Exodus 13:2, 12, 15.

ᵈ 2:24, Leviticus 12:8.

ᵉ 2:25, **behold:** Absent from D(05).

ᶠ 2:27, **Jesus:** Absent from ℵ(01).

ᵍ 2:28, **the:** ℵ(01) B(03) W(032) NA28 SBLGNT THGNT ‖ Some manuscripts read "his." A(02) D(05).

ʰ 2:28, **in the arms:** Absent from Latin(ff²).

ⁱ 2:32, **to the nations:** Or Gentiles. Absent from D(05).

ʲ 2:33, **his father:** ℵ(01) B(03) D(05) W(032) NA28 SBLGNT THGNT ‖ Some manuscripts read "Joseph." A(02) N(022) BYZ TR.

ᵏ 2:33, **the:** B(03) D(05) W(032) NA28 SBLGNT THGNT ‖ Some manuscripts read "his." ℵ(01) A(02) Latin(it) BYZ TR.

ˡ 2:37, **until she was eighty-four:** Some manuscripts read "of about eighty-four years." W(032) BYZ TR.

ᵐ 2:38, **herself:** Included in BYZ TR.

ⁿ 2:38, **God:** Some manuscripts read "the Lord." BYZ TR.

ᵒ 2:38, **the redemption of:** Some manuscripts read "redemption in." BYZ TR.

39 And when they had completed {everything}[a] according to the law of the Lord, they returned to Galilee, to their own city of Nazareth. [[As it was said through the prophet, "He will be called a Nazarene."]][b]

40 The child [[Jesus]][c] grew and became strong [[in spirit]][d], {filled with}[e] wisdom, and the grace of God was upon him.

41 And his parents were traveling to Jerusalem every year for the feast of the Passover.

42 And when he was twelve years old, {they}[f] went up [[to Jerusalem]][g] [[having him with them]][h] according to the custom of the feast [[of Unleavened Bread]].[i]

43 And when the days were completed, as they were returning, [Jesus][j] the boy stayed behind in Jerusalem, and {his parents}[k] did not know. 44 But supposing him to be in the company, they went a day's journey and sought him among their relatives and acquaintances. 45 And not finding [[him]],[l] they returned to Jerusalem, seeking him.

46 And it happened that after three days they found him in the temple, sitting in the midst of the teachers, listening to them and asking them questions. 47 And all [who heard him][m] were amazed at his understanding and his answers. 48 And when they saw him, they were astonished, and his mother said to him, "Child, why have you treated us like this? [Behold, your father and I,][n] In distress [[and sorrowful]],[o] we were seeking you."

49 And he said to them, "Why were you looking for me? Did you not know that I must be in the things[p] of {my}[q] Father?" 50 And they did not understand the word that he spoke [to them].[r]

51 And he went down [with them][s] [and came][t] to Nazareth and was submissive to them. And his mother kept all these words in her heart.

52 And Jesus advanced in wisdom and stature, and in favor with God and [[with]][u] men.

---

a 2:39, **everything:** ℵ(01) B(03) W(032) NA28 SBLGNT THGNT ‖ Some manuscripts read "all things." A(02) D(05) BYZ TR.

b 2:39, **As it was said through the prophet, "He will be called a Nazarene":** Included in D(05) Latin(a).

c 2:40, **Jesus:** Included in D(05).

d 2:40, **in spirit:** Included in A(02) BYZ TR ‖ Absent from ℵ(01) B(03) D(05) W(032) NA28 SBLGNT.

e 2:40, **filled with:** B(03) W(032) NA28 SBLGNT THGNT ‖ Some manuscripts read "full of." ℵ(01) A(02) D(05) BYZ TR.

f 2:42, **they:** Some manuscripts read "his parents." D(05) Latin(e).

g 2:42, **to Jerusalem:** Included in A(02) C(04) Latin(it) BYZ TR ‖ Absent from ℵ(01) B(03) D(05) W(032) NA28 SBLGNT THGNT.

h 2:42, **having him with them:** Included in D(05) Latin(e).

i 2:42, **of Unleavened Bread:** Included in D(05) Latin(a, c, e).

j 2:43, **Jesus** Absent from ℵ(01).

k 2:43, **his parents:** ℵ(01) B(03) D(05) W(032) NA28 SBLGNT THGNT ‖ Some manuscripts read "Joseph and his mother." A(02) C(04) BYZ TR.

l 2:45, **him:** Included in A(02) BYZ TR. ‖ Absent from ℵ(01) B(03) C(04) D(05) W(032) Latin(it) NA28 SBLGNT THGNT.

m 2:47, **who heard him:** Absent from B(03) W(032).

n 2:48, **Behold, your father and I** Absent from Latin(a b ff2).

o 2:48, **and sorrowful:** Included in D(05) Latin(a e ff2it) Syriac(syc).

p 2:49, **things:** Or "business."

q 2:49, **my:** W(032) reads "the."

r 2:50, **to them:** Absent from Latin(e).

s 2:51, **with them:** Absent from C(04).

t 2:51, **and came:** Absent from C(04) D(05).

u 2:52, **with:** Included in D(05).

3 1 In the fifteenth year of the reign of Tiberius Caesar, when Pontius Pilate was governor [of Judea],ᵃ and Herod [was tetrarch of Galilee],ᵇ and his brother Philip was tetrarch [of the region of {Iturea}ᶜ and Trachonitis,]ᵈ and Lysanias was tetrarch of Abilene, 2 during the high priesthood of Annas and Caiaphas, the word of God came to John, the son of Zechariah, in the wilderness.

3 And he went into all the region around the Jordan, proclaiming a baptism of repentance [for the forgiveness of sins],ᵉ 4 as it is written in the book of the words of Isaiah the prophet, [[saying]]ᶠ "The voice of one crying in the wilderness, Prepare the way of the Lord, make {his}ᵍ paths straight.

5 "Every valley shall be filled, and every mountain and hill shall be made low, and the crooked shall become straight, and the rough places shall become smooth ways; 6 and all flesh shall see the salvation of {God}.ʰ⁾ⁱ

7 So he said to the crowds coming out to be baptized {by}ʲ him, "You brood ᵏ of vipers, who warned you {to flee from}ˡ the impending [wrath]?ᵐ 8 Produce {fruit}ⁿ worthy of repentance, and do not begin to say to yourselves, 'We have Abraham as our father.' For I say to you that God is able to raise up children for Abraham from these stones. 9 Indeed, the axe is already laid at the root of the trees; therefore, every tree not producing [good]ᵒ fruit is cut down and thrown into the fire."

10 And the crowds were questioning him, saying, "What [then]ᵖ should we do [[so that we may be saved]]?"q 11 In response, he said to them, "Whoever has two tunics should share with the one who has none, and whoever has food should do likewise."

ᵃ 3:1, **of Judea:** Absent from ℵ(01).

ᵇ 3:1, **was tetrarch of Galilee:** Absent from D(05).

ᶜ 3:1, **Iturea:** W(32) reads "Judah." D(05) reads "With the tetrarchy of Judea."

ᵈ 3:1, **of the region of Iturea and Trachonitis, and:** Absent from ℵ(01).

ᵉ 3:3, **for the forgiveness of sins:** Absent from Latin(a b ff²).

ᶠ 3:4, **saying:** Included in BYZ TR.

ᵍ 3:4, **his:** D(05) reads "your."

ʰ 3:6, **God:** Some manuscripts read "the Lord." D(05) Syriac(syˢ syᶜ).

ⁱ 3:4-6, Isaiah 40:3-5 LXX.

ʲ 3:7, **by:** Some manuscripts read "before." D(05) Latin(it).

ᵏ 3:7, **brood:** Or offspring.

ˡ 3:7, **to flee from:** Some manuscripts read "of." W(032).

ᵐ 3:7, **impending:** Absent from W(032).

ⁿ 3:8, **fruit (plural):** Some manuscripts read "fruit" (singular). D(05) W(032) Latin(e).

ᵒ 3:9, **good:** Absent from 𝔓4 Latin(a ff²).

ᵖ 3:10, **then:** Absent from D(05).

q 3:10, **so that we may be saved:** Included in D(05). ‖ Some Latin manuscripts read "so that we may live." Latin(b).

12 Tax collectors also came to be
baptized and said to him, "Teacher,
what should we do [[to be saved]]?"[a]
13 [And he said [to them],[b]][c] "Do
nothing more than what is commanded
to you [[to do]]."[d]

14 And the soldiers also asked
[him],[e] saying, "And what should we
do [[to be saved]]?"[f] He said to them,
"Do not extort money from anyone, nor
accuse anyone falsely, and be content
with your wages."

15 While the people were waiting
and all were pondering in their hearts
about John, whether he might be
the Christ,[g] 16 [[recognizing their
thoughts,]][h] {John answered},[i] [saying
to them all,][j] "I [indeed][k] baptize
you with water [[for repentance]];[l]
but one who is more powerful than I
is coming, I am not worthy to untie
the strap of {his}[m] sandals. He will
baptize you with the Holy Spirit[n] and
fire. 17 His winnowing fork is in his
hand {to clear}[o] his threshing floor
and to gather the wheat into {his}[p]
storehouse, but the chaff he will burn
with unquenchable fire."

18 And with many other
exhortations, he preached good news to
the people.

19 But Herod the tetrarch, being
rebuked by him concerning Herodias,
his {brother's}[q] wife, and for all the evil
things that Herod had done, 20 added
this also to them all: [and][r] he locked
up John in prison.

21 Now it happened that when all
the people were being baptized, and
Jesus was baptized and praying, the
heavens were opened, 22 and the Holy
Spirit[s] descended in bodily form like a
dove {upon}[t] him, and a voice came
from heaven, "{You are my beloved
Son; in you I am well pleased}."[u]

---

[a] 3:12, **to be saved:** Included in D(05) Latin(a).
[b] 3:13 , **to them:** Absent from ℵ(01) Latin(a b ff²).
[c] 3:13, **And he said to them:** Absent from ℵ(01).
[d] 3:13, **to do:** Included in D(05).
[e] 3:14, **him:** Absent from D(05).
[f] 3:14, **to be saved:** Included in D(05).
[g] 3:15, **Christ:** See footnote for Christ in Luke 2:11.
[h] 3:16, **Recognizing their thoughts:** Included in D(05).
[i] 3:16, **John answered:** Some manuscripts read "He said." D(05) Latin(a b ff²).
[j] 3:16, **saying to them all:** Absent from D(05).
[k] 3:16, **indeed:** Absent from D(05).
[l] 3:16, **for repentance:** Included in C(04) D(05) Latin(a b e ff² it).
[m] 3:16, **his:** Some manuscripts read "the." D(05) Latin(a e d ff²).
[n] 3:16, **Spirit:** See footnote for Spirit in Luke 1:15.
[o] 3:17, **to clear:** 𝔓4 ℵ(01) B(03) NA28 SBLGNT THGNT ‖ Some manuscripts read "And he will clear." A(02) C(04) D(05) BYZ TR.
[p] 3:17, **his:** Some manuscripts read "the." D(05) Latin(e).
[q] 3:19, **brother's:** Some manuscripts read "brother Phillip's." A(02) C(04) W(032) TR Latin(e).
[r] 3:20, **and:** A(02) C(04) W(032) BYZ TR NA28[] SBLGNT ‖ Absent from 𝔓75 ℵ(01) B(03) D(05) Latin(b e) THGNT.
[s] 3:22, **Spirit:** See footnote for Spirit in Luke 1:15.
[t] 3:22, **upon:** D(05) reads "into."
[u] 3:22, **You are my beloved Son; in you I am well pleased:** Some manuscripts read "You are my Son, today I have begotten you," corresponding to Psalm 2. D(05) Latin(a b ff²).

23 And Jesus [himself][a] was about thirty years old when he began, being the son (as was supposed) of Joseph[b]

[[, of Jacob, of Matthew, of Eleazar, of Eliud, of Iachin, of Sadok, of Azor, of Eliakim, the of Abiud, of Zorobabel, of Shealtiel, of Jehoiakim, of Joakim, of Eliakim, of Joseph, of Amos, of Manasseh, of Hezekiah, of Achaz, of Joathan, of Oziah, of Amasiah, of Joas, of Ochozias, of Joram, of Josaphat, of Asa, of Abiud, of Roboam, of Solomon, of David.]][c]

[, of {Eli},[d] 24 of Matthew, of Levi, of Melchi, of {Jannai},[e] of Joseph, 25 of Mattathias, of Amos, of Nahum, of {Hesli},[f] of Naggai, 26 [of Maath,][g] of Mattathias, of {Semein},[h] of {Josech},[i] of {Joda},[j] 27 of {Joanan},[k] of Rhesa, of Zerubbabel, of Shealtiel, of Neri, 28 of Melchi, of Addi, of Cosam, of {Elmadam},[l] of Er, 29 of {Joshua},[m] of Eliezer, of {Jorim},[n] of Matthat, [of Levi,][o] 30 of {Simeon},[p] of Judah, of Joseph, of {Jonam},[q] of Eliakim, 31 [of Melea,][r] [of Menna,][s] of Mattatha, of Nathan, of David,][t]

32 [of Jesse, of {Jobed},[u] of Boaz, of {Sala},[v] of Nahshon, 33 {of Amminadab, of Admin, of Arni},[w] of Hezron, [of Perez,][x] of Judah, 34 of Jacob, of Isaac, of Abraham, of Terah, of Nahor, 35 of {Serug},[y] of Reu, of Peleg, of Eber, of Sala, 36 of Cainan, of Arphaxad, of Shem, of Noah, of Lamech, 37 of Methuselah, of Enoch, of {Jaret},[z] of Mahalalel, of Cainan, 38 of Enos, of Seth, of Adam, of God].[a]

---

[a] 3:23, **himself:** Absent from D(05).

[b] 3:23-38, The genealogy that follows in verses 23c-38 is absent from a some manuscripts. W(032). D(05) is more consistent with the genealogy of Matthew 1:6-16 in an inverted order, and with different spelling for some names starting with of Jacob. The genealogy also exhibits a large number of textual variants, the most notable being verse 33.

[c] 3:23, **of Jacob…:** D(05) includes a genealogy to David starting with Jacob being the father of Joseph, consistent with Matthew 1:16.

[d] 3:23, **Eli:** Some manuscripts read "Heli." THGNT.

[e] 3:24, **Jannai:** Some manuscripts read "Janna." BYZ TR.

[f] 3:25, **Hesli:** Some manuscripts read "Esli." BYZ TR THGNT.

[g] 3:26, **of Maath:** Absent from Latin(a b e).

[h] 3:26, **Semein:** Some manuscripts read "Seme" or "Semei." BYZ TR.

[i] 3:26, **Josech:** Some manuscripts read "Joseph." BYZ TR.

[j] 3:26, **Joda:** Some manuscripts read "Judah." BYZ TR.

[k] 3:27, **Joanan:** TR reads "Joanna."

[l] 3:28, **Elmadam:** Some manuscripts read "Elmodam." BYZ TR.

[m] 3:29, **Joshua:** Some manuscripts read "Jose." BYZ TR.

[n] 3:29, **Jorim:** Some manuscripts read "Joreim." BYZ TR THGNT.

[o] 3:29, **Levi:** Absent from Latin(b).

[p] 3:30, **Simeon:** Or Symeon.

[q] 3:30, **Jonam:** Some manuscripts read "Jonan." BYZ TR.

[r] 3:31, **of Melea:** Absent from Latin(a b e).

[s] 3:31, **of Menna:** Absent from A(02). Some manuscripts read "Mainan." BYZ TR.

[t] 3:24-31 Verses 24-31 are absent from some manuscripts. D(05) W(032).

[u] 3:32, **Jobed:** or "Jobel." Some manuscripts read "Obed." BYZ TR.

[v] 3:32, **Sala:** Some manuscripts read "Salmon." BYZ TR.

[w] 3:33, **Amminadab, of Admin, of Arni:** NA28 SBLGNT THGNT ‖ Some manuscripts read "of Adam, of Admin, of Arni." 𝔓4 ℵ(01) ‖ Some manuscripts read "of Admin, of Arni." B(03). ‖ Some manuscripts read "of Amminadab, of Aram." A(02) D(05) BYZ TR. According to Metzger, "there is a confusing variety of readings here; but the reading in the text, followed by most translations, seems to be the least unsatisfactory; and it was known in the Alexandrian church at an early period." (R. L. Omanson and B. M. Metzger, *A Textual Guide to the Greek New Testament: An Adaptation of Bruce M. Metzger's Textual commentary for the Needs of Translators* [Stuttgart: Deutsche Bibelgesellschaft, 2006], 113).

[x] 3:33, **of Perez:** Absent from A(02).

[y] 3:35, **Serug:** TR reads "Sarug."

[z] 3:37, **Jaret:** Some manuscripts read "Jared." BYZ TR.

[a] 3:32-38, Verses 32-38 are absent from some manuscripts. W(032).

4 ¹ But Jesus, full of the Holy Spirit[a] [, returned][b] from the Jordan and was led [by the Spirit][c] {in}[d] the wilderness ² for forty days, being tempted by {the devil}.[e] And he ate nothing during those days, and when they were finished, [[afterwards,]][f] he was hungry.

³ The devil said to him, "If you are the Son of God, command {this stone}[g] to become bread." ⁴ Jesus answered [him][h] [[saying]],[i] "It is written, 'Man shall not live by bread alone [[but by every word of God]].'"[j]

⁵ And {he}[k] having led him up [[into a high mountain]],[l] showed him all the kingdoms of the world[m] in a moment of time, ⁶ and said to him, "To you I will give all this authority and their glory, for it has been delivered to me, and I give it to whomever I wish. ⁷ Therefore, if you [[fall down and]][n] worship before me, all will be yours." ⁸ Jesus answered him, [["get behind me Satan! For"]][o] "It is written, 'You shall worship the Lord your God and serve him alone.'"[p]

⁹ And he led him to Jerusalem and he stood [[him]][q] on the pinnacle of the temple and said [to him],[r] "If you are the Son of God,[s] throw yourself down [from here];[t] ¹⁰ for it is written, 'He will command his angels concerning you, to guard you,' ¹¹ and [that][u] 'On their hands they will bear you up, lest you strike your foot against a stone.'"[v]

¹² And Jesus answered him, "It is {said},[w] 'You shall not put the Lord your God to the test.'"[x]

¹³ And after completing every temptation, the devil departed from him for a time.

¹⁴ And Jesus returned in the power of the Spirit to Galilee, and a report went out through all the surrounding region about him. ¹⁵ And he was teaching in {their}[y] synagogues, being glorified[z] by all.

---

a 4:1, **Spirit:** See footnote for Spirit in Luke 1:15.

b 4:1, **returned:** Absent from ℵ(01).

c 4:1, **by the Spirit:** Absent from Latin(b).

d 4:1, **in:** 𝔓4 𝔓7 𝔓75 ℵ(01) B(03) D(05) W(032) NA28 SBLGNT THGNT ‖ Some manuscripts read "into." A(02) BYZ TR.

e 4:2, **the devil:** Some manuscripts read "Satan." D(05) Latin(e) Syriac(sy^c).

f 4:2, **afterwards:** Included in A(02) Latin(b ff²) BYZ TR ‖ Absent from 𝔓4 ℵ(01) B(03) W(032) Latin(a e) NA28 SBLGNT THGNT.

g 4:3, **this stone:** Some manuscripts read "these stones." D(05).

h 4:4, **him:** Absent from D(05).

i 4:4, **saying** Included in A(02) BYZ TR ‖ Some manuscripts include "he said." D(05) Latin(a b e ff²) ‖ Absent from ℵ(01) B(03) W(032) NA28 SBLGNT THGNT.

j 4:4, **but by every word of God:** Included in A(02) D(05) BYZ TR ‖ Absent from ℵ(01) B(03) W(032) NA28 SBLGNT THGNT.

k 4:5, **he:** Some manuscripts read "the devil." A(02) Latin(a b) BYZ TR.

l 4:5, **into a high mountain:** Included in Latin(e ff²) BYZ TR ‖ W(032) includes "mountain."

m 4:5, **world:** Or inhabited earth.

n 4:7, **fall down and:** Included in Latin(a b ff²).

o 4:8, **get behind me Satan! For:** Included in A(02) Latin(b e) BYZ TR ‖ Absent from ℵ(01) B(03) D(05) W(032) NA28 SBLGNT THGNT.

p 4:8, Deuteronomy 6:13 LXX.

q 4:9, **him:** Included in A(02) D(05) (W032) Latin(a b ff²) BYZ TR ‖ Absent from ℵ(01) B(03) Latin(e) NA28 SBLGNT THGNT.

r 4:9, **to him:** Absent from Latin(e).

s 4:9, **the Son of God:** Or a son of God.

t 4:9 , **from here:** Absent from Latin(a).

u 4:11, **that:** Absent from D(05) BYZ.

v 4:11, Psalm 91:11-12.

w 4:12, **said:** Some manuscripts read "written." D(05) W(032) Latin(a b e ff²).

x 4:12, Deuteronomy 6:16.

y 4:15, **their:** Some manuscripts read "the." D(05) Latin(a b).

z 4:15, **glorified:** Or, being honored.

16 And he came to Nazareth, where he {had been brought up},[a] and he entered, as was {his}[b] custom, on the Sabbath day into the synagogue and stood up to read. 17 And [the scroll of][c] the prophet Isaiah was given to him, and unrolling the scroll, he found [the place][d] where it was written, 18 "The Spirit of the Lord is upon me, because he has anointed[e] me to bring good news to the poor; he has sent me [[to heal those who are brokenhearted,]][f] to proclaim release to the captives and recovery of sight to the blind, to send out those who are broken in release,[g] 19 to proclaim the acceptable year [[and day of retribution]][h] of the Lord."[i]

20 And folding the scroll, he gave it back to the attendant and sat down; and the eyes of all in the synagogue were fixed on him. 21 He began to say to them [that],[j] "Today this scripture has been fulfilled in your hearing."

22 And all were bearing witness to him and marveling at the words of grace that were coming out of his mouth, and they said, "Is this not the son of Joseph?" 23 And he said to them, "Surely you will say to me this proverb: 'Physician, heal yourself; whatever we have heard done in Capernaum, do also here in your hometown.'"

24 And he said, "Truly [[Truly]][k] I say to you, no prophet is accepted in his hometown."

25 "[But][l] In truth, I say to you, [[that]][m] there were many widows in Israel in the days of Elijah, when the heavens were shut up [for][n] three years and six months, and a [great][o] famine came upon all the land, 26 and Elijah was sent to none of them but only to Zarephath, in the land of Sidon, to a woman who was a widow. 27 And there were many lepers in Israel in the time of Elisha the prophet, and none of them was cleansed, but only Naaman the Syrian."

28 And all in the synagogue were filled with wrath when they heard these things, 29 and they rose up and they cast [him][p] out of the city and led him to the brow of the hill on which their city was built [{so that they might}[q] throw him down].[r] 30 But he passed through the midst of them and went on his way.

31 And he went down to Capernaum, a city of Galilee, [[the coastal region in the territories of Zebulun and

---

a 4:16, **had been brought up:** D(05) reads "was."

b 4:16, **his:** Some manuscripts read "the." D(05).

c 4:17, **the scroll of:** Absent from D(05).

d 4:17, **the place:** Absent from Latin(e).

e 4:18, **anointed:** The Greek word means anoint in our literature only in a figurative sense of an anointing by God setting a person apart for special service under divine direction... God anoints (a) David, (b) Jesus, the Christ for his work or mission, (c) the prophets, (d) the apostles or, more probably, all Christians (at baptism or through the Spirit) 1 Cor 1:21. (BDAG, χρίω).

f 4:18, **to heal those who are brokenhearted:** Included in A(02) BYZ TR ‖ Absent from ℵ(01) B(03) D(05) W(032) Latin(a b e ff²) NA28 SBLGNT THGNT.

g 4:18, **to send out those who are broken in release:** Or "set at liberty those who are oppressed."

h 4:19, **and day of retribution:** Included in Latin(e ff²) ‖ Some manuscripts read "and the day of recompense." Latin(b) ‖ Some manuscripts read "and the day of redemption." Latin(a).

i 4:19, **to proclaim the acceptable year of the Lord:** Or "to proclaim the year of the Lord's acceptance." Isaiah 61:1-2 LXX/Dead Sea Scrolls, Isaiah 58:6 LXX.

j 4:21, **that:** Absent from D(05) W(032) Syriac(sy^s).

k 4:24, **Truly:** Included in D(05) Latin(ff²).

l 4:25, **But:** Absent from D(05).

m 4:25, **that:** Included in ℵ(01) W(032) Latin(e).

n 4:25, **for:** Absent from B(03) D(05).

o 4:25, **great:** Absent from Latin(e).

p 4:29, **him:** Absent from ℵ(01).

q 4:29, **so that they might:** 𝔓4 ℵ(01) B(03) D(05) W(032) NA28 SBLGNT THGNT ‖ Some manuscripts read "in order to." A(02) C(04) BYZ TR.

r 4:29, **so that they might throw him down:** Absent from Latin(a b e ff²).

Naphtali,]][a] and he was teaching them on the Sabbath; 32 and they were astonished at his teaching, for his word was with authority.

33 And in the synagogue there was a man having an unclean {demonic}[b] spirit, and he cried out with a loud voice, 34 [[saying]][c] "[Ha!][d] What have we to do with you, Jesus of Nazareth? Have you come to destroy us? I know who you are, the Holy One of God." 35 And Jesus rebuked him, saying, "Be silent and come out of him." And the demon throwing him [into the midst][e] [[cried out and]][f] came out of him [without harming him].[g] 36 And there was [[great]][h] amazement upon all, and they spoke with one another, saying, "What is this word, that with authority and power he commands the unclean spirits and they come out?"

37 And the report about him went out into every place of the surrounding region.

38 But rising up {from}[i] the synagogue, he entered into the house of Simon [[and Andrew]].[j] Now Simon's mother-in-law was suffering from a great fever, and they asked him about her. 39 And standing over her, he rebuked the fever, and it left her; immediately {she rose up and served them}.[k]

40 As the sun was setting, all those who had any sick with various diseases brought them to him; and he laid his hands on each one [of them][l] and healed them. 41 And demons were also coming out [from many],[m] crying out and saying, "You are [[the Christ]][n] the Son of God." And rebuking them, he did not allow them to speak, because they knew him to be the Christ.

42 And when it was day, he went out and proceeded to a deserted place; and the crowds were seeking him, and they came to him and tried to keep him from leaving them. 43 But he said to them, "I must also proclaim the kingdom of God to the other cities, {because}[o] for this I was sent." 44 And he was preaching in the synagogues of {Judea}.[p]

5 1 Now it happened that while the crowd was pressing around him and to hear the word of God, he was standing by the Lake of Gennesaret,[q] 2 and he saw two boats standing by the lake; but the fishermen [had gotten out of them and][r] were {washing}[s] their nets. 3 Stepping into {one of the boats},[t] which was Simon's, he asked him to put out a little from the land. And sitting down in the boat, he taught the crowds.

---

a 4:31, **the coastal region in the territories of Zebulun and Naphtali:** Included in D(05).

b 4:33, **demonic:** Some manuscripts read "demon." D(05).

c 4:34, **saying:** Included in A(02) D(05) Latin(a b e ff²) BYZ TR.

d 4:34, **Ha:** Absent from D(05).

e 4:35, **into the midst:** Absent from Latin(a b ff²).

f 4:35, **cried out and:** Included in D(05).

g 4:35, **without harming him:** Absent from W(032).

h 4:36, **great:** Included in D(05) Latin(b) Syriac(sy^p).

i 4:38, **from:** Some manuscripts read "out of." BYZ TR.

j 4:38, **and Andrew:** Included in D(05) Latin(b e ff² it).

k 4:39, **she rose up and served them:** Some manuscripts read "so that they raised her up to serve." D(05).

l 4:40, **of them:** Absent from D(05) Latin(e).

m 4:41, **from many:** Absent from ℵ(01) Latin(b).

n 4:41, **the Christ:** Included in A(02) BYZ TR.

o 4:43, **because:** Some manuscripts read "indeed." D(05).

p 4:44, **Judea:** 𝔓75 ℵ(01) B(03) C(04) W(032) NA28 SBLGNT THGNT ‖ Some manuscripts read "Galilee." A(02) D(05) BYZ TR.

q 5:1, **Lake of Gennesaret:** Also known as the Sea of Galilee.

r 5:2, **had gotten out of them:** Absent from Latin(e).

s 5:2, **washing:** Some manuscripts read "washing off." A(02) BYZ TR.

t 5:3, **one of the boats:** Some manuscripts read "a boat." BYZ TR.

4 When he had finished speaking, he said to Simon, "Put out into the deep and let down your nets for a catch." 5 And Simon answered and said [[to him]],[a] "{Master},[b] we worked hard all night and caught nothing, but at your word I will {let down the {nets}[c]}."[d] 6 {When they had done this},[e] they enclosed a great quantity of fish, {but their nets were torn apart};[f] 7 so they signaled to their partners [[those]][g] in the other boat to come and help them. And they [came and][h] filled both the boats, so that they began to sink.

8 But when Simon [Peter][i] saw this, he fell down at {Jesus' knees},[j] saying, "Go away from me, for I am a sinful man [, Lord]!"[k] 9 For amazement had seized him [and all those with him][l] because of the catch of fish which they had taken; 10 {and likewise also James and John, sons of Zebedee, who were partners with Simon. And Jesus said to Simon, "Do not fear, from now on you will be catching men}."[m]

11 {When they had brought their boats to land, they left everything}[n] and followed him.

12 {But}[o] it happened, while he was in one of the cities, behold, a man full of leprosy; [and when he saw Jesus,][p] he fell on his face [and he pleaded with him],[q] saying, "Lord, if you are willing, you can make me clean." 13 And stretching out his hand, he touched him, saying, "I am willing, be cleansed;" and immediately {the leprosy left him}.[r] 14 And he commanded [him][s] to tell no one, but "Go, show yourself to the priest and offer for your cleansing, as Moses commanded, as a testimony to them." [[But he went out and began to proclaim and spread the word, so that he could no longer openly enter a city, but was out in deserted places. And they came to him, and he returned to Capernaum.]][t]

---

a 5:5, **to him:** Some manuscripts include A(02) C(04) D(05) W(032) BYZ TR ‖ Absent from 𝔓75 ℵ(01) B(03).

b 5:5, **Master:** Some manuscripts read "Teacher." D(05) Latin(a b e ff²).

c 5:5, **nets:** Some manuscripts read "net." BYZ TR.

d 5:5, **let down the nets:** Some manuscripts read "not disobey." BYZ TR.

e 5:6, **When they had done this:** Some manuscripts read "And immediately, having let down the nets." D(05).

f 5:6, **but their nets were torn apart:** 𝔓75 ℵ(01) B(03) NA28 SBLGNT THGNT ‖ Some manuscripts read "But their net was breaking." A(02) C(04) BYZ TR ‖ Some manuscripts read "So that the nets were tearing." D(05) Latin(e f).

g 5:7, **those:** 𝔓4 ℵ(01) B(03) D(05) W(032) ‖ Absent from A(02) C(04) BYZ TR.

h 5:7, **came and:** Absent from Latin(b).

i 5:8, **Peter:** Absent from D(05) W(032) Latin (a b e).

j 5:8, **Jesus' knees:** D(05) reads "Jesus feet."

k 5:8, **Lord:** Absent from ℵ(01) Latin(b e ff²).

l 5:9, **and all those with him:** Absent from D(05).

m 5:10, **and likewise also James…:** Some manuscripts read "And when he saw them, James and John, the sons of Zebedee, he said to them, Come, and do not become fishermen of fish, for I will make you fishermen of men." D(05) Latin(e).

n 5:11, **When they had…:** Some manuscripts read "And those who heard left everything on the earth." D(05) Latin(e).

o 5:12, **But:** ℵ(01) B(03) NA28 ‖ Some manuscripts read "and." A(02) C(04) D(05) BYZ TGR SBLGNT THGNT.

p 5:12, **and when he saw Jesus:** Absent from Latin(a b ff²).

q 5:12, **and he pleaded with him:** Absent from D(05) Latin (e).

r 5:13, **the leprosy left him:** Some manuscripts read "he was cleansed." D(05) Latin(e).

s 5:14, **him:** Absent from W(032) Latin(e).

t 5:14, **But he went out…:** Included in D(05).

15 But the word about him spread even more, and many crowds gathered to hear and to be healed [[by him]]ᵃ of their infirmities. 16 But he would withdraw to desolate places and pray.

17 And it happened {on one of the days, andᵇ he was teaching, and there were [sitting]ᶜ Pharisees and teachers of the law who}ᵈ had come from every village of Galilee and Judea [and Jerusalem]ᵉ {; and the power of the Lord was *present* for him to heal}.ᶠ

18 And behold, men were carrying on a bed a man who was paralyzed, and they were seeking to bring him in and lay [him]ᵍ before him. 19 And not finding a way to bring him in because of the crowd, they went up on the roof and {let him down with the {bed}ʰ through the tiles}ⁱ [into the middle]ʲ in front of {Jesus}.ᵏ 20 {And seeing {their}ˡ faith, he said [[to him]],ᵐ "Man, your sins are forgiven you."}ⁿ

21 And the scribes and the Pharisees began to reason [[in their hearts]],º saying, "Who is this who speaks blasphemies? Who can forgive sins {but God alone}?"ᵖ

22 But Jesus, perceiving their thoughts, [answered and]�q said to them, "Why do you ponder [[evil]]ʳ in your hearts? 23 Which is easier, to say, 'Your sins are forgiven [you],ˢ' or to say, 'Rise and walk'? 24 But that you may know that the Son of Man has authority on earth to forgive sins;" he said to the paralyzed man, "I say to you, rise, [take up your mat,]ᵗ and go to your house."

25 And immediately he rose up before them, took up what he had been lying on, and went to his house, glorifying God. 26 [And amazement seized them all, and they glorified God.]ᵘ And they were filled with fear, saying [that],ᵛ "We have seen extraordinary things today."

ᵃ 5:15, **by him:** Included in A(02) BYZ TR.

ᵇ 5:17, **and:** Or "also."

ᶜ 5:17, **sitting:** Absent from D(05) Latin(e).

ᵈ 5:17, **on one of the days…:** Some manuscripts read "one day, while he was teaching, the Pharisees and teachers of the law gathered." D(05) Latin(e).

ᵉ 5:17 , **and Jerusalem:** Absent from D(05).

ᶠ 5:17, **and the power of the Lord was present:** Some manuscripts read "to be healed." D(05).

ᵍ 5:18, **him:** B(03) NA28[] ‖ Absent from ℵ(01) A(02) C(04) D(05) W(032) Latin(a b e ff²) BYZ TR SBLGNT THGNT.

ʰ 5:19, **bed:** Some manuscripts read "mat." D(05) Latin(b).

ⁱ 5:19, **let him down…:** D(05) reads "having removed the tiles where he was lying, they lowered the mat with the paralytic."

ʲ 5:19, **into the middle:** Absent from Latin(a e).

ᵏ 5:19, **Jesus:** Some manuscripts read "all." B(03).

ˡ 5:20, **their:** Some manuscripts read "the." Latin(b ff²).

ᵐ 5:20, **to him:** Included in A(02) W(032) Latin(e) BYZ TR ‖ D(05) reads "to the paralytic."

ⁿ 5:20, **And seeing their…:** Some manuscripts read "Seeing their faith, Jesus says to the paralytic man, 'Your sins are forgiven.'" D(05).

º 5:21, **in their hearts:** Included in D(05) Latin(a e it).

ᵖ 5:21, **but God alone:** D(05) reads "except one, God."

q 5:22, **answered and:** Absent from C(04) D(05) Latin(a b ff²).

ʳ 5:22, **evil:** Included in D(05) Latin(it).

ˢ 5:23, **you:** A(02) B(03) BYZ TR NA28 SBLGNT THGNT ‖ Absent from ℵ(01) D(05) W(032).

ᵗ 5:24, **take up your mat:** Absent from Latin(e).

ᵘ 5:26, **And amazement seized them all, and they glorified God:** Absent from D(05) W(032) Latin(e).

ᵛ 5:26, **that:** Absent from D(05).

27 [[And coming again by the sea, the crowd following him, he taught.]]ᵃ {And after this, he went out and saw a tax collector named Levi sitting at the tax booth, and he said to him},ᵇ "Follow me." 28 And leaving [everything],ᶜ he rose and followed him.

29 And Levi made a [great]ᵈ feast for him in his house, and there was a large crowd of tax collectors [and others]ᵉ who were reclining [with them].ᶠ 30 And {the Pharisees and their scribes}ᵍ grumbled at his disciples, saying, "Why {do you}ʰ eat and drink with tax collectors [and sinners]?"ⁱ

31 And {Jesus}ʲ answered and said to them, "Those who are well have no need of a physician, but those who are sick; 32 I have not come to call the righteous, but sinners to repentance."

33 And they said to him, "[[Why do]]ᵏ the disciples of John [[and the disciples of the Pharisees]]ˡ {often fast and offer prayers, likewise also the Pharisees},ᵐ but {yours eat and drink}."ⁿ

34 {Jesus}ᵒ said to them, "Can [you make]ᵖ the sons of the bridechamber fast {while the bridegroom is}ᑫ [with them].ʳ 35 But days will come, and when the bridegroom is taken away from them, then they will [fast]ˢ in those days."

36 He also told them a parable: "No one tears a piece from a new garment [and sews it]ᵗ on an old one; otherwise, the new will tear and the patch from the new will not match the old. 37 And no one puts [new]ᵘ wine into old wineskins; otherwise, the new wine will burst the [[old]]ᵛ wineskins and it will be spilled, and the wineskins will

---

ᵃ 5:27, **And coming again...:** Included in D(05).
ᵇ 5:27, **And after this:** Some manuscripts read "And passing by, he saw Levi, the son of Alphaeus, sitting at the tax booth, and he says to him." D(05).
ᶜ 5:28, **everything:** Absent from Latin(a).
ᵈ 5:29, **great:** Absent from D(05).
ᵉ 5:29, **and others:** Absent from ℵ(01) ‖ Some manuscripts read "and sinners." W(032).
ᶠ 5:29, **with them:** Absent from D(05) Latin(e).
ᵍ 5:30, **the Pharisees and their scribes:** B(03) C(04) W(032) NA28 SBLGNT THGNT ‖ Some manuscripts read "their scribes and the Pharisees." A(02) BYZ TR ‖ Some manuscripts read "the Pharisees and the scribes." ℵ(01) D(05).
ʰ 5:30, **do you:** Some manuscripts read "does he." D(05).
ⁱ 5:30, **and sinners:** Absent from C(04) D(05).
ʲ 5:31, **Jesus:** W(032) reads "he."
ᵏ 5:33, **Why do:** Included in ℵ(01) A(02) C(04) D(05) BYZ TR ‖ Absent from 𝔓4 B(03) W(032) Latin(a b e ff²) NA28 SBLGNT THGNT.
ˡ 5:33, **and the disciples of the Pharisees:** Included in D(05).
ᵐ 5:33, **often fast and...:** Some manuscripts read "and the disciples of the Pharisees fast often and make prayers." D(05) Latin(it).
ⁿ 5:33, **yours eat and drink:** Some manuscripts read "your disciples do none of these things." D(05) Latin(e).
ᵒ 5:34, **Jesus:** 𝔓4 ℵ(01) B(03) C(04) D(05) W(032) NA28 THGNT ‖ Some manuscripts read "he." A(02) Latin(a b e ff²) SBLGNT BYZ TR.
ᵖ 5:34, **you make:** Absent from ℵ(01) D(05) Latin(it).
ᑫ 5:34, **while the bridegroom is:** Some manuscripts read "for as long as they have the bridegroom." D(05) Latin(e).
ʳ 5:34, **with them:** Absent from Latin(b ff²).
ˢ 5:35, **fast:** Absent from Latin(b).
ᵗ 5:36, **and sews it:** Absent from Latin(b ff²).
ᵘ 5:37, **new:** Absent from ℵ(01).
ᵛ 5:37, **old:** Included in D(05).

be destroyed. 38 But [new][a] wine must
be put into fresh wineskins [[and both
are preserved]].[b] 39 [[And][c] No one after
drinking old wine [[immediately]][d]
desires new; for he says, 'The old is
{good}.'[e]]"[f]

6 1 Now it happened {on a Sabbath}[g]
that he was passing through
grainfields, and his disciples {were
plucking and eating the heads of
grain rubbing them in their hands}.[h]
2 But some of the Pharisees said [[to
them]],[i] "{Why are you}[j] doing what is
not lawful [[to do]][k] on the Sabbath?"

3 And Jesus answered them, "Have
you not read what David did when he
and {those [who were][l] with him}[m]
were hungry, 4 {[how][n] he entered the
house of God [and took][o] and}[p] ate the
bread of the Presence, and [[also]][q]
gave it to those with him, which is not
lawful to eat except the priests alone?"
[[On the same day, seeing someone
working on the Sabbath, he said to him,
"Man, if you know what you are doing,
you are blessed; but if you do not know,
you are cursed and a transgressor of the
law."]][r]

5 And he said to them [[that]],[s]
"The Son of Man is lord [[even]][t] of the
Sabbath."[u]

---

a 5:38, **new:** Absent from Latin(a).

b 5:38, **and both are preserved:** A(02) C(04) D(05) BYZ TR Latin(latt) Syriac(sy) || Absent from 𝔓4 𝔓75 א(01) B(03) W(032).

c 5:39, **and:** Absent from 𝔓4 B(03) BYZ TR.

d 5:39, **immediately:** Included in A(02) BYZ TR.

e 5:39, **good:** 𝔓4 א(01) B(03) W(032) NA28 SBLGNT THGNT || Some manuscripts read "better." A(02) C(04) BYZ TR.

f 5:39, Verse 39 is absent from some manuscripts. D(05) Latin(a b e ff^{2} it).

g 6:1, **on a Sabbath:** 𝔓4 א(01) B(03) W(032) Latin (b) NA28 SBLGNT THGNT || Some manuscripts read "On the second-first Sabbath." A(02) C(04) D(05) Latin (a ff^{2}) BYZ TR.

h 6:1, **were plucking and eating...:** 𝔓4 𝔓75 א(01) B(03) W(032) NA28 SBLGNT THGNT || Some manuscripts read "were plucking the heads of grain and eating them, rubbing them in their hands." A(02) W(032) BYZ TR. || Some manuscripts read "began to pluck the heads of grain, and rubbing them in their hands, they were eating." D(05) Latin(e, f) Syriac(sy^{p}).

i 6:2, **to them:** Included in A(02) Latin (a e ff^{2}) BYZ TR || D(05) reads "to him." || Absent from 𝔓4 𝔓75 א(01) B(03) C(04) W(032) NA28 SBLGNT THGNT.

j 6:2, **Why are you:** D(05) reads "Look your disciples are."

k 6:2, **to do:** Included in א(01) A(02) C(04) BYZ TR || Absent in 𝔓4 𝔓75 B(03) Latin(a b e ff^{2}) NA28 SBLGNT THGNT.

l 6:3, **who were:** A(02) C(04) BYZ TR NA28[] SBLGNT || Absent from 𝔓4 א(01) B(03) D(05) Latin(a b c e ff^{2}) THGNT.

m 6:3, **those [who were] with him:** Some manuscripts read "his *men*." D(05).

n 6:4, **how:** א(01) A(02) C(04) W(032) Latin(a b e ff^{2}) NA28 SBLGNT THGNT || Absent from 𝔓4 B(03) D(05).

o 6:4, **and took:** 𝔓4 B(03) C(04) BYZ TR NA28 SBLGNT THGNT || Absent from א(01) D(05) W(032).

p 6:4, **how he entered the...:** Some manuscripts read "Entering into the house of God, he." D(05).

q 6:4, **also:** Included in א(01) A(02) D(05) BYZ TR || Absent from B(03) W(032) NA28 SBLGNT THGNT.

r 6:4, **On the same day...:** Included in D(05).

s 6:5, **that:** Included in A(02) D(05) Latin(a b e) BYZ TR || Absent from 𝔓4 א(01) B(03) W(032) Latin(ff^{2}) NA28 SBLGNT THGNT.

t 6:5, **even:** Included in A(02) D(05) BYZ TR || Absent from א(01) B(03) W(032) NA28 SBLGNT THGNT.

u 6:5, **And he said...:** In D(05), verse 5 is located after verse 10.

6 {Now [[also]]ᵃ it happened on another Sabbath that he entered the synagogue [and was teaching].ᵇ And there was a man there whose [right]ᶜ hand was withered}.ᵈ 7 [But]ᵉ The scribes and the Pharisees were watching [him]ᶠ closely to see if he would heal on the Sabbath, so that they might find a reason to accuse him. 8 But he knew their thoughts, and said to the {man}ᵍ [with the withered hand],ʰ "Get up and stand in the middle."ⁱ And he got up and stood.

9 [Therefore]ʲ Jesus said to them, "I ask you, {is it}ᵏ lawful on the {Sabbath}ˡ to do good or to do harm, to save a life or to {destroy it}?"ᵐ [[But they were silent.]]ⁿ 10 And looking around at them all [[in anger]],ᵒ he said to {him},ᵖ "Stretch out your hand." And he {did so},ᑫ and his hand was restored [[healthy]]ʳ [[as the other]].ˢ [[And he said to them, "The Son of Man is Lord even of the Sabbath."]]ᵗ 11 But they were filled with senselessness and discussed with one another {what they might do to Jesus}.ᵘ

12 Now it happened in those days that he went out to the mountain to pray, and he spent the night in prayer [to God].ᵛ

13 And when it was day, he {called}ʷ his disciples, and from them he chose twelve, whom he also named apostles: 14 [[First]]ˣ Simon, whom he also named Peter, and Andrew his brother, and James and John [[his brother, whom he named Boanerges, which is Sons of Thunder,]]ʸ and Philip [and Bartholomew],ᶻ 15 and Matthew and Thomas [[the one called Didyhmus]]ᵃ and James the son of Alphaeus and Simon called the Zealot, 16 and Judas the son of James, and Judas Iscariot, who [[also]]ᵇ became a traitor.

ᵃ 6:6, **also:** Included in BYZ TR.

ᵇ 6:6, **and was teaching:** Absent from D(05).

ᶜ 6:6, **right:** Absent from D(05).

ᵈ 6:6, **Now it happened on ...:** D(05) reads, "And when he entered again into the synagogue on the Sabbath, there was a man there who had a withered hand."

ᵉ 6:7, **But:** Absent from D(05).

ᶠ 6:7, **him:** 𝔓4 ℵ(01) B(03) D(05) W(032) TR NA28 THGNT ‖ Absent from A(02) BYZ SBLGNT.

ᵍ 6:8, **man:** D(05) reads "one."

ʰ 6:8, **with the withered hand:** Absent from Latin(e).

ⁱ 6:8, **in the middle:** Or "in the midst."

ʲ 6:9, **Therefore:** Included in A(02) BYZ TR.

ᵏ 6:9, **is it:** Some manuscripts read "what is." A(02) BYZ TR.

ˡ 6:9, **Sabbath:** Some manuscripts read "Sabbaths." BYZ TR.

ᵐ 6:9, **destroy it:** 𝔓4 ℵ(01) B(03) D(05) W(032) TR NA28 SBLGNT THGNT ‖ Some manuscripts read "kill." A(02) BYZ.

ⁿ 6:9, **But they were silent:** Included in D(05).

ᵒ 6:10, **in anger:** Included in D(05) Latin(b).

ᵖ 6:10, **him:** Some manuscripts read "the man." D(05) TR.

ᑫ 6:10, **did so:** Some manuscripts read "stretched it out." BYZ TR.

ʳ 6:10, **healthy:** Included in BYZ TR.

ˢ 6:10, **as the other:** Included in A(02) Latin(b) BYZ TR ‖ Absent from 𝔓4 ℵ(01) B(03) Latin(a e ff²) NA28 SBLGNT THGNT.

ᵗ 6:10, **And he said to them...:** D(05) includes this statement here rather than in verse 5.

ᵘ 6:11, **what they might do to Jesus:** D(05) reads "how they might destroy him."

ᵛ 6:12, **to God:** Absent from D(05).

ʷ 6:13, **called:** D(05) reads "addressed."

ˣ 6:14, **First:** Included in D(05) Latin(a).

ʸ 6:14, **his brother...:** Included in D(05) Latin(ff²).

ᶻ 6:14, **Bartholomew:** Absent from ℵ(01).

ᵃ 6:15, **the one called Didyhmus:** Included in D(05).

ᵇ 6:16, **also:** Included in A(02) D(05) BYZ TR.

17 And coming down with them, he stood on a level place, and a [large]ᵃ crowd of his disciples, and a great multitude [of the people]ᵇ from all Judea and Jerusalem [[and the region beyond]]ᶜ and {the coastal region of Tyre and Sidon,}ᵈ 18 who came to hear him and to be healed of their diseases; and those who were troubled by unclean spirits were being healed, 19 and all the crowd sought to touch him, for power came out from him and healed them all.

20 And lifting up his eyes to {his}ᵉ disciples, he said,

"Blessed are the poor [[in spirit]],ᶠ for yours is the kingdom of God.

21 "Blessed are those who hunger now, for you will be satisfied.

["Blessed are those who weep now, for you will laugh.]ᵍ

22 "Blessed are you when men hate you, and [when]ʰ they exclude you and insult you and reject your name as evil, because of the Son of Man.

23 "Rejoice in that day and leap for joy, for [behold,]ⁱ your reward is [great]ʲ in heaven; [for]ᵏ their fathers did [the same]ˡ to the prophets.

24 "But woe to you who are rich, for you have received your consolation.

25 "Woe to you who are full [now],ᵐ for you will be hungry.

"Woe [[to you,]]ⁿ those who laugh now, for you will mourn and weep.

26 "Woe [[to you]]ᵒ when [all]ᵖ men speak well of you; [for]�q {their fathers}ʳ did the same to the false prophets.

27 "But I say to you who hear [[me]],ˢ love your enemies, do good to those who hate you, 28 bless those who curse you, pray for those who mistreat you.

29 "To the one who strikes you on the [[right]]ᵗ cheek, offer [to him]ᵘ the other also, and from the one who takes away your cloak, do not withhold your tunic either.

30 "Give to everyone who asks you, and from the one who takes your things, do not demand them back.

31 "And just as you want men to do to you, [[also you]]ᵛ do [likewise]ʷ to them.

ᵃ 6:17, **large:** Absent from A(02) D(05) Latin(a b e ff²) BYZ TR.

ᵇ 6:17, **of the people:** Absent from ℵ(01).

ᶜ 6:17, **and the region beyond:** Included in ℵ(01) W(032).

ᵈ 6:17, **the coastal region of Tyre and Sidon:** Some manuscripts read "of Perea and of the coast." W(032) Latin(a b e ff²) ‖ ℵ(01) reads "of Piraeus and the coast." D(05) reads "of other cities."

ᵉ 6:20, **his:** D(05) reads "the."

ᶠ 6:20, **in spirit:** Included in Latin(a).

ᵍ 6:21, **Blessed are those who weep now, for you will laugh:** Absent from D(05).

ʰ 6:22, **when:** Absent from W(032).

ⁱ 6:23, **behold:** Absent from D(05).

ʲ 6:23, **great:** Absent from Latin(e).

ᵏ 6:23, **for:** Absent from D(05) Latin(a ff²).

ˡ 6:23, **the same:** Absent from Latin(a).

ᵐ 6:25, **now:** Absent from A(02) D(05) BYZ TR.

ⁿ 6:25, **you:** Included in 𝔓75 A(02) D(05) Latin(a b e ff²) BYZ TR ‖ Absent from ℵ(01) B(03) W(032) NA28 SBLGNT THGNT.

ᵒ 6:26, **to you:** Included in D(05) W(032) Latin(b) Syriac(syˢ syᵖ) TR ‖ Absent from 𝔓75 ℵ(01) A(02) B(03) W(032) NA28 SBLGNT THGNT.

ᵖ 6:26, **all:** Absent from D(05) Syriac(syˢ, syᵖ).

q 6:26, **for:** Absent from D(05) Latin(a b e ff²).

ʳ 6:26, **their fathers** Absent from some manuscripts which otherwise read "they." 𝔓75 B(03).

ˢ 6:27, **me:** Included in W(032).

ᵗ 6:29, **right:** Included in ℵ(01).

ᵘ 6:29, **to him:** Included in D(05) Latin(a b e ff²).

ᵛ 6:31, **also you:** Included in ℵ(01) A(02) D(05) W(032) BYZ TR THGNT ‖ Absent from 𝔓75 B(03) Latin(a b e ff²) NA28 SBLGNT.

ʷ 6:31, **likewise:** Absent from D(05) Latin(a e).

32 "And if you love those who love you, what credit is that to you? For even sinners [[do this;]][a] love those who love them.

33 "And [indeed][b] if you do good to those who do good to you, what grace[c] is that to you? [[For]][d] Even sinners do the same.

34 "And if you lend to those from whom you hope to receive, what grace [is][e] to you? [[For]][f] Even sinners lend to sinners {in order to receive back [an equal amount][g]}.[h]

35 "But love your enemies, and do good, and lend, expecting nothing in return; and your reward will be great [[in the heavens]],[i] and you will be sons of the Most High, for he is kind to the ungrateful and the wicked.

36 "Be merciful [[therefore]],[j] just as [also][k] your Father is merciful.

37 "And do not judge, {and you}[l] will not be judged; and do not condemn, {and you}[m] will not be {condemned}.[n] Release, and you will be released.[o]

38 "Give, and it will be given to you; a good measure, pressed down, shaken together, running over, will be poured into your lap. For with the [[same]][p] measure [[that you use]],[q] it will be measured [back][r] to you."

39 And he [also][s] told them a parable: "Can a blind person guide a blind person? Will not both fall into a pit?

40 "A disciple is not above {the}[t] teacher; but [everyone][u] when fully trained, will be like his teacher.

41 "[But][v] Why do you see the speck in your brother's eye, but do not notice the log[w] in your own eye?

42 "How can you say to your brother, '[Brother,][x] Let me take out the speck in your eye,' {when you yourself do not see}[y] the log in your own eye? Hypocrite, first take the log out of your own eye, and then you will see clearly

---

a 6:32, **do this:** Included in D(05).

b 6:33, **indeed:** ℵ(01) B(03) NA28[] THGNT. || Absent from some manuscripts A(02) D(05) W(032) BYZ TR Latin(a b e ff2) Syriac(sy) SBLGNT.

c 6:33, **grace:** Or credit.

d 6:33, **For:** Included in A(02) D(05) BYZ TR THGNT.

e 6:34, **is:** Absent from 𝔓45 𝔓75 B(03) Latin(e).

f 6:34, **For:** Included in A(02) D(05) BYZ TR THGNT.

g 6:34, **an equal amount:** Absent from D(05) Latin(a b e ff2 it) Syriac(sys).

h 6:34, **in order to receive back an equal amount:** Some manuscripts read "to receive as much again." D(05).

i 6:35, **in the heavens:** Included in A(02) Latin(a).

j 6:36, **therefore:** Included in BYZ TR.

k 6:36, **also:** A(02) D(05) BYZ TR NA28[] THGNT || Absent from ℵ(01) B(03) W(032) SBLGNT.

l 6:37, **and you:** Some manuscripts read "so that you." A(02) D(05) W(032) Latin(a, c, e, f) Syriac(sys).

m 6:37, **and you:** Some manuscripts read "so that you." D(05) W(032) Latin(it) Syriac(sys).

n 6:37, **condemned:** Some manuscripts read "judged." 𝔓75 B(03).

o 6:37, **Release, and you will be released:** Or "Forgive, and you will be forgiven."

p 6:38, **same:** Included in 𝔓45 A(02) C(04) BYZ TR || Absent from ℵ(01) B(03) D(05) W(032) NA28 SBLGNT THGNT.

q 6:38, **that you use:** ℵ(01) B(03) D(05) W(032) NA28 SBLGNT THGNT || Included in 𝔓75 A(02) C(04) BYZ TR.

r 6:38, **back:** Absent from B(03) Latin(b e).

s 6:39, **also:** Absent from A(02) BYZ TR.

t 6:40, **the:** 𝔓75 ℵ(01) B(03) D(05) W(032) Latin (a be ff2) NA28 SBLGNT THGNT || Some manuscripts read "his." A(02) C(04) BYZ TR.

u 6:40, **everyone:** Absent from ℵ(01) Latin(b).

v 6:41, **But:** Absent from 𝔓75.

w 6:41-43, **log:** Or beam.

x 6:42, **brother:** Absent from D(05) Latin(a b e ff2).

y 6:42, **when you yourself do not see:** Some manuscripts read "and behold." D(05) Latin(it) Syriac(sys syp).

to remove the speck from your brother's eye.

43 "For there is no good tree producing rotten[a] fruit, nor [again][b] a rotten tree producing good fruit.

44 "[For][c] Each tree is known by its [own][d] fruit; for they do not gather figs from thorns, nor do they pick grapes from a bramble bush.

45 "The good person out of the good treasure of {the}[e] heart brings forth good, and the evil [[person]][f] out of the evil [[treasure of his heart]][g] brings forth evil; for out of the abundance of the heart the mouth speaks.

46 "Why do you call me, Lord, Lord, and do not do what I say?

47 "Everyone who comes to me and hears my words and does them, I will show you what he is like; 48 he is like a man building a house who dug deep and laid the foundation on the rock;

when a flood came, the river beat against that house, but it could not shake it [because it was {well built}[h]].[i]

49 "But the one who hears and does not do is like a man[j] who built a house on the ground without a foundation, against which the river beat, and it [immediately][k] fell,[l] and the ruin of that house was great."

7 1 {After he had finished [all][m] his sayings in the hearing of the people, he entered Capernaum}.[n]

2 {A certain centurion had a servant who}[o] was ill and about to die, was highly valued by him. 3 Having heard about Jesus, he sent [to him][p] elders of the Jews, asking him to come and save his servant. 4 When they came [to Jesus],[q] they earnestly pleaded with him, saying [[to him]],[r] "He is worthy for you to grant this, 5 [for][s] he loves our nation and he himself built our synagogue for us."

---

a 6:43, **rotten:** Or bad.

b 6:43, **again:** Absent from A(02) C(04) D(05) Latin(a e ff²) BYZ TR.

c 6:44, **For:** Absent from D(05) Latin(a b e ff² it) Syriac(sy^s).

d 6:44, **own:** Absent from D(05).

e 6:45, **the:** 𝔓75 ℵ(01) B(03) D(05) W(032) NA28 THGNT ‖ Some manuscripts read "his." A(02) C(04) D(05) W(032) Latin(a b e ff²) BYZ TR SBLGNT.

f 6:45, **person:** Or men, Included in W(032) Latin(a e ff²) BYZ TR.

g 6:45, **treasure of his heart:** Included in A(02) C(04) Latin(e) BYZ TR ‖ Absent from 𝔓75 ℵ(01) B(03) D(05) Latin(a ff²) NA28 SBLGNT THGNT. ‖ Some manuscripts read "treasure." Latin(b).

h 6:48, **well built:** Some manuscripts read "founded on the rock." A(02) C(04) D(05) BYZ TR.

i 6:48, **because it was well built:** 𝔓75 ℵ(01) B(03) W(032) NA28 SBLGNT THGNT ‖ Absent from 𝔓45 Syriac(sy^s) ‖ Some manuscripts read "for it had been founded on the rock." A(02) C(04) D(05) BYZ TR.

j 6:49, **man:** Or person.

k 6:49, **immediately:** Absent from D(05) Latin(a).

l 6:49, **fell:** Or collapsed.

m 7:1, **all:** Absent from ℵ(01) Latin(a b e ff²).

n 7:1, **After he had finished...:** Some manuscripts read, "And it happened when he had finished these words, he came to Capernaum." D(05) Latin(a b e ff² it).

o 7:2, **A certain centurion...:** Some manuscripts read, "Of a certain centurion, someone." BYZ TR.

p 7:3, **to him:** Absent from D(05) Latin(a b e ff² it) BYZ TR.

q 7:4, **to Jesus:** Some manuscripts read "to him." C(04) ‖ Absent in some manuscripts. D(05) Latin(a c it).

r 7:4, **to him:** Absent from A(02) C(04).

s 7:5, **for:** Absent from A(02).

⁶So Jesus went with them. Already, not far from his house, the centurion sent friends [[to him]],ᵃ saying [to him],ᵇ "Lord, do not trouble yourself, for I am not worthy to have you come under my roof. ⁷[Therefore, I did not even consider myself worthy to come to you.]ᶜ But [[just]]ᵈ say the word, and my servant will be healed. ⁸For I too am a man under authority, having soldiers under me; and I say to this one, 'Go,' and he goes, and to another, 'Come,' and he comes, and to my servant, 'Do this,' and he does it."

⁹When Jesus heard these things, he marveledᵉ [at him],ᶠ and {turning to the crowd [following him],ᵍ he said, "[[Truly]]ʰ I say to you, not even in Israel have I found such faith."}ⁱ

¹⁰{And returning to the house, the ones sent found the [[sick]]ʲ servant in good health.}ᵏ

¹¹And {it happened in the following,}ˡ he went into a city [called]ᵐ Nain and his disciples were accompanying [him],ⁿ [[a considerable number,]]ᵒ along with a large crowd. ¹²[[And it happened that]]ᵖ As he approached the city gate, [behold],ᑫ a [dead]ʳ only son was being carried out, his mother was a widow; and a considerable crowd from the city was with her. ¹³{And seeing her, the Lord}ˢ had compassion on her and said to her, "Do not weep."

¹⁴And coming forward, he touched the bierᵗ, and those carrying it stood still, and he said, "Young man, [[Young man,]]ᵘ I say to you, arise."

¹⁵And the dead man sat up and began to speak, and he gave him to his mother. ¹⁶Fear seized everyone, and they glorified God, saying, "A prophet has risen among us," and "God [[for his good]]ᵛ has visited his people." ¹⁷And this word spread throughout all Judea and all the surrounding region.

¹⁸{And John's disciples reported to him about all these things. And [John]ʷ calling}ˣ two of his disciples, ¹⁹{sent

---

ᵃ 7:6, **to him:** Included in C(04) D(05) W(032) BYZ TR.

ᵇ 7:6, **to him:** Absent from ℵ(01) Latin(b).

ᶜ 7:7, **Therefore, I did not...:** Absent from D(05) Latin (a b e ff² it) Syriac(syˢ).

ᵈ 7:7, **just:** Included in C(04).

ᵉ 7:9, **marveled:** Or "was amazed."

ᶠ 7:9, **at him:** Absent from D(05) Latin(a b e ff²).

ᵍ 7:9, **following him:** Absent from W(032).

ʰ 7:9, **Truly:** Included in D(05) Latin(a e).

ⁱ 7:9, **turning to the crowd...:** D(05) reads "turning around, said to the following crowd, 'Truly I say to you, I have never found such faith in Israel.'."

ʲ 7:10, **sick:** Included in A(02) C(04) D(05) BYZ TR ‖ Absent from 𝔓75 ℵ(01) B(03) W(032) Latin(a b e ff²) NA28 SBLGNT THGNT.

ᵏ 7:10, **And returning ...:** Some manuscripts read "And the servants who were sent, returning to the house, found the sick man healthy." D(05).

ˡ 7:11, **it happened in the following:** Some manuscripts read "the next day." D(05) Latin(e).

ᵐ 7:11, **called:** Absent from ℵ(01).

ⁿ 7:11, **him:** Absent from A(02).

ᵒ 7:11, **a considerable number:** Included in A(02) C(04) Latin (b) BYZ TR ‖ Absent from 𝔓75 ℵ(01) B(03) D(05) W(032) Latin(a e ff²) NA28 SBLGNT THGNT.

ᵖ 7:12, **And it happened that:** Included in D(05) Latin(a b e ff² it).

ᑫ 7:12, **behold:** Absent from D(05).

ʳ 7:12, **dead:** Absent from A(02).

ˢ 7:13, **And seeing her, the Lord:** Some manuscripts read "Seeing this, Jesus." D(05) W(032) Syriac(syˢ syᵖ).

ᵗ 7:14, **bier:** Also translated "open coffin."

ᵘ 7:14, **Young man:** Some manuscripts include a second time. D(05) Latin (a ff²).

ᵛ 7:16, **for his good:** Included in Latin(a b e ff²).

ʷ 7:18, **John:** Absent from D(05).

ˣ 7:18, **And John's disciples...:** Some manuscripts read "In which also until John the Baptist, who also having called." D(05) Latin(e).

them to {the Lord},^a saying,}^b "Are you the one who is to come, or should we expect {someone else}?"^c

20 When the men came to him, they said, "John the Baptist has sent us to you, saying, 'Are you the one who is coming, or should we expect someone else?'" 21 In that [[very]]^d hour, he healed many from diseases and afflictions and evil spirits, and {to many blind he granted sight}.^e 22 And in response {he}^f said to them, "Go and report to John what you have seen [[with your eyes]]^g and [[your ears have]]^h heard: [[for]]ⁱ the blind receive sight, the lame walk, the lepers are cleansed, [and]^j the deaf hear; the dead are raised; the poor have good news preached to them. 23 And blessed is the one who is not offended by me."

24 After the messengers of John had departed, he began to speak to the crowds about John,

"What did you go out into the wilderness to see? A reed shaken by the wind?

25 "But what did you go out to see? A man dressed in soft clothing? Behold, those who are in splendid clothing and luxury are in the palaces.

26 "But what did you go out to see? A prophet? [Yes,]^k I say to you, and more than [a prophet].^l [[For no one is greater among those born of women than the prophet John the Baptist.]]^m

27 "This is the one about whom it is written, 'Behold, I send my messenger before your face, who will prepare your way [before you].ⁿ"^o

28 "[[Truly,]]^p I say to you [[that]]^q [, among those born of women, there is no one like [[the prophet]]^r John [[the baptist]];^s but]^t the least in the kingdom of God is greater than he."

29 And all the people who heard this, and the tax collectors, justified^u God, having been baptized with the baptism of John; 30 but the Pharisees and the lawyers rejected the counsel of God [for themselves],^v not being baptized [by him].^w

---

a 7:19, **the Lord:** B(03) NA28 SBLGNT THGNT ‖ Some manuscripts read "Jesus." ℵ(01) A(02) W(032) BYZ TR.

b 7:19, **sent them to the Lord, saying:** Some manuscripts read "he says, Go tell him." D(05) Latin(e).

c 7:19, **someone else:** A(02) D(05) BYZ TR NA28 SBLGNT ‖ Some manuscripts read "another." ℵ(01) B(03) W(032) THGNT.

d 7:21, **very:** 𝔓75 ℵ(01) B(03) W(032) NA28 SBLGNT THGNT ‖ Included in A(02) D(05) BYZ TR.

e 7:21, **to many blind he granted sight:** Some manuscripts read "he made the blind see." BYZ TR.

f 7:22, **he:** Some manuscripts read "Jesus." A(02) Latin(ff²) BYZ TR.

g 7:22, **with your eyes:** Included in D(05) Latin(e).

h 7:22, **your ears have:** Included in D(05) Latin(e).

i 7:22, **for:** Included in A(02) D(05) BYZ TR ‖ Absent from 𝔓75 ℵ(01) B(03) W(032) NA28 SBLGNT THGNT.

j 7:22, **and:** 𝔓75 ℵ(01) B(03) D(05) W(032) NA28 THGNT ‖ Absent from A(02) BYZ TR SBLGNT.

k 7:26, **Yes:** Absent from Latin(ff²).

l 7:26, **a prophet:** Absent from Latin(ff²).

m 7:26, **For no one is greater among those born of women than the prophet John the Baptist:** Included in D(05) Latin(a).

n 7:27, **before you:** Absent from D(05) Latin(a it).

o 7:27, Malachi 3:1.

p 7:28, **Truly:** Included in ℵ(01) ‖ Some manuscripts read "For." A(02) BYZ TR ‖ Some manuscripts read "But." D(05) W(032) Latin(a b e ff²). ‖ Absent from 𝔓75 ℵ(01) A(03) Syriac(sy^s sy^p) NA28 SBLGNT THGNT.

q 7:28, **that:** Included in W(032) Latin(e).

r 7:28, **the prophet:** Included in A(02) BYZ TR.

s 7:28, **the baptist:** Included in A(02) Latin(a b e ff²) BYZ TR.

t 7:28, **among those born of women...:** Absent from D(05) which includes a similar statement in verse 26.

u 7:29, **justified:** Or Praised.

v 7:30, **for themselves:** Absent from ℵ(01) D(05).

w 7:30, **by him:** Absent from Latin(a b e ff²).

31 [[And the Lord said,]][a] "To
what then will I compare the people
of this generation, and what are they
like? 32 They are like children sitting
in the marketplace and calling to one
another [[and]][b] saying, 'We played the
flute for you, and you did not dance;
we mourned [[to you]],[c] and you did
not weep.'

33 "For John the Baptist has come
neither eating [bread][d] nor drinking
[wine],[e] and you say, 'He has a demon.'
34 The Son of Man has come eating
and drinking, and you say, 'Look, a
glutton and a drunkard, a friend of tax
collectors and sinners!' 35 And Wisdom
is justified by [all][f] her children."

36 Now one of the Pharisees asked
him to eat with him, and he went into
the Pharisee's house and reclined at the
table. 37 And behold, a woman who was
a sinner in the city, and knowing that
he was reclining in the house of the
Pharisee, brought an alabaster jar of
ointment 38 and standing behind him at
his feet, weeping, she began to wet his
feet with her tears and wiped them with
the hair of her head, and kissed his feet
and anointed them with the ointment.

39 {But when}[g] the Pharisee {who
had invited him}[h] saw this, he said to
himself [saying],[i] "If this man were a
prophet, he would have known who
and what sort of woman this is who is
touching him, for she is a sinner."

40 And Jesus, answering, said to
him, "Simon, I have something to say
to you." And he said, "Teacher, say it."
41 [[He said,]][j] "There were two debtors
to a certain moneylender; one owed
five hundred denarii[k], and the other
fifty [[denarii]].[l] 42 [[But]][m] since they
had nothing to pay, he forgave them
both. Which [of them,][n] [[he said,]][o]
will love him more?" 43 [[But]][p] Simon
answered, "I suppose the one to whom
he forgave more." And {he}[q] said to
him, "You have judged rightly."

44 Then, turning to the woman, he
said to Simon, "Do you see this woman?
I entered your house; you gave me no
water for my feet, but she has wet my
feet with her tears and wiped them with
{her hair}.[r] 45 You gave me no kiss, but
she, since the time I came in, has not
ceased to kiss my feet. 46 You did not
anoint my head with oil, but she has
anointed [my feet][s] with ointment.

47 "[[Not]][t] For this reason I say to
you, {her many sins are forgiven}.[u] [For
she loved much; but to whom little is
forgiven, loves little.]"[v] 48 And he said to
her, "Your sins are forgiven."

[a] 7:31, **And the Lord said:** Included in TR.
[b] 7:32, **and:** Included in A(02) BYZ TR.
[c] 7:32, **to you:** Included in A(02) Latin(a b ff^2) BYZ TR.
[d] 7:33, **bread:** Absent from D(05) Latin(a b e ff^2 it) Syriac(sy^s sy^c).
[e] 7:33, **wine:** Absent from D(05) Latin(a b e ff^2 it) Syriac(sy^s sy^c).
[f] 7:35, **all:** Absent from D(05).
[g] 7:39, **But when:** Some manuscripts read "Seeing this." D(05).
[h] 7:39, **who had invited him:** Some manuscripts read "who was reclining with him." D(05) Latin(e).
[i] 7:39, **saying:** Absent from D(05).
[j] 7:41, **He said:** Included in D(05) Latin(ff^2).
[k] 7:41, **denarii:** A denarius was a day's wage for a laborer.
[l] 7:41, **denarii:** Included in D(05) Latin(a).
[m] 7:42, **but:** Included in 𝔓3 ℵ(01) A(02) W(032) BYZ TR || Absent from B(03) D(05) NA28 SBLGNT THGNT.
[n] 7:42, **of them:** Absent from D(05).
[o] 7:42, **he said:** Included in A(02) BYZ TR.
[p] 7:43, **But:** Included in 𝔓3 ℵ(01) A(02) BYZ TR THGNT || Absent from B(03) NA28 SBLGNT.
[q] 7:43, **he:** Some manuscripts read "Jesus." W(032) Latin(ff^2).
[r] 7:44, **her hair:** Some manuscripts read "the hairs of her head." BYZ TR.
[s] 7:46, **my feet:** Absent from D(05) W(032) Latin(a b e ff^2 it).
[t] 7:47, **Not:** Included in D(05).
[u] 7:47, **her many sins are forgiven:** Some manuscripts read "many are forgiven her." D(05) Latin(ff^2).
[v] 7:47, **For she loved much; but to whom little is forgiven, loves little:** Absent from D(05) Latin(e).

49 And those who were reclining
with him began to say among
themselves, "Who is this who even
forgives sins?"

50 And he said to the woman,
"[[Woman,]][a] Your faith has saved you;
go in peace."

8

1 And it came to pass afterward,
that he went throughout every city
and village, preaching and showing
the good news of the kingdom of God,
and the twelve [were][b] with him,
2 and certain women, who had been
healed of evil spirits and infirmities,
Mary called Magdalene, out of whom
went seven demons, 3 and Joanna,
the wife of Chuza, Herod's steward,
and Susanna, and many others,[c] who
[[also]][d] served {them}[e] from their
possessions.

4 As a large crowd was gathering
and people from town after town were
coming to him, he spoke {through a
parable}:[f]

5 "The sower went out to sow his
seed. And while [he was][g] sowing, some
fell by the road and was trampled, and
the birds [of the sky][h] ate {it}.[i] 6 [[But]]
Also some fell upon a rock, and as
soon as it grew, it withered away,
because it had no moisture. 7 And some
fell among thorns, and the thorns
grew up and choked {it}.[j] 8 And other
fell on[k] the good [[and beautiful]][l]
ground, and sprang up, and bore fruit a
hundredfold."

And when he had said these things,
he cried, "He who has ears to hear, let
him hear."

9 And his disciples were asking him
[[saying]],[m] "What might this parable
be?"

10 But he said, "To you it has been
given to know the mysteries [of the
kingdom][n] of God, but to the rest in
parables, so that seeing they may
not see and hearing they may not
understand."[o]

11 "Now this is the parable: The
seed is the word of God. 12 Those by the
wayside are the ones who {have heard;
then}[p] the devil comes and takes away
the word from their hearts, lest they
should believe and be saved.

13 "Those on the rock are the ones
who, when they hear, receive {the
word}[q] with joy; and [these][r] have no
root, who believe for a while and in
time of temptation fall away.[s]

---

[a] 7:50, **Woman:** Included in D(05).
[b] 8:1, **were:** Absent from D(05).
[c] 8:3, **and many others:** "And many others" is feminine indicating that these others were all women.
[d] 8:3, **also:** Included in D(05) Latin(it).
[e] 8:3, **them:** B(03) D(05) W(032) BYZ NA28 SBLGNT THGNT || Some manuscripts read "him." ℵ(01) A TR.
[f] 8:4, **through a parable:** Some manuscripts read "such a parable to them." D(05) Latin(it).
[g] 8:5, **he was:** Absent from D(05).
[h] 8:5, **of the sky:** Absent in some manuscripts. D(05) W(032) Latin(a b e ff^2 it) Syriac(sy^s sy^c sy^p).
[i] 8:5, **it:** Some manuscripts read "them." 𝔓75 B(03).
[j] 8:7, **it:** Some manuscripts read "them." 𝔓75.
[k] 8:8, **on:** Greek "into."
[l] 8:8, **and beautiful:** Included in D(05) Latin (a e) Syriac(sy^p).
[m] 8:9, **saying:** Included in A(02) BYZ TR.
[n] 8:10, **of the kingdom:** Absent from W(032) Latin(ff^2).
[o] 8:10, Isaiah 6:9 LXX.
[p] 8:12, **have heard; then:** D(05) manuscripts read "who follow, of whom."
[q] 8:13, **the word:** ℵ(01) reads "God."
[r] 8:13, **these:** Absent from D(05) Latin(e).
[s] 8:13, **fall away:** Or "stumble."

14 "The ones that fell among thorns are those who, when they have heard [[the word]],[a] [go out and][b] are choked with cares, [and][c] wealth, and pleasures of life, and bring no fruit to maturity.

15 "But the ones on the good ground, these are the ones who, having heard the word [[of God]][d] with a [good and][e] noble heart, hold it fast and bear fruit with patience.

16 "No one, after lighting a lamp, covers it with a vessel or puts it under [a bed],[f] but {puts it}[g] on a lampstand [, so that those who enter may see the light].[h]

17 "[For][i] Nothing is hidden that will not be revealed, nor anything secret that will not be known and come to light.

18 "Therefore, be careful how you listen; for whoever has, to them will be given; and whoever does not have, even what they think they have will be taken away from them."

19 But his mother and his brothers came to him, but they could not reach him because of the crowd. 20 And it was reported to him [[that,]][j] "Your mother and your brothers are standing outside, {wanting to see you}."[k] 21 But he answered and said to them, "My mother and my brothers, these are the ones {hearing and doing the word of God}."[l]

22 {Now}[m] it happened one of those days that he got into a boat with his disciples, and he said to them, "Let us go over to the other side of the lake." And they set out. 23 As they were sailing, he fell asleep. And a [[great]][n] windstorm came down on the lake, and [{they were}[o] filling *with water* and][p] they were in danger.

24 Approaching, they woke him up, saying, "{Master, Master},[q] we are perishing!" But {having been awakened},[r] he rebuked the wind and the wave [of the water];[s] and they ceased, and there was a calm.

25 He said to them, "Where is your faith?" And they were afraid and marveled, saying to one another, "Who then is this, that he commands even the winds and the water, and they obey him?"

26 And they sailed to the country of the {Gerasenes},[t] which is opposite Galilee.

---

a 8:14, **the word:** Included in Latin(a) Syriac(sy^c sy^p).

b 8:14, **go out and:** Absent from Latin(e).

c 8:14, **and:** Absent from D(05).

d 8:15, **of God:** Included in D(05).

e 8:15, **good and:** Absent from D(05) Latin(it).

f 8:16, **a bed:** Absent from Latin(b).

g 8:16, **puts it:** 𝔓75 ℵ(01) B(03) D(05) NA28 SBLGNT THGNT ‖ Some manuscripts read "sets it." A(02) W(032) BYZ TR.

h 8:16, **so that those who enter may see the light:** Absent from 𝔓75 B(03).

i 8:17, **For:** Absent from W(032).

j 8:20, **that:** Included in ℵ(01) D(05) Latin(a b e ff2 it) ‖ Some manuscripts read "saying." A(02) BYZ TR ‖ Absent from 𝔓75 B(03) W(032) NA28 SBLGNT THGNT.

k 8:20, **wanting to see you:** Some manuscripts read "seeking you." D(05).

l 8:21, **hearing and doing the word of God:** Some manuscripts read "who hear the word of God and do it." 𝔓75 BYZ TR.

m 8:22, **Now:** Some manuscripts read "And." BYZ TR.

n 8:23, **great:** Included in D(05).

o 8:23, **they were:** Some manuscripts read "the ship was." Latin(b ff2).

p 8:23, **they were filling with water and:** Absent from Latin(e).

q 8:24, **Master, Master:** Some manuscripts read "Lord, Lord." D(05) Syriac(sy^c) ‖ Some manuscripts read "Master" once. W(032).

r 8:24, **having been awakened:** Some manuscripts read "having risen." D(05).

s 8:24, **of the water:** Absent from D(05).

t 8:26, **Gerasenes:** Some manuscripts read "Gadarenes." A(02) W(032) BYZ TR.

27 When {he}[a] went out [onto the land],[b] a [certain][c] man [from the city][d] met him, {who had demons, and for a considerable time he did not wear a garment},[e] and he did not stay in a house, but in the tombs. 28 Seeing Jesus, {he cried out}[f] [and fell before him,][g] {and with a loud voice said [[to him]][h]},[i] "What have I to do with you, [Jesus,][j] Son of the Most High [God]?[k] I beg you, do not torment me." 29 For he had commanded the unclean spirit to come out of the man. For many times it had seized him, {and}[l] he was kept bound with chains and shackles, but he would break the chains {and be}[m] driven [by the demon][n] into the wilderness. 30 Jesus asked him [[saying,]][o] "What is your name?" And he said, {"Legion," because many demons had entered him}.[p] 31 {And they were begging [him][q] not to}[r] command them to go into the abyss.

32 There was a herd of pigs there, [a considerable number,][s] feeding [on the mountain];[t] and they begged him to allow them to enter {those};[u] and {he}[v] allowed them.

33 And the demons, having come out of the man, {entered}[w] into the pigs; and the herd rushed down the cliff into the lake and were drowned.

34 And when the herdsmen saw [what had happened],[x] they fled and reported it in the city and in the fields. 35 {And they came to see what had happened, and they came to Jesus, and found the man from whom the demons had gone out},[y] clothed and in his right mind, sitting at the feet of Jesus; [and][z] they were afraid. 36 {And

---

a 8:27, **he:** D(05) reads "they." BYZ TR.

b 8:27, **onto the land:** Absent from Latin(a ff²).

c 8:27, **certain:** Absent from D(05) Latin(a).

d 8:27, **from the city:** Absent from Latin(a ff²).

e 8:27, **who had demons, and for a considerable time he did not wear a garment:** NA28 SBLGNT THGNT ‖ Some manuscripts read "who had demons for a considerable time. He did not wear a garment." D(05) Latin (e)BYZ TR.

f 8:28, **he cried out:** Some manuscripts read "and crying out." BYZ TR.

g 8:28, **and fell before him:** Absent from D(05) Latin(e).

h 8:28, **to him:** Included in W(032).

i 8:28, **and with a loud voice said:** Some manuscripts read "with a loud voice and said." D(05).

j 8:28, **Jesus:** Absent from 𝔓75 D(05) Latin(e).

k 8:28, **God:** Absent from D(05).

l 8:29, **and:** Some manuscripts read "for." D(05) BYZ TR.

m 8:29, **and be:** Some manuscripts read "for he was." D(05) Latin(e).

n 8:29, **by the demon:** Absent from Latin(ff²).

o 8:30, **saying:** Included in A(02) C(04) D(05) W(032) BYZ TR ‖ Absent from 𝔓75 ℵ(01) B(03) Latin(a b e ff²) NA28 SBLGNT THGNT.

p 8:30, **Legion, because...:** Some manuscripts read "Legion is my name, for we are many demons." BYZ TR.

q 8:31, **him:** Absent from D(05) W(032) Latin(ff²).

r 8:31, **And they were begging him not to:** Some manuscripts read "But he was begging that he would not." BYZ TR ‖ Some manuscripts read "But they were begging that he would not." D(05).

s 8:32, **a considerable number:** Absent from D(05).

t 8:32, **on the mountain:** Absent from Latin(a b ff²).

u 8:32, **those:** Some manuscripts read "the pigs." D(05) Latin(c it).

v 8:32, **he:** W(032) reads "Jesus."

w 8:33, **entered:** Some manuscripts read "rushed." D(05).

x 8:34, **what had happened:** Absent from Latin(a).

y 8:35, **And they came:** D(05) reads "But when they came from the city and saw the demon-possessed man."

z 8:35, **and:** Absent from D(05).

they [who saw it][a] reported to them
how the demon-possessed man had
been healed}.[b]

37 And {the whole crowd}[c] of the
region of the {Gerasenes}[d] asked {him}[e]
to depart from them, for they were
seized with great fear; but he, having
entered [into {a}[f] boat],[g] returned.

38 [But the man from whom the
demons had gone out was begging
him to be with him;][h] But {he}[i] sent
him away, saying, 39 "{Return to your
house and tell}[j] what God has done [for
you]."[k]

And {he went throughout the
[whole][l] city, proclaiming what}[m] Jesus
had done for him.

40 But when Jesus was returning [[it
happened that]][n] the crowd welcomed
him, for they were all expecting him.

41 [And behold,][o] A man [[of the
synagogue]][p] [named Jairus][q] came;
[and he was][r] a ruler of the synagogue.
And falling at the feet of Jesus, he
pleaded with him to come to his house,
42 for he had an only daughter, [about][s]
twelve years old, [and she][t] was dying.
As he was going, the crowds were
pressing against him.

43 And a [[certain]][u] woman
who had a flow of blood for twelve
years, [having spent all her life on
physicians][v] {was not able to be healed
by anyone},[w] 44 approaching [from
behind],[x] she touched [the fringe of][y]
his garment,[z] and immediately her flow
of blood ceased.

45 And Jesus [[knowing that power
had gone out from him,]][a] {said},[b]
"Who touched me?" When all denied
it, Peter [[and those with him]][c] said,
"Master, the crowds surround you and

---

[a] 8:36, **who saw it:** Absent from Syriac(sy^{s} sy^{c}).
[b] 8:36, **And they...:** D(05) reads "For those who saw reported to them how the man of the legion was saved."
[c] 8:37, **the whole crowd:** D(05) reads "everyone."
[d] 8:37, **Gerasenes:** Some manuscripts read "Gadarenes." A(02) BYZ TR.
[e] 8:37, **him:** D(05) reads "Jesus."
[f] 8:37, **a:** Some manuscripts read "the." A(02) W(032) BYZ TR.
[g] 8:37, **into a boat:** Absent from D(05).
[h] 8:38, **begging him to be:** Absent from W(032).
[i] 8:38, **he:** 𝔓75 ℵ(01) B(03) D(05) Latin(b ff^{2}) || Some manuscripts read "Jesus." A(02) C(04) Latin(a) BYZ TR.
[j] 8:39, **Return to your house and tell:** D(05) reads "Go to your house, telling."
[k] 8:39, **you:** Absent from Latin(b).
[l] 8:39, **whole:** Absent from D(05).
[m] 8:39, **he went throughout the whole city, proclaiming what:** D(05) reads "having gone throughout the city, he proclaimed all that."
[n] 8:40, **it happened that:** Included in ℵ(01) A(02) C(04) D(05) W(032) Latin(a b ff^{2}) BYZ TR || Absent from 𝔓75 B(03) NA28 SBLGNT THGNT.
[o] 8:41, **And behold:** Absent from D(05).
[p] 8:41, **of the synagogue:** Absent from D(05).
[q] 8:41, **named Jairus:** Absent from D(05).
[r] 8:41, **and he was:** Absent from D(05) Latin(a ff^{2}).
[s] 8:42, **about:** Absent from D(05).
[t] 8:42, **and she:** Absent from D(05).
[u] 8:43, **certain:** Included in Latin(a b ff^{2}).
[v] 8:43, **having spent all her life on physicians:** ℵ(01) A(02) C(04) W(032) Latin(a b ff^{2}) BYZ TR NA28[] SBLGNT THGNT || Absent from 𝔓75 B(03) D(05).
[w] 8:43, **was not able to be healed by anyone:** D(05) reads "and no one could heal her."
[x] 8:44, **behind:** Absent from D(05).
[y] 8:44, **the fringe of:** Or hem. Absent from D(05) Latin(a ff^{2} it).
[z] 8:44, **garment:** Or cloak.
[a] 8:45, **knowing that power had gone out from him:** Included in D(05) Latin(a).
[b] 8:45, **said:** Some manuscripts read "asked." D(05) Latin(a).
[c] 8:45, **and those with him:** Included in ℵ(01) A(02) C(04) D(05) W(032) BYZ TR THGNT || Absent from 𝔓75 B(03) NA28 SBLGNT.

press in on you. [[And you say, ‘Who
touched me?’]]”[a] 46 But {Jesus}[b] said,
“Someone touched me, for I knew
power had gone out from me.”

47 [But the woman realizing that
she had not gone unnoticed, came
{trembling}[c]][d] and falling down at his
feet, she explained in front of all [the
people][e] [why she had touched him
and][f] how she had been immediately
healed. 48 And {he}[g] said to her,
“Daughter, [[take heart]][h] your faith
has saved you; go in peace.”

49 While he was still speaking,
{someone}[i] came from the ruler of the
synagogue's house, saying [[to him]],[j]
“Your daughter is dead; do not trouble
the Teacher.” 50 But Jesus, having
heard [[the word]],[k] responded to him
[[saying]],[l] “Do not fear; only believe,
and she will be saved.”

51 {But when he came into}[m] the
house, he did not allow anyone to
enter [with him],[n] except Peter, {John,
and James},[o] and the girl's father and
mother. 52 And all were weeping and
mourning for her. But he said, “Do not
weep, for she is not dead but sleeping.”
53 And they laughed at him, knowing
that she was dead. 54 But he [[having
sent everyone out,]] [p]taking her by the
hand, called out saying, “Child, arise.”

55 And her spirit returned, [and she
rose immediately,][q] and he directed
that something should be given her
to eat.

56 And her parents [[observing,]][r]
were amazed, but he charged them to
tell no one what had happened.

9 1 And having called together {the}[s]
twelve [[apostles]],[t] he gave
them power and authority over all the
demons and to heal diseases, 2 and he
sent them to proclaim the kingdom of
God and to heal [the sick].[u]

3 And he said to them, “Take
nothing for the journey, neither a staff,
nor a bag, nor bread, nor money, nor
[even][v] two tunics to wear. 4 And into
whatever house you enter, there stay
and from there depart. 5 And whoever
does not receive you, when you leave
that city, shake off [[even]][w] the dust
from your feet as a testimony against
them.”

---

a 8:45, **and you say, Who touched me?:** Included in A(02) C(04) D(05) W(032) BYZ TR || Absent from 𝔓75 א(01) B(03) NA28 SBLGNT THGNT.

b 8:46, **Jesus:** Some manuscripts read “he.” D(05) Latin(a).

c 8:47, **trembling:** D(05) reads “being in awe.”

d 8:47, **But the woman realizing...:** Absent from א(01).

e 8:47, **the people:** Absent from Latin (b).

f 8:47, **why she had touched him and:** Absent from א(01).

g 8:48, **he:** Some manuscripts read “Jesus.” C(04).

h 8:48, **take heart:** Included in A(02) C(04) W(032) BYZ TR || Absent from 𝔓75 א(01) B(03) D(05) Latin(a b ff^2) NA28 SBLGNT THGNT.

i 8:49, **someone:** Absent from some manuscripts which would be rendered “they.” D(05) Latin(a b).

j 8:49, **to him:** Included in A(02) C(04) D(05) W(032) Latin (a b) BYZ TR || Absent from א(01) B(03) NA28 Latin(e) SBLGNT THGNT.

k 8:50, **having heard:** Included in D(05) Latin(a b e ff^2).

l 8:50, **saying:** Included in A(02) C(04) D(05) W(032) BYZ TR.

m 8:51, **But when he came into:** Some manuscripts read “But entering.” D(05).

n 8:51, **with him:** Absent from A(02) W(032) BYZ TR.

o 8:51, **John, and James:** Some manuscripts read “James, and John.” א(01) A(02).

p 8:54, **having sent everyone out:** Included in A(02) C(04) BYZ TR.

q 8:55, **and she rose immediately:** Absent from א(01).

r 8:56, **observing:** Included in D(05).

s 9:1, **the:** Some manuscripts read “his.” TR Latin(b ff^2).

t 9:1, **apostles:** Included in א(01) C(04) Latin(a e) || Others read “disciples.” Latin(b ff^2) TR || Absent from 𝔓75 A(02) B(03) D(05) W(032) BYZ NA28 SBLGNT THGNT.

u 9:2, **the sick:** Absent from B(03).

v 9:3, **even:** A(02) D(05) W(032) BYZ TR NA28[] THGNT || Absent from א(01) B(03) C(04) Latin(a b e ff^2) SBLGNT.

w 9:5, **even:** 𝔓75 א(01) B(03) C(04) D(05) W(032) NA28 SBLGNT THGNT || Included in A(02) BYZ TR.

6 And going out, they went {through the villages},ᵃ preaching the gospel and healing everywhere.

7 But Herod the tetrarch heard about [all]ᵇ these things [[by him]],ᶜ and he was perplexed because some were saying that John had been raised from the dead. 8 But some [[were saying]]ᵈ that Elijah had appeared, and by others that one of the ancient prophets had risen.

9 Herod said [[that]],ᵉ "John I beheaded; but who is this about whom I hear such things?" And he sought to see him.

10 And the apostles, having returned, reported to him all that they had done. And taking them with him, he withdrew privately [[into a desert place]]ᶠ [of a city]ᵍ [called Bethsaida].ʰ 11 But the crowds, having learned of it, followed him; and welcoming them, he spoke to them about the kingdom of God, and healed {those in need of healing}.ⁱ

12 Now the day began to decline; and the twelve, having approached, said to him, "Dismiss the crowd, so that they may go into the surrounding villages and fields and find lodging [and provisions],ʲ for we are here in a desolate place."

13 But {he}ᵏ said to them, "You give them something to eat." And they said, "We have no more than five loaves and two fish, unless we go and buy food for all these people." 14 For there were about five thousand men. And he said to {his}ˡ disciples, "Have them sit down in groups of [about]ᵐ fifty each." 15 And they did so. [And they made them all sit down.]ⁿ

16 Having taken the five loaves and the two fish, he looked up to heaven and blessed [them].ᵒ [And he broke *them*]ᵖ And he gave *them* to the disciples to set before the crowd. 17 And they all ate and were satisfied, and the leftover fragments filled twelve baskets.

ᵃ 9:6, **through the villages:** D(05) reads "from city to city." ‖ Some manuscripts read "through cities and villages." Latin(a b ff² it).

ᵇ 9:7, **all:** Absent from D(05) Latin(a b e ff²).

ᶜ 9:7, **by him:** Included in A(02) W(032) BYZ TR ‖ Absent from 𝔓75 ℵ(01) B(03) C(04) D(05) NA28 SBLGNT THGNT.

ᵈ 9:8, **were saying:** Included in W(032).

ᵉ 9:9, **that:** Included in C(04) D(05).

ᶠ 9:10, **into a desert place:** Included in ℵ(01) A(02) C(04) W(032) Latin(a b e ff²) BYZ TR ‖ Absent from 𝔓75 B(03) D(05) NA28 SBLGNT THGNT.

ᵍ 9:10, **of a city:** Absent from 𝔓75 ℵ(01) B(03) SBLGNT ‖ Some manuscripts read "of a village." D(05).

ʰ 9:10, **called Bethsaida:** Absent from ℵ(01) Syriac(syᶜ).

ⁱ 9:11, **those in need of healing:** D(05) reads "all of their diseases."

ʲ 9:12, **and provisions:** Absent from D(05).

ᵏ 9:13, **he:** Some manuscripts read "Jesus." C(04) Latin(ff²).

ˡ 9:14, **his:** Some manuscripts read "the." Latin(b e).

ᵐ 9:14, **about:** ℵ(01) B(03) C(04) D(05) NA28[] SBLGNT THGNT ‖ Absent from A(02) W(032) Latin(a b ff²) BYZ TR.

ⁿ 9:15, **And they made them all sit down:** Absent from D(05).

ᵒ 9:16, **them:** Absent from ℵ(01).

ᵖ 9:16, **and he broke them:** Absent from D(05).

18 And it happened that [while]ᵃ he was [praying]ᵇ alone, {the}ᶜ disciples {were with}ᵈ him, and {he}ᵉ asked them, saying, "Who do the crowds say that I am?" 19 But they answered, saying, "John the Baptist, but others say Elijah; {others yet that a certain prophet of the ancients has risen}."ᶠ 20 He said to them, "But who do you say that I am?" Peter answered and said, "The Christᵍ [[, Son]]ʰ of God."

21 And he, having rebuked them, commanded them not to tell this to anyone, 22 saying that the Son of Man must suffer many things and be rejected by the elders and chief priests and scribes, and be killed, and {on the third [day]ⁱ be raised}.ʲ

23 He said to all, "If anyone wishes to follow me, let him deny himself [and take up his cross]ᵏ [daily]ˡ and follow me. 24 For whoever wishes to save {his}ᵐ life will lose it, but whoever loses his life for my sake, this one will save it. 25 For what does it profit a man to gain the whole world, but lose or forfeit himself?

26 "For whoever is ashamed of me and those [words]ⁿ of mine, the Son of Man will be ashamed of him when he comes in his glory and the glory of {the}ᵒ Father and the holy angels.

27 "Truly I say to you, [[truly]]ᵖ there are some standing here who will not taste death until they see the {kingdom of God}."ᑫ

28 Now it happened after these words, about eight days [and]ʳ taking Peter, John, and James, he went up on the mountain to pray. 29 And it happened while he was praying, the appearance of his face changed and his clothing became dazzling white.

30 And behold, two men were talking with him, who were Moses and Elijah, 31 who, appearing in glory, spoke of his departure,ˢ which he was about to fulfill [in Jerusalem].ᵗ

32 But Peter and those with him were weighed down with sleep; having fully awakened, they saw his glory and the two men standing with him.

ᵃ 9:18, **while:** Absent from Latin(a b e ff²).

ᵇ 9:18, **praying:** Absent from D(05) Latin (a e) Syriac(syᶜ).

ᶜ 9:18, **the:** Some manuscripts read "his." W(032) Latin(a).

ᵈ 9:18, **were with:** literally "understood with him." That is, "were reasoning with him." ‖ Some manuscripts read "met with." B(03).

ᵉ 9:18, **he:** Some manuscripts read "Jesus." ℵ(01).

ᶠ 9:19, **others yet that a certain prophet of the ancients has risen:** Some manuscripts read "or one of the prophets." D(05) Latin(e).

ᵍ 9:20, **Christ:** See footnote for Christ in Luke 2:11.

ʰ 9:20, **Son:** Included in D(05) Latin(e).

ⁱ 9:22, **day:** Absent from 𝔓75.

ʲ 9:22, **on the third day be raised:** Some manuscripts read "after three days rise again." D(05) Latin(it).

ᵏ 9:23, **and take up his cross:** Absent from D(05) Latin (a).

ˡ 9:23, **daily:** Absent from C(04) D(05) Latin(a b e ff² it) Syriac(syˢ).

ᵐ 9:24, **his:** W(032) reads "the."

ⁿ 9:26, **words:** Absent from D(05) Latin(a e) Syriac(syᶜ).

ᵒ 9:26, **the:** D(05) reads "his."

ᵖ 9:27, **truly:** Included in 𝔓45 D(05).

ᑫ 9:27, **kingdom of God:** D(05) reads "Son of Man coming in his glory."

ʳ 9:28, **and:** A(02) C(04) D(05) W(032) BYZ TR NA28[] THGNT ‖ Absent from 𝔓45 ℵ(01) B(03) THGNT.

ˢ 9:31, **departure:** The Greek word for *departure* is defined by BDAG as: (1) movement from one geographical area to another, departure, path, course or (2) departure from among the living (BDAG, ἔξοδος).

ᵗ 9:31, **in Jerusalem:** Absent from Latin(e).

33 And it happened as they were parting from him, Peter said [to Jesus],[a] "Master, it is good for us to be here, and let us make three tents, one for you, one for Moses, and one for Elijah," not knowing what he was saying.

34 While he was saying these things, a cloud came and overshadowed them; and they were afraid as they entered the cloud. 35 And a voice came from the cloud, [saying],[b] "This is my {chosen}[c] Son [[, in whom I am well pleased]];[d] listen to him." 36 And [[it happened]][e] when {the voice}[f] had occurred, Jesus was found alone. They reported to no one in those days, [nothing][g] of what they had seen.

37 Now it happened {on the next day},[h] when they had come down from the mountain, that a large crowd met him.

38 And behold, a man from the crowd cried out, saying, "Teacher, I beg you to look at my son, for he is my only child. 39 {And behold, a spirit seizes him, and he suddenly cries out and it convulses him},[i] with foam, and it hardly departs from him crushing[j] him. 40 I asked your disciples to cast it out, but they were not able."

41 Jesus [answered and][k] said, "O faithless and perverse generation, how long will I be with you and bear with you? Bring your son [here]."[l]

42 While he was still approaching, the demon tore him and convulsed him. But Jesus rebuked the unclean spirit, {healed the boy},[m] and gave him back to his father.

43 But all were astonished at the greatness of God. And while everyone was marveling at all the things that {he was doing},[n] {he}[o] said to his disciples, 44 "Put these words into your ears: for the Son of Man is about to be delivered into the hands of men." 45 But they did not understand this statement, and it was concealed from them so that they would not perceive it; and they were afraid to ask [him][p] about this statement.

---

a 9:33, **to Jesus:** Absent from Latin(a b ff²).

b 9:35, **saying:** Absent from 𝔓45 Latin(b).

c 9:35, **chosen:** 𝔓45 𝔓75 ℵ(01) B(03) NA28 SBLGNT THGNT ‖ Some manuscripts read "beloved." A(02) C(04) D(05) W(032) BYZ TR.

d 9:35, **in whom I am well pleased:** Included in D(05).

e 9:36, **it happened:** Included in 𝔓45.

f 9:36, **the voice:** Latin(e) reads "this."

g 9:36, **nothing:** Absent from 𝔓45 D(05).

h 9:37, **on the next day:** Some manuscripts read "during the day." 𝔓45 D(05) Latin(a b e ff² it) Syriac(sy^s).

i 9:39, **And behold, a spirit seizes him, and he suddenly cries out and it convulses him:** Some manuscripts read "For a spirit seizes him suddenly, and he shrieks and convulses." D(05) Latin(a e ff²).

j 9:39, **crushing:** Or "bruising."

k 9:41, **answered and:** Absent from C(04).

l 9:41, **here:** Absent from D(05).

m 9:42, **healed the boy:** D(05) and an early Latin manuscript (e) reads "And it left him."

n 9:43, **he was doing:** 𝔓75 ℵ(01) B(03) D(05) ‖ Some manuscripts read "Jesus did" or "Jesus was doing." A(02) C(04) W(032) BYZ TR.

o 9:43, **he:** Some manuscripts read "Jesus." A(02) W(032) BYZ TR.

p 9:45, **him:** Absent from D(05) Latin(e).

46 [But a dispute arose among them
as to][a] {"What might be greater than
these?"}[b] 47 But Jesus, {knowing}[c] the
thoughts of their hearts, took a child
and placed it by himself 48 and said [to
them],[d] "Whoever receives this child in
my name receives me; and [whoever
receives me, receives][e] the one who
sent me; for the one who is least among
all of you, this one {is}[f] great."

49 But John answered, "Master, we
saw someone casting out demons in
your name, and we tried to stop him,
because he does not follow with us."

50 Jesus said [to him],[g] "Do not
hinder [him]."[h] For {whoever is not
against you, is for you.}[i]

51 Now it came to pass, when the
days were approaching for him to be
taken up, that he set his face to go [to
Jerusalem].[j] 52 And he sent messengers
ahead [of him.][k] [And they [went and][l]
entered a village of the Samaritans to
make preparations for him;][m] 53 but they
did not receive him, because his face
was set toward Jerusalem.

54 Seeing this, {the}[n] disciples James
and John said, "Lord, do you want
us to call down fire from heaven and
consume them [[just as Elijah did]]?"[o]
55 But he turned and rebuked them.
[[And he said, "You do not know what
manner of spirit you are of;]][p] [[for
the Son of Man came not to destroy
people's lives but to save them."]][q]
56 And they went on to another village.

57 And [[it happened]][r] as they
were going on the road, someone said
to him,"[[Lord]][s] I will follow you
wherever you go." 58 And Jesus said to
him, "The foxes have dens and the birds
of the sky have nests, but the Son of
Man has nowhere to lay his head."

59 He said to another, "Follow me."
But he said, "[Lord,][t] allow me [first][u]
to go and bury my father."

60 But {he}[v] said to him, "Let the
dead to bury their own dead, but you
go and proclaim the kingdom of God."

---

a 9:46, **But a dispute arose among them as to:** Absent from D(05).

b 9:46, **What might be greater than these:** Or "Who might be the greatest among them."

c 9:47, **knowing:** ℵ(01) B(03) NA28 SBLGNT THGNT || Some manuscripts read "seeing." A(02) C(04) D(05) W(032) BYZ TR.

d 9:48, **to them:** Absent from 𝔓45 D(05) Latin(a b e ff^{2}) Syriac(sy^{s} sy^{c}).

e 9:48, **whoever receives me, receives:** Absent from D(05).

f 9:48, **is:** 𝔓45 𝔓75 ℵ(01) B(03) C(04) NA28 SBLGNT THGNT || Some manuscripts read "will be." A(02) D(05) W(032) BYZ TR.

g 9:50, **to him:** Absent from D(05) Latin(e).

h 9:50, **him:** Absent from C(04) D(05).

i 9:50, **whoever is not against you, is for you:** 𝔓45 reads "it is not against you, nor for you."

j 9:51, **to Jerusalem:** Absent from Latin(b).

k 9:52, **of him:** Absent from 𝔓45 Latin(e).

l 9:52, **went and:** Absent from Latin(e).

m 9:52, **and they went and entered...:** Absent from Latin(e).

n 9:54, **the:** 𝔓45 𝔓75 ℵ(01) B(03) Latin(e) NA28 SBLGNT THGNT || Some manuscripts read "his." A(02) C(04) D(05) W(032) Latin(a b) BYZ TR.

o 9:54, **just as Elijah did:** Included in A(02) C(04) D(05) W(032) BYZ TR || Absent from 𝔓45 𝔓75 ℵ(01) B(03) NA28 SBLGNT THGNT.

p 9:55, **And he said, You do not know what manner of spirit you are of:** Included in D(05) Latin(it) Syriac(sy^{c} sy^{p}) BYZ TR.

q 9:55, **for the Son of Man came not to destroy people's lives but to save them:** Included in Latin(it) Syriac(sy^{c} sy^{p}) BYZ TR.

r 9:57, **it happened:** Included in A(02) D(05) W(032) Latin(a b e) BYZ TR.

s 9:57, **Lord:** Included in A(02) C(04) W(032) BYZ TR || Absent from 𝔓45 𝔓75 ℵ(01) B(03) D(05).

t 9:59, **Lord:** 𝔓45 𝔓75 ℵ(01) A(02) C(04) W(032) BYZ TR NA28[] SBLGNT THGNT || Absent from B(03) D(05) Syriac(sy^{s}).

u 9:59, **first:** Absent from W(032).

v 9:60, **he:** Some manuscripts read "Jesus." A(02) C(04) W(032) Latin(b e) BYZ TR.

61 Another also said, "I will follow you, Lord; but first allow me to say goodbye to those in my house." 62 But Jesus said [to him],ᵃ "No one {who puts {the}ᵇ hand to the plow and looks back}ᶜ is fit for the kingdom of God."

10 1 [After this,]ᵈ {The Lord}ᵉ appointed {seventy-two}ᶠ others and sent [them]ᵍ two by two ahead of him; [two]ʰ to every town and place where he was about to go.

2 [[Therefore]]ⁱ He said to them, "[Indeed,]ʲ The harvest is plentiful, but the workers are few; [therefore],ᵏ pray to [the Lord]ˡ of the harvest to send out workers into his harvest.

3 "Go; behold, I am sending you out as lambs among wolves. 4 Do not carry a money bag, do not *carry* a sack, do not *wear* sandals, [and]ᵐ greet no one on the road.

5 "When you enter a house, [first]ⁿ say, 'Peace to this house.' 6 And if [[indeed]]ᵒ a son of peace is there, your peace will rest on him; if not, it will return to you. 7 Stay in that house, eating [and drinking]ᵖ what they provide, for the worker is worthy of his wages. Do not move from house to house. 8 When you enter a town and they welcome you, eat what is set before you 9 and heal the sick there, and say to them, 'The kingdom of God has come near to you.'

10 "But when you enter a town and they do not welcome you, go out into its streets and say, 11 'And the dust [that clung to us]�q from {your}ʳ city, we wipe off [against you]ˢ [from our feet].'ᵗ But know this, that it has drawn near; [[upon you]]ᵘ the kingdom of God has come. 12 [[But]]ᵛ I say to you, that it will be more bearable for Sodom {on that day}ʷ than for that city.

ᵃ 9:62, **to him:** ℵ(01) A(02) C(04) D(05) W(032) BYZ TR NA28[] THGNT ‖ Absent from 𝔓45 𝔓75 B(03) SBLGNT.

ᵇ 9:62, **the:** 𝔓75 B(03) NA28 SBLGNT ‖ Some manuscripts read "his." 𝔓45 ℵ(01) A(02) C(04) D(05) W(032) BYZ TR THGNT.

ᶜ 9:62, **who puts the hand to the plow and looks back:** Some manuscripts read "having put his hand to the plow and looking back." 𝔓45 D(05) Latin(it).

ᵈ 10:1, **After this:** Absent from D(05) Latin(a b e it).

ᵉ 10:1, **The Lord:** Some manuscripts read "he." D(05) Latin(a e it).

ᶠ 10:1, **seventy-two:** B(03) D(05) Latin(a b e) NA28[] SBLGNT ‖ Some manuscripts read "seventy." ℵ(01) A(02) C(04) W(032) Syriac(syˢ syᶜ) BYZ TR THGNT.

ᵍ 10:1, **them:** Absent from 𝔓75 B(03) Latin(e).

ʰ 10:1, **two:** B(03) NA28[] SBLGNT ‖ Absent from ℵ(01) A(02) C(04) D(05) W(032) BYZ TR THGNT.

ⁱ 10:2, **Therefore:** Included in BYZ TR.

ʲ 10:2, **indeed:** Absent from D(05) Latin(a e).

ᵏ 10:2, **therefore:** Absent from D(05).

ˡ 10:2, **the Lord:** D(05) reads "God."

ᵐ 10:4, **and:** Absent from ℵ(01).

ⁿ 10:5, **first:** Absent from Latin(e).

ᵒ 10:6, **indeed:** Included in TR.

ᵖ 10:7, **and drinking:** Absent from W(032).

q 10:11, **that clung to us:** Absent from 𝔓45.

ʳ 10:11, **your:** Some manuscripts read "the." 𝔓45 W(032).

ˢ 10:11, **against you:** Absent from 𝔓45.

ᵗ 10:11, **from our feet:** Absent from BYZ TR.

ᵘ 10:11, **upon you:** Included in A(02) C(04) W(032) BYZ TR. ‖ Absent from 𝔓45 𝔓75 ℵ(01) B(03) D(05) Latin(a b e) NA28 SBLGNT THGNT.

ᵛ 10:12, **But:** Included in ℵ(01) D(05) TR.

ʷ 10:12, **on that day:** Some manuscripts read "in the kingdom of God." D(05) Latin(e).

13 "Woe to you, Chorazin! {Woe to you,}[a] Bethsaida! For if the miracles that were done in you had been done in Tyre and Sidon, long ago, [sitting][b] in sackcloth and ashes, they would have repented 14 {But it will be more bearable for Tyre and Sidon [in the judgment][c] than for you.}[d]

15 "And you, Capernaum, {will you be exalted to heaven?}[e] You will {descend}[f] to Hades.

16 "{The one hearing you hears me, and the one rejecting you rejects me; but the one rejecting me rejects the one who sent me}."[g]

17 And the {seventy-two}[h] returned with joy, saying, "Lord, even the demons are subject to us in your name." 18 And he said to them, "I saw Satan fall like lightning from heaven. 19 Behold, {I have given}[i] you authority to tread on serpents and scorpions, and over all the power of the enemy, and nothing will [by no means][j] harm you.

20 "However, do not rejoice in this, that the {spirits}[k] are subject to you, but [[rather]][l] rejoice that your names are written in the heavens."

21 At that very hour, {he}[m] rejoiced [in][n] the [Holy][o] Spirit and said, "I thank you,[p] Father, Lord of heaven [and earth],[q] because you have hidden these things from the wise and intelligent and revealed them to infants; yes, Father, {for this was well-pleasing in your sight}.[r]

22 [[And turning to the disciples, he said,]][s] "All things have been handed over to me by {my}[t] Father, and no one knows who the Son is except the Father, and who the Father is except the Son and to whom the Son chooses to reveal him."

---

a 10:13, **Woe to you:** Some manuscripts read "and." D(05) Latin(it).

b 10:13, **sitting:** Absent from Latin(e).

c 10:14, **in the judgment:** Absent from 𝔓45 D(05) Latin(e).

d 10:14, **But it will be more bearable…:** D(05) reads "But for Tyre and Sidon it will be more tolerable than for us."

e 10:15, **will you be exalted to heaven:** 𝔓45 𝔓75 ℵ(01) B(03) D(05) NA28 SBLGNT THGNT ‖ Some manuscripts read "It was lifted up to the heaven." A(02) C(04) W(032) BYZ TR.

f 10:15, **descend:** 𝔓75 B(03) D(05) NA28 ‖ Some manuscripts read "brought down." 𝔓45 ℵ(01) A(02) C(04) W(032) BYZ TR SBLGNT THGNT.

g 10:16, **The one hearing…:** Some manuscripts read "The one who hears you hears me, and the one who rejects you rejects me. And the one who hears me hears the one who sent me." D(05) Latin(it). ‖ Some manuscripts include this statement in addition to "but the one rejecting me rejects the one who sent me." Syriac(sy^s sy^c).

h 10:17, **seventy-two:** B(03) D(05) Latin(a b e) Syriac(sy^s) NA28[] SBLGNT ‖ Some manuscripts read "seventy." ℵ(01) A(02) C(04) W(032) Syriac(sy^c sy^p) BYZ TR THGNT.

i 10:19, **I have given:** 𝔓75 ℵ(01) B(03) NA28 SBLGNT THGNT ‖ Some manuscripts read "I give." 𝔓45 A(02) D(05) BYZ TR.

j 10:19, **by no means:** Absent from ℵ(01) D(05).

k 10:20, **spirits:** Some manuscripts read "demons." D(05) Latin(e) Syriac(sy^s sy^c sy^p).

l 10:20, **rather:** Included in TR.

m 10:21, **he:** 𝔓45 𝔓75 ℵ(01) B(03) D(05) Latin(a b) Syriac(sy^s sy^c) NA28 SBLGNT THGNT ‖ Some manuscripts read "Jesus." A(02) C(04) W(032) Latin(e ff²) Syriac(sy^p) BYZ TR.

n 10:21, **in:** 𝔓45 ℵ(01) D(05) NA28[] ‖ Absent from 𝔓75 A(02) B(03) C(04) NA28 SBLGNT THGNT.

o 10:21, **Holy:** 𝔓75 ℵ(01) B(03) C(04) D(05) Latin(a b e ff²) NA28[] SBLGNT THGNT ‖ Absent from 𝔓45 A(02) W(032) BYZ TR.

p 10:21, **I thank you:** Or "I praise you."

q 10:21, **and earth:** Absent from 𝔓45.

r 10:21, **for this was well-pleasing in your sight:** D(05) reads "for such was your gracious will."

s 10:22, **And turning to the disciples, he said:** Included in A(02) C(04) W(032) Latin(ff²) BYZ TR ‖ Absent from 𝔓45 𝔓75 ℵ(01) B(03) D(05) Latin(a b e) Syriac(sy^s sy^c) NA28 SBLGNT THGNT.

t 10:22, **my:** Some manuscripts read "the." D(05) Latin(a) Syriac (sy^s).

23 And turning to the disciples
[privately],[a] he said [[to them]],[b]
"Blessed are the eyes that see what
you see [[and hear what you hear]].[c]
24 [For][d] I say to you that many prophets
[[and righteous men]][e] [and kings][f]
desired to see what you see, and did
not see, and to hear what you hear, and
they did not hear."

25 [And behold,][g] A certain
lawyer stood up, testing him, saying,
"[Teacher,][h] What shall I do to inherit
eternal life?" 26 And he said to him,
"{What}[i] is written in the law? How do
you read it?"

27 And he answered, "You shall
love the Lord [your][j] God with all your
heart; [and][k] with all your soul, and
with all your strength [, and with all
your mind];[l] and your neighbor as
yourself."[m]

28 And {he}[n] said to him, "You have
answered correctly; do this and you
will live."

29 But he, wanting to justify
himself, said to Jesus, "And who is my
neighbor?"

30 [But][o] Jesus, taking this up, said
[[to him]],[p] "A certain man was going
down from Jerusalem to Jericho, and
fell among robbers, who both stripped
him and inflicted wounds on him,
then they went away, leaving him half
dead [[as it happens]].[q] 31 Now [by
coincidence][r] a certain priest was going
down that road, and when he saw
him, he passed by on the other side.
32 [Likewise, a Levite also, {[arriving][s]
[at the place],[t] [came and][u] saw
[[him]],[v] but}[w] passed by on the other
side.][x]

33 "But a certain Samaritan, as he
journeyed, came where he was, and
seeing [him],[y] he had compassion.
34 And he went to him and bound up
his wounds, pouring on oil and wine,
and he set him on his own animal, and
brought him to an inn, and took care
of him. 35 And on the next day, [[when

---

a 10:23, **privately:** Absent from D(05) Latin(a b e ff^{2} i) Syriac(sy^{s} sy^{c}).
b 10:23, **to them:** Included in D(05) Latin(e).
c 10:23, **and hear what you hear:** Included in D(05) Latin(e).
d 10:24, **For:** Absent from 𝔓75 Syriac(sy^{c}).
e 10:24, **and righteous men:** Included in Latin(b).
f 10:24, **and kings:** Absent from D(05) Latin(a b e ff^{2} i it).
g 10:25, **And behold:** Absent from D(05) Latin(e).
h 10:25, **Teacher:** Absent from D(05).
i 10:26, **What:** D(05) reads "It" as a statement rather than a question.
j 10:27, **your:** Absent from B(03).
k 10:27, **and:** Absent from 𝔓75 B(03).
l 10:27, **and with all your mind:** Absent from D(05) Latin(it).
m 10:27, Deuteronomy 6:5, Leviticus 19:18.
n 10:28, **he:** Some manuscripts read "Jesus." Latin(ff^{2}).
o 10:30, **But:** Included in A(02) D(05) W(032) BYZ TR SBLGNT || Absent from 𝔓75 ℵ(01) B(03) C(04) NA28 THGNT.
p 10:30, **to him:** Included in D(05).
q 10:30, **as it happens:** Included in A(02) C(04) W(032) BYZ TR || Absent from 𝔓45 𝔓75 ℵ(01) B(03) D(05) Latin(a b e ff^{2} i) NA28 SBLGNT THGNT.
r 10:31, **by coincidence:** Absent from Latin(it) || D(05) reads "by chance."
s 10:32, **arriving:** 𝔓45 A(02) D(05) BYZ TR NA28[] || Absent from 𝔓75 B(03) SBLGNT THGNT.
t 10:32, **at the place:** Absent from ℵ(01) Latin(e).
u 10:32, **came and:** Absent from 𝔓45 D(05) Latin(a b e ff^{2} i).
v 10:32, **him:** Included in A(02) D(05) Latin(a b e ff^{2} i).
w 10:32, **arriving at the place, came and saw him, but:** D(05) reads "having come to the place and seeing him."
x 10:32, Verse 32 is absent from ℵ(01).
y 10:33, **him:** Included in A(02) C(04) W(032) Latin(a ff^{2}) BYZ TR || Absent from 𝔓45 𝔓75 ℵ(01) B(03) D(05) Latin(b i) NA28 SBLGNT THGNT.

he departed,]][a] having taken out two
denarii, he gave them to the innkeeper
and said [[to him]],[b] 'Take care of
him; and whatever you spend beyond
that, I will repay [you][c] when I return.'
36 [[Therefore,]][d] {Which}[e] [[of these
three,]][f] do you think, {proved to be}[g]
a neighbor to the man who fell among
the robbers?" 37 He said, "The one who
showed mercy on him." [But][h] Jesus
said [to him],[i] "Go and do likewise."

38 And [[it happened that,]][j] as
{they were}[k] traveling, he entered a
certain village; and a certain woman
named Martha welcomed him [[into
her house]].[l] 39 And there was a sister
called Mary, [who][m] also sat at {the
Lord's feet}[n] and listened to {his}[o]
word. 40 But Martha was distracted
with much serving; and she came up
and said, "Lord, do you not care that
my sister has left me to serve alone?
Therefore, tell her then to help me."

41 But {the Lord}[p] answered her,
"Martha, Martha, you are [anxious
and][q] troubled [about many things];[r]
42 [but one thing is necessary;][s]
[for][t] Mary has chosen the good
portion, which will not be taken away
from her."

---

[a] 10:35, **when he departed:** Included in A(02) C(04) W(032) BYZ TR || Absent from 𝔓45 𝔓75 ℵ(01) B(03) D(05) Latin(a b e ff^{2} i) NA28 SBLGNT THGNT.

[b] 10:35, **to him:** Included in ℵ(01) A(02) C(04) W(032) Latin(a) BYZ TR || Absent from 𝔓45 𝔓75 B(03) D(05) Latin(b e ff^{2} i) NA28 SBLGNT THGNT.

[c] 10:35, **you:** Absent from D(05).

[d] 10:36, **Therefore:** Included in A(02) C(04) W(032) TR.

[e] 10:36, **Which:** Some manuscripts read "who." D(05) Latin(e).

[f] 10:36, **of these three:** Absent from D(05).

[g] 10:36, **proved to be:** Some manuscripts read "became." D(05) Latin(e).

[h] 10:37, **But:** 𝔓45 𝔓75 ℵ(01) B(03) C(04) D(05) NA28 SBLGNT THGNT || Some manuscripts read "Therefore." A(02) W(032) BYZ TGR.

[i] 10:37, **to him:** Absent from D(05) W(032).

[j] 10:38, **it happened:** Included in A(02) C(04) D(05) W(032) Latin(a b e ff^{2} i latt) BYZ TR || Absent from 𝔓45 𝔓75 ℵ(01) B(03) NA28 SBLGNT THGNT.

[k] 10:38, **they were:** D(05) reads "he was."

[l] 10:38, **into her house:** Included in 𝔓3 A(02) C(04) D(05) W(032) Latin(a b e ff^{2} i) BYZ TR THGNT || Absent from 𝔓45 𝔓75 B(03) NA28 SBLGNT.

[m] 10:39, **who:** A(02) B(03) C(04) D(05) W(032) BYZ TR NA28[] SBLGNT || Absent from 𝔓45 𝔓75 ℵ(01) THGNT.

[n] 10:39, **the Lord's feet:** 𝔓3 ℵ(01) D(05) NA28 || Some manuscripts read "the feet of Jesus." 𝔓45 𝔓75 A(02) W(032) BYZ TR SBLGNT THGNT.

[o] 10:39, **his:** D(05) reads "the."

[p] 10:41, **the Lord:** 𝔓3 𝔓45 𝔓75 ℵ(01) B(03) NA28 SBLGNT THGNT || Some manuscripts read "Jesus." A(02) B(03) C(04) D(05) W(032) Latin(it) Syriac(sy^{s}) BYZ TR.

[q] 10:41, **anxious and:** Absent from D(05) Latin(a b e ff^{2} i).

[r] 10:41, **about many things:** Absent from D(05) Latin(a b e ff^{2} i).

[s] 10:42, **one thing is necessary:** 𝔓45 𝔓75 C(04) W(032) BYZ TR NA28 THGNT || Absent from D(05) Latin(a b e ff^{2} i). || Some manuscripts read "few things are needed, or just one." 𝔓3 ℵ(01) B(03) SBLGNT.

[t] 10:42, **for:** 𝔓3 𝔓75 B(03) NA28 SBLGNT THGNT || Absent from D(05) Latin(a b e ff^{2} i) Syriac(sy^{s} sy^{c})/ || Some manuscripts read "but." A(02) C(04) W(032) BYZ TR.

11 [1] And it happened that while he was in a certain place praying, when he stopped, one of his disciples said to him, "Lord, teach us to pray, just as John[a] also taught his disciples."

[2] And he said to them, "[[When you pray, do not babble as the rest do, for some think that they will be heard because of their many words.]][b] When you pray, say, '[[Our]][c] Father [[who is in the heavens]],[d] may your name be sanctified.[e] Your kingdom come; [[Your will be done, as in heaven, also on earth;]][f] [3] Give us {each day}[g] our daily bread; [4] And forgive us our {sins},[h] {for we ourselves also forgive everyone who is indebted to us};[i] and do not lead us into temptation [[but deliver us from evil]].'"[j]

[5] And he said [to them][k], "Which of you will have a friend and will go to him at midnight and say to him, 'Friend, lend me three loaves, [6] for a friend [of mine][l] has come {[to me][m] [from his journey][n]},[o] and I have nothing to set before him'? [7] And he from within will answer, 'Do not bother me; {the}[p] door is now shut, and {my}[q] children are with me in bed. [I cannot get up and give you anything.][r] [8] I say to you, [even if][s] he will not give him, rising because he is his friend, yet because of his persistence he will rise and give [him][t] as much as he needs.

[9] "I say to you, ask, and it will be given to you; seek, and you will find; knock, and it will be opened to you. [10] For everyone who asks receives, and the one who seeks finds, and to the one who knocks it will be opened.

[11] "{Which of you fathers},[u] if his son [[asks for bread, he will not give him a stone will he? Or if he]][v] asks for a fish, will instead of a fish give him a serpent? Will he? [12] Or if he asks for an egg, will give him a scorpion?

---

[a] 11:1, **John:** Absent from ℵ(01).

[b] 11:2, **When you pray...:** Included in D(05).

[c] 11:2, **Our:** Included in A(02) C(04) D(05) W(032) BYZ TR ‖ Absent from 𝔓75 ℵ(01) B(03) NA28 SBLGNT THGNT.

[d] 11:2, **who is in the heavens:** Included in A(02) C(04) D(05) W(032) Latin(a b e ff²) Syriac(syᶜ syᵖ) BYZ TR ‖ Absent in 𝔓75 ℵ(01) B(03) Syriac(syˢ) NA28 SBLGNT THGNT.

[e] 11:2, **may your name be sanctified:** Or "hallowed be your name."

[f] 11:2, **Your will be done, as in heaven, also on earth:** Included in ℵ(01) A(02) C(04) D(05) W(032) Latin(b e ff² i) BYZ TR ‖ Absent from 𝔓75 B(03) NA28 SBLGNT THGNT. ‖ Latin(a) reads "your will be done."

[g] 11:3, **each day:** Some manuscripts read "today." D(05) Latin(it).

[h] 11:4, **sins:** Some manuscripts read "debts." D(05) Latin(b c ff²).

[i] 11:4, **for we ourselves also forgive everyone who is indebted to us:** D(05) reads "as we also forgive our debtors."

[j] 11:4, **but deliver us from evil:** Included in A(02) C(04) D(05) W(032) BYZ TR ‖ Absent from 𝔓75 ℵ(01) B(03) NA28 SBLGNT THGNT.

[k] 11:5, **to them:** Absent from D(05).

[l] 11:6, **of mine:** Absent from C(04) Latin(b) BYZ.

[m] 11:6, **to me:** Absent from D(05) Latin(i).

[n] 11:6, **from his journey:** Absent from Latin(b).

[o] 11:6, **to me from his journey:** D(05) "come from the field."

[p] 11:7, **the:** 𝔓75 reads "my."

[q] 11:7, **my:** Some manuscripts read "the." C(04) Latin(b ff² i).

[r] 11:7, **I cannot get up and give you anything:** Absent from Latin(b).

[s] 11:8, **even if:** Absent from D(05).

[t] 11:8, **him:** Absent from D(05).

[u] 11:11, **Which of you fathers:** Some manuscripts read "Who among you." ℵ(01) Latin (b ff² i).

[v] 11:11, **asks for bread, he will not give him a stone will he? Or if he:** Included in ℵ(01) A(02) C(04) D(05) W(032) BYZ TR ‖ Absent from 𝔓45 𝔓75 B(03) NA28 SBLGNT THGNT.

13 "If you then, being evil, know how to give good gifts to your children, how much more will {the}[a] Father [who is][b] in heaven give the {Holy Spirit}[cd] to those who ask him!"

14 {And he was casting out a demon and it was mute; [and it happened],[e] when the demon had gone out, the [mute][f] man spoke, and the crowds were [[all]][g] amazed.}[h]

15 But some of them said, "By {Beelzebul},[i] the prince of demons, he casts out the demons." [[But he answered and said, "How can Satan cast out Satan?"]][j]

16 Others, testing him, sought a sign from heaven from him.

17 But knowing their thoughts, he said to them, "Every kingdom divided against itself is laid waste, and a house falls upon a house.[k]

18 "If Satan also is divided against himself, how will his kingdom stand? Because you say [that][l] I cast out demons by {Beelzebul}.[m] 19 If I cast out demons by Beelzebul, by whom do your sons cast them out? Therefore, they will be your judges. 20 But if I cast out demons by the finger of God, then the kingdom of God has come upon you.

21 "When the strong man, fully armed, guards his own courtyard, his possessions are in peace; 22 but when one stronger [than he][n] attacks [and overcomes][o] him, he takes away his armor in which he trusted and distributes {his}[p] spoils.

23 "He who is not with me is against me, and he who does not gather [with me][q] scatters.

24 "[[But]][r] When the unclean spirit goes out from a man, it passes through waterless places seeking rest and not finding it. [Then][s] It says, 'I will return to my house from which I came out.' 25 And having come, it finds it [at rest,][t] swept and decorated. 26 [Then][u] It goes and takes with it seven other spirits more evil than itself, and they enter and dwell [there];[v] and the last state of that man becomes worse than the first."

---

a 11:13, **the:** Some manuscripts read "your." BYZ TR.

b 11:13, **who is:** Absent from 𝔓75 ℵ(01).

c 11:13, **Holy Spirit:** Some manuscripts read "Good Spirit." 𝔓45 ‖ Some manuscripts read "Good gift." D(05) ‖ See footnote for Spirit in Luke 1:15 for the BDAG definition.

d 11:13, **Spirit:** See footnote for Spirit in Luke 1:15.

e 11:14, **and it happened:** Absent from D(05) Latin(b ff² i).

f 11:14, **mute:** Absent from 𝔓45.

g 11:14, **all:** Included in D(05) Latin(b ff² i).

h 11:14, **And he was casting...:** D(05) reads "While he was saying these things, they brought to him a demon-possessed man who was mute. And when he had cast it out, everyone was amazed."

i 11:15, **Beelzebul:** Some manuscripts read "Beelzebub." Syriac (sy).

j 11:15, **But he answered...:** Included in A(02) D(05).

k 11:17, **and a house falls upon a house:** Understood as "a house divided against itself falls."

l 11:18, **that:** Absent from Latin(ff² i).

m 11:18, **Beelzebul:** Latin(b ff² i) reads "the chief of demons."

n 11:22, **than he:** Absent from 𝔓45 𝔓75 D(05).

o 11:22, **and overcomes:** Absent from D(05).

p 11:22, **his:** Some manuscripts read "the." D(05) Latin(b).

q 11:23, **with me:** Absent from 𝔓45.

r 11:24, **but:** Included in 𝔓45 𝔓75 D(05) W(032) Latin(b).

s 11:24, **then:** 𝔓75 B(03) NA28[] Latin(b) ‖ Absent from 𝔓45 ℵ(01) A(02) C(04) D(05) W(032) Latin(ff² i) BYZ THGNT SBLGNT THGNT.

t 11:25, **at rest:** Included in B(03) C(04) ‖ Absent from 𝔓75 ℵ(01) A(02) D(05) W(032) BYZ TR NA28 SBLGNT THGNT.

u 11:26, **Then:** Absent from D(05).

v 11:26, **there:** Absent from C(04) D(05) Latin(a b e ff² i).

27 And it happened, while he was speaking [these things],ᵃ a certain woman from the crowd, raising her voice, said to him, "Blessed is the womb that bore you and the breasts at which you nursed." 28 But he said, "On the contrary,ᵇ blessed are those who hear the word of God and keep {it}ᶜ."

29 As the crowds were increasing, he began to say, "This generation is {an evil generation};ᵈ it seeks a sign, and no sign will be given to it except the sign of [[the prophet]]ᵉ Jonah. 30 [For]ᶠ just as Jonah became a sign to the Ninevites, so [also]ᵍ will the Son of Man be a sign to this generation. [[And just as Jonah was in the belly of the whale for three days and three nights, so also will the Son of Man be in the earth.]]ʰ

31 "The Queen [of the South]ⁱ will rise upʲ [at the judgment]ᵏ with the men of this generation and condemn them, for she came from the ends of the earth to hear the wisdom of Solomon,

and behold, something greater than Solomon is here.

32 ["The men of Nineveh will rise up in the judgment with this generation and condemn it, for they repented at the preaching of Jonah, and behold, something greater than Jonah is here.]ˡ

33 "[[But]]ᵐ No one, after lighting a lamp, puts it in a hidden place [nor under a basket],ⁿ but on a lampstand, so that those who enter may see the light.

34 "The lamp of {the}ᵒ body is your eye.ᵖ [[Therefore]]ᑫ when your eye is clear,ʳ your whole body is full of light; but when it is evil, your body is full of darkness. 35 {Therefore, be careful that the light within you is not darkness}.ˢ 36 [If your whole body is full of light, having no part dark, it will be completely illuminated, as when a lamp with its bright shining gives you light.]"ᵗ

37 [Now as he spoke,]ᵘ A [[certain]]ᵛ Pharisee asked him to dine with him; so he went in and reclined. 38 But the

---

ᵃ 11:27, **these things:** Absent from 𝔓75.

ᵇ 11:28, **On the contrary:** Or "Indeed."

ᶜ 11:28, **it:** ℵ(01) reads "the word of God."

ᵈ 11:29, **an evil generation:** 𝔓45 𝔓75 ℵ(01) A(02) B(03) ‖ Some manuscripts read "evil." C(04) W(032) BYZ TR.

ᵉ 11:29, **the prophet:** Included in A(02) C(04) W(032) Latin(e) Syriac(syˢ syᴾ) BYZ TR ‖ Absent from 𝔓45 𝔓75 ℵ(01) B(03) D(05) Latin(a b ff² i) NA28 SBLGNT THGNT.

ᶠ 11:30, **for:** Absent from ℵ(01).

ᵍ 11:30, **also:** Absent from 𝔓45.

ʰ 11:30, **And just as Jonah...:** Included in D(05) Latin(a e ff²).

ⁱ 11:31, **of the South:** Absent from D(05).

ʲ 11:31, **rise up:** Or be raised.

ᵏ 11:31, **at the judgment:** Absent from 𝔓45 D(05).

ˡ 11:32, Verse 32 is absent from D(05).

ᵐ 11:33, **But:** Included in A(02) W(032) Latin(b ff²).

ⁿ 11:33, **nor under a basket:** ℵ(01) A(02) B(03) C(04) D(05) W(032) Latin(a b e ff² i) BYZ TR NA28 SBLGNT THGNT ‖ Absent from 𝔓45 𝔓75 Syriac(syˢ).

ᵒ 11:34, **the:** Some manuscripts read "your." D(05) Latin(a b e ff²).

ᵖ 11:34, **the lamp of the body is your eye:** Or, "inward lamp" and "inward eye." The discourse shifts from the ordinary lamp, which gives light from the outside, to a figurative extension of the word 'lamp', here called 'the lamp of the body', which gives light from within. (UBS Handbooks for New Testament (20 Vols.)).

ᑫ 11:34, **Therefore:** Included in A(02) C(04) BYZ TR ‖ Absent from 𝔓45 𝔓75 ℵ(01) B(03) D(05) W(032) NA28 SBLGNT THGNT.

ʳ 11:34, **clear:** Or healthy. The Greek word for *clear* is defined by BDAG as: being motivated by singleness of purpose so as to be open and aboveboard, without guile, sincere, straightforward, i.e. without a hidden agenda. (BDAG, ἁπλοῦς).

ˢ 11:35, **Therefore, be careful...:** Some manuscripts read "So if the light in you is darkness, how great is that darkness." D(05) Latin(it).

ᵗ 11:36, **If your whole body...:** Absent from D(05) Latin(a b e ff² i).

ᵘ 11:37, **Now as he spoke:** Absent from D(05) Syriac(syˢ syᶜ).

ᵛ 11:37, **certain:** Included in A(02) C(04) W(032) Latin(b e).

Pharisee, {seeing this, marveled that he had not first washed}ᵃ before the meal.

39 The Lord said to him, "Now you Pharisees [[hypocrites]]ᵇ clean the outside of the cup and the dish, but the inside of you is full of greed and wickedness. 40 Fools, did not the one who made the outside also make the inside? 41 But give as charity what is inside, and behold {everything is}ᶜ clean for you.

42 "But woe to you Pharisees; [for]ᵈ you tithe mint and rue and every herb, and pass by justice and {the love of God}.ᵉ [[But]ᶠ these things you ought to have done without neglecting the others.]ᵍ

43 "Woe to you Pharisees, for you love the best seats in the synagogues and the greetings in the marketplaces. [[And the places of honor at banquets.]]ʰ

44 "Woe to you [[Scribes and Pharisees.]]ⁱ [[Hypocrites!]]ʲ For you are [as]ᵏ unmarked graves, and the men walking above do not know."

45 But one of the lawyers answered him, "Teacher, by saying these things you also insult us."

46 And he said, "Woe to you lawyers [as well],ˡ for you load men with [[heavy]]ᵐ burdens hard to bear, and you [yourselves]ⁿ do not touch [it]ᵒ [the burdens]ᵖ with one of your fingers.

47 "Woe to you, for you build the tombs of the prophets, and your fathers killed them. 48 Therefore, you are witnesses and you approve of the deeds of your fathers, for they indeed killed them, but you build [[their tombs]].�q 49 Therefore, for this reason [the Wisdom of God said,]ʳ 'I will send them prophets and apostles, and some of them they will kill and {persecute},'ˢ 50 so that the blood of all the prophets, shed from the foundation of the world, may be required of this generation, 51 from the blood of Abel [[the righteous]]ᵗ to the blood of Zechariah, [[son of Barachiah,]]ᵘ {who perished}ᵛ between the altar and the

---

ᵃ 11:38, **seeing this, marveled that he had not first washed:** Some manuscripts read "began to question within himself, saying, Why was he not first baptized." D(05) Latin(a b e ff² i) Syriac(syᶜ).

ᵇ 11:39, **hypocrites:** Included in D(05) Latin(b).

ᶜ 11:41, **everything is:** Some manuscripts read "everything will be." 𝔓45 D(05).

ᵈ 11:42, **for:** Absent from 𝔓45.

ᵉ 11:42, **the love of God:** B(03) reads "love."

ᶠ 11:42, **but:** 𝔓45 𝔓75 B(03) C(04) ‖ Absent from ℵ(01) A(02) W(032) BYZ TR.

ᵍ 11:42, **but these you ought to have done without neglecting the others:** 𝔓75 B(03) NA28 SBLGNT THGNT ‖ Absent from D(05). ‖ Some manuscripts read "without leaving the others undone." 𝔓45 ℵ(01) A(02) C(04) W(032) BYZ TR.

ʰ 11:43, **And the places of honor at banquets:** Included in C(04) D(05) Latin(b).

ⁱ 11:44, **Scribes and Pharisees:** Included in A(02) D(05) W(032) Latin(b i) BYZ TR ‖ Absent from 𝔓45 𝔓75 ℵ(01) B(03) C(04) Latin(a e ff²) Syriac(syˢ syᶜ) NA28 SBLGNT THGNT.

ʲ 11:44, **hypocrites!:** Included in A(02) W(032) Latin(b) BYZ TR ‖ Absent from 𝔓45 𝔓75 ℵ(01) B(03) C(04) D(05) Latin(a e i) Syriac(syˢ syᶜ) NA28 SBLGNT THGNT.

ᵏ 11:44, **as:** Absent from D(05) Latin(a b e ff² i).

ˡ 11:46, **as well:** Absent from D(05).

ᵐ 11:46, **heavy:** Included in C(04).

ⁿ 11:46, **yourselves:** Absent from 𝔓75 B(03).

ᵒ 11:46, **it:** Absent from 𝔓75.

ᵖ 11:46, **the burdens:** Absent from D(05) Latin(b) Syriac(syˢ syᶜ).

q 11:48, **their tombs:** Included in A(02) C(04) W(032) BYZ TR ‖ Absent from 𝔓75 ℵ(01) B(03) D(05) Latin(a b e i) Syriac(syˢ syᶜ) NA28 SBLGNT THGNT.

ʳ 11:49, **and the Wisdom of God said:** Absent from D(05) Latin(b).

ˢ 11:49, **persecute:** 𝔓45 B(03) NA28 SBLGNT THGNT ‖ Some manuscripts read "drive out." 𝔓75 ℵ(01) A(02) C(04) D(05) W(032) BYZ TR.

ᵗ 11:51, **the righteous:** Included in Latin(e i).

ᵘ 11:51, **son of Barachiah:** Included in D(05).

ᵛ 11:51, **who perished:** Some manuscripts read "they murdered." D(05) Latin(a) Syriac(syˢ syᶜ syᵖ).

sanctuary. Yes, I say to you, it will be required of this generation.

52 "Woe to you lawyers, for you have taken away the key of knowledge; you yourselves did not enter."

53 {And as he went away from there},[a] {the scribes and the Pharisees began to press him hard and to provoke him to speak about many things, 54 [lying in wait][b] [for him,][c] [[seeking]][d] to catch something from his mouth}[e] [[that they might accuse him]].[f]

12 1 Among which, {when the multitudes of the crowd had gathered together, so that they were trampling on one another,}[g] he began to say to {his}[h] disciples first, "Beware of the leaven, which is hypocrisy, of the Pharisees.

2 "But there is nothing concealed that will not be revealed [and hidden that will not be known].[i]

3 "For what was said in the darkness will be heard in the light, and what was spoken to the ear[j] [in the storerooms][k] will be proclaimed on the rooftops.

4 "And I say to you, my friends, do not fear those who kill the body and after that no more that they can do. 5 But I will show you whom to fear; [fear][l] the one who, after killing, has authority to cast into Gehenna[m]. Yes, I say to you, fear this one.

6 "Are not five sparrows sold for two pennies?[n] And not one of them is forgotten before God. 7 But even the hairs of your head are all numbered. [[Therefore,]][o] Do not fear; [[for]][p] you are worth more than many sparrows.

8 "[But][q] I say to you, [[that]][r] everyone who acknowledges[s] me before men, the son of man will also acknowledge[t] him before the angels of God. 9 [But whoever denies me before

---

a 11:53, **And as he went away from there:** 𝔓45 𝔓75 ℵ(01) B(03) C(04) NA28 SBLGNT THGNT ‖ Some manuscripts read "Saying these things to them." A(02) D(05) W(032) Syriac(sy) BYZ TR.

b 11:54, **lying in wait:** Absent from D(05) Latin(a b e i).

c 11:54, **for him:** Absent from ℵ(01).

d 11:54, **seeking:** Included in A(02) C(04) D(05) W(032) BYZ TR ‖ Absent from 𝔓45 𝔓75 ℵ(01) B(03) Latin(a b e i) NA28 SBLGNT THGNT.

e 11:54, **the scribes and...:** Some manuscripts read "the Pharisees and the lawyers began to be greatly distressed and to question him about many things, seeking some opportunity to seize him so that they might find a reason to accuse him." D(05) Latin(it) Syriac(sy^s sy^c).

f 11:54, **that they might accuse him:** Included in A(02) C(04) D(05) W(032) Syriac(sy^c) BYZ TR ‖ Absent from 𝔓45 𝔓75 ℵ(01) B(03) NA28 SBLGNT THGNT.

g 12:1, **when the multitudes...:** Some manuscripts read "with many crowds pressing around so that they were choking each other." D(05).

h 12:1, **his:** D(05) reads "the."

i 12:2, **and hidden that will not be known:** Absent from 𝔓45.

j 12:3, **spoken to the ear:** Or "whispered."

k 12:3, **in the storerooms:** Absent from Latin(b).

l 12:5, **fear:** Absent from ℵ(01) D(05) Latin(a) Syriac(sy^p).

m 12:5, **Gehenna:** Often translated hell. Gehenna is originally a transliteration of the Hebrew "Valley of Hinnom." This is a valley southwest of Jerusalem, where human sacrifices had once been offered and where garbage from the city was constantly burning. It was known as the valley of slaughter and the place of divine punishment (Jeremiah 19). Later this picture was combined with the idea of God's judgment, and so the notion of a fiery hell developed. In the New Testament it is the place of punishment of the wicked after the final judgment. (*UBS Handbooks for the New Testament* [20 Vols.] [American Bible Society, 2021]. Matthew 5:22 and James 3:6).

n 12:6, **pennies:** Greek "assaria."

o 12:7, **therefore:** Included in BYZ TR.

p 12:7, **for:** Included in D(05).

q 12:8, **But:** Absent from 𝔓45 Latin(a b ff² i).

r 12:8, **that:** Included in ℵ(01) D(05).

s 12:8, **acknowledges:** Or "confess in."

t 12:8, **acknowledge:** Or "confess in."

men will be denied before the angels of
God.][a]

10 "And everyone who speaks
a word against the Son of man, it
will be forgiven him; {but he who
blasphemes}[b] against the Holy Spirit,[c]
it will not be forgiven. [[Neither in this
age nor in the one to come.]][d]

11 "[But] When they {bring}[e]
you {before the synagogues and the
rulers and the authorities},[f] do not
worry about how [or what][g] you
should defend or what you should say;
12 for the Holy Spirit[h] will teach you in
that very hour what must be said."

13 Someone in the crowd said to
him, "Teacher, tell my brother to divide
the inheritance with me." 14 But he said
to him, "Man, who appointed me a
judge [or divider][i] [over you]?"[j]

15 And he said to them, "Watch out
and guard against all greed, because
[one's][k] life does not consist in the
abundance of possessions."

16 He told them a parable, saying,
"The land of a certain rich man
produced plentifully. 17 And he thought
to himself, saying, 'What shall I do,
for I have nowhere to store my crops?'
18 And he said, 'I will do this: I will tear
down my barns and build larger ones,
and there I will gather {all my grain}[l]
[and my goods].[m] 19 And I will say to my
soul, "Soul, you have many goods [laid
up for many years; rest, eat, drink];[n] be
merry."' 20 But God said to him, 'Fool,
this night your soul is required of you;
and the things you have prepared,
whose will they be?'" 21 [So is the one
who stores up treasure for himself and
is not rich toward God.][o]

22 But he said to {his}[p] disciples,
"Therefore, [I say to you,][q] do not
worry about [[your]][r] life, what you
will eat, nor about {the}[s] body, what
you will wear. 23 [For][t] The life[u] is more
than food, and the body more than
clothing."

---

a 12:9, **But whoever denies me before men will be denied before the angels of God:** Absent from 𝔓45 Latin(e) Syriac(sy^s^).

b 12:10, **but he who blasphemes:** D(05) reads "To him, however, against."

c 12:10, **Spirit:** See footnote for Spirit in Luke 1:15.

d 12:10, **Neither in this age nor in the one to come:** Included in D(05) Latin (e).

e 12:11, **bring:** Some manuscripts read "offer." BYZ TR.

f 12:11, **before the synagogues and the rulers and the authorities:** Some manuscripts read "into the synagogues, and before the authorities and powers." ℵ(01) D(05) Latin(b e ff^2).

g 12:11, **or what:** Absent from D(05) Latin(it) Syriac(sy^c sy^p).

h 12:12, **Spirit:** See footnote for Spirit in Luke 1:15.

i 12:14, **or divider:** Absent from D(05) Latin(a).

j 12:14, **over you:** Absent from Latin(a).

k 12:15, **one's:** Absent from D(05).

l 12:18, **grain:** B(03) NA28 SBLGNT THGNT || Some manuscripts read "crops." ℵ(01) A(02) D(05) W(032) Latin(it) Syriac(sy^s sy^c sy^p) BYZ TR.

m 12:18, **and my goods:** Absent from ℵ(01) D(05) Latin (it) Syriac (sy^s sy^c).

n 12:19, **laid up for many years; rest, eat, drink:** Absent from D(05) Latin(it).

o 12:21, **So is the one...:** Absent from D(05) Latin(a b).

p 12:22, **his:** ℵ(01) A(02) D(05) W(032) BYZ TR NA28[] THGNT || Some manuscripts read "the." 𝔓45 𝔓75 B(03) Latin(e) SBLGNT.

q 12:22, **I say to you:** Absent from Latin(i).

r 12:22, **your:** Included in 𝔓45 Latin(a e) Syriac(sy^c sy^p) BYZ TR || Absent from 𝔓75 ℵ(01) A(02) B(03) D(05) W(032) Latin(b ff^2 i) Syriac(sy^s) NA28 SBLGNT THGNT.

s 12:22, **the:** Some manuscripts read "your." B(03) Latin(a).

t 12:23, **For:** 𝔓75 ℵ(01) B(03) D(05) Latin(b e) NA28 SBLGNT THGNT || Absent from 𝔓45 A(02) W(032) Latin(a ff^2 i) BYZ TR.

u 12:23, **life:** Or soul.

24 “Consider the {ravens},[a] that they
neither sow nor reap, for which there
is no [storehouse nor][b] barn, and God
feeds {them};[c] {how much more do you
surpass the birds!}[d] 25 {And which of
you [by worrying][e] can add {a}[f] cubit to
his stature}?[g] 26 [If then you are not able
to do even the least;][h] And concerning
the rest, why do you worry?

27 “Consider the lilies [[of the
field]],[i] how [they grow;][j] they neither
toil nor spin; yet I say to you [[that]],[k]
even Solomon in all his glory was not
arrayed like one of these.

28 “But if God so clothes the grass
[of the field],[l] is today and tomorrow is
thrown into the oven, how much more
[[then]][m] will he clothe you, You of
little faith!

29 “And you, do not seek what you
will eat {and}[n] what you will drink, and
do not be anxious. 30 For all these things
the nations of the world seek, but your
Father knows that you need [[all]][o]
these things.

31 “But seek [[first]][p] [his
kingdom],[q] and [[all]][r] these things will
be added to you.

32 “Do not fear, little flock, for it {is
your Father's good pleasure}[s] to give
you the kingdom.

33 “Sell your possessions and give
to charity; make for yourselves purses
that do not wear out, an inexhaustible[t]
treasure in heaven, where no thief
comes near nor moth destroys;

34 “For where your treasure is, there
your heart will be also.

35 “Let your waists be girded[u] and
your lamps burning; 36 and be like
men waiting for their master when he
returns from the wedding feast, so that
when he comes and knocks, they may
immediately open to him.

37 “Blessed are those servants whom
the master finds awake when he comes;
truly, I say to you, he will gird[v] himself

---

a 12:24, **ravens:** Some manuscripts read “birds of the sky.” D(05) Latin(e). || 𝔓45 reads “The birds of the sky and the ravens.”

b 12:24, **storehouse nor:** Absent from Latin(e).

c 12:24, **them:** Some manuscripts read “these.” 𝔓45 D(05) Latin(f).

d 12:24, **how much more do you surpass the birds!:** D(05) reads “are you not worth more than the birds?.”

e 12:25, **by worrying:** Absent from D(05).

f 12:25, **a:** 𝔓45 𝔓75 ℵ(01) B(03) D(05) NA28 SBLGNT THGNT || Some manuscripts read “one.” A K W(032) BYZ TR.

g 12:25, **And which of you...:** Some manuscripts read “Who among you is able to add a cubit to his lifespan?” D(05) W(032).

h 12:26, **If then you are not able to do even the least:** Absent from D(05) Latin(a b e ff^{2} i it).

i 12:27, **Of the field:** Included in Latin(a b e i).

j 12:27, **they grow:** Absent from D(05) Latin(a) Syriac(sy^{s} sy^{c}).

k 12:27, **that:** Included in ℵ(01) A(02) D(05) Latin(a b e ff^{2} i it) || Absent from 𝔓45 𝔓75 B(03) W(032) BYZ TR NA28 SBLGNT THGNT.

l 12:28, **of the field:** Absent from D(05).

m 12:28, **then:** Included in 𝔓45.

n 12:29, **and:** 𝔓45 ℵ(01) B(03) NA28 SBLGNT THGNT || Some manuscripts read “or.” 𝔓75 A(02) D(05) W(032) BYZ TR.

o 12:30, **all:** Included in Latin(a b).

p 12:31, **first:** Included in Latin(i).

q 12:31, **his kingdom:** ℵ(01) B(03) D(05) NA28 Latin (a) SBLGNT THGNT || Absent from 𝔓75. || Some manuscripts read “the kingdom of God.” 𝔓45 A(02) W(032) Latin(b e ff^{2} i) Syriac(sy) BYZ TR.

r 12:31, **all:** Included in A(02) D(05) W(032) Latin(b ff^{2} i) BYZ TR || Absent from 𝔓45 𝔓75 ℵ(01) B(03) Latin(a e) Syriac(sy^{s} sy^{c}) NA28 SBLGNT THGNT.

s 12:32, **is your Father's good pleasure:** D(05) reads “pleased your Father.”

t 12:33, **inexhaustible:** Or unfailing.

u 12:35, **girded:** Or, dressed for service. The Greek word means to (1) put a belt or sash around, (2) gird oneself. Girding is an indication that one is prepared for some activity. (BDAG, περιζώννυμι).

v 12:37, **gird:** See the footnote for verse 35.

and have them recline at table [and he will come and serve them].ᵃ

₃₈ "{And if in the second or in the third watch he comes and finds them so, [those]ᵇ [[servants]]ᶜ they are blessed.}ᵈ

₃₉ "But know this, that if the master of the house had known at what hour the thief was coming, he would [[have stayed awake and]]ᵉ not have [let his house be broken into].ᶠ

₄₀ "[[Therefore]]ᵍ You also must be ready, for the Son of Man is coming at an hour you do not expect."ʰ

₄₁ But Peter said [[to him]],ⁱ "Lord, are you telling this parable for us [or for everyone]?"ʲ

₄₂ {And}ᵏ the Lord said, "Who then is the faithful; the wise; [the good;]ˡ that the Lord will establish upon his service to give out food at the proper time? ₄₃ Blessed is that servant, whom {the}ᵐ lord finds doing so when he comes. ₄₄ [Truly I say to you,]ⁿ [that]ᵒ He will put him in charge of all his possessions.

₄₅ "But if that servant says in his heart, 'My lord is taking a long time to come,' and begins to beat the male and female servants, and to eat and drink and get drunk, ₄₆ the lord of {that servant}ᵖ will come on a day when he does not expect and at an hour he does not know, and will cut him in two and assign him a place with the unbelievers.

₄₇ "That servant who knew his lord's will and did not�q {prepare or do}ʳ according to his will, will be beaten with [many]ˢ blows.

₄₈ "But the one who did not know, and did things deserving of blows, will be beaten with few.

"[But]ᵗ from everyone to whom much was given, much will be demanded from him; and to whom much was entrusted, more will be {asked}ᵘ of him.

ᵃ 12:37, **and he will come and serve them:** Absent from ℵ(01).

ᵇ 12:38, **those:** Absent from ℵ(01) Latin(it).

ᶜ 12:38, **servants:** Included in A(02) W(032) BYZ TR ‖ Absent from 𝔓75 ℵ(01) B(03) D(05) Latin(it) NA28 SBLGNT THGNT.

ᵈ 12:38, **second or in the third…:** Some manuscripts read "And if he comes in the evening watch and finds it so, he will do likewise. And if in the second and third, blessed are those there." D(05) Latin(b ff² i it) Syriac(syᶜ).

ᵉ 12:39, **have stayed awake and:** Included in A(02) B(03) W(032) Latin(b ff²) BYZ TR ‖ Absent from 𝔓75 ℵ(01) D(05) Latin (e i) Syriac(syˢ syᶜ) NA28 SBLGNT THGNT.

ᶠ 12:39, **let his house be broken into:** Absent from D(05).

ᵍ 12:40, **Therefore:** Included in A(02) W(032) BYZ TR ‖ Absent from 𝔓75 ℵ(01) B(03) Latin(b e ff² i) NA28 SBLGNT THGNT.

ʰ 12:40, Verse 40 is absent from the f1 family of manuscripts.

ⁱ 12:41, **to him:** Included in ℵ(01) A(02) W(032) BYZ TR ‖ Absent from 𝔓75 B(03) D(05) Latin(b e ff² i) NA28 SBLGNT THGNT.

ʲ 12:41, **or for everyone:** Absent from D(05).

ᵏ 12:42, **And:** Some manuscripts read "But." BYZ TR.

ˡ 12:42, **the good:** Included in D(05) Latin(e) Syriac(syᶜ).

ᵐ 12:43, **the:** Some manuscripts read "his." D(05) Latin(i).

ⁿ 12:44, **Truly I say to you:** Absent from Latin(e).

ᵒ 12:44, **that:** Absent from W(032) Latin(b ff² i).

ᵖ 12:46, **that servant:** Some manuscripts read "him." D(05).

q 12:47, **did not:** Absent from 𝔓45.

ʳ 12:47, **prepare or do:** 𝔓75 ℵ(01) B(03) NA28 SBLGNT THGNT ‖ Some manuscripts read "Prepare." W(032) Latin(b e ff² i it) Syriac(syˢ syᶜ syᵖ) ‖ Some manuscripts read "do." 𝔓45 D(05) ‖ Some manuscripts read "prepare nor do." A(02) BYZ TR.

ˢ 12:47, **many:** Absent from Latin(ff²).

ᵗ 12:48, **But:** Absent from 𝔓45 ℵ(01).

ᵘ 12:48, **asked:** Some manuscripts read "demanded." D(05) Latin(e ff²).

49 "I have come to cast fire upon the earth, and what do I desire if it has [already]^a been kindled.

50 "But I have a baptism to be baptized with, and how am I constrained until it is accomplished?

51 "Do you think that I came to {give}^b peace [on earth]?^c No, I say to you, but rather division.

52 "For from now on {there will be five in one house divided},^d [three against two]^e and two against three.

53 "They will be divided, father against his son and son [[divided]]^f against his father, mother against daughter and daughter against mother, mother-in-law against [her]^g daughter-in-law and daughter-in-law against [[her]]^h mother-in-law."

54 And he said also to the crowds, that "When you see [the]ⁱ cloud rising {in}^j the west, you immediately say [that]^k rain is coming, and so it happens.

55 "And [[behold,]]^l when you see the south wind blowing, you say [that]^m there will be a scorching heat, and it happens.

56 "Hypocrites, you know how to discern the appearance of the earth and the sky, {but how do you [not]ⁿ know how to discern the time}?^o

57 "{Why do you not judge for yourselves what is right?}^p

58 "For as you are going with your adversary to the magistrate, make an effort on the way to be released from him, lest he drag you to the judge, and the judge hand you over to the officer, and the officer throw you into prison.

59 "I say to you, you will not get out of there until you have paid the last penny."^q

13 1 Now there were some present at that time who told [him]^r about the Galileans whose blood Pilate had mixed with their sacrifices.

2 And in response [{he}^s said to them],^t "Do you think that these Galileans were sinners more than all the other Galileans, because they suffered [these things]?^u 3 No, I say to you,

---

a 12:49, **already:** Absent from Latin(b e ff² i).

b 12:51, **give:** Some manuscripts read "do." D(05) Latin(e) Syriac(sy^c).

c 12:51, **on earth:** Absent from Latin(e).

d 12:52, **there will be five in one house divided:** Some manuscripts read "in one house there will be five divided." 𝔓45 D(05).

e 12:52, **three against two:** Absent from Latin(ff²).

f 12:53, **divided:** Included in D(05) Latin(e ff² i).

g 12:53, **her:** Absent from 𝔓75 ℵ(01).

h 12:53, **her:** Included in A(02) W(032) BYZ TR ‖ Absent from 𝔓45 𝔓75 ℵ(01) B(03) D(05) NA28 SBLGNT THGNT.

i 12:54, **the:** 𝔓45 D(05) W(032) BYZ TR NA28[] ‖ Some manuscripts read "a." 𝔓75 ℵ(01) A(02) B(03) SBLGNT THGNT.

j 12:54, **in:** 𝔓75 ℵ(01) B(03) NA28 SBLGNT THGNT ‖ Some manuscripts read "from." 𝔓45 A(02) D(05) W(032) BYZ TR.

k 12:54, **that:** Absent from D(05) W(032) Latin(b ff² i) Syriac(sy^p) TR BYZ.

l 12:55, **behold:** Included in 𝔓45 Latin(b ff² i).

m 12:55, **that:** Absent from 𝔓45 ℵ(01) D(05) Syriac(sy^p).

n 12:56, **not:** Absent from Latin(ff²).

o 12:56, **but how do you not know how to discern the time?:** 𝔓75 ℵ(01) B(03) NA28 SBLGNT THGNT ‖ Some manuscripts read "but this time, how do you not test?" 𝔓45 A(02) W(032) BYZ TR ‖ Some manuscripts read "but this time you do not discern?" D(05) Latin(it) Syriac(sy^c).

p 12:57, **Why do you not judge...:** Some manuscripts read "And from yourselves, you do not judge what is right." BYZ TR.

q 12:59, **penny:** Greek "lepton."

r 13:1, **him:** Absent from 𝔓75.

s 13:2, **he:** 𝔓75 ℵ(01) B(03) Latin(a b e i) NA28 SBLGNT THGNT ‖ Some manuscripts read "Jesus." A(02) D(05) W(032) Latin(ff²) Syriac(sy) BYZ TR.

t 13:2, **he:** Absent from W(032).

u 13:2, **these things:** Absent from Latin(a e).

but unless you repent, you will [all]ᵃ likewise perish."

₄"Or those {eighteen}ᵇ on whom the tower in Siloam fell and killed them, do you think that they became debtors above all the other people living in Jerusalem? ₅No, I say to you, but unless you repent, you will all likewise perish."

₆And he told this parable: "A man had a fig tree planted in his vineyard, and he came seeking fruit on it and found none. ₇So he said to the vineyard worker, 'Look, for three years I have come seeking fruit on this fig tree and find none. [[Bring the axe,]]ᶜ Cut it down [then],ᵈ why should it even waste the ground?'

₈"But he answered and said to him, 'Sir, leave it also for this year, until I dig around it and put on manure. ₉And if indeed it bears fruit [in the future],ᵉ well; but if not, you shall cut it down.'"

₁₀Now he was teaching in one of the synagogues on the Sabbath. ₁₁And behold, [[there was]]ᶠ a woman having a spirit of infirmity for {eighteen}ᵍ years, and she was bent over and not able to straighten up completely. ₁₂Seeing her, {Jesus}ʰ [called out]ⁱ and said to her, "Woman, you are freed from your infirmity."

₁₃And he laid his hands on her, and immediately she was made straight, and she glorified God.

₁₄[But]ʲ The ruler of the synagogue, indignant because Jesus had healed on the Sabbath, said to the people [that],ᵏ "There are six days [in which]ˡ work ought to be done. Come on those days and be healed, and not on the Sabbath day."

₁₅{But}ᵐ {the Lord}ⁿ answered him and said, "You hypocrites! Does not each of you [on the Sabbath]ᵒ untie his ox or his donkey from the manger and lead it away to water it? ₁₆And this daughter of Abraham, whom Satan has bound for eighteen years, should she not have been set free from this bond on the Sabbath day?"

₁₇And [as he was saying these things,]ᵖ [all] q those opposing him were put to shame, and all the people rejoiced at [all]ʳ the glorious things that were done by him.

₁₈He said therefore: "What is the kingdom of God like, and to what shall I compare it?"

₁₉"It is like a mustard seed, which a man took and planted in his garden, and it grew and became a [large]ˢ tree, and the birds of the sky nested in its branches."

ᵃ 13:3, **all:** Absent from Latin(ff²).

ᵇ 13:4, **eighteen:** Some manuscripts read "ten and eight." A(02) W(032) Latin(a b e ff² i) BYZ TR.

ᶜ 13:7, **Bring the axe:** Included in D(05).

ᵈ 13:7, **then:** 𝔓75 A(02) Latin(a b ff² i) NA28[] THGNT ‖ Absent from ℵ(01) B(03) D(05) W(032) Latin(e) SBLGNT BYZ TR.

ᵉ 13:9, **in the future:** Absent from D(05).

ᶠ 13:11, **there was:** Absent from A(02) Latin(e) BYZ TR.

ᵍ 13:11, **eighteen:** Some manuscripts read "ten and eight." BYZ TR.

ʰ 13:12, **Jesus:** Some manuscripts read "he." 𝔓45 Latin(b i).

ⁱ 13:12, **called out:** Absent from D(05) Latin(e).

ʲ 13:14, **But:** Absent from 𝔓75.

ᵏ 13:14, **that:** Absent from 𝔓45 A(02) D(05) W(032) Latin(a b e ff² i) BYZ TR.

ˡ 13:14, **in which:** Absent from ℵ(01) B(03).

ᵐ 13:15, **But:** Some manuscripts read "therefore." BYZ TR.

ⁿ 13:15, **the Lord:** Some manuscripts read "Jesus." D(05) Syriac(syˢ syᶜ syᵖ).

ᵒ 13:15, **on the Sabbath:** Absent from ℵ(01).

ᵖ 13:17, **as he was saying these thing:** Absent from D(05) Latin(e).

q 13:17, **all:** Absent from 𝔓45 D(05) Latin(b e ff² i it).

ʳ 13:17, **all:** Absent from Latin(b ff² i).

ˢ 13:19, **large:** Included in 𝔓45 A(02) W(032) BYZ TR ‖ Absent from 𝔓75 ℵ(01) B(03) D(05) Latin(a b ff² i) NA28 SBLGNT THGNT.

20 [And again he said,][a] [["To what
is the kingdom of God like?"]][b] "To
what shall I compare the kingdom of
God? 21 It is like leaven that a woman
took and hid in three measures of flour,
until it was [all][c] leavened."[d]

22 And he went on his way through
towns and villages, teaching and
journeying toward Jerusalem.

23 And someone said to him, "Lord,
{will those who are saved be few}?"[e]
And {he said to them},[f] 24 "Strive to
enter through the narrow {door}.[g] For
many, [I say to you,][h] will seek to enter
and will not be able."

25 "From the time master of the
house has {risen}[i] and shut the door,
and you begin [to stand outside and][j]
to knock [at the door],[k] saying, 'Lord,
[[Lord]][l] open to us,' then he will
answer you, 'I do not know where you
are from.'

26 "Then you will begin to say,
'[Lord][m] We ate and drank in your
presence, and you taught in our streets.'

27 "And he [will say][n] to you, '{I
do not know [you][o]}[p] [where you are
from];[q] depart from me, all workers of
{unrighteousness}.'[r]

28 "In that place there will be
weeping and gnashing of teeth, when
you see Abraham and Isaac and Jacob
and all the prophets in the kingdom of
God but you yourselves cast out.[s]

29 "And people will come from east
and west, and [from][t] north and south,
and recline at the table in the kingdom
of God.

30 "And behold, some are last who
will be first, and some are first who will
be last."

31 {At that very hour}[u] some
Pharisees came and said to him, "Get
away from here, for Herod wants to
kill you."

32 And he said to them, "Go and tell
that fox, 'Behold, I cast out demons and
perform healings today and tomorrow,
and the third [[day]][v] I finish my
course.'"

33 "Nevertheless, I must go [on
my way today and tomorrow and the
day following],[w] for it cannot be that

---

a 13:20, **And again he said:** Absent from D(05).
b 13:20, **To what is the kingdom of God like:** Included in D(05) Latin(a ff^2).
c 13:21, **all:** Absent from Latin(a).
d 13:21, The phrase is literally translated as "hid in three measures of meal" or "mixed into about sixty pounds of flour." The term "σάτα" (*sata*) is a measure of volume, and the exact conversion can vary.
e 13:23, **will those who are saved be few:** D(05) reads "are there few who are saved."
f 13:23, **he said to them:** D(05) reads "He answered, saying."
g 13:24, **door:** 𝔓45 𝔓75 ℵ(01) B(03) D(05) NA28 SBLGNT THGNT || Some manuscripts read "gate." A(02) W(032) BYZ TR.
h 13:24, **I say to you:** Absent from D(05).
i 13:25, **risen:** Some manuscripts read "entered." D(05) Latin(a ff^2 i).
j 13:25, **to stand outside and:** Absent from ℵ(01).
k 13:25, **at the door:** Absent from D(05) Latin(a).
l 13:25, **Lord:** Some manuscripts include a second time. A(02) D(05) W(032) Latin(b e ff^2 i it) Syriac(sy^c sy^p) BYZ TR || Absent from 𝔓75 ℵ(01) B(03) Syriac(sy^s) NA28 SBLGNT THGNT.
m 13:26, **Lord:** Absent from D(05).
n 13:27, **will say:** Absent from ℵ(01) Latin(a b e ff^2 i).
o 13:27, **you:** ℵ(01) A(02) W(032) NA28[] THGNT || Absent from 𝔓75 ℵ(01) B(03) SBLGNT.
p 13:27, **I do not know you:** Some manuscripts read "I never knew you." D(05) Latin(e).
q 13:27, **where you are from:** Absent from D(05) Latin(e).
r 13:27, **unrighteousness:** Some manuscripts read "lawlessness." D(05).
s 13:28, **but you yourselves cast out:** Absent from Syriac(sy^s).
t 13:29, **from:** 𝔓75 B(03) || Absent from ℵ(01) A(02) D(05) W(032) BYZ.
u 13:31, **At that very hour:** 𝔓75 ℵ(01) B(03) D(05) NA28 SBLGNT TR || Some manuscripts read "On that very day." BYZ TR.
v 13:32, **day:** Included in B(03) Latin(b e).
w 13:33, **following:** Absent from Latin(b ff^2 i).

a prophet should perish away from Jerusalem.

34 "O Jerusalem, Jerusalem, the one killing the prophets and stoning those sent to her!

"How often would I have gathered your children together, just as a {hen}[a] [gathers her chicks under her wings],[b] and you were not willing!

35 "Behold, your house is left to you [[desolate]].[c]

"[But][d] I say to you [[that]],[e] you will not see me until [the time comes when][f] you say, 'Blessed is he who comes in the name of the Lord!'"

14 1 And it happened that when he went into the house of one of the rulers [of the][g] Pharisees on the Sabbath to eat bread, they were watching him closely. 2 And behold, there was a man with dropsy[h] before him.

3 And Jesus, having responded, said to the lawyers and Pharisees, [saying][i] "Is it lawful to heal on the Sabbath [or not]?"[j] 4 But they remained silent. And taking hold [of him],[k] he healed him and sent him away.

5 And [[answering]][l] he said to them, "Which of you, if your {son}[m] or ox falls into a well, will not immediately pull him out on the Sabbath day?" 6 {And they were not able to}[n] respond [[to him]][o] [to these things].[p]

7 He also told a parable to the invited guests, noticing how they were choosing the places of honor, saying [to them],[q] 8 "When you are invited [by someone][r] [to a wedding feast,][s] do not recline in the place of honor, lest someone more distinguished [than you][t] {has been invited [by him][u]},[v] 9 and the one who invited both you and him will come and say to you, 'Give this person your place,' and then you will begin with shame to take the lowest place. 10 But when you are invited, [go and][w] recline in the lowest place, so that when the one who invited you

---

a 13:34, **hen:** Some manuscripts read "bird." ℵ(01) D(05) W(032).

b 13:34, **gathers her chicks under her wings:** Absent from 𝔓75.

c 13:35, **desolate:** Included in D(05) Latin(a b) Syriac(sy^c sy^p) BYZ TR ‖ Absent from 𝔓45 𝔓75 ℵ(01) A(02) B(03) Latin(e ff^2 i) Syriac(sy^s) NA28 SBLGNT THGNT.

d 13:35, **But:** 𝔓75 A(02) B(03) D(05) W(032) ‖ Absent from 𝔓45 ℵ(01) ‖ Latin(a e) reads "for." ‖ TR reads "truly."

e 13:35, **that:** Absent from A(02) W(032) Latin(a) BYZ TR.

f 13:35, **the time comes when:** A(02) D(05) W(032) BYZ TR NA28[] SBLGNT‖ Absent from 𝔓45 𝔓75 ℵ(01) B(03) Latin(e i) THGNT.

g 14:1, **of the:** A(02) D(05) W(032) BYZ TR NA28[] SBLGNT ‖ Absent from 𝔓45 𝔓75 ℵ(01) THGNT.

h 14:2, **dropsy:** An illness characterized by the swelling of the feet, ankles, and legs with possible puffiness visible in the hands and face.

i 14:3, **saying:** Absent from D(05) Latin(a e).

j 14:3, **or not:** 𝔓75 ℵ(01) B(03) D(05) Latin(b e) NA28 SBLGNT THGNT ‖ Absent from 𝔓45 A(02) W(032) Latin (a ff^2 i) BYZ TR.

k 14:4, **of him:** Absent from Latin (b e ff^2 i).

l 14:5, **answering:** Included in A(02) W(032) BYZ TR ‖ Absent from 𝔓45 𝔓75 B(03) D(05) Latin (a b e ff^2 i) NA28 SBLGNT THGNT.

m 14:5, **son:** 𝔓45 𝔓75 B(03) W(032) BYZ NA28 SBLGNT THGNT ‖ Some manuscripts read "donkey." ℵ(01) Latin(a b ff^2 i) TR ‖ D(05) reads "sheep."

n 14:6, **And they were not able to:** D(05) reads "But they did not."

o 14:6, **to him:** Included in A(02) W(032) BYZ TR.

p 14:6, **to these things:** Absent from Latin(a).

q 14:7, **to them:** Absent from Latin(e).

r 14:8, **by someone:** Absent from D(05) Latin(a e i).

s 14:8, **to a wedding feast:** Absent from 𝔓75 Latin(b).

t 14:8, **than you:** Absent from 𝔓75 Latin(e).

u 14:8, **by him:** Absent from 𝔓75 D(05) Latin(a b ff^2 i).

v 14:8, **has been invited by him:** D(05) reads "comes."

w 14:10, **go and:** Absent from D(05).

comes, he {will}[a] say [to you],[b] 'Friend, move up higher'; then glory will be yours in the presence of [all][c] who are at table [with you].[d]

11 "For everyone who exalts himself will be humbled, and he who humbles himself will be exalted."

12 He also said to the one who had invited him, "When you make a lunch or dinner, do not invite [your][e] friends, nor your brothers, [nor [your][f] relatives,][g] nor {your rich neighbors},[h] lest they also invite you in return and repayment be made to you. 13 But when you make a feast, invite the poor, the crippled, the lame, the blind; 14 and you will be blessed, because they cannot repay you. For you will be repaid at the resurrection of the righteous."

15 When one of those who reclined at table with him heard [these things],[i] he said [to him],[j] "Blessed is the one who will eat {bread}[k] in the kingdom of God!"

16 But he said to him, "A certain man prepared a [great][l] feast and invited many. 17 And he sent his servant at the hour of the dinner to say to those who were invited, 'Come, because it [[all]][m] is already prepared.' 18 And they all alike began to make excuses. The first said [to him],[n] 'I have bought a field, and I need to go and see it; I ask you, consider me excused.' 19 And another said, 'I have bought five yoke of oxen, and I am going to try them out; {I ask you, consider me excused}.'[o] 20 And another said, 'I have married a wife, and {for this reason}[p] I cannot come.' 21 [And][q] The servant came and reported [[all]][r] [these things][s] to his lord.

"Then the master of the house became angry and said to his servant, 'Go out quickly into the streets and lanes of the city, and bring in the poor and crippled and blind [and lame].'[t] 22 And the servant said [[to him]],[u] '[Lord,][v] {What}[w] you commanded has been done, and still there is room.' 23 And the lord said to {the}[x] servant, 'Go out to the highways and hedges and compel people to come in, that my house may be filled. 24 For I say to you, none of {those} [y]men who were invited

---

a 14:10, will: 𝔓75 𝔓97 ℵ(01) B(03) NA28 SBLGNT THGNT ‖ Some manuscripts read "may." A(02) D(05) W(032) BYZ TR.

b 14:10, to you: Absent from Latin(a i).

c 14:10, all: 𝔓75 ℵ(01) A(02) B(03) NA28 SBLGNT THGNT ‖ Absent from 𝔓97 D(05) W(032) Latin(a b e ff2 i) Syriac(sys) BYZ TR.

d 14:10, with you: Absent from D(05) Latin(a b e ff2 i).

e 14:12, your: Absent from D(05) Latin(a).

f 14:12, your: Absent from ℵ(01) D(05) Latin(a b ff2).

g 14:12, nor your relatives: Absent from Latin(a e).

h 14:12, your rich neighbors: D(05) reads "the rich."

i 14:15, these things: Absent from ℵ(01).

j 14:15, to him: Absent from Latin(i).

k 14:15, bread: Some manuscripts read "dinner." A(02) W(032) BYZ.

l 14:16, great: Absent from Latin(e).

m 14:17, all: Included in A(02) D(05) W(032) Latin(a e) BYZ TR ‖ Absent from 𝔓75 ℵ(01) B(03) Latin(b ff2 i it) NA28 SBLGNT THGNT.

n 14:18, to him: Absent from D(05) Latin(a b e ff2 i).

o 14:19, I ask you, consider me excused: Some manuscripts read "therefore, I cannot come." D(05) Latin(it).

p 14:20, for this reason: Some manuscripts read "therefore." D(05) Latin (a b e i) Syriac(sys syc).

q 14:21, And: Absent from 𝔓75.

r 14:21, all: Included in D(05).

s 14:21, these things: Absent from Latin(b e).

t 14:21, and lame: Absent from A(02).

u 14:22, to him: Included in A(02).

v 14:22, Lord: Absent from D(05) Latin (e).

w 14:22, what: Some manuscripts read "as." BYZ TR.

x 14:23, the: Some manuscripts read "his." 𝔓75 D(05) Latin (a b) Syriac(sys syc syp).

y 14:24, those: D(05) reads "the."

shall taste my dinner.' [[For many are called, but few are chosen.]]"[a]

25 And [many][b] crowds were traveling together [with him],[c] and he turned and said to them, 26 "If anyone comes to me and does not hate his [own][d] father and mother, and [[his]][e] wife and children, and brothers and sisters, yet, even his own life; he cannot be my disciple.

27 "[[And]][f] Whoever [[therefore]][g] does not carry his {own}[h] cross[i] and follow me, cannot be my disciple.

28 "[For][j] Which of you, desiring to build a tower, does not first sit down and count the cost, whether he has enough to complete it? 29 Lest ever, {after he has}[k] laid the foundation {and is not able to finish,}[l] all who see it {begin to mock him,[m] 30 saying that}, 'This man began to build and was not able to finish.'

31 "Or what king, going out to meet another king in battle, will not [[immediately]][n] sit down first and consider whether he is able with ten thousand to confront the one coming [against him][o] with twenty thousand? 32 And if not, while the other is yet a great way off, he sends a delegation and asks for terms of peace.

33 "[Therefore,][p] {Any one of you}[q] who does not renounce all his possessions cannot be my disciple.

34 "[Therefore][r] Salt is good; but if [even][s] the salt becomes foolish, with what will it be seasoned?

35 "Neither into earth nor into dung is it suitable; they throw it out.

"He who has ears to hear, let him hear."

15 1 Now [all][t] the tax collectors and sinners were coming near to listen [to him].[u] 2 And the Pharisees and the scribes were grumbling, saying, "This one welcomes sinners and eats with them."

---

a 14:24, **For many are called, but few are chosen:** Included in BYZ.

b 14:25, **many:** Absent from D(05) Latin(b e ff² it) Syriac(syᶜ).

c 14:25, **with him:** Absent from 𝔓75.

d 14:26, **own:** Absent from Latin(e).

e 14:26, **his:** Included in D(05).

f 14:27, **And:** Included in A(02) D(05) W(032) BYZ TR ‖ Absent from 𝔓45 𝔓75 ℵ(01) B(03) NA28 SBLGNT THGNT.

g 14:27, **therefore:** Included in B(03).

h 14:27, **own:** Absent from D(05) BYZ TR THGNT.

i 14:27, **Cross:** BDAG gives the definition as (1) a pole to be placed in the ground and used for capital punishment, *cross* (2) the cross, with focus on the fate of Jesus Christ or (3) the suffering/death which believers endure in following the crucified Lord, *cross* . (BDAG, σταυρός).

j 14:28, **For:** Absent from Latin(a b ff²) ‖ Some manuscripts read "But." D(05) Latin(e).

k 14:29, **after he has:** Some manuscripts read "having." Latin(a b e ff² i).

l 14:29, **and is not able to finish:** Some manuscripts read "He was not able to build and." D(05) Latin(e).

m 14:29-30, **begin to mock him, saying that:** Some manuscripts read "will be about to say." D(05) Latin(a b e ff² i).

n 14:31, **immediately:** Included in D(05).

o 14:31, **against him:** Absent from Latin(e).

p 14:33, **Therefore:** Absent from W(032).

q 14:33, **any one of you:** D(05) reads "also from you, everyone." ‖ Some manuscripts read "from you." Latin(b ff² i).

r 14:34, **Therefore:** 𝔓75 ℵ(01) B(03) NA28 SBLGNT THGNT ‖ Absent from A(02) D(05) W(032) Latin(a b e ff² i) Syriac(sy) BYZ TR.

s 14:34, **even:** ℵ(01) B(03) D(05) NA28 SBLGNT THGNT ‖ Absent from 𝔓75 A(02) W(032) BYZ TR.

t 15:1, **all:** Absent from W(032).

u 15:1, **to him:** Absent from ℵ(01).

3 So he told them this parable, [saying,][a] 4 "Which man among you, having a hundred sheep and [losing one of them,][b] does not leave the ninety-nine in the wilderness and go after the one that is lost until he finds it? 5 And finding, he places it on his shoulders, rejoicing. 6 And when he comes home, he calls together his friends and neighbors, saying to them, 'Rejoice with me, for I have found my lost sheep.'

7 "[[But]][c] I say to you [that][d] in this way there will be joy in heaven over one sinner repenting, *more* than over ninety-nine righteous ones who have no need of repentance.

8 "Or what woman, having ten [silver coins],[e] if she loses one coin, does not light a lamp and sweep the house and search carefully until [when][f] she finds it? 9 And when she has found it, she calls together her friends and neighbors, saying, 'Rejoice with me, for I have found the coin that I had lost.'

10 "Thus, I say to you, there is joy in the presence of the angels of God over one sinner who repents."

11 And he said, "A certain man had two sons. 12 And the younger of them said to his father, '[Father,][g] Give me the share of the property that falls to me.' {So}[h] he divided his livelihood between them. 13 And not many days later, the younger son gathered everything together and traveled to a distant country, and there he squandered his {property}[i] by living recklessly. 14 And when he had spent everything, a severe famine arose in that country, and he began to be in need. 15 So he went and joined himself to one of the citizens of that country, who sent him into {his}[j] fields to feed pigs. 16 And he longed {to be satisfied}[k] with the pods that the pigs were eating, but no one gave him anything.

17 "But when he came to himself, he said, 'How many of my father's hired servants have more than enough bread, but I am perishing here with hunger! 18 I will arise and go to my father, and I will say to him, Father, I have sinned against heaven and before you, 19 I am no longer worthy to be called your son; treat me as one of your hired servants.'

20 "And he arose and came to his father. But while he was still far off, his father saw him and was filled with compassion, and ran and embraced him and kissed him. 21 And the son said to him, 'Father, I have sinned against heaven and before you; [[and]][l] I am no longer worthy to be called your son. [[Make me like one of your hired men.]][m]'

---

a 15:3, **saying:** Absent from D(05) Latin(b e) Syriac(sy^s sy^c sy^p).

b 15:4, **losing one of them:** Absent from Latin(i).

c 15:7, **But:** Included in D(05).

d 15:7, **that:** Absent from Latin(e).

e 15:8, **silver coins:** Or "drachmas." Absent from D(05) Latin(a b e ff² i).

f 15:8, **when:** Absent from D(05) Latin(b e ff² i).

g 15:12, **Father:** Absent from ℵ(01).

h 15:12, **So:** A(02) B(03) NA28 SBLGNT THGNT ‖ Some manuscripts read "And." ℵ(01) D(05) W(032) Latin (a b e ff² i) BYZ TR ‖ Absent from 𝔓75.

i 15:13, **property:** D(05) reads "life."

j 15:15, **his:** D(05) reads "the."

k 15:16, **to be satisfied:** 𝔓75 ℵ(01) B(03) D(05) NA28 THGNT ‖ Some manuscripts read "fill his stomach." A(02) Latin(b ff² i) BYZ TR SBLGNT ‖ W(032) reads "fill the stomach and to be satisfied."

l 15:21, **and:** Included in BYZ TR.

m 15:21, **Make me like one of your hired men:** Included in ℵ(01) B(03) D(05) ‖ Absent from 𝔓75 A(02) W(032) Latin(a b e ff² i) BYZ TR NA28 SBLGNT THGNT.

22 “But the father said to his
servants, ‘[Quickly],[a] bring out the
best robe [and put it on him],[b] and put
a ring on his hand and sandals [on
his feet],[c] 23 and {bring}[d] the fattened
calf and sacrifice it, and eating, let us
rejoice, 24 for this son of mine was dead
and has come to life; [[and]][e] [he was
lost and has been found.]’[f] And they
began to celebrate.

25 “Now his older son was in
the field; and as he was coming, he
approached the house, he heard music
and dancing. 26 And calling one of the
servants, he inquired what these things
might be.

27 “But he said [to him][g] [[that]],[h]
‘Your brother has come, and your father
has killed the fattened calf, because he
has received him back safe and sound.’
28 [But][i] he was angry and did not want
to go in. {But}[j] his father came out and
pleaded with him.

29 “But he answered {his}[k] father,
‘Look, these many years I have served
you, and I never disobeyed your
command, yet you never gave me a
young goat [[from your flock]],[l] that
I might {celebrate}[m] with my friends.
30 {But when this son of yours came,
who has squandered your livelihood
with prostitutes, you sacrificed [for
him][n] the fattened calf}!’[o]

31 “And he said to him, ‘[Son,][p]
You are always with me, and all that is
mine is yours. 32 But it was necessary
to rejoice and be glad, because this
brother of yours was dead and has
come to life; he was lost and has
been found.’”

16 1 He also said to {the}[q] disciples,
“There was a rich man who had
a manager, and this one was accused
to him of squandering his possessions.
2 And calling [him],[r] he said to him,
‘What is this I hear about you? Give
an account of your management,
for you can no longer be manager.’
3 And the manager said to himself,
‘What shall I do, since my lord is taking
the management away from me? I am
not strong enough to dig, and I am
ashamed to beg. 4 I know what I will do,
so that when I am removed from the
management, they will receive me into
their houses.’

---

a 15:22, **Quickly:** 𝔓75 א(01) B(03) D(05) NA28 SBLGNT THGNT || Absent from A(02) W(032) BYZ TR.
b 15:22, **and put it on him:** Absent from Latin(e).
c 15:22, **on his feet:** Absent from Latin(e).
d 15:23, **bring:** Some manuscripts read “having brought.” A(02) W(032) BYZ TR.
e 15:24, **and:** Included in BYZ TR.
f 15:24, **he was lost and has been found:** Absent from W(032).
g 15:27, **to him:** Absent from D(05).
h 15:27, **that:** Absent from W(032) Latin (ff^{2} i).
i 15:28, **But:** Some manuscripts read “Therefore.” BYZ TR.
j 15:28, **But:** Some manuscripts read “Therefore.” BYZ TR.
k 15:29, **his:** 𝔓75 A(02) B(03) D(05) Latin(a b e ff^{2} i) NA28 SBLGNT || Some manuscripts read “the.” א(01) W(032) BYZ TR THGNT.
l 15:29, **from your flock:** Included in D(05).
m 15:29, **celebrate:** D(05) reads “dine.”
n 15:30, **for him:** Absent from D(05) Latin(a e).
o 15:30, **But when this son...:** D(05) reads “But to your son, who has consumed everything with prostitutes and upon his return, you have sacrificed the fattened calf.”
p 15:31, **son:** Absent from D(05) Latin(a).
q 16:1, **the:** Some manuscripts read “his.” A(02) W(032) Latin(a b ff^{2} i) BYZ TR.
r 16:2, **to him:** Absent from D(05).

5 "And he called in each one of his master's debtors and said to the first, 'How much do you owe my master?' 6 And he said [[to him]],ᵃ 'A hundred {baths}ᵇ of oil.' {And}ᶜ he said [to him],ᵈ 'Take your bills, and [quickly sitting down,]ᵉ write fifty.' 7 Then he said to another, ['And how much do you owe?' He said,]ᶠ 'A hundred measures of wheat.' [And]ᵍ he said to him, 'Take your bill and write eighty.' 8 And the lord praised the dishonest manager because he had acted shrewdly; [[therefore, I say to you]]ʰ for the sons of this age are more shrewd in dealing with their own generation than the sons of light."

9 "[And]ⁱ I say to you, make friends for yourselves from the unrighteous wealth, so that when {it}ʲ fails, they may receive you into the eternalᵏ dwellings.

10 "One who is faithful in a very little is also faithful in much, and one who is dishonest in a very little is also dishonest in much.

11 "If then you have not been faithful in the unrighteous wealth, who will entrust to you the true riches?

12 "And if you have not been faithful in that which is another's, who will give to you [that which is your own]?ˡ

13 "No servant can serve two masters; for either he will hate the one and love the other, or he will be devoted to the one and despise the other.

"You cannot serve God and {wealth}."ᵐ

14 They were hearing [all]ⁿ these things, [[also]]ᵒ [Pharisees]ᵖ who were lovers of money, and they were ridiculing him. 15 And he said to them, "You are those who justify yourselves before men, but God knows your hearts; for what is exalted among men is an abomination in the sight of {God}.ᑫ

16 "The law and the prophets {were}ʳ until John; since then the kingdom of God is preached [; and everyone forces his way into it].ˢ

17 "But it is easier for heaven and earth to pass away than for one stroke of the law to fall.

18 "Everyone who divorces his wife and marries another commits adultery, and {he}ᵗ who marries a woman divorced [from a man]ᵘ commits adultery."

ᵃ 16:6, **to him:** Included in ℵ(01).

ᵇ 16:6, **baths:** D(05) reads "jars."

ᶜ 16:6, **And:** Some manuscripts read "But." BYZ TR.

ᵈ 16:6, **to him:** Absent from W(032) Latin(e).

ᵉ 16:6, **quickly sitting down:** Absent from D(05).

ᶠ 16:7, **And how much do you owe? He said:** Absent from D(05).

ᵍ 16:7, **And:** 𝔓75 B(03) NA28 SBLGNT THGNT ‖ Included in A(02) W(032) BYZ TR ‖ Some manuscripts read "But." ℵ(01) D(05).

ʰ 16:8, **therefore, I say to you:** Included in D(05) Latin(a).

ⁱ 16:9, **And:** Absent from D(05) BYZ TR.

ʲ 16:9, **it:** Some manuscripts read "you." BYZ TR.

ᵏ 16:9, **eternal:** Or "lasting." The primary meaning of the Greek word pertains to a long period of time. (BDAG, αἰώνιος).

ˡ 16:12, **that which is your own:** Absent from some manuscripts Latin(b).

ᵐ 16:13, **wealth:** Greek "mammon."

ⁿ 16:14, **all:** Absent from D(05) Latin(i).

ᵒ 16:14, **also:** Included in A(02) W(032) BYZ TR.

ᵖ 16:14, **Pharisees:** Absent from ℵ(01).

ᑫ 16:15, **God:** B(03) reads "the Lord."

ʳ 16:16, **were:** Some manuscripts read "prophesied until John." D(05) Syriac(syᶜ).

ˢ 16:16, **and everyone forces his way into it:** Absent from ℵ(01).

ᵗ 16:18, **he:** 𝔓75 B(03) D(05) Latin(a b e ff² i) Syriac(syˢ syᶜ) NA28 SBLGNT THGNT ‖ Some manuscripts read "everyone." ℵ(01) A(02) W(032) Syriac(syᵖ) BYZ TR.

ᵘ 16:18, **from a man:** Absent from D(05) Syriac(syˢ syᶜ syᵖ).

19 [[He also told another parable:]][a]
"There was a certain rich man [[named
Neues]],[b] and he dressed in purple and
fine linen, rejoicing splendidly every
day. 20 But a certain poor man named
Lazarus was laid at his gate, covered
with sores, 21 who desired to be fed with
{what}[c] fell from the rich man's table;
moreover, the dogs came and licked
his sores.

22 "And it happened that the poor
man died and was carried away by the
angels into Abraham's bosom. The rich
man also died and was buried; 23 and in
Hades, being in torment, he lifted up
his eyes and saw Abraham far off and
Lazarus in his bosom [[resting]].[d]
24 And he called out, 'Father Abraham,
have mercy upon me, and send Lazarus
to dip the end of his finger in water and
cool my tongue; for I am in anguish in
this flame.'

25 "But Abraham said [[to him]],[e]
'Son, remember that you in your
lifetime received your good things, and
Lazarus in like manner evil things; but
now he is comforted here, and you are
in anguish. 26 And {in}[f] all these things,
a great chasm has been established
between us and you, so that those who
want to cross over [from here][g] to you
cannot, {nor can they cross over from
there to us}.'"[h]

27 "But he said, '[Therefore],[i] I ask
you, [father,][j] [[Abraham,]][k] {that you
might}[l] send him to my father's house,
28 for I have five brothers, so that he
may warn them, lest they also come
into this place of torment.'

29 "But Abraham said [[to him]],[m]
'They have Moses and the prophets; let
them listen to them.' 30 And he said, 'No,
father Abraham; but if someone goes to
them from the dead, they will repent.'
31 He said to him, 'If they do not hear
Moses and the prophets, neither will
they be convinced if someone rises from
the dead [[and goes to them]].'"[n]

17 1 And he said to {his}[o] disciples,
"It is inevitable that stumbling
blocks come, but woe to {the one}
through whom they come!

2 "[[But]][p] It would be better for
him if a millstone were hung around his
neck and he were thrown into the sea,
rather than causing one of these little
ones to stumble.

3 "Be on your guard! If your brother
sins [[against you]],[q] rebuke him; and if
he [[indeed]][r] repents, forgive him.

---

a 16:19, **He also told another parable:** Included in D(05) Syriac(sy^{c}).
b 16:19, **named Neues:** Included in 𝔓75.
c 16:21, **what:** 𝔓75 ℵ(01) B(03) Latin(b e ff^{2} i) Syriac(sy^{s} sy^{c}) NA28 SBLGNT THGNT || Some manuscripts read "the crumbs that." A(02) D(05) W(032) Latin(a) Syriac(sy^{p}) BYZ TR.
d 16:23, **resting:** Included in D(05) Latin(b e it).
e 16:25, **to him:** Included in Latin (a b ff^{2} i).
f 16:26, **in:** 𝔓75 ℵ(01) B(03) NA28 SBLGNT THGNT || Some manuscripts read "upon." A(02) D(05) BYZ TR.
g 16:26, **from here:** Absent from D(05) W(032) Latin(e).
h 16:26, **nor can they cross over from there to us:** Some manuscripts read "Neither from there to here to cross over." D(05).
i 16:27, **therefore:** Absent from W(032) Latin(e f).
j 16:27, **father:** Absent from Latin(e).
k 16:27, **Abraham:** Included in D(05) Syriac(sy^{c}).
l 16:27, **that you might:** Some manuscripts read "to." D(05) Latin(a b e i).
m 16:29, **to him:** Included in A(02) D(05) W(032) Latin(a) Syriac($sy^{c\ p}$) BYZ TR || Absent from 𝔓75 ℵ(01) B(03) Latin(b ff^{2} i) Syriac(sy^{s}) NA28 SBLGNT THGNT.
n 16:31, **and goes to them:** Included in D(05) Latin(a b ff^{2} i).
o 17:1, **his:** Some manuscripts read "the." W(032) Latin(e) BYZ TR.
p 17:2, **But:** Included in D(05). || Some manuscripts read "However." Latin(a b ff^{2} i).
q 17:3, **against you:** Included in D(05) Latin(e) BYZ TR.
r 17:3, **indeed:** Included in A(02).

4“And if he sins against you seven
times a day, and returns [to you][a] seven
times [[in a day]],[b] saying, ‘I repent,’
you shall forgive him.”

5The apostles said to the Lord,
“Increase our faith!” 6But {the Lord}[c]
said [to them],[d] “If you had faith like a
mustard seed, [[you would say to this
mountain, 'Move from here to there,'
and it would move. And]][e] you would
say to {this}[f] {mulberry}[g] tree, ‘[Be
uprooted and][h] Be planted in the sea;’
and it would obey you.

7“But which of you, having a
servant plowing or tending sheep, will
say [[to him]][i] when he has come in
from the field, ‘Come [immediately][j]
and sit down to eat’? 8But will he [not][k]
say to him, ‘Prepare something for me
to eat, and, having girded yourself,
serve me until I eat and drink; and
afterward you will eat and drink’?
9Does he thank [{the}[l] servant][m]
because he did what was commanded
[[to him]]?[n] [[I think not!]][o] 10[So][p]
[You][q] Also, when you {have done [all][r]
[[these things]][s] what was commanded
to you},[t] {[you say][u] [that][v] ‘We are
unworthy servants; [[because]][w] we
have done only what we were obligated
to do.’”}[x]

11And it happened that while [[he
was]][y] on the way to Jerusalem, he
passed through the midst of Samaria
and Galilee. 12And as he entered
into a certain village, {ten leprous
men met}[z] [him],[a] [who stood][b] at
a distance; 13and they {raised their
voices, saying,}[c] “Jesus, Master, have
mercy on us.”

---

a 17:4, **to you:** Absent from W(032) BYZ.
b 17:4, **in a day:** Included in A(02) W(032) Latin(e) BYZ TR.
c 17:6 , **the Lord:** Some manuscripts read “he.” D(05).
d 17:6, **to them:** Included in D(05).
e 17:6, **you would say to this mountain...:** Included in D(05).
f 17:6, **this:** A(02) B(03) W(032) Latin(a b e i) NA28[] SBLGNT || Some manuscripts read “the.” 𝔓75 ℵ(01) D(05) Latin(ff^2) BYZ TR THGNT.
g 17:6, **mulberry:** Some manuscripts read “fig.” D(05).
h 17:6, **Be uprooted and:** Absent from D(05).
i 17:7, **to him:** Absent from A(02) W(032) BYZ TR.
j 17:7, **immediately:** Absent from Latin(a b ff^2 i).
k 17:8, **not:** Absent from D(05) Latin(a b e ff^2 i).
l 17:9, **the:** Some manuscripts read “that.” W(032) Latin(e) BYZ TR.
m 17:9, **the servant:** Absent from ℵ(01).
n 17:9, **to him:** Included in D(05) Latin(b ff^2 i) TR.
o 17:9, **I think not!:** Included in A(02) D(05) W(032) Latin(b ff^2 i) Syriac(sy^p) BYZ TR || Absent from 𝔓75 B(03) NA28 SBLGNT THGNT.
p 17:10, **So:** Absent from Latin(b ff^2 i).
q 17:10, **You:** Absent from D(05).
r 17:10, **all:** Absent from D(05) Latin(a b e ff^2 i).
s 17:10, **these things:** Included in A(02).
t 17:10, **have done all what was commanded to you:** D(05) reads “do all that I say.”
u 17:10, **you say:** Absent from Latin(it) Syriac(sy^s sy^c).
v 17:10, **that:** Absent from A(02) W(032) Latin(a b e ff^2 i).
w 17:10, **because:** Included in W(032) Latin(b e ff^2 i) BYZ TR.
x 17:10, **you say that...:** D(05) reads “it is said that we are servants, useless, we have done what we ought to have done.”
y 17:11, **he was:** Included in A(02) D(05) W(032) BYZ TR.
z 17:12, **ten leprous men met:** D(05) reads “there were ten men with leprosy.”
a 17:12, **him:** ℵ(01) A(02) W(032) NA28[] THGNT BYZ TR || Absent from 𝔓75 B(03) D(05) SBLGNT.
b 17:12, **who stood:** Absent from ℵ(01). || B(03) reads “they rose up.”
c 17:13, **raised their voices, saying:** Some manuscripts read “cried out with a loud voice.” D(05) Latin(e).

14 And seeing [[them]],ᵃ he said to them, "[[Be healed,]]ᵇ Go and show yourselves to the priests." And it happened that as they went, they were cleansed.

15 And one of them, when he saw that he was healed, turned back, and with a loud voice glorified God, 16 and fell down [on his face]ᶜ at his feet [, giving thanks to him];ᵈ and he was a Samaritan.

17 And Jesus answered [[to them]],ᵉ "{Were not the ten cleansed?}ᶠ [But]ᵍ Where are the nine? 18 {Were there none found who returned}ʰ to give glory to God except this foreigner?" 19 And he said to him, "Rise and go." [[For]]ⁱ [Your faith has saved you.]ʲ

20 And when asked by the Pharisees when the kingdom [of God]ᵏ would come, he answered them and said, "The kingdom of God does not come with observation, 21 nor will they say, 'Look, here!' Or, [['Look']]ˡ 'There!' [[Do not believe it]]ᵐ for behold, the kingdom of God is within you."ⁿ

22 He [[therefore]]ᵒ said to {the}ᵖ disciples, "Days will come when you will desire [to see]ᑫ one of {the}ʳ days of the Son of Man,ˢ and you will not see it. 23 And they will say to you, 'Look, there! [Or,]ᵗ Look, here!' Do not go awayᵘ, nor pursue.

24 "For just as the lightning flashes from [under]ᵛ heaven [to what is under heaven],ʷ so [[also]]ˣ will {the Son of Man}ʸ [be in his day].ᶻ

25 "But first must he suffer many things, and be rejected of this generation.

ᵃ 17:14, **them:** Included in D(05) Latin(a e).

ᵇ 17:14, **Be healed:** Included in D(05).

ᶜ 17:16, **on his face:** Absent from Latin(ff²).

ᵈ 17:16, **giving thanks to him:** Absent from D(05).

ᵉ 17:17, **to them:** Included in D(05).

ᶠ 17:17, **Were not the ten cleansed:** Some manuscripts read "These ten were cleansed,." D(05) Latin(a b e ff² i it) Syriac(syˢ syᶜ).

ᵍ 17:17, **But:** Absent from A(02) D(05) Latin (a b e ff² i).

ʰ 17:18, **Were there none found who returned:** Some manuscripts read "None of them was found returning." D(05) Latin(it) Syriac(syˢ syᶜ).

ⁱ 17:19, **for:** Included in D(05) Latin(a b e ff²).

ʲ 17:19, **Your faith has saved you:** Absent from B(03).

ᵏ 17:20, **of God:** Absent from Latin(a i).

ˡ 17:21, **Look:** Included in A(02) D(05) W(032) Latin(a b) BYZ TR ‖ Absent from 𝔓75 ℵ(01) B(03) Latin(e ff² i) NA28 SBLGNT THGNT.

ᵐ 17:21, **Do not believe it:** Included in D(05).

ⁿ 17:21, **within you:** Or, in your midst.

ᵒ 17:22, **therefore:** Included in D(05).

ᵖ 17:22, **the:** Some manuscripts read "his." A(02) Latin(a b ff² i) BYZ TR.

ᑫ 17:22, **to see:** Absent from D(05).

ʳ 17:22, **the:** D(05) read "these."

ˢ 17:22, **one of the days of the Son of Man:** Or, the revealing of the Son of Man. See verse 30.

ᵗ 17:23, **or:** 𝔓75 A(02) B(03) NA28[] THGNT BYZ TR ‖ Absent from ℵ(01) D(05) W(032) SBLGNT.

ᵘ 17:23, **Do not go away:** Or, after them.

ᵛ 17:24, **under:** Absent from Latin(a b e).

ʷ 17:24, **to what is under heaven:** Absent from D(05) Latin(a ff² it).

ˣ 17:24, **also:** Included in TR.

ʸ 17:24, **the son of Man:** D(05) reads "men."

ᶻ 17:24, **be in his day:** ℵ(01) A(02) W(032) Syriac(sy) BYZ TR NA28[] SBLGNT THGNT ‖ Absent from 𝔓75 B(03) D(05) Latin(a b e ff² i it).

26 “And just as it happened in the
days of Noah, so it will be also in the
days of the Son of Man. 27 They were
eating, they were drinking, they were
marrying, they were being given in
marriage, until the day that Noah
entered into the ark, and the flood
{came},[a] and {destroyed}[b] them all.

28 “Likewise [as][c] it happened in
the days of Lot; they were eating, they
were drinking, buying, selling, planting,
building; 29 [but][d] the same day Lot
left Sodom, fire and sulfur rained
from heaven, and destroyed everyone.
30 It will be the same on the day the Son
of Man is revealed.

31 “On that day, whoever is on the
roof and their belongings in {the}[e]
house, let him not go down to take
them, and likewise, the one in the field
should not turn [to what is][f] behind.

32 “Remember Lot's wife.
33 {Whoever seeks [to preserve][g] his life
will lose it},[h] {but}[i] whoever loses it
will {give it life}.[j]

34 “I say to you, in that night there
shall be two in [one][k] bed; [the][l] one
will be taken, and the other will be left.
35 [There will be two in the same place,
[the][m] one will be taken, the other will
be left.][n] 36 [[Two men will be in the
field; one will be taken and the other
left.]]”[o]

37 And they responded, saying [to
him],[p] “Where, Lord?” And he said
[to them],[q] “{Where}[r] the body is,
[also][s] the eagles[t] will {be gathered
together}.”[u]

18 1 [[There they will be gathered
for their terrible fate;]][v] [He
was telling them a parable to the effect
that [they][w] ought][x] Always pray and
do not lose heart; 2 [saying,][y] “In a
certain city there was a judge who
neither feared God nor respected man.

---

[a] 17:27, **came:** Some manuscripts read “happened.” D(05) Latin(e).
[b] 17:27, **destroyed:** ℵ(01) reads “took.”
[c] 17:28, **as:** Absent from Latin(b ff^{2}).
[d] 17:29, **but:** Absent from D(05) Latin(a e).
[e] 17:31, **the:** ℵ(01) reads “his.”
[f] 17:31, **to what is:** Absent from Latin(a b e ff^{2} i).
[g] 17:33, **to preserve:** 𝔓75 B(03) NA28 SBLGNT THGNT || Absent from D(05). || Some manuscripts read “save.” ℵ(01) A(02) W(032) Latin(a b e ff^{2} i) BYZ TR.
[h] 17:33, **Whoever seeks to preserve his life will loose it:** 𝔓75 B(03) NA28 SBLGNT THGNT || Some manuscripts read “Whoever seeks to save his life will lose it.” ℵ(01) A(02) W(032) BYZ TR || Some manuscripts read “Whoever wishes to bring life to his soul will lose it.” D(05) Syriac(sy^{s} sy^{c} sy^{p}).
[i] 17:33, **but:** 𝔓75 ℵ(01) B(03) NA28 SBLGNT THGNT || Some manuscripts read “and.” A(02) D(05) W(032) BYZ TR.
[j] 17:33, **give it life:** Some manuscripts read “save it.” Latin(a b ff^{2} i).
[k] 17:34, **one:** Absent from B(03).
[l] 17:34, **the:** 𝔓75 ℵ(01) B(03) TR NA28 SBLGNT THGNT || Absent from A(02) D(05) W(032) BYZ.
[m] 17:35, **the:** Absent from A(02) W(032).
[n] 17:35, **There will be two...:** Verse 35 is absent from ℵ(01).
[o] 17:36, **Two men will be in the field...:** Some manuscripts include verse 36. D(05).
[p] 17:37, **to him:** Absent from D(05).
[q] 17:37, **to them:** Absent from Latin(b e ff^{2} i).
[r] 17:37, **Where:** Some manuscripts read “Wherever it may happen.” Latin(a b ff^{2} i).
[s] 17:37, **also:** Absent from D(05) BYZ TR.
[t] 17:37, **eagles:** Or vultures.
[u] 17:37, **be gathered together:** Some manuscripts read “will gather.” A(02) D(05) W(032).
[v] 18:1, **There they will be gathered there for their terrible fate:** Included in D(05).
[w] 18:1, **they:** Absent from D(05) Latin(a b e ff^{2} i) BYZ TR.
[x] 18:1, **He was telling them a parable...:** Absent from D(05).
[y] 18:2, **saying:** Absent from D(05).

3 "And there was a widow in that city who kept coming to him and saying, 'Give me justice against my adversary.' 4 And he {did not want to}[a] for a [some][b] time. But after these things, {he said to himself}[c] , 'Even if I do not fear God, {nor}[d] regard men, 5 indeed, because this widow causes [me][e] trouble, I will grant her justice, so that she may not wear me out in the end by her constant coming.'"

6 And the Lord said, "[Hear][f] What the judge of unrighteousness says:[g] 7 And will not God bring about justice for his chosen ones who cry out [to him][h] day and night, and is he {slow to respond to them}?[i] 8 I say to you [that][j] he will bring about their vindication quickly.

"{However},[k] when the Son of Man comes, will he find the faith on the earth?"

9 But he [also][l] told [this parable][m] to some who trusted in themselves [that they were righteous,][n] and despised {others}.[o]

10 "Two men went up into the temple to pray, one a Pharisee and the other [one][p] a tax collector. 11 The Pharisee, standing [by himself][q], prayed thus: 'God, I thank you that I am not like other men, extortioners, unjust, adulterers, or even like this tax collector. 12 I fast twice a week; I give tithes of all that I get.'

13 "[But][r] The tax collector, standing far off, would not even lift up his eyes to heaven, but beat his breast, saying, '[God,][s] Be merciful to me, a sinner!' 14 I say to you [[that]],[t] this man went down [to his house][u] justified, rather than {the other}.[v]

"For everyone who exalts himself will be humbled, but he who humbles himself will be exalted."

15 Now they were [also][w] bringing {babies}[x] to him that he might touch them. And when the disciples saw this, they rebuked them. 16 But Jesus called [them],[y] saying, "Let the children come to me, and do not hinder them, for to such belongs the kingdom {of God}.[z]

---

a 18:4, **did not want to:** Some manuscripts read "refused."

b 18:4, **some:** Included in D(05).

c 18:4, **he said to himself:** Some manuscripts read "he came to himself and says."

d 18:4, **nor:** ℵ(01) B(03) NA28 SBLGNT THGNT ‖ Some manuscripts read "and do not." A(02) D(05) W(032) BYZ TR.

e 18:5, **me:** Absent from W(032).

f 18:6, **Hear:** Absent from ℵ(01).

g 18:6, **says:** Or "indicates."

h 18:7, **to him:** Absent from Latin(a b ff² i).

i 18:7, **slow to respond to them:** Some manuscripts read "patient with them." D(05).

j 18:8, **that:** Absent from D(05) Latin(b ff² i).

k 18:8, **However:** D(05) reads "So."

l 18:9, **also:** Absent from BYZ.

m 18:9, **this parable:** Absent from D(05).

n 18:9, **that they were righteous:** Absent from Latin(i).

o 18:9, **others:** D(05) manuscripts reads "the rest of men."

p 18:10, **one:** Included in D(05) Latin(c e ff²).

q 18:11, **by himself:** Absent from ℵ(01) Latin(b ff² i).

r 18:13, **But:** Absent from BYZ TR.

s 18:13, **God:** Absent from ℵ(01).

t 18:14, **that:** Included in Latin(a b ff² i).

u 18:14, **to his house:** Absent from D(05) Latin(a b ff² i).

v 18:14, **the other:** Some manuscripts read "that Pharisee." D(05) Latin(a b ff² i).

w 18:15, **also:** Absent from D(05).

x 18:15, **babies:** D(05) reads "children."

y 18:16, **them:** Absent from B(03).

z 18:16, **of God:** Some manuscripts read "of the heavens." BYZ TR.

17 "[[For]]ᵃ Truly, I say to you, whoever does not receive the kingdom of God like a child will not enter it."

18 And a ruler asked him, [saying,]ᵇ "Good Teacher, what must I do to inherit eternal life?" 19 And {Jesus}ᶜ said to him, "Why do you call me good? No one is good except God alone.ᵈ 20 You know the commandments."

[[But he said, "Which ones?" Jesus said,]]ᵉ

"Do not commit adultery, [Do not murder,]ᶠ Do not steal, Do not bear false witness, Honor your father and [[your]]ᵍ mother."ʰ

21 And he said [[to him]],ⁱ "All these I have kept from [my]ʲ youth."

22 When Jesus heard [these things],ᵏ he said to him, "One thing you still lack. Sell all that you have and distribute to the poor, and you will have treasure in {the heavens};ˡ and come, follow me."

23 But when he heard [[all]]ᵐ these things, he became very sad, for he was extremely rich.

24 {But seeing him, Jesus [becoming very distressed],ⁿ said},ᵒ "How difficult it is for those who have wealth to enter the kingdom of God!

25 "[For]ᵖ It is easier for a camel to {enter} q the eye of a needle than for a rich man [to enter]ʳ the kingdom of God."

26 But those who heard said, "And who can be saved?" 27 But {he}ˢ said, "What is impossible with man is possible with God."

28 And Peter said, "Behold, we have left {our own things};ᵗ [[and]]ᵘ we have followed you."

ᵃ 18:17, **For:** Included in D(05).

ᵇ 18:18, **saying:** Absent from D(05).

ᶜ 18:19, **Jesus:** Some manuscripts read "he." D(05).

ᵈ 18:19, **God alone:** Or "one, God."

ᵉ 18:20, **But he said, Which ones? Jesus said:** Included in D(05). Latin(a e) includes part of this. This is a parallel with Matthew 19:18.

ᶠ 18:20, **Do not murder:** Absent from Latin(e).

ᵍ 18:20, **your:** Included in ℵ(01) Latin(a b) Syriac(syˢ syᶜ syᵖ) BYZ TR ‖ Absent from A(02) B(03) D(05) W(032) Latin(e ff² i) NA28 SBLGNT THGNT.

ʰ 18:20, Exodus 20:12-16, Deuteronomy 5:16-20.

ⁱ 18:21, **to him:** Included in Latin(ff² i).

ʲ 18:21, **my:** ℵ(01) A(02) W(032) Latin(a b e ff² i) BYZ TR SBLGNT THGNT ‖ Absent from B(03) D(05) NA28.

ᵏ 18:22, **these things:** A(02) W(032) BYZ TR ‖ Absent from ℵ(01) B(03) D(05) Latin(a b ff² i) NA28 SBLGNT THGNT.

ˡ 18:22, **the heavens:** ℵ(01) A(02) B(03) D(05) NA28 SBLGNT THGNT ‖ Some manuscripts read "heaven." W(032) BYZ TR.

ᵐ 18:23, **all:** Included in ℵ(01).

ⁿ 18:24, **becoming very distressed:** A(02) D(05) W(032) BYZ TR NA28[] ‖ Absent from ℵ(01) B(03) Syriac(sy) SBLGNT THGNT.

ᵒ 18:24, **But seeing him, Jesus...:** Some manuscripts read "Seeing him become very distressed, Jesus said." D(05) Latin(b ff² i).

ᵖ 18:25, **For:** Absent from Latin (b i).

q 18:25, **enter:** Some manuscripts read "pass through." A(02) D(05).

ʳ 18:25, **to enter:** Absent from Latin(a e ff² i).

ˢ 18:27, **he:** Some manuscripts read "Jesus." Latin(b ff² i).

ᵗ 18:28, **our own things:** B(03) Latin(b ff² i) NA28 SBLGNT THGNT ‖ Some manuscripts read "all." ℵ(01) A(02) W(032) BYZ TR ‖ Some manuscripts read "all our own things." D(05) Latin(a e).

ᵘ 18:28, **and:** Included in ℵ(01) A(02) BYZ TR ‖ Absent from B(03) D(05) NA28 SBLGNT THGNT.

29 And he said to them, "Truly, I
say to you, [that][a] there is no one who
has left house or {wife or brothers or
parents}[b] or children, for the sake of the
kingdom of God, 30 who will not receive
{many times}[c] more in this time, and in
the coming age, [[will inherit]][d] eternal
life."

31 Taking the twelve [[disciples]],[e]
{he}[f] said to them, "Behold, we are
going up to Jerusalem, and all that is
written through the prophets about
the Son of Man will be accomplished.
32 For he will be handed over to the
Gentiles,[g] and will be mocked, [and
insulted,][h] and spat upon. 33 And after
flogging him, they will kill him, and on
the third day he will rise again."

34 And they understood none of
these things, and {this}[i] word was
hidden from them, and they did not
understand the things being said.

35 As he approached Jericho, a
blind man was sitting by the road
begging. 36 Hearing a crowd passing
by, he inquired what this might be.
37 They told him, "Jesus of Nazareth is
passing by." 38 And he cried out, saying,
"[Jesus,][j] Son of David, have mercy
on me!"

39 But those leading rebuked him, so
that he would be silent; but he cried out
[more],[k] "[[Jesus,]][l] Son of David, have
mercy on me!"

40 Jesus stopped and ordered
the man to be brought [to him].[m]
When he came near, Jesus asked him,
41 [[Saying,]][n] "What do you want me to
do for you?" He said, "Lord, that I may
regain my sight."

42 [[And answering,]][o] {Jesus}[p] said
to him, "Regain your sight; your faith
has saved you." 43 And immediately he
regained his sight and followed him,
glorifying God. And all the people,
when they saw it, gave {praise}[q]
to God.

19 1 And entering, {he}[r] passed
through Jericho. 2 And behold, a
man [named][s] Zacchaeus, and he was a
chief tax collector; [and he was][t] rich.
3 And he sought to see who Jesus was,
but could not because of the crowd, for
he was short in stature. 4 And having
{run ahead}[u] [to the][v] front, he climbed
up into a sycamore tree in order to see
him, for he was about to pass that way.

---

[a] 18:29, **that:** Absent from ℵ(01) D(05).

[b] 18:29, **wife or brothers or parents:** ℵ(01) B(03) Latin(a b e ff^{2} i) NA28 SBLGNT THGNT ‖ Some manuscripts read "parents or brothers or wife." A(02) W(032) BYZ TR ‖ Some manuscripts read "parents or brothers or sisters or wife." D(05).

[c] 18:30, **many times:** Some manuscripts read "sevenfold." D(05) Latin(a b e ff^{2} i) BYZ.

[d] 18:30, **will inherit:** Included in Latin(a b ff^{2} i).

[e] 18:31, **disciples:** Included in Latin(a ff^{2} i).

[f] 18:31, **he:** Some manuscripts read "Jesus." Latin(ff^{2} i).

[g] 18:32, **Gentiles:** Or "nations."

[h] 18:32, **and insulted:** Absent from D(05) Latin(it) Syriac(sy^{p}).

[i] 18:34, **this:** Some manuscripts read "the." D(05) Latin(a b e ff^{2} i it) Syriac(sy^{s} sy^{c}).

[j] 18:38, **Jesus:** Absent from A(02).

[k] 18:39, **more:** Absent from D(05).

[l] 18:39, **Jesus:** Included in ℵ(01).

[m] 18:40, **to him:** Absent from D(05) Latin(a e ff^{2} i it) Syriac(sy^{s} sy^{c}).

[n] 18:41, **saying:** Included in A(02) W(032) Latin(a ff^{2} i) BYZ TR ‖ Absent from ℵ(01) B(03) D(05) Latin(e) NA28 SBLGNT THGNT.

[o] 18:42, **And answering:** Included in D(05) Latin(a b e ff^{2} i).

[p] 18:42 , **Jesus:** Some manuscripts read "he." D(05).

[q] 18:43, **praise:** Some manuscripts read "glory." D(05).

[r] 19:1, **he:** Some manuscripts read "Jesus." Latin(e).

[s] 19:2, **named:** Absent from D(05) Latin(a b ff^{2} i).

[t] 19:2, **and he was:** Absent from D(05) Latin(e).

[u] 19:4, **run ahead:** D(05) reads "gone ahead." ‖ W(032) reads "running up."

[v] 19:4, **to the:** ℵ(01) B(03) NA28 SBLGNT THGNT ‖ Absent in some manuscripts. A(02) D(05) W(032) Latin(a b e ff^{2} i) BYZ TR.

5 And {when he came to the place,}[a] [Jesus looked up and][b] [[he saw him and]][c] he said to him, "Zacchaeus, hurry and come down, for today I must stay at your house." 6 And he hurried and came down and received him joyfully. 7 And when they saw it, they all grumbled, [saying,][d] "He has gone in to be the guest of a man who is a sinner."

8 And Zacchaeus stood and said to {the Lord},[e] "Behold, [Lord,][f] half of my possessions I give to the poor, and if I have defrauded anyone of anything, I restore it fourfold."

9 And Jesus said to him, "Today salvation has come to this house, since he also is a son of Abraham.

10 "For the Son of Man came to seek and to save the lost."

11 As they were listening to these things, he added and said a parable, because he was near to Jerusalem, and they thought that the kingdom of God was to appear immediately.

12 {He said [therefore],[g] "A nobleman went into}[h] a far country to receive [for himself][i] a kingdom and then return. 13 Calling ten {of his}[j] servants, he gave them ten minas,[k] and said to them, 'Engage in business until I come.' 14 But his citizens hated him and sent a delegation after him, saying, 'We do not want this man to reign over us.' 15 And it happened, upon his return after receiving the kingdom, he ordered {those}[l] servants, to whom he had given the money, to be called [to him][m] so that he might know what they had done.

16 "The first came before him, saying, 'Lord, your mina[n] has made ten minas.' 17 And he said to him, 'Well done, good servant! Because you have been faithful in a very little, you shall have authority over ten cities.'

18 "And the {second}[o] came, [saying, 'Lord, Your mina has made five minas.' 19 And he said to him, 'And you are [to become][p] over five cities.'

20 "And the {the other}[q] came,][r] saying, 'Lord, behold, your mina which I had [put away][s] in a handkerchief; 21 for I was afraid of you, because you are a severe man. You take what you did not deposit, and reap what you did not sow.'

---

a 19:5, **when he came to the place:** Some manuscripts read "it happened, as he was passing by." D(05) Latin(it).

b 19:5, **Jesus looked up and:** Absent from D(05).

c 19:5, **saw him and:** Included in A(02) D(05) W(032) Syriac(sy^p) BYZ TR ‖ Absent from ℵ(01) B(03) NA28 SBLGNT THGNT.

d 19:7, **saying:** Absent from D(05) Latin(a e ff² i it) Syriac(sy^c).

e 19:8, **the Lord:** Some manuscripts read "Jesus." Latin(e).

f 19:8, **Lord:** Absent from Latin(e i).

g 19:12, **therefore:** Absent from D(05) Latin(e).

h 19:12, **He said therefore, "A nobleman went into":** Some manuscripts read "A certain nobleman said, 'I am going to.'" BYZ TR.

i 19:12, **for himself:** Absent from D(05) Latin(a b e i).

j 19:13, **of his:** Absent from D(05) Latin(b ff²).

k 19:13, **mina:** About three months' wages.

l 19:15, **those:** Some manuscripts read "the." D(05) Latin(b e ff² i).

m 19:15, **to him:** Absent from W(032) Latin(a b ff² i).

n 19:16-20, **mina:** singular.

o 19:18, **second:** Some manuscripts read "the other came." D(05) Latin(b ff² i) Syriac(sy^s) ‖ Some manuscripts read "another." Latin(a e).

p 19:19, **to become:** Absent from D(05).

q 19:20, **the other:** Some manuscripts read "another." A(02) W(032) BYZ TR.

r 19:20, The account of a servant with five minas in verses 18-20 is absent from Latin(i).

s 19:20, **put away:** Absent from Latin(e).

22 “[[But]][a] He said to him, ‘I will
judge by your own words, you wicked
servant! You knew that I was a strict
man, taking what I did not deposit and
reaping what I did not sow? 23 Why then
did you not put my money in the bank,
and I, coming, would have collected it
with interest?’ 24 And he said to those
standing by, ‘Take [the mina][b] from
him, and {give it}[c] to the one who has
the ten minas.’ 25 [And they said to him,
‘[Lord,][d] He has ten minas!’][e]

26 “[[And he said to them,]][f]
‘[[For]][g] I say [to you][h] [that][i] to
everyone who has, more will be given,
but from the one who does not have,
even what he has will be taken away
[[from him]].[j] 27 But those enemies
of mine, who did not want me to
reign over them, bring them here and
slaughter them before me. [[And cast
out the worthless servant into the outer
darkness; there will be weeping and
gnashing of teeth.]]’”[k]

28 And having said these things,
he went on [ahead],[l] going up to
Jerusalem. 29 And it happened, when he
approached Bethphage and Bethany,
near the mount [called Olivet],[m] he
sent two of {the}[n] disciples, 30 saying,
“Go into the village opposite, in which
as you enter you will find a colt [tied,
on which no one [of men][o] has [ever][p]
sat; [and][q] having untied it, bring it
here].[r] 31 And if anyone asks you, [‘Why
are you untying it?’][s] You shall say
[[to him]][t] [[that]] ‘The Lord has need
of it.’”

32 [[And they departed]][u] [And
those who were sent went away and
found it [[standing]][v] just as he had
told them. 33 And as they were untying
the colt, its owners said to them, “Why
are you untying the colt?” 34 But they
said, [Because][w] “The Lord has need of
it.”][x]

35 And they brought {it}[y] [to Jesus],[z]
and throwing their garments on the
colt, they set Jesus on it.

36 And as he was going, they spread
their garments [on the road].[a]

---

a 19:22, **But:** Included in A(02) W(032) BYZ TR.
b 19:24, **the mina:** Absent from D(05) Latin (a e).
c 19:24, **give it:** Some manuscripts read “carry it away.” D(05).
d 19:25, **Lord:** Absent from B(03) D(05) Latin(b e ff^2).
e 19:25, **And they said to him, Lord, he has ten minas:** Absent from D(05) W(032) Latin(b e ff^2) Syriac(sy^s sy^c).
f 19:26, **And he said to them:** Some manuscripts read “And he said to them.” Latin(i).
g 19:26, **For:** Included in A(02) D(05) W(032) BYZ TR.
h 19:26, **to you:** Absent from ℵ(01).
i 19:26, **that:** Absent from Latin(a b ff^2 i).
j 19:26, **from him:** Included in A(02) D(05) W(032) Latin(a e ff^2) BYZ TR || Absent from ℵ(01) B(03) Latin(i) NA28 SBLGNT THGNT.
k 19:27, **And cast out the worthless servant...:** Included in D(05).
l 19:28, **ahead:** Absent from D(05) Latin(a e ff^2 i).
m 19:29, **called Olivet:** Absent from B(03). || Some manuscripts read “of Olives.” Latin(e) Syriac(sy^s).
n 19:29, **the:** Some manuscripts read “his.” B(03) D(05) W(032) Latin(a ff^2 i) BYZ TR.
o 19:30, **of men:** Absent from D(05) Latin(a ff^2 i).
p 19:30, **ever:** Absent from D(05) Latin(a e ff^2 i) Syriac(sy^s sy^c).
q 19:30, **and:** B(03) D(05) NA28 SBLGNT THGNT || Absent from ℵ(01) A(02) ℵ(01) W(032) BYZ TR.
r 19:30, **tied, on which no one...:** Absent from D(05).
s 19:31, **Why are you untying it?:** Absent from D(05) Latin(e ff^2).
t 19:31, **to him:** Included in A(02) W(032) Latin(a) BYZ TR || Absent from ℵ(01) B(03) D(05) Latin(e ff^2 i) NA28 SBLGNT THGNT.
u 19:32, **And they departed:** Included in D(05).
v 19:32, **standing:** Included in Latin(e ff^2 i).
w 19:34, **Because:** Absent from Latin(e ff^2 i) BYZ TR.
x 19:34, Verses 32-34 is absent from D(05).
y 19:35, **it:** D(05) reads “the colt.”
z 19:35, **to Jesus:** Absent from D(05).
a 19:36, **on the road:** Absent from D(05).

37 As {he was}[a] [already][b] approaching the descent of the Mount of Olives, all the multitude [of the disciples][c] began to rejoice and praise God [with a loud voice][d] for [all][e] the {mighty works}[f] that they had seen, 38 saying, "Blessed is {the one coming, the king}[g] in the name of the Lord; [[Blessed is the king;]][h] peace in heaven and glory in the highest." 39 And some of the Pharisees in the crowd said to him, "Teacher, rebuke your disciples." 40 And he answered and said [[to them]],[i] "I say you, [that][j] if these become silent, the stones will cry out."

41 And when he drew near and saw the city, he wept over it, 42 saying, "If you had known on [this day],[k] even you, the things that make for [[your]][l] peace! [But now][m] They are hidden from your eyes. 43 For the days will come upon you when your enemies will cast up a trench against you and surround you and hem you in on every side, 44 and they will level you to the ground and your children [within you],[n] and they will not leave one stone upon stone in [[all of]][o] you, because you did not recognize the time of your visitation."

45 And entering the temple, he began to drive out those who sold [[and those who bought]],[p] [[and he poured out the tables of the money changers and the seats of those selling the doves,]][q] 46 saying to them, "It is written [[that]],[r] 'My house will be [[called]][s] a house of prayer,' but you have made it a den of robbers."[t]

47 And he was teaching daily [in the temple].[u] But the chief priests and the scribes sought to destroy him, and the leaders of the people, 48 and they could not find what to do [to him],[v] for all the people were hanging on his words.

---

a 19:37, **he was:** Some manuscripts read "they were." D(05) Syriac(sy^s sy^c).

b 19:37, **already:** Absent from D(05) Latin(a e).

c 19:37, **of the disciples:** Absent from Latin(a ff² i).

d 19:37, **with a loud voice:** Absent from D(05).

e 19:37, **all:** Absent from Latin(ff² i).

f 19:37, **mighty works:** D(05) reads "things happening."

g 19:38, **the one coming, the king:** B(03) NA28 ‖ Some manuscripts read "the coming king." A(02) BYZ TR SBLGNT THGNT ‖ Some manuscripts read "the one coming." D(05) W(032) Latin(a e ff² i it) ‖ Some manuscripts read "the king." ℵ(01).

h 19:38, **Blessed is the king:** Included in D(05) Latin(a e ff² i).

i 19:40, **to them:** Included in A(02) D(05) W(032) Latin(a e) BYZ TR ‖ Absent from ℵ(01) B(03) Latin(ff² i) NA28 SBLGNT THGNT.

j 19:40, **that:** ℵ(01) A(02) D(05) BYZ TR SBLGNT THGNT ‖ Absent from B(03) W(032) Latin(a ff²) NA28.

k 19:42, **this day:** ℵ(01) B(03) NA28 SBLGNT THGNT ‖ Some manuscripts read "at least in this your day." A(02) W(032) BYZ TR.

l 19:42, **your:** Included in A(02) D(05) W(032) Latin(a e ff² i) BYZ TR ‖ Absent from ℵ(01) B(03) NA28 SBLGNT THGNT.

m 19:42, **But now:** Absent from A(02) Latin (a e i).

n 19:44, **within you:** Absent from D(05).

o 19:44, **all of:** Included in some manuscripts D(05).

p 19:45, **and those who bought:** Included in A(02) D(05) W(032) (Latin a e ff² i) BYZ TR ‖ Absent from ℵ(01) B(03) NA28 SBLGNT THGNT.

q 19:45, **and he poured out the tables...:** Included in D(05) Latin(a e ff² i it).

r 19:46, **that:** Included in A(02) C(04) D(05) W(032).

s 19:46, **called:** Included in Latin(e).

t 19:46, Isaiah 56:7, Jeremiah 7:11.

u 19:47, **in the temple:** Absent from ℵ(01).

v 19:48, **to him:** Absent from D(05) Latin(ff² i) Syriac(sy^s sy^c sy^p).

20 ¹ And it happened on one of {the}ᵃ days while teaching the people in the temple and preaching the good news, the {chief priests}ᵇ and the scribes, along with the elders, confronted him. ² And they said [, saying]ᶜ to him, "[Tell us]ᵈ By what authority you do these things, or who is the one who gave you this authority?"

³ And {he}ᵉ answered and said to them, "I will also ask you [{a}ᶠ question],ᵍ and you tell me; ⁴ Was the baptism of John from heaven or from men?" ⁵ And they reasoned among themselves, saying [that],ʰ "If we say, 'From heaven,' he will say [[to us]],ⁱ 'Why [[therefore]]ʲ did you not believe him?' ⁶ But if we say, 'From men,' all the people will stone us, for they are convinced that John was a prophet." ⁷ And they answered that they did not know where it was from. ⁸ And Jesus said to them, "Neither will I say to you by what authority I do these things."

⁹ [But]ᵏ He began to tell [ᶦthe people] this parable: "A man planted a vineyard and leased it to vine-growers and went away for a long time. ¹⁰ And at the right time, he sent a servant to the vine-growers so that they would give him some of [the fruit]ᵐ of the vineyard; [but the vine-growers,]ⁿ they sent him away empty-handed {after beating him}.ᵒ

¹¹ "And he {proceeded to send}ᵖ another servant to them; but they also beat [and dishonored]�q him and sent him away empty-handed. ¹² And he {proceeded to send}ʳ a third; but they also wounded him and threw him out.

¹³ "And the lord of the vineyard said, '[What shall I do?]ˢ I will send my beloved son; perhaps [when they see him,]ᵗ they will respect him.' ¹⁴ Seeing [him],ᵘ [the vine-growers,]ᵛ they reasoned [[among themselves]],ʷ saying, 'This is the heir; [[Come!]]ˣ Let us kill him, so that the inheritance may become ours.' ¹⁵ And having thrown him out of the vineyard, they killed him.

ᵃ 20:1, **the:** ℵ(01) B(03) D(05) NA28 SBLGNT THGNT ‖ Some manuscripts read "those." A(02) C(04) W(032) BYZ TR.

ᵇ 20:1, **chief priests :** ℵ(01) B(03) C(04) D(05) NA28 SBLGNT THGNT ‖ Some manuscripts read "priests." A(02) W(032) BYZ.

ᶜ 20:2, **saying:** Absent from C(04) D(05) Latin(e).

ᵈ 20:2, **Tell us:** Absent from ℵ(01) C(04).

ᵉ 20:3, **he:** Some manuscripts read "Jesus." Latin(ff² i).

ᶠ 20:3, **a:** ℵ(01) B(03) W(032) NA28 SBLGNT THGNT ‖ Some manuscripts read "one." C(04) D(05) BYZ TR.

ᵍ 20:3, **a question:** Absent from Latin(a e ff² i).

ʰ 20:5, **that:** Absent from C(04) Latin(e ff² i).

ⁱ 20:5, **to us:** Included in C(04) Latin(a).

ʲ 20:5, **therefore:** Included in A(02) C(04) D(05) TR.

ᵏ 20:9, **But:** A(02) W(032) BYZ TR NA28 SBLGNT THGNT ‖ Absent from ℵ(01) B(03) C(04) D(05).

ˡ 20:9, **the people:** Absent from D(05) Latin(a e).

ᵐ 20:10, **the fruit:** Absent from ℵ(01).

ⁿ 20:10, **but the vine-growers:** Absent from D(05) Latin(a e).

ᵒ 20:10, **after beating him:** ℵ(01) B(03) BYZ TR NA28 SBLGNT THGNT ‖ Some manuscripts read "with insults." A(02) C(04) W(032) Latin(it) Syriac(syᵖ).

ᵖ 20:11, **proceeded to send:** Some manuscripts read "sent." D(05) Latin(e).

q 20:11, **and dishonored:** Absent from Latin(a).

ʳ 20:12, **proceeded to send:** Some manuscripts read "sent." D(05) Latin(e).

ˢ 20:13, **What shall I do:** Absent from B(03).

ᵗ 20:13, **when they see him:** ℵ(01) B(03) C(04) D(05) NA28 SBLGNT THGNT ‖ Included in A(02) W(032) BYZ TR.

ᵘ 20:14, **him:** Absent from ℵ(01) Latin(a ff² i).

ᵛ 20:14, **the vine-growers** Absent from D(05) Latin(e).

ʷ 20:14, **among themselves:** ℵ(01) B(03) D(05) NA28 SBLGNT THGNT ‖ Some manuscripts read "among themselves." A(02) C(04) W(032) BYZ TR.

ˣ 20:14, **Come!:** Included in ℵ(01) C(04) D(05) Latin(e) Syriac(syˢ syᶜ syᵖ) BYZ TR ‖ Absent from A(02) B(03) W(032) Latin(a ff² i) NA28 SBLGNT THGNT.

"What then will the lord of the vineyard do [to them]?[a] 16 He will come and destroy {these}[b] [vine-growers][c] and give the vineyard to others."

{But when they heard this, they said,}[d] "May it never be!" 17 But he, looking at them, said, "What then is this that is written: 'The stone which the builders rejected, this has become the cornerstone'?[e] 18 Everyone who falls on that stone will be broken to pieces; but on whomever it falls, it will crush him."

19 And the {scribes and the chief priests}[f] sought to lay hands on him at that very hour, but they feared [the people,][g] for they knew that he had spoken this parable against them.

20 And {they watched him and}[h] sent spies who pretended to be righteous, in order that they might catch him in a statement, {so as to}[i] deliver him to the [authority and power][j] of the governor.

21 And they questioned him, saying, "Teacher, we know that you speak [and teach][k] rightly, and you {do not show partiality},[l] but teach [the way][m] of God in truth: 22 Is it lawful for us to pay taxes to Caesar, or not?" 23 But {perceiving}[n] their {craftiness},[o] he said to them, [["Why are you testing me?"]][p] 24 "Show me {a denarius}.[q] [[And they showed and he said,]][r] Whose image and inscription does it have?" And [[answering]][s] they said, "Caesar's." 25 And he said [to them],[t] "Then render to Caesar the things that are Caesar's, and to God the things that are God's."

---

a 20:15, **to them:** Absent from D(05) Latin(a e).

b 20:16, **these:** Some manuscripts read "the." D(05) Latin(e) Syriac(sy[s]).

c 20:16, **vine-growers:** Absent from ℵ(01).

d 20:16, **But when they heard this, they said:** Some manuscripts read "And those who heard said." BYZ TR.

e 20:17, Psalm 118:22.

f 20:19, **scribes and the chief priests:** A(02) B(03) W(032) NA28 SBLGNT THGNT ‖ Some manuscripts read "chief priests and the scribes." ℵ(01) D(05) BYZ TR.

g 20:19, **the people:** Absent from TR.

h 20:20, **they watched him and:** Some manuscripts read "having departed, they." D(05) Latin(it).

i 20:20, **so as to:** ℵ(01) B(03) C(04) D(05) NA28 SBLGNT THGNT ‖ Some manuscripts read "in order to." A(02) W(032) BYZ TR.

j 20:20, **authority and power:** Absent from D(05) Latin(e) Syriac(sy[c]).

k 20:21, **and teach:** Absent from Latin(a ff² i).

l 20:21, **do not show partiality:** Some manuscripts read "show partiality to no one." D(05) Syriac(sy[s] sy[c]).

m 20:21, **the way:** Absent from Latin(e).

n 20:23, **perceiving:** Some manuscripts read "recognizing." D(05) Latin(e).

o 20:23, **craftiness:** Some manuscripts read "wickedness." C(04) D(05) Latin(a e) Syriac(sy[s] sy[c]).

p 20:23, **Why are you testing me?:** Included in A(02) C(04) D(05) W(032) BYZ TR Latin(a i) Syriac(sy) ‖ Absent from ℵ(01) B(03) Latin(e) NA28 SBLGNT THGNT.

q 20:24, **a denarius:** Some manuscripts read "the coin." D(05).

r 20:24, **And they showed and he said:** Included in ℵ(01) C(04).

s 20:24, **answering:** Included in A(02) C(04) D(05) W(032) Latin(a ff² i) BYZ TR SBLGNT ‖ Absent from ℵ(01) B(03) Syriac(sy[p]) NA28 THGNT.

t 20:25, **to them:** Absent from Latin(a).

26 And they were not able to grasp {his}[a] word in front of the people, and marveling at his response, they fell silent.

27 Some of the Sadducees, who {deny}[b] that there is a resurrection, came forward and asked him, 28 saying, "Teacher, Moses wrote for us that if a man's brother dies having {a wife, and this one is childless},[c] his brother should take the wife [of him][d] and raise up offspring for his brother.[e] 29 There were seven brothers [[with us]];[f] and the first, having taken a wife, died childless; 30 and the second [[took her as wife, and he died childless,]][g] 31 and the third [took her][h] [[in the same way]];[i] [but also][j] likewise all seven [[also]][k] left no children [and died].[l] 32 [Later,][m] [The woman also died.][n]

33 "So [the woman],[o] in the resurrection, whose wife [of them][p] will she be? For all seven had her as wife."

34 {Jesus}[q] [[answering]][r] said to them, "The sons of this age [[are born and they give birth,]][s] they marry and are given in marriage, 35 but those who are considered worthy to attain to that age and the resurrection from the dead, neither marry nor are given in marriage; 36 for they {cannot die anymore},[t] for they are like angels [and are sons][u] of God, being sons of the resurrection.

---

a 20:26, **his:** A(02) C(04) D(05) W(032) NA28 BYZ TR ‖ Some manuscripts read "the." ℵ(01) B(03) SBLGNT THGNT.

b 20:27, **deny:** A(02) W(032) BYZ TR NA28 SBLGNT ‖ Some manuscripts read "say." ℵ(01) B(03) C(04) D(05) THGNT.

c 20:28, **a wife, and this one is childless:** Some manuscripts read "a childless wife." D(05) Latin(e).

d 20:28, **of him:** Included in Latin(a e).

e 20:28, Deuteronomy 25:5-6.

f 20:29, **with us:** Included in D(05) Latin(ff²).

g 20:30, **took her as wife, and he died childless:** Included in A(02) W(032) Latin(a i) Syriac(syᶜ) BYZ TR ‖ Absent from ℵ(01) B(03) D(05) Latin(e ff²) NA28 SBLGNT THGNT.

h 20:31, **took her:** Absent from D(05) Latin(a e).

i 20:31, **in the same way:** Included in BYZ.

j 20:31, **but also:** Absent from D(05).

k 20:31, **also:** Included in W(032) Latin(a).

l 20:31, **and died:** Absent from Latin(ff² i).

m 20:32, **Later:** Absent from some manuscripts Latin(e i). ‖ Some manuscripts read "Last of all." A(02) W(032) BYZ TR.

n 20:32, **The woman also died:** Absent from Latin(e). ‖ Some manuscripts read "But all men died, and the woman." A(02) W(032) Latin(ff² i).

o 20:33, **the woman:** B(03) NA28 SBLGNT THGNT ‖ Absent from A(02) D(05) W(032) Latin(a e ff² i) Syriac(syˢ syᶜ) BYZ TR.

p 20:33, **of them:** Absent from ℵ(01) Latin(e ff²).

q 20:34, **Jesus:** Some manuscripts read "he." D(05) Latin(e i).

r 20:34, **answering:** Included in A(02) W(032) BYZ TR ‖ Absent from ℵ(01) B(03) D(05) Latin(a ff² i) NA28 SBLGNT THGNT.

s 20:34, **are born and they give birth:** That is, they are born and reproduce. Included in D(05) Latin(a it) Syriac(syˢ syᶜ).

t 20:36, **cannot die anymore:** ℵ(01) A(02) B(03) W(032) BYZ TR NA28 SBLGNT THGNT ‖ Some manuscripts read "are no longer destined to die." D(05) W(032) ‖ Some manuscripts read "will not die again." Latin(e ff² i).

u 20:36, **and are sons:** Absent from D(05) Latin(a e ff² i it) Syriac(syˢ).

37 "{But that the dead are raised, even Moses showed, in the passage about the bush, where}[a] he calls the Lord the God of Abraham, and [the God][b] of Isaac[c] [, and [the God][d] of Jacob].[e] 38 [Now][f] He is not God of the dead, but of the living, for all live to him."

39 Some of the scribes answered [[to him]],[g] "Teacher, you have spoken well." 40 {For}[h] they no longer dared to ask him any question.

41 He said to them, "How can {they}[i] say that the Christ is David's son? 42 {For}[j] David himself says in the Book of Psalm, 'The Lord said to my Lord, "Sit at my right hand, 43 until I {make your enemies a footstool for}[k] your feet."[l] 44 David [thus][m] calls him Lord; [so][n] how is he his son?"

45 In the hearing of all the people he said to {the}[o] disciples, 46 "Beware of the scribes, who like to walk around in long robes, and love greetings in the marketplaces and the best seats in the synagogues and the places of honor at banquets; 47 those who devour widows' houses; [and][p] for a show make long prayers; they will receive the greater condemnation."

21 1 Looking up, {he}[q] saw the rich putting their gifts into the treasury. 2 And he saw a poor widow putting [there][r] two {small copper coins.}[s]

3 And he said, "Truly I say to you, this poor widow has put in more than all of them; 4 for all these people have put in their gifts [[of God]][t] out of their abundance, but she out of her poverty has put in all the living that she had."

5 Some were talking about the temple, that it was adorned with beautiful stones and gifts; he said, 6 "These things which you see, days will come in which not a stone will be left upon a stone [[in the wall]][u] [[here]][v] that will not be torn down."

7 And {they}[w] asked him, saying "Teacher, when [then][x] will these things be, and what will be the sign

---

a 20:37 , **But that the dead are raised...:** Some manuscripts read "For indeed, Moses demonstrated that the dead are raised, at the bush, as." D(05).

b 20:37, **the God:** Absent from W(032) Latin(e).

c 20:37, Exodus 3:6, 15.

d 20:37, **the God:** Absent from Latin(a e).

e 20:37, **and the God of Jacob:** Absent from W(032).

f 20:38, **Now:** Absent from D(05).

g 20:39, **to him:** Absent from ℵ(01).

h 20:40, **For:** ℵ(01) B(03) NA28 SBLGNT THGNT ‖ Some manuscripts read "And." A(02) D(05) W(032) Latin(a e ff² i) Syriac(sy) BYZ TR.

i 20:41, **they:** Some manuscripts read "some." A(02).

j 20:42, **For:** ℵ(01) B(03) NA28 SBLGNT THGNT ‖ Some manuscripts read "And." A(02) D(05) W(032) BYZ TR.

k 20:43, **make your enemies a footstool for:** Some manuscripts read "put your enemies under." D(05) Latin(it) Syriac(sy^c sy^p).

l 20:43, Psalm 110:1.

m 20:44, **thus:** Absent from D(05) Latin(a e ff² i).

n 20:44, **So:** Absent from D(05) Latin(e ff² i).

o 20:45, **the:** B(03) D(05) SBLGNT ‖ Some manuscripts read "his." ℵ(01) A(02) W(032) Latin(a e ff² i) BYZ TR NA28[] THGNT.

p 20:47, **and:** Absent from D(05) Latin(a i).

q 21:1, **he:** Some manuscripts read "Jesus." Latin(a ff²).

r 21:2, **there:** Included in D(05) Latin(a e ff² i).

s 21:2, **small copper coins:** Some manuscripts read "two lepta, which is a quadrans." D(05) Latin(a).

t 21:4, **of God:** Included in A(02) D(05) W(032) Latin(a e ff² i) BYZ TR ‖ Absent from ℵ(01) B(03) NA28 SBLGNT THGNT.

u 21:6, **in the wall:** Included in D(05) Latin(a it).

v 21:6, **here:** Included in ℵ(01) B(03) D(05) Latin(a e ff² i it) Syriac(sy^c).

w 21:7, **they:** Some manuscripts read "the disciples." D(05).

x 21:7, **then:** Absent from D(05) Latin(a e ff² i).

{when these things are about to happen}?"[a]

8 But he said, "Watch that you are not deceived; for many will come in my name, saying [[that]],[b] 'I am [he],'[c] and, ['The time is near.'][d] [[Therefore]][e] do not follow them.

9 "But when you hear of wars and disturbances, do not be {alarmed};[f] for these things must happen first, but the end will not come immediately."

10 [Then he said to them,][g] "[[For]][h] Nation will rise against nation, and kingdom against kingdom.

11 "There will be great earthquakes, and in various places famines and plagues; and there will be terrifying events and great signs from heaven.

12 "But before all this occurs, they will arrest you and persecute you; they will hand you over to synagogues and prisons, and you will be brought before kings and governors because of my name.

13 "[[But]][i] This will give you an opportunity to testify. 14 [Therefore,][j] {Place}[k] in your hearts not to premeditate a defense.

15 "For I will give you a mouth and wisdom, which all your adversaries will not be able to resist [or contradict].[l]

16 "You will be betrayed [even][m] by {parents and brothers and relatives and friends};[n] and they will put some of you to death.

17 "And you will be hated by all because of my name.

18 "But not a hair of your head will perish.

19 "In your endurance, acquire your souls.[o]

20 "But when you see Jerusalem surrounded by armies, then know that its desolation has come near.

21 "Then those in Judea should flee to the mountains, and those inside the city should leave it, and those out in the surrounding areas should not enter it;

22 "For these are days of vengeance, as a fulfillment of all that is written.

23 "Woe to those who are pregnant and [to those][p] who are nursing infants in those days! [For][q] [[In those days]][r] There will be great distress on the earth and wrath against this people;

24 "They will fall by the edge of the sword and be taken away as captives among all nations; and Jerusalem will be trampled on by the Gentiles, until the times [of the Gentiles][s] are fulfilled.

---

a 21:7, **when these things are about to happen:** D(05) reads "of your coming."

b 21:8, **that:** Included in A(02) D(05) W(032) Latin(a e ff² i) BYZ TR ‖ Absent from ℵ(01) B(03) NA28 SBLGNT THGNT.

c 21:8, **he:** Some manuscripts read "Christ." Latin(e ff² i).

d 21:8, **The time is near:** Absent from ℵ(01).

e 21:8, **Therefore:** Included in A(02) W(032) BYZ TR ‖ Absent from ℵ(01) B(03) D(05) Latin(a e ff² i) NA28 SBLGNT THGNT.

f 21:9, **alarmed:** Some manuscripts read "afraid." D(05).

g 21:10, **Then he said to them:** Absent from D(05) Latin(a e ff² i it) Syriac(sy^s sy^c sy^p).

h 21:10, **For:** Included in D(05) Latin(it) Syriac(sy^s sy^c sy^p).

i 21:13, **But:** Included in A(02) W(032) Latin(e) BYZ TR ‖ Absent from ℵ(01) B(03) D(05) NA28 SBLGNT THGNT.

j 21:14, **Therefore:** Absent from ℵ(01).

k 21:14, **place:** Some manuscripts read "set yourselves." BYZ TR.

l 21:15, **or contradict:** Absent from D(05) Latin(a ff² i it) Syriac(sy^s sy^c sy^p).

m 21:16, **even:** Absent from Latin(ff² i).

n 21:16 **parents and brothers and relatives and friends:** Some manuscripts read "And of relatives and friends." Latin(a) ‖ Some manuscripts read "And of brothers and friends." Latin(e).

o 21:19, **acquire your souls:** Or "you will gain your lives."

p 21:23, **to those:** Absent from W(032).

q 21:23, **For:** Absent from ℵ(01).

r 21:23, **in those days:** Included in ℵ(01).

s 21:24, **of the Gentiles:** Absent from D(05).

25 "There will be signs in the sun, the moon, and the stars, and on the earth distress among nations confused by the roaring of the sea and the waves, 26 men fainting from fear and the expectation of what is coming on the world, for the powers of the heavens will be shaken.

27 "And then they will see the Son of Man coming in a cloud with great power and glory.ᵃ

28 "But when these things begin to take place, [stand up and]ᵇ lift up your heads, because [your] redemption is drawing near."

29 And he told them a parable: "Look at the fig tree and all the trees; 30 when they {put forth leaves},ᶜ you [see for yourselves and]ᵈ know [that]ᵉ summer already is near. 31 {In this way also you},ᶠ when you see these things [happening],ᵍ know that the kingdom of God is near.

32 "Truly I say to you this generation will not pass away until all [[these]]ʰ things take place. 33 Heaven and earth will pass away, but my words will not pass away.

34 "[But]ⁱ Be on guard for yourselves, lest your hearts be weighed down with dissipation and drunkenness and the worries of life, and that day come upon you suddenly 35 {like a trap};ʲ for it will come upon [all]ᵏ those who dwell on the face of the whole earth.

36 "{But}ˡ be alert at all times, praying that you may {have strength}ᵐ to escape all [these things]ⁿ that are about to happen and {to stand}ᵒ before the Son of Man."

37 He was teaching in the temple during the day, [and during the nights]ᵖ he would [go out and]ᵍ {lodge}ʳ on the mountain {called}ˢ Olives. 38 And all the people would rise up early to listen to him in the temple.ᵗ

22 1 Now the Feast of Unleavened Bread, called the Passover, was approaching. 2 And the chief priests and the scribes were seeking how to destroy him, for they feared the people.

ᵃ 21:27, Daniel 7:13.

ᵇ 21:28, **stand up:** Absent from Latin(e).

ᶜ 21:30, **put forth leaves:** Some manuscripts read "produce their fruit." D(05) Syriac(syˢ syᶜ).

ᵈ 21:30, **see for yourselves and:** Absent from D(05) Latin(a i).

ᵉ 21:30, **that:** Absent from Latin(a).

ᶠ 21:31, **In this way also you:** Some manuscripts read "Thus." D(05) Latin(a).

ᵍ 21:31, **happening:** Absent from D(05) Latin(a).

ʰ 21:32, **these:** Included in D(05) Syriac(syˢ syᶜ syᵖ).

ⁱ 21:34, **But:** Absent from ℵ(01) D(05).

ʲ 21:35, **like a trap:** ℵ(01) B(03) D(05) NA28 Latin(it) SBLGNT THGNT ‖ Some manuscripts read "Like a trap" starting a new sentence, rather than "like a trap;" as a continuation of the previous sentence. A(02) C(04) W(032) Syriac(sy) BYZ TR.

ᵏ 21:35, **all:** Absent from Latin(ff²).

ˡ 21:36, **But:** ℵ(01) B(03) D(05) NA28 SBLGNT THGNT ‖ Some manuscripts read "therefore." A(02) C(04) W(032) BYZ TR.

ᵐ 21:36, **have strength:** Some manuscripts read "be counted worthy." A(02) C(04) D(05) Latin(latt) Syriac(sy).

ⁿ 21:36, **these things:** Absent from ℵ(01) BYZ.

ᵒ 21:36, **to stand:** Some manuscripts read "you will stand." D(05) Latin(it) Syriac(sy).

ᵖ 21:37, **and during the nights:** Absent from D(05).

ᵍ 21:37, **go out and:** Absent from W(032).

ʳ 21:37, **lodge:** Some manuscripts read "rest." D(05).

ˢ 21:37, **called:** Some manuscripts read "of." Latin(e).

ᵗ 21:38, The f¹³ family of manuscripts add the Pericope of the Adulteress (John 7:53-8:11) following verse 38.

3 Then Satan entered into Judas {called}[a] Iscariot, who was of the number of the twelve. 4 And he went away and discussed with the chief priests [[and scribes]][b] [and officers][c] [[of the temple]][d] how he might betray him [to them].[e] 5 And they [were glad and][f] agreed to give [him][g] money. 6 [And he consented.][h] And he was seeking an opportunity to betray him [to them][i] in the absence of a crowd.

7 Then came the day of {Unleavened Bread},[j] [on][k] which the Passover lamb had to be sacrificed. 8 And he sent Peter and John, saying, "Go and prepare the Passover for us, that we may eat."

9 They said to him, "Where do you want us to prepare [[for you]]?"[l] 10 He said [to them],[m] "Behold, as you enter the city, a man carrying a jar [of water][n] will meet you. Follow him into the house that he enters, 11 And you will say to the master of the house, 'The Teacher says [to you],[o] "Where is {the}[p] guest room where I may eat the Passover with my disciples?"' 12 And he will show you a [large][q] upper room furnished; there prepare."

13 And they went and found it just as he had told them, and they prepared the Passover.

14 And when the hour came, he reclined at table, and the [[twelve]][r] apostles with him. 15 And he said to them, "I have earnestly desired to eat this Passover with you before I suffer; 16 for I say to you [that][s] I will not eat of it [[again]][t] until it is fulfilled in the kingdom of God."

17 And having taken the cup, having given thanks, "Take [this];[u] [and][v] divide it among yourselves. 18 For I say to you [that][w] [from now on][x] I will not drink of the fruit of the vine until the kingdom of God comes."

---

a 22:3, **called:** א(01) B(03) D(05) W(032) NA28 SBLGNT THGNT ‖ Some manuscripts read "surnamed." A(02) C(04) BYZ TR.

b 22:4, **and scribes:** Included in C(04) Latin(a b e ff² i it) Syriac(sy).

c 22:4, **and officers:** Absent from D(05) Latin(a b e ff² i it) Syriac(sy).

d 22:4, **of the temple:** Included in C(04).

e 22:4, **to them:** Absent from D(05) Latin(a e ff² i).

f 22:5, **were glad and:** Absent from Latin(b ff² i).

g 22:5, **him:** Absent from Latin(a).

h 22:6, **And he consented:** Absent from א(01) C(04) Latin(a b ff² i it) Syriac(syˢ).

i 22:6, **to them:** Absent from D(05) Latin(e).

j 22:7, **Unleavened Bread:** Some manuscripts read "the Passover." D(05) Latin(it) Syriac(syˢ syᶜ).

k 22:7, **on:** א(01) A(02) W(032) BYZ TR NA28 SBLGNT THGNT ‖ Absent from 𝔓75 B(03) C(04) D(05).

l 22:9, **for you:** Included in B(03) D(05) Latin(e).

m 22:10, **to them:** Absent from D(05) Latin(e).

n 22:10, **of water:** Absent from א(01).

o 22:11, **to you:** Absent from some manuscripts D(05) Syriac(syˢ syᶜ syᵖ).

p 22:11, **the:** Some manuscripts read "my." א(01).

q 22:12, **large:** Absent from D(05).

r 22:14, **twelve:** Included in A(02) C(04) W(032) BYZ TR ‖ Absent from 𝔓75 א(01) B(03) D(05) Latin(a b e ff² i) NA28 SBLGNT THGNT.

s 22:16, **that:** Absent from C(04) D(05).

t 22:16, **again:** Absent from C(04) W(032) TR.

u 22:17, **this:** Absent from א(01) Latin(e).

v 22:17, **and:** Absent from D(05) Latin(e) Syriac(syˢ syᶜ).

w 22:18, **that:** א(01) A(02) W(032) BYZ TR NA28[] ‖ Absent from 𝔓75 B(03) C(04) D(05) SBLGNT THGNT.

x 22:18, **from now on:** 𝔓75 א(01) B(03) D(05) W(032) Latin(e) Syriac(syˢ syᶜ) BYZ TR NA28 SBLGNT THGNT ‖ Absent from A(02) C(04) BYZ TR.

19 And he took bread, and when he had given thanks, he broke it and gave it to them, saying, "[[Take]]ᵃ This is my body. [Which is given for you. Do this in remembrance of me.]"ⁿᵇ

20 [And likewise the cup after they had eaten, saying, "This cup is the new covenant in my blood, which is poured out for you."]ᶜ

21 "But behold, the hand of him who betrays me is [with me]ᵈ upon the table. 22 {For}ᵉ the Son of Man goes as it has been determined, but woe [to that man]ᶠ by whom he is betrayed!"

23 And they began to question one another, who [among themselves]ᵍ could be the one to do this.

24 There also arose a dispute among them; {as to which of them was considered to be greatest}.ʰ 25 But {he}ⁱ said to them, "The kings of the nations rule over them, and those who exercise authority over them are called benefactors. 26 But you are not so, but let the greater among you become as the younger,ʲ and the leader as the one who serves.

27 "{For who is greater, the one reclining at the table or the one serving? Is it not the one reclining at the table? Yet I am among you as the one serving}.ᵏ

28 "You {are}ˡ those who have stayed with me in my trials, 29 And I {appoint for you,}ᵐ as my Father has appointed for me, a kingdom, 30 so that you may eat and {drink}ⁿ at my table in {my}ᵒ kingdom and you will sit on

---

ᵃ 22:19, **Take:** Absent from A(02).

ᵇ 22:19b-20, Verses 19b-20 are absent from some manuscripts. D(05) Latin(a b e ff² i it). ‖ The text is supported by 𝔓75 ℵ(01) A(02) B(03) C(04) W(032) BYZ TR NA28 SBLGNT THGNT. ‖ It is double bracketed in the critical edition of Westcott-Hort. ‖ According to Metzger, "Considerations in favor of the originality of the longer text include the following: (a) The external evidence supporting the shorter reading represents only part of the Western text-type, whereas the other representatives of the Western text join with witnesses belonging to all the other ancient text-types in support of the longer reading. (b) It is easier to suppose that the editor of manuscript D(05), puzzled by the order of cup-bread-cup, eliminated the second mention of the cup without being concerned about the reversed order of cup-bread, than that the editor of the longer version brought in from Paul the second mention of the cup in order to correct the order and let the first mention of the cup remain. (c) The rise of the shorter version can be accounted for in terms of the theory of disciplina arcana, that is, in order to protect the Eucharist from being profaned, one or more copies of the Gospel according to Luke, prepared for circulation among non-Christian readers, omitted the sacramental formula after the beginning words. Considerations in favor of the originality of the shorter text include the following: (a) Generally in NT textual criticism the shorter reading is to be preferred. (b) Since the words in vv. 19b and 20 are suspiciously similar to Paul's words in 1 Cor 11:24b-25, it appears that Paul's letter was the source for the addition into the shorter text. (c) Verses 19b-20 contain several linguistic features that are not characteristic of Luke's style." (R. L. Omanson and B. M. Metzger, *A Textual Guide to the Greek New Testament: An Adaptation of Bruce M. Metzger's Textual commentary for the Needs of Translators* [Stuttgart: Deutsche Bibelgesellschaft, 2006], 149.).

ᶜ 22:20 See prior footnote.

ᵈ 22:21, **with me:** Absent from D(05).

ᵉ 22:22, **For:** 𝔓75 ℵ(01) B(03) NA28 SBLGNT THGNT ‖ Some manuscripts read "Indeed." A(02) D(05) W(032) Latin(b ff² i) BYZ TR.

ᶠ 22:22, **to that man:** Absent from D(05) Latin(e) Syriac(syˢ syᶜ).

ᵍ 22:23, **among themselves:** Absent from D(05) Latin(a b e ff² i).

ʰ 22:24, **as to which of them was considered to be greatest:** Some manuscripts read "who might be greater." D(05) Latin(a).

ⁱ 22:25, **he:** Some manuscripts read "Jesus." Latin(ff²).

ʲ 22:26, **younger:** Or "lesser."

ᵏ 22:27, **For who is greater…:** D(05) reads "Rather, he who reclines, for I came among you not as one who reclines but as one who serves."

ˡ 22:28, **are:** D(05) reads "have grown in my service, as the one serving."

ᵐ 22:29, **appoint for you:** Some manuscripts read "am making a covenant with you." A(02).

ⁿ 22:30, **drink:** D(05) reads "be hungry."

ᵒ 22:30, **my:** D(05) reads "the."

thrones judging the [twelve]^a tribes of Israel.

31 [[And the Lord said,]]^b "Simon, [Simon,]^c behold, Satan has demanded to sift you like wheat; 32 but I have prayed for you that your faith may not fail; and when you have turned back, strengthen your brothers."

33 He said to him, "Lord, I am [ready]^d to go with you both to prison and to death." 34 But {he}^e said [[to him]],^f "I say to you, Peter, the rooster will not crow today {until}^g you deny three times that you know me."

35 And he said to them, "When I sent you out without a purse, bag, or sandals, did you lack anything?" They said, "Nothing." 36 {But}^h he said [to them],ⁱ "But now, let the one who has a purse take it, and likewise a bag. And let the one who has no sword sell his cloak and buy one. 37 For I say [to you]^j that this which is written must be fulfilled in me, 'And he was reckoned with lawless ones.' And [indeed,]^k the end concerning me is at hand."^l

38 They said [[to him]],^m "[Lord,]ⁿ Look, here are two swords." He said [to them],^o "It is enough."

39 And he went out and proceeded as was his custom to the Mount of Olives; [and]^p {the}^q disciples followed him. 40 When he arrived [to the place],^r he said to them, "Pray not [to enter]^s into temptation."

41 And he withdrew from them about a stone's throw, and knelt down and prayed, 42 saying, "Father, {if you are willing, remove this cup from me; yet not my will, but yours be done}."^t

43 [[And there appeared to him an angel from heaven, strengthening him. 44 And being in agony, he prayed more earnestly; and his sweat became like great drops of blood falling down to the ground.]]^u

45 And rising from prayer, coming to {the}^v disciples, he found them sleeping from sorrow, 46 and he said to them, "Why are you sleeping? Get up and pray, so that you may not enter into temptation."

---

a 22:30, **twelve:** Absent from Latin(e).

b 22:31, **And the Lord said:** Included in ℵ(01) A(02) D(05) W(032) Latin(a b ff² i) Syriac(sy^c sy^p) BYZ TR THGNT ‖ Absent from 𝔓75 B(03) Syriac(sy^s) NA28 SBLGNT.

c 22:31, **Simon:** The second occurrence is absent from some manuscripts. ℵ(01) Latin(e).

d 22:33, **ready:** Absent from W(032).

e 22:34, **he:** Some manuscripts read "Jesus." Latin(ff²).

f 22:34, **to him:** Included in Latin(ff²).

g 22:34, **until:** ℵ(01) B(03) D(05) NA28 SBLGNT THGNT ‖ Some manuscripts read "before." A(02) W(032) BYZ TR.

h 22:36, **But:** 𝔓75 ℵ(01) B(03) D(05) NA28 SBLGNT THGNT ‖ Some manuscripts read "Therefore." A(02) W(032) BYZ TR.

i 22:36, **to them:** Absent from D(05).

j 22:37, **to you:** Absent from D(05) Latin(b).

k 22:37 , **indeed:** Absent from D(05) Syriac(sy^s sy^c).

l 22:37, Isaiah 53:12.

m 22:38, **to him:** Included in Latin(b).

n 22:38, **Lord:** Absent from ℵ(01) Latin(i).

o 22:38, **to them:** Absent from Latin(e).

p 22:39, **and:** Absent from B(03).

q 22:39, **the:** Some manuscripts read "his." Latin(a b e ff² i) BYZ TR.

r 22:40, **to the place:** Absent from Latin(e).

s 22:40, **to enter:** Absent from B(03).

t 22:42, **if you are willing...:** Some manuscripts read "not my will, but yours be done. If you wish, remove this cup from me." D(05) Latin(a c e ff²).

u 22:43-44, ℵ(01) D(05) BYZ TR NA28[[]] SBLGNT THGNT ‖ Verses 43-44 are absent from some manuscripts. P75, A(02), B(03) W(032) Syriac(sy^s). ‖ The verses are double bracketed in NA28 and the critical edition of Westcott-Hort.

v 22:45, **the:** Some manuscripts include "his." Latin(a b e ff² i) BYZ TR.

⁴⁷[[But]]ᵃ While he was still speaking, behold, a [[large]]ᵇ crowd, and the one called Judas [[Iscariot]],ᶜ one of the twelve, was leading them and approached {Jesus to kiss him}.ᵈ [[For he had given them this sign, "Whomever I kiss, he is the one.]]ᵉ ⁴⁸But {Jesus}ᶠ said to {him},ᵍ "Judas, are you betraying the Son of Man with a kiss?"

⁴⁹Seeing the things about to happen, they said [[to him]],ʰ "Lord, shall we strike with the sword?" ⁵⁰And one of them struck the servant of the high priest and cut off his right ear. ⁵¹[But]ⁱ Jesus answered and said, "Let it be until this point." And [[stretching out his hand,]]ʲ {touching his ear, he healed him}.ᵏ

⁵²But {Jesus}ˡ said to the chief priests and officers of the temple and elders who had come against him, "Have you come out as against a robber, with swords and clubs? ⁵³Every day when I was with you in the temple, you did not lay hands on me, but this is your hour and the power of darkness."

⁵⁴And having seized him, they led [away and brought]ᵐ him to the house of the high priest; but Peter was following at a distance.

⁵⁵And when they had kindled a fire in the middle of the courtyard and sat down together, [[and]]ⁿ Peter was sitting among them [[, warming himself]].ᵒ ⁵⁶But a certain servant girl, seeing him sitting in the light and looking intently at him, said, "This man was also with him." ⁵⁷But he denied {it},ᵖ saying, "I do not know him [, woman]."�q

⁵⁸And after a short while another seeing him said [[the same,]]ʳ ["You also are one of them."]ˢ But {Peter}ᵗ said, "[Man,]ᵘ I am not."

⁵⁹And after a short time another seeing him insisted "Truly [[, I say]]ᵛ This one also was with him, for he is a Galilean." ⁶⁰But Peter said, "Man, I do not know what you are saying." And immediately, while he was still speaking, a rooster crowed.

⁶¹{{And the Lord}ʷ turned and looked at Peter}.ˣ And {Peter}ʸ remembered the word of the Lord, how

ᵃ 22:47, **But:** Included in D(05) BYZ TR.
ᵇ 22:47, **large:** Included in D(05) Syriac(syˢ syᶜ).
ᶜ 22:47, **Iscariot:** Included in D(05).
ᵈ 22:47, **Jesus to kiss him:** Some manuscripts read "he kissed Jesus." D(05).
ᵉ 22:47, **For he had given…:** Included in D(05) Latin(b c) Syriac(syᵖ).
ᶠ 22:48, **Jesus:** Latin(e) reads "he."
ᵍ 22:48, **him:** Some manuscripts read "Judas." D(05).
ʰ 22:49, **to him:** Included in A(02) W(032) Latin(a b e ff² i) BYZ TR.
ⁱ 22:51, **But:** Absent from A(02).
ʲ 22:51, **stretching out his hand:** Included in D(05).
ᵏ 22:51, **touching his ear, he healed him:** Some manuscripts read "he touched him, and his ear was restored." D(05) Latin(it).
ˡ 22:52, **Jesus:** Some manuscripts read "he." D(05).
ᵐ 22:54, **away and brought:** Absent from D(05) Latin(a b e ff² i) Syriac(syˢ syᶜ syᵖ).
ⁿ 22:55, **and:** Included in D(05) Latin(it) Syriac(syᵖ).
ᵒ 22:55, **warming himself:** Included in D(05).
ᵖ 22:57, **it:** 𝔓75 א(01) B(03) Latin(a b e ff² i it) Syriac(syˢ syᶜ syᵖ) NA28 SBLGNT THGNT ‖ Some manuscripts read "him." A(02) D(05) W(032) BYZ TR.
q 22:57, **woman:** Absent from D(05).
ʳ 22:58, **the same:** Included in D(05) Syriac(syᶜ).
ˢ 22:58, **You also are one of them:** Absent from D(05) Syriac(syᶜ).
ᵗ 22:58, **Peter:** Some manuscripts read "he." 𝔓69 D(05) Latin(b ff² i) Syriac(syˢ).
ᵘ 22:58, **Man:** Absent from Latin(a b e ff² i).
ᵛ 22:59, **I say:** Absent from D(05).
ʷ 22:61, **And the Lord:** Some manuscripts read "But Jesus." D(05) Syriac(syˢ syᵖ).
ˣ 22:61, **And the Lord turned and looked at Peter:** 𝔓69 reads "Peter turned and looked at him."
ʸ 22:61, **Peter:** Some manuscripts read "he." D(05).

he had said to him [that],[a] "Before the rooster crows [today],[b] you will deny me three times [[not knowing me]][c]." [62] [And going out, {he}[d] wept bitterly.][e]

[63] And the men who were holding {him}[f] mocked [him],[g] [beating him,][h] [64] and [they covered him;][i] [[they struck his face and]][j] they were [asking,][k] saying, "Prophesy! Who is it that struck you?" [65] And many other things, blaspheming,[l] they said against him.

[66] And when day came, the assembly of the elders of the people gathered together, both chief priests and scribes, and they led him away to their council, [67] saying, "If you are the Christ[m] [tell us]."[n] [But][o] He said to them, "If I tell [you],[p] you will not believe; [68] [But][q] [[even]][r] If I ask, you will not answer [[or let me go]].[s] [69] [But][t] From now on, the Son of Man will be seated at the right hand of the power of God."

[70] And they all said, "Are you then the Son of God?" And he replied to them, "You say that I am." [71] And they said, "What further need do we have of {testimony}?"[u] We have heard it ourselves from his own mouth."

23 [1] And having risen, [the [whole][v] multitude of them][w] led him to Pilate.

[2] They began to accuse him, saying, "We found this man [perverting {our}[x] nation,][y] forbidding to pay taxes to Caesar, and saying that he himself is Christ, a king."

[3] And Pilate {asked}[z] [him],[a] saying, "Are you the king of the Jews?" And he, answering him, said, "You say so." [4] Pilate said to the chief priests and the crowds, "I find no guilt in this man."

---

a 22:61, **that:** Absent from 𝔓69 D(05) Latin(a b e ff² i).

b 22:61, **today:** 𝔓75 ℵ(01) B(03) Latin(b ff²) Syriac(sy^s) NA28 SBLGNT THGNT ‖ Absent from A(02) D(05) W(032) Syriac(sy^c sy^p) BYZ TR.

c 22:61, **not knowing me:** Included in D(05) Latin(a b).

d 22:62, **he:** Some manuscripts read "Peter." A(02) W(032) BYZ TR.

e 22:62, **And going out, he wept bitterly:** Absent from Latin(a b e ff² i).

f 22:63, **him:** Some manuscripts read "Jesus." BYZ TR.

g 22:63, **him:** Absent from Latin(ff²).

h 22:63, **beating him** Absent from D(05) Latin(it).

i 22:64, **they covered him:** 𝔓75 ℵ(01) B(03) NA28 SBLGNT THGNT ‖ Absent from Latin(b e) ‖ Some manuscripts read "They covered his face." Latin(a f) Syriac(sy^s sy^c sy^p).

j 22:64, **they struck his face:** Included in A(02) W(032) BYZ TR.

k 22:64, **asking:** Absent from D(05) Syriac(sy^p).

l 22:65, **blaspheming:** Or, hurling abuse. The Greek word means to speak in a disrespectful way that demeans, denigrates, maligns (BDAG, βλασφημέω).

m 22:67, **Christ:** See footnote for Christ in Luke 2:11.

n 22:67, **tell us:** Absent from D(05).

o 22:67, **but:** Absent from D(05) Latin(a b e ff² i).

p 22:67, **you:** Absent from ℵ(01).

q 22:68, **But:** Absent from D(05).

r 22:68, **even:** Included in A(02) W(032) Latin(f).

s 22:68, **or let me go:** Included in A(02) D(05) W(032) Latin(b ff² i) Syriac(sy^s sy^c sy^p) BYZ TR ‖ Absent from 𝔓75 ℵ(01) B(03) NA28 SBLGNT THGNT.

t 22:69, **But:** Absent from W(032) BYZ TR.

u 22:71, **testimony:** Some manuscripts read "witnesses." D(05) Syriac(sy^p).

v 23:1, **whole:** Absent from Latin(e).

w 23:1, **the whole multitude of them:** Absent from D(05).

x 23:2, **our:** 𝔓75 ℵ(01) B(03) D(05) Syriac(sy) NA28 SBLGNT THGNT ‖ Some manuscripts read "the." A(02) W(032) Latin(a) BYZ TR.

y 23:2, **perverting our nation:** Absent from Latin(a).

z 23:3, **asked:** 𝔓78 ℵ(01) B(03) NA28 SBLGNT THGNT ‖ Some manuscripts read "questioned." A(02) D(05) W(032) BYZ TR.

a 23:3, **him:** Absent from 𝔓75 W(032).

5 But they insisted, saying [that],[a] "He stirs up the people, [teaching][b] throughout all {Judea},[c] beginning from Galilee even to this place."

6 When Pilate heard {this},[d] he asked whether the man was [a Galilean].[e] 7 And recognizing that he is under Herod's jurisdiction, he sent him to Herod, who was [also][f] in Jerusalem during these days.

8 But Herod, seeing Jesus, was very glad, for he had wanted to see him for a long time because he had heard [[many things]][g] about him and hoped to see some miracle performed by him. 9 He questioned him with many words, but he answered him nothing.

10 The chief priests and the scribes stood there, vehemently accusing him. 11 But Herod, with his soldiers, treated him with contempt [and][h] mocked him. Dressing him in bright clothing, he sent him back to Pilate. 12 {That same day, Herod and Pilate became friends with each other [, for before this they had been at enmity with each other]}[i].[j]

13 Pilate, however, having summoned the chief priests and the rulers and [[all]][k] the people, 14 said to them, "You brought this man to me as one who was leading the people astray, and behold, I, having examined him in your presence, found nothing guilty in this man [of the charges you accuse him of].[l] 15 But not even Herod, for {he sent him back to us};[m] and [behold,][n] nothing deserving of death has been done by him. 16 Therefore, having disciplined him, I will release him 17 [[for he was obligated to release one to them at the festival.]][o]

18 But they all cried out together, saying, "Take this one away, [[take this one away,]][p] and release to us Barabbas;" 19 who had been [thrown][q] in prison for a certain insurrection in the city and for murder.

20 [[Therefore,]][r] Again, Pilate addressed them, wanting to release Jesus. 21 But they {kept shouting}[s] [saying,][t] "Crucify [, Crucify][u] him!"

22 He said to them for the third time, "What evil has this man done?

---

a 23:5, **that:** Absent from D(05) Latin(a b e ff² i).

b 23:5, **teaching:** Absent from ℵ(01) Latin(b e i).

c 23:5, **Judea:** Some manuscripts read "the earth." D(05).

d 23:6, **this:** 𝔓75 ℵ(01) B(03) NA28 SBLGNT THGNT ‖ Some manuscripts read "of Galilee." A(02) D(05) W(032) Latin(latt) Syriac(sy) BYZ TR.

e 23:6, **a Galilean:** Absent from D(05).

f 23:7, **also:** Absent from D(05) Latin(a b e ff² i).

g 23:8, **many things:** Included in A(02) W(032) Latin(a b e ff² i) BYZ TR ‖ Absent from 𝔓75 ℵ(01) B(03) D(05) NA28 SBLGNT THGNT.

h 23:11, **and:** 𝔓75 ℵ(01) Latin(a d) NA28[] SBLGNT THGNT ‖ Absent from A(02) B(03) D(05) W(032) BYZ TR.

i 23:12, **for before this...:** Absent from D(05) Latin (b e ff²).

j 23:12, **That same day...:** D(05) reads "However, Pilate and Herod, being in a state of annoyance, became friends on that day."

k 23:13, **all:** Included in D(05) BYZ TR.

l 23:14, **of the charges you accuse him of:** Absent from D(05).

m 23:15, **he sent him back to us:** 𝔓75 ℵ(01) B(03) NA28 SBLGNT THGNT ‖ Some manuscripts read "I sent you back to him." A(02) D(05) W(032) Latin(a b ff²) BYZ TR.

n 23:15, **behold:** Absent from D(05) Latin(ff²).

o 23:17, Some manuscripts include verse 17. ℵ(01) W(032) Latin(b e ff²) BYZ TR ‖ Absent from 𝔓75 A(02) B(03) Latin(a) NA28 SBLGNT THGNT.

p 23:18, **take this one away:** Included in D(05) a second time.

q 23:19, **thrown:** Absent from ℵ(01).

r 23:20, **Therefore:** Included in BYZ TR.

s 23:21, **kept shouting:** Some manuscripts read "cried out." D(05).

t 23:21, **saying:** Absent from D(05).

u 23:21, **Crucify:** Absent from W(032).

[[Therefore]]ᵃ I found {nothing}ᵇ deserving of death in him; therefore, having disciplined him, I will release him." 23 But they were insistent, demanding with loud voices that he be crucified, and {their}ᶜ voices [[and those of the chief priests]]ᵈ prevailed. 24 So Pilate decided that their demand should be granted.

25 He released [[to them]]ᵉ the one who for insurrection and murder had been thrown into prison [, whom they asked for].ᶠ But Jesus he delivered up to their will.

26 And as they led him away, they seized a certain Simon of Cyrene, who was coming from the country, and laid on him the cross [to carry]ᵍ behind Jesus.

27 And a [great]ʰ multitude of the people and women were following him, who were beating their breasts and mourning for him. 28 But Jesus turning to them said, "Daughters of Jerusalem, do not weep for me, [[nor morn,]]ⁱ but weep for yourselves and for your children. 29 For [behold],ʲ the days are coming when they will say, 'Blessed are the barren and the wombs that never bore and the breasts that never nursed!' 30 Then they will begin to say to the mountains, 'Fall on us,' and to the hills, 'Cover us.'ᵏ 31 For if they do these things when the wood is green, what will happen when it is dry?"

32 And there were also two other criminals led with him to be executed. 33 And when they {came}ˡ to the place that is called The Skull, there they crucified him, and the criminals [[together]],ᵐ one on the right and the other on the left. 34 [[And Jesus said, "Father, forgive them, for they know not what they are doing."]]ⁿ

ᵃ 23:22, **Therefore:** Included in Latin(b).

ᵇ 23:22, **nothing:** Some manuscripts read "no cause." D(05).

ᶜ 23:23, **their:** Some manuscripts include "and of the high priests." A(02) D(05) W(032).

ᵈ 23:23, **and those of the chief priests:** Included in A(02) D(05) W(032) Syriac(sy) BYZ TR ‖ Absent from 𝔓75 ℵ(01) B(03) Latin(a b e ff²) NA28 SBLGNT THGNT.

ᵉ 23:25, **to them:** Included in Latin(a b e ff²).

ᶠ 23:25, **whom they asked for:** Absent from Latin(a b e ff²).

ᵍ 23:26, **to carry:** Absent from ℵ(01).

ʰ 23:27, **great:** Absent from Latin(b e ff²).

ⁱ 23:28, **nor morn:** Included in D(05).

ʲ 23:29, **Behold:** Absent from 𝔓75 D(05) Latin(a b e ff² it) Syriac(syˢ syᶜ).

ᵏ 23:30, Hosea 10:8.

ˡ 23:33, **came:** 𝔓75 ℵ(01) B(03) C(04) D(05) NA28 SBLGNT THGNT ‖ Some manuscripts read "departed." A(02) W(032) BYZ TR.

ᵐ 23:33, **together:** Included in D(05).

ⁿ 23:34, **And Jesus said, Father, forgive them, for they know not what they are doing:** Included in C(04) BYZ TR NA28[[]] SBLGNT, THGNT ‖ Absent from 𝔓75 B(03) D(05) W(032) Latin(a) Syriac(syˢ). This verse is double bracketed both in NA28 and the critical edition of Westcott-Hort.

Dividing up his garments, they cast [lots]^a.^b 35 And the people stood by {watching. But the rulers also}^c [[with them]]^d sneered, [saying,]^e "[He saved others;]^f Let him save himself, {if this is the Christ^g [[, the Son]]^h of God, the Chosen One}."ⁱ

36 And the soldiers [also]^j mocked him, approaching and offering him vinegar 37 [and]^k saying, {"If you are the King of the Jews, save yourself!}"^l [[They put on him a crown of thorns.]]^m

38 And there was [also]ⁿ an inscription [[written]]^o over him [[in Greek, Roman, and Hebrew letters]],^p "This is the King of the Jews."

39 But one of the criminals [who were hanged there]^q was blaspheming^r [him,]^s [saying,]^t "[{Are you not the Christ?}^u Save yourself and us]."^v

40 But the other, rebuking him, said, "Do you not fear God, since you are under the same sentence of condemnation [[we are]]?^w [[And we indeed are.]]^x 41 And we indeed justly, for we are receiving the due reward of our deeds; but this man has done nothing wrong."

42 And [[turning towards the Lord,]]^y he said, {"Jesus,}^z [[Lord]]^a Remember me {when you come in your kingdom}."^b 43 And {he}^c said to him,

---

^a 23:34, **lots:** Absent from Latin(b).

^b 23:34, Psalm 22:18.

^c 23:35, **watching. But the rulers also:** Some manuscripts read "and the rulers with them." A(02) W(032) ‖ Some manuscripts read "watching and." D(05).

^d 23:35, **with them:** Included in B(03) W(032) BYZ TR.

^e 23:35, **saying:** Absent from D(05).

^f 23:35, **He saved others:** Absent from Latin(b e ff²).

^g 23:35, **Christ:** See footnote for Christ in Luke 2:11.

^h 23:35, **the Son:** Included in A(02) BYZ TR.

ⁱ 23:35, **if this is the Christ of God, the Chosen One:** Some manuscripts read "if this is the Christ, the Chosen One of God." BYZ TR ‖ Some manuscripts read "if this is the Christ, the Son of God." 𝔓75 ‖ Some manuscripts read "If Christ is the son of God." B(03) ‖ Other Manuscripts read "save yourself if you are the Son of God. If you are the Christ." D(05).

^j 23:36, **also:** Absent from ℵ(01).

^k 23:37, **and** Absent from D(05) Latin(b e ff²).

^l 23:37, **If you are the King of the Jews, save yourself!:** Some manuscripts read "Hail, King of the Jews!" D(05) Latin(a) Syriac(sy^s sy^c).

^m 23:37, **They put on him a crown of thorns:** Included in D(05).

ⁿ 23:38, **also:** Absent from Latin(a b e ff²).

^o 23:38, **written:** Included in ℵ(01) A(02) D(05) W(032) Latin(ff²) BYZ TR ‖ Absent from 𝔓75 B(03) C(04) Latin(a b e) NA28 SBLGNT THGNT.

^p 23:38, **in Greek, Roman, and Hebrew letters:** Included in ℵ(01) A(02) D(05) W(032) Latin(ff²) Syriac(sy^s) BYZ TR ‖ Absent from 𝔓75 B(03) C(04) Latin(a b e) Syriac(sy^s sy^c) NA28 SBLGNT THGNT.

^q 23:39, **who were hanged there:** Absent from D(05).

^r 23:39, **blaspheming:** Or hurling abuse. The Greek word for *blaspheming* is defined by BDAG as: to speak in a disrespectful way that demeans, denigrates, maligns (BDAG, βλασφημέω).

^s 23:39, **him:** Absent from Latin(ff²).

^t 23:39, **saying:** Absent from B(03) D(05) Latin(e).

^u 23:39, **Are you not the Christ?:** Some manuscripts read "If you are the Christ." BYZ TR.

^v 23:39, **Are you not the Christ? Save yourself and us:** Absent from D(05) Latin(e).

^w 23:40, **we are:** Included in C(04) D(05) W(032) Syriac(sy^s sy^c).

^x 23:40, **And we indeed are:** Included in D(05).

^y 23:42, **turning towards the Lord:** Included in D(05).

^z 23:42, **Jesus:** Some manuscripts read "to him." D(05) Latin(e ff²).

^a 23:42, **Lord:** Included in A(02) W(032) BYZ TR ‖ Absent from 𝔓75 B(03) NA28 SBLGNT THGNT.

^b 23:42, **when you come into your kingdom:** Some manuscripts read "on the day of your coming." D(05).

^c 23:43, **he:** 𝔓75 ℵ(01) B(03) C(04) Latin(a b e ff²) NA28 SBLGNT THGNT ‖ Some manuscripts read "Jesus." A(02) C(04) D(05) W(032) Latin(it) Syriac(sy) BYZ TR.

"Truly, I say to you [[that]],[a] today you will be with me in paradise."[b]

44 And it was [already][c] about the sixth hour, and there was darkness over the whole land until the ninth hour, 45 {With the sun having faded,}[d] the curtain of the temple was torn in two.[e]

46 Then, calling out with a loud voice, {Jesus}[f] said, "Father, into your hands I commit my spirit!"[g] And having said this, he breathed his last.

47 [But seeing what happened,][h] The centurion glorified God, saying [[that]],[i] "Truly this man was righteous!"

48 And all [the crowds][j] that had assembled for this spectacle, when they saw [what had happened,][k] they returned beating their breasts [[and their foreheads]][l] [[saying, "Woe to us for what has happened today because of our sins; for the desolation of Jerusalem has indeed drawn near."]][m]

49 But all his acquaintances stood at a distance, and the women who followed [him][n] from Galilee stood at a distance watching these things.

50 And behold, a man named Joseph, who was a member of the council, {[and][o] a good [and][p] righteous man},[q] 51 (This man was not in agreement with their counsel and action) from the city of Arimathea of the Jews, {who accepted}[r] the kingdom of God. 52 {This man}[s] went to Pilate and asked for the body of Jesus.

53 And having taken him down, he wrapped [[the body]][t] [of him][u] in a linen cloth and placed him in a {hewn tomb}[v] {where no one had yet been laid}.[w] [[And after placing him, he put a stone on the tomb, which barely twenty men could roll.]][x]

---

a 23:43, **that:** Included in Latin(b).

b 23:43, **I say to you, today you will be with me in paradise:** Or "I tell to you today, you will be with me in paradise."

c 23:44, **already:** 𝔓75 B(03) C(04) NA28 SBLGNT THGNT ‖ Absent from ℵ(01) A(02) D(05) W(032) Latin(a b e ff²) Syriac(sy^s sy^c sy^p) BYZ TR.

d 23:45, **With the sun having faded:** 𝔓75 ℵ(01) B(03) C(04) NA28 SBLGNT THGNT ‖ Some manuscripts read "And the sun was darkened." A(02) D(05) W(032) Latin(a b e) BYZ TR.

e 23:45, **the curtain of the temple was torn in two:** D(05) includes this at the end of verse 46.

f 23:46, **Jesus:** Latin(ff²) reads "he."

g 23:46, Psalm 31:5.

h 23:47, **But seeing what happened:** Absent from Latin(a). D(05) reads "Having called out."

i 23:47, **that** Included in ℵ(01).

j 23:48, **the crowds:** Absent from D(05).

k 23:48, **what had happened:** Absent from A(02).

l 23:48, **and their foreheads:** Included in D(05).

m 23:48, **saying, Woe to us...:** Included in Syriac(sy^s sy^c) Latin(g¹ [8th-century]).

n 23:49, **him:** Absent from A(02) C(04) W(032).

o 23:50, **and:** 𝔓75 ℵ(01) NA28[] ‖ Absent from A(02) B(03) W(032) BYZ TR SBLGNT THGNT.

p 23:50, **and:** Absent from B(03).

q 23:50, **and a good and righteous man:** Some manuscripts read "good and righteous." D(05) Latin(a b e ff² it).

r 23:51, **who accepted:** 𝔓75 ℵ(01) B(03) C(04) D(05) Latin(a b e ff² it) NA28 BYZ TR ‖ Some manuscripts read "And he also accepted." A(02) W(032) BYZ TR.

s 23:52, **This man:** D(05) reads "he."

t 23:53, **the body:** Included in D(05).

u 23:53, **him:** Absent from W(032) Latin(b e) ‖ Some manuscripts read "Jesus." D(05).

v 23:53, **hewn tomb:** Some manuscripts read "a tomb cut out of rock." D(05).

w 23:53, **where no one had yet been laid:** 𝔓75 A(02) B(03) D(05) NA28 SBLGNT THGNT ‖ Some manuscripts read "there was not yet anyone lying." ℵ(01) C(04) W(032) BYZ TR.

x 23:53, **And after placing him...:** Included in D(05) Sahidic(sa) ‖ The f¹³ family of manuscripts read "and he rolled a large stone against the door of the tomb."

54 And it was the day {of Preparation, and the Sabbath was beginning}.[a] 55 But [the][b] women who had [[also]][c] come [with him][d] from Galilee followed and saw the tomb [and how his body was laid].[e] 56 Having returned, they prepared spices and perfumes.

And indeed, they rested on the Sabbath [according to the commandment].[f]

24 1 But on the first day of the week, at early dawn, they came to the tomb bringing the spices which they had prepared [[and some were with them]].[g] [[They were wondering among themselves, "Who will indeed roll away the stone?"]][h] 2 [[And having come]][i] They found the stone rolled away from the tomb, 3 but when they entered, they did not find the body [of the Lord][j] [Jesus].[k]

4 And it happened, as they were perplexed about this, behold, two men stood by them in {dazzling apparel}.[l] 5 But when they became fearful and bowed their faces to the ground, they said to them, "Why do you seek the living among the dead? 6 [He is not here, but has risen.][m] Remember {how}[n] he spoke to you while he was still in Galilee, 7 saying that the Son of Man must be delivered into the hands of [sinful][o] men, be crucified, and on the third day rise again." 8 And they remembered his words.

9 And having returned [from the tomb],[p] they reported all these things to the eleven and to all the rest. 10 [Now there were][q] Mary Magdalene, and Joanna, and Mary the mother of James, and the others with them. They told these things to the apostles, 11 and {these}[r] words seemed to them like nonsense, and they did not believe them.

12 [But Peter, having risen, ran to the tomb and stooping down, he sees the linen cloths [[lying]][s] [alone],[t] and he went away to himself, marveling at what had happened.][u]

---

a 23:54, **of Preparation, and the Sabbath was beginning:** Some manuscripts read "before the Sabbath." D(05).

b 23:55, **The:** 𝔓75 B(03) ‖ Absent from ℵ(01) A(02) C(04) W(032) BYZ TR ‖ Some manuscripts read "two." D(05) Latin(it).

c 23:55, **also:** Included in TR.

d 23:55, **with him:** Absent from D(05) Latin(a b e ff2).

e 23:55, **and how his body was laid:** Absent from D(05).

f 23:56, **according to the commandment:** Absent from D(05).

g 24:1, **and some were with them:** Included in A(02) D(05) W(032) Syriac(sy) BYZ TR ‖ Absent from 𝔓75 ℵ(01) B(03) C(04) Latin(a b e ff2) NA28 SBLGNT THGNT.

h 24:1, **They were wondering...:** Included in D(05).

i 24:2, **And having come:** Included in D(05) Latin(b e ff2).

j 24:3, **of the Lord:** Absent from D(05) Latin(a b e ff2 it) SBLGNT.

k 24:3, **Jesus:** Absent from D(05) Latin(a b e ff2 it) Syriac(sys syc syp) SBLGNT.

l 24:4, **dazzling apparel:** 𝔓75 ℵ(01) B(03) D(05) NA28 SBLGNT THGNT ‖ Some manuscripts read "flashing garments." A(02) C(04) W(032) BYZ TR.

m 24:6, **he is not here, but has risen:** Absent from D(05) Latin(a b e ff2 it). Double bracketed in Westcott-Hort critical edition.

n 24:6, **how:** Some manuscripts read "what." D(05) Syriac(sys syc).

o 24:7, **sinful:** Absent from D(05) Latin(a b e ff2).

p 24:9, **from the tomb:** Absent from D(05).

q 24:10, **And there were:** Absent from A(02) D(05) W(032) and some early Syriac witnesses. Double bracketed in Tregelles critical edition.

r 24:11, **these:** 𝔓75 ℵ(01) B(03) D(05) NA28 SBLGNT THGNT ‖ Some manuscripts read "their." A(02) W(032) BYZ TR.

s 24:12, **lying:** Included in A(02) BYZ TR.

t 24:12, **alone:** Absent from ℵ(01) A(02).

u 24:12, Verse 12 is absent in from some manuscripts. D(05) Latin(e it) This verse is double bracketed in Tregelles and Westcott-Hort critical editions.

13 And [behold,]ᵃ two of them on that very day were going to a village [[one hundred]]ᵇ sixty stadia away from Jerusalem, named {Emmaus}.ᶜ 14 and they were talking [with each other]ᵈ about all these things that had happened. 15 And it happened that as they were talking and discussing, Jesus [himself]ᵉ came near and went with them, 16 but their eyes were kept from recognizing him.

17 But he said [to them],ᶠ "What are these words that you are exchanging with each other as you walk [[, looking sad]]?"ᵍ [And they stood still, looking sad.]ʰ

18 But {one named}ⁱ Cleopas, answered him, "Are you the only one living in Jerusalem who does not know the things that have happened there in these days?"

19 And he said to them, "What things?"

[But they said]ʲ [to him,]ᵏ "The things about Jesus {of Nazareth},ˡ who became a man, a prophet powerful {deed and word}ᵐ before God and all the people, 20 {just as}ⁿ the high priests and our rulers handed [him]ᵒ over for the judgment of death and crucified him. 21 But {were hoping}ᵖ that he {is}ᵠ the one to redeem Israel.

"[And]ʳ Indeed, with all these things, {this}ˢ is the third day since these things happened. 22 But also some women, [from among us,]ᵗ astonished us, having gone early in the morning to the tomb; 23 and when they did not find his body, they came back saying [also]ᵘ that they had even seen a vision of angels, who said that he was alive. 24 Some of those who were with us went to the tomb and found it just as the women had said, but they did not see him."

25 And he said to them, "O foolish men, and slow of heart [to believe]ᵛ concerning all that the prophets have spoken! 26 {Was it not necessary that the Christ}ʷ should suffer these things}ˣ and to enter into his {glory}?"ʸ

ᵃ 24:13, **behold:** Absent from D(05).

ᵇ 24:13, **one hundred:** Included in some manuscripts. ℵ(01).

ᶜ 24:13, **Emmaus:** Some manuscripts read "Ullammas." D(05).

ᵈ 24:14, **with each other:** Absent from Latin(a b ff²).

ᵉ 24:15, **himself:** Absent from D(05) Latin(a).

ᶠ 24:17, **to them:** Absent from D(05).

ᵍ 24:17, **looking sad:** Included in D(05).

ʰ 24:17, **And they stood still, looking sad:** 𝔓75 ℵ(01) A(02) B(03) NA28 SBLGNT THGNT ‖ Absent from D(05). ‖ Some manuscripts read "And why are you sad?" W(032) Syriac(syˢ syᶜ) BYZ TR.

ⁱ 24:18, **one named:** 𝔓75 ℵ(01) B(03) Latin(b) NA28 SBLGNT THGNT ‖ Some manuscripts read "one, whose name was." A(02) D(05) W(032) BYZ TR.

ʲ 24:19, **And he said:** Absent from D(05).

ᵏ 24:19, **to him:** Absent from D(05) Latin(a b e ff²).

ˡ 24:19, **of Nazareth:** Or "the Nazarene."

ᵐ 24:19, **deed and word:** Some manuscripts read "word and deed." ℵ(01) D(05) Syriac(syᵖ).

ⁿ 24:20, **just as:** D(05) reads "as this one."

ᵒ 24:20, **handed:** Absent from D(05).

ᵖ 24:21, **were hoping:** ℵ(01) A(02) B(03) D(05) W(032) BYZ TR NA28 SBLGNT THGNT ‖ Some manuscripts read "had hoped." 𝔓75.

ᵠ 24:21, **is:** Some manuscripts read "was." D(05) Latin(e).

ʳ 24:21, **And:** Absent from BYZ TR.

ˢ 24:21, **this:** Some manuscripts read "today." A(02) D(05) W(032) BYZ TR.

ᵗ 24:22, **from among us:** Absent from D(05).

ᵘ 24:23 , **also:** Absent from D(05) Latin(e) Syriac(syˢ syᶜ syᵖ).

ᵛ 24:25, **to believe:** Absent from D(05).

ʷ 24:26, **Christ:** See footnote for Christ in Luke 2:11.

ˣ 24:26, **Was it not necessary...:** Some manuscripts read "For these things had to be suffered by the Christ." D(05) Latin(it).

ʸ 24:26, **glory:** 𝔓75 reads "kingdom."

27 {And beginning with Moses and from all the Prophets, he interpreted}[a] to them in [all][b] the Scriptures the things concerning himself.

28 And they drew near to the village where they were going, and he made as though to go further. 29 And they urged him, saying, "Stay with us, for it is toward evening and the day has [already][c] declined." And he went in [to stay][d] with them.

30 And it happened that, when he reclined [with them],[e] he took the bread, blessed it, and [breaking it,][f] gave it to them. 31 And [[having taken the bread from them,]][g] their eyes were opened [and they recognized him];[h] and he became invisible to them.

32 And they said to each other, "Was not our heart burning [within us][i] as he spoke to us on the way, [[and]][j] as he opened the Scriptures to us?"

33 And rising up that very hour, they returned to Jerusalem [[in sorrow]][k] and found the eleven and those with them gathered together, 34 saying, "The Lord has [truly][l] been raised and has appeared to Simon." 35 And they were explaining the things on the road and how he was recognized by them in the breaking of the bread.

36 While they were saying these things, {he}[m] himself stood among them. [And he said to them, "Peace to you,"][n] [["It is I; do not be afraid."]][o]

37 But having been startled and becoming frightened, they thought the were seeing a {spirit}.[p]

38 And he said to them, "Why are you troubled, and why do doubts arise in your {heart}?[q] 39 See my hands and [my][r] feet, that I am he; touch [me][s] and see, for a spirit does not have flesh and bones as you see me having." 40 [And when he had said this, he showed them his hands and his feet.][t]

---

a 24:27, **And beginning...**: D(05) reads "And he began, starting from Moses and all the prophets, to interpret."

b 24:27, **all**: Absent from ℵ(01) D(05).

c 24:29, **already**: 𝔓75 ℵ(01) B(03) NA28 SBLGNT THGNT ‖ Absent from A(02) D(05) W(032) BYZ TR.

d 24:29, **to stay**: Absent from Latin(ff²).

e 24:30, **with them**: Absent from D(05) Latin(e) Syriac(sy^s sy^c).

f 24:30, **breaking it**: Absent from D(05).

g 24:31, **having taken the bread from them**: Included in D(05).

h 24:31, **and they recognized him**: Absent from ℵ(01).

i 24:32, **within us**: Absent from 𝔓75 B(03) D(05) Syriac(sy^s sy^c).

j 24:32, **and**: Included in A(02) W(032) BYZ TR.

k 24:33, **in sorrow**: Included in D(05).

l 24:34, **truly**: Absent from W(032).

m 24:36, **he**: 𝔓75 ℵ(01) B(03) D(05) NA28 SBLGNT THGNT ‖ Some manuscripts read "Jesus." A(02) W(032) BYZ TR.

n 24:36, **and said to them, "peace to you."**: Absent from D(05) Latin(a b e ff² it) SBLGNT. Double bracketed in Westcott-Hort critical edition.

o 24:36, **it is I; do not be afraid**: Included in W(032) Syriac(sy^p).

p 24:37, **spirit**: D(05) reads "ghost."

q 24:38, **heart**: 𝔓75 B(03) D(05) Latin(it) NA28 SBLGNT THGNT ‖ Some manuscripts read "hearts." ℵ(01) A(02) W(032) Syriac(sy) BYZ TR.

r 24:39, **my**: Absent from 𝔓75 W(032).

s 24:39, **me**: Absent from D(05) W(032) Latin(a b e ff²) Syriac(sy^s sy^c).

t 24:40, **And when he had...**: Verse 40 is absent in from some manuscripts. D(05) Latin(a b e ff² it) Syriac(sy^s sy^c) ‖ Bracketed with single brackets in SBLGNT and double brackets in Tregelles and Westcott-Hort critical editions.

41 And while they still did not
believe for joy, and marveling, he said
[to them],[a] "Do you have any food
here?" 42 And they gave him a piece of
broiled fish [[and some honeycomb]].[b]
43 And taking it, he ate it in their
presence. [[He took the leftovers and
gave them to them.]][c]

44 And he said to them, "These
are {my}[d] words which I spoke to
you while I was still with you, that
everything written about me in the Law
of Moses and [[in]][e] the Prophets and
the Psalm must be fulfilled."

45 Then he opened their minds to
understand the Scriptures, 46 and said to
them, "Thus it is written [[and thus it
was necessary]][f] that the Christ should
suffer and rise [from the dead][g] on
the third day, 47 and that repentance
{for}[h] the forgiveness of sins should be
proclaimed in his name to all nations,
beginning from Jerusalem. 48 [[But]][i]
You are witnesses of these things.

49 "And [behold][j] I am sending the
promise {of my Father}[k] upon you.
But stay in the city [[of Jerusalem]][l]
until you are clothed with power from
on high."

50 And he led them {out as far as}[m]
Bethany, and lifting up {his}[n] hands,
he blessed them. 51 And it happened
that, as he was blessing them, he parted
from them [, and was carried up into
heaven].[o]

52 And they, [having worshiped
him,][p] returned to Jerusalem with
[great][q] joy, 53 and were continually [in
the temple,][r] {blessing}[s] God. [[Amen]][t]

---

a 24:41, **to them:** Absent from D(05).

b 24:42, **and some honeycomb:** Included in BYZ TR || Absent from 𝔓75 ℵ(01) A(02) B(03) D(05) W(032) Latin(a b e ff²) NA28 SBLGNT THGNT.

c 24:43, **He took the leftovers and gave them to them:** Included in Syriac(syᶜ) f¹³ family.

d 24:44, **my:** Some manuscripts read "the." ℵ(01) W(032) Latin(a b e ff²) BYZ TR.

e 24:44, **in:** Included in ℵ(01).

f 24:46, **and thus it was necessary:** Included in A(02) W(032) Syriac(syˢ) BYZ TR || Absent from 𝔓75 ℵ(01) B(03) C(04) D(05) Latin(a b e ff² it) NA28 SBLGNT THGNT.

g 24:46, **from the dead:** Absent from D(05) Sahidic(sa).

h 24:47, **for:** 𝔓75 ℵ(01) B(03) Syriac(syᵖ) NA28 || Some manuscripts read "and." A(02) C(04) D(05) W(032) Syriac(syˢ) BYZ TR SBLGNT THGNT.

i 24:48, **But:** Included in A(02) W(032) BYZ TR || D(05) includes "And."

j 24:49, **behold:** A(02) B(03) C(04) NA28[] SBLGNT BYZ TR || Absent from 𝔓75 ℵ(01) D(05) Syriac(syˢ syᵖ) THGNT.

k 24:49, **of my Father:** Some manuscripts read "of me." D(05) Latin(e).

l 24:49, **of Jerusalem:** Included in A(02) W(032) Syriac(syᵖ) BYZ TR || Absent from 𝔓75 ℵ(01) B(03) C(04) D(05) Latin(a b e ff²) Syriac(syˢ) NA28 SBLGNT THGNT.

m 24:50, **out as far as:** A(02) W(032) BYZ TR NA28[] || Some manuscripts read "as far as." 𝔓75 ℵ(01) B(03) C(04) Latin(a b e ff²) SBLGNT THGNT || Some manuscripts read "out towards." D(05).

n 24:50, **his:** Some manuscripts read "the." D(05) W(032) Latin(ff²).

o 24:51, **and was carried up into heaven:** Absent from ℵ(01) D(05) Latin(it) Syriac(syˢ) || Double bracketed in Westcott-Hort.

p 24:52, **having worshiped him:** Absent from D(05) Latin(it) Syriac(syˢ) || Double bracketed in the critical edition of Westcott-Hort. BDAG gives meaning of the Greek word translated "worship" as to express in attitude or gesture one's complete dependence on or submission to a high authority figure, *(fall down and) worship, do obeisance to, prostrate oneself before, do reverence to, welcome respectfully*. BDAG states "Frequently used to designate the custom of prostrating oneself before persons and kissing their feet or the hem of their garment, the ground, etc." (BDAG, προσκυνέω).

q 24:52, **great:** Absent from B(03).

r 24:53, **in the temple:** Absent from A(02).

s 24:53, **blessing:** 𝔓75 ℵ(01) A(02) C(04) D(05) W(032) Syriac(syˢ) NA28 SBLGNT THGNT || Some manuscripts read "praising and blessing." W(032) Syriac(syᵖ) BYZ TR || some manuscripts read "praising." D(05) Latin(a b e ff² it).

t 24:53, **Amen:** Included in A(02) B(03) Syriac(syᵖ) BYZ TR || Absent from 𝔓75 ℵ(01) C(04) D(05) W(032) Latin(a b e ff² it) NA28 Syriac(syˢ) SBLGNT THGNT.

John[a]

1 [1] In the beginning was the Word[b], and the Word was with[c] God, and the Word was God.[d]

[2] This was in the beginning with God.

[3] All things were made through it,[e] and without it not even one thing was made.

{What has been made [4] in it {was}[f] life, and the life was the light of men.}[g]

[5] And the light shines in the darkness, and the darkness did not overcome[h] it.

[6] There was a man, sent from {God},[i] whose name was John.

[7] This one came for a testimony, to testify about the light, so that all might believe through him.

[8] He was not the light, but came to testify about the light.

---

a 1:0, **Title ("John"):** Absent from ℵ(01) B(03). ‖ Latin(e) BYZ reads "According to John." ‖ 𝔓66 𝔓75 A(02) D(05) Latin(ff²) reads "Gospel According to John." ‖ TR reads "The Holy Gospel According to John."

b 1:1, **Word:** The Greek word *Logos* is defined as (1) a communication whereby the mind finds expression, *word*, (2) *computation, reckoning*, or (3) the independent personified expression of God, *the Logos* (BDAG, λόγος). GPT-4 capitalized "Word" as a neutral rendering consistent with the English convention of capitalizing specific names, titles, and concepts. For example, the word *Torah* is typically capitalized to reflect its broader meaning as divine instruction encompassing law, ethics, and wisdom, not just a set of written texts. In English, capitalization can signal the significance or distinct nature of a concept, beyond simply marking proper nouns.

c 1:1, **with:** The Greek word is a preposition that, with the accusative, is a marker of movement or orientation toward someone or something. (BDAG, πρός).

d 1:1, **the Word was God:** The interpretation of this phrase will depend on the theological perspective of the reader. Some see this as a statement of ontology (the word having the very nature of God) and others see the Word as being described as divine in some other sense (a noun used as an adjective). The emerging consensus is that when two nouns are connected by the verb "to be" and only one of those nouns has a definite article, then the noun without the definite article functions as an adjective (Dustin R. Smith, *Wisdom Christology in the Gospel of John* [Eugene, OR: Wipf & Stock, 2024], 58).

e 1:3, **it:** The Greek word αὐτός is used with masculine nouns, even when they don't refer to persons. Its masculine form is grammatical and does not indicate personal gender unless the context clearly refers to a person. The pronoun may be rendered "him" or "it," depending on whether Logos is interpreted as a person, a personification, or an abstract aspect of God. GPT-4 rendered "it" as the most theologically neutral choice in English, accommodating all three interpretations. This translation is also found in several 16th-century Bibles, including Tyndale, Coverdale, Matthew's, the Great Bible, the Bishops' Bible, and the Geneva Bible.

f 1:4, **was:** Some manuscripts read "is." ℵ(01) D(05) Latin(a b e ff² it).

g 1:3-4, **What has been made in it...:** Manuscripts that punctuate verses 3-4 as shown include 𝔓75 (punctuation added later) C(04) D(05) W(032) (supplemented) Syriac(sy^c) Latin(b) NA28 SBLGNT. Additional early witnesses that attest to this are the Sadhic text, Ptolemy according to Irenaeus, Theophilus of Alexandria, Irenaeus, Tertullian, Clement of Alexandria and Origen of the third through fourth centuries (NA28). The English translations of NRSV, NAB and NABRE exhibit this punctuation. ‖ Other manuscripts punctuate with the separation occurring at the start of verse 4, as exhibited in most English translations, with the reading, "In him/it was life and the light was the light of men." This includes ℵ(01) (punctuation added later), BYZ, TR, and THGNT. ‖ Manuscripts with no or uncertain punctuation include 𝔓66, A(02), and B(03). Note that early manuscripts did not have verse numbers.

h 1:5, **overcome:** Or comprehend.

i 1:6, **God:** D(05) reads "the Lord."

9 The true light, which enlightens every person, was coming into the world.[a]

10 He[b] was in the world,[c] and the world came into being through him,[d] yet the world did not know him.

11 He came to his own, and his own did not receive him.

12 [But][e] To all who received him, he gave them the right to become children of God, to those who believe in his name, 13 who were born not of blood, nor of the will of the flesh, [nor of the will of a man,][f] but of God.

14 And the Word became flesh and dwelt among us, and we have beheld his glory, glory as of the unique[g] one from the Father, full of grace and truth.

15 John bears witness concerning him and has cried out, [saying,][h] "This was he of whom [I said],[i] 'He who comes after me has become before me, because he was before me.'"[j]

16 {For}[k] from his fullness we have all received, grace upon grace.

17 For the law was given through Moses; [[But]][l] Grace and truth came through Jesus [Christ].[m]

---

a 1:9, **world:** The Greek word can mean (1) that which serves to beautify through decoration, adornment, adorning, (2) condition of orderliness, orderly arrangement, order, (3) the sum total of everything here and now, the world, the (orderly) universe, (4) the sum total of all beings above the level of the animals, the world, (5) planet earth as a place of inhabitation, the world, (6) humanity in general, the world, (7) the system of human existence in its many aspects, the world, or (8) collective aspect of an entity, totality, sum total. (BDAG, κόσμος).

b 1:10, **him:** Verses 10–18 clearly refer to the Word after becoming flesh, that is, to the person Jesus Christ, through whom grace and truth came (v. 17), who was in the world (v. 10), and who came to his own, though they did not receive him (v. 11). In this context, the masculine pronoun αὐτός is more appropriately rendered "him" than in verses 3–4, where the referent is less clearly personal.

c 1:10, **world:** See the footnote of verse 9 for the meaning of the Greek word for instances of "world."

d 1:10, **the world came into being through him:** Judaism consistently portrayed the Creator God making all things through his creative word (Gen 1:3; Ps 33:6; Wis 9:1) and through the word's close synonym, wisdom (Ps 104:24; Prov 3:19; Wis 9:2). While verses 1-4 describe the Word in a more abstract sense, verses 10-14 go further in associating the Word with Jesus. The interpretation of John 1:10, and how the Word relates to Christ, varies according to different theological perspectives. A common interpretation is that Jesus existed from the beginning and was actively involved in the creation of the world. An alternative interpretation, consistent with the Jewish understanding of the Word and Wisdom of God, is Wisdom Christology (D. Smith, *Wisdom Christology in the Gospel of John*). Others suggest that the world was made in view of Christ or with him in mind. Additionally, some interpreters have proposed that the Word represents God's plan, of which Christ is central, existing before the world and serving as the framework through which the world was created.

e 1:12, **But:** Absent from D(05) Latin(e).

f 1:13, **nor of the will of a man:** Absent from B(03).

g 1:14, **unique:** Although traditionally translated "only-begotten" the meaning of the Greek word is (1) being the only one of its kind within a specific relationship, *one and only, only,* or (2) to being the only one of its kind or class, *unique (in kind).* (BDAG, μονογενής).

h 1:15, **saying:** Absent from א(01) D(05) Latin(b).

i 1:15, **I said:** Absent from א(01).

j 1:15, **he was before me:** The interpretation will depend on the theological perspective of the reader. The phrase can be interpreted in a few different ways: (1) Chronological precedence: This interpretation emphasizes the aspect of time, suggesting that Jesus existed before John the Baptist. (2) Superior rank or status: Some scholars interpret this phrase to indicate that Jesus has a higher rank or status than John the Baptist. (3) Priority in function or role: Another interpretation is that Jesus has a more important function or role than John the Baptist.

k 1:16, **For:** 𝔓66 𝔓75 א(01) B(03) C(04) D(05) Latin(a b e ff²) NA28 SBLGNT THGNT ‖ Some manuscripts read "And." A(02) Syriac(sy) BYZ TR.

l 1:17, **But:** Included in P66 Latin(a b ff²).

m 1:17, **Christ:** Absent from א(01). ‖ The Greek word for Christ means (1) fulfiller of Israelite expectation of a deliverer, the Anointed One, the Messiah, the Christ, or (2) the personal name ascribed to Jesus, Christ. (BDAG, Χριστός).

18 No one has ever seen God; unique[a] {Son},[b] [who is][c] in the bosom of the Father, that one has made known.

19 And this is the testimony of John, when the Jews sent [to him][d] from Jerusalem priests and Levites to ask him, "Who are you?" 20 And he did not deny, [and he confessed,][e] "I am not the Christ."

21 And they asked him [[again]],[f] "What then? [Are you][g] Elijah?" [And][h] He says, "I am not." "[[What then,]][i] Are you the prophet?" And {he answered, "No."}[j]

22 So they said to him, "Who are you? That we may give an answer to those who sent us. What do you say about yourself?"

23 He said, "I am the voice of one crying out in the wilderness, 'Make straight the way of the Lord,' as the prophet Isaiah said."[k]

24 And {they were sent}[l] from the Pharisees; 25 [And they asked him][m] [and said to him,][n] "Why then do you baptize if you are not the Christ, nor Elijah, nor the prophet?" 26 John answered them, [saying,][o] "I [[indeed]][p] baptize [[you]][q] with water; [[but]][r] among you stands one whom you do not know, 27 [[he is]][s] {the one}[t] coming after me [[who was before me,]][u] of whom I am not {worthy}[v] to untie the strap of his sandal."

---

a 1:18, **unique:** See the footnote for verse 14.

b 1:18, **Son:** A(02) Latin (a b e ff²) Syriac(sy^c) BYZ TR THGNT ‖ Some manuscripts read "God." P66 P75 ℵ(01) B(03) C(04) SBLGNT NA28 ‖ "Son" is selected over "God" from the critical editions as it is the more theologically neutral. Although the most commonly attested reading is "the unique Son," found in A(02) and many other Greek manuscripts, there are a number of different readings exhibited in early manuscripts, including "the unique God" (P75), and "unique God" (P66, A(02) B(03) C(04)). The BDAG entry of the Greek word for "God" states, "Some writing in our literature uses the word θεός in reference to Christ without necessarily equating Christ with the Father, and therefore in harmony with the Shema of Israel. Dt 6:4." BDAG further gives a fourth definition of θεός : "4 that which is nontranscendent but considered worth of special reverence or respect, god ... of humans θεοί John 10:34f; humans are called θεός in the Old Testament" (BDAG, θεός).

c 1:18, **who is:** Absent from ℵ(01) Latin(a).

d 1:19, **to him:** B(03) C(04) Latin(a b) NA28[] THGNT ‖ Absent from 𝔓66 𝔓75 ℵ(01) A(02) Latin(e ff²) BYZ TR SBLGNT.

e 1:20, **and he confessed:** Absent from ℵ(01) Latin(e) Sahidic.

f 1:21, **again:** Included in ℵ(01) Latin(a b e ff²) Syriac(sy^p).

g 1:21, **are you:** Absent from ℵ(01) Latin(a).

h 1:21, **And:** Absent from ℵ(01) Latin(a b).

i 1:21, **What then:** Included in Latin(a b ff²).

j 1:21, **he answered, "No":** Some manuscripts read "he says, 'I am not.'" Latin(e).

k 1:23, Isaiah 40:3 LXX.

l 1:24, **they were sent:** Some manuscripts read "those who were sent were" BYZ TR.

m 1:25, **And they asked him:** Absent from ℵ(01) Syriac(sy^C) Latin(a e).

n 1:25, **and said to him:** Absent from 𝔓119. "To him" absent from Latin(e ff²).

o 1:26, **saying:** Absent from 𝔓75 𝔓120 Latin(e).

p 1:26, **indeed:** Included in Latin(b ff²).

q 1:26, **you:** Included in Latin(a b ff²).

r 1:26, **but:** Included in A(02) Latin(a b e ff²) Syriac(sy) BYZ TR ‖ Absent from 𝔓59 𝔓66 𝔓75 𝔓120 ℵ(01) B(03) C(04) NA28 SBLGNT THGNT.

s 1:27, **he is:** Included in A(02) Latin (b e ff²) BYZ TR ‖ Absent from 𝔓66 𝔓75 𝔓120 ℵ(01) B(03) Latin(a) NA28 SBLGNT THGNT.

t 1:27, Some manuscripts read "It is he" as a new sentence rather than "the one" as a continuation of verse 26. A(02) Latin (b) BYZ TR.

u 1:27, **who was before me:** Included in A(02) BYZ TR ‖ Some manuscripts read "he has come before me." Latin(a b) ‖ Absent from 𝔓5 𝔓66 𝔓75 ℵ(01) B(03) C(04) Latin(b) NA28 SBLGNT THGNT.

v 1:27, **worthy:** Some manuscripts read "sufficient." 𝔓66 𝔓75.

28 These things [[indeed]][a] took
place in {Bethany}[b] across the Jordan
[[River]],[c] where John was baptizing
[[first]].[d]

29 The next day {he}[e] sees Jesus
coming [toward him] and says,
"Behold, the Lamb of God who takes
away the sin of the world.

30 "This is the one {about}[f] whom I
said, 'After me comes a man who has
become before me, because he was first
with respect to me.'[g] 31 And I did not
know him, but in order that he might
be revealed to Israel, for this reason I
came baptizing in water."

32 And John testified, [saying,][h] "I
have seen the Spirit descending like a
dove from heaven and remaining upon
him. 33 And I did not know [him],[i] but
the one who sent me to baptize in water
said to me, 'Upon whom you see the
Spirit descending and remaining upon
him, this is the one who baptizes in
the Holy Spirit.'[j] 34 And I have seen and
have testified that this is the {chosen}[k]
of God."

35 On the next day, John was
[standing][l] [again][m] with two of his
disciples, 36 And looking at Jesus
walking, he says, "Behold, the Lamb of
God. [[The one taking away the sin of
the world.]]"[n]

37 [And][o] {The}[p] two disciples heard
him speaking [and][q] followed Jesus.

38 [But][r] Jesus, having turned and
seen them following [[him]],[s] says [to
them],[t] "What are you seeking?" And
they said to him, "Rabbi (which is
translated as 'Teacher'), where are you
staying?" 39 He says to them, "Come and
see." [So][u] They went and saw where
he was staying, and they stayed with
him that day; it was about the tenth
hour. 40 Andrew, the brother of Simon
Peter, was one of the two who heard
from John and followed him.

41 He finds first his own brother
Simon and says to him, "We have
found the Messiah," which is translated
Christ.[v]

42 [[Therefore,]][w] He brought him to
Jesus. Looking at him, Jesus said, "You
are Simon, the son of {John};[x] you will
be called Cephas," which is translated
as Peter.[y]

43 The next day {he}[z] wanted to
go out to Galilee and found Philip.

---

a 1:28, **indeed:** Included in Latin(a).
b 1:28, **Bethany:** Some manuscripts read "Bethabara." Syriac(sy^s sy^c) TR.
c 1:28, **River:** Included in ℵ(01).
d 1:28, **first:** Included in C(04).
e 1:29, **he:** Some manuscripts read "John." Latin (b e ff^2) TR.
f 1:30, **about:** Some manuscripts read "of." A(02) BYZ TR.
g 1:30, **he was first with respect to me:** See the note for verse 15.
h 1:32, **saying:** Absent from 𝔓106 ℵ(01) Latin(e).
i 1:33, **him:** Absent from A(02).
j 1:33, **Spirit:** See footnote for Spirit in Luke 1:15.
k 1:34, **chosen:** 𝔓106 ℵ(01) Latin(b e ff^2) Syriac(sy^s sy^c) SBLGNT ‖ Some manuscripts read "Son." 𝔓5 𝔓66 𝔓75 𝔓120 A(02) B(03) C(04) BYZ TR NA28 THGNT.
l 1:35, **standing:** Absent from Latin(b).
m 1:35, **again:** Absent from 𝔓75 Latin(b e).
n 1:36, **The one taking away the sin of the world:** Included in P66 C(04) Latin(a ff^2).
o 1:37, **And:** Absent from ℵ(01).
p 1:37, **The:** Some manuscripts read "His." Latin(e ff^2) TR.
q 1:37, **and:** Absent from 𝔓120 Latin(e).
r 1:38, **but:** Absent from ℵ(01).
s 1:38, **him:** Included in 𝔓66 C(04) Latin(a b e ff^2).
t 1:38, **to them:** Absent from ℵ(01) D(05).
u 1:39, **So:** Absent from Latin(ff^2) TR BYZ.
v 1:41, **Christ:** See footnote for verse 1:17.
w 1:42, **Therefore:** Included in Latin(b e).
x 1:42, **John:** Some manuscripts read "Jonah." A(02) Syriac(sy) BYZ TR.
y 1:42, **Peter:** Meaning a rock.
z 1:43, **he:** TR reads "Jesus." TR.

And {Jesus}[a] says to him, "Follow me." [44] [Now][b] Philip was from Bethsaida, the city of Andrew and Peter.

[45] Philip finds Nathanael and says to him, "We have found the one whom Moses wrote about in the law and the prophets, Jesus {son}[c] of Joseph from Nazareth." [46] [And][d] Nathanael said to him, "Can anything good come out of Nazareth?" Philip said to him, "Come and see."

[47] Jesus saw Nathanael coming toward him and says about {him},[e] "Behold, truly an Israelite in whom there is no deceit." [48] Nathanael says to him, "From where do you know me?" Jesus answered and said to him, "Before Philip called you, being under the fig tree, I saw you."

[49] Nathanael answered him [[and said to him]],[f] "Rabbi, you are [[truly]][g] the son of God,[h] you are the king of Israel."

[50] Jesus answered and said to him, "Because I said to you [that][i] I saw you under the fig tree, do you believe? You will see greater things than these." [51] And he says to him, "Truly, truly I say to you [[hereafter]],[j] you will see the heaven opened and the angels of God ascending and descending upon the Son of Man."

2 [1] And on the third day a wedding took place in Cana of Galilee, and the mother of Jesus was there; [2] And Jesus was [also][k] invited, and his disciples, to the wedding.

[3] And when the wine ran out [[, the wine of the wedding was gone]];[l] {The mother of Jesus}[m] says to him, "{They have}[n] no wine." [4] [And][o] Jesus says to her, "What is it to me and to you, woman? My hour has not yet come."

[5] [[Therefore]][p] His mother says to the servants, "Whatever he says to you, do it."

[6] Now there were six stone water jars there for the Jewish purification [standing],[q] each holding two or three measures.[r] [7] [[And]][s] Jesus says to them, "Fill the jars with water." And they filled them up to the top. [8] [And][t] {He}[u] says to them, "Draw out [now][v] and bring to the master of the feast;" and they brought.

[9] But when the master of the feast tasted the water now become wine, and did not know where it came from (though the servants who had drawn the water knew), the master of the feast called the bridegroom. [10] And he says [to him],[w] "Every man first puts the good wine, and when they are

---

[a] 1:43, **Jesus:** Some manuscripts read "he." Latin(e) TR.

[b] 1:44, **Now:** Absent from ℵ(01).

[c] 1:45, **son:** Some manuscripts read "the son." A(02) BYZ TR.

[d] 1:46, **And:** Absent from ℵ(01) Latin(a b e).

[e] 1:47, **him:** Some manuscripts read "Nathanael." ℵ(01) Latin(a).

[f] 1:49, **and said to him:** Included in A(02) Latin(a ff²).

[g] 1:49, **truly:** Included in 𝔓66.

[h] 1:49, **you are the son of God:** Absent from some later manuscripts including the f13 family.

[i] 1:50, **that:** Absent from Latin(e ff²) TR BYZ.

[j] 1:51, **hereafter:** Included in A(02) Latin(e) BYZ TR Syriac(sy).

[k] 2:2, **also:** Absent from 𝔓66 Latin(e it).

[l] 2:3, **the wine of the wedding was gone:** Included in ℵ(01) Latin (a b ff²).

[m] 2:3, **The mother of Jesus:** Some manuscripts read "His mother." Latin(a).

[n] 2:3, **They have:** ℵ(01) reads "There is."

[o] 2:4, **and:** 𝔓66 A(02) B(03) Latin(b e ff²) Syriac(syᵖ) NA28[] SBLGNT ‖ Absent from 𝔓75 ℵ(01) Latin(a) BYZ TR THGNT.

[p] 2:5, **Therefore:** Included in Latin(e).

[q] 2:6, **standing:** Absent from ℵ(01) Latin(a e ff²) f13.

[r] 2:6, **two or three measures:** This corresponds to 20 or 30 gallons.

[s] 2:7, **And:** Included in ℵ(01) Latin(e ff²).

[t] 2:8, **And:** Absent from Latin(a b ff²).

[u] 2:8, **he:** Some manuscripts read "Jesus." Latin(a b ff²).

[v] 2:8, **now:** Absent from Latin(a e).

[w] 2:10, **to him:** Absent from ℵ(01).

intoxicated, [[then]]ᵃ the lesser; you have kept the good wine until now." ¹¹ The [[first]]ᵇ beginning of the signs Jesus did in Cana of Galilee, and he revealed his glory; and his disciples believed in him.

¹² After this he went down to Capernaum, with his mother and {his}ᶜ brothers [and {his}ᵈ disciples],ᵉ and they stayed there for a few days.

¹³ And the Passover of the Jews was near, and Jesus went up to Jerusalem. ¹⁴ And he found in the temple those selling oxen and sheep and doves, and the money changers sitting. ¹⁵ And making a whip out of cords, he drove all, both the sheep and the oxen out of the temple, [and he poured out the coins of the money changers]ᶠ and overturned their tables, ¹⁶ and to those selling the doves he said, "Take these things away from here; do not make my Father's house a house of trade." ¹⁷ [[And]]ᵍ his disciples remembered that it is written, "The zeal for your house will consume me."ʰ

¹⁸ Therefore, the Jews answered and said to him, "What sign do you show [us]ⁱ that you do these things?"

¹⁹ Jesus answered and said to them, "Destroy this temple, and in three days I will raise it up." ²⁰ So the Jews said, "This temple was built in forty-six years, and you will raise it up in three days?" ²¹ But he was speaking about the temple of {his}ʲ body. ²² Therefore, when he was raised from the dead, his disciples remembered that he had said this [[to them]],ᵏ and they believed the Scripture and the word which Jesus had spoken.

²³ But when he was in Jerusalem during the Passover, during the feast, many believed in his name, seeing the signs which he did; ²⁴ But {Jesus}ˡ himself did not {entrust himself to them},ᵐ because he knew all men, ²⁵ And [because]ⁿ he had no need that anyone should testify about man; for he himself knew what was in man.

3 ¹ There was a man of the Pharisees, named Nicodemus, a ruler of the Jews; ² this one came to {him}ᵒ at night and said to him, "Rabbi, we know that you have come from God as a teacher; for no one can do these signs that you do, unless God is with him."

³ Jesus answered [and said to him],ᵖ "Truly, truly, I say to you, unless one is born from above,ᑫ he cannot see the kingdom of God."

⁴ Nicodemus says to him, "How can a man be born when he is old? Can he enter a second time into his mother's womb and be born?"

⁵ Jesus answered, "Truly, [truly,]ʳ I say to you, unless one is born of water and the Spirit, he cannot {enter}ˢ the kingdom of {God}.ᵗ

ᵃ 2:10, **then:** Included in A(02) Latin(b) BYZ TR.

ᵇ 2:11, **first:** Included in 𝔓66 Latin(b).

ᶜ 2:12, **his:** Some manuscripts read "the." 𝔓66 P75 B(03) Latin(a e).

ᵈ 2:12, **his:** Some manuscripts read "the." Latin(a e).

ᵉ 2:12, **and his disciples:** Absent from ℵ(01) Latin(b ff² it).

ᶠ 2:15, **and he poured out the coins of the money changers:** Absent from Latin(e).

ᵍ 2:17, **And:** Included in A(02) Latin(b e ff²) BYZ TR.

ʰ 2:17, Psalm 69:9.

ⁱ 2:18, **us:** Absent from 𝔓75.

ʲ 2:21, **his:** Some manuscripts read "the." ℵ(01).

ᵏ 2:22, **to them:** Included in TR.

ˡ 2:24, **Jesus:** Some manuscripts read "he." Latin(e).

ᵐ 2:24, **entrust himself to them:** Some manuscripts read "trust them." 𝔓75.

ⁿ 2:25, **because:** Absent from A(02).

ᵒ 3:2, **him:** Some manuscripts read "Jesus." Latin(a e) TR.

ᵖ 3:3, **and said to him:** Absent from ℵ(01).

ᑫ 3:3, **born from above:** Or "born again."

ʳ 3:5, **truly:** Absent from A(02).

ˢ 3:5, **enter:** Some manuscripts read "see." BYZ TR.

ᵗ 3:5, **God:** Some manuscripts read "the heavens." ℵ(01) Latin(e).

6 "That which is born of the flesh is flesh, and that which is born of the Spirit is spirit.

7 "Do not be amazed that I said to you,[a] 'You must be born from above.'[b]

8 "The wind blows where it wishes and you hear its sound, but you do not know where it comes from {and}[c] where it goes; so is everyone who is born of the [[water and the]][d] Spirit."

9 Nicodemus answered and said to him, "How can these things be?"

10 Jesus answered and said to him, "Are you the teacher of Israel and you do not understand these things?"

Possible Narrator Interjection[e]

11 Truly, truly, I say to you, we speak what we know and testify what we have seen, and you[f] do not receive our testimony

12 If I have told you earthly things and you do not believe, how will you believe if I tell you heavenly things?[g]

13 And no one has ascended into heaven except the one who descended from heaven, the Son of Man [[who is in heaven]].[h]

14 And just as Moses lifted up the serpent in the wilderness, thus it is necessary for the Son of Man to be lifted up, 15 so that everyone who believes in him may [[not perish but]][i] have eternal life.

16 For God so loved the world, that he gave {the}[j] unique Son [[into the world]],[k] so that everyone who believes in him should not perish but have eternal life.

17 For God did not send {the}[l] Son into the world in order to judge the world, but in order that the world might be saved through him.

---

a 3:7, **you:** "You" is in the plural.

b 3:7, **born from above:** Or "born again."

c 3:8, **and:** Some manuscripts read "or." A(02) Latin(a b).

d 3:8, **water and the:** Included in ℵ(01) Latin(a b e ff² it) Syriac(sy^s sy^c).

e 3:11-21, It is disputed whether verses 11-21 are Jesus' words or a narrative interlude by the author. Most regard all of the verses 13-21 are quoting Jesus, while some believe a narrative interpolation begins at verse 11, 13, or at verse 16. The indication that it might begin here is (1) "you" is in the plural both in verses 11 and 12, (2) "we speak what we know and testify what we have seen" contains 4 plural verbs and, (3) "our" is plural in reference to "our testimony." According to *UBS Handbooks for New Testament (20 Vols.)* (John 3:11), "The shift from singular to plural should be carefully noted. The verse begins with the first person singular (I) addressing the second person singular (you). The shift is then made to the first-person plural (we... our) addressing the second person plural (none of you). A number of theories exist as to why this shift is made, but the most probable solution is that John has shifted the time perspective from Jesus' day to the time in which he writes his Gospel. If so, then 'we' represents the Christian believers of John's own day who are in dialogue with the Jews represented by 'you' (plural)."

f 3:11, **you:** You is plural.

g 3:12, **you:** "You" throughout this verse is plural, so it must not only be addressed to Nicodemus (*UBS Handbooks for New Testament (20 Vols.)*, John 3:12).

h 3:13, **who is in heaven:** Included in A(02) Latin(a b e ff²) BYZ TR.

i 3:15, **not perish but:** Included in 𝔭63 A(02) Latin(b e ff²) BYZ TR.

j 3:16, **the:** 𝔭66 𝔭77 ℵ(01) B(03) NA28 SBLGNT THGNT ‖ Some manuscripts read "his." 𝔭63 A(02) Latin(a b e ff²) BYZ TR.

k 3:16, **into the world:** Included in 𝔭63 Latin(e).

l 3:17, **the:** 𝔭66 𝔭75 ℵ(01) B(03) NA28 SBLGNT THGNT ‖ Some manuscripts read "his." 𝔭63 A(02) Latin(a b e ff²) Syriac(sy) BYZ TR.

18 The one who believes in him is not judged; [but]ᵃ the one who does not believe [[in him]]ᵇ has already been judged, because he has not believed in the name of the uniqueᶜ Son of God.

19 And this is the judgment: that [the]ᵈ light has come into the world, and men loved the darkness rather than the light; for their deeds were evil.

20 [For]ᵉ Everyone who does evil hates the light [and does not come to the light,]ᶠ so that their deeds may not be exposed [[as evil]].ᵍ

21 [[But]ʰ The one who does the truth comes to the light, in order that their deeds may be revealed, that they have been done in God.]ⁱ [[For in God is peace established.]]ʲ

22 After this, Jesus and his disciples came into the land of Judea, and there he spent time with them and baptized. 23 Now John also was baptizing in Aenon near Salim, because there was much water there, and people came and were baptized; 24 for John had not yet been thrown into prison.

25 Then a dispute arose between John's disciples and {a Jew}ᵏ about purification. 26 And they came to John and said to him, "Rabbi, he who was with you beyond the Jordan, to whom you have testified, behold, this one is baptizing and all are coming to him." 27 John answered and said, "A person cannot receive even one thing unless it has been given to him from heaven. 28 You yourselves testify to me [that]ˡ I said, 'I am not the Christ, but I have been sent before that one.'

29 "The one who has the bride is the bridegroom; but the friend of the bridegroom, who stands and hears him, rejoices with joy because of the bridegroom's voice. This joy of mine has been fulfilled. 30 That one must increase, but I must decrease."

*Possible Narrator Interjection*ᵐ

31 The one who comes from above is above all; he who is {of}ⁿ the earth is from the earth° [and speaks from the earth].ᵖ The one coming from heaven

---

ᵃ 3:18, **but:** Absent from ℵ(01) B(03) Latin(ff²).

ᵇ 3:18, **in him:** Included in Latin(ff²).

ᶜ 3:18, **unique:** The meaning of the Greek word is (1) being the only one of its kind within a specific relationship, *one and only, only,* or (2) to being the only one of its kind or class, *unique (in kind).* (BDAG, μονογενής), **unique:** The meaning of the Greek word is (1) being the only one of its kind within a specific relationship, *one and only, only,* or (2) to being the only one of its kind or class, *unique (in kind).* (BDAG, μονογενής).

ᵈ 3:19, **the:** Absent from 𝔓66.

ᵉ 3:20, **for:** Absent from Latin(a).

ᶠ 3:20, **and does not come to the light:** Absent from ℵ(01).

ᵍ 3:20, **as evil:** Included in 𝔓66.

ʰ 3:21, **But:** Absent from 𝔓66.

ⁱ 3:21, **But the one who does the truth…:** Absent from ℵ(01).

ʲ 3:21, **For in God is peace established:** Included in ℵ(01).

ᵏ 3:25, **a Jew:** Some manuscripts read "Jews." 𝔓66 ℵ(01) Latin(a b d e ff²) TR.

ˡ 3:28, **that:** 𝔓66 𝔓75 Latin(a ff²) NA28[] ‖ Absent from ℵ(01) A(02) D(05) Latin(b) BYZ TR SBLGNT THGNT.

ᵐ 3:31-36, It is disputed whether verses 31-36 are John's words or a narrative interlude by the author. Some translators regard all of verses 13-36 are quoting John while others believe these verses are a narrative interpolation including RSV, NRSV and NEB which omits quotation marks around verses 31-36. With respect to John 3:31-36, the UBS Handbooks for New Testament (20 Vols.) notes, "It is possible that these words are the comments of the author of the Gospel. This is the opinion held by TEV, NEB, and RSV. If this is the case, there is a parallel between verses 14-21 (or 16-21) and the present passage. That is, the earlier section represents the author's commentary on Jesus' dialogue with Nicodemus, while this passage serves as a commentary on the relationship between Jesus and John the Baptist."

ⁿ 3:31, **of:** Some manuscripts read "on." B(01) Latin(a, e) Some manuscripts read "upon." D(05).

° 3:31, **earth:** Or "land."

ᵖ 3:31, **and speaks from the earth:** Absent from 𝔓66.

[is above all]^a $_{32}$[[And]]^b what he has seen and heard, [this]^c he testifies, and no one receives his testimony.

$_{33}$The one who has received his testimony has sealed^d that God is true.

$_{34}$For the one whom God has sent speaks the words of God, for {he}^{e} does not give by measure [the Spirit].^{f}

$_{35}$The Father loves the Son and has given all things into his hand.

$_{36}$The one who believes in the Son has eternal life; [but]^g the one who disobeys the Son will not see life, but the wrath of God remains on him. [[And after these things, John was handed over.]]^h

4 $_1$So when {Jesus}^{i} knew that the Pharisees had heard that Jesus was making more disciples and baptizing than John $_2$although Jesus himself was not baptizing, but his disciples were. $_3$He left {Judea}^{j} and went back [again]^k to Galilee. $_4$But he had to pass through Samaria.

$_5$He comes to {a city of Samaria}^{l} called Sychar, near the plot of ground that Jacob had given to his son Joseph; $_6$and Jacob's well was there. So Jesus, tired from his journey, sat down by the well; it was about the sixth hour.

$_7$A woman from Samaria came to draw water. Jesus said to her, "Give me a drink"; $_8$for his disciples had gone away into the city to buy food. $_9$[So]^m The Samaritan woman says to him, "How is it that you, a Jew, ask for a drink from me, a Samaritan [woman]?"^{n} [For Jews have no dealings with Samaritans.]^o

$_{10}$Jesus answered her, "If you knew the gift of God, and who it is that is saying to you, 'Give me a drink,' you would have asked him, and he would have given you living water."

$_{11}$She says to him [the woman],^{p} "Sir, you have neither a bucket and the well is deep; where [then]^q do you get the living water? $_{12}$Are you greater than our father Jacob, who gave us {the}^{r} well and drank from it himself, as well as his sons and his livestock?"

$_{13}$Jesus answered her, "Everyone who drinks of this water will thirst again; $_{14}$but {the one who}^{s} drinks from the water that I will give him [will never thirst again. The water that I will give him]^t will become in him a spring of water welling up to eternal life."

---

^{a} 3:31, **is above all:** 𝔓36 𝔓66 A(02) B(03) Latin(a b e ff²) Syriac(sy^s) BYZ TR NA28[] SBLGNT THGNT ‖ Absent from 𝔓75 ℵ(01) D(05) Latin(it) Syriac(sy^c).

^{b} 3:32, **And:** Included in A(02) BYZ TR.

^{c} 3:32, **this:** Absent from ℵ(01) D(05) Latin(a b d e ff²) Syriac(sy^s sy^c sy^p).

^{d} 3:33, **sealed:** Or "certified."

^{e} 3:34, **he:** Some manuscripts read "God." A(02) D(05) Latin(a d) BYZ TR.

^{f} 3:34, **the Spirit:** Absent from B(03).

^{g} 3:36, **but:** Absent from ℵ(01) Latin(a e ff²).

^{h} 3:36, **And after these things, John was handed over:** Included in Latin(e).

^{i} 4:1, **Jesus:** ℵ(01) D(05) Latin(a b d e ff²) Syriac(sy^c sy^p) SBLGNT NA28 ‖ Other Manuscripts read "the Lord." 𝔓66 𝔓75 A(02) B(03) C(04) Syriac(sy^s) BYZ TR THGNT.

^{j} 4:3, **Judea:** Some manuscripts read "Judean land." D(05) Latin(a b d e ff²).

^{k} 4:3, **again:** Absent from A(02) B(03) BYZ.

^{l} 4:5, **a city of Samaria:** Absent from some manuscripts which otherwise reads "a place." 𝔓75 ℵ(01).

^{m} 4:9, **So:** Absent from ℵ(01) Syriac(sy^s sy^c sy^p).

^{n} 4:9, **woman:** Absent from ℵ(01) Latin(a b).

^{o} 4:9, **For Jews have no dealings with Samaritans:** Absent from some manuscripts ℵ(01) D(05) Latin(a b d e).

^{p} 4:11, **the woman:** Absent from 𝔓75 B(03).

^{q} 4:11, **then:** Absent from ℵ(01) D(05) Latin(a b d e ff²).

^{r} 4:12, **the:** Some manuscripts read "this." Latin(a e ff²).

^{s} 4:14, **the one who:** Some manuscripts read "whoever." ℵ(01) D(05).

^{t} 4:14, **will never thirst again...:** Absent from C(04).

15 The woman says to him, "Sir, give me this water, so that I will not be thirsty or have to come here to draw water." 16 {He}[a] says to her, "Go, call your husband and come here." 17 The woman answered and said [to him],[b] "I have no husband." Jesus says to her, "You have said well that 'I have no husband'; 18 for you have had five husbands, and the one you now have is not your husband; this you have said truly."

19 The woman says to him, "[Lord,][c] I perceive that you are a prophet. 20 Our fathers worshiped on this mountain; and you[d] say that in Jerusalem is [the place][e] where people ought to worship."

21 Jesus says to her, "Believe me, woman, the hour is coming when neither on this mountain nor in Jerusalem will you[f] worship the Father. 22 You[g] worship what you do not know; we worship what we know, for salvation is from the Jews.

23 "But the hour is coming, and now is, when the true worshipers will worship the Father in spirit and truth; for the Father seeks such as these to worship him [[in spirit]].[h] 24 God is spirit, and those who worship [him][i] must worship in spirit and truth."

25 The woman says to him, "I know that Messiah is coming, the one called Christ;[j] when that one comes, he will tell us all things." 26 Jesus says to her, "I am, the one speaking to you."

27 And [upon this,][k] his disciples came and {were amazed}[l] that he was speaking with a woman; yet no one said [[to him]],[m] "What are you seeking?" or "Why are you speaking with her?"

28 So the woman left her water jar and went into the city and tells the people, 29 "Come, see a man who told me everything I ever did. Could this be the Christ?" 30 They [[therefore]][n] went out of the city and came to him.

31 In the meantime, {the}[o] disciples were asking [him],[p] saying, "Rabbi, eat." 32 [But][q] He said to them, "I have food to eat that you do not know about." 33 [So][r] The disciples were saying to {one another},[s] "Did someone bring him something to eat?"

34 Jesus says to them, "My food is to do the will of the one who sent me and to complete his work.

35 "Do you not say, '[Yet][t] There are four months, and then comes the harvest'? Behold, I say to you, lift up your eyes and look at the fields, for they are white for harvest. {Already}[u]

---

a 4:16, **he:** 𝔓66 𝔓75 B(03) C(04) Latin(a) ‖ Some manuscripts read "Jesus." ℵ(01) A(02) D(05) Latin(b d e ff²) BYZ TR THGNT.

b 4:17, **to him:** Absent from ℵ(01).

c 4:19, **Lord:** Absent from ℵ(01).

d 4:20, **you:** Plural.

e 4:20, **the place:** Absent from ℵ(01).

f 4:21, **you:** Plural.

g 4:22, **you:** Plural.

h 4:23, **in spirit:** Included in Latin(a b).

i 4:24, **him:** Absent from ℵ(01) D(05) Latin(ff²).

j 4:25, **Christ:** See footnote for Christ in Luke 2:11.

k 4:27, **upon this:** Absent from Latin(a b e ff²) ‖ Some manuscripts read "in this." ℵ(01) D(05).

l 4:27, **were amazed:** Some manuscripts read "marveled." D(05) BYZ TR.

m 4:27, **to him:** Included in ℵ(01) D(05) Latin(a b ff²) Syriac(sy^s sy^c).

n 4:30, **therefore:** Included in 𝔓66 ℵ(01) Latin(e ff²) TR.

o 4:31, **the:** Some manuscripts read "his." Latin(e).

p 4:31, **him** Absent from some manuscripts Latin(a ff²).

q 4:32, **But:** Absent from Latin(a).

r 4:33, **So:** Absent from ℵ(01) Latin (d e) ‖ Some manuscripts read "but." D(05) Latin(a b).

s 4:33, **one another:** D(05) reads "themselves."

t 4:35, **Yet:** Absent from 𝔓75 D(05) Latin(d).

u 4:35, **Already:** Some manuscripts include "already" as part of verse 36 as "Already the one who reaps..." 𝔓66 ℵ(01) A(02) B(03) C(04) D(05) Syriac(sy^s sy^c) TR THGNT ‖ Other manuscripts

36 the one who reaps receives wages and gathers fruit for eternal life, so that [[also]]ᵃ that the one sowing may rejoice together with the one reaping. 37 For in this the saying is true: 'One sows and another reaps.' 38 I sent you to reap what you have not labored for; others have labored, and you have entered [into]ᵇ their labor."

39 But from that city many of the Samaritans believed [in him]ᶜ because of the woman's testimony, saying, "He told me everything [I have ever done]."ᵈ 40 So when the Samaritans {came to}ᵉ him, they asked him to stay with them; and he stayed there two days. 41 And many more believed [[in him]]ᶠ because of his word, 42 and they said to the woman [that],ᵍ "We no longer believe because of your {words},ʰ for we have heard [[from him]]ⁱ for ourselves and know that this one is [truly]ʲ [[the Christ]]ᵏ the Savior of the world."

43 After two days, {he departed from there}ˡ to Galilee. 44 For Jesus himself testified that a prophet has no honor in his own country.

45 So {when}ᵐ he came to Galilee, [the Galileans welcomed him,]ⁿ the men who had seen all that he had done in Jerusalem at the feast; for they too had gone to the feast.

46 So {he}ᵒ came again to Cana of Galilee, where he had made the water wine. And there was a certain royal official whose son was sick in Capernaum. 47 [This one,]ᵖ Hearing that Jesus came from Judea into Galilee, went [to him]ᑫ and was asking [him]ʳ that he might come down and heal his son, for he was about to die. 48 [Therefore]ˢ Jesus said to him, "Unless you see signs and wonders, you will not believe."ᵗ 49 The royal official says to him, "Lord, come down before {my}ᵘ child dies."

---

include "already" as part of the previous sentence as "...they are white for the harvest already." 𝔓75 BYZ Syriac(syᵖ) NA28 SBLGNT.

ᵃ 4:36, **also:** Included in ℵ(01) A(02) D(05) Latin(a b d ff²) Syriac(syᵖ) BYZ TR ‖ Absent from 𝔓66 𝔓75 B(03) C(04) Latin(e) NA28 SBLGNT THGNT.

ᵇ 4:38, **into:** Absent from C(04).

ᶜ 4:39, **in him:** Absent from ℵ(01) Latin(a e).

ᵈ 4:39, **I have ever done:** Absent from 𝔓66.

ᵉ 4:40, **came to:** Some manuscripts read "gathered together with." B(03) Latin(e).

ᶠ 4:41, **in him:** Included in Latin(b).

ᵍ 4:42 , **that:** Absent from B(03) Latin(b) Syriac(syᶜ).

ʰ 4:42, **words:** Some manuscripts read "testimony." ℵ(01) D(05) Latin(b d).

ⁱ 4:42, **from him:** Included in ℵ(01).

ʲ 4:42, **truly:** Absent from Latin(ff²).

ᵏ 4:42, **the Christ:** Included in A(02) D(05) Latin(d e) BYZ TR ‖ Absent from 𝔓66 𝔓75 ℵ(01) B(03) C(04) Latin(a b ff²) Syriac(syᶜ) NA28 SBLGNT THGNT.

ˡ 4:43, **he departed from there:** Some manuscripts read "he left from there and departed." A(02) BYZ TR.

ᵐ 4:45, **when:** Some manuscripts read "then." ℵ(01) D(05).

ⁿ 4:45, **the Galileans welcomed him:** Absent from ℵ(01).

ᵒ 4:46, **he:** Some manuscripts read "Jesus." A(02) BYZ TR.

ᵖ 4:47, **This one:** Absent from ℵ(01).

ᑫ 4:47, **to him:** Absent from 𝔓75.

ʳ 4:47, **him:** Included in A(02) Latin(b ff²) BYZ TR.

ˢ 4:48, **Therefore:** Absent from 𝔓66.

ᵗ 4:48, **you:** In the plural twice here.

ᵘ 4:49, **my:** Some manuscripts read "the." D(05) Latin(b d e ff²).

50 Jesus says to him, "Go, your son lives." The man believed the word that Jesus spoke [to him]^a and [went on his way];^b 51 But already as {he was coming down, his servants}^c met him, {saying}^d that his {child}^e lives. 52 [So]^f He asked them the hour when he began to get better; they said [to him],^g "Yesterday at the seventh hour the fever left {him}."^h

53 {The}^i father knew that it was at that hour when {Jesus}^j had said to him, "Your son lives," and he believed, he and his whole household.

54 This [then]^k again a second sign Jesus did, coming from Judea into Galilee.

5 1 After this there was {a}^l feast of the Jews, and Jesus went up to Jerusalem.

2 {[Now there is in Jerusalem]^m By the Sheep Gate there is a pool},^n which is called in Hebrew Bethesda, having five porticoes. 3 [[Therefore]]^o In these lay a [[great]]^p multitude of those who were sick, blind, lame, and {withered}^q [[waiting for the moving of the water. 4 For an angel went down at certain seasons into the pool and stirred up the water; then whoever stepped in first, after the stirring up of the water, was made well from whatever disease he had.]]^r

5 And a certain man was there [who had been]^s in [his]^t sickness for thirty-eight years. 6 When Jesus saw him lying there, and knew that he had been there a long time [already],^u he says to him, "Do you want to be made well?" 7 The sick man {answered}^v him, "Sir, I have no one to put me into the pool when the water is stirred up; but while I am coming, another steps down before me." 8 Jesus says to him, "Rise, [[and]]^w take up your bed, and walk."

9 And [immediately]^x the man was made well, and he [[rose and]]^y took up his bed and walked.

---

a 4:50, **to him**: Absent from 𝔓75 ℵ(01) Latin(d).

b 4:50, **went on his way**: Absent from Latin(e).

c 4:51, **he was coming down, his servants**: Some manuscripts read "his servants met him, saying." ℵ(01) D(05) Latin(a b e ff²).

d 4:51, **saying**: 𝔓75 B(03) NA28 SBLGNT THGNT ‖ Some manuscripts read "and they reported, saying." 𝔓66 A(02) C(04) D(05) Latin(a b d e ff²) BYZ TR ‖ Some manuscripts read "and they reported to him." ℵ(01) D(05) Latin(b) ‖ Latin(a) reads "and they reported to him, saying."

e 4:51, **child**: Some manuscripts read "son." D(05) Latin(a b d e ff²) Syriac(sy^c sy^p).

f 4:52, **So**: Absent from Latin(a).

g 4:52, **to him**: Absent from 𝔓45 Latin(a b).

h 4:52, **him**: Some manuscripts read "her." B(03).

i 4:53, **The**: Some manuscripts read "His." 𝔓66 C(04) Latin(e).

j 4:53, **Jesus**: Some manuscripts read "he." ℵ(01).

k 4:54, **then**: 𝔓66 𝔓75 B(03) C(04) NA28[] SBLGNT THGNT ‖ Absent from ℵ(01) A(02) D(05) Latin(a b d ff²) Syriac(sy) BYZ TR.

l 5:1, **a**: Some manuscripts read "the." ℵ(01) C(04) BYZ.

m 5:2, **Now there is in Jerusalem**: Absent from Latin(b).

n 5:2, **Now there is in Jerusalem by the Sheep Gate there is a pool**: ℵ(01) reads "In a certain place in Jerusalem, there is a sheep pool."

o 5:3, **Therefore**: Included in D(05).

p 5:3, **great**: Included in A(02) BYZ TR.

q 5:3, **withered**: Some manuscripts read "paralyzed." D(05) Latin(a b d e ff²) BYZ TR.

r 5:3-4, Some manuscripts include verse 3c and verse 4. A(02) D(05) Latin(a b e ff²) Syriac(sy^p) BYZ TR ‖ Absent from 𝔓66 𝔓75 ℵ(01) B(03) C(04) Syriac(sy^p) NA28 SBLGNT THGNT.

s 5:5, **who had been**: Absent from ℵ(01).

t 5:5, **his**: Absent from A(02) Latin(b) BYZ TR.

u 5:6, **already**: Absent from 𝔓66 ℵ(01) Latin(e).

v 5:7, **answered**: Some manuscripts read "says to." D(05).

w 5:8, **and**: Included in A(02) D(05) Latin(a b d e ff²).

x 5:9, **immediately**: Absent in some manuscripts. ℵ(01) D(05).

y 5:9, **rose and**: Included in ℵ(01) Latin(a b e) ‖ Some manuscripts read "having risen." D(05) Latin(d ff²).

Now it was the Sabbath [on that day].[a] 10 So the Jews said to the one who had been healed, "It is the Sabbath, and it is not lawful for you to carry {the}[b] bed."

11 [But][c] He answered them, "The one who made {me}[d] well said to me, 'Take up {your}[e] bed and walk.'" 12 [[Therefore]][f] [They asked [him],[g] "Who is the man who said to you, 'Take up [[your bed]][h] and walk'?"][i] 13 [But][j] the one who was {healed}[k] did not know who it was, {for}[l] Jesus had slipped away, there being a crowd in the place.

14 Afterward Jesus found {him}[m] in the temple and said to him, "See, you have been made well; do not sin anymore, so that nothing worse happens to you." 15 [[Therefore]][n] The man went away and {reported to}[o] the Jews [[and said to them]][p] that it was Jesus who had made him well. 16 [And][q] For this reason the Jews persecuted Jesus [[and sought to kill him]],[r] because he did these things on the Sabbath.

17 But {he}[s] answered them, "My Father is working until now, and I am working." 18 [Therefore,][t] for this reason, the Jews sought all the more to kill him, because he not only broke the Sabbath, but also called God his own Father, making himself equal to God.

19 {Jesus therefore answered and}[u] said to them, "Truly, [truly,][v] I say to you, the Son [[of Man]][w] {can do nothing}[x] of himself, unless he sees the Father doing [something];[y] for {whatever}[z] the Father does, the Son does likewise.

20 "For the Father loves the Son and shows him {all that he himself is doing};[a] and he will show him greater works than these, so that you may marvel.

21 "Just as the Father raises the dead and gives life, so also the Son gives life to whom he wishes.

22 "For the Father judges no one, but has given all judgment to the Son, 23 so that all men may honor the Son, just as they honor the Father.

---

[a] 5:9, **on that day:** Absent from D(05) Latin(d e).

[b] 5:10, **the:** A(02) B(03) Latin(e) TR SBLGNT THGNT ‖ Some manuscripts read "your." 𝔓66 𝔓75 ℵ(01) C(04) D(05) Latin(a b d ff²) Syriac(sy) NA28.

[c] 5:11, **But:** Absent from D(05) Latin(a b d e ff²) BYZ TR.

[d] 5:11, **me:** Some manuscripts read "you." 𝔓66.

[e] 5:11, **your:** Absent from ℵ(01) which otherwise reads "the."

[f] 5:12, **Therefore:** Included in 𝔓75 C(04) BYZ TR.

[g] 5:12, **him:** Absent from some manuscripts 𝔓75.

[h] 5:12, **your bed:** Some manuscripts include D(05) Latin(a d e ff²) Syriac(sy) BYZ TR.

[i] 5:12, **They asked him...:** Absent from A(02) W(032) Latin(b).

[j] 5:13, **But:** Absent from D(05) Latin(d).

[k] 5:13, **healed:** Some manuscripts read "weak." D(05) Latin(b d).

[l] 5:13, **for:** Some manuscripts read "but." 𝔓75 Latin(ff²).

[m] 5:14, **him:** ℵ(01) reads "the healed man."

[n] 5:15, **Therefore:** Included in D(05) Latin(d).

[o] 5:15, **reported to:** Some manuscripts read "said to." ℵ(01) C(04) Latin(a e).

[p] 5:15, **and said to them:** Included in W(032).

[q] 5:16, **And:** Absent from Latin(a ff²).

[r] 5:16, **and sought to kill him:** Included in A(02) Latin(e) BYZ TR.

[s] 5:17, **he:** 𝔓75 ℵ(01) B(03) W(032) SBLGNT THGNT ‖ Some manuscripts read "Jesus." 𝔓66 A(02) D(05) Latin(a b e ff²) Syriac(sy^s) BYZ TR NA28 [].

[t] 5:18, **Therefore:** Absent from ℵ(01) D(05) Latin(a b d e it) Syriac(sy^p).

[u] 5:19, **Jesus therefore answered and:** Some manuscripts read "And Jesus." 𝔓75 B(03).

[v] 5:19, **truly:** Second occurrence absent from ℵ(01).

[w] 5:19, **of Man:** Included in D(05).

[x] 5:19, **can do nothing:** D(05) reads "cannot do anything."

[y] 5:19, **something:** Absent from W(032) Latin(a d e).

[z] 5:19, **whatever:** Some manuscripts read "what." A(02) D(05).

[a] 5:20, **all that he himself is doing:** Some manuscripts read "everything that he himself does." D(05).

"He who does not honor the
Son does not honor the Father who
sent him.

24 "Truly, truly, I say to you, [that][a]
whoever hears my word and believes in
the one who sent me has eternal life,
and does not come into judgment, but
has passed from death to life.

25 "Truly, truly, I say to you, the
{hour}[b] is coming, [and now is,][c] when
the dead will hear the voice of the Son
of God, and those who hear will live.

26 "For [just][d] as the Father has
life in himself, [so he has granted
the Son also to have life in himself,][e]
27 he has given him authority [[also]][f] to
execute judgment, because he is the Son
of Man.

28 "Do not marvel at this; for the
hour is coming when all who are in the
tombs will hear his voice 29 and come
out, those who have done good to the
resurrection of life, and those who
have done evil to the resurrection of
judgment.

30 "I can do nothing on my own; as I
hear, I judge; and my judgment is just,
because I do not seek my own will but
the will of the {one}[g] who sent me.

31 "If I testify about myself, my
testimony is not true;[h] 32 there is
another who testifies about me [, and
I know that {the}[i] testimony which he
{testifies} about me is true].[j]

33 "You have sent to John, and he
has testified to the truth; 34 But I do
not accept the testimony from men,
but I say these things so that you may
be saved.

35 "That one was the lamp that
was burning and shining, and you
were willing to rejoice for a while in
his light.

36 "But I have testimony greater
than that of John; for the works which
the Father has given me to accomplish,
{these very}[k] works [that I do],[l] testify
[about me][m] that the Father has
sent me.

37 "And the Father who sent me,
he has [[himself]][n] testified about me.
You have never heard his voice nor
seen {his}[o] form, 38 and you do not have
his word abiding in you, because the
one whom he sent, you do not believe
in him.

39 "You search the Scriptures,
because you think that in them you
have eternal life; and {these are they}[p]
which testify about me; 40 and you are
not willing to come to me so that you
may have life.

41 "I do not receive glory from men,
42 but I know you, that you do not have
the love of God in yourselves.

43 "[[But]][q] I have come in my
Father's name, and you do not receive
me; if another comes in his own name,
him you will receive.

44 "How can you believe, receiving
glory from one another, and not seeking

---

a 5:24, **that:** Absent from D(05) Latin(d).
b 5:25, **hour:** 𝔓75 reads "time."
c 5:25, **and now is:** Absent from ℵ(01) Latin(a b).
d 5:26, **just:** Absent from ℵ(01) D(05) W(032).
e 5:26, **so he has granted the Son also to have life in himself:** Absent from ℵ(01).
f 5:27, **also:** Included in D(05) BYZ TR.
g 5:30, **one:** Some manuscripts read "Father." Latin(b ff²) BYZ TR.
h 5:31, **true:** Or "valid."
i 5:32, **the:** Some manuscripts read "his." Latin(b d) || Some manuscripts read "my." D(05) Latin(e).
j 5:32, **and I know that the testimony which he testifies about me is true:** Absent from Latin(ff²).
k 5:36, **these very:** Some manuscripts read "the." 𝔓96.
l 5:36, **that I do:** Absent from Latin (a ff²).
m 5:36, **about me:** Absent from Latin(a).
n 5:37, **himself:** Included in D(05) Latin(d).
o 5:37, **his:** Some manuscripts read "any." W(032) Latin(b).
p 5:39, **these are they:** Some manuscripts read "they are the ones." D(05) Latin(d).
q 5:43, **But:** Included in 𝔓66.

the glory that comes from the only [God]?[a]

45 "Do not think that I will accuse you to the Father; there is one who accuses you [[before the Father]],[b] Moses, in whom you have put your hope. 46 For if you believed Moses, you would believe me; for he wrote about me. 47 But if you do not believe his writings, how will you believe my words?"

6 1 After this, Jesus went across the Sea of Galilee [{which is the}[c] Tiberias].[d] 2 And a large crowd was following him, [because][e] they {were observing}[f] the signs which he was performing on the sick.

3 Jesus went up on the mountain and sat [there][g] with his disciples. 4 Now the Passover, the festival of the Jews, was near.

5 Therefore, [Jesus,][h] lifting up his eyes and seeing that a large crowd was coming towards him, he said to Philip, "Where can we buy bread so that these men may eat?" 6 He said this to test him, {for}[i] he himself knew what he was going to do.

7 [[Therefore]][j] Philip answered him, "Two hundred denarii worth of bread would not be enough for them, so that each [[of them]][k] might receive a little [something]."[l]

8 One of his disciples, Andrew, Simon Peter's brother, says to him, 9 "There is {a}[m] boy [[here]][n] who has five barley loaves and two fish. But what are they among so many people?" 10 [[But]][o] Jesus said, "Make the people sit down." There was plenty of {grass}[p] in the place. So the men sat down, about five thousand in number.

11 {Therefore},[q] Jesus took the [[five]][r] loaves, and having given thanks, he distributed them [[to his disciples, and the disciples]][s] [to those who were seated],[t] [[but]][u] [likewise][v] also from the fish, as much as they wanted. 12 When they were satisfied, he told his disciples, "Gather up the fragments left over, so that nothing may be lost [[from among them]]."[w] 13 {So}[x] they gathered them up, and from the five barley loaves left by those who had eaten, they filled twelve baskets.

---

[a] 5:44, **God:** Absent from 𝔓66 𝔓75 B(03) W(032) Latin(a b).

[b] 5:45, **before the Father:** Included in C(04).

[c] 6:1, **which is the:** Some manuscripts read "to the region of the." D(05) Latin(b d e).

[d] 6:1, **which is the Tiberias:** Absent from 𝔓66.

[e] 6:2, **because:** Absent from W(032).

[f] 6:2, **were observing:** Some manuscripts read "saw." 𝔓66 ℵ(01) BYZ TR THGNT.

[g] 6:3, **there:** Absent from ℵ(01).

[h] 6:5, **Jesus:** Absent from some manuscripts Latin(e).

[i] 6:6, **for:** Some manuscripts read "but." ℵ(01) Latin (d ff²).

[j] 6:7, **Therefore:** Included in 𝔓66 ℵ(01).

[k] 6:7, **of them:** Included in D(05) BYZ TR.

[l] 6:7, **something:** Absent from 𝔓75 B(03) D(05).

[m] 6:9, **a:** Some manuscripts read "one."

[n] 6:9, **here:** Included in A(02) Latin(ff²) Syriac(sys syc syp) BYZ TR.

[o] 6:10, **But:** Some manuscripts include A(02) W(032) Latin(b) BYZ TR ‖ Some manuscripts read "Therefore." 𝔓66 D(05) Latin(d e ff²).

[p] 6:10, **grass:** Some manuscripts read "space." ℵ(01).

[q] 6:11, **Therefore:** Some manuscripts read "But/And (δε)." (01) Latin(b) TR BYZ.

[r] 6:11, **five:** Included in D(05).

[s] 6:11, **to his disciples, and the disciples:** Included in D(05) Latin(b d e) BYZ TR.

[t] 6:11, **to those who were seated:** Absent from Latin(ff²)

[u] 6:11, **but:** Included in some manuscripts. D(05).

[v] 6:11, **likewise:** Absent from Latin(ff²).

[w] 6:12, **from among them:** Included in D(05) Latin (d).

[x] 6:13, **So:** Some manuscripts read "But/And (δὲ)." D(05) Latin(b d).

14 [When the men, having seen {what sign that}[a] {he}[b] performed, said [that][c] "This is [truly][d] the prophet who is to come into the world."][e]

15 Therefore, Jesus knowing that they were about to come and seize him to make him king, he {withdrew}[f] [again][g] to the mountain {by himself}.[h] [[And there he prayed.]][i]

16 When evening came, {his disciples}[j] went down to the sea, 17 got into a boat, they were going across the sea to Capernaum. {And it was already dark},[k] and Jesus had not yet come to them. 18 And the sea was stirred up by a great wind blowing.

19 When they had rowed about twenty-five or thirty {stadia},[l] they saw Jesus walking on the sea and coming near the boat, and they were frightened. 20 But he says to them, "It is I; do not be afraid." 21 Then they wanted to take him into the boat, [and immediately][m] the boat was on the land to which they were going.

22 The next day, the crowd that had stayed on the other side of the sea saw that there was no other boat there, except one [[that his disciples had entered]],[n] and that Jesus had not entered the boat with his disciples, but only his disciples had gone away alone.

23 {But other boats came}[o] from Tiberias [near the place][p] where they ate the bread [after the Lord had given thanks].[q] 24 {So when the crowd saw}[r] that neither Jesus nor his disciples were there, they themselves got into the boats and went to Capernaum seeking Jesus. 25 And [not][s] finding him on the other side of the sea, they said to him, "Rabbi, when did you get here?"

26 Jesus said to them, "Truly, truly, I say to you, [you are looking for me,][t] not because you saw signs, but because you ate your fill of the loaves.

27 "{Do not work for the food that perishes, but for the food}[u] that endures to eternal life, which the Son of Man {will give}[v] you. For on him God the Father has set his seal."

28 They said [therefore][w] to him, "What must we do to perform the works of God?"

29 Jesus answered them, "This is the work of God, that you believe in the one whom he has sent."

---

a 6:14, **what sign that:** Some manuscripts read "what signs." 𝔓75 Latin(a).

b 6:14, **he:** Some manuscripts read "Jesus." A(02) Syriac(sy^p) BYZ TR.

c 6:14, **that:** Absent from ℵ(01) ℵ(01) W(032) Latin(a b e).

d 6:14, **truly:** Absent from ℵ(01) D(05).

e 6:14, **When the men...:** Verse 14 is absent from Latin(e).

f 6:15, **withdrew:** Some manuscripts read "fled." ℵ(01) Latin(a ff²).

g 6:15, **again:** Absent from W(032) BYZ.

h 6:15, **by himself:** Some manuscripts read "alone." Latin(b ff²).

i 6:15, **And there he prayed:** Included in some manuscripts. D(05) Latin(d).

j 6:16, **his disciples:** W(032) reads "they."

k 6:17, **And it was already dark:** Some manuscripts read "But darkness overtook them." ℵ(01) D(05) Latin(d).

l 6:19, **stadia:** Some manuscripts read "stadium." ℵ(01) D(05).

m 6:21, **and immediately:** Absent from Latin(e).

n 6:22, **that his disciples had entered:** Included in Latin(e) Syriac(sy) BYZ TR ‖ Some manuscripts read "that the disciples of Jesus had entered." ℵ(01) D(05) Latin(a d) ‖ Absent 𝔓75 A(02) B(03) W(032) Latin(ff²) NA28 SBLGNT THGNT.

o 6:23, **But other boats came:** ℵ(01) reads "When the boats had come."

p 6:23, **near the place:** Absent from W(032).

q 6:23, **after the Lord had given thanks:** Absent from D(05) Latin(a, e) Syriac(sy^s sy^c).

r 6:24, **So when the crowd saw:** Some manuscripts read "And seeing." ℵ(01) Syriac(sy^s).

s 6:25, **not:** Included in C(04).

t 6:26, **you are looking for me:** Absent from ℵ(01).

u 6:27, **Do not work for the food that perishes, but for the food:** ℵ(01) reads "Work for food, not the perishable one, but the one."

v 6:27, **will give:** ℵ(01) reads "gives to."

w 6:28, **therefore:** Absent from A(02).

30 [So]ᵃ they said to him, "What sign are you going to give us then, so that we may see it and believe you? What work are you performing? 31 Our fathers ate the manna in the wilderness; as it is written, 'He gave them bread from heaven to eat.'"

32 [Therefore]ᵇ Jesus said to them, "Truly, truly, I say to you, it was not Moses who gave you the bread from heaven, but it is my Father who gives you the true bread from heaven.ᶜ 33 For the bread of God is that which comes down from heaven and gives life to the world."

34 They said therefore to him, "Lord, always give us this bread."

35 [Therefore]ᵈ Jesus said to them, "I am the bread of life; the one coming to me will never be hungry, and the one believing in me will never be thirsty. 36 But I said to you that [even]ᵉ you have seen [me]ᶠ and do not believe [[me]].ᵍ 37 Everything that the Father gives me will come to me, and I will not cast out the one who comes to me. 38 For I have {come down from heaven, not}ʰ to do my will but the will of the {one}ⁱ who sent me;

39 "[This is the will of the {one}ʲ who sent me,]ᵏ That I should lose nothing of all that he has given me, but raise it up {on}ˡ the last day. 40 [For this is the will]ᵐ Of {my Father},ⁿ that everyone who sees the Son and believes in him may have eternal life, and I will raise him up on the last day."

41 [So]ᵒ The Jews grumbled about him because he said, "I am the bread that came down from heaven," 42 and they said, "Is not this [Jesus, the son of Joseph,]ᵖ whose father [and mother]ᑫ we know? How can he [now]ʳ say [that],ˢ 'I have come down from heaven?'"

43 Jesus [[therefore]]ᵗ answered and said to them, "Do not grumble among yourselves. 44 No one can come to me unless [the Father]ᵘ who sent me draws him [[to me]],ᵛ and I will raise him up on the last day. 45 It is written in the prophets, 'And they will all be taught by God.'ʷ [[Therefore,]]ˣ Everyone who has heard and learned [[the truth]]ʸ from the Father comes to me.

ᵃ 6:30, **So:** Absent from ℵ(01).

ᵇ 6:32, **Therefore:** Absent from Latin(a e).

ᶜ 6:32, Psalm 78:24 LXX, Exodus 16:4, Nehemiah 9:15.

ᵈ 6:35, **Therefore:** Included in ℵ(01) D(05) Latin(d).

ᵉ 6:36, **even:** Absent from Latin(e).

ᶠ 6:36, **me:** Absent from ℵ(01) A(02) Syriac(syˢ syᶜ) Latin(a b e).

ᵍ 6:36, **me:** Included in A(02) W(032).

ʰ 6:38, **come down from heaven, not:** Some manuscripts read "not come down from heaven." ℵ(01) Latin(b e).

ⁱ 6:38, **one:** Some manuscripts read "Father." D(05) Latin(a d e ff²).

ʲ 6:39, **one:** Some manuscripts read "Father." Latin(a ff²) BYZ TR.

ᵏ 6:39, **This is the will of the one who sent me:** Absent from ℵ(01) C(04).

ˡ 6:39, **in:** Some manuscripts read "on." 𝔓66 𝔓75 B(03) C(04) W(032) Latin(e) BYZ SBLGNT.

ᵐ 6:40, **For this is the will:** Absent from 𝔓66.

ⁿ 6:40, **my Father:** Some manuscripts read "the one who sent me." A(02) BYZ TR.

ᵒ 6:41, **So:** D(05) reads "But."

ᵖ 6:42, **Jesus, the son of Joseph:** Absent from Latin(b).

ᑫ 6:42, **and mother:** Absent from ℵ(01) W(032) Latin(b) Syriac(syˢ syᶜ).

ʳ 6:42, **now:** Absent from Latin(a e).

ˢ 6:42, **that:** Absent from ℵ(01) D(05) Latin(d).

ᵗ 6:43, **therefore:** Included in ℵ(01) A(02) D(05) W(032) Latin(b d ff²) BYZ TR.

ᵘ 6:44, **the Father:** Absent from A(02). ‖ 𝔓66 reads "my Father."

ᵛ 6:44, **to me:** Included in W(032).

ʷ 6:45, Isaiah 54:13.

ˣ 6:45, **Therefore:** Included in A(02) Syriac(syᶜ syᵖ) BYZ TR.

ʸ 6:45, **the truth:** Included in A(02).

⁴⁶"Not that anyone has seen the Father except the one who is from {God};ᵃ this one has seen {the Father}.ᵇ

⁴⁷"Truly, truly, I say to you [that],ᶜ the one believing [[in me]]ᵈ has eternal life.

⁴⁸"I am the bread of life. ⁴⁹Your fathers ate the {manna in the wilderness,}ᵉ and they died. ⁵⁰This is the bread that comes down from heaven, so that [if]ᶠ one may eat of it and not die.

⁵¹"I am the living bread that came down from heaven. [[Therefore]]ᵍ If anyone eats of this bread, he will live forever, and the bread that I will give is my flesh [[which I shall give]]ʰ for the life of the world."

⁵²The Jews then disputed among themselves, saying, "How [[then]]ⁱ can this man give us [his]ʲ flesh to eat?"

⁵³So Jesus said to them, "Truly, truly, I say to you, unless you eat the flesh of the Son of Man and drink his blood, you do not have [[eternal]]ᵏ life in yourselves.

⁵⁴"The one who eats {my}ˡ flesh and drinks my blood has eternal life, and I will raise him up on the last day.

⁵⁵"[For]ᵐ my flesh is {true}ⁿ {food}ᵒ [and my blood is {true} drink].ᵖ ⁵⁶The one who eats my flesh and drinks my blood abides in me, and I in him. [[Just as the Father is in me and I in the Father. Truly, truly, I say to you, unless you take the body of the Son of Man as the bread of life, you do not have life in him.]]�q

⁵⁷"Just as the living Father sent me, and I live because of {the}ʳ Father, so the one who {feeds on}ˢ me, he also will live because of me.

⁵⁸"This is the bread that came down from heaven, not like the bread {the fathers ate}ᵗ and died. The one who eats this bread will live forever."

⁵⁹He said these things while teaching in the synagogue in Capernaum [[on the Sabbath]].ᵘ

⁶⁰Therefore, many of {his}ᵛ disciples, when they heard this, said, "This teaching is difficult; who can listen to it?"

⁶¹{But}ʷ Jesus, knowing in himself that his disciples were grumbling about this, said to them, "Does this offend you? ⁶²[Therefore]ˣ If you see the Son of Man ascending to where he was before?

ᵃ 6:46, **God:** ℵ(01) reads "the Father."

ᵇ 6:46, **the Father:** Some manuscripts read "God." ℵ(01) D(05) Latin(a b d e).

ᶜ 6:47, **that:** Included in ℵ(01).

ᵈ 6:47, **in me:** Included in A(02) D(05) Latin(a b d e ff²) BYZ TR.

ᵉ 6:49, **manna in the wilderness:** Some manuscripts read "bread in the wilderness, the manna." D(05) Latin(a b d e).

ᶠ 6:50, **if:** Some manuscripts include Latin(a b d ff²).

ᵍ 6:51, **Therefore:** Included in D(05).

ʰ 6:51, **which I shall give:** Included in BYZ TR.

ⁱ 6:52, **then:** Absent from ℵ(01).

ʲ 6:52, **his:** Absent from 𝔓75 ℵ(01) C(04) D(05) W(032) Latin(d ff²) BYZ TR THGNT.

ᵏ 6:53, **eternal:** Included in ℵ(01).

ˡ 6:54, **my:** Some manuscripts read "his." D(05) Latin(d e).

ᵐ 6:55, **For:** Absent from Latin(a d).

ⁿ 6:55, **true:** Some manuscripts read "truly" in both places.

ᵒ 6:55, **food:** Some manuscripts read "drink." ℵ(01).

ᵖ 6:55, **and my blood is true drink:** Absent from ℵ(01) D(05) Latin(d).

q 6:56, **Just as the Father…:** Included in D(05) Latin(d).

ʳ 6:57, **the:** Some manuscripts read "my." 𝔓75.

ˢ 6:57, **feeds on:** Some manuscripts read "receives." D(05) Latin(d).

ᵗ 6:58, **the fathers ate:** Some manuscripts read "your fathers ate the manna." Latin(a b) BYZ TR.

ᵘ 6:59, **on the Sabbath:** Included in D(05) Latin(a d ff²).

ᵛ 6:60, **his:** Some manuscripts read "the." 𝔓66.

ʷ 6:61, **But:** Some manuscripts read "Therefore." ℵ(01) Latin(a e ff²).

ˣ 6:62, **Therefore:** Absent from ℵ(01).

63 "The spirit is what gives life; the flesh profits nothing. The words that I have spoken to you are spirit and life.

64 "But there are some of you who do not believe." For {Jesus}[a] knew from the beginning who {[[who were the ones not believing and]][b] who was the one to betray him.}[c] 65 And he said, "For this reason I have told you [that][d] no one can come to me unless it has been given [to him][e] from {the}[f] Father."

66 [Therefore][g] From this time many of {his}[h] disciples turned back and no longer walked with him.

67 {Then}[i] Jesus said to the twelve [[disciples]],[j] "Do you also want to leave?" 68 Simon Peter {answered}[k] him, "Lord, to whom shall we go? You have the words of eternal life, 69 and we have believed and come to know that you are the {Holy One}[l] of [[the living]][m] God."

70 Jesus answered [[and said to]][n] [them],[o] "Did I not choose you, the twelve? And yet one of you is a devil."

71 He spoke of {Judas, the son of Simon Iscariot},[p] for he was going to betray him, one of the twelve.

7 1 [And][q] After this, Jesus was walking in Galilee; for he did not {want}[r] to walk in Judea, because the Jews were seeking to kill him.

2 Now the feast of the Jews, the Feast of Tabernacles, was near. 3 Therefore his brothers said to him, "Leave here and go to {Judea},[s] so that your disciples also may see the works you are doing; 4 for no one does anything in secret and seeks [himself][t] to be in openness. If you do these things, reveal [yourself][u] to the world." 5 For even his brothers did not believe in him [[then]].[v]

6 Jesus [then][w] says to them, "My time has not yet come, but your time is always ready. 7 The world cannot hate you, but it hates me because I testify [of it,][x] that its works are evil.

---

[a] 6:64, **Jesus:** Some manuscripts read "he." ℵ(01).

[b] 6:64, **who were the ones not believing and:** Absent from 𝔓66 Latin(e).

[c] 6:64, **who were the ones...:** ℵ(01) reads "which of them were believers, and who was going to betray him."

[d] 6:65, **that:** Absent from W(032) Latin(a).

[e] 6:65, **to him:** Absent from ℵ(01).

[f] 6:65, **the:** Some manuscripts read "my." Latin(c e) BYZ TR.

[g] 6:66, **Therefore:** Included in 𝔓66 ℵ(01) D(05) Latin(b d ff²).

[h] 6:66, **his:** Some manuscripts read "the." ℵ(01).

[i] 6:67, **Then:** Some manuscripts read "But." D(05) Latin(b d).

[j] 6:67, **disciples:** Included in Latin(e ff²).

[k] 6:68, **answered:** ℵ(01) reads "said to."

[l] 6:69, **Holy One:** Some manuscripts read "Christ, the Son." Latin(a e ff²) BYZ TR. ‖ Some manuscripts read "Christ, the Holy One." 𝔓66.

[m] 6:69, **the living** Included in Latin(ff²) BYZ TR.

[n] 6:70, **and said to:** Included in ℵ(01) Latin(a ff²).

[o] 6:70, **them:** Absent from ℵ(01) D(05) Latin(a b d e ff²).

[p] 6:71, **Judas, the son of Simon Iscariot:** Some manuscripts read "Judas Iscariot, the son of Simon." D(05) Latin(a b d e ff²) ‖ Some manuscripts read "Judas of Simon from Kerioth." ℵ(01).

[q] 7:1, **And:** Absent from 𝔓66 ℵ(01) D(05) Latin(a b e ff²) Syriac(sy^s sy^c sy^p).

[r] 7:1, **want:** Some manuscripts read "have authority." W(032) Latin(a b ff²) Syriac(sy^c).

[s] 7:3 , **Judea:** D(05) reads "Galilee."

[t] 7:4, **himself:** Absent from Latin(b e).

[u] 7:4, **yourself:** Absent from Latin(a e).

[v] 7:5, **then:** Included in D(05) Latin(it) Syriac(sy^s sy^c).

[w] 7:6, **then:** Absent from ℵ(01) D(05) W(032) Latin(e) Syriac(sy^s sy^c sy^p).

[x] 7:7, **of it:** Absent from ℵ(01).

8 "You go up to {the}[a] feast; I am not [[yet]][b] going up to this feast, for my time has not yet been fulfilled." 9 [And][c] Having said these things [[to them]],[d] he remained in Galilee.

10 But when his brothers had gone up to the feast, then he also went up, not openly, but [as it were][e] in secret. 11 So the Jews sought him at the feast and said, "Where is that man?" 12 And there was [much][f] murmuring among the people concerning him. Some said, "He is good"; others [however][g] said, "No, but he deceives the people." 13 However, no one spoke openly about him for fear of the Jews.

14 Now about the middle of the feast, Jesus went up into the temple and taught. 15 And the Jews marveled, saying, "How does this man know letters, having never learned?"

16 Jesus [then][h] answered them and said, "My teaching is not mine, but his who sent me. 17 If anyone desires [to do][i] his will, he shall know whether the teaching is from God or whether I speak on my own authority.

18 "He who speaks from himself seeks his own [glory];[j] but he who seeks the glory of the one who sent {him},[k] this one is true, and no unrighteousness is in him.

19 "Did not Moses give you the law [, and yet none of you keeps the law]?[l] Why do you seek to kill me?" 20 [The crowd answered [[and said]],[m] "You have a demon; who is seeking to kill you?"][n]

21 Jesus answered and said [to them],[o] "I did one work, and you [all][p] marvel. 22 [For this reason,][q] Moses gave you circumcision, not that it is from Moses, but from the fathers, and on the Sabbath, you circumcise a man. 23 [So][r] If a man receives circumcision on the Sabbath so that the law of Moses may not be broken, [[why]][s] are you angry with me because I made a man completely well on the Sabbath? 24 Do not judge according to appearance, but judge with righteous judgment."

25 [Therefore][t] Some of the people of Jerusalem said, "Is this not the one they seek to kill? 26 And behold, he speaks openly, and they say nothing [to him].[u] Could it be that the rulers truly knew that this is [[truly]][v] the Christ? 27 But we know where this man is from; [but][w] when the Christ comes, no one will know where he is from."

28 Then Jesus cried out, as he taught in the temple, saying, "You both know me, and you know where I am from;

---

[a] 7:8, **the:** Some manuscripts read "this." ℵ(01) BYZ TR.

[b] 7:8, **yet:** Included in 𝔓66 𝔓75 B(03) W(032) BYZ TR THGNT.

[c] 7:9 , **And:** Absent from ℵ(01) D(05) Latin(a b d ff²).

[d] 7:9, **to them:** Included in 𝔓75 B(03) Latin(a ff²) BYZ TR.

[e] 7:10, **as it were:** Absent from ℵ(01) D(05) Latin(a b d e) Syriac(sy^s sy^c).

[f] 7:12, **much:** Absent from 𝔓66 D(05) Latin(a d e ff²).

[g] 7:12, **however:** Absent from 𝔓66 ℵ(01) D(05) BYZ.

[h] 7:16, **then:** Absent from D(05) Latin(a d e ff²) BYZ TR.

[i] 7:17, **to do:** Absent from 𝔓75.

[j] 7:18, **glory:** Absent from 𝔓75.

[k] 7:18, **him:** Some manuscripts read "me." 𝔓66 Latin(e).

[l] 7:19, **and yet none of you keeps the law:** Absent from Latin(ff²).

[m] 7:20, **and said:** Included in D(05) Latin(a d e ff²) BYZ TR.

[n] 7:20, **The crowd answered...:** Absent from Latin(b).

[o] 7:21, **to them:** Absent from D(05) Latin(d e).

[p] 7:21, **all:** Absent from D(05) Latin(d).

[q] 7:22, **For this reason:** Absent from ℵ(01).

[r] 7:23, **So:** Included in D(05) Latin(a d).

[s] 7:23, **why:** Absent from D(05) Latin(d).

[t] 7:25, **Therefore:** Absent from La.

[u] 7:26, **to him:** Absent from Latin(ff²).

[v] 7:26, **truly:** Included in BYZ TR.

[w] 7:27, **but:** Absent from ℵ(01) Latin(e).

and I have not come of myself, but he
who sent me is true, whom you do not
know. 29 [But][a] I know him, for I am
from him, and he sent me."

30 [Therefore][b] they were seeking
to take him; but no one laid a hand
on him, because his hour had not
yet come.

31 And many from the crowd
believed in him and said, [that][c] "When
the Christ comes, will he do more [[of
these]][d] signs than these which this
man has done?"

32 [[But]][e] The Pharisees heard the
crowd murmuring [these things][f] about
him, and [the chief priests and the
Pharisees][g] sent officers to arrest him.

33 Therefore Jesus said [[to them]],[h]
"For a little while longer I am with you,
and then I go to the one who sent me.
34 You will seek me and not find [me],[i]
and where I am, you cannot come
[[there]]."[j]

35 So the Jews said [to themselves],[k]
"Where is this man going to go that we
will not find him? Does he intend to
go to the Dispersion among the Greeks
and teach the Greeks? 36 What is this
statement that he said, 'You will seek
me and not find [me],[l] and where I am,
you cannot come?'"

37 On the last day [, the great day][m]
of the feast, Jesus stood and cried out,
saying, "If anyone is thirsty, let him
come [to me][n] and drink. 38 The one
who believes in me, as the Scripture
said, 'Out of his belly will flow rivers of
living water.'"

39 But this he said about the Spirit,
which those who believed in him were
[about][o] to receive; for the [[Holy]][p]
Spirit was not yet [[upon them]],[q]
because Jesus was not yet glorified.

40 {Some}[r] of the crowd, therefore,
when they heard these words[s] [[of
him]][t] were saying, [[that]][u] "This
is truly the prophet." 41 Others said,
[[that]][v] ["This is the Christ," but
{some}[w] said,][x] "Does the Christ come
from Galilee? 42 Has not the Scripture
said that the Christ comes from the
seed of David and from Bethlehem, the
village where David was?"[y]

43 So a division occurred in the
crowd because of him. 44 And some of
them wanted to arrest him, but no one
laid hands on him.

---

[a] 7:29, **But:** Included in 𝔓66 א(01) D(05) BYZ TR Latin(b d ff^{2}).
[b] 7:30, **Therefore:** Absent from 𝔓66 א(01).
[c] 7:31, **that:** Included in BYZ TR.
[d] 7:31, **of these:** Included in BYZ TR.
[e] 7:32, **But:** Included in 𝔓66 א(01) D(05) Latin(d e) || Some manuscripts read "Therefore." Latin(a ff^{2}).
[f] 7:32, **these things:** Absent from D(05) Latin(a b d e ff^{2}).
[g] 7:32, **the chief priests and the Pharisees:** Absent from Latin(b e).
[h] 7:33, **to them:** Included in TR.
[i] 7:34, **me:** 𝔓75 B(03) NA28[] || Absent from 𝔓66 א(01) D(05) W(032) Latin(a b d e ff^{2}) Syriac(sy^{s} sy^{c}) BYZ TR THGNT SBLGNT.
[j] 7:34, **there:** Included in B(03).
[k] 7:35, **to themselves:** Absent from א(01) Latin(e).
[l] 7:36, **me:** 𝔓75 B(03) || Absent from 𝔓66 א(01) D(05) W(032) Latin(a b d e ff^{2}) BYZ TR SBLGNT.
[m] 7:37, **the great day:** Absent from W(032).
[n] 7:37, **to me:** Absent from 𝔓66 א(01) D(05) Latin(b d e).
[o] 7:39, **about:** Absent from W(032).
[p] 7:39, **Holy:** Included in 𝔓66 B(03) W(032) Latin(e d) BYZ TR.
[q] 7:39, **upon them:** Absent from D(05).
[r] 7:40, **some:** Some manuscripts read "many." 𝔓66 BYZ TR.
[s] 7:40, **these words:** Some manuscripts read "the word." BYZ TR.
[t] 7:40, **of him:** Included in 𝔓66 א(01) D(05) Latin(d).
[u] 7:40, **that:** Included in B(03) D(05) Latin(d).
[v] 7:41, **that:** Included in D(05) Latin(d).
[w] 7:41, **some:** Some manuscripts read "others."
[x] 7:41, **This is the Christ, but some said:** Absent from Latin(b).
[y] 7:42, Micah 5:2.

45 So the officers then came to the chief priests and Pharisees, and they said to them, "Why did you not bring him?" 46 The servants answered [[and said]],[a] "Never has a man spoken [[in this way]]."[b] 47 [So][c] The Pharisees answered [[them]],[d] "Have you also been deceived? 48 Has any of the rulers or the Pharisees believed in him? 49 But these crowds, who do not know the law, are accursed."[e]

50 Nicodemus, [who had come to him [earlier][f] [[by night]],[g]][h] being one of them, says to them, 51 "Does not our law judge a man unless it [first][i] hears [from him][j] and {knows what he is doing}[k] ?"

52 They answered and said to him, "Are you also from Galilee? Search [[the scriptures]][l] and see that no prophet {arises}[m] from Galilee."[n]

53 [[And each went to his own house.]][o]

Pericope Adulterae Interpolation[p]

8 1 [[But Jesus went to the Mount of Olives. 2 Early in the morning he {came}[q] again to the temple. All the people came to him, [[and he sat down and taught them]].[r] 3 The scribes and the Pharisees brought [[to him]][s] a woman who had been caught in {adultery},[t] and placing her in the midst 4 they say to him, [[testing,]][u] [[so that they might have an accusation against him,]][v] "Teacher, this woman has been caught in the act of adultery. 5 {Now in the Law, Moses commanded

---

a 7:46, **and said:** Included in Latin(a e).

b 7:46, **in this way:** Included in D(05) Latin(d ff²) ‖ Some manuscripts read "like this man speaks." 𝔓66 ℵ(01) ‖ Some manuscripts read "like this man." Latin(e) BYZ TR ‖ Absent from 𝔓75 B(03) W(032) NA28 SBLGNT THGNT.

c 7:47, **So:** Absent from ℵ(01) D(05) Latin(a d e ff²).

d 7:47, **them:** Absent from B(03).

e 7:49, **accursed:** Or "cursed."

f 7:50, **earlier:** Absent from ℵ(01) D(05) BYZ TR SBL.

g 7:50, **by night:** Some manuscripts include D(05) Latin(d ff²) BYZ TR.

h 7:50, **who had come...:** Absent from ℵ(01).

i 7:51, **first:** Absent from Latin(e).

j 7:51, **from him:** Absent from ℵ(01).

k 7:51, **knows what he is doing:** Some manuscripts read "recognized what he did." D(05) Latin(d).

l 7:52, **the scriptures:** Included in W(032) Latin(a e ff²).

m 7:52, **arises:** Some manuscripts read "has risen."

n 7:52, This discourse continues in chapter 8 verse 12.

o 7:53, **And each went to his own house:** D(05) Latin(d e) BYZ TR ‖ Absent from most early manuscripts including 𝔓66 𝔓75 ℵ(01) A(02) B(03) C(04) W(032) Latin(a ff²) Syriac(sy).

p 8:1 Verses 7:53-8:11, known as the *Pericope Adulterae*, is absent from the earliest manuscripts including 𝔓66, 𝔓75, ℵ(01), A(02), B(03), C(04) W(032) Latin(a) and Syriac(sy). Absent from THGNT ‖ Double bracketed in NA28 and SBLGNT. ‖ Included in D(05) Latin(d e ff²) BYZ and TR. *UBS Handbooks for New Testament (20 vol.)* states regarding the pericope, "is not found in the earlier and better Greek manuscripts, it differs in style and vocabulary from the rest of John's Gospel, and it interrupts the sequence of 7.52 and 8.12 and following. But it was evidently a widely circulated account in certain parts of the early church and finally found its place in various ancient manuscripts. In terms of style and vocabulary, it is closer to the Lukan writings than it is to John, and in some ancient manuscripts it is even found after Luke 21.38." The UBS committee regards this passage as original history, though not originally located within John's gospel.

q 8:2, **came:** D(05) reads "comes."

r 8:2, **and he sat down and taught them:** Absent from D(05) that includes the Pericope Adulterae.

s 8:3, **to him:** Some manuscripts include "to him." Latin(ff²) BYZ TR.

t 8:3, **adultery:** D(05) reads "sin."

u 8:4, **testing:** Included in BYZ SBLGNT.

v 8:4, **so that they might have an accusation against him:** Included in D(05).

us}[a] to stone such. So what do you say?" 6 [[This they said to test him, that they might have some charge to bring against him.]] [b]

Jesus bent down and wrote with his finger on the ground [[not pretending]].[c] 7 And as they continued to ask [[him]],[d] he stood up and said to them, "Let him who is without sin among you be the first to throw a stone at her." 8 And once more he bent down and wrote on the ground. 9 But {when they heard it},[e] they went away one by one [[convicted by their conscience]],[f] beginning with the elders [[so that all may go out]][g] [[to the last]],[h] and {he}[i] was left alone, and the woman in the middle. 10 Jesus having stood up [[and seeing no one but the woman]][j] and said to {her, "Woman,}[k] where are {they}?[l] Has no one condemned you?" 11 She said [[to him]],[m] "No one, Lord." And {Jesus}[n] said [[to her]],[o] "Neither do I condemn you; go, and from now on sin no more."]][p]

Continuation from John 7:52

12 [Again][q] Jesus spoke to them, saying, "I am the light of the world. Whoever follows me will not walk in darkness, but will have the light of life."

13 So the Pharisees said to him, "You are bearing witness about yourself; your testimony is not true."

14 Jesus [answered and][r] said to them, "Even if I do bear witness about myself, my testimony is true, for I know where I came from and where I am going; [but][s] you do not know where I come from or where I am going.

15 "You judge according to the flesh; [[but]][t] I judge no one. 16 [And][u] If I do judge, my judgment is true, for I am not alone, but I and the {Father}[v] who sent me.

17 "[And][w] In your Law it is written that the testimony of two men is true.[x] 18 I am the one who bears witness about myself, and the Father who sent me bears witness about me."

---

[a] 8:5, **Now in the law, Moses commanded us:** Some manuscripts read "Moses, however, commanded in the law." D(05) Latin(d).

[b] 8:6, **This they said to test him..:** Absent from D(05) that includes the *Pericope Adulterae*.

[c] 8:6, **not pretending:** Included in BYZ SBLGNT.

[d] 8:7, **him:** Absent from D(05) that includes the *Pericope Adulterae*.

[e] 8:9, **when they heard it:** D(05) reads "each of the Jews."

[f] 8:9, **convicted by their conscience:** Included in BYZ TR.

[g] 8:9, **so that all may go out:** Included in D(05) Latin(d).

[h] 8:9, **to the last:** Included in TR.

[i] 8:9, **he:** Some manuscripts read "Jesus." Latin(e) BYZ TR.

[j] 8:10, **and seeing no one but the woman:** Included in BYZ TR.

[k] 8:10, **her, "Woman:"** Latin(e ff²) TR NA28[[]] ‖ Some manuscripts read "her." BYZ ‖ D(05) reads "the woman." SBLGNT[[]].

[l] 8:10, **they:** Some manuscripts read "those accusers of yours." Latin(ff²) BYZ TR.

[m] 8:11, **to him:** Included in D(05) Latin(d).

[n] 8:11, **he:** D(05) reads "he."

[o] 8:11, **to her:** Included in Latin(ff²) TR.

[p] 8:11, See first footnote for chapter 8.

[q] 8:12, **Again:** Absent from Latin(ff²).

[r] 8:14, **answered:** Absent from ℵ(01).

[s] 8:14, **but:** Absent from ℵ(01) Latin(a).

[t] 8:15, **but:** Included in 𝔓75 Latin(d).

[u] 8:16, **And:** Absent from some manuscripts W(032).

[v] 8:16, **Father:** Some manuscripts read "one." ℵ(01) D(05) Latin(d) Syriac(sy^s sy^c).

[w] 8:17, **And:** Absent from Latin (a b).

[x] 8:17, Deuteronomy 19:15.

19 They said to him therefore, "Where is your Father?" Jesus answered [[and said]]ᵃ [[to him]],ᵇ "You know neither me nor my Father. If you knew me, you would know {my}ᶜ Father also."

20 These words {he}ᵈ spoke in the treasury [teaching in the temple];ᵉ but no one arrested him, because his hour had not yet come.

21 So {he}ᶠ said to them [again],ᵍ "I am going away, and you will seek me, and you will die in your sin. Where I am going, you cannot come." 22 So the Jews said, "Will he kill himself, since he says, 'Where I am going, you cannot come'?"

23 And he was saying to them, "You are from below; I am from above. You are of this world; I am not of this world. 24 [Therefore]ʰ I told you [that]ⁱ you would die in your sins, for unless you believe that I am, you will die in your sins."

25 So they said to him, "Who are you?" Jesus said to them, "Just what I have been telling you from the beginning. 26 I have much to say about you and much to judge, but he who sent me [[the Father]]ʲ is true, and I declare to the world what I have heard from him."

27 They did not understand that he had been speaking to them about the Father [[, the God]].ᵏ 28 Therefore, Jesus said [to them]ˡ [[again]]ᵐ [[that]],ⁿ "When you have lifted up the Son of Man, then you will know that I am he, and I do nothing of myself, but as {the Father}ᵒ taught me, I speak these things. 29 And the one who sent me is with me; {he}ᵖ has not left me alone, because I always do what is pleasing to him."

30 As he was saying these things, many believed in him.

31 Jesus then said to the Jews who had believed in him, "If you remain in my word, truly you are [my]�q disciples, 32 and you will know the truth, and the truth will set you free."

33 {They}ʳ answered him [[and said]],ˢ "We are offspring of Abraham and have never been enslaved to anyone. How can you say [that]ᵗ we will become free?" 34 Jesus answered [them],ᵘ "Truly, truly, I say to you, everyone who practices sin is a slave [to sin].ᵛ 35 The slave does not remain in the house forever; the son remains forever. 36 [So]ʷ If the son sets you free, you will be free indeed.

ᵃ 8:19, **and said:** Included in ℵ(01) D(05) Latin(b e d).

ᵇ 8:19, **to him:** Included in D(05) Latin(b d).

ᶜ 8:19, **the:** ℵ(01) reads "the."

ᵈ 8:20, **he:** Some manuscripts read "Jesus." BYZ TR.

ᵉ 8:20, **teaching in the temple:** Absent from ℵ(01).

ᶠ 8:21, **he:** Some manuscripts read "Jesus." Latin (a ff²) BYZ TR.

ᵍ 8:21, **again:** Absent from ℵ(01).

ʰ 8:24, **Therefore:** Absent from 𝔓(66) ℵ(01) Latin(a e).

ⁱ 8:24, **that:** Absent from 𝔓66 W(032) Latin (a e) Syriac(syˢ syᵖ).

ʲ 8:26, **the Father:** Included in ℵ(01).

ᵏ 8:27, **the God:** Included in ℵ(01) D(05) Latin (a d e ff²) ‖ Absent from 𝔓66 𝔓75 B(03) W(032) Latin(b) BYZ TR NA28 SBLGNT THGNT.

ˡ 8:28, **to them:** Absent from 𝔓66 B(03) SBLGNT Latin(a).

ᵐ 8:28, **again:** Included in ℵ(01) D(05) Latin(d).

ⁿ 8:28, **that:** Included in 𝔓66 𝔓75 B(03).

ᵒ 8:28, **the Father:** W(032) reads "he."

ᵖ 8:29, **he:** Some manuscripts read "the Father." BYZ TR.

q 8:31, **my:** Absent from ℵ(01).

ʳ 8:33, **They:** Some manuscripts read "the Jews." Latin(a b e ff²).

ˢ 8:33, **and said:** Included in D(05).

ᵗ 8:33, **that:** Absent from W(032) Latin(b ff²).

ᵘ 8:34, **them:** Absent from 𝔓75 Latin(b e).

ᵛ 8:34, **to sin:** Absent from D(05) Latin(b d).

ʷ 8:36, **So:** Absent from 𝔓75 Latin(a e ff²).

37 "I know that you are offspring of Abraham; yet you seek to kill me because my word finds no place in you. 38 What I have seen with {the}[a] Father, I speak [[these things]];[b] and therefore, what you have {heard}[c] from {the}[d] father, do [[these things]]."[e]

39 [[Therefore]][f] They answered and said to him, "Our father is Abraham." Jesus says [to them],[g] "If you {are}[h] children of Abraham, you would be doing the works of Abraham, 40 but now you seek to kill me, a man who has told you the truth that I heard from God. This is not what Abraham did."

41 [[But]][i] You do the works of your father. They said [then][j] to him, "We were not born of sexual immorality; we have one father, God."

42 [[Therefore]][k] Jesus said to them, "If God were your Father, you would love me, for I {came}[l] forth from God and I am here. I came not of my own accord, but he sent me.

43 "{Why do you not understand what I say? Because}[m] you are unable to hear my word. 44 You are of [your father][n] the devil, and your will is to do your father's desires. He was a murderer from the beginning, and {does not stand}[o] in the truth, because there is no truth in him. When he lies, he speaks out of his own character, for he is a liar and the father of lies. 45 But because I tell the truth [[to you]],[p] you do not believe me.

46 "[Which one of you convicts me of sin? If I tell the truth, why do you not believe me?][q] 47 Whoever is of God hears the words of God. {The reason why you do not hear them is that you are not of God}."[r]

48 [[Therefore]][s] The Jews answered him, "Are we not right in saying that you are a Samaritan and have a demon?"

49 Jesus answered [[and said]],[t] "I do not have a demon, but I honor my Father, and you dishonor me. 50 Yet I do not seek my own glory; there is one who seeks it; [and][u] he is the judge.

---

a 8:38, **the:** Some manuscripts read "my."

b 8:38, **these things:** Included in D(05) Latin(b d).

c 8:38, **heard:** 𝔓75 B(03) C(04) NA28 SBLGNT THGNT ‖ Some manuscripts read "seen." 𝔓66 ℵ(01) D(05) Latin(a b d e ff²) BYZ TR.

d 8:38, **the:** 𝔓66 𝔓75 B(03) NA28 SBLGNT THGNT, Some manuscripts read "your." ℵ(01) C(04) D(05) Latin(a b d e ff²) BYZ TR.

e 8:38, **these things:** Included in D(05).

f 8:39, **Therefore:** Included in 𝔓66 D(05) Latin (b d e).

g 8:39, **to them:** Absent from D(05) Latin(d e).

h 8:39, **are:** 𝔓66 𝔓75 ℵ(01) B(03) D(05) Latin(d ff²) NA28 SBLGNT THGNT ‖ Some manuscripts read "were." C(04) W(032) Latin(a b e) BYZ TR.

i 8:41, **But:** Included in D(05) Latin(b d e).

j 8:41, **then:** 𝔓66 𝔓75 C(04) D(05) Latin (d) BYZ TR N28[] ‖ Absent from ℵ(01) B(03) W(032) Latin(a b e ff²) SBLGNT THGNT.

k 8:42, **Therefore:** Included in ℵ(01) D(05) Latin(d) BYZ TR.

l 8:42, **came:** 𝔓66 reads "have come."

m 8:43, **Why do you not understand what I say? Because:** D(05) reads "Because you do not know my truth, that."

n 8:44, **your father:** Absent from Syriac(sy^s).

o 8:44, **does not stand:** Some manuscripts read "has not stood."

p 8:45, **to you:** Included in C(04) Latin(b).

q 8:46, **Which one...:** Verse 46 is absent from D(05) Latin(d).

r 8:47, **The reason why...:** Some manuscripts read "For this reason, you do not hear." D(05) Latin(d).

s 8:48, **therefore:** Included in BYZ TR.

t 8:49, **and said:** Included in ℵ(01).

u 8:50, **and:** Absent from 𝔓66.

51 "Truly, truly, I say to you, {if anyone}[a] keeps my word, he will certainly not see death into the age."[b]

52 The Jews [therefore][c] said to him, "Now we know that you have a demon! Abraham died, as did the prophets, yet you say, 'If anyone keeps my word, he will never taste death into the age.' 53 Are you greater than [our father][d] Abraham, {who}[e] died? And the prophets died! Who do you make yourself to be?"

54 Jesus answered, "If I glorify myself, my glory is nothing. It is my Father who glorifies me, of whom you say, 'He is {our}[f] God.' 55 Yet you have not known him, but I know him. If I were to {say}[g] that I do not know him, I would be a liar like you, but I do know him and I keep his word.

56 "Abraham your father rejoiced to {see}[h] my day, and he saw it and was glad."

57 So the Jews said to him, "You are not yet fifty years old, and Abraham {has}[i] seen you?"

58 [[Therefore]][j] Jesus said to them, "Truly, truly, I say to you, before Abraham [was],[k] I am."

59 So they picked up stones to throw at him; [but][l] Jesus hid himself and went out of the temple [[going through the midst of them, and so passed by]].[m]

9 1 And passing by, he saw a man blind from birth [[sitting]].[n] 2 And his disciples asked him, [saying,][o] "Rabbi, who sinned, this one or his parents, that he should be born blind?"

3 Jesus answered [[and he said to them]],[p] "Neither this one sinned nor his parents, but so that the works of God might be revealed in him.

4 "We[q] must work the works of the one who sent me while it is day; night is coming when no one can work.

5 "As long as I am in the world, I am the light of the world."

6 Having said these things, he spat on the ground and made mud from the saliva and [he][r] smeared [the mud][s] on his eyes [[of the blind man]].[t] 7 And he said [to him],[u] "Go, [wash][v] in the pool of Siloam" (which is translated, Sent).

---

a 8:51, **if anyone:** Some manuscripts read "whoever." D(05) Syriac(sy^s sy^p).

b 8:51, **into the age:** Or "forever."

c 8:52, **therefore:** 𝔓75 D(05) Latin(d ff²) BYZ TR NA28[] ‖ Absent from 𝔓66 ℵ(01) B(03) C(04) W(032) Latin (a b e) Syriac(sy^s sy^p) SBLGNT THGNT.

d 8:53, **our father:** Absent from D(05) W(032) Latin(a b d e ff²).

e 8:53, **who:** Some manuscripts read "that." 𝔓66 D(05) Latin(a d).

f 8:54, **our:** Some manuscripts read "your." ℵ(01) B(03) D(05).

g 8:55, **say:** 𝔓75 reads "tell you."

h 8:56, **see:** Some manuscripts read "have seen." ℵ(01) A(02) B(03) W(032).

i 8:57, **has:** Some manuscripts read "would have." 𝔓75 ℵ(01).

j 8:58, **Therefore:** Included in D(05) Latin(d).

k 8:58, **was:** Absent from D(05) Latin(a b e ff²).

l 8:59, **but:** Absent from B(03) W(032).

m 8:59, **going through the midst of them, and so passed by:** Included in A(02) C(04) BYZ TR ‖ Absent from 𝔓66 𝔓75 ℵ(01) B(03) D(05) W(032) Latin(a b d e ff² it) Syriac(sy^s) NA28 SBLGNT THGNT.

n 9:1, **sitting:** Included in D(05) Latin(d).

o 9:2, **saying:** Absent from D(05) Latin (d e).

p 9:3, **and he said to them:** Included in Latin (b e).

q 9:4, **we:** 𝔓66 𝔓75 ℵ(01) C(04) D(05) NA28 SBLGNT THGNT ‖ Some manuscripts read "I." A(02) C(04) Latin(a b e ff²) Syriac(sy) BYZ TR.

r 9:6, **he:** Absent from C(04) W(032) Latin(e) BYZ TR.

s 9:6, **the mud:** Absent from Latin(a e).

t 9:6, **of the blind man:** Some manuscripts include A(02) C(04) W(032) Latin(b) BYZ TR.

u 9:7, **to him:** Absent from D(05) Latin(a d e).

v 9:7, **wash:** Absent from A(02) Latin(a b e).

So he went [and washed and came back]ᵃ seeing.

8 Then {the}ᵇ neighbors and those who had seen him before as a {beggar}ᶜ said, "Is not this the one who used to sit and beg?" 9 Some said [that],ᵈ "This is he," {others said, "No, but}ᵉ he is like him." [[But]]ᶠ He said [that],ᵍ "I am."

10 [So]ʰ {They}ⁱ said to him [then],ʲ "How then were your eyes opened?" 11 He answered [[and said]],ᵏ "The man called Jesus made mud and anointed my eyes and said to me, 'Go to [[the pool of]]ˡ Siloam and wash'; so I went and {washed and received my sight}."ᵐ

12 {And}ⁿ they said to him, "Where is he?" He says [[to them]]ᵒ "I do not know."

13 They brought to the Pharisees the man who had formerly been blind. 14 It was the Sabbath [on the day]ᵖ when Jesus made the mud and opened his eyes. 15 So the Pharisees again asked him how he had received his sight. And he said to them, "He put mud on my eyes, and I washed, and I see."

16 Some of the Pharisees said, "This man is not from God, for he does not keep the Sabbath." [But]ᵠ Others said, "How can a sinful man do such signs?" And there was a division among them. 17 So they said to the [[once]]ʳ blind man again, "What do you say about him, since he has opened your eyes?" He said, "He is a prophet."

18 [So]ˢ The Jews did not believe [that he had been blind and had received his sight]ᵗ until they called the parents [[of him]]ᵘ [of the one who had received his sight]ᵛ 19 and asked them, [saying]ʷ "Is this your son, who you say was born blind? How [then]ˣ does he now see?"

ᵃ 9:7, **and washed and came back:** Absent from C(04).
ᵇ 9:8, **the:** Some manuscripts read "his." 𝔓66 Latin(a b ff²).
ᶜ 9:8, **beggar:** Some manuscripts read "blind man." BYZ TR.
ᵈ 9:9, **that:** Absent from 𝔓66 ℵ(01) W(032) Latin(a b e ff²).
ᵉ 9:9, **others said, "no, but.":** Some manuscripts read "But others that."
ᶠ 9:9, **But:** Included in 𝔓66 ℵ(01) A(02) Latin(a b e ff² it).
ᵍ 9:9, **that:** Absent from 𝔓66 Latin(a b e ff²).
ʰ 9:10, **So:** Absent from 𝔓66.
ⁱ 9:10, **they:** ℵ(01) reads "the Jews."
ʲ 9:10, **then:** ℵ(01) C(04) D(05) Latin (a d) NAS28[] ‖ Absent from 𝔓75 A(02) B(03) W(032) Latin(b e ff²) BYZ TR SBLGNT THGNT.
ᵏ 9:11, **and said:** Included in A(02) Latin(a b) BYZ TR.
ˡ 9:11, **the pool of:** Some manuscripts include, "the pool of." A(02) Latin(e) BYZ TR.
ᵐ 9:11, **washed and received my sight:** Some manuscripts read "when I washed, I could see." D(05) Latin(b d).
ⁿ 9:12, **And:** Some manuscripts read "therefore." 𝔓66 D(05) Latin(a b d ff²) BYZ TR.
ᵒ 9:12, **to them:** Included in D(05) Latin (b d).
ᵖ 9:14, **on the day:** Absent from A(02) D(05) Latin(d) BYZ TR.
ᵠ 9:16, **But:** Absent from 𝔓66 𝔓75 A(02) Latin(a b e ff²) BYZ TR SBLGNT.
ʳ 9:17, **once:** Included in ℵ(01).
ˢ 9:18, **So:** Absent from D(05) Latin(a d).
ᵗ 9:18, **that he had been blind and had received his sight:** Absent from D(05) Latin(d).
ᵘ 9:18, **of him:** Absent from D(05) Latin(ff²).
ᵛ 9:18, **of the one who had received his sight:** Absent from 𝔓66 Latin(a b e ff²).
ʷ 9:19, **saying:** Absent from W(032) Latin(a b ff²).
ˣ 9:19, **then:** Absent from Latin(a e).

20 [So][a] [[To them]][b] His parents
answered them, "We know that this is
our son and that he was born blind;
21 but how he [now][c] sees we do not
know, nor do we know who opened his
eyes. [Ask him;][d] He is of age. [He will
speak for himself.]"[e]

22 His parents said these things
because they feared the Jews; for the
Jews had already agreed that if anyone
should confess him as Christ, he was to
be put out of the synagogue. 23 Because
of this, his parents said, [that][f] "He is of
age, ask him."

24 So for the second time they called
{the man}[g] who had been blind and
said to him, "Give glory to God. We
know that this man is a sinner."

25 So he answered [[and said]],[h]
"Whether he is a sinner I do not know;
one thing I know, that though I was
blind, now I see."

26 [Therefore][i] They said to him
[[again]],[j] "What did he do to you?
[[And]][k] How did he open your eyes?"

27 He answered them, "I have told
you already, and you would not listen.
Why do you want to hear it again? Do
you [[therefore]][l] also want to become
his disciples?"

28 [And][m] They reviled him, saying,
"You are his disciple, but we are
disciples of Moses. 29 [[But]][n] We know
that God has spoken to Moses [[, and
that God does not listen to sinners]];[o]
but we do not know where this man
is from."

30 [[But]][p] The man answered
and said [to them],[q] "{For this is the
astonishing thing},[r] that you do not
know where he is from, and yet he
opened my eyes. 31 [[But]][s] We know
that God does not listen to sinners,
but if anyone is a worshiper of God
and does his will, God listens to him.
32 Never since the world began has it
been heard that anyone opened the eyes
of a man born blind. 33 If this man were
not from God, he could do nothing."

34 They answered him, "You were
born in utter sin, and would you teach
us?" And they cast him out.

35 [[But]][t] Jesus heard that they had
cast him out, and when he found him,
he said [[to him]],[u] "Do you believe in

a 9:20, **So:** 𝔓66 P75 ℵ(01) B(03) NA28 SBLGNT THGNT || Absent from D(05) W(032) Latin(a b e d ff^{2}) TR BYZ || Some manuscripts read "But." A(02).

b 9:20, **To them:** Included in D(05) Latin(b) BYZ TR.

c 9:21, **now:** Absent from Latin(e ff^{2}).

d 9:21, **Ask him:** Absent from 𝔓75 ℵ(01) W(032).

e 9:21, **He will speak for himself:** Absent from ℵ(01) W(032) Latin(b).

f 9:23, **that:** Absent from D(05) Latin(a d e).

g 9:24, **the man:** Some manuscripts read "him." BYZ TR.

h 9:25, **and said:** Included in BYZ TR.

i 9:26, **Therefore:** 𝔓66 P75 B(03) D(05) W(032) Latin(b d ff^{2}) NA28 SBLGNT THGNT || Absent from ℵ(01) Latin(a e) || Some manuscripts read "But." A(02) BYZ TR.

j 9:26, **again:** Included in 𝔓66 A(02) BYZ TR.

k 9:26, **And:** Included in D(05).

l 9:27, **therefore:** Included in 𝔓75 B(03) Latin(b ff^{2}).

m 9:28, **And:** 𝔓75 ℵ(01) B(03) W(032) NA28 || Absent from 𝔓66 A(02) Latin(a b d e) BYZ SBLGNT THGNT || Some manuscripts read "But." D(05) || Some manuscripts read "Therefore." Latin(ff^{2}) TR.

n 9:29, **But:** Included in 𝔓75.

o 9:29, **and that God does not listen to sinners:** Included in D(05) Latin(d).

p 9:30, **But:** Included in 𝔓75.

q 9:30, **to them:** Absent from 𝔓66 D(05) Latin(b d e ff^{2}).

r 9:30, **For this is the astonishing thing:** D(05) reads "In this, then, is something amazing."

s 9:31, **But:** Included in A(02) W(032) Latin(ff^{2}) BYZ TR.

t 9:35, **But:** Included in W(032) Latin (b ff^{2}).

u 9:35, **to him:** Included in 𝔓66 A(02) Latin(a b d ff^{2}) BYZ TR.

the Son of {Man}?"[a] [36] [He answered][b] [and said,][c] "Who is {the Lord,}[d] that I may believe in him?" [37] [[But]][e] Jesus {said}[f] to him, "You have both seen him, and it is he who is talking with you." [38] [Then he said, "I believe, Lord," and he worshiped[g] him. [39] And Jesus said,][h] "I came into this world for judgment, that those who do not see may see, and that those who see may become blind."

[40] [[And]][i] The ones with him, having heard [these things][j] from the Pharisees, said to him, "Are we also blind?" [41] Jesus [[therefore]][k] said to them, "If you were blind, you would have no sin; but now you say, 'We see.' [[And]][l] [[Therefore]][m] Your sins remain."

10 [1] "Truly, truly, I say to you, the one not entering through the door into the sheepfold but climbing up from elsewhere, that one is a thief and a robber; [2] But the one who enters through the door, he is the shepherd of the sheep. [3] To this one the doorkeeper opens, and the sheep hear the voice of that one, and that one calls the sheep by name and leads them out. [4] [[And]][n] When he has brought out {[all][o] his own},[p] he goes ahead of them, and the sheep follow him, because they know his voice; [5] but they will not follow a stranger, but will flee from the stranger because they do not know the voice of strangers."

[6] Jesus spoke this parable to them, but they did not understand what [it was][q] that he was saying to them.

[7] [So][r] Jesus said [again][s] [[to them,]][t] "Truly, truly, [For][u] I say to you, [that][v] I am the door of the sheep. [8] {All}[w] who came [before me][x] are thieves and robbers, but the sheep did not listen to them. [9] I am the door; if anyone enters through me, they will be saved and will go in [and go out][y] and find pasture.

---

[a] 9:35, **Man:** 𝔭666 𝔭75 ℵ(01) B(03) D(05) W(032) Latin(d) Syriac(sy[s]) NA28 SBLGNT THGNT ‖ Some manuscripts read "God." A(02) Latin(a b e ff[2]) Syriac(sy[p]) BYZ TR.

[b] 9:36, **He answered:** Absent from 𝔭75 B(03) W(032).

[c] 9:36, **and said:** Absent from 𝔭66 𝔭75 A(02) B(03) W(032).

[d] 9:36, **the Lord:** Some manuscripts read "it, Lord." BYZ TR 𝔭66 𝔭75 B(03) W(032).

[e] 9:37, **But:** Included in A(02) BYZ TR.

[f] 9:37, **said:** Some manuscripts read "answered." D(05) Latin(d).

[g] 9:38, **worshiped:** See footnote for worship in Luke 22:52.

[h] 9:38-39a, **Then he said, "I believe, Lord," and he worshiped him. 39 And Jesus said:** Absent from 𝔭75 ℵ(01) W(032) Latin(b).

[i] 9:40, **And:** Included in A(02) Latin(a b e ff[2]) BYZ TR ‖ Some manuscripts read "But." D(05) Latin(d) ‖ Absent from 𝔭66 𝔭75 ℵ(01) B(03) W(032) NA28 THGNT SBLGNT.

[j] 9:40, **these things:** Absent from ℵ(01) D(05) Latin(a b d e ff[2]) Syriac(sy[s]).

[k] 9:41, **therefore:** Included in D(05) Latin(d).

[l] 9:41, **And:** Included in 𝔭75.

[m] 9:41, **Therefore:** Included in A(02) Latin(a) BYZ TR.

[n] 10:4, **And:** Included in A(02) D(05) Latin(a d e ff[2]) BYZ TR.

[o] 10:4, **all:** Absent from ℵ(01).

[p] 10:4, **all his own:** Some manuscripts read "his own sheep." A(02) BYZ TR.

[q] 10:6, **it was:** Absent from 𝔭66.

[r] 10:7, **So:** Absent from 𝔭66 Latin(e) Syriac(sy[s]).

[s] 10:7, **again:** Absent from 𝔭45, 𝔭66 W(032) Latin (e ff[2]).

[t] 10:7, **to them:** Included in 𝔭45 𝔭66 ℵ(01) A(02) W(032) Latin(b d) BYZ TR SBLGNT THGNT ‖ Absent from 𝔭6 𝔭75 B(03).

[u] 10:7, **for:** Absent from 𝔭66 ℵ(01) Latin(e).

[v] 10:7, **that:** Absent from 𝔭75 B(03) Latin(a).

[w] 10:8, **All:** D(05) reads "As many as."

[x] 10:8, **before me:** Absent from 𝔭75 ℵ(01) Latin(a b e ff[2]) BYZ.

[y] 10:9, **and go out:** Absent from W(032).

10 "The thief comes only to steal and kill and destroy; [[But]]ᵃ I came that they may have [[eternal]]ᵇ life [and have it abundantly].ᶜ

11 "I am the good shepherd. The good shepherd lays down his life for the sheep; 12 [[But]]ᵈ The hired hand, who is not a shepherd and does not own the sheep, sees the wolf [coming]ᵉ and leaves the sheep and flees. And the wolf snatches them and scatters them [[the sheep]];ᶠ 13 [[But the hired hand flees]]ᵍ because he is a hired hand and does not care about the sheep.

14 "I am the good shepherd, and I know my own and my own know me, 15 just as the Father knows me and I know the Father; and I lay down my life for the sheep.

16 "And I have other sheep that are not of this fold; I must {lead}ʰ them also, and they will listen to my voice, and there will be one flock, one shepherd.

17 "For this reason the Father loves me, because I lay down my life in order to take it up again.

18 "No one takes it from me [but I lay it down of my own accord].ⁱ I have authority to lay it down, and I have authority to {receive}ʲ it again; this command I received from {my}ᵏ Father."

19 [[Therefore]]ˡ A division [again]ᵐ occurred among the Jews because of these words. 20 {But}ⁿ many of them said, [[that]]ᵒ "He has a demon and is insane; why do you listen to him?" 21 [[But]]ᵖ Others said, "These are not the words of one who is demon-possessed; can a demon open the eyes of the blind?"

22 {Then}�q the Feast of Dedicationʳ took place in Jerusalem. [[And]]ˢ It was winter, 23 and Jesus was walking in the temple, in the portico of Solomon. 24 So the Jews gathered around him and said to him, "How long will you keep us in suspense? If you are the Christ,ᵗ tell us plainly."

25 Jesus answered [them],ᵘ "I told you, and you do not believe [[me]];ᵛ the works that I do in my Father's name, these testify about me; 26 but you do not believe because you are not of my sheep [[as I said to you]].ʷ

ᵃ 10:10, **But:** Included in 𝔓45 D(05) Latin(a d).

ᵇ 10:10, **eternal:** Included in ℵ(01).

ᶜ 10:10, **and have it abundantly:** Absent from 𝔓66 D(05) Latin(d ff²).

ᵈ 10:12, **But:** Included in 𝔓66 ℵ(01) A(02) D(05) Latin(b d e ff²) BYZ TR.

ᵉ 10:12, **coming:** Absent from A(02).

ᶠ 10:12, **the sheep:** Included in A(02) Latin(a b e ff²) BYZ TR.

ᵍ 10:13, **But the hired hand flees:** Included in A(02) Latin(a b ff²) BYZ TR ‖ Absent from 𝔓45 𝔓66 𝔓77 ℵ(01) B(03) D(05) W(032) Latin(d e) NA28 SBLGNT THGNT.

ʰ 10:16, **lead:** Or "bring." 𝔓66 reads "to gather together."

ⁱ 10:18, **but I lay it down of my own accord:** Absent from D(05) Latin(d).

ʲ 10:18, **receive:** D(05) reads "take."

ᵏ 10:18, **my:** Some manuscripts read "the." D(05) Latin(a b d ff²).

ˡ 10:19, **Therefore:** Included in 𝔓66 A(02) D(05) Latin(d ff²) BYZ TR.

ᵐ 10:19, **again:** Absent from D(05) Latin(d ff²).

ⁿ 10:20, **But:** Some manuscripts read "Therefore." ℵ(01) D(05) Latin(d).

ᵒ 10:20, **that:** Included in 𝔓45 D(05) Latin(d).

ᵖ 10:21, **But:** Included in 𝔓66 ℵ(01) W(032) Latin(d).

q 10:22, **Then:** 𝔓75 B(03) NA28 SBLGNT THGNT ‖ Some manuscripts read "And." 𝔓66 ℵ(01) A(02) D(05) Latin(d e ff²) BYZ TR ‖ Absent from Latin(a b).

ʳ 10:22, **Feast of Dedication:** Or Hanukkah.

ˢ 10:22, **And:** Included in A(02) Latin(a e) BYZ TR.

ᵗ 10:24, **Christ:** See footnote for Christ in Luke 2:11.

ᵘ 10:25, **them:** Absent from 𝔓66 ℵ(01) B(03) D(05).

ᵛ 10:25, **me:** Included in D(05).

ʷ 10:26, **as I said to you:** Included in 𝔓66 A(02) D(05) Latin(a b e ff²) BYZ TR ‖ Absent from 𝔓75 ℵ(01) B(03) NA28 SBLGNT THGNT.

27 [[Because]][a] My sheep hear my voice,
and I know them, and they follow me;
28 and I give them eternal life, and
they will never perish, and no one will
snatch them out of my hand.

29 "{My}[b] Father, who has given
[me][c] everything, is greater than all,
and no one is able to snatch anything
from {the}[d] Father's hand."

30 "I and {the}[e] Father are one."

31 [[So]][f] [Again][g] The Jews picked
up stones to stone him.

32 Jesus answered them, "I have
shown you many [good][h] works from
{the}[i] Father; [[therefore]][j] for which of
them are you going to stone me?"

33 The Jews answered him
[[saying]],[k] "It is not for a good work
that we are going to stone you but for
blasphemy, because you, being a man,
make yourself God."[l]

34 Jesus answered them [[and
said]],[m] "Is it not written in [[the
Scripture,]][n] {your}[o] law, [that][p] 'I said,
you are gods'?[q]

35 "If he called them gods [to
whom the word of God came],[r] and
it cannot be broken, [the Scripture,][s]
36 do you say of him whom the Father
consecrated and sent into the world,
'You are blaspheming,'[t] because I said,
'I am the Son of God'?

37 "If I am not doing the works of
my Father, do not believe me; 38 but if
I do them, even though you do not
[[want to]][u] believe me, believe the
works, that you may {know}[v] [and
understand][w] that the Father is in me
and I am in {the Father}."[x]

39 [Therefore][y] They sought [again][z]
to arrest him, but he escaped from
their hands.

---

a 10:27, **Because:** Included in 𝔓66.

b 10:29, **My:** Some manuscripts read "The." ℵ(01) Latin(a b e ff^2) Syriac(sy^s).

c 10:29, **me:** Absent from 𝔓66.

d 10:29, **the:** 𝔓66 ℵ(01) B(03) NA28 SBLGNT THGNT || Some manuscripts read "my." A(02) D(05) W(032) Latin(a b e d ff^2) BYZ TR.

e 10:30, **the:** Some manuscripts read "my." W(032) Latin(e).

f 10:31, **So:** Included in 𝔓66 A(02) D(05) Latin(a b d e) BYZ TR SBLGNT || Absent from 𝔓45 ℵ(01) B(03) W(032) Latin(ff^2) NA28 THGNT.

g 10:31, **Again:** Absent from 𝔓45 D(05) Latin(a b d e ff^2).

h 10:32, **good:** Absent from W(032) Latin(b).

i 10:32, **the:** ℵ(01) B(03) D(05) Latin(d e) NA28 SBLGNT || Some manuscripts read "my." 𝔓66 A(02) W(032) Latin(a b ff^2) BYZ TR THGNT.

j 10:32, **therefore:** Included in 𝔓66 W(032).

k 10:33, **saying:** Included in D(05) Latin(d e) BYZ TR.

l 10:33, **God:** "God" here usually lacks the definite article in the Greek so it can be interpreted as "a god."

m 10:34, **and said:** Included in 𝔓66 D(05) Latin(d).

n 10:34, **the scripture:** Included in 𝔓45.

o 10:34, **your:** Some manuscripts read "the." 𝔓45 ℵ(01) D(05) Latin(b d e ff^2).

p 10:34, **that:** Absent from A(02) BYZ TR.

q 10:34, Psalm 82:6.

r 10:35, **To whom the word of God came:** Absent from 𝔓45.

s 10:35, **the Scripture:** Absent from 𝔓45 Latin(e).

t 10:36, **blaspheming:** The Greek word means to speak in a disrespectful way that demeans, denigrates, maligns (BDAG, βλασφημέω).

u 10:38, **want to:** Included in D(05).

v 10:38, **know:** W(032) reads "read."

w 10:38, **and understand:** Absent from D(05) Latin(a b d e ff^2) || Some manuscripts read "and believe." ℵ(01) A(02) BYZ TR.

x 10:38, **the Father:** 𝔓75 ℵ(01) B(03) D(05) W(032) Latin(a d e) NA28 SBLGNT THGNT || Some manuscripts read "him." 𝔓45 A(02) Latin(b ff^2) BYZ TR || 𝔓66 reads "him, the Father."

y 10:39, **Therefore:** Absent from 𝔓45 𝔓75 B(03) D(05) Latin(d).

z 10:39, **again:** Absent from ℵ(01) D(05) Latin(a b e d ff^2).

40 He went away [again]ᵃ across the Jordan [to the place]ᵇ where John had been baptizing at first, and there he remained. 41 And many came to him and they said, [that]ᶜ "John did no sign, but everything that {John}ᵈ said about this man was true." 42 {And}ᵉ many believed in him [there].ᶠ

11 1 Now there was a certain man who was sick, Lazarus from Bethany, the village of Mary and her sister [Martha].ᵍ 2 {It was}ʰ Mary who anointed the Lord with ointment and wiped his feet with her hair, [[and]]ⁱ whose brother Lazarus was sick. 3 So {the sisters}ʲ sent to him, saying, "Lord, the one whom you love is sick."

4 But when Jesus heard it, he said, "{This}ᵏ sickness is not unto death, but for the glory of [[his]]ˡ God, so that the Son of God may be glorified through it."

5 Now Jesus loved Martha and her sister and Lazarus. 6 So when he heard that he was sick, {he}ᵐ stayed in the place where he was for two days.

7 Then after this he says [to {the}ⁿ disciples],ᵒ "Let us go into Judea [again]."ᵖ 8 {The}�q disciples said to him, "Rabbi, the Jews were just now seeking to stone you, and are you going there again?"

9 Jesus answered, "Are there not twelve hours in the day? If anyone walks in the day, they do not stumble, because they see the light of this world; 10 but if anyone walks in the night, they stumble, because the light is not in them." 11 These things he said, and after this he says to them, "Lazarus our friend has fallen asleep; but I am going so that I may awaken him."

12 So his disciples said to him, "Lord, if he has fallen asleep, he will be saved."ʳ

13 Now Jesus had spoken about his {death},ˢ but they thought [that]ᵗ he was speaking about the rest of sleep.

14 [Then]ᵘ Jesus told them plainly, "Lazarus [[our friend]]ᵛ has died, 15 and for your sake I am glad that I was not there, so that you may believe. But let us go to him."

16 So Thomas, called the Twin, said to {the}ʷ fellow disciples, "Let us also go, that we may die with him."

17 When Jesus arrived [[in Bethany]],ˣ he found that Lazarus had [already]ʸ been in the tomb for

---

ᵃ 10:40, **again:** Absent from 𝔓66 Latin(e).

ᵇ 10:40, **to the place:** Absent from ℵ(01).

ᶜ 10:41, **that:** Absent from ℵ(01) D(05) Latin(d e).

ᵈ 10:41, **he:** W(032) reads "he."

ᵉ 10:42, **And:** W(032) reads "Therefore."

ᶠ 10:42, **there:** Absent from Latin(a b e ff²).

ᵍ 11:1, **Martha:** Absent from A(02).

ʰ 11:2, **It was:** Some manuscripts read "This is the." 𝔓45 Latin(e).

ⁱ 11:2, **and:** Included in ℵ(01) D(05).

ʲ 11:3, **the sisters:** 𝔓66 reads "Martha."

ᵏ 11:4, **This:** Some manuscripts read "His." D(05) Latin(d).

ˡ 11:4, **his:** Included in 𝔓66.

ᵐ 11:6, **he:** Some manuscripts read "Jesus." D(05) Latin(b d ff²).

ⁿ 11:7, **the:** Some manuscripts read "his." A(02) D(05) Latin(b d ff²).

ᵒ 11:7, **to the disciples:** Absent from 𝔓45 Latin(e) ‖ 𝔓66 reads "to them."

ᵖ 11:7, **again:** Absent from ℵ(01).

q 11:8, **The:** Some manuscripts read "His." D(05) Latin(a d e).

ʳ 11:12, **saved:** Or, get well.

ˢ 11:13, **death:** 𝔓(75) reads "sleep."

ᵗ 11:13, **that:** Absent from 𝔓75.

ᵘ 11:14, **Then:** Absent from A(02) W(032) Latin(a).

ᵛ 11:14, **our friend:** Included in D(05) Latin(d).

ʷ 11:16, **the:** Some manuscripts read "his." D(05) Latin(d).

ˣ 11:17, **in Bethany:** Included in D(05) Latin(d).

ʸ 11:17, **already:** Absent from A(02) D(05).

four days. 18 Now Bethany was near Jerusalem, about two miles away.

19 And many of {the Jews}[a] had come to [[those around]][b] Martha and Mary to console them concerning their brother.

20 So when Martha heard that Jesus was coming, she went and met him, but Mary remained seated in {the}[c] house.

21 Martha said to {Jesus},[d] "[Lord,][e] If you had been here, my brother would not have died. 22 [But][f] Even now I know that whatever you ask from God, God will give you."

23 Jesus says to her, "Your brother will rise." 24 Martha says to him, "I know that he will rise again in the resurrection on the last day."

25 [[So]][g] Jesus said to her, "I am the resurrection [and the life].[h] Whoever believes in me, though they die, shall live, 26 and everyone who lives and believes [in me][i] shall never die. Do you believe this?" 27 She says to him, "Yes, Lord; I believe that you are the Christ, the Son of God, who is coming into the world."

28 And having said {this},[j] she went away and {secretly}[k] called Mary her sister, saying, [[that]][l] "The teacher is here and is calling for you." 29 [But][m] When she heard this, she got up quickly and went to him. 30 Now Jesus had not yet come {into}[n] the village, but was [still][o] in the place where Martha had met him.

31 So when the Jews who were with her in the house, comforting her, saw Mary get up quickly and go out, they followed her, {thinking highly of her}[p] that she was going to the tomb to weep there.

32 Then Mary, when she came to where Jesus was and saw [him],[q] fell at his feet, saying [to him],[r] "Lord, if you had been here, my brother would not have died." 33 When Jesus saw her weeping, and the Jews who had come with her also weeping, he was deeply moved in spirit and troubled himself. 34 And he said, "Where have you laid him?" They said to him, "[Lord,][s] come and see."

35 Jesus wept. 36 So the Jews said, "See how he loved him!" 37 But some of them said, "Could not he who opened the eyes of the blind man also have kept this man from dying?"

---

a 11:19, **the Jews:** Some manuscripts read "of Jerusalem." D(05) Latin (d).

b 11:19, **those around:** Included in 𝔓45, A(02) BYZ, TR.

c 11:20, **the:** 𝔓66 reads "her."

d 11:21, **Jesus:** 𝔓66 reads "the Lord."

e 11:21, **Lord:** Absent from B(03).

f 11:22, **But:** Absent from 𝔓75 ℵ(01) B(03) C(04) Latin(a) SBLGNT.

g 11:25, **So:** Included in 𝔓75 ‖ Some manuscripts read "But." ℵ(01) Latin(d).

h 11:25, **and the life:** Absent from 𝔓45 Syriac(sy^s).

i 11:26, **in me:** Absent from W(032).

j 11:28, **this:** Some manuscripts read "these things."

k 11:28, **secretly:** Some manuscripts read "in silence." D(05) Latin (a b d e ff²).

l 11:28, **that:** Included in 𝔓66 D(05) W(032) Latin(d).

m 11:29, **But:** Absent from 𝔓66 A(02) D(05) Latin(a d e) BYZ TR.

n 11:30, **into:** Some manuscripts read "upon." 𝔓45 𝔓66.

o 11:30, **still:** Absent from 𝔓45 A(02) D(05) BYZ TR Latin(d).

p 11:31, **thinking highly of her:** 𝔓45 𝔓75 ℵ(01) B(03) C(04) D(05) Latin(d) NA28 SBLGNT THGNT ‖ Some manuscripts read "saying." 𝔓66 A(02) Latin (a b e ff²) BYZ TR.

q 11:32, **him:** Absent from D(05) Latin(d).

r 11:32, **to him:** Absent from 𝔓66 D(05) Latin(a d).

s 11:34, **Lord:** Absent from 𝔓66.

38 Jesus, [therefore,]ᵃ again deeply moved within himself, came to the tomb. It was a cave, and a stone {lay upon it}.ᵇ 39 Jesus says, "Remove the stone." Martha, [the sister of the deceased,]ᶜ says to him, "[Lord,]ᵈ There is already a stench, [for]ᵉ he has been dead four days."

40 Jesus says to her, "Did I not tell you [that]ᶠ if you believed, you would see the glory of God?" 41 So they took away the stone [[from where the dead man was lying]].ᵍ And Jesus lifted [up]ʰ his eyes and said, "Father, I thank you that you have heard me. 42 [But]ⁱ I knew that you always hear me, but I said this on account of the people standing around, that they may believe that you sent me."

43 When he had said these things, he cried out with a loud voice, "Lazarus, come out." 44 [[And]]ʲ [[immediately,]]ᵏ The man who had died came out, his hands and feet bound with linen strips, and his face wrapped with a cloth. Jesus says to them, "Unbind him, and let him go."

45 [Therefore,]ˡ Many of the Jews, who had come with Mary, [and]ᵐ having seen what {he}ⁿ did, believed in him. 46 But some of them went to the Pharisees and told them what Jesus had done.

47 So the chief priests and the Pharisees gathered the council and said, "What are we to do? For this man performs many signs. 48 If we let him go on like this, everyone will believe in him, and the Romans will come and take away both our place and our nation."

49 But one of them, Caiaphas, who was high priest that year, said to them, "You know nothing at all. 50 Nor do you consider that it is to {your}ᵒ advantage that one man should die for the people, and not that the whole nation should perish." 51 He did not say this of his own accord, but being high priest [of that year]ᵖ he prophesied that Jesus would die for the nation, 52 and not for the nation only, but also to gather into one the children of God who are scattered abroad.

53 From that day on, they plotted to kill him. 54 Therefore, Jesus no longer walked openly among the Jews, but went [from there]�q to the region [[of Samphourein]]ʳ near the wilderness, to a city called Ephraim, and there he {stayed}ˢ with {the}ᵗ disciples.

55 Now the Passover of the Jews was near, and many went up to Jerusalem

---

ᵃ 11:38, **therefore:** Absent from Latin (a b e ff²).

ᵇ 11:38, **lay upon it:** Some manuscripts read "was lying against it." ℵ(01) Latin(a b e ff²).

ᶜ 11:39, **the sister of the deceased:** Absent from Latin(b e ff²) Syriac(syˢ).

ᵈ 11:39, **Lord:** Absent from 𝔓66.

ᵉ 11:39, **for:** Absent from D(05) Latin(d).

ᶠ 11:40, **that:** Absent from 𝔓66.

ᵍ 11:41, **from where the dead man was lying:** Included in BYZ TR.

ʰ 11:41, **up:** Absent from Latin (b e).

ⁱ 11:42, **But:** Absent from D(05) Latin(d) ‖ Some manuscripts read "And." Latin (a e ff²).

ʲ 11:44, **And:** Included in ℵ(01) A(02) D(05) W(032) Latin(a b d e ff²).

ᵏ 11:44, **immediately:** Included in D(05) Latin(d).

ˡ 11:45, **Therefore:** Absent from 𝔓45. ‖ ℵ(01) reads "But."

ᵐ 11:45 , **and:** Absent from 𝔓45 𝔓66 D(05) Latin(a b d).

ⁿ 11:45, **he:** Some manuscripts read "Jesus." ℵ(01) D(05) Latin(a d ff²) BYZ TR.

ᵒ 11:50, **your:** 𝔓45 𝔓66 B(03) D(05) Latin(a b d e ff²) Syriac(sy) ‖ Some manuscripts read "our." A(02) W(032) BYZ TR ‖ Absent from ℵ(01).

ᵖ 11:51, **of that year:** Absent from 𝔓45 Latin(e) Syriac(syˢ).

q 11:54, **from there:** Absent from 𝔓66 D(05) Latin (a b c d e ff²).

ʳ 11:54, **of Samphourein:** Included in D(05) Latin(d).

ˢ 11:54, **stayed:** 𝔓66 𝔓75 ℵ(01) B(03) W(032) NA28 SBLGNT THGNT ‖ Some manuscripts read "spent time." A(02) D(05) Latin (a b d e ff²) BYZ TR.

ᵗ 11:54, **the:** 𝔓45 𝔓66 ℵ(01) B(03) D(05) W(032) Latin(d) NA28 SBLGNT THGNT ‖ Some manuscripts read "his." A(02) Latin (a b e ff²) Syriac(sy) BYZ TR.

from the region before the Passover
to purify themselves. 56 So they were
looking for Jesus and said to one
another as they stood in the temple,
“What do you think? That he will not
come to the feast?” 57 And the chief
priests and the Pharisees had given
orders that if anyone knew where he
was, they should report it, so that they
might seize him.

12 1 Therefore, Jesus came to
Bethany {six}[a] days before the
Passover, where Lazarus was [[who had
been dead]],[b] whom Jesus had raised
from the dead. 2 They made a dinner
for him there, and Martha served, but
Lazarus was one of those {reclining}[c]
with him.

3 Then Mary, taking a pound of
[very costly][d] pure [nard][e] perfume,
anointed the feet of Jesus and wiped his
feet with her hair; and the house was
filled with the fragrance of the perfume.

4 {But}[f] Judas {Iscariot}[g] [[son of
Simon]],[h] one of his disciples, the one
who was going to betray him, says,
5 “Why was this perfume not sold for
three hundred denarii and given to the
poor?” 6 He said this not because he
cared about the poor, but because he
was a thief and, having the money box,
he used to take what was put into it.

7 Jesus therefore said, “Leave her
alone, {so that she may keep it}[i] for the
day of [my][j] burial. 8 [For you always
have the poor with you, but you do not
always have me].”[k]

9 A large crowd of the Jews {then
knew}[l] that he was there, and they
came not [only][m] because of Jesus, but
also to see Lazarus, whom {he}[n] had
raised [from the dead].[o] 10 But the chief
priests planned to put Lazarus to death
as well, 11 because on account of him
many of the Jews were [going away
and][p] believing in Jesus.

12 On the next day, the large crowd
that had come to the feast, when
they heard that Jesus was coming
to Jerusalem, 13 took the branches of
the palm trees and went out to meet
him, and they cried out, [[saying,]][q]
“Hosanna! Blessed is the one who
comes in the name of the Lord, [and][r]
the king of Israel.”

14 And Jesus, having found a young
donkey, sat on it, as it is written, 15 “Do
not fear, daughter of Zion; behold,
{your}[s] king is coming, seated on a
donkey's colt.”[t]

---

[a] 12:1, **six:** 𝔓66 reads “five.”
[b] 12:1, **who had been dead:** Included in 𝔓66 A(02) D(05) Latin(d) Syriac(sy^{s}) BYZ TR || Absent from ℵ(01) B(03) W(032) Latin (a b e ff^{2}) NA28 SBLGNT THGNT.
[c] 12:2, **reclining:** Some manuscripts read “being gathered together.” W(032) TR.
[d] 12:3, **very costly:** Absent from Latin(a b e ff^{2}).
[e] 12:3, **nard:** Absent from D(05) Latin (d e).
[f] 12:4, **But:** 𝔓66 ℵ(01) B(03) W(032) Latin(b ff^{2}) NA28 SBLGNT THGNT || Some manuscripts read “Therefore.” A(02) D(05) Latin (d) BYZ TR || Absent from Latin(a e).
[g] 12:4, **Iscariot:** Some manuscripts read “of Kerioth.” (05) Latin(d).
[h] 12:4, **son of Simon:** Included in BYZ TR.
[i] 12:7, **so that she may keep it:** Some manuscripts read “she has kept this.” A(02) BYZ TR.
[j] 12:7, **my:** Absent from D(05) Latin(d).
[k] 12:8, **For you always...:** Absent from D(05) Latin(d) Syriac(sy^{s}) || 𝔓75 reads “For you always have the poor.” || “For” is absent from some additional manuscripts. 𝔓66 Latin(e).
[l] 12:9, **then knew:** Some manuscripts read “heard.” D(05) Latin(a b d e ff^{2}).
[m] 12:9, **only:** Absent from D(05) Latin(b d e) Syriac(sy^{s}).
[n] 12:9, **he:** Some manuscripts read “Jesus.” A(02) D(05) Latin(d).
[o] 12:9, **from the dead:** Absent from W(032).
[p] 12:11, **going away and:** Absent from 𝔓66.
[q] 12:13, **saying:** Included in 𝔓66 ℵ(01) A(02) D(05) Latin(a d ff^{2}) Syriac(sy^{s}).
[r] 12:13, **and:** Absent from 𝔓66 A(02) D(05) Latin(a b d e ff^{2}) BYZ TR.
[s] 12:15, **your:** A(02) reads “the.”
[t] 12:15, Zechariah 9:9.

16 His disciples did not understand these things at first, but when Jesus was glorified, [then]ᵃ they remembered that these things were written about him and that they had done these things to him.

17 So the crowd that was with him when he called Lazarus out of the tomb and raised him from the dead bore witness. 18 For this reason the [[large]]ᵇ crowd [also]ᶜ met him, because they heard that he had performed this sign.

19 The Pharisees then said to one another, "You see that you are gaining nothing. Look, the [[whole]]ᵈ world has gone after him."

20 There were [[also]]ᵉ some Greeks among those who went up to worship at the feast. 21 [So]ᶠ These men came to Philip, who was from Bethsaida in Galilee, and asked him, saying, "Sir, we wish to see Jesus." 22 Philip comes and tells Andrew, {Andrew and Philip come and they tell Jesus}.ᵍ

23 And Jesus answers them, saying, "The hour has come for the Son of Man to be glorified.

24 "Truly, truly, I say to you, unless a grain of wheat falls into the earth and dies, it remains alone; but if it dies, it bears much fruit.

25 "The one who loves his life {destroys it},ʰ and the one who hates his life in this world will keep it for eternal life.

26 "If anyone serves me, they must follow me; and where I am, [there]ⁱ will my servant be also. [[And]]ʲ If anyone serves me, the Father will honor them.

27 "Now my soul is troubled, and what shall I say? 'Father, save me from this hour'? But for this purpose I have come to this hour. 28 Father, glorify {your}ᵏ name [[in the glory that I had with you before the world came into being]]."ˡ Then a voice came from heaven, [[saying,]]ᵐ "I have glorified it, and I will glorify it again."

29 [So]ⁿ The crowd that stood there and heard it said [that]ᵒ it had thundered. [[But]]ᵖ Others said [[that]],�q "An angel has spoken to him."

30 Jesus answered [and said],ʳ "This voice has come for your sake, not mine.

31 "Now is the judgment of this world; now the ruler of this world will be cast out. 32 And I, when I am lifted up from the earth, will draw all people to myself." 33 He said this to show by what kind of death he was going to die.

34 [So]ˢ The crowd answered him, "We have heard from the Law that the Christ remains forever. How can you say [that]ᵗ the Son of Man must be

---

ᵃ 12:16, **then:** Absent from 𝔓66, W(032) Latin(b e ff²).
ᵇ 12:18, **large:** Included in ℵ(01).
ᶜ 12:18, **also:** Absent from 𝔓66 𝔓75 Latin(a b e ff²).
ᵈ 12:19, **whole:** Included in D(05) Latin(a b d e ff²).
ᵉ 12:20, **also:** Included in D(05) Latin(d).
ᶠ 12:21, **So:** Absent from Latin(a e).
ᵍ 12:22, **Andrew and Philip come and they tell Jesus:** Some manuscripts read "and again Andrew and Philip told Jesus." 𝔓66 ℵ(01) D(05) W(032) Latin (d) BYZ TR.
ʰ 12:25, **destroys it:** Some manuscripts read "will destroy it." A(02) D(05) BYZ TR.
ⁱ 12:26, **There:** Absent from D(05) Latin(d).
ʲ 12:26, **And:** Included in A(02) BYZ TR.
ᵏ 12:28, **your:** B(03) reads "my."
ˡ 12:28, **in the glory that I had with you before the world came into being:** Included in D(05).
ᵐ 12:28, **saying:** Included in D(05) Latin(a d e) Syriac(syˢ).
ⁿ 12:29, **So:** Absent from B(03) Latin(a) ‖ Some manuscripts read "But." W(032).
ᵒ 12:29, **that:** Absent from D(05) Latin(d).
ᵖ 12:29, **But:** Included in W(032).
q 12:29, **that:** Included in D(05) Latin(d).
ʳ 12:30, **and said:** Absent from ℵ(01).
ˢ 12:34, **So:** Absent from A(02) D(05) Latin (a b d e ff²) BYZ TR.
ᵗ 12:34, **that:** Absent from 𝔓75 BYZ.

lifted up? [Who [[then]]^a is this Son of Man?]"^b

35 So Jesus said to them, "The light is {among}^c you for a little while longer. Walk while you have the light, lest darkness overtake you; and the one who walks in the darkness does not know where he is going. 36 While you have the light, believe in the light, so that you may become children of light." Jesus spoke these things, and going away, he hid himself [from them].^d

37 Although he had performed so many signs before them, they did not believe in him, 38 so that the word of Isaiah the prophet might be fulfilled, [which he said,]^e "Lord, who has believed our report? And to whom has the arm of the Lord been revealed?" ^f

39 For this reason they could not believe, because again Isaiah said, 40 "Their {eyes have been blinded and their heart has been hardened},^g so that they may not see with their eyes and understand with their heart and turn, and I would heal them."^h

41 Isaiah said these things {because}ⁱ he saw {his glory},^j and he spoke about him.

42 Nevertheless, many of the rulers believed in him, but because of the Pharisees they did not confess him, so that they would not be put out of the synagogue; 43 for they loved the glory of men more than the glory of God.

44 Jesus [[therefore]]^k cried out and said, "Whoever believes in me does not believe in me, but in the one who sent me. 45 [And whoever sees me sees the one who sent me.]^l

46 "I have come as a light into the world, so that everyone who believes in me should not remain in darkness.

47 "And if anyone hears my words and does not {keep them},^m I do not judge him; for I did not come to judge the world, but to save the world. 48 The one who rejects me and does not receive my words has a judge; the word that I have spoken will judge him on the last day. 49 For I have not spoken on my own, but the Father who sent me has himself given me a commandment about what to say and what to speak. 50 And I know that his commandment is eternal life. What I speak, just as the Father has told me, thus I speak."

13 1 Now before the feast of the Passover, Jesus, knowing that his hour had come to depart from this world to the Father, having loved his own who were in the world, he loved them to the end.

2 And during supper, the devil having already put into the heart that Judas, son of Simon Iscariot, to betray him.

---

^a 12:34, **then:** Included in D(05) Latin(d).

^b 12:34, **Who is this Son of Man:** Absent from 𝔓75.

^c 12:35, **among:** Some manuscripts read "with." A(02)Syriac(sy^s) BYZ TR.

^d 12:36, **from them:** Absent from Latin(a e).

^e 12:38, **which he said:** Absent from 𝔓75.

^f 12:38, Isaiah 53:1 LXX.

^g 12:40, **eyes have been blinded and their heart has been hardened:** Some manuscripts read "heart has been blinded." D(05) Latin(d).

^h 12:40, Isaiah 6:10 LXX.

ⁱ 12:41, **because:** Some manuscripts read "when." D(05) Latin(a b d ff²) BYZ TR ‖ W(032) reads "since."

^j 12:41, **his glory:** Some manuscripts read "the glory of his God." D(05) Latin(d) ‖ Other manuscripts including the f13 family read "the glory of God."

^k 12:44, **therefore:** Included in D(05) Latin(d).

^l 12:45, **And whoever sees me sees the one who sent me:** Absent from Latin(b) and six later Greek texts (030 178 579 703 825 944).

^m 12:47, **keep them:** Some manuscripts read "believe." BYZ TR.

3 [[Jesus]][a] knowing that the Father
had given all things into his hands, and
that he had come from God and was
going to God, 4 rose from supper, laid
aside his garments, and taking a towel,
girded himself. 5 Then he poured water
into a basin and began to wash [the][b]
disciples' feet and to wipe them with
the towel with which he was girded.

6 So he comes to Simon Peter; he
says to him, "[Lord,][c] are you washing
my feet?" 7 Jesus answered and said
to him, "What I am doing you do not
understand now, but you will know
after this."

8 Peter says to him, "[[Lord,]][d]
You shall never wash my feet." Jesus
answered him, "If I do not wash you,
you have no part with me." 9 [Simon][e]
Peter says to him, "[Lord,][f] Not my feet
only, but also my hands and my head."

10 "The one who has bathed does
not need to wash, [except for his feet,][g]
but is completely clean; and you are
clean, but not all." 11 For he knew who
would betray him. [Therefore [he][h]
said, "Not all of you are clean."][i]

12 So when he had washed their feet,
and taken his garments, [and sat down
again, he said to them,][j] "Do you know
what I have done to you? 13 You call me
Teacher and Lord, and you say well,
for so I am. 14 If I then, your Lord and
Teacher, have washed your feet, [[how
much more]][k] you also ought to wash
one another's feet. 15 [For][l] I have given
you an example, that as I have done to
you, you also should do.

16 "Truly, truly, I say to you, a
servant is not greater than his master,
nor is an apostle [greater][m] than the
one who sent him. 17 If you know these
things, blessed are you if you do them.

18 "I do not speak concerning all of
you; I know whom I have chosen; but
that the Scripture may be fulfilled, 'He
who eats {bread with me}[n] has lifted up
his heel against me.'[o]

19 "[From now on I tell you before][p]
It happens, so that you may believe
when it happens that I am. 20 Truly,
truly, I say to you, he who receives
whomever I send receives me; and he
who receives me receives the one who
sent me."

21 After saying these things, Jesus
was troubled in spirit, and testified
and said, "Truly, truly, I say to you,
one of you will betray me." 22 {{The}[q]
disciples [[therefore]][r] were looking at
one another, perplexed about whom he
was speaking.}[s]

---

a 13:3, **Jesus:** Included in A(02) Syriac(sy^s) BYZ TR.
b 13:5, **the:** Some manuscripts read "his." D(05) Latin(d).
c 13:6, **Lord:** Absent from ℵ(01).
d 13:8, **Lord:** Included in D(05) Latin(d).
e 13:9, **Simon:** Absent from D(05) Latin(d).
f 13:9, **Lord:** Absent from ℵ(01).
g 13:10, **except for his feet:** Absent from ℵ(01).
h 13:11, **he:** Some manuscripts read "Jesus." D(05) Latin(d).
i 13:11, **Therefore he said...:** Absent from D(05) Latin(d).
j 13:12, **and sat down again, he said to them:** Absent from A(02).
k 13:14, **how much more:** Included in D(05) Latin(a d ff^2).
l 13:15, **For:** Absent from 𝔓66 Latin(d).
m 13:16, **greater:** Absent from 𝔓66.
n 13:18, **bread with me:** B(03) C(04) NA28 SBLGNT THGNT ‖ Some manuscripts read "my bread." 𝔓66 ℵ(01) A(02) D(05) W(032) Latin(a b d e ff^2) Syriac(sy) BYZ TR.
o 13:18, Psalm 41:9.
p 13:19, **From now on I tell you before:** Absent from 𝔓66.
q 13:22, **The:** Some manuscripts read "His." 𝔓66 Latin(a).
r 13:22, **therefore:** Included in 𝔓66 ℵ(01) A(02) D(05) W(032) Latin(b d ff^2) BYZ TR. ‖ Absent from B(03) D(05) Latin(e) NA28 SBLGNT THGNT.
s 13:22, **The disciples...:** ℵ(01) reads "So the Jews were looking at each other, the disciples were perplexed about what he was saying."

23 One of his disciples, whom Jesus loved, was reclining at the table at Jesus' side. 24 [So]ᵃ Simon Peter signals to this one {to find out who it might be about whom he is speaking}.ᵇ 25 [So,]ᶜ Having leaned back on Jesus' chest, he says to him, "Lord, who is it?"

26 Jesus answered [[and said]],ᵈ "That one is to whom I will {dip the bread and give it to him.}"ᵉ So when he had dipped the bread, he gave it to Judas, son of Simon {Iscariot}.ᶠ 27 [And after the bread,]ᵍ [Then]ʰ Satan entered into him. So Jesus says to him, "What you are doing, do quickly."

28 [But]ⁱ No one at the table knew why he said this to him. 29 For some thought, since Judas had the money box, that Jesus was telling him, "Buy what we need for the festival," or to give something to the poor. 30 So, having received the morsel, he immediately went out. And it was night.

31 [Therefore,]ʲ When he went out, Jesus says, "Now the Son of Man has been glorified, and God has been glorified in him. 32 [If God was glorified in him,]ᵏ God will also glorify him in himself. [And immediately, he will glorify him.]ˡ

33 "Little children, I am with you a little while longer; you will seek me, and just as I said to the Jews, 'Where I am going, you cannot come,' I say to you now.

34 "A new commandment I give to you, that you love one another. [Just as I have loved you, you also should love one another.]ᵐ 35 [For]ⁿ In this all men will know that you are my disciples, if you have love for one another."

36 Simon Peter says to him, "Lord, where are you going?" Jesus answered [him],ᵒ "Where I am going, you cannot follow me [now],ᵖ but you will follow [[me]]ۋ later." 37 {Peter}ʳ says to him, "[Lord,]ˢ Why can't I follow you [now]?ᵗ I will lay down my life for you." 38 Jesus answered [him]ᵘ [[and said to him]],ᵛ "Will you lay down your life for me? Truly, truly, I say to you, [that]ʷ the rooster will not crow until you have denied me three times.

ᵃ 13:24, **So:** Absent from C(04).

ᵇ 13:24, **to find out who:** Some manuscripts read "And he says to him, 'Tell, who is it?'" 𝔓66 B(03) C(04) Latin(b ff²).

ᶜ 13:25, **So:** Absent from A(02) B(03) C(04) Latin (ff²) BYZ TR SBLGNT.

ᵈ 13:26, **and said:** Included in ℵ(01) D(05) Latin(d).

ᵉ 13:26, **dip the bread and give it to him:** B(03) C(04) NA28 SBLGNT THGNT ‖ Some manuscripts read "give the dipped bread." 𝔓66 ℵ(01) A(02) D(05) Latin(a b d e ff²) BYZ TR ‖ W(032) reads "to whom I shall dip this piece of bread and give it to him."

ᶠ 13:26, **Iscariot:** Some manuscripts read "of Karyot." D(05) Latin(d).

ᵍ 13:27, **And after the bread:** Absent from D(05) Latin(d e).

ʰ 13:27, **Then:** Absent from ℵ(01) D(05) Latin(a b d ff²).

ⁱ 13:28, **But:** Absent from B(03) W(032).

ʲ 13:31, **Therefore:** Absent from A(02) BYZ TR.

ᵏ 13:32, **if God was glorified in him:** B(03) Latin (e) BYZ TR NA28[] SBLGNT THGNT ‖ Absent from 𝔓66 ℵ(01) B(03) C(04) D(05) W(032) Latin(a b d ff²).

ˡ 13:32, **And immediately, he will glorify him:** Absent from W(032).

ᵐ 13:34, **Just as I have loved you, you also should love one another.:** Absent from C(04) f13 family.

ⁿ 13:35, **For:** Absent from D(05) Latin(d).

ᵒ 13:36, **him:** Absent from B(03) C(04) Latin(a b e ff²) SBLGNT.

ᵖ 13:36, **now:** Absent from D(05) Latin(d).

ۋ 13:36, **me:** Included in Latin(b d) BYZ TR.

ʳ 13:37, **Peter:** Some manuscripts read "he." D(05) Latin(d).

ˢ 13:37, **Lord:** Absent from ℵ(01).

ᵗ 13:37, **now:** Absent from C(04).

ᵘ 13:38, **him:** Included in Latin(b) BYZ TR.

ᵛ 13:38, **and said to him:** Included in D(05) Latin(d ff²).

ʷ 13:38, **that:** Included in D(05) Latin(d).

14 [[And he said to his disciples,]]^a "Do not let your hearts be troubled; believe in God and believe in me. ²In my Father's house are many dwelling places; if it were not so, would I have told you [that]^b I go to prepare a place for you? ³[And]^c If I go and prepare a place for you, I will come again and take you to myself, so that where I am, you may be also. ⁴And where I am going, you know [, and you know]^d the way."

⁵Thomas [[who is called Didymus,]]^e says to him, "Lord, we do not know where you are going; [[and]]^f how can we know the way?" ⁶Jesus says to him, "I am the way, and the truth, and the life; no one comes to the Father except through me. ⁷If you have know [me],^g you will also know my Father. From now on you do know him and have seen [him]."^h

⁸Philip says to him, "Lord, show us the Father, and we will be satisfied." ⁹Jesus says to him, "Have I been with you all this time, and you still do not know me, Philip? Whoever has seen me has seen the Father. How can you say, 'Show us the Father'?

¹⁰"Do you not believe that I am in the Father and the Father is in me? The words that I say to you I do not speak on my own; but the Father who dwells in me {does his}^i works. ¹¹Believe me that I am in the Father and the Father is in me; but if not, believe [[in me]]^j because of the works themselves.

¹²"Truly, truly, I say to you, he who believes in me will also do the works that I do, [and greater works than these will he do,]^k because I am going to {the}^l Father.

¹³"And whatever you ask [[the Father]]^m in my name, I will do [this],^n that the Father may be glorified in the Son.

¹⁴["If you ask anything [of me]^o in my name, [[this]]^p I will do it.]^q

¹⁵"If you love me, you will keep my commandments. ¹⁶And I will ask the Father, and he will give you another Advocate,^r {so that it^s may be} 'with you forever, ¹⁷the Spirit of truth, which the world cannot receive, because it does not perceive it nor knows [[it]].^u [[But]]^v You know it, because it remains with you and will be {in}^w you.

---

^a 14:1, **And he said to his disciples:** Included in D(05) Latin(a d).
^b 14:2, **that:** Absent from 𝔓66 Latin(a e) BYZ TR.
^c 14:3, **And:** Absent from A(02) D(05) W(032) Latin(d).
^d 14:4, **and you know:** Included in A(02) D(05) Latin(b d e ff²) BYZ TR.
^e 14:5, **who is called Didymus:** Included in D(05) Latin(d).
^f 14:5, **and:** Included in ℵ(01) A(02) D(05) Latin(d e ff²) BYZ TR.
^g 14:7, **me:** Absent from ℵ(01).
^h 14:7, **him:** Absent from B(03).
^i 14:10, **does his:** Some manuscripts read "he does the."
^j 14:11, **in me:** Included in A(02) B(03) Latin(a b ff²) BYZ TR.
^k 14:12, **and greater works than these will he do:** Absent from Latin(e).
^l 14:12, **the:** Some manuscripts read "my." Latin(e) BYZ TR.
^m 14:13, **the Father:** Included in Latin(b).
^n 14:13, **this:** Absent from Latin(b ff²).
^o 14:14, **of me:** Absent from A(02) D(05) Latin(a d e ff²) TR.
^p 14:14, **this:** Included in 𝔓75 A(02) B(03).
^q 14:14, Verse 14 is absent from some manuscripts. Latin(b) Syriac(sy^s) f1 family.
^r 14:16, **Advocate:** The Greek word *paraclete* is often translated as Comforter, Helper, or Counselor. BDAG states "In the few places where the word is found in pre-Christian and extra-Christian literature as well it has for the most part a more general sense: one who appears in another's behalf, mediator, intercessor, helper." (BDAG, παράκλητος).
^s 14:16-17, **it:** "It" is the neutral rendering of GPT-4 that encompasses interpretations of the subject being a person, personification, or thing. In English, "it" can refer to either a person or a thing.
^t 14:16, **so that it may be:** Some manuscripts read "to be." D(05) Latin(d).
^u 14:17, **it:** Or "this.", Included in A(02) Latin(b d e ff²) BYZ TR.
^v 14:17, **But:** Included in A(02) D(05) Latin(d e ff²) BYZ TR.
^w 14:17, **in:** Some manuscripts read "with." Latin(b ff²).

18 "I will not leave you as orphans; I am coming to you.

19 "Yet a little while and the world will see me no more, but you will see me. Because I live, you also will live. 20 {In}[a] That day you will know that I am in my Father, and you in me, and I in you.

21 "Whoever has my commandments and keeps them, he it is who loves me. And he who loves me will be loved by my Father, and I will love him and manifest myself to him."

22 Judas (not {Iscariot}[b]) says to him, "Lord, {[And]c how is it that you will}[d] reveal yourself to us, and not to the world?"

23 Jesus answered him, "If anyone loves me, he will keep my word, and my Father will love him, and we will come to him and make our dwelling with him. 24 Whoever does not love me does not keep my words. And the word that you hear is not mine but the Father's who sent me.

25 "These things I have spoken to you while I am still with you. 26 But the Advocate, the Holy Spirit,[e] which {the}[f] Father will send in my name, that one will teach you all things [and remind you of all][g] that I have said to you.

27 "[[My]][h] Peace I leave with you; my peace I give to you. [Not as the world gives do I give to you.][i] Let not your hearts be troubled, neither let them be afraid. 28 You heard that I said to you, 'I am going away, and I will come to you.' If you loved me, you would have rejoiced, because [[I said]][j] I am going to {the}[k] Father, for {the}[l] Father is greater than I.

29 "[And][m] Now I have told you before it takes place, so that when it does take place you may believe.

30 "I will no longer talk much with you, for the ruler of this world is coming. And he has nothing [[to find]][n] in me, 31 but I do as the Father has {commanded me},[o] so that the world may know that I love the Father. Rise, let us go from here."

15 1 "I am the true vine, and my Father is the gardener. 2 Every branch in me that does not bear fruit, he takes away; and every branch that bears fruit, he prunes it so that it may bear more fruit.

3 "You are already clean because of the word which I have spoken to you.

4 "[Abide in me, and I in you.][p] Just as the branch cannot bear fruit by itself unless it abides in the vine, so neither can you unless you abide in me.

---

a 14:20, **In:** Absent from W(032) Latin(a).

b 14:22, **Iscariot:** Some manuscripts read "The one from Kerioth." D(05) Latin(d).

c 14:22, **and:** Absent from 𝔓66 𝔓75 A(02) B(03) D(05) Latin(a b d e ff²) BYZ TR.

d 14:22, **how is it that you will:** Some manuscripts read "what is the reason that you are going to." D(05) Latin(b).

e 14:26, **Spirit:** The Greek word is given the following definitions by BDAG: (1) air in movement, *blowing, breathing,* (2) that which animates or gives life to the body, *breath, (life-)spirit,* (3) a part of human personality, *spirit,* (4) an independent noncorporeal being, in contrast to a being that can be perceived by the physical senses, *spirit,* or (5) God's being as controlling influence, with focus on association with humans, *Spirit, spirit...* (c) Because of its heavenly origin and nature this Spirit is called (the) Holy Spirit. (BDAG, πνεῦμα).

f 14:26, **the:** Some manuscripts read "my." D(05) Latin(d).

g 14:26, **and remind you of all:** Absent from Latin(b).

h 14:27, **My:** Included in Latin(a e ff²).

i 14:27, **Not as the world gives do I give to you:** Absent from Latin(e).

j 14:28, **I said:** Included in BYZ TR.

k 14:28, **the:** Some manuscripts read "my." ℵ(01) Latin(a) BYZ TR.

l 14:28, **the:** Some manuscripts read "my." BYZ TR.

m 14:29, **and:** Absent from Latin(b ff²).

n 14:30, **to find:** Included in D(05) Latin(a d).

o 14:31, **commanded me:** Some manuscripts read "has given a command." D(05) Latin(d e).

p 15:4, **Abide in me, and I in you:** Absent from D(05) Latin(d).

5 "[[For]]ᵃ I am the vine, you are the branches. Whoever abides in me and I in him, this one bears much fruit, for apart from me you can do nothing.

6 "If anyone does not abide in me, he is thrown away like a branch and withers; and they gather them and throw them into the fire, and they are burned.

7 "[[But]]ᵇ If you abide in me and my words abide [in you],ᶜ {ask}ᵈ whatever you wish, and it will be done [for you].ᵉ

8 "In this my Father is glorified, that you bear much fruit and {become}ᶠ my disciples.

9 "Just as the Father has loved me, so I have loved you; abide in my love.

10 "[If you keep my commandments, you will {abide}ᵍ in my love,]ʰ Just as I have kept {my}ⁱ Father's commandments and abide in his love.

11 "[[But]]ʲ These things I have spoken to you, that my joy may {be}ᵏ in you, and that your joy may be full.

12 "This is my commandment, that you love one another as I have loved you.

13 "No one has greater love than this, that he lay down his life for his friends.

14 "[[For]]ˡ You are my friends if you do {what}ᵐ I command you. 15 No longer do I call you servants, for the servant does not know what his master is doing; but I have called you friends, for all that I have heard from my Father I have made known to you.

16 "You did not choose me, but I chose you and appointed you so that you might go and bear fruit, fruit that will last, so that whatever you ask the Father in my name, he may give it to you.

17 "These things I command you, that you love one another. 18 If the world hates you, know that it has hated me first [before you].ⁿ

19 "If you were of the world, the world would love its own. [But]ᵒ Because you are not of the world, but I chose you out of the world, therefore the world hates you.

20 "Remember the word that I said to you, 'A servant is not greater than his master.' If they persecuted me, they will also persecute you; if they kept my word, they will also keep yours. 21 But [all]ᵖ these things they will do [to you]�q on account of my name, because they do not know the one who sent me.

22 "If I had not come and spoken to them, they would not have sin; but now they have no excuse for their sin. 23 Whoever hates me hates my Father [also].ʳ

24 "If I had not done among them the works that no one else did, they would not have sin; but now they have seen and hated both me and my Father. 25 But this is to fulfill the word that is

---

ᵃ 15:5, **for:** Included in D(05) Latin(a d).
ᵇ 15:7, **But:** Included in D(05) Latin(d).
ᶜ 15:7, **in you:** Absent from ℵ(01).
ᵈ 15:7, **ask:** Some manuscripts read "you will ask." ℵ(01) BYZ TR.
ᵉ 15:7, **for you:** Absent from some manuscripts 𝔓66 D(05) Latin(d e).
ᶠ 15:8, **become:** Some manuscripts read "you will become." BYZ TR.
ᵍ 15:10, **abide:** Or "remain."
ʰ 15:10, **If you keep my commandments...:** Absent from ℵ(01).
ⁱ 15:10, **my:** Some manuscripts read "the." 𝔓66 Latin(e).
ʲ 15:11, **But:** Included in D(05) Latin(d).
ᵏ 15:11, **be:** Some manuscripts read "remain." ℵ(01) BYZ TR.
ˡ 15:14, **For:** Included in ℵ(01) D(05) Latin(d).
ᵐ 15:14, **what:** Some manuscripts read "as much as."
ⁿ 15:18, **before you:** Absent from ℵ(01) D(05) Latin(a b d e ff²).
ᵒ 15:19, **But:** Absent from D(05) Latin(d e).
ᵖ 15:21, **all:** Absent from D(05) Latin(d).
q 15:21, **to you:** Absent from ℵ(01).
ʳ 15:23, **also:** Absent from 𝔓66 D(05) Latin(a d e ff²).

written in their law, 'They hated me without a cause.'[a]

26 "[[But]][b] When the Advocate[c] comes, which I will send to you from {the}[d] Father, the Spirit[e] of truth that proceeds from {the}[f] Father, that one will bear witness about me. 27 [But][g] You also will bear witness, because you have been with me from the beginning."

16 1 "I have spoken these things to you so that you may not be caused to stumble.

2 "They will make you outcasts from the synagogue; but an hour is coming when everyone who kills [you][h] will think they are offering service to God. 3 They will do these things because they have not known the Father or me. 4 [But][i] I have spoken these things to you, so that when {their}[j] time comes, you may remember [them],[k] that I told you. But I did not tell you these things from the beginning, because I was with you.

5 "But now I am going to the one who sent me, and none of you asks me, 'Where are you going?' 6 [But][l] Because I have spoken these things to you, sorrow has filled your heart.

7 "But I tell you the truth, it is to your advantage that I go away. For if I do not go away, the Advocate[m] will not come to you. [But if I go, I will send it[n] to you.][o]

8 "And when that one comes, it will convict the world concerning sin, and concerning righteousness, and concerning judgment; 9 concerning sin, because they do not believe in me; 10 concerning righteousness, because I am going to {the}[p] Father and you will see me no longer; 11 concerning judgment, because the ruler of this world has been judged.

12 "I still have many things to say to you, but you cannot bear them now. 13 [But][q] When that one, the Spirit of truth, comes, {it}[r] will guide you into [all][s] truth; for it will not speak on its own, but whatever it hears, it will speak, and it will declare to you the things that are to come. 14 That one will glorify me, because it will take from what is mine and declare it to you.

15 ["All that the Father has is mine; for this reason I said that {it takes}[t] from what is mine and will declare it to you.][u]

---

a 15:25, Psalm 35:19, 69:4.

b 15:26, **But:** Included in A(02) D(05) BYZ TR Latin(a b d ff²).

c 15:26, **Advocate:** For the definition of the Greek word, see the footnote of 14:16.

d 15:26, **the:** Some manuscripts read "my." D(05) Latin(a d ff²).

e 15:26, **Spirit:** For the definition of the Greek word, see the footnote of 14:26

f 15:26, **the:** Some manuscripts read "my." D(05) Latin(a d ff²).

g 15:27, **But:** Absent from Latin(a b d e ff²).

h 16:2, **you:** Absent from B(03).

i 16:4, **But:** Absent from D(05) Latin(a d e).

j 16:4, **their:** Some manuscripts read "the." ℵ(01) D(05) BYZ TR Latin(a d ff²).

k 16:4, **them:** Absent from ℵ(01) D(05) Latin(a b d e ff²) BYZ TR.

l 16:6, **But:** Absent from A(02).

m 16:7, **Advocate:** For the definition of the Greek word, see the footnote of 14:16.

n 16:7-8, **it:** "It" is the neutral rendering of GPT-4 that encompasses interpretations of the subject being a person, personification, or thing. In English, "it" can refer to either a person or a thing.

o 16:7, **But if I go, I will send…:** Absent from 𝔓66.

p 16:10, **the:** Some manuscripts read "my." A(02) BYZ TR.

q 16:13, **But:** Absent from D(05) W(032) Latin(d e).

r 16:13-15, **it:** "It" is the neutral rendering of GPT-4 that encompasses interpretations of the subject being a person, personification, or thing. In English, "it" can refer to either a person or a thing.
∥ Some manuscripts read "that one." D(05) Latin(a d).

s 16:13, **all:** Absent from ℵ(01).

t 16:15, **it takes:** Some manuscripts read "it will take." A(02) TR.

u 16:15 Verse 15 is absent from some manuscripts. 𝔓66 ℵ(01) and early Sahidic and Bohairic witnesses.

16 "A little while, and you will see me {no longer};[a] and again a little while, and you will see me [[because I go to the Father]]."[b]

17 So the disciples said to one another, "What is this that he says to us, 'A little while and you will not see me, and again a little while and you will see me'; and, 'Because I am going to the Father'?" 18 [They were saying,][c] "What is this that [he says][d] 'the little while'? We do not know [what he speaks]."[e]

19 Jesus [[therefore]][f] knew that they wanted to ask him, so he said [to them],[g] "Are you discussing among yourselves what I meant when I said, 'A little while, and you will not see me, and again a little while, and you will see me'?

20 "Truly, truly, I say to you, you will weep and mourn, but the world will rejoice. [[But]][h] You will be sorrowful, but your sorrow will turn into joy.

21 "When a woman is giving birth, she has sorrow because her hour has come, but when she has delivered the child, she no longer remembers the anguish, for joy that a person has been born into the world.

22 "So also you have sorrow now, but I will see you again, and your hearts will rejoice, and no one will take your joy away from you.

23 "[And][i] [On][j] That day you will not ask [me][k] anything. Truly, truly I say to you, {if}[l] you ask the Father for anything {in my name, he will give it to you}.[m] 24 Until now you have asked for nothing in my name; ask and you will receive, so that your joy may be complete.

25 "I have said these things to you in figures of speech. [[But]][n] The hour is coming when I will no longer speak to you in parables but will tell you plainly about {the}[o] Father.

26 "In that day you will ask in my name, and I do not say to you that I will ask {the}[p] Father [on your behalf];[q] 27 for the Father himself loves you, because you have loved me and have believed that I came from {God}.[r]

28 "{[I came forth {from}[s] the Father][t] And}[u] I have come into the world; Again, I leave the world and go to the Father."

---

a 16:16, **no longer:** Some manuscripts read "not." A(02) Latin(a d e) BYZ TR.

b 16:16, **because I go to the Father:** Included in A(02) BYZ TR.

c 16:18, **They were saying:** Absent from D(05) Latin (a b d e) Syriac(sy^s).

d 16:18, **he says:** Absent from 𝔓66, ℵ(01) D(05) W(032) Latin(a b d e ff²).

e 16:18, **what he speaks:** Absent from B(03).

f 16:19, **therefore:** Included in A(02) Latin(ff²) BYZ TR.

g 16:19, **to them:** Absent from A(02).

h 16:20, **But:** Included in A(02) W(032) BYZ TR.

i 16:23, **And:** Absent from Latin(e).

j 16:23, **On:** Absent from W(032).

k 16:23, **me:** Absent from Latin(e ff²).

l 16:23, **if:** Some manuscripts read "whatever." M*(01) Latin(a) BYZ TR.

m 16:23, **in my name, he will give it to you:** NA28 ‖ Some manuscripts read "he will give you in my name." 𝔓5 ℵ(01) B(03) C(04) SBLGNT THGNT.

n 16:25, **But:** Included in A(02) Latin(ff²) BYZ TR.

o 16:25, **the:** Some manuscripts read "my." 𝔓66.

p 16:26, **the:** Some manuscripts read "my." D(05) Latin(d).

q 16:26, **on your behalf:** Absent from 𝔓5 𝔓66 Latin(b e).

r 16:27, **God:** Some manuscripts read "the Father." B(03) C(04) D(05) Latin(d).

s 16:28, **from:** 𝔓5 𝔓22 ℵ(01) A(02) BYZ TR NA28 SBLGNT THGNT ‖ Some manuscripts read "out of" or "of." B(03) C(04). This variant is classified with {C} in the UBS-5 critical apparatus, which states, "The letter C indicates that the Committee had difficulty in deciding which variant to place in the text."

t 16:28, **I came forth from the Father:** Absent from D(05) W(032) Latin(b ff²) Syriac(sy^s) Also absent from Lycopolitanic and proto-Bohairic (NA-28).

u 16:28, **I came forth from the Father and:** Some manuscripts read "From the Father." Latin(a b).

29 {His}[a] disciples say [[to him]],[b] "See, now you speak plainly and not using any parables. 30 Now we know that you know everything and do not need anyone to question you; in this we believe that you came from God."

31 Jesus answered them, "Do you now believe? 32 Behold, the hour is coming, indeed it has [[now]][c] come, when you [[all]][d] will be scattered, each to his own home, and will leave me alone. Yet I am not alone, for the Father is with me.

33 "[[But]][e] These things I have spoken to you, so that in me you may have peace. [In the world {you have}[f] tribulation.][g] But take heart, I have overcome the world."

17 1 Jesus spoke these things, and lifting up his eyes to heaven, he said, "Father, the hour has come; glorify your Son, so that {the}[h] Son [[also]][i] may glorify you, 2 just as you have given him authority over all flesh, so that {he may give eternal life to all whom you have given him}.[j]

3 "And this is eternal life, that they may know [you,][k] the only true God, and the one whom you have sent, Jesus Christ [[into this world]].[l]

4 "I have glorified you on the earth, [{having}[m] finished][n] {the}[o] work which you have given me to do; 5 And now, glorify me, Father, with yourself, with the glory {which I had before the world was, with you}.[p]

6 "I have made your name known to the men whom you gave me from {the}[q] world. They were yours, and you gave them to me, and they have kept your word. 7 [And][r] Now they have known that all things which you have given to me are from you; 8 for [the][s] words that you gave to me I have given to them, and they [have received them {and}[t] know in truth}[u] that I came from you; and they have believed that you sent me.

9 "I am asking on their behalf; I am not asking on behalf of the world, but on behalf of those whom you have given me, for they are yours. 10 {All mine are yours, and yours are mine;}[v] and {I have been glorified in them}.[w]

---

[a] 16:29, **His:** Some manuscripts read "The." W(032) Latin(a).
[b] 16:29, **to him:** Included in 𝔓5 A(02) W(032) Latin(a b d ff²) Syriac(sy^s sy^p).
[c] 16:32, **now:** Included in Latin(e) BYZ TR.
[d] 16:32, **all:** Included in 𝔓66.
[e] 16:33, **But:** Included in 𝔓66.
[f] 16:33, **you have:** Some manuscripts read "you will have." א(01) W(032).
[g] 16:33, **In the world you have tribulation:** Absent from some manuscripts 𝔓66.
[h] 17:1, **the:** Some manuscripts read "your." A(02) D(05) Latin(a b) Syriac(sy) BYZ TR.
[i] 17:1, **also:** Included in BYZ TR.
[j] 17:2, **he may give eternal life to all whom you have given him:** Some manuscripts read "so that everything you have given him may have eternal life." D(05) Latin(d).
[k] 17:3, **you:** Absent from W(032).
[l] 17:3, **into this world:** Included in D(05) Latin(d).
[m] 17:4, **having:** Some manuscripts read "and have." D(05).
[n] 17:4, **having finished:** Absent from Latin(a).
[o] 17:4, **the:** W(032) reads "your."
[p] 17:5, **which I had before the world was, with you:** Some manuscripts read "which I had with you before the world existed." 𝔓66 Latin(a) ‖ Some manuscripts read "that I had with you before the world came into being." D(05) Latin(d).
[q] 17:6, **the:** Some manuscripts read "this." 𝔓66 Latin(a b d).
[r] 17:7, **And:** Included in Latin(b ff²).
[s] 17:8, **the:** Some manuscripts read "your." D(05) Latin(d).
[t] 17:8, **have received them and:** Absent from 𝔓66.
[u] 17:8, **know in truth:** Some manuscripts read "truly." א(01) A(02) D(05) W(032) Latin(a d e).
[v] 17:10, **All mine are yours, and yours are mine:** א(01) reads "To me, you have given them."
[w] 17:10, **I have been glorified in them:** Some manuscripts read "you have glorified me." D(05) Latin(d).

11 "And I am {no longer}ᵃ in {the}ᵇ world, and they are in the world, and I am coming to you. [[I am no longer in the world. And in the world,]]ᶜ Holy Father, keep them in {your}ᵈ name which you have given me. [[And when I was with them, I was keeping them in your name.]]ᵉ [So that they may be one as we are].ᶠ

12 "When I was with them [[in the world]],ᵍ I kept them in {your}ʰ name [, which you have given me]ⁱ [[, so that they may be one as we are]].ʲ [And]ᵏ I guarded them, and none of them perished except the son of destruction, so that the scripture might be fulfilled.

13 "But now I am coming to you, and I speak these things in {the}ˡ world so that they may have my joy made complete in {themselves}.ᵐ 14 [[But]]ⁿ I have given them your word, and the world has hated them, because they are not of {the}ᵒ world [, just as I am not of the world].ᵖ

15 "I am not asking that you take them out of the world, but that you keep them from the evil one.

16 "They are not of {the}ᑫ world, just as I am not of the world. 17 Sanctify them in {the}ʳ truth. [Your word is truth.]ˢ 18 As you have sent me into {the}ᵗ world, so I have sent them into {the}ᵘ world. 19 And for their sake I sanctify myself, so that they also may be sanctified in truth.

20 "Not concerning these only do I ask, but also concerning those who believe in me through their word, 21 that they may all be [one],ᵛ as you, Father, are in me and I am in you, may they also be [[one]]ʷ in us, so that the world may believe that you have sent me.

22 "And {the}ˣ glory that you have given me I have given them, so that they may be one in us, just as we are one, 23 I in them and you in me, that they may become completely one, {so that}ʸ the world may know that you have sent me and have loved them even as you have loved me.

24 "Father, I desire that those also, whom you have given me, may be with me where I am, to see {my}ᶻ glory, which you have given me because you

---

ᵃ 17:11, **no longer:** A(02) reads "yet."

ᵇ 17:11, **the:** Some manuscripts read "this." D(05) Latin(a b d ff²).

ᶜ 17:11, **I am no longer in the world. And in the world:** Included in 𝔓107 D(05) Latin(a d).

ᵈ 17:11, **your:** 𝔓66 reads "my."

ᵉ 17:11, **And when I was with them, I was keeping them in your name:** Included in D(05).

ᶠ 17:11, **so that they may be one as we are:** Some manuscripts contain this in verse 12 after "which you have given me." 𝔓66 Latin(b e ff²).

ᵍ 17:12, **in the world:** Included in A(02) BYZ TR.

ʰ 17:12, **your:** 𝔓66 reads "my."

ⁱ 17:12, **which you have given me:** Absent from 𝔓66 ℵ(01).

ʲ 17:12, **so that they may be one as we are:** Included in ℵ(01).

ᵏ 17:12, **And:** Absent from A(02) D(05) Latin(a b e ff²) BYZ TR.

ˡ 17:13, **the:** Some manuscripts read "this." D(05) Latin(a b d ff²).

ᵐ 17:13, **themselves:** C(04) reads "in their own hearts."

ⁿ 17:14, **But:** Included in D(05) Latin(d).

ᵒ 17:14, **the:** Some manuscripts read "this." D(05) Latin(a d).

ᵖ 17:14, **just as I am not of the world:** Absent from 𝔓66 ℵ(01) Latin (b d e).

ᑫ 17:16, **the:** Some manuscripts read "this." D(05) Latin(b d).

ʳ 17:17, **the:** Some manuscripts read "your." BYZ TR.

ˢ 17:17, **Your word is truth:** Absent from ℵ(01).

ᵗ 17:18, **the:** Some manuscripts read "this." D(05) Latin(a b d).

ᵘ 17:18, **the:** Some manuscripts read "this." D(05) Latin(b d).

ᵛ 17:21, **one:** Absent from C(04).

ʷ 17:21, **one:** Included in ℵ(01) A(02) BYZ TR THGNT.

ˣ 17:22, **the:** W(032) reads "my."

ʸ 17:23, **so that:** Some manuscripts read "and." 𝔓66 ℵ(01) W(032) Latin(b) ∥ Some manuscripts read "and so that." A(02) BYZ TR.

ᶻ 17:24, **my:** Some manuscripts read "the." D(05) Latin(d).

loved [me][a] before the foundation of
the world.

25 “Righteous Father, {the}[b] world
does not know you. [But][c] I know you;
and these know that you have sent me.
26 I made your name known to them,
and I will make it known, so that the
love with which you have loved me
may be in them, and I in them.”

18 1 After saying these things, Jesus
went out with his disciples
across the Kidron ravine, where there
was a garden, into which he and his
disciples entered. 2 Now Judas, the one
betraying him, also knew the place,
because Jesus had often gathered there
with {his}[d] disciples.

3 So Judas, having taken the cohort
and servants from the chief priests and
[from the][e] Pharisees, comes there with
lanterns and torches and weapons.

4 {Therefore},[f] Jesus, knowing all
the things coming upon him, went
out and said to them, “Whom are you
seeking?” 5 They answered him, “Jesus
the Nazarene.” {He}[g] says to them, “I
am [[Jesus]].”[h] Now Judas, [the one
betraying him],[i] was also standing with
them. 6 [So][j] When he said [to them],[k]
[[that]][l] “I am,” they stepped back and
fell to the ground.

7 Again he asked them [[saying]],[m]
“Whom are you seeking?” And they
said [[again]],[n] “Jesus of Nazareth.”
8 {Jesus}[o] answered [[them]],[p] “I told
you that I am. So if you are seeking me,
let these others go,” 9 in order to fulfill
the word he had spoken, “Of those you
have given me, {I have not lost any of
them}.”[q]

10 Then Simon Peter, having a
sword, drew it and struck the high
priest's servant, cutting off his right ear.
The servant's name was Malchus.

11 So Jesus said to Peter, “Put your
sword back into its sheath. Shall I not
drink the cup that {the}[r] Father has
given me?”

12 So the cohort and the commander
and the officers of the Jews arrested
Jesus and bound him. 13 They led
him first to Annas, for he was the
father-in-law of Caiaphas, who was
high priest that year. 14 {Now}[s] Caiaphas
was the one who had advised the Jews
that it was beneficial for one man to die
on behalf of the people.

---

[a] 17:24, **me:** Absent from Latin(e).
[b] 17:25, **the:** Some manuscripts read “this.” D(05) Latin(d).
[c] 17:25, **But:** Absent from A(02).
[d] 18:2, **his:** Some manuscripts read “the.” 𝔓66 Latin(e).
[e] 18:3, **from the:** 𝔓66 𝔓108 ℵ(01) D(05) Latin(a) NA28 SBLGNT THGNT || Absent from A(02) C(04) W(032) Latin(b e) BYZ TR.
[f] 18:4, **Therefore:** Some manuscripts read “But.” ℵ(01) D(05) Latin(a b).
[g] 18:5, **he:** Some manuscripts read “Jesus.” BYZ TR.
[h] 18:6, **Jesus:** Included in B(03) Latin(a) Syriac(sy^s) This variant is classified with {C} in the UBS-5 critical apparatus, which states, “The letter C indicates that the Committee had difficulty in deciding which variant to place in the text.”
[i] 18:5, **the one betraying him:** Absent from 𝔓66.
[j] 18:6, **so:** Absent from A(02).
[k] 18:6, **to them:** Absent from ℵ(01).
[l] 18:6, **that:** Included in C(04) BYZ TR.
[m] 18:7, **saying:** Included in D(05).
[n] 18:7, **again:** Included in D(05).
[o] 18:8, **Jesus:** Some manuscripts read “he.” 𝔓60.
[p] 18:8, **them:** Included in D(05).
[q] 18:9, **I have not lost any of them:** Some manuscripts read “of them, I have lost none.” D(05) Latin(d).
[r] 18:11, **the:** Some manuscripts read “my.” 𝔓66.
[s] 18:14, **Now:** Some manuscripts read “And.” C(04).

15 Simon Peter and {another}[a] disciple followed {Jesus}.[b] [But that disciple was known to the high priest,][c] And he went with Jesus into the courtyard of the high priest.

16 But Peter was standing outside at the door. So the [other][d] disciple, who was known to the high priest, went out and spoke to the doorkeeper and brought Peter in. 17 The servant girl at the door says to Peter, "Are you also one of this man's disciples?" He said, "I am not."

18 Now the servants and officers had made a charcoal fire because it was cold, and they were warming themselves. Peter also was standing with them and warming himself.

19 The high priest questioned Jesus about his disciples and his teaching. 20 Jesus answered [him],[e] "I have spoken openly to the world. I always taught in synagogues and in the temple, where all the Jews come together, and I have said nothing in secret. 21 Why do you ask me? Ask those who have heard what I said to them; they know what I said."

22 When he had said these things, one of the officers standing by struck Jesus, saying, "Is that how you answer the high priest?" 23 [[But]][f] Jesus {answered}[g] him, "If I have spoken wrongly, testify about the wrong; but if rightly, why do you strike me?"

24 [So][h] Annas sent him bound to Caiaphas the high priest.[i]

25 Now Simon Peter was standing and warming himself. They said [to him],[j] "Are you not also one of his disciples?" He denied it and said, "I am not." 26 One of the servants of the high priest, a relative of the man whose ear Peter had cut off, says, "Did I not see you in the garden with him?" 27 Peter denied it again, and immediately a rooster crowed.

28 So they led Jesus from Caiaphas to the governor's headquarters; it was early morning. They themselves did not enter the headquarters, so that they would not be defiled but could eat the Passover. 29 Pilate then went [out][k] to them and said, "What accusation do you bring [against][l] this man?"

30 They answered and said to him, "If this one were not {doing evil},[m] we would not have handed him over to you." 31 [[Therefore]][n] Pilate said to them, "Take him yourselves and judge [him][o] according to your law." [[So]][p] The Jews said to him, "It is not lawful for us to put {anyone}[q] to death," 32 so that the word of Jesus might be fulfilled, [which he spoke][r] signifying what kind of death he was going to die.

---

a 18:15, **another:** Some manuscripts read "the other."

b 18:15, **Jesus:** C(04) reads "them."

c 18:15, **But that disciple was known to the high priest:** Absent from 𝔓66.

d 18:16, **other:** Absent from 𝔓66.

e 18:20, **him:** Absent from C(04) Latin(a b).

f 18:23, **But:** Included in ℵ(01) W(032).

g 18:23, **answered:** Some manuscripts read "said to." ℵ(01) W(032).

h 18:24, **So:** Absent from A(02) BYZ TR ‖ Some manuscripts read "But." ℵ(01) Syriac(sy^s).

i 18:13-24, Old Syriac (sy^s) has a different sequence of verses 13-24 in the order: 13, 24, 14, 15, 19-23, 16-18.

j 18:25, **to him:** Absent from C(04).

k 18:29, **out:** Absent from A(02) D(05) BYZ TR.

l 18:29, **against:** Absent from ℵ(01) B(03) Latin(e).

m 18:30, **doing evil:** Some manuscripts read "an evildoer." A(02) Latin(b ff²) BYZ TR.

n 18:31, **Therefore:** Included in 𝔓66.

o 18:31, **him:** Absent from ℵ(01) W(032).

p 18:31, **So:** Included in 𝔓60 ℵ(01) W(032) Latin(a b ff²) BYZ TR ‖ Some manuscripts read "But." A(02).

q 18:31, **anyone:** ℵ(01) reads "any Jew."

r 18:32, **which he spoke:** Absent from ℵ(01).

33 So {Pilate}[a] entered the headquarters again, called [Jesus],[b] and said to him, "Are you the king of the Jews?" 34 Jesus answered [[him]],[c] "Do you say this of your own accord, or did others tell you about me?" 35 Pilate answered, "Am I a Jew? Your own nation and the chief priests have handed you over to me; what have you done?"

36 Jesus answered, "My kingdom is not of this world; if my kingdom were of this world, my servants would have been fighting [perhaps][d] that I might not be delivered over to the Jews; but now my kingdom is not from here."

37 Pilate said to him, "So you are a king?" Jesus answered, "You say that I am a king. I was born for this and I have come into the world for this, to testify {to}[e] the truth. Everyone who is of the truth hears my voice."

38 Pilate says to him, "What is truth?" And having said this, he went out again to the Jews and said to them, "I find no guilt in him. 39 But you have a custom that I should release one man for you at the Passover; do you want me to release for you the king of the Jews?"

40 They cried out again, [saying,][f] "Not this one, but Barabbas!" Now Barabbas was a robber.

19 1 Then Pilate took Jesus and had him flogged. 2 And the soldiers twisted together a crown of thorns and put it on his head and wrapped him in a purple robe. 3 [And they came up to him,][g] And they said, "Hail, King of the Jews!" and struck him with their hands.

4 {And}[h] Pilate went out again and says to them, "Look, I am bringing him out to you, so that you may know that I find no guilt [in him]."[i]

5 So Jesus came out, wearing the crown of thorns and the purple robe. [And he says to them, "Behold the man!"][j]

6 So when the chief priests and the officers saw him, they cried out [saying,][k] "Crucify [, crucify][l] [[him]]."[m] Pilate said [to them],[n] "You take him and crucify him; for I find no fault in him." 7 The Jews answered [him],[o] "We have a law, and according to {that}[p] law he ought to die because he made himself the Son of God."

---

a 18:33, **Pilate:** 𝔓60 reads "he."

b 18:33, **Jesus:** Absent from 𝔓60.

c 18:34, **him:** Included in ℵ(01) BYZ TR.

d 18:36, **perhaps:** Absent from B(03) Latin(a b e).

e 18:37, **to:** D(05) reads "about."

f 18:40, **saying:** Absent from 𝔓66 Latin(b e ff²).

g 19:3, **they came up to him:** Absent from A(02) BYZ TR.

h 19:4, **And:** Some manuscripts read "So." 𝔓66 W(032) Latin(b ff²) BYZ TR ‖ Absent from ℵ(01) Latin(a e).

i 19:4, **in him:** Absent from ℵ(01).

j 19:5, **And he says to them, Behold, the man:** Absent from 𝔓66 Latin(a e ff²).

k 19:6, **saying:** Absent from ℵ(01) Latin(a b e).

l 19:6, **crucify:** Absent from 𝔓66 𝔓90 Latin(a e).

m 19:6, **him:** Included in ℵ(01) A(02) BYZ Latin(b ff²).

n 19:6, **to them:** Absent from 𝔓66.

o 19:7, **him:** Absent from 𝔓66 ℵ(01) W(032) Latin(a b e ff²).

p 19:7, **that:** Some manuscripts read "our." A(02) BYZ TR.

8 When Pilate heard this statement, he was even more afraid, 9 and he entered the governor's headquarters [again]ᵃ and says to Jesus, "Where are you from?" But Jesus gave him no answer. 10 [So]ᵇ Pilate says to him, "You will not speak to me? Do you not know that I have authority to release you and authority to crucify you?" 11 Jesus answered him, "You would have no authority over me at all unless it had been given you from above. Therefore he who delivered me over to you has the greater sin." 12 From then on Pilate sought to release him, but {the Jews}ᶜ cried out [saying],ᵈ "If you release this man, you are not Caesar's friend. Everyone who makes himself a king opposes Caesar."

13 So when Pilate heard these words, he brought Jesus out and sat down on the judgment seat at a place called The Stone Pavement, and in Aramaic, Gabbatha. 14 Now it was the day of Preparation of the Passover. It was about the sixth hour. He says to the Jews, "Behold your King!" 15 {They cried out},ᵉ "Away with him, [away with him,]ᶠ crucify him!" Pilate says to them, "Shall I crucify your King?" The chief priests answered, "We have no king but Caesar."

16 Then he handed him over to them to be crucified. So they took Jesus [[and led him away]],ᵍ 17 and [he went out, bearing his [own]ʰ cross,]ⁱ he went out to the place called Skull Place, which is called Golgotha in Hebrew.ʲ 18 There they {crucified}ᵏ him, and with him two others, one on either side, and Jesus between them.

19 Pilate also wrote an inscription and put it on the cross. It read, "Jesus of Nazareth, the King of the Jews." 20 [Many of the Jews read this inscription, for the place where Jesus was crucified was near the city, and it was written in Aramaic, {in Latin, and in Greek}.ˡ]ᵐ

21 [So the chief priests of the Jews said to Pilate, "Do not write, 'The King of the Jews,']ⁿ But rather, he said, 'I am King of the Jews.'" 22 Pilate answered, "What I have written, I have written."

23 When the soldiers had crucified Jesus, they took his garments and divided them into four parts, one part for each soldier; [also his tunic.]ᵒ But the tunic was seamless, woven in one piece from top to bottom. 24 So they said to one another, "Let us not tear it, but cast lots for it to see whose it shall be." This was to fulfill the Scripture [which says],ᵖ "They divided my garments among them, and for my clothing they cast lots."�q So the soldiers did these things.

25 But standing by the cross [of Jesus]ʳ were his mother and his mother's sister, Mary the wife of Clopas, and Mary Magdalene.

ᵃ 19:9, **again:** Absent from ℵ(01).

ᵇ 19:10, **So:** Absent from ℵ(01) A(02).

ᶜ 19:12, **the:** 𝔓60 reads "they."

ᵈ 19:12, **saying:** Absent from ℵ(01).

ᵉ 19:15, **They cried out:** Some manuscripts read "But they were saying." 𝔓66 ℵ(01) W(032).

ᶠ 19:15, **away with him:** The second occurrence is absent from some manuscripts. 𝔓66.

ᵍ 19:16, **and led him away:** Included in 𝔓60 𝔓66 ℵ(01) W(032) TR.

ʰ 19:17, **own:** Absent from B(03) BYZ TR SBLGNT.

ⁱ 19:17, **he went out, bearing his own cross:** Absent from 𝔓66.

ʲ 19:17, **Hebrew:** Hebrew/Aramaic (BDAG, Ἑβραϊστί).

ᵏ 19:18, **crucified:** 𝔓66 reads "crowned."

ˡ 19:20, **Latin, and in Greek:** Some manuscripts swap the order of to read "Greek, and in Latin." A(02) BYZ TR.

ᵐ 19:20, **and:** Absent from ℵ(01).

ⁿ 19:21, **So the chief priests...:** Absent from ℵ(01).

ᵒ 19:23, **also his tunic:** Absent from ℵ(01) Latin(a b ff²).

ᵖ 19:24, **which says:** Absent from ℵ(01) B(03) Latin(a b e ff²).

q 19:24, Psalm 22:18.

ʳ 19:25, **of Jesus:** Absent from W(032).

26 When Jesus saw his mother and
the disciple whom he loved standing
nearby, he says to his mother, "Woman,
behold, your son!" 27 Then he says to the
disciple, "Behold, your mother!" And
from that {hour}[a] the disciple took her
to his own home.

28 After this, Jesus, knowing that
all was now finished, says [(to fulfill
the Scripture),][b] "I thirst."[c] 29 [So][d] A
vessel full of sour wine was lying there;
so they {put a sponge full of the sour
wine on hyssop}[e] and brought it to his
mouth. 30 So when {Jesus}[f] had received
the sour wine, he said, "It is finished,"
and he bowed his head and gave up
his spirit.

31 So the Jews, since it was the day
of Preparation, in order not to leave the
bodies on the cross during the Sabbath
(for that Sabbath was a great day),
asked Pilate to have their legs broken
and removed. 32 The soldiers came and
broke the legs of the first and the other
who had been crucified with him.
33 But when they came to Jesus and saw
that he was already dead, they did not
break his legs, 34 but one of the soldiers
pierced his side with a spear, and
immediately blood and water came out.

35 And the one who has seen has
testified, and his testimony is true,
[and][g] he knows that he speaks the
truth, so that you [also][h] may believe.
36 For these things happened so that
the Scripture would be fulfilled,
"Not a bone of his will be broken."[i]
37 And again another Scripture says,
"They will look on the one whom they
pierced."[j]

38 After these things, Joseph from
Arimathea, who was a disciple of Jesus,
but secretly for fear of the Jews, asked
Pilate that he might take away the body
of Jesus. [And Pilate permitted it.][k] So
he came and took {his body}[l] away.
39 And Nicodemus also came, the one
who had first come to {him}[m] at night,
bringing a mixture of myrrh and aloes,
about a hundred pounds.

40 They took the body of {Jesus}[n]
and wrapped it in linen cloths with the
spices, as {is}[o] the custom of the Jews
for burial.

41 Now in the place where he was
crucified there was a garden, and in the
garden a new tomb in which no one
had yet been laid. 42 Therefore, because
of the preparation of the Jews, since the
tomb was nearby, they laid Jesus there.

20 1 On the first day of the week,
Mary Magdalene came [early,][p]
while it was still dark, to the tomb and
saw the stone removed from [[the door
of]][q] the tomb. 2 So she ran and came to
Simon Peter and to the other disciple
whom Jesus loved and says to them,
"They have taken the Lord out of the
tomb, and we do not know where they
have laid him."

---

a 19:27, **hour:** Some manuscripts read "day." A(02).
b 19:28, **to fulfill the Scripture:** Absent from 𝔓66.
c 19:28, Psalm 22:15, 69:21.
d 19:29, **So:** Included in BYZ TR || ℵ(01) reads "But."
e 19:29, **put a sponge full of the sour wine on hyssop:** Some manuscripts read "and the filled a sponge with vinegar, and put it on hyssop." A(02) BYZ TR.
f 19:30, **Jesus:** Some manuscripts read "he." ℵ(01) Latin(a).
g 19:35, **and:** Absent from ℵ(01) A(02) BYZ TR.
h 19:35, **also:** Absent from BYZ TR.
i 19:36, Exodus 12:46, Numbers 9:12, Psalm 34:20.
j 19:37, Zechariah 12:10 (Hebrew text).
k 19:38, **And Pilate permitted it:** Absent from 𝔓66. || A(02) reads "And Pilate turned away."
l 19:38, **his body:** Some manuscripts read "him." ℵ(01) W(032) Latin(a b e ff^2).
m 19:39, **him:** Some manuscripts read "Jesus." Latin(a b e ff^2) BYZ TR.
n 19:40, **Jesus:** A(02) reads "God."
o 19:40, **is:** Some manuscripts read "was." ℵ(01) W(032).
p 20:1, **early:** Absent from W(032) Latin(a b).
q 20:1, **the door of:** Included in ℵ(01) W(032) Latin(d).

3 So Peter and the other disciple went out [and came to the tomb].[a]

4 The two were running together, {and the other disciple}[b] outran Peter and came first to the tomb, 5 and stooping down, he saw the linen cloths lying there [, but he did not go in].[c]

6 So Simon Peter [also][d] comes, following him, and he enters into the tomb, and he sees the linen cloths lying there, 7 and the face cloth, which had been on his head, not lying with the linen cloths but rolled up in a place by itself.

8 Then the other disciple, who had come first to the tomb, also went in, and he saw and believed; 9 for they did not yet understand the Scripture, that he must rise from the dead. 10 So the disciples went away again to their own homes.

11 But Mary stood outside the tomb weeping. As she wept, she bent over to look into the tomb, 12 and she saw [two][e] angels in white sitting, one at the head and one at the feet, where the body of Jesus had lain. 13 [And][f] They say to her, "Woman, why are you weeping? [[Who are you seeking?]]"[g] She says to them, "They have taken away my Lord, and I do not know where they have laid him."

14 [[And]][h] Having said this, she turned around and saw Jesus standing there, but she did not know that it was {Jesus}.[i] 15 Jesus says to her, "Woman, why are you weeping? Whom are you seeking?" She, thinking that he is the gardener, says to him, "Sir, if you have carried him away, tell me where you have laid him, and I will take him away."

16 Jesus says to her, "Mary." She turns and says to {him}[j] [in Hebrew],[k] "Rabboni," which means Teacher.

17 Jesus says to her, "Do not touch me, for I have not yet ascended to {the}[l] Father; but go to {my}[m] brothers and say to them, '[[Behold,]][n] I am ascending to my Father and your Father, and to my God and your God.'"

---

a 20:3, **and came to the tomb:** Absent from ℵ(01).

b 20:4, **and the other disciple:** ℵ(01) reads "but he."

c 20:5, **but he did not go in:** Absent from ℵ(01).

d 20:6, **also:** Absent from A(02) BYZ TR Latin(a b d ff²).

e 20:12, **two:** Absent from ℵ(01) Latin(e).

f 20:13, **And:** Absent from ℵ(01) Latin(a b d ff²).

g 20:13, **Who are you seeking:** Absent from A(02) D(05) Latin(d).

h 20:14, **And:** Included in BYZ TR.

i 20:14, **Jesus:** Some manuscripts read "the Lord." 𝔓66 Latin(b).

j 20:16, **him:** Some manuscripts read "Lord." D(05) Latin(d e ff²).

k 20:16, **in Hebrew:** Absent from A(02) Latin(a) BYZ TR.

l 20:17, **the:** Some manuscripts read "my." 𝔓66 A(02) Latin(a ff²) BYZ TR.

m 20:17, **the:** Some manuscripts read "my." ℵ(01) D(05) W(032) Latin(d e).

n 20:17, **behold:** Included in ℵ(01).

18 Mary Magdalene came, {announcing to the disciples, "I have seen the Lord},"[a] and that he had said these things to her.

19 On the evening of that day, the first day of the week, the doors being locked where the disciples were [[assembled]][b] for fear of the Jews, Jesus came and stood among them and said [to them],[c] "Peace be with you." 20 When he had said this, he showed them his hands and his side. Then the disciples rejoiced when they saw the Lord.

21 Then {Jesus}[d] said to them again, "Peace be with you. As the Father has sent me, even so I am sending you." 22 [And][e] Having said this, he breathed on them and says to them, "Receive the Holy Spirit;

23 "If you forgive the sins of any, they are forgiven them; if you retain the sins of any, they are retained."

24 Now Thomas, one of the twelve, called the Twin, was not with them when Jesus came. 25 [So][f] The other disciples told him, "We have seen the Lord." [But][g] He said to them [[that]],[h] "Unless I see in his hands the mark of the nails, and place my finger into the mark of the nails, and place my hand into his side, I will not believe."

26 Eight days later, his disciples were inside again, and Thomas was with them. Jesus came, the doors being locked, and stood in their midst and said, "Peace be with you." 27 Then he says to Thomas, "Put your finger here and see my hands; and bring your hands, and put it in my side. Do not be unbelieving, but believing."

28 Thomas answered and said to him, "My Lord and my God!"[i] 29 [[But]][j] Jesus says to him, "because you have seen me, you have believed? Blessed are those who have not seen and yet have believed."

30 Now Jesus did many other signs in the presence of {the}[k] disciples, which are not written in this book; 31 but these are written so that you may believe that Jesus is the Christ,[l] the Son of God, and that by believing you may have [[eternal]][m] life in his name.

---

a 20:18, **announcing to the disciples, "I have seen the Lord":** Some manuscripts read "reporting to his disciples that she had seen the Lord." D(05) Latin(d e).

b 20:19, **assembled:** Included in Latin(b e ff²) BYZ TR.

c 20:19, **to them:** Absent from ℵ(01).

d 20:21, **Jesus:** Some manuscripts read "he." ℵ(01) D(05) W(032) Latin(a d e) Syriac(sy^s).

e 20:22, **And:** Absent from D(05) Latin(a).

f 20:25, **So:** Absent from ℵ(01).

g 20:25, **but:** Absent from ℵ(01).

h 20:25, **that:** Included in D(05) Latin(d).

i 20:28, **God:** The BDAG entry of the Greek word for "God" states, "Some writing in our literature uses the word θεός in reference to Christ without necessarily equating Christ with the Father, and therefore in harmony with the Shema of Israel. Dt. 6:4." BDAG further gives a fourth definition of θεός : "4 that which is nontranscendent but considered worth of special reverence or respect, *god* ... of humans θεοί John 10:34f; humans are called θεός in the Old Testament" (BDAG, θεός).

j 20:29, **But:** Included in ℵ(01) W(032) Latin(e).

k 20:30, **the:** A(02) B(03) SBLGNT ‖ Some manuscripts read "his." 𝔓66 ℵ(01) C(04) D(05) Latin(a b d e) Syriac(sy^s) BYZ TR NA28[] THGNT.

l 20:31, **Christ:** See footnote for Christ in Luke 2:11.

m 20:31, **eternal:** Included in ℵ(01) C(04) D(05) Latin(b d e).

21 1 After this, {Jesus}[a] revealed
himself again to {the}[b] disciples
by the Sea of Tiberias;[c] and he revealed
himself in this way. 2 Simon Peter,
Thomas called the Twin, Nathanael of
Cana in Galilee, the sons of Zebedee,
and two others of his disciples were
together. 3 Simon Peter says to them,
"I am going fishing." They say to him,
"We are coming with you as well."
They went out and got into the boat
[[immediately]],[d] and that night they
caught nothing. 4 Just as day was
breaking, Jesus stood [on the shore; yet
the disciples did not know that it was
Jesus].[e]

5 Jesus therefore says to them,
"[Children,][f] Do you have any fish?"
They answered him, "No." 6 [But][g]
He said to them, "Cast the net on the
right side of the boat, and you will
find some." [[But they said: "We have
toiled all night and caught nothing;
But at your word, we will cast."]][h] So
they cast it, and now they were not able
to haul it in, because of the quantity
of fish.

7 Therefore, that disciple whom
Jesus loved says to Peter, "It is {the}[i]
Lord." So when Simon Peter heard that
it was the Lord, he put on his outer
garment, for he was naked, and threw
himself into the sea. 8 But the other
disciples came in the boat, for they
were not far from the land, but about
two hundred cubits away, dragging the
net of fish.

9 When they got out on land, they
saw a charcoal fire in place, with fish
laid out on it, and bread. 10 Jesus says
to them, "Bring some of the fish that
you have just caught." 11 [So][j] Simon
Peter went aboard and hauled the net
ashore, full of large fish, 153 of them.
And although there were so many, the
net was not torn.

12 Jesus says to them, "Come and
have breakfast." [But][k] no one of the
disciples dared to question him, "Who
are you?" They knew it was the Lord.

13 [[Therefore]][l] Jesus came and
took the bread and [[having given
thanks]][m] he gives it to them, and so
with the fish.

14 This was now the third time that
{Jesus}[n] was revealed to {the}[o] disciples
after he was raised from the dead.

15 So when they had eaten breakfast,
Jesus says to Simon Peter, "Simon, son
of {John},[p] do you love me [more than
these]?"[q] He says to him, "Yes, Lord [,
you know that I love you]."[r] {He}[s] says
to him, "Feed my lambs."

---

a 21:1, **Jesus:** Some manuscripts read "he." D(05) Latin(d e).
b 21:1, **the:** Some manuscripts read "his." D(05) BYZ Latin(a b).
c 21:1, **Sea of Tiberias:** Another term for the Sea of Galilee.
d 21:3, **immediately:** Included in A(02) BYZ TR.
e 21:4, **on the shore; yet the disciples did not know that it was Jesus:** Absent from W(032).
f 21:5, **Children:** Absent from A(02) Latin(a).
g 21:6, **But:** Absent from ℵ(01) W(032).
h 21:6, **But they said...:** Included in 𝔓66.
i 21:7, **the:** Some manuscripts read "our." D(05) Latin(d).
j 21:11, **So:** Absent from A(02) D(05) Latin(a b d e ff^{2}) BYZ TR.
k 21:12, **But:** Absent from B(03) C(04).
l 21:13, **Therefore:** Included in A(02) Latin(ff^{2}) BYZ TR.
m 21:13, **having given thanks:** Included in D(05) Latin(d).
n 21:14, **Jesus:** Some manuscripts read "he." 𝔓122 W(032).
o 21:14, **the:** Some manuscripts read "his." D(05) Latin(b d) BYZ TR.
p 21:15, **John:** Some manuscripts read "Jonah." B(03) Syriac(sy) BYZ TR.
q 21:15, **more than these:** Absent from Latin(a b e ff^{2}).
r 21:15, **you know that I love you:** Absent from Latin(a e).
s 21:15, **He:** Some manuscripts read "Jesus." D(05) Latin(d).

16 {He}[a] says to him [again][b] [a second time],[c] "Simon, son of {John},[d] do you love me?" He says to him, "[Yes,][e] Lord, you know that I love you." He says to him, "Shepherd my sheep."

17 He says to him the third time, "Simon, son of {John},[f] do you love me?" Peter was grieved because he said to him the third time, "Do you love me?" [And][g] He says to him, "Lord, you know all things; you know that I love you." {Jesus}[h] says to him, "Tend my sheep."

18 "Truly, truly, I say to you, when you were young, you used to dress yourself and walk wherever you wanted, but when you are old, [you will stretch out your hands, and][i] another will dress you and {carry}[j] you where you do not want to go." 19 This he said, signifying by what kind of death he would glorify God. And having said this, he says to him, "Follow me."

20 [But][k] Peter turned and saw the disciple whom Jesus loved [following],[l] the one who also had leaned back against him during the supper and had said [[to him]],[m] "[Lord,][n] Who is it that is going to betray you?"

21 [When][o] Peter saw him, he says to Jesus, "[Lord,][p] What about this man?" 22 Jesus says to him, "If it is my will that he remain until I come, what is that to you? You follow me!"

23 So the saying spread abroad among the brothers [[and they thought]][q] that this disciple was not to die; yet Jesus did not say to him [that][r] he was not to die, but, "If it is my will that he remain until I come, [what is that to you]?"[s]

24 This is the disciple who [[also]][t] testifies about these things and who wrote these things, and we know that his testimony is true.

25 [But there are also many other things that [[Christ]][u] Jesus did, which if they were written one by one, I do not think the world itself could contain the books that would be written.][v] [[Amen]][wx]

---

[a] 21:16, **He:** D(05) reads "The Lord."
[b] 21:16, **again:** Absent from D(05) Latin(e).
[c] 21:16, **a second time:** Absent from ℵ(01) Latin(a b ff²).
[d] 21:16, **John:** Some manuscripts read "Jonah." B(03) Syriac(sy) BYZ TR.
[e] 21:16, **Yes:** Absent from ℵ(01).
[f] 21:17, **John:** Some manuscripts read "Jonah." B(03) Syriac(sy) BYZ TR.
[g] 21:17, **And:** Absent from A(02) Latin(a b).
[h] 21:17, **he:** Some manuscripts read "he." BYZ TR.
[i] 21:18, **you will stretch out your hands:** Absent from Latin(e).
[j] 21:18, **carry:** Some manuscripts read "take." 𝔓59 𝔓109 W(032) ‖ Some manuscripts read "lead." D(05) Latin(a b).
[k] 21:20, **But:** Included in 𝔓59 ℵ(01) D(05) BYZ TR.
[l] 21:20, **following:** Absent from ℵ(01) W(032) Latin(ff²).
[m] 21:20, **to him:** Included in ℵ(01) C(04) D(05) W(032) Latin(d ff²).
[n] 21:20, **Lord:** Absent from C(04).
[o] 21:21, **When:** Absent from A(02) W(032) BYZ TR.
[p] 21:21, **Lord:** Absent from ℵ(01).
[q] 21:23, **and they thought:** Included in D(05) Latin(d).
[r] 21:23, **that:** Absent from D(05) Latin(a b e).
[s] 21:23, **what is that to you?:** Absent from ℵ(01) Latin(a e).
[t] 21:24, **also:** Included in B(03) C(04) W(032).
[u] 21:25, **Christ:** Included in D(05) Latin(d).
[v] 21:25, **But there are also many other things…:** Absent from ℵ(01).
[w] 21:25, **Amen:** Included in BYZ TR.
[x] 21:25 Some manuscripts include the postscript "According to John." A(02) C(04) B(03) W(032).
[a] 1:0, **Title ("Acts of the Apostles"):** D(05) BYZ ‖ Absent from 𝔓56 ℵ(01) A(02) B(03) ‖ TR reads "Acts of the Holy Apostles."

Acts of the Apostles[a]

1 [1] I composed the first account about all things, O Theophilus,[b] which Jesus began both to do and to teach, [2] until the day when, having given instructions to the apostles through the Holy Spirit[c] whom he had chosen, he was taken up [[and he commanded to proclaim the gospel]].[d] [3] To them he also presented himself alive after his suffering, with many convincing proofs, appearing to them over a period of forty days and speaking about the kingdom of God.

[4] And while he was with them, he commanded them not to depart from Jerusalem, but to wait for the promise of the Father, which, he said, "you heard {from me};[e] [5] for John baptized with water, but you will be baptized with the Holy Spirit[f] [[and that which is about to be received]][g] not many days from now [[, until Pentecost]]."[h]

[6] So when they had come together, they asked him, "Lord, will you at this time restore the kingdom to Israel?" [7] He said to them, "It is not for you to know the times or seasons that the Father has fixed by his own authority, [8] but you will receive power when the Holy Spirit has come upon you, and you will be my witnesses in Jerusalem and in all Judea and Samaria, and to the end of the earth."

[9] And when he had said these things, as they were looking on, [he was lifted up,][i] and a cloud took him out of their sight [[and he was taken up]].[j] [10] And as they were gazing into heaven as he went, behold, two men stood by them in white robes, [11] and said, "Men of Galilee, why do you stand looking into heaven? This Jesus, who was taken up from you [into heaven],[k] will come in the same way as you saw him go into heaven."

[12] Then they returned to Jerusalem from the mount called Olivet, which is near Jerusalem, a Sabbath day's journey away. [13] And when they had entered, they went [up][l] to the upper room, where they were staying, Peter and John and James and Andrew, Philip and Thomas, Bartholomew and Matthew, James the son of Alphaeus and Simon the Zealot and Judas the son of James.

---

[b] 1:1, **Theophilus:** Related to the word θεοφιλής which means (be)loved by God or loving God (BDAG, θεοφιλής). There are numerous theories among scholars to the identity of Theophilus. These include (1) a Roman official or nobleman, (2) a wealthy patron, (3) a generic title for believers, (4) a new convert (catechumen), (5) a Jewish priest or leader, or (6) a title used for literary purposes (literary device). Each of these theories has varying degrees of acceptance among scholars, and without concrete historical evidence, the true identity of Theophilus remains a matter of interpretation and conjecture.

[c] 1:2, **Spirit:** See footnote for Spirit in Luke 1:15.

[d] 1:2, **and he commanded to proclaim the gospel:** Included in D(05).

[e] 1:4, **from me:** D(05) reads "through my mouth."

[f] 1:5, **Spirit:** See footnote for Spirit in verse 2.

[g] 1:5, **and that which is about to be received:** Included in D(05).

[h] 1:5, **until Pentecost:** Included in D(05).

[i] 1:9, **he was lifted up:** Absent from D(05).

[j] 1:9, **and he was taken up:** Included in D(05).

[k] 1:11, **into heaven:** Absent from D(05).

[l] 1:13, **up:** Absent from א(01).

14 All these with one accord were devoting themselves to prayer [[and supplication]],ᵃ together with the women [[and children]]ᵇ and Mary the mother of Jesus, and [with]ᶜ his brothers.

15 In those days Peter stood up among the {brothers}ᵈ (the company of persons was in all about 120) and said, 16 "Brothers, {the}ᵉ Scripture had to be fulfilled, which the Holy Spiritᶠ spoke beforehand by the mouth of David concerning Judas, who became a guide to those who arrested Jesus. 17 For he was numbered among us and was allotted his share in this ministry."

18 "This one, therefore, acquired a field from the wages of [[his]]ᵍ unrighteousness, and falling headlong,ʰ burst open in the middle, and [all]ⁱ his entrails poured out. 19 And it became known to all the inhabitants of Jerusalem, so that the field was called in their [own]ʲ language Akeldama, that is, Field of Blood. 20 For it is written in the book of Psalm, 'Let his dwelling place become desolate,' and 'let there be no one living in it;' and, 'Let another take his position of oversight.' 21 Therefore, of the men who have accompanied us during all the time that the Lord Jesus went in and out among us, 22 beginning from the baptism of John until the day when he was taken up from us, one of these must become a witness with us of his resurrection."

23 And they put forward two, Joseph called Barsabbas, who was also called Justus, and Matthias. 24 And they prayed and said, "[You,]ᵏ Lord, who know the hearts of all, show which one of these two you have chosen 25 to take the place in this ministry and apostleship from which Judas turned aside to go to his own place." 26 And they cast lots for them, and the lot fell on Matthias, and he was numbered with the eleven apostles.

2 1 And [[it happened in those days]]ˡ when the day of Pentecost was fully come, {they were [all]ᵐ together}ⁿ in one place. 2 And suddenly there came from heaven a sound like a violent rushing wind, and it filled the whole house where they were sitting. 3 And there appeared to them tongues as of fire, being distributed, and it sat upon each of them, 4 and they were all filled with the Holy Spiritᵒ and began to speak with other tongues, as the Spirit gave them utterance.

5 Now there were dwelling in Jerusalem Jews, devout men from every nation under heaven. 6 And when this sound occurred, the multitude came together and were confounded, because each one heard them speaking in his [own]ᵖ language.

7 And they were [[all]]�q amazed and marveled, saying [[to one another]],ʳ "Are not all these who are speaking Galileans? 8 And how is it that we each

---

ᵃ 1:14, **and supplication:** Included in BYZ TR.
ᵇ 1:14, **and children:** Included in D(05).
ᶜ 1:14, **with:** SBLGNT THGNT‖ Absent from NA28.
ᵈ 1:15, **brothers:** Some manuscripts read "disciples." D(05) BYZ TR.
ᵉ 1:16, **the:** Some manuscripts read "this." D(05) BYZ TR.
ᶠ 1:16, **Spirit:** See footnote for Spirit in verse 2.
ᵍ 1:18, **his:** Included in D(05).
ʰ 1:18, **falling headlong:** Or "swelling up."
ⁱ 1:18, **all** Absent from A(02).
ʲ 1:19, **own** Absent from ℵ(01) B(03) D(05).
ᵏ 1:24, **You:** Absent from D(05).
ˡ 2:1, **it happened in those days:** Included in D(05).
ᵐ 2:1, **all:** Absent from ℵ(01).
ⁿ 2:1, **they were all together:** Some manuscripts read "they were all with one accord."
ᵒ 2:4, **Spirit:** See footnote for Spirit in Luke 1:15.
ᵖ 2:6, **own:** Absent from D(05).
q 2:7, **all:** Included in ℵ(01) A(02) C(04) BYZ TR.
ʳ 2:7, **to one another:** Included in D(05) BYZ TR.

hear them in our [own]ᵃ language in which we were born? ⁹Parthians and Medes [and Elamites],ᵇ and those dwelling in Mesopotamia, Judea and Cappadocia, Pontus and Asia, ¹⁰Phrygia and Pamphylia, Egypt and the parts of Libya near Cyrene, and visitors from Rome, ¹¹both Jews and proselytes, Cretans and Arabians, we hear them speaking in our own tongues the mighty works of God."

¹²And they were all amazed and perplexed, saying one to another [[about what had happened]],ᶜ "What does this mean?" ¹³But others, mocking, said, "They are filled with sweet wine."

¹⁴But Peter, standing up with {the eleven},ᵈ lifted up his voice [[first]]ᵉ and {addressed them},ᶠ "Men of Judea and all who dwell in Jerusalem, let this be known to you and give ear to my words. ¹⁵For these are not drunk, as you suppose, since it is only the third hour of the day.

¹⁶"But this is what was spoken by the prophet [Joel]:ᵍ ¹⁷'And it shall come to pass {in the last days},ʰ says {God},ⁱ that I will pour out of my Spirit upon all flesh; and {your}ʲ sons and {your}ᵏ daughters shall prophesy, and {your}ˡ young men shall see visions, [and your old men shall dream dreams];ᵐ ¹⁸and on my servants and on my handmaidens I will pour out in those days of my Spirit [, and they shall prophesy].ⁿ ¹⁹And I will show wonders in heaven [above]ᵒ and signs on the earth beneath [, blood and fire and vapor of smoke];ᵖ ²⁰the sun shall be turned into darkness and the moon into blood, before the great [and manifest]�q day of the Lord comes. ²¹[And it will be that whoever calls on the name of the Lordʳ shall be saved.]ˢ,ᵗ

²²"Men of Israel, listen to these words: Jesus the Nazarene, a man attested to you by God with miracles and wonders and signs which God performed through him in your midst, just as you yourselves know, ²³this one, by the predetermined plan and foreknowledge of God, [[having received,]]ᵘ you have taken and, by the hands of lawless men, nailed to a cross and killed; ²⁴whom God raised up, having released the pains of {death},ᵛ because it was not possible for him to be held by it.

ᵃ 2:8, **own:** Absent from D(05).
ᵇ 2:9, **and Elamites:** Absent from ℵ(01).
ᶜ 2:12, **about what had happened:** Included in D(05).
ᵈ 2:14, **the eleven:** D(05) reads "ten apostles."
ᵉ 2:14, **first:** Included in D(0).
ᶠ 2:14, **addressed them:** D(05) reads "said."
ᵍ 2:16, **Joel:** Absent from D(05).
ʰ 2:17, **in the last days:** B(03) read "after this."
ⁱ 2:17, **God:** Some manuscripts read "Lord." D(05).
ʲ 2:17, **your:** D(05) reads "their."
ᵏ 2:17, **your:** D(05) reads "their."
ˡ 2:17, **your:** D(05) reads "their."
ᵐ 2:17, **and your old men shall dream dreams:** Absent from D(05).
ⁿ 2:18, **and they shall prophesy:** Absent from D(05).
ᵒ 2:19, **above:** Absent from A(02).
ᵖ 2:19, **blood and fire and vapor of smoke:** Absent from D(05).
q 2:20, **and manifest:** Absent from ℵ(01) D(05).
ʳ 2:21, **Lord:** In reference to the Greek word for Lord, BDAG states, "The principal meaning relates to the possession of power or authority, in various senses... (1) one who is in charge by virtue of possession, *owner*, (2) one who is in a position of authority, *lord, master*... in some places it is not clear whether God or Christ is meant." (BDAG, κύριος).
ˢ 2:21, **And it will be...:** Absent from ℵ(01).
ᵗ 2:17-21, Joel 2:28-32 LXX.
ᵘ 2:23, **having received:** Absent from D(05) BYZ TR.
ᵛ 2:24, **death:** D(05) reads "Hades."

25 "For David says concerning him,
'I saw {the}[a] Lord always before me, for
he is at my right hand so that I will not
be shaken. 26 Therefore my heart was
glad and my tongue rejoiced; Moreover
my flesh also will dwell in hope,
27 because you will not abandon my soul
to Hades, nor will you allow your Holy
One to see corruption. 28 You have made
known to me the ways of life; you will
fill me with joy in your presence.'[b]

29 "Men and brothers, I may say
to you with confidence about the
patriarch David that he both died and
was buried, and his tomb is with us
to this day. 30 So being a prophet, and
knowing that God had sworn an oath to
him that from the fruit of his {loins}[c]
[[to raise up the Christ according to
the flesh]],[d] he would seat one upon his
throne,[e] 31 [foreseeing, he spoke about][f]
the resurrection [of the Christ],[g] that he
was not abandoned to Hades, nor did
his flesh see corruption.

32 "This Jesus God raised up, of
which we all are witnesses. 33 Being
therefore exalted at the right hand of
God, and having received from the
Father the promise of the Holy Spirit,[h]
he has poured out this which you
[[now]][i] [also][j] see and hear.

34 "For David did not ascend into
the heavens, but he himself says, 'The
Lord said to my Lord, "Sit at my right
hand, 35 until I make your enemies a
footstool for your feet."'[k]

36 "Therefore let all the house of
Israel know for certain that God has
made him both Lord[l] and Christ,[m] this
Jesus whom you crucified."

37 Now [[all who had gathered
together,]][n] when they heard this,
they were pierced to the heart, and
[[some]][o] said to Peter and [the rest
of][p] the apostles, "What shall we do,
men, brothers?" [[Declare to us.]][q]

38 But Peter [says][r] to them,
"Repent, and let each of you be
baptized in[s] the name of [[the Lord]][t]
Jesus Christ for the forgiveness of
[your][u] sins; and you will receive the
gift of the Holy Spirit.[v]

39 "For the promise is for you and
for your children and for all who are
far off, as many as the Lord our God
will call."

40 And with many other words
he testified and exhorted [them],[w]

---

a 2:25, **the:** Some manuscripts read "my." א(01) D(05).
b 2:25-28, Psalm 16:8-11 LXX.
c 2:30, **loins:** Some manuscripts read "heart." D(05).
d 2:30, **to raise up the Christ according to the flesh:** Included in D(05) BYZ TR.
e 2:30, Psalm 132:11.
f 2:31, **foreseeing, he spoke about:** Absent from D(05).
g 2:31, **of the Christ:** Absent 𝔓91. **Christ:** See footnote for Christ in Luke 2:11.
h 2:33, **Spirit:** See footnote for Spirit in verse 4.
i 2:33, **now:** Included in BYZ TR.
j 2:33, **also:** B(03) D(05) || Absent from א(01) A(02) C(04) BYZ TR.
k 2:34-35, Psalm 110:4.
l 2:36, **Lord:** In reference to the Greek word for Lord, BDAG states, "The principal meaning relates to the possession of power or authority, in various senses... (1) one who is in charge by virtue of possession, *owner*, (2) one who is in a position of authority, *lord, master*... in some places it is not clear whether God or Christ is meant." (BDAG, κύριος).
m 2:36, **Christ:** See footnote for verse 31.
n 2:37, **all who had gathered together:** Included in D(05).
o 2:37, **some:** Included in D(05).
p 2:37, **the rest of:** Absent from D(05).
q 2:37, **Declare to us:** Included in D(05).
r 2:38, **says:** א(01) A(02) C(04) NA28[] THGNT || Absent from B(03) D(05) BYZ TR SBLGNT.
s 2:38, **in:** Literally "upon" (ἐπὶ). Some manuscripts read "in" (ἐν).
t 2:38, **the Lord:** Included in D(05).
u 2:38, **your:** Absent from D(05) BYZ TR.
v 2:38, **Spirit:** See footnote for Spirit in verse 4.
w 2:40, **them:** Absent from BYZ TR.

saying, "Be saved from this crooked
generation." 41 So then, those who had
[[gladly]][a] {received}[b] his word were
baptized; and that day about three
thousand souls were added.

42 And they were continually
devoting themselves to the teaching of
the apostles [[in Jerusalem]][c] and to
fellowship, to the breaking of bread and
to prayers.

43 And fear came upon every
soul, and many wonders and signs
were done through the apostles
[[in Jerusalem, and great fear was
upon all]].[d] 44 Now all the believers
[were][e] together and had everything
in common, 45 and they were selling
their possessions and belongings and
distributing them [[daily]][f] to all, as
anyone had need.

46 Day by day continuing [with one
mind][g] in the temple, and breaking
bread from house to house, they
were taking their meals together
with gladness and sincerity of heart,
47 praising God and having favor with
all the people. And the Lord was adding
daily those who were being saved
together [[into the church]].[h]

3 1 Now [[in these days]][i] Peter
and John were going up to
the temple [[in the evening]][j] at
the hour of prayer, the ninth hour.
2 And [[behold]][k] a certain man, lame
from his mother's womb, was being
carried, whom they laid daily at
the gate of the temple that is called
Beautiful, to ask for alms from those
entering the temple.

3 Seeing Peter and John about to
go into the temple, he asked to receive
alms. 4 And Peter directed his gaze at
him, as did John, and said, "Look at
us." 5 And he fixed his {attention}[l] on
them, expecting to receive something
from them.

6 But Peter said, "I have no silver
and gold, but what I do have I give to
you. In the name of Jesus Christ of
Nazareth, [rise up and][m] walk."

7 And he took him by the right hand
and raised him up, and immediately
his feet and ankles were [[made firm
and]][n] strengthened. 8 And leaping up,
he stood and began walking, and he
entered with them into the temple,
{walking and leaping}[o] and praising
God. 9 And all the people saw him
walking and praising {God},[p] 10 and they
recognized him, that he was the one
who used to sit for alms at the Beautiful
Gate of the temple, and they were filled
with amazement and astonishment at
what had happened to him.

11 And as {he}[q] was holding on to
Peter and John, {all the people ran
together to them at}[r] the portico called
Solomon's, utterly amazed.

---

[a] 2:41, **gladly:** Included in BYZ TR.
[b] 2:41, **received:** Some manuscripts read "believed." D(05).
[c] 2:42, **in Jerusalem:** Included in D(05).
[d] 2:43, **in Jerusalem, and great fear was upon all:** Included in ℵ(01) A(02) C(04).
[e] 2:44, **were:** Absent from B(03).
[f] 2:45, **daily:** Included in D(05).
[g] 2:46, **with one mind:** Absent from D(05).
[h] 2:47, **into the church:** Included in D(05).
[i] 3:1, **in these days:** Included in D(05).
[j] 3:1, **in the evening:** Included in D(05).
[k] 3:2, **behold:** Included in D(05).
[l] 3:5, **attention:** D(05) reads "gaze."
[m] 3:6, **rise up and:** Absent from ℵ(01) B(03) D(05) SBLGNT.
[n] 3:7, **made firm and:** Included in D(05).
[o] 3:8, **walking and leaping:** D(05) reads "rejoicing."
[p] 3:9, **God:** C(04) reads "Lord."
[q] 3:11, **he:** Some manuscripts read "the lame man who was healed." BYZ TR.
[r] 3:11, **all the people ran together to them at:** D(05) reads "and they, being astonished, stood in."

12 And when Peter saw it he addressed the people: "Men of Israel, why do you wonder at this, or why do you stare at us, as though by our own power or piety we have made him walk? 13 The God of Abraham, [the God][a] of Isaac, and [the God][b] of Jacob, the God of our fathers, has glorified his servant Jesus [[Christ]],[c] whom you [indeed][d] delivered over [[to judgment]][e] and denied [[him]][f] in the presence of Pilate, when he had decided to release him [[, wanting to do so]].[g]

14 "But you denied the Holy and Righteous One, and asked for a murderer to be granted to you, 15 and you killed the Author of life, whom God raised from the dead. To this we are witnesses. 16 And on the basis of faith in his name, this one whom you see and know, his name has made strong, and the faith that comes through him has given him this complete healing in the presence of you all.

17 "And now, brothers, {I}[h] know that you acted in ignorance, as did also your rulers. 18 But what God foretold by the mouth of all the prophets, [ʰthat {his}ʲ Christ would suffer,] he thus fulfilled.

19 "Repent therefore, and turn back, that your sins may be blotted out, 20 that times of refreshing may come from the presence of the Lord, and that he may send the Christ appointed for you, Jesus, 21 whom it is necessary for heaven to receive until the times of restoration of all things, of which God spoke through the mouth of [[all]][k] his holy prophets [from of old].[l]

22 "Moses indeed said [[to our fathers]],[m] 'The Lord [your][n] God will raise up for you a prophet like me from your brothers. You shall listen to him in whatever he tells you.[o] 23 And it shall be that every soul who does not listen to that prophet shall be destroyed from the people.'

24 "[And][p] All the prophets who have spoken, from Samuel and those who came after him, also proclaimed these days.

25 "You are the sons of the prophets and of the covenant that God made with your fathers, saying to Abraham, 'And in your offspring shall all the families of the earth be blessed.'[q] 26 God, having raised up his servant [[Jesus]],[r] sent [him][s] to you first, to bless you by turning every one of you from [your][t] wickedness."

4 1 While they were speaking to the people [[these words]],[u] the priests, [[the captain of the temple,]][v] and the Sadducees came upon them, 2 being

---

a 3:13, **the God:** ℵ(01) A(02) C(04) D(05) NA28[] ‖ Absent from B(03) BYZ TR SBLGNT THGNT.

b 3:13, **the God:** Absent from B(03) BYZ TR SBLGNT THGNT.

c 3:13, **Christ:** Included in D(05).

d 3:13, **indeed:** Absent from D(05) TR.

e 3:13, **to judgment:** Included in D(05).

f 3:13, **him:** Included in BYZ TR.

g 3:13, **wanting to do so:** Included in D(05).

h 3:17, **I:** Some manuscripts read "we." D(05).

i 3:18, **that his Christ would suffer:** Absent from A(02).

j 3:18, **his:** Some manuscripts read "the." BYZ TR.

k 3:21, **all:** Included in BYZ TR.

l 3:21, **from of old:** Absent from D(05).

m 3:22, **to our fathers:** Included in D(05) BYZ TR.

n 3:22, **your:** Absent from B(03).

o 3:22-23, Deuteronomy 18:15-19.

p 3:24, **and:** Absent from D(05).

q 3:25, Genesis 22:18, 26:4.

r 3:26, **Jesus:** Included in A(02) BYZ TR.

s 3:26, **him:** Absent from D(05).

t 3:26, **you:** Absent from B(03).

u 4:1, **these words:** Included in D(05).

v 4:1, **the captain of the temple:** Absent from D(05).

greatly disturbed because they were teaching the people and proclaiming in Jesus the resurrection from the dead. 3 They laid hands on them and put them in custody until the next day, for it was already evening. 4 But many of those who had heard [the word]ᵃ believed, and the number of the men came to be [about]ᵇ five thousand.

5 On the next day, their rulers, elders, and scribes were gathered together in Jerusalem, 6 along with Annas the high priest, Caiaphas, John, Alexander, and all who were of the high-priestly family. 7 When they had placed them in the center, they began to inquire, "By what power or in what name have you done this?"

8 Then Peter, filled with the Holy Spirit, said to them, "Rulers of the people and elders [[of Israel]],ᶜ 9 if we are being examined [[by you]]ᵈ today concerning a good deed done to a crippled man, by what means this person has been healed, 10 let it be known to all of you and to all the people of Israel that by the name of Jesus Christ the Nazarene, whom you crucified, whom God raised from the dead; by him this man is standing before you well. 11 This is the stone that was rejected by you, the builders, which has become the cornerstone. 12 And there is no [salvation]ᵉ in any other, for there is no other name under heaven given among men by which we must be saved."

13 Now when they saw the boldness of Peter and John, and perceived that they were uneducated [and ordinary],ᶠ they marveled. And they recognized that they had been with Jesus. 14 And seeing the man who had been healed standing with them, they had nothing to [[do or]]ᵍ say in opposition.

15 [But]ʰ When they had commanded them to go aside out of the council, they conferred among themselves, 16 saying, "What shall we do with these men? For, indeed, a notable miracle has been done through them, as evident to all who dwell in Jerusalem, and we cannot deny it. 17 [But]ⁱ So that it does not spread any further among the people, let us warn them [[with a threat]]ʲ to speak no more to anyone in this name." 18 And [[as they were agreeing with the opinion,]]ᵏ they called them and commanded [[them]]ˡ not to speak at all nor teach in the name of Jesus.

19 But Peter and John answered and said to them, "Whether it is right in the sight of God to listen to you more than to God, you judge. 20 For we cannot but speak the things which we have seen and heard." 21 So when they had further threatened them, they let them go, finding no way to punish them, because of the people, for all glorified God for what had been done. 22 For the man on whom this sign of healing had been performed was more than forty years old.

23 And when they were released, they went to their own people and reported everything the chief priests and the elders had said to them. 24 And when they heard it [[and recognized the working of God]],ᵐ they lifted their voices together to God

---

ᵃ 4:4, **the word:** Absent from A(02).

ᵇ 4:4, **about:** Absent from ℵ(01) A(02).

ᶜ 4:8, **of Israel:** Included in D(05) BYZ TR.

ᵈ 4:9, **by you:** Included in D(05).

ᵉ 4:12, **salvation:** Absent from D(05).

ᶠ 4:13, **and ordinary:** Absent from D(05).

ᵍ 4:14, **do or:** Included in D(05).

ʰ 4:15, **But:** Absent from D(05).

ⁱ 4:17, **But:** Absent from D(05).

ʲ 4:17, **with a threat:** Included in D(05) BYZ TR.

ᵏ 4:18, **as they were agreeing with the opinion:** Included in D(05).

ˡ 4:18, **them:** Included in BYZ TR.

ᵐ 4:24, **and recognized the working of God:** Absent from D(05).

and said, "Master, you [[God]]ᵃ are the one who made the heaven and the earth and the sea and everything in them, ₂₅ who, through the mouth of [our father]ᵇ David your servant, said [through the Holy Spirit]:ᶜ 'Why did the nations rage and the peoples plot in vain? ₂₆ The kings of the earth took their stand, and the rulers were gathered together against the Lord and against his Anointed.'ᵈ

₂₇ "For truly [in this city]ᵉ there were gathered together against your holy servant Jesus, whom you anointed,ᶠ both Herod and Pontius Pilate, along with the Gentiles and the peoples of Israel, ₂₈ To do whatever your hand and [your]ᵍ plan predestined to happen. ₂₉ And now, Lord, look upon their threats and grant to your servants to speak your word with all boldness, ₃₀ While you stretch out your hand for healing, and that signs and wonders may take place through the name of your holy servant Jesus."

₃₁ And when they had prayed, the place in which they were gathered together was shaken, and they were all filled with the Holy Spirit and spoke the word of God with boldness [to everyone who wants to believe].ʰ

₃₂ Now the multitude of those who had believed were of one heart and soul, and [[there was no division at all among them,]]ⁱ and no one said that any of the things he possessed was his own, but they had everything in common.

₃₃ And with great power the apostles were giving their testimony to the resurrection of the Lord Jesus [[Christ]],ʲ and great grace was upon them all. ₃₄ For there was not a needy person among them, for as many as were owners of lands or houses were selling them and bringing the proceeds of what was sold. ₃₅ and laid it at the apostles' feet, and it was distributed to each as any had need.

₃₆ Joseph, who was also called by the apostles Barnabas (which means son of encouragement), a Levite, a native of Cyprus, ₃₇ sold a field that belonged to him and brought the money and laid it at the apostles' feet.

5 ₁ Now a man named Ananias, together with his wife Sapphira, sold a piece of property ₂ and kept back part of the proceeds, with his wife's knowledge, and brought only a portion of it and laid it at the apostles' feet.

₃ But Peter said, "Ananias, why has Satan filled your heart to lie to the Holy Spirit and to steal for yourself from the price of the field? ₄ While it remained unsold, did it not remain your own? And after it was sold, was it not at your disposal? Why have you conceived this deed in your heart [[to do]]?ᵏ You have not lied to men but to God." ₅ And hearing these words, [[immediately]]ˡ Ananias fell down and breathed his last, and great fear came upon all who heard [[these things]].ᵐ ₆ The young men rose and wrapped him up, and carried him out and buried him.

ᵃ 4:24, **God:** Included in D(05) BYZ TR.

ᵇ 4:25, **our father:** Absent from D(05) BYZ TR.

ᶜ 4:25, **through the Holy Spirit:** Absent from BYZ TR.

ᵈ 4:25-26, Psalm 2:1-2 LXX.

ᵉ 4:27, **in this city:** Absent from BYZ TR.

ᶠ 4:27, **anointed:** Setting a person apart for special service under divine direction... God anoints (a) David, (b) Jesus, the Christ for his work or mission, (c) the prophets, (d) the apostles or, more probably, all Christians (at baptism or through the Spirit) 1 Cor 1:21. (BDAG, χρίω).

ᵍ 4:28, **your:** Absent from A(02) B(03) SBLGNT.

ʰ 4:31, **to everyone who wants to believe:** Absent from D(05).

ⁱ 4:32, **there was no division at all among them:** Included in D(05).

ʲ 4:33, **Christ:** Included in ℵ(01) A(02) D(05).

ᵏ 5:4, **to do:** Included in 𝔓75 D(05).

ˡ 5:5, **immediately:** Included in D(05).

ᵐ 5:5, **these things:** Included in BYZ TR.

7 About three hours later, his wife, not knowing what had happened, came in. 8 But Peter {asked}ᵃ her, "{Tell me,}ᵇ did you sell the land for this much?" She said, "[Yes,]ᶜ for that much." 9 But Peter [[said]]ᵈ to her, "Why is it that it was agreed by you to test the Spirit of the Lord? Look, the feet of those who buried your husband are at the door, and they will carry you out." 10 Immediately, she fell down at his feet and breathed her last. The young men came in and found her dead, and they carried her out and buried her beside her husband. 11 And great fear came upon the whole church and upon all who heard these things.

12 Now, many signs and wonders were done among the people through the hands of the apostles. And they were all together [[in the temple]]ᵉ in Solomon's Portico. 13 Of the rest, no one dared to join them [, but the people magnified them].ᶠ

14 And more and more believers were added to the Lord, multitudes of both men and women, 15 so that they [even]ᵍ carried out {the}ʰ sick into the streets and laid them on cots and mats, in order that Peter's shadow might fall on some of them as he passed by. [[For they were being freed from every sickness among them, each one according to what he had.]]ⁱ

16 The people [also]ʲ gathered from the towns around Jerusalem, bringing the sick and those being tormented by unclean spirits, and they were all healed.

17 Then the high priest and all those with him, the sect of the Sadducees, were filled with jealousy 18 and they laid their hands on the apostles and put them in public custody. [[And each one went to his own.]]ᵏ

19 But an angel of the Lord opened the prison doorsˡ during the night, brought them out, and said, 20 "Go, stand in the temple and speak to the people all the words of this life."

21 But having heard, they entered the temple at daybreak and were teaching. Now when the high priest and those with him arrived, [[having risen in the morning]]ᵐ they called together the Sanhedrin and all the elders of the sons of Israel, they sent to the prison to have them brought. 22 But the officers, having arrived, did not find them in the prison; and having returned, they reported it, 23 saying, "We [[indeed]]ⁿ found the prison securely locked and the guards standing at the doors, but when we opened them, we found no one inside."

24 When they heard these words, both the chief priest and the commander of the temple [[and the high priests]],ᵒ they were perplexed about them, wondering what this might lead to. 25 Then someone came and told them [[saying]],ᵖ "Look! The men whom you put in prison are in

---

ᵃ 5:8, **asked:** D(05) reads "said to."
ᵇ 5:8, **Tell me:** D(05) reads "I will ask you whether, then."
ᶜ 5:8, **Yes:** Absent from A(02).
ᵈ 5:9, **said:** Included in A(02) BYZ TR.
ᵉ 5:12, **in the temple:** Included in D(05).
ᶠ 5:13, **but the people magnified them:** Absent from 𝔓45.
ᵍ 5:15, **even:** Absent from D(05) BYZ TR.
ʰ 5:15, **the:** D(05) reads "their."
ⁱ 5:15, **For they were being freed...:** Included in D(05).
ʲ 5:16, **also:** Absent from D(05).
ᵏ 5:18, **And each one went to his own:** Included in D(05).
ˡ 5:19, **an angel of the Lord opened the prison doors:** The irony here is the Sadducees did not believe in angels.
ᵐ 5:21, **having risen in the morning:** Included in D(05).
ⁿ 5:23, **indeed:** Included in BYZ TR.
ᵒ 5:24, **and the high priests:** Included in BYZ TR.
ᵖ 5:25, **saying:** Included in TR.

the temple [standing and]ᵃ teaching the people."

26 Then the captain went with the officers and brought them, but not by force, for they were afraid of being stoned by the people.

27 When they had brought them, they had them stand before the council. The high priest questioned them, 28 saying, "Did we not strictly order you not to teach in this name? Yet here you have filled Jerusalem with your teaching, and you intend to bring this man's blood upon us."

29 But Peter and the apostles answered, "We must obey God rather than men. 30 The God of our ancestors raised up Jesus, whom you had killed by hanging him on a tree. 31 God exalted him at his right hand as Leader and Savior, to give repentance to Israel and forgiveness of sins [[in him]].ᵇ 32 And we are witnesses of [[all]]ᶜ these words, and also the Holy Spirit,ᵈ which God gave to those who obey him."

33 But when they heard this, they were enraged and wanted to kill them.

34 However, a Pharisee named Gamaliel, a respected teacher of the law, stood up in the council and ordered the {men}ᵉ to be put outside for a short time. 35 He said to {them},ᶠ

"Men of Israel, be careful what you are about to do with these men. 36 [For]ᵍ Before these days, Theudas rose up, claiming to be somebody [[great]],ʰ and a number of men, about four hundred, joined him. He was {killed},ⁱ and all who followed him [dispersed and]ʲ were brought to nothing. 37 After him, Judas the Galilean rose up in the days of the census and led [[a considerable number of]]ᵏ people after him; he also perished, and [all]ˡ who followed him were scattered. 38 So now I say [to you]ᵐ [[brothers]],ⁿ withdraw from these men and leave them alone [[not defiling your hands]];ᵒ for if this plan or this work is of human origin, it will be overthrown; 39 but if it is of God, you will not be able to overthrow them, lest you be found fighting against God. [[Neither you nor kings nor tyrants should therefore keep away from these men.]]"ᵖ

They were persuaded by him, 40 and after calling the apostles, they had them flogged, ordered them not to speak [[to them]]�q in the name of Jesus, and released [[them]].ʳ

41 So {they}ˢ went on their way from the presence of the council, rejoicing that they were considered worthy to suffer dishonor for {the name}.ᵗ

ᵃ 5:25, **standing and:** Absent from ℵ(01).

ᵇ 5:31, **in him:** Included in D(05).

ᶜ 5:32, **all:** Included in D(05).

ᵈ 5:32, **Spirit:** See footnote for Spirit in Luke 1:15.

ᵉ 5:34, **men:** Some manuscripts read "apostles." D(05) BYZ TR.

ᶠ 5:35, **them:** Some manuscripts read "the rulers and the Sanhedrin." D(05).

ᵍ 5:36, **For:** Absent from 𝔓45.

ʰ 5:36, **great:** Included in D(051).

ⁱ 5:36, **killed:** Some manuscripts read "destroyed, he himself by himself." D(05).

ʲ 5:36, **dispersed and:** Absent from D(05).

ᵏ 5:37, **a considerable number of:** Included in D(05) BYZ TR.

ˡ 5:37, **all:** Absent from 𝔓45 D(05).

ᵐ 5:38, **to you:** Absent from ℵ(01).

ⁿ 5:38, **brothers:** Included in D(05).

ᵒ 5:38, **not defiling your hands:** Included in D(05).

ᵖ 5:39, **Neither you nor kings nor tyrants:** Included in D(05).

q 5:40, **to them:** Included in A(02).

ʳ 5:40, **them:** Included in D(05) BYZ TR.

ˢ 5:41, **they:** Some manuscripts read "the Apostles." D(05).

ᵗ 5:41, **the name:** Some manuscripts read "his name." TR ‖ BYZ reads "the name of Jesus."

42 And every day, in the temple and from house to house, they did not cease teaching and proclaiming[a] the Christ, Jesus.[b]

6 1 Now in those days, when the number of the disciples was multiplying, there arose a complaint by the Hellenists against the Hebrews, because their widows were being overlooked in the daily distribution [[in the service of the Hebrews]].[c] 2 But the twelve, having called together the multitude of the disciples, said [[to them]],[d] "It is not desirable for us, having left the word of God, to serve at tables. 3 Therefore, [brothers],[e] select from among you seven men of good reputation, full of the [[Holy]][f] Spirit and wisdom, whom we will appoint over this need. 4 But we will devote ourselves to prayer and to the ministry of the word."

5 And {the}[g] word was pleasing before the whole multitude [[of the disciples]],[h] and they chose Stephen, a man full of faith and the Holy Spirit, and Philip, Prochorus, Nicanor, Timon, Parmenas, and Nicolas, a proselyte from Antioch, 6 whom they set before the apostles; and when they had prayed, they laid their hands on them.

7 And the word of {God}[i] increased, and the number of the disciples multiplied greatly in Jerusalem, and a great many of the {priests}[j] were obedient to the faith.

8 And Stephen, full of {grace}[k] and power, was performing great wonders and signs among the people [[through the name of the Lord Jesus Christ]].[l]

9 But some of those from the synagogue called the Freedmen, and of the Cyrenians, and of the Alexandrians, and of those from Cilicia [and Asia],[m] rose up and disputed with Stephen, 10 and they could not withstand the wisdom [[which was in him]][n] and the Spirit by which he spoke [[because they were being refuted by him with all boldness, not being able to look directly at the truth]].[o]

11 Then they secretly induced men to say, "We have heard him speak blasphemous words against Moses and God." 12 And they stirred up the people, the elders, and the scribes, and they [came upon him,][p] seized him, and brought him to the council. 13 They also set up false witnesses [[against him]][q] who said, "This man does not cease to speak {words}[r] against [this][s] holy place and the law; 14 for we have heard him say that this Jesus of Nazareth will destroy this place and change the customs which Moses handed down to us."

---

a 5:42, **proclaiming:** Or evangelizing.
b 5:42, **the Christ, Jesus:** Some manuscripts read "Jesus the Christ" (Jesus as the Christ) BYZ TR ‖ C(04) reads "the Lord Jesus." ‖ D(05) reads "the Lord Jesus Christ." See footnote for Christ in Luke 2:11.
c 6:1, **in the service of the Hebrews:** Included in D(05).
d 6:2, **to them:** Included in D(05).
e 6:3, **brothers:** Absent from A(02) D(05).
f 6:3, **Holy:** Included in A(02) C(04) BYZ TR.
g 6:5, **the:** Some manuscripts read "this." D(05).
h 6:5, **of the disciples:** Included in D(05).
i 6:7, **God:** Some manuscripts read "the Lord." D(05).
j 6:7, **priests:** א(01) reads "Jews."
k 6:8, **grace:** Some manuscripts read "faith." BYZ TR.
l 6:8, **through the name of the Lord Jesus Christ:** Included in D(05).
m 6:9, **and Asia:** Absent from A(02).
n 6:10, **which was in him:** Included in D(05).
o 6:10, **because they were:** Included in D(05).
p 6:12, **came upon him:** Absent from א(01).
q 6:13, **against him:** Included in D(05).
r 6:13, **words:** Some manuscripts read "blasphemous words." BYZ TR.
s 6:13, **this:** Absent from A(02) SBLGNT THGNT.

15 And all who sat in the council, looking intently at him, saw his face as the face of an angel [[standing in the midst of them]].ª

7 1 Then the high priest [[with the crown]]ᵇ said, "Are [[then]]ᶜ these things so?"

2 And he replied, "Men, brothers, and fathers, listen. The God of glory appeared to our father Abraham when he was in Mesopotamia, before he lived in Haran, 3 and said to him, 'Leave your country and your relatives, and come to the land that I will show you.'

4 "Then {he}ᵈ left the land of the Chaldeans and settled in Haran. From there, after his father died, God moved him to this land in which you now live [[, you lived, and our fathers who were before us]].ᵉ 5 Yet he gave him no inheritance in it, not even a foot of ground, but promised to give it to him as a possession and to his descendants after him, even though he had no child.

6 "God spoke [to him]ᶠ in this way: that his descendants would be strangers in a foreign land, and they would enslave and mistreat them for four hundred years; 7 'And the nation to which they will be in bondage I will judge,'ᵍ God said, 'And after that they will come out and serve me in this place.'ʰ 8 And he gave him the covenant of circumcision; and so Abraham fathered Isaac and circumcised him on the {eighth}ⁱ day, and Isaac fathered Jacob, and Jacob the twelve patriarchs.

9 "The patriarchs, jealous of Joseph, sold him into Egypt. But God was with him 10 and rescued him from all his troubles, and gave [him]ʲ favor and wisdom before Pharaoh, king of Egypt, who made him ruler over Egypt and [over]ᵏ his entire household. 11 Then a famine came over all Egypt and Canaan, and great distress, and our fathers could find no food.

12 "But when Jacob heard that there was grain in Egypt, he sent our fathers there the first time. 13 On the second visit, Joseph made himself known to his brothers, and Pharaoh *learned of* {Joseph's}ˡ family. 14 Then Joseph sent for his father Jacob and all his relatives, seventy-five persons in all. 15 So Jacob went down to Egypt, and he and our fathers died, 16 and they were carried back to Shechem and laid in the tomb that Abraham had bought for a sum of money from the sons of Hamor in Shechem.

17 "But as the time of the promise which God had declared to Abraham was drawing near, the people increased and multiplied in Egypt. 18 until another king arose [[over Egypt]]ᵐ who did not know Joseph. 19 This one, having deceived our race, mistreated {our}ⁿ fathers by making their infants exposed so that they would not be kept alive. 20 At this time Moses was born, and he was beautiful in the sight of God. He was brought up for three months in his father's house, 21 and when he had been laid out, Pharaoh's daughter took him and brought him up as her own

---

ª 6:15, **standing in the midst of them:** Included in D(05).

ᵇ 7:1, **with the crown** Included in D(05).

ᶜ 7:1, **then:** Included in D(05) BYZ TR.

ᵈ 7:4, **he:** Some manuscripts read "Abraham." D(05).

ᵉ 7:4, **you lived, and our fathers who were before us:** Included in D(05).

ᶠ 7:6, **to him:** Included in D(05).

ᵍ 7:6-7b, Genesis 15:13-14.

ʰ 7:7, Exodus 3:12.

ⁱ 7:8, **eighth:** ℵ(01) reads "seventh."

ʲ 7:10, **him:** Absent from A(02).

ᵏ 7:10, **over:** Absent from B(03) D(05) BYZ TR SBLGNT THGNT.

ˡ 7:13, **Joseph's:** Some manuscripts read "his." ℵ(01) A(02).

ᵐ 7:18, **over Egypt:** Absent from D(05) BYZ TR.

ⁿ 7:19, **our:** Absent from some manuscripts which read "the Fathers." ℵ(01) B(03) D(05) SBLGNT THGNT.

son. 22 Moses was educated [in]^a all the wisdom of the Egyptians and was powerful in [his]^b words and deeds.

23 "When he was forty years old, it came into his heart to visit his brothers, the sons of Israel. 24 Seeing one of them being wronged [[from the race]],^c he defended the oppressed man and avenged him by striking down the Egyptian [[and hid him in the sand]].^d 25 He supposed that [his]^e brothers would understand that God was giving them deliverance through his hand, but they did not understand. 26 The next day he appeared to them as they were fighting [[, he saw them acting unjustly]]^f and tried to reconcile them in peace, saying, '[[What are you doing?]]^g Men, you are brothers; why do you wrong each other?' 27 But the one who was wronging his neighbor pushed him away, saying, 'Who made you a ruler and a judge over us? 28 Do you want to kill me as you killed the Egyptian yesterday?' ^h 29 Then Moses fled because of this statement and became a sojourner in the land of Midian, where he fathered two sons.

30 "And [[after these things]]^i when forty years had passed, an angel [[of the Lord]]^j appeared to him in the wilderness of Mount Sinai, in a flame of fire in a bush. 31 When Moses saw it, he marveled [at the vision];^k and as he approached to look more closely, {there came the voice of the Lord}^l [[to him]]:^m 32 'I am the God of your fathers, the God of Abraham, [[the God of]]^n Isaac, and [[the God of]]^o Jacob.' Moses became terrified and did not dare to look.^p 33 {Then the Lord said to him},^q 'Take off the sandals from {your}^r feet, for the place [where]^s you are standing is holy ground.^t 34 [[For having seen,]]^u I have certainly seen the oppression of {my}^v people who are in Egypt, and have heard their groaning, and I have come down to deliver them; and now come, I will send you to Egypt.'^w

35 "This Moses, whom they rejected, saying, 'Who made you a ruler and judge [[over us]]?'^x This one God [also]^y sent as ruler and deliverer by the hand of an angel who appeared to him in the bush. ^z 36 This man led them out, performing wonders and signs in the land of Egypt, and in the Red Sea, and in the wilderness for forty years.

---

a 7:22, in: Absent from SBLGNT THGNT B(03) BYZ TR SBLGNT.

b 7:22, his: Absent from BYZ TR.

c 7:24, from the race: Included in D(05).

d 7:24, and hid him in the sand: Included in D(05).

e 7:25, his: Some manuscripts read "the." א(01) B(03) C(04) SBLGNT.

f 7:26, he saw them acting unjustly: Absent from D(05).

g 7:26, What are you doing?: Included in D(05).

h 7:27-28, Exodus 2:14 LXX.

i 7:30, after these things: Included in D(05).

j 7:30, of the Lord: Included in D(05) BYZ TR.

k 7:31, at the vision: Absent from A(02).

l 7:31, there came the voice of the Lord: D(05) reads "the Lord said."

m 7:31, to him: Some manuscripts include C(04) D(05) BYZ TR.

n 7:32, the God of: Included in D(05) BYZ TR.

o 7:32, the God of: Included in D(05) BYZ TR.

p 7:32, Exodus 3:6.

q 7:33, Then the Lord said to him: D(05) reads "and a voice came to him."

r 7:33, your: B(03) reads "the."

s 7:33, where: Absent from D(05).

t 7:33, Exodus 3:5.

u 7:34, For having seen: Included in D(05).

v 7:34, my: D(05) reads "the."

w 7:34, Exodus 3:7-8, 10.

x 7:35, over us: Included in א(01) C(04) D(05).

y 7:35, also Absent from 𝔓45 א(01) A(02) C(04) BYZ TR.

z 7:35, Exodus 2:14.

37 "This is the Moses who said to the sons of Israel, '[[the Lord]]ᵃ [[your]]ᵇ God will raise up for you a prophet like me from your brothers; [[to him shall you listen]]'ᶜᵈ

38 "This is the one who was in the assembly in the wilderness with the angel who spoke to him on Mount Sinai, and with our fathers; the one who received living oracles to give to us, 39 to whom our fathers were unwilling to be obedient, but pushed him away and turned back in their hearts to Egypt, 40 saying to Aaron, 'Make for us gods who will go before us; for this Moses, who led us out of the land of Egypt, we do not know what has happened to him.'ᵉ 41 And they made a calf in those days, and brought a sacrifice to the idol, and were rejoicing in the works of their hands. 42 But God turned away and delivered them up to serve the host of heaven, as it is written in the book of the prophets: 'Did you offer to me slain beasts and sacrifices for forty years in the wilderness, O house of Israel? [[Says the Lord]]ᶠ 43 You also took up the tabernacle of Moloch and the star of {the god}ᵍ Rephan, the images which you made to worship them; and I will remove you beyond Babylon.'ʰ

44 "Our fathers had the tabernacle of testimony in the wilderness, just as He who spoke to Moses directed him to make it according to the pattern which he had seen. 45 And having received it in their turn, our fathers brought it in with Joshua when they took possession of the nations whom God drove out before our fathers, until the days of David, 46 who found favor in the sight of God and asked to find a dwelling place for the {house}ⁱ of Jacob. 47 But it was Solomon who built a house for him.

48 "But the Most High does not dwell in {things}ʲ made by hands, just as the prophet says, 49 'Heaven is my throne, and the earth is the footstool of my feet; what kind of house will you build for me, says the Lord, or what place is there for my rest? 50 Did not my hand make all these things?'ᵏ

51 "You stiff-necked and uncircumcised in {heart}ˡ and ears, you always resist the Holy Spirit; as your fathers did, so do you. 52 Which of the prophets did your fathers not persecute? They killed [[them,]]ᵐ those who had previously announced the coming of the Righteous One, whose betrayers and murderers you have now become; 53 you who received the law as ordained by angels, and yet did not keep it."

54 Now when they heard these things, they were infuriated in their hearts and gnashed their teeth at him.

55 But being full of [[faith and]]ⁿ the Holy Spirit, he gazed intently into heaven and saw the glory of God, and [[the Lord]]ᵒ Jesus standing at the right hand of God; 56 and he said, "Behold, I see the heavens opened up and the Son of Man standing at the right hand of {God}."ᵖ

ᵃ 7:37, **the Lord:** Included in C(04) BYZ TR.

ᵇ 7:37, **your:** Included in BYZ TR.

ᶜ 7:37, **to him shall you listen:** Included in C(04) D(05) TR.

ᵈ 7:37, Deuteronomy 18:15.

ᵉ 7:40, Exodus 31:1, 23.

ᶠ 7:42, **Says the Lord:** Included in C(04).

ᵍ 7:43, **the god:** B(03) D(05) SBLGNT ‖ Some manuscripts read "your god." ℵ(01) A(02) C(05) NA28[] THGNT BYZ TR.

ʰ 7:42-43, Amos 5:25-27.

ⁱ 7:46, **house:** ℵ(01), B(03) D(05) ‖ Some manuscripts read "God." A(02) C(04) BYZ TR.

ʲ 7:48, **things:** Some manuscripts read "temples." BYZ TR.

ᵏ 7:49-50, Isaiah 66:1-2.

ˡ 7:51, **heart:** ℵ(01) reads "your hearts."

ᵐ 7:52, **them:** Included in D(05).

ⁿ 7:55, **faith and:** Included in 𝔓45 ℵ(01).

ᵒ 7:55, **the Lord:** Included in D(05).

ᵖ 7:56, **God:** C(04) reads "him."

57 But crying out with a loud voice, they covered their ears and rushed at him with one accord. 58 And having cast him out of the city, they began to stone him. And the witnesses laid down [their]^a garments at the feet of a young man named Saul. 59 And they stoned Stephen as he called out and said, "Lord Jesus, receive my spirit."

60 Then falling on his knees, he cried out [with a loud voice],^b "Lord, do not hold this sin against them!"

Having said this, he fell asleep.

8 1 Now Saul was consenting to his death. And on that day a great persecution [[and afflictions]]^c arose against the church in Jerusalem, and all were scattered throughout the regions of Judea and Samaria, except the apostles [who remained in Jerusalem].^d

2 Devout men buried Stephen and made great lamentation over him.

3 But Saul was ravaging the church, entering house after house, and dragging off men and women, he committed them to prison.

4 Now those who were scattered went about preaching the word. 5 Philip went down to the city of Samaria and proclaimed the Christ to them. 6 And the crowds with one accord paid attention to what was being said by Philip when they heard and saw the signs that he did. 7 For many of those who had unclean spirits, crying out with a loud voice, came out, and many who were paralyzed and lame were healed. 8 So there was much joy in that city.

9 But there was a man named Simon who had previously practiced magic in the city and amazed the people of Samaria, saying that he himself was someone great. 10 They [all]^e paid attention to him, from the least to the greatest, saying, "This is the power of God that is called Great." 11 And they paid attention to him because for a long time he had amazed them with his magic. 12 But when they believed Philip as he preached good news about the kingdom of God and the name of Jesus Christ, they were baptized, both men and women. 13 Even Simon himself believed, and after being baptized, he continued with Philip. And seeing signs and great miracles performed, he was amazed.

14 Now when the apostles at Jerusalem heard that Samaria had received the word of God, they sent to them Peter and John, 15 who came down and prayed for them that they might receive the Holy Spirit,^f 16 for it had not yet fallen on any of them, but they had only been baptized in the name of the Lord Jesus. 17 Then they laid their hands on them and they received the Holy Spirit.

18 Now when Simon saw that the [[Holy]]^g Spirit was given through the laying on of the apostles' hands, he offered them money, 19 [[urging and]] ^h saying, "Give me also this power so that anyone on whom I lay my hands may receive the Holy Spirit." 20 But Peter said to him, "May your silver perish with you, because you thought you could obtain the gift of God with money! 21 You have neither part nor lot in this matter, [for]^i your heart is not right before God. 22 Repent, therefore, of this wickedness of yours, and pray to {the Lord}^j that, if possible, the intent of your heart may be forgiven you. 23 For I see you

---

a 7:58, **their:** Absent from BYZ.

b 7:60, **with a loud voice:** Absent from ℵ(01).

c 8:1, **and afflictions:** Included in D(05).

d 8:1, **who remained in Jerusalem:** Included in D(05).

e 8:10, **all:** Absent from BYZ.

f 8:15, **Spirit:** See footnote for Spirit in Luke 1:15.

g 8:18, **Holy:** Included in 𝔓45 A(02) C(04) D(05) BYZ TR THGNT ‖ Absent from ℵ(01) B(03) NA28 SBLGNT.

h 8:19, **urging:** Included in D(05).

i 8:21, **for:** Absent from D(05).

j 8:22, **the Lord:** Some manuscripts read "God." BYZ TR.

being in the gall of bitterness and the bond of unrighteousness." 24 And Simon answered, "[[I urge you toward them,]]ᵃ Pray for me to {the Lord},ᵇ that nothing of what you have said may come upon me."

25 So when they had testified and spoken the word of the Lord, they returned to Jerusalem, preaching the gospel to many villages of the Samaritans.

26 But an angel of the Lord spoke to Philip, saying, "Get up and go south to the road the one [[that is called]]ᶜ that goes down from Jerusalem to Gaza, which is a desert." 27 So he got up and went. And behold, there was an Ethiopian eunuch, a high official of Candace, queen of the Ethiopians, who was in charge of all her treasury, who had come to worship in Jerusalem. 28 He was returning and sitting in {his}ᵈ chariot [and]ᵉ reading the prophet Isaiah.

29 The Spirit said to Philip, "Go and join this chariot." 30 So Philip ran up and heard him reading Isaiah the prophet, and said [[to the eunuch]],ᶠ "Do you understand what you are reading?" 31 He replied, "How can I, unless someone guides me?" And he invited Philip to come up and sit with him. 32 Now the passage of Scripture he was reading was this: "Like a sheep he was led to the slaughter, and like a lamb silent before its shearer, so he does not open his mouth. 33 In his humiliation [his]ᵍ judgment was taken away; who will declare his generation? For his life is taken from the earth."ʰ

34 The eunuch answered Philip and said, "I ask you, about whom does the prophet say this? About himself or about someone else?" 35 Then Philip opened his mouth, and beginning with this Scripture, he preached Jesus to him.

36 As they went along the road, they came to some water, and the eunuch said, "[Look, here is water!] ⁱWhat prevents me from being baptized?" 37 [[And Philip said, "If you believe with all your heart, you can." And he answered him, "I believe Jesus Christ is the Son of God."]]ʲ 38 So he ordered the chariot to stop, and both Philip and the eunuch went down into the water, and he baptized him. 39 When they came up out of the water, the [[Holy]]ᵏ Spirit [[fell upon the eunuch, but an angel]]ˡ of the Lord snatched Philip away, and the eunuch saw him no more, and went on his way rejoicing.

40 But Philip was found at Azotus; and as he passed through, he preached the gospel to all the cities until he came to Caesarea.

9 1 Now Saul, still breathing threats and murder against the disciples of the Lord, approached the high priest 2 and asked for letters to the synagogues in Damascus, so that if he found any belonging to the Way, both men and women, he might bring them bound to Jerusalem.

3 And as he journeyed, it happened that he drew near to Damascus, and suddenly a light from heaven shone around him. 4 Falling to the ground, he heard a voice saying to him, "Saul, Saul, why are you persecuting me?" 5 He said, "Who are you, Lord?" But {he

---

ᵃ 8:24, **I urge you toward them:** Included in D(05).
ᵇ 8:24, **the Lord:** Some manuscripts read "God." D(05).
ᶜ 8:26, **that is called:** Included in ℵ(01).
ᵈ 8:28, **his:** D(05) reads "the."
ᵉ 8:28, **and:** Absent from ℵ(01) A(02) D(05).
ᶠ 8:30, **to the eunuch:** Included in 𝔓50.
ᵍ 8:33, **his:** Absent from ℵ(01) A(02) B(03).
ʰ 8:33, Isaiah 53:7-8 LXX.
ⁱ 8:36, **Look, here is water!:** Absent from 𝔓45.
ʲ 8:37, TR includes verse 37.
ᵏ 8:39, **Holy:** Included in A(02).
ˡ 8:39, **fell upon the eunuch, but an angel:** Included in A(02).

said},[a] "I am Jesus [[the Nazarene]],[b] whom you are persecuting. [[Is it hard for you to kick against goads?]][c] 6 But [[the Lord said to him]][d] get up and go into the city, and you will be told what you must do."

7 The men who were traveling with him stood speechless, hearing the voice but seeing no one. 8 Saul got up from the ground, and though his eyes were open, he could see nothing; so they led him by the hand and brought him into Damascus. 9 For three days he was without sight, and neither ate nor drank.

10 Now there was a disciple in Damascus named Ananias, and the Lord said to him in a vision, "Ananias." He said, "Here I am, Lord." 11 The Lord said to him, "Get up and go to the street called Straight, and inquire at the house of Judas for a man from Tarsus named Saul; for he is praying, 12 and he has seen [in a vision][e] a man named Ananias come in and lay his hands on him so that he might regain his sight."

13 But Ananias answered, "Lord, I have heard from many about this man, how much harm he has done to your saints in Jerusalem; 14 and here he has authority from the chief priests to bind all who call on your name."

15 But the Lord said to him, "Go, for this man is a chosen instrument of mine to carry my name before Gentiles and kings and the sons of Israel; 16 for I will show him how much he must suffer for the sake of my name."

17 So Ananias went and entered the house, and laying his hands on him he said, "Brother Saul, the Lord Jesus, who appeared to you on the road by which you came, has sent me so that you may regain your sight and be filled with the Holy Spirit." 18 And immediately something like scales fell from his eyes, and he [[immediately]][f] regained his sight; and getting up, he was baptized. 19 And after taking some food, he was strengthened.

{He}[g] spent some days with the disciples in Damascus, 20 and immediately he began to proclaim {Jesus}[h] in the synagogues, saying, "This is the Son of God."

21 All who heard were amazed and said, "Is not this the man who ravaged those who called on this name in Jerusalem and came here for this purpose, to bring them bound before the chief priests?"

22 But Saul was increasingly empowered [[by the word]][i] and confounded the Jews who lived in Damascus by proving that this is the Christ. 23 When many days had passed, the Jews plotted to kill him, 24 but their plot became known to Saul. They were also watching the gates day and night so that they might kill him; 25 but his disciples took him by night and let him down through an opening in the wall, lowering him in a basket.

26 When {he}[j] had come to Jerusalem, he attempted to join the disciples; and they were all afraid of him, for they did not believe that he was a disciple. 27 But Barnabas took him and brought him to the apostles and described to them how on the road he had seen the Lord, who had spoken to him, and how in Damascus he had spoken boldly in the name {of Jesus}.[k]

---

a 9:5, **he said:** Some manuscripts read "the Lord said." BYZ TR ‖ Absent from ℵ(01).

b 9:5, **the Nazarene:** Included in A(02) C(04).

c 9:5, **Is it hard for you to kick against goads:** Included in TR.

d 9:6, **the Lord said to him:** Included in TR.

e 9:12, **in a vision:** Absent from ℵ(01) A(02).

f 9:18, **immediately:** Included in BYZ TR.

g 9:19, **He:** Some manuscripts read "Saul." BYZ TR.

h 9:20, **Jesus:** Some manuscripts read "Christ." BYZ TR.

i 9:22, **by the word:** Included in C(04).

j 9:26, **he:** Some manuscripts read "Saul." BYZ TR.

k 9:27, **Jesus:** Some manuscripts read "the Lord." A(02).

28 So he went in among them in Jerusalem, speaking boldly in the name of the Lord [[Jesus]],ᵃ 29 and he spoke and debated with the Hellenists; but they were trying to kill him.

30 When the brothers learned of it, they brought him down to {Caesarea}ᵇ and sent him off to Tarsus.

31 So the church throughout all Judea, Galilee, and Samaria had peace and was being built up. And walking in the fear of the Lord and in the comfort of the Holy Spirit, it multiplied.

32 Now, as Peter went here and there among them all, he came down also to the saints who lived at Lydda. 33 There he found a man named Aeneas, who had been bedridden for eight years, for he was paralyzed. 34 And Peter said to him, "Aeneas, [[the Lord]]ᶜ Jesus [[the]]ᵈ Christ heals you; rise and make your bed." And immediately he rose. 35 And all the residents of Lydda and {Sharon}ᵉ saw him, and they turned to the Lord.

36 Now in Joppa there was a disciple named Tabitha, which, translated, means Dorcas. She was full of good works and acts of charity. 37 In those days she became ill and died, and when they had washed her, they laid [her]ᶠ in an upper room. 38 Since Lydda was near Joppa, the disciples, hearing that Peter was there, sent [two men]ᵍ to him, urging him, "Please come to us without delay." 39 So Peter rose and went with them. And when he arrived, they took him to the upper room.

All the widows stood beside him weeping and showing tunics and other garments that Dorcas made while she was with them. 40 But Peter put them all outside, and knelt down and prayed; and turning to the body he said, "Tabitha, rise." She opened her eyes, and when she saw Peter she sat up. 41 And he gave her his hand and raised her up. Then calling the saints and widows, he presented her alive. 42 And it became known throughout all Joppa, and many believed in the Lord.

43 And he stayed in Joppa for many days with a certain Simon, a tanner.

10 ¹ There was a certain man in Caesarea named Cornelius, a centurion of what was called the Italian Regiment, 2 devout and fearing God with all his household, doing many acts of charity to the people and praying to God continually.

3 He saw in a vision clearly about the ninth hour of the day an angel of God coming in to him and saying to him, "Cornelius." 4 And he, gazing intently at him and becoming fearful, said, "What is it, Lord?" And he said to him, "Your prayers and your acts of charity have ascended [as a memorial]ʰ before God. 5 Now send men to Joppa and summon [a certain]ⁱ Simon who is called Peter; 6 he is staying with a certain Simon, a tanner, whose house is by the sea."

7 When the angel who spoke to him had departed, he called two of his servants and a devout soldier from among those who attended him, 8 and having explained everything to them, he sent them to Joppa.

9 The next day, as they were on their journey and approaching the city, Peter went up on the housetop to pray, about the sixth hour [[of the day]].ʲ 10 And he became hungry and wanted to eat. But while they were preparing, he fell into a trance 11 and saw the

---

ᵃ 9:28, **Jesus:** Included in BYZ TR.
ᵇ 9:30, **Caesarea:** A(02) reads "Jerusalem."
ᶜ 9:34, **the Lord:** Included in A(02).
ᵈ 9:34, **the:** Included in A(02) BYZ TR.
ᵉ 9:35, **Sharon:** Some manuscripts read "Assaron." 𝔓45 𝔓53 ℵ(01) A(02) BYZ TR.
ᶠ 9:37, **her:** Absent from B(03).
ᵍ 9:38, **two men:** Absent from BYZ TR.
ʰ 10:4, **as a memorial:** Absent from ℵ(01).
ⁱ 10:5, **a certain:** Absent from ℵ(01) BYZ TR.
ʲ 10:9, **of the day:** Included in A(02).

heavens opened and something like a [great]ᵃ sheet descending [[upon him]],ᵇ [[having been bound and]]ᶜ being let down by its four corners upon the earth. 12 In it were all kinds of four-footed animals and reptiles of the earth and birds of the sky [[and wild beasts]].ᵈ

13 And a voice came to him, "Rise, [Peter;]ᵉ kill and eat." 14 But Peter said, "By no means, Lord; for I have never eaten anything common and unclean."

15 [And]ᶠ a voice came to him again a second time, "What God has made clean, do not call common."

16 This happened three times, and [immediately]ᵍ the sheet was taken up to heaven.

17 Now as Peter was perplexed in himself as to what the vision that he had seen might mean, [[and]]ʰ behold, the men who were sent by Cornelius, having made inquiry for Simon's house, stood at the gate 18 and called out to ask whether Simon who was called Peter was lodging there.

19 While Peter was pondering the vision, the Spirit said [to him],ⁱ "Behold, [three]ʲ men are looking for you. 20 But rise and go down and accompany them without hesitation, for I have sent them."

21 {And}ᵏ Peter went down to the men [[who had been sent from Cornelius]]ˡ and said, "Behold, I am the one you are looking for. [[What do you want?]]ᵐ What is the reason for your coming?" 22 And they said, "Cornelius, a centurion, an upright and God-fearing man, who is well spoken of by the whole Jewish nation, was directed by a holy angel to send for you to come to his house and to hear words from you." 23 Therefore, [[Peter]]ⁿ having summoned them, he showed hospitality.

On the next day {he rose and}ᵒ went away with them, and some of the brothers from Joppa accompanied him. 24 And on the following day they entered Caesarea. Cornelius was expecting them and had called together his relatives and close friends. 25 {When Peter entered,}ᵖ Cornelius [[having leapt up and]]�q met him and fell down at his feet and worshiped [[him]].ʳ 26 But Peter lifted him up, saying, "Stand up; I too am [[as you are also]]ˢ a man." 27 And [as he talked with him,]ᵗ he went in and found many persons gathered.

---

a 10:11, **great:** Absent from 𝔓45.

b 10:11, **upon him:** Included in BYZ TR.

c 10:11, **having been bound and:** Included in BYZ TR.

d 10:12, **and wild beasts:** Included in C(04) BYZ TR.

e 10:13, **Peter:** Absent from 𝔓45.

f 10:15, **And:** D(05) reads "But."

g 10:16, **immediately:** Absent from 𝔓45. ‖ Some manuscripts read "again." D(05) BYZ TR.

h 10:17 , **and:** Included in C(04) D(05) BYZ TR.

i 10:19, **to him:** Absent from B(03).

j 10:19, **three:** Absent from D(05) BYZ. ‖ B(03) reads two.

k 10:21, **And:** Some manuscripts read "Then." D(05).

l 10:21, **who had been sent from Cornelius:** Included in TR.

m 10:21, **What do you want?:** Included in D(05).

n 10:23, **Peter:** Included in D(05).

o 10:23, **he rose and:** Some manuscripts read "Peter." BYZ TR.

p 10:25, **When Peter entered:** D(05) reads "And as Peter was approaching Caesarea, one of the servants ran ahead and reported that he had arrived; and."

q 10:25, **having leapt up and** Included in D(05).

r 10:25, **him:** Included in D(05).

s 10:26, **as you are also:** Included in D(05).

t 10:27, **as he talked with him:** Absent from D(05).

28 And he said to them, “You
yourselves know how unlawful it is
for a Jew to associate with or to visit
anyone of another nation, but God has
shown me that I should not call any
person common or unclean. 29 So when I
was sent for [[by you]],[a] I came without
objection. Therefore, I ask, what reason
did you sent for me.”

30 {And}[b] Cornelius said, “Four
days ago [[I was fasting]],[c] about this
hour, I was praying in my house at
the ninth hour, and behold, a man
stood before me in bright clothing
31 and said, ‘Cornelius, your prayer has
been heard and your acts of charity
have been remembered before God.
32 Send therefore to Joppa and ask for
Simon who is called Peter. He is staying
in the house of Simon, a tanner, by the
sea, [[who, when he comes, will speak
to you.]]’[d] 33 So I sent for you at once
[[urging you to come]],[e] and you have
been kind enough to come [[quickly]].[f]
Now therefore {we are all here}[g] {in the
presence of God}[h] to hear all that you
have been commanded by {the Lord}.”[i]

34 Opening [his mouth],[j] Peter said,
“In truth, I understand that God is
not a respecter of persons, 35 but in
every nation, the one who fears him
and works righteousness is acceptable
to him.

36 “[[For]][k] The word [which][l] was
sent to the sons of Israel, preaching
peace through Jesus Christ, this one
is Lord of all, 37 You know {the word
that}[m] that took place throughout all
Judea, beginning from Galilee after
the baptism which John proclaimed,
38 Jesus from Nazareth, how God
anointed[n] him with the Holy Spirit[o]
and with power, who went about
doing good and healing all who were
oppressed by the devil, because God
was with him.

39 “And we [[indeed]][p] are witnesses
of [all][q] the things he did both in
the country of the Jews [and in
Jerusalem].[r] They [also][s] killed him,
hanging him on a tree, 40 but God raised
him {on}[t] the third day and made him
to appear, 41 not to all the people, but to
[witnesses][u] [[us]][v] chosen beforehand
by God, [to us,][w] who ate and drank
with him [[and associated with him]][x]
after he rose from the dead [[for forty

---

a 10:29, **by you:** Included in D(05).
b 10:30, **And** 𝔓50 reads “But.”
c 10:30, **I was fasting:** Included in BYZ TR.
d 10:32, **Who, when he comes, will speak to you:** Included in C(04) D(05) BYZ TR.
e 10:33, **urging you to come:** Included in 𝔓127 D(05).
f 10:33, **quickly:** Included in 𝔓127 D(05).
g 10:33, **we are all here:** 𝔓127 reads “behold.”
h 10:33, **in the presence of God:** Some manuscripts read “in your presence.” 𝔓127 D(05).
i 10:33, **the Lord:** Some manuscripts read “God.” 𝔓127 D(05) BYZ TR.
j 10:34, **his mouth:** Absent from 𝔓127.
k 10:36, **For:** Included in C(04) D(05).
l 10:36, **which:** Absent from A(02) B(03).
m 10:37, **the word that:** D(05) reads “what.”
n 10:38, **anointed:** The Greek word means anoint in our literature only in a figurative sense of an anointing by God setting a person apart for special service under divine direction... God anoints (a) David, (b) Jesus, the Christ for his work or mission, (c) the prophets, (d) the apostles or, more probably, all Christians (at baptism or through the Spirit) 1 Cor 1:21.
o 10:38, **Spirit:** See footnote for Spirit in Luke 1:15.
p 10:39, **indeed:** Included in 𝔓45.
q 10:39, **all:** Absent from D(05).
r 10:39, **and in Jerusalem:** Absent from 𝔓45.
s 10:39, **also:** Absent from BYZ TR.
t 10:40, **on:** Some manuscripts read “after.” D(05).
u 10:41, **witnesses:** Absent from 𝔓127.
v 10:41, **us:** Included in C(04).
w 10:41, **to us:** Absent from C(04).
x 10:41, **and associated with him** Included in 𝔓127 D(05).

days]].[a] 42 And he commanded us to preach to the people and to testify that {this one}[b] is the one appointed by [[the plan and foreknowledge of]][c] God as judge of the living and the dead. 43 [To this one][d] All the prophets bear witness that everyone who believes in him will receive forgiveness of sins through his name."

44 While Peter was still speaking these words, the Holy Spirit[e] fell upon all those who were listening to the message. 45 And the believers from the circumcision who had come with Peter were amazed, because the gift of the Holy Spirit had been poured out even on the Gentiles. 46 For they heard them speaking in tongues and magnifying God.

Then Peter responded, 47 "Can anyone withhold the water for these not to be baptized, who have received the Holy Spirit just as we have?" 48 And he ordered them to be baptized in the name of {Jesus Christ}.[f]

Then they asked him to stay for a few days.

11 1 Now the apostles and the brothers who were throughout Judea heard that the Gentiles also had received the word of God.

2 So {when Peter went up}[g] to Jerusalem, [[and having called out to the brothers and having strengthened them, speaking at length while passing through the regions, teaching them. He also came to them and reported to them the grace of God.]][h] [[But the brothers from]][i] the circumcision party criticized him, 3 saying [that],[j] "You went to uncircumcised men and ate with them."

4 But Peter began and {explained it to them in order}:[k] 5 "I was in [the city of][l] Joppa [praying],[m] and in a trance I saw a vision, something like a great sheet descending, being let down from heaven by its four corners, and it came down to me. 6 Looking at it closely, and saw the four-footed animals of the earth and the wild [beasts][n] and reptiles and birds of the sky. 7 And I [also][o] heard a voice saying to me, 'Rise, Peter; kill and eat.' 8 But I said, 'By no means, Lord; for nothing common or unclean has ever entered my mouth.' 9 But the voice {answered}[p] [[me]][q] a second time from heaven, 'What God has made clean, do not call common.' 10 [And][r] This happened three times, and all was drawn up again into heaven.

11 "And behold, at that very moment three men arrived at the house in which we were, sent to me from Caesarea. 12 And the Spirit told me to go with them [not doubting at all].[s] These six brothers also accompanied me, and we entered the man's house. 13 And he told

---

a 10:41, **for forty days:** Included in 𝔓127 D(05).

b 10:42, **this one:** Some manuscripts read "he."

c 10:42, **the plan and foreknowledge of:** Included in 𝔓127.

d 10:43, **To this one:** Absent from 𝔓127.

e 10:44, **Spirit:** See the footnote for Spirit in verse 38.

f 10:48, **Jesus Christ:** D(05) reads "the Lord Jesus Christ." ‖ Some manuscripts read "the Lord" BYZ TR.

g 11:2, **when Peter went up:** D(05) "therefore, after a considerable time wished to go."

h 11:2, **and having called out...:** Included in D(05) ‖ 𝔓127 reads "Passing through the regions, teaching them, he also arrived in Jerusalem and reported to them the grace of God."

i 11:2, **But the brothers from:** Included in 𝔓127 D(05).

j 11:3, **that:** Absent from 𝔓45.

k 11:4, **explained it to them in order:** Some manuscripts read "said to them." 𝔓127.

l 11:5, **the city of:** Absent from 𝔓127.

m 11:5, **praying:** Absent from 𝔓127 ℵ(01).

n 11:6, **beasts:** Absent from A(02).

o 11:7, **also:** Absent from A(02) D(05) BYZ TR.

p 11:9, **answered:** Some manuscripts read "happened." BYZ TR.

q 11:9, **me:** Included in BYZ TR.

r 11:10, **And:** Absent from 𝔓45.

s 11:12, **not doubting at all:** Absent from 𝔓45 D(05).

us how he had seen the angel standing in his house and saying [[to him]],[a] 'Send to Joppa [men][b] and bring Simon who is called Peter; 14 he will declare to you a message by which you will be saved, you and all your household.' 15 As I began to speak [[to them]],[c] the Holy Spirit[d] fell upon them [just][e] as it did upon us at the beginning. 16 And I remembered the word of the Lord, how he said, 'John baptized with water, but you will be baptized with the Holy Spirit.'[f]

17 "If then {God}[g] gave the same gift to them as he gave to us when we believed in the Lord Jesus Christ, who was I that I could stand in God's way [[from giving to them the Holy Spirit, having believed upon him]]?"[h]

18 When they heard these things they fell silent. And they glorified God, saying, "Then to the Gentiles also God has granted repentance that leads to life."

19 Now those who were scattered because of the persecution that arose over Stephen traveled as far as Phoenicia and Cyprus and Antioch, speaking the word to no one except Jews.

20 But there were some of them, men of Cyprus and Cyrene, who, on coming to Antioch spoke to the Hellenists [also],[i] preaching the Lord Jesus [[Christ]].[j] 21 And the hand of the Lord was with them, and a great number who believed turned to the Lord.

22 The report of this {came to}[k] the ears of the church in Jerusalem, and they sent Barnabas to [go through][l] as far as Antioch. 23 When he came and saw the grace of God, he was glad, and he exhorted them all to remain faithful to the Lord with steadfast purpose, 24 for he was a good man, full of the Holy Spirit and of faith. And a great many people were added [to the Lord].[m]

25 {And {he}[n] went out to Tarsus to seek Saul},[o] 26 {and when he had found him},[p] he brought him to Antioch. {And it happened to them [also][q] for}[r] a whole year they met with [the church and taught][s] a great many people. And in Antioch the disciples were first called Christians.

27 Now in these days prophets came down from Jerusalem to Antioch [[there was much rejoicing]][t]. 28 And one of them named Agabus stood up and foretold by the Spirit that there would be a great famine over all the world (this took place in the days of Claudius [[Caesar]])[u]. 29 So the disciples determined, everyone according to his

---

a 11:13, **to him:** Included in D(05) BYZ TR.

b 11:13, **men:** Included in BYZ TR.

c 11:15, **to them:** Included in D(05).

d 11:15, **Spirit:** See footnote for Spirit in Luke 1:15.

e 11:15, **just:** Absent from D(05).

f 11:16, **Spirit:** See the footnote for Spirit in verse 15.

g 11:17, **God:** D(05) reads "his."

h 11:17, **from giving to them the Holy Spirit, having believed upon him:** Included in D(05).

i 11:20, **also:** Absent from D(05) BYZ TR.

j 11:20, **Christ:** Included in D(05).

k 11:22, **came to:** Some manuscripts read "was heard in." A(02) D(05) BYZ TR.

l 11:22, **go through:** Absent from 𝔓74 ℵ(01) A(02) SBLGNT.

m 11:24, **to the Lord:** Absent from B(03).

n 11:25, **he:** Some manuscripts read "Barnabas." BYZ TR.

o 11:25, **And he went out to Tarsus to seek Saul:** D(05) reads "But having heard that Saul is in Tarsus, he went out searching for him."

p 11:26, **and when he had found him:** D(05) reads "Having met [him], he urged [him] to come."

q 11:26, **also:** Absent from D(05) BYZ TR.

r 11:26, **And it happened to them also for:** D(05) reads "Who, having arrived, [spent]."

s 11:26, **the church and taught:** Absent from D(05).

t 11:27, **there was much rejoicing:** Included in D(05).

u 11:28, **Caesar:** Included in BYZ TR.

ability, to send relief to the brothers living in Judea. 30 And they did so, sending it to the elders by the hand of Barnabas and Saul.

12 1 At that time, Herod the king laid hands on some of the church [[in Judea]]ᵃ to mistreat them. 2 He killed James, the brother of John, with the sword. 3 When he saw that it pleased the Jews, {he proceeded to arrest Peter as well}.ᵇ It was during the days of Unleavened Bread - 4 and when he had seized him, he put him in prison, handing him over to four squads of soldiers to guard him, intending to bring him out to the people after the Passover.

5 So Peter was kept in [[much]]ᶜ prison, but fervent prayer was being made [to God]ᵈ by the church on his behalf.

6 On the very night when Herod was about to bring him out, Peter was sleeping between two soldiers, bound with two chains, and guards in front of the door were watching the prison. 7 And behold, an angel of the Lord stood by {him},ᵉ and a light shone [[upon him]]ᶠ in the cell; and striking Peter's side, he woke him, saying, "Get up quickly." And the chains fell off his hands. 8 The angel said to him, "Tie your sandals and put them on." And he did so. Then he said to him, "Wrap your cloak around you and follow me." 9 And going out, he followed him, not knowing that what was happening through the angel was real; he thought he was seeing a vision. 10 Passing the first and second guard, they came to the iron gate leading into the city, which opened for them by itself; and going out, they [[went down the seven steps]]ᵍ and approached a street, and immediately the angel left him. 11 And Peter, coming to himself, said, "Now I truly know that the Lord has sent his angel and rescued me from the hand of Herod and from all that the Jews [of the people]ʰ were expecting." 12 When he realized this, he went to the house of Mary, the mother of John who was called Mark, where many were gathered together and were praying. 13 When he knocked at the door of the gateway, a servant girl named Rhoda came to answer. 14 Recognizing Peter's voice, in her joy she did not open the gate but ran in and reported that Peter was standing at the gate. 15 They said to her, "[[It might be so.]]ⁱ You are out of your mind." But she insisted that it was so. They said, "It is his angel." 16 But {Peter}ʲ continued knocking; and when they opened, they saw him and were amazed. 17 But motioning to them with his hand to be silent, he explained [to them]ᵏ how the Lord had led him out of the prison. And he said, "Tell James and the brothers these things." And he went out and went to another place.

18 When day came, there was [no small]ˡ disturbance among the soldiers as to what had become of Peter. 19 Herod, after searching for him and not finding him, examined the guards and ordered them to be led away. And he went down from Judea to Caesarea and stayed there.

ᵃ 12:1, **in Judea:** Included in 𝔓127 D(05).
ᵇ 12:3, **he proceeded to arrest Peter as well:** Some manuscripts read "His action was directed against the faithful; he also wanted to seize Peter." 𝔓127 D(05).
ᶜ 12:5, **much:** Included in D(05).
ᵈ 12:5, **to God:** Absent from B(03).
ᵉ 12:7, **him:** Some manuscripts read "Peter." 𝔓127.
ᶠ 12:7, **upon him:** Included in 𝔓127.
ᵍ 12:10, **went down the seven steps:** Included in D(05).
ʰ 12:11, **of the people:** Absent from A(02).
ⁱ 12:15, **It might be so:** Absent from D(05).
ʲ 12:16, **Peter:** Some manuscripts read "he." D(05).
ᵏ 12:17, **to them:** Absent from 𝔓45 ℵ(01) A(02).
ˡ 12:18, **no small:** Absent from D(05).

20 Now {he}[a] was angry with the people of Tyre and Sidon; and they came to him with one accord [[from both cities]],[b] and having won over Blastus, the king's chamberlain, they asked for peace, because their country was fed by the king's country.

21 On an appointed day, Herod, dressed in royal robes, sat on his throne and delivered an oration to them. 22 And the people shouted, "The voice of a god, and not of a man!" 23 Immediately an angel of the Lord struck him down, because he did not give the glory to God; and he was {eaten by worms and}[c] breathed his last.

24 But the word of {God}[d] grew and multiplied. 25 Barnabas and Saul returned to Jerusalem, [having completed their ministry,][e] and they took with them John, who was called Mark.

13 1 Now there were [[some]][f] in Antioch, in the existing church, prophets and teachers: both Barnabas and Simeon called Niger, and Lucius the Cyrenian, Manaen the foster brother of Herod the tetrarch, and Saul. 2 And as they were ministering to the Lord and fasting, the Holy Spirit said, "Set apart for me Barnabas and Saul for the work to which I have called them." 3 Then, having [[all]][g] fasted and prayed and laid their hands on them, they sent them off.

4 So, being sent out by the Holy Spirit, they went down to Seleucia, and from there they sailed to Cyprus. 5 When they arrived in Salamis, they proclaimed the word of God in the synagogues of the Jews. And they had John as their assistant.

6 Having traveled through the [whole][h] island as far as Paphos, they found a certain [man, a][i] magician, a false prophet, a Jew whose name was Bar-Jesus, 7 who was with the proconsul, Sergius Paulus, a man of understanding. This man, having called for Barnabas and Saul, sought to hear the word of God.

8 But Elymas the magician (for so his name is translated) withstood them, seeking to turn the proconsul away from the faith [[since he was most gladly listening to them]].[j] 9 But Saul, who is also called Paul, filled with the Holy Spirit, looked intently at him 10 and said, "O full of [all][k] deceit and all fraud, you son of the devil, you enemy of all righteousness, will you not cease perverting the straight ways of the Lord?

11 "And now, behold, the hand of the Lord is upon you, and you shall be blind, not seeing the sun for a time." And immediately a mist and darkness fell upon him, and he went about seeking those to lead him by the hand.

12 Then the proconsul, when he saw what had happened, {believed},[l] being astonished at the teaching of {the Lord}.[m]

13 Now when Paul and his party set sail from Paphos, they came to Perga in Pamphylia; and John, departing from them, returned to Jerusalem. 14 But when they departed from Perga, they came to Antioch in Pisidia, and

---

a 12:20, **he:** Some manuscripts read "Herod." BYZ TR.

b 12:20, **from both cities:** Included in D(05).

c 12:23, **eaten by worms and:** D(05) reads "eaten by worms, still living, and in this way."

d 12:24, **God:** Some manuscripts read "Lord."

e 12:25, **having completed their ministry:** Absent from D(05).

f 13:1, **some:** Included in BYZ TR.

g 13:3, **all:** Included in D(05).

h 13:6, **whole:** Absent from BYZ TR.

i 13:6, **man:** Absent from BYZ TR.

j 13:8, **since he was most gladly listening to them:** Included in D(05).

k 13:10, **all:** Absent from D(05).

l 13:12, **believed:** D(05) reads "marveled and believed in God."

m 13:12, **the Lord:** C(04) reads "God." BYZ TR.

[having] entered the synagogue on the Sabbath day, they sat down.

15 And after the reading of the Law and the Prophets, the rulers of the synagogue sent to them, saying, "Men and brethren, if there is a word of exhortation for the people, speak."

16 Then Paul stood up, and motioning with his hand said, "Men of Israel, and those who fear God, listen: 17 The God of this people [Israel][a] chose our fathers, and exalted the people when they dwelt as strangers in the land of Egypt, and with an uplifted arm he brought them out of it. 18 And for about forty years he [bore][b] with them in the wilderness. 19 [And][c] When he had destroyed seven nations in the land of Canaan, He distributed their land [[to them]][d] by allotment 20 as four hundred and fifty years. And after these things, he gave judges until Samuel the prophet. 21 And afterward they asked for a king; so God gave them Saul the son of Kish, a man of the tribe of Benjamin, for forty years. 22 And when He had removed him, He raised up for them David as king, to whom also he gave testimony and said, 'I have found David the son of Jesse, a man after my own heart, who will do all my will.'[e]

23 "Of this one, God, [from {the}[f] seed][g] according to the promise, {brought}[h] to Israel {a Savior, Jesus};[i] 24 having been proclaimed by John before the face of his entrance a baptism of repentance to [all][j] [the people of][k] Israel. 25 And as John was completing his course, he said, 'Who do you think I am? I am not he. But behold, there comes one after me, whose sandals of his feet I am not worthy to untie.'

26 "Men, brothers, sons of the family of Abraham and those among you fearing God, to us the word of [this][l] salvation has been sent. 27 For those who dwell in Jerusalem, and their rulers, because they did not know him, nor even the voices of the {Prophets}[m] which are read every Sabbath, have fulfilled them in condemning him. 28 And though they found no cause for death [in him],[n] [[after judging him]][o] they asked Pilate that he should be put to death. 29 Now when they had fulfilled all that was written concerning him, [[they kept asking Pilate for this one indeed to be crucified, and having succeeded again,]][p] they took him down from the tree and laid him in a tomb. 30 But God raised him [from the dead].[q] 31 He was seen [for many days][r] by those who came up with him from Galilee to Jerusalem [[for more days]],[s] who are [now][t] his witnesses to the people.

---

a 13:17, **Israel:** Absent from BYZ.

b 13:18, **bore:** The Greek word means to bear/put up with (someone's) manner, moods etc. (BDAG, τροποφορέω). Some manuscripts read "cared for them." ‖ Absent from D(05).

c 13:19, **And** Absent from some B(03).

d 13:19, **to them:** Included in A(02) C(04) BYZ TR ‖ D(05) reads "to the Gentiles."

e 13:22, Psalm 89:20, 1 Samuel 13:14.

f 13:23, **the:** Some manuscripts read "his." D(05).

g 13:23, **from the seed:** Absent from ℵ(01).

h 13:23, **brought:** Some manuscripts read "raised." C(04) D(05) TR.

i 13:23, **a Savior, Jesus:** Some manuscripts read "salvation." BYZ.

j 13:24, **all:** Absent from BYZ.

k 13:24, **the people of:** Absent from ℵ(01) A(02) BYZ.

l 13:26, **this:** Absent from C(04).

m 13:27, **Prophets:** Some manuscripts read "Scriptures." BYZ TR.

n 13:28, **in him:** Absent from D(05).

o 13:28, **after judging him:** Included in D(05).

p 13:29, **they kept asking Pilate for this one indeed to be crucified, and having succeeded again:** Included in D(05).

q 13:30, **from the dead:** Absent from D(05).

r 13:31, **for many days:** Absent from D(05).

s 13:31, **for more days:** Included in D(05).

t 13:31, **now** Absent from B(03) BYZ TR ‖ D(05) reads "remaining until now."

³²"And we proclaim to you the promise made to {the}ᵃ fathers, ³³God has fulfilled this for us their children, in that he has raised up [[the Lord]]ᵇ {Jesus} ᶜ[[Christ]].ᵈ As it is also written in the [second]ᵉ Psalm: 'You are My Son, today I have begotten You.ᶠ [[Ask from me, and I will give you the nations as your inheritance, and the ends of the earth as your possession.]]'ᵍ

³⁴"But that he raised him from the dead, no more to return to corruption, he has spoken in this way, 'I will give you the holy and sure blessings of David.'ʰ ³⁵For also in another it says, 'You will not allow your Holy One to see decay.'ⁱ

³⁶"[For]ʲ [indeed]ᵏ David, after he had served the purpose of God in his own generation, fell asleep and was laid with his fathers and saw corruption, ³⁷but he whom God raised up did not see corruption.

³⁸"Therefore, let it be known to you, men, brothers, that through this one forgiveness of sins is proclaimed to you, [and]ˡ [[repentance]]ᵐ from all things from which you could not be justified in the law of Moses, ³⁹in this one everyone who believes is justified [[by God]].ⁿ

⁴⁰"Therefore, see that the thing spoken of in the prophets does not come [upon you]:ᵒ ⁴¹'Look, you scoffers, be amazed and perish, for I am doing a work in your days, [a work]ᵖ that you will not believe, even if someone tells it to you.'"�q

⁴²As they [[from the synagogue of the Jews]]ʳ went out, {they}ˢ urged to speak these words to them on the next Sabbath. ⁴³And when the synagogue was dismissed, many of the Jews and devout converts followed Paul and Barnabas, who, speaking [to them],ᵗ persuaded them to {continue}ᵘ in the grace of God. [[Now it happened that throughout the whole city the word of God was being spread.]]ᵛ

⁴⁴On the coming Sabbath almost the whole city gathered to hear the word [[, and Paul had spoken many words]]ʷ {of the Lord}.ˣ ⁴⁵But when the Jews saw the crowds, they were filled with jealousy and began to

---

ᵃ 13:32, **the:** D(05) reads "our."

ᵇ 13:33, **the Lord:** Included in D(05).

ᶜ 13:33, **Jesus:** A(02) reads "from death."

ᵈ 13:33, **Christ** Included in D(05).

ᵉ 13:33, **second:** Absent from D(05).

ᶠ 13:33, Psalm 2:7.

ᵍ 13:33, **Ask from me...:** Included in D(05).

ʰ 13:34, Isaiah 55:3 LXX.

ⁱ 13:35, Psalm 16:10 LXX.

ʲ 13:36, **For:** Absent from D(05).

ᵏ 13:36, **indeed:** Absent from D(05).

ˡ 13:38, **and:** Absent from א(01) A(02) C(04).

ᵐ 13:38, **repentance:** Included in D(05).

ⁿ 13:39, **by God:** Absent from D(05).

ᵒ 13:40, **upon you:** Included in A(02) C(04) BYZ TR.

ᵖ 13:41, **a work:** Absent from D(05) BYZ.

q 13:41, Habakkuk 1:5 LXX.

ʳ 13:42, **from the synagogue of the Jews:** Included in BYZ TR.

ˢ 13:42, **they:** Some manuscripts read "the Gentiles." BYZ TR.

ᵗ 13:43, **to them:** Absent from BYZ.

ᵘ 13:43, **continue:** Some manuscripts read "remain." BYZ TR.

ᵛ 13:43, **Now it happened...:** Included in D(05).

ʷ 13:44, **and Paul had spoken many words:** Included in D(05).

ˣ 13:44, **the Lord:** Some manuscripts read "God." B(03) C(04) BYZ TR.

contradict {the things}[a] spoken by Paul, [[contradicting and]][b] blaspheming.[c]

46 And Paul and Barnabas spoke out boldly and said [[to them]],[d] "It was necessary that the word of God be spoken to you first; since you thrust it aside and judge yourselves unworthy of eternal life, behold, we are turning to the Gentiles. 47 For so the Lord has commanded [us],[e] saying, 'I have set you as a light for the Gentiles, that you may bring salvation to the ends of the earth.'"[f]

48 And when the Gentiles heard this, they began rejoicing and glorifying the word of {the Lord},[g] and as many as were appointed to eternal life believed.

49 And the word of the Lord was spreading throughout the whole region. 50 But the Jews incited the devout women of high standing and the leading men of the city, stirred up [[great tribulation and]][h] persecution against Paul and Barnabas, and drove them out of {their}[i] district. 51 But they shook off the dust from their feet against them and went to Iconium.

52 And the disciples were filled with joy and the Holy Spirit.

14 1 Now it happened in Iconium that they entered together into the synagogue [of the Jews],[j] and spoke in such a way [[to them]][k] that a great number of both Jews and Greeks believed. 2 But the Jews who refused to believe {stirred up}[l] and poisoned the minds of the Gentiles against the brothers. [[But the Lord gave swift peace.]][m]

3 So they spent a considerable time there, speaking boldly for the Lord, who bore witness to the word of his grace, granting signs and wonders to be done through their hands.

4 But the people of the city were divided; some sided with the Jews, and some with the apostles [[being joined because of the word of God]].[n]

5 When an attempt was made by both Gentiles and Jews, with their rulers, to mistreat them and to stone them, 6 they became aware of it and fled to the cities of Lycaonia, Lystra and Derbe, and the [[whole]][o] surrounding region. 7 And there they continued to preach the good news [[and the whole crowd was stirred up by the teaching, but Paul and Barnabas stayed on in Lystra]].[p]

---

a 13:45, **the things:** D(05) reads "the words." BYZ TR.

b 13:45, **contradicting and:** Included in D(05) BYZ TR.

c 13:45, **blaspheming:** The Greek word means to speak in a disrespectful way that demeans, denigrates, maligns. In relation to humans: "slander," "revile," or "defame." (BDAG, βλασφημέω).

d 13:46, **to them** Included in D(05).

e 13:47, **us:** Absent from D(05).

f 13:47, Isaiah 49:6.

g 13:48, **the Lord:** Some manuscripts read "God." B(03) D(05).

h 13:50, **great tribulation and:** Absent from D(05).

i 13:50, **their** B(03) reads "the."

j 14:1, **of the Jews:** Absent from ℵ(01).

k 14:1, **to them:** Included in D(05).

l 14:2, **stirred up:** D(05) reads "and the rulers of the synagogue stirred up persecution against the righteous for them."

m 14:2, **But the Lord gave swift peace:** Included in D(05).

n 14:4, **being joined because of the word of God:** Included in D(05).

o 14:6, **whole:** Included in D(05).

p 14:7, **and the whole crowd...:** Included in D(05).

8 And a certain man was sitting [in Lystra],[a] disabled in his feet [, lame][b] from his mother's womb, who had never walked. 9 This one heard Paul speaking; who, [[being in fear, but Paul]][c] having fixed his gaze on him and seeing that he had faith to be healed, 10 said with a loud voice, "[[I say to you in the name of the Lord Jesus Christ]][d] Stand upright on your feet." And [[immediately at once]][e] he sprang up and began to walk.

11 And when the crowds saw what Paul had done, they lifted up their voices, saying in Lycaonian, "The gods have come down to us in human form!" 12 Barnabas they called Zeus, and Paul, Hermes, because he was the chief speaker. 13 The priest of Zeus, whose temple was at the entrance to the city, brought oxen and garlands to the gates and wanted to offer sacrifice with the crowds.

14 But when [the apostles][f] Barnabas and Paul heard of it, they tore their clothes and rushed out into the crowd, shouting, 15 "Men, why are you doing these things? We [also][g] are men, of like nature with you, and we bring you good news, that you should turn away from these vain things to {a living God},[h] who made the heaven and the earth and the sea and all that is in them.

16 "In past [generations][i] he allowed all the nations to walk in their own ways. 17 Yet he did not leave himself without witness, for he did good by giving you rains from heaven and fruitful seasons, satisfying your hearts with food and gladness."

18 Even with these words they scarcely restrained the people from offering sacrifice to them [[but for each to go to his own things]].[j]

19 But [[while they were staying and teaching,]][k] Jews came from Antioch and Iconium, and having persuaded the crowds [[to turn away from them, saying that they speak nothing true but everything they say is false]],[l] they stoned Paul and dragged him out of the city, supposing that he was dead. 20 But when the disciples gathered about him, he rose up and entered the city, and on the next day he went on with Barnabas to Derbe.

21 And when they had preached the gospel to that city and had made many disciples, they returned to Lystra and to Iconium and to Antioch, 22 strengthening the souls of the disciples, encouraging them to continue in the faith, and saying that through many tribulations we must enter the kingdom of God.

23 And when they had appointed elders for them in every church, with prayer and fasting they committed them to the Lord in whom they had believed.

24 Then they passed through Pisidia and came to Pamphylia. 25 And when they had spoken the word [[of the Lord]][m] in Perga, they went down to Attalia, [[proclaiming good news to them,]][n] 26 and from there [they sailed][o] to Antioch, where they had been

---

a 14:8, **in Lystra:** Absent from D(05).

b 14:8, **lame:** Absent from D(05). ‖ Some manuscripts read "being lame." BYZ TR.

c 14:9, **being in fear, but Paul:** Included in D(05).

d 14:10, **I say to you in the name of the Lord Jesus Christ:** Included in C(04) D(05).

e 14:10, **immediately at once:** Included in D(05).

f 14:14, **the apostles:** Absent from D(05).

g 14:15, **also:** Absent from 𝔓45 D(05).

h 14:15, **a living God:** Some manuscripts read "the living God." 𝔓45 D(05) BYZ TR.

i 14:16, **generations** Absent from 𝔓45.

j 14:18, **but for each to go to his own things:** Included in C(04).

k 14:19, **while they were staying and teaching:** Included in C(04) D(05).

l 14:19, **to turn away from them... :** Include in C(04).

m 14:25, **of the Lord:** Included in ℵ(01) A(02) C(04).

n 14:25, **proclaiming good news to them:** Included in D(05).

o 14:26, **they sailed:** Absent from B(03).

commended to the grace of God for the work that they had fulfilled.

27 And when they arrived and gathered the church together, they declared all that God had done with them [[with their souls]],[a] and how he had opened a door of faith to the Gentiles.

28 And they spent a long time [[there]][b] with the disciples.

15 ¹ And some men came down from Judea and were teaching the brothers, "Unless you are circumcised according to the custom of Moses, you cannot be saved." ² And when Paul and Barnabas had no small dissension and debate with them, [[for Paul was saying to remain in this way as they had believed, insisting strongly,]][c] they appointed Paul and Barnabas [and certain others of them][d] to go up to the apostles and elders in Jerusalem [[so it might be decided]][e] concerning this matter.

³ So, being sent on their way by the church, they passed through both Phoenicia and Samaria, describing the conversion of the Gentiles, and brought great joy to all the brothers. ⁴ When they came to Jerusalem, they were welcomed by the church and the apostles and the elders, and they declared all that God had done with them [[and how he had opened a door of faith to the Gentiles.]][f]

⁵ But some believers who belonged to the party of the Pharisees rose up and said, "It is necessary to circumcise them and to order them to keep the law of Moses."

⁶ The apostles and the elders were gathered together to consider this matter. ⁷ And after there had been much {debate}[g] [[by Paul and Barnabas with them, they appointed Paul and Barnabas and certain others of them to go up to the apostles and elders]],[h] Peter stood up [[in the Spirit]][i] and said to them, "Brothers, you know that in the early days God made a choice among you, that by my mouth the Gentiles should hear the word of the gospel and believe.

⁸ "And the heart-knowing God bore witness to them, giving the Holy Spirit[j] [[to them]][k] just as also to us. ⁹ And he made no distinction between us and them, having cleansed their hearts by faith.

10 "[Now,][l] Therefore, why are you putting God to the test by placing [a yoke][m] on the neck of the disciples that neither our fathers nor we have been able to bear?

11 "But we believe that we will be saved through the grace of the Lord Jesus [[Christ]],[n] just as they will."

12 And all the assembly fell silent, and they listened to Barnabas and Paul as they related what signs and wonders God had done through them among the Gentiles.

---

a 14:27, **with their souls:** Included in D(05).

b 14:28, **there:** Included in BYZ TR.

c 15:2, **or Paul was saying to remain in this way as they had believed, insisting strongly:** Included in D(05).

d 15:2, **and certain others of them:** Absent from D(05).

e 15:2, **so it might be decided:** Included in D(05).

f 15:4, **and how he had opened a door of faith to the Gentiles:** Included in D(05).

g 15:7, **debate:** Some manuscripts read "discussion." C(04) D(05) BYZ TR.

h 15:7, **by Paul and Barnabas with them...:** Included in 𝔓45.

i 15:7, **in the Spirit:** Included in D(05).

j 15:8, **Spirit:** See footnote for Spirit in Luke 1:15.

k 15:8, **to them:** Included in C(04) D(05) BYZ TR.

l 15:10, **Now:** Absent from C(04).

m 15:10, **a yoke:** Absent from ℵ(01).

n 15:11, **Christ:** Included in C(04) D(05) TR.

13 After they finished speaking, James replied, "Brothers, listen to me. 14 Simeon has related how God first visited the Gentiles, to take from them a people for his name. 15 And with this the words of the prophets agree, just as it is written, 16 'After this I will return, and I will rebuild the tent of David that has fallen; I will rebuild its ruins, and I will restore it, 17 that the remnant of mankind may seek the Lord, and [all][a] the Gentiles who are called by my name, says the Lord, who makes these things 18 {known from of old}.'[bc]

19 "Therefore my judgment is that we should not trouble those of the Gentiles who turn to God, 20 but should write to them to abstain from the things polluted by idols, and from sexual immorality,[d] and from what has been strangled, and from blood [[and whatever they do not want to happen to themselves, do not do to others]].[e] 21 For from ancient generations Moses has had [in every city][f] those who proclaim him, for he is read every Sabbath in the synagogues."

22 Then it seemed good to the apostles and the elders, with the whole church, to choose men [from among them][g] and send them to Antioch with Paul and Barnabas. They sent Judas called Barsabbas, and Silas, leading men among the brothers, 23 having written by their own hand [[these things]][h] [[a letter containing the following]][i] : "The brothers, both the apostles and the elders, to the brothers who are of the Gentiles in Antioch and Syria and Cilicia, greetings.

24 "Since we have heard that some persons [have gone out][j] from us and troubled you with words, unsettling your minds [[saying, "Be circumcised and keep the law]],"[k] although we gave them no instructions, 25 it has seemed good to us, having come to one accord, to choose men and send them to you with our beloved Barnabas and Paul, 26 men who have risked their lives for the name of our Lord Jesus Christ [[into every trial]].[l] 27 We have therefore sent Judas and Silas, who themselves will tell you the same things by word of mouth.

28 "For it has seemed good to the Holy Spirit and to us to lay on you no greater burden than these requirements: 29 that you abstain from what has been sacrificed to idols, and from blood, [and from what has been strangled,][m] and from sexual immorality [[, and whatever you do not want to happen to yourselves, do not do to another]].[n] If you keep yourselves from these, you will do well [[led by the Holy Spirit]].[o] [Farewell.]"[p]

30 So when they were sent off, [[after a few days,]][q] they went down to Antioch, and having gathered the

---

a 15:17, **all:** Included in BYZ TR.

b 15:18, **known from of old:** Some manuscripts read "known to God from of old are all his works." A(02) D(05) BYZ TR.

c 15:16-18, Amos 9:11-12 LXX.

d 15:20, **Sexual immorality:** Absent from P45.

e 15:20, **and whatever they do not want to happen to themselves, do not do to others:** Included in D(05).

f 15:21, **in every city:** Absent from 𝔓45.

g 15:22, **from among them:** Absent from A(02).

h 15:23, **these things:** Included in C(04) D(05) BYZ TR.

i 15:23, **a letter containing the following:** Included in C(04) D(05).

j 15:24, **have gone out:** Absent from ℵ(01) B(03).

k 15:24, **saying, "Be circumcised and keep the law:** Included in C(04) BYZ TR.

l 15:26, **into every trial:** Included in D(05).

m 15:29, **and from what has been strangled:** Absent from D(05).

n 15:29, **and whatever you do not want to happen to yourselves, do not do to another:** Included in D(05).

o 15:29, **led by the Holy Spirit:** Included in D(05).

p 15:29, **Farewell:** Absent from 𝔓127.

q 15:30, **after a few days:** Included in D(05).

multitude, they delivered the letter. 31 And when they had read it, they rejoiced over the encouragement. 32 Judas and Silas, also being [[full of the Holy Spirit,]]^a prophets themselves, encouraged the brothers with [many]^b words [and strengthened them].^{c} 33 And after spending some time, they were sent off in peace from the brothers to {those who had sent [them].^{d}}^{e} 34 [[But it seemed good to Silas to remain there.]]^f

35 But Paul and Barnabas stayed in Antioch, teaching and preaching the word [of the Lord],^{g} with many others also.

36 And after some days, Paul said to Barnabas, "Let us return and visit {the} ^{h}brothers in every city where we have proclaimed the word of the Lord, and see how they are doing."

37 Barnabas {wanted}^{i} to take with them [also]^j John, called Mark. 38 But Paul {thought it best not to take with them the one who had withdrawn from them in Pamphylia and had not gone with them to the work}.^{k}

39 And there arose a sharp disagreement, so that they separated from one another. Barnabas took Mark and sailed to Cyprus.

40 But Paul chose Silas and departed, having been commended by the brothers to the grace of {the Lord}.^{l} 41 And he went through {Syria and [the]^m Cilicia},^{n} strengthening the churches [[delivering the commands from the apostles and the elders for them to keep]].^{o}

16 1 [[Handing over the commandments of the elders, and having gone through these nations]]^p But they [also]^q came to Derbe and Lystra. And behold, there was a certain disciple there [named]^r Timothy, the son of a [[certain]]^s believing Jewish woman [[, but his father was a Greek]].^{t} 2 He was well spoken of by the brothers in Lystra and Iconium.

3 Paul wanted this one to go with him, and he took and circumcised him because of the Jews who were in those places [, for they all knew that his father was a Greek].^{u}

---

^{a} 15:32, **full of the Holy Spirit:** Included in D(05).

^{b} 15:32, **words:** Absent from D(05).

^{c} 15:32, **and strengthened them:** Absent from ℵ(01).

^{d} 15:33, **them:** Absent from ℵ(01).

^{e} 15:33, **those who had sent them:** Some manuscripts read "the apostles." BYZ TR.

^{f} 15:34, **But it seemed good to Silas to remain there:** Included in C(04) D(05) BYZ TR.

^{g} 15:35, **of the Lord:** Absent from D(05).

^{h} 15:36, **the:** Some manuscripts read "our." BYZ TR.

^{i} 15:37, **wanted:** Some manuscripts read "planned." D(05) BYZ TR.

^{j} 15:37, **also:** Absent from D(05) BYZ TR.

^{k} 15:38, **thought it best not to take with them…:** Some manuscripts read "was not willing, saying that the one who had departed from them from Pamphylia and had not gone with them to the work to which they had been sent, this one was not to be with them." 𝔓127 D(05).

^{l} 15:40, **the Lord:** ℵ(01) A(02) B(03) NA28 SBLGNT THGNT ‖ Some manuscripts read "God." 𝔓45 C(04) BYZ TR.

^{m} 15:41, **the:** 𝔓45 B(03) D(05) NA28[] SBLGNT ‖ Absent from ℵ(01) A(02) C(04) BYZ TR THGNT.

^{n} 15:41, **Stria and the Cilicia:** 𝔓127 reads "Syrophoenicia."

^{o} 15:41, **delivering the commands from the apostles and the elders for them to keep:** Included in 𝔓127 D(05).

^{p} 16:1, **Handing over the commandments of the elders, and having gone through these nations:** Included in D(05).

^{q} 16:1, **also:** Absent from 𝔓74 ℵ(01) C(04) D(05) BYZ TR.

^{r} 16:1, **named:** Absent from 𝔓45.

^{s} 16:1, **certain:** Included in BYZ TR.

^{t} 16:1, **but his father was a Greek:** Absent from 𝔓127.

^{u} 16:3, **for they all knew that his father was a Greek** Absent from 𝔓127.

⁴And as they went through the cities, {they delivered to them the decrees to keep, which had been determined by}ᵃ the apostles and elders who were in Jerusalem.

⁵So the churches were strengthened in [the faith]ᵇ and increased in number daily.

⁶And they went through the region of Phrygia and Galatia, having been forbidden by the Holy Spirit to speak [[to no one]]ᶜ the word [[of God]]ᵈ in Asia. ⁷And when they had come up to Mysia, they {attempted}ᵉ to go into Bithynia, but the Spirit {of Jesus}ᶠ did not allow them.

⁸So, passing by Mysia, they went down to Troas. ⁹And a vision appeared to Paul in the night: a man of Macedonia was standing there [[before him]],ᵍ urging him and saying, "Come over to Macedonia and help us." ¹⁰{And when he had seen the vision, immediately we sought to go on into Macedonia, concluding that Godʰ had called us to preach the gospel to them}.ⁱ

¹¹{But having setting sail}ʲ from Troas, we made a direct voyage to Samothrace, and the following day to Neapolis, ¹²and from there to Philippi, which is a leading city of the district of Macedonia and a Roman colony.

We remained in this city some days.

¹³And on the Sabbath day we went outside the gateᵏ to the riverside, where we supposed there was a place of prayer, and we sat down and spoke to the women who had come together. ¹⁴One who heard us was a woman named Lydia, a seller of purple goods from the city of Thyatira, who worshiped {God}.ˡ The Lord opened her heart [to pay attention]ᵐ to what was said by Paul. ¹⁵And when she was baptized, and [[all]]ⁿ her household as well, she urged us, saying, "If you have judged me to be faithful [to the Lord],ᵒ come to my house and stay." And she prevailed upon us.

¹⁶Now [it happened]ᵖ as we were going to the place of prayer, a certain slave girl having a spirit [of Python met us],�q who provided much profit to her masters by fortune-telling.ʳ ¹⁷She followed Paul [and us],ˢ crying out, "These [men]ᵗ are servants of the Most High [God],ᵘ who proclaim to you the way of salvation." ¹⁸And this she kept doing for many days. Paul, having become greatly annoyed, turned and said to the spirit, "I command you in

---

ᵃ 16:4, **they delivered to them the decrees to keep, which had been determined by:** Some manuscripts read "they were proclaiming the Lord Jesus Christ with boldness, together handing over also the commandments of." 𝔓127 D(05).

ᵇ 16:5, **the faith:** Absent from ℵ(01).

ᶜ 16:6, **to no one:** Included in D(05).

ᵈ 16:6, **of God:** Included in D(05).

ᵉ 16:7, **attempted:** D(05) reads "wanted."

ᶠ 16:7, **of Jesus:** C(04) reads "the Lord." ‖ Absent from BYZ TR.

ᵍ 16:9, **before him:** Included in D(05).

ʰ 16:10, **God:** Some manuscripts read "the Lord." D(05) BYZ TR.

ⁱ 16:10, **And when he had seen the vision…:** D(05) reads "Then, having been awakened, he related the vision to us, and we understood that the Lord had called us to proclaim the good news to those in Macedonia."

ʲ 16:11, **But having setting sail:** D(05) reads "But on the next day, having been brought."

ᵏ 16:13, **gate:** Some manuscripts read "city."

ˡ 16:14, **God:** D(05) reads "the Lord."

ᵐ 16:14, **to pay attention:** Absent from 𝔓127.

ⁿ 16:15, **all:** Included in D(05).

ᵒ 16:15, **to the Lord:** Absent from 𝔓127.

ᵖ 16:16, **it happened:** Absent from 𝔓127.

q 16:16, **of Python met us:** Absent from 𝔓127.

ʳ 16:16, **fortune-telling:** Or divination.

ˢ 16:17, **us:** Absent from 𝔓127.

ᵗ 16:17, **men:** Absent from 𝔓127 D(05).

ᵘ 16:17, **God:** Absent from 𝔓127.

the name of Jesus Christ to come out of
her." [And it came out that very hour.][a]

19 But when {her owners}[b] saw that
their hope of gain [[through her]][c] was
gone, they seized Paul and Silas and
dragged them into the marketplace
[before the rulers].[d] 20 And when they
had brought them to the magistrates,
they said, "These men are Jews, and
they are disturbing our city. 21 They
advocate customs that are not lawful
for us as Romans to accept or practice."

22 The crowd joined in attacking
them [[shouting out]],[e] and the
magistrates tore the garments off them
and gave orders to beat them with rods.
23 And when they had inflicted many
blows [upon them],[f] they threw them
into prison, ordering the jailer to keep
them safely.

24 Having received this [order],[g]
he put them into the inner prison and
fastened their feet in the stocks.

25 About midnight Paul and Silas
were praying and singing hymns to
God, and the prisoners were listening to
them. 26 And suddenly there was a great
earthquake, so that the foundations
of the prison were shaken. And
[immediately][h] all the doors were
opened, and everyone's bonds were
unfastened.

27 When the jailer woke and saw
that the prison doors were open, he
drew his sword and was about to kill
himself, supposing that the prisoners
had escaped. 28 But Paul cried [with a
loud voice],[i] "Do not {harm yourself},[j]
for we are all here." 29 And the jailer
called for lights and rushed in, and
trembling with fear he fell down [[at
the feet]][k] before Paul and Silas.

30 Then he brought them out and
[[after securing the rest, he went in
and]][l] said, "Sirs, what must I do to
be saved?" 31 And they said [to him],[m]
"Believe in the Lord Jesus [[Christ]],[n]
and you will be saved [together with all
those in his household]."[o] 32 And they
spoke the word of {the Lord}[p] [[Jesus]][q]
to him and [to all who were in his
house][r].

33 And he took them the same hour
of the night and washed their wounds;
and he was baptized at once, he and all
his house.

34 And having brought them up into
{the}[s] house, he set a table before them,
and rejoiced with his whole household,
having believed in God.

---

[a] 16:18, **And it came out that very hour:** Absent from 𝔓127. ‖ D(05) reads "And immediately it came out."
[b] 16:19, **her owners:** D(05) reads "the owner of the servant girl."
[c] 16:19, **through her:** Included in D(05).
[d] 16:19, **before the rulers:** Absent from 𝔓127.
[e] 16:22, **shouting out:** Included in 𝔓127 D(05).
[f] 16:23, **upon them:** Absent from 𝔓127.
[g] 16:24, **order:** Absent from 𝔓127.
[h] 16:26, **immediately:** Absent from B(03).
[i] 16:28, **with a loud voice:** Absent from B(03).
[j] 16:28, **harm yourself:** 𝔓127 reads "be troubled."
[k] 16:29, **at the feet** Included in D(05).
[l] 16:30, **After securing the rest, he went in and:** Absent from 𝔓127 D(05).
[m] 16:31, **to him:** Included in 𝔓127.
[n] 16:31, **Christ:** Included in C(04) D(05) BYZ TR.
[o] 16:31, **together with all those in his household:** Absent from 𝔓127.
[p] 16:32, **the Lord:** Some manuscripts read "God." ℵ(01) B(03).
[q] 16:32, **Jesus:** Included in A(02).
[r] 16:32, **to all who were in his house:** Absent from 𝔓127.
[s] 16:34, **the:** Some manuscripts read "his." ℵ(01) A(02) D(05) BYZ TR.

35 But when it became day, the
commanders [[at the same place
into the marketplace, and having
remembered the earthquake that
had happened, they were afraid and
they]][a] sent the officers, saying [[to the
jailer]],[b] "Release those men [[whom
you took in yesterday]]."[c]

36 And [[having entered]][d] the jailer
reported [{these}[e] words][f] to {Paul},[g]
saying, "The commanders have sent to
release you; now therefore, go out and
proceed [in peace]."[h] 37 But Paul said
to them, "Having beaten us publicly
without trial, men who are Romans,
they threw us into prison; and now do
they cast us out secretly? [No, indeed!][i]
Let them come themselves and bring
us out."

38 The officers reported these words
to the commanders, [and they were
afraid][j] when {they}[k] heard that they
were Romans.

39 And having come [[with many
friends at the prison]],[l] they urged
them, and having brought them out,
they {asked them to depart from the
city}.[m]

40 And having {gone out of the
prison},[n] they went to Lydia, and
when they saw the brothers, {they
encouraged them and departed}.[o]

17 1 Now when they came
through Amphipolis and [went
down into][p] Apollonia, they came to
Thessalonica [, where there was a
synagogue of the Jews].[q] 2 And Paul
went in [[the synagogue of the Jews]][r]
as was his custom, and on three
Sabbath days he reasoned with them
from the Scriptures, 3 explaining and
proving that it was necessary for the
Christ to suffer and to rise from the
dead, and saying, "This is the Christ,[s]
[the] Jesus whom I proclaim to you."
[[Many attended the teaching.]][t]

4 And some of them were persuaded
and joined Paul and Silas, as did a great
many of the devout Greeks and not a
few of the leading women.

5 But the [[disobeying]][u] Jews were
jealous, and taking some wicked men
of the rabble, they formed a mob, set
the city in an uproar, and attacked
the house of Jason, seeking to bring
them out to the people. 6 And when
they could not find them, they dragged
Jason and some of the brothers before
the city authorities, shouting [[and
saying]],[v] "These men who have turned
the world upside down have come here

---

[a] 16:35, **at the same place into the marketplace, and having remembered the earthquake that had happened, they were afraid and they:** Included in some manuscripts. 𝔓127 D(05).
[b] 16:35, **to the jailer:** Absent from 𝔓127.
[c] 16:35, **whom you took in yesterday:** Included in 𝔓127 D(05).
[d] 16:36, **having entered:** Included in 𝔓127 D(05).
[e] 16:36, **these:** Some manuscripts read "the." 𝔓45 B(03) C(04) D(05).
[f] 16:36, **these words:** Absent from 𝔓127.
[g] 16:36, **Paul:** Some manuscripts read "him." 𝔓127.
[h] 16:36, **in peace:** Absent from some 𝔓127 D(05).
[i] 16:37, **No, indeed:** Absent from 𝔓127.
[j] 16:38, **and they were afraid:** Absent from 𝔓127 D(05).
[k] 16:38, **they:** Some manuscripts read "the officers." 𝔓127 D(05).
[l] 16:39, **with many friends at the prison:** Absent from 𝔓127 C(05).
[m] 16:39, **asked them to depart from the city:** Some manuscripts read "urged them again, saying, Leave this city, lest they again associate with us, shouting out against you." 𝔓127 D(05).
[n] 16:40, **gone out of the prison:** Some manuscripts read "been released." BYZ TR.
[o] 16:40, **they encouraged them and departed:** Some manuscripts read "they recounted all that the Lord had done for them, and after encouraging them." 𝔓127 D(05).
[p] 17:1, **went down into:** Included in D(05).
[q] 17:1, **where there was a synagogue of the Jews:** Absent from 𝔓127.
[r] 17:2, **the synagogue of the Jews:** Included in 𝔓127.
[s] 17:3, **Christ:** See footnote for Christ in Luke 2:11.
[t] 17:3, **many attended the teaching:** Included in D(05).
[u] 17:5, **disobeying:** Included in TR.
[v] 17:6, **and saying:** Included in 𝔓127 D(05).

also, 7 and Jason has received them, and they are all acting against the decrees of Caesar, saying that there is another king, Jesus."

8 And the people and the city authorities were disturbed when they heard these things. 9 And having received the sufficient amount from Jason and the rest, they released them.

10 The brothers [immediately]ᵃ sent Paul and Silas away by night to Berea, and when they arrived, [they went]ᵇ into the synagogue of the Jews. 11 Now these Jews were more noble than those in Thessalonica; they received the word with all eagerness, examining the Scriptures daily to see if these things were so.

12 Many of them therefore believed, {with not a few Greek women of high standing as well as men}.ᶜ

13 But when the Jews from Thessalonica learned that the word of God was proclaimed by Paul at Berea also, they came there too, agitating [and stirring up]ᵈ the crowds [[, they were not ceasing]].ᵉ 14 Then the brothers [immediately]ᶠ sent Paul off on his way to the sea, but Silas and Timothy remained there. 15 Those who conducted Paul brought him as far as Athens, [[, and he passed through Thessaly, for he had been prevented from proclaiming the word to them]];ᵍ and after receiving a command [[from Paul]]ʰ for Silas and Timothy to come to him as soon as possible, they departed.

16 Now while Paul was waiting for them at Athens, his spirit was provoked within him as he saw that the city was full of idols. 17 So he reasoned in the synagogue with the Jews and the devout persons, and in the marketplace every day with those who happened to be there. 18 Now some of the Epicurean and Stoic philosophers also conversed with him, and some said, "What does this babbler want to say?" Others said, "He seems to be a proclaimer of foreign deities," [because he was preaching the good news of Jesus and the resurrection].ⁱ

19 [[And after some days]]ʲ They took him and brought him to the Areopagus, [[questioning and]]ᵏ saying, "May we know what this new teaching is that you are presenting? 20 For you bring some strange {things}ˡ to our ears. We wish to know therefore what these things mean." 21 Now all the Athenians and the foreigners who lived there would spend their time in nothing except telling or hearing something new.

22 So Paul, standing in the midst of the Areopagus, said: "Men of Athens, I perceive that in every way you are very religious. 23 For as I passed along and observed the objects of your worship, I found also an altar with this inscription: 'To an unknown god.' What therefore you worship as unknown, this I proclaim to you.

24 "The God who made the world and everything in it, being Lord of heaven and earth, does not live in temples made by hands, 25 nor is he served by human hands, as though he needed anything, since he himself gives to all mankind life and breath and everything. 26 And he made from

ᵃ 17:10, **immediately:** Absent from 𝔓127.
ᵇ 17:10, **they went:** Absent from 𝔓45.
ᶜ 17:12, **with not a few Greek women...** D(05) reads " but some disbelieved, and of the Greeks, both prominent men and women, a considerable number believed."
ᵈ 17:13, **and stirring up:** Absent from 𝔓45 BYZ TR.
ᵉ 17:13, **they were not ceasing:** Included in D(05).
ᶠ 17:14, **immediately:** Absent from D(05).
ᵍ 17:15, **and he passed through Thessaly:** Included in D(05).
ʰ 17:15, **from Paul:** Included in D(05).
ⁱ 17:18, **because he was preaching...:** Absent from D(05).
ʲ 17:19, **And after some days:** Included in D(05).
ᵏ 17:19, **questioning and:** Absent from D(05).
ˡ 17:20, **things:** D(05) reads "words."

one [[blood]]^a every nation of men to dwell on the face of the earth, having determined allotted periods and the boundaries of their habitation, 27 that they should [[especially]]^b seek {God},^{c} and perhaps feel their way toward him and find him. Yet he is actually not far from each one of us, 28 For 'in him we live and move and have our being [[, day by day]]',^{d} as also some of your own [poets]^e have said, 'For we are also his offspring.'

29 "Being then the offspring of God, we ought not to think that the divine nature is like gold or silver or stone, an image formed by the art and thought of man.

30 "The times of ignorance God overlooked, but now he commands all men everywhere to repent, 31 because he has fixed a day on which he will judge the world in righteousness by a man whom he has appointed, having provided assurance to all by raising him from the dead."

32 Now when they heard of the resurrection of the dead, some mocked, while others said, "We will hear you again concerning this." 33 So Paul went out from among them.

34 But some men joined him and believed, among whom also were Dionysius the Areopagite {and a woman named Damaris},^{f} and others with them.

18 1 After this, {he}^{g} left Athens and went to Corinth. 2 There he found a Jew named Aquila, a native of Pontus, who had recently come from Italy with his wife Priscilla, because {Claudius}^{h} had ordered all the Jews to leave Rome. He went to see them, [[those who had settled in Achaia,]]^i 3 and because of their shared trade, he stayed with them and worked [; for they were tentmakers by trade].^{j}

4 Every Sabbath he reasoned [[and set forth the name of the Lord Jesus]]^k in the synagogue, trying to persuade {Jews and Greeks}.^{l}

5 But when both Silas and Timothy came down from Macedonia, Paul was occupied {with the word},^{m} testifying to {the Jews}^{n} that {the Christ was Jesus}.^{o}

6 But when they opposed and insulted him, {he}^{p} shook out his clothes in protest and said to them, "Your blood be on your own heads! I am innocent of it. From now on I will go to the Gentiles."

7 Then he left there and went to the house of a man named [Titius]^q Justus, a worshiper of God, whose house was next door to the synagogue. 8 Crispus, the synagogue leader, and his entire household believed in the Lord; and many of the Corinthians who heard Paul believed and were baptized [[, believing in God through the name of our Lord Jesus Christ]].^{r}

---

^{a} 17:26, **blood:** Included in D(05) BYZ TR.
^{b} 17:27, **especially:** Absent from D(05).
^{c} 17:27, **God:** Some manuscripts read "the Lord." BYZ TR.
^{d} 17:28, **day by day:** Included in D(05).
^{e} 17:28, **poets:** Absent from D(05).
^{f} 17:34, **and a woman named Damaris:** D(05) reads "of high standing."
^{g} 18:1, **he:** Some manuscripts read "Paul." A(02) BYZ TR.
^{h} 18:2, **Claudius:** Some manuscripts read "he." BYZ TR.
^{i} 18:2, **those who had settled in Achaia:** Included in D(05).
^{j} 18:3, **for they were tentmakers by trade:** Absent from D(05).
^{k} 18:4, **and set forth the name of the Lord Jesus:** Included in D(05).
^{l} 18:4, **Jews and Greeks:** D(05) reads "not only Jews, but also."
^{m} 18:5, **with the word:** Some manuscripts read "in the Spirit." BYZ TR.
^{n} 18:5, **the Jews:** A(02) reads "them."
^{o} 18:5, **the Christ was Jesus:** D(05) reads "Jesus is the Christ, the Lord."
^{p} 18:6, **he:** Some manuscripts read "Paul." D(05).
^{q} 18:7, **Titius:** Absent from A(02) BYZ TR.
^{r} 18:8, **believing in God through the name of our Lord Jesus Christ:** Included in D(05).

9 [One night]ᵃ The Lord spoke to Paul in a vision: "Do not be afraid; keep on speaking, do not be silent. 10 For I am with you, and no one is going to attack and harm you, because I have many people in this city."

11 So Paul stayed in Corinth for a year and a half, teaching them the word of God.

12 But when Gallio was proconsul of Achaia, the Jews, with one accord, [[having conferred among themselves]]ᵇ rose up against Paul and brought him to the tribunal, 13 [[shouting and]]ᶜ saying, "This man is persuading people to worship God contrary to the law."

14 Just as Paul was about to speak, Gallio said to the Jews, "If [[indeed]]ᵈ it were a matter of wrongdoing or wicked crime, O [[men,]]ᵉ Jews, I would have reason to put up with you. 15 But if it is a question of words and names and your own law, see to it yourselves. [[For]]ᶠ I do not want to be a judge of such matters." 16 And he drove them from the tribunal.

17 Then {they all}ᵍ seized Sosthenes, the synagogue leader, and beat him in front of the tribunal. But Gallio showed no concern whatever.

18 Paul stayed on in Corinth for some time. Then he left the brothers and sailed for Syria, accompanied by Priscilla and Aquila. Before he sailed, he had his hair cut off at Cenchreae because of a vow he had taken.

19 And they arrived at Ephesus, and he left them there [[on the coming Sabbath]];ʰ but he himself, having entered the synagogue, reasoned with the Jews. 20 But when they asked him to stay [[with them]]ⁱ for a longer time, he did not consent, 21 but taking leave of them and saying, "I will return to you again, if God wills. [[I must certainly observe the upcoming feast in Jerusalem.]]"ʲ He set sail from Ephesus.

22 When he landed at Caesarea, he went up to greet the church and then went down to Antioch. 23 After spending some time in Antioch, Paul set out from there and traveled from place to place throughout the region of Galatia and Phrygia, strengthening all the disciples.

24 Meanwhile a Jew named Apollos, a native of Alexandria, came to Ephesus. He was a learned man, with a thorough knowledge of the Scriptures. 25 He had been instructed in the way of the Lord [[in his homeland]],ᵏ and he spoke with great fervor and taught about {Jesus}ˡ accurately, though he knew only the baptism of John. 26 He began to speak boldly in the synagogue. When Priscilla and Aquila heard him, they invited him to their home and explained to him the way [of God]ᵐ more accurately.

ᵃ 18:9, **One night:** Absent from A(02).
ᵇ 18:12, **having conferred among themselves:** Included in D(05).
ᶜ 18:13, **shouting and:** Included in D(05).
ᵈ 18:14, **indeed:** Included in BYZ TR.
ᵉ 18:14, **men:** Included in D(05).
ᶠ 18:15, **For:** Included in BYZ TR.
ᵍ 18:17, **they all:** Some manuscripts read "all the Greeks." D(05) BYZ TR.
ʰ 18:19, **on the coming Sabbath:** Included in D(05).
ⁱ 18:20, **with them:** Included in D(05) BYZ TR.
ʲ 18:21, **I must certainly observe the upcoming feast in Jerusalem:** Included in D(05) BYZ TR.
ᵏ 18:25, **in his homeland:** Included in D(05).
ˡ 18:25, **Jesus:** Some manuscripts read "the Lord." BYZ TR.
ᵐ 18:26, **of God:** Absent from D(05).

27 {But when he wanted to go into Achaia, the brothers, having encouraged him, wrote to the disciples to welcome him; when he arrived, he greatly helped those who had believed through grace.}[a] 28 For he vigorously refuting the Jews in public, [[reasoning and]][b] proving from the Scriptures that Jesus was the Christ.

19 1 Now it happened that while Apollos was in Corinth, Paul passed through the upper regions and came to Ephesus, [and found some disciples].[c]

2 He said to them, "Did you receive the Holy Spirit[d] when you believed?" They replied, "No, we have not even heard that {there is}[e] a Holy Spirit."

3 He asked [[them]],[f] "Then into what were you baptized?" They said, "Into John's baptism."

4 Paul said, "John baptized with a baptism of repentance, telling the people to believe in the one who was to come after him, that is, in {Jesus}."[g]

5 Having heard [[this]],[h] they were baptized in the name of the Lord Jesus [[Christ for the forgiveness of sin]].[i]

6 And when Paul laid his hands on them, [[immediately]][j] the Holy Spirit[k] came upon them, and they spoke in tongues and prophesied.

7 There were about twelve men in all.

8 Entering the synagogue, {he}[l] spoke boldly for three months, discussing and persuading them about the kingdom of God. 9 [But when][m] Some [[of them indeed therefore]][n] became stubborn and refused to believe, speaking evil of the Way before the multitude [[of the Gentiles]],[o] {he}[p] withdrew from them and separated the disciples, discussing daily in the school of Tyrannus [[from the fifth hour until the last]].[q] 10 This continued for two years, so that all who lived in Asia heard the word of the Lord [[Jesus]],[r] both Jews and Greeks.

11 God performed extraordinary miracles through the hands of Paul, 12 so that even handkerchiefs or aprons that had touched his skin were carried away to the sick, and their diseases left them and the evil spirits came out of them.

13 Some of the itinerant Jewish exorcists also tried to invoke the name of the Lord Jesus over those who had evil spirits, saying, "I adjure you by the Jesus whom Paul proclaims." 14 {And there were seven sons of a certain Sceva, a Jewish chief priest, doing

---

a 18:27, **But when he wanted...:** D(05) reads "Now certain Corinthians who were staying in Ephesus, having heard him, were urging him to go with them to their homeland; and when he consented, the Ephesians wrote to the disciples in Corinth to receive the man, who, having arrived in Achaia, greatly contributed among the churches." 𝔓38 is in agreement with D(05) in some areas where the manuscript is extant.

b 18:28, **reasoning and:** Included in 𝔓38 D(05).

c 19:1, **and found some disciples:** Absent from 𝔓38.

d 19:2, **Spirit:** See footnote for Spirit in Luke 1:15.

e 19:2, **there is:** Some manuscripts read "some receive." 𝔓38 D(05).

f 19:3, **them:** Included in 𝔓38 BYZ TR.

g 19:4, **Jesus:** Some manuscripts read "Christ Jesus." BYZ TR ‖ D(05) reads "Christ."

h 19:5, **this:** Included in D(05).

i 19:5, **Christ for the forgiveness of sin:** Included in P38 D(05).

j 19:6, **immediately:** Included in 𝔓38 D(05).

k 19:6, **Spirit:** See the footnote for Spirit in verse 2.

l 19:8, **he:** Some manuscripts read "Paul." D(05).

m 19:9, **But when:** Absent from D(05).

n 19:9, **of them indeed therefore:** Included in D(05).

o 19:9, **of the Gentiles:** Included in D(05).

p 19:9, **he:** D(05) reads "Paul."

q 19:9, **from the fifth hour until the last:** Included in D(05).

r 19:10, **Jesus:** Included in BYZ TR.

this}.^a ¹⁵But the evil spirit answered [them],^b "I know [indeed]^c Jesus and I am acquainted with Paul, but who are you?" ¹⁶And the man in whom the evil spirit was leaped on them, overpowered both of them, and prevailed against them, so that they fled out of that house naked and wounded.

¹⁷This became known to all Jews and Greeks living in Ephesus, and fear fell upon them all, and the name of the Lord Jesus was magnified. ¹⁸Many of those who had believed came confessing and disclosing their practices.

¹⁹A considerable number of those who had practiced magic arts brought their books together and burned them in the presence of everyone. And they counted the value of them and found it came to fifty thousand pieces of silver.

²⁰Thus, by the power of the Lord, {the word grew and strengthened}^d

²¹When these things were accomplished, Paul resolved in the Spirit to pass through Macedonia and Achaia and go to Jerusalem, saying, "After I have been there, I must also see Rome." ²²So he sent two of his helpers, Timothy and Erastus, to Macedonia, while he himself stayed for a while in Asia [[a short time]].^e

²³About that time there arose no small disturbance concerning the Way.

²⁴For a man named Demetrius, a silversmith who made silver shrines of Artemis, brought no little business to the craftsmen. ²⁵He gathered them together, along with the workmen in similar trades, and said [[to them]],^f "Men, [[fellow craftsmen]]^g you know that our prosperity depends on this business. ²⁶You see and hear that not only in Ephesus but [[also]]^h in almost all of Asia this Paul has [persuaded and]ⁱ turned away a considerable number of people, saying that [[these]]^j gods made with hands are not gods. ²⁷Not only is there danger that this trade of ours will fall into disrepute, but also that the temple of the great goddess Artemis will be counted as nothing, and she [[is about to be brought down]]^k whom all Asia and the world worship will {be dethroned from her magnificence}."^l

²⁸When they heard this and were filled with rage [[having run into the street]],^m they began to shout, "Great is Artemis of the Ephesians!" ²⁹The [[whole]]ⁿ city was filled with confusion, and they rushed with one accord into the theater, dragging along Gaius and Aristarchus, Macedonians who were Paul's traveling companions.

³⁰Paul wanted to go into the crowd, but the disciples would not let him. ³¹Some of the Asiarchs, who were friends of his, sent word to him and urged him not to venture into the theater. ³²Some were shouting one thing, some another; for the assembly

---

^a 19:14, **And there were seven... :** 𝔓38 and D(05) reads "Among them also, the sons of Sceva, a certain priest, attempted to do the same; they had the custom of exorcising such persons. And having entered into the one possessed by a demon, they began to invoke the name, saying, We command you by Jesus, whom Paul proclaims, to come out."

^b 19:15, **them:** Absent from BYZ TR.

^c 19:15, **indeed:** Absent from ℵ(01) A(02) D(05) BYZ TR.

^d 19:20, **the word grew and strengthened:** D(05) reads "and the faith in God was strengthened."

^e 19:22, **a short time:** Included in D(05).

^f 19:25, **to them:** Included in D(05).

^g 19:25, **fellow craftsmen:** Included in D(05).

^h 19:26, **also:** Included in A(02) D(05).

ⁱ 19:26, **persuaded:** Absent from ℵ(01).

^j 19:26, **these:** Included in D(05).

^k 19:27, **is about to be brought down:** Included in D(05).

^l 19:27, **be dethroned from her magnificence:** Some manuscripts read "have her magnificence destroyed."

^m 19:28, **having run into the street:** Included in D(05).

ⁿ 19:29, **whole:** Included in D(05) BYZ TR.

was in confusion, and most of them did not know why they had come together.

33 But from the crowd they put forward Alexander, the Jews having pushed him forward; and Alexander, having motioned with his hand, wanted to make a defense to the people. 34 But when they recognized that he was a Jew, a single outcry arose from them all for about two hours, shouting, "Great is Artemis of the Ephesians!"

35 The city clerk, having quieted the crowd, said, "Men of Ephesus, who is there among men who does not know that {the city of the Ephesians}ᵃ is the temple guardian of the great [[goddess]]ᵇ Artemis and of the image that fell from heaven? 36 Since these [things]ᶜ are undeniable, you ought to be calm and do nothing rash. 37 For you have brought these men here who are neither temple robbers nor blasphemers of our goddess. 38 If, then, Demetrius and the craftsmen with him have a complaint against anyone, the courts are open and there are proconsuls; let them bring charges against one another. 39 But if you seek anything further, it shall be settled in the lawful assembly. 40 For indeed, we are in danger of being accused of insurrection concerning today, there being no cause, about which we will not be able to give a reason regarding this gathering."

41 And having said these things, he dismissed the assembly.

20 1 After the uproar had ceased, Paul, having sent for the disciples and [encouraged them],ᵈ greeted themᵉ and {departed to go}ᶠ to Macedonia.

2 Passing through [[all]]ᵍ those regions and offering much encouragement to them, he came to Greece 3 and spent three months there.

When a plot was made against him by the Jews as he was about to set sail for Syria, he decided to return through Macedonia. 4 He was accompanied [[as far as Asia]]ʰ by Sopater of Berea, the son [of Pyrrhus];ⁱ Aristarchus and Secundus from Thessalonica; Gaius of Derbe; Timothy; and the Asians Tychicus and Trophimus. 5 [But]ʲ These went on ahead and were waiting for us in Troas. 6 We sailed away from Philippi after the days of Unleavened Bread, and in five days we joined them in Troas, where we stayed for seven days.

7 On the first day of the week, when {we}ᵏ were gathered together to break bread, Paul talked with them, intending to depart on the next day, and he prolonged his speech until midnight. 8 There were many lamps in the upper room where we were gathered.

9 Now a certain young man named Eutychus, sitting at the window, was overcome by a deep sleep as Paul spoke at length; falling down from the third story, he was picked up dead. 10 But Paul went down, fell on him, and embracing him said, "Do not be alarmed, for his life is in him." 11 Then going up and breaking the bread and tasting it, he conversed for a considerable time until dawn; so he departed. 12 And [[as they were greeting]]ˡ they brought the boy alive and were greatly comforted.

13 We went ahead to the ship and set sail for Assos, intending to take Paul aboard there, for so he had

---

ᵃ 19:35, **the city of the Ephesians:** D(05) reads "our city."

ᵇ 19:35, **goddess:** Included in BYZ TR.

ᶜ 19:36, **things:** Absent from ℵ(01).

ᵈ 20:1, **encouraged them:** Absent from BYZ TR.

ᵉ 20:1, **greeted them:** Or, said farewell.

ᶠ 20:1, **departed to go:** D(05) reads "went out."

ᵍ 20:2, **all:** Included in D(05).

ʰ 20:4, **as far as Asia:** Included in A(02) D(05) BYZ TR.

ⁱ 20:4, **of Pyrrhus:** Absent from BYZ TR.

ʲ 20:5, **But:** Absent from D(05) BYZ TR.

ᵏ 20:7, **we:** Some manuscripts read "the disciples." BYZ TR.

ˡ 20:12, **as they were greeting:** Included in D(05).

arranged, intending himself to go by
land. 14 And when he met us at Assos,
we took him on board and went to
Mitylene. 15 And sailing from there, we
came the following day opposite Chios;
the next day we touched at Samos
[[after remaining at Trogylium]];[a]
and the day after that we went to
Miletus. 16 For Paul had decided to
sail past Ephesus, so that he might
not have to spend time in Asia, for he
was hastening to be at Jerusalem, if
possible, on the day of Pentecost.

17 From Miletus he sent to Ephesus
and called the elders of the church
to come to him. 18 And when they
came to him, [[he swore while they
were present,]][b] he said to them, "You
yourselves know [[brothers]][c] how
I lived among you [[for about three
years or even more, in what manner,]][d]
from the first day that I set foot in Asia,
19 serving the Lord [[with you]][e] with all
humility and with [[many]][f] tears and
with trials that happened to me through
the plots of the Jews; 20 how I did not
shrink from declaring to you anything
that was profitable, and teaching you
in public and from house to house,
21 testifying both to Jews and to Greeks
of repentance toward God and of faith
in our Lord Jesus [[Christ]].[g]

22 "And now, behold, I am bound
by the Spirit to go to Jerusalem, not
knowing what will happen to me there,
23 except that the Holy Spirit testifies [to
me][h] in every city that imprisonment
and afflictions await me.

24 "{But I do not account my life of
any value nor as precious to myself},[i]
so that I may finish my course [[with
joy]][j] and the ministry [[of the word]][k]
that I received from the Lord Jesus,
to testify to the gospel [[to Jews and
Greeks]][l] of the grace of God.

25 "And now, behold, I know that
you all, among whom I went about
preaching the kingdom [[of God]],[m]
will no longer see my face. 26 Therefore,
{I testify to you this day}[n] that I am
innocent of the blood of all men; 27 for I
did not shrink back from declaring to
you the whole counsel of God.

28 "[[Therefore,]][o] Take heed to
yourselves and to all the flock, in which
the Holy Spirit has made you overseers,
to shepherd the church of {God},[p]
which he [[himself]][q] obtained with
{the blood of his own}.[r]

29 "{I know}[s] that after my
departure, savage wolves will come
in among you, not sparing the flock;
30 and from among your own selves men
will arise, speaking perverse things, to
draw away the disciples after them.

---

a 20:15, **after remaining at Trogylium:** Included in D(05) BYZ TR.
b 20:18, **he swore while they were present:** Included in A(02) D(05).
c 20:18, **brothers:** Included in D(05).
d 20:18, **for about three years or even more, in what manner:** Included in D(05).
e 20:19, **with you:** Included in C(04).
f 20:19, **many:** Included in C(04) BYZ TR.
g 20:21, **Christ:** Included in א(01) A(02) C(04) TR.
h 20:23, **to me:** Absent from BYZ TR.
i 20:24, **But I do not account my life of any value nor as precious to myself:** Some manuscripts read "But none of these things move me, nor do I count my life precious to myself."
j 20:24, **with joy:** Included in C(04) BYZ TR.
k 20:24, **of the word:** Included in D(05).
l 20:24, **to Jews and Greeks:** Included in D(05).
m 20:25, **of God:** Included in BYZ TR || D(05) reads "Jesus." D(05).
n 20:26, **I testify to you this day:** Some manuscripts read "up to this day." D(05).
o 20:28, **Therefore:** Included in C(04) BYZ TR.
p 20:28, **God:** א(01) B(03) TR NA28 SBLGNT || Other early manuscripts read "the Lord." A(02) C(04) D(05) THGNT || Some manuscripts read "the Lord and God." BYZ.
q 20:28, **himself:** Included in D(05).
r 20:28, **the blood of his own:** א(01) A(02) C(04) D(05) NA28 SBLGNT || Some manuscripts read "with his own blood." BYZ TR.
s 20:29, **I know:** Some manuscripts read "for I know this." BYZ TR.

31 "Therefore, be on the alert, remembering that for three years, night and day, I did not cease to admonish each one with tears. 32 And now I commend you [[brothers]]ᵃ to {God}ᵇ and to the word of his grace, which is able to build you up and to give [[you]]ᶜ the inheritance [[from him]]ᵈ among all those who are sanctified.

33 "I have coveted no one's silver or gold or clothing. 34 You yourselves know that these hands ministered to my own needs and to [[all]]ᵉ those who were with me.

35 "In everything I showed you that by working hard in this manner you must help the weak and remember the words of the Lord Jesus, that he himself said, 'It is more blessed to give than to receive.'"

36 And when he had said these things, he knelt down with them all and prayed.

37 And there was much weeping by everyone, and they embraced Paul and kissed him, 38 being especially grieved by the word which he had spoken, that they would not see his face again.

And they accompanied him to the ship.

21 1 But when it happened for us [to set sail],ᶠ having been torn away from them, we ran a straight course to Cos, and the next day to Rhodes, and from there to Patara [[and Myra]],ᵍ 2 and finding a ship crossing over to Phoenicia, we went aboard and set sail.

3 After sighting Cyprus and leaving it on the left, we sailed on to Syria and landed at Tyre, for there the ship was to unload its cargo.

4 And having found the disciples, we stayed there seven days; who told Paul through the Spirit not to go up to Jerusalem.

5 When our days there were ended, we [left and]ʰ continued on our journey, while all of them, with their wives and children, accompanied us outside the city. Kneeling down on the beach, we prayed 6 and said farewell to one another. Then we went on board the ship, and they returned home.

7 After completing the voyage from Tyre, we arrived at Ptolemais, and after greeting the brothers, we stayed with them for one day.

8 But on the next day, having departed, {we came}ⁱ to Caesarea, and entering the house of Philip the evangelist, who was one of the seven, we stayed with him.

9 Now this man had four virgin daughters who prophesied.

10 As we stayed there for many days, a prophet named Agabus came down from Judea. 11 Coming to us, he took Paul's belt, bound his own feet and hands, and said, "This is what the Holy Spirit says: 'In this way, the Jews in Jerusalem will bind the man to whom this belt belongs, and they will hand him over to the Gentiles.'"

12 When we heard this, both we and the local residents urged {him}ʲ not to go up to Jerusalem. 13 Then Paul {answered},ᵏ "What are you doing, weeping and breaking my heart? For I am ready not only to be bound, but also to die in Jerusalem for the name of

---

ᵃ 20:32, **brothers:** Included in C(04) BYZ TR.

ᵇ 20:32, **God:** Some manuscripts read "the Lord." B(03).

ᶜ 20:32, **you:** Included in C(04) BYZ TR.

ᵈ 20:32, **from him:** Included in A(02).

ᵉ 20:34, **all:** Included in D(05).

ᶠ 21:1, **to set sail:** Absent from A(02).

ᵍ 21:1, **and Myra:** Included in D(05).

ʰ 21:5, **left and:** Absent from A(02).

ⁱ 21:8, **we came:** Some manuscripts read "those around Paul came." BYZ TR.

ʲ 21:12, **him:** D(05) reads "Paul."

ᵏ 21:13, **answered:** Some manuscripts read "answered and said." ℵ(01) A(02) ‖ D(05) reads "said to us."

the Lord Jesus [[Christ]]."ᵃ ¹⁴Since he would not be persuaded, we remained silent, saying [[to one another]],ᵇ "The Lord's will be done."

¹⁵After these days, having made preparations, we went up to Jerusalem. ¹⁶And some of the disciples from Caesarea also came with us, bringing a certain Mnason of Cyprus, an early disciple,ᶜ with whom we were to stay.

¹⁷When we arrived in Jerusalem, the brothers welcomed us gladly. ¹⁸The next day, Paul went with us to see James, and all the elders were {present}.ᵈ ¹⁹After greeting them, he related one by one the things that God had done among the Gentiles through his ministry.

²⁰When they heard this, they glorified {God}ᵉ and said to him, "You see, brother, how many thousands there are among the Jews who have believed, and they are all zealous for the law. ²¹But they have been informed about you, that you teach apostasy from Moses to [all]ᶠ the Jews among the nations, [saying]ᵍ not to circumcise their children nor to walk according to the customs. ²²What then is to be done? Certainly [[the multitude will gather.]]ʰ They will hear that you have come.

²³"So do what we tell you: We have four men who have taken a vow upon themselves. ²⁴Take these men and purify yourself along with them, and pay their expenses so that they may shave their heads. Then everyone will know that there is nothing in what they have been told about you, but that you yourself also live in observance of the law.

²⁵"As for the Gentiles who have believed, we have sent our decision that they should {abstain}ⁱ from food sacrificed to idols, from blood, [from what is strangled,]ʲ and from sexual immorality."

²⁶Then Paul took the men, and the next day he purified himself along with them and went into the temple, giving notice of the completion of the days of purification, until the offering was presented for each one of them.

²⁷Now when the seven days were about to be completed, the Jews from Asia, having seen him in the temple, stirred up the whole crowd and laid hands on him, ²⁸crying out, "Men of Israel, help! This is the man who is teaching everyone everywhere against the people and the law and this [[holy]]ᵏ place. Moreover, he even brought Greeks into the temple and has defiled this holy place." ²⁹For they had previously seen Trophimus the Ephesian with him in the city, and they supposed that Paul had brought him into the temple.

³⁰Then the whole city was aroused, and the people rushed together. They seized Paul and dragged him out of the temple, and immediately the doors were shut. ³¹And when they were seeking to kill him, a report went up to the commander of the cohort that all Jerusalem was in confusion. ³²Who, having taken soldiers and centurions from him, ran down upon them; and when they saw the chief captain and the soldiers, they stopped beating Paul.

ᵃ 21:13, **Christ:** Included in C(04) D(05).

ᵇ 21:14, **to one another:** Included in D(05).

ᶜ 21:16, **early disciple:** Or, old disciple.

ᵈ 21:18, **present:** D(05) reads "gathered together with him."

ᵉ 21:20, **God:** Some manuscripts read "the Lord." D(05) BYZ TR.

ᶠ 21:21, **all:** Absent from A(02).

ᵍ 21:21, **saying:** Absent from D(05).

ʰ 21:22, **The multitude will gather:** Included in ℵ(01) A(02) D(05) BYZ TR.

ⁱ 21:25, **abstain:** Some manuscripts read "To observe nothing of the sort except to keep themselves." C(04) D(05) BYZ TR.

ʲ 21:25, **from what is strangled:** Absent from D(05).

ᵏ 21:28, **holy:** Included in A(02).

33 Then the chief captain came near, took hold of him, and commanded him to be bound with two chains; and inquired who he might be and what he had done.

34 Some in the crowd shouted one thing, some another. And as he could not learn the facts because of the uproar, he ordered him to be brought into the barracks. 35 When he came to the steps, {he}ᵃ was actually carried by the soldiers because of the violence of the crowd, 36 for the multitude [of the people]ᵇ followed, crying out, "Away with him!"

37 As Paul was about to be brought into the barracks, he said to the commander, "May I say something to you?" And he replied, "Do you know Greek? 38 Are you not [then]ᶜ the Egyptian who, before these days, stirred up a revolt and led the four thousand men of the assassins out into the wilderness?"

39 But Paul said, "I am a man, a Jew from Tarsus in Cilicia, a citizen of no insignificant city; and I beg you, allow me to speak to the people."

40 When he had given him permission, Paul, standing on the steps, motioned with his hand to the people. And when there was a great silence, he addressed them in the Hebrew language, saying,

22 1 "Men, brothers, and fathers, listen to my defense before you now." 2 When they heard that he was addressing [them]ᵈ in the Hebrew language, they became even more quiet. And he says, 3 "[[Indeed]]ᵉ I am a Jewish man, born in Tarsus of Cilicia, but brought up in this city, educated at the feet of Gamaliel according to the strictness of our ancestral law, [being]ᶠ zealous for God just as all of you are today.

4 "I persecuted this Way to the point of death, binding and putting both men and women into prisons, 5 as also the high priest and the whole council of elders can testify about me. From them I also received letters to the brothers in Damascus, and I went there in order to bring those who were there bound to Jerusalem to be punished.

6 "Now as I was going and approaching Damascus around noon, suddenly a great light from heaven flashed around me, 7 and I fell to the ground and heard a voice saying to me, 'Saul, Saul, why are you persecuting me?' 8 I answered [[and said]],ᵍ 'Who are you, Lord?' And he said to me, 'I am Jesus the Nazarene, whom you are persecuting.' 9 Those who were with me saw the light [[and were afraid]]ʰ but did not hear the voice of the one speaking to me. 10 I said, 'What shall I do, Lord?' And {the Lord}ⁱ said to me, 'Get up and go to Damascus, and there you will be told about everything that has been assigned for you to do.' 11 But since I could not see because of the brightness of that light, I was led by the hand by those who were with me and came to Damascus.

12 "Now a certain Ananias, a [devout]ʲ man according to the law, well spoken of by all the Jews who lived there, 13 came to me and standing by me said, 'Saul, brother, regain your sight.' And at that very hour I looked up at him. 14 And he said, 'The God of our fathers has appointed you to know his will and to see the Righteous One and to hear a voice from his mouth, 15 for you will be a witness for him to all

---

ᵃ 21:35, **he:** D(05) reads "Paul."
ᵇ 21:36, **of the people:** Absent from D(05).
ᶜ 21:38, **then:** Absent from D(05).
ᵈ 22:2, **them:** Absent from some D(05).
ᵉ 22:3, **indeed:** Included in BYZ TR.
ᶠ 22:3, **being:** Absent from D(05).
ᵍ 22:8, **and said:** Included in ℵ(01).
ʰ 22:9, **and were afraid:** Included in D(05) BYZ TR.
ⁱ 22:10, **the Lord:** D(05) reads "he."
ʲ 22:12, **devout:** Absent from A(02).

men of what you have seen and heard. 16 And now why do you wait? Rise and be baptized and wash away your sins, calling on {his}[a] name.'

17 "And it happened to me, when I returned to Jerusalem and was praying in the temple, that I fell into a trance 18 and saw him saying to me, 'Hurry and leave Jerusalem quickly, because they will not accept your testimony about me.' 19 And I said, 'Lord, they themselves know that I was imprisoning and beating those who believed in you in the synagogues, 20 and when the blood of your witness [Stephen][b] was being shed, I myself was standing by and approving [[of his death]],[c] and guarding the clothes of those who were killing him.' 21 And he said to me, 'Go, for I will send you far away to the nations.'"[d]

22 They listened to him until this word, and they raised their voices saying, "Remove such a person from the earth, for it is not fitting for him to live." 23 And as they were shouting and throwing off their cloaks and tossing dust into the air, 24 the commander ordered that he be brought into the barracks, saying that he should be examined by flogging, in order to find out the reason why they were shouting against him like this.

25 But when they had stretched him out for the whips, {Paul}[e] said to the centurion who was standing by, "Is it lawful for you to flog a man who is a Roman citizen and uncondemned?" 26 But when the centurion heard [[that he says he is a Roman]],[f] he went

to the commander and reported it, saying, "{What are you about to do?}[g] For this man is a Roman." 27 And the commander came and said to him, "Tell me, are you a Roman?" And he said, "Yes." 28 But the commander answered [[and said]],[h] "I acquired this citizenship for a large sum of money." Paul said, "But I was born a citizen." 29 [Immediately,][i] Those who were about to examine him withdrew from him, and the commander was also afraid when he realized that he was a Roman and that he had bound him.

30 But on the next day, wanting to know the certainty, the reason why he was accused by the Jews, he released him [[from his bonds]][j] and ordered the chief priests and the whole council to assemble, and after bringing Paul down, he stood him before them.

23 1 Looking intently at the council, Paul said, "Men, brothers, I have lived my life with a clear conscience before God up to this day."

2 But the high priest Ananias ordered those standing near [him][k] to strike his mouth. 3 Then Paul said to him, "God is going to strike you, you whitewashed wall! And you sit there judging me according to the law, and yet you order me to be struck contrary to the law?"

4 Those standing nearby said, "Do you insult the high priest of God?" 5 Paul replied, "I did not know, brothers, that he is the high priest; for it is written, 'You shall not speak evil of a ruler of your people.'"

---

a 22:16, **his:** Some manuscripts read "the Lord's." BYZ TR.

b 22:20, **Stephen:** Absent from A(02).

c 22:20, **of his death:** Included in BYZ TR.

d 22:21, **nations:** Or, the Gentiles.

e 22:25, **Paul:** D(05) reads "he."

f 22:26, **that he says he is a Roman:** Included in D(05).

g 22:26, **What are you about to do:** Some manuscripts read "Take heed what you are about to do." BYZ TR.

h 22:28, **and said:** Included in D(05).

i 22:29, **Immediately:** Absent from D(05).

j 22:30, **from his bonds:** Included in BYZ TR.

k 23:2, **him:** Absent from ℵ(01).

6 But when Paul realized that one part were Sadducees and the other Pharisees, he cried out in the council, "Men, brothers, I am a Pharisee, a son of Pharisees; concerning the hope and resurrection of the dead I am being judged."

7 {Upon him saying this},ᵃ there arose a dissension between the Pharisees [and Sadducees],ᵇ and the assembly was divided. 8 For the Sadducees say that there is no resurrection, neither angel nor spirit, but the Pharisees confess both.

9 But there arose a great outcry, and some [of the scribes of the party]ᶜ of the Pharisees stood up and argued [[with one another]],ᵈ saying, "We find nothing wrong in this man; but if a spirit or an angel has spoken to him? [[let us not fight against God]]"ᵉ

10 And when there was a great dissension, the commander, fearing that Paul might be torn apart by them, ordered the soldiers to go down and take him away [from among them]ᶠ and bring him into the barracks.

11 The following night, the Lord stood by him and said, "Take courage [[Paul]];ᵍ for as you have testified about me in Jerusalem, so you must also testify in Rome."

12 When day came, [[some of]]ʰ the Jews made a conspiracy and bound themselves with an oath, [saying]ⁱ that they would neither eat nor drink until they had killed Paul. 13 Now there were more than forty who formed this conspiracy, 14 who, having approached the chief priests and the elders, said, "We have bound ourselves under a curse to taste nothing [[at all]]ʲ until we have killed Paul. 15 Now therefore [[we urge you, do this for us: summon the council]],ᵏ you make it clear to the commander [along with the council]ˡ that he should bring him down to you [[tomorrow]],ᵐ as though you were going to investigate more accurately the things concerning him; and we, before he comes near, are ready to kill him [[if it be necessary, even to die]]."ⁿ

16 And when the son of Paul's sister heard of the ambush, he went and entered the barracks and reported it to Paul. 17 Paul called one of the centurions and said, "Take this young man to the commander, for he has something to report to him." 18 So he took him and brought him to the commander and said, "The prisoner Paul called me and asked me to bring this young man to you; he has something to tell you." 19 The commander took him by the hand, withdrew privately, and asked, "What is it that you have to report to me?" 20 He said, "The Jews have agreed to ask you to bring Paul down to the council tomorrow, as though they were going to inquire more thoroughly about him. 21 Therefore, do not be persuaded by them; for more than forty men among them are lying in wait for him, who have bound themselves under a curse neither to eat nor to drink until they have killed him, and now they

---

ᵃ 23:7, **Upon him saying this:** ℵ(01) A(02) NA28 THGNT ‖ Some manuscripts read "While he was saying this." B(03) C(04) BYZ TR SBLGNT.

ᵇ 23:7, **and Sadducees:** Absent from BYZ.

ᶜ 23:9, **of the scribes of the party:** Absent from A(02).

ᵈ 23:9, **with one another:** Included in ℵ(01).

ᵉ 23:9, **let us not fight against God:** Included in BYZ TR.

ᶠ 23:10, **from among them:** Absent from ℵ(01).

ᵍ 23:11, **Paul:** Included in BYZ TR.

ʰ 23:12, **some of:** Included in 𝔓48 BYZ TR.

ⁱ 23:12, **saying:** Absent from C(04).

ʲ 23:14, **at all:** Included in 𝔓48.

ᵏ 23:15, **we urge you, do this for us: summon the council:** Included in 𝔓48.

ˡ 23:15, **along with the council:** Absent from 𝔓48.

ᵐ 23:15, **tomorrow:** Included in BYZ TR.

ⁿ 23:15, **if it be necessary, even to die:** Included in 𝔓48.

are ready, waiting for the promise^a from you."

²² So the commander released the young man, ordering *him* not to speak to anyone that he had revealed these things to me.

²³ Then he summoned two of the centurions and said, "Get ready to leave by the third hour of the night with two hundred soldiers, seventy horsemen, and two hundred spearmen to go as far as Caesarea. ²⁴ Also provide mounts for Paul to ride and bring him safely to Felix the governor."

²⁵ [[For he was afraid that the Jews, having seized him by force, might kill him, and that he himself might have a charge laid against him, as if he had taken a bribe;]]^b He wrote a letter to this effect:

²⁶ "Claudius Lysias to his Excellency the governor Felix, greetings. ²⁷ This man was seized by the Jews and was about to be killed by them, but when I had learned that he was a Roman citizen, I came with the troops and rescued him [[as he was crying out and speaking]].^c ²⁸ Wanting to know the charge for which they accused him [, I brought him down to their council].^d ²⁹ I found that he was accused concerning questions of their law, but had nothing [[more]]^e charged against him deserving of death or imprisonment. ³⁰ When I was informed {of a plot to be laid against the man},^f I sent him to you at once, ordering his accusers also to state before you what they have against him. [[Farewell.]]"^g

³¹ So the soldiers, according to their instructions, took Paul and brought him by night to Antipatris.

³² The next day they let the horsemen go on with him, while they returned to the barracks. ³³ When they came to Caesarea and delivered the letter to the governor, they presented Paul also before him. ³⁴ On reading the letter, {he}^h asked what province he was from. And when he learned that he was from Cilicia, ³⁵ he said, "I will give you a hearing when your accusers arrive." Then he ordered [[him]]ⁱ that he be kept under guard in Herod's Praetorium.

24 ¹ After five days, the high priest Ananias came down with some elders and a certain orator named Tertullus, who presented their case against Paul to the governor.

² When he was called, Tertullus began to accuse him, saying, "Through you, we enjoy much peace, and {reforms}^j are taking place for this nation through your foresight. ³ In every way and everywhere, we accept this, most excellent Felix, with all gratitude. ⁴ But, not to detain you further, I beg you to hear us briefly with your indulgence. ⁵ For we have found this man to be a plague, stirring up riots among all the Jews throughout the world, and a ringleader of the sect of the Nazarenes. ⁶ He even tried to profane the temple, and we seized him [[and according to our law, we wanted to judge, ⁷ But Lysias the commander came with great force and took him out of our hands, ⁸ commanding his accusers to come to you,]]^k from whom you can yourself examine and learn

---

^a 23:21, **waiting for the promise:** Or, what was promised.

^b 23:25, **For he was afraid that the Jews…:** Included in 𝔓48.

^c 23:27, **as he was crying out and speaking:** Included in 𝔓48.

^d 23:28, **I brought him down to their council:** Absent from B(03).

^e 23:29, **more:** Included in 𝔓48.

^f 23:30, **of a plot to be laid against the man:** Some manuscripts read "the Jews lay in wait for the man." BYZ TR.

^g 23:30, **Farewell:** Included in BYZ TR.

^h 23:34, **he:** Some manuscripts read "the governor." BYZ TR.

ⁱ 23:35, **him:** Included in BYZ TR.

^j 24:2, **reforms:** Some manuscripts read "very worthy deeds." BYZ TR.

^k 24:6-8, Some manuscripts include to verses 6, 7 and 8. BYZ TR.

about all these things of which we accuse him." 9 The Jews also joined in the attack, asserting that these things were so.

10 Then Paul, after the governor had signaled for him to speak, responded, "Knowing that you have been a judge for this nation for many years, I gladly make my defense concerning myself, 11 as you can ascertain that it is not more than twelve days since I went up to worship in Jerusalem. 12 And neither in the temple did they find me speaking with anyone or causing a commotion among the crowd, nor in the synagogues, nor throughout the city, 13 Nor can they prove [to you]ᵃ the charges they now bring against me.

14 "But I confess this to you, that according to the Way which they call a sect, so I worship the God of our ancestors, believing {everything}ᵇ written in the Law and the Prophets, 15 having hope in God, which these *men* themselves also await, that there is going to be a resurrection [[of the dead]]ᶜ of both the righteous and the unrighteous.

16 "In this, I also strive to maintain a blameless conscience before God and men at all times.

17 "Now after several years, I came to bring alms to my nation and offerings, 18 in which they found me purified in the temple, not with a crowd nor with commotion. 19 But some Jews from Asia, who ought to be present before you and bring charges if they have anything against me. 20 Or let these men themselves say what wrongdoing they found [[in me]]ᵈ when I stood before the council, 21 or concerning this one statement that I cried out while standing among them: 'Concerning the

resurrection of the dead, I am being judged before you today.'"

22 But Felix, [[when he heard these things]],ᵉ having a more accurate knowledge of the Way, adjourned them, saying, "When Lysias the commander comes down, I will decide your case." 23 And he ordered the centurion to keep {him}ᶠ in custody, but to grant him some freedom and not to prevent any of his own people from serving him [[or coming to him]].ᵍ

24 After some days, Felix came with his wife Drusilla, who was a Jewish woman, and he sent for Paul and listened to him speak about faith in Christ [Jesus].ʰ

25 While he was discussing righteousness, self-control, and the coming judgment, Felix became frightened and replied, "Go away for now; when I have an opportunity, I will summon you." 26 At the same time, he was hoping that money would be given to him by Paul [[so that he might release him]];ⁱ therefore, he sent for him more frequently and conversed with him.

27 But when two years had passed, Felix was succeeded by Porcius Festus; and desiring to do the Jews a favor, Felix left Paul bound.ʲ

25 1 So Festus, having arrived in the province, after three days went up to Jerusalem from Caesarea. 2 The chief priests and the leaders of the Jews brought charges against Paul, and they were urging him, 3 asking as a favor against Paul that he might summon him to Jerusalem, planning an ambush to kill him on the way.

4 Festus then answered that Paul was being kept in Caesarea and that

---

ᵃ 24:13, **to you:** Absent from BYZ TR.
ᵇ 24:14, **everything:** B(03) reads "the things." B(03).
ᶜ 24:15, **of the dead:** Included in BYZ TR.
ᵈ 24:20, **in me:** Included in C(04) BYZ TR.
ᵉ 24:22, **when he heard these things:** Included in BYZ TR.
ᶠ 24:23, **him:** Some manuscripts read "Paul." BYZ TR.
ᵍ 24:23, **or coming to him:** Included in BYZ TR.
ʰ 24:24, **Jesus:** Absent from A(02) BYZ TR.
ⁱ 24:26, **so that he might release him:** Included in BYZ TR.
ʲ 24:27, **bound:** Or, in prison.

he himself was about to leave shortly. 5 "Therefore," he said, "let the men of authority among you go down with me, and if there is anything wrong about the man, let them bring charges against him."

6 After he had spent not more than [eight or]^a ten days among them, he went down to Caesarea, and the next day he took his seat on the tribunal and ordered Paul to be brought.

7 When he had arrived, the Jews who had come down from Jerusalem stood around [him],^{b} bringing many and serious charges against {him}^{c} that they could not prove. 8 {Paul}^{d} argued in his defense, "Neither against the law of the Jews, nor against the temple, nor against Caesar have I committed any offense."

9 But Festus, wishing to do the Jews a favor, said to Paul, "Do you wish to go up to Jerusalem and there be judged concerning these things before me?" 10 But Paul said, "I am standing before Caesar's tribunal, where I ought to be judged. To the Jews I have done no wrong, as you also know very well. 11 If then I am a wrongdoer and have committed anything worthy of death, I do not refuse to die. But if there is nothing to their charges against me, no one can give me up to them. I appeal to Caesar."

12 Then Festus, when he had conferred with his council, answered, "You have appealed to Caesar; to Caesar you shall go."

13 Now after some days had passed, King Agrippa and Bernice arrived in Caesarea, greeting Festus. 14 And as they stayed there many days, Festus laid Paul's case before the king, saying, "There is a man left prisoner by Felix, 15 and when I was at Jerusalem, the chief priests and the elders of the Jews laid out their case against him, asking for a {sentence}^{e} of condemnation against him. 16 I answered them that it was not the custom of the Romans to give up anyone [[to destruction]]^f before the accused met the accusers face to face and had opportunity to make his defense concerning the charge laid against him. 17 So when they came together here, I made no delay, but on the next day took my seat on the tribunal and ordered the man to be brought. 18 Concerning whom, when the accusers stood up, they brought no charge of the [wicked]^g things I had suspected. 19 Rather they had certain points of dispute with him about their own religion and about a certain Jesus, who was dead, but whom Paul asserted to be alive. 20 Being at a loss how to investigate these questions, I asked whether he wanted to go to Jerusalem and be judged there regarding them. 21 But when Paul had appealed to be kept in custody for the decision of the emperor, I ordered him to be held until I could send him to Caesar."

22 Agrippa [said]^h to Festus, "I would also like to hear the man myself." "Tomorrow," said he, "you will hear him."

23 So on the next day Agrippa and Bernice came with great pomp, and they entered the audience hall with the military tribunes and the prominent men of the city. Then, at the command of Festus, Paul was brought in.

---

^{a} 25:6, **eight or:** Absent from BYZ TR.
^{b} 25:7, **him:** Absent from BYZ TR.
^{c} 25:7, **him:** Some manuscripts read "Paul." BYZ TR.
^{d} 25:8, **Paul:** Some manuscripts read "he." BYZ TR.
^{e} 25:15, **sentence:** Some manuscripts read "punishment." BYZ TR.
^{f} 25:16, **to destruction:** Included in BYZ TR.
^{g} 25:18, **wicked:** Absent from BYZ TR.
^{h} 25:22, **said:** Included in C(04) BYZ TR.

24 And Festus said, "King Agrippa and all who are present with us, you see this man about whom the whole Jewish people petitioned me, both in Jerusalem and here, shouting [[loudly]]ᵃ that he ought not to live any longer. 25 But I found that he had done nothing deserving death. And as he himself appealed to the Emperor, I decided to send him. 26 But I have nothing definite to write to my lord about him. Therefore, I have brought him before you all, and especially before you, King Agrippa, so that, after we have examined him, I may have something to write. 27 For it seems to me unreasonable, in sending a prisoner, not to indicate the charges against him."

26 1 Agrippa said to Paul, "You are permitted to speak for yourself." Then Paul, extending his hand, began his defense:

2 "Concerning all the things of which I am accused by the Jews, King Agrippa, I consider myself fortunate to be able to defend myself before you today, 3 especially since you are familiar with [all]ᵇ the customs and [[knowing about]]ᶜ controversies among the Jews. Therefore, I beg [[you]]ᵈ to listen to me patiently.

4 "All the Jews know my way of life from my youth, which from the beginning was spent among my own nation and in Jerusalem. 5 They have known me for a long time, if they are willing to testify, that according to the strictest sect of our religion, I lived as a Pharisee. 6 And now I stand on trial because of the hope in the promise made by God to {our}ᵉ fathers, 7 to which our twelve tribes hope to attain, as they earnestly serve God night and day. Concerning this hope, I am accused by the Jews [, O king]ᶠ [[Agrippa]].ᵍ

8 "[Why is it considered incredible among you]ʰ if God raises the dead? 9 I myself was convinced that I ought to do many things in opposition to the name of Jesus of Nazareth. 10 And this is what I did in Jerusalem; I not only locked up many of the saints in prison, having received authority from the chief priests, but when they were put to death I cast my vote against them. 11 And I punished them often in all the synagogues and tried to make them blaspheme; and in raging fury against them, I persecuted them even to foreign cities.

12 "In this connection, I journeyed to Damascus with the authority and commission {of}ⁱ the chief priests. 13 [At midday,]ʲ O king, I saw on the way a light from heaven, brighter than the sun, shining around me and those who journeyed with me.

14 "And when we had all fallen to the ground, I heard a voice speaking to me [[and saying]]ᵏ in the Hebrew language, 'Saul, Saul, why are you persecuting me? It is hard for you to kick against the goads.'ˡ 15 And I said, 'Who are you, Lord?' And [the Lord]ᵐ said, 'I am Jesus whom you are persecuting. 16 But rise [and stand]ⁿ upon your feet; for this purpose I have

---

ᵃ 25:24, **loudly:** Included in C(04) BYZ TR.

ᵇ 26:3, **all:** Absent from A(02).

ᶜ 26:3, **knowing about:** Included in A(02) C(04).

ᵈ 26:3, **you:** Included in BYZ TR.

ᵉ 26:6, **our** Some manuscripts read "the." BYZ TR.

ᶠ 26:7, **O king:** Absent from A(02).

ᵍ 26:7, **Agrippa:** Included in BYZ TR.

ʰ 26:8, **Why is it considered incredible among you:** Absent from 𝔓29.

ⁱ 26:12, **of:** Some manuscripts read "from." C(04) BYZ TR.

ʲ 26:13, **At midday:** Absent from ℵ(01).

ᵏ 26:14, **and saying:** Included in BYZ TR.

ˡ 26:14, **goads:** Or, sharp objects.

ᵐ 26:15, **the Lord:** Absent from some manuscripts which would be otherwise translated as "he." BYZ TR.

ⁿ 26:16, **and stand:** Absent from B(03).

appeared to you, to appoint you as a servant and a witness of what you have seen [of me]ᵃ and what I will reveal to you, 17 rescuing you from the people and from the nations to which I am sending you, 18 to open their eyes, to turn them from darkness to light and from the power of Satan to God, so that they may receive forgiveness of sins and a share among those who are sanctified by faith in me.'

19 "Therefore, King Agrippa, I was not disobedient to the heavenly vision, 20 But to those in Damascus first, and also in Jerusalem, and throughout [all the region]ᵇ of Judea, and to the Gentiles, I proclaimed repentance and turning to God, performing deeds worthy of repentance. 21 Because of these things, Jews seized me [being]ᶜ in the temple and tried to kill me. 22 To this day I have had the help that comes from God, and so I stand here testifying both to small and great, saying nothing but what the prophets and Moses said would come to pass: 23 that the Christ must suffer and that, by being the first to rise from the dead, he would proclaim light [both] to our people and to the Gentiles."

24 But as he was making his defense, Festus {said} with a loud voice, "You are out of your mind, Paul! Your great learning is driving you mad." 25 But [Paul]ᵈ said, "I am not out of my mind, most excellent Festus, but I am speaking words of truth and sound judgment. 26 For the king knows about these things, to whom also I speak boldly; For I am persuaded that none of these things has escaped his notice, for this has not been done in a corner. 27 King Agrippa, do you believe the prophets? I know that you believe."

28 And Agrippa said to Paul, "In a short time you would persuade me to be a Christian." 29 But Paul [[said]],ᵉ "I would pray to God that whether {in a short time or a long time},ᶠ not only you but also all who hear me today might become such as I am, except for these chains."

30 [[And as he was saying these things]]ᵍ The king and the governor got up, as well as Bernice and those sitting with them, 31 And having withdrawn, they spoke to one another, saying, "This person does nothing worthy of death or chains." 32 And Agrippa said to Festus, "This man could have been set free if he had not appealed to Caesar." [[And thus the governor decided to refer him.]]ʰ

27 1 But when it was decided that we should sail for Italy, they handed over Paul and some other prisoners to a centurion named Julius, of the Augustan Cohort. 2 Boarding a ship from Adramyttium {that was about to sail to the ports along the coast of Asia, we put out to sea}, accompanied by Aristarchus, a Macedonian from Thessalonica. 3 The next day we landed at Sidon; and Julius treated Paul kindly and allowed him to go to his friends to be cared for.

4 From there we put out to sea again and sailed under the lee of Cyprus because the winds were against us. 5 After we had sailed across the open sea off the coast of Cilicia and Pamphylia, we landed at Myra in Lycia. 6 There the centurion found an Alexandrian ship sailing for Italy and put us on board. 7 We sailed slowly for a number of days and arrived with difficulty off Cnidus, and as the wind did not allow us to go farther, we sailed under the lee of Crete off Salmone. 8 Sailing past it with

---

ᵃ 26:16, **of me:** B(03) C(04) ‖ Absent from ℵ(01) A(02) BYZ TR.

ᵇ 26:20, **all the region:** Absent from 𝔓29.

ᶜ 26:21, **being:** Absent from A(02) B(03) BYZ TR.

ᵈ 26:25, **Paul:** Absent from some manuscripts which would be otherwise translated as "he." BYZ TR.

ᵉ 26:29, **said:** Included in BYZ TR.

ᶠ 26:29, **in a short time or a long time:** Some manuscripts read "with a little or much." BYZ TR.

ᵍ 26:30, **And as he was saying these things:** Included in BYZ TR.

ʰ 26:32, **And thus the governor decided to refer him:** Included in 𝔓112.

difficulty, we came to a place called Fair Havens, near the city of Lasea.

9 Much time had been lost, and sailing had already become dangerous because by now it was after the Day of Atonement. So Paul warned them, 10 "Men, I can see that our voyage is going to be disastrous and bring great loss to ship and cargo, and to our own lives also."

11 But the centurion, instead of listening to what Paul said, followed the advice of the pilot and of the owner of the ship.

12 But since the harbor was unsuitable for wintering, the majority decided to set sail from there, if somehow they could reach Phoenix, a harbor of Crete facing southwest and northwest, to spend the winter.

13 When a gentle south wind began to blow, they thought they had obtained what they wanted; so they weighed anchor and sailed along the shore of Crete.

14 Before very long, a wind of hurricane force, called the Northeastern, swept down from the island. 15 And when the ship was caught and could not face the wind, we gave way and were driven along.

16 As we passed to the lee of a small island called {Cauda},ᵃ we were hardly able to make the lifeboat secure, 17 so the men hoisted it aboard. Then they passed ropes under the ship itself to hold it together. Because they were afraid they would run aground on the sandbars of Syrtis, they lowered the sea anchor and let the ship be driven along.

18 We took such a violent battering from the storm that the next day they began to throw the cargo overboard.

19 On the third day, they threw the ship's tackle overboard with their own hands.

20 When neither sun nor stars appeared for many days and the storm continued raging, we [finally]ᵇ gave up all hope of being saved.

21 After they had gone a long time without food, Paul stood up before them and said: "Men, you should have taken my advice not to sail from Crete; then you would have spared yourselves this damage and loss. 22 But now I urge you to keep up your courage, because not one of you will be lost; only the ship will be destroyed. 23 For this night an angel of the God to whom I belong and whom I serve stood before me 24 and said, 'Do not be afraid, Paul. You must stand trial before Caesar; and God has graciously given you the lives of all who sail with you.' 25 So keep up your courage, men, for I have faith in God that it will happen just as he told me. 26 Nevertheless, we must run aground on some island."

27 But when the fourteenth night came, as we were being driven about in the Adriatic Sea, about midnight the sailors began to suspect that they were approaching some land. 28 And having cast, they found twenty fathoms; and having gone a little farther, they cast again and found fifteen fathoms. 29 Fearing that we might run aground on the rocky coast, they cast four anchors from the stern and prayed for day to come.

30 But the sailors seeking to escape from the ship, and having lowered the boat into the sea, under the pretext of intending to extend anchors from the bow, 31 Paul said to the centurion and the soldiers, "Unless these men remain in the ship, you cannot be saved." 32 Then the soldiers cut away the ropes of the boat and let it go.

33 As day was about to dawn, Paul urged them all to take some food, saying, "Today is the fourteenth day that you have been in suspense and have continued without food, having taken nothing. 34 Therefore, I urge you to take some food; for this is for your

---

ᵃ 27:16, **Cauda:** Some manuscripts read "Clauda." ℵ(01) A(02) BYZ TR.

ᵇ 27:20, **finally:** Absent from B(03).

safety, for not a hair from the head of any of you will {perish}."ᵃ

₃₅ And when he had said this, he took bread and gave thanks to God in the presence of all, and he broke it and began to eat. ₃₆ And all becoming cheerful, they themselves also took food.

₃₇ We were in all two hundred seventy-six persons in the ship. ₃₈ And when they had eaten enough, they lightened the ship by throwing the wheat into the sea.

₃₉ When day came, they did not recognize the land, but they noticed a bay with a beach, on which they planned to run the ship ashore if they could. ₄₀ And casting off the anchors, they left them in the sea, at the same time loosening the ropes of the rudders and hoisting the foresail to the blowing wind, they held course for the beach. ₄₁ But striking a reef, they ran the ship aground; the bow stuck and remained immovable, but the stern was being broken up by the force [of the waves].ᵇ

₄₂ The soldiers' plan was to kill the prisoners, lest any should swim away and escape.

₄₃ But the centurion, wishing to save Paul, kept them from carrying out their plan. He ordered those who could swim to throw themselves overboard first and make for the land, ₄₄ and the rest on planks or on pieces of the ship.

And so it was that all were brought safely to land.

28 ₁ And when we were saved, we then learned that the island was called Malta. ₂ The natives showed us extraordinary kindness, for they kindled a fire and welcomed us [all],ᶜ because of the rain that was falling and because of the cold.

₃ But when Paul had gathered a bundle of sticks and laid them on the fire, a viper came out because of the heat and fastened on his hand.

₄ When the natives saw the creature hanging from his hand, they said to one another, "Certainly this man is a murderer, whom, though he has escaped from the sea, justice has not allowed to live."

₅ However, he shook off the creature into the fire and suffered no harm.

₆ They were expecting him to swell up or suddenly fall down dead. But after they had waited a long time and saw no misfortune come to him, they changed their minds and said that he was a god.

₇ Now in the neighborhood of that place were lands belonging to the chief man of the island, named Publius, who received us and entertained us hospitably for three days.

₈ It happened that the father of Publius lay sick with fever and dysentery; and Paul went in to him, and after praying, he laid his hands on him and healed him.

₉ And when this had taken place, the rest of the people on the island who had diseases also came and were cured.

₁₀ They also honored us greatly, and when we were about to sail, they put on board whatever we needed.

₁₁ After three months we set sail in a ship that had wintered in the island, an Alexandrian ship with the Twin Brothers as its figurehead.

₁₂ Putting in at Syracuse, we stayed there for three days. ₁₃ And from there we made a circuit and arrived at Rhegium. And after one day a south wind sprang up, and on the second day we came to Puteoli. ₁₄ There we found brothers and were invited to stay with them for seven days. And so we came to Rome. ₁₅ And the brothers there, when they heard about us, came as far as the Forum of Appius and Three Taverns to meet us. On seeing them, Paul thanked God and took courage.

ᵃ 27:34, **perish:** Some manuscripts read "fall." BYZ TR.
ᵇ 27:41, **of the waves:** C(04) BYZ TR NA28 THGNT ‖ Absent from ℵ(01) A(02) B(03) SBLGNT.
ᶜ 28:2, **all:** Absent from A(02).

16 When we entered Rome, [[the centurion delivered the prisoners to the captain of the guard, but]]ᵃ Paul was allowed to stay by himself with the soldier guarding him.

17 After three days, he called together the leading men of the Jews. When they had gathered, he said to them, "Men, brothers, I have done nothing against our people or the customs of our ancestors, yet I was delivered as a prisoner from Jerusalem into the hands of the Romans. 18 They examined me and wanted to release me because there was no cause for the death penalty in my case. 19 But when the Jews objected, I was compelled to appeal to Caesar, not because I had any charge to bring against my nation. 20 For this reason, I have asked to see you and speak with you, for it is because of the hope of Israel that I am wearing this chain."

21 They replied, "We have received no letters about you from Judea, nor have any of the brothers come here and reported or spoken anything evil about you. 22 But we ask to hear from you what you think; for indeed, concerning this sect, it is known to us that it is spoken against everywhere."

23 They set a day to meet with him, and they came to him at his lodging in greater numbers. From morning until evening, he expounded to them, testifying about the kingdom of God and trying to persuade them about Jesus from both the Law of Moses and the Prophets.

24 Some were convinced by what he said, while others disbelieved. 25 But disagreeing with one another, they began to leave after Paul had spoken one word:

"Well did the Holy Spirit speak through Isaiah the prophet to our fathers, 26 saying, 'Go to this people and say, You will indeed hear but never understand, and you will indeed see but never perceive. 27 For this people's heart has grown dull, and with their ears they can barely hear, and their eyes they have closed; lest they should see with their eyes and hear with their ears [and understand with their heart]ᵇ and turn, and I would heal them.'ᶜ

28 "Therefore, let it be known to you that {this}ᵈ salvation of God has been sent to the Gentiles; they will listen." 29 [[And having said these things, the Jews departed, having much discussion among themselves.]]ᵉ

30 {He}ᶠ lived there two whole years at his own expense and welcomed all who came to him, 31 proclaiming the kingdom of God and teaching about the Lord Jesus [Christ]ᵍ with all boldness and without hindrance.ʰ

ᵃ 28:16, **the centurion delivered the prisoners to the captain of the guard, but:** Included in BYZ TR.

ᵇ 28:27, **and understand with their heart:** Absent from ℵ(01).

ᶜ 28:27, Isaiah 6:9-10 LXX.

ᵈ 28:28, **this:** Absent from BYZ TR.

ᵉ 28:29, Some manuscripts include verse 29. BYZ TR ‖ Absent from ℵ(01) A(02) B(03).

ᶠ 28:30, **He:** Some manuscripts read "Paul." BYZ TR.

ᵍ 28:31, **Christ:** Absent from ℵ(01).

ʰ 28:31, Some manuscripts include the postscript "Acts of Apostles." ℵ(01) B(03).

Romans[a]

1 [1] Paul, a servant of {Christ[b] Jesus}[c], called to be an apostle, set apart for the gospel of God; [2] Which he promised beforehand through his prophets in the holy Scriptures, [3] concerning his Son, who was descended from David according to the flesh, [4] and was declared to be the Son of God in power according to the Spirit of holiness by his resurrection from the dead, Jesus Christ our Lord, [5] through whom we have received grace and apostleship to bring about the obedience of faith for the sake of his name among all the nations, [6] [among whom you also are the called][d] of Jesus Christ.

[7] To all those in Rome who are loved by God and called to be saints: Grace to you and peace from God our Father and the Lord {Jesus Christ}.[e]

[8] First, I thank my God [through Jesus Christ][f] for all of you, because your faith is proclaimed in all the world. [9] For God is my witness, whom I serve with my spirit in the gospel of his Son, that without ceasing I mention you [10] always in my prayers, asking that somehow by God's will I may now at last succeed in coming to you. [11] For I long to see you, so that I may impart to you some spiritual gift for your strengthening, [12] and this is to be mutually encouraged among you through the faith in one another, both yours and mine.

[13] I want you to know, brothers, that I have often intended to come to you (but thus far have been prevented), in order that I may reap some harvest among you as well as among the rest of the nations. [14] I am under obligation both to Greeks and to barbarians, both to the wise and to the foolish. [15] So I am eager to preach the gospel to you also who are in Rome.

[16] For I am not ashamed of the gospel [[of Christ]],[g] for it is the power of God for salvation to everyone who believes, to the Jew [first][h] and also to the Greek. [17] For in it the righteousness of God is revealed from faith for faith, as it is written, "The righteous shall live by faith."[i]

[18] For the wrath of God is revealed from heaven against all ungodliness and unrighteousness of men, who by their unrighteousness suppress the truth.

[19] For what can be known about God is plain to them, because God has shown it to them. [20] For his invisible attributes, namely, his eternal power and divine nature, have been clearly perceived, ever since the creation of the world, in the things that have been made. So they are without excuse.

[21] For although they knew God, they did not honor him as God {or give}[j] thanks to him, but they became futile in their thinking, and their foolish hearts were darkened.

---

[a] 1:0, **Title ("Romans"):** Absent from 𝔓10 ℵ(01) B(03) ‖ A(02) C(04) BYZ reads "To the Romans." ‖ TR reads "The letter of Paul the apostle to the Romans."

[b] 1:1, **Christ:** The Greek word for *Christ* means (1) fulfiller of Israelite expectation of a deliverer, *the Anointed One, the Messiah, the Christ,* (2) the personal name ascribed to Jesus, *Christ.* (BDAG, Χριστός).

[c] 1:1, **Christ Jesus:** 𝔓10 B(03) NA28 SBLGNT ‖ Some manuscripts read "Jesus Christ." 𝔓26 ℵ(01) A(02) THGNT BYZ TR.

[d] 1:6, **among whom you also are the called:** Absent from 𝔓10.

[e] 1:7, **Jesus Christ:** 𝔓10 reads "Christ Jesus."

[f] 1:8, **through Jesus Christ:** Absent from ℵ(01).

[g] 1:16, **of Christ:** Included in BYZ TR.

[h] 1:16, **first:** Absent from B(03).

[i] 1:17, Habakkuk 2:4.

[j] 1:21, **or give:** A(02) reads "giving."

22 Claiming to be wise, they became fools, 23 and exchanged the glory of the immortal God for images resembling mortal man and birds and animals and creeping things.

24 Therefore {God}[a] gave them up in the lusts of their hearts [to impurity],[b] to the dishonoring of their bodies among {them},[c] 25 because they exchanged the truth about God for a lie and worshiped and served the creature rather than the Creator, who is blessed forever! Amen.

26 For this reason God, gave them up to dishonorable passions. For their women exchanged natural relations for those that are contrary to nature. 27 And the men likewise gave up natural relations with women and were consumed with passion for one another, men committing shameless acts with men and receiving in themselves the due penalty for their error.

28 And since they did not see fit to acknowledge [God],[d] {God}[e] gave them up to a debased mind to do what ought not to be done.

29 They were filled with all manner of unrighteousness, evil, covetousness, malice [immorality].[f]

They are full of envy, murder, strife, [deceit,][g] maliciousness. They are gossips, 30 slanderers, haters of God, insolent, haughty, boastful, inventors of evil, disobedient to parents, 31 foolish, faithless, heartless, ruthless [[unforgiving]].[h]

32 Though they know God's righteous decree that those who practice such things deserve to die, they not only do them but give approval to those who practice them.

2 1 Therefore [[by judgment]][i] you are without excuse, O man, every one of you who judges. For in passing judgment on another you condemn yourself, because you, the judge, practice the very same things. 2 We know that the judgment of God rightly falls on those who practice such things.

3 But consider this, O man who judges those practicing such things and doing them, that you will escape the judgment of God?

4 Or do you presume on the riches of his kindness and forbearance and patience, not knowing that God's kindness is meant to lead you to repentance?

5 But because of your hard and impenitent heart you are storing up wrath for yourself on the day of wrath [[and]][j] when God's righteous judgment will be revealed.

6 He will render to each one according to his works. 7 To those who by patience in well-doing seek for glory and honor and immortality, he will give eternal life. 8 But for those who are self-seeking and [[indeed]][k] disobeying the truth, but obey unrighteousness, there will be {wrath and anger}.[l]

9 There will be tribulation and distress for every human being who does evil, the Jew first and also the Greek, 10 but glory and honor and peace for everyone who does good, the Jew first and also the Greek.

---

a 1:24, **he:** C(04) reads "God."

b 1:24, **to impurity:** Absent from A(02).

c 1:24, **them:** Some manuscripts read "themselves." BYZ TR.

d 1:28, **God:** Absent from ℵ(01) A(02).

e 1:28, **God:** Some manuscripts read "he." ℵ(01) A(02).

f 1:29, **immorality:** Included in BYZ TR.

g 1:29, **deceit:** Absent from A(02).

h 1:31, **unforgiving:** Included in C(04) BYZ TR.

i 2:1, **by judgment:** Included in C(04).

j 2:5, **and:** Included in A(02) BYZ TR.

k 2:8, **indeed:** Included in A(02) BYZ TR.

l 2:8, **wrath and anger:** Some manuscripts read "anger and wrath." BYZ TR.

11 For there is no partiality with God. 12 For as many as have sinned[a] without law, will also perish without law, and as many as have sinned in the law, will be judged by the law. 13 For it is not the hearers of the law who are righteous before God, but the doers of the law who will be justified.

14 For when Gentiles, which do not have the law by nature, do the things of the law, these, not having the law, are a law to themselves; 15 who show the work of the law written in their hearts, their conscience bearing witness, and their thoughts *alternately* accusing or even defending them, 16 on the day when God judges the hidden things of men according to my gospel {through}[b] {Christ Jesus}.[c]

17 {But if you}[d] call yourself a Jew and rely on the law and boast in God, 18 and know his will and approve the things that are superior, being instructed from the law, 19 and are confident that you yourself are a guide to the blind, a light to those in darkness, 20 an instructor of the foolish, [a teacher of infants,][e] having the form of knowledge and truth in the law; 21 you then who teach others, do you not teach yourself? While you preach against stealing, do you steal? 22 You who say that one must not commit adultery, do you commit adultery? You who abhor idols, do you rob temples? 23 You who boast in the law dishonor God by breaking the law.

24 For, as it is written, "The name of God is blasphemed among the Gentiles because of you."[f]

25 For circumcision indeed is of value if you obey the law, but if you break the law, your circumcision becomes uncircumcision.

26 So, if a man who is uncircumcised keeps the precepts of the law, {will not}[g] his uncircumcision be regarded as circumcision?

27 And will not the physically uncircumcised, if he keeps the law, judge you who, having the written code and circumcision, are a transgressor of the law? 28 For no one is a Jew who is merely one outwardly, nor is circumcision outward and physical. 29 But the one in the hidden place is a Jew, and circumcision is of the heart, in spirit not in letter, whose praise is not from men but from God.

3 1 What then is the advantage of the Jew, or what is the benefit of circumcision? 2 Much in every way. First of all, they were entrusted with the oracles of God.

3 What if some were unfaithful? Will their unfaithfulness nullify the faithfulness of God?

4 By no means! Let God be true, and every man a liar, as it is written: "So that you may be justified in your words and prevail when you are judged."[h]

5 But if our unrighteousness serves to show the righteousness of God, what shall we say? Is God unjust to inflict [[his]][i] wrath? I am speaking in human terms.

6 By no means! For then how could God judge the world?

---

a 2:12, **sinned:** Or "fouled." The word for sin in a general sense means to "miss the mark, error, do wrong" (BDAG, ἁμαρτάνω).

b 2:16, **through** ℵ(01) reads "of."

c 2:16, **Christ Jesus:** ℵ(01) B(03) NA28 SBLGNT ‖ Some manuscripts read "Jesus Christ." A(02) THGNT BYZ TR.

d 2:17, **But if you:** Some manuscripts read "Behold you." BYZ TR.

e 2:20, **a teacher of infants:** Absent from A(02).

f 2:24, Isaiah 52:5 LXX.

g 2:26, **will not:** Some manuscripts read "Is it not." BYZ TR.

h 3:4, Psalm 51:4 LXX.

i 3:5, **his:** Included in ℵ(01).

7 But if through my falsehood God's truth abounds to his glory, why am I still being condemned as a sinner? 8 And why not say, as some people slander us by claiming that we say, Let us do evil that good may come? Their condemnation is just.

9 What then? Are we any better off? Not at all! For we have already charged that both Jews [[first]]ᵃ and Greeks are all under sin,ᵇ 10 as it is written: "There is no one righteous, not even one; 11 there is no one who understands, no one who seeks God. 12 All have turned away, together they have become worthless; there is no one who does good, not even one.ᶜ 13 Their throat is an open grave; they deceive with their tongues; the venom of asps is under their lips;ᵈ 14 their mouth is full of curses and bitterness.ᵉ 15 Their feet are swift to shed blood, 16 ruin and misery mark their ways, 17 and the way of peace they have not known.ᶠ 18 There is no fear of God before their eyes."ᵍ

19 Now we know that whatever the law says, it speaks to those who are under the law, so that every mouth may be silenced and the whole world held accountable to God.

20 Therefore no one will be declared righteous in his sight by works of the law; for through the law comes the knowledge of sin.ʰ

21 But now, apart from the law, the righteousness of God has been revealed, being witnessed by the Law and the Prophets, 22 the righteousness of God through faith in Jesus Christⁱ for all [[and upon all]]ʲ who believe. For there is no distinction, 23 for all have sinnedᵏ and fall short of the glory of God, 24 being justified freely by his grace through the redemption that is in Christ Jesus, 25 whom God set forth as a propitiation through [the faith]ˡ in his blood, for a demonstration of his righteousness because of the passing over of the sins previously committed, 26 in the forbearance of God, for the demonstration of his righteousness in the present time, so that he might be justifier of the one who has faith in Jesus.ᵐ

27 Where then is boasting? It is excluded. By what kind of law? Of works? No, but by a law of faith. 28 {For}ⁿ we maintain that a person is justified by faith apart from works of the law.

29 Or is God the God of Jews only? Is he not the God of Gentiles too? Yes, of Gentiles too, 30 {if indeed}ᵒ there is one God who will justify the circumcised by faith and the uncircumcised through faith. 31 Do we then nullify the law by this faith? By no means! Rather, we uphold the law.

4 1 What shall we say then that Abraham, our forefather, [was found]ᵖ according to the flesh, ? 2 For if Abraham was justified by works, he

---

ᵃ 3:9, **first:** Included in A(02).

ᵇ 3:9, **sin:** Or error. The word for sin in a general sense means to "miss the mark, error, do wrong" (BDAG, ἁμαρτάνω).

ᶜ 3:12, Psalm 14:1-3, 53:1-3 LXX.

ᵈ 3:13, Psalm 5:9 LXX.

ᵉ 3:14, Psalm 10:7 LXX.

ᶠ 3:15-17, Isaiah 59:7-8.

ᵍ 3:18, Psalm 36:1.

ʰ 3:20, **sin:** Or, what is error. The word for sin in a general sense means to "miss the mark, error, do wrong" (BDAG, ἁμαρτάνω).

ⁱ 3:22, **faith in Jesus Christ:** Or "faithfulness of Jesus" as the construction is genitive.

ʲ 3:22, **and upon all:** Included in BYZ TR.

ᵏ 3:23, **sinned:** Or fouled. The word for sin in a general sense means to "miss the mark, error, do wrong" (BDAG, ἁμαρτάνω). Here the Greek word is in the aorist case.

ˡ 3:25, **the faith:** Absent from A(02).

ᵐ 3:26, **faith in Jesus:** Or "faithfulness of Jesus" as the construction is genitive.

ⁿ 3:28, **For:** Some manuscripts read "Therefore." BYZ TR.

ᵒ 3:30, **if indeed:** Some manuscripts read "since indeed." BYZ TR.

ᵖ 4:1, **was found:** Absent from B(03).

has something to boast about, but not before God. ₃For what does the Scripture say? "Abraham believed God, and it was credited to him as righteousness."ᵃ

₄Now to the one working, the reward is not credited according to grace, but according to debt. ₅But to the one {not working},ᵇ but believing in the one who justifies the ungodly, that one's faith is credited for righteousness; ₆[just as David also speaks]ᶜ of the blessing of the person to whom God credits righteousness apart from works: ₇Blessed are those whose lawless deeds are forgiven, and whose sins are covered; ₈blessed is the man against whom the Lord will not count his sin.ᵈ

₉Is this blessing then on the circumcised, or on the uncircumcised also? For we say [[that]], ᵉ"Faith was credited to Abraham as righteousness." ₁₀How then was it credited? While he was circumcised, or uncircumcised? Not in circumcision, but in uncircumcision.

₁₁And he received the sign of circumcision, a seal of the righteousness of the faith which he had while still uncircumcised, so that he might be the father of all who believe without being circumcised, that righteousness might be credited to them [also],ᶠ ₁₂and the father of circumcision to those who not only are of the circumcision, but who also follow in the steps [of the faith]ᵍ of our father Abraham which he had while still uncircumcised.

₁₃For the promise to Abraham or to his offspring, that he would be heir of the world, was not through the law, but through the righteousness of faith. ₁₄For if those who are of the law are heirs, faith is made void and the promise is nullified; ₁₅for the law produces wrath; {but}ʰ where there is no law, there is no transgression.

₁₆Therefore it is of faith, that it might be according to grace, so that the promise might be sure to all the descendants, not only to those who are of the law, but also to those who are of the faith of Abraham, who is the father of us all, ₁₇as it is written, "I have made you a father of many nations," in the presence of the God in whom he believed, who gives life to the dead and calls into existence the things that do not exist. ₁₈In hope against hope he believed, so that he might become a father of many nations according to that which had been spoken, "So shall your descendants be."ⁱ

₁₉And not weakening in faith, {he considered}ʲ his own body [already]ᵏ as good as dead, being about a hundred years old, and the deadness of Sarah's womb; ₂₀yet, with respect to the promise of God, he did not waver in unbelief but grew strong in faith, giving glory to God, ₂₁and being fully convinced that what was promised, he is able also to do. ₂₂Therefore [also]ˡ it was credited to him as righteousness.

₂₃It was not written for his sake alone that it was credited to him, ₂₄but also for our sake, to whom it will be credited, to those who believe in the one who raised Jesus our Lord from the dead, ₂₅who was handed over for our trespasses and was raised for our justification.

ᵃ 4:3, Genesis 15:6.

ᵇ 4:5, **not working:** 𝔭40 reads "working, the wage is not credited according to grace."

ᶜ 4:6, **Just as David also speaks:** Absent from 𝔭40.

ᵈ 4:8, Psalm 32:1-2.

ᵉ 4:9, **that:** Included in A(02) C(04) BYZ TR.

ᶠ 4:11, **also:** C(04) BYZ TR NA28[] ‖ Absent from ℵ(01) A(02) B(03) SBLGNT THGNT.

ᵍ 4:12, **of the faith:** Absent from ℵ(01).

ʰ 4:15, **but:** Some manuscripts read "for." BYZ TR.

ⁱ 4:17-18, Genesis 17:5, 15:5.

ʲ 4:19, **he considered:** ℵ(01) A(02) B(03) C(04) NA28 SBLGNT THGNT ‖ Some manuscripts read "he did not consider." BYZ TR.

ᵏ 4:19, **already:** ℵ(01) A(02) C(04) NA28[] THGNT BYZ TR ‖ Absent from B(03) SBLGNT.

ˡ 4:22, **also:** ℵ(01) A(02) C(04) NA28[] THGNT BYZ TR ‖ Absent from B(03) SBLGNT.

5 ¹Therefore, having been justified by faith, {let us have}ᵃ peace with God through our Lord Jesus Christ, ²through whom we have also obtained access [by faith]ᵇ into this grace in which we stand, and we rejoice in the hope of the glory of God.

³Not only that, but we also rejoice in our sufferings, knowing that suffering produces endurance, ⁴and endurance produces character, and character produces hope. ⁵And hope does not disappoint, because the love of God has been poured out into our hearts through the Holy Spiritᶜ that has been given to us.

⁶[For]ᵈ While we were [still]ᵉ weak, at the right time Christ died for the ungodly. ⁷Indeed, rarely will someone die for a righteous person; though perhaps for a good person someone might even dare to die. ⁸But God demonstrates his own love for us, in that while we were still sinners, Christ died for us.

⁹Much more then, having now been justified by his blood, we shall be saved from the wrath through him.

¹⁰For if, while we were enemies, we were reconciled to God through the death of his Son, much more, having been reconciled, we shall be saved by his life. ¹¹Not only that, but we also rejoice in God through our Lord Jesus [Christ],ᶠ through whom we have now received the reconciliation.

¹²Therefore, just as through one man sinᵍ entered into the world, and death through sin, and so death spread to all men, because all sinned;ʰ ¹³for until the law, sin was in the world, but sin is not counted when there is no law.

¹⁴Nevertheless, death reigned from Adam until Moses, even over those who had not sinned in the likeness of the transgression of Adam, who is a type of the one to come.

¹⁵But the free gift is not like the trespass; for if by the trespass of the one the many died, [therefore]ⁱ much more did the grace of God and the gift by the grace of the one man, Jesus Christ, abound to the many. ¹⁶And the gift is not like the result of one sin; for indeed the judgment from one sin led to condemnation, but the gift from many trespasses led to justification.

¹⁷For if by the trespass of the one, death reigned through the one, much more will those who receive the abundance of grace and [the gift]ʲ [of righteousness]ᵏ reign in life through the one, {Jesus Christ}.ˡ

¹⁸Consequently [[of man]],ᵐ just as one trespass led to condemnation for all men, so also one act of righteousness leads to justification and life for all men.

¹⁹For just as through the disobedience of the one man the many were made sinners, so also through the

---

ᵃ 5:1, **let us have:** ℵ(01) A(02) B(03) C(04) THGNT ‖ Some manuscripts read "we have." NA28 SBLGNT BYZ TR.

ᵇ 5:2, **by faith:** Absent from B(03).

ᶜ 5:5, **Spirit:** See footnote for Spirit in Luke 1:15.

ᵈ 5:6, **For:** Absent from B(03).

ᵉ 5:6, **still:** Absent from BYZ TR.

ᶠ 5:11, **Christ:** Absent from B(03).

ᵍ 5:12, **sin:** Or "error." The word for sin in a general sense means to "miss the mark, error, do wrong" (BDAG, ἁμαρτάνω).

ʰ 5:12, **sinned:** Or "erred." The word for sin in a general sense means to "miss the mark, error, do wrong" (BDAG, ἁμαρτάνω).

ⁱ 5:15, **therefore:** Included in A(02).

ʲ 5:17, **the gift:** Absent from B(03).

ᵏ 5:17, **of righteousness:** Absent from C(04).

ˡ 5:17, **Jesus Christ:** Some manuscripts read "Christ Jesus." B(03).

ᵐ 5:18, **of man:** Included in ℵ(01).

obedience of the one the many will be made righteous.

20 Now the law came in so that the transgression might increase; but where sin increased, grace abounded all the more, 21 so that, just as sin reigned in death, so also grace might reign through righteousness to eternal life through Jesus Christ our Lord.

6 1 What shall we say then? Shall we continue in sin, so that grace may abound? 2 By no means! How can we who died to sin still live in it?

3 Or do you not know that as many of us as were baptized into Christ [Jesus]ᵃ were baptized into his death? 4 Therefore, we were buried with him through baptism into death, so that just as Christ was raised from the dead through the glory of the Father, so also we might walk in newness of life.

5 For if we have become united with him in the likeness of his death, we shall also be in the likeness of his resurrection; 6 knowing this, that our old manᵇ was crucified with him, so that the body of sin might be rendered powerless, that we should no longer be slaves to sin; 7 For the one who has died has been justifiedᶜ from sin.

8 Now if we died with Christ, we believe that we shall also live with him, 9 knowing that Christ, having been raised from the dead, dies no more. Death no longer has dominion over him.

10 For what has died, has died to sin once for all; but what lives, lives to God. 11 So also you, consider yourselves [to be]ᵈ dead indeed to sin, but living to God in Christ Jesus [[our Lord]].ᵉ

12 Therefore, do not let sin reign in your mortal body so that you obey {its desires},ᶠ 13 and do not present your members as instruments of unrighteousness to sin, but present yourselves to God as being alive from the dead, and your members as instruments of righteousness to God. 14 For sin shall not have dominion over you, for you are not under law but under grace.

15 What then? Shall we sin because we are not under law but under grace? By no means! 16 Do you not know that when you present yourselves as slaves for obedience, you are slaves to the one you obey, either of sin leading to death, or of obedience leading to righteousness? 17 But thanks be to God that though you were slaves of sin, you have obeyed from the heart the pattern of teaching to which you were entrusted.

18 Having been freed from sin, you became slaves to righteousness.

19 I am speaking in human terms because of the weakness of your flesh. For just as you presented your members as slaves to impurity and to lawlessness [into lawlessness],ᵍ so now present your members as slaves to righteousness into sanctification.

20 For when you were slaves of sin, you were free in regard to righteousness. 21 What fruit did you have then in the things of which you are now ashamed? For the end of those things is death.

22 But now, having been set free from sin and having become slaves to God, you have your fruit into sanctification, and the end, eternal life. 23 For the wages of sin is death, but the gift of God is eternal life in Christ Jesus our Lord.

ᵃ 6:3, **Jesus:** Absent from B(03).

ᵇ 6:6, **our old man:** Or self. BDAG gives the definition of the Greek word in the context of the two sides of human nature as "the outer being" or "the inner being" (BDAG, ἄνθρωπος). The Hebrew word for "man" is āḏām. Adam is treated as a separate entry in BDAG under Ἀδάμ.

ᶜ 6:7, **justified:** Or vindicated or released.

ᵈ 6:11, **to be:** Absent from 𝔓46 A(02).

ᵉ 6:11, **our Lord:** Included in BYZ TR.

ᶠ 6:12, **its desires:** Some manuscripts read "it in its desires." BYZ TR. ‖ 𝔓46 reads "this."

ᵍ 6:19, **into lawlessness:** Absent from B(03).

7 1 Or do you not know, brothers, for I am speaking to those who know the law, that the law has authority over a person as long as they live? 2 For a married woman is bound by law to her living husband; but if her husband dies, she is released from the law concerning her husband. 3 So then, if she is joined to another man while her husband is alive, {she}ᵃ will be called an adulteress; but if her husband dies, she is free from the law, so that she is not an adulteress, though she is joined to another man.

4 So then, my brothers, you also were put to death in relation to the law through the body of Christ, so that you might belong to another, to the one who was raised from the dead, in order that we might bear fruit for God. 5 For when we were in the flesh, the sinful passions that came through the law were at work in our members, so that we bore fruit for death. 6 But now we have been released from the law, having died to that which held [us]ᵇ captive, so that we serve in the newness of the Spirit and not in the oldness of the letter.

7 What then shall we say? Is the law sin? By no means! But I would not have known sin except through the law; for I would not have known desireᶜ if the law had not said, "You shall not desire."ᵈ 8 But sin, seizing an opportunity through the commandment, produced in me every kind of desire; for apart from the law, sin is dead.

9 I was once alive apart from the law, but when the commandment came, sinᵉ came to life 10 and I died. The commandment that was meant to bring life, in fact, brought death. 11 For sin, seizing an opportunity through the commandment, deceived me and through it killed me. 12 So then, the law is holy, and the commandment is holy and righteous and good.

13 Did that which is good, then, become death to me? By no means! But sin, in order that it might be shown to be sin, was producing death in me through what is good, so that sin might become exceedingly sinful through the commandment.

14 For we know that the law is spiritual, but I am of the flesh, sold under sin. 15 For I do not understand my own actions. For I do not do what I want, but I do the very thing I hate.

16 Now, if I do what I do not want, I agree with the law, that it is good. 17 So now it is no longer I who do it, but sin that dwells within me. 18 For I know that good does not dwell in me, that is, in my flesh; for the willing is present with me, but {the doing of the good is not}.ᶠ 19 For I do not do the good I want, but the evil I do not want is what I keep on doing. 20 Now if I do what I do not want, it is no longer I who do it, but sin that dwells within me.

21 So I find it to be a law that when I want to do right, evil lies close at hand; 22 For I delight in the law of God, in my inner being, 23 but I see another law in my members warring against the law of my mind and taking me captive [in the law of sin that is in]ᵍ my members.

24 Wretched man that I am! Who will deliver me from this body of death?

25 [[But]]ʰ Thanks to God through Jesus Christ our Lord. So then, I myself with the mind serve the law of God, but with the flesh the law of sin.

ᵃ 7:3, **she:** Some manuscripts read "the woman." A(02).

ᵇ 7:6, **us:** Absent from B(03).

ᶜ 7:7, **desire:** Or, to covet.

ᵈ 7:7, Exodus 20:17, Deuteronomy 5:21.

ᵉ 7:9, **sin:** The word for sin in a general sense means to "miss the mark, error, do wrong" (BDAG, ἁμαρτάνω).

ᶠ 7:18, **the doing of the good is not:** ℵ(01) A(02) B(03) C(04) NA28 SBLGNT THGNT ‖ Some manuscripts read "I cannot find how to do it." BYZ TR.

ᵍ 7:23, **in the law of sin that is in:** Absent from A(02).

ʰ 7:25, **But:** Some manuscripts read "I give." ℵ(01) A(02) BYZ TR THGNT ‖ Absent from B(03), , and SBLGNT.

8 1 Therefore, there is now no condemnation for those in Christ Jesus [[who do not walk according to the flesh]]ᵃ [[but according to the Spirit]].ᵇ

2 For the law of the Spirit of life in Christ Jesus has set {you}ᶜ free from the law of sin and death.

3 For what was impossible for the law, in that it was weak through the flesh, God, sending his own Son in the likeness of sinful flesh and for sin, condemned sin in the flesh, 4 so that the requirement of the law might be fulfilled in us, who do not walk according to the flesh but according to the Spirit.

5 For those who are according to the flesh set their minds on the things of the flesh, but those who are according to the Spirit, the things of the Spirit.

6 For the mindset of the flesh is death, but the mindset of the Spirit is life and peace; 7 because the mindset of the flesh is hostile to God, for it does not submit to the law of God, nor is it able to; 8 and those who are in the flesh cannot please God.

9 But you are not in the flesh, but in the Spirit, if indeed the Spirit of God dwells in you. And if anyone does not have the Spirit of Christ, this one is not of him.

10 But if Christ is in you, the body is dead because of sin, but the Spirit is life because of righteousness.

11 And if the Spirit of the one who raised Jesus from the dead dwells in you, the one who raised Christ [Jesus]ᵈ from the dead will [also]ᵉ give life to your mortal bodies through his spirit dwelling in you.

12 So then, brothers, we are debtors, not to the flesh, to live according to the flesh; 13 for if you live according to the flesh, you are about to die; but if by the Spirit you put to death the deeds of the body, you will live. 14 For all who are led by the Spirit of God, these are sons of God.

15 For you did not receive a spirit of slavery leading to fear again, but you received a spirit of adoption, by which we cry out, "Abba, Father."

16 The Spirit itself bears witness with our spirit that we are children of God. 17 And if children, [then heirs;]ᶠ heirs of God and fellow heirs with Christ, if indeed we suffer with him so that we may [also]ᵍ be glorified with him.

18 For I consider that the sufferings of this present time are not worthy to be compared with the glory that is to be revealed to us.

19 For the eager expectation of the creation awaits the revelation of the sons of God. 20 For the creation was subjected to futility, not willingly, but because of the one who subjected it, in hope 21 that creation itself will also be set free from the bondage of corruption into the freedom of the glory of the children of God.

22 For we know that all creation groans together and suffers birth pains until now; 23 And not only this, but [also we ourselves,]ʰ having the firstfruits of the Spirit, [we]ⁱ also groan within ourselves, awaiting [adoption,]ʲ the redemption of our body.

ᵃ 8:1, **who do not walk according to the flesh:** Included in A(02) BYZ TR.

ᵇ 8:1, **but according to the Spirit:** Included in BYZ TR.

ᶜ 8:2, **you:** ℵ(01) B(03) NA28 SBLGNT ‖ Some manuscripts read "me." A(02) THGNT BYZ TR.

ᵈ 8:11, **Jesus:** ℵ(01) A(02) C(04) SBLGNT ‖ Absent from B(03) BYZ TR NA28 THGNT.

ᵉ 8:11, **also:** Absent from ℵ(01) A(02).

ᶠ 8:17, **then heirs:** Absent from 𝔓46.

ᵍ 8:17, **also:** Absent from 𝔓46.

ʰ 8:23, **also we ourselves:** Absent from 𝔓46.

ⁱ 8:23, **we:** Absent from B(03).

ʲ 8:23, **adoption:** Absent from 𝔓46.

24 For in hope we have been saved; but hope that is seen is not hope; {for who hopes for what he sees}?[a] 25 But if we hope for what we do not see, we eagerly wait for it with perseverance.

26 Likewise, the Spirit also helps in our weakness; for we do not know what we should pray for as we ought, but the Spirit itself intercedes [[for us]][b] with inexpressible groanings; 27 and the one searching the hearts knows what the mind of the Spirit is, because it intercedes for the saints according to God.

28 And we know that for those who love God, {all things work}[c] together for good, for those who are called according to his purpose. 29 For those whom he foreknew, he also predestined to be conformed to the image of his Son, so that he would be the firstborn among many brothers; 30 and those whom he predestined, he also called; and those whom he called, he also justified; and those whom he justified, he also glorified.

31 What then shall we say to these things? If God is for us, who can be against us? 32 Indeed, who did not spare *his* own son, but delivered him up for us all, how will he not also with him graciously give us all things?

33 Who will bring a charge against God's elect? It is God who justifies. 34 Who is the one who condemns? [[But if also]][d] Christ [Jesus],[e] the one who died, rather, who was raised, who also is at the right hand of God, who also intercedes on our behalf.

35 Who will separate us from the love of {Christ}?[f] Tribulation or distress or persecution or famine or nakedness or danger or sword? 36 As it is written, "For your sake we are being put to death all day long; we were considered as sheep for slaughter."[g]

37 No, in all these things we are more than conquerors through him who loved us. 38 For I am convinced that neither death nor life, neither angels {nor rulers, nor things present nor things to come, nor powers, 39 nor height}[h] nor depth, nor any other created thing, will be able to separate us from the love of God that is in Christ Jesus our Lord.

9 1 I am speaking the truth in Christ, I am not lying, my conscience bears witness with me in the Holy Spirit, 2 that there is great sorrow and unceasing pain in my heart. 3 For I could wish that I myself were cursed and cut off from Christ for the sake of [my brothers,][i] my kinsmen according to the flesh, 4 who are Israelites, to whom belong the adoption, the glory, the covenants, the giving of the law, the worship, and the promises, 5 of whom the fathers and from whom is the Christ according to the flesh, the one being over all, God blessed into the ages,[j] amen.

6 Not as though the word of God has failed. For not all those from Israel

---

a 8:24, **for who hopes for what he sees?:** 𝔓46 B(03) NA28 SBLGNT ‖ Some manuscripts read "for what a man sees, why does he also hope for it?" ℵ(01) A(02) C(04) THGNT BYZ TR.

b 8:26, **for us:** Included in C(04) BYZ TR.

c 8:28, **all things work:** ℵ(01) C(04) NA28 SBLGNT THGNT BYZ TR ‖ Some manuscripts read "God works all things." 𝔓46 A(02) B(03).

d 8:34, **But if also:** Included in 𝔓46.

e 8:34, **Jesus:** ℵ(01) A(02) C(04) NA28 [ ] ‖ Absent from B(03) SBLGNT THGNT BYZ TR.

f 8:35, **Christ:** ℵ(01) reads "God." ‖ B(03) reads "of God, the one in Christ Jesus."

g 8:36, Psalm 44:22.

h 8:39, **nor rulers, nor things present nor things to come, nor powers, nor height:** Some manuscripts read "rulers nor powers nor things present nor things to come nor height." BYZ TR ‖ C(04) reads "nor rulers nor authorities nor things present nor things to come nor powers nor height."

i 9:3, **my brothers:** Absent from B(03).

j 9:5, **over all, God blessed into the ages:** GPT-4 rendered the output of this verse, often associated with a high level of syntactical ambiguity, consistently as "over all, God blessed into the ages." The word for "blessed" (εὐλογητὸς) is an adjective rather than a verb. Different translations punctuate this verse differently.

are Israel; [7] nor because they are the offspring of Abraham are they all children, but, "your offspring will be reckoned."[a]

[8] This means that it is not the children of the flesh who are the children of God, but the children of the promise are counted as offspring.

[9] For this is the word of promise: "At this time I will come, and Sarah shall have a son."[b]

[10] And not only this, but also Rebecca, having conceived by one, Isaac our father; [11] For not yet having been born, nor having done anything good or bad, so that the purpose of God according to election might remain, [12] not by works, but by the one who calls, it was said to her, "The greater shall serve the lesser,"[c] [13] just as it is written, "Jacob I loved, but Esau I hated."[d]

[14] What shall we say then? Is there injustice on God's part? By no means! [15] For he says to Moses, "I will have mercy on whom I have mercy, and I will have compassion on whom I have compassion."[e] [16] So then it depends not on human will or exertion, but on God, who has mercy. [17] For the Scripture says to Pharaoh, "For this very purpose I have raised you up, that I might show my power in you, and that my name might be proclaimed in all the earth."[f] [18] So then he has mercy on whomever he wills, and he hardens whomever he wills.

[19] You will say to me then, Why [then][g] does he still find fault? For who can resist his will? [20] But who are you, O man, to answer back to God? Will what is molded say to its molder, "Why have you made me like this?"[h] [21] Or does not the potter have authority over the clay, from the same lump to make one vessel for honor and another for dishonor?

[22] What if God, desiring to show his wrath and to make known his power, endured with much patience vessels of wrath prepared for destruction, [23] in order to make known the riches of his glory for vessels of mercy, which he has prepared beforehand for glory; [24] even us whom he has called, not from the Jews only but also from the Gentiles?

[25] As indeed he says in Hosea, "Those who were not my people I will call my people, and her who was not beloved I will call 'beloved.'"[i] [26] "And it will be in the place where [it was said to them, 'You are not my people,'][j] there they will be called 'sons of the living God.'"[k]

[27] And Isaiah cries out concerning Israel: "Though the number of the sons of Israel be as the sand of the sea, only a remnant of them will be saved, [28] For he is completing and cutting short the word [[in righteousness, because a word having been shortened]],[l] the Lord will do upon the earth."[m]

[29] And just as Isaiah had foretold, "If the Lord of Hosts had not left us offspring, we would have become like Sodom and would have been made like Gomorrah."[n]

---

[a] 9:7, Genesis 21:12.
[b] 9:9, Genesis 18:10, 14.
[c] 9:12, Genesis 25:23.
[d] 9:13, Malachi 1:2-3.
[e] 9:15, Exodus 33:19.
[f] 9:17, Exodus 9:16 LXX.
[g] 9:19, **then:** 𝔓46 B(03) NA28[] SBLGNT ‖ Absent from ℵ(01) A(02) BYZ TR THGNT.
[h] 9:20, Isaiah 29:16, 45:9.
[i] 9:25, Hosea 2:23 LXX.
[j] 9:26, **it was said to them, You are not my people:** Absent from 𝔓46.
[k] 9:26, Hosea 1:10.
[l] 9:28, **in righteousness, because a word having been shortened:** Included in BYZ TR.
[m] 9:27-28, Isaiah 10:22-23 LXX.
[n] 9:29, Isaiah 1:9 LXX.

30 What shall we say then?
That Gentiles who did not pursue
righteousness have attained it, that
is, a righteousness that is by faith;
31 but Israel who pursued a law that
would lead to righteousness did not
succeed in reaching that law [[of
righteousness]].[a]

32 Why? Because it was not from
faith but as from works [[of the law]];[b]
[[for]][c] they stumbled over the stone
of stumbling, 33 just as it is written,
"Behold, I am laying in Zion a stone of
stumbling and a rock of offense, and
{the one}[d] who believes in him will not
be put to shame."[e]

10 1 Brothers, the desire of my
heart and my prayer to God
for {them}[f] is for salvation. 2 For I
testify about them that they have a
zeal for God, but not according to
knowledge. 3 For, being ignorant of the
righteousness of God and seeking to
establish their own [righteousness],[g]
they did not submit to the righteousness
of God.

4 For Christ is the end of the law
for righteousness to everyone who
believes. 5 For Moses writes about the
righteousness that is from the law, that
the man who does these things will live
by {them}.[hi]

6 But the righteousness from faith
speaks in this way, "Do not say in your
heart, 'Who will ascend into heaven?'"
- That is, to bring Christ down - 7 or,
"Who will descend into the abyss?"
- that is, to bring Christ up from the
dead. 8 But what does it say? "The word
is near you, in your mouth and in your
heart;"[j] that is, the word of faith which
we proclaim.

9 For if you confess[k] [[the word]][l]
with your mouth the Lord Jesus
[[Christ]][m] and believe in your heart
that God raised him from the dead,
you will be saved; 10 for with the heart
one believes unto righteousness, and
with the mouth confession is made unto
salvation.

11 For the Scripture says, "Whoever
believes in him will not be put to
shame."[n]

12 For there is no distinction
between Jew and Greek, for the same
Lord[o] is Lord of all, rich to all who call
upon him; 13 For "whoever calls on the
name of the Lord[p] shall be saved."[q]

14 How then will they call on the
one in whom they have not believed?
And how will they believe in whom
they have not heard? And how will
they hear without someone preaching?
15 And how will they preach unless

---

a 9:31, **of righteousness:** Included in BYZ TR.
b 9:32, **of the law:** Included in BYZ TR.
c 9:32, **for:** Included in BYZ TR.
d 9:33, **the one:** Some manuscripts read "everyone." BYZ TR.
e 9:33, Isaiah 8:14 Masoretic, Isaiah 28:16 LXX.
f 10:1, **them:** Some manuscripts read "Israel." BYZ TR.
g 10:3, **righteousness:** 𝔓46 ℵ(01) BYZ TR || Absent from A(02) B(03).
h 10:5, **them:** 𝔓46 B(03) BYZ TR || Some manuscripts read "it." ℵ(01) A(02) .
i 10:5, Leviticus 18:5.
j 10:6-8, Deuteronomy 30:12-14.
k 10:9, The Greek word means (1) to commit oneself to do something for someone, promise, assure, (2) to share a common view or be of common mind about a matter, agree, (3) to concede that something is factual or true, grant, admit, confess, or (4) to acknowledge something, ordinarily in public, acknowledge, claim, profess, praise. (BDAG, ὁμολογέω).
l 10:9, **the word:** Included in B(03).
m 10:9, **Christ:** Included in 𝔓46 A(02).
n 10:11, Isaiah 28:16 LXX.
o 10:12, **Lord:** In reference to the Greek word for Lord, BDAG states, "The principal meaning relates to the possession of power or authority, in various senses... (1) one who is in charge by virtue of possession, *owner*, (2) one who is in a position of authority, *lord, master*... in some places it is not clear whether God or Christ is meant." (BDAG, κύριος).
p 10:13, **Lord:** See footnote for verse 12.
q 10:13, Joel 2:32b.

they are sent? As it is written, "How beautiful are the feet of those who proclaim the good news [[of peace, those who proclaim good news of the good things]]."[a]

16 But not all obeyed the gospel. {For Isaiah says},[b] "Lord, who has believed our report?"[c] 17 So faith comes from hearing, and hearing through the word of {Christ}.[d]

18 But I say, did they not hear? Indeed they did: "Their voice has gone out to all the earth, and their words to the ends of the world."[e]

19 But I say, did Israel not know? First Moses says, "I will provoke you to jealousy by those who are not a nation; By a nation without understanding I will anger you."[f]

20 And Isaiah boldly says, "I was found by those who did not seek me; I became manifest to those who did not ask for me."[g]

21 But to Israel he says, "All day long I have stretched out my hands to a disobedient and contrary people."[h]

11 1 I say then, has God rejected his people [[whom he foreknew]]?[i] By no means! For I myself am an Israelite, of the seed of Abraham, of the tribe of Benjamin.

2 God has not rejected his people whom he foreknew. Or do you not know what the Scripture says in the passage about Elijah, how he pleads with God against Israel? [[saying]][j] 3 "Lord, they have killed your prophets, they have demolished your altars, and I alone am left, and they seek my life."[k] 4 But what does the divine response say to him? "I have reserved for myself seven thousand men who have not bowed the knee to Baal."[l]

5 So too, at the present time there is a remnant according to the election of grace. 6 And if by grace, then it is no longer of works; otherwise grace would no longer be grace. [[But if it is by works, it is no longer grace, since the work is no longer work.]][m]

7 What then? Israel failed to obtain what it was seeking, but the elect obtained it, and the rest were hardened, 8 just as it is written, "God gave them a spirit of stupor, eyes not to see and ears not to hear, until this very day."[n] 9 {And}[o] David says, "Let their table become a snare and a trap, a stumbling block and a retribution for them; 10 Let their eyes be darkened so that they cannot see, and bend their back continually."[p]

11 I say then, have they stumbled so as to fall? By no means! But by their transgression, salvation has come to the Gentiles, to provoke them to jealousy. 12 But if their transgression is the riches of the world, and their loss the riches of the nations, how much more will their fullness be.

13 {But}[q] I am speaking to you Gentiles. Inasmuch then as I am an apostle to the Gentiles, I magnify my

a 10:15, **of peace, those who proclaim good news of the good things:** Included in BYZ TR.
b 10:16, **For Isaiah says:** 𝔓46 reads "as it is written in Isaiah."
c 10:16, Isaiah 53:1 LXX.
d 10:17, **Christ:** 𝔓46 B(03) C(04) ℵ(01) NA28 SBLGNT THGNT || Some manuscripts read "God." A(02) BYZ TR.
e 10:18, Psalm 19:4 LXX.
f 10:19, Deuteronomy 32:21.
g 10:20, Isaiah 65:1 LXX and Dead Sea Scrolls.
h 10:21, Isaiah 65:2 LXX.
i 11:1, **whom he foreknew:** Included in 𝔓46 A(02).
j 11:2, **saying:** ℵ(01) BYZ TR || Absent in A(02) B(03) C(04) NA28.
k 11:3, 1 Kings 19:10, 14.
l 11:4, 1 Kings 19:18.
m 11:6, **But if it is by works...:** Included in B(03) BYZ TR.
n 11:8, Isaiah 29:10.
o 11:9, **And:** C(04) reads "just as also."
p 11:9-10, Psalm 69:22-23.
q 11:13, **But:** ℵ(01) A(02) B(03) || Some manuscripts read "For." BYZ TR.

ministry 14 if somehow I might provoke to jealousy my own flesh and save some of them. 15 For if their rejection means the reconciliation of the world, what will their acceptance be but life from the dead? 16 Now if the firstfruits are holy, so is the lump; and if the root [is holy],ᵃ so are the branches.

17 But if some of the branches were broken off, and you, a wild olive shoot, were grafted in among them and have become a partaker of [the root and]ᵇ the richness of the olive tree, 18 do not boast over the branches. But if you do boast, remember it is not you who support the root, but the root that supports you.

19 You will say then, Branches were broken off so that I might be grafted in. 20 Or, true. They were broken off because of their unbelief, but you stand by faith. Do not be arrogant, but fear; 21 for if God did not spare the natural branches, [perhaps]ᶜ he will not spare you either.

22 Behold then the kindness and severity of God: severity toward those who have fallen, but [God's]ᵈ kindness to you, provided you continue in his kindness; otherwise you too will be cut off. 23 And those also, if they do not persist in unbelief, will be grafted in; for God is able to graft them in again. 24 For if you were cut from what is by nature a wild olive tree, and grafted, contrary to nature, into a cultivated olive tree, how much more will these, the natural branches, be grafted back into their own olive tree.

25 Lest you be wise in your own sight, I do not want you to be unaware of this mystery, brothers: a partial hardening has come upon Israel, until the fullness of the Gentiles has come in. 26 And in this way all Israel will be [[also]]ᵉ saved, just as it is written, "The Deliverer will come from Zion, he will turn away ungodliness from Jacob." 27 "And this is the covenant for them from me, when I take away their sins."ᶠ

28 As for the gospel, they are enemies for your sake; but as for the election, they are beloved for the sake of the fathers. 29 For the gifts and the calling of God are irrevocable.

30 [Just as you were once disobedient to God, but now have received mercy through their disobedience,]ᵍ 31 So they too have now been disobedient in order that, by the mercy shown to you, they also [now]ʰ may receive mercy. 32 For God has consigned all to disobedience, so that he may have mercy on all.

33 Oh, the depth of the riches and wisdom and knowledge of God! How unsearchable are his judgments and how unsearchableⁱ are his ways!

34 For who has known the mind of the Lord, or who has been his counselor?ʲ 35 Or who has given a gift to him that he might be repaid?ᵏ 36 For from him and through him and to him are all things. To him be glory forever. Amen.

12 1 Therefore, I urge you, brothers, through the mercies of God, to present your bodies as a living, holy, and pleasing sacrifice to God, your rationalˡ service.

ᵃ 11:16, **is holy:** Absent from 𝔓46.

ᵇ 11:17, **the root and:** Absent from 𝔓46.

ᶜ 11:21, **perhaps:** 𝔓46 NA28[] BYZ TR ‖ Absent from ℵ(01) A(02) B(03) C(04) SBLGNT THGNT.

ᵈ 11:22, **God's:** Absent from BYZ TR.

ᵉ 11:26, **also:** Included in BYZ TR.

ᶠ 11:26-27, Isaiah 59:20-21 LXX, 27:9 LXX, Jeremiah 31:33-34.

ᵍ 11:30, **Just as you were once disobedient to God, but now have received mercy through their disobedience:** Absent from ℵ(01).

ʰ 11:31, **now:** ℵ(01) B(03) NA28[] SBLGNT ‖Absent from 𝔓46 A(02) THGNT BYZ TR.

ⁱ 11:33, **unsearchable:** Or "incomprehensible."

ʲ 11:34, Isaiah 40:13 LXX, Jeremiah 23:18.

ᵏ 11:35, Isaiah 40:13 LXX, Job 41:11 Masoretic.

ˡ 12:1, **rational:** Pertaining to being carefully thought through, thoughtful (BDAG, λογικός).

2 And do not be conformed to this age, but be transformed by the renewal of {the}ᵃ mind, so that you may discern what is the will of God, the good and pleasing and perfect.

3 For I say, through the grace given to me, to everyone who is among you, not to think more highly than one ought to think, but to think so as to be sober-minded, as God has allotted to each a measure of faith.

4 [For]ᵇ Just as in one body we have many members, and not all the members have the same function, 5 so we, though many, are one body in Christ, and individually members of one another.

6 Having gifts that differ according to the grace given to us, let us use them: if prophecy, in proportion to our faith; 7 if service, in our serving; the one who teaches, in his teaching; 8 the one who exhorts, in his exhortation; the one who contributes, in generosity; the one who leads, with zeal [; the one who does acts of mercy, with cheerfulness].ᶜ

9 Let love be genuine.

Abhor what is evil; hold fast to what is good.

10 Love one another with brotherly affection.

Outdo one another in showing honor.

11 Do not be slothful in zeal, be fervent in spirit, serve the Lord.

12 Rejoice in hope, be patient in tribulation, be constant in prayer.

13 Contribute to the needs of the saints and seek to show hospitality.

14 Bless those who persecute [you];ᵈ [bless]ᵉ and do not curse them.

15 Rejoice with those who rejoice, [[and]]ᶠ weep with those who weep.

16 Live in harmony with one another. Do not be haughty, but associate with the lowly. Do not be wise in your own estimation.

17 Do not repay anyone evil for evil, taking thought for what is honorable in the sight of [all]ᵍ people.

18 If possible, so far as it depends on you, be at peace with all people.

19 Do not take revenge, beloved, but leave room for wrath; for it is written, "Vengeance is mine, I will repay, says the Lord."ʰ

20 {But}ⁱ if your enemy is hungry, feed him; if he is thirsty, give him something to drink; for by doing this you will heap burning coals on his head.

21 Do not be overcome by evil, but overcome evil with good.

ᵃ 12:2, **the:** Some manuscripts read "your." ℵ(01) BYZ TR.
ᵇ 12:4, **For:** Absent from 𝔓46.
ᶜ 12:8, **the one who does acts of mercy, with cheerfulness:** Absent from 𝔓46.
ᵈ 12:14, **you:** ℵ(01) A(02) NA28[] THGNT BYZ TR ‖ Absent from 𝔓46 B(03) SBLGNT.
ᵉ 12:14, **bless:** Absent from 𝔓46.
ᶠ 12:15, **and:** Included in A(02) BYZ TR.
ᵍ 12:17, **all:** Absent from 𝔓46 A(02).
ʰ 12:19, Deuteronomy 32:35.
ⁱ 12:20, **But:** Some manuscripts read "Therefore." BYZ TR.

13 ¹ Let every soul be subject to the superior[a] authorities. For there is no authority except from God, and those [[authorities]][b] that exist have been ordained by God. ² Therefore, whoever resists the authority resists the ordinance of God, and those who resist will bring judgment on themselves. ³ For rulers are not a terror to good works, but to evil. But do you wish not to fear the authority? Do what is good, and you will have praise from it; ⁴ for it is a servant of God to you for good. But if you do evil, be afraid; for it does not bear the sword in vain; for it is a servant of God, an avenger to execute wrath on the one who practices evil. ⁵ Therefore, it is necessary to be subject, not only because of wrath, but also for the sake of conscience.

⁶ For this reason, also pay taxes; for they are servants of God, attending to this very thing.

⁷ [[Therefore]][c] Pay to all what is owed to them: to the one the tax, the tax; to the one the custom, the custom; to the one the fear, the fear; to the one the honor, the honor.

⁸ Owe no one anything except to love one another, for he who loves another has fulfilled the law. ⁹ For the commandments, "You shall not commit adultery," "You shall not murder," "You shall not steal," [["You shall not bear false witness,"]][d] "You shall not covet," and any other commandment, are summed up in this word: "You shall love your neighbor as {yourself}[e]."[f] ¹⁰ [Love does no harm to a neighbor; therefore,][g] Love is the fulfillment of the law.

¹¹ And this knowing the time, that it is already the hour for {you}[h] to awaken from sleep, for [now][i] our salvation is nearer than when we first believed. ¹² The night is far gone, the day is near. Let us then cast off the works of darkness, and let us put on the armor of light.

¹³ As in the day, let us walk decently, not in revelries and drunkenness, not in sexual immorality and debauchery, not in strife and jealousy, ¹⁴ but put on [the Lord][j] Jesus Christ, and do not make provision for the desires of the flesh.

14 ¹ Accept the one who is weak in faith, but not for the purpose of quarreling over opinions.

² One person believes they may eat anything, while the weak person eats only vegetables. ³ The one who eats must not {despise}[k] the one who abstains, and the one who abstains must not judge the one who eats, for God has accepted them.

⁴ Who are you to judge someone else's servant? To their own master they stand or fall; and they will stand, for {the Lord}[l] is able to make them stand.

---

a 13:1, **superior:** The Greek word for *superior* means (1) to be at a point higher than another on a scale of linear extent, *rise above, surpass, excel* (2) to be in a controlling position, *have power over, be in authority (over), be highly placed* (3) to surpass in quality or value, *be better than, surpass, excel.* (BDAG, ὑπερέχω).

b 13:1, **authorities:** Included in BYZ TR.

c 13:7, **Therefore:** Included in BYZ TR.

d 13:9, **You shall not bear false witness:** Included in ℵ(01) BYZ TR ‖ Absent from 𝔓46 A(02) B(03) NA28 SBLGNT THGNT BYZ.

e 13:9, **yourself:** TR reads "himself."

f 13:9, Exodus 20:13-15, 17, Deuteronomy 5:17-19, 21, Leviticus 19:18.

g 13:10, **Love does no harm to a neighbor; therefore:** Absent from A(02).

h 13:11, **you:** ℵ(01) A(02) B(03) C(04) NA28 SBLGNT THGNT ‖ Some manuscripts read "us." 𝔓46 BYZ TR.

i 13:11, **now:** Absent from C(04).

j 13:14, **the Lord:** Absent from B(03).

k 14:3, **despise:** A(02) reads "judge."

l 14:4, **the Lord:** 𝔓46 ℵ(01) A(02) B(03) C(04) NA28 SBLGNT THGNT ‖ Some manuscripts read "God." BYZ TR.

5 [For]ᵃ Some judge one day to be better than another, while others judge all days to be alike. Let each be fully convinced in their own mind.

6 The one who observes the day, observes it in honor of the Lord [[and he who does not observe the day, to the Lord he does not observe it]].ᵇ [And]ᶜ The one who eats, eats in honor of the Lord, since they give thanks to God; and the one who abstains, abstains in honor of the Lord and gives thanks to God.

7 For none of us lives for oneself, and none dies for oneself; 8 If we live, we live for the Lord; and if we die, we die for the Lord. So, whether we live or die, we belong to the Lord. 9 For to this end Christ died [[and rose]]ᵈ and lived again, so that he might be Lord of both the dead and the living.

10 Why do you judge your brother? Or why do you despise your brother? For we will all stand before the judgment seat of {God},ᵉ 11 for it is written, "As I live, says the Lord, every knee shall bow to me, and every tongue shall confess to God."ᶠ

12 So [therefore]ᵍ each of us will give an account of ourselves [to God].ʰ

13 Therefore, let us no longer judge one another; but rather decide this, not to put a [stumbling block or]ⁱ a trapʲ before a brother.

14 I know and am persuaded in the Lord Jesus that nothing is unclean in itself; but it is unclean for anyone who thinks it unclean.

15 {For}ᵏ if your brother is grieved because of food, you are no longer walking in love; do not destroy that one with your food, for whom Christ died. 16 Therefore, do not let your good be blasphemed.

17 For the kingdom of God is not a matter of eating and drinking, but of righteousness, peace, and joy in the Holy Spirit.ˡ

18 Whoever serves {Christ}ᵐ in {this way}ⁿ is pleasing to God and approved by men.

19 So then, let us pursue what makes for peace and for mutual edification. 20 Do not destroy the work of God for the sake of food. All things are indeed clean, but it is wrong for anyone to cause another to stumble by what they eat. 21 It is good not to eat meat or drink wine or *do anything* by which your brother stumbles, [or to be offended or made weak].ᵒ

ᵃ 14:5, **For:** Absent from 𝔓46 B(03) BYZ TR.

ᵇ 14:6, **and he who does not observe the day, to the Lord he does not observe it:** Included in BYZ TR.

ᶜ 14:6, **And:** Absent from 𝔓46 TR.

ᵈ 14:9, **and rose:** Included in BYZ TR.

ᵉ 14:10, **God:** Some manuscripts read "Christ." BYZ TR.

ᶠ 14:11, Isaiah 49:18, 45:23 LXX.

ᵍ 14:12, **therefore:** ℵ(01) A(02) C(04) NA28[] THGNT BYZ TR ‖ Absent in some manuscripts. B(03) SBLGNT.

ʰ 14:12, **to God:** ℵ(01) A(02) C(04) NA28[] THGNT BYZ TR ‖ Absent from B(03) SBLGNT.

ⁱ 14:13, **stumbling block or:** Absent from B(03).

ʲ 14:13, **trap:** Or, a temptation.

ᵏ 14:15, **For:** Some manuscripts read "But." BYZ TR.

ˡ 14:17, **Spirit:** See footnote for Spirit in Luke 1:15.

ᵐ 14:18, **Christ:** B(03) reads "God."

ⁿ 14:18, **this way:** Some manuscripts read "these things." BYZ TR.

ᵒ 14:21, **or to be offended or made weak:** 𝔓46 B(03) SBLGNT THGNT BYZ TR ‖ Absent from ℵ(01) A(02) C(04) NA28.

22 {You have faith, [which]ᵃ you have [before God],ᵇ keep to yourself.}ᶜ Blessed is the one who does [not]ᵈ judge oneself in what one approves; 23 But the one who doubts, if they eat, they are condemned, because it is not from faith; and everything that is not from faith is sin.ᵉ

15 1 Now we who are strong ought to bear the weaknesses of those who are not strong, and not to please ourselves.

2 Let each of us please our neighbor [for their good],ᶠ for the purpose of building them up. 3 For even Christ did not please himself, but as it is written, "The reproaches of those who reproached you fell upon me."ᵍ

4 For {whatever}ʰ was written [beforehand]ⁱ was written for our instruction, so that through perseverance and the encouragement of the Scriptures, we might have hope.

5 Now may the God of perseverance and encouragement grant you to be of the same mind with one another according to Christ Jesus, 6 so that with one accord and with one voice you may glorify the God and Father of our Lord Jesus Christ.

7 Therefore, accept one another, just as Christ also accepted you, for the glory of God.

8 For I say that Christ [[Jesus]]ʲ has become a servant of the circumcision on behalf of the truth of God, to confirm the promises given to the fathers, 9 and for the Gentiles to glorify God for his mercy; as it is written [[of the prophet]],ᵏ "For this reason I will praise you among the Gentiles, and sing to your name."ˡ

10 And again it says, "Rejoice, you Gentiles, with his people."ᵐ

11 And [it says]ⁿ again , "Praise the Lord, all you Gentiles, and {let all the peoples praise him}."ᵒᵖ

12 And again Isaiah says, "There will be the root of Jesse and the one rising up to rule nations, on him nations will hope."�q

13 Now may the God of hope fill you with all joy and peace in believing, [so that you may abound]ʳ in hope by the power of the Holy Spirit.

14 Now I am convinced, [my]ˢ brothers, that you yourselves are full

---

ᵃ 14:22, **which:** Absent from BYZ TR.

ᵇ 14:22, **before God:** Absent from ℵ(01).

ᶜ 14:22, **You have faith, which you have before God, keep to yourself:** Some manuscripts read, "Do you have faith? Have it to yourself before God." TR ‖ Faith in this context is in reference to confidence in eating foods that others may be convicted not to eat.

ᵈ 14:22, **not:** Absent from some manuscripts. BYZ TR

ᵉ 14:23, BYZ includes "Now to him who is able to strengthen you according to my gospel and the proclamation of Jesus Christ, according to the revelation of the mystery that was kept silent for eternal times, but now has been revealed through prophetic writings by the command of the eternal God, to bring about the obedience of faith, to all the nations made known, to the only wise God, through Jesus Christ, to whom be the glory forever. Amen."

ᶠ 15:2, **for their good:** Absent from ℵ(01).

ᵍ 15:3, Psalm 69:9.

ʰ 15:4, **whatever:** Some manuscripts read "all that." B(03).

ⁱ 15:4, **beforehand:** Absent from B(03).

ʲ 15:8, **Jesus:** Included in BYZ TR.

ᵏ 15:9, **of the prophet:** Absent from ℵ(01).

ˡ 15:9, 2 Samuel 22:50, Psalm 18:49.

ᵐ 15:10, Deuteronomy 32:43.

ⁿ 15:11, **it says:** Included in B(03).

ᵒ 15:11, **let all the peoples praise him:** Some manuscripts read "praise him, all you peoples." BYZ TR.

ᵖ 15:11, Psalm 117:1.

q 15:12, Isaiah 11:10 LXX.

ʳ 15:13, **so that you may abound:** Absent from B(03).

ˢ 15:14, **my:** ℵ(01) A(02) B(03) C(04) BYZ TR ‖ Absent from some manuscripts 𝔭46.

of goodness, filled with all [the]^a knowledge, able [also]^b to admonish one another.

15 But I have written to you more boldly [[brothers]]^c on some points, as a reminder [to you],^d because of the grace given to me by God 16 to be a minister of {Christ Jesus}^e [to the Gentiles],^f ministering as a priest the gospel of God, so that the offering of the Gentiles may become acceptable, sanctified by the Holy Spirit.

17 Therefore, I have my boasting in Christ [Jesus]^g in things pertaining to God. 18 For I will not dare to speak of anything that Christ has not accomplished through me for the obedience of the Gentiles, by word and deed, 19 in the power of signs and wonders, in the power of the {Spirit of God};^h so that from Jerusalem and all around as far as Illyricum, I have fully preached the gospel of Christ.

20 And thus I aspired to preach the gospel, not where Christ was already named, so that I would not build on another's foundation, 21 but as it is written, "They who had no news of him shall see, and they who have not heard shall understand."ⁱ

22 For this reason I have often been hindered from coming to you; 23 but now, having no further place in these regions, and since I have had a longing to come to you for many years, 24 {As I may go to Spain};^j [[I will come to you,]]^k for I hope, passing through, to see you and to be sent on my way there by you, if first I may be somewhat filled by you.

25 But now I am going to Jerusalem, serving the saints. 26 For Macedonia and Achaia have been pleased to make a contribution for the poor among the saints in Jerusalem. 27 Yes, [they were pleased to do so, and]^l they are indebted to them. For if the Gentiles have shared in their spiritual things, they are indebted to minister to them also in material things.

28 Therefore, when I have finished this, and have put my seal on this fruit of theirs, I will go on by way of you to Spain. 29 I know that when I come to you, I will come in the fullness of the blessing [[of the gospel]]^m of Christ.

30 I urge you, [brothers,]ⁿ by our Lord Jesus Christ and by the love of the Spirit, to strive together with me in your prayers to God on my behalf, 31 that I may be delivered from the disobedient in Judea, and that my ministry for Jerusalem may be acceptable to the saints, 32 so that, coming to you with joy by the will of {God}^o [, I may find rest with you].^p

33 Now may the God of peace be with you all. [Amen.]^q

---

a 15:14, **the:** א(01) B(03) NA28[] THGNT ‖ Absent from some manuscripts 𝔓46 A(02) C(04) SBLGNT BYZ TR.

b 15:14, **also:** Absent from 𝔓46.

c 15:15, **brothers:** א(01) A(02) B(03) C(04) NA28 SBLGNT THGNT ‖ Included in 𝔓46 BYZ TR.

d 15:15, **to you:** Absent from 𝔓46.

e 15:16, **Christ Jesus:** Some manuscripts read "Jesus Christ." 𝔓46 BYZ TR.

f 15:16, **to the Gentiles:** Absent from B(03).

g 15:17, **Jesus:** Absent from 𝔓46.

h 15:19, **Spirit of God:** 𝔓46 א(01) BYZ TR NA28[] THGNT ‖ Some manuscripts read "Spirit." B(03) SBLGNT ‖ Some manuscripts read "Holy Spirit." A(02).

i 15:21, Isaiah 52:15 LXX.

j 15:24, **As I may go to Spain:** Some manuscripts read "If I go to Spain, I will come to you." BYZ TR.

k 15:24, **I will come to you:** Included in BYZ TR.

l 15:27, **they were pleased to do so, and:** Absent from 𝔓46.

m 15:29, **of the gospel:** Included in BYZ TR.

n 15:30, **brothers:** Absent from 𝔓46 B(03).

o 15:32, **God:** א(01) reads "Christ Jesus." ‖ B(03) reads "the Lord Jesus."

p 15:32, **I may find rest with you:** Absent from 𝔓46 B(03).

q 15:33, **Amen:** Absent from 𝔓46 A(02).

16

¹I commend to you our sister Phoebe, who is [also]ᵃ a servant of the church in Cenchreae, ²that you may welcome her in the Lord in a manner worthy of the saints, and assist her in whatever matter she may need from you; for she has been a benefactor of many, including myself.

³Greet {Prisca}ᵇ and Aquila, my fellow workers in Christ Jesus, ⁴who risked their own necks for my life, to whom not only I give thanks, but also all the churches of the Gentiles, ⁵and the church that meets in their house.

Greet my beloved Epaenetus, who is the firstfruits of {Asia}ᶜ for Christ.

⁶Greet Mary, who has worked hard for {you}.ᵈ

⁷Greet Andronicus and Junia, my relatives and fellow prisoners, who are notable among the apostles, and who were in Christ before me.

⁸Greet {Ampliatus},ᵉ my beloved in the Lord. ⁹Greet Urbanus, our fellow worker in {Christ},ᶠ and my beloved Stachys.

¹⁰Greet Apelles, who is approved in Christ. Greet those who belong to the household of Aristobulus.

¹¹Greet Herodion, my relative.

Greet those who belong to the household of Narcissus, who are in the Lord.

¹²Greet Tryphaena and Tryphosa, who have labored in the Lord. Greet my beloved Persis, who has worked hard in the Lord.

¹³Greet Rufus, chosen in the Lord, and his mother, who has been a mother to me as well.

¹⁴Greet Asyncritus, Phlegon, Hermes, Patrobas, Hermas, and the brothers who are with them.

¹⁵Greet Philologus and Julia, Nereus and his sister, and Olympas, and [all]ᵍ the saints who are with them.

¹⁶Greet one another with a holy kiss. [All]ʰ The churches of Christ greet you.

¹⁷Now I urge you, brothers, to watch out for those who cause divisions and create obstacles contrary to the teaching that you have learned; avoid them.

¹⁸For such people do not serve our Lord [[Jesus]]ⁱ Christ, but their own appetites, and by smooth talk and flattery they deceive the hearts of the naive.

¹⁹For your obedience has become known to all. Therefore, I rejoice over you, but I want you to be wise [[indeed]]ʲ in what is good, and innocent in what is evil.

²⁰The God of peace will soon crush Satan under your feet.

The grace of our Lord Jesus [Christ]ᵏ be with you.

²¹Timothy, my fellow worker, greets you, as do Lucius, Jason, and Sosipater, my relatives [[and all the churches in Christ]].ˡ

²²I, Tertius, who wrote this letter, greet you in the Lord.

ᵃ 16:1, **also:** 𝔓46 B(03) C(04) NA28[] SBLGNT ‖ Absent from ℵ(01) A(02) THGNT BYZ TR.
ᵇ 16:3, **Prisca:** TR reads "Priscilla."
ᶜ 16:5, **Asia:** Some manuscripts read "Achaia." BYZ TR.
ᵈ 16:6, **you:** Some manuscripts read "us." BYZ TR.
ᵉ 16:8, **Ampliatus:** Some manuscripts read "Amplias." BYZ TR.
ᶠ 16:9, **Christ:** Some manuscripts read "the Lord." C(04).
ᵍ 16:15, **all:** Absent from 𝔓46.
ʰ 16:16, **all:** Absent from BYZ TR.
ⁱ 16:18, **Jesus:** Included in BYZ TR.
ʲ 16:19, **indeed:** Included in ℵ(01) A(02) C(04) BYZ TR.
ᵏ 16:20, **Christ:** 𝔓46 ℵ(01) B(03) SBLGNT BYZ TR ‖ Absent from A(02) C(04) NA28 THGNT.
ˡ 16:21, **and all the churches in Christ:** Included in .

23 Gaius, my host and the host of the whole church, greets you. Erastus, the city treasurer, and our brother Quartus greet you.

24 [The grace of our Lord Jesus Christ be with you all, Amen.]ᵃ

25 [Now to him who is able to strengthen you according to my gospel [and the proclamation]ᵇ of [Jesus Christ],ᶜ according to the revelation of the mystery that was kept secret for long ages, 26 but has now been disclosed through the prophetic writings by the command of the eternal God, to bring about the obedience of faith among all the nations, 27 to the only wise God, through {Jesus Christ},ᵈ to whom be glory forever [[and ever]].ᵉ Amen.]ᶠᵍ

ᵃ 16:24, **The grace of our Lord Jesus Christ be with you all, Amen:** SBLGNT BYZ TR ‖ Absent from 𝔓46 𝔓61 ℵ(01) A(02) B(03) C(04) NA28 THGNT.

ᵇ 16:25, **and the proclamation:** Absent from ℵ(01).

ᶜ 16:25, **Jesus Christ:** B(03) reads "Christ Jesus." ‖ ℵ(01) reads "the Lord Jesus Christ."

ᵈ 16:27, **Jesus Christ:** Some manuscripts read "Christ Jesus." B(03).

ᵉ 16:27, **and ever:** Included in 𝔓61 ℵ(01) A(02) ‖ Absent from 𝔓46 B(03) C(04) NA28 SBLGNT THGNT BYZ TR.

ᶠ 16:25-27, The doxology of Rom 16:25-27 is placed after Rom 14:23 in A(02) and after Rom 15:33 in 𝔓46.

ᵍ 16:27, TR includes the postscript, "To the Romans [it] was written from Corinth through Phoebe, the servant of the church in Cenchreae."

First Corinthians[a]

1 [1] Paul, [called as][b] an apostle of {Christ[c] Jesus}[d] by the will of God, and Sosthenes the brother, [2] to the church of God that is in Corinth, to those sanctified in Christ Jesus, called as saints, together with all those who call upon the name of our Lord Jesus [Christ][e] in every place, both theirs and ours.

[3] Grace to you and peace from God our Father and the Lord[f] Jesus Christ.

[4] I always give thanks to [my][g] God for you because of the grace of God that was given to you in Christ Jesus, [5] for in every way you were enriched in him, in all speech and all knowledge, [6] just as the testimony of {Christ}[h] was confirmed among you, [7] so that you are not lacking in any spiritual gift as you eagerly await the revelation of our Lord Jesus Christ; [8] who will also confirm you until the end, blameless on the day of our Lord Jesus [Christ].[i]

[9] God is faithful, through whom you were called into the fellowship of his Son, Jesus Christ our Lord.

[10] Now I appeal to you, brothers, by the name of our Lord Jesus Christ, that all of you agree and that there be no divisions among you, but that you be united in the same mind and the same purpose.

[11] For it has been reported [to me][j] about you, my brothers, by those of Chloe's household, that there are quarrels among you. [12] What I mean is that each of you says, "I belong to Paul," or "I belong to Apollos," or "I belong to Cephas," or "I belong to Christ."

[13] Is Christ divided? Was Paul crucified for you? Or were you baptized in the name of Paul?

[14] I give thanks [to God][k] that I baptized none of you except Crispus and Gaius, [15] so that no one can say that {you were}[l] baptized in my name.

[16] I did baptize also the household of Stephanas; beyond that, I do not know whether I baptized anyone else.

[17] For Christ did not send me to baptize but to preach the gospel, and not with eloquent wisdom, so that the cross of Christ might not be emptied of its power.

[18] For the message of the cross is foolishness to those who are perishing, but to us who are being saved it is the power of God.

[19] For it is written, "I will destroy the wisdom of the wise, and the discernment of the discerning I will thwart."[m]

---

a 1:0, **Title ("First Corinthians"):** Absent from ℵ(01) B(03) ‖ 𝔓46 A(02) C(04) BYZ reads "To Corinthians One." ‖ TR reads "The first letter of Paul the apostle to the Corinthians."

b 1:1, **called as:** Absent from A(02).

c 1:1, **Christ:** See footnote for Christ in Luke 2:11.

d 1:1, **Christ Jesus:** 𝔓61 B(03) NA28 SBLGNT ‖ Some manuscripts read "Jesus Christ." ℵ(01) A(02) THGNT BYZ TR.

e 1:2, **Christ:** Absent from A(02).

f 1:3, **Lord:** In reference to the Greek word for Lord, BDAG states, "The principal meaning relates to the possession of power or authority, in various senses... (1) one who is in charge by virtue of possession, *owner*, (2) one who is in a position of authority, *lord, master*... in some places it is not clear whether God or Christ is meant." (BDAG, κύριος).

g 1:4, **my:** Absent from ℵ(01) B(03).

h 1:6, **Christ:** B(03) reads "God."

i 1:8, **Christ:** Absent from 𝔓46 B(03).

j 1:11, **to me:** Absent from 𝔓46 C(04).

k 1:14, **to God:** Absent from ℵ(01) B(03).

l 1:15, **you were:** 𝔓46 ℵ(01) A(02) B(03) C(04) ‖ Some manuscripts read "I had." BYZ TR.

m 1:19, Isaiah 29:14 LXX.

20 Where is the wise? Where is the scribe? Where is the debater of this age? Has not God made foolish the wisdom of the world?

21 For since, in the wisdom of {God},ª the world did not know God through wisdom, God was pleased through the foolishness of preaching to save those who believe.

22 For Jews demand {signs}ᵇ and Greeks seek wisdom, 23 but we preach Christ crucified, a stumbling block to Jews and foolishness to {Gentiles}.ᶜ

24 But to those who are called, both Jews and Greeks, Christ the power of God and the wisdom of God;

25 For the foolishness of God is wiser than human wisdom, and the weakness of God is stronger than human strength.

26 Consider your own calling, brothers: not many of you were wise by human standards, not many were powerful, not many were of noble birth.

27 But God chose the foolish things of the world to shame the wise; And God chose the weak things of the world to shame the strong; 28 God chose the lowly things of the world and the despised things, [[also]]ᵈ the things that are not, to nullify the things that are, 29 so that no one may boast in the presence of {God}.ᵉ

30 It is because of him that you are in Christ Jesus, who became for us wisdom from God, and righteousness and sanctification and redemption,

31 so that, as it is written, "Let the one who boasts, boast in the Lord."ᶠ

2 1 And when I came to you, brothers, I did not come with superiority of speech or wisdom, proclaiming to you the {mystery}ᵍ of God. 2 For I determined not to know anything among you except Jesus Christ and him crucified.

3 And I was with you in weakness and in fear and in much trembling, 4 And my word and my proclamation were not with persuasive [words]ʰ of [[human]]ⁱ wisdom, but with a demonstration of the Spirit and of power, 5 so that your faith might not be in the wisdom of men but in the power of God.

6 Yet we do speak wisdom among the mature, but not the wisdom of this age or of the rulers of this age, who are being brought to nothing. 7 But we speak God's wisdom in a mystery, the hidden wisdom which God predestined before the ages for our glory, 8 which none of the rulers of this age has understood; for if they had known it, they would not have crucified {the}ʲ Lord of glory.

9 [But]ᵏ As it is written, "What no eye has seen, nor ear heard, nor the heart of man imagined, what God has prepared for those who love him."ˡ

10 {But}ᵐ God has revealed it to us through {the}ⁿ Spirit; for the Spirit searches all things, even the depths of God.

ª 1:21, **God:** 𝔓46 reads "the world."

ᵇ 1:22, **signs:** Some manuscripts read "a sign." BYZ TR.

ᶜ 1:23, **Gentiles:** Some manuscripts read "Greeks." BYZ TR.

ᵈ 1:28, **also:** Included in B(03) BYZ TR.

ᵉ 1:29, **God:** Some manuscripts read "him." C(04) TR.

ᶠ 1:31, Jeremiah 9:24.

ᵍ 2:1, **mystery:** 𝔓46 ℵ(01) A(02) C(04) NA28 ‖ Some manuscripts read "testimony." B(03) SBLGNT THGNT BYZ TR.

ʰ 2:4, **words:** ℵ(01) A(02) B(03) C(04) NA28[] THGNT BYZ TR ‖ Absent from 𝔓46 SBLGNT.

ⁱ 2:4, **human:** Included in A(02) C(04) BYZ TR.

ʲ 2:8, **the:** 𝔓46 reads "their."

ᵏ 2:9, **But:** Absent from A(02).

ˡ 2:9, Isaiah 64:4.

ᵐ 2:10, **But:** ℵ(01) A C(04) NA28 THGNT BYZ TR ‖ Some manuscripts read "For." 𝔓46 B(03) SBLGNT.

ⁿ 2:10, **the:** Some manuscripts read "his." BYZ TR.

11 For who [among men][a] knows the things of a man except the spirit of the man which is in him? Likewise, no one has known the things of God except the Spirit of God.

12 Now we have received not the spirit of the world, but the Spirit which is from God, that we might know the things freely given to us by God.

13 And we speak of these things not in words taught by human wisdom, but in words taught by the [[Holy]][b] Spirit, comparing spiritual things with spiritual.

14 But the natural man does not accept the things of the Spirit of God; for they are foolishness to him, and he cannot understand them, because they are spiritually discerned. 15 But the spiritual person judges all things, yet he himself is judged by no one.

16 For who has known the mind of the Lord, who will instruct him? But we have the mind of {Christ}.[c]

3 1 And I, brothers, was not able to speak to you as spiritual people, but as people of the flesh, as infants in Christ. 2 I fed you with milk, not solid food; for you were not yet able to receive it. But even now you are {not}[d] able, 3 for you are still of the flesh. For where there is jealousy and strife [[and divisions]][e] among you, are you not of the flesh and walking according to human ways?

4 For when someone says, "I am of Paul," and [another,][f] "I am of Apollos," are you not {men}?[g]

5 What then is Apollos? What is Paul? [[But]][h] Servants through whom you believed, and to each as the Lord has given. 6 I planted, Apollos watered, but God gave the growth. 7 So [neither][i] the one who plants nor the one who waters is anything, but only God who gives the growth. 8 The one planting and the one watering are one, but each will receive their own reward according to their own labor. 9 For we are God's coworkers; you are God's field, God's building.

10 According to the grace [of God][j] given to me, like a skilled master builder I laid a foundation, and someone else is building upon it. Let each one take care how they build upon it. 11 For no one can lay a foundation other than the one that is laid, which is [Jesus][k] Christ. 12 Now if anyone builds on {the}[l] foundation with gold, silver, precious stones, wood, hay, straw, 13 each one's work will become manifest, for the day will disclose it, because it will be revealed by fire, and the fire will test what sort of work each one has done.

14 If the work that anyone has built on the foundation survives, they will receive a reward. 15 If anyone's work is burned up, they will suffer loss, though they themselves will be saved, but only as through fire.

16 Do you not know that you are God's temple and that the Spirit of God dwells in you?[m] 17 If anyone destroys God's temple, God will destroy that person. For God's temple is holy, and you are that temple.

---

[a] 2:11, **among men:** Absent from A(02).

[b] 2:13, **Holy:** Included in BYZ TR.

[c] 2:16, **Christ:** Some manuscripts read "the Lord." B(03).

[d] 3:2, **not:** Some manuscripts read "not yet" (BYZ) or "still not." (TR).

[e] 3:3, **and divisions:** Included in 𝔓46 BYZ TR.

[f] 3:4, **another:** Absent from A(02).

[g] 3:4, **men:** Some manuscripts read "fleshly." BYZ TR.

[h] 3:5, **But:** Included in BYZ TR.

[i] 3:7, **neither:** Absent from A(02).

[j] 3:10, **of God:** Absent from 𝔓46.

[k] 3:11, **Jesus:** Absent from C(04).

[l] 3:12, **the:** Some manuscripts read "this." BYZ TR.

[m] 3:16, **you:** "You" in both places is second person plural.

18 Let no one deceive themselves. If anyone among you thinks that they are wise in this age, let them become a fool so that they may become wise.

19 For the wisdom of this world is foolishness beside God. For it is written, "He catches the wise in their craftiness,"[a] 20 and again, "The Lord knows the thoughts of the wise, that they are futile."[b]

21 So let no one boast in men. For all things are yours, 22 whether Paul or Apollos or Cephas or the world or life or death or the present or the future, all are yours, 23 and you are Christ's, and Christ is God's.

4 1 So let men consider us as servants of Christ and stewards of the mysteries of God.

2 So then it is required of stewards that they be found faithful. 3 But it is of little importance to me that I should be judged by you or by any human court; I do not even judge myself. 4 For I am not aware of anything against myself, but I am not thereby acquitted; the one who judges me is the Lord.

5 Therefore, do not judge anything before the time, until the Lord comes, who will both bring to light the hidden things of darkness and reveal the intentions of the hearts; and then praise will come to each one from God.

6 Now, brothers, I have applied these things to myself and Apollos for your benefit, so that you may learn from us the saying, "Do not go beyond what is written [[to think]],"[c] so that none of you may be puffed up in favor of one against another.

7 For who makes you different? And what do you have that you did not receive? But if you did receive it, why do you boast as if you had not received it? 8 Already you are filled, already you have become rich, apart from us you have begun to reign; and indeed, I wish you had begun to reign, so that we also might reign with you.

9 For I think [[that]][d] God has exhibited us, the apostles, last of all, as men condemned to death, because we have become a spectacle to the world, both to angels and to men.

10 We are fools for Christ's sake, but you are wise in Christ; we are weak, but you are strong; you are honored, but we are dishonored. 11 To this very hour we are hungry and thirsty, [we are poorly clothed,][e] we are beaten, and we are homeless. 12 We labor, working with our own hands; when reviled, we bless; when persecuted, we endure; 13 when {slandered},[f] we entreat; we have become as the scum of the world, the dregs of all things, even until now. 14 I do not write these things to shame you, but as my beloved children, I admonish [you]. 15 [For][g] Though you have ten thousand tutors in Christ, yet you do not have many fathers; for in Christ [Jesus],[h] through the gospel, I have begotten you.[i]

16 Therefore, I urge you, be imitators of me.

17 For this reason, I have sent Timothy to you, who is my beloved and faithful child in the Lord, who will remind you of my ways in Christ [Jesus],[j] just as I teach everywhere in every church.

18 Some are puffed up, as though I were not coming to you. 19 But I will come to you soon, if the Lord wills, and I will know, not the word of those who are puffed up, but the power.

---

a 3:19, Job 5:13 Masoretic text.

b 3:20, Psalm 94:11.

c 4:6, **to think:** Included in BYZ TR.

d 4:9, **that:** Included in BYZ TR.

e 4:11, **we are poorly clothed:** Absent from A(02).

f 4:13, **slandered:** 𝔓46 ℵ(01) A(02) C(04) ‖ Some manuscripts read "blasphemed." B(03) BYZ TR.

g 4:15, **For:** Absent from 𝔓46.

h 4:15, **Jesus:** Absent from B(03).

i 4:15, **I have begotten you:** Or, "I have become your father."

j 4:17, **Jesus:** 𝔓46 ℵ(01) NA28[] SBLGNT ‖ Absent from A(02) B(03) BYZ TR THGNT.

20 For the kingdom of God is not in word, but in power.

21 What do you want? Shall I come to you with a rod, or in love and a spirit of gentleness?

5 1 It is actually reported that there is sexual immorality among you, and such sexual immorality as is not even [[named]]ᵃ among the Gentiles, so that one has his father's wife. 2 And you are puffed up, and did not rather mourn, so that he who has done this deed might be taken away from among you? 3 For I, indeed, [[as]]ᵇ though I am being absent in body but present in spirit, have already judged, as though I were present, him who has so done this thing. 4 In the name of {our}ᶜ Lord Jesus [[Christ]],ᵈ when you are gathered together, along with my spirit, with the power of {our}ᵉ Lord Jesus [[Christ]],ᶠ 5 to deliver such a one to Satan for the destruction of the flesh, that his spirit may be saved in the day of the Lord [[Jesus]].ᵍ

6 Your boasting is not good. Do you not know that a little leaven leavens the whole lump? 7 Clean out [[therefore]]ʰ the old leaven, that you may be a new lump, just as you are unleavened. For indeed, our Passover, Christ, has been sacrificed [[on our behalf]].ⁱ

8 Therefore let us celebrate the feast, not with old leaven, nor with the leaven of malice and wickedness, but with the unleavened bread of sincerity and truth.

9 I wrote to you in my letter not to associate with sexually immoral people, 10 not at all *meaning* the sexually immoral of this world, or the greedy and swindlers, or idolaters, since then you would need to go out of the world.

11 But now I have written to you not to associate with anyone who is called a brother if he is sexually immoral, or greedy, or an idolater, or a reviler, or a drunkard, or a swindler; with such a person do not even eat.

12 For what have I to do with judging those who are outside? Do you [not]ʲ judge those who are inside? 13 But those who are outside, God judges. {Remove}ᵏ the wicked person from among yourselves.

6 1 Does any of you, having a dispute with another, dare to be judged by the unrighteous and not by the saints?

2 [Or]ˡ Do you not know that the saints will judge the world? And if the world is judged by you, are you unworthy of the smallest judgments? 3 Do you not know that we will judge angels, [not to mention] matters of this life?

4 So if you have judgments concerning matters of this life, do you appoint those who are despised in the church to judge? 5 I say this to your shame. Is it so, that there is not among you one wise who will be able to judge between his brother? 6 But brother goes to law against brother, and that before unbelievers!

ᵃ 5:1, **named:** Included in BYZ TR.
ᵇ 5:3, **as:** Included in BYZ TR.
ᶜ 5:4, **our:** Some manuscripts read "the." ℵ(01) A(02).
ᵈ 5:4, **Christ:** Included in BYZ TR.
ᵉ 5:4, **our:** 𝔓46 reads "the."
ᶠ 5:4, **Christ:** Included in BYZ TR.
ᵍ 5:5, **Jesus:** Included in ℵ(01) A(02) BYZ TR. ‖ Absent from 𝔓46 B(03).
ʰ 5:7, **therefore:** Included in C(04) TR.
ⁱ 5:7, **on our behalf:** Included in BYZ TR ‖ Absent from 𝔓46 ℵ(01) A(02) B(03) C(04) NA28 SBLGNT TH.
ʲ 5:12, **not:** Absent from 𝔓46.
ᵏ 5:13, **Remove:** Some manuscripts read "And you shall remove." BYZ TR.
ˡ 6:2, **Or:** Absent from BYZ TR.

7 Now therefore [indeed],[a] it is already a complete defeat for you that you have lawsuits with one another. Why not rather be wronged? Why not rather be defrauded?

8 But you yourselves do wrong and defraud, and that to your brothers.

9 Or do you not know that the unrighteous will not inherit the kingdom of God? Do not be deceived: neither the sexually immoral, nor idolaters, nor adulterers, nor effeminate, nor homosexuals, 10 nor thieves, nor the greedy, nor drunkards, nor revilers, nor swindlers will inherit the kingdom of God.

11 And such were some of you; but you were washed, but you were sanctified, but you were justified in the name of the Lord Jesus [Christ][b] and in the Spirit of our God.

12 All things are lawful for me, but not all things are profitable; all things are lawful for me, but I will not be mastered by anything.

13 Food is for the stomach and the stomach for food, but God will destroy both it and them. Now the body is not for sexual immorality, but for the Lord, and the Lord for the body. 14 And God raised up the Lord and will also raise us up by His power.

15 Do you not know that your bodies are members of Christ? Shall I then take the members of Christ and make them members of a prostitute? May it never be!

16 Or do you not know that the one who joins himself to a prostitute is one body with her? For [he says],[c] "The two shall become one flesh." 17 But the one who joins himself to the Lord is one spirit with Him.

18 Flee sexual immorality. Every sin that a person commits is outside the body, but the one who commits sexual immorality sins against his own body.

19 Or do you not know that your body is a temple of the Holy Spirit within you, which you have from God, and you are not your own? 20 For you were bought with a price; therefore glorify God in your body [[and in your spirit, which are God's]].[d]

7 1 Now concerning the matters about which you wrote [[to me]],[e] it is good for a man not to touch a woman, 2 but because of sexual immorality, each man should have his own wife and each woman her own husband.

3 The husband should give to his wife her due [[affection]],[f] and likewise the wife to her husband.

4 The wife does not have authority over her own body, but the husband does; and likewise the husband does not have authority over his own body, but the wife does. 5 Do not deprive one another, except perhaps by agreement for a limited time, that you may devote yourselves to [[fasting and]][g] prayer; but then come together again, so that Satan may not tempt you because of [your][h] lack of self-control.

6 Now I say this as a concession, not as a command. 7 I wish that all men were as I am. But each has his own gift from God, one in this manner, and another in that.

8 To the unmarried and the widows I say that it is good for them to remain single as I am. 9 But if they cannot exercise self-control, they should marry. For it is better to marry than to burn with passion.

---

[a] 6:7, **indeed:** Absent from 𝔓46 ℵ(01) .

[b] 6:11, **Christ:** Absent from A(02) BYZ TR.

[c] 6:16, **he says:** Absent from A(02).

[d] 6:20, **and in your spirit, which are God's:** Included in BYZ TR.

[e] 7:1, **to me:** Included in A(02) BYZ TR ‖ Absent from 𝔓46 ℵ(01) B(03) C(04) NA28 SBLGNT THGNT.

[f] 7:3, **affection:** Included in BYZ TR.

[g] 7:5, **fasting and:** Included in BYZ TR.

[h] 7:5, **your:** Absent from B(03).

10 To the married I give this charge (not I, but the Lord): the wife should not separate from her husband 11 (but if she does, she should remain unmarried or else be reconciled to her husband), and the husband should not divorce his wife.

12 To the rest I say (I, not the Lord): if any brother has a wife who is an unbeliever, if she is willing to live with him, let him not send her away. 13 And if any woman has a husband who is an unbeliever, and he consents to live with her, she should not divorce him.

14 For the unbelieving husband is sanctified in the wife, and the unbelieving wife is sanctified in the {brother};[a] otherwise your children would be unclean, but now they are holy.

15 But if the unbelieving partner separates, let it be so. In such cases the brother or sister is not enslaved. God has called {you}[b] to peace. 16 For how do you know, wife, whether you will save your husband? Or how do you know, husband, whether you will save your wife?

17 Only let each person lead the life that {the Lord}[c] has assigned to him, and to which {God}[d] has called him. This is my rule in all the churches.

18 Was anyone at the time of his call already circumcised? {Let him} not seek to remove the marks of circumcision. Was anyone at the time of his call uncircumcised? Let him not seek circumcision. 19 For neither circumcision counts for anything nor uncircumcision, but keeping the commandments of God.

20 Each one should remain in the condition in which he was called. 21 Were you a slave when called? Do not be concerned about it. But if you can gain your freedom, avail yourself of the opportunity.

22 For he who was called in the Lord as a slave is a freedman of the Lord. Likewise he who was free when called is a slave of Christ. 23 You were bought with a price; do not become slaves of men.

24 So, brothers, in whatever condition each was called, there let him remain with God.

25 Now concerning virgins, I have no command from the Lord, but I give my opinion as one who has received mercy from the Lord to be trustworthy.

26 I think, therefore, that this is good because of the present distress: that it is good for a man to be as he is. 27 Are you bound to a wife? Do not seek to be released. Are you released from a wife? Do not seek a wife.

28 But if you marry, you have not sinned; and if a virgin marries, she has not sinned. Yet such will have trouble in the flesh, and I would spare you.

29 But this I say, brothers, the time is short; from now on, let those who have wives be as though they had none, 30 and those who weep as though they did not weep, and those who rejoice as though they did not rejoice, and those who buy as though they did not possess, 31 and those who use {the}[e] world as though they did not make full use of it; for the form of this world is passing away.

---

a 7:14, **brother:** Some manuscripts read "husband" and clarify the obvious intent of Paul. BYZ TR.

b 7:15, **you:** ℵ(01) A(02) C(04) NA28 ‖ Some manuscripts read "us." 𝔓46 B(03) SBLGNT THGNT BYZ TR.

c 7:17, **Lord:** 𝔓46 ℵ(01) A(02) B(03) C(04) NA28 SBLGNT THGNT ‖ Some manuscripts read "God." BYZ TR.

d 7:17, **God:** 𝔓46 ℵ(01) A(02) B(03) C(04) NA28 SBLGNT THGNT ‖ Some manuscripts read "the Lord." BYZ TR.

e 7:31, **the:** Some manuscripts read "this." BYZ TR.

32 But I want you to be free from concern. The unmarried person is concerned about the things of the Lord, how to please the Lord; 33 But the one who marries is concerned with the things of the world, how to please his wife, 34 {and is divided.[a] The unmarried woman and the virgin} are concerned about the things of the Lord, that they may be holy both in body and in spirit; but the married woman is concerned [about the things of the world,][b] how she may please her husband.

35 Now I say this for your own benefit, not to put a restraint upon you, but to promote what is appropriate and to secure undistracted devotion to the Lord.

36 If anyone thinks he is acting improperly toward his virgin, if she is past the bloom of youth and it must be so, let him do what he wishes; he does not sin. Let them marry.

37 But the one who stands firm in his heart, having no necessity, but has authority over his own will, and has decided this in his own heart, to keep his own virgin, he will do well. 38 So then, he who marries [his own virgin][c] does well, and he who does not marry her will do better.

39 A woman is bound [[by law]][d] as long as her husband lives; but if her husband falls asleep, she is free to marry whom she wishes, only in the Lord.

40 But in my opinion, she is happier if she remains as she is; and I think that I also have the Spirit of {God}.[e]

8 1 Now concerning food offered to idols, we know that we all have knowledge. Knowledge puffs up, but love builds up.

2 [[But]][f] If anyone thinks they know something, he {does not yet know}[g] as he ought to know. 3 But if anyone loves [God],[h] this one is known [by him].[i]

4 So then, about eating food sacrificed to idols, we know that an idol is nothing in the world and that there is no [[other]][j] God but one. 5 For even if there are so-called gods, whether in heaven or on earth (as indeed there are many gods and many lords), 6 [but][k] for us *there is* one [God, the][l] Father, from whom *are* all things and we *are* for him, and one Lord, Jesus Christ, through whom *are* all things and we *are* through him.[m]

7 But not all men have this knowledge. Some, still accustomed to idols, eat food as if it were sacrificed to an idol, and their conscience, being weak, is defiled.

8 But food will not bring us closer to God; we are no worse if we do [not][n] eat, and no better if we do.

---

a 7:34, **and is divided...:** Some manuscripts read "the woman and the virgin are divided. The unmarried woman." BYZ TR.

b 7:34, **about the things of the world:** Absent from B(03).

c 7:38, **his own virgin:** Absent from BYZ TR.

d 7:39, **by law:** Included in BYZ TR.

e 7:40, **God:** 𝔓15 reads "Christ." BYZ TR.

f 8:2, **But:** Included in BYZ TR.

g 8:2, **does not yet know:** Some manuscripts read "has not yet known anything." BYZ TR.

h 8:3, **God:** Absent from 𝔓46.

i 8:3, **by him:** Absent from 𝔓46 ℵ(01).

j 8:4, **other:** Included in BYZ TR.

k 8:6, **but:** Absent from 𝔓46 B(03).

l 8:6, **God, the** Absent from ℵ(01).

m 8:6, A 12th century manuscripts (1315) adds: "And one Holy Spirit, in whom are all things and we in him."

n 8:8, **not:** Absent from ℵ(01) BYZ TR.

9 [But]ᵃ Be careful, however, that the exercise of [your]ᵇ rights does not become a stumbling block to the weak. 10 For if someone with a weak conscience sees you, who have this knowledge, eating in an idol's temple, won't that person be emboldened to eat what is sacrificed to idols? 11 {For}ᶜ the one who is weak is destroyed by your knowledge, the brother for whom Christ died. 12 Thus, sinning against the brothers and wounding their conscience [being weak],ᵈ you sin against Christ.

13 Therefore, if food causes my brother to stumble, I will never eat meat, so that I may not cause my brother to stumble.

9 1 Am I not free? Am I not an apostle? Have I not seen Jesus [[Christ]]ᵉ our Lord? Are you not my work in the Lord?

2 If to others I am not an apostle, at least I am to you; for you are the seal of my apostleship [in the Lord].ᶠ

3 This is my defense to those who would examine me. 4 Do we not have the right to eat and drink? 5 Do we not have the right to take along a believing wife, as do the other apostles and the brothers of the Lord and Cephas? 6 Or is it only I and Barnabas who do not have the right to refrain from working?

7 Who ever serves as a soldier at his own expense? Who plants a vineyard and does not eat its fruit? Or who tends a flock and does not drink the milk of the flock?

8 Do I say [these things]ᵍ on human authority? Does not the law also say the same? 9 For it is written in the Law [of Moses],ʰ "You shall not muzzle an ox when it is treading out the grain."ⁱ Is it for oxen that God is concerned?

10 Or is he saying this certainly for us? For it was written for us that the one who plows should plow in hope, and the one threshing in hope should partake [[in hope]].ʲ

11 If we have sown spiritual things among you, is it too much if we reap material things from you?

12 If others share this rightful claim on you, do not we still more? Nevertheless, we have not made use of this right, but we endure anything rather than put an obstacle in the way of the gospel of {Christ}.ᵏ

13 Do you not know that those who perform the sacred duties *eat* from the temple, those who attend to the altar share in the altar? 14 In the same way, the Lord commanded that those who proclaim the gospel should get their living by the gospel.

15 But I have made no use of any of these rights, nor am I writing these things to secure any such provision. For to me, it is better to die than; no one will nullify my boasting. 16 [For]ˡ If I preach the gospel, that gives me no ground for {boasting}.ᵐ For necessity is laid upon me. {For}ⁿ woe to me if I do not preach the gospel!

ᵃ 8:9, **But:** Absent from 𝔓46.

ᵇ 8:9, **your:** Absent from 𝔓46.

ᶜ 8:11, **For:** Some manuscripts read "And." BYZ TR.

ᵈ 8:12, **being weak:** Absent from 𝔓46.

ᵉ 9:1, **Christ:** Included in BYZ TR.

ᶠ 9:2, **in the Lord:** Absent from A(02).

ᵍ 9:8, **these things:** Absent from 𝔓46.

ʰ 9:9, **of Moses:** Absent from 𝔓46.

ⁱ 9:9, Deuteronomy 25:4.

ʲ 9:10, **in hope:** Included in BYZ TR.

ᵏ 9:12, **Christ:** C(04) reads "the Lord."

ˡ 9:16, **For:** Absent from 𝔓46.

ᵐ 9:16, **boasting:** 𝔓46 A(02) B(03) C(04) NA28 SBLGNT THGNT ‖ Some manuscripts read "grace." ℵ(01).

ⁿ 9:16, **For:** Some manuscripts read "But." BYZ TR.

17 For if I do this of my own will, I have a reward; but if not of my own will, I am entrusted with a commission. 18 What then is my reward? That in my preaching I may present the gospel {of Christ}[a] free of charge, so as not to make full use of my right in the gospel.

19 For though I am free from all, I have made myself a servant to all, that I might win more of them.

20 [To the Jews I became as a Jew, in order to win Jews. To those under the law I became as one under the law [(though not being myself under the law)][b] that I might win those under the law.][c]

21 To those outside the law I became as one outside the law (not being outside the law of God but under the law of Christ) that I might win those outside the law.

22 To the weak I became [[as]][d] weak, that I might win the weak. I have become all things to all people, that by all means I might save some.

23 I do it all for the sake of the gospel, that I may share with them in its blessings.

24 Do you not know that those who run in a stadium all run, but only one receives the prize? So run that you may obtain it.

25 And everyone who competes exercises self-control in all things; they then do it to receive a perishable wreath, but we an imperishable.

26 So I run in this way, not aimlessly; I box in this way, not beating the air; 27 but I discipline my body and bring it into subjection, lest after preaching to others, I myself should be disqualified.

10 1 {For}[e] I do not want you to be unaware, brothers, that our fathers were all under the cloud and all passed through the sea, 2 and all were baptized into Moses in the cloud and in the sea, 3 and all ate the same spiritual food, 4 and all drank the same spiritual drink. For they drank from the spiritual rock that followed them, and the rock was Christ.[f]

5 But with most of them God was not pleased, for they were struck down in the wilderness. 6 Now these things took place as examples for us, so that we might not desire evil as they did. 7 Do not become idolaters as some of them did; as it is written, "The people sat down to eat and drink and rose up to play."[g] 8 We must not indulge in sexual immorality as some of them did, and twenty-three thousand fell in a single day. 9 We must not put {the Lord}[h] to the test, as some of them did and were destroyed by serpents. 10 And do not grumble as some of them did and were destroyed by the Destroyer.

11 Now [[all]][i] these things happened to them as examples, and they were written down as warnings for us, on whom the culmination of the ages has come.

12 Therefore let anyone who thinks that he stands take heed lest he fall. 13 No temptation has overtaken you that is not common to man. God is faithful, and he will not let you be tempted beyond your ability, but with the temptation he will also provide the way of escape, {to be}[j] able to endure it.

---

a 9:18, **of Christ:** Included in C(04) BYZ TR.

b 9:20, **though not being myself under the law:** Absent from BYZ TR.

c 9:20, **To the Jews...:** Verse 20 is absent from 𝔓46.

d 9:22, **as:** Included in C(04) BYZ TR.

e 10:1, **For:** Some manuscripts read "But." BYZ TR.

f 10:4, **Christ:** Or "the Anointed One." See footnote for Christ in Luke 2:11.

g 10:7, Exodus 32:6.

h 10:9, **the Lord:** ℵ(01) B(03) C(04) THGNT ‖ Some manuscripts read "Christ." 𝔓46 BYZ TR NA28 SBLGNT ‖ A(02) reads "God."

i 10:11, **all:** Included in ℵ(01) C(04) BYZ TR.

j 10:13, **to be:** Some manuscripts read "that you may." BYZ TR.

14 Therefore, my beloved, flee from idolatry. 15 I speak as to sensible people; judge for yourselves what I say. 16 The cup of blessing that we bless, is it not a participation in the blood of Christ? The bread that we break, is it not a participation in the body of Christ? 17 Because there is one bread, we who are many are one body, for we all partake of the one bread.

18 Consider the people of Israel; are not those who eat the sacrifices participants in the altar?

19 What then am I saying? That an idol sacrifice is something [, or that an idol is something]?ᵃ 20 But what {they}ᵇ sacrifice, they sacrifice to demons and not to God [they sacrifice];ᶜ I do not want you to become sharers with demons. 21 You cannot drink the cup of the Lord and the cup of demons. You cannot partake of the table of the Lord and the table of demons.

22 Or are we provoking the Lord to jealousy? Are we stronger than he?

23 All things are lawful [[for me]],ᵈ but not all things are helpful. All things are lawful [[for me]],ᵉ but not all things build up.

24 Let no one seek his own good, but [[each]]ᶠ the good of his neighbor.

25 Eat whatever is sold in the meat market without raising any question on the ground of conscience. 26 For "the earth is the Lord's, and the fullness thereof."ᵍ

27 If one of the unbelievers invites you to dinner and you are disposed to go, eat whatever is set before you without raising any question on the ground of conscience. 28 But if someone says to you, "This is offered to an idol," do not eat it, for his sake [of the one who informed you and for conscience's sake]ʰ [[for the earth is the Lord's, and all its fullness]].ⁱ 29 But I am speaking of conscience, not his own, but the other's. For why is my freedom judged by another's conscience?

30 [[But]]ʲ If I partake with thankfulness, why am I denounced because of that for which I give thanks? 31 Whether then you eat or drink or whatever [you do],ᵏ do all things for the glory of God.

32 Give no offense to Jews or to Greeks or to the church of God, 33 just as I try to please everyone in everything I do, not seeking my own advantage, but that of many, that they may be saved.

11 1 Be imitators of me, just as I also am of Christ.

2 Now I praise you [[brothers]]ˡ because you remember me in everything and hold fast to the traditions just as I delivered them to you.

3 But I want you to understand that the head of every man is Christ, and the head of a woman is her husband, and the head of Christ is God.

ᵃ 10:19, **or that an idol is something:** Absent From some manuscripts. 𝔓46 ℵ(01) A(02) C(04).
ᵇ 10:20, **they:** B(03) NA28 SBLGNT ‖ Some manuscripts read "the Gentiles." 𝔓46 ℵ(01) A(02) C(04) BYZ TR THGNT.
ᶜ 10:20, **they sacrifice:** NA28[] SBLGNT THGNT ‖ Absent from BYZ TR.
ᵈ 10:23, **for me:** Included in BYZ TR ‖ Absent from 𝔓46 ℵ(01) A(02) B(03) C(04) NA28 SBLGNT THGNT.
ᵉ 10:23, **for me:** Included in BYZ TR ‖ Absent from 𝔓46 ℵ(01) A(02) B(03) C(04) NA28 SBLGNT THGNT.
ᶠ 10:24, **each:** Included in BYZ TR ‖ Absent from 𝔓46 ℵ(01) A(02) B(03) C(04) NA28 SBLGNT THGNT.
ᵍ 10:26, Psalm 24:1.
ʰ 10:28, **of the one who informed you and for conscience's sake:** Absent from 𝔓46.
ⁱ 10:28, **for the earth is the Lord's, and all its fullness:** Included in BYZ TR ‖ Absent from ℵ(01) A(02) B(03) C(04) NA28 SBLGNT THGNT.
ʲ 10:30, **But:** Some manuscripts read. TR.
ᵏ 10:31, **you do:** Absent from 𝔓46.
ˡ 11:2, **brothers:** Included in BYZ TR ‖ Absent from 𝔓46 ℵ(01) A(02) B(03) C(04) NA28 SBLGNT THGNT.

4 Every man who prays or prophesies with his head covered dishonors his head. 5 But every woman who prays or prophesies with her head uncovered dishonors {her own}[a] head, for it is one and the same as if she were shaved. 6 For if a woman does not cover her head, let her also have her hair cut off; but if it is disgraceful for a woman to have her hair cut off or her head shaved, let her cover her head.

7 For a man ought not to have his head covered, since he is the image and glory of God; but the woman is the glory of man.

8 For man does not originate from woman, but woman from man; 9 for indeed man was not created for the woman's sake, but woman for the man's sake. 10 Therefore the woman ought to have a symbol of authority on her head, because of the angels.[b]

11 However, in the Lord, neither is {woman independent of man, nor is man independent of woman}.[c] 12 For as the woman originates from the man, so also the man has his birth through the woman; and all things originate from God.

13 Judge for yourselves: is it proper for a woman to pray to God with her head uncovered? 14 Does not even nature itself teach you that if a man has long hair, it is a dishonor to him, 15 but if a woman has long hair, it is a glory to her? For her hair is given to her for a covering.

16 But if one is inclined to be contentious, we have no such practice, nor do the churches of God.

17 But in giving this instruction, I do not praise you, because you come together not for the better but for the worse.

18 For, in the first place, when you come together as a church, I hear that there are divisions among you; and in part I believe it. 19 For there must [also][d] be factions among you, so that those who are approved may become evident [among you].[e]

20 [Therefore][f] When you meet together, it is not to eat the Lord's Supper, 21 for in your eating each one takes his own supper first; and one is hungry and another is drunk.

22 What! Do you not have houses in which to eat and drink? Or do you despise the church of God and shame those who have nothing? What shall I say to you? Shall I praise [you]?[g] In this I will not praise you.

23 For I received from the Lord that which I also delivered to you, that the Lord [Jesus][h] in the night in which he was betrayed took bread; 24 And having given thanks, he broke it and said, [["Take, eat]][i] this is my body which is [[broken]][j] for you; do this in remembrance of me." 25 In the same way he took the cup also after supper, saying, "This cup is the new covenant in my blood; do this, as often as you drink it, in remembrance of me."[k] 26 For as often as you eat this bread [and

---

a 11:5, **her:** Some manuscripts read "her own." 𝔓46 B(03) BYZ TR.

b 11:10, **angels:** This context likely refers to human messengers. The Greek word can mean (1) a human messenger serving as an envoy, an envoy, one who is sent or (2) a transcendent power who carries out various missions or tasks, messenger, angel (BDAG, ἄγγελος).

c 11:11, Some manuscripts reverse the occurrences of "woman" and "man." BYZ TR.

d 11:19, **also:** 𝔓46 B(03) NA28[] SBLGNT ‖ Absent from ℵ(01) A(02) C(04) THGNT BYZ TR.

e 11:19, **among you:** Absent from 𝔓46 C(04).

f 11:20, **Therefore:** Absent from 𝔓46.

g 11:22, **you:** Absent from 𝔓46.

h 11:23, **Jesus:** Absent from B(03).

i 11:24, **Take, eat:** Included in BYZ TR ‖ Absent from 𝔓46 ℵ(01) A(02) B(03) C(04) NA28 SBLGNT THGNT.

j 11:24, **broken:** Included in BYZ TR ‖ Absent from 𝔓46 ℵ(01) A(02) B(03) C(04) NA28 SBLGNT THGNT.

k 11:25, Luke 22:19-20.

drink]^a {the}^b cup, you proclaim the Lord's death until he comes.

27 Therefore, whoever eats the bread or drinks {the}^c cup of the Lord in an manner unworthy [[of the Lord]],^d shall be guilty of the body and the blood of {the Lord}.^e

28 But a man must examine himself, and in so doing he is to eat of the bread and drink of the cup. 29 For the one eating and drinking [[in an unworthy manner]]^f brings judgment upon oneself, eating and drinking without discerning the body [[of the Lord]].^g

30 For this reason many among you are weak and sick, and a number sleep. 31 {But}^h if we judged ourselves rightly, we would not be judged. 32 But when we are judged, we are disciplined by the Lord so that we will not be condemned along with the world.

33 So then, my brethren, when you come together to eat, wait for one another. 34 [[But]]ⁱ If anyone is hungry, let him eat at home, so that you will not come together for judgment. The remaining matters I will arrange when I come.

12 1 Now concerning spiritual matters, brothers, I do not want you to be uninformed. 2 You know that [when]^j you were Gentiles, you were led astray to mute idols, however you were led. 3 Therefore I want you to understand that no one speaking in the Spirit of God ever says "Jesus is accursed!" and no one can say "Jesus is Lord" except in the Holy Spirit.

4 Now there are varieties of gifts, but the same Spirit; 5 and there are varieties of services, but the same Lord; 6 And there are varieties of activities, but it is the same God who activates all things in everyone.

7 To each is given the manifestation of the Spirit for the common good.

8 To one indeed, through the Spirit, is given a word of wisdom, and to another a word of knowledge according to the same Spirit, 9 to another faith in the same Spirit, and to another gifts of healing [in the {one}^k Spirit],^l 10 to another workings of powers, [[but]]^m to another prophecy, [[but]]ⁿ to another discernment of spirits, to another kinds of tongues [, and to another interpretation of tongues].^o

11 But all these things are worked by the one and the same Spirit, distributing to each one individually as it wills.

12 For just as the body is one and has many members, and all the members of the [[one]]^p body, though many, are one body, so also is the {Christ}.^q 13 For indeed in one spirit we all were baptized into one body, whether Jews or Greeks, whether slaves or free, and we all were made to drink

---

^a 11:26, **and drink:** Absent from 𝔓46.

^b 11:26, **the:** Some manuscripts read "this." 𝔓46 BYZ TR.

^c 11:27, **the:** Some manuscripts read "this." BYZ TR.

^d 11:27, **of the Lord:** Included in ℵ(01) BYZ.

^e 11:27, **the Lord:** A(02) reads "Christ."

^f 11:29, **in an unworthy manner:** Included in BYZ TR ‖ Absent from 𝔓46 ℵ(01) A(02) B(03) C(04) NA28 SBLGNT THGNT.

^g 11:29, **of the Lord:** Included in BYZ TR ‖ Absent from 𝔓46 ℵ(01) A(02) B(03) C(04) NA28 SBLGNT THGNT.

^h 11:31, **But:** Some manuscripts read "For." C(04) BYZ TR.

ⁱ 11:34, **But:** Included in BYZ TR.

^j 12:2, **when:** Absent from TR.

^k 12:9, **one:** Some manuscripts read "the same." ℵ(01) A(02) B(03) BYZ TR.

^l 12:9, **in the one Spirit:** Absent from C(04).

^m 12:10, **but:** ℵ(01) A(02) B(03) C(04) NA28[] SBLGNT THGNT ‖ Absent from 𝔓46 B(03) BYZ TR.

ⁿ 12:10, **but:** ℵ(01) A(02) B(03) C(04) NA28[] SBLGNT THGNT ‖ Absent from 𝔓46 B(03) BYZ TR.

^o 12:10, **and to another interpretation of tongues:** Absent from B(03).

^p 12:12, **one:** Included in BYZ TR.

^q 12:12, **Christ:** C(04) reads "the Lord."

[[into]]ᵃ one spirit. ¹⁴For the body is not one member, but many.

¹⁵If the foot should say, Because I am not a hand, I do not belong to the body, that would not make it any less a part of the body. ¹⁶And if the ear should say, because I am not an eye, I do not belong to the body, that would not make it any less a part of the body. ¹⁷If the whole body were an eye, where would be the sense of hearing? If the whole body were an ear, where would be the sense of smell? ¹⁸But as it is, God arranged the members in the body, each one of them, as he chose.

¹⁹If all were a single member, where would the body be? ²⁰As it is, there are many parts, [yet]ᵇ one body. ²¹The eye cannot say to the hand, I have no need of you, nor again the head to the feet, I have no need of you. ²²On the contrary, the parts of the body that seem to be weaker are indispensable, ²³and on those parts of the body that we think less honorable we bestow the greater honor, and our unpresentable parts are treated with greater modesty, ²⁴which our more presentable parts do not require. But God has so composed the body, giving greater [honor]ᶜ to the part that lacked it, ²⁵that there may be no division in the body, but that the members may have the same care for one another.

²⁶If {one}ᵈ member suffers, all suffer together; if {one}ᵉ member is honored, all rejoice together.

²⁷Now you are the body of Christ and individually members of it. ²⁸And God has appointed in the church first apostles, second prophets, third teachers, then miracles, then gifts of healing, helping, administrating, and various kinds of tongues.

²⁹Not all are apostles, are they? Not all are prophets, are they? Not all are teachers, are they? Not all have powers? ³⁰Do not all have gifts of healing? Do not all speak in tongues? Not all interpret, do they? ³¹But strive for the {greater}ᶠ gifts.ᵍ

And I will show you a still more excellent way.

13 ¹If I speak in the tongues of men and of angels, but do not have love, I have become a sounding brass or a clanging cymbal.

²And if I have prophecy and know all mysteries and all knowledge, and if I have all faith so as to move mountains, but do not have love, I am nothing.

³And if I give away all my possessions and [if]ʰ I hand over my body so that I may {boast},ⁱ but do not have love, I gain nothing.

⁴Love is patient, love is kind, it does not envy, [love]ʲ does not boast, it is not puffed up, ⁵it does not behave indecently, it does not seek its own, it is not provoked, it does not keep a record of wrongs, ⁶it does not rejoice in unrighteousness, but rejoices with the truth; ⁷it bears all things, believes all things, hopes all things, endures all things.

⁸Love never {fails};ᵏ [but]ˡ whether there are prophecies, they will be done away with; whether there are tongues, they will cease; whether there

---

ᵃ 12:13, **into:** Included in BYZ TR.

ᵇ 12:20, **yet:** Absent from 𝔓46 B(03).

ᶜ 12:24, **honor:** Absent from B(03).

ᵈ 12:26, **one:** A(02) reads "a."

ᵉ 12:26, **one:** Some manuscripts read "a." 𝔓46 ℵ(01) A(02) B(03).

ᶠ 12:31, **greater:** Some manuscripts read "better." BYZ TR.

ᵍ 12:31, **But strive for the greater gifts:** Possibly this is not an imperative but a question, "But are you striving for the greater gifts?."

ʰ 13:3, **if:** Absent from 𝔓46 B(03) C(04).

ⁱ 13:3, **boast:** 𝔓46 ℵ(01) A(02) B(03) NA28 SBLGNT THGNT ‖ Some manuscripts read "be burned." C(04) BYZ TR.

ʲ 13:4, **Love:** Absent from B(03).

ᵏ 13:8, **fails:** Some manuscripts read "falls away." BYZ TR.

ˡ 13:8, **but:** Absent from 𝔓46.

is knowledge, it will be done away with. 9 [For]ᵃ We know in part and we prophesy in part; 10 but when the perfect comes, [[then]]ᵇ the partial will be done away with.

11 When I was a child, I spoke as a child, I thought as a child, I reasoned as a child; [[but]]ᶜ when I became a man, I put away childish things. 12 For [now]ᵈ we see through a mirror, in a riddle, but then face to face; now I know in part, but then I will know fully, just as I also have been fully known.

13 And now these three remain: faith, hope, love; but the greatest of these is love.

14 1 Pursue love, and earnestly desire spiritual gifts, especially that you may prophesy.

2 For the one who speaks in a tongue does not speak to people but to God; for no one understands, but in the Spirit one speaks mysteries. 3 But the one who prophesies speaks to men for edification and encouragement and consolation.

4 The one speaking in a tongue builds up oneself; but the one prophesying builds up the assembly.

5 I wish that you all spoke in tongues, but even more that you would prophesy; for the one who prophesies is greater than the one who speaks in tongues, unless they interpret, so that the church may receive edification.

6 Now, brothers, if I come to you speaking in tongues, how will I benefit you unless I speak to you either by revelation or by knowledge or by prophecy or by teaching? 7 Likewise,

lifeless things that produce sound, whether flute or harp, if they do not give distinction to the notes, how will what is played on the flute or the harp be recognized? 8 For if the trumpet gives an indistinct sound, who will prepare for battle?

9 So also you, through the tongue, if you do not give a clear word, how will what is spoken be known? For you will be speaking into the air. 10 There are, perhaps, many [kinds of]ᵉ languages in the world, and none [[of them]]ᶠ is without meaning. 11 Therefore, if I do not know the meaning of the language, I will be a foreigner to the speaker, and the speaker will be a foreigner to me.

12 In this way also you, since you are zealous for spirits,ᵍ seek for the building up of the church so that you may abound.

13 Therefore, the one who speaks in a tongue should pray that they may interpret.

14 [For]ʰ If I pray in a tongue, my spirit prays, but my understanding is unfruitful.

15 What then? I will pray with the spirit, and I will also pray with the understanding; I will sing with the spirit, and I will also sing with the understanding.

16 For if you bless in the spirit, how will the one filling the place of the unlearned say the Amen upon your thanksgiving? Since what you say, they do not know. 17 For you indeed give thanks well, but the other person is not built up.

ᵃ 13:9, **For:** BYZ reads "but."
ᵇ 13:10, **then:** Included in BYZ TR.
ᶜ 13:11, **but:** Included in BYZ TR.
ᵈ 13:12, **now:** Absent from 𝔓46.
ᵉ 14:10, **kinds of:** Absent from 𝔓46.
ᶠ 14:10, **of them:** Included in BYZ TR.
ᵍ 14:12, **spirits:** Or, spiritual gifts.
ʰ 14:14, **For:** Absent from 𝔓46 B(03).

18 I thank [[my]]ᵃ God, more than all of you, [that I speak]ᵇ in tongues. 19 [But]ᶜ In the church, I would rather speak five words {with}ᵈ my mind, so that I may instruct others also, rather than ten thousand [words]ᵉ in a tongue.

20 Brothers, do not be children in your thinking; be infants in evil, but in your thinking be mature.

21 In the Law it is written, "By people of strange tongues and by the lips of others will I speak to this people, and even then they will not listen to me, says the Lord."ᶠ 22 Therefore, tongues are a sign not for believers but for unbelievers, while prophecy is not for unbelievers but for believers.

23 If, therefore, the whole church comes together and all speak in tongues, and outsiders [or unbelievers]ᵍ enter, will they not say that you are out of your minds? 24 But if all prophesy, and an unbeliever or uninformed person enters, they are convicted by all, they are examined by all, 25 [[And thus]]ʰ the secrets of their heart become evident, and thus falling on their face, they will worship God, declaring that [[indeed]]ⁱ God is among you.

26 What then, brothers? When you come together, each one [[of you]]ʲ has a hymn, a teaching, a revelation, a tongue, an interpretation; let all things be done for building up.

27 If anyone speaks in a tongue, let it be by two or at most three, and each in turn, and let one interpret; 28 but if there is no interpreter, let the speaker be silent in the assembly, and let them speak to themselves and to God.

29 Let two or three prophets speak, and let the others discern; 30 [but]ᵏ if a revelation is made to another who is seated, let the first be silent. 31 For you can all prophesy one by one, so that all may learn and all may be encouraged. 32 And the spirits of prophets are subject to prophets, 33 for God is not a God of disorder but of peace, as in all the churches of the saints.

34 [Let {the}ˡ women be silent in the churches; for they are not permitted to speak, but let them be subject [[to the men]],ᵐ as the law also says. 35 If they desire [to learn]ⁿ anything, let them ask their own husbands at home; for it is shameful for a woman to speak in the assembly.]ᵒ 36 Or did the word of God originate from you? Or did it reach only you?

37 If anyone thinks they are a prophet or spiritual, let them recognize that what I am writing to you is a command of [the Lord];ᵖ 38 but if anyone is ignorant, let them be ignorant.

39 So then, brothers [of mine],ᵍ strive to prophesy and do not forbid speaking in tongues. 40 [But]ʳ Let all things be done decently and in order.

ᵃ 14:18, **my:** Included in BYZ TR.

ᵇ 14:18, **that I speak:** Absent from A(02).

ᶜ 14:19, **But:** Absent from ℵ(01).

ᵈ 14:19, **with:** Some manuscripts read "through." BYZ TR.

ᵉ 14:19, **words:** Absent from 𝔓46.

ᶠ 14:21, Isaiah 28:11-12.

ᵍ 14:23, **or unbelievers:** Absent from B(03).

ʰ 14:25, **And thus:** Included in BYZ TR.

ⁱ 14:25, **indeed:** Included in BYZ TR.

ʲ 14:26, **of you:** Included in BYZ TR.

ᵏ 14:30, **but:** Absent from 𝔓46.

ˡ 14:34, **the:** Some manuscripts read "your." BYZ TR.

ᵐ 14:34, **to the men:** Included in A(02).

ⁿ 14:35, **to learn:** Absent from A(02).

ᵒ 14:35, Some manuscripts of the Western tradition including D(06) place verses 34-35 after verse 40.

ᵖ 14:37, **the Lord:** Some manuscripts read "God." A(02).

ᵍ 14:39, **of mine:** ℵ(01) A(02) B(03) NA28 SBLGNT THGNT ‖ Absent from 𝔓46 BYZ TR.

ʳ 14:40, **But:** Absent from BYZ TR.

15

¹Now I make known to you, brothers, the gospel which I preached to you, which you also received, in which you also stand, ²Through which also you are being saved, by what word I preached to you [to hold fast],ᵃ if you hold fast, unless you believed in vain.

³For I delivered to you as of first importance what I also received, that Christ died for our sins according to the Scriptures, ⁴and that he was buried, and that he was raised on the third day according to the Scriptures, ⁵and that he appeared to Cephas, then to the twelve.

⁶After that, he appeared to more than five hundred brothers at once, of whom the majority remain until now, but some have [[also]]ᵇ fallen asleep; ⁷then he appeared to James, then to all the apostles; ⁸and last of all, as to one untimely born, he appeared also to me. ⁹For I am the least of the apostles, who am not worthy to be called an apostle, because I persecuted the church of God. ¹⁰But by the grace of God I am what I am, and his grace toward me did not prove vain; but I labored more than all of them, yet not I, but the grace of God [that is]ᶜ with me. ¹¹Whether then it was I or they, so we preach and so you believed.

¹²Now if Christ is preached, that he has been raised from the dead, how do some among you say [that]ᵈ there is no resurrection of the dead? ¹³[But]ᵉ If there is no resurrection of the dead, not even Christ has been raised; ¹⁴But if Christ has not been raised, then our preaching is [also]ᶠ in vain, [[but]]ᵍ also your faith is in vain.

¹⁵Moreover, we are even found to be false witnesses of God, because we testified against God that he raised Christ, whom he did not raise [, if in fact the dead are not raised].ʰ

¹⁶For if the dead are not raised, not even Christ has been raised; ¹⁷and if Christ has not been raised, your faith is worthless; you are [[also]]ⁱ still in your sins. ¹⁸Then those also who have fallen asleep in Christ have perished.

¹⁹If we have hoped in Christ in this life only, we are of all men most to be pitied.

²⁰But now Christ has been raised from the dead, [[and become]]ʲ the firstfruits of those who have fallen asleep.

²¹For since by a man came death, by a man also came the resurrection of the dead. ²²For as in Adam all die, so also in Christ all will be made alive. ²³[But]ᵏ Each in their own order: Christ the firstfruits, then those of Christ at his coming, ²⁴Then the end, when he delivers the kingdom to the God and Father, when he abolishes all rule and all authority and power.

²⁵For he must reign until he has put all his enemies under his feet. ²⁶The last enemy that will be abolished is death. ²⁷[For he has put all things in subjection under his feet.]ˡ But when he says [that],ᵐ "All things are put in subjection,"ⁿ it is evident that he is excepted who put all things in subjection to him.

ᵃ 15:2, **to hold fast:** Included in 𝔓46.
ᵇ 15:6, **also:** Included in BYZ TR.
ᶜ 15:10, **that is:** Absent from ℵ(01) B(03) THGNT.
ᵈ 15:12, **that:** Absent from 𝔓46.
ᵉ 15:13, **But:** Absent from ℵ(01).
ᶠ 15:14, **also:** Absent from ℵ(01) B(03) BYZ TR.
ᵍ 15:14, **but:** Included in BYZ TR.
ʰ 15:15, **if in fact the dead are not raised:** Absent from D(06) and Syriac Peshitta.
ⁱ 15:17, **also:** Included in ℵ(01) A(02).
ʲ 15:20, **and become:** Included in BYZ TR.
ᵏ 15:23, **But:** Absent from ℵ(01).
ˡ 15:27, **For he has put all things in subjection under his feet:** Absent from some ℵ(01).
ᵐ 15:27, **that:** Absent from 𝔓46 B(03).
ⁿ 15:27, Psalm 8:6.

28 [But when all things are subjected to him,]ᵃ Then the Son himself [also]ᵇ will be subjected to the one who subjected all things to him, so that God may be all in all.

29 What will those who are baptized for the dead do? If the dead are not raised at all, why are they baptized for {them}?ᶜ 30 Why do we also risk ourselves every hour?

31 I die every day, by your boasting, [brothers]ᵈ which I have in Christ Jesus {our}ᵉ Lord.

32 If I fought with wild animals in Ephesus for merely human reasons, what benefit is it to me? If the dead are not raised, "Let us eat and drink, for tomorrow we die." ᶠ

33 Do not be deceived: Bad company corrupts good morals.

34 Wake upᵍ to righteousness and do not sin, for some have ignorance of God; I speak this to your shame.

35 But someone will say, How are the dead raised? And with what kind of body do they come? 36 Foolish one, what you sow does not come to life unless it dies; 37 and what you sow, you do not [sow]ʰ the body that will be, but a bare grain, perhaps of wheat or of some other kind; 38 but God gives it a body as he has chosen, and to each of the seeds his own body.

39 Not all flesh is the same flesh, but there is one [flesh]ⁱ of men, another flesh of animals, another [flesh]ʲ of birds, and another of fish. 40 There are also heavenly bodies and earthly bodies; but the glory of the heavenly is one, and the glory of the earthly is another. 41 There is one glory of the sun, another glory of the moon, and another glory of the stars; for one star differs from another star in glory.

42 So also is the resurrection of the dead. It is sown in corruption, it is raised in incorruption; 43 it is sown in dishonor, it is raised in glory; it is sown in weakness, it is raised in power; 44 It is sown a physical body, it is raised a spiritual body. {If there is a physical body, there is also a spiritual one}.ᵏ 45 So it is written, "The first [man]ˡ Adam became a living soul,"ᵐ the last [Adam]ⁿ became a life-giving spirit.

46 However, the spiritual is not first, but the natural, and afterward the spiritual.

47 The first man [[Adam]]° was of the earth, made of dust; the second man is [[spiritual]]ᵖ from heaven. 48 As the earthly one, so also are the earthly ones, and as the heavenly one, so [[also]]�q are the heavenly ones. 49 And just as we have borne the image of the earthly one, we will also bear the image of the heavenly one.

50 Now this I say, brothers, that flesh and blood cannot inherit the kingdom of God; nor does corruption inherit incorruption.

ᵃ 15:28, **But when all things are subjected to him:** Absent from ℵ(01).

ᵇ 15:28, **also:** Absent from B(03).

ᶜ 15:29, **them:** Some manuscripts read "the dead." BYZ TR.

ᵈ 15:31, **brothers:** Absent from 𝔓46 BYZ TR.

ᵉ 15:31, **our:** 𝔓46 reads "the."

ᶠ 15:32, Isaiah 22:13.

ᵍ 15:34, **Wake up:** The Greek word means become sober, figuratively to come to one's senses (BDAG, ἐκνήφω).

ʰ 15:37, **sow:** Absent from ℵ(01).

ⁱ 15:39, **flesh:** Included in TR.

ʲ 15:39, **flesh:** Absent from A(02).

ᵏ 15:44, **If there is a physical body, there is also a spiritual one:** Some manuscripts read "There is a physical body, and there is a spiritual body." BYZ TR.

ˡ 15:45, **man:** Absent from B(03).

ᵐ 15:45, Genesis 2:7.

ⁿ 15:45, **Adam:** Absent from 𝔓46.

° 15:47, **Adam** Absent from ℵ(01).

ᵖ 15:47, **spiritual:** 𝔓46 includes. ‖ Other manuscripts include "the Lord." BYZ TR.

q 15:48, **also:** Absent from C(04).

51 Behold, I tell you a mystery: [[Indeed]]ᵃ We shall notᵇ all sleep, but we shall all be changed, 52 in a moment, [[as]]ᶜ in the twinkling of an eye, at the last trumpet. For the trumpet will sound, and the dead will {be raised}ᵈ incorruptible, and we shall be changed.

53 For this corruptible must put on incorruption, and this mortal must put on immortality. 54 So when [[this corruptible has put on incorruption, and]]ᵉ this mortal has put on immortality, then shall be brought to pass the saying that is written: "Death is swallowed up in victory."ᶠ

55 "[O Death, where is your victory?]ᵍ {O Death, where is your sting?}ʰⁱ 56 The sting of death is sin, and the power of sin is the law.

57 But thanks be to God, who gives us the victory through our Lord Jesus Christ.

58 Therefore, my beloved brothers, be steadfast, immovable, always abounding in the work of the Lord, knowing that your labor is not in vain in the Lord.

16 1 Now concerning the collection for the saints, as I directed the churches of Galatia, so you also are to do. 2 On the first day of every week, each of you is to put something aside and store it up, as he may prosper, so that there will be no collecting when I come. 3 And when I arrive, I will send those whom you approve with letters to carry your gift to Jerusalem. 4 If it is fitting that I should go also, they will accompany me.

5 I will visit you after passing through Macedonia, for I intend to pass through Macedonia, 6 [but]ʲ perhaps I will stay with you or [even]ᵏ spend the winter, so that you may help me on my journey, wherever I go.

7 [For]ˡ I do not want to see you now just in passing. I hope to spend some time with you, if the Lord permits.

8 But I will stay in Ephesus until Pentecost, 9 for a wide door for effective work has opened to me, and there are many adversaries.

10 If Timothy comes, see that he may be with you without fear, for he is doing the work of the Lord, as I also am. 11 Let no one despise him. Help him on his way in peace, that he may return to me, for I am expecting him [with the brothers].ᵐ

12 Now concerning our brother [Apollos],ⁿ I strongly urged him to visit you with the other brothers, but it was not at all his will to come now. He will come when he has opportunity.

13 Be watchful, stand firm in the faith, act like men, be strong.

14 Let all that you do be done in love.

ᵃ 15:51, **indeed:** Included in ℵ(01) A(02) BYZ TR ‖ Absent from 𝔓46 B(03) C(04) NA28 SBLGNT THGNT.

ᵇ 15:51, **not:** Absent from ℵ(01). Likely an error.

ᶜ 15:52, **as:** Included in C(04).

ᵈ 15:52, **be raised:** Some manuscripts read "rise up." A(02).

ᵉ 15:54, **this corruptible has put on incorruption, and:** Absent from 𝔓46 ℵ(01) C(04).

ᶠ 15:54, Isaiah 25:8.

ᵍ 15:55, **O Death, where is your victory:** Absent from ℵ(01) A(02).

ʰ 15:55, **O Death, where is your sting:** Some manuscripts read "O Hades, where is your victory." BYZ TR.

ⁱ 15:55 Hosea 13:14 LXX.

ʲ 16:6, **but:** Absent from 𝔓46.

ᵏ 16:6, **even:** Absent from 𝔓46 B(03).

ˡ 16:7, **For:** Some manuscripts read "But." BYZ TR.

ᵐ 16:11, **with the brothers:** Absent from B(03).

ⁿ 16:12, **Apollos:** Absent from ℵ(01).

15 I urge you, brothers and sisters; you know the household of Stephanas, [[and Fortunatus, and Achaicus,]]ᵃ that it is the firstfruits of Achaia and they have devoted themselves to the service of the saints; 16 so that you also may submit to such people and to everyone who works and labors.

17 I rejoice at the coming of Stephanas and Fortunatus and Achaicus, because they have made up for your absence, 18 for they refreshed my spirit as well as yours. Give recognition to such people.

19 [[All]]ᵇ [The churches of Asia]ᶜ [send you greetings.]ᵈ Aquila and {Prisca},ᵉ together with the church in their house, greet you much in the Lord.

20 All the brothers {send you greetings}.ᶠ Greet one another with a holy kiss.

21 I, Paul, write this greeting with my own hand.

22 If anyone does not love the Lord [[Jesus Christ]],ᵍ let that person be cursed. Maranatha.ʰ

23 The grace of the Lord Jesus [[Christ]]ⁱ be with you.

24 My love be with you all in Christ Jesus. [[Amen]]ʲᵏ

ᵃ 16:15, **and Fortunatus, and Achaicus:** Included in C(04).

ᵇ 16:19, **All:** Included in C(04).

ᶜ 16:19, **The churches of Asia:** Absent from 𝔓46.

ᵈ 16:19, **send you greetings:** Absent from 𝔓46 A(02).

ᵉ 16:19, **Prisca:** 𝔓46 ℵ(01) B(03) NA28 SBLGNT THGNT ‖ Some manuscripts read "Priscilla." C(04) BYZ TR.

ᶠ 16:20, **send you greetings:** A(02) reads "greet you."

ᵍ 16:22, **Jesus Christ:** Included in BYZ TR.

ʰ 16:22, **Maranatha:** An Aramaism meaning "Come, O Lord."

ⁱ 16:23, **Christ:** Included in A(02) C(04) BYZ TR ‖ Absent from ℵ(01) B(03).

ʲ 16:24, **Amen:** Included in ℵ(01) A(02) C(04) THGNT BYZ TR ‖ Absent from B(03) NA28 SBLGNT.

ᵏ 16:24 TR includes the postscript, "First letter to the Corinthians was written from Philippi through Stephanas and Fortunatus and Achaicus and Timothy."

Second Corinthians[a]

1 [1] Paul, an apostle of {Christ[b] Jesus}[c] by the will of God, and Timothy our brother, to the church of God that is in Corinth, together with all the saints who are in the whole of Achaia:

[2] Grace to you and peace from God our Father and the Lord Jesus Christ.

[3] Blessed is the God and Father of our Lord Jesus Christ, the Father of mercies and God of all comfort, [4] who comforts us in all our affliction so that we may be able to comfort those in any affliction with the comfort with which we ourselves are comforted by God.

[5] For just as the sufferings of Christ abound in us, so also through Christ [our][d] comfort abounds.

[6] Whether we are afflicted, it is for your encouragement [and salvation];[e] [Whether we are encouraged,][f] It is for your encouragement which is at work in the endurance of the same sufferings [of which we also suffer.][g] [7] [And our hope for you is firm, knowing that as you are sharers of the sufferings,][h] so also *you are* of the encouragement.[i] [[And our hope is firm concerning you; whether we are comforted, it is for your encouragement and salvation.]][j]

[8] For we do not want you to be ignorant, brothers, concerning our affliction that happened [[to us]][k] in Asia, that we were burdened excessively, beyond our strength, so that we despaired even of living. [9] But we ourselves have held the sentence of death within us, so that we might not[l] trust in ourselves but in God who raises the dead, [10] who has delivered us from such a deadly peril [, and he will deliver us];[m] in him we have placed our hope [that][n] he will also yet deliver us, [11] as you [also][o] help together by prayer for us, so that the gift to us by means of many persons may be thankfully acknowledged by many on our behalf.

[12] For our boasting is this, the testimony of our conscience, that in simplicity and sincerity of God, [and][p] not in fleshly wisdom but in the grace of God, we conducted ourselves in the world, and more abundantly toward you. [13] For we write no other things to you than what you read [or][q] also recognize; and I hope that you will recognize them fully [[even]][r] until the end, [14] Just as you also recognized us in part, that we are your boast, just as

---

[a] 1:0, **Title ("Second Corinthians"):** Absent from ℵ(01) B(03). ‖ 𝔓46 A(02) reads "To Corinthians Two." ‖ TR reads "Of Paul the apostle, the second letter to the Corinthians."

[b] 1:1, **Christ:** See footnote for Christ in Luke 2:11.

[c] 1:1, **Christ Jesus:** Some manuscripts read "Jesus Christ." BYZ TR.

[d] 1:5, **our:** Absent from 𝔓46.

[e] 1:6, **and salvation:** Absent from B(03).

[f] 1:6, **Whether we are encouraged:** Absent from B(03) BYZ TR.

[g] 1:6, **of which we also suffer:** Absent from 𝔓46.

[h] 1:7, **And our hope for you is firm, knowing that as you are sharers of the sufferings:** Absent from 𝔓45.

[i] 1:7, The word order of verses 6-7 varies between BYZ, TR and earlier manuscripts.

[j] 1:7, **And our hope is firm…:** Included in TR.

[k] 1:8, **to us:** Included in BYZ TR.

[l] 1:9, **not:** Absent from 𝔓46. Likely an error.

[m] 1:10, **and he will deliver us:** Absent from A(02).

[n] 1:10, **that:** Absent from 𝔓46 B(03).

[o] 1:11, **also:** Absent from 𝔓46.

[p] 1:12, **and:** 𝔓46 B(03) NA28[] ‖ Absent from ℵ(01) A(02) C(04) BYZ TR SBLGNT THGNT.

[q] 1:13, **or:** Absent from 𝔓46.

[r] 1:13, **even:** Included in BYZ TR.

you also are ours, in the day of [our]ᵃ Lord Jesus.

15 And in this confidence I intended to come to you [before],ᵇ so that you might have a second grace, 16 and through you to pass into Macedonia, and again from Macedonia to come to you, and to be sent on my way to Judea by you.

17 Therefore, when I was intending this, did I use lightness? Or do I plan according to the flesh, so that with me there should be "Yes, yes" and "No, no"? 18 But as God is faithful, that our word to you is not [[become]]ᶜ "Yes" and "No." 19 For the Son of God, {Jesus Christ},ᵈ who was preached among you by us, by me and Silvanus and Timothy, was not "Yes" and "No," but in him has been "Yes." 20 For as may of the promises of God in him are "Yes"; therefore also {through}ᵉ him is the "Amen" to the glory of God through us.

21 Now the one who establishes us together with you in Christ and anointedᶠ us is God, 22 who also sealed us and gave the down payment of the Spirit in our hearts.

23 But I call upon God as witness against my soul, that to spare you I did not come again to Corinth. 24 Not that we lord it over your faith, but we are fellow workers for your joy; for by faith you stand.

2 1 {For}ᵍ I decided this for myself, not to come again to you in sorrow. 2 For if I cause you sorrow, who is there to cheer me if not the one who is made sorrowful by me?

3 And I wrote [[to you]]ʰ this very thing, so that when I come, I may not have sorrow from those who ought to make me rejoice, having confidence in all of you that my joy is the joy of all of you. 4 For out of much affliction and anguish of heart I wrote to you with many tears, not that you should be grieved, but that you might know the love which I have more abundantly for you.

5 But if anyone has caused sorrow, it is not me they have caused sorrow, but to some extent (that I may not be a burden)ⁱ all of you.

6 Sufficient for such a one is this punishment which was inflicted by the majority, 7 so that on the contrary you should [rather]ʲ forgive and comfort, lest somehow such a one be overwhelmed by excessive sorrow. 8 Therefore I urge you to reaffirm your love for him. 9 For to this end also I wrote, in order that I might know your proven character, whether you are obedient in all things.

10 To whom you forgive anything, I also forgive. For indeed, what I have forgiven, if I have forgiven anything, it was for your sake in the presence of Christ, 11 so that we might not be taken advantage of by Satan; for we are not ignorant of his schemes.

12 Now when I came to Troas for the gospel of Christ and a door was opened for me in the Lord, 13 I had no rest in my spirit because I did not find Titus my brother; but taking my leave of them, I went on to Macedonia.

ᵃ 1:14, **our:** Absent from A(02) C(04) BYZ TR.

ᵇ 1:15, **before:** Absent from ℵ(01).

ᶜ 1:18, **become:** Absent from BYZ TR.

ᵈ 1:19, **Jesus Christ:** Some manuscripts read "Christ Jesus." ℵ(01) A(02) C(04).

ᵉ 1:20, **through:** Some manuscripts read "in." C(04) BYZ TR.

ᶠ 1:21, **anointed:** The Greek word means anoint in our literature only in a figurative sense of an anointing by God setting a person apart for special service under divine direction... God anoints (a) David, (b) Jesus, the Christ for his work or mission, (c) the prophets, (d) the apostles or, more probably, all Christians (at baptism or through the Spirit) 1 Cor 1:21. (BDAG, χρίω).

ᵍ 2:1, **For:** Some manuscripts read "But." ℵ(01) A(02) C(04) BYZ TR.

ʰ 2:3, **to you:** Included in 𝔓46 ℵ(01) A(02) BYZ TR.

ⁱ 2:5, **that I may not be a burden:** Or, "that I am not being severe."

ʲ 2:7, **rather:** Absent from A(02) B(03).

14 [[But]]ᵃ Thanks be to God, who always leads us in triumph in Christ [[Jesus]],ᵇ and manifests through us the fragrance of the knowledge of him in every place. 15 For we are the aroma of Christ to God among those who are being saved and among those who are perishing, 16 to the one an aroma from death to death, to the other an aroma from life to life. And who is sufficient for these things?

17 For we are not like the {many},ᶜ peddling the word of God, but as from sincerity, but as from God, before God, in Christ we speak.

3 1 Do we begin again to commend ourselves? {Or do we}ᵈ need, as some do, letters [[of recommendation]]ᵉ to you or from you?

2 You are our letter, written on our hearts, known and read by all men; 3 being revealed that you are a letter of Christ, ministered by us, [[and]]ᶠ written not with ink but with the Spirit of the living God, not on tablets of stone but on tablets of human hearts.

4 Such confidence we have through Christ toward God.

5 Not that we are sufficient of ourselves to think anything [as]ᵍ of ourselves, but our sufficiency is from God, 6 who also made us sufficient as ministers of a new covenant, not of the letter but of the Spirit; for the letter kills, but the Spirit gives life.

7 Now if the ministry of {death},ʰ engraved in letters on stones, came with glory, so that the sons of Israel could not look intently at the face of Moses because of the glory of his face, which was fading away, 8 how will the ministry of the Spirit not be even more glorious? 9 For if the ministry of condemnation had glory, much more does the ministry of righteousness abound in glory.

10 For indeed, what had been glorious in this case has not been glorified on account of the surpassing glory. 11 For if that which fades away was with glory, much more that which remains is in glory.

12 Therefore, having such a hope, we use great boldness, 13 and not like Moses, who put a veil over his face so that the sons of Israel would not look intently {at the end}ⁱ of what was fading away. 14 But their minds were hardened. For until this very day the same veil remains upon the reading of the old covenant, not being unveiled, because it is abolished in Christ. 15 But to this day, whenever Moses is read, a veil lies over their hearts; 16 but whenever one turns to the Lord, the veil is taken away.

17 Now the Lord is the Spirit; and where the Spirit of the Lord is, there is freedom.

18 And we [all],ʲ with unveiled faces, beholding the glory of the Lord as in a mirror, are being transformed into the same image from glory to glory, just as from the Lord, the Spirit.

ᵃ 2:14, **but:** Absent from 𝔓46.

ᵇ 2:14, **Jesus:** Included in 𝔓46.

ᶜ 2:17, **many:** Some manuscripts read "others." 𝔓46 BYZ.

ᵈ 3:1, **Or do we:** Some manuscripts read "If we do." A(02) BYZ TR.

ᵉ 3:1, **of recommendation:** Included in BYZ TR.

ᶠ 3:3, **and:** Included in 𝔓46 B(03).

ᵍ 3:5, **as:** Absent from C(04).

ʰ 3:7, **death:** ℵ(01) reads "God."

ⁱ 3:13, **at the end:** A(02) reads "toward the face."

ʲ 3:18, **all** Absent from 𝔓46.

4 ¹ Therefore, having this ministry, as we have received mercy, we do not lose heart.

² But we have renounced the hidden things of shame, not walking in craftiness nor handling the word of God deceitfully, but by the manifestation of the truth commending ourselves to every man's conscience in the sight of God.

³ [And]ᵃ Even if our gospel is veiled, it is veiled to those who are perishing, ⁴ in whom the god of this age has blinded the minds of the unbelieving, so that they might not see the light of the gospel of the glory of {Christ},ᵇ who is the image of God.

⁵ For we do not proclaim ourselves, but {Christ Jesus}ᶜ as Lord, and ourselves as your servants for Jesus' sake.

⁶ For God, who said, "Out of darkness light shall shine,"ᵈ is the one who shone in our hearts for the illumination of the knowledge of the glory of {God}ᵉ in the face [of Jesus]ᶠ Christ.

⁷ But we have this treasure in earthen vessels, so that the surpassing power may be of God and not from us; ⁸ being pressed in every way but not crushed, being perplexed {but}ᵍ not in despair, ⁹ being persecuted but not abandoned, being struck down but not destroyed, ¹⁰ always carrying around in the body the dying of [[the Lord]]ʰ Jesus, so that the life of Jesus [[Christ]]ⁱ may also be revealed in our body.

¹¹ For we who live are always being delivered over to death for Jesus' sake, so that the life of {Jesus}ʲ [also]ᵏ may be manifested in our mortal flesh. ¹² So then, [[indeed]]ˡ death is at work in us, but life in you.

¹³ And having the same spirit of faith, according to what is written, "I believed, therefore I spoke,"ᵐ we also believe, therefore we also speak, ¹⁴ knowing that he who raised [the Lord]ⁿ Jesus will raise us also {with}ᵒ Jesus and will present us with you.

¹⁵ For all things are for your sake, so that the grace, having abounded through the many, may cause thanksgiving to overflow to the glory of God.

¹⁶ Therefore we do not lose heart, but even if our outer person is being destroyed, yet {our}ᵖ inner person is being renewed day by day.

¹⁷ For {our}ᵠ momentary light affliction is producing for us, beyond all measure [unto surpassing measure],ʳ an eternal weight of glory, ¹⁸ as we look not at the things which are seen, but at the things which are not seen; for the things which are seen are temporary, but the things which are not seen are eternal.

ᵃ 4:3, **And:** Absent from 𝔓46.

ᵇ 4:4, **Christ:** C(04) reads "Lord."

ᶜ 4:5, **Christ Jesus:** Some manuscripts read "Jesus Christ." B(03) BYZ TR NA28.

ᵈ 4:6, Genesis 1:3, Psalm 112:4.

ᵉ 4:6, **God:** Some manuscripts read "him." 𝔓46 C(04).

ᶠ 4:6, **of Jesus:** Absent from A(02) B(03) SBLGNT.

ᵍ 4:8, **but:** 𝔓46 reads "and."

ʰ 4:10, **the Lord:** Included in BYZ TR.

ⁱ 4:10, **Christ:** Included in 𝔓46.

ʲ 4:11, **Jesus:** 𝔓46 reads "the Son."

ᵏ 4:11, **also:** Included in C(04).

ˡ 4:12, **indeed:** Included in BYZ TR.

ᵐ 4:13, Psalm 116:10 LXX.

ⁿ 4:14, **the Lord:** Absent from 𝔓46 B(03).

ᵒ 4:14, **with:** Some manuscripts read "through." BYZ TR.

ᵖ 4:16, **our:** Some manuscripts read "the." BYZ TR.

ᵠ 4:17, **our:** Some manuscripts read "the." 𝔓46 B(03).

ʳ 4:17, **unto surpassing measure:** Absent from ℵ(01).

5 ¹For we know that if our earthly house, the tent, is destroyed, we have a building from God, a house not made with hands, eternal in the heavens. ²And indeed, in this we groan, longing to put on our dwelling from heaven, ³if indeed, having {taken it off},ᵃ we will not be found naked.

⁴For indeed, we who are in this tent groan, being burdened, because we do not want to be unclothed but clothed, so that the mortal may be swallowed up by life.

⁵Now the one who has prepared us for this very thing is God, who has given us the down payment of the Spirit.

⁶Therefore, we are always confident and know that while we are at home in the body, we are away from the Lord; ⁷for we walk by faith, not by sight.

⁸We are confident, yes, and prefer rather to be away from the body and to be at home with the Lord. ⁹Therefore, we [also]ᵇ make it our aim, whether at home or away, to be pleasing to him.

¹⁰For we must all appear before the judgment seat of Christ, so that each one may receive what is due for what he has done inᶜ the body, whether good or {bad}.ᵈ

¹¹Knowing therefore the fear of the Lord, we persuade men, but we are made manifest to God; and I hope also to be made manifest in your consciences.

¹²[[For]]ᵉ We are not commending ourselves to you again, but giving you an opportunity for boasting on our behalf, so that you may have something to say to those who boast in appearance and not in heart. ¹³For if we are out of our minds, it is for God; if we are in our right minds, it is for you.

¹⁴For the love of {Christ}ᶠ compels us, having concluded this: that [[if]]ᵍ one died for all, therefore all [died];ʰ ¹⁵And He died for all , so that those who live should no longer live for themselves, but for the one who died and was raised for them.

¹⁶So from now on, we regard no one according to the flesh; even if we have known Christ according to the flesh, yet now we know him in this way no longer.

¹⁷So if anyone is in Christ, a new creation; the old things have passed away, behold, {new things have come}.ⁱ ¹⁸And all these things are from God, who reconciled us to himself through [[Jesus]]ʲ Christ and gave us the ministry of reconciliation, ¹⁹as that God was in Christ reconciling the world to himself, not counting their trespasses against them and entrusting to us the {message}ᵏ of reconciliation.

²⁰[Therefore,]ˡ We are ambassadors for Christ, as though God were making his appeal through us; we implore you on behalf of Christ, be reconciled to God.

²¹[[For]]ᵐ The one not knowing sin, for our sake, was made sin, so that we might become the righteousness of God in him.

ᵃ 5:3, **taken it off:** Some manuscripts read "put on it." 𝔓46 ℵ(01) B(03) BYZ TR.

ᵇ 5:9, **also:** Absent from 𝔓46.

ᶜ 5:10, **in:** Or "through."

ᵈ 5:10, **bad:** Some manuscripts read "evil." 𝔓46 B(03) BYZ TR.

ᵉ 5:12, **For:** Included in BYZ TR.

ᶠ 5:14, **Christ:** C(04) reads "God."

ᵍ 5:14, **if:** Included in C(04) BYZ TR.

ʰ 5:14, **died:** Absent from 𝔓46.

ⁱ 5:17, **new things have come:** Some manuscripts read "all things have become new." BYZ TR.

ʲ 5:18, **Jesus:** Included in BYZ TR.

ᵏ 5:19, **message:** 𝔓46 reads "Gospel" meaning good news.

ˡ 5:20, **Therefore:** Absent from 𝔓46.

ᵐ 5:21, **For:** Included in BYZ TR.

6 ¹ And working together, we also urge you not to receive the grace of God in vain; ² for he says, "In an acceptable time I listened to you, and in a day of salvation I helped you."ᵃ

Behold, now is the favorable time; behold, now is the day of salvation: ³ giving no cause for offense in anything, so that the ministry may not be discredited, ⁴ but in everything commending ourselves as servants of God, in great endurance, in afflictions, in hardships, in distresses, ⁵ in beatings, in imprisonments, in disturbances, in labors, in sleeplessness, in fastings, ⁶ in purity, in knowledge, in patience, in kindness, in the Holy Spirit, in genuine love, ⁷ in the word of truth, in the power of God; with the weapons of righteousness for the right hand and the left, ⁸ through glory and dishonor, through slander and praise; as deceivers and [[behold]]ᵇ yet true, ⁹ as unknown and yet well-known, as dying and behold, we live, as disciplined and yet not put to death, ¹⁰ as sorrowful yet always rejoicing, as poor yet making many rich, as having nothing and yet possessing everything.

¹¹ Our mouth has spoken openly to you, Corinthians, our heart is wide open. ¹² You are not restricted by us, but you are restricted in your own affections. ¹³ Now in the same way as a fair exchange, I speak as to children, open wide your hearts also.

¹⁴ Do not be unequally yoked with unbelievers; for what partnership have righteousness and lawlessness, {or}ᶜ what fellowship has light with darkness?

¹⁵ What agreement has Christ with Belial,ᵈ or what portion does a believer share with an unbeliever?

¹⁶ What agreement has the temple of God with idols? For {we}ᵉ are the temple of the living God; just as God said, "I will dwell in them and walk among them; and I will be their God, and they shall be my people."ᶠ

¹⁷ "Therefore, come out from among them and be separate," says the Lord, and "do not touch anything unclean; and I will receive you."ᵍ

¹⁸ "And I will be a Father to you, and you shall be sons and daughters to me," says the Lord Almighty.ʰ

7 ¹ Therefore, having these promises, beloved, let us cleanse ourselves from every defilement of flesh and spirit, perfecting holiness in the fear of God.

² Make room for us; we have wronged no one, we have corrupted no one, we have taken advantage of no one. ³ I do not say this to condemn; for I have said before that you are in our hearts, to die together and to live together. ⁴ Great is my boldness toward you, great is my boasting on your behalf; I am filled with encouragement, I am overflowing with joy in all our affliction.

⁵ For when we came into Macedonia, our flesh had no rest, but we were afflicted in every way: battles on the outside, fears within. ⁶ But God, who comforts the humble, comforted us by the coming of Titus, ⁷ and not only by his coming but also by the comfort with which he was comforted by you, as he told us of your longing, your mourning, your zeal for me, so that I rejoiced still more.

⁸ For even if I caused you sorrow with my letter, I do not regret it; even if I did regret it, I see [for]ⁱ that letter,

---

ᵃ 6:2, Isaiah 49:8 LXX.

ᵇ 6:8, **behold:** Included in 𝔓46.

ᶜ 6:14, **or:** Some manuscripts read "and." BYZ TR.

ᵈ 6:15, **Belial:** Or Beliar. A term occurring in the Hebrew Bible and later Jewish and Christian texts to refer to the devil or a wicked person. It is often used as a personification of wickedness.

ᵉ 6:16, **we:** Some manuscripts read "you." 𝔓46 BYZ TR.

ᶠ 6:16, Leviticus 26:12, Jeremiah 32:38, Ezekiel 37:27.

ᵍ 6:17, Isaiah 52:11, Ezekiel 20:34, 41.

ʰ 6:18, 2 Samuel 7:8, 14.

ⁱ 7:8, **for:** Absent from 𝔓46 𝔓117 B(03).

even if for a short time, caused you sorrow. 9 As it is, I rejoice, not because you were grieved, but because you were grieved into repentance; for you felt a godly grief, so that you suffered no loss through us.

10 For godly grief {works}[a] a repentance that leads to salvation without regret, whereas worldly grief produces death.

11 For see what earnestness this godly grief has produced in you, but also what eagerness to clear yourselves, what indignation, what fear, what longing, what zeal, what punishment! At every point you have proved yourselves innocent in the matter. 12 So although I wrote to you, it was not on account of the one who did the wrong, nor on account of the one who suffered the wrong, but in order that your earnestness for us might be revealed to you in the sight of God. 13 Because of this, we are comforted.

And besides {our}[b] own comfort, we rejoiced still more at the joy of Titus, because his spirit has been refreshed by you all. 14 For whatever boast I made to him about you, I was not put to shame; but just as everything we said to you was true, so also our boasting before Titus has proved true. 15 And his affection for you is even greater, as he remembers the obedience of you [all],[c] how you received him with fear and trembling. 16 I rejoice, because I have complete confidence in you.

8 1 Now we make known to you, brothers, the grace of God that has been given in the churches of Macedonia, 2 that in a great trial of affliction, the abundance of their joy and their deep poverty overflowed in the wealth of their generosity.

3 For according to their ability, I testify, and beyond their ability, they gave voluntarily, 4 with much urging, requesting from us [[to receive]][d] the grace and the fellowship of the ministry to the saints, 5 and not as we had hoped, but they gave themselves first to {the Lord}[e] and to us by the will of God, 6 so that we might encourage Titus, that as he had begun, so he would also complete among you this gracious work.

7 But just as in everything you excel, in faith and word and knowledge and all eagerness and the love from {us in you},[f] so that you may also excel in this grace.

8 Not by command do I say this, but through the eagerness of others and testing the genuineness of your love; 9 for you know the grace of our Lord Jesus [Christ],[g] that for your sake he became poor, being rich, so that you through his poverty might become rich.

10 And in this matter I give my advice: for this is advantageous for you, who not only began to do, but also to desire from last year. 11 Now also complete the doing, so that just as there was the eagerness to desire, so also there may be the completion from what you have.

12 For if the eagerness is present, it is acceptable according to what one has, not according to what one does not have. 13 For it is not that there should be relief for others and affliction for you, but rather from equality; 14 at the present time your abundance for their need, so that their abundance may also be for your need, in order that there may be equality, 15 as it is written, "He who gathered much did not have too much, and he who gathered little did not have too little."[h]

---

a 7:10, **works:** Some manuscripts read "produces." BYZ TR.
b 7:13, **our:** Some manuscripts read "your." BYZ TR.
c 7:15, **all:** Absent from ℵ(01).
d 8:4, **to receive:** Included in TR.
e 8:5, **the Lord:** 𝔓45 reads "God."
f 8:7, **us in you:** Some manuscripts read "you in us." ℵ(01) C(04) BYZ TR.
g 8:9, **Christ:** Absent from B(03).
h 8:15, Exodus 16:18.

16 But thanks be to God who put the same earnest care for you into the heart of Titus, 17 for he not only accepted the exhortation, but being more diligent, he went to you of his own accord.

18 And we have sent with him the brother whose praise is in the gospel throughout all the churches, 19 not only that, but also having been appointed by the churches as {our}[a] traveling companion, together {with}[b] this grace that is being ministered by us for the glory of the Lord and {our}[c] eagerness, 20 taking precaution in this, so that no one may find fault with us in this generous undertaking being administered by us; 21 [for][d] we are intent on doing what is right, not only in the sight of {the Lord},[e] but also in the sight of men.

22 We have sent with them our brother, whom we have tested many times in many ways as being diligent, but now [much][f] more diligent because of the great confidence he has in you. 23 Whether for Titus, my partner and fellow worker for you; or for our brothers, apostles of the churches, the glory of {Christ}.[g]

24 Therefore, show the proof of your love and our boasting about you to them, in the presence of the churches.

9 ¹ Now concerning the ministry to the saints, it is superfluous[h] for me to write to you; 2 for I know your eagerness, which I boast about on your behalf to the Macedonians, that Achaia has been prepared since last year, and your zeal has stirred up most of them.

3 So I sent the brothers, in order that our boasting about you might not be made empty in this respect, so that, just as I was saying, you would be prepared, 4 lest perhaps, if Macedonians come with me and find you unprepared, we (not to mention you) would be put to shame in this confidence [[of boasting]].[i] 5 Therefore, I considered it necessary to urge the brothers to go ahead to you and arrange in advance the generous gift you have promised beforehand, so that it may be ready as a generous gift and not as an act of greed.

6 The point is this: whoever sows sparingly will also reap sparingly, and whoever sows bountifully will also reap bountifully. 7 Each one must give as he {has decided}[j] in his heart, not reluctantly or under compulsion, for God loves a cheerful giver.

8 And God is able to make all grace abound to you, so that in all things at all times, having all sufficiency, you may abound in every good work, 9 as it is written, "He has scattered abroad, he has given to the poor, his righteousness endures forever."[k]

10 Now the one who supplies seed to the sower and bread for food will supply and multiply your seed and increase the harvest of your righteousness; 11 being enriched in everything for all generosity, which produces thanksgiving to God through us; 12 For the ministry of this service is not only supplying the needs of the saints, but also overflowing through many thanksgivings to {God}.[l]

13 Through the proof of this ministry, they glorify God for your submission to the confession of the gospel of Christ and for the simplicity of your fellowship with them and with

---

a 8:19, **our:** C(04) reads "your."

b 8:19, **with:** B(03) reads "in."

c 8:19, **our:** TR reads "your."

d 8:21, **for:** Absent from BYZ TR.

e 8:21, **the Lord:** 𝔓46 reads "God."

f 8:22, **much:** Absent from 𝔓46.

g 8:23, **Christ:** C(04) reads "the Lord."

h 9:1, **superfluous:** Or, unnecessary

i 9:4, **of boasting:** Included in BYZ TR.

j 9:7, **has decided:** Some manuscripts read "decides." BYZ TR.

k 9:9, Psalm 112:9.

l 9:12, **God:** B(03) reads "Christ."

all. 14 And in their prayers for you, they long for you because of the surpassing grace of God upon you. 15 [[But]]ᵃ Thanks to God for his indescribable gift.

10 1 But I myself, Paul, urge you by the gentleness and forbearance of Christ, who in presence am humble among you, but being absent am bold toward you; 2 and I ask that when I am not present, I may be bold with the confidence with which I think to be daring against some who consider us as walking according to the flesh.

3 For though we walk in the flesh, we do not wage war according to the flesh, 4 for the weapons of our warfare are not of the flesh but powerful for God for the demolition of strongholds, destroying reasoningsᵇ 5 and every high thing that is exalted against the knowledge of God, and taking captive every thought to the obedience of Christ, 6 And being ready to punish every disobedience, whenever your obedience is fulfilled [[beforehand]].ᶜ

7 Look at what is before your eyes. If anyone {is}ᵈ confident inᵉ himself to be of Christ, let him consider this again in himself, that just as he is of Christ, so also are we [[Christ's]].ᶠ 8 For if indeed I should boast somewhat more about our authority, which the Lord gave [[us]]ᵍ for building up and not for tearing you down, I will not be ashamed.

9 So that I may notʰ appear as if I were trying to frighten you with my letters. 10 Because as he says, "The letters are weighty and strong, but his bodily presence is weak, and his speech is of no account." 11 Let such a person consider this, that what we are in word through letters when absent, such we will be in deed when present.

12 For we do not dare to classify {or compare ourselves}ⁱ with some of those who commend themselves, [[putting themselves to death,]]ʲ [but they, measuring themselves]ᵏ by themselves and comparing themselves with themselves, do not understand. 13 But we will not boast beyond limits, but according to the measure of the ruleˡ which God has apportioned to us, a measure to reach even to you.

14 For we are not overextending ourselves, as though we did not reach you, for we were the first to come even as far as you in the gospel of Christ. 15 We do not boast beyond measure in the labors of others, but we have hope that as your faith increases, our influence among you may be greatly enlarged, according to our rule, 16 so as to preach the gospel in the regions beyond you, not to boast in another's rule of things already accomplished.

17 But let the one who boasts, boast in the Lord;ᵐ 18 for it is not the one who commends oneself who is approved, but the one whom the Lord commends.

ᵃ 9:15, **But:** Included in BYZ TR.

ᵇ 10:4, **reasonings:** Or sophistries. That is, thoughts and sentiments. In this context "sophistries," is an appropriate meaning (BDAG). Later manuscripts include "destroying reasonings" at the beginning of verse 5.

ᶜ 10:6, **beforehand:** Included in C(04).

ᵈ 10:7, **is:** B(03) reads "seems to be."

ᵉ 10:7, **in:** Some manuscripts read "from." C(04) BYZ TR.

ᶠ 10:7, **Christ's:** Included in BYZ TR.

ᵍ 10:8, **us:** Included in BYZ TR.

ʰ 10:9, **So that I may not:** That is, "I would rather not."

ⁱ 10:12, **or compare ourselves:** 𝔓46 reads "themselves."

ʲ 10:12, **putting themselves to death:** Included in 𝔓46.

ᵏ 10:12, **but they, measuring themselves:** Absent from 𝔓46.

ˡ 10:13, **rule:** Or "sphere."

ᵐ 10:17, Jeremiah 9:24.

11 1 I wish you would bear with me in a little foolishness; but indeed, bear with me. 2 For I am jealous for you with a godly jealousy; for I betrothed you to one husband, to present you as a pure virgin to Christ. 3 But I am afraid that, as the serpent deceived Eve by his cunning, [[thus]]ᵃ your thoughts may be corrupted from the simplicity [and the purity]ᵇ that is in Christ.

4 For if the one coming proclaims another Jesus whom we did not proclaim, or you receive a different spirit which you did not receive, or a different gospel which you did not accept, you put up with it well.

5 For I consider myself not at all inferior to the most eminent apostles. 6 But even if I am unskilled in speech, yet not in knowledge [; but in every way we have made this evident to you in all things].ᶜ

7 Or did I commit a sin by humbling myself so that you might be exalted, because I preached the gospel of God to you without charge? 8 I robbed other churches by taking support from them for your service, 9 [and]ᵈ when I was with you and in need, I did not burden anyone; for my need was supplied by the brothers who came from Macedonia, and in everything I kept myself from being a burden to you, and I will continue to do so.

10 As the truth of Christ is in me, this boasting of mine will not be stopped in the regions of Achaia. 11 Why? [Because]ᵉ I do not love you? God knows.

12 What I do, and will do, is to cut off the opportunity [of those who desire an opportunity],ᶠ so that in what they boast, they may be found just as we are. 13 For such people are false apostles, deceitful workers, disguising themselves as apostles of Christ. 14 And no wonder, for even Satan disguises himself as an angel of light. 15 Therefore it is not surprising if his servants also disguise themselves as servants of righteousness, whose end will be according to their deeds.

16 Again I say, let no one think me to be foolish; but if you do, accept me as foolish, so that I too may boast a little. 17 What I speak, I do not speak according to the Lord, but as in foolishness, in this confidence of boasting. 18 Since many boast according to the flesh, I too will boast.

19 For you, being so wise, gladly bear with the foolish. 20 For you bear with it if someone enslaves you, if someone devours you, if someone takes from you, if someone exalts themselves, if someone strikes [[you]]ᵍ in the face.

21 I speak in foolishness, as though we have become weak. But in whatever anyone else dares to boast (I am speaking foolishly) I also dare. 22 Are they Hebrews? So am I. Are they Israelites? So am I. Are they descendants of Abraham? So am I. 23 Servants of Christ are they? (I speak as one beside himself) I am more so: in labors more abundantly, in prisons more abundantly, in stripes exceedingly,ʰ in deaths many times.

24 Five times I received from the Jews forty lashes minus one, 25 three times I was beaten with rods, once I was stoned, three times I was shipwrecked, a night and a day I have spent in the deep; 26 on frequent journeys, in dangers from rivers, dangers from robbers, dangers from my own people, dangers from the Gentiles, dangers in the city, dangers in the

---

ᵃ 11:3, **thus:** Included in BYZ TR.

ᵇ 11:3, **and the purity:** Absent from 𝔓46 BYZ TR.

ᶜ 11:6, **but in every way we have made this evident to you in all things:** Absent from 𝔓46.

ᵈ 11:9, **and:** Absent from 𝔓46.

ᵉ 11:11, **Because:** Absent from B(03).

ᶠ 11:12, **of those who desire an opportunity:** Absent from 𝔓46.

ᵍ 11:20, **you:** Included in BYZ TR.

ʰ 11:23, **stripes exceedingly:** Or, severe beatings.

wilderness, dangers at sea, dangers among false brothers; 27 {with}[a] toil and hardship, through many sleepless nights, in hunger and thirst, often without food, in cold and exposure. 28 Apart from other things, there is the daily pressure on me of my concern for all the churches. 29 Who is weak, and I am not weak? Who is caused to stumble,[b] and I do not kindle?[c]

30 If it is necessary to boast, I will boast in [my][d] weaknesses.

31 The God and Father of {the}[e] Lord Jesus [[Christ]],[f] who is blessed forever, knows that I am not lying.

32 In Damascus, the ethnarch of King Aretas was guarding the city of the Damascenes [[waiting]][g] to seize me, 33 and through a window in a basket I was let down through the wall and escaped his hands.

12 1 {Boasting is necessary, though not beneficial};[h] , but I will proceed to visions and revelations of the Lord.

2 I know a man in Christ who fourteen years ago - whether in the body I do not know, or out of the body I do not know, God knows - such a one was caught up to the third heaven. 3 And I know such a man; whether in the body or {apart}[i] from the body [I do not know],[j] God knows 4 that he was caught up into Paradise and heard inexpressible words, which a man is not permitted to speak. 5 On behalf of such a one I will boast; but I will [not][k] boast about myself, except in {the}[l] weaknesses.

6 For if I should choose to boast, I will not be foolish, for I will speak the truth; but I refrain, lest anyone should think of me above what they see me or hear from me. 7 And because of the surpassing greatness of the revelations, [therefore,][m] so that I would not become conceited, a thorn in the flesh was given to me, an angel of Satan, to torment me [, so that I would not become conceited].[n] 8 Concerning this, I pleaded with the Lord three times that it might depart from me.

9 And he has said to me, "My grace is sufficient for you, for [[my]][o] power is perfected in weakness." Therefore, I will most gladly boast in [my][p] weaknesses, so that the power of Christ may dwell upon me. 10 For this reason, I take pleasure in weaknesses, in insults, in necessities, [in persecutions, {and}[q] distresses][r] for the sake of Christ; for when I am weak, then I am strong.

---

[a] 11:27, **with:** Some manuscripts read "in." BYZ TR.

[b] 11:29, **stumble:** Or, be offended.

[c] 11:29, **kindle:** Or, to inflame.

[d] 11:30, **my:** Absent from B(03).

[e] 11:31, **the:** TR reads "our."

[f] 11:31, **Christ:** Included in BYZ TR.

[g] 11:32, **waiting:** Included in ℵ(01) BYZ TR.

[h] 12:1, **Boasting is necessary, though not beneficial:** Some manuscripts read "Indeed, boasting does not benefit me." BYZ TR.

[i] 12:3, **apart:** Some manuscripts read "outside." ℵ(01) BYZ TR.

[j] 12:3, **I do not know:** Absent from B(03).

[k] 12:5, **not:** Absent from ℵ(01).

[l] 12:5, **the:** Some manuscripts read "my." ℵ(01) BYZ TR.

[m] 12:7, **therefore:** Absent from 𝔓46 BYZ TR.

[n] 12:7, **so that I would not become conceited:** Absent from ℵ(01) A(02).

[o] 12:9, **the:** Some manuscripts read "my." BYZ TR.

[p] 12:9, **my:** Absent from 𝔓46.

[q] 12:10, **and:** Some manuscripts read "in." A(02) BYZ TR.

[r] 12:10, **in persecutions and distresses:** Absent from A(02).

11 I have become a fool [[in boasting]],[a] you compelled me. For I ought to have been commended by you; for I was not inferior to the most eminent apostles, even though I am nothing. 12 Indeed, the signs of an apostle were performed among you with all perseverance, {by}[b] signs and wonders and mighty deeds.

13 For in what respect were you treated as inferior to the rest of the churches, except that I myself did not burden you? Forgive me this wrong!

14 Here for this third time I am ready to come to you, and I will not be a burden [[to you]];[c] for I do not seek what is yours, but you; for children are not responsible to save up for their parents, but parents for their children. 15 I will most gladly spend and be expended for your souls. If [[even]][d] I love you more, am I to be loved less? 16 But be that as it may, I did not burden you myself; But being crafty, I took you by deceit.

17 Did I take advantage of you through any of those whom I have sent to you? 18 I urged Titus to go, and I sent the brother with him. Did Titus take advantage of you? Did we not walk in the same spirit? Did we not follow the same footsteps?

19 [[For a long time,]][e] Do you think that we have been defending ourselves to you. We speak before God [in Christ];[f] but all things, beloved, are for your edification. 20 For I fear that perhaps when I come, I may not find you as I wish, and I may be found by you as you do not wish; perhaps there will be strife, jealousy, anger, selfishness, slander, gossip, arrogance, and disorder. 21 I fear that when I come again, my God may humble me before you, and I may mourn for many who have sinned before and have not repented of the impurity, sexual immorality, and sensuality that they have practiced.

13 1 [[Behold]][g] This is the third time I am coming to you; by the mouth of two or three witnesses every word shall be established.[h]

2 I have said beforehand and I say again, as being present the second time and being absent now, [[I write them]][i] to those who have sinned before and to all the rest, that if I come again I will not spare anyone, 3 since you seek a proof of the Christ speaking in me, who is not weak toward you but is powerful in you. 4 For indeed [[if]][j] he was crucified out of weakness, but he lives by the power of God. For we also are weak {in}[k] him, but we will live with him by the power of God [toward you].[l]

5 Test yourselves to see if you are in the faith [; examine yourselves!][m] Or do you not recognize yourselves, that {Jesus Christ}[n] is in you? Unless perhaps you are disqualified? 6 But I hope that you will realize that we are not disqualified.

---

a 12:11, **in boasting:** Included in BYZ TR.

b 12:12, **by:** Some manuscripts read "in." BYZ TR.

c 12:14, **to you:** Included in BYZ TR.

d 12:15, **even:** Included in BYZ TR.

e 12:19, **For a long time:** Some manuscripts read "Again." BYZ TR.

f 12:19, **in Christ:** Absent from 𝔓46.

g 13:1, **Behold:** Included in A(02).

h 13:1, Deuteronomy 19:15.

i 13:2, **I write them:** Included in BYZ TR.

j 13:4, **if:** Included in A(02) BYZ TR.

k 13:4, **in:** Some manuscripts read "with." ℵ(01) A(02).

l 13:4, **toward you:** Absent from B(03).

m 13:5, **examine yourselves:** Absent from A(02).

n 13:5, **Jesus Christ:** Some manuscripts read "Christ Jesus." ℵ(01) A(02).

7 Now {we}[a] pray to God that you do no evil, not that we may appear approved, but that you may do what is right, even though we may appear disqualified. 8 For we have no power against the truth, but only for the truth.

9 For we rejoice when we are weak and you are strong; and this we also pray for, your equipping. 10 For this reason, I write these things while absent, so that when present, I may not use severity according to the authority which the Lord gave me for building up and not for tearing down.

11 Finally, brothers, rejoice, be perfected, be encouraged, [be of the same mind,][b] be in peace, and the God of love and peace will be with you.

12 Greet one another with a holy kiss.

13 [[All the saints greet you.]][c]

14 The grace of the Lord Jesus [Christ],[d] and the love of God, and the fellowship of the [Holy][e] Spirit be with you all. [[Amen]][fg]

---

a 13:7, **we:** Some manuscripts read "I." BYZ TR.
b 13:11, **be of the same mind:** Absent from A(02).
c 13:13, **All the saints greet you:** Included in BYZ. What follows is verse 14 in BYZ
d 13:14, **Christ:** Absent from B(03).
e 13:14, **Holy:** Absent from 𝔓46.
f 13:14, **Amen:** Included in BYZ TR.
g 13:14 TR includes the postscript, "The second letter to the Corinthians was written from Philippi, a city of Macedonia, by Titus and Luke."

Galatians[a]

1 [1] Paul, an apostle not from {men}[b] nor through man, but through Jesus Christ[c] and God the Father who raised him from the dead, [2] and all the brothers with me, to the churches of Galatia:

[3] Grace to you and peace from God our Father and the Lord Jesus Christ, [4] who gave himself for our sins, so that he might deliver us from the present evil age, according to the will of our God and Father, [5] to whom *is* the glory forever and ever,[d] amen.

[6] I am astonished that you are so quickly turning away from the one who called you in the grace [of Christ][e] to a different gospel, [7] which is not another; except there are some who are troubling you [and wanting][f] to distort the gospel of Christ.

[8] But even if we or an angel from heaven should preach [to you][g] a gospel contrary to the one we preached to you, let them be under a curse. [9] As we have said before, so now I say again: if anyone is preaching to you a gospel contrary to the one you received, let them be under a curse.

[10] For am I now seeking the approval of men, or of God? Or am I trying to please men? [[For]][h] if I were still trying to please men, I would not be a servant of Christ.

[11] For I make known to you, brothers, the gospel that was [preached][i] by me, that it is not according to man; [12] for I did not receive it from any man, nor was I taught it, but it came through a revelation of Jesus Christ.

[13] For you have heard of my former life in Judaism, how I persecuted the church of God beyond measure and tried to destroy it; [14] And I was advancing in Judaism beyond many of my contemporaries in my nation, being more exceedingly zealous for the traditions of my fathers.

[15] But when it pleased [God,][j] the one who set me apart from my mother's womb [and called me through his grace],[k] [16] to reveal His Son in me so that I might preach Him among the Gentiles, I did not immediately consult with flesh and blood, [17] Nor did I go up to Jerusalem to those who were apostles before me, but I went away to Arabia and again returned to Damascus.

[18] Then after three years I went up to Jerusalem to visit {Cephas}[l] and stayed with him fifteen days. [19] But I saw none of the other apostles except James, the Lord's brother. [20] What I am writing to you, behold, before God, I am not lying.

---

a 1:0, **Title ("Galatians"):** Absent from ℵ(01) B(03) ‖ 𝔓46 A(02) 016 BYZ reads "To the Galatians."
‖ TR reads "The letter of Paul the apostle to the Galatians."

b 1:1, **man:** Some manuscripts read "saints." I016

c 1:1, **Christ:** See footnote for Christ in Luke 2:11.

d 1:5, **forever and ever:** Or "unto the ages of the ages."

e 1:6, **of Christ:** Absent from ℵ(01) A(02) B(03).

f 1:7, **and wanting:** Absent from ℵ(01).

g 1:8, **to you:** Absent from ℵ(01).

h 1:10, **For:** Included in BYZ TR.

i 1:11, **preached:** Absent from 𝔓46.

j 1:15, **God:** Absent from 𝔓46 B(03).

k 1:15, **and called me through his grace:** Absent from 𝔓46.

l 1:18, **Cephas:** Some manuscripts read "Peter." BYZ TR.

21 Then I went into the regions of Syria and Cilicia. 22 And I was still unknown by face to the churches of Judea that are in Christ. 23 But they were only hearing that "The one who once persecuted us is now preaching the faith he once tried to destroy." 24 And they glorified God because of me.

2 ¹ Then after fourteen years, I went up again to Jerusalem with Barnabas, taking Titus along also. 2 But I went up according to a revelation, and I laid before them the gospel which I proclaim among the nations, but privately to those who are esteemed, lest somehow I run or had run in vain.

3 But not even Titus, [who was with me,]ᵃ being a Greek, was compelled to be circumcised; 4 but because of the false brothers secretly brought in, who slipped in to spy out our freedom which we have in Christ Jesus, in order to bring us into bondage, 5 to whom we did not yield [in submission]ᵇ even for an hour, so that the truth of {the gospel}ᶜ might remain with you.

6 But from those who seemed to be something - whatever they were, it makes no difference to me; God does not show favoritism to people - for those who seemed important added nothing to me, 7 but on the contrary, when they saw that I had been entrusted with the gospel of the uncircumcision, just as Peter with the circumcision, 8 for the one [who worked in Peter for the apostleship of the circumcision]ᵈ also worked in me for the Gentiles, 9 and when they recognized the grace that was given to me, James [and Cephas]ᵉ and John, those who seemed to be pillars, gave the right hand of fellowship to me and Barnabas, that we should [[indeed]]ᶠ go to the Gentiles and they to the circumcision; 10 only they asked us to remember the poor, which I also was eager to do.

11 But when {Cephas}ᵍ came to Antioch, I opposed him to his face, because he was condemned. 12 For before certain men came from James, he was eating with the Gentiles; but when they came, he withdrew and separated himself, fearing those from the circumcision. 13 And they played the hypocrite with him [and]ʰ [[all]]ⁱ the rest of the Jews, so that even Barnabas was carried away with their hypocrisy. 14 But when I saw that they were not straightforward about the truth of the gospel, I said to {Cephas}ʲ in front of them all, "If you, being a Jew, live like the Gentiles [and not like the Jews],ᵏ how do you compel the Gentiles to live [like Jews]?"ˡ

15 We are by nature Jews and not sinners from among the Gentiles; 16 knowing [however]ᵐ that a person is not justified by works of the law but through faith inⁿ {Jesus Christ},ᵒ we also have believed in {Christ Jesus},ᵖ in order that we might be {justified by faith in Christ}�q and not by works of the

---

ᵃ 2:3, **who was with me**: Absent from 𝔓46.

ᵇ 2:5, **in submission**: Absent from 𝔓46.

ᶜ 2:5, **the gospel**: 𝔓46 reads "God."

ᵈ 2:8, **who worked in Peter for the apostleship of the circumcision**: Absent from ℵ(01).

ᵉ 2:9, **and Cephas**: Absent from A(02).

ᶠ 2:9, **indeed**: Included in A(02) BYZ.

ᵍ 2:11, **Cephas**: Some manuscripts read "Peter." BYZ TR.

ʰ 2:13, **and**: Absent from 𝔓46 B(03).

ⁱ 2:13, **all**: Included in ℵ(01).

ʲ 2:14, **Cephas**: Some manuscripts read "Peter." BYZ TR.

ᵏ 2:14, **and not like the Jews**: Absent from 𝔓46.

ˡ 2:14, **like Jews**: Absent from 𝔓46.

ᵐ 2:16, **however**: Absent from 𝔓46 A(02) BYZ TR.

ⁿ 2:16, **through faith in**: Or "faithfulness of" as the phrase is a genitive construction.

ᵒ 2:16, **Jesus Christ**: Some manuscripts read "Christ Jesus." A(02) B(03).

ᵖ 2:16, **Christ Jesus**: Some manuscripts read "Jesus Christ." 𝔓46 B(03).

q 2:16, **justified by faith in Christ**: Or "justified by the faithfulness of Jesus Christ" as the phrase is a genitive construction.

law, because by works of the law no
flesh will be justified.

17 But if, in seeking to be justified
in Christ, we ourselves are found to be
sinners, is Christ then a servant of sin?
Certainly not! 18 For if I rebuild what I
have destroyed, I prove myself to be a
transgressor.

19 For through the law I died to the
law, so that I might live to God. I have
been crucified with Christ; 20 and it is no
longer I who live, but Christ lives in
me; and the life which I now [live][a] in
the flesh, I live by faith in[b] {the Son of
God},[c] who loved me and gave himself
for me.

21 I do not nullify the grace of God;
for if righteousness comes through the
law, then Christ died for nothing.

3 1 O foolish Galatians, who has
bewitched you [[that you should
not obey the truth]],[d] before whose eyes
Jesus Christ was publicly portrayed
as crucified [[among you]]?[e] 2 This
only I want to learn from you: Did you
receive the Spirit by works of the law
or by hearing with faith? 3 Are you so
foolish? Having begun with the Spirit,
are you now being perfected by the
flesh? 4 Did you suffer so many things in
vain, if indeed [even][f] it was in vain?

5 So then, the one supplying the
Spirit to you and working miracles
among you, is it from works of the law
[[you received the Spirit]][g] or from
hearing with faith? 6 Just as Abraham
believed God, and it was credited to
him as righteousness.[h]

7 Therefore, know that those of
faith, these are sons of Abraham.

8 But the Scripture, foreseeing that
God would justify the nations by faith,
announced the good news beforehand
to Abraham, saying, "In you all the
nations will be blessed."[i] 9 So then,
those who are of faith are blessed with
faithful Abraham.

10 For as many as are of works of the
law are under a curse; for it is written
[that],[j] "Cursed is everyone who does
not abide {by}[k] all things written in the
book of the law, to do them."[l] 11 Now it
is evident that no one is justified before
God by the law, for "The righteous shall
live by faith."[m] 12 [But][n] The law is not
of faith; rather, "The {one}[o] who does
these things will live by them."[p]

13 Christ redeemed us from the curse
of the law by becoming a curse for us,
for it is written, "Cursed is everyone
who hangs on a tree,"[q] 14 in order that
the blessing of Abraham might come to
the Gentiles in {Christ Jesus},[r] so that
we might receive the promise of the
Spirit through faith.

---

a 2:20, **live:** Absent from A(02).
b 2:20, **I live by faith:** Or "I live by faithfulness of" as the phrase is a genitive construction.
c 2:20, **the Son of God:** Some manuscripts read "God and Christ." 𝔓46 B(03).
d 3:1, **that you should not obey the truth:** Included in C(04) BYZ TR.
e 3:1, **among you:** Included in BYZ TR.
f 3:4, **even:** Absent from 𝔓46.
g 3:5, **you received the Spirit:** Included in A(02).
h 3:6, Genesis 15:6.
i 3:8, Genesis 12:3, 18:18.
j 3:10, **that:** Absent from BYZ TR.
k 3:10, **by:** Some manuscripts read "in." A(02) C(04) BYZ TR.
l 3:10, Deuteronomy 27:26 LXX.
m 3:11, Habakkuk 2:4.
n 3:12, **But:** Absent from 𝔓46.
o 3:12, **one:** Some manuscripts read "man." BYZ TR.
p 3:12, Leviticus 18:5.
q 3:13, Deuteronomy 21:23 LXX.
r 3:14, **Christ Jesus:** Some manuscripts read "Jesus Christ." א(01) B(03).

15 Brothers, I speak in human terms: even a human covenant, once ratified, no one sets aside or adds to it. 16 But to Abraham were the promises spoken and to his seed.ᵃ It does not say, "And to seeds," as referring to many, but as referring to one, "And to your seed," who is Christ.ᵇ

17 This is what I mean: the law, which came 430 years afterward, does not annul a covenant previously ratified by God [[in Christ]],ᶜ so as to make the promise void. 18 For if the inheritance comes by the law, it no longer comes by promise; but God granted it to Abraham by a promise.

19 Why then the law? [It was added]ᵈ Because of transgressions, until the offspring should come to whom the promise had been made, and it was ordained through angels by the hand of a mediator. 20 Now a mediator is not for one party alone, but God is one.

21 Is the law then contrary to the promises [of God]?ᵉ Certainly not! For if a law had been given that could give life, then righteousness would indeed be by the law. 22 But the Scripture has confined all things under sin, so that the promise by faith in Jesus Christ might be given to those who believe.

23 But before faith arrived, we were guarded under the law, confined to the faith that was about to be disclosed. 24 So then, the law was our guardian until Christ came, in order that we might be justified by faith. 25 But now that faith has come, we are no longer under a guardian.

26 For you are all sons of God through faith [in]ᶠ Christ Jesus.

27 For as many of you as were baptized into Christ have put on Christ.

28 There is neither Jew nor Greek, there is neither slave nor free, there is no male and female; [for]ᵍ you are all one in Christ Jesus.

29 And if you belong to Christ, then you are Abraham's seed, heirs [[also]]ʰ according to the promise.

4 ¹ I say, for as long a time as the heir is an infant, he is no different from a slave, though being lord of all, 2 but is under guardians and stewards until the time appointed by the father.

3 In the same way, when we were infants, we were enslaved under the basic principles of the world; 4 But when the fullness of time came, God sent forth his Son, born of a woman, born under the law, 5 In order to redeem those under the law, so that we might receive the adoption as sons.

6 And because you are sons, [God]ⁱ sent the Spirit [of his Son]ʲ into {our}ᵏ hearts, crying, "Abba, Father!" 7 So you are no longer a slave, but a son; and if a son, then an {heir through God}.ˡ

8 But at that time, not knowing God, you served those who by nature are not gods; 9 But now, having come to know God, or rather, being known by God, how can you turn back again to the weak and poor elements, to which you want to be enslaved once more?

10 You observe days and months and seasons and years. 11 I fear for you,

---

ᵃ 3:16, **seed:** Or offspring.

ᵇ 3:16, Genesis 12:7.

ᶜ 3:17, **in Christ:** Included in BYZ TR.

ᵈ 3:19, **It was added:** Absent from 𝔓46.

ᵉ 3:21, **of God:** Absent from 𝔓46 B(03).

ᶠ 3:26, **through faith in:** Or "through the faithfulness of Christ Jesus," as the phrase is a genitive construction. ‖ "in" is absent from 𝔓46.

ᵍ 3:28, **for:** Absent from 𝔓46.

ʰ 3:29, **also:** Included in BYZ TR.

ⁱ 4:6, **God:** Absent from B(03).

ʲ 4:6, **of his Son:** Absent from 𝔓46.

ᵏ 4:6, **our:** Some manuscripts read "your." BYZ TR.

ˡ 4:7, **heir through God:** Some manuscripts read "heir of God through Christ." BYZ TR.

that perhaps I have labored over you in vain.

12 Become as I am, because I also am as you are, brothers, I beg of you. You have not wronged me; 13 But you know that because of a weakness of the flesh I preached the gospel to you the first time, 14 And you did not[a] despise [nor reject][b] the trial in my flesh, but you received me as an angel[c] of God, as if I were Christ Jesus.

15 {Where then is}[d] your blessedness? For I testify to you that, if possible, you would have gouged out your eyes and given them to me. 16 Have I then become your enemy by telling you the truth?

17 They are zealous for you, but not in a good way; they want to exclude you, so that you may be zealous for them.

18 But it is good to be zealous in a good thing always, and not only when I am present with you. 19 My [[children]],[e] for whom I am again in labor until Christ is formed in you; 20 And I would like to be present with you now and to change my tone, for I am perplexed about you.

21 Tell me, you who want to be under the law, do you not listen to the law? 22 For it is written that Abraham had two sons, one by the slave woman and one by the free woman. 23 But [on the one hand][f] the one from the slave woman was born according to the flesh, while the one {from}[g] the free woman was born through [[the]][h] promise.

24 Which things are allegorized; for these are two covenants, one indeed from Mount Sinai, giving birth to slavery, which is Hagar. 25 {Now Hagar is Mount Sinai in Arabia; and she}[i] corresponds to the present Jerusalem, {for}[j] she is in slavery with her children. 26 But the Jerusalem above is free, which is {our mother};[k]

27 For it is written, "Rejoice, barren one who does not give birth; break forth and cry out, you who do not travail; because many are the children of the desolate, more than of her who has the husband."[l]

28 Now {you},[m] brothers, like Isaac, are children of the promise. 29 But just as at that time the one born according to the flesh persecuted the one according to the Spirit, so also now. 30 But what does the Scripture say? "Cast out the slave woman and her son; for the son of the slave woman shall not[n] inherit with the son of the free woman."[o]

31 {Therefore,}[p] brothers, we are not children of the slave woman, but of the free woman.

---

a 4:14, **not:** Absent from ℵ(01). Likely an error.

b 4:14, **nor reject:** Absent from 𝔓46.

c 4:14, **angel:** That is, messenger. The Greek word can mean (1) a human messenger serving as an envoy, an envoy, one who is sent or (2) a transcendent power who carries out various missions or tasks, messenger, angel (BDAG, ἄγγελος).

d 4:15, **Where then is:** Some manuscripts read "What has become of." BYZ TR.

e 4:19, **children:** Some manuscripts read "little children." BYZ TR.

f 4:23, **on the one hand:** Absent from 𝔓46 B(03).

g 4:23, **from:** Some manuscripts read "of." 𝔓46 B(03).

h 4:23, **the:** Included in BYZ TR.

i 4:25, **Now Hagar is Mount Sinai in Arabia; and she:** Some manuscripts read "For Sinai is a mountain in Arabia; and it." 𝔓46 ℵ(01) C(04).

j 4:25, **for:** Some manuscripts read "but." BYZ TR.

k 4:26, **our mother:** Some manuscripts read "the mother of us all." A(02) BYZ TR.

l 4:27, Isaiah 54:1 LXX.

m 4:28, **you:** Some manuscripts read "we." ℵ(01) A(02) C(04) BYZ TR.

n 4:30, **not:** Absent from 𝔓46.

o 4:30, Genesis 21:10.

p 4:31, **Therefore:** Some manuscripts read "But." A(02) C(04).

5 1 {For freedom, Christ set us free; stand firm therefore}[a] and do not be subject again to a yoke of slavery.

2 Behold, I, [Paul,][b] say to you that if you are circumcised, Christ will not benefit you at all.

3 I testify again to every man who receives circumcision [that][c] he is obligated to keep the whole law.

4 You have been severed from Christ, you who are seeking to be justified by the law; you have fallen from grace.

5 For we, through the Spirit, by faith, [eagerly][d] await the hope of righteousness.

6 [For][e] In Christ [Jesus][f] neither circumcision nor uncircumcision means anything, but faith working through love.

7 You were running well; who hindered you from obeying the truth? 8 This persuasion is not from the one who calls you. 9 A little leaven leavens the whole lump.

10 I have confidence in you [in the Lord][g] that you will take no other view, and the one who is troubling you will bear the judgment, whoever he may be.

11 But if I, brothers, still preach circumcision, why am I still being persecuted? In that case, the offense of the cross [[of Christ]][h] has been removed.

12 I wish those who unsettle you would even cut themselves off.

13 For you were called to freedom, brothers; only do not use your freedom as an opportunity for the flesh, but through love serve one another. 14 For the whole law is fulfilled in one word: "You shall love your neighbor as yourself."

15 But if you bite and devour one another, watch out that you are not consumed by one another.

16 But I say, walk by the Spirit, and you will not carry out the desire of the flesh.

17 For the flesh desires against the Spirit, and the Spirit against the flesh; for these are opposed to each other, so that you may not do what you want. 18 But if you are led by the Spirit, you are not under the law.

19 Now the works of the flesh are evident: [[adultery]][i] sexual immorality, impurity, sensuality, 20 idolatry, sorcery, enmities, strife, jealousy, outbursts of anger, selfish ambitions, dissensions, factions, 21 envies, [[murders]],[j] drunkenness, carousing,[k] and things like these. I warn you, as I [[also]][l] warned you [before],[m] that those who practice such things will not inherit the kingdom of God.

22 But the fruit of the Spirit is love, joy, peace, patience, kindness, goodness, faithfulness, 23 gentleness, self-control; against such things there is no law.

---

a 5:1, **For freedom, Christ set us free; stand firm therefore:** Some manuscripts read "Stand firm, therefore, in the freedom with which Christ has set us free,." BYZ TR.

b 5:2, **Paul:** Absent from ℵ(01).

c 5:3, **that:** Absent from ℵ(01).

d 5:5, **eagerly:** Absent from 𝔓46 ℵ(01).

e 5:6, **For:** Absent from 𝔓46.

f 5:6, **Jesus:** Absent from B(03).

g 5:10, **in the Lord:** Absent from 𝔓46 C(04).

h 5:11, **of Christ:** Included in A(02) C(04).

i 5:19, **adultery:** Included in BYZ TR.

j 5:21, **murders:** Included in A(02) C(04) BYZ TR.

k 5:21, **carousing:** Or, excessive feasting.

l 5:21, **also:** Absent from A(02) C(04) BYZ TR.

m 5:21, **before:** Absent from ℵ(01).

24 And those who belong to [[the Lord]]ᵃ Christ [Jesus]ᵇ have crucified the flesh with its passions and desires.

25 If we live by the Spirit, let us [also]ᶜ keep in step with the Spirit.

26 Let us not become conceited, provoking one another, envying one another.

6 1 Brothers, if a person is caught in any wrongdoing, you who are spiritual should restore such a one in a spirit of gentleness, watching yourself so that you too may not be tempted.

2 Carry one another's burdens, and you will fulfill the law of Christ. 3 For if someone thinks [[himself]]ᵈ to be something, being nothing, they deceive themselves.

4 But let each one examine their own work, and then their reason for boasting will be in themselves alone and not in another; 5 for each will bear their own load.

6 Let the one who is taught the word share all good things with the one who teaches. 7 Do not be deceived: God is not mocked. For whatever a person sows, this they will also reap; 8 because the one sowing to their own flesh will reap corruption from the flesh, but the one sowing to the Spirit will reap eternal life from the Spirit.

9 And let us not grow weary in doing good, for in due time we will reap if we do not give up. 10 So then, as we have opportunity, let us work for the good of all, especially for those of the household of faith.

11 See with what large letters I have written to you with my own hand. 12 Those who want to make a good impression in the flesh, these are the ones who compel you to be circumcised, only so that they may not be persecuted for the cross of Christ [[Jesus]].ᵉ

13 For even those who are circumcised do not themselves keep the law, but they want you to be circumcised so that they may boast in your flesh. 14 But may it never be that I would boast, except in the cross of our Lord Jesus Christ, through whom the world has been crucified to me, and I to the world.

15 For [[in Christ Jesus]]ᶠ neither circumcision {is anything},ᵍ nor uncircumcision, but a new creation. 16 And as many as will walk by this rule, peace be upon them and mercy, andʰ upon the Israel of God.

17 From now on, let no one cause me trouble, for I bear the marks of [[the Lord]]ⁱ Jesus [[Christ]]ʲ on my body.

18 The grace of {our}ᵏ Lord Jesus Christ be with your spirit, brothers. Amen.ˡ

ᵃ 5:24, **the Lord:** Included in ℵ(01).

ᵇ 5:24, **Jesus:** Absent from 𝔓46 BYZ TR.

ᶜ 5:25, **also:** Absent from 𝔓46.

ᵈ 6:3, **himself:** Included in BYZ TR.

ᵉ 6:12, **Jesus:** Included in ℵ(01) B(03).

ᶠ 6:15, **in Christ Jesus:** Included in ℵ(01) A(02) C(04) BYZ TR.

ᵍ 6:15, **is anything:** Some manuscripts read "has any power." BYZ TR.

ʰ 6:16, **and:** Or even.

ⁱ 6:17, **the Lord:** Included in ℵ(01) BYZ TR.

ʲ 6:17, **Christ:** Included in ℵ(01).

ᵏ 6:18, **our:** Absent from ℵ(01).

ˡ 6:18, TR includes the postscript, "To the Galatians written from Rome."

Ephesians[a]

1 [1] Paul, an apostle of {Christ[b] Jesus}[c] by the will of God, to [[all]][d] the saints who are [in Ephesus][e] and[f] faithful in Christ Jesus, [2] grace to you and peace from God our Father and the Lord Jesus Christ.

[3] Blessed be the {God and Father}[g] [of our Lord [[and savior]][h] Jesus Christ],[i] who has blessed us with every spiritual blessing in the heavenly places in Christ, [4] just as he chose us in him before the foundation of the world to be holy and blameless before him in love, [5] having predestined us for adoption {through}[j] Jesus Christ to himself, according to the good pleasure of his will, [6] to the praise of the glory of his grace, {by}[k] which he freely bestowed on us in the Beloved.

[7] In him we have redemption through his blood, the forgiveness of our trespasses, according to the riches of his grace [8] which he lavished upon us, in all wisdom and insight, [9] making known to us the mystery of his will, [[so that we might be to the praise of his glory]][l] according to his good pleasure which he purposed in him [10] for the administration of the fullness of the times, to gather up all things in Christ, [[both]][m] things in the heavens and things on earth in him.

[11] In him we have [also][n] obtained an inheritance, having been predestined according to the purpose of him who works all things according to the counsel of his will, [12] so that we who were the first to hope in Christ might be to the praise of his glory.

[13] In him you also, when you heard the word of truth, the gospel of your salvation, and believed in him, were sealed with the promised Holy Spirit,[o] [14] which is the pledge of our inheritance, for the redemption of the possession, for the praise of his glory.

---

[a] 1:0, **Title ("Ephesians"):** Title originally absent from ℵ(01) B(03) ‖ 𝔓46 A(02) BYZ reads "To the Ephesians." ‖ TR reads "The letter of Paul the apostle to the Ephesians."

[b] 1:1, **Christ:** See footnote for Christ in Luke 2:11.

[c] 1:1, **Christ Jesus:** 𝔓46 B(03) NA28 SBLGNT ‖ Some manuscripts read "Jesus Christ." ℵ(01) A(02) BYZ TR THGNT.

[d] 1:1, **all:** Included in A(02).

[e] 1:1, **in Ephesus:** Absent from 𝔓46 ℵ(01) B(03).

[f] 1:1, **and:** Or even/yet.

[g] 1:3, **God and Father:** 𝔓46 reads "Father." ‖ B(03) reads "God."

[h] 1:3, **and savior:** Included in ℵ(01).

[i] 1:3, **of our Lord [[and savior]] Jesus Christ:** Absent from 𝔓46.

[j] 1:5, **through:** Absent from 𝔓46 which could be rendered "of" due to "Jesus Christ" being in the genitive.

[k] 1:6, **by:** Some manuscripts read "in." BYZ TR.

[l] 1:9, **so that we might be to the praise of his glory:** Included in A(02).

[m] 1:10, **both:** Included in TR.

[n] 1:11, **also:** Absent from 𝔓92.

[o] 1:13, **Spirit:** See footnote for Spirit in Luke 1:15.

15 For this reason, I too, having heard of the faith among you in {the}[a] Lord Jesus and {the love for}[b] all the saints, 16 do not cease giving thanks for you, making mention of you in my prayers, 17 that the God of our Lord Jesus Christ, the Father of glory, may give you a spirit of wisdom and revelation in the knowledge of him, 18 having the eyes of your heart enlightened to know what is the hope of his calling, [[and]][c] what is the wealth of the glory of his inheritance among the saints, 19 and what is the surpassing greatness of his power toward us who believe, according to the working[d] of the might of his strength, 20 which he worked in Christ, raising him from the dead and {having sat down}[e] at his right hand in the heavenly places, 21 far above all rule and authority and power and lordship and every name that is named, not only in this age but also in the one to come; 22 and he put all things under his feet and gave him as head over all things to the church, 23 which is his body, the fullness of him who fills all in all.

2 1 And you, being dead in [your][f] trespasses and sins, 2 in which you once walked according to the age of this world, according to the ruler of the authority of the air, the spirit now working in the sons of disobedience; 3 Among whom we all also once conducted ourselves in the desires of our flesh, doing the will of the flesh and of the thoughts, and we were by nature children of wrath, just as the rest.

4 But God, being rich in mercy, because of {his}[g] great love with which he loved us, 5 even when we were dead in {trespasses},[h] made us alive together with Christ, – by grace you have been saved – 6 and raised us up together, and seated us together in the heavenly places in Christ Jesus 7 [, so that in the ages to come he might show the exceeding riches of his grace in kindness toward us in Christ Jesus].[i]

8 For by grace you have been saved through [[the]][j] faith; and this is not of yourselves, it is the gift of God; 9 not of works, lest anyone should boast.

10 For we are {his workmanship}[k] , created in Christ Jesus for good works, which God prepared beforehand, that we should walk in them.

11 Therefore, remember that once you, the Gentiles in the flesh, were called "uncircumcision" by those called "circumcision," which is made in the flesh by hands. 12 At that time you were without Christ, alienated from the commonwealth of Israel and strangers to the covenants of promise, having no hope and without God in the world. 13 But now in Christ Jesus, you who once were far off have been brought near by the blood of Christ. 14 For he is our peace, who has made both one and has broken down the dividing wall of hostility, in his flesh, 15 by abolishing the law of commandments [in ordinances],[l] that he might create in himself one new man in place of the two, so making peace, 16 and might reconcile both in one body to God through the cross, having put to death the hostility in him.

---

a 1:15, **the:** Some manuscripts read "the." 𝔓46.

b 1:15, **the love for:** Some manuscripts read "that which is toward." 𝔓46 ℵ(01) A(02).

c 1:18, **and:** Included in BYZ TR.

d 1:19, **working:** The Greek word *energeia* pertains to metaphysical working, operation, action (BDAG, ἐνέργεια).

e 1:20, **having sat down:** Some manuscripts read "he seated." ℵ(01) A(02).

f 2:1, **your:** Absent from BYZ TR.

g 2:4, **his:** 𝔓46 reads "the."

h 2:5, **trespasses:** 𝔓46 reads "the body." ‖ B(03) reads "the transgressions and the desires."

i 2:7, Verse 7 is absent in ℵ(01).

j 2:8, **the:** Included in A(02) BYZ TR.

k 2:10, **his workmanship:** ℵ(01) reads "the work of God."

l 2:15, **in ordinances:** Absent from 𝔓46.

17 And coming, he proclaimed peace to you who are far away and [peace][a] to those who are near. 18 For through him we both[b] have access in one spirit to the Father.

19 So then you are no longer strangers and aliens, but [you are][c] fellow citizens with the saints and members of the household of God, 20 built on the foundation of the apostles and prophets, with {Christ Jesus}[d] himself as the cornerstone, 21 in whom the whole structure, being joined together, grows into a holy temple in the Lord. 22 In him you also are being built together into a dwelling place {for God}[e] in the Spirit.

3 1 For this reason, I, Paul, the prisoner of Christ [Jesus][f] on behalf of you Gentiles – 2 if indeed you have heard of the stewardship of {God's}[g] grace given to me for you, 3 [that][h] by revelation the mystery {it was}[i] made known to me, as I wrote briefly before, 4 by which, when you read, you can understand my insight into the mystery of Christ, 5 which in other generations was not made known to the sons of men, as it has now been revealed to his {holy apostles}[j] and prophets by the Spirit, 6 that the Gentiles are fellow heirs and fellow members of the body, and fellow partakers of {the}[k] promise in Christ [Jesus][l] through the gospel, 7 of which I became a servant according to the gift of God's grace given to me according to the working[m] of {his}[n] power.

8 To me, the very least of all [the saints],[o] this grace was given, to preach {to}[p] the Gentiles the unsearchable riches of Christ 9 and to enlighten [all] as to what is the administration of the mystery which has been hidden from the ages in God, who created all things [[through Jesus Christ]],[q] 10 so that now, through the church, the manifold wisdom of God might be made known to the rulers and authorities in the heavenly realms, 11 according to the purpose of the ages which he made in Christ [Jesus][r] our Lord, 12 in whom we have boldness and access with confidence through faith in him.[s]

13 Therefore, I ask you not to lose heart at my tribulations on your behalf, which is {your}[t] glory.

---

a 2:17, **peace:** Absent from BYZ TR.

b 2:18, **both:** That is, both Jews and Gentiles.

c 2:19, **you are:** Absent from BYZ TR.

d 2:20, **Christ Jesus:** Some manuscripts read "Jesus Christ." C(04) BYZ TR. ‖ ℵ(01) reads "Christ."

e 2:22, **for God:** B(03) reads "of Christ." BYZ TR.

f 3:1, **Jesus:** Absent from ℵ(01).

g 3:2, **God's:** Some manuscripts read "his." A(02).

h 3:3, **that:** Absent from 𝔓46 B(03).

i 3:3, **it was:** Some manuscripts read "he." BYZ TR.

j 3:5, **holy apostles:** B(03) reads "saints."

k 3:6, **the:** Some manuscripts read "his." BYZ TR.

l 3:6, **Jesus:** Absent from BYZ TR.

m 3:7, **working:** The Greek word *energeia* pertains to metaphysical working, operation, action (BDAG, ἐνέργεια).

n 3:7, **his:** 𝔓46 reads "God's."

o 3:8, **the saints:** Absent from 𝔓46.

p 3:8, **to:** Some manuscripts read "among." BYZ TR.

q 3:9, **through Jesus Christ:** Included in BYZ TR.

r 3:11, **Jesus:** Absent from 𝔓46.

s 3:12, **faith in him:** Or, "his faithfulness," as the construction is genitive.

t 3:13, **your:** Some manuscripts read "our." 𝔓46 C(04).

14 For this reason, I bow my knees before the Father [[of our Lord Jesus Christ]],[a] 15 from whom every family in heaven and on earth is named, 16 so that, according to the riches of his glory, he may grant you to be strengthened with power through his Spirit in the inner person, 17 That Christ may dwell in your hearts through faith, rooted and grounded in love, 18 that you may have strength to comprehend with all the saints what is the breadth and length and height and depth, 19 and to know the love of Christ that surpasses knowledge, that you may be filled with all the fullness of God.

20 Now to him who is able to do far more abundantly than all that we ask or think, according to the power at work within us, 21 to him be glory in the church [and][b] in Christ Jesus throughout all generations, forever and ever. Amen.

4 1 Therefore, I, the prisoner in {the Lord},[c] urge you to walk worthily of the calling with which you were called, 2 with all humility and gentleness, with patience, bearing with one another in love, 3 making every effort to maintain the unity of the Spirit in the bond of peace.

4 There is one body and one Spirit, just as you were [also][d] called in one hope of your calling; 5 one Lord,[e] one faith, one baptism, 6 one God and Father of all, who is over all and through all and in [[us]][f] all.

7 But to each one of us grace was given according to the measure of the gift of Christ.

8 Therefore it says, "When he ascended on high, he led captivity captive, [[and]][g] he gave gifts to men."[h] 9 But what does "he ascended" mean, if not that he also [[first]][i] descended into the lower [parts][j] of the earth? 10 The one who descended is also the one who ascended far above all the heavens, in order to fill[k] all things.

11 And it is this one who gave some as apostles, some as prophets, some as evangelists, and some as pastors and teachers, 12 for the equipping of the saints for the work of ministry, for the building up of the body of Christ, 13 until we all attain to the unity of the faith and of the knowledge of the Son of God, to a mature man, to the measure of the stature of the fullness of Christ, 14 so that we may no longer be infants, tossed back and forth by {every wind of}[l] teaching, by the trickery of men, by craftiness in deceitful scheming [[of the devil]],[m] 15 but speaking the truth in love, we are to grow up in all aspects into him who is the head, Christ, 16 From whom the whole body, being joined together and being held together by every supporting ligament,

---

a 3:14, **of our Lord Jesus Christ:** Included in BYZ TR.

b 3:21, **and:** Absent from 𝔓132 BYZ TR.

c 4:1, **the Lord:** ℵ(01) reads "Christ."

d 4:4, **also:** Absent from B(03).

e 4:5, **Lord:** In reference to the Greek word for Lord, BDAG states, "The principal meaning relates to the possession of power or authority, in various senses... (1) one who is in charge by virtue of possession, *owner*, (2) one who is in a position of authority, *lord, master...* in some places it is not clear whether God or Christ is meant." (BDAG, κύριος).

f 4:6, **us:** Included in BYZ ‖ TR includes "you."

g 4:8, **and:** Included in BYZ TR.

h 4:8, Psalm 68:18.

i 4:9, **first:** Included in B(03) BYZ TR.

j 4:9, **parts:** Absent from P46.

k 4:10, **fill:** Or fulfill. According to BDAG the Greek word can mean (1) to make full, fill, (2) to complete a period of time, fill (up), complete, (3) to bring to completion that which has already begun, complete, finish. (BDAG, πληρόω).

l 4:14, **every wind of:** C(04) reads "all my."

m 4:14, **of the devil:** Included in A(02).

{according}[a] to the working[b] in the measure of each individual part, causes the growth of the body for the building up of itself in love.

17 Therefore, I say this and testify in the Lord, that you no longer walk as the [[rest of the]][c] nations also walk, in the futility of their mind, 18 being dead in their thinking, alienated from the life of God because of the ignorance that is in them, due to the hardness of their hearts, 19 who, having become callous, have given themselves over to sensuality into [the working of][d] every kind of impurity with greediness.

20 But you did not learn Christ in this way, 21 if indeed you have heard [about] him and were taught in him, just as truth is in Jesus, 22 To put off, according to the former way of life, the old man, who is being corrupted according to the desires of deceit, 23 and be renewed in the spirit of your mind, 24 and put on the new person, created according to God in righteousness and holiness of the truth.

25 [Therefore,][e] Putting away falsehood, speak the truth, each one with their neighbor, for we are members of one another.[f]

26 Be angry and do not sin; do not let the sun go down on your anger,[g] 27 nor give place to the devil.

28 Let the thief no longer steal, but rather let him labor, working for the good with his [own][h] hands, so that he may have something to share with those in need.

29 Let no corrupting talk come out of your mouths, but only such as is good for building up, as fits the occasion, that it may give grace to those who hear.

30 And do not[i] grieve the Holy Spirit[j] of God, by which you were sealed for the day of redemption.

31 Let all bitterness and wrath and anger and clamor[k] and slander be put away from you, along with all malice.

32 [But][l] Be kind to one another, tenderhearted, forgiving one another, as [also][m] God in Christ forgave {you}.[n]

5 1 Therefore, be imitators of God, as beloved children; 2 and walk in love, just as Christ also loved us and gave himself up for us, an offering and a sacrifice to God as a fragrant aroma.

3 But sexual immorality and all impurity or greed must not even be named among you, as is proper for saints; 4 and there must be no filthiness, foolish talk, or coarse jesting, which are not {permitted},[o] but rather giving of thanks.

5 For this you know, understanding that every sexually immoral person or impure person or greedy person, which is an idolater, does not have an inheritance in the kingdom of [Christ and][p] God.

---

a 4:16, **according:** 𝔓46 reads "and."

b 4:16, **working:** The Greek word *energeia* pertains to metaphysical working, operation, action (BDAG, ἐνέργεια).

c 4:17, **rest of the:** Included in BYZ TR.

d 4:19, **the working of:** Absent from A(02).

e 4:25, **Therefore:** Absent from 𝔓46.

f 4:25, Zechariah 8:16.

g 4:26, Psalm 4:4 LXX.

h 4:28, **own:** Absent from 𝔓46 𝔓49 B(03) BYZ TR.

i 4:30, **not:** Absent from 𝔓46. Likely an error.

j 4:30, **Spirit:** See footnote for Spirit in Luke 1:15.

k 4:31, **clamor:** Meaning a loud cry or shout. In this verse, people shouting back and forth in a quarrel. (BDAG, κραυγή).

l 4:32, **But:** Absent from 𝔓46 B(03).

m 4:32, **also:** Absent from 𝔓49.

n 4:32, **you:** N Some manuscripts read "us."𝔓49 B(03) BYZ.

o 5:4, **permitted:** Some manuscripts read "fitting." BYZ TR.

p 5:5, **Christ and:** Absent from 𝔓46.

6 Let no one deceive you with empty words; [for]^a because of these things the wrath of God comes upon the sons of disobedience.

7 Therefore, do not become partakers with them; 8 for you were once darkness, but now you are light in the Lord.

Walk as children of light 9 - for the fruit of the {light}^b is in all goodness and righteousness and truth - 10 testing what is pleasing to {the Lord},^c 11 and do not participate in the unfruitful works of darkness, but rather [even]^d expose them.

12 For it is shameful even to speak of the things done by them in secret, 13 but all things exposed by the light become visible, 14 for everything that becomes visible is light. Therefore, it says, "Awake, O sleeper, and arise from the dead, and Christ will shine on you."

15 Therefore see [[, brothers,]]^e carefully how you walk, not as unwise but as wise, 16 redeeming the time, because the days are evil. 17 For this reason, do not be foolish, but understand what the {will}^f of {the Lord}^g is.

18 And do not get drunk with wine, in which there is debauchery, but be filled with the Spirit, 19 speaking to one another [in]^h psalms and hymns and [spiritual]ⁱ songs, singing and making melody [[with grace]]^j in your hearts to the Lord, 20 giving thanks always for everything in the name of {our}^k Lord {Jesus Christ}^l to the God and Father.

21 Submit to one another in the fear of {Christ}.^m

22 Wives, [be subject]ⁿ to your own husbands as to the Lord, 23 for a man is the head of the woman, just as Christ is the head of the church, [[and]]^o he himself is the savior of the body.

24 But {as}^p the church submits to Christ, so also wives to their [[own]]^q husbands in everything.

25 Men, love your [[own]]^r wives, just as Christ also loved the church and gave himself up for her, 26 in order to sanctify her, having cleansed her by the washing of water with the word, 27 so that he might present her to himself the glorious church, not having spot or wrinkle or any such thing, but that she might be holy and blameless.

28 In this way [also],^s men ought to love their wives as their own bodies. He who loves his own wife loves himself.

29 For no one ever hated his own flesh, but nourishes and cherishes it, just as {Christ}^t also does the church, 30 because we are members of his body [[of his flesh and of his bones]].^u

---

a 5:6, **for**: Absent from ℵ(01).

b 5:9, **light**: Some manuscripts read "Spirit." 𝔓46 BYZ TR.

c 5:10, **the Lord**: 𝔓49 reads "Christ."

d 5:11, **even**: Absent from 𝔓46.

e 5:15, **brothers**: Included in A(02).

f 5:17, **will**: ℵ(01) reads "mindset."

g 5:17, **the Lord**: A(02) reads "God." ‖ B(03) reads "our Lord."

h 5:19, **in**: Absent from ℵ(01) A(02) BYZ TR.

i 5:19, **spiritual**: Absent from 𝔓46 B(03).

j 5:19, **with grace**: Included in A(02).

k 5:20, **our**: ℵ(01) reads "the."

l 5:20, **Jesus Christ**: B(03) reads "Christ Jesus."

m 5:21, **Christ**: TR reads "God."

n 5:22, **be subject**: Included in ℵ(01) A(02) BYZ TR. ‖ Absent from 𝔓46 B(03).

o 5:23, **and**: Included in BYZ TR.

p 5:24, **as**: 𝔓46 reads "that." ‖ Absent from B(03).

q 5:24, **own**: Included in A(02) BYZ TR.

r 5:25, **own**: Included in BYZ TR.

s 5:28, **also**: Absent from ℵ(01) BYZ TR.

t 5:29, **Christ**: Some manuscripts read "the Lord." BYZ TR.

u 5:30, **of his flesh and of his bones**: Included in BYZ TR.

31 For this reason a man will leave [[his]]ᵃ father and mother and be joined to his wife, and the two will become one flesh. 32 This mystery is great, but I am speaking with reference to Christ and the church. 33 Nevertheless, you, each one of you, should love his own wife in this way, as himself, and the wife should respect her husband.

6 1 Children, obey your parents [in the Lord];ᵇ for this is right.

2 Honor your father and mother, which is the first commandment with a promise, 3 so that it may go well with you and you may live long on the earth.ᶜ

4 And fathers, do not provoke your children, but bring them up in the discipline and instruction of the Lord.

5 Slaves,ᵈ obey your earthly masters with fear and trembling, in sincerity of heart, as to {Christ},ᵉ 6 not with eye-service as people-pleasers, but as slaves of Christ, doing the will of God from the soul, 7 serving with goodwill as to the Lord and not to men, 8 {knowing that each one, if he does something good},ᶠ will receive this from the Lord, whether slave or free.

9 And masters, do the same to them, giving up threatening, knowing that both their Master and yours is in heaven, and there is no partiality with him.

10 Finally [[my brothers]],ᵍ be strong in the Lord and in the strength of his power.

11 Put on the full armor of God, [for you]ʰ to be able to stand against the schemes of the devil;

12 For our struggle is not against blood and flesh, but against the {rulers},ⁱ [against the authorities,]ʲ against the world powers of {this darkness},ᵏ against the spiritual forces of evil [in the heavenly places].ˡ

13 Therefore take up the whole armor of God, so that you may be able to withstand on the evil day, and having done everything, to stand.

14 Stand therefore, and fasten the belt of truth around your waist, and put on the breastplate of righteousness.

15 As shoes for your feet put on whatever will make you ready to proclaim the gospel of peace.

16 {In all},ᵐ taking up the shield of faith, with which you will be able to extinguish all the flaming arrows of the evil one;

17 And take the helmet of salvation, and the sword of the Spirit, which is the word of God.

ᵃ 5:31, **his:** Included in A(02) BYZ TR.

ᵇ 6:1, **in the Lord:** Absent from B(03).

ᶜ 6:3, Exodus 20:12, Deuteronomy 5:16.

ᵈ 6:5, **Slaves:** *Servant* in normal usage at the present time. i.e., one who works for another (employee).

ᵉ 6:5, **Christ:** A(02) reads "the Lord."

ᶠ 6:8, **knowing that each one, if he does something good:** Some manuscripts read "knowing that whatever good each one does." BYZ TR.

ᵍ 6:10, **my brothers:** Included in BYZ TR.

ʰ 6:11, **for you:** Absent from 𝔓46.

ⁱ 6:12, **rulers:** 𝔓46 reads "schemes."

ʲ 6:12, **against the authorities:** Absent from 𝔓46.

ᵏ 6:12, **this darkness:** Some manuscripts read "the darkness of the age." BYZ TR.

ˡ 6:12, **in the heavenly places:** Absent from 𝔓46.

ᵐ 6:16, **in all:** Some manuscripts read "above all." A(02) BYZ TR.

18 Through every prayer and supplication praying at all times in Spirit, and to this keeping watch with all perseverance and supplication for all the saints, 19 and for me, that a word may be given to me in the opening of my mouth, to make known with boldness the mystery [of the gospel],ª 20 for which I am an ambassador in chains. Pray that I may declare it boldly, as I must speak.

21 So that you [also]ᵇ may know about my circumstances, what I am doing, Tychicus, the beloved brother and faithful [servant]ᶜ in the Lord, will make everything known to you. 22 Whom I have sent to you for this very purpose, that you may know our circumstances and that he may encourage {your}ᵈ hearts.

23 Peace to the {brothers}ᵉ and sisters, and {love}ᶠ with faith, from God the Father and the Lord Jesus Christ.

24 Grace be with all who love our Lord Jesus Christ in incorruptibility.ᵍ [[Amen]]ʰⁱ

ª 6:19, **of the gospel:** Absent from B(03).

ᵇ 6:21, **also:** Absent from 𝔓46.

ᶜ 6:21, **servant:** Absent from ℵ(01).

ᵈ 6:22, **your:** 𝔓46 reads "our."

ᵉ 6:23, **brothers:** 𝔓46 reads "saints."

ᶠ 6:23, **love:** A(02) reads "mercy."

ᵍ 6:24, **incorruptibility:** Or, with undying love. BDAG defines the Greek word as "the state of not being subject to decay/dissolution/interruption, incorruptibility, immorality." (BDAG, ἀφθαρσία).

ʰ 6:24, **Amen:** Included in BYZ TR.

ⁱ 6:24, TR includes the postscript "To the Ephesians it was written from Rome through Tychicus." ‖ B(03) includes the postscript "To the Ephesians it was written from Rome."

Philippians[a]

1 ¹Paul and Timothy, servants of {Christ Jesus},[b] to all the saints in Christ[c] Jesus who are in Philippi, with the overseers and deacons: ²Grace to you and peace from God our Father and the Lord Jesus Christ.

³I thank my God for every remembrance of you, ⁴always in every prayer of mine for you all, making my prayer with joy, ⁵because of your partnership in the gospel from the first day until now, ⁶being confident of this very thing, that the one who began a good work in you will complete it until the day of {Christ Jesus};[d] ⁷Just as it is right for me to think this about all of you, because I have you in my heart, both in my chains and in the defense and confirmation of the gospel, all of you being {fellow}[e] partakers with me of grace.

⁸For God is [my][f] witness, how I long for you all with the affection of {Christ Jesus}.[g] ⁹And this I pray, that your love may abound yet more and more in knowledge and all discernment, ¹⁰so that you may approve the things that are excellent, in order to be sincere and blameless for the day of Christ, ¹¹being filled with the {fruit}[h] of righteousness which comes through {Jesus Christ},[i] to the glory and praise of God.

¹²I want you to know, brothers, that what has happened to me has really served to advance the gospel, ¹³so that it has become known throughout the whole imperial guard and to everyone else that my imprisonment is for Christ. ¹⁴And most of the brothers, having become confident in the Lord by my imprisonment, are much more bold to speak the word [[of God]][j] without fear.

¹⁵Some indeed preach Christ from envy and strife, but others from goodwill. ¹⁶Some indeed preach Christ from love, knowing that I am set for the defense of the gospel, ¹⁷but others proclaim Christ out of selfish ambition, not sincerely, thinking to {stir up}[k] trouble for me in my imprisonment.

¹⁸What then? [Only][l] That in every way, whether in pretense or in truth, Christ is proclaimed, {and}[m] in this I rejoice. Yes, and I will rejoice, ¹⁹{for}[n] I know that this will turn out for my deliverance through your prayers and the provision of the Spirit of {Jesus Christ},[o] ²⁰according to my eager expectation and hope, that I will not be put to shame in anything, but that with all boldness, as always, so now also Christ will be magnified in my body, whether through life or through death.

---

[a] 1:0 , **Title ("Philippians"):** Absent from ℵ(01) B(03). ‖ 𝔓46 A(02) BYZ reads "To the Philippians." ‖ TR reads "the letter of Paul the apostle to the Philippians."

[b] 1:1, **Christ Jesus:** Some manuscripts read "Jesus Christ." BYZ TR.

[c] 1:1, **Christ:** See footnote for Christ in Luke 2:11.

[d] 1:6, **Christ Jesus:** 𝔓46 B(03) ‖ Some manuscripts read "Jesus Christ." ℵ(01) A(02) BYZ TR.

[e] 1:7, **fellow:** 𝔓46 reads "also."

[f] 1:8, **my:** Absent from 𝔓46.

[g] 1:8, **Christ Jesus:** Some manuscripts read "Jesus Christ." BYZ TR.

[h] 1:11, **fruit:** Some manuscripts read "fruits." BYZ TR.

[i] 1:11, **Jesus Christ:** Some manuscripts read "Jesus Christ." 𝔓46.

[j] 1:14, **of God:** Included in ℵ(01) A(02) B(03). ‖ Absent from 𝔓46 BYZ TR.

[k] 1:17, **stir up:** Some manuscripts read "cause." BYZ TR.

[l] 1:18, **Only:** Absent from B(03).

[m] 1:18, **and:** B(03) reads "but also."

[n] 1:19, **for** Some manuscripts read "but." 𝔓46 B(03).

[o] 1:19, **Jesus Christ:** 𝔓46 read "Christ Jesus."

21 For to me, to live is Christ and to die is gain.

22 But if I live on in the flesh, this will mean fruit from my labor; yet what I shall choose I do not know.

23 {But}[a] I am hard pressed between the two, having a desire to depart and be with Christ, [for][b] this is [far][c] better. 24 Yet to remain in the flesh is more necessary for your sake.

25 And being confident of this, I know that I will remain and continue with all of you for your progress and joy in [[your]][d] faith, 26 that your rejoicing for me may be more abundant in Christ Jesus by my coming to you again.

27 Only conduct yourselves in a manner worthy of the gospel [of Christ],[e] so that whether I come and see you or remain absent, I may hear of you, that you are standing firm in one spirit, with one soul striving together for the faith of the gospel. 28 And in no way frightened by {your}[f] opponents, which is [[indeed]][g] a sign of destruction for them, but {of your}[h] salvation, and this from God.

29 For it has been granted to {you}[i] on behalf of Christ, not only to believe in him, but also to suffer for him,

30 having the same struggle which you saw in me and now hear [is in me].[j]

2 1 Therefore, if there is any encouragement in Christ, if any consolation of love, if any fellowship of the Spirit, if any affection and compassion, 2 fulfill my joy by thinking the same way, having the same love, being united in spirit, and having one purpose.

3 Do nothing from selfish ambition or conceit, but in humility regard one another as surpassing yourselves, 4 not looking out for each one's own interests, but also for the interests of others.

5 [[For]][k] Let this mindset be in you, which also was in Christ Jesus, 6 who, existing[l] in the form[m] of God, did not consider equality with God as something to be seized,[n] 7 but emptied *himself*, taking the form of a servant, being made in the likeness of men; and in appearance, being found in appearance as a man,[o] 8 he humbled himself, becoming obedient to the point of death, even death on a cross.

9 Therefore, God highly exalted him and gave him {the}[p] name that is above every name, 10 so that at the name of Jesus [[Christ]][q] every knee should bow, of those in heaven and on earth

a 1:23, **But:** TR reads "For."
b 1:23, **for:** Absent from ℵ(01) BYZ TR.
c 1:23, **far:** Absent from 𝔓46.
d 1:25, **your:** Included in ℵ(01).
e 1:27, **Christ:** Absent from ℵ(01).
f 1:28, **your:** C(04) reads "our."
g 1:28, **indeed:** Included in BYZ TR.
h 1:28, **of your:** Some manuscripts read "to you." BYZ TR.
i 1:29, **you:** Some manuscripts read "up." A(02).
j 1:30, **is in me:** Absent from 𝔓46.
k 2:5, **For:** Included in 𝔓46 BYZ TR.
l 2:6, **existing:** The Greek word is in the present active case.
m 2:6, **form:** The Greek word means form, outward appearance, shape (BDAG, μορφή).
n 2:6, **seized:** The Greek word means (1) a violent seizure of property, robbery or (2) something to which one can claim or assert title by gripping or grasping, something claimed. BDAG also notes "only the context and an understanding of Paul's thought in general can decide whether it means holding fast to something already obtained... or the appropriation to oneself of something that is sought after" (BDAG, ἁρπαγμός).
o 2:7, J. Jeremias gives the alternate punctuation: "but emptied himself, taking the form of a servant. Being made in the likeness of men, and being found in appearance as a man," J. Jeremias, "Zur Gedankenführung in den paulinischen Briefen," in Studia Paulina in honorem Johannis de Zwaan septuagenarii (ed. J.N. Sevenster and W.C. van Unnik; Haarlem: Bohn, 1953) 146–155, 154.
p 2:9, **the:** Some manuscripts read "a." BYZ TR.
q 2:10, **Christ:** Absent from ℵ(01).

and under the earth, 11 and every tongue confess that Jesus Christ is Lord, to the glory of God the Father.

12 So then, my beloved, just as you have always obeyed, not only in my presence but now much more in my absence, work out your own salvation with fear and trembling; 13 For God is the one working [[powers]]^a in you, both to will and to work for his good pleasure.

14 Do everything without grumbling and disputing, 15 so that you {may become}^b blameless and innocent, children of God blameless in the midst of a crooked and twisted generation, among whom you shine as lights in the world, 16 holding fast to the word of life, so that I may boast on the day of Christ that I did not run in vain or labor in vain.

17 But even if I am being poured out as a drink offering upon the sacrifice and service of your faith, I rejoice [and share my joy]^c with you all. 18 Likewise, you also should rejoice [and share your joy]^d with me.

19 I hope in {the Lord}^e Jesus to send Timothy to you soon, so that I also may be encouraged when I learn of your situation. 20 For I have no one like him, who will genuinely care for your concerns, 21 for they all seek their own interests, not those of {Jesus Christ}.^f 22 But you know his proven character, that as a son with his father he has served with me in [[the chains of]]^g the gospel.

23 Therefore, I hope to send him as soon as I see how things go with me;

24 and I trust in the Lord that I myself also will come [[to you]]^h soon.

25 But I thought it necessary to send to you Epaphroditus, my brother, fellow worker, and fellow soldier, who is also your messenger and minister to my need, 26 since he has been longing {for you all}^i and was distressed because you heard that he was sick. 27 For indeed, he was sick, nearly unto death; but God had mercy on him, and not only on him but also on me, so that I would not have sorrow upon sorrow. 28 Therefore, I am sending him all the more eagerly, so that when you see him again you may rejoice and I may be less anxious.

29 Receive him then in the Lord with all joy, and hold such people in honor, 30 because for the work {of Christ}^j he came close to death, risking his life to make up for the help you could not give me.

3 1 Finally, [my]^k brothers, rejoice in the Lord. To write the same things to you is not tiresome for me, but for you it is safe.^l

2 Watch out for the dogs, watch out for the evil workers, watch out for those who mutilate the flesh. 3 For we are the circumcision, those who worship by the Spirit [of God]^m and boast in Christ Jesus and do not put confidence in the flesh, 4 even though I myself have confidence also in the flesh. If anyone else thinks he has confidence in the flesh, I more so: 5 circumcised on the eighth day, of the nation of Israel, of the tribe of Benjamin, a Hebrew of Hebrews; as to the law, a Pharisee; 6 as to zeal, persecuting the church; as

---

a 2:13, **powers:** Included in A(02).

b 2:15, **may become:** Absent from 𝔓46 A(02).

c 2:17, **and share my joy:** Absent from ℵ(01).

d 2:18, **and share your joy:** Absent from 𝔓46.

e 2:19, **the Lord:** C(04) reads "Christ."

f 2:21, **Jesus Christ:** Some manuscripts read "Christ Jesus." B(03) BYZ TR.

g 2:22, **the chains of:** Included in C(04).

h 2:24, **to you:** Included in ℵ(01) A(02) C(04).

i 2:26, **for you all:** 𝔓46 reads "to send to you."

j 2:30, **of Christ:** ℵ(01) reads "the Lord." ‖ Absent from C(04).

k 3:1, **my:** Absent from 𝔓46.

l 3:1, **safe:** Or, pertaining to being in someone's best interest (BDAG).

m 3:3, **of God:** Absent from 𝔓46.

to the righteousness which is in the law,
blameless. 7 [But][a] whatever things were
gain to me, these I have considered loss
for the sake of Christ.

8 But indeed, I [also][b] consider
everything to be a loss because of the
surpassing knowledge of {Christ Jesus}[c]
{my}[d] Lord, for whom I have suffered
the loss of all things, and I consider
them [[to be]][e] rubbish, so that I may
gain Christ 9 and be found in him, not
having a righteousness of my own that
comes from the law, but that which
comes through faith in Christ,[f] the
righteousness from God that depends
on faith, 10 that I may know him and
the power of his resurrection, and the
fellowship of his sufferings, [being
conformed to his death,][g] 11 that by any
means I may attain the resurrection
{from}[h] the dead.

12 Not that I have already obtained
this [[or already have been justified]][i]
or have already reached perfection, but
I press on to make it my own, because
Christ [Jesus][j] has made me his own.

13 Brothers, I do {not}[k] consider that
I have made it my own. But one thing
I do: forgetting what lies behind and
straining forward to what lies ahead,
14 I pursue according to the goal for the
prize of the upward calling of God [in
Christ Jesus].[l]

15 Therefore, as many as are
perfect,[m] let us think this way; and if
you think differently, God will reveal
this to you as well. 16 However, to what
we have already attained, let us walk
by the same rule. [[Let us be of the
same mind.]][n]

17 Become imitators of me, brothers,
and observe those who walk in this
way, just as you have us as an example.
18 For many walk, of whom I often told
you, [and][o] now even weeping I say, as
enemies of the cross of Christ, 19 whose
end is destruction, whose god is their
belly, and whose glory is in their
shame, who set their minds on earthly
things.

20 For our citizenship exists in the
heavens, from which [we also eagerly
await][p] a savior, the Lord Jesus Christ,
21 who will transform the body of our
humiliation {to be}[q] conformed to the
body of his glory, according to the
working[r] by which he is able even to
subject all things to {him}.[s]

4 1 Therefore, my beloved and
longed-for brothers, my joy and
crown, stand firm in the Lord in this
way, beloved.

2 I urge Euodia and I urge Syntyche
to have the same mindset in the Lord.
3 {Yes},[t] I ask you also, true companion,
help these women who have labored
with me in the gospel, along with

---

a 3:7, **But:** Absent from 𝔓46 ℵ(01) A(02).
b 3:8, **and:** Absent from 𝔓46 ℵ(01).
c 3:8, **Christ Jesus:** A(02) reads "Jesus Christ."
d 3:8, **my:** A(02) reads "our."
e 3:8, **to be:** Included in A(02) BYZ TR.
f 3:9, **through faith in Christ:** Or "through faithfulness of Christ" as the phrase is in the genitive case.
g 3:10, **being conformed to his death:** Absent from 𝔓46.
h 3:11, **from:** Some manuscripts read "of." BYZ TR.
i 3:12, **or already have been justified:** Included in 𝔓46.
j 3:12, **Jesus:** Absent from B(03).
k 3:13, **not:** Some manuscripts read "not yet." ℵ(01) A(02).
l 3:14, **in Christ Jesus:** Absent from 𝔓46.
m 3:15, **perfect:** Or, as many are near perfection.
n 3:16, **let us be of the same mind:** Included in BYZ TR.
o 3:18, **and:** Absent from 𝔓46.
p 3:20, **we also eagerly await:** Absent from 𝔓46.
q 3:21, **to be:** Some manuscripts read "to become." BYZ TR.
r 3:21, **working:** The Greek word *energeia* pertains to metaphysical working, operation, action (BDAG, ἐνέργεια).
s 3:21, **him:** Some manuscripts read "himself." BYZ TR.
t 4:3, **Yes:** TR reads "And."

Clement and the rest of my fellow workers [and of the others],[a] whose names are in the book of life.

4 Rejoice in the Lord always; again I will say, rejoice.

5 Let your gentleness be known to all men.

The Lord is near. 6 Do not be anxious about anything, but in everything by prayer and supplication with thanksgiving let your requests be made known to God. 7 And the peace {of God},[b] which surpasses all understanding, will guard your hearts and your minds [[and bodies]][c] in {Christ}[d] Jesus.

8 Finally, brothers, whatever is true, whatever is honorable, whatever is just, whatever is pure, whatever is lovely, whatever is commendable, if there is any excellence,[e] if there is anything worthy of praise, think about these things. 9 What you have learned and received and heard and seen in me; practice these things, and the God of peace will be with you.

10 I rejoiced greatly in the Lord that at last you renewed your concern for me. Indeed, you were concerned, but you had no opportunity to show it. 11 I am not saying this because I am in need, for I have learned to be content whatever the circumstances.

12 I know how to be brought low, and I know how to abound. In everything and in all, I have learned the secret of facing plenty and hunger, abundance and need. 13 I can do all things through {the one}[f] who strengthens me.

14 Yet it was kind of you to share in my affliction. 15 And you Philippians yourselves know that in the beginning of the gospel, when I left Macedonia, no church entered into partnership with me in giving and receiving, except you only, 16 for even in Thessalonica you sent me help for my needs once and again.

17 Not [that I seek the gift,][g] but I seek the fruit that abounds to your account. 18 But I have received everything in full and have an abundance; I am fully satisfied, having received [from Epaphroditus][h] the things sent from you, a fragrant aroma, an acceptable sacrifice, pleasing to God.

19 And my God will fulfill every need of yours according to his riches in glory in Christ Jesus.

20 But to our God and Father be the glory forever and ever, amen.

21 Greet every saint in Christ Jesus. The brothers who are with me greet you.

22 All the saints greet you, especially those of Caesar's household.

23 The grace of {the}[i] Lord Jesus Christ be with {your spirit}.[j] [[Amen]][kl]

---

a 4:3, **and of the others** Absent from 𝔓16 ℵ(01).

b 4:7, **of God:** A(02) reads "Christ."

c 4:7, **and bodies:** Included in 𝔓16.

d 4:7, **Christ:** 𝔓46 reads "the Lord."

e 4:8, **excellence:** That is, uncommon character worthy of praise. (BDAG).

f 4:13, **the one:** Some manuscripts include "Christ." BYZ TR.

g 4:17, **that I seek the gift:** Absent from 𝔓46.

h 4:18, **from Epaphroditus:** Absent from A(02).

i 4:23, **the:** Some manuscripts read "our." 𝔓46 TR.

j 4:23, **your spirit:** Some manuscripts read "you all." BYZ TR.

k 4:23, **Amen:** Included in 𝔓46 ℵ(01) A(02) BYZ TR.

l 4:23, TR includes the postscript, "To the Philippians written from Rome by Epaphroditus."

Colossians[a]

1 [1] Paul, an apostle of {Christ[b] Jesus}[c] by the will of God, and Timothy the brother, [2] to the saints and faithful brothers in Christ [[Jesus]][d] at Colossae: grace to you and peace from God our Father {and the Lord Jesus Christ}.[e]

[3] We give thanks to the God and Father of our Lord Jesus [Christ],[f] always praying for you, [4] having heard of your faith in {Christ}[g] Jesus and the love [which you have][h] for all the saints, [5] because of the hope laid up for you in the heavens, which you heard before in the word of truth, the gospel [6] that has come to you, just as it [[also]][i] is bearing fruit [and growing][j] in the whole world, as it is also among you, since the day you heard and knew the grace of God in truth;

[7] Just as you [[also]][k] learned from Epaphras, our beloved fellow servant, who is a faithful minister of Christ on {your}[l] behalf, [8] and who also made known to us your love in the Spirit.

[9] For this reason, we also, since the day we heard, do not cease praying for you [and asking][m] that you may be filled with the knowledge of his will in all wisdom and spiritual understanding, [10] {to walk}[n] worthy of the Lord, pleasing in every way, bearing fruit in every good work and growing in the knowledge of God, [11] being strengthened with all power according to his glorious might for all endurance and patience, with joy [12] [[and]][o] giving thanks [[at the same time]][p] to [[God]][q] the Father, who has [[called and]][r] qualified {you}[s] for the share of the inheritance of the holy ones in the light; [13] who delivered us from the power of darkness and transferred us into the kingdom of the beloved Son, [14] in whom we have redemption [[through his blood]],[t] the forgiveness of sins; [15] who is the image of the invisible God, the firstborn of all creation, [16] because in him all things were created, [[those]][u] in the heavens and on the earth, the visible and the invisible, whether thrones or dominions or rulers or authorities; [[that]][v] all things have been created through him and for him.

---

[a] 1:0, **Title ("Colossians")**: Absent from ℵ(01) B(03) ‖ 𝔓46 A(02) C(04) reads "To the Colossians." ‖ TR reads "the letter of Paul the apostle to the Colossians."

[b] 1:1, **Christ**: See footnote for Christ in Luke 2:11.

[c] 1:1, **Christ Jesus**: Some manuscripts read "Jesus Christ." BYZ TR.

[d] 1:2, **Jesus**: Included in A(02).

[e] 1:2, **and the Lord Jesus Christ**: Included in ℵ(01) C(04) BYZ TR.

[f] 1:3, **Christ**: Absent from B(03).

[g] 1:4, **Christ**: Some manuscripts read "the Lord." ℵ(01) A(02).

[h] 1:4, **which you have**: Absent from B(03).

[i] 1:6, **also**: Included in BYZ TR.

[j] 1:6, **and growing**: Absent from TR.

[k] 1:7, **also**: Included in BYZ TR.

[l] 1:7, **your**: Some manuscripts read "our." 𝔓46 ℵ(01) A(02) B(03).

[m] 1:9, **and asking**: Absent from B(03).

[n] 1:10, **to walk**: Some manuscripts read "for you to walk." BYZ TR.

[o] 1:12, **and**: Included in 𝔓46.

[p] 1:12, **at the same time**: Included in 𝔓46 B(03).

[q] 1:12, **God**: Included in ℵ(01). ‖ Absent from 𝔓46 A(02) B(03) C(04) BYZ TR.

[r] 1:12, **called and**: Included in B(03).

[s] 1:12, **you**: Some manuscripts read "us." A(02) C(04) BYZ TR.

[t] 1:14, **through his blood**: Included in TR.

[u] 1:16, **those**: Included in A(02) C(04) BYZ TR.

[v] 1:16, **that**: Included in 𝔓46.

17 And he is before all things, and [in]^a him all things hold together.

18 And he is the head of the body, the church; who is the beginning,^b the firstborn from the dead, so that he might come to have first place in everything, 19 because in him all the fullness was pleased to dwell 20 and through him to reconcile all things to him, having made peace through the blood of {his} ^ccross, [through him]^d whether things on earth or things in the heavens.

21 And you, who once were alienated and hostile in mind, engaged in evil deeds, 22 he has now reconciled in the body of his flesh through [[his]]^e death, to present you holy and blameless and above reproach before him.

23 If indeed you continue in the faith, grounded and steadfast, [[and]]^f not shifting from the hope of the gospel that you heard, which has been proclaimed in all creation^g under heaven, of which I, Paul, became a {servant}.^h

24 Now I rejoice in {the}ⁱ sufferings for your sake, and in my flesh I complete what is lacking in Christ's afflictions for the sake of his body, that is, the church, 25 of which I [[Paul]]^j became a minister according to the stewardship from God that was given to me for you, to make the word of God fully known, 26 the mystery hidden for ages and generations but now revealed to his saints.

27 To them God chose to make known how great among the Gentiles are the riches [of the glory]^k of this mystery, which is Christ in you, the hope of glory;

28 We proclaim this one, admonishing every person and teaching every person with all wisdom, so that we may present every person mature in Christ [[Jesus]];^l

29 For this I toil, struggling with his energy^m that powerfully works within me.

---

^a 1:17, **in:** Absent from 𝔓46.

^b 1:18, **beginning:** Or ruler. The Greek word means (1) the commencement of something as an action, process, or state of being, beginning, (2) one with whom a process begins, beginning, (3) the first cause, the beginning, (4) a point at which two surfaces or lines meet, corner, (5) a basis for further understanding, beginning, (6) an authority figure who initiates activity or process, ruler, authority, or (7) the sphere of one's official activity, rule, office. (BDAG, ἀρχή).

^c 1:20, **his:** 𝔓46 reads "the."

^d 1:20, **through him:** Absent from B(03).

^e 1:22, **his:** Included in ℵ(01) A(02).

^f 1:23, **and:** Absent from 𝔓46.

^g 1:23, **creation:** the Greek word for "creation" can also mean "creature."

^h 1:23, **servant:** ℵ(01) reads "herald and apostle." ‖ A(02) reads "herald and apostle and servant."

ⁱ 1:24, **the:** TR reads "my."

^j 1:25, **Paul:** Included in ℵ(01) A(02).

^k 1:27, **of the glory:** Absent from 𝔓46.

^l 1:28, **Jesus:** Included in BYZ TR.

^m 1:29, **energy:** The Greek word *energeia* pertains to metaphysical working, operation, action (BDAG, ἐνέργεια).

2 ¹ For I want you to know how great a struggle I have for you and for those in Laodicea, and for all who have not seen my face [in the flesh],ᵃ ² that their hearts may be encouraged, being knit together in love, and attaining to all the wealth that comes from the full assurance of understanding, to the knowledge of the mystery of {the God, Christ},ᵇ ³ in whom are hidden all the treasures of wisdom and [[the]]ᶜ knowledge.

⁴ {I say this, so that no one}ᵈ may deceive you with persuasive words.

⁵ For even though I am absent in the flesh, yet in the spirit I am with you, rejoicing and observing your order and the firmness of your faith in Christ.

⁶ Therefore, as you received Christ Jesus the Lord, walk in him, ⁷ rooted and built up in him and established in the faith, just as you were taught [[in it]],ᵉ abounding in thanksgiving.

⁸ See to it that no one takes you captive through philosophy and empty deceit, according to human tradition, according to the elemental spirits of the world, and not according to Christ.

⁹ For in him dwells all the fullness of deity bodily, ¹⁰ and you have been filled in him, who is the head of all rule and authority.

¹¹ In him also you were circumcised with a circumcision made without hands, by putting off the body [[of the sins]]ᶠ of the flesh, in the circumcision of Christ, ¹² {Buried}ᵍ with him in baptism, in which you were also raised with him through faith in the activityʰ of God, who raised him from the dead;

¹³ And you, being dead [in]ⁱ your trespasses and the uncircumcision of your flesh, made you alive together with him, having forgiven us all our trespasses. ¹⁴ By canceling the record of debt that stood against us with its legal demands, he set it aside, nailing it to the cross. ¹⁵ Having disarmed the rulers and authorities, he made a public spectacle of them, triumphing over them in himself.

¹⁶ Therefore, let no one judge you in fold and in drink, or in part of a feast, or a new moon, or Sabbaths; ¹⁷ these are a shadow of the things to come, but the body belongs to [the]ʲ Christ.

¹⁸ Let no one disqualify you, insisting on humility and worship of angels [[about to come]],ᵏ claiming to have seen visions he has [[not]]ˡ seen, puffed up without reason by their fleshly mind, ¹⁹ and not holding the head, from whom the whole body, through the joints and ligaments, being nourished and knit together, grows with the growth of God.

ᵃ 2:1, **in the flesh:** Absent from ℵ(01).

ᵇ 2:2, **the God, Christ:** 𝔓46 ℵ(01) B(03) NA28 SBLGNT ‖ Some manuscripts read "the God and Father of the Christ." A(02) C(04) THGNT ‖ Some manuscripts read "the God and Father and of the Christ." BYZ TR.

ᶜ 2:3, **the:** Included in BYZ TR.

ᵈ 2:4, **I say this, so that no one:** Some manuscripts read "But I say this lest anyone." C(04) BYZ TR.

ᵉ 2:7, **in it:** Included in A(02) B(03) C(04) BYZ TR.

ᶠ 2:11, **of the sins:** Included in BYZ TR.

ᵍ 2:12, **buried:** Some manuscripts read "having been buried." BYZ TR.

ʰ 2:12, **activity:** The Greek word *energeia* pertains to metaphysical working, operation, action (BDAG, ἐνέργεια).

ⁱ 2:13 , **in:** Absent from ℵ(01) B(03).

ʲ 2:17, **the:** Absent from 𝔓46 A(02).

ᵏ 2:18, **about to come:** Included in ℵ(01).

ˡ 2:18, **not:** Included in C(04) BYZ TR.

20 [[Therefore]]ᵃ If you died with Christ from the elements of the world, why, as though living in the world, do you subject yourselves to regulations? 21 Do not handle, do not taste, do not touch, 22 all if which are destined for destruction with use, according to the commandments and teachings of men, 23 which indeed have an appearance of wisdom in self-made religion and humility and severe treatment of the body, but are of no value against the indulgence of the flesh.

3 1 If then you were raised {with Christ},ᵇ seek the things above, where Christ is, seated at the right hand of God.

2 Set your minds on things above, not on things on the earth. 3 For you have died, and your life is hidden with Christ in God.

4 When Christ, {your}ᶜ life, is revealed, then [together]ᵈ you also will be revealed with him in glory.

5 Therefore, put to death your earthly members: sexual immorality, impurity, passion, [evil]ᵉ desire, and greed, which is idolatry. 6 Because of these things, the wrath of God comes [upon the sons of disobedience].ᶠ

7 In {these things}ᵍ you also once walked, when you lived in them.

8 But now [you also]ʰ put away all these things: anger, wrath, malice, blasphemy, and shameful speech from your mouth.

9 Do not lie to one another, having stripped off the old manⁱ with his practices 10 and having put on the new, the one being renewed for knowledge according to the image of the one who created him, 11 where there is neither Greek nor Jew, circumcision nor uncircumcision, Barbarian, Scythian, slave nor free, but [the]ʲ all and in all is Christ.

12 Therefore, as God's chosen ones, holy and beloved, put on {compassion, mercy,}ᵏ kindness, humility, gentleness, patience, 13 bearing with one another and forgiving each other if anyone has a complaint against anyone. Just as {the Lord}ˡ forgave you, so also should you. 14 Above all these, love, which is the bond of perfection.

15 And let the peace of {Christ}ᵐ rule in your hearts, to which also you were called in [one]ⁿ body; and be thankful.

ᵃ 2:20, **Therefore:** Included in TR.

ᵇ 3:1, **with Christ:** Absent from some 𝔓46. ‖ ℵ(01) reads "God."

ᶜ 3:4, **your:** Some manuscripts read "our." B(03) BYZ TR.

ᵈ 3:4, **together:** Absent from A(02).

ᵉ 3:5, **evil:** Absent from 𝔓46.

ᶠ 3:6, **upon the sons of disobedience:** Absent from some manuscripts, including P46 B(03).

ᵍ 3:7, **these things:** Some manuscripts read "them." BYZ TR.

ʰ 3:8, **you also:** Absent from ℵ(01).

ⁱ 3:9, **man:** Or self. BDAG gives the definition of the Greek word in the context of the two sides of human nature as "the outer being" or "the inner being" (BDAG, ἄνθρωπος). The Hebrew word for "man" is ādām. Adam is treated as a separate entry in BDAG under Ἀδάμ.

ʲ 3:11, **the:** Absent from ℵ(01) A(02) C(04).

ᵏ 3:12, **compassion, mercy:** NA28 SBLGNT TR ‖ Some manuscripts read "compassion of mercy" or "merciful compassion." THGNT BYZ.

ˡ 3:13, **the Lord:** 𝔓46 A(02) B(03) ‖ Some manuscripts read "Christ." C(04) BYZ TR. ‖ ℵ(01) reads "God."

ᵐ 3:15, **Christ:** Some manuscripts read "God." BYZ TR.

ⁿ 3:15, **one:** Absent from 𝔓46 B(03).

16 Let the word of {Christ}[a] dwell in you richly, teaching and admonishing one another in all wisdom, singing psalms and hymns and spiritual songs, with [the][b] grace in your {hearts to God}.[c] 17 And whatever you do, in word or deed, do everything in the name of {the Lord Jesus},[d] giving thanks to God [[and]][e] the Father through him.

18 Wives, submit to your [[own]][f] husbands as is fitting in the Lord.

19 Husbands, love your wives and do not be embittered against them.

20 Children, obey your parents in everything, for this is pleasing in {the Lord}.[g]

21 Fathers, do not provoke your children, so that they do not become discouraged.

22 Slaves[h] obey [in all things][i] your masters according to the flesh, not with eye-service as people-pleasers, but in singleness of heart, fearing {the Lord}.[j]

23 [[And]][k] Whatever you do, work heartily, as for [[serving]][l] the Lord and not for men, 24 Knowing that from the Lord you will receive {the}[m] inheritance as your reward. [[For]][n] You are serving the Lord Christ.

25 {For}[o] the one who does wrong will be repaid for the wrong he has done, and there is no partiality.

4 1 Masters, provide what is right and fair to your slaves,[p] knowing that you also have a master[q] in {heaven}.[r]

2 Devote yourselves to prayer, being watchful [in it][s] with thanksgiving, 3 praying at the same time for us, that God may open a door for the word, to speak [[with boldness]][t] the mystery of {Christ},[u] for which I am also in chains, 4 so that I may reveal it as I ought to speak.

5 Walk in wisdom toward those who are outside, redeeming the time.

6 Let your speech always be with grace, seasoned with salt, so that you may know how you ought to answer each one.

---

a 3:16, **Christ:** Some manuscripts read "God." A(02) C(04) ‖ א(01) reads "the Lord."

b 3:16, **the:** 𝔓46 B(03) ‖ Absent from א(01) A(02) C(04) BYZ TR.

c 3:16, **hearts to God:** Some manuscripts read "heart to the Lord." BYZ TR.

d 3:17, **the Lord Jesus:** Some manuscripts read "Jesus Christ." A(02) C(04) ‖ א(01) reads "the Lord Jesus Christ."

e 3:17, **and:** Included in BYZ TR.

f 3:18, **own:** Included in BYZ TR.

g 3:20, **the Lord:** TR reads "God."

h 3:22, **Slaves:** *Servant* in normal usage at the present time. i.e., one who works for another (employee).

i 3:22, **in all things:** Absent from 𝔓46.

j 3:22, **the Lord:** Some manuscripts read "God." 𝔓46 BYZ TR.

k 3:23, **And:** Included in BYZ TR.

l 3:23, **serving:** Included in A(02).

m 3:24, **the:** C(04) reads "your."

n 3:24, **For:** Included in BYZ TR.

o 3:25, **For:** Some manuscripts read "But." BYZ TR.

p 4:1, **slaves:** *Servant* in normal usage at the present time. i.e., one who works for another (employee).

q 4:1, **master:** Or Lord.

r 4:1, **heaven:** Some manuscripts read "the heavens." BYZ TR.

s 4:2, **in it:** Absent from א(01).

t 4:3, **with boldness:** Included in A(02).

u 4:3, **Christ:** B(03) reads "God."

7 Tychicus, the beloved brother and faithful servant [and fellow slave]ᵃ in the Lord, will make known to you all things concerning me, 8 whom I sent to you for this very purpose, that you may know our circumstances and he may encourage your hearts, 9 together with Onesimus, the faithful and beloved brother, who is one of you. They will make known to you all things here.

10 Aristarchus, my fellow prisoner, greets you, as does Mark, the cousin of Barnabas (concerning whom you have received instructions: if he comes to you, welcome him), 11 and Jesus who is called Justus. These are the only men of the circumcision who are my fellow workers for the kingdom of God, and they have been a comfort to me.

12 Epaphras, one of you, a servant of Christ [Jesus],ᵇ greets you, always struggling on your behalf in his prayers, that you may stand mature and fully {assured}ᶜ in all the will of God. 13 For I bear him witness that he has {worked hard}ᵈ for you and for those in Laodicea and in Hierapolis.

14 Luke, the beloved physician, and Demas greet you.

15 Greet the brothers in Laodicea, and Nympha and the church in {her}ᵉ house.

16 And when this [letter]ᶠ has been read among you, have it also read in the church of the Laodiceans; and see that you also read the letter from Laodicea.ᵍ

17 And say to Archippus, "See to the ministry that you have received in the Lord, that you may fulfill it."

18 The greeting with my own hand, Paul's. Remember my chains. Grace be with you. [[Amen]]ʰⁱ

ᵃ 4:7, **and fellow slave:** Absent from ℵ(01).
ᵇ 4:12, **Jesus:** Absent from 𝔓46 BYZ TR.
ᶜ 4:12, **assured:** Some manuscripts read "fulfilled." 𝔓46 BYZ TR.
ᵈ 4:13, **worked hard:** Some manuscripts read "a great zeal." BYZ TR.
ᵉ 4:15, **her:** Some manuscripts read "his." BYZ TR.
ᶠ 4:16, **letter:** Absent from B(03).
ᵍ 4:16, **Laodicea:** Possibly referring to Ephesians.
ʰ 4:18, **Amen:** Included in BYZ TR.
ⁱ 4:18, TR includes the postscript, "To the Colossians, written from Rome by Tychicus and Onesimus."

First Thessalonians[a]

1 [1] Paul, Silvanus, and Timothy, to the church of the Thessalonians in God {the}[b] Father and the Lord Jesus Christ:[c] Grace to you and peace [[from God our Father and the Lord Jesus Christ]].[d]

[2] We always give thanks to God for all [of you],[e] making remembrance [[of you]][f] in our prayers [[unceasingly]],[g] [3] remembering your work of faith and labor of love and endurance [[of hope]][h] in our Lord Jesus Christ, before our God and Father, [4] knowing, beloved brothers, loved by God, your election, [5] for our gospel [[of God]][i] did not come to you in word only, but also in power, and in the Holy Spirit, and [with][j] much assurance, just as you know what kind of men we became [among][k] you for your sake.

[6] And you became imitators of us and of {the Lord},[l] receiving the word in much affliction, with joy of the Holy Spirit, [7] so that you became an example referring to all the believers in Macedonia and in Achaia. [8] [For the word of {the Lord}[m] has sounded forth from you, not [only][n] in Macedonia and Achaia,][o] but in every place your faith toward God has gone out, so that we have no need to say anything.

[9] For they themselves report about us what kind of reception we had among you, and how you turned to God from idols to serve the living and true God, [10] and to {wait}[p] for his Son from heaven, whom he raised from [the] dead, Jesus who rescues us from the coming wrath.

2 [1] For you yourselves know, brothers, that our coming to you was not in vain, [2] but [[also]][q] having suffered and been mistreated, as you know, in Philippi, we had the courage in our God to speak to you the gospel of God in much struggle.

[3] For our exhortation was not from error, nor from impurity, nor in deceit, [4] but just as we have been tested by God to be entrusted with the good news, so we speak, not as pleasing men, but God who tests our hearts.

---

a 1:0, **Title ("First Thessalonians"):** Absent from ℵ(01) A(02) B(03) BYZ ‖ 𝔓46 BYZ reads "To the Thessalonians, first." ‖ TR reads "of Paul the apostle, the first letter to the Thessalonians."

b 1:1, **the:** A(02) reads "our."

c 1:1, **Christ:** See footnote for Christ in Luke 2:11.

d 1:1, **from God our Father and the Lord Jesus Christ:** Included in ℵ(01) A(02) BYZ TR.

e 1:2, **of you:** Absent from C(04).

f 1:2, **of you:** Included in C(04) BYZ TR.

g 1:2, **unceasingly:** Absent from BYZ TR.

h 1:3, **of hope:** Absent from A(02).

i 1:5, **of God:** Included in ℵ(01) C(04).

j 1:5, **in:** NA28[] SBLGNT THGNT BYZ TR. ‖ Absent from ℵ(01) B(03).

k 1:5, **among:** NA28[] SBLGNT THGNT BYZ TR. ‖ Absent from ℵ(01) A(02) C(04).

l 1:6, **the Lord:** A(02) reads "God."

m 1:8, **the Lord:** ℵ(01) reads "God."

n 1:8, **only:** Absent from A(02).

o 1:8, **For the word of the Lord...:** Absent from A(02).

p 1:10, **wait:** 𝔓46 reads "endure."

q 2:2, **also:** Included in BYZ TR.

5 For we never came with flattering speech, as you know, nor a pretext for greed, God is witness, 6 nor seeking glory from men, neither from {you}ᵃ nor from others, 7 though we could have been a burden as apostles of Christ, but we became {infants}ᵇ among you. Just as a nurse cherishes her own children.

8 In this way, longing for you, we were pleased to share with you not only the gospel of God but also our own souls, because you became beloved to us.

9 For you remember, brothers, our labor and toil; [[For]]ᶜ working night and day so as not to be a burden to any of you, we preached to you the gospel of God.

10 You are witnesses, and so is God, how devoutly and justly and blamelessly we behaved ourselves toward you believers; 11 Just as you know, how each one of you, as a father his own children, 12 encouraging you and comforting [and testifying]ᵈ for you to walk worthily of God, the one calling you into his own kingdom and glory.

13 [And]ᵉ For this reason we also give thanks to God unceasingly, for when you received the word of God which you heard from us, you accepted it not as the word of men, but as it [truly]ᶠ is, the word of God, which also is at work in you who believe.

14 For you became imitators, brothers, of the churches of God that are in Judea in Christ Jesus, because you suffered the same things from your own countrymen as they did from the Jews, 15 who killed both the Lord Jesus and {the}ᵍ prophets, and drove us out, and displease God, and oppose all men,

16 hindering us from speaking to the Gentiles that they might be saved, so as always to fill up the measure of their sins. But wrath has come upon them at last.

17 But we, brothers, being separated from you for a short time, in presence not in heart, were all the more eager to see your face with great desire. 18 {Because}ʰ we wanted to come to you, I, Paul, both once and twice, but Satan hindered us.

19 For what is our hope, or joy, or crown of {boasting}?ⁱ Is it not even you, before our Lord Jesus [[Christ]]ʲ at his coming? 20 For you are our glory and joy.

3 1 Therefore, no longer able to bear it, we decided to be left behind in Athens alone, 2 and we sent Timothy, our brother and servant of God [[and our fellow worker]]ᵏ in the gospel of Christ, to strengthen you and encourage you concerning your faith, 3 so that no one would be shaken by these afflictions. For you yourselves know that we are destined for this. 4 Indeed, when we were with you, we kept telling you that we were going to be afflicted, just as it happened, and you know.

5 For this reason, I could no longer bear it and sent to know your faith, lest somehow the tempter had tempted you and our labor would be in vain.

6 But now, having come to us from you, Timothy has brought us good news of your faith and love, and that you always have good memories of us, longing to see us just as we also long to see you. 7 For this reason, we were comforted, brothers, in you in all

---

ᵃ 2:6, **you:** Some manuscripts read "us." A(02).

ᵇ 2:7, **infants:** NA28 ‖ Some manuscripts read "gentile." A(02) BYZ TR.

ᶜ 2:9, **For:** Included in BYZ TR.

ᵈ 2:12, **and testifying:** Absent from A(02).

ᵉ 2:13, **And:** Absent from BYZ TR.

ᶠ 2:13, **truly:** Absent from ℵ(01).

ᵍ 2:15, **the:** Some manuscripts read "their own." BYZ TR.

ʰ 2:18, **Because:** Some manuscripts read "Therefore." BYZ TR.

ⁱ 2:19, **boasting:** A(02) reads "exultation."

ʲ 2:19, **Christ:** Included in TR.

ᵏ 3:2, **and our fellow worker:** Included in BYZ TR.

{our}[a] distress and affliction through your faith. 8 For now we live, if you stand firm in the Lord. 9 For what thanksgiving can we return to {God}[b] for you, for all the joy with which we rejoice for your sake before our {God},[c] 10 night and day praying exceedingly that we might see your face and complete what is lacking in your faith?

11 Now may our God and Father himself, and our Lord Jesus [[Christ]],[d] direct our way to you;

12 And may {the Lord}[e] cause you to increase and abound in love for one another and for all, just as we also do for you, 13 to strengthen your hearts blameless in holiness before our God and Father at the coming of our Lord Jesus [[Christ]][f] with all his holy ones [amen].[g]

4 1 Finally then, brothers, we ask and urge you in the Lord Jesus, [that][h] as you received from us how you ought to walk and please God, just as you are walking, [so that you may abound].[i]

2 For you know what instructions we gave you through the Lord Jesus. 3 For this is the will of God, your sanctification: that you abstain from sexual immorality; 4 that each one of you know how to control his own body in holiness and honor, 5 not in the passion of lust like the Gentiles who do not know God; 6 that no one transgress and wrong his brother in this matter, because the Lord is an avenger in all these things, as we [also][j] told you beforehand and solemnly warned you.

7 For God has not called us for impurity, but in holiness. 8 Therefore, the one who disregards this does not disregard a man, but God, who [also][k] gives His Holy Spirit to {you}.[l]

9 Now concerning brotherly love, you have no need for anyone to write to you, for you yourselves have been taught by God to love one another, 10 for indeed you do this to all the brothers who are throughout Macedonia. But we urge you, brothers, to do this more and more, 11 and to aspire to live quietly, and to mind your own affairs, and to work with your [own][m] hands, as we instructed you, 12 so that you may walk properly before outsiders and be dependent on no one.

13 But {we}[n] do not want you to be ignorant, brothers, about those who {are asleep},[o] so that you may not grieve as others do who have no hope. 14 For if we believe that Jesus died and rose again, in the same way, God will bring with him those who have fallen asleep through Jesus.

15 For this we declare to you by a word from the Lord, that we who are alive, who are left until the coming of the Lord, will not precede those who have fallen asleep. 16 For the Lord himself will descend from heaven with a cry of command, with the voice of an archangel, and with the sound of the trumpet of God. And the dead in Christ will rise first. 17 Then we who are alive, who are left, will be caught up together with them in the clouds to meet the

---

a 3:7, **our:** A(02) reads "your."

b 3:9, **God:** א(01) reads "the Lord."

c 3:9, **God:** א(01) reads "Lord."

d 3:11, **Christ:** Included in BYZ TR.

e 3:12, **the Lord:** A(02) reads "God."

f 3:13, **Christ:** Included in BYZ TR.

g 3:13, **Amen:** א(01) A(02) ‖ Absent from B(03) BYZ TR.

h 4:1, **that:** Absent from א(01) A(02) BYZ TR.

i 4:1, **so that you may abound:** Absent from BYZ TR.

j 4:6, **also:** Absent from A(02).

k 4:8, **also:** Absent from A(02) B(03).

l 4:8, **you:** Some manuscripts read "us." A(02) TR.

m 4:11, **own:** Absent from א(01) B(03).

n 4:13, **we:** TR reads "I."

o 4:13, **are asleep:** Some manuscripts read "have fallen asleep." BYZ TR.

Lord in the air, and so we will always be with the Lord.[a]

18 Therefore, encourage one another with these words.

5 1 Concerning the times and the seasons, brothers, you have no need for anything to be written to you. 2 For you yourselves know precisely that the day of the Lord comes like a thief in the night.

3 [[For]][b] When they say, "Peace and safety," then sudden destruction comes upon them, as labor pains upon a pregnant woman, and they shall not escape.

4 But you, brothers, are not in darkness, so that the day would overtake you like a thief; 5 [for][c] you are all sons of light and sons of the day. We are not of the night nor of darkness.

6 So then, let us not sleep as the others do, but let us stay awake and be sober.

7 For those who sleep, sleep at night, and those who get drunk, get drunk at night. 8 But since we are of the day, let us be sober, putting on the breastplate of faith [and love],[d] and as a helmet, the hope of salvation.

9 For God has not destined us for wrath, but for obtaining salvation through our Lord Jesus [Christ],[e] 10 who died for us, so that whether we are awake or asleep, we may live together with him.

11 Therefore encourage one another and build up one another, just as you also are doing.

12 Now we ask you, brothers, to recognize those who labor among you and are over you in the Lord and admonish you, 13 and to esteem them very highly in love because of their work.

Be at peace among yourselves.

14 We urge you, brothers, admonish the unruly, encourage the fainthearted, help the weak, be patient with everyone.

15 See that no one repays evil for evil, but always pursue what is good [and][f] for one another and for all.

16 Rejoice always.

17 Pray without ceasing.

18 In everything give thanks; for this is the will of God in Christ Jesus for you.

19 Do not quench the Spirit.

20 Do not despise prophecies, 21 [but][g] test everything; hold fast to what is good.

22 Abstain from every form of evil.

23 Now may the God of peace himself sanctify you entirely; and may your spirit and soul and body be preserved blameless at the coming of our Lord Jesus Christ. 24 The one who calls you is faithful, who will also do it.

25 Brothers, pray [also][h] for us.

26 Greet all the brothers with a holy kiss.

27 I adjure you by the Lord to have this letter read to all the [[holy]][i] brothers.

28 The grace of our Lord Jesus Christ be with you. [[Amen]][jk]

---

a 4:15-17, Matthew 24:30-31, Mark 13:26-27, Luke 21:27-28.

b 5:3, **For:** Absent from BYZ TR.

c 5:5, **for:** Absent from BYZ TR.

d 5:8, **and love:** Absent from ℵ(01).

e 5:9, **Christ:** Absent B(03).

f 5:15, **and:** Absent from ℵ(01) A(02).

g 5:21, **but:** Absent from ℵ(01) A(02) TR.

h 5:25, **also:** Absent from ℵ(01) A(02) BYZ TR.

i 5:27, **holy:** Included in A(02) BYZ TR.

j 5:28, **Amen:** Included in A(02) BYZ TR.

k 5:28, TR includes the postscript, "To the Thessalonians, the first letter written from Athens."

Second Thessalonians[a]

1 ¹Paul, Silvanus, and Timothy, to the church of the Thessalonians in God our Father and the Lord Jesus Christ,[b] ²Grace to you and peace from God {our}[c] Father and of the Lord Jesus Christ.

³We ought to give thanks to God always for you, brothers, as it is fitting, because your faith is growing abundantly and the love of each one of you all for one another is increasing, ⁴so that, they may boast about us in your presence in the churches of God for your endurance and faith in all your persecutions and in the afflictions that you are enduring, ⁵a clear sign of the righteous judgment of God, that you may be considered worthy of the kingdom of God, for which you also suffer,

⁶Since indeed it is just for God to repay with affliction those who afflict you, ⁷and to give relief to you who are afflicted as well as to us, when the Lord Jesus is revealed from heaven with his mighty angels ⁸in a flame of fire, inflicting vengeance on those who do not know God and on those who do not obey the gospel of our Lord Jesus [[Christ]],[d] ⁹who will suffer the penalty of eternal destruction, away from the presence of the Lord and from the glory of his might, ¹⁰when he comes to be glorified in his saints and to be marveled at among all who have believed, because our testimony to you was believed, on that day.

¹¹For this we also pray always for you, that our God may deem you worthy of the calling and may fulfill every desire for goodness and work of faith with power, ¹²so that the name of our Lord Jesus may be glorified in you, and you in him, according to the grace of our God and of the Lord Jesus [[Christ]].[e]

2 ¹We ask you, brothers, concerning the coming of {our}[f] Lord Jesus Christ and our gathering to him, ²not to be quickly shaken from your mind or alarmed, neither by a spirit, nor by a message, nor by a letter as if from us, as though the day of {the Lord}[g] has come.

³Let no one deceive you in any way. For it will not be, unless the rebellion comes first, and the man of {lawlessness}[h] is revealed, the son of destruction, ⁴who opposes and exalts himself against all that is called God or that is worshiped, so that he sits in the temple of God, [[as God]][i] showing himself that he is God.

⁵Do you not remember that when I was still with you, I told you these things?

---

a 1:0, **Title ("Second Thessalonians"):** Absent from א(01) B(03). ‖ 𝔓30 A(02) BYZ reads "to the Thessalonians, second." ‖ TR reads "of Paul the apostle, the second letter to the Thessalonians."

b 1:1, **Christ:** See footnote for Christ in Luke 2:11.

c 1:2, **our:** B(03) reads "the."

d 1:8, **Christ:** Included in BYZ TR.

e 1:12, **Christ:** Included in BYZ TR.

f 2:1, **our:** Some manuscripts read "the." B(03).

g 2:2, **the Lord:** Some manuscripts read "Christ." BYZ TR.

h 2:3, **lawlessness:** Some manuscripts read "sin." BYZ TR.

i 2:4, **as God:** Included in BYZ TR.

6 And now you know what is restraining, for it to be revealed in its own time. 7 For the mystery of lawlessness is already at work; only the one who now restrains will do so until he is out of the way. 8 And then the lawless one will be revealed, whom the Lord [Jesus]ᵃ will destroy with the breath of his mouth and will bring to nothing by the appearance of his coming, 9 whose coming is in accordance with the workingᵇ of Satan, with all power and signs and false wonders, 10 and with all wicked deception {for those}ᶜ who are perishing, because they did not receive the love of the truth so as to be saved.

11 And because of this, God {sends}ᵈ them a workingᵉ of delusion, for them to believe the falsehood, 12 so that all may be judged who did not believe the truth but took pleasure in unrighteousness.

13 But we ought to always give thanks to God for you, brothers loved by the Lord, because God chose you as the firstfruits for salvation through sanctification by the Spirit and faith in the truth. 14 For this purpose [also]ᶠ he called {you}ᵍ through our gospel, for the obtaining of the glory of our Lord Jesus Christ.

15 So then, brothers, stand firm and hold to the traditions which you were taught, whether by word or by our letter.

16 Now may our Lord {Jesus Christ}ʰ himself and [our]ⁱ God the Father, who loved us and gave us eternal comfort and good hope by grace, 17 comfort your hearts and strengthen [[you]]ʲ in every good work and word.

3 1 Finally, pray for us, brothers, that the word of the Lord may run and be glorified, just as it is with you, 2 and that we may be delivered from perverse and evil men; for not all have faith.

3 But {the Lord}ᵏ is faithful, who will establish you and guard you from the evil one.

4 But we have confidence in the Lord concerning you, that you are doing and will do the things we command. 5 May the Lord direct your hearts into the love of God and into the endurance of Christ.

ᵃ 2:8, **Jesus:** Absent from ℵ(01) B(03) BYZ TR.
ᵇ 2:9, **working:** The Greek word *energeia* pertains to metaphysical working, operation, action (BDAG, ἐνέργεια).
ᶜ 2:10, **for those:** Some manuscripts read "among." BYZ TR.
ᵈ 2:11, **sends:** Some manuscripts read "will send." BYZ TR.
ᵉ 2:11, **working:** The Greek word *energeia* pertains to metaphysical working, operation, action (BDAG, ἐνέργεια).
ᶠ 2:14, **also:** Absent from B(03) BYZ TR.
ᵍ 2:14, **you:** Some manuscripts read "us." A(02) B(03).
ʰ 2:16, **Jesus Christ:** B(03) reads "Christ Jesus."
ⁱ 2:16, **our:** Absent from ℵ(01).
ʲ 2:17, **you:** Included in BYZ TR.
ᵏ 3:3, **the Lord:** A(02) reads "God."

6 We instruct you, brothers, in the name of {our}[a] Lord Jesus Christ, to keep away from every brother who is living in disorder and not according to the tradition that they received from us.

7 For you yourselves know how you ought to imitate us, because we were not disorderly[b] referring among you, 8 nor did we eat bread as a gift from anyone, but in labor and hardship, working throughout night and day, so as not to burden any of you; 9 not because we do not have the right, but in order to provide ourselves as a model for you to imitate us.

10 For even when we were with you, we commanded you this: If anyone will not work, neither shall he eat.

11 For we hear that some among you are leading an undisciplined life, doing no work at all, but are busybodies.

12 Now such persons we command and exhort {in the}[c] Lord Jesus Christ to work in quietness and eat their own bread.

13 But you, brothers, do not grow weary in doing good.

14 And if anyone does not obey our word in this letter, note that person, [[and]][d] do not keep company with him, that he may be ashamed. 15 Yet do not count him as an enemy, but admonish him as a brother.

16 Now may the Lord of peace Himself give you peace always in every way. The Lord be with you all.

17 The greeting is in my own hand, Paul's, which is a sign in every letter; so I write.

18 The grace of our Lord Jesus Christ be with you all. [[Amen]][ef]

---

a 3:6, **our:** B(03) reads "the."

b 3:7, **disorderly:** Or undisciplined. The Greek word means to violate prescribed or recognized order, behave inappropriately. (BDAG, ἀτακτέω).

c 3:12, **in the:** Some manuscripts read "through our." BYZ TR.

d 3:14, **and:** Included in BYZ TR.

e 3:18, **Amen:** Included in A(02) BYZ TR.

f 3:18, TR includes the postscript "To the Thessalonians, a second letter written from Athens."

First Timothy[a]

1 [1]Paul, an apostle of Christ[b] Jesus by the command of God our savior and of {Christ Jesus}[c] our hope, [2]To Timothy, my true child in the faith: Grace, mercy, and peace from God {the}[d] Father and Christ Jesus our Lord.

[3]As I urged you when I was going to Macedonia, remain in Ephesus so that you may instruct certain men not to teach different doctrine, [4]nor to pay attention to myths and endless genealogies, which promote disputes rather than God's administration in faith.

[5]The aim of our charge is love that issues from a pure heart and a good conscience and sincere faith. [6]Some have swerved from these and have turned aside to fruitless discussion, [7]desiring to be teachers of the law, without understanding either what they are saying or the things about which they make confident assertions.

[8]We know, however, that the law is good, if one uses it lawfully, [9]knowing this, that the law is not laid down for the righteous, but for the lawless and disobedient, for the ungodly and sinners, for the unholy and profane, for those who strike their father and mother, for murderers of men, [10]for the sexually immoral, men who practice homosexuality, enslavers, liars, perjurers, and whatever else is contrary to [sound][e] doctrine, [11]in accordance with the gospel of the glory of the blessed God, which was entrusted to me.

[12]I am grateful to the one who has strengthened me, Christ Jesus our Lord, because he considered me trustworthy, putting me into service, [13]even though I was formerly a blasphemer, a persecutor, and a man of violence. But I received mercy because I had acted ignorantly in unbelief, [14]and the grace of our Lord overflowed for me with the faith and love that are in Christ Jesus.

[15]The saying is trustworthy and deserving of full acceptance, that Christ Jesus came into the world to save sinners - of whom I am the foremost. [16]But for that very reason I received mercy, so that in me, as the foremost, {Christ Jesus}[f] might display the utmost patience, making me an example to those who would come to believe in him for eternal life.

[17]To the king of the ages, immortal, invisible, the only [[wise]][g] God, be honor and glory forever and ever. Amen.

[18]This command I entrust to you, child Timothy, in accordance with the prophecies previously made about you, so that by them you may wage the good warfare, [19]having faith and a good conscience, which some having rejected concerning the faith have suffered shipwreck, [20]of whom are Hymenaeus and Alexander, whom I have handed over to Satan, so that they may be taught not to blaspheme.

---

[a] 1:0, **Title ("First Timothy"):** Absent from ℵ(01). ‖ A(02) BYZ reads "to Timothy, first." ‖ TR reads "Of Paul the apostle, the first letter to Timothy."

[b] 1:1, **Christ:** See footnote for Christ in Luke 2:11.

[c] 1:1, **Christ Jesus:** Some manuscripts read "the Lord Jesus Christ." A(02) BYZ TR.

[d] 1:2, **the:** Some manuscripts read "our." BYZ TR.

[e] 1:10, **sound:** Absent from A(02).

[f] 1:16, **Christ Jesus:** Some manuscripts read "Jesus Christ." ℵ(01) BYZ TR.

[g] 1:17, **wise:** Included in ℵ(01) BYZ TR.

2 ¹ Therefore, I urge first of all that requests, prayers, intercessions, and thanksgivings be made for all men, ² for kings and all those in authority, that we may lead a quiet and peaceful life in all godliness and dignity.

³ [[For]]ᵃ This is good and acceptable in the sight of God our savior, ⁴ who desires all men to be saved and to come to the knowledge of the truth.

⁵ For there is one God, and one mediator between God and men, the man Christ Jesus, ⁶ who gave himself as a ransom for all, [the testimony]ᵇ at the proper time.

⁷ For this I was appointed a herald and an apostle - I am telling the truth [[in Christ]],ᶜ I am not lying - a teacher of the Gentiles in {faith}ᵈ and truth.

⁸ Therefore, I desire that men pray in every place, lifting up holy hands without anger and argument.

⁹ Likewise, [also]ᵉ women should adorn themselves in modest attire, with respect and self-control, not with braids {and}ᶠ gold or pearls or expensive clothing, ¹⁰ but with what is proper for women who profess godliness, through good works.

¹¹ A woman should learn in quietness and full submission.

¹² But I do not permit a woman to teach or to exercise authority over a man, but to be in quietness.

¹³ For Adam was formed first, then Eve.

¹⁴ And Adam was not deceived, but the woman, being {deceived},ᵍ fell into transgression.

¹⁵ But she will be saved through childbearing, if they continue in faith, love, and holiness, with self-control.

3 ¹ The word is trustworthy. If anyone aspires to the office of overseer, they desire a noble task. ² Therefore, an overseer must be above reproach, the husband of one wife, sober-minded, self-controlled, respectable, hospitable, able to teach, ³ not given to drunkenness, not violent, [[not greedy for gain]]ʰ but gentle, not quarrelsome, not a lover of money.

⁴ They must manage their own household well, with all dignity keeping their children submissive

⁵ But if someone does not know how to manage his own household, how will he care for the church of God? ⁶ Not a recent convert, lest they become conceited and fall into the condemnation of the devil.

⁷ Moreover, {one}ⁱ must also have a good reputation with those outside, so as not to fall into disgrace and the snare of the devil.

⁸ Likewise, deacons should be dignified, not double-tongued, not addicted to much wine, not greedy for dishonest gain, ⁹ holding the mystery of the faith with a clear conscience.

¹⁰ And let these also first be tested, then let them serve, being without accusation.

¹¹ Likewise, women should be dignified, not slanderous, sober-minded, faithful in all things.

¹² Deacons must be husbands of one wife, managing their children and their own households well.

ᵃ 2:3, **For:** Included in BYZ TR.

ᵇ 2:6, **the testimony:** Absent from A(02).

ᶜ 2:7, **in Christ:** Included in ℵ(01) BYZ TR.

ᵈ 2:7, **faith:** Some manuscripts read "knowledge." ℵ(01).

ᵉ 2:9, **also:** Absent from ℵ(01) A(02).

ᶠ 2:9, **and:** Some manuscripts read "or." BYZ TR.

ᵍ 2:14, **deceived:** Some manuscripts read "led astray." BYZ TR.

ʰ 3:3, **not greedy for gain:** Included in BYZ TR.

ⁱ 3:7, **one:** Included in BYZ TR.

13 For those who have served well as deacons acquire a good standing for themselves and great confidence in the faith that is in Christ Jesus.

14 I am writing these things to you, hoping to come [to you]ᵃ soon; 15 but if I delay, you may know how one ought to behave in the house of God, which is the assembly of the living God, the pillar and foundation of truth.

16 And without a doubt, the mystery of godliness is great: {who}ᵇ was revealed in the flesh, was justified in the spirit, was seen by angels, was proclaimed among the nations, was believed in the world, was taken up in glory.

4 1 The Spirit clearly says that in later times some will abandon the faith and follow deceiving spirits and teachings of demons, 2 through the insincerity of liars whose consciences are seared, 3 who forbid marriage and require abstinence from foods that God created to be received with thanksgiving by those who believe and know the truth.

4 For everything created by God is good, and nothing is to be rejected if it is received with thanksgiving, 5 for it is made holy by the word of God and prayer.

6 If you put these things before the brothers, you will be a good servant of {Christ Jesus},ᶜ being nourished in the words of the faith and of the good teaching that you have followed; 7 but the profane ones and {silly myths},ᵈ reject.

8 For while bodily training is of some value, godliness is of value in every way, as it holds promise for the present life and also for the life to come.

9 The saying is trustworthy and deserving of [full]ᵉ acceptance.

10 For this reason, we [[also]]ᶠ labor and {strive},ᵍ because we have put our hope in the living God, who is the savior of all men, most of all, of the faithful.

11 Command these things and teach them.

12 Let no one despise you for your youth, but become an example to the believers in word, in conduct, in love, [[in spirit,]]ʰ in faith, in purity.

13 Until I come, pay attention to the reading, the exhortation, the teaching.

14 Do not neglect the gift within you, which was given to you through prophecy with the laying on of hands by the elders.

15 Meditate on these things, immerse yourself in them, so that your progress may be evident to all.

16 Pay attention to yourself and to the teaching; persist in it, for by doing this you will save both yourself and those hearing [you].ⁱ

5 1 Do not rebuke an older man, but encourage him as a father, younger men as brothers, 2 older women as mothers, younger women as sisters, in all purity.

3 Honor {widows}ʲ who are truly widows.

4 But if any widow has children or grandchildren, let them first learn to show piety at home and to repay their parents; for this is [[good and]]ᵏ acceptable in the sight of God.

ᵃ 3:14, **to you:** Absent from 𝔓133.
ᵇ 3:16, **who:** Some manuscripts read "God." BYZ TR.
ᶜ 4:6, **Christ Jesus:** Some manuscripts read "Jesus Christ." BYZ TR.
ᵈ 4:7, **silly myths:** Greek "old wives tales." ‖ C(04) reads silly wraths.
ᵉ 4:9, **full:** Absent from ℵ(01).
ᶠ 4:10, **also:** Absent from BYZ TR.
ᵍ 4:10, **strive:** Some manuscripts read "are reproached." BYZ TR.
ʰ 4:12, **in spirit:** Included in BYZ TR.
ⁱ 4:16, **you:** Absent from ℵ(01).
ʲ 5:3, **widows:** Absent from ℵ(01).
ᵏ 5:4, **good and:** Included in TR.

5 Now she who is truly a widow, and left alone, puts her hope in {God}[a] and continues in supplications and prayers night and day, 6 but she who is self-indulgent is dead even while she lives.

7 Prescribe these things as well, so that *they may be* blameless above reproach.

8 But if anyone does not provide for his own, and especially for those of his household, he has denied the faith and is worse than an unbeliever.

9 Let a widow be enrolled if she is not less than sixty years old, having been the wife of one husband, 10 having a reputation for good works; and if she has brought up children, if she has shown hospitality to strangers, if she has washed the saints' feet, if she has assisted those in distress, and if she has devoted herself to every good work.

11 But refuse younger widows; for when they feel sensual desires in disregard of Christ,[b] they want to marry 12 and incur judgment because they have set aside their first faith;

13 At the same time they also learn to be idle, as they go around from house to house; and not merely idle, but also gossips and busybodies, talking about things not proper to mention.

14 Therefore, I want younger widows to get married, bear children, keep house, and give the enemy no occasion for reproach; 15 for some have already turned aside to follow Satan.

16 If any believing {woman}[c] has relatives who are widows, let her assist them, and the church must not be burdened, so that it may assist those who are truly widows.

17 Let the elders who rule well be considered worthy of double honor, especially those who labor in the word and in teaching. 18 For the scripture says, "You shall not muzzle an ox when it is treading out the grain," and, "The worker is worthy of his wages."[d]

19 Do not accept an accusation against an elder, except on the evidence of two or three witnesses.

20 Rebuke those who sin in the presence of all, so that the rest may also have fear.

21 I solemnly charge you in the presence of God and {Christ Jesus}[e] and the chosen angels, that you keep these things without prejudice, doing nothing by partiality.

22 Do not quickly lay hands on anyone, nor participate in others' sins; keep yourself pure.

23 No longer drink only water, but use a little wine for the sake of your stomach and your frequent ailments.

24 The sins of some men are clearly evident, leading to judgment, but for others, they appear later. 25 In the same way, good deeds are obvious, and those [[that are]][f] otherwise cannot be hidden.

6 1 All who are under the yoke as slaves, let them consider their own masters as worthy of all honor, so that the name of God and the teaching may not be blasphemed. 2 And those who have believing masters should not disrespect them because they are brothers, but rather they should serve them, because those who benefit by their good service are believers and beloved.

Teach and encourage these things. 3 If anyone teaches otherwise and does not agree with the sound words of our Lord {Jesus Christ}[g] and the teaching that is in accordance with

---

a 5:5, **God:** ℵ(01) reads "the Lord."

b 5:11, **feel sensual desires in disregard of Christ:** Or want to seduce the anointed one.

c 5:16, **woman:** Some manuscripts read "man or woman." BYZ TR.

d 5:18, Deuteronomy 25:4, Luke 10:7.

e 5:21, **Christ Jesus:** Some manuscripts read "the Lord Jesus Christ." BYZ TR.

f 5:25, **that are:** Included in BYZ TR.

g 6:3, **Jesus Christ:** Some manuscripts read "Christ Jesus." 𝔓61.

godliness, 4he has become conceited, understanding nothing. He has an unhealthy craving for controversy and for quarrels about words, which produce envy, dissension, slander, evil suspicions, 5constant friction among people who are depraved in mind and deprived of the truth, imagining that godliness is a means of gain.ᵃ Withdraw from such people.ᵇ

6But there is great gain in godliness with contentment; 7for we brought nothing into the world, and [[it is clear]]ᶜ we cannot take anything out of it.

8But if we have food and clothing, with these we will be content.

9But those who desire to be rich fall into temptation and a trap and many foolish and harmful desires, which plunge men into ruin and destruction. 10For the love of money is a root of all kinds of evil, and some by longing for it have wandered away from the faith and pierced themselves with many griefs.

11But you, O man of God, flee from these things; pursue righteousness, [godliness,]ᵈ faith, love, endurance, gentleness. 12Fight the good fight of faith, take hold of the eternal life to which you were called and you confessed the good confession in the presence of many witnesses.

13I charge [you]ᵉ in the presence of God, who gives life to all things, and of {Christ Jesus},ᶠ who testified the good confession before Pontius Pilate, 14to keep the instruction unstained and free from reproach until the appearing of our Lord {Jesus Christ},ᵍ 15whom, at the proper time, the blessed and only Sovereign will reveal, the King of kings and Lord of lords, 16who alone has immortality, dwelling in unapproachable light, whom no one has ever seen or can see; to him be honor and eternal dominion. Amen.

17Instruct those who are rich in this present age not to be haughty, nor to set their hope on the uncertainty of wealth, but on [[the living]]ʰ God, to the one providing us with all things richly for enjoyment. 18They should do good, be rich in good works, be generous and ready to share, 19storing up for themselves a good foundation for the future, so that they may take hold of the life that is {truly}ⁱ life.

20O Timothy, guard the deposit entrusted to you, turning away from the profane empty chatter and contradictions of falsely named knowledge, 21which some professing have missed the mark concerning the faith.

Grace be with you. [[Amen]]ʲᵏ

ᵃ 6:5, **gain:** Or, material or worldly gain.
ᵇ 6:5, **Withdraw from such people:** Included in BYZ TR.
ᶜ 6:7, **it is clear:** Included in BYZ TR.
ᵈ 6:11, **godliness:** Absent from ℵ(01).
ᵉ 6:13, **you:** Absent from ℵ(01).
ᶠ 6:13, **Christ Jesus:** ℵ(01) reads "Jesus Christ."
ᵍ 6:14, **Jesus Christ:** ℵ(01) reads "Christ Jesus."
ʰ 6:17, **the living:** Included in BYZ TR.
ⁱ 6:19, **truly:** Some manuscripts read "eternal." BYZ TR.
ʲ 6:21, **Amen:** Included in BYZ TR.
ᵏ 6:21 TR includes the postscript, "To Timothy, the first letter written from Laodicea, which is the metropolis of Phrygia Pacatiana."

Second Timothy[a]

1 [1]Paul, an apostle of {Christ[b] Jesus}[c] by the will of God, according to the promise of life that is in Christ Jesus.

[2]To Timothy, my beloved child: Grace, mercy, and peace from God the Father and Christ Jesus our Lord.

[3]I thank God, whom I serve with a clear conscience as my ancestors did, as I constantly remember you in my prayers night and day, [4]longing to see you, remembering your tears, so that I may be filled with joy, [5]Having received remembrance of the sincere faith that is in you, which first dwelt in your grandmother Lois and your mother Eunice, and I am convinced is in you as well.

[6]For this reason, I remind you to rekindle the {gift}[d] of God, which is in you through the laying on of my hands. [7]For God did not give us a spirit of fear, but of power, and love, and self-control.

[8]Therefore, do not be ashamed of the testimony [of our Lord],[e] nor of me, his prisoner, but share in suffering for the gospel according to the power of God, [9]who saved us and called us with a holy calling, not according to our works, but according to his own purpose and grace, which was given to us in Christ Jesus before the ages began, [10]but has now been revealed through the appearing of our Savior {Christ Jesus},[f] who abolished death and brought life and immortality to light through the gospel, [11]for which I was appointed a preacher and an apostle and a teacher [[of the Gentiles]],[g] [12]for which reason I also suffer these things.

But I am not ashamed, for I know whom I have believed and I am convinced that he is able to guard my deposit[h] until that day.

[13]Hold the pattern of sound words which you have heard from me, in faith and love which are in Christ Jesus. [14]Guard the good deposit through the Holy Spirit[i] in us.

[15]You know this, that all who are in Asia have turned away from me, among whom are {Phygelus}[j] and Hermogenes. [16]May the Lord grant mercy to the household of Onesiphorus, for he often refreshed me and was not ashamed of my chains, [17]but when he arrived in Rome, he diligently searched for me and found me. [18]May the Lord grant him to find mercy from the Lord on that day! And you know very well how much service he rendered in Ephesus.

2 [1]Therefore, my child, be strong in the grace that is in Christ Jesus, [2]and what you have heard from me through many witnesses, entrust these things to faithful men, who will be able to teach others also.

---

a 1:0, **Title ("Second Timothy")**: Absent from ℵ(01). ‖ A(02) BYZ reads "To Timothy, Second." ‖ TR reads "The second letter of Paul the apostle to Timothy."

b 1:1, **Christ**: See footnote for Christ in Luke 2:11.

c 1:1, **Christ Jesus**: Some manuscripts read "Jesus Christ." A(02) BYZ TR.

d 1:6, **gift**: ℵ(01) reads "will."

e 1:8, **of our Lord**: Absent from ℵ(01).

f 1:10, **Christ Jesus**: Some manuscripts read "Jesus Christ." C(04) BYZ TR.

g 1:11, **of the Gentiles**: Included in C(04) BYZ TR.

h 1:12, **deposit**: That is, property entrusted to another (BDAG, παραθήκη).

i 1:14, **Spirit**: See footnote for Spirit in Luke 1:15.

j 1:15, **Phygelus**: Some manuscripts read "Phygellus." A(02) TR.

3 [[You, therefore,]]ᵃ Endure hardship with me, as a good soldier of {Christ Jesus}.ᵇ 4 No one serving as a soldier gets entangled in the affairs of everyday life, so that he may please the one who enlisted him.

5 If indeed someone competes, they are not crowned unless they compete according to the rules. 6 The hardworking farmer ought to be the first to receive a share of the crops. 7 Understand what I am saying; {for}ᶜ the Lord will give you insight in all things.

8 Remember Jesus Christ, raised from the dead, from the seed of David, according to my gospel, 9 in which I suffer hardship to the point of chains as a criminal, but the word of God is not bound.

10 For this reason, I endure all things for the sake of the chosen ones, so that they too may obtain the salvation that is in Christ Jesus, with eternal glory.

11 This saying is trustworthy: For if we died together, we will also live together; 12 if we endure, we will also reign together; if we deny him, he also will deny us; 13 if we are faithless, he remains faithful; [for]ᵈ he cannot denyᵉ himself.

14 Remind them of these things, solemnly testifying before {God}ᶠ not to quarrel about words, which is of no use and leads to the ruin of the hearers.

15 Strive to present yourself approved to {God},ᵍ an unashamed worker, rightly dividing the word of truth.

16 But avoid irreverent, empty speech, for this will lead to more and more ungodliness, 17 and their words will spread like gangrene. Among them are Hymenaeus and Philetus, 18 who have deviated from the truth, saying [the]ʰ resurrection has already occurred, and they are overturning the faith of some.

19 However, the solid foundation of {God}ⁱ stands, having this seal: "The Lord knows [[all]]ʲ those who are his," and, "Let everyone who names the name of {the Lord}ᵏ depart from iniquity."ˡ

20 In a large house there are not only gold and silver vessels, but also wooden and clay ones, and some are for honor, others for dishonor. 21 Therefore, if anyone cleanses himself from these things, he will be [a vessel for honor,]ᵐ sanctified, [[and]]ⁿ useful to the Master, prepared for every good work.

22 But flee youthful desires, and pursue righteousness, faith, love, peace, along with {all} ᵒthose who call on the Lord from a pure heart.

23 But avoid foolish and uneducated disputes, knowing that they generate strife.

ᵃ 2:3, **You, therefore:** Included in BYZ TR.

ᵇ 2:3, **Christ Jesus:** Some manuscripts read "Jesus Christ." BYZ TR.

ᶜ 2:7, **for:** Some manuscripts read "may." BYZ TR.

ᵈ 2:13, **for:** Absent from BYZ TR.

ᵉ 2:13, **deny:** Or disregard. The Greek word means (1) to refuse consent to something, refuse, disdain, (2) the state that something is not true, deny (3) to disclaim association with a person or event, deny, repudiate, disown, or (4) refuse to pay any attention to, disregard, renounce (BDAG, ἀρνέομαι).

ᶠ 2:14, **God:** ℵ(01) C(04) ‖ Some manuscripts read "the Lord." A(02) BYZ TR.

ᵍ 2:15, **God:** A(02) reads "Christ."

ʰ 2:18, **the:** Absent from ℵ(01).

ⁱ 2:19, **God:** ℵ(01) reads "the Lord."

ʲ 2:19, **all:** Included in ℵ(01).

ᵏ 2:19, **the Lord:** TR reads "Christ."

ˡ 2:19, Numbers 16:5 LXX, Numbers 16:26, Isaiah 52:11 LXX.

ᵐ 2:21, **a vessel for honor:** Absent from ℵ(01).

ⁿ 2:21, **and:** Included in C(04) BYZ TR.

ᵒ 2:22, **all:** Included in A(02) C(04).

24 A servant of the Lord must not quarrel but be gentle to all, able to teach, patient, 25 correcting those who oppose him with gentleness, so that perhaps God may grant them [repentance]ᵃ leading to the knowledge of the truth, 26 and they may come to their senses and escape from the snare of the devil, having been taken captive by him to do his will.

3 1 But know this, that in the last days difficult times will come; 2 for men will be lovers of themselves, lovers of money, boastful, arrogant, blasphemers, disobedient to parents, ungrateful, unholy, 3 unloving, [irreconcilable,]ᵇ slanderers, without self-control, brutal, not lovers of good, 4 traitorous, reckless, conceited, lovers of pleasure rather than lovers of God, 5 having a form of godliness but denying its power; and avoid such people.

6 For among them are those who creep into households and captivate weak women, burdened with sins, led away by various desires [[and pleasures]],ᶜ 7 always learning and never able to come to the knowledge of the truth.

8 Just as {Jannes}ᵈ and Jambresᵉ opposed Moses, so these also oppose the truth, men corrupted in mind, disqualified concerning the faith. 9 But they will not make further progress; for their {folly}ᶠ will be obvious to all, just as theirs was.

10 But you have followed my teaching, conduct, purpose, faith, patience, [love,]ᵍ endurance, 11 persecutions, and sufferings, such as happened to me in Antioch, Iconium, and Lystra; what persecutions I endured, and out of them all the Lord rescued me.

12 And indeed, all who desire to live a godly life in Christ Jesus will be persecuted.

13 But evil men and impostors will proceed from bad to worse, deceiving and being deceived.

14 But you, remain in what you have learned and have become convinced of, knowing from whom you learned it, 15 and that from infancy you have known, [the]ʰ sacred writings, which are able to make you wise for salvation through faith in Christ Jesus.

16 Every scripture is God-breathedⁱ and beneficial for teaching, for reproof, for correction, and for training in righteousness, 17 so that the person of God may be complete, equipped for every good work.

4 1 [[Therefore,]]ʲ I solemnly charge you in the presence of God and [[of the Lord]]ᵏ {Christ Jesus},ˡ who is to judge the living and the dead, {and by}ᵐ his appearing and his kingdom: 2 Preach the word; be ready in season and out of season; reprove, rebuke, and exhort, with complete patience and teaching.

ᵃ 2:25, **repentance:** Absent from ℵ(01).

ᵇ 3:3, **irreconcilable:** Absent from ℵ(01).

ᶜ 3:6, **and pleasures:** Absent from A(02).

ᵈ 3:8, **Jannes:** C(04) reads "John."

ᵉ 3:8, **Jannes and Jambres:** While these names do not appear in the Old Testament, Jewish tradition and extra-biblical sources, such as the Targum and writings like the Book of Jannes and Jambres, identify them as Egyptian magicians who opposed Moses during the events described in Exodus 7:8-13, when Pharaoh's magicians attempted to replicate the miracles performed by Moses and Aaron.

ᶠ 3:9, **folly:** A(02) reads "mind."

ᵍ 3:10, **love:** Absent from A(02).

ʰ 3:15, **the:** Absent from ℵ(01).

ⁱ 3:16, **God-breathed:** Or, inspired by God.

ʲ 4:1, **Therefore:** Included in BYZ TR.

ᵏ 4:1, **of the Lord:** Included in BYZ TR.

ˡ 4:1, **Christ Jesus:** Some manuscripts read "Jesus Christ." BYZ TR.

ᵐ 4:1, **and by:** Some manuscripts read "according." BYZ TR.

3 For there will be a time when they will not endure sound teaching, but according to their [own]^a desires, they will accumulate for themselves teachers, itching to hear something new. 4 And indeed, they will turn away from hearing the truth, but will be diverted to myths.

5 But you, be sober in all things, [endure hardship,]^b do the work of an evangelist, fulfill your ministry.

6 For I am already being poured out, and the time of my departure has come.

7 I have fought the good fight, I have finished the race, I have kept the faith;

8 Finally, there is laid up for me the crown of righteousness, which the Lord, the righteous judge, will award to me on that day, and not only to me, but also to all who have loved his appearing.

9 Do your best to come to me soon. 10 For Demas, in love with this present world, has deserted me and gone to Thessalonica. Crescens has gone to Galatia, Titus to Dalmatia. 11 Luke alone is with me. Get Mark and bring him with you, for he is very useful to me for ministry. 12 Tychicus I have sent to Ephesus.

13 The cloak that I left at Troas with Carpus, when you come, bring it, and the books, especially the parchments.

14 Alexander the coppersmith did me great harm; {the Lord will}^c repay according to his deeds. 15 Beware of him yourself, for he {stood against}^d our message.

16 In my first defense, no one {came to me},^e but all deserted me; may it not be counted against them.

17 But the Lord stood by [me]^f and strengthened me, so that through me the message might be fully proclaimed and all the Gentiles might hear it. So I was rescued from the lion's mouth.

18 The Lord will rescue me from every evil deed and bring me safely into his heavenly kingdom. To him be the glory forever and ever. Amen.

19 Greet Prisca and Aquila, and the household of Onesiphorus.

20 Erastus remained at Corinth, and I left Trophimus, who was ill, at Miletus.

21 Do your best to come before winter.

Eubulus sends greetings to you, as do Pudens and Linus and Claudia and [all]^g the brothers.

22 The Lord [[Jesus Christ]]^h be with your spirit. Grace be with you. [[Amen]]^ij

---

a 4:3, **own:** Absent from BYZ TR.

b 4:5, **endure hardship:** Absent from ℵ(01).

c 4:14, **the Lord will:** Some manuscripts read "may the Lord." BYZ TR.

d 4:15, **stood against:** Some manuscripts read "opposed." BYZ TR.

e 4:16, **came to me:** Some manuscripts read "stood with me." BYZ TR.

f 4:17, **me:** Absent from A(02).

g 4:21, **all:** Absent from ℵ(01).

h 4:22, **Jesus Christ:** Included in C(04) BYZ TR ‖ A(02) reads "Jesus."

i 4:22, **Amen:** Included in BYZ TR.

j 4:22, TR includes the postscript "To Timothy, second of the Ephesian church, first ordained bishop, was written from Rome when Paul appeared for the second time before Caesar Nero."

Titus[a]

1 ¹Paul, a servant of God, and an apostle of {Jesus Christ[b]},[c] according to the faith of God's chosen and the knowledge of the truth that is in accordance with godliness, ²in hope of eternal life, which God, who does not lie, promised before eternal times, ³but revealed in due times his word through the proclamation, which I was entrusted with according to the command of God our savior,

⁴To Titus, a genuine child according to a common faith,

Grace [[mercy and]][d] and peace from God the Father and [[the Lord]][e] {Christ Jesus} our savior.[f]

⁵For this reason I left you in Crete, so that you might put in order what remains and appoint elders in every town, as I directed you, ⁶if anyone is above reproach, the husband of one wife, having faithful children not accused of wild living or disobedience. ⁷For an overseer must be blameless as God's steward, not arrogant, not quick-tempered, not given to drunkenness, not violent, not greedy for dishonest gain, ⁸but hospitable, a lover of good, self-controlled, righteous, holy, and disciplined, ⁹holding firm to the trustworthy word as taught, so that he may be able to {give instruction in the sound teaching}[g] and also to refute those who oppose it.

¹⁰For there are many [also][h] who are insubordinate, empty talkers and deceivers, [[but]][i] especially those of the circumcision, ¹¹whom it is necessary to silence, who overturn whole households, teaching things they ought not for the sake of shameful gain.

¹²[[But]][j] One of them, a prophet of their own, said, "Cretans are always liars, evil beasts, lazy gluttons." ¹³This testimony is true. For this reason, rebuke them sharply, so that they may be healthy in [the][k] faith, ¹⁴not paying attention to Jewish myths and commands of men who turn away from the truth.

¹⁵To the pure, all things [[indeed]][l] are pure, but to those who are corrupted and unbelieving, nothing is pure, but their minds and consciences are corrupted.

¹⁶They profess to know God, but by their deeds they deny him, being detestable and disobedient, and disqualified for any good work.

---

[a] 1:0, **Title ("Titus")**: Absent from ℵ(01). ‖ A(02) BYZ reads "to Titus." ‖ TR reads "The letter of Paul the apostle to Titus."

[b] 1:1, **Christ**: See footnote for Christ in Luke 2:11.

[c] 1:1, **Jesus Christ**: Some manuscripts read "Christ Jesus." A(02).

[d] 1:4, **mercy and**: Included in A(02) BYZ TR. ‖ Absent from ℵ(01) C(04).

[e] 1:4, **the Lord**: Included in BYZ TR.

[f] 1:4, **Christ Jesus**: Some manuscripts read "Jesus Christ." BYZ TR.

[g] 1:9, **give instruction in the sound teaching**: A(02) reads "exhort those in every affliction."

[h] 1:10, **also**: Absent from ℵ(01) A(02) C(04).

[i] 1:10, **but**: Included in C(04).

[j] 1:12, **But**: Included in ℵ(01).

[k] 1:13, **the**: Absent from ℵ(01).

[l] 1:15, **indeed**: Included in BYZ TR.

2 1 But you, speak what is fitting for sound teaching.

2 Older men should be temperate, dignified, self-controlled, sound in faith, love, and endurance.

3 Likewise, older women should be reverent in behavior, not slanderers, not enslaved to much wine, teachers of what is good, 4 so that they may encourage the young women to love their husbands, to love their children, 5 to be sensible, pure, workers at home,[a] kind, being subject to their own husbands, so that the word of God [[and the teaching]][b] will not be dishonored.

6 Likewise, encourage the younger men to be self-controlled.

7 In everything, present yourself as an example of good works, in teaching demonstrating integrity, dignity, incorruptibility, [[purity]][c] 8 sound in speech which is beyond reproach, so that the opponent will be put to shame, having nothing bad to say about {us}.[d]

9 Slaves should be submissive to their own masters in all things, pleasing them, not talking back, 10 not stealing, but showing all good [faith],[e] so that they may adorn the teaching of our Savior God in all things.

11 For the grace of God has appeared, bringing salvation to all men, 12 instructing us, so that, denying ungodliness and worldly desires, we might live sensibly, righteously, and godly in the present age,

13 Awaiting the blessed hope and appearance of the glory of our great God[f] and {Jesus Christ}[g] our savior,[h] 14 who gave himself for us, to redeem us from all lawlessness and to purify for himself a people for his own possession, zealous for good works.

15 {Speak}[i] these things, encourage, and rebuke with all authority. Let no one disregard you.

3 1 [[But]][j] Remind them to be submissive to rulers and authorities, to obey, to be ready for every good work, 2 to slander no one, to avoid quarreling, to be gentle, showing all humility to all men.

3 For we were once also foolish, disobedient, deceived, enslaved to various desires and pleasures, living in malice and envy, detestable, hating one another.

4 But when the kindness and love for mankind of God our savior appeared, 5 not by works of righteousness which we have done, but according to his mercy, he saved us through the washing of regeneration and renewing of the Holy Spirit,[k] 6 which he poured out on us abundantly through Jesus Christ our savior, 7 that having been justified by [his][l] grace, we should become heirs according to the hope of eternal life.

---

a 2:5, **workers at home:** Pertaining to carrying out household responsibilities (BDAG, οἰκουργός). Some manuscripts read "keepers" rather than "workers." BYZ TR.

b 2:5, **and the teaching:** Included in C(04).

c 2:7, **purity:** Included in C(04).

d 2:8, **us:** A(02) reads "you."

e 2:10, **faith:** Absent from ℵ(01).

f 2:13, **God:** The BDAG entry of the Greek word for "God" includes the statement: "Some writing in our literature uses the word θεός in reference to Christ without necessarily equating Christ with the Father, and therefore in harmony with the Shema of Israel. (Dt 6:4)." BDAG further gives a fourth definition of θεός : "that which is nontranscendent but considered worth of special reverence or respect, god ... of humans θεοί John 10:34f; humans are called θεός in the Old Testament" (BDAG, θεός).

g 2:13, **Jesus Christ:** ℵ(01) reads "Christ Jesus."

h 2:13, GPT-4 gives the additional variation "the glory of the great God and our savior Jesus Christ" on account of syntactical ambiguity.

i 2:15, **Speak:** A(02) reads "Teach."

j 3:1, **But:** Included in A(02).

k 3:5, **Spirit:** See footnote for Spirit in Luke 1:15.

l 3:7, **his:** Absent from ℵ(01).

8 The saying is trustworthy; and concerning these things, I want you to insist, so that those who have believed in God may be careful to devote themselves to good works. These things are good and beneficial for men.

9 But avoid foolish disputes and genealogies and arguments and quarrels about the law, for they are unprofitable and useless.

10 Reject a divisive person after a first and second warning, 11 knowing that such a person is warped and sinning, being self-condemned.

12 When I send Artemas to you, or Tychicus, be diligent to come to me at Nicopolis, for I have decided to spend the winter there.

13 Send Zenas the lawyer and Apollos on their journey diligently, so that nothing may be lacking for them.

14 And let our people also learn to maintain good works, to meet necessary needs, that they may not be unfruitful.

15 All who are with me greet you.

Greet those who love us in faith.

Grace be with you all. [[Amen]][ab]

---

a 3:15, **Amen:** Included in BYZ TR.

b 3:15, TR includes the postscript "To Titus, first ordained bishop of the church of the Cretans, written from Nicopolis of Macedonia."

Philemon[a]

1 Paul, a prisoner of Christ[b] Jesus and Timothy our brother, to Philemon our beloved fellow worker, 2 and to Apphia our {sister},[c] and to Archippus our fellow soldier, and to the church in your house,

3 Grace to you and peace from God {our}[d] Father and the Lord Jesus Christ.

4 I always thank my God when I mention you in my prayers, 5 hearing of your love and faith, which you have {towards}[e] the Lord Jesus and towards all the saints, 6 so that the fellowship of your faith may become effective in the knowledge of every good thing that is in {you}[f] for Christ [[Jesus]].[g]

7 For {I have had}[h] great joy [and encouragement][i] in your love, because the hearts of the saints have been refreshed through you, brother.

8 Therefore, having great boldness in Christ to command you what is proper, 9 I appeal more out of love, being such as Paul, an elder, but now also a prisoner of {Christ Jesus};[j]

10 I appeal to you for my child, whom I have begotten[k] while in {these}[l] chains, Onesimus, 11 who once was useless to you, but now is [also][m] useful to you and to me, 12 whom I have sent to you, [[receive him,]][n] that is, my own heart; 13 I would have liked to keep him with me, so that he might serve me on your behalf during my imprisonment for the gospel, 14 but I did not want to do anything without your consent, so that your goodness would not be, as it were, by compulsion, but of your own free will.

15 For perhaps this is why he was separated for a while, so that you might have him back forever, 16 no longer as a slave, but more than a slave, a beloved [brother],[o] especially to me, but how much more to you, both in the flesh and in the Lord.

17 If then you consider me a partner, receive him as you would me. 18 But if he has wronged you in any way or owes you anything, charge that to my account.

---

a 1:0, **Title ("Philemon"):** Absent from ℵ(01). ‖ A(02) BYZ reads "To Philemon." ‖ TR reads "The letter of Paul the apostle to Philemon."

b 1:1, **Christ:** See footnote for Christ in Luke 2:11.

c 1:2, **sister:** Some manuscripts read "beloved" BYZ TR.

d 1:3, **our:** ℵ(01) reads "the."

e 1:5, **towards:** Some manuscripts read "in" ℵ(01) A(02) B(04).

f 1:6, **you:** Some manuscripts read "us." ℵ(01) TR.

g 1:6, **Jesus:** Included in BYZ TR.

h 1:7, **I have had:** Some manuscripts read "we have." BYZ TR.

i 1:7, **and encouragement:** Absent from ℵ(01).

j 1:9, **Christ Jesus:** Some manuscripts read "Jesus Christ." BYZ TR.

k 1:10, **begotten:** That is, become a father to.

l 1:10, **these:** Some manuscripts read "my." C(04) BYZ TR.

m 1:11, **also:** ℵ(01) ‖ Absent from A(02) C(04) BYZ TR.

n 1:12, **receive him:** Included in C(04) BYZ TR.

o 1:16, **brother:** Absent from ℵ(01).

19 I, Paul, have written with my own hand, I will repay it; not to mention to you that you owe me even yourself. 20 Yes, brother, let me benefit from you in the Lord; refresh my heart in {Christ}.[a]

21 Trusting in your obedience, I wrote to you, knowing that you will do even more than what I say.

22 But at the same time, also prepare a guest room for me, for I hope that through your prayers I will be graciously given to you.

23 Epaphras, my fellow prisoner in Christ Jesus, greets you, 24 as do Mark, Aristarchus, Demas, and Luke, my fellow workers.

25 The grace of {the}[b] Lord Jesus Christ be with {your spirit}.[c] [Amen][de]

---

a 1:20, **Christ:** Some manuscripts read "the Lord." BYZ TR.

b 1:25, **the:** ℵ(01) ‖ Some manuscripts read "our." A(02) C(04) BYZ TR.

c 1:25, **your spirit:** 𝔓87 reads "you."

d 1:25, **Amen:** Some manuscirpts include. ℵ(01) C(04) BYZ TR. ‖ Absent from 𝔓87 A(02).

e 1:25, TR includes the postscript "To Philemon, written from Rome by Onesimus, a servant."

Hebrews[a]

1 [1] In many parts[b] and in many ways, God long ago spoke to {the}[c] fathers through the prophets.

[2] In these last days, he has spoken to us in a son, whom he appointed heir of all things, through whom [also][d] he made the ages; [3] who, being the radiance[e] of glory and the exact representation[f] of his essence,[g] upholding all things by the word of [his][h] power, having made purification for [[our]][i] sins [[through himself]],[j] he sat down at the right hand of the Majesty on high, [4] having become as much superior to [the][k] angels, as he has inherited a name more distinguished than theirs.

[5] For to which of the angels did he ever say, "You are my Son, today I have begotten you"?[l]

And again, "I will be a Father to him, and he will be a Son to me"?[m]

[6] And when he again brings the firstborn into the world, he says, "And let all the angels of God worship him."[n]

[7] And of the angels he says, "He makes his angels spirits, and his ministers a flame of fire."[o]

---

[a] 1:0, **Title ("Hebrews")**: Absent from 𝔓12 ℵ(01) B(03). ‖ 𝔓46 A(02) BYZ TR reads "To the Hebrews." ‖ TR reads "The letter of Paul the apostle to the Hebrews."

[b] 1:1, **In many parts**: Or, of prophetic writings.

[c] 1:1, **the**: 𝔓12 reads "our."

[d] 1:2, **also**: Absent from 𝔓46.

[e] 1:3, **radiance**: Or reflection. The Greek word means radiance, effulgence in the sense of brightness from a source or reflection in the passive sense as brightness shining back. (BDAG, ἀπαύγασμα).

[f] 1:3, **representation**: The Greek word used means (1) a mark or impression placed on an object, (2) something produced as a representation, reproduction, representation, (3) characteristic trait or manner, distinctive mark, or (4) an impression that is made, outward aspect, outward appearance, form. (BDAG, χαρακτήρ).

[g] 1:3, **essence**: The Greek word used has a wide range of meanings for this word including, (1) the essential or basic structure/nature of an entity (Or, underlying structure, representation, realization) (2) a plan that one devises for action (3) situation, condition, frame of mind, or (4) guarantee of ownership/entitlement, title deed. (BDAG, ὑπόστασις).

[h] 1:3, **his**: Absent from 𝔓46.

[i] 1:3, **our**: Included in BYZ TR.

[j] 1:3, **through himself**: Included in 𝔓46 BYZ TR.

[k] 1:4, **the**: Absent from 𝔓46 B(03).

[l] 1:5, Psalm 2:7.

[m] 1:5, 2 Samuel 7:14, 1 Chronicles 17:13.

[n] 1:6, Deuteronomy 32:43 LXX /Dead Sea Scrolls, Psalm 97:7.

[o] 1:7, Psalm 104:4 LXX.

8 But of the Son, "Your throne, O God,[a] is forever [and ever];[b] [and][c] the scepter of uprightness is the scepter of {your}[d] kingdom. 9 You have loved righteousness and hated lawlessness; therefore God, your God, has anointed[e] you with the oil of gladness beyond your companions."[f]

10 And, "You, Lord, laid the foundation of the earth in the beginning, and the heavens are the work of your hands; 11 they will perish, but you remain; and they will all grow old like a garment, 12 and like a garment you will roll them up, and [[like a garment]][g] they will be changed; but you are the same, and your years will never end."[h]

13 And to which of the angels has he ever said, "Sit at my right hand, until I make your enemies a footstool for your feet"?[i]

14 Are they not all ministering spirits, sent out to serve for the sake of those who are to inherit salvation?

2 1 For this reason, we must pay much closer attention to what we have heard, lest we drift away.

2 For if the message spoken through angels proved to be reliable, and every transgression and disobedience received a just retribution, 3 how will we escape if we neglect such a great salvation, which began to be spoken through the Lord and was confirmed to us by those who heard, 4 with God bearing witness by signs and wonders and various miracles and {distributions}[j] of the Holy Spirit according to his own will?

5 For it is not to angels that {he}[k] subjected the world to come, about which we are speaking.

6 But someone has testified somewhere, saying, "What is man that you remember him, or the son of man that you care for him? 7 You made him a little lower than the angels; you crowned him with glory and honor, [[and you have set him over the works of your hands,]][l] 8 and subjected everything under his feet."[m]

---

a 1:8, **God:** The BDAG entry of the Greek word for "God" includes the statement: "Some writing in our literature uses the word θεός in reference to Christ without necessarily equating Christ with the Father, and therefore in harmony with the Shema of Israel. Dt 6:4." BDAG further gives a fourth definition of θεός : "that which is nontranscendent but considered worth of special reverence or respect, god ... of humans θεοί John 10:34f; humans are called θεός in the Old Testament" (BDAG, θεός). Capitalization of "God" is not intended to suggest a particular theological perspective. Some translations, including the Revised English Bible and the James Moffatt translation, render the phrase as "God is your throne." Supporters of this alternate rendering argue that the nominative reading is grammatically possible, suggesting that God serves as the basis or foundation of the throne rather than the addressee being explicitly called "God."

b 1:8, **and ever:** Absent from B(03).

c 1:8, **and:** Absent from BYZ TR.

d 1:8, **your:** A(02) BYZ TR ‖ Some manuscripts read "his." 𝔓46 ℵ(01) B(03).

e 1:9, **anointed:** The Greek word means anoint in our literature only in a figurative sense of an anointing by God setting a person apart for special service under divine direction... God anoints (a) David, (b) Jesus, the Christ for his work or mission, (c) the prophets, (d) the apostles or, more probably, all Christians (at baptism or through the Spirit) 1 Cor 1:21. (BDAG, χρίω).

f 1:8-9, Psalm 45:6-7 LXX.

g 1:12, **like a garment:** Absent from BYZ TR.

h 1:10-12, Psalm 102:25-27 LXX/Dead Sea Scrolls.

i 1:13, Psalm 110:1.

j 2:4, **distributions:** ℵ(01) reads "harvests."

k 2:5, **he:** C(04) reads "God."

l 2:7, **and you have set him over the works of your hands:** Included in ℵ(01) A(02) C(04) TR. ‖ Absent from 𝔓46 B(03).

m 2:8, Psalm 8:4-6 LXX.

For in subjecting [to him]^a [all]^b things, he left nothing unsubjected to him. But now we do not yet see all things subjected to him;

9 But we do see Jesus, who was made a little lower than the angels, crowned with glory and honor because of the suffering of death, so that by the grace of God he might taste death for everyone.

10 For it was fitting for him, for whom are all things and through whom are all things, having led many sons into glory, to perfect the pioneer of their salvation through sufferings. 11 For both the one who sanctifies and those who are being sanctified all come from one.^c For this reason, he does not feel shame to call them brothers, 12 saying, "I will declare your name to my brothers; in the midst of the assembly I will sing your praise."^d 13 And again, "I will put my trust in him." And again, "Behold, I and the children whom God has given me."^e

14 Therefore, since the children have shared in blood and flesh, he likewise partook of the same, so that through death he might render powerless the one having the power of death, that is, the devil, 15 and might set free these, as many as were subject to slavery all their lives by the fear of death.

16 For surely it is not angels that he helps, but he helps the offspring of Abraham.

17 Therefore, it was necessary for him to become like the brothers in every way, so that he might become merciful and a faithful high priest in relation to God, to make propitiation for the sins of the people. 18 For in that he himself has suffered [being tempted],^f he is able to help those who are being tempted.

3 1 Therefore, holy brothers, partakers of a heavenly calling, consider the apostle and high priest of our confession, {Jesus [[Christ]]},^gh 2 being faithful to the one who made him, just as Moses also was in [all]^i his house.

3 For this one has been deemed worthy of more glory than Moses, inasmuch as the one who built the house has more honor than the house itself; 4 for every house is built by someone, but God is the builder of everything.

5 And Moses indeed was faithful in all his house as a servant, for a testimony of those things which were to be spoken, 6 but Christ,^j as a son over his house; of which we are the house, if indeed we hold fast to the confidence and the boast of hope [[until the end]].^k

7 Therefore, as the Holy Spirit says, "Today, if you hear his voice, 8 do not harden your hearts as in the rebellion, on the day of testing in the wilderness, 9 where your fathers tested me {by trial}^l and saw my works 10 for forty years. Therefore, I was provoked with {this}^m generation, and I said, 'They always go astray in their hearts, and they have not known my ways.' 11 As I

---

^a 2:8, **to him:** Absent from 𝔓46 B(03).

^b 2:8, **all:** Absent from 𝔓46.

^c 2:11, **from one:** One person or thing.

^d 2:12, Psalm 22:22 LXX.

^e 2:13, 2 Samuel 22:3; Isaiah 8:17 LXX, 8:18.

^f 2:18, **being tempted:** Absent from ℵ(01).

^g 3:1, **Christ:** Included in BYZ TR.

^h 3:1, **Jesus Christ:** TR reads "Christ Jesus."

^i 3:2, **all:** Absent from 𝔓13 𝔓46 B(03).

^j 3:6, **Christ:** The Greek word for Christ means (1) fulfiller of Israelite expectation of a deliverer, the Anointed One, the Messiah, the Christ, or (2) the personal name ascribed to Jesus, Christ. (BDAG, Χριστός).

^k 3:6, **until the end:** Included in ℵ(01) A(02) C(04) BYZ TR.

^l 3:9, **by trial:** Some manuscripts read "the tried me." BYZ TR.

^m 3:10, **this:** Some manuscripts read "that." C(04) BYZ TR.

swore in my wrath, 'They will not enter my rest.'"[a]

12 Be careful, brothers, lest there be in any of you an evil, unbelieving heart, leading you to fall away from the living God. 13 But exhort one another every day, as long as it is called "Today," that none of you may be hardened by the deceitfulness of sin. 14 For we have become partakers of Christ, if indeed we hold fast the beginning of {the}[b] confidence firm to the end. 15 As it is said, "Today, if you hear his voice, do not harden your hearts as in the rebellion."[c]

16 For who were those who heard and yet rebelled? Was it not all those who left Egypt led by Moses? 17 And with whom was he provoked for forty years? Was it not with those who sinned, whose bodies fell in the wilderness? 18 And to whom did he swear that they would not enter his rest, but to those who were disobedient? 19 And we see that they were unable to enter because of unbelief.

4 1 Therefore, let us fear, lest anyone of you should seem to have fallen short of the promise of entering into His rest, having been left behind.

2 For we have been given the good news just as they were; but the word they heard did not benefit them, because it was not mixed with faith in those who heard.

3 {For}[d] we who have believed enter into [the][e] rest, just as he has said, "As I swore in my wrath, 'They shall not enter into my rest,'"[f] although his works were finished from the foundation of the world.

4 For somewhere it has said about the seventh day in this way, "And God rested [on the seventh day][g] from all his works,"[h] 5 and in this again, "If they will enter into my rest."[i]

6 Therefore, since it remains for some to enter into it, and those who were previously told the good news did not enter because of disobedience, 7 again, he designates a certain [day],[j] "Today," saying in David after so much time, as it has been [previously][k] said, "[Today] If you hear his voice, do not harden your hearts."[l]

8 For if Joshua had given them rest, he would not have spoken afterward about another day. 9 [So then, there remains a Sabbath rest for the people of God.][m]

10 For the one who has entered into his rest has also rested from his works, just as God did from his own.

11 Let us therefore strive to enter that rest, so that no one may fall by the same sort of disobedience.

12 For the word of God is living and active, sharper than any two-edged sword, and piercing as far as the division of [[both]][n] soul and spirit, of joints and marrow, and discerning the thoughts and intentions of the heart.

13 And there is no creature hidden from his sight, but all things are naked and laid bare to the eyes of him to whom we must give account.

---

a 3:7-11, Psalm 95:7-11 LXX.

b 3:14, **the:** A(02) reads "his."

c 3:15, Psalm 95:7-8 LXX.

d 4:3, **For:** Some manuscripts read "therefore:." ℵ(01) A(02) C(04).

e 4:3, **the:** NA28[] THGNT BYZ TR ‖ Absent from SBLGNT B(03).

f 4:3, Psalm 95:11.

g 4:4, **on the seventh day:** Absent from A(02).

h 4:4, Genesis 2:2.

i 4:5, Psalm 95:11.

j 4:7, **day:** Absent from 𝔓46.

k 4:7, **previously:** Absent from 𝔓46.

l 4:7, Psalm 95:7-8 LXX.

m 4:9, **So then, there remains a Sabbath rest for the people of God:** Absent from ℵ(01).

n 4:12, **both:** Included in BYZ TR.

14 Therefore, having a great high priest who has passed through the heavens, Jesus the son of God, let us hold fast to our confession.

15 For we do not have a high priest who is unable to sympathize with our weaknesses, but one who has been tempted in every way, just as we are, yet without sin.

16 Therefore, let us approach the throne of grace with boldness, so that we may receive mercy and [find]ᵃ grace to help in time of need.

5 1 For every high priest, being taken from among men, is appointed on behalf of men in matters pertaining to God, so that he may offer [both]ᵇ gifts and sacrifices for sins;

2 He is able to deal gently with those who are ignorant and going astray, since he himself is also surrounded by weakness. 3 And because of it he is obligated, just as for the people, so also for himself, to offer for sins.

4 And no one takes this honor for oneself, but only when called by God, just as Aaron was.

5 So also Christ did not glorify himself to become a high priest, but the one who said to him, "You are my Son, today I have begotten you."ᶜ 6 As he also says in another place, "You are a priest forever according to the order of Melchizedek."ᵈ

7 In the days of his flesh, he offered up prayers and supplications with loud cries and tears to the one who was able to save him from death, and he was heard because of his reverence. 8 Although he was a son, he learned obedience through what he suffered. 9 And having been made perfect, he became the cause of eternal salvation for all who obey him, 10 being designated by God {as}ᵉ a high priest according to the order of Melchizedek.

11 Concerning this, we have much to say and it is hard to explain, since you have become dull in understanding. 12 For though by this time you ought to be teachers, you need someone to teach you again the basic principles of the oracles of God. You need milk, [and]ᶠ not solid food!

13 For everyone who lives on milk is unskilled in the word of righteousness, since he is a child.

14 But solid food is for the mature, for those who have their powers of discernment trained by constant practice to distinguish good from evil.

6 1 Therefore, leaving the elementary teaching about Christ, let us press on to maturity, not laying again a foundation of repentance from dead works and of faith toward God, 2 of instruction about baptisms, laying on of hands, the resurrection of the dead, and eternal judgment. 3 And this we will do, if God permits.

4 For it is impossible for those who were once enlightened, and have tasted of the heavenly gift, and were made partakers of the Holy Spirit, 5 and have tasted the good word of God, and the powers of the world to come, 6 if they shall fall away, to renew them again unto repentance, crucifying for themselves the son of God and making a public spectacle.

7 For the earth, which drinks in the rain that often comes upon it, and produces vegetation suitable for those for whom it is also cultivated, partakes of a blessing from God. 8 But if it bears thorns and thistles, it is worthless and near to being cursed, its end is to be burned.

ᵃ 4:16, **find:** Absent from B(03).
ᵇ 5:1, **both:** Absent from 𝔓46 B(03).
ᶜ 5:5, Psalm 2:7.
ᵈ 5:6, Psalm 110:4.
ᵉ 5:10, **as:** 𝔓46 reads "you are."
ᶠ 5:12, **and:** Absent from 𝔓46 ℵ(01) C(04).

9 But we are convinced of better things concerning you, {beloved},[a] and things that accompany salvation, though we speak in this manner. 10 For God is not unjust to forget your work and the [[labor of]][b] love which you have shown toward his name, having served the saints and continuing to serve.

11 [But][c] We desire each of you to show the same diligence for the full assurance of hope until the end, 12 so that you may not become sluggish, but imitators of those who through faith and patience inherit the promises.

13 For when God made a promise to Abraham, since he could swear by no one greater, he swore by himself, 14 saying, "Indeed, I will bless you and I will surely multiply you."[d]

15 And thus, having patiently endured, he obtained the promise.

16 For [[indeed]][e] men swear by the greater, and for them an oath is the end of all dispute as a confirmation;

17 In which God, desiring to show more abundantly to the heirs of the promise the unchangeable nature of his purpose, interposed with an oath, 18 so that by two unchangeable things, in which it is impossible for God to lie, we who have fled for refuge might have strong encouragement to hold fast to the hope set before us. 19 We have this as a sure and steadfast anchor of the soul, a hope that enters into the inner place behind the curtain, 20 where Jesus has gone as a forerunner on our behalf, having become a high priest forever after the order of Melchizedek.

7 1 For this Melchizedek, king of Salem, priest of the Most High God, who met Abraham returning from the slaughter of the kings and blessed him, 2 to whom also Abraham apportioned a tenth part of all, first being translated as king of righteousness, and [then also][f] king of Salem, which is king of peace,[g] 3 without father, without mother, without genealogy, having neither beginning of days nor end of life, but made like the Son of God, remains a priest perpetually.

4 Now consider how great this one was, to whom [even][h] the patriarch Abraham gave a tenth of the choicest spoils. 5 And those indeed of the sons of Levi who receive the priestly office have commandment in the Law to collect a tenth from the people, [that is,][i] from their brethren, although these are descended from the loins of Abraham; 6 but the one whose genealogy is not traced from them collected a tenth from Abraham and blessed the one who had the promises. 7 And without any dispute the lesser is blessed by the greater.

8 In this case mortal men receive tithes, but there it is testified that he lives. 9 And, so to speak, through Abraham even Levi, who received tithes, paid tithes, 10 {for he was still}[j] in the loins of his father when Melchizedek met him.

11 Now if perfection was through the Levitical priesthood ([for][k] the people have received the Law based upon it), what further need was there for another priest to arise according to the order of Melchizedek, and not be designated according to the order of Aaron? 12 For when the priesthood is

---

a 6:9, **beloved:** ℵ(01) reads "brothers."
b 6:10, **labor of:** Included in BYZ TR.
c 6:11, **But:** Absent from 𝔓46.
d 6:14, Genesis 22:16-17.
e 6:16, **indeed:** Included in C(04) BYZ TR.
f 7:2, **then also:** Absent from 𝔓46.
g 7:1-2, Genesis 14:17-20.
h 7:4, **even:** Absent from 𝔓46 B(03).
i 7:5, **that is:** Absent from B(03).
j 7:10, **for he was still:** ℵ(01) reads "he was."
k 7:11, **for:** Absent from 𝔓46.

changed, of necessity there also takes place a change [of law].[a]

13 For the one concerning whom these things are spoken belongs to another tribe, from which no one has officiated at the altar. 14 For it is evident that our Lord was descended from Judah, a tribe about which Moses said nothing concerning {priests}.[b]

15 And it is even more evident if another priest arises according to the likeness of Melchizedek, 16 who has become such not on the basis of a law of physical requirement, but according to the power of an indestructible life.

17 For it is attested of him, "You are a priest forever according to the order of Melchizedek."[c]

18 For there is, indeed, a setting aside of the preceding commandment due to its weakness and uselessness - 19 for the Law perfected nothing - but the introduction of a better hope, through which we draw near to God.

20 And inasmuch as it was not without an oath; for indeed, those have become priests without an oath, 21 [but][d] this one with an oath through the one who said to him: "The Lord has sworn and will not change his mind, 'You are a priest [forever][e] [[after the order of Melchizedek]]."[f,g] 22 In this way [also],[h] Jesus has become the guarantor of a better covenant.

23 And indeed, many have become priests, because death prevents them from continuing. 24 But because he remains forever, the priesthood is unchangeable. 25 Therefore, he is [also][i] able to save completely those who approach God through him, always living to intercede for them.

26 For such a high priest was fitting for us, holy, innocent, unstained, separated from sinners and having become higher than the heavens, 27 who does not need daily, like those high priests, to offer up [sacrifices],[j] first for his own sins and then for the sins of the people; for this, he did by offering himself once for all.

28 For the Law appoints men as high priests who have weakness, but the word of the oath, which came after the Law, appoints a son, into the age completed.[k]

8 1 Now, concerning what has been said, we have such a high priest, who has taken a seat at the right hand of the throne of Majesty in the heavens, 2 [[for he is]][l] a minister of the holy things and of the true tabernacle, which the Lord set up, [[and]][m] not man.

3 For every high priest is appointed to offer both gifts and sacrifices; therefore, it is necessary for this one [also][n] to have something to offer.

4 If indeed he were on earth, he would not even be a priest, since there are {those}[o] who offer the gifts according to the Law; 5 who serve a copy and shadow of the heavenly things, just as Moses was instructed when he was about to complete the tabernacle; for he says, "See [that

---

a 7:12, **of law:** Absent from B(03).
b 7:14, **priests:** Some manuscripts read "priesthood." BYZ TR.
c 7:17, Psalm 110:4.
d 7:21, **but:** Absent from 𝔓46.
e 7:21, **forever:** Absent from ℵ(01).
f 7:21, **after the order of Melchizedek:** Included in A(02) BYZ TR.
g 7:21, Psalm 110:4.
h 7:22, **Also:** Absent from 𝔓46 A(02) BYZ TR.
i 7:25, **also:** Absent from 𝔓46.
j 7:27, **sacrifices:** Absent from 𝔓46.
k 7:28, **completed:** Or brought to full measure, fulfilled, made perfect. (BDAG, τελειόω).
l 8:2, **for he is:** Included in 𝔓46.
m 8:2, **and:** Included in A(02) BYZ TR.
n 8:3, **also:** Absent from ℵ(01).
o 8:4, **those:** Some manuscripts read "the priests." BYZ TR.

you make]ᵃ everything according to the pattern shown to you on the mountain."ᵇ

6 But now [he] has obtained a more excellent ministry [, inasmuch as he is also the mediator of a better covenant, which has been enacted on better promises].ᶜ

7 For if that first one had been faultless, there would have been no occasion sought for {a second}.ᵈ 8 For finding fault with them, he says, "[Behold, the days are coming, says]ᵉ the Lord, when I will make a new covenant with the house of Israel and with the house of Judah, 9 Not like the covenant that I made with their fathers on the day when I took them by the hand to bring them out of the land of Egypt, because they did not remain in my covenant, and I disregarded them, says the Lord. 10 For this is {the}ᶠ covenant that I will make with the house of Israel after those days, says the Lord: I will put my laws into their minds and write them on their hearts, and I will be their God, and they shall be my people. 11 And they will not teach, each one his citizen, and each one his brother, saying, 'Know the Lord,' for they will all know me, from {the least}ᵍ to the greatest. 12 [For I will be merciful to their iniquities,]ʰ And their sins [[and their lawlessness]]ⁱ I will remember no more."ʲ

13 In speaking of a new covenant, he has made the first one obsolete; and what is becoming obsolete and growing old is near to disappearing.

9 1 So then [also]ᵏ the first [[tent]]ˡ had regulations for worship and an earthly sanctuary. 2 For a tabernacle was prepared, the first one, in which were the lampstand and the table and the presentation of the loaves [[and the golden alter]],ᵐ which is called the {Holy Place}.ⁿ 3 And behind the second curtain, the tabernacle called the Holy of Holies, 4 [having a golden altar]ᵒ and the ark of the covenant covered on all sides with gold, in which was a golden jar holding the manna, and Aaron's rod that budded, and the tablets of the covenant. 5 Above it were the cherubim of glory overshadowing the mercy seat; of these things we cannot now speak in detail.

6 Now with these things prepared in this way, the priests continually enter the first tabernacle, performing their services, 7 but into the second only the high priest enters once a year, not without blood, which he offers for himself and for the people's unintentional sins, 8 the Holy Spirit indicating this, that the way into the holy places had not yet been disclosed while the first tabernacle was still standing, 9 which is a symbol for the present time, in which both gifts and sacrifices are offered that cannot perfect the conscience of the worshiper, 10 but deal only with food and drink and various washings, regulations for the flesh imposed until the time of reformation.

11 But when Christ appeared as a high priest of the good things {that

---

ᵃ 8:5, **that you make:** Absent from 𝔓46.

ᵇ 8:5, Exodus 25:40.

ᶜ 8:6, **inasmuch as he is also the mediator...:** Absent from (01).

ᵈ 8:7, **a second:** B(03) read "another."

ᵉ 8:8, **Behold, the days are coming, says:** Absent from 𝔓46.

ᶠ 8:10, **the:** A(02) reads "my."

ᵍ 8:11, **the least:** Some manuscripts read "their smallest." BYZ TR.

ʰ 8:12, **For I will be merciful to their iniquities:** Absent from 𝔓46.

ⁱ 8:12, **and their lawlessness:** Some manuscripts read add. BYZ TR.

ʲ 8:8-12, Jeremiah 31:31-34 LXX.

ᵏ 9:1, **also:** Absent from 𝔓46 B(03).

ˡ 9:1, **tent:** Included in TR.

ᵐ 9:2, **and the golden alter:** Included in B(03).

ⁿ 9:2, **Holy Place:** Some manuscripts read "Holy of Holies." 𝔓46 A(02).

ᵒ 9:4, **having a golden altar:** Absent from B(03).

have come},[a] through the greater and more perfect tabernacle not made with hands, that is, not of this creation, 12 he entered once for all into the holy places, not by means of the blood of goats and calves but by means of his own blood, thus securing an eternal redemption. 13 For if the blood of goats and bulls, and the sprinkling of defiled persons with the ashes of a heifer, sanctify for the purification of the flesh, 14 how much more will the {blood}[b] of Christ, who through the Holy Spirit offered himself without blemish to God [, purify {our}[c] conscience from dead works to serve the living [[true]][d] God].[e]

15 And for this reason he is the mediator of a new covenant, so that those who are called may receive the promised eternal inheritance, since a death has occurred that redeems them from the transgressions committed under the first covenant. 16 For where a covenant is, there must of necessity be the death of the one who made it. 17 For a covenant is valid only when people are dead, since it is never in force while the one who made it is alive. 18 Therefore not even the first covenant was inaugurated without blood. 19 For when every commandment had been spoken by Moses to all the people according to the Law, he took the blood of calves [and of goats],[f] with water and scarlet wool and hyssop, and sprinkled both the book itself and all the people, 20 saying, "This is the blood of the covenant that God {commanded}[g] for you."[h] 21 And in the same way he sprinkled with the blood both the tabernacle and all the vessels of the ministry. 22 Indeed, under the Law almost everything is purified with blood, and without the shedding of blood there is no forgiveness of sins.

23 Thus it was necessary for the copies of the heavenly things to be purified with these rites, but the heavenly things themselves with better sacrifices than these. 24 For Christ has entered, not into holy places made with hands, which are copies of the true things, but into heaven itself, now to appear in the presence of God on {our}[i] behalf. 25 Nor was it to offer himself repeatedly, as the high priest enters the holy places every year with blood not his own, 26 for then he would have had to suffer repeatedly since the foundation of the world. But as it is, he has appeared once for all at the end of the ages to put away sin by the sacrifice of himself. 27 And just as it is appointed for men to die once, and after that comes judgment, 28 so also[j] Christ, having been offered once to bear the sins of many, will appear a second time, not to deal with sin but to save [[through faith]][k] those who are eagerly waiting for him.

10 1 For the Law, having a shadow of the good things to come, [not][l] the very image of the things, can never with the same sacrifices, which they offer continually year by year, is never able to perfect those who draw near. 2 For then would they not have ceased to be offered, because the worshipers, once purified, would have had no more consciousness of sins? 3 But in those sacrifices there is a reminder of sins every year.

4 For it is impossible for the blood of bulls and goats to take away sins.

---

a 9:11, **that have come:** Some manuscripts read "to come." ℵ(01) A(02) BYZ TR.
b 9:14, **blood:** 𝔓46 reads "Spirit."
c 9:14, **our:** Some manuscripts read "your." ℵ(01) BYZ TR.
d 9:14, **true:** Included in A(02).
e 9:14, **purify our conscience...:** Absent from 𝔓46.
f 9:19, **and of goats:** Absent from 𝔓46.
g 9:20, **commanded:** Some manuscripts read "decreed." BYZ TR.
h 9:20, Exodus 24:8.
i 9:24, **our:** C(04) read "your."
j 9:28, **also:** Absent from TR.
k 9:28, **through faith:** Included in A(02).
l 10:1, **not:** Absent from 𝔓46.

5 Therefore, when entering into the world, it says, "You did not desire sacrifice and offering, but you prepared a body for me;[a] 6 You did not take pleasure in burnt offerings and sin offerings. 7 Then I said, 'Behold, [I have come;][b] in the scroll of the book it is written about me, to do, O God, your will'"[c]

8 Saying above, "You did not desire or take pleasure in sacrifices, offerings, burnt offerings, and sin offerings" (which are offered according to the Law), 9 then he said, "Behold, I have come to do your will [[O God]]."[d] He abolishes the first in order to establish the second, 10 in which we are sanctified, those [[ones]][e] through the offering of the body of Jesus Christ once for all.

11 And every {priest}[f] stands daily at his service, offering repeatedly the same sacrifices, which can never take away sins. 12 But {this one},[g] having offered one sacrifice for sins, sat down at the right hand of God, 13 waiting from that time until his enemies should be made a footstool for his feet.

14 For by a single offering he has perfected for all time those who are being sanctified.

15 And the Holy Spirit also bears witness to us; for after having {said}[h] 16 "[[But]][i] This is the covenant that I will make with them after those days, says the Lord: I will put my laws upon their hearts and I will write them on their minds," 17 and, "And {their}[j] sins and their lawless deeds I will remember no more."[k] 18 Where there is forgiveness [of these],[l] there is no longer any offering for sin.

19 Therefore, brothers, since we have confidence to enter the holy places by the blood of Jesus, 20 by the new and living way that he inaugurated for us through the curtain, that is, through his flesh, 21 and since we have a great priest over the house of God, 22 let us draw near with a true heart in full assurance of faith, with our hearts sprinkled clean from an evil conscience and our body washed with pure water.

23 Let us hold fast the confession of [our][m] hope without wavering, for he who promised is faithful. 24 And let us consider how to stir up one another unto love and to good works, 25 not neglecting to meet together, as is the habit of some, but encouraging one another, and all the more as you see the Day drawing near.

26 [For][n] If we sin deliberately after receiving the knowledge of the truth, there no longer remains a sacrifice for sins, 27 but a fearful expectation of judgment and a fury of fire that will consume the adversaries.

28 If someone disregards the Law of Moses, they die without mercy on the testimony of two or three witnesses. 29 How much worse punishment, do you think, will be deserved by the one who has trampled underfoot the Son of God, and has profaned the blood of the covenant [by which they were sanctified,][o] and has outraged the Spirit of grace?

---

a 10:5, Psalm 40:6-8 LXX.
b 10:7, I have come: Absent from ℵ(01).
c 10:5-7, Psalm 40:6-8 LXX.
d 10:9, O God: Included in BYZ TR.
e 10:10, ones: Included in BYZ TR.
f 10:11, priest: Some manuscripts read "high priest." A(02) C(04).
g 10:12, this one: Some manuscripts read "he." BYZ TR.
h 10:15, said: Some manuscripts read "previously said." BYZ TR.
i 10:16, But: Included in 𝔓13.
j 10:17, their: Some manuscripts read "the." 𝔓13 𝔓46.
k 10:16-17, Jeremiah 31:33-34 LXX.
l 10:18, of these: Absent from ℵ(01).
m 10:23, our: Absent from ℵ(01).
n 10:26, For: Absent from 𝔓46.
o 10:29, by which they were sanctified: Absent from A(02).

30 For we know him who said, "Vengeance is mine; I will repay [[says the Lord]]."ᵃ And again, "The Lord will judge his people."ᵇ

31 It is a fearful thing to fall into the hands of the living God.

32 But remember {the}ᶜ former days, in which, after being enlightened, you endured a great struggle with sufferings, 33 partly by being made a public spectacle through reproaches and tribulations, and partly by becoming partners with those who were so treated.

34 For you sympathized with {those in prison}ᵈ and joyfully accepted the confiscation of your property, knowing that you yourselves have a better and enduring possession [[in the heavens]].ᵉ 35 Therefore, do not throw away your confidence, which has a great reward.

36 For you have need of endurance, so that having done the will of God, you may receive the promise.

37 [For]ᶠ Yet a little while, how very little, the one who is coming will come and will not delay; 38 "But {my}ᵍ righteous one will live by faith, and if he shrinks back, my soul takes no pleasure in them."ʰ 39 But we are not of those who [shrink back and]ⁱ are destroyed, but of those who have faith and preserve their souls.

11 1 [Now]ʲ Faith is the assuranceᵏ of things hoped for, the conviction of things not seen. 2 For by it the men of old gained approval.

3 By faith we understand that the ages were prepared by the word of God, so that what is seen was not made out of things which are visible.

4 By faith Abel offered to God a better sacrifice than Cain, through which he was attested to be righteous, [God]ˡ bearing witness over his gifts, and through it, though he is dead, he still speaks.

5 By faith Enoch was taken up so that he would not see death, and he was not found because God took him up; for before [[his]]ᵐ being taken up, he was attested to have been pleasing to God.

6 And without faith it is impossible to please him, for he who comes to God must believe that he exists and that he is a rewarder of those who seek him.

7 By faith Noah, being warned about things not yet seen, in reverence prepared an ark for the salvation of his household, by which he condemned the world, and became an heir of the righteousness which is according to faith.

8 By faith Abraham, when he was called, obeyed by going out to {a}ⁿ place which he was to receive for an inheritance; and he went out, not knowing where he was going.

9 By faith he lived as an alien in the land of promise, as in a foreign land, dwelling in tents with Isaac and Jacob, fellow heirs of the same promise; 10 for he was looking for the city which

---

ᵃ 10:30, **says the Lord:** Included in A(02) BYZ TR.

ᵇ 10:30, Deuteronomy 32:35-36, Psalm 135:14.

ᶜ 10:32, **the:** Some manuscripts read "your." ℵ(01).

ᵈ 10:34, **those in prison:** Some manuscripts read "my chains." ℵ(01) BYZ TR.

ᵉ 10:34, **in the heavens:** Included in BYZ TR.

ᶠ 10:37, **For:** Absent from 𝔓13.

ᵍ 10:38, **my:** Some manuscripts read "the." 𝔓13 BYZ TR.

ʰ 10:38, Habakkuk 2:3-4 LXX.

ⁱ 10:39, **shrink back and:** Absent from 𝔓46.

ʲ 11:1, **Now:** Absent from 𝔓46.

ᵏ 11:1, **assurance:** The Greek word *hypostasis* means (1) the essential or basic structure/nature of an entity, (2) a plan that one devises for action, plan, project, undertaking, endeavor, (3) situation, condition, or (4) guarantee of ownership/entitlement, title deed. (BDAG, ὑπόστασις).

ˡ 11:4, **God:** Absent from 𝔓13.

ᵐ 11:5, **him:** Included in BYZ TR.

ⁿ 11:8, **a:** Some manuscripts read "the." BYZ TR.

has foundations, whose architect and builder is God.

11 By faith, Sarah herself, [being barren,]ᵃ received power to conceive, and beyond the time of age, [[gave birth,]]ᵇ since she considered the one who had promised to be faithful. 12 Therefore there were born even of one man, and him as good as dead at that, as many descendants as the stars of heaven in number, and innumerable {as}ᶜ the sand {which is by the seashore}ᵈ.ᵉ

13 By faith, these all died, not having {received}ᶠ the promises, but from afar they saw them [[and were persuade]]ᵍ and greeted them, and confessed that they are strangers and sojourners on the earth. 14 For those who say such things make it clear that they are seeking a homeland.

15 And indeed if they had were remembering that from which they had departed, they would have had an opportunity to return. 16 But now they desire a better, that is, a heavenly one. Therefore, God is not ashamed to be called their God; for He has prepared a city for them.

17 By faith, {Abraham}ʰ offered up Isaac when he was tested, and he who had received the promises was offering up his only begotten, 18 to whom it was said, "In Isaac your offspring will be named,"ⁱ 19 considering [that]ʲ God is able to raise even from the dead, from which he also received him in a parable.

20 [And]ᵏ By faith Isaac blessed Jacob and Esau, regarding things to come.

21 By faith Jacob, as he was dying, blessed each of the sons of Joseph, and worshiped, leaning on the top of his staff.ˡ

22 By faith Joseph, when he was dying, made mention of the exodus of the sons of Israel, and gave orders concerning his bones.

23 By faith Moses, when he was born, was hidden for three months by his parents, because they saw he was a beautiful child; and they were not afraid of the king's edict.

24 By faith Moses, when he had grown up, refused to be called the son of Pharaoh's daughter, 25 choosing rather to endure ill-treatment with the people of God than to enjoy the passing pleasures of sin, 26 considering the reproach of Christ greater riches than the treasures of Egypt; for he was looking to the reward.

27 By faith, he left Egypt, not fearing the king's wrath; for he endured as seeing the invisible one.

28 By faith he kept the Passover and the sprinkling of the blood, so that he who destroyed the firstborn would not touch them.

29 By faith they passed through the Red Sea as though they were passing through dry land; and the Egyptians, when they attempted it, were drowned.

30 By faith the walls of Jericho fell down after they had been encircled for seven days.

31 By faith Rahab the harlot did not perish along with those who were disobedient, after she had welcomed the spies in peace.

ᵃ 11:11, **being barren:** Absent from 𝔓13 ℵ(01) A(02) BYZ TR.

ᵇ 11:11, **gave birth:** Included in BYZ TR.

ᶜ 11:12, **as:** TR reads "like."

ᵈ 11:12, **which is by the seashore:** 𝔓46 reads "of the sea."

ᵉ 11:12, Genesis 22:17.

ᶠ 11:13, **received:** Some manuscripts read "having welcomed." ℵ(01) A(02).

ᵍ 11:13, **and were persuade:** Included in TR.

ʰ 11:17, **Abraham:** 𝔓46 reads "he."

ⁱ 11:18, Genesis 21:12.

ʲ 11:19, **that:** Absent from 𝔓46.

ᵏ 11:20, **And:** Absent from ℵ(01) BYZ TR.

ˡ 11:21, Genesis 47:31 LXX.

32 And what more shall I say? For time will fail me if I tell of Gideon, Barak, {Samson, Jephthah},[a] of David and Samuel and the prophets, 33 who through faith conquered kingdoms, performed acts of righteousness, obtained promises, shut the mouths of lions, 34 quenched the power of fire, escaped the edge of the sword, from weakness were made strong, became mighty in war, turned to flight foreign armies.

35 Women received their dead by resurrection; others were tortured, not accepting release, so that they might obtain a better resurrection. 36 And others experienced mockings and scourgings, and even chains and imprisonment.

37 They were stoned, they were sawn in two [[they were tempted]],[b] they died by the sword, they wandered about in sheepskins, in goatskins, being destitute, afflicted, ill-treated, 38 of whom the world was not worthy, wandering in deserts and mountains and caves and the holes of the earth.

39 And all [these],[c] having gained approval through their faith, did not receive the promise, 40 since God had foreseen something better for us, so that apart from us they would not be made perfect.

12 1 Therefore, we also, having such a great cloud of witnesses surrounding us, having laid aside every weight and the sin that so easily ensnares us, let us run with endurance the race that is set before us, 2 looking to Jesus, the pioneer and perfecter of faith, who for the joy set before him endured the cross, despising its shame, and has taken his seat at the right hand of the throne [of God].[d]

3 Consider him who endured such opposition from sinful men, so that you will not grow weary and lose heart.

4 You have not yet resisted to the point of shedding [blood][e] in your struggle against sin.

5 And you have forgotten the exhortation that addresses you as sons: "My son, do not make light of the Lord's discipline, or lose heart when he rebukes you, 6 For whom the Lord loves, he disciplines, and he scourges every son whom he accepts."[f]

7 Endure hardship as discipline; God is treating you as sons. For {what}[g] son is not disciplined by his father? 8 But if you are without discipline (and everyone undergoes discipline) then you are illegitimate children and not sons.

9 Then indeed, we had our earthly fathers as disciplinarians and we respected them; [but][h] shall we not much more be subject to the Father of spirits and live? 10 [For][i] Our fathers disciplined us for a little while as they thought best; but God disciplines us for our good, that we may share in his holiness.

11 Now, all discipline for the present does not seem to be of joy, but of sorrow; yet afterwards, it yields the peaceful fruit of righteousness to those who have been trained by it.

12 Therefore, lift up the drooping hands and the weakened knees, 13 and make straight paths for your feet, so that what is lame may not be put out of joint, but rather be healed.[j]

14 Pursue peace with everyone, and holiness, without which no one will see the Lord, 15 watching that no one falls short of the grace of God, that no

---

a 11:32, **Samson, Jephthah:** Some manuscripts read "and also Samson, and Jephthah." BYZ TR.
b 11:37, **they were tempted:** Included in 𝔓13 ℵ(01) A(02) BYZ TR. ‖ 𝔓46.
c 11:39, **these:** Absent from 𝔓46.
d 12:2, **of God:** Absent from 𝔓46.
e 12:4, **blood:** Absent from 𝔓46.
f 12:5-6, Proverbs 3:11-12 LXX.
g 12:7, **what:** Some manuscripts read "who is the." BYZ TR.
h 12:9, **but:** Absent from ℵ(01) A(02) BYZ TR.
i 12:10, **For:** Absent from 𝔓46.
j 12:13, Proverbs 4:26.

root of bitterness springs up and causes trouble, and through it many become defiled, 16 that no one is sexually immoral or unholy like Esau, who sold his birthright for a single meal. 17 For you know that even afterwards, when he wanted to inherit the blessing, he was rejected, for he found no place for repentance, though he sought it with tears.

18 For you have not come to a touchable [[mountain]]^a and burning fire, and darkness, and gloom, and storm, 19 to a trumpet blast or to such a voice speaking words, which those who heard begged that no^b further word be added to them, 20 because they could not bear what was commanded: "If even an animal touches the mountain, it must be stoned [[or shot with an arrow]]."^{cd} 21 The sight was so terrifying that Moses said, "{I am trembling with fear}."^{ef}

22 But you have come to Mount Zion, to the heavenly Jerusalem, the city of the living God. You have come to thousands upon thousands of angels in joyful assembly, 23 to the church of the firstborn, whose names are written in heaven. You have come to God, the judge of [all]^g men, to the spirits of righteous men made perfect, 24 to Jesus [[Christ]]^h the mediator of a new covenant, and to the sprinkled blood that speaks a better word than the blood of Abel.

25 See to it that you do not refuse him who speaks. If they did not escape when they refused him who warned them on earth, how much less will we, if we turn away from him who warns us from the heavens, 26 whose voice then shook the earth.

But now it has been promised, saying, "Yet once more I will shake not only the earth, but also the heaven."ⁱ 27 But the phrase, "Yet once more," indicates the removal of things that are shaken, that is, things that have been made, [so that {what}^j cannot be shaken may remain].^k

28 Therefore, since we are receiving a kingdom that cannot be shaken, let us be thankful, and so worship God acceptably with {reverence and fear}.^l

29 For indeed, our God is a consuming fire.^m

13 1 Let brotherly love continue.

2 Do not neglect hospitality, for through it some have unknowingly entertained angels.

3 Remember those who are in prison, as if you were bound with them, and those who are mistreated, since you also are in the body.

4 Marriage is honorable among all, and the bed undefiled; {for}ⁿ God will judge the sexually immoral and adulterers.

5 Keep your lives free from the love of money, and be content with what you have; for he has said, "I will never leave you nor will I ever forsake you,"^o 6 so that we may confidently say, "The

---

a 12:18, **mountain:** Included in BYZ TR.

b 12:19, **no:** Absent from ℵ(01). Likely an error.

c 12:20, **or shot with an arrow:** Included in TR.

d 12:20, Exodus 19:12-13.

e 12:21, **I am trembling with fear:** Or "I am terrified and trembling."

f 12:21, Deuteronomy 9:19.

g 12:23, **all:** Absent from 𝔓46.

h 12:24, **Christ:** Included in 𝔓46.

i 12:26, Haggai 2:6 LXX.

j 12:27, **what:** Some manuscripts read "the things which." BYZ TR.

k 12:27, **so that what cannot be shaken may remain:** Absent from A(02).

l 12:28, **reverence and fear:** Some manuscripts read "respect and reverence." BYZ TR.

m 12:29, Deuteronomy 4:24.

n 13:4, **for:** Some manuscripts read "but." C(04) BYZ TR.

o 13:5, Deuteronomy 31:6, 8; Joshua 1:5.

Lord is my helper; [and]^a I will not fear, what can man do to me?"^{b}

$_7$ Remember [your]^c leaders, who spoke the word of God to you; considering the outcome of their way of life, imitate their faith.

$_8$ Jesus Christ is the same yesterday, today, [and]^d into the ages.

$_9$ Do not be carried away by various and strange teachings; for it is good for the heart to be strengthened by grace, not by foods, in which those who walk have not benefited. $_{10}$ We have an altar from which those who serve the tent have no right to eat.

$_{11}$ [For]^e The blood of animals, which is brought [for sin]^f into the holy places by the high priest, their bodies are burned outside the camp.

$_{12}$ Therefore, Jesus also, in order to sanctify the people through his own blood, suffered outside the {gate}.^{g}

$_{13}$ Therefore, let us go out to him outside the camp, bearing his disgrace; $_{14}$ for we do not have a city here that remains, but we are seeking the one to come.

$_{15}$ Through him [then]^h let us continually offer up a sacrifice of praise to God, that is, the fruit of lips that confess his name.

$_{16}$ [And]^i Do not neglect to do good and to share what you have; for with such sacrifices God is pleased.

$_{17}$ Obey your leaders and submit to them, for they keep watch over your souls as those who will give an account, so that they may do this with joy and not with groaning; for that would be unprofitable for you.

$_{18}$ Pray for us; for we are persuaded that we have a good conscience, desiring to conduct ourselves well in all things. $_{19}$ I urge you more earnestly to do this, so that I may be restored to you sooner.

$_{20}$ Now the God of peace, who brought up from the dead the great shepherd of the sheep through the blood of the eternal covenant, our Lord Jesus, $_{21}$ may he equip you in every good {thing}^{j} to do his will, doing in us [[for him]]^k what is pleasing in his sight, through Jesus Christ, to whom be the glory for the ages [of the ages],^{l} Amen.

$_{22}$ I urge you, brothers, bear with this word of exhortation, [for]^m I have written to you briefly.

$_{23}$ Know that [our]^n brother Timothy has been released, with whom I will see you if he comes soon.

$_{24}$ Greet [all]^o your leaders [and all the saints].^{p} Those from Italy send you greetings.

$_{25}$ Grace be with all [of you].^{q} [[Amen]]^{rs}

---

^{a} 13:6, **and:** Absent from ℵ(01).

^{b} 13:6, Psalm 118:6 LXX.

^{c} 13:7, **your:** Absent from 𝔓46.

^{d} 13:8, **and:** Absent from 𝔓46.

^{e} 13:11, **For:** Absent from 𝔓46.

^{f} 13:11, **for sin:** Absent from A(02).

^{g} 13:12, **gate:** 𝔓46 reads "camp." ‖ 𝔓126 reads "gate of the camp."

^{h} 13:15, **then:** Absent from 𝔓46 ℵ(01).

^{i} 13:16, **And:** Absent from 𝔓46.

^{j} 13:21, **thing:** Some manuscripts read "work." BYZ TR.

^{k} 13:21, **for him:** Included in 𝔓46 ℵ(01) A(02) C(04).

^{l} 13:21, **of the ages:** Absent from 𝔓46.

^{m} 13:22, **for:** Absent from ℵ(01).

^{n} 13:23, **our:** Absent from BYZ TR.

^{o} 13:24, **all:** Absent from 𝔓46.

^{p} 13:24, **and all the saints:** Absent from 𝔓46.

^{q} 13:25, **of you:** Absent from 𝔓46.

^{r} 13:25,

^{s} 13:25, TR includes the postscript, "To the Hebrews, written from Italy by Timothy."

James[a]

1 [1] James,[b] a servant of God and of the Lord Jesus Christ,[c] to the twelve tribes in the Dispersion: Greetings.

[2] Consider it all joy, my brothers, when you encounter various trials, [3] knowing that the testing of your faith produces endurance. [4] And let endurance have its perfect work, so that you may be perfect and complete, lacking in nothing.

[5] But if any of you lacks wisdom, let him ask of the God who gives to all generously and without reproach, and it will be given to him.

[6] But let him ask in faith, with no doubting, for the one who doubts is like a wave of the sea driven and tossed by the wind. [7] For that person must not suppose that he will receive anything from the Lord, [8] a double-minded man, unstable in all his ways.

[9] Let the lowly brother boast in his exaltation, [10] and the rich in his humiliation, because like a flower of the grass he will pass away. [11] For the sun rises with its scorching heat and withers the grass; its flower falls, and its beauty perishes. So [also][d] will the rich man fade away in the midst of his pursuits.

[12] Blessed is the man who endures temptation, because when he has been tested, He will receive the crown of life, which {he}[e] promised to those who love him.

[13] Let no one say when he is tempted, "I am being tempted by God," for God cannot be tempted with evil, and He himself tempts no one. [14] But each person is tempted when he is lured and enticed by his own desire. [15] Then desire, when it has conceived, gives birth to sin, and sin, when it is fully grown, brings forth death.

[16] Do not be deceived, my beloved brothers.

[17] Every good gift and every perfect gift is from above, coming down from the Father of lights, with whom there is no variation or shadow due to change. [18] Of his own will he brought us forth by the word of truth, that we should be a kind of firstfruits of his creatures.

---

[a] 1:0, **Title ("James")**: Absent from 𝔓74 ℵ(01) A(02) B(03) ‖ BYZ reads "James." ‖ TR reads "Of James the apostle, the general letter." ‖ Or "Jacob." The translation of Ἰάκωβος as Jacob is valid since the name originates from the Hebrew Yaʻaqov and is linguistically consistent in Greek as Ἰάκωβος or Ἰακώβ. The use of "James" in English is a later development tied to linguistic tradition rather than fidelity to the original text.

[b] 1:1, **James**: Or "Jacob." The translation of Ἰάκωβος as Jacob is valid since the name originates from the Hebrew Yaʻaqov and is linguistically consistent in Greek as Ἰάκωβος or Ἰακώβ. The use of "James" in English is a later development tied to linguistic tradition rather than fidelity to the original text.

[c] 1:1, **Christ**: See footnote for Christ in Luke 2:11.

[d] 1:11, **also**: Absent from some 𝔓23.

[e] 1:12, **he**: Some manuscripts read "the Lord." C(04) BYZ TR.

19 {Know this},ᵃ my beloved brothers: [but]ᵇ let every man be quick to hear, slow to speak, slow to anger; 20 for the anger of man does {not work}ᶜ the righteousness of God. 21 Therefore, put away all filthiness and rampant wickedness and receive with meekness the implanted word, which is able to save your souls.

22 But be doers of the word, and not hearers only, deceiving yourselves.

23 For if anyone is a hearer of the word and not a doer, he is like a man who looks intently at his natural face in a mirror; 24 for he looks at himself and goes away and at once forgets what he was like.

25 But the one who looks into the perfect law, the law of liberty, and perseveres, [[this one]]ᵈ not a hearer who forgets but a doer who acts, he will be blessed in his doing.

26 If anyone [[among you]]ᵉ thinks he is religious and does not bridle his tongue but deceives his heart, this person's religion is worthless.

27 Religion that is pure and undefiled before God the Father is this: to visit orphans and widows in their affliction, and to {keep oneself unstained from the world}.ᶠ

2 1 My brothers, do not hold the faith of our Lord Jesus Christ, the glory, with partiality.

2 For if a man with a gold ring and fine clothing enters your assembly, and a poor man in dirty clothing also enters, 3 {but}ᵍ you look upon the one wearing the fine clothing and say [[to him]],ʰ You sit here in a good place, and to the poor man, You stand there, or sit [[here]]ⁱ under {my footstool},ʲ 4 [[and]]ᵏ have you not made distinctions among yourselves and become judges with evil thoughts?

5 Listen, my beloved brothers: Has not God chosen the poor in {the}ˡ world to be rich in faith and heirs of the {kingdom}ᵐ which he promised to those who love him? 6 But you have dishonored the poor man. Do not the rich oppress you and drag you into courts? 7 Do they {not}ⁿ blaspheme the good name by which you are called?

8 If you fulfill the royal law according to the Scripture, "You shall love your neighbor as yourself," you do well;ᵒ 9 but if you show partiality, you commit sin, being convicted by the law as transgressors.

10 For whoever keeps the whole law but stumbles in one point has become guilty of all. 11 For he who said, "Do not commit adultery," also said, "Do not murder."ᵖ Now if you do not commit adultery but do murder, you have become a transgressor of the law.

ᵃ 1:19, **know this:** Some manuscripts read "Therefore." BYZ TR.

ᵇ 1:19, **but:** Absent from BYZ TR.

ᶜ 1:20, **not work:** NA27 SBLGNT THGNT ‖ Some manuscripts read "not produce." NA28 BYZ TR.

ᵈ 1:25, **this one:** Included in BYZ TR.

ᵉ 1:26, **among you:** Included in BYZ TR.

ᶠ 1:27, **keep oneself unstained from the world:** Some manuscripts read "defend them." 𝔓74.

ᵍ 2:3, **but:** Some manuscripts read "and." ℵ(01) A(02) BYZ TR.

ʰ 2:3, **to him:** Included in BYZ TR.

ⁱ 2:3, **here:** Included in 𝔓74 ℵ(01) BYZ TR.

ʲ 2:3, **my footstool:** A(02) reads "the footstool under my feet."

ᵏ 2:4, **and:** Included in BYZ TR.

ˡ 2:5, **the:** TR reads "this."

ᵐ 2:5, **kingdom:** Some manuscripts read "promise." ℵ(01) A(02) .

ⁿ 2:7, **not:** Some manuscripts read "and." 𝔓74 A(02).

ᵒ 2:8, Leviticus 19:18.

ᵖ 2:11, Exodus 20:13, 14, Deuteronomy 5:17, 18.

12 So speak and so act as those who will be judged by the {law}[a] of liberty.

13 For judgment is merciless to the one who has not shown mercy; [[and]][b] mercy triumphs over judgment.

14 What [is the][c] benefit, my brothers, if someone says he has faith but does not have works? Can faith save him?

15 [[But]][d] If a brother or sister is naked and [[might be]][e] lacking daily food, 16 and one of you says to them, Go in peace, be warmed and filled, but you do not give them the things needed for the body, what is the profit? 17 In the same way, faith also, if it does not have works, is dead by itself.

18 But someone will say, You have faith, and I have works. Show me your faith {without the}[f] works, and I will show you my faith from {the}[g] works.

19 You believe that God is one.[h] You do well. Even the demons believe and tremble!

20 But do you want to know, O empty man, that faith apart from works is {useless}?[i]

21 Was not Abraham our father justified by works when he offered Isaac his son on the altar? 22 You see that faith worked with his works, and by works faith was made perfect, 23 and the Scripture was fulfilled which says, "Abraham believed God, and it was credited to him as righteousness." And he was called the friend of God.[j]

24 [[Therefore]][k] You see that a person is justified by works and not by faith alone.

25 {Likewise},[l] was not Rahab the prostitute also justified by works when she received the messengers and sent them out another way?

26 [For][m] just as the body without the spirit[n] is dead, also faith without [[the]][o] works is dead.

3 1 Not many *of you* should become teachers, my brothers, knowing that we will receive greater judgment.

2 For we all stumble in many ways. If anyone does not stumble in speech, this one is a perfect man, able to control the whole body as well.

3 {But if}[p] we put bits into the mouths of horses to make them obey us, we also guide their whole body.

4 Behold, even the ships, being so large and driven by strong winds, are directed by a very small rudder wherever the impulse of the one steering desires. 5 So also the tongue is a small member and boasts great things.

See how {great a forest a}[q] fire ignites!

---

a 2:12, **law:** 𝔓74 reads "word."

b 2:13, **and:** Included in TR. ‖ A(02) reads "but."

c 2:14, **is the:** Absent from B(03) C(04) SBLGNT.

d 2:15, **But:** Included in A(02) C(04) BYZ TR.

e 2:15, **might be:** Included in A(02) BYZ TR.

f 2:18, **without the:** Some manuscripts read "from your." C(04) BYZ TR.

g 2:18, **the:** Some manuscripts read "my." 𝔓74 A(02) BYZ TR.

h 2:19, **God is one:** Or, there is one God.

i 2:20, **useless:** Some manuscripts read "dead." ℵ(01) A(02) BYZ TR. ‖ 𝔓74 reads "empty."

j 2:23, Genesis 15:6.

k 2:24, **Therefore:** Included in BYZ TR.

l 2:25, **Likewise:** C(04) reads "Thus."

m 2:26, **For:** Absent from B(03).

n 2:26, **Spirit:** Or breath. The Greek word means (1) air in movement, blowing, breathing, (2) that which animates or gives life to the body, breath, (life-)spirit (3) a part of human personality, spirit, (4) an independent noncorporeal being, in contrast to a being that can be perceived by the physical sense, spirit, or (5) God's being as controlling influence, with focus on association with humans, Spirit, spirit. (BDAG, πνεῦμα).

o 2:26, **the:** Included in A(02) C(04) BYZ TR.

p 3:3, **But if:** Some manuscripts read "Behold." C(04) BYZ TR.

q 3:5, **great a forest a:** Some manuscripts read "a forest a small." A(02) BYZ TR.

6 And the tongue is a fire. The world of unrighteousness, the tongue, is set among our members, staining the whole body and setting on fire the wheel of [[our]]ᵃ existence, and is set on fire by Gehenna.

7 For every kind of beast and bird, of reptile and sea creature, can be tamed and has been tamed by human nature, 8 but no one can tame the tongue; it is a {unstable}ᵇ evil, full of deadly poison.

9 With it we bless {the Lord}ᶜ and Father, and with it we curse men who are made in the likeness of God.

10 From the same mouth come blessing and cursing. My brothers, these things ought not to be so.

11 Does a spring pour forth from the same opening both fresh and bitter water?

12 Can a fig tree, my brothers, produce olives, or a grapevine produce figs? {Neither can salt water produce fresh}.ᵈ

13 Who is wise and understanding among you? Let him show by his good conduct his works in the meekness of wisdom.

14 But [[then]]ᵉ if you have bitter jealousy and selfish ambition in your hearts, do not boast and be false to the truth. 15 This is not the wisdom that comes down from above, but is earthly, unspiritual, demonic. 16 For where jealousy and selfish ambition exist, there will be disorder and every vile practice.

17 But the wisdom from above is first pure, then peaceable, gentle, open to reason, full of mercy and {good fruits},ᶠ impartial, [[and]]ᵍ sincere.

18 And the fruit of righteousness is sown in peace by those who make peace.

4 1 Where do wars and [where do]ʰ fights among you come from? Is it not from your pleasures that wage war in your members? 2 You desire and do not have, you murder and are envious and cannot obtain, you fight and wage war, [[but]]ⁱ you do not have because you do not ask.

3 You ask and do not receive, because you ask wrongly, to {spend}ʲ it on your pleasures.

4 [[Adulterers and]]ᵏ Adulteresses, do you not know that friendship with {the}ˡ world is enmity with God? Whoever wishes to be a friend of the world becomes an enemy of God.

5 Or do you think that the Scripture says in vain, "The spirit {that dwells}ᵐ in us yearns with envy"? 6 But it gives greater grace; therefore it says, "God opposes the proud, but gives grace to the humble."ⁿ

7 Submit yourselves therefore to God, [but]ᵒ resist the devil, and he will flee from you.

ᵃ 3:6, **our:** Included in ℵ(01).

ᵇ 3:8, **unstable:** Some manuscripts read "uncontrollable." C(04) BYZ TR.

ᶜ 3:9, **the Lord:** Some manuscripts read "God." BYZ TR.

ᵈ 3:12, **neither can salt water produce fresh:** Some manuscripts read "Thus, no spring yields both salt water and fresh." ℵ(01) BYZ TR.

ᵉ 3:14, **then:** Included in A(02).

ᶠ 3:17, **good fruits:** C(04) reads "fruits of good works."

ᵍ 3:17, **and:** Included in 𝔓100 BYZ TR.

ʰ 4:1, **where do:** Absent from BYZ TR.

ⁱ 4:2, **but:** Included in TR.

ʲ 4:3, **spend:** ℵ(01) reads "squander."

ᵏ 4:4, **Adulterers and:** Included in BYZ TR.

ˡ 4:4, **the:** ℵ(01) reads "this."

ᵐ 4:5, **that dwells:** Some manuscripts read "that dwelled." BYZ TR.

ⁿ 4:6, Proverbs 3:34 LXX.

ᵒ 4:7, **but:** Absent from TR.

8 Draw near to God, and he will draw near to you. Cleanse your hands, sinners, and purify your hearts, you double-minded.

9 Be miserable and mourn and weep. Let your laughter be turned to mourning and your joy to gloom. 10 Humble yourselves [[then]]ᵃ before the Lord, and he will exalt you.

11 Do not speak against one another, [[my]]ᵇ brothers. He who speaks against a brother {or}ᶜ judges his brother speaks against the law and judges the law; but if you judge the law, you are not a doer of the law but a judge. 12 There is one lawgiver [and judge]ᵈ who is able to save and to destroy; but who are you to judge {your neighbor}?ᵉ

13 Come now, you who say, Today or tomorrow {we will go}ᶠ to such and such a city, spend {a}ᵍ year [there],ʰ engage in business, and make a profit, 14 [[for]]ⁱ you who do not know what will happen tomorrow. [For]ʲ What is your life? It [is a vapor that]ᵏ appears for a little while [[but]]ˡ also disappearing. 15 Instead, you should say, If the Lord wills, {we will}ᵐ live and do this or that.

16 But now you boast in your arrogance; all such boasting is evil.

17 Therefore, to him who knows to do good and does not do it, to him it is sin.

5 1 Come now, you who are rich, weep and wail over the miseries that are coming upon you.

2 Your wealth has rotted, and your garments have become moth-eaten. 3 Your gold and silver have corroded, and their corrosion will be a witness against you and will consume your flesh like fire. You have stored up treasure in the last days.

4 Behold, the wages of the laborers who mowed your fields, which you kept back by fraud, cry out, and the cries of the harvesters have reached the ears of the Lord of Hosts.

5 You have lived on the earth in luxury and self-indulgence; you have fattened your hearts [[as]]ⁿ in a day of slaughter.

6 You have condemned and murdered the righteous one; he does not resist you.

7 Therefore, be patient, brothers, until the coming of the Lord. Behold, the farmer waits for the precious fruit of the earth, being patient over it, until it might receive [[rain]] °early and late.

8 [[Therefore]]ᵖ You also, be patient. Strengthen your hearts, for the coming of the Lord is near.

ᵃ 4:10, **then:** Included in ℵ(01).

ᵇ 4:11, **my:** Included in A(02).

ᶜ 4:11, **or:** Some manuscripts read "and." BYZ TR.

ᵈ 4:12, **and judge:** Absent from 𝔓74 BYZ TR.

ᵉ 4:12, **your neighbor:** Some manuscripts read "another." BYZ TR.

ᶠ 4:13, **we will go:** Some manuscripts read "let us go." A(02) BYZ TR.

ᵍ 4:13, **a:** Some manuscripts read "one." A(02) BYZ TR.

ʰ 4:13, **there:** Absent from A(02).

ⁱ 4:14, **for:** Included in 𝔓74 𝔓100 A(02) BYZ TR.

ʲ 4:14, **For:** Absent from ℵ(01) A(02).

ᵏ 4:14, **is a vapor that:** Absent from ℵ(01).

ˡ 4:14, **but:** Included in BYZ TR.

ᵐ 4:15, **we will:** Some manuscripts read "let us." BYZ TR.

ⁿ 5:5, **as:** Included in BYZ TR.

° 5:7, **rain:** Included in A(02) BYZ TR.

ᵖ 5:8, **Therefore:** Included in 𝔓74 ℵ(01).

⁹Do not grumble against one another, [[my]]ᵃ brothers, so that you may not be {judged};ᵇ behold, the judge is standing at the doors.

¹⁰Take as an example of suffering and patience, [[my]]ᶜ brothers, the prophets who spoke in the name of the Lord.

¹¹Behold, we consider those blessed who remained steadfast. You have heard of the steadfastness of Job, and you have seen the purpose of the Lord, how [the Lord,]ᵈ he is compassionate and merciful.

¹²Above all, my brothers, do not swear, neither by heaven nor by earth nor by any other oath: But let your "Yes" be yes and your "No" be no, so that you may not fall under judgment.

¹³Is anyone among you suffering? Let him pray. Is anyone cheerful? Let him sing praise.

¹⁴Is anyone among you weak?ᵉ Let him call for the elders of the church, and let them pray over him, anointing him with oil in the name of the Lord.

¹⁵And the prayer of faith will save the one who is weary, and the Lord will raise him up. And if he has committed sins, he will be forgiven.

¹⁶[Therefore],ᶠ confess your sins to one another and pray for one another, that you may be healed. The prayer of a righteous person has great power as it is working.

¹⁷Elijah was a man with a nature like ours, and he prayed fervently that it might not rain, and for three years and six months it did not rain on the earth. ¹⁸Then he prayed again, and heaven gave rain, and the earth bore its fruit.

¹⁹[My]ᵍ brothers, if anyone among you wanders from [[the way of]]ʰ the truth and someone brings him back, ²⁰[let him know that]ⁱ whoever brings back a sinner from his wandering will save his soul from death and will cover a multitude of sins.

ᵃ 5:9, **my:** Included in A(02).

ᵇ 5:9, **judged:** Some manuscripts read "condemned." BYZ TR.

ᶜ 5:10, **my:** Included in ℵ(01) BYZ TR.

ᵈ 5:11, **the Lord:** Absent from BYZ.

ᵉ 5:14, **weak:** Or sick. The Greek word means (1) to suffer a debilitating illness, be sick, (2) to experience some personal incapacity or limitation, be weak, or (3) to experience lack of material necessities, be in need. (BDAG, ἀσθένεια).

ᶠ 5:16, **Therefore:** Absent in some manuscripts. BYZ TR.

ᵍ 5:19, **my:** Absent from BYZ TR.

ʰ 5:19, **the way of:** Included in ℵ(01).

ⁱ 5:20, **let him know that:** Absent from 𝔓74.

First Peter[a]

1 ¹Peter, an apostle of Jesus Christ,[b] to the elect sojourners of the Dispersion in Pontus, Galatia, Cappadocia, [Asia,][c] [and Bithynia,][d] ²according to the foreknowledge of God the Father, in the sanctification of the Spirit, for obedience and sprinkling of the blood of Jesus Christ: Grace to you and peace be multiplied.

³Blessed be the [God and][e] Father of our Lord Jesus Christ, who according to his abundant mercy has begotten us again to a living hope through the resurrection of Jesus Christ from the dead, ⁴to an inheritance incorruptible and undefiled and unfading, reserved in the heavens for {you},[f] ⁵who are guarded by the power of God through faith for a salvation ready to be revealed in the last time.

⁶[In this][g] You greatly rejoice, though now for a little while, if need be, you have been grieved by various trials, ⁷that the genuineness of your faith, more precious than gold that perishes, though it is tested by fire, may be found to result in praise, glory, and honor at the revelation of Jesus Christ, ⁸whom having not {seen}[h] you love; and though now you do not see him, yet believing, you rejoice with joy inexpressible and full of glory, ⁹receiving the end of [your][i] faith, the salvation of souls.

¹⁰Concerning this salvation, the prophets who prophesied about the grace that would come to you searched and carefully investigated, ¹¹seeking to know what person or time the Spirit [of Christ][j] within them was indicating when it testified beforehand the sufferings of Christ and the glories that would follow. ¹²To whom it was revealed that not for themselves, but {for you},[k] they were serving these things which now have been announced to you through those who preached the good news to you by the Holy Spirit sent from heaven, into which things angels desire to look.

¹³Therefore, having girded up the loins of your mind, being sober, set your hope fully on the grace that is being brought to you at the revelation of Jesus Christ; ¹⁴as obedient children, not conforming yourselves to the former lusts in your ignorance; ¹⁵but as he who called you is holy, you also be holy in all your conduct, ¹⁶For it is written [that],[l] "{You will be}[m] holy, for I am holy."[n]

---

a 1:0, **Title ("First Peter"):** Absent from ℵ(01) B(03) ‖ BYZ reads "Of Peter One." ‖ 𝔓72 A(02) reads "Letter of Peter One." ‖ TR reads "Of Peter the apostle, the first general letter."

b 1:1, **Christ:** See footnote for Christ in Luke 2:11.

c 1:1, **Asia:** Absent from ℵ(01).

d 1:1, **and Bithynia:** Absent from B(03).

e 1:3, **God and:** Absent from 𝔓72.

f 1:4, **you:** Some manuscripts read "us." 𝔓72 TR.

g 1:6, **In this:** Absent from 𝔓72.

h 1:8, **seen:** Some manuscripts read "known." A(02) BYZ TR.

i 1:9, **your:** Absent from B(03).

j 1:11, **of Christ:** Absent from B(03).

k 1:12, **for you:** TR reads "for us."

l 1:16, **that:** Absent from 𝔓72 ℵ(01) A(02) C(04) BYZ TR.

m 1:16, **You will be:** Some manuscripts read "Become." BYZ TR.

n 1:16, Leviticus 19:2.

17 And if you call upon the Father,
who judges impartially according to
each one's work, conduct yourselves in
fear [[therefore]][a] during the time of
your exile; 18 knowing that you were not
redeemed with perishable things, with
silver or gold, from your futile way of
life handed down from your ancestors,
19 but with the precious blood of Christ,
like that of a lamb without blemish
or spot.

20 He was foreknown before the
foundation of the world but was made
manifest in the last times for your sake,
21 who through him {are faithful to}[b]
God, who raised him from the dead and
gave him glory, so that your faith and
hope are in God.

22 Having purified your souls by
obedience to the truth [[through the
Spirit]][c] for sincere brotherly love, love
one another earnestly from [a pure][d]
heart. 23 Having been born again, not
from perishable seed but imperishable,
through the living and word of God,
enduring [[forever]],[e] 24 for "All flesh
is as grass, and {all its glory}[f] is like
the flower [of the grass].[g] The grass
withers, and {the}[h] flower falls,
25 but [the word of][i] the Lord endures
forever."[jk]

This is the message that was preached to you.

2 1 Therefore, putting away all
wickedness and all deceit and
{hypocrisies}[l] and envies and [all][m]
slander, 2 like newborn infants, long for
the pure spiritual milk, so that by it you
may grow [into salvation],[n] 3 {if}[o] you
{have tasted}[p] that the Lord is good.

4 As you come to him, a living
stone rejected by men but chosen
and precious in the sight of God,
5 and you, as living stones, are being
built up [into][q] a spiritual house, to be
a holy priesthood, to offer [spiritual][r]
sacrifices[s] acceptable to God through
Jesus Christ.

---

[a] 1:17, **therefore:** Included in 𝔓72.
[b] 1:21, **faithful to:** Some manuscripts read "believing in." 𝔓72 ℵ(01) C(04) BYZ TR.
[c] 1:22, **through the Spirit:** Included in BYZ TR.
[d] 1:22, **a pure:** Absent from some manuscripts which imply "the." A(02) B(03).
[e] 1:23, **forever:** Included in BYZ TR || The Greek word αἰών can mean (1) a long period of time, without ref. to beginning or end, *eternity* (2) a segment of time as a particular unit of history, *age* (3) the world as a spatial concept, *the world.* (BDAG, αἰών).
[f] 1:24, **all its glory:** Some manuscripts read "all the glory of men." BYZ TR.
[g] 1:24, **of the grass:** Absent from 𝔓72.
[h] 1:24, **the:** Some manuscripts read "its." BYZ TR.
[i] 1:25, **the word of:** Absent from A(02).
[j] 1:25, **forever:** Lit. into the age (αἰών).
[k] 1:24-25, Isaiah 40:6-8 LXX.
[l] 2:1, **hypocrisies:** Some manuscripts read "hypocrisy." B(03).
[m] 2:1, **slander:** Absent from 𝔓75 A(02).
[n] 2:2, **into salvation:** Absent from BYZ TR.
[o] 2:3, **if:** Some manuscripts read "if indeed." BYZ TR.
[p] 2:3, **have tasted:** 𝔓72 reads "believed to taste."
[q] 2:5, **into:** Absent from BYZ TR.
[r] 2:5, **spiritual:** Absent from ℵ(01).
[s] 2:5, **sacrifices:** Absent from 𝔓72.

6 For it is [[also]][a] contained in
[[the]][b] Scripture: "Behold, I am laying
in Zion a stone, a cornerstone chosen
and precious, and whoever believes in
him will not be put to shame."[c] 7 So the
honor is for you who believe, but for
those who do not {believe},[d] "The stone
that the builders rejected has become
the cornerstone,"[e] 8 and "A stone of
stumbling, and a rock of offense." They
stumble because they disobey the word,
as they were destined to do.

9 But you are a chosen race, a royal
priesthood, a holy nation, a people
for his own possession, that you may
proclaim the excellencies of him who
called you out of darkness into {his}[f]
marvelous light.[g] 10 Once you were not
{a}[h] people, but now you are God's
people; once you had not received
mercy, but now you have received
mercy.

11 Beloved, I urge you as sojourners
and exiles to abstain from the fleshly
desires which wage war against the
soul; 12 keep your conduct among the
Gentiles honorable, so that when they
speak against you as evildoers, they
may, by observing your good deeds,
glorify [[your]][i] God on the day of
visitation.

13 [[Therefore]][j] Submit to every
human institution for the sake of the
Lord, whether to a king as supreme,
14 whether to rulers as being sent
through him for the punishment
[[indeed]][k] of wrongdoers, but praise
for those who do good, 15 For this is the
will of God, that by doing good you
should put to silence the ignorance of
foolish people.

16 Live as people who are free,
not using your freedom as a cover-up
for evil, but living as servants of
God. 17 Honor everyone. Love the
brotherhood. Fear God. Honor
the emperor.

18 Servants, be subject to [[your]][l]
masters with all respect, not only to
the good and gentle but [also][m] to the
unjust. 19 For this is grace [[with God]],[n]
when, mindful of {God},[o] one endures
sorrows while suffering unjustly.

20 For what credit is it if, when you
sin and are beaten for it, you endure?
But if when you do good and suffer
for it [you endure],[p] [[for]][q] this is a
gracious thing in the sight of God.

21 For to this you have been called,
because Christ also suffered for {you},[r]
leaving you an example, so that you
might follow in his steps.

---

a 2:6, **also:** Included in TR.
b 2:6, **the:** Included in C(04) BYZ TR.
c 2:6, Isaiah 28:16 LXX.
d 2:7, **believe:** Some manuscripts read "obey." BYZ TR.
e 2:7, Psalm 118:22.
f 2:9, **his:** 𝔓72 reads "his."
g 2:9, Isaiah 43:20 LXX, Exodus 19:16 LXX.
h 2:10, **a:** 𝔓125 reads "my."
i 2:12, **your:** Included in 𝔓72.
j 2:13, **Therefore:** Included in BYZ TR.
k 2:14, **indeed:** Included in C(04) TR.
l 2:18, **your:** Included in ℵ(01).
m 2:18, **also:** Absent from 𝔓72.
n 2:19, **with God:** Included in C(04).
o 2:19, **God:** 𝔓72 reads "God's goodness." || Some manuscripts read "goodness." A(02) C(04).
p 2:20, **you endure:** Absent from C(04).
q 2:20, **for:** Included in A(02).
r 2:21, **you:** Some manuscripts read "us." BYZ TR.

22 He committed no sin, neither was deceit found in his mouth.[a] 23 When he was reviled, he did not revile in return; when he suffered, he did not threaten, but continued entrusting himself to him who judges justly, 24 who bore {our}[b] sins in the body on the tree, so that we might die to [[our]][c] sins and live for righteousness; by whose wounds[d] [[you]][e] were healed. 25 [For][f] You were like wandering sheep, but now you have returned to the shepherd and guardian of your souls.

3 1 Likewise, wives, being submissive to your own husbands, so that [even][g] if some are disobedient to the word, they may be won over without a word by the conduct of their wives, 2 observing your pure conduct in reverence. 3 Let your adornment not be the external braiding [of hair][h] and the wearing of gold jewelry or fine clothes, 4 but the hidden person of the heart, with the imperishable quality of a gentle and quiet spirit, which is precious in the sight of God.

5 For in this way, in former times, the holy women who hoped in God also adorned themselves, submitting to their own husbands, 6 just as Sarah obeyed Abraham, calling him lord. You have become her children by doing good and not fearing any intimidation.

7 Husbands, likewise, live with your wives in an understanding way, as with a weaker vessel, the female, giving honor as co-heirs of the [[manifold]][i] grace of life, so that your prayers may not be hindered.

8 Finally, all of you, be like-minded, sympathetic, brotherly, tender-hearted, humble-minded, 9 not repaying evil for evil or insult for insult, but on the contrary, blessing, [[knowing]][j] for to this you were called, that you might inherit a blessing.

10 For whoever desires to love life and see good days, let him keep {the}[k] tongue from evil and {the}[l] lips from speaking deceit; 11 [[but]][m] let him turn away from evil and do good; let him seek peace and pursue it. 12 For the eyes of the Lord are on the righteous, and his ears are open to their prayers; but the face of the Lord is against those who do evil.[n]

13 And who is there to harm you if you are {zealous}[o] for what is good? 14 But even if you should suffer for righteousness sake, you are blessed. Do not fear their intimidation, nor be troubled, 15 but sanctify {Christ}[p] as Lord in your hearts, always being ready to give a defense to everyone who asks you for a reason for the hope that is in you, 16 but with gentleness and reverence, having a good conscience, so that in what they slander [[you as evildoers]],[q] those who revile your good conduct in Christ may be put to shame. 17 For it is better to suffer for doing good, if it is God's will, than for doing evil.

---

[a] 2:22, Isaiah 53:9 LXX.

[b] 2:24, **our:** Some manuscripts read "your." 𝔓72 B(03).

[c] 2:24, **our:** Included in A(02).

[d] 2:24, **wounds:** Or bruises.

[e] 2:24, **you:** Included in ℵ(01) BYZ TR.

[f] 2:25, **For:** Absent from B(03).

[g] 3:1, **even:** Absent from 𝔓81 B(03).

[h] 3:3, **of hair:** Absent from 𝔓72.

[i] 3:7, **manifold:** Included in ℵ(01) A(02).

[j] 3:9, **knowing:** Included in BYZ TR.

[k] 3:10, **the:** Some manuscripts read "his." ℵ(01) BYZ TR.

[l] 3:10, **the:** Some manuscripts read "his." BYZ TR.

[m] 3:11, **but:** Absent from ℵ(01) BYZ TR.

[n] 3:10-12, Psalm 34:12-16.

[o] 3:13, **zealous:** Some manuscripts read "imitators." BYZ TR.

[p] 3:15, **Christ:** Some manuscripts read "God." BYZ TR.

[q] 3:16, **you as evildoers:** Included in ℵ(01) A(02) C(04) BYZ TR. ‖ Absent from 𝔓72 B(03).

18 For Christ [also]ᵃ {suffered}ᵇ once for [[our]]ᶜ sins, the righteous for the unrighteous, that he might bring {you}ᵈ [to God],ᵉ being put to death in the flesh [but]ᶠ made alive in the spirit; 19 in which he went and proclaimed to the spirits [[confined]]ᵍ in prison, 20 who formerly did not obey, when [[once]]ʰ God's patience waited in the days of Noah, while the ark was being prepared, in which a few, that is, [eight]ⁱ souls, were saved through water.

21 This also, as an antitype, now saves {you},ʲ baptism, not a removal of the filth of the flesh, but an appeal for a good conscience toward God, through the resurrection of Jesus Christ, 22 who has gone into heaven and is at the right hand of God, with angels, authorities, and powers having been subjected to him.

4 1 Therefore, since Christ suffered [[for us]]ᵏ in the flesh, arm yourselves also with the same mindset, because the one who has suffered in the flesh has ceased from sin, 2 so as to live the remaining time in the flesh no longer for human desires, but for the will of {God}.ˡ

3 For sufficient [[for us]]ᵐ the time [[of life]]ⁿ that has passed to have carried out the desire of the Gentiles, having walked in licentiousness, lusts, drunkenness, carousing, drinking parties, and unlawful idolatry.ᵒ

4 In this they are surprised that you do not run with them into the same flood of debauchery, blaspheming.

5 [They will give [an account]ᵖ to]ᑫ The one {having readiness}ʳ to judge the living and the dead.

6 For this reason, the gospel was also preached to the dead, so that they might be judged according to men in the flesh, but live according to God in the spirit.

ᵃ 3:18, **also:** Absent from 𝔓72 ℵ(01).
ᵇ 3:18, **suffered:** Some manuscripts read "died." 𝔓72 ℵ(01) A(02) C(04) .
ᶜ 3:18, **our:** Included in 𝔓72 ℵ(01) A(02) C(04).
ᵈ 3:18, **you:** TR reads "us."
ᵉ 3:18, **to God:** Absent from B(03).
ᶠ 3:18, **but:** Absent from 𝔓72 A(02).
ᵍ 3:19, **confined:** Included in C(04).
ʰ 3:20, **once:** Included in TR.
ⁱ 3:20, **eight:** Absent from 𝔓72.
ʲ 3:21, **you:** Some manuscripts read "us." C(04) BYZ TR.
ᵏ 4:1, **for us:** Some manuscripts include BYZ TR.
ˡ 4:2, **God:** ℵ(01) reads "man."
ᵐ 4:3, **for us:** Included in ℵ(01) BYZ TR.
ⁿ 4:3, **of life:** Included in BYZ TR.
ᵒ 4:3, **Licentiousness:** Sexual indulgence or debauchery. "Carousing" is excessive feasting.
ᵖ 4:5, **an account:** Absent from 𝔓72 ℵ(01).
ᑫ 4:5, **They will give an account to:** Absent from ℵ(01).
ʳ 4:5, **having readiness:** Some manuscripts read "ready." 𝔓72 B(03) C(04).

7 But the end of all things has drawn
near. Therefore, be self-controlled and
sober-minded for [[the]][a] prayers.

8 [[But]][b] Above all, maintain
fervent love for one another, because
love {covers}[c] a multitude of sins.

9 Be hospitable to one another
without grumbling.

10 As each one has received a gift,
use it to serve one another, as good
stewards of the varied grace of God.

11 If anyone speaks, let it be as the
oracles of God; if anyone serves, let it
be as from the strength {that}[d] God
supplies, so that in all things God may
be glorified through Jesus Christ, to
whom belong [the][e] glory and [the][f]
dominion forever and ever. Amen.

12 Beloved, do not be surprised at
the fiery ordeal among you, which
comes upon you for your testing,
as though something strange were
happening to you.

13 But to the degree that you share
in the sufferings of Christ, rejoice, so
that at the revelation of his glory you
may also rejoice and be glad.

14 If you are insulted for the name
of Christ, blessed are you, because the
spirit of glory and [[of power and]][g] of
God rests upon you. [[On their part he
is blasphemed, but on your part he is
glorified.]][h]

15 Let none of you suffer as a
murderer, or [[as]][i] a thief, or an
evildoer, or as a meddler.

16 But if anyone suffers [as][j] a
Christian, let him not be ashamed, but
let him glorify God in this {name}.[k]

17 For {the time has come}[l] for
judgment to begin with the house of
God; and if it begins with us first, what
will be the end of those who do not
obey the {gospel of God}?[m]

18 And [[indeed]][n] if the righteous
are scarcely saved, where will the
ungodly and the sinner appear?[o]

19 Therefore, those suffering
according to the will of God should
entrust [their][p] souls [[as]][q] to a faithful
Creator in doing good.

---

a 4:7, **the:** Included in BYZ TR.
b 4:8, **But:** Included in BYZ TR.
c 4:8, **covers:** Some manuscripts read "will cover." א(01) BYZ TR.
d 4:11, **that:** Some manuscripts read "as." BYZ.
e 4:11, **the:** Absent from 𝔓72.
f 4:11, **the:** Absent from 𝔓72.
g 4:14, **of power and:** Included in א(01) A(02).
h 4:14, **On their part he is blasphemed, but on your part he is glorified:** Included in BYZ MT.
i 4:15, **as:** Included in 𝔓72.
j 4:16 , **as:** Absent from 𝔓72.
k 4:16, **name:** Some manuscripts read "part." BYZ TR || Likely in reference to the term Christian.
l 4:17, **the time has come:** Some manuscripts read "it is time."
m 4:17, **gospel of God:** א(01) reads "word of God's gospel."
n 4:18, **indeed:** Included in 𝔓72.
o 4:18, Proverbs 11:31 LXX.
p 4:19, **their:** Absent from B(03).
q 4:19, **as:** Included in BYZ TR.

5 ¹ [Therefore]ᵃ I exhort the elders among you, as fellow elder and witness of the sufferings of {Christ},ᵇ and a partaker of the glory that is to be revealed: ² Shepherd the flock of God among you, [overseeing]ᶜ not by compulsion but willingly [according to God];ᵈ not for shameful gain, but eagerly; ³ [not as domineering over those in your charge, but being examples to the flock.]ᵉ ⁴ And when the Chief Shepherd appears, you will receive the unfading crown of glory.

⁵ Likewise, younger men, submit yourselves to the elders.

And all of you, [[submit]]ᶠ to one another, clothe yourselves with humility; for God opposes the proud but gives grace to the humble.ᵍ

⁶ Therefore, humble yourselves under the mighty hand of God, so that he may exalt you in a time [[of visitation]],ʰ ⁷ casting all your anxieties on him, because he cares for {you}.ⁱ

⁸ Be sober-minded, be watchful. [[Because]]ʲ Your adversary the devil prowls around like a roaring lion, seeking {someone}ᵏ to devour.

⁹ Resist him, firm in your faith, knowing that the same kinds of suffering are being experienced by your brotherhood throughout the world.

¹⁰ The God of all grace, who has called {you}ˡ to his eternal glory in Christ [Jesus],ᵐ having suffered a little, he himself will restore [you],ⁿ will strengthen, [will make strong,]ᵒ [will establish].ᵖ

¹¹ To him be [[the glory and]]�q the dominion forever [and ever].ʳ Amen.

¹² Through Silvanus, a faithful brother as I regard him, I have written briefly, exhorting and testifying that this is the true grace of God in which you stand.

¹³ The co-elect [[church]]ˢ in Babylon greets you, and Mark my son.

¹⁴ Greet one another with {a kiss of love}.ᵗ

[Peace to all of you who are in Christ]ᵘ [[Jesus. Amen]].ᵛ

ᵃ 5:1, **Therefore:** Absent from BYZ TR.

ᵇ 5:1, **Christ:** Absent from 𝔓72.

ᶜ 5:2, **overseeing:** Absent from ℵ(01) B(03).

ᵈ 5:2, **according to God:** Absent from B(03) BYZ TR.

ᵉ 5:3, **not as domineering…:** Absent from B(03).

ᶠ 5:5, **submit:** Included in BYZ TR.

ᵍ 5:5, Proverbs 3:34 LXX.

ʰ 5:6, **of visitation:** Included in A(02).

ⁱ 5:7, **you:** ℵ(01) reads "us."

ʲ 5:8, **because:** Included in 𝔓72.

ᵏ 5:8, **someone:** Absent from B(03).

ˡ 5:10, **you:** TR reads "us."

ᵐ 5:10, **Jesus:** Absent from ℵ(01) B(03).

ⁿ 5:10, **you:** Included in BYZ TR.

ᵒ 5:10, **will make strong:** Absent from 𝔓72.

ᵖ 5:10, **will establish:** Absent from A(02) B(03).

q 5:11, **the glory and:** Included in ℵ(01) BYZ TR.

ʳ 5:11, **and ever:** Included in ℵ(01) A(02) BYZ TR.

ˢ 5:13, **church:** Included in ℵ(01).

ᵗ 5:14, **a kiss of love:** Some manuscripts read "a holy kiss."

ᵘ 5:14, **Peace to all of you who are in Christ:** Absent from 𝔓72.

ᵛ 5:14, **Jesus. Amen:** Included in ℵ(01) BYZ TR.

ᵃ 1:0, **Title ("Second Peter"):** Absent from ℵ(01) A(02) B(03) ‖ BYZ reads "Of Peter Two." ‖ 𝔓72 reads "Letter of Peter Two." ‖ TR reads "Of Peter the apostle, the second general letter."

Second Peter^a

1 ¹Simeon Peter, a servant and apostle of Jesus Christ,^b to those who have obtained a faith of equal standing with ours in the righteousness of our {God}^c and Savior Jesus Christ:^d

²May grace and peace be multiplied to you in the knowledge of [God and of Jesus]^e [[Christ]]^f our Lord.

³His divine power has granted to us all things that pertain to life and godliness, through the knowledge of him who called us {to}^g his own glory and virtue, ⁴by which the precious and greatest promises have been given to {us},^h so that through these you may become partakers of the divine nature, having escaped the corruption that is in the world through desire.

⁵For this very reason, having brought in [all]ⁱ diligence supply in your faith virtue, and virtue with knowledge, ⁶and knowledge with self-control, and self-control with steadfastness, and steadfastness with godliness, ⁷and godliness with brotherly affection, and brotherly affection with love.

⁸For if these qualities are yours and are increasing, they keep you from being ineffective or unfruitful in the knowledge of our Lord Jesus Christ.

⁹For whoever lacks these qualities is so nearsighted that he is blind, having forgotten that he was cleansed from his former sins.

¹⁰Therefore, brothers, be all the more diligent [[through good works]]^j to confirm your calling and election, for if you practice these qualities you will never fall. ¹¹For in this way there will be richly provided for you an entrance into the eternal kingdom of our Lord and Savior Jesus Christ.

¹²Therefore I will [[not]]^k neglect always to remind you concerning these things, though you know them and are established in the truth that you have. ¹³[I think it right, as long as I am in this body, to stir you up]^l By way of reminder, ¹⁴since I know that the putting off of my body will be soon, as [our Lord]^m Jesus Christ made clear to me. ¹⁵And I will be diligent [also]ⁿ so that after my departure you may be able at any time to recall these things.

---

^b 1:1, **Christ:** See footnote for Christ in Luke 2:11.

^c 1:1, **God:** ℵ(01) reads "Lord."

^d 1:1, **our God and Savior Jesus Christ:** Or "our God, and the Savior Jesus Christ."

^e 1:2, **God and of Jesus:** Absent in some manuscripts. P(024).

^f 1:2, **Christ:** Included in ℵ(01) A(02).

^g 1:3, **to:** Some manuscripts read "by." BYZ TR.

^h 1:4, **us:** A(02) reads "you."

ⁱ 1:5, **all:** Absent from C(04).

^j 1:10, **through good works:** Included in ℵ(01) A(02).

^k 1:12, **not:** Included in 𝔓72 BYZ TR.

^l 1:13, **I think it right...:** Absent from ℵ(01).

^m 1:14, **our Lord:** Absent from ℵ(01).

ⁿ 1:15, **also:** Absent from 𝔓72.

16 For we did not follow cleverly devised myths when we made known to you the power and coming of our Lord Jesus Christ, but we were eyewitnesses of his majesty. 17 For when he received honor and glory from God the Father, and the voice was borne to him by the Majestic Glory, "This is my beloved Son with whom I am well pleased," 18 we ourselves heard this very voice borne from heaven, for we were with him on the holy mountain.

19 And we have the prophetic word more fully confirmed, to which you will do well to pay attention as to a lamp shining in a dark place, until the day dawns and the morning star rises in your hearts, 20 knowing this first of all, that no prophecy of Scripture comes from someone's own interpretation. 21 For prophecy was never brought about by the will of men, but carried along by the Holy Spirit,[a] {men spoke from God}.[b]

2 1 But there were also false prophets among the people, just as there will be false teachers among you, who will secretly introduce destructive heresies, even denying the Master who bought them, bringing swift destruction upon themselves. 2 Many will follow their {licentiousness},[c] and because of them the way of truth will be blasphemed. 3 In their greed, they will exploit you with fabricated words; for whom the judgment from long ago is not idle, and their destruction is not asleep.

4 For if God did not spare angels when they sinned, but having cast them into Tartarus[d] with chains of darkness, delivering them to be {kept}[e] for judgment; 5 and if he did not spare the ancient world, but preserved Noah, a herald of righteousness, with seven others, when he brought a flood upon the world of the ungodly; 6 and the cities of Sodom and Gomorrah, having reduced them to ashes, he condemned them [to destruction],[f] Setting forth an example of those who are to be ungodly. 7 And if he rescued righteous Lot, who was distressed by the depraved conduct of the lawless 8 (for that righteous man, living among them day after day, was tormented in his righteous soul by the lawless deeds he saw and heard.)

9 The Lord knows how to deliver the godly out of temptation,[g] but reserves the unrighteous for the day of judgment to be punished, 10 especially those who follow after the flesh in the desire of defilement and despise authority.

Bold and arrogant, they do not tremble as they blaspheme the glorious ones. 11 Yet even angels, being greater in [strength and][h] power, do not bring a slanderous judgment against them [from the Lord].[i]

---

a 1:21, **Spirit:** See footnote for Spirit in Luke 1:15.

b 1:21, **men spoke from God:** Some manuscripts read "holy men of God spoke." ℵ(01) A(02) BYZ TR.

c 2:2, **licentiousness:** TR reads "destruction."

d 2:4, **Tartarus:** This is the only occurrence of this word in the New Testament. In A(02), the word Τάρταρος (Tartarus) appears in a unique expansion of Job 40:20. However, it is not found in all versions of the LXX. Tartarus, thought of by the Greeks as a subterranean place lower than Hades where divine punishment was meted out, and so regarded in Israelite apocalyptic as well. (BDAG, ταρταρόω).

e 2:4, **kept:** Some manuscripts read "punished." ℵ(01) A(02).

f 2:6, **to destruction:** Absent from 𝔓72 C(04).

g 2:9, **temptation:** The Greek word means (1) an attempt to learn the nature or character of something, *test, trial,* or (2) an attempt to make one do something wrong *temptation, enticement* to sin (BDAG, πειρασμός). Some manuscripts read "temptations" rather than "temptation."

h 2:11, **strength and:** Absent from 𝔓72.

i 2:11, **from the Lord:** Absent in manuscripts. A(02).

12 But these people, like irrational animals, creatures of instinct, [born]ᵃ to be caught and destroyed, blaspheme in matters they do not understand, in their destruction they will also be destroyed, 13 {suffering}ᵇ harm as the wages of their wrongdoing. They consider it a pleasure to revel in the daytime, blots and blemishes, [[hidden reefs]]ᶜ reveling in their {deceptions}ᵈ while they feast with you; 14 having eyes [full]ᵉ of adultery and insatiable for sin, enticing unstable souls, having a heart trained in greed,ᶠ cursed children.

15 Having left the straight path, they have gone astray, following the way of Balaam son of {Bosor},ᵍ who loved the wages of unrighteousness. 16 But he received a rebuke for his own transgression; a mute beast, speaking with a human voice, restrained the prophet's madness.

17 These people are springs without water and {mists}ʰ driven by a storm, for whom the gloom of darkness has been reserved [[forever]].ⁱ

18 For, speaking with inflated vanity, they entice by fleshly desires, with debauchery, those who are truly escaping from those who live in error,

19 Promising them freedom, they themselves are [[also]]ʲ slaves of corruption; for whatever someone is defeated by, to this they are enslaved.

20 If they have escaped the corruption of the world by knowing {the}ᵏ Lord and Savior Jesus Christ and are again entangled in it and are overcome, they are worse off at the end than they were at the beginning.

21 For it would have been better for them not to have known the way of righteousness, than having known it, to turn back [[to the things behind,]]ˡ from the holy commandment delivered to them.

22 [[But]]ᵐ Of them the proverbs are true: "A dog returns to its vomit," and, "A pig that is washed goes back to rolling in the mire."ⁿ

3 1 This is now, beloved, the second letter I am writing to you, in which I am stirring up your sincere mind by way of reminder, 2 Remember the words spoken beforehand by the holy prophets, and the commandment of {your}ᵒ Lord and Savior given by your apostles.

ᵃ 2:12, **born:** Absent from 𝔓72.
ᵇ 2:13, **suffering:** Some manuscripts read "receiving." A(02) C(04) BYZ TR.
ᶜ 2:13 , **hidden reefs:** Included in C(04).
ᵈ 2:13, **deceptions:** B(03) reads "love feasts."
ᵉ 2:14, **full:** Absent from 𝔓72.
ᶠ 2:14, **greed:** The Greek word refers to "the state of desiring to have more than one's due, *greediness, insatiableness, avarice, covetousness*" (BDAG, πλεονεξία).
ᵍ 2:15, **Bosor:** B(03) reads "Beor."
ʰ 2:17, **mists:** Some manuscripts read "clouds." BYZ TR.
ⁱ 2:17, **forever:** Included in A(02) C(04) BYZ TR.
ʲ 2:19, **also:** Included in A(02) C(04) BYZ TR.
ᵏ 2:20, **the:** B(03) BYZ TR SBLGNT THGNT ‖ Some manuscripts read "our." 𝔓72 ℵ(01) A(02) C(04) NA27 [].
ˡ 2:21, **to the things behind:** Included in ℵ(01) A(02).
ᵐ 2:22, **But:** Included in C(04) BYZ TR.
ⁿ 2:22, Proverbs 26:11.
ᵒ 3:2, **your:** TR reads "our."

3 Firstly, know this, that in the last days scoffers will come, walking according to their own desires [in mockery]^a 4 and saying, Where is the promise of his coming? For ever since the fathers fell asleep, all things continue as they were from the beginning of creation.

5 For when they maintain this, it escapes their notice that by the word of God the heavens existed long ago and the earth was formed out of water and by water, 6 through which the world at that time was destroyed, being flooded with water.

7 But the present heavens and earth, by the same word, are stored up for fire, being kept for the day of judgment and destruction of ungodly men.

8 But do not let this one fact escape your notice, beloved, that with the Lord one day is like a thousand years, [and a thousand years]^b like one day.

9 The Lord is not slow about his promise, as some count slowness, but is patient toward {you},^c not wishing for any to perish but for all to come to repentance.

10 But the day of the Lord will come like a thief [[in the night]],^d in which the heavens will pass away with a roar and the elements will be destroyed with intense heat, and the earth and its works will {be found}.^e

11 With all these things {thus}^f being dissolved what sort of men ought {you}^g to be in holy conduct and godliness? 12 looking for [and hastening]^h the coming of the day of {God},ⁱ because of which the heavens will be destroyed by burning, and the elements will melt with intense heat!

13 But according to his {promise}^j we are looking for new heavens and a new earth, in which righteousness dwells.

14 Therefore, beloved, since you look for these things, be diligent to be found by him in peace, spotless and blameless, 15 and regard the patience of our Lord as salvation; just as also our beloved brother Paul, according to the wisdom given him, wrote to you, 16 as also in all his letters, speaking in them of these things, in which are some things hard to understand, which the untaught and unstable distort, as they do also the rest of the Scriptures, to their own destruction.

17 You therefore, beloved, knowing this beforehand, be on your guard so that you are not carried away by the error of unprincipled men and fall from your own steadfastness, 18 but grow in the grace and knowledge of our Lord and Savior Jesus Christ.

To him be the glory, both now and to the day of eternity. [Amen.]^k

---

a 3:3, **in mockery:** Absent from BYZ TR.

b 3:8, **and a thousand years:** Absent from 𝔓72 ℵ(01).

c 3:9, **you:** Some manuscripts read "us." BYZ TR.

d 3:10, **in the night:** Included in C(04) BYZ TR.

e 3:10, **be found:** ℵ(01) B(03) ‖ A(02) BYZ TR reads "be burned up." ‖ 𝔓72 reads "be found dissolved." ‖ C(04) reads "disappear."

f 3:11, **thus:** Some manuscripts read "therefore." ℵ(01) A(02) B(03) C(04) BYZ TR.

g 3:11, **you:** ℵ(01) reads "us." ‖ Absent from 𝔓72 B(03).

h 3:12, **and hastening:** Absent from ℵ(01).

i 3:12, **God:** C(04) reads "the Lord."

j 3:13, **promise:** ℵ(01) A(02) reads "promises."

k 3:18, **Amen:** Absent from B(03).

First John [a]

1 [1] What was from the beginning, what we have heard, what we have seen with our eyes, what we have looked at and our hands have touched concerning the word of life – [2] and the life was revealed, and we have seen and testify and proclaim to you the eternal life which was with the Father and was revealed to us.

[3] What we have seen and heard, we proclaim to you [also], [b] so that you too may have fellowship with us. And indeed our fellowship is with the Father and with his Son Jesus Christ. [c]

[4] And we write these things so that {our} [d] joy may be complete.

[5] And this is the {message} [e] we have heard from him and announce to you, that God is light and in him there is no darkness at all.

[6] [[For]] [f] If we say that we have fellowship with him and walk in the darkness, we lie and do not practice the truth;

[7] But if we walk in the light, as he is in the light, we have fellowship with one another, and the blood of Jesus [[Christ]] [g] his Son cleanses us from all sin.

[8] If we say that we have no sin, we deceive ourselves and the truth is not in us.

[9] If we confess our sins, he is faithful and just to forgive us our sins and to cleanse us from all unrighteousness.

[10] If we say that we have not sinned, we make him a liar, and his word is not in us.

2 [1] My children, I write these things to you so that you may not sin.

And if anyone sins, we have an advocate with the Father, Jesus Christ the righteous;

[2] And he is the atoning sacrifice for our sins, and not for ours only but also for the whole world.

[3] By this we know that we have come to know him, if we {keep} [h] his commandments.

[4] Whoever says [that], [i] I have come to know him, and does not keep his commandments, is a liar, and in such a person the truth [[of God]] [j] does not exist;

[5] But whoever keeps his word, in this person the love of God has truly been perfected.

By this we know that we are in him. [6] Whoever says he abides in him ought to walk, [just] [k] as he walked.

[7] {Beloved}, [l] I am not writing you a new commandment, but an old commandment that you have had from the beginning; the old commandment is the word that you have heard [[from the beginning]]. [m]

---

a 1:0, **Title ("First John"):** Absent from ℵ(01) B(03) C(04) ‖ BYZ reads "Of John One." ‖ TR reads "Of John the apostle, the first general letter."

b 1:3, **also:** Absent from BYZ TR.

c 1:3, **Christ:** See footnote for Christ in Luke 2:11.

d 1:4, **our:** ℵ(01) B(03) NA28 SBLGNT THGNT BYZ TR ‖ Some manuscripts read "your." A(02) C(04).

e 1:5, **message:** Some manuscripts read "promise." C(04) TR.

f 1:6, **For:** Included in A(02).

g 1:7, **Christ:** Included in A(02) BYZ TR.

h 2:3, **keep:** ℵ(01) reads "guards."

i 2:4, **that:** Absent from C(04) BYZ TR.

j 2:4, **of God:** Included in ℵ(01).

k 2:6, **just:** Absent from A(02) B(03).

l 2:7, **Beloved:** Some manuscripts read "Brothers." BYZ TR.

m 2:7, **from the beginning:** Included in BYZ TR.

8 Again, I am writing you a new commandment, which is true in him and in you, because the darkness is passing away and the true light is already shining.

9 Whoever says he is in the light and hates his brother is [a liar and][a] in the darkness until now.

10 Whoever loves his brother abides in the light, and there is no cause for stumbling in him;

11 But whoever hates his brother is in the darkness and walks in the darkness, and does not know where he is going, because the darkness has blinded his eyes.

12 I write to you, children, because your sins are forgiven for his name's sake.

13 I write to you, fathers, because you have known him who is from the beginning.

I write to you, young men, because you have overcome the evil one.

14 I have written to you, children, because you have known the Father.

I have written to you, fathers, because you have known him who is from the beginning.

I have written to you, young men, because you are strong, and the word [of God][b] abides in you, and you have overcome the evil one.

15 Do not love the world or the things in the world.

If anyone loves the world, the love of {the Father}[c] is not in him; 16 for all that is in the world, the lust of the flesh and the lust of the eyes and the boastful pride of life, is not from the Father but is from the world.

17 And the world is passing away, and the lust of it; but the one who does the will of God abides forever.

18 Children, it is the last hour; and just as you have heard that the antichrist is coming, even now many antichrists have arisen, by which we know that it is the last hour.

19 They went out from us, but they were not of us; for if they had been of us, they would have remained with us; but they went out, so that it might be shown that they all are not of us.

20 And you have an anointing from the Holy One, and you all know.

21 I have not written to you because you do not know the truth, but because you know it, and because no lie is of the truth.

22 Who is the liar but the one who denies that Jesus is the Christ? This is the antichrist, the one who denies the Father and the Son.

23 Whoever denies the Son does not have the Father[; the one who confesses the Son has the Father also].[d]

24 [[Therefore]][e] As for you, let what you heard from the beginning abide in you. If what you heard from the beginning abides in you, you also will abide in the Son and in the Father.

25 And this is the promise that he himself made to us: eternal life.

26 These things I have written to you concerning those who are trying to deceive you.

27 As for you, the anointing that you received from him abides in you, and you have no need that anyone should teach you; but [as][f] his anointing teaches you about all things, and is true and is not a lie, and just as it has taught you, abide in him.

---

a 2:9, **a liar and:** Included in ℵ(01).

b 2:14, **of God:** Absent from B(03).

c 2:15, **the Father:** Some manuscripts read "God." A(02) C(04).

d 2:23, **the one who confesses the Son has the Father also:** Absent from BYZ TR.

e 2:24, **Therefore:** Included in BYZ TR.

f 2:27, **as:** Absent from B(03).

28 [And now, little children, abide in him,]ᵃ so that when he appears, we may have confidence and not be ashamed before him at his coming.

29 If you know that he is righteous, you know that [also]ᵇ everyone who practices righteousness has been born of him.

3 1 See what great love the Father has given us, that we should be called children of God[, and we are].ᶜ For this reason, the world does not know {us},ᵈ because it did not know him.

2 Beloved, now we are children of God, and it has not yet been revealed what we will be. [[But]]ᵉ We know that when he is revealed, we will be like him, for we will see him as he is.

3 And everyone who has this hope in him purifies himself, just as he is pure.

4 Everyone who commits sin also commits lawlessness, and sin is lawlessness.

5 And you know that this one was revealed, in order to take away [[our]]ᶠ sins, and in this one there is no sin.

6 Whoever abides in him does not sin; whoever sins has neither seen him nor known him.

7 Little children, let no one deceive you; the one who practices righteousness is righteous, just as he is righteous; 8 the one who commits sin is of the devil, for the devil has been sinning from the beginning.

For this purpose, the Son of God was revealed to destroy the works of the devil.

9 Whoever is born of God does not commit sin, for his seed remains in him, and he cannot sin, because he is born of God.

10 In this, the children of God and the children of the devil are manifest: whoever does not practice righteousness is not of God, nor is the one who does not love his brother.

11 For this is the message that you heard from the beginning, that we should love one another, 12 not as Cain, who was of the evil one and murdered his brother. And why did he murder him? Because his works were evil, and his brother's works were righteous.

13 [And]ᵍ Do not be surprised, [[my]]ʰ brothers, if the world hates you.

14 We know that we have passed from death to life because we love {the}ⁱ brothers. He who does not love [[the brother]]ʲ remains in death.

15 Everyone who hates his brother is a murderer, and you know that no murderer has eternal life abiding in {him}.ᵏ

16 In this we have come to know love, that he laid down his life for us, and we also ought to lay down our lives for the brothers.

17 But whoever has this world's goods and sees his brother in need, and shuts up his heart from him, how does the love of God abide in him?

18 [[My]]ˡ Little children, let us not love in word or in tongue, but in deed and in truth.

ᵃ 2:28, **And now, little children, abide in him:** Absent from ℵ(01).

ᵇ 2:29, **also:** Absent from B(03) BYZ TR.

ᶜ 3:1, **and we are:** Absent from BYZ TR.

ᵈ 3:1, **us:** Some manuscripts read "you." ℵ(01) C(04) BYZ.

ᵉ 3:2, **But:** Included in BYZ TR.

ᶠ 3:5, **our:** Included in ℵ(01) C(04) BYZ TR ‖ Absent from A(02) B(03) NA28 SBLGNT THGNT.

ᵍ 3:13, **And:** ℵ(01) C(04) NA28 ‖ Absent from A(02) B(03) BYZ TR SBLGNT THGNT .

ʰ 3:13, **my:** Included in BYZ TR.

ⁱ 3:14, **the:** ℵ(01) reads "us."

ʲ 3:14, **the brother:** Included in C(04) BYZ TR.

ᵏ 3:15, **him:** Some manuscripts read "himself." ℵ(01) A(02) C(04) BYZ.

ˡ 3:18, **My:** Included in BYZ TR.

19 [And]^a In this we {know}^{b} that we are of the truth, and shall assure our {heart}^{c} before him. 20 For if our heart condemns us, {God}^{d} is greater than our heart, and knows all things.

21 Beloved,^{e} if {the}^{f} heart does not condemn [us],^{g} we have confidence toward God.

22 And whatever we ask, we receive from him, because we keep his commandments and do those things that are pleasing in his sight.

23 And this is his commandment: that we should believe in the name of [the Son]^h Jesus Christ and love one another, as he gave [us]^i *the* commandment.

24 And he who keeps his commandments abides in him, and he in him. [And]^j By this we know that he abides in us, by the Spirit which he has given us.

4 1 Beloved, do not believe every spirit, but test the spirits to see if they are from God, because many false prophets have gone out into the world.

2 By this {you know the Spirit of God}:^{k} every spirit that confesses {Jesus Christ}^{l} has come in the flesh is from God, 3 and every spirit that does not confess Jesus [[having come in the flesh]]^m is not from God; and this is the spirit of the antichrist, which you have heard is coming, and is now already in the world.

4 You are from God, children, and have overcome them, because the one who is in you is greater than the one who is in the world.

5 They are from the world; therefore they speak from the world, and the world listens to them.

6 We are from God; the one who knows God listens to us; the one who is not from God does not listen to us. By this we know the spirit of truth and the spirit of error.

7 Beloved, let us love one another, because love is from God, and everyone who loves has been born of God and knows God.

8 [The one who does not love does not know God,]^n because God is love.

9 In this the love of God was revealed among us, that God sent his only Son into the world, so that we might live through him.

10 In this is love, not that we loved God, but that he loved us and sent his Son as an atoning sacrifice for our sins.

11 Beloved, if God so loved us, we also ought to love one another.

12 No one has ever seen God; if we love one another, God abides in us and his love is perfected in us.

13 By this we know that we abide in him and he in us, because he has given us of his Spirit.

---

a 3:19, **And:** Absent from A(02) B(03).

b 3:19, **know:** Some manuscripts read "will know." BYZ TR.

c 3:19, **heart:** Some manuscripts read "hearts." ℵ(01) BYZ TR.

d 3:20, **God:** C(04) reads "the Lord."

e 3:21, **Beloved:** ℵ(01) reads "Brothers."

f 3:21, **the:** A(02) B(03) SBLGNT THGNT ‖ Some manuscripts read "our." ℵ(01) C(04) NA27[] NA28 BYZ TR.

g 3:21, **us:** Absent from B(03).

h 3:23, **the Son:** Absent from A(02).

i 3:23, **us:** Absent from BYZ.

j 3:24, **And:** Absent from ℵ(01).

k 4:2, **you know the Spirit of God:** BYZ reads "the Spirit of God is known."

l 4:2, **Jesus Christ:** Some manuscripts read "Christ Jesus." C(04).

m 4:3, **having come in the flesh:** Included in ℵ(01) BYZ TR.

n 4:8, **The one who does not love does not know God:** Absent from ℵ(01).

14 And we have seen and testify that the Father has sent the Son as the Savior of the world.

15 Whoever confesses that Jesus [[Christ]]ᵃ is the Son of God, God abides in him and he in God.

16 And we have come to know and have believed the love that {God}ᵇ has for us. God is love, and the one who abides in love abides in God, and God [abides]ᶜ in him.

17 In this love is perfected with us [[in us]],ᵈ so that we may have confidence in the {day}ᵉ of judgment, because as he is, so also are we in this world.

18 There is no fear in love, but perfect love casts out fear, because fear involves punishment, and the one who fears has not been perfected in love.

19 [[Therefore,]]ᶠ We love [[him]]ᵍ because he first loved us.

20 If someone says, I love God, and hates his brother, he is a liar; for the one who does not love his brother whom he has seen, {cannot love God}ʰ whom he has not seen.

21 And this commandment we have from him, that the one who loves God should also love his brother.

5 1 Everyone who believes that Jesus is the Christ has been born of God, and everyone who loves the one who gave birth [also]ⁱ loves the one who has been born from him.

2 By this we know that we love the children of God, when we love God and {obey}ʲ his commands.

3 For this is the love of God, that we keep his commandments; and his commandments are not burdensome.

4 For whatever is born of God overcomes the world; and this is the victory that has overcome the world, our faith.

5 [And]ᵏ who is the one who overcomes the world, except the one who believes that Jesus is the Son of God?

6 This is the one who came by water and blood [[and Spirit]],ˡ Jesus Christ, not in the water only, but with the water and [in]ᵐ the {blood}ⁿ ; and the Spirit is the one bearing witness, because the Spirit is the truth.

7 For there are three that testify [[in heaven, the Father, the Word, and the Holy Spirit; and these three are one. 8 And there are three that testify on earth]] the Spirit, the water, and the blood; and the three are in agreement.ᵒ

ᵃ 4:15, **Christ:** Included in B(03).

ᵇ 4:16, **God:** 𝔓9 reads "Christ."

ᶜ 4:16, **abides:** Absent from A(02) TR.

ᵈ 4:17, **in us:** Included in ℵ(01).

ᵉ 4:17, **day:** ℵ(01) reads "love."

ᶠ 4:19, **Therefore:** Included in A(02).

ᵍ 4:19, **him:** Included in BYZ TR ‖ ℵ(01) reads "God." ‖ Absent from A(02) B(03) NA28 SBLGNT THGNT.

ʰ 4:20, **cannot love God:** Some manuscripts read "how can he love God...?" BYZ TR.

ⁱ 5:1, **also:** Absent from B(03).

ʲ 5:2, **obey:** B(03) NA28 SBLGNT THGNT ‖ Some manuscripts read "keep." ℵ(01) A(02) BYZ TR.

ᵏ 5:5, **and:** Absent from A(02) BYZ TR.

ˡ 5:6, **and Spirit:** Included in ℵ(01) A(02).

ᵐ 5:6, **in:** Absent from ℵ(01) BYZ TR.

ⁿ 5:6, **blood:** A(02) reads "Spirit."

ᵒ 5:7-8, **in heaven, the Father, the Word, and the Holy Spirit; and these three are one. 8 And there are three that testify on earth:** Included in TR ‖ This later addition is known as the Comma Johanneum, one of the most famous textual variants in the New Testament. Although present in the Latin Vulgate, this expanded text is not found as the base text in any Greek manuscript before the 12th century.

9 If we accept the testimony of {men},[a] the testimony of God is greater; for this is the testimony of God, {that}[b] he has testified concerning his Son.

10 The one who believes in the Son of God has the testimony [[of God]][c] in {him};[d] the one who does not believe {God}[e] has made him a liar, because he has not believed in the testimony that God has testified concerning his Son.

11 And this is the testimony, that God has given us eternal life, and this life is in his Son.

12 The one who has the Son has the life; the one who does not have the Son of God does not have the life.

13 These things I have written to you, so that you may know that you have eternal life, {to those who}[f] believe in the name of the Son of God.

14 And this is the confidence that we have before him, that if we ask anything according to his will, he hears us. 15 [And if we know that he hears us][g] In whatever we ask, we know that we have the requests that we have asked {of}[h] him.

16 If anyone sees his brother committing a sin not leading to death, he shall ask, and he will give him life, to those who commit sins not leading to death. There is a sin leading to death; I do not say that one should pray for that. 17 All unrighteousness is sin, and there is sin not leading to death.

18 We know that everyone who has been born of God does not sin, but the one who was born of God keeps {himself},[i] and the evil one does not touch him.

19 We know that we are of God, and the whole world lies in the power of the evil one.

20 And we know that the Son of God has come and has given us understanding, so that we may know the true {one},[j]

And we are in the true one, in his Son [Jesus Christ].[k]

This one is the true God and eternal life.

21 Little children, guard yourselves from idols. [[Amen]][l]

---

a 5:9, **men:** A(02) reads "God."
b 5:9, **that:** Some manuscripts read "which." BYZ TR.
c 5:10, **of God:** Included in 𝔓74 A(02).
d 5:10, **him:** A(02) B(03) SBLGNT BYZ TR ‖ Some manuscripts read "himself." ℵ(01) NA28.
e 5:10, **God:** A(02) reads "the Son."
f 5:13, **to those who:** Some manuscripts read "and so that you may." BYZ TR.
g 5:15, **And if we know that he hears us:** Absent from ℵ(01) A(02).
h 5:15, **of:** Some manuscripts read "from." A(02) BYZ TR.
i 5:18, **himself:** Some manuscripts read "him." A(02) B(03) SBLGNT.
j 5:20, **one:** A(02) reads "God."
k 5:20, **Jesus Christ:** Absent from A(02).
l 5:21, **Amen:** Included in BYZ TR.

Second John[a]

1 The elder to the chosen lady and her children, whom I love in truth, and not only I, but also all who know the truth, 2 because of the truth that {abides} [b]in us and will be with us forever.

3 Grace, mercy, and peace [will be with us][c] from God the Father and from [[the Lord]][d] Jesus Christ,[e] the Son of the Father, in truth and love.

4 I rejoiced greatly to find some of your children walking in the truth, just as we received commandment from the Father. 5 And [[a commandment]][f] now I ask you, lady, not as though I were writing you a new commandment, but the one we have had from the beginning, that we love one another.

6 And this is love, that we walk according to his commandments; this is the commandment, just as you have heard from the beginning, so that you should walk in it.

7 For many deceivers {have gone out}[g] into the world, those who do not confess Jesus Christ as coming in the flesh; this is the deceiver and the antichrist.

8 Watch yourselves, so that [you][h] may not lose what we have worked for, but may receive a full reward.

9 Everyone who {goes ahead}[i] and does not abide [[and not]][j] in the teaching of Christ[k] does not have God; whoever abides in the teaching [[of Christ]][l] has both the Father and the Son.

10 If anyone comes to you and does not bring this teaching, do not receive him into your house or give him any greeting; 11 for whoever greets him takes part in his wicked works.

12 Having much to write to you, I did not want to do so with paper and ink, {but}[m] I hope to come to you and speak face to face, so that {our}[n] joy may be complete.

13 The children of your chosen sister greet you. [[Amen]][o]

---

a 1:0, **Title ("Second John")**: Absent from ℵ(01) B(03) C(04) ‖ BYZ reads "Of John Two." ‖ TR reads "Of John the apostle, the second general letter."

b 1:2, **abides**: A(02) reads "dwells."

c 1:3, **will be with us**: Absent from A(02).

d 1:3, **the Lord**: Included in ℵ(01) BYZ TR.

e 1:3, **Christ**: See footnote for Christ in Luke 2:11.

f 1:5, **a commandment**: Included in ℵ(01).

g 1:7, **have gone out**: Some manuscripts read "have entered into." BYZ TR.

h 1:8, **you**: Some manuscripts read "we." BYZ TR.

i 1:9, **goes ahead**: Some manuscripts read "goes beyond." BYZ TR.

j 1:9, **and not**: Included in ℵ(01).

k 1:9, **the teaching of Christ**: This is likely referring to the teaching about Christ of verse 7 as an objective genitive Greek phrase.

l 1:9, **of Christ**: Included in BYZ TR.

m 1:12, **but**: A(02) reads "for."

n 1:12, **our**: Some manuscripts read "your." A(02) B(03) SBLGNT.

o 1:13, **Amen**: Included in BYZ TR.

Third John[a]

1 The elder to Gaius the beloved, whom I love in truth.

2 Beloved, I pray that in all things you may prosper and be in good health, just as your soul prospers. 3 [For][b] I rejoiced greatly when brothers came and testified of your truth, just as you walk in the truth.

4 I have no greater joy than to hear that my children are walking in the truth.

5 Beloved, you are faithful in whatever you do for the brothers {and also}[c] strangers 6 who have testified of your love before the church. You will do well to send them on their journey in a manner worthy of God. 7 For they went out for the sake of the Name, accepting nothing from the Gentiles.[d] 8 Therefore, we ought to {support}[e] such men, so that we may be fellow workers for the {truth}.[f]

9 I wrote [something][g] to the church, but Diotrephes, who loves to be first among them, does not accept us. 10 For this reason, if I come, I will call attention to his deeds which he does, slandering us with wicked words. And not content with that, he himself does not receive the brothers, and he forbids those who want to do so and expels them from the church.

11 Beloved, do not imitate what is evil, but what is good. The one who does good is of God; the one who does evil has not seen God.

12 Demetrius has received a good testimony from everyone, and from [[the church and]][h] the truth itself; and we also testify, and you know that our testimony is true.

13 I had much to write [to you],[i] but I do not want to write to you with ink and pen; 14 but I hope to see you soon, and we will speak face to face.

15 Peace to you. The friends greet you. Greet the friends by name.

---

a 1:0, **Title ("Third John"):** Absent from ℵ(01) A(02) ‖ B(03) BYZ reads "Of John Three." ‖ TR reads "Of John the apostle, the third general letter."

b 1:3, **For:** Absent from ℵ(01).

c 1:5, **and also:** Some manuscripts read "and to." BYZ TR.

d 1:7, **Gentiles:** Or "nations."

e 1:8, **support:** Some manuscripts read "welcome." BYZ TR.

f 1:8, **truth:** ℵ(01) A(02) read "church."

g 1:9, **something:** Absent from C(04) BYZ TR.

h 1:12, **the church and:** Included in 𝔓74 C(04).

i 1:13, **to you:** Absent from BYZ TR.

Jude[a]

1 Jude, a servant of Jesus Christ[b] and brother of James, to those who are {loved}[c] in God the Father and kept for Jesus Christ, called: 2 May mercy, peace, and love be multiplied to you.

3 Beloved, while I was making every effort to write to you about our common salvation [[and life]],[d] I felt the necessity to write to you urging you to contend earnestly for the faith which was once for all handed down to the saints. 4 For certain men have crept in unnoticed, those who were long beforehand marked out for this condemnation, ungodly persons who turn the grace of our God into licentiousness and deny {our only Master and Lord},[e] Jesus Christ.

5 Now I desire to remind you, [[brothers]][f] knowing {once for all}[g] that {the Lord},[h] having saved a people out of the land of Egypt, the second time destroyed those who did not believe.

6 And angels who did not keep their own domain, but abandoned their proper abode, He has kept in eternal bonds under darkness for the judgment of the great day, 7 just as Sodom and Gomorrah and the cities around them, since they in the same way as these indulged in gross immorality and went after strange flesh, are exhibited as an example in undergoing the punishment of eternal fire.

8 Likewise, however, these people, while dreaming, defile the flesh, they reject authority, and blaspheme glories.[i] 9 But Michael the archangel, when he disputed with the devil and argued about the body of Moses, did not dare pronounce against him a railing judgment, but said, "{The Lord}[j] rebuke you!"

10 These men, indeed, blaspheme in matters they do not understand; and in things they know by instinct, like unreasoning animals, they are destroyed in these things.

11 Woe to them! For they have gone the way of Cain, and for pay they have rushed headlong into the error of Balaam, and perished in the rebellion of Korah.

1:0, **Title ("Jude"):** Absent from ℵ(01) B(03) ‖ BYZ reads "Jude." ‖ 𝔓72 A(02) reads "Letter of Jude." ‖ TR reads "Of Jude the apostle, the general letter."

1:1, **Christ:** See footnote for Christ in Luke 2:11.

1:1, **loved:** Some manuscripts read "sanctified." BYZ TR.

1:3, **and life:** Included in ℵ(01).

1:4, **our only Master and Lord:** Some manuscripts read "And denying the only Master, God, and our Lord Jesus Christ." BYZ TR ‖ 𝔓72 reads "the law of us, our Master and Lord."

1:5, **brothers:** Included in 𝔓78.

1:5, **once for all:** Some manuscripts read "that you once knew everything."

1:5, **the Lord:** ℵ(01) C(04) BYZ TR NA27 ‖ Some manuscripts read "Jesus." A(02) B(03) NA28 SBLGNT THGNT ‖ This was changed from "Lord" in NA-27 to "Jesus" in NA28. In UBS-5 this variant is classified with {C} which indicates that the Committee had difficulty in deciding which variant to place in the text. 𝔓72 is a third-century manuscript that contains the unique reading "Christ." In 𝔓72, a later corrector also added "God" before "Christ." "Lord" is selected over "Jesus" from the critical editions as that is the more theologically neutral option. "The Lord" is also attested by the critical editions of Wescott Hort, Tregelle, and the Greek text underlying the NIV translation.

1:8, **glories:** Or "glorious ones."

1:9, **the Lord:** ℵ(01) reads "God."

12 [These are]ᵃ [[grumblers, malcontents, following after their own lusts,]]ᵇ blemishesᶜ in your love feasts, feasting with you without fear, tending to themselves, waterless clouds carried along by winds, autumn trees without fruit, twice dead, uprooted, 13 wild waves of the sea, foaming up their own shame; wandering stars, for whom the gloom of darkness has been reserved forever.

14 It was also about these men that Enoch, in the seventh generation from Adam, prophesied, saying, "Behold, the Lord came with many thousands of His holy ones, 15 To execute judgment against all, and to convict {every soul}ᵈ concerning all the works [of their ungodliness],ᵉ and concerning all the harsh {things}ᶠ which ungodly sinners have spoken against him."ᵍ

16 These are grumblers, finding fault, following after {their}ʰ desires; they speak arrogantly, flattering people for the sake of gaining an advantage.

17 But you, beloved, ought to remember the words that were spoken beforehand by the apostles of our Lord Jesus Christ, 18 that they were saying to you, [[that]]ⁱ "At the end of time there will be mockers, following after their own ungodly lusts." 19 These are the ones who cause divisions, worldly-minded, devoid of the Spirit.

20 But you, beloved, building yourselves up on your most holy faith, praying in the Holy Spirit,ʲ 21 keep yourselves in the love of God, waiting anxiously for the mercy of our Lord Jesus Christ to eternal life.

22 [And have mercy on some, who are doubting; 23 save others, snatching them]ᵏ out of the fire; [but others have mercy on with fear,]ˡ hating even the garment polluted by the flesh.

24 Now to him [who is able to keep {you}ᵐ from stumbling, and to make you stand in the presence of his glory]ⁿ blameless with great joy, 25 to the only [[wise]]ᵒ God [our Savior],ᵖ [through Jesus Christ our Lord,]ᑫ be glory, majesty, dominion and authority, [before all ages],ʳ and now and forever. Amen.

ᵃ 1:12, **These are:** Absent from C(04).

ᵇ 1:12, **grumblers, malcontents, following after their own lusts:** Included in א(01).

ᶜ 1:12, **blemishes:** The Greek word has two meanings: (1) a rocky hazard hidden by waves, *a rock washed by the sea, a (hidden) reef* or (2) that which soil or discolors, *spit, stain* (BDAG, σπιλάς).

ᵈ 1:15, **every soul:** 𝔓72 א(01) NA28 ‖ Some manuscripts read "all the ungodly." A(02) B(03) C(04) SBLGNT THGNT ‖ BYZ TR read "all of their ungodly."

ᵉ 1:15, **of their ungodliness:** Absent from א(01).

ᶠ 1:15, **things:** א(01) reads "words."

ᵍ 1:15, 1 Enoch 1:9.

ʰ 1:16, **their:** א(01) A(02) BYZ TR SBLGNT THGNT ‖ Some manuscripts read "there own." B(03) C(04) NA28.

ⁱ 1:18, **that:** Absent from א(01) B(03).

ʲ 1:20, **Spirit:** See footnote for Spirit in Luke 1:15.

ᵏ 1:23-24, **And have mercy on some...:** Absent from 𝔓72.

ˡ 1:23, **but others have mercy on with fear:** Absent from C(04) BYZ TR.

ᵐ 1:24, **you:** Some manuscripts read "them." BYZ TR.

ⁿ 1:24, **who is able to keep...:** Absent from 𝔓72.

ᵒ 1:25, **wise:** Included in BYZ TR.

ᵖ 1:25, **our Savior:** Absent from 𝔓72.

ᑫ 1:25, **through Jesus Christ our Lord:** Absent from BYZ TR.

ʳ 1:25, **before all ages:** Absent from 𝔓72 BYZ TR.

Revelation[a]

1 [1] The revelation of Jesus Christ,[b] which God gave to him, to show his {servants}[c] what must soon take place; and he made it known by sending his angel to his servant John, [2] who bore witness to the word of God and to the testimony of Jesus Christ, as much as he saw.

[3] Blessed is the one who reads, and those who hear {the}[d] {words}[e] of this prophecy and keep what is written in it, for the time is near.

[4] John, to the seven churches in Asia: Grace to you and peace from {the one}[f] who is and who was and who is to come, and from the seven spirits that are before his throne, [5] and from Jesus Christ, the faithful witness, the firstborn of the dead, and the ruler of the kings of the earth; to the one {loving}[g] us and {to the one who set [us][h] free}[i] from [our][j] sins by his blood, [6] and[k] he has made {us}[l] {a kingdom, priests}[m] to his God and Father; to him be glory and dominion forever [and ever].[n] Amen.

[7] Behold, he is coming {with}[o] the clouds,[p] and every eye will see him, even those who pierced [him],[q] and all the tribes of the earth will mourn over him. Yes, amen.

[8] "I am the Alpha and the Omega, [[the Beginning and the End]]"[r] says the Lord God,[s] "the one who is and who was and who is to come, the Almighty."

[9] I, John, your brother and fellow partaker in the tribulation and [[in the]][t] kingdom and perseverance {in}[u] [[Christ]][v] {Jesus},[w] was on the island called Patmos because of the word of God and [[for]][x] the testimony of Jesus [[Christ]].[y]

---

[a] 1:0, **Title ("Revelation")**: Absent from ℵ(01) A(02) ‖ BYZ NA28 SBLGNT reads "Revelation of John." ‖ TR reads "Revelation of John the Theologian."

[b] 1:1, **Christ**: The Greek word for Christ means (1) fulfiller of Israelite expectation of a deliverer, *the Anointed One, the Messiah, the Christ*, (2) the personal name ascribed to Jesus, *Christ*. (BDAG, Χριστός).

[c] 1:1, **servants**: ℵ(01) reads "saints."

[d] 1:3, **the**: C(04) reads "these."

[e] 1:3, **words**: ℵ(01) reads "word."

[f] 1:4, **the one**: Some manuscripts read "God." BYZ ‖ Absent from 𝔓18 ℵ(01) A(02) C(04) TR NA28 SBLGNT THGNT.

[g] 1:5, **loving**: Some manuscripts read "who loved." TR.

[h] 1:5, **us**: Absent from ℵ(01).

[i] 1:5, **to the one who set us free**: 𝔓18 ℵ(01) A(02) C(04) NA28 SBLGNT THGNT ‖ Some manuscripts read "to the one who washed us." BYZ TR.

[j] 1:5, **our**: Absent from A(02).

[k] 1:6, **and**: Or also.

[l] 1:6, **us**: Some manuscripts read "to us." A(02).

[m] 1:6, **a kingdom, priests**: Some manuscripts read "kings and priests." TR.

[n] 1:6, **and ever**: C(04) BYZ TR NA28[] SBLGNT THGNT ‖ Absent from 𝔓18 A(02).

[o] 1:7, **with**: 𝔓18 ℵ(01) A(02) BYZ TR NA28 SBLGNT THGNT ‖ C(04) reads "upon."

[p] 1:7, Mark 13:26, Luke 21:27.

[q] 1:7, **him**: Absent from ℵ(01).

[r] 1:8, **the Beginning and the End**: Included in TR.

[s] 1:8, **God**: Absent from TR.

[t] 1:9, **in the**: Included in TR.

[u] 1:9, **in**: Some manuscripts read "of." TR.

[v] 1:9, **Christ**: Included in A(02) (instead of "Jesus") BYZ (before "Jesus") TR (after "Jesus").

[w] 1:9, **Jesus**: Some manuscripts read "Christ" rather than "Jesus." A(02).

[x] 1:9, **for**: Included in ℵ(01) TR BYZ THGNT ‖ Absent from A(02) C(04) NA28 SBLGNT.

[y] 1:9, **Christ**: Included in BYZ TR.

10 I was in the Spirit on the Lord's day, and I heard behind me a loud voice like a trumpet 11 saying, "[[I am Alpha and Omega, the first and the last and]]ᵃ What you see, write in a book and send it to the seven churches [[in Asia]]:ᵇ to Ephesus, to Smyrna, to Pergamum, to Thyatira, to Sardis,ᶜ to Philadelphia, and to Laodicea."

12 And [[there]]ᵈ I turned to see the voice that {was speaking}ᵉ with me, and having turned I saw seven golden lampstands 13 and in the midst of the [[seven]]ᶠ lampstands one like a son of man, clothed with a long robe and with a golden sash around his chest. 14 His head and his hair were white like white wool, like snow, and his eyes were like a flame of fire; 15 and his feet were like burnished bronze, refined in a furnace; and his voice was like the sound of many waters. 16 He had in his right hand seven stars, and out of his mouth came a sharp, double-edged sword, and his face was like the sun shining in its strength.

17 And when I saw him, I fell at his feet as though dead, and he placed his right [[hand]]ᵍ on me, saying [[to me]],ʰ "[Do not be afraid;]ⁱ I am the {first}ʲ and the last, 18 [and]ᵏ the living one, and I was dead, and behold, I am alive forever and ever [[amen]],ˡ and I have the keys of {death and of Hades}.ᵐ 19 [Therefore],ⁿ write the things which you have seen, and the things which are, and the things which will take place after these.

20 "The mystery of the seven stars which you saw {on}ᵒ my right hand, and the seven golden lampstands: the seven stars [are]ᵖ the angels of the seven churches, and the seven lampstands [[which you saw]] q are the seven churches."

2 1 To the angel of the church {in}ʳ Ephesus write: "These things says the one who holds the seven stars in his right [[hand]],ˢ who walks in the midst of the seven golden lampstands:

2 "I know your works, {the}ᵗ labor, and your endurance, and that you cannot bear evil ones, and you have tested those {saying themselves}ᵘ apostles and are not, and have found them to be false; 3 and you have endurance, [[and have borne all tribulations,]]ᵛ and have labored for my name's sake, and you {have not grown weary}.ʷ

4 "But I have this against you, that you have left your first love. 5 Remember therefore from where you have fallen, and repent, and do

---

ᵃ 1:11, **I am Alpha and Omega, the first and the last and:** Included in TR ‖ Absent from ℵ(01) A(02) C(04) NA28 SBLGNT THGNT BYZ.

ᵇ 1:11, **in Asia:** Included in TR.

ᶜ 1:11, **to Sardis:** Absent from ℵ(01).

ᵈ 1:12, **there:** Included in BYZ.

ᵉ 1:12, **was speaking:** Some manuscripts read "spoke." TR.

ᶠ 1:13, **seven:** Included in ℵ(01) BYZ TR THGNT.

ᵍ 1:17, **hand:** Included in TR.

ʰ 1:17, **to me:** Included in TR.

ⁱ 1:17, **Do not be afraid:** Absent from ℵ(01).

ʲ 1:17, **first:** A(02) reads "firstborn" (πρωτοτοκος) rather than "first" (πρῶτος).

ᵏ 1:18, **and:** Absent from ℵ(01).

ˡ 1:18, **Amen:** Included in BYZ TR. ‖ Absent in 𝔓98 ℵ(01) A(02) C(04) BYZ TR NA28 SBLGNT THGNT.

ᵐ 1:18, **death and of Hades:** Some manuscripts read "Hades and death." TR.

ⁿ 1:19, **Therefore:** Absent from TR.

ᵒ 1:20, **on:** A(02) reads "in."

ᵖ 1:20, **are:** Absent from ℵ(01).

q 1:20, **which you saw:** Included in BYZ TR.

ʳ 2:1, **in:** TR reads "of."

ˢ 2:1, **hand:** Included in ℵ(01).

ᵗ 2:2, **the:** Some manuscripts read "your." ℵ(01) BYZ TR.

ᵘ 2:2, **saying themselves:** TR reads "claiming to be."

ᵛ 2:3, **and have borne all tribulations:** Included in ℵ(01).

ʷ 2:3, **have not grown weary:** Some manuscripts read "did not grow weary." BYZ.

the first works; or else I will come to you [[quickly]]^a and remove your lampstand from its place, unless you repent. 6 But this you have, that you hate the works of the Nicolaitans, which I also hate.

7 "Let the one who has ears hear what the Spirit says to the [[seven]]^b churches. To the one who overcomes, I will give to eat from the tree of life, which is in [[the midst of]]^c the paradise of [[my]]^d God."

8 And to the angel of the church in Smyrna write: "These things says the {first}^e and the last, who was dead and came to life:

9 "I know [[your works and]]^f your tribulation and your poverty (but you are rich) and the blasphemy^g {from}^h those who say they are Jews and are not, but are a synagogue of Satan.

10 "Do not fear what you are about to suffer. Behold [[indeed]],ⁱ the devil is about to throw [[some of]]^j you into prison, that you may be tested, and you will have tribulation for ten days. [Be]^k faithful unto death, and I will give you the crown of life.

11 "Let the one who has ears hear what the Spirit says to the churches.

"The one who conquers^l will not be harmed by the second death."

12 And to the angel of the church in Pergamum write: "These things says the one who has the sharp, double-edged sword:

13 "I know [[your works and]]^m where you dwell, where Satan's throne is, and you hold fast to my name, and did not deny {my}ⁿ faith [even]^o in the days of Antipas {my witness, my faithful one},^p who was killed among you, where Satan dwells.

14 "But I have this [against you],^q because you have there those who hold the doctrine of Balaam, who taught [Balak]^r to put a stumbling block before the sons of Israel, to eat food sacrificed to idols, and to commit sexual immorality.^s 15 So you also have those who hold the doctrine of [the]^t Nicolaitans {in the same way}.^u

16 "Repent [therefore];^v or else I will come to you quickly and will make war against them with the sword of my mouth.

17 "Let the one who has ears hear what the Spirit says to the churches.

---

^a 2:5, **quickly:** Included in BYZ TR.
^b 2:7, **seven:** Included in A(02) C(04).
^c 2:7, **the midst of:** Included in BYZ TR.
^d 2:7, **my:** Included in BYZ
^e 2:8, **first:** A(02) reads "firstborn."
^f 2:9, **works and:** Included in ℵ(01) BYZ TR.
^g 2:9, **blasphemy:** Or "slander."
^h 2:9, **from:** TR reads "of."
ⁱ 2:10, **indeed:** Included in BYZ.
^j 2:10, **some of:** Included in TR.
^k 2:10, **Be:** Absent from ℵ(01).
^l 2:11, **conquers:** Or "overcomes."
^m 2:13, **your works and:** Included in BYZ TR SBLGNT ‖ Absent from ℵ(01) A(02) C(04) NA28 THGNT.
ⁿ 2:13, **my:** ℵ(01) reads "your."
^o 2:13, **even:** Absent from ℵ(01) BYZ.
^p 2:13, **my witness, my faithful one:** Some manuscripts read "my faithful witness." ℵ(01) BYZ TR THGNT.
^q 2:14, **against you:** Absent from ℵ(01).
^r 2:14, **Balak:** Absent from ℵ(01).
^s 2:14, **immorality:** Or fornication as in breaking covenant by assimilating with fallen culture. The Greek word means (1) to engage in sexual immorality, engage in illicit sex, to fornicate, to whore, or (2) engagement in polytheistic cult, fornicate. (BDAG, πορνεύω).
^t 2:15, **the:** ℵ(01) NA28[] THGNT BYZ TR ‖ Absent from A(02) C(04) SBLGNT.
^u 2:15, **in the same way:** Some manuscripts read "which I hate." TR.
^v 2:16, **therefore:** Absent from ℵ(01) TR.

"To the one who conquers, I will
give [to him][a] [[to eat]][b] some of the
hidden manna, and [I will give him][c] a
white stone, with a new name written
on the stone that no one knows except
the one who receives it."

18 And to the angel [of the church][d]
in Thyatira write: "These things says
the Son of God, who has eyes like
a flame of fire, and his feet are like
fine brass:

19 "I know your works, your love,
your faith, [your service,][e] and your
endurance, [[and]][f] your last works are
more than the first.

20 "But I have [[a few things]][g]
against you, that you {have left}[h] {the}[i]
woman Jezebel, who {calls herself}[j]
a prophetess and teaches and leads
my servants astray to commit sexual
immorality[k] and to eat food sacrificed
to idols. 21 And I gave her time to repent
[, and she does not want to repent][l] of
her sexual immorality. 22 Behold, I am
throwing her {into a bed,}[m] and those
committing adultery with her into
great tribulation, unless they repent
from {her}[n] works. 23 [And][o] I will kill
her children with death, and all the
churches shall know that I am the one
who searches the minds and hearts.
And I will give to each one of you
according to [your][p] works.

24 "But I say to the rest of you in
Thyatira, those who do [not][q] hold
this teaching, [[and]][r] who have not
known the deep things[s] of Satan (as
they say), I will not put upon you any
other burden. 25 However, what you
have, hold on to until I come.

26 "And the one who conquers, and
keeps my works until the end, to him I
will give authority over the nations,
27 And he will shepherd them with an
iron rod, as the ceramic vessels {are
shattered}[t] [[by it]],[u] 28 just as I also
have received from my Father; and I
will give him the morning star.

29 "Let the one who has ears hear
what the Spirit says to the churches."

3 1 And to the angel of the church in
Sardis write: "These things says the
one who has the [seven][v] spirits of God
and the seven stars: I know your deeds,
that you have {a}[w] name that you live,
and you are dead.

---

a 2:17, **to him:** Absent from ℵ(01).
b 2:17, **to eat:** Included in BYZ TR.
c 2:17, **I will give him:** Absent from ℵ(01).
d 2:18, **of the church:** Absent from A(02).
e 2:19, **your service:** Absent from ℵ(01).
f 2:19, **and:** Included in TR.
g 2:20, **a few things:** Included in ℵ(01) TR.
h 2:20, **have left:** Or, have left here in place. Some manuscripts read "tolerate." TR.
i 2:20, **the:** Some manuscripts read "your." A(02) Syriac(sy) BYZ.
j 2:20, **calls herself:** Some manuscripts read "says she is." BYZ.
k 2:20, **immorality:** See footnote for 2:14.
l 2:21, **and she does not want to:** Absent from ℵ(01).
m 2:22, **into a bed:** Or, "on a sickbed." A(02) reads "into prison." The Greek text says only "I throw her on a bed," but this is obviously a punishment in the form of an illness. (*UBS Handbooks for the New Testament* [20 Vols.] [American Bible Society, 2021]. Revelation 2:22).
n 2:22, **her:** Some manuscripts read "their." TR.
o 2:23, **And:** Absent from A(02).
p 2:23, **your:** Absent from ℵ(01).
q 2:24, **not:** Absent from ℵ(01).
r 2:24, **and:** Included in TR.
s 2:24, **deep things:** Or "depths."
t 2:27, **are shattered:** Some manuscripts read "will be shattered." BYZ.
u 2:27, **by it:** Included in 𝔓115.
v 3:1, **seven:** Absent from TR(1550).
w 3:1, **a:** TR reads "the."

2 "Be alert and strengthen the remaining things which you were about to {die};[a] for I have not found your works complete in the sight of [my][b] God.

3 "Remember, [therefore,][c] how you have received and heard, and keep it, and repent. If, therefore, you do not watch, I will come [[upon you]][d] like a thief, and you will not know at what hour I will come upon you.

4 "[But][e] you [[also]][f] have a few names in Sardis who have not defiled their garments; and they shall walk with me in white, for they are worthy.

5 "The one who conquers[g] {thus}[h] shall be clothed in white garments, and I will not blot out their name from the Book of Life; but I will confess their name before my Father and before his angels.

6 "Let the one who has ears hear what the Spirit says to the churches"

7 And to the angel of the church in Philadelphia write: "These things says the Holy One, the True One, the one who has the key of David, the one who opens and no one will shut, and shuts and no one opens:

8 "I know your works, behold, I have set before you an open door, which no one is able to shut; for you have little strength and you have kept my word and have not denied my name.

9 "Behold, I will make those of the synagogue of Satan, who say they are Jews and are not, but lie. Indeed I will make them come and worship before your feet, and to know that I have loved you.

10 "{Because}[i] you have kept the word of my patience, I also [will keep][j] you from the hour of trial which shall come upon the whole world, to test those who dwell on the earth.

11 "[[Behold]][k] I am coming quickly. Hold fast what you have, that no one may take your crown.

12 "The one who conquers, I will make them a pillar in the temple of my God, and they shall not go out [anymore].[l] I will write [on him][m] the name of my God and the name of the city of my God, the New Jerusalem, {descending}[n] from heaven from my God, and {my}[o] new name.

13 "Let the one who has ears hear what the Spirit says to the churches."

14 And to the angel of the church {in}[p] Laodicea write: "These things says the Amen, the faithful and true witness, the beginning[q] of the {creation}[r] of God:

---

a 3:2, **die:** Some manuscripts read "cast off." BYZ.

b 3:2, **my:** Absent from Syriac(Philoxeniana) TR.

c 3:3, **therefore:** Absent from ℵ(01).

d 3:3, **upon you:** Included in ℵ(01) BYZ TR.

e 3:4, **but:** Absent from TR.

f 3:4, **also:** Included in TR.

g 3:5, **conquers:** Or "overcomes."

h 3:5, **thus:** Some manuscripts read "this one." BYZ TR.

i 3:10, **because:** A(02) reads "And."

j 3:10, **will keep:** Absent from ℵ(01).

k 3:11, **Behold:** Included in TR.

l 3:12, **anymore:** Absent from ℵ(01).

m 3:12, **on him:** Absent from C(04).

n 3:12, **descending:** Some manuscripts read "which descends." BYZ.

o 3:12, **my:** ℵ(01) reads "the."

p 3:14, **in:** Some manuscripts read "of." TR THGNT.

q 3:14, **beginning:** Or ruler. The Greek word means (1) the commencement of something as an action, process, or state of being, beginning, (2) one with whom a process begins, beginning, (3) the first cause, the beginning, (4) a point at which two surfaces or lines meet, corner, (5) a basis for further understanding, beginning, (6) an authority figure who initiates activity or process, ruler, authority, or (7) the sphere of one's official activity, rule, office. (BDAG, ἀρχή).

r 3:14, **creation:** ℵ(01) reads "church."

15 "I know your works, that you are neither cold nor hot. [I wish that you were cold or hot.]ᵃ 16 Thus, because you are lukewarm, and {neither}ᵇ {hot nor cold},ᶜ [I am about to spit you out]ᵈ of my mouth. 17 For you say [that],ᵉ 'I am rich, I have prospered, and I need {nothing},'ᶠ and you do not know that you are wretched and pitiable and poor and blind and naked;

18 "I advise you to buy from me gold refined by fire so that you may become rich, and white garments so that you may clothe yourself and the shame of your nakedness may not be revealed, and apply ointment {to}ᵍ your eyes so that you may see.

19 "As many as I love, I reprove and discipline; therefore, be zealous and repent.

20 "Behold, I stand at the door and knock. If anyone hears my voice and opens the door, [also]ʰ I will come in to them and dine with them, and they with me.

21 "To the one who conquers I will grant to sit with me on my throne, as I also overcame and sat down with my Father on his throne.

22 "Let the one who has ears hear what the Spirit says to the churches."

4 1 After these things, I saw, and behold, a door was opened in heaven, and the first voice which I heard was like a trumpet speaking with me, saying, "Come up here, and I will show you what must take place."

After these things 2 [[and]]ⁱ immediately I was in the Spirit, and behold, a throne was set in heaven, and one seated on the throne, 3 [and the one seated]ʲ [[was]]ᵏ like the appearance of jasper and carnelian, and a rainbow around the throne, [like the appearance of an emerald].ˡ

4 [And around the throne were]ᵐ twenty-four thrones, and on the thrones [[I saw]]ⁿ twenty-four [[thrones and]]ᵒ elders seated, clothed in white garments, and [[they had]]ᵖ on their heads golden crowns.

5 And from {the}�q throne proceed flashes of lightning, voices, and peals of thunder, and seven lamps of fire burning before the throne, [which are the seven]ʳ spirits of God, 6 and before the throne there was something like a sea of glass, like crystal.

In the midst of the throne and around the throne were four living creatures full of eyes in front and behind.

7 The first living creature was like a lion, the second living creature like a calf, the third living creature had a face like [[similar to]]ˢ a man, and the fourth living creature was like a flying eagle.

ᵃ 3:15, **I wish that you were cold or hot:** Absent from A(02).
ᵇ 3:16, **neither:** Some manuscripts read "not." BYZ.
ᶜ 3:16, **hot nor cold:** Some manuscripts read "cold nor hot." TR.
ᵈ 3:16, **I am about to spit you out:** Absent from ℵ(01).
ᵉ 3:17, **that:** Absent from ℵ(01) BYZ.
ᶠ 3:17, **nothing:** Some manuscripts read "no one." BYZ TR.
ᵍ 3:18, **to:** BYZ reads "for."
ʰ 3:20, **also:** ℵ(01) NA28[] SBLGNT THGNT BYZ ‖ Absent from A(02) TR.
ⁱ 4:2, **And:** Included in BYZ TR.
ʲ 4:3, **and the one seated:** Absent from BYZ.
ᵏ 4:3, **was:** Included in TR.
ˡ 4:3, **like the appearance of an emerald:** Absent from ℵ(01).
ᵐ 4:4, **And around the throne were:** Absent from ℵ(01).
ⁿ 4:4, **I saw:** Included in TR.
ᵒ 4:4, **thrones and:** Included in ℵ(01).
ᵖ 4:4, **they had:** Included in TR.
q 4:5, **the:** Some manuscripts read "his." BYZ.
ʳ 4:5, **which are the seven:** Absent from ℵ(01).
ˢ 4:7, **similar to:** Included in ℵ(01).

8 The four living creatures, each [of them][a] having six wings, full of eyes around and within, and they do not rest day and night, saying, "Holy, holy, holy, [[holy, holy, holy, holy, holy,]][b] Lord God Almighty, who was and is and is to come."

9 And when the creatures give [glory and][c] honor and thanks to the one seated on the throne, the one who lives forever and ever, [[amen,]][d] 10 the twenty-four elders [[also]][e] will fall down before the one seated on the throne and worship the one who lives forever and ever, [[amen,]][f] and they will cast their crowns before the throne, saying, 11 "You are worthy, our Lord and God,[g] [[the Holy One,]][h] to receive glory, honor, and power, for you created all things, and by your will they {existed}[i] [and were created]."[j]

5 1 And I saw on the right hand of the one seated on the throne [a book written][k] {inside}[l] and {on the back},[m] sealed with seven seals.

2 And I saw a strong angel proclaiming {in}[n] a loud voice, "Who [[is]][o] worthy to open the book and to break its seals?" 3 And no one was able in heaven [[above]][p] or on the earth [or under the earth][q] to open the book or to look at it. 4 [[And]][r] {they}[s] wept greatly, because no one was found worthy to open the book [[and read]][t] or to look at it.][u]

5 And one of the elders says to me, "Do not weep, behold, the lion [who][v] from the tribe of Judah, the root of David, has overcome[w] to open the book and [[loosen]][x] its seven seals."

6 And I saw [[and behold]][y] in the midst of the throne and of the four living creatures, and in the midst of the elders, a Lamb standing as though it had been slain, having seven horns and seven eyes, which are the [seven][z] spirits of God sent out into all the earth. 7 And he came and took [[the book]][a] from the right hand of the one seated on the throne.

8 And when he had taken the book, the four living creatures and the twenty-four elders fell down before the Lamb, each holding a harp and golden bowls full of incense, which are the prayers of the saints.

---

a 4:8, **of them:** Absent from BYZ.

b 4:8, **holy, holy, holy, holy, holy:** Some manuscripts include. ℵ(01)

c 4:9, **glory and:** Absent from ℵ(01).

d 4:9, **amen:** Included in ℵ(01).

e 4:10, **also:** Included in ℵ(01).

f 4:10, **amen:** Included in ℵ(01).

g 4:11, **and God:** Absent from TR.

h 4:11, **the holy One:** Included in BYZ.

i 4:11, **existed:** Or "were." TR reads "are."

j 4:11, **and were created:** Absent from A(02).

k 5:1, **a book written:** Or, "a scroll written." Absent from ℵ(01)

l 5:1, **inside:** ℵ(01) reads "in front of."

m 5:1, **on the back:** BYZ reads "outside."

n 5:2, **in:** TR reads "with."

o 5:2, **is:** Included in BYZ TR.

p 5:3, **above:** Included in BYZ.

q 5:3, **or under the earth:** Absent from ℵ(01).

r 5:4, **And:** Absent from A(02).

s 5:4, **they:** ℵ(01) NA28 THGNT ‖ Some manuscripts read "I." BYZ TR SBLGNT.

t 5:4, **and read:** Included in TR.

u 5:4, **And they wept greatly…:** Verse 4 is absent from A(02).

v 5:5, **who:** Included in TR.

w 5:5, **overcome:** Or "triumphed."

x 5:5, **loosen:** Included in ℵ(01) BYZ TR.

y 5:6, **and behold:** Included in TR.

z 5:6, **seven:** Absent from A(02).

a 5:7, **the book:** Included in TR.

9 And they sing a new song, saying,
"Worthy are you to take the book and
to open its seals, because you were
slain and you purchased [[us]][a] to
God by your blood out of every tribe
and tongue and people and nation,
10 and you have made {them}[b] {a
kingdom}[c] and priests [to our God],[d]
and {they}[e] shall reign on the earth."

11 And I saw, and I heard [[as]][f]
the voice of many angels around the
throne and the living creatures and
the elders, and their number was
myriads of myriads and thousands of
thousands, 12 saying with a loud voice,
"Worthy is the Lamb who was slain to
receive power and wealth and wisdom
and might and honor and glory and
blessing!"

13 And I heard every creature [[that
is]][g] in heaven and on earth [and under
the earth][h] and [[what is]][i] in the sea,
and all that is in them, saying, "To the
one seated on the throne and to the
Lamb be blessing and honor and glory
and might forever and ever! [[Amen]]"[j]

14 And the four living creatures
{said},[k] "Amen." And the
[[twenty-four]][l] elders fell down and
worshiped [[him who lives for ever and
ever]].[m]

6

1 And I saw {when}[n] the Lamb
opened one of the {seven seals,}[o]
and I heard one of the four living
creatures saying with a voice like
thunder [[saying]],[p] "Come [[and
see]]."[q]

2 [And I saw,][r] and behold, a white
horse, and the one seated on it had a
bow, and a crown was given to him,
and he went out conquering and {to
conquer}.[s]

3 And when he opened the second
seal, I heard the second living creature
saying, "Come [[and see]]."[t] 4 And [[I
saw, and behold]][u] another horse, fiery
red, went out, and to the one seated
on it was given [to him][v] to take peace
[from][w] the earth, [and][x] that they
{will}[y] slaughter one another, and a
great sword was given to him.

5 And when he opened the third
seal, I heard the third living creature
saying, "Come [[and see]]."[z] And
behold, a black horse, and the one
seated on it had a scale in his hand.
6 And I heard [something like][a] a
voice in the midst of the four living

---

[a] 5:9, **us:** Some manuscripts include. ℵ(01) BYZ TR.
[b] 5:10, **them:** TR reads "us."
[c] 5:10, **a kingdom:** Some manuscripts read "kings." BYZ TR.
[d] 5:10, **to our God:** Absent from A(02).
[e] 5:10, **they:** TR reads "we."
[f] 5:11, **as:** Or like. Included in ℵ(01) BYZ.
[g] 5:13, **that is:** Some manuscripts include. BYZ TR.
[h] 5:13, **and under the earth:** Absent from ℵ(01).
[i] 5:13, **what is:** Included in A(02) BYZ TR THGNT.
[j] 5:13, **Amen:** Included in BYZ.
[k] 5:14, **said:** Some manuscripts read "were saying." BYZ.
[l] 5:14, **twenty-four:** Included in TR.
[m] 5:14, **him who lives for ever and ever:** Included in TR.
[n] 6:1, **when:** Some manuscripts read "that." BYZ.
[o] 6:1, **seven seals:** A(02) C(04) BYZ NA28 SBLGNT THGNT || TR reads "seals." || ℵ(01) reads "seven."
[p] 6:1, **saying:** Included in A(02).
[q] 6:1, **and see:** Included in ℵ(01) BYZ TR.
[r] 6:2, **and I saw:** Absent from BYZ.
[s] 6:2, **to conquer:** ℵ(01) reads "conquered."
[t] 6:3, **and see:** Included in ℵ(01) TR.
[u] 6:4, **I saw, and behold:** Some manuscripts include. ℵ(01)
[v] 6:4, **to him:** Absent from A(02).
[w] 6:4, **from:** Absent from A(02)
[x] 6:4, **and:** Or "also." Absent from BYZ.
[y] 6:4, **will:** Some manuscripts read "might." ℵ(01) BYZ TR.
[z] 6:5, **and see:** Included in ℵ(01) TR.
[a] 6:6, **something like:** Absent from BYZ TR.

creatures saying, "A quart of wheat for a denarius, and three quarts of barley for a denarius, and do not harm the oil and the wine."

7 And when he opened the fourth seal, I heard [the voice of][a] the fourth living creature saying, "Come [[and see]]."[b] 8 And [I saw,][c] and behold, a pale horse, and the name of the one seated on [it][d] was Death, and Hades followed [with][e] him.

And authority was given to {them}[f] over a fourth of the earth, to kill with sword and [with][g] famine and with death and [[fourth]][h] by the beasts of the earth.

9 And when the [fifth][i] seal was opened, I saw beneath the altar the souls of {those}[j] who had been slain because of the word of God and [because of][k] the testimony they held [[of the Lamb]].[l]

10 And they cried out with a loud voice, saying, "How long, O Lord, holy and true, will you not judge and avenge [[for]][m] our blood from those who dwell on the earth?" 11 And a white robe was given to each [of them],[n] and it was said to them that they should rest a [little][o] while longer, until both their fellow servants and their brothers, who were about to be killed [[by them]][p] as they [[also]][q] were, [[until they]][r] should be completed.

12 And I saw when he opened the sixth seal, and [[behold]][s] there was a great earthquake, and the sun became black as sackcloth of hair, and the [whole][t] moon became like blood, 13 and the stars of {heaven}[u] fell to the earth, as a fig tree drops its figs when shaken by a great wind. 14 And the heaven receded like a book[v] being rolled up, and every mountain and island was moved out of [their][w] place.

15 [And][x] The kings of the earth, the great men, the commanders, the rich, the mighty, and every slave [and [[every]][y] free man][z] hid themselves in the caves and in the rocks of the mountains, 16 and they said to the mountains and the rocks, "Fall on us and hide us from the face of the one seated on the throne and from the wrath of the Lamb, 17 for the great day of {their}[a] wrath has come, and who is able to stand?"

---

a 6:7, **the voice of:** Absent from C(04) BYZ.

b 6:7, **and see:** Included in ℵ(01) TR.

c 6:8, **I saw:** Absent from BYZ.

d 6:8, **it** Absent from C(04).

e 6:8, **with:** Absent from BYZ.

f 6:8, **them:** Some manuscripts read "him." BYZ.

g 6:8, **with:** Absent from ℵ(01).

h 6:8, **fourth:** Some manuscripts include. ℵ(01)

i 6:9, **fifth:** Absent from ℵ(01).

j 6:9, **those:** Some manuscripts read "the men." ℵ(01).

k 6:9, **because of:** Absent from A(02).

l 6:9, **of the Lamb:** Included in BYZ.

m 6:10, **for:** Included in ℵ(01).

n 6:11, **of them:** Absent from TR.

o 6:11, **little:** Absent from BYZ.

p 6:11, **by them:** Included in ℵ(01).

q 6:11, **also:** Included in BYZ.

r 6:11, **until they:** Some manuscripts include. BYZ.

s 6:12, **behold:** Included in A(02) TR.

t 6:12, **whole:** Absent from TR.

u 6:13, **heaven:** A(02) reads "God."

v 6:14, **book:** Or "scroll."

w 6:14, **their:** Absent from ℵ(01).

x 6:15, **And:** Absent from A(02).

y 6:15, **every:** Some manuscripts include. BYZ TR.

z 6:15, **and free man:** Absent from ℵ(01).

a 6:17, **their:** ℵ(01) C(04) NA28 SBLGNT THGNT ‖ Some manuscripts read "his." A(02) BYZ TR.

7 1 [[And]]ᵃ After {this}ᵇ I saw four angels standing at the four corners of the earth, holding back the four winds of the earth so that no wind would blow [on the earth]ᶜ neither on the sea or upon {every}ᵈ tree.

2 And I saw another angel {ascending}ᵉ from the rising of the sun, having the seal of the living God; and he cried out with a loud voice to the four angels to whom it was granted to harm the earth and the sea, 3 saying, "Do not harm the earth or the sea or the trees until we have [[not]]ᶠ sealed the servants of our God on their foreheads."

4 [And I heard the number of those who were sealed,]ᵍ One hundred [[and]]ʰ forty-four thousand, sealed from every tribe of the sons of Israel:

5 From the tribe of Judah twelve thousand were sealed, from the tribe of Reuben twelve thousand, [from the tribe of Gad twelve thousand [[were sealed]],ⁱ]ʲ 6 from the tribe of Asher twelve thousand, from the tribe of Naphtali twelve thousand, from the tribe of Manasseh twelve thousand [[were sealed]],ᵏ 7 from the tribe of Simeon twelve thousand,ˡ from the tribe of Levi twelve thousand, from the tribe of Issachar twelve thousand

[[were sealed]],ᵐ 8 from the tribe of Zebulun twelve thousand, from the tribe of Joseph twelve thousand, from the tribe of Benjamin twelve thousand were sealed [[were sealed]].ⁿ

9 After these things I looked, [and behold,]ᵒ a great multitude which no one could count, from every nation and all tribes and peoples and tongues, standing {before}ᵖ the throne and before the Lamb, clothed in white robes, and palm branches were in their hands; 10 and they cry out with a loud voice, saying, "Salvation {to our God, to the one [who sits]�q upon the throne},ʳ and to the Lamb [[forever and ever. Amen]]."ˢ

11 And all the angels were standing around {the}ᵗ throne and the elders and the four living creatures; and they fell on {their faces}ᵘ before the throne and worshiped God, 12 saying, "Amen, blessing and glory [and wisdom]ᵛ and thanksgiving and honor and power and might be to our God forever and ever. [Amen.]"ʷ

13 Then one of the elders answered, saying to me, "These who are clothed in the white robes, who are they, and where have they come from?" 14 And I

ᵃ 7:1, **And:** Included in ℵ(01) BYZ TR.

ᵇ 7:1, **this:** TR reads "these."

ᶜ 7:1, **on the earth:** Absent from A(02).

ᵈ 7:1, **every:** Some manuscripts read "any." A(02) C(04) BYZ.

ᵉ 7:2, **ascending:** TR reads "having ascended."

ᶠ 7:3, **not** Included in TR.

ᵍ 7:4, **And I heard the number of those who were sealed:** Absent from A(02).

ʰ 7:4, **and:** Included in BYZ.

ⁱ 7:5, **were sealed:** Included in TR.

ʲ 7:5, **from the tribe of Gad…:** Absent from ℵ(01).

ᵏ 7:6, **were sealed:** Included in TR.

ˡ 7:7, **from the tribe of Simeon twelve thousand:** Absent from ℵ(01).

ᵐ 7:7, **were sealed:** Included in TR.

ⁿ 7:8, **were sealed:** Included in TR.

ᵒ 7:9, **and behold:** Absent from A(02) C(04).

ᵖ 7:9, **before:** A(02) reads "upon."

q 7:10, **who sits:** Absent from ℵ(01).

ʳ 7:10, **to our God, to the who sits upon the throne:** TR reads "to the one seated upon the throne of our God."

ˢ 7:10, **forever and ever. Amen:** Included in ℵ(01).

ᵗ 7:11, **the:** BYZ reads "his."

ᵘ 7:11, **their faces:** TR reads "the face."

ᵛ 7:12, **and wisdom:** Absent from A(02).

ʷ 7:12, **Amen:** Absent from C(04).

said to him, "{My lord},[a] you know." And he said to me, "These are the ones {who come}[b] out of the great tribulation, and they have washed their robes and made [them][c] white in the blood of the Lamb. 15 For this reason, they are before the throne of God and serve him day and night in his temple; and he who sits on the throne will spread his tabernacle over[d] them.

16 "They will not hunger [anymore][e] nor thirst anymore, nor will the sun [[not]][f] fall on them, nor any heat; 17 for the Lamb in the midst of the throne will be their shepherd, and will guide them to springs of the water of life; and God will wipe away every tear from their eyes."

8 1 And when he opened the seventh seal, there was silence in heaven for about half an hour. 2 And I saw the seven angels who stand before God, and seven trumpets were given to them.

3 And another angel came and stood at the altar, having a golden censer, and much incense was given to him, that he should offer it with the prayers of all the saints upon the golden altar which was before the throne. 4 And the smoke of the incense, with the prayers of the saints, ascended up before God out of the angel's hand. 5 And the angel took the censer, and filled it with fire from the altar, and cast it onto the earth, and there were thunders, and voices, and lightnings, and an earthquake.

6 And the seven angels who had the seven trumpets prepared {them}[g] to sound them.

7 And the first [[angel]][h] sounded, and there was hail and fire mixed with blood, and it was cast upon the earth, [and a third part of the earth was burnt up,][i] and a third part of the trees was burnt up, and all green grass was burnt up.

8 And the second [angel][j] sounded, and as it were a great mountain burning [with fire][k] was cast into the sea, and a third part of the sea became blood; 9 And a third [[part]][l] of the creatures which were in the sea, and had life, died; and a third part of the ships were destroyed.

10 And the third angel sounded, and there fell a great star from heaven, burning as it were a lamp, and it fell upon a third part of the rivers; [and upon the springs of the waters;][m] 11 And the name of the star is called Wormwood, and a third part of the waters became wormwood; and many men died of the waters, because they were made bitter.

12 And the fourth angel sounded, and a third part of the sun was smitten, and a third part of the moon, and a third part of the stars, so as a third part of them was darkened, and the day did not shine for a third part of it, and the night likewise.

13 And I saw, and I heard an {eagle}[n] flying in mid-heaven, saying with a loud voice, "Woe, woe, woe to the inhabitants of the earth by reason of the other voices of the trumpet of the three angels, who are yet to sound!"

---

a 7:14, **my lord:** Some manuscripts read "Lord." A(02) TR.

b 7:14, **who come:** Or "are coming."

c 7:14, **them:** TR reads "their garments."

d 7:15, **spread his tabernacle over:** Or "shelter."

e 7:16, **anymore:** Absent from ℵ(01).

f 7:16, **not:** Included in BYZ.

g 8:6, **them:** Some manuscripts read "themselves." 𝔓115 BYZ TR.

h 8:7, **angel:** Included in TR.

i 8:7, **and a third part of the earth was burnt up:** Absent from TR.

j 8:8, **angel:** Absent from ℵ(01).

k 8:8, **with fire:** Absent from BYZ.

l 8:9, **part:** Included in ℵ(01).

m 8:10, **upon the springs of the waters:** Absent from A(02).

n 8:13, **eagle:** TR reads "angel."

9 ¹ And the fifth angel sounded; and I saw a star fallen from heaven to the earth, and the key of the bottomless well[a] was given to him. ² And [he opened the well of the abyss, and][b] smoke rose from the well [like][c] the smoke of a {great}[d] furnace, and the sun and the air were darkened by the smoke of the well. ³ [And][e] From the smoke came locusts upon the earth, and power was given to them as the scorpions of the earth have power.

⁴ And it was said to them that they should not harm the grass of the earth, [nor any green thing,][f] nor any tree, but [[only]][g] the men who do not have the seal of God on {the}[h] foreheads. ⁵ And it was given to them that they should not kill them, but that they should be tormented for five months, and their torment was as the torment of a scorpion when it strikes a man.

⁶ And in those days, men will seek death and will not find it, and they will desire to die, and death {flees}[i] from them.

⁷ And the likenesses of the locusts were like horses prepared for battle, and on their heads were {crowns like gold},[j] and their faces were like the faces of men, ⁸ and they had hair like the hair of women, and their teeth were like those of lions, ⁹ and they had breastplates [like breastplates][k] of iron, and the sound of their wings was like the sound of many chariots with horses running into battle, ¹⁰ and they have tails like scorpions and stingers, and in their tails {is their}[l] power to harm men for five months. ¹¹ [[And]][m] {They have}[n] as king [[the ruler]][o] over them the angel of the abyss; {his}[p] name in Hebrew is Abaddon, {and}[q] in Greek he has the name Apollyon.

¹² The first woe is past; behold, there are still two woes to come after this.

¹³ [And][r] The sixth angel sounded; and I heard a voice [from the [four][s] horns][t] of the golden altar before God, ¹⁴ Saying to the [sixth][u] angel, {the one having}[v] the trumpet, "Release the [four][w] angels who are bound at the great river Euphrates." ¹⁵ And the four angels who had been prepared for the hour and [[into the]][x] [day and][y] month and year were released, so that they

---

a 9:1, **well:** The Greek word indicates (1) a construction consisting of a vertical shaft, covered with stone, for water supply, *a well*, or (2) an opening that leads to the depths of the nether world, *pit, shaft* (BDAG, φρέαρ).

b 9:2, **he opened the well of the abyss, and:** Absent from ℵ(01).

c 9:2, **like:** Absent from A(02).

d 9:2, **great:** Some manuscripts read "burning." BYZ.

e 9:3, **And:** Absent from ℵ(01).

f 9:4, **nor any green thing:** Absent from ℵ(01).

g 9:4, **only:** Included in TR.

h 9:4, **the:** Some manuscripts read "their." BYZ TR.

i 9:6, **flees:** Some manuscripts read "will flee." BYZ TR.

j 9:7, **crowns like gold:** Some manuscripts read "golden crowns." BYZ.

k 9:9, **like breastplates:** Absent from uncial 0207 (4th century, Aland category III).

l 9:10, **is their:** BYZ reads "they had."

m 9:11, **And:** Included in TR.

n 9:11, **They have:** Some manuscripts read "having." BYZ.

o 9:11, **the ruler:** Included in A(02).

p 9:11, **his:** 𝔓47 reads "the."

q 9:11, **and:** BYZ reads "but."

r 9:13, **And:** Absent from 𝔓47 ℵ(01).

s 9:13, **four:** 𝔓115 BYZ TR NA28[] ‖ Absent from 𝔓47 ℵ(01) A(02) SBLGNT THGNT.

t 9:13, **from the four horns:** Absent from ℵ(01).

u 9:14, **sixth:** Absent from A(02).

v 9:14, **the one having:** Some manuscripts read "who had." TR.

w 9:14, **four:** Absent from 𝔓47.

x 9:15, **into the:** Included in BYZ.

y 9:15, **day and:** Absent from ℵ(01).

might [[not]][a] kill a third of mankind.
16 And the number of the armies of the
[[two]][b] horsemen was two myriads of
myriads;[c] [[and]][d] I heard the number
of them.

17 And thus I saw the horses in
the vision and those who sat on
them, having breastplates of fire and
hyacinth[e] and sulfur,[f] and the heads of
the horses were like the heads of lions,
and from their mouths came fire and
smoke and sulfur.

18 From {these}[g] [three][h] [plagues][i]
a third of mankind was killed, by the
fire and the smoke and the sulfur[j]
coming out of {their}[k] mouths.
19 For the power of {the horses}[l] is in
their mouths [and in their tails];[m] for
their tails are like serpents, having
heads, and with them they do harm.

20 And the rest of mankind, who
were not killed by these plagues [[of
theirs]],[n] did not repent of the works
of their hands, so as not to worship
demons [and idols][o] of gold and silver
and bronze and stone and wood, which
can neither see nor hear nor walk,
21 and they did not repent of their
murders, nor of their {drugs},[p] nor of
their sexual immorality [nor of their
thefts].[q]

10 1 And I saw [another][r] strong
angel coming down from
heaven, wrapped in a cloud, and a
rainbow was over his head, and his
face was like the sun, and his feet like
pillars of fire, 2 And holding in his hand
a {little book}[s] [which was opened].[t]
And he placed his [right][u] foot upon
the sea, and the left upon the land,
3 and he cried out with a loud voice, as
a lion roars. And when it cried out, the
[seven][v] thunders spoke their voices.
4 And when [[I heard]][w] the [seven][x]
thunders spoke [[their own voices]],[y] I
was about to write, but I heard a voice
from heaven saying [[to me]],[z] "Seal up
what the [seven][a] thunders have said,
and do not write it down."

---

[a] 9:15, **not:** Included in ℵ(01).
[b] 9:16, **two:** Some manuscripts include. 𝔓47 ℵ(01) TR
[c] 9:16, **two myriads of myriads:** Or "twenty thousands times ten thousand." Or, two hundred million.
[d] 9:16, **and:** Included in BYZ TR.
[e] 9:17, **hyacinth:** Or Sapphire. A flower of a vibrant color. Likely dark blue or violet. (BDAG, ὑακίνθινος).
[f] 9:17, **sulfur:** A vibrant yellow color. Or brimstone.
[g] 9:18, **these:** Some manuscripts read "the." 𝔓47.
[h] 9:18, **three:** Absent from ℵ(01).
[i] 9:18, **plagues:** Absent from TR.
[j] 9:18, **sulfur:** Greek "divine."
[k] 9:18, **their:** 𝔓47 reads "the."
[l] 9:19, **the horses:** TR reads "them."
[m] 9:19, **and in their tails:** Absent from TR(1550).
[n] 9:20, **of theirs:** Included in 𝔓47 ℵ(01).
[o] 9:20, **and idols:** Absent from 𝔓47.
[p] 9:21, **drugs:** Or "potions." 𝔓47 ℵ(01) C(04) NA28 SBLGNT THGNT || Some manuscripts read "sorcery." A(02) BYZ TR.
[q] 9:21, **nor of their thefts:** Absent from 𝔓47 Syriac(Philoxeniana).
[r] 10:1, **another:** Absent from BYZ.
[s] 10:2, **little book:** Or little scroll. BYZ reads "book."
[t] 10:2, **which was opened:** Absent from A(02).
[u] 10:2, **right:** Absent from C(04).
[v] 10:3, **seven:** Absent from 𝔓47.
[w] 10:4, **I heard:** Included in 𝔓47.
[x] 10:4, **seven:** Absent from 𝔓47.
[y] 10:4, **their own voices:** Included in TR.
[z] 10:4, **to me:** Included in TR.
[a] 10:4, **seven:** Absent from 𝔓47 C(04).

5 And the angel, whom I saw standing on the sea and on the earth, raised his [right]^a hand to heaven 6 and swore {by}^b the one who lives forever and ever, who created heaven and what is in it, [and the earth and what is in it, and the sea and what is in it,]^c that there would be no more delay, 7 but in the days of the voice of the seventh angel, when he is about to sound, the mystery of God will be completed, just as he proclaimed to his servants [[and]]^d the prophets.

8 And the voice which I heard from heaven, speaking again with me and saying, "Go, take the {book}^e that is opened [in the hand]^f of the angel who is standing on the sea and on the earth." 9 And I went to the angel, telling him to give me the {little book}.^g And he said to me, "Take and eat [[it]];^h it will make your stomach bitter, but in your mouth it will be sweet as honey."

10 And I took the {little book}^i from the hand of the angel and ate it, and it was in my mouth as sweet as honey, and when I ate it, my stomach was {made bitter}.^j 11 And {they say}^k to me, "You must prophesy again about peoples and [[about]]^l nations and languages and many kings."

11 1 And a reed like a rod was given to me [[and the angel stood]],^m saying, "Rise and measure the temple of God and the altar and those who worship in it. 2 And [the courtyard]^n which is outside the temple, throw it out outside and do not measure it, for it has been given to the nations, and they will trample the holy city for forty-two months.

3 "And I will grant authority to my two witnesses, and they will prophesy for 1,260 days, clothed in sackcloth." 4 These are the two olive trees and the two lampstands standing before {the Lord}^o of the earth. 5 And if anyone wants to harm them, fire comes out of their mouth and consumes their enemies; and if anyone wants to harm them, [thus]^p he must be killed.

6 These have the power to shut the sky, so that no rain falls during the days of {their}^q prophecy, and they have power over the waters to turn them into blood and to strike the earth with every kind of plague, as often as they desire.

7 And when they have finished their testimony, the [[fourth]]^r beast that rises from the abyss will make war with them and conquer them and kill them. 8 And their corpse *will be* in the street of the great city, which is called spiritually Sodom and Egypt, where [also]^s {their}^t lord was crucified. 9 And they see from the peoples and tribes and tongues and nations their {corpse}^u for three and a half days, and they {do not

---

a 10:5, **right:** Absent from A(02) TR.

b 10:6, **by:** Some manuscripts read "to." 𝔓47 ℵ(01).

c 10:6, **and the earth and what is in it…:** Absent from A(02).

d 10:7, **and:** Some manuscripts include. 𝔓47 𝔓85 ℵ(01).

e 10:8, **book:** Some manuscripts read "little book." ℵ(01) BYZ TR.

f 10:8, **in the hand:** Absent from C(04).

g 10:9, **little book:** Some manuscripts read "book." 𝔓47 ℵ(01).

h 10:9, **it:** Included in 𝔓85.

i 10:10, **little book:** Some manuscripts read "book." ℵ(01) BYZ.

j 10:10, **made bitter:** Some manuscripts read "filled." 𝔓115 ℵ(01).

k 10:11, **they say:** Some manuscripts read "he says." BYZ TR.

l 10:11, **about:** Included in BYZ.

m 11:1, **and the angel stood:** Included in KJV but absent in BYZ and TR.

n 11:2, **the court:** Absent from 𝔓47.

o 11:4, **the Lord:** TR reads "God."

p 11:5, **thus:** Absent from A(02).

q 11:6, **their:** Absent from TR.

r 11:7, **fourth:** Included in A(02).

s 11:8, **also:** Absent from ℵ(01).

t 11:8, **their:** Some manuscripts read "the." 𝔓47 ℵ(01) ‖ TR reads "our."

u 11:9, **corpse:** Some manuscripts read "corpses." BYZ TR.

allow}[a] their corpses to be placed into {a tomb}.[b] 10 And those dwelling on the earth {rejoice}[c] over them and {are glad},[d] and they {will send}[e] gifts to one another, because {these}[f] two prophets tormented those dwelling on the earth.

11 And after the three and a half days, the breath of life from God entered {in}[g] them, and they stood on their feet, and great fear fell upon those who saw them. 12 And {they heard}[h] a loud voice from heaven saying [to them],[i] "Come up here." And they went up to heaven in a cloud, and their enemies watched them. 13 And at {that}[j] {hour}[k] there was a great earthquake, and a tenth of the city fell; {and}[l] 7,000 people were killed in the earthquake, and the rest were terrified and gave glory to the God of heaven.

14 The second woe has passed; behold, the third woe is coming soon.

15 And the seventh angel sounded; and there were loud voices in heaven, saying, "The {kingdom}[m] of the world has become the kingdom of our Lord and of his Christ, and he shall reign forever and ever. [[Amen]]"[n]

16 And the twenty-four elders who sit [on their thrones][o] [who are][p] before [[the throne of]][q] God fell on their faces and worshiped God, 17 saying, "We give thanks to you, Lord God [[the God]][r] Almighty, who is and who was, [[and who comes]][s] for you have taken your great power and have begun to reign. 18 The nations raged, but your wrath has come, and the time for the dead to be judged, and to give the reward to your servants the prophets and to the saints and to those who fear your name, both small and great, and to destroy those who destroy the earth."

19 And the temple of God in heaven was opened, and the ark of his covenant was seen in {his temple},[t] and there were flashes of lightning and voices and thunder [and an earthquake][u] and great hail.

12 1 And a great sign appeared in heaven: a woman clothed with the sun, and the moon under her feet, and on her head a crown of twelve stars; 2 and she was with child; [and][v] she cried out, being in labor and in pain to give birth.

3 And another sign appeared in heaven: and behold, a great red dragon having seven heads and ten horns, and on his heads were seven diadems; 4 and his tail swept away a third of the stars of heaven and threw them to the earth. And the dragon stood before the

---

a 11:9, **do not allow:** Some manuscripts read "will not allow." BYZ TR.

b 11:9, **a tomb:** TR reads "tombs."

c 11:10, **rejoice:** TR reads "will rejoice."

d 11:10, **are glad:** Some manuscripts read "will be glad." BYZ TR.

e 11:10, **will send:** Some manuscripts read "will give." BYZ.

f 11:10, **these:** 𝔓47 reads "the."

g 11:11, **in:** Some manuscripts read "into." 𝔓47 ℵ(01) BYZ. ‖ TR reads "upon."

h 11:12, **they heard:** Some manuscripts read "I heard." 𝔓47 BYZ.

i 11:12, **to them:** Absent from A(02).

j 11:13, **that:** 𝔓47 reads "this."

k 11:13, **hour:** Some manuscripts read "day." ℵ(01) BYZ.

l 11:13, **and:** C(04) reads "So that."

m 11:15, **kingdom:** TR reads "kingdoms."

n 11:15, **Amen:** Included in ℵ(01).

o 11:16, **on their thrones** Absent from 𝔓47.

p 11:16, **who are:** Absent from 𝔓47 A(02).

q 11:16, **the throne of:** Included in BYZ.

r 11:17, **the God:** Included in 𝔓47.

s 11:17, **and who comes:** Included in TR.

t 11:19, **his temple:** A(02) C(04) TR NA28 SBLGNT THGNT ‖ Some manuscripts read "the temple of the Lord." BYZ ‖ Some manuscripts read "the temple of God." 𝔓47 ℵ(01).

u 11:19, **and an earthquake:** Absent from BYZ.

v 12:2, **and:** Absent from BYZ TR.

woman who was about to give birth, so that when she gave birth he might devour her child. 5 And she gave birth to a son, a male, who is destined to shepherd all the nations with an iron rod. And her child was snatched up to God and {to}[a] his throne. 6 And the woman fled into the wilderness where she had a place prepared by God, so that there she would be nourished for one thousand two hundred and sixty days.

7 And there was war in heaven, Michael and his angels waging war {with}[b] the dragon. The dragon and his angels waged war, 8 And they did not prevail [[against him]],[c] nor was a place found [for them][d] any longer in heaven. 9 And the great dragon was thrown down, the serpent [of old][e] who is called the devil and Satan, who deceives the whole world; he was thrown down to the earth, and {his}[f] angels were thrown down with him.

10 And I heard a loud voice in heaven saying, "Now has come the salvation and the power and the kingdom of our God, and the authority of his {Christ},[g] because the accuser of our brothers has been {cast out},[h] the one who accuses them before our God day and night. 11 And they overcame him because of the blood of the Lamb and because [of the word][i] of

their testimony, and they did not love their life even when faced with death. 12 For this reason, rejoice, [O][j] heavens and you who dwell in them. Woe to the [[inhabitants of]][k] earth and the sea, because the devil has come down to you, having [great][l] wrath, knowing that he has only a short time."

13 And when the dragon saw that he was thrown down to the earth, he {persecuted}[m] the woman who gave birth to the male child. 14 And [the][n] two wings of {the}[o] great eagle were given to the woman, so that she might fly into the wilderness, into her place, where she is nourished there for a time, and times, and half a time, away from the face of the serpent.

15 And the serpent poured water like a river out of his mouth after the woman, so that he might cause her to be swept away with the flood. 16 But the earth helped the woman, and [the earth][p] opened its mouth and swallowed up the {river}[q] which the dragon had poured out of his mouth.

17 And the dragon was enraged {at}[r] the woman, and went off to make war with the rest of her seed,[s] who keep the commandments of God and hold to the testimony of {Jesus}[t] [[Christ]].[u] 18 And he stood on the sand of the seashore.

---

a 12:5, **to:** Absent from TR.

b 12:7, **with:** TR reads "against."

c 12:8, **against him:** Include in ℵ(01)

d 12:8, **for them:** Absent from ℵ(01).

e 12:9, **of old:** Absent from 𝔓47.

f 12:9, **his:** 𝔓47 reads "the."

g 12:10, **Christ:** C(04) reads "Lord."

h 12:10, **cast out:** TR reads "cast down."

i 12:11, **of the word:** Absent from C(04).

j 12:12, **O:** Absent from ℵ(01) C(04).

k 12:12, **inhabitants of:** Included in TR.

l 12:12, **great:** Absent from ℵ(01).

m 12:13, **persecuted:** 𝔓47 reads "went away to persecute."

n 12:14, **the:** Absent from 𝔓47 BYZ TR.

o 12:14, **the:** ℵ(01) reads "a."

p 12:16, **the earth:** Absent from 𝔓47.

q 12:16, **river:** A(02) reads "water."

r 12:17, **at:** Some manuscripts and read "with" since the Greek word ἐπί is absent. 𝔓47 C(04).

s 12:17, **seed:** Or "offspring."

t 12:17, **Jesus:** ℵ(01) reads "God."

u 12:17, **Christ:** Included in TR.

13 1 And I saw a beast rising out
of the sea, having ten horns
and seven heads, and on its horns ten
diadems, and on its heads {names}[a] of
blasphemy. 2 And the beast that I saw
[was][b] like a leopard, and its feet were
like a bear's, and its mouth was like the
mouth of a lion. And the dragon gave
it his power and his throne and great
authority. 3 And [[I saw]][c] one of its
heads seemed to have been slain unto
death, and its death wound was healed.
And the whole earth marveled after the
beast. 4 And they worshiped the dragon,
because it gave authority to the beast,
and they worshiped the beast, saying,
"Who is like the beast, and who can
wage war against it?"

5 And a mouth was given to it,
speaking great things and blasphemies,
and [authority][d] was given to it {to
act}[e] for forty-two months. 6 And it
opened [its mouth][f] for {blasphemies}[g]
against God, to blaspheme his name
and his dwelling, [those who dwell][h]
in heaven.

7 [And it was given to him to make
war with the saints and to conquer[i]
them,][j] And authority was given to
it over every tribe [and people][k] and
language and nation.

8 And all the inhabitants of the
earth will worship it, whose {name}[l]
has not been written in the book of life
of the Lamb who was slain from the
foundation of the world.

9 If anyone has ears, let him hear.

10 If anyone {is to go into}[m]
captivity, [into captivity][n] they go. If
anyone is to be killed with the sword,
with the sword they will be killed.
Here is the endurance and the faith[o] of
the saints.

11 And I saw another beast rising
out of the earth, and it had two horns
like a lamb and it spoke like a dragon.
12 And it exercises all the authority
of the first beast in its presence, and
{makes}[p] the earth and those dwelling
in it {so that they will}[q] worship the
first beast, whose [death][r] wound was
healed. 13 And it performs great signs,
{so that he even makes fire}[s] come
down from heaven to earth in the sight
of men, 14 and it deceives [[my own]][t]
those who dwell on the earth by the
signs that it was allowed to perform
in the presence of the beast, telling
those who dwell on the earth to make
an image for the beast, which has the
wound of the sword and yet lived.

---

a 13:1, **names:** Some manuscripts read "name." 𝔓47 ℵ(01).
b 13:2, **was:** Absent from 𝔓47.
c 13:3, **I saw:** Included in TR.
d 13:5, **authority:** Absent from ℵ(01).
e 13:5, **to act:** ℵ(01) reads "to act as he wishes." || Some manuscripts read "to wage war." BYZ.
f 13:6, **its mouth:** Absent from some manuscripts. ℵ(01)
g 13:6, **blasphemies:** Some manuscripts read "blasphemy." BYZ TR. || 𝔓47 reads "to blaspheme."
h 13:6, **those who dwell:** Absent from 𝔓47.
i 13:7, **conquer:** Or "overcome."
j 13:7, **And it was given to it to make war with the saints and to conquer them:** Absent from 𝔓47 A(02) C(04).
k 13:7, **and people:** Absent from 𝔓47 TR.
l 13:8, **name:** Some manuscripts read "names." 𝔓47 ℵ(01) TR
m 13:10, **is to go into:** TR reads "leads."
n 13:10, **into captivity:** Absent from 𝔓47(NA28) ℵ(01) C(04) BYZ THGNT.
o 13:10, **faith:** Or "faithfulness."
p 13:12, **makes:** BYZ reads "made."
q 13:12, **so that they will:** ℵ(01) reads "to."
r 13:12, **death:** Absent from A(02).
s 13:13, **so that he even makes fire:** Some manuscripts read "and fire so that it." BYZ.
t 13:14, **my own:** Included in BYZ.

15 [And it was given to it to give spirit[a] to the image of the beast,][b] so that the image of the beast might also speak and [that][c] it {might cause}[d] [as many as do not worship the image of the beast][e] [[that]][f] they should be killed. 16 And it causes all, both small and great, both rich and poor, both free and slave, to be given a mark {to them}[g] on the right hand or {the forehead},[h] 17 [and][i] so that[j] no one can buy or sell unless he has the mark, {the name of the beast}[k] or the number of its name.

18 Here is wisdom. Let him who has understanding calculate the number of the beast, for it is the number of a man, [and its number is][l] {six hundred sixty-six}.[m]

14 1 And I saw, and behold, the Lamb standing on Mount Zion, and with him [[a number of]][n] {one hundred forty-four thousand},[o] having

[his name and][p] the name of his father written on their foreheads.

2 And I heard a voice from heaven like the sound of many waters and like the sound of a [great][q] thunder, and the voice I heard [was][r] [[a voice]][s] [like][t] harpists playing on {their}[u] harps.

3 And they sing [as][v] a new song before the throne and before the four living creatures, [and [[before]][w] the elders,][x] and no one could learn the song except the {one hundred forty-four}[y] thousand, those who were purchased from the earth; 4 [these are][z] the ones who have not defiled themselves with women, for they are virgins. These are the ones who follow the Lamb wherever it goes. These were purchased [[by Jesus]][a] [from among men][b] as firstfruits to God and to the Lamb, 5 and in their mouth, no {lie}[c] was found, [[for]][d] they are blameless [[before the throne of God]].[e]

---

a 13:15, **spirit:** Or "breath."

b 13:15, **And it was given…:** Absent from C(04).

c 13:15, **that:** Absent from ℵ(01) C(04) BYZ TR.

d 13:15, **might cause:** ℵ(01) reads "will cause." ‖ Absent from C(04).

e 13:15, **as many as do not worship…:** Absent from C(04).

f 13:15, **that:** Included in TR.

g 13:16, **them:** ℵ(01) read "him."

h 13:16, **the forehead:** Some manuscripts read "their foreheads." 𝔓47 BYZ TR.

i 13:17, **and:** Absent from ℵ(01) C(04).

j 13:17, **and so that:** Or "so that also."

k 13:17, **the name of the beast:** ℵ(01) reads "of the beast or its name."

l 13:18, **and its number is:** Absent from 𝔓47 ℵ(01).

m 13:18, **six hundred sixty-six:** 𝔓115 reads "616."

n 14:1, **a number of:** Included in BYZ.

o 14:1, **one hundred forty-four thousand:** 𝔓47 reads "thousands."

p 14:1, **his name and:** Absent from TR.

q 14:2, **great:** Absent from ℵ(01).

r 14:2, **was:** Absent from 𝔓47 TR.

s 14:2, **a voice:** Included in 𝔓47.

t 14:2, **as:** Absent from TR.

u 14:2, **their:** C(04) reads "the."

v 14:3, **as:** Absent from 𝔓47 ℵ(01) BYZ.

w 14:3, **before:** Included in ℵ(01).

x 14:3, **and the elders:** Absent from C(04).

y 14:3, **One hundred forty-four:** C(04) reads "one hundred forty." ‖ ℵ(01) reads "one hundred forty-one."

z 14:4, **these are:** Absent from A(02).

a 14:4, **by Jesus:** Included in BYZ.

b 14:4, **from among men:** Absent from C(04).

c 14:5, **lie:** Some manuscripts read "deceit." TR.

d 14:5, **for:** Included in 𝔓47 ℵ(01) BYZ TR.

e 14:5, **before the throne of God:** Included in TR.

6 And I saw [another]ᵃ angel flying in midheaven, having an eternal gospel to preach to those who dwell on the earth and to every nation and tribe and language and people, 7 [saying]ᵇ with a loud voice, "Fear {God}ᶜ and give him glory, for the hour of his judgment has come, and worship {the one}ᵈ who made the heaven and the earth and [[the]]ᵉ sea and springs of water."

8 And another [angel],ᶠ [a second]ᵍ followed, [saying, "Fallen, [fallen]ʰ is Babylon the great, who has made all the nations drink of the wine of the wrath of her immorality."]ⁱ

9 [And [another]ʲ angel, a third one, followed them,]ᵏ saying with a loud voice, "If anyone worships the beast and its image, [and]ˡ receives a mark on their forehead or on their hand, 10 they too will drink of the wine of the wrath of God, which is mixed undiluted in the cup of his anger, and they will be tormented with fire and sulfur in the presence of the [holy]ᵐ angels and in the presence of the Lamb. 11 And the smoke of their torment goes up forever and ever, and they have no rest day and night, those who worship the beast and its image, and whoever receives the mark of its name."

12 Thus [the]ⁿ endurance of the saints, [[here are]]ᵒ those who keep the commandments of God and the faithᵖ of Jesus.

13 And I heard a voice from heaven saying [[to me]],�q "Write: Blessed are the dead who die in {the Lord}ʳ from now on. [Yes,]ˢ says the Spirit, so that they may rest from their labors, {for}ᵗ their deeds follow with them."

14 [And I saw,]ᵘ And behold, a white cloud, and on the cloud one seated like a son of men, having on his head a golden crown and in his hand a sharp sickle. 15 And another angel came out of the temple, crying with a loud voice to the one seated on the cloud, "Send your sickle and reap, [for the hour has come [[for you]]ᵛ to reap,]ʷ because the harvest of the earth is ripe." 16 And the one seated on the cloud swung his sickle over the earth, and the earth was reaped.

17 And another angel came out of the temple in heaven, and it too had a sharp sickle.

18 And another angel [came out]ˣ from the altar, [he]ʸ having authority over fire, and called with a loud

---

ᵃ 14:6, **another:** Absent from 𝔓47 ℵ(01) BYZ.

ᵇ 14:7, **saying:** Absent from ℵ(01).

ᶜ 14:7, **God:** Some manuscripts read "the Lord." BYZ.

ᵈ 14:7, **the one:** Some manuscripts read "him." BYZ.

ᵉ 14:7, **the:** Included in 𝔓47 ℵ(01) BYZ.

ᶠ 14:8, **angel:** Absent from 𝔓47.

ᵍ 14:8, **a second:** Absent from TR.

ʰ 14:8, **fallen:** Absent from C(04).

ⁱ 14:8, **saying, Fallen, fallen is Babylon...:** Absent from ℵ(01).

ʲ 14:9, **another:** Absent from TR.

ᵏ 14:9, **And another angel, a third one, followed them:** Absent from ℵ(01).

ˡ 14:9, **and:** Absent from C(04).

ᵐ 14:10, **holy:** Absent from A(02).

ⁿ 14:12, **the:** Absent from TR.

ᵒ 14:12, **here are:** Included in BYZ TR.

ᵖ 14:12, **faith:** Or "faithfulness."

q 14:13, **to me:** Included in BYZ TR.

ʳ 14:13, **the Lord:** C(04) reads "Christ."

ˢ 14:13, **Yes:** Absent from 𝔓47 ℵ(01).

ᵗ 14:13, **for:** Some manuscripts read "but." BYZ TR.

ᵘ 14:14, **And I saw:** Absent from ℵ(01).

ᵛ 14:15, **for you:** Included in TR.

ʷ 14:15, **for the hour has come to reap:** Absent from 𝔓47.

ˣ 14:18, **came out:** Absent from 𝔓47 A(02) SBLGNT.

ʸ 14:18, **he:** Absent from 𝔓47 ℵ(01) BYZ TR.

{voice}[a] to the one who had the sharp sickle, saying, "Send your sharp sickle and gather the clusters of the vine of the earth, for its grapes are ripe." 19 And the angel swung his sickle into the earth and gathered the vine of the earth, and threw it into the great winepress of the wrath of God. 20 And the winepress was trodden outside the city, and blood flowed from the winepress up to the horses' bridles, for a distance of {sixteen}[b] hundred stadia.

15 1 And I saw another great and marvelous sign in heaven, seven angels having seven plagues, the last ones, because in them the wrath of God was completed.

2 And I saw something like a sea of glass mixed with fire, and those who had conquered the beast and its image [[from his mark and]][c] from the number of its name standing beside the sea of glass with harps of {the Lord}[d] God. 3 [And they sing the song of Moses, the servant of God, and][e] the song of the Lamb, saying, "Great and marvelous are your works, Lord God Almighty; just and true are your ways, King of the {nations}.[f] 4 Who will [not][g] fear

[[you,]][h] the Lord, and glorify your name? For you alone are [holy].[i] For all the nations will come and worship before you [[Lord]],[j] for your righteous acts have been revealed [[before you]]."[k]

5 And after these things I saw, [[and behold,]][l] the temple of the tabernacle of the testimony in heaven was opened, 6 and the seven angels {who had}[m] the seven plagues came out of the temple, [[who were]][n] clothed in {pure, bright linen}[o] and girded around their chests with golden sashes.

7 And {one of}[p] the four [living][q] creatures gave the seven angels [seven][r] golden bowls full of the wrath of God who lives forever and ever. [[Amen]][s] 8 And the temple was filled with smoke from the glory of God and from his power, and no one could enter the temple until the seven plagues of the seven angels were completed.

16 1 And I heard a loud voice from the temple saying to the seven angels, "Go and pour out the [seven][t] bowls of God's wrath [on the earth]."[u]

2 [So the first went and poured out his bowl {on}[v] the earth],[w] [and a harmful][x] and an evil sore came

---

[a] 14:18, **voice:** Some manuscripts read "cry." 𝔓47 C(04) BYZ TR.

[b] 14:20, **sixteen:** 𝔓115 reads "two."

[c] 15:2, **from his mark and:** Included in TR.

[d] 15:2, **the Lord:** Included in ℵ(01).

[e] 15:3, **And they sing the song of Moses...:** Absent from C(04).

[f] 15:3, **nations:** A(02) BYZ NA28 THGNT ‖ Some manuscripts read "ages." 𝔓47 ℵ(01) SBLGNT ‖ Some manuscripts read "saints." TR.

[g] 15:4, **not:** Absent from ℵ(01).

[h] 15:4, **you:** Included in 𝔓47 ℵ(01) BYZ TR ‖Absent from A(02) C(04) NA28 SBLGNT THGNT.

[i] 15:4, **holy:** Absent from 𝔓47.

[j] 15:4, **Lord:** Included in A(02).

[k] 15:4, **before you:** Included in ℵ(01).

[l] 15:5, **and behold:** Included in TR.

[m] 15:6, **who had:** A(02) C(04) BYZ NA28[] SBLGNT THGNT ‖ Some manuscripts read "having." 𝔓47 ℵ(01) TR.

[n] 15:6, **who were:** Included in BYZ.

[o] 15:6, **pure, bright linen:** TR reads "linen, pure and bright."

[p] 15:7, **one of:** 𝔓47 and ℵ(01) reads "from" as the Greek word ἐν is absent.

[q] 15:7, **living:** Absent from 𝔓47.

[r] 15:7, **seven:** Absent from ℵ(01).

[s] 15:7, **Amen:** Included in ℵ(01).

[t] 16:1, **seven:** Absent from TR.

[u] 16:1, **on the earth:** Absent from 𝔓47.

[v] 16:2, **on:** Some manuscripts read "upon." TR.

[w] 16:2, **So the first went...:** Absent from ℵ(01).

[x] 16:2, **and a harmful:** Absent from A(02).

{upon}[a] the men who had the mark of the beast and who worshiped its image.

3 [The second [[angel]][b] poured out][c] his bowl into the sea, and it became blood like that of a dead man, and every living soul died in the sea.

4 The third [[angel]][d] poured out his bowl into the rivers and [[upon]][e] the springs of water, and they became blood.

5 And I heard the angel of the waters saying, "You are righteous [[Lord]],[f] the One who is and who was, [[and]][g] the Holy One, because you have judged these things, 6 for they have shed the blood of saints and prophets, and you have given them blood to drink; [[for]][h] they are deserving."

7 And I heard [[another from]][i] the altar saying, "Yes, Lord God Almighty, true and just are your judgments."

8 And the fourth [[angel]][j] poured out his bowl upon the sun, and it was given [to him][k] to scorch men with fire. 9 And men were scorched with great heat, and {they}[l] blasphemed {the name}[m] of God who has authority over these plagues, and they did not repent to give him glory.

10 And the fifth [[angel]][n] poured out his bowl upon the throne of the beast, and its kingdom became darkened, and they gnawed {their}[o] tongues because of the pain, 11 and they blasphemed the God of heaven because of their pains and their sores, and they did not repent [of their deeds].[p]

12 And the sixth [[angel]][q] poured out his bowl upon the great river, [the][r] Euphrates, and its water was dried up, so that the way of the kings from the east of the sun might be prepared.

13 And I saw from the mouth [of the dragon, and from the mouth of the beast, and from the mouth][s] of the false prophet, three unclean spirits like frogs; 14 For there are spirits of demons performing signs, which go out to the kings [[of the Earth and]][t] of the whole world to gather them for the battle on {the}[u] great day of God, the Almighty.

15 Behold, I am coming like a thief. Blessed is the one who stays awake and keeps his garments, so that he may not walk naked and they see his shame. 16 And gathered them together into the {place}[v] which is called in Hebrew Armageddon.[w]

---

a 16:2, **upon:** Some manuscripts read "on." TR.

b 16:3, **angel:** Included in BYZ TR.

c 16:3, **The second poured out:** Absent from ℵ(01).

d 16:4, **angel:** Included in BYZ TR.

e 16:4, **upon:** Included in 𝔓47. ‖ BYZ TR reads "into."

f 16:5, **Lord:** Included in TR.

g 16:5, **and:** Included in 𝔓47 TR.

h 16:6, **for:** Included in TR.

i 16:7, **another from:** Included in TR.

j 16:8, **angel:** Included in ℵ(01) BYZ TR.

k 16:8, **to him:** Absent from 𝔓47.

l 16:9, **they:** BYZ reads "the men."

m 16:9, **the name:** A(02) reads "in the presence of."

n 16:10, **angel:** Included in BYZ TR.

o 16:10, **their:** 𝔓47 reads "the."

p 16:11, **of their deeds:** Absent from ℵ(01).

q 16:12, **angel:** Included in BYZ TR.

r 16:12, **the:** Absent from ℵ(01) BYZ .

s 16:13, **of the dragon...:** Absent from ℵ(01).

t 16:14, **of the Earth and:** Included in TR.

u 16:14, **the:** Some manuscripts read "that." BYZ TR.

v 16:16, **place** A(02) reads "river."

w 16:16, **Armageddon:** Or Har-Magedon, a Hebraism of Mount Megiddo. Some manuscripts read Ar-mageddon, a Hebraism City of Megiddo.

17 And {the seventh}[a] [[angel]][b] poured out his bowl {upon}[c] the air, and a [great][d] voice came {out}[e] of the temple [[of heaven]][f] from {the throne},[g] saying, "It is done." 18 And there were flashes of lightning, and voices, and thunders, and a great earthquake occurred, such as had not occurred since men were upon the earth, so great an earthquake, so mighty. 19 And the great city was divided into three parts, and the cities of the nations fell. And Babylon the great was remembered before God, to give her the cup of the wine of the wrath of {his}[h] anger. 20 And every island fled away, and the mountains were not found.

21 And great hail, [as][i] heavy as a talent, came down from heaven upon men, and men blasphemed God because of the plague of the hail, for its plague is exceedingly great.

17 1 And one of the seven angels who had the seven bowls came and spoke with me, saying [[to me]],[j] "Come, I will show you the judgment of the great prostitute who sits on [[the]][k] many waters, 2 with her the kings of the earth committed sexual immorality, and the inhabitants of the earth were intoxicated with the wine of her sexual immorality."

3 And he carried me away in the spirit into a wilderness. And I saw a woman sitting on a scarlet beast, full of blasphemous names, having seven heads and ten horns. 4 And the woman was clothed in purple and scarlet, and adorned with gold and precious stones and pearls, having a golden cup in her hand, filled with abominations and the impurities of her immorality. 5 And [[on the earth and]][l] on her forehead a name was written, a mystery: "Babylon the great, the mother of prostitutes and of the abominations of the earth."

6 And I saw the woman drunk with the blood of the saints and with the blood of the witnesses of Jesus. And I was greatly amazed when I saw her. 7 And the angel said to me, "Why are you amazed? I will tell you the mystery of the woman and of the beast that carries her, which has the seven heads and the ten horns.

8 "The beast that you saw was, and is not, and is about to rise from the abyss and go to destruction. And the inhabitants of the earth will be amazed, those whose {name}[m] has not been written in the book of life from the foundation of the world, when they see the beast, because it was and is not and [[again]][n] {will be present}.[o]

9 "Here is the mind that has wisdom. The seven heads are seven mountains on which the woman sits, and they are seven kings; 10 five have fallen, [[and]][p] one is, the other has not yet come; and when he comes, he must remain for a little while.

11 "And the beast that was and is not, is himself [also][q] an eighth and is of the seven, and he goes to destruction. 12 And the ten horns that you saw are

a 16:17, **the seventh:** ℵ(01) reads "when."

b 16:17, **angel:** Included in TR.

c 16:17, **upon:** Some manuscripts read "into." TR.

d 16:17, **great:** Absent from A(02).

e 16:17, **out:** Some manuscripts read "from." BYZ TR.

f 16:17, **of heaven:** Included in BYZ TR.

g 16:17, **the throne:** ℵ(01) reads "God."

h 16:19, **his:** Some manuscripts read "the." ℵ(01).

i 16:21, **as:** Absent from ℵ(01).

j 17:1, **to me:** Included in BYZ TR.

k 17:1, **the:** Included in BYZ TR.

l 17:5, **on the earth and:** Included in ℵ(01).

m 17:8, **name:** Some manuscripts read "names." ℵ(01) BYZ TR.

n 17:8, **again:** Included in ℵ(01).

o 17:8, **will be present:** TR reads "yet it is."

p 17:10, **and:** Included in TR.

q 17:11, **also:** Absent from ℵ(01).

ten kings who have not yet received a kingdom, but they receive authority as kings with the beast for one hour. 13 These have one purpose, and {they give}[a] their power and authority to the beast. 14 These will wage war against the Lamb, and the Lamb will conquer them, because he is Lord of lords and King of kings, and those with him are the called and chosen and faithful."

15 And he said to me, "{The waters}[b] that you saw, where the prostitute sits, are peoples and multitudes and nations and languages. 16 And the ten horns that you saw, {and}[c] the beast, they will hate the prostitute and will make her desolate and [[they will make her]][d] naked, and they will eat her flesh and will burn her up with fire. 17 For God has put it into their hearts to carry out his purpose [and to be of one mind,][e] and to give their kingdom to the beast, until the words of God are fulfilled. 18 And the woman whom you saw is the great city, which reigns over the kings of the earth."

18 1 [[And]][f] After these things, I saw [another][g] angel coming down from heaven, having great authority, and the earth was illuminated by his glory. 2 And he cried out with a mighty [[loud]][h] voice, saying, "Fallen, [fallen][i] is Babylon the great, and it has become a dwelling place of demons and a prison of every unclean [[and detestable]][j] spirit, [and a prison of every unclean and hated bird,][k] [and a prison of every unclean and hated beast],[l] 3 because all the nations have drunk [of the wine][m] of the wrath of her immorality, and the kings of the earth have committed immorality with her, and the merchants of the earth [[with whom they committed fornication]][n] have become rich from the power of her luxury."

4 And I heard another voice from heaven, saying, "Come out of her, my people, so that you will not participate in her sins and receive her plagues; 5 for her sins have {piled}[o] up to heaven, and God has remembered her iniquities. 6 Repay her as she has repaid [[you]];[p] [and][q] double [[to her]][r] the double according to her deeds; in {the}[s] cup which she has mixed, mix a double portion for her. 7 As much as {she}[t] was glorified and lived luxuriously, give her that much torment and mourning. For in her heart she says, '[Because][u] I sit as a queen, I am not a widow, and I will never see mourning.'

---

a 17:13, **they give:** TR reads "therefore they will give."

b 17:15, **the waters:** ℵ(01) reads "these things."

c 17:16, **and:** TR reads "on."

d 17:16, **they will make her:** Included in BYZ.

e 17:17, **and to be of one mind:** Absent from A(02).

f 18:1, **And:** Included in BYZ TR.

g 18:1, **another:** Absent from TR.

h 18:2, **loud:** Included in TR.

i 18:2, **fallen:** The second occurrence is absent from some manuscripts. ℵ(01).

j 18:2, **and detestable:** Included in A(02).

k 18:2, **and a prison of every unclean and hated bird:** Absent from A(02).

l 18:2, **and a prison of every unclean and hated beast:** A(02) NA28[] (-and hated) SBLGNT ‖ Absent from ℵ(01) C(04) BYZ TR THGNT.

m 18:3, **the wine:** Absent from A(02) C(04).

n 18:3, **with whom they committed fornication:** Included in ℵ(01).

o 18:5, **piled:** TR reads "followed her."

p 18:6, **you:** Included in BYZ TR.

q 18:6, **and:** Absent from ℵ(01).

r 18:6, **to her:** Included in BYZ TR.

s 18:6, **the:** Some manuscripts read "her." ℵ(01).

t 18:7, **she:** Some manuscripts read "herself." ℵ(01) BYZ TR.

u 18:7, **Because:** Absent from TR.

8 "For this reason her plagues will come in one day, death and mourning and famine, and she will be burned up with fire; for [the Lord God][a] who judges her is strong.

9 "And the kings of the earth who committed immorality [and lived luxuriously][b] with her will weep and wail over her when they see the smoke of her {burning},[c] 10 standing at a distance for fear of her torment, saying, 'Woe, woe, the great city, Babylon, the mighty city! For in one hour your judgment [has come].'[d]

11 "And the merchants of {the}[e] earth {weep}[f] and mourn over her, because no one buys their merchandise anymore: 12 gold and silver and precious stone and pearls and fine linen [and purple][g] and silk and scarlet, and all thyine wood and all ivory vessels and all vessels of most precious wood and bronze and iron [and marble],[h] 13 and cinnamon [and spice][i] and incense [and perfume][j] and frankincense and wine and oil and fine flour and wheat and cattle and sheep, and horses and chariots and slaves, and human souls. 14 And the fruit of your soul's desire has departed from you, and all the rich and the bright things have {perished}[k] from you, and {they}[l] will no longer find them.

15 "The merchants of these things, who became rich from her, will stand at a distance because of the fear of her torment, weeping and mourning, 16 [[and]][m] saying, 'Woe, woe, the great city, she who was clothed in fine linen and purple and scarlet, and adorned with gold and precious stones and {a pearl};[n] 17 for in one hour such great wealth has been laid waste.' And every shipmaster {and everyone who sails to a place,}[o] and sailors and as many as work the sea, stood from afar, 18 and {were crying out}[p] as they saw the {smoke}[q] of her burning, saying, '{Who is like the great city?}'[r] 19 And they threw dust on their heads and were crying out, [weeping and mourning,][s] saying, 'Woe, [woe,][t] the great city, in which all who had ships at sea became rich by her wealth, for in one hour she has been laid waste.'

20 "Rejoice over her, O heaven, and the saints, [and the][u] apostles and the prophets, because God has pronounced judgment for you against her."

21 Then a [strong][v] angel took up a stone like a great {millstone}[w] and threw it into the sea, saying, "{So}[x]

---

a 18:8, **the Lord God:** Absent from A(02).
b 18:9, **and lived luxuriously:** Absent from א(01).
c 18:9, **burning:** א(01) reads "downfall."
d 18:10, **has come:** Absent from A(02).
e 18:11, **the:** א(01) reads "your."
f 18:11, **weep:** Some manuscripts read "will weep." BYZ.
g 18:12, **and purple:** Absent from A(02).
h 18:12, **and marble:** Absent from א(01).
i 18:13, **and spice:** Absent from BYZ TR.
j 18:13, **and perfume:** Absent from C(04).
k 18:14, **perished:** TR reads "departed."
l 18:14, **they:** Some manuscripts read "you." BYZ TR.
m 18:16, **and:** Included in BYZ TR.
n 18:16, **a pearl:** Some manuscripts read "pearls." BYZ TR.
o 18:17, **everyone who sails to a place:** TR reads "the crowd [was] on the boats."
p 18:18, **were crying out:** א(01) BYZ TR NA28 || Some manuscripts read "cried out." A(02) C(04) SBLGNT THGNT.
q 18:18, **smoke:** A(02) reads "place."
r 18:18, **Who is like the great city?:** C(04) reads "Like this great city!"
s 18:19, **weeping and mourning:** Absent from A(02).
t 18:19, **woe:** Absent from א(01).
u 18:20, **and the:** Absent from C(04) TR.
v 18:21, **strong:** Absent from א(01).
w 18:21, **millstone:** א(01) reads "stone."
x 18:21, **So:** א(01) reads "For thus."

will Babylon, the great city, be thrown down with violence, and will not be found any longer [[in it]].[a] 22 [And][b] The sound of harpists and musicians and flute players and trumpeters will not be heard in you any longer; and no craftsman [of any craft][c] will be found in you any longer; [and the sound of a mill will not be heard in you any longer;][d] 23 [and the light of a lamp will not shine in you any longer;][e] and the voice of the bridegroom and [[voice of the]][f] bride will not be heard in you any longer; for your merchants were the great men of the earth, because all the nations were deceived by your sorcery. 24 And in her was found the blood of prophets and saints and of all who have been slain on the earth."

19 1 [[And]][g] After this, I heard what sounded [like][h] a loud voice of a great multitude in heaven, saying, "Hallelujah! Salvation, [glory][i] [[and honor]][j] and power belong to [[the Lord]][k] our God, 2 for his judgments are true and just; for he has judged the great prostitute who corrupted the earth with her immorality, and has avenged the blood of his servants at her hand."

3 And again they said, "Hallelujah! Her smoke goes up forever and ever."

4 And the twenty-four elders and the four [living][l] creatures fell down and worshiped God who is seated on the throne, saying, "Amen. Hallelujah!"

5 And a voice came {from}[m] the throne, saying, "Praise our God, all you his servants, [and][n] those who fear him, both small and great."

6 And I heard what sounded [like][o] a voice of a great multitude, like the sound of many waters and like the sound of mighty thunder, saying, "Hallelujah! For the Lord, [our][p] God, the Almighty, reigns. 7 Let us rejoice and be glad, and give him the glory, for the marriage of the Lamb has come, and his bride has made herself ready; 8 it was granted her to be clothed in {bright, pure linen},"[q] for the linen is the righteous deeds of the saints.

9 And he said to me, "Write: Blessed are those who are invited to the [marriage][r] supper of the Lamb." And he said [to me,][s] "These are the true words of God."

10 Then {I fell down}[t] at his feet to worship him, but he said to me, "You must not do that! I am a fellow servant [with you][u] and your brothers who hold the testimony of Jesus. Worship God. For the testimony of Jesus is the spirit of prophecy."

---

a 18:21, **in it:** Included in א(01).

b 18:22, **And:** Absent from א(01).

c 18:22, **of any craft:** Absent from א(01) A(02).

d 18:22, **and the sound of a mill will not be heard in you any longer:** Absent from א(01).

e 18:23, **and the light of a lamp...:** Absent from A(02).

f 18:23, **voice of the bride:** Included in C(04).

g 19:1, **And:** Included in BYZ TR.

h 19:1, **like:** Absent from TR.

i 19:1, **glory:** Absent from א(01).

j 19:1, **and honor:** Included in TR.

k 19:1, **the Lord:** Included in TR.

l 19:4, **living:** Absent from א(01).

m 19:5, **from:** Some manuscripts read "out of." BYZ TR.

n 19:5, **and:** Absent from א(01) C(04).

o 19:6, **like:** Absent from A(02)

p 19:6, **our:** Absent from A(02) TR SBLGNT.

q 19:8, **bright, pure linen:** Some manuscripts read "linen, bright and pure." BYZ TR.

r 19:9, **marriage:** Absent from א(01).

s 19:9, **to me:** Included in א(01).

t 19:10, **I fell down:** TR reads "they fell down."

u 19:10, **with you:** Absent from א(01).

11 And I saw heaven opened, and behold, a white horse! And the one sitting on it [called]ᵃ Faithful and True, and in righteousness judges and makes war. 12 But his eyes [were like]ᵇ a flame of fire, and on his head were many diadems, having [[names written and]]ᶜ a name [written which]ᵈ no one knows except himself, 13 and {wrapped}ᵉ in a robe dipped in blood, and his name {has been}ᶠ called the Word of God.

14 And the armies [that are]ᵍ in heaven were following it on white horses, dressed in {pure white linen}.ʰ 15 From his mouth comes a sharp [[double edge]]ⁱ sword, so that with it {he will strike}ʲ the nations; and he himself will shepherd them with an iron rod. He will tread the winepress of the fury {of}ᵏ the wrath of God the Almighty. 16 [On his robe]ˡ And on his thigh he has {a}ᵐ name written: "King of kings and Lord of lords."

17 And I saw {an}ⁿ angel standing in the sun, and he cried out {with}ᵒ a loud voice, saying to all the birds flying in midheaven, "Come, [[and]]ᵖ gather for the great feast of God, 18 to eat the flesh of kings, the flesh of commanders, the flesh of the mighty, the flesh of horses and their riders, and the flesh of all men, [both]�q free and slave, [[both]]ʳ small and great."

19 And I saw the beast and the kings of the earth with their armies gathered to make [the]ˢ war against him who was sitting on the horse and against his army. 20 And the beast was captured, and with it the false prophet who had performed the signs in its presence, by which he deceived those who had received the mark of the beast and those who worshiped its image.

These two were thrown alive into the lake of fire that burns with sulfur. 21 And the rest were slain by the sword of the one seated on the horse, {which came out}ᵗ of his mouth; and all the birds were filled with their flesh.

20 1 And I saw an angel coming down [from heaven],ᵘ having the key to the abyss and a great chain in his hand. 2 And he seized the dragon, the ancient serpent, who is the Devil and Satan, [[the one deceiving the whole world]],ᵛ and bound him for a thousand years, 3 and threw him into the abyss, and shut {it}ʷ and sealed it {over}ˣ him, so that he would not deceive the nations any longer until the thousand years were completed.

ᵃ 19:11, **called:** Absent from A(02).

ᵇ 19:12, **were like:** Absent from ℵ(01) BYZ.

ᶜ 19:12, **names written and:** Included in BYZ.

ᵈ 19:12, **written which:** Absent from ℵ(01).

ᵉ 19:13, **wrapped:** ℵ(01) reads "having been clothed."

ᶠ 19:13, **has been:** Some manuscripts read "is." BYZ TR.

ᵍ 19:14, **that are:** Absent from ℵ(01) A(02) TR(1550).

ʰ 19:14, **pure white linen:** Some manuscripts read "linen, pure and white." ℵ(01) TR(1550).

ⁱ 19:15, **double edge:** Included in BYZ.

ʲ 19:15, **he will strike:** Some manuscripts read "he strikes." TR.

ᵏ 19:15, **of:** TR reads "and."

ˡ 19:16, **on his robe:** Absent from A(02).

ᵐ 19:16, **a:** TR reads "the."

ⁿ 19:17, **an:** ℵ(01) reads "another."

ᵒ 19:17, **with:** A(02) BYZ TR SBLGNT THGNT ‖ Some manuscripts read "in." ℵ(01) NA28[].

ᵖ 19:17, **and:** Included in TR.

q 19:18, **both:** Absent from TR.

ʳ 19:18, **both:** Included in BYZ.

ˢ 19:19, **the:** Absent from BYZ TR.

ᵗ 19:21, **which came out:** TR reads "the one that comes out."

ᵘ 20:1, **from heaven:** Absent from ℵ(01).

ᵛ 20:2, **the one deceiving the whole world:** Included in BYZ.

ʷ 20:3, **it:** Some manuscripts read "him." TR.

ˣ 20:3, **over:** A(02) reads "steadfastly toward."

[[And]]^a After that, he must be released for a short time.

4 And I saw thrones, and they sat on them, and judgment was given to them,^{b} and [[I saw]]^c the souls of those who had been beheaded because of the testimony of Jesus and because of the word of God, and those who had not^d worshiped the beast or its image, and had not received the mark on their forehead and on their hand. And they lived and reigned with Christ for a thousand years.

5 [[And]]^e [The rest of the dead did not {live}^{f} until the thousand years were completed.]^g

This is the first resurrection. 6 Blessed and holy is the one who has a part in the first resurrection; over these the second death has no power, but they will be priests of God and of Christ and will reign with him {a}^{h} thousand years.

7 And when^i the thousand years are completed, Satan will be released from his prison 8 and will go out to deceive [[all]]^j the nations [which are]^k in the four corners [of the earth],^{l} Gog and Magog, to gather them together for [the]^m war; {their}^{n} number is like the sand of the sea. 9 And they went up on the breadth of the earth and surrounded the camp of the saints and the beloved city, and fire came down [from heaven]^o [[from God]]^p [and devoured them].^{q}

10 And the devil who deceived them was thrown [into the lake of]^r fire and sulfur, [and]^s where the beast and the false prophet are; and [[where]]^t they will be tormented day and night forever and ever.^{u}

11 And I saw a great white throne and the one seated on it, from whose face earth and heaven fled away, and no place was found for them.

12 And I saw the dead, the great and the small, standing [before]^v {the throne},^{w} and books were opened; [and another book was opened,]^x which is of life. And the dead were judged from the things which were written in the books, according to their deeds.

---

^{a} 20:3, **And:** Included in BYZ TR.

^{b} 20:4, **judgment was given to them:** Or "judgment was given for them" (That is, they were vindicated).

^{c} 20:4, **I saw:** Included in Italic in KJV.

^{d} 20:4, **not:** Absent from ℵ(01).

^{e} 20:5, **And:** Included in BYZ ‖ TR adds "But."

^{f} 20:5, **live:** TR reads "revive."

^{g} 20:5, **The rest of the dead did not live until the thousand years were completed:** Absent from some manuscripts including ℵ(01) and the Syriac Philoxeniana (first Syriac version to include Revelation).

^{h} 20:6, **a:** A(02) BYZ TR SBLGNT ‖ Some manuscripts read "the." ℵ(01) NA28[] THGNT.

^{i} 20:7, **when:** Or whenever.

^{j} 20:8, **all:** Included in ℵ(01).

^{k} 20:8, **which are:** Absent from ℵ(01).

^{l} 20:8, **of the earth:** Absent from ℵ(01).

^{m} 20:8, **the:** Absent from TR.

^{n} 20:8, **their:** TR reads "the."

^{o} 20:9, **from heaven:** Absent from ℵ(01).

^{p} 20:9, **from God:** Included in BYZ TR.

^{q} 20:9, **and devoured them:** Absent from ℵ(01).

^{r} 20:10, **into the lake of:** Absent from ℵ(01).

^{s} 20:10, **and:** Absent from ℵ(01) TR.

^{t} 20:10, **where:** Included in ℵ(01).

^{u} 20:10, **forever and ever:** Or "to the ages of the ages."

^{v} 20:12, **before:** Absent from ℵ(01).

^{w} 20:12, **the throne:** TR reads "God."

^{x} 20:12, **and another book was opened:** Absent from ℵ(01).

13 And the sea gave up the dead [who were]^a in it, and Death and Hades gave up the dead who were in them; and they were {judged},^{b} each one according to their deeds.

14 And Death and Hades were thrown into the lake of fire. This is the second death, [the lake of fire].^{c} 15 And if anyone's name was not found written in the book of life, he was thrown into the lake of fire.

21 1 And I saw a new heaven and a new earth. For the first heaven and the first earth had passed away, and the sea is no more. 2 And [[I John saw]]^d the holy city, new Jerusalem, descending from {heaven from God,}^{e} prepared as a bride adorned for her husband.

3 And [I heard]^f a loud voice from {the throne}^{g} saying, "Behold, the dwelling of God is with men, and he will dwell with them, and they will be his people, and God himself will be with them [as their God],^{h} 4 and {he}^{i} will wipe away every tear from their eyes, and death shall be no more, neither shall there be mourning, nor crying[, nor pain]^j anymore, [for]^k the former things have passed away."

5 And he who was seated on the throne said, "Behold, I am make all things new." And he says [[to me]],^{l} "Write, for these words are trustworthy and true." 6 And he said to me, "It is done. I {am}^{m} the Alpha and the Omega, the beginning and the end. I will give to the one who thirsts [from the spring]^n of the water of life freely. 7 The one who conquers will inherit {these}^{o} things, and I will be {his}^{p} God and he will be my son."

8 But as for the cowardly, the faithless, [[the sinful,]]^q the detestable, the murderers, the sexually immoral, the sorcerers, the idolaters, and all liars, their portion will be in the lake that burns with fire and sulfur, which is the second death.

9 And one of the seven angels who had the seven bowls full of the seven last plagues came [[to me]]^r and spoke with me, saying, "Come, I will show you the bride, the wife of the Lamb." 10 And he carried me away in the Spirit to a great and high mountain, and showed me [[the great]]^s the holy city, Jerusalem coming down out of heaven from God, 11 having the glory of God, [[and]]^t its light was like a most precious stone, like a jasper stone, clear as crystal.

---

a 20:13, **who were:** Absent from TR.

b 20:13, **judged:** ℵ(01) reads "condemned."

c 20:14, **the lake of fire:** Absent from some manuscripts including TR and all Syriac versions.

d 21:2, **I John saw:** Included in TR.

e 21:2, **heaven from God:** TR reads "from God out of heaven."

f 21:3, **I heard:** Absent from ℵ(01).

g 21:3, **the throne:** Some manuscripts read "heaven." BYZ TR.

h 21:3, **as their God:** A(02) TR NA28[] THGNT ‖ Absent from ℵ(01) BYZ SBLGNT.

i 21:4, **he:** Some manuscripts read "God." A(02) TR.

j 21:4, **nor pain:** Absent from ℵ(01).

k 21:4, **for:** BYZ TR NA28[] ‖ Absent from A(02) SBLGNT THGNT.

l 21:5, **to me:** Included in ℵ(01) BYZ TR.

m 21:6, **am:** TR NA28[] THGNT ‖ The Greek word εἰμι is absent from ℵ(01) BYZ SBLGNT. Without the Greek word "am" is implied. An alternative reading of the sentence is "I, the Alpha and the Omega, the beginning and the end, will give to the one who thirsts of the water of life freely."

n 21:6, **from the spring:** Absent from A(02).

o 21:7, **these:** TR(1550) reads "all."

p 21:7, **his:** A(02) reads "the."

q 21:8, **the sinful:** Included in BYZ.

r 21:9, **to me:** Included in TR.

s 21:10, **the great:** Included in BYZ TR.

t 21:11, **and:** Included in TR.

12 It had a great and high wall, with twelve gates, [and at the gates twelve angels,]ᵃ and [[their]]ᵇ names {inscribed},ᶜ which are [the names]ᵈ of the twelve tribes of the sons of Israel; 13 on the east three gates, [and]ᵉ on the north three gates, [and] on the south three gates, [and] on the west three gates. 14 And the wall of the city had twelve foundations, and on them were the [twelve]ᶠ names of the twelve apostles of the Lamb.

15 And the one speaking with me had a golden [measuring]ᵍ rod, in order to measure the city and its gates and its wall. 16 The city lies foursquare, and its length is as much as [also]ʰ its width. And he measured the city with his rod, twelve thousand stadia; its length and width and height are equal. 17 He also measured its wall, one hundred forty-four cubits by human measurement, which is also an angel's measurement.

18 The wall was built of jasper, while the city was pure gold, like clear glass. 19 The foundations of the wall of the city were adorned with every kind of precious stone. The first foundation was jasper, the second sapphire, the third chalcedony, the fourth emerald, 20 the fifth sardonyx, the sixth carnelian, the seventh chrysolite, the eighth beryl, the ninth topaz, the tenth chrysoprase, the eleventh jacinth, the twelfth amethyst. 21 And the twelve gates were twelve pearls, each of the gates made of a single pearl, and the street of the city was pure gold, transparent as glass.

22 And I saw no temple in the city, for the Lord God the Almighty and the Lamb are its temple. 23 And the city has no need of sun or moon to shine on it, for the glory of God gives it light, and its lamp is the Lamb.

24 And the nations [[of those being saved]]ⁱ will walk by its light, and the kings of the earth will bring their glory [[and honor]]ʲ into it, 25 and its gates will never be shut by day and there will be no night there. 26 They will bring the glory and the honor of the nations into it.

27 And nothing unclean will ever enter into it, also [one]ᵏ who practices abomination and falsehood, except those whose names are written in the book of life {of the Lamb}.ˡ

22 1 And he showed me a [[pure]]ᵐ river of the water of life, clear as crystal, flowing from the throne of God and of the Lamb. 2 In the middle of its street and on either side of the river [was the tree of life],ⁿ producing twelve kinds of fruit, yielding its fruit each [[in one]]ᵒ month; and the leaves of the tree were for the healing of the nations.

3 There will be no more curse; and the throne of God and of the Lamb will be in it, and his servants will serve him. 4 They will see his face, and his name will be on their foreheads.

ᵃ 21:12, **and at the gates twelve angels:** Absent from A(02).
ᵇ 21:12, **their:** Included in ℵ(01).
ᶜ 21:12, **inscribed:** ℵ(01) reads "written."
ᵈ 21:12, **the names:** A(02) NA28[] THGNT ‖ Absent from ℵ(01) BYZ TR SBLGNT.
ᵉ 21:13, **and:** Absent from some manuscripts in three places. TR.
ᶠ 21:14, **twelve:** Absent from TR.
ᵍ 21:15, **measuring:** Absent from TR.
ʰ 21:16, **also:** A(02) NA28[] THGNT ‖ Absent from ℵ(01) BYZ SBLGNT.
ⁱ 21:24, **of those being saved:** Included in TR.
ʲ 21:24, **and honor:** Included in BYZ TR.
ᵏ 21:27, **one:** TR NA28[] ‖ Absent from ℵ(01) A(02) BYZ SBLGNT THGNT.
ˡ 21:27, **of the Lamb:** ℵ(01) reads "of the name."
ᵐ 22:1, **pure:** Included in BYZ TR.
ⁿ 22:2, **was the tree of life:** Absent from ℵ(01).
ᵒ 22:2, **in one:** Included in TR.

5 And there will be no night, and
they will have no need of [the light of][a]
a lamp or sunlight, because the Lord
God will illumine them; and they will
reign forever and ever.

6 And {he said}[b] to me, "These
words are faithful and true; and the
Lord, the God of {the spirits of},[c] the
prophets sent his angel to show his
servants what must soon take place."

7 "[And][d] Behold, I am coming
quickly. Blessed is the one who
keeps the words of the prophecy of
this book."

8 And I, John, am the one seeing
and hearing these things. And when I
heard and saw, I fell down to worship
at the feet of the angel who showed me
these things.
9 But he said to me, "See
do not; [[for]][e] I am a fellow servant of
yours and of your brothers the prophets
and of those who keep the words of this
book. Worship God."

10 And he said to me, "Do not seal
up the words of {the}[f] prophecy of this
book, {for}[g] the time is near."[h]

11 Let the one who does wrong still
do wrong; [and let the filthy one still be
made filthy;][i] and let the righteous one
still {practice righteousness},[j] and let
the holy one still be made holy.

12 [[And]][k] Behold, I am coming
quickly, and my reward is with me, to
give to each one as his {work is}.[l]

13 "I {am}[m] the Alpha and the
Omega, {the first and the last, the
beginning and the end.}"[n][o]

14 Blessed are those who {wash
their robes},[p] so that they may have
the {right to}[q] the tree of life, and may
enter by the gates into the city.

15 [[But]][r] Outside are the dogs and
the sorcerers and the sexually immoral
and the murderers and the idolaters,
and everyone who loves and practices
falsehood.

16 "I, Jesus, have sent my angel
to testify to you these things for
the churches. I am the root[s] and
the descendant of David, the bright
morning star."

17 And the Spirit and the bride say,
"Come." And let the one who hears say,
"Come." And let the one who is thirsty
come; And let the one who wishes take
the water of life freely.

---

a 22:5, **the light of:** Absent from BYZ TR.
b 22:6, **he said:** Some manuscripts read "he says." BYZ.
c 22:6, **the spirits of:** TR reads "holy."
d 22:7, **and:** Absent from TR.
e 22:9, **for:** Included in TR.
f 22:10, **the:** א(01) reads "this."
g 22:10, **for:** TR reads "because."
h 22:10, It is not clear when the angel stops speaking and when a narrative summary begins, which may be at verse 11 or 12 or some later verse. Verses 11-21 appear to be an epilogue that provides an end summary with highlights from what precedes it.
i 22:11, **and let the filthy one still be made filthy:** Absent from A(02).
j 22:11, **practice righteousness:** TR reads "be justified."
k 22:12, **And:** Included in TR.
l 22:12, **work is:** Some manuscripts read "work will be." BYZ TR.
m 22:13, **am:** TR adds "am" (εγω + ειμι) which is otherwise implied.
n 22:13, **the first and the last, the beginning and the end:** A(02) reads "beginning and end, the first and the last." || TR reads "the beginning and the end, the first and the last."
o 22:12-13 Verses 12-13 are a parallel with Revelation 1:7-8.
p 22:14, **wash their robes:** Some manuscripts read "do his commandments." BYZ TR.
q 22:14, **right to:** א(01) reads "authority over."
r 22:15, **But:** Included in TR.
s 22:16, **root:** Can also mean "shoot" (cf. Isaiah 11:1).

18 [[For]]ᵃ {I testify}ᵇ to everyone who hears the words of the prophecy of this book: if anyone adds to {them},ᶜ God will add [to him]ᵈ the [[seven]]ᵉ plagues which are written in this book; 19 and if anyone takes away from {the}ᶠ words of the book of this prophecy, God will remove his part from the {tree}ᵍ of life and [from]ʰ the holy city, [[and]]ⁱ which are written in this book.

20 The one who testifies to these things says, "Yes, I am coming quickly." [Amen.]ʲ [[Yes,]]ᵏ Come, Lord Jesus.

21 The grace of {the}ˡ Lord Jesus [[Christ]]ᵐ be with all [[of the saints]].ⁿ [[Amen]]ᵒᵖ

ᵃ 22:18, **For:** Included in TR.
ᵇ 22:18, **I testify:** TR reads "I join in testifying."
ᶜ 22:18, **them:** TR reads "these."
ᵈ 22:18, **to him:** Absent from A(02).
ᵉ 22:18, **seven:** Some manuscripts include. BYZ
ᶠ 22:19, **the:** ℵ(01) reads "these."
ᵍ 22:19, **tree:** TR reads "book."
ʰ 22:19, **from:** Absent from A(02).
ⁱ 22:19, **and:** Included in TR.
ʲ 22:20, **Amen:** Absent from ℵ(01).
ᵏ 22:20, **Yes:** Included in BYZ TR.
ˡ 22:21, **the:** Some manuscripts read "our." TR.
ᵐ 22:21, **Christ:** Included in BYZ TR(1550).
ⁿ 22:21, **of the saints:** Included in ℵ(01) Syriac(Philoxeniana) BYZ THGNT ‖ Absent from A(02) NA28 SBLGNT ‖ TR reads "of you."
ᵒ 22:21, **Amen:** Included in ℵ(01) BYZ TR THGNT ‖ Absent from A(02) NA28 SBLGNT.
ᵖ 22:21, Some manuscripts include the postscript "Revelation of John." ℵ(01) A(02) ‖ TR reads "End."

Josiah E Verkaik, founder of Integrity Syndicate, is a researcher with a background in engineering. Josiah offers numerous contributions to the field of New Testament studies as an innovator and analytical thinker. He is the architect of the AICNT and directed all aspects of its development.

Dustin Smith, PhD, is a New Testament scholar and Research Manager at Spartanburg Methodist College. He is the author or editor of nine books, including *A Systematic Theology of the Early Church, Wisdom Christology in the Gospel of John, The Son of God: Three Views of the Identity of Jesus,* and *Paradoxical Conquering in the Apocalypse of John.* Dr. Smith has taught Biblical Greek for over a decade at the undergraduate and graduate levels. Additionally, he has served on the editorial boards of two scholarly journals.

INTEGRITY SYNDICATE

Established in 2020, Integrity Syndicate publishes critical resources at the core of the New Testament.

integritysyndicate.com

www.ingramcontent.com/pod-product-compliance
Lightning Source LLC
Chambersburg PA
CBHW050226270326
41914CB00003BA/585